1,000,000 Books

are available to read at

www.ForgottenBooks.com

Read online
Download PDF
Purchase in print

ISBN 978-0-331-01911-7
PIBN 11106645

This book is a reproduction of an important historical work. Forgotten Books uses state-of-the-art technology to digitally reconstruct the work, preserving the original format whilst repairing imperfections present in the aged copy. In rare cases, an imperfection in the original, such as a blemish or missing page, may be replicated in our edition. We do, however, repair the vast majority of imperfections successfully; any imperfections that remain are intentionally left to preserve the state of such historical works.

Forgotten Books is a registered trademark of FB &c Ltd.
Copyright © 2018 FB &c Ltd.
FB &c Ltd, Dalton House, 60 Windsor Avenue, London, SW19 2RR.
Company number 08720141. Registered in England and Wales.

For support please visit www.forgottenbooks.com

1 MONTH OF
FREE
READING

at

www.ForgottenBooks.com

By purchasing this book you are eligible for one month membership to ForgottenBooks.com, giving you unlimited access to our entire collection of over 1,000,000 titles via our web site and mobile apps.

To claim your free month visit:

www.forgottenbooks.com/free1106645

* Offer is valid for 45 days from date of purchase. Terms and conditions apply.

English
Français
Deutsche
Italiano
Español
Português

www.forgottenbooks.com

Mythology Photography **Fiction** Fishing Christianity **Art** Cooking Essays Buddhism Freemasonry Medicine **Biology** Music **Ancient Egypt** Evolution Carpentry Physics Dance Geology **Mathematics** Fitness Shakespeare **Folklore** Yoga Marketing **Confidence** Immortality Biographies Poetry **Psychology** Witchcraft Electronics Chemistry History **Law** Accounting **Philosophy** Anthropology Alchemy Drama Quantum Mechanics Atheism Sexual Health **Ancient History** **Entrepreneurship** Languages Sport Paleontology Needlework Islam **Metaphysics** Investment Archaeology Parenting Statistics Criminology **Motivational**

4 Apr 1913

KEYSTONE ELECTRIC COMPANY

ERIE — — PENNA.

ELECTRICAL TRANSMISSION

THE BEST AND MOST PRACTICAL METHOD FOR DRIVING

CEMENT MACHINERY.

PLANT OF THE WHITEHALL PORTLAND CEMENT COMPANY, CEMENTON, PENNA.

ELECTRICALLY DRIVEN THROUGHOUT BY

KEYSTONE MACHINERY

GENERATORS: 900 K. W.
MOTORS: 1720 H. P.

SWITCHBOARD AT THE WHITEHALL PORTLAND CEMENT COMPANY'S PLANT

FAIRBANKS

CEMENT TESTING MACHINE

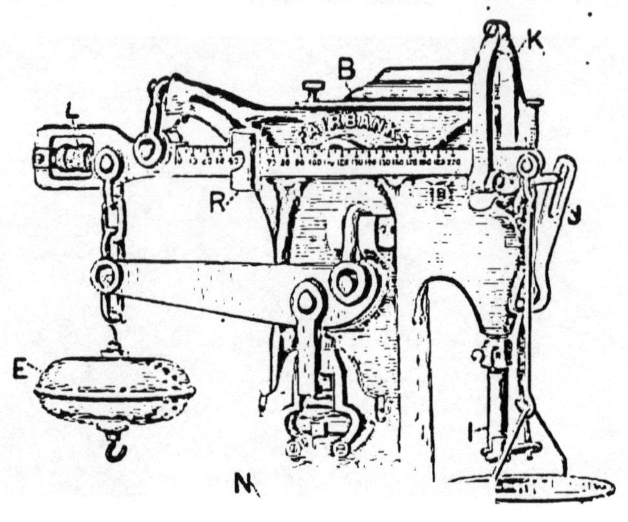

DIRECTORY

RAILROAD GAZ

OF

AMERICAN CEMENT INDUSTRIES

AND

HAND-BOOK FOR CEMENT USERS

EDITED BY

CHARLES CARROLL BROWN

M. AM. SOC. C. E.

PUBLISHED BY

MUNICIPAL ENGINEERING COMPANY

INDIANAPOLIS, IND.

NEW YORK, N. Y.

1901

THE NEW YORK
PUBLIC LIBRARY
549504
ASTOR, LENOX AND
TILDEN FOUNDATIONS.
R 1913 L

COPYRIGHT 1901
BY
MUNICIPAL ENGINEERING COMPANY

CONTENTS.

ADVERTISERS' INDEX

PREFACE

The publication of the Directory of American Cement Industries and Hand Book of Cement Users is the direct result of the many demands for information upon all questions connected with the manufacture, sale and use of cement which have been made upon Municipal Engineering Magazine and of the conclusion drawn from close observation, that the time has now arrived for the publication of such a book giving, more particularly from the practical and commercial standpoints, the answers to all the classes of questions which those interested in cement are asking.

The introductory chapter gives a short sketch of the development of the cement industry in this country, beginning with the manufacture of natural hydraulic cement and culminating in the manufacture of the best Portland cement at the lowest price ever reached. The principles of the various processes which are in use are stated in the course of this history. The descriptions of individual works follow. These descriptions are carried to sufficient detail to give the information regarding the materials and processes used and the care taken, necessary to form a judgment of the conditions under which the cement is manufactured, without revealing the economic methods followed to enable the factories to produce the cement at the lowest possible cost. It will be seen that the same general description will answer for all the factories in a class and thus it is only necessary to give one lengthy description and give in other cases the differences in design.

An examination of these descriptions will give the reader a general knowledge of all the processes used and many ideas of the differences in detail made necessary by variations in material and local conditions, or introduced for economic reasons.

The chapter on the uses of cement is not small, but it is not complete. The extension of the use of cement has been so rapid in the last few years that it is difficult to keep pace with it. The chapter tries to confine itself to such uses as have stood the test of time and is believed to fill the field it attempts to cover satisfactorily. It will be extended in future editions as may seem desirable.

The chapter on specifications gives samples of standard specifications for the various uses of cement which are known to give satisfaction. Variations with conditions of climate, soil, materials, etc., are shown in the differences in specification. The author and the locality for which the specification is made are given whenever it seemed desirable.

Enough is given regarding testing laboratories to show what the facilities in such laboratories should be, and the work which they may be expected to do. Municipal and government laboratories do not usually make tests on materials beyond their own requirements, but occasionally arrangements for such tests or the use of the machinery can be made. A number of the colleges in the country have facilities for partial physical tests of cement and concrete and for chemical analysis, and with most of them arrangements can be made for special tests. But few are open at all times for testing on a commercial basis.

There are also a number of private laboratories with which arrangements can be made for partial tests and analyses of cements. But few of these are on a permanent commercial basis.

There has been no attempt at completeness in the list beyond the laboratories which may be considered to be always ready for making tests and analyses on a commercial basis.

There were some potent reasons for issuing the book at the earliest possible moment and it has all been prepared since November 1st. This haste in preparation has not been permitted to interfere with the accuracy of the work, but the shortness of the time has prevented the receipt of the information desired from some of those who should be represented. It is believed that what is thus omitted will not detract from the value of the book as a whole.

Some managers of cement works have refused to give the information requested from reasons of business policy which seem sufficient to them and will not therefore be criticised. It has been necessary, however, to make the proper notation to this effect that the reason for the lack of information in such cases may be clearly understood.

The formation of new companies for the manufacture of cement is proceeding with so much rapidity that some of these companies which have not yet begun the erection of works are doubtless omitted. Not a few are omitted because the preliminary steps have not been followed up, from failure of material to show the requisite quality and failure to interest the necessary capital.

The list of brands or names under which cement is sold is large, larger than the actual number of different cements which are manufactured. It is believed that the book is successful in listing each brand of American Portland cement under at least one of its names. The large number of small scattered plants for the manufacture of natural hydraulic cement and the fact that in such districts as that about Louisville the product of many mills is marketed by one company, makes it probable that every brand of natural hydraulic cement is not listed. All those of more than local reputations are included in the list, but less attention has been paid to this class of cements, except so far as the leading manufacturers are concerned than to the American Portland cements. The circulars requesting information concerning cement contained a request for information regarding foreign cements sold in the American market, which has been overlooked by some of the agents and importers to which they were sent. As the sale of these cements is at a standstill or is diminishing, strong effort to make the list of foreign cements complete has not been made.

The list of sales agents will be found convenient. It includes all the distributers of American cements and some of the larger dealers as well as most of the agents and importers of foreign cements. Cement manufacturing companies who market their own products are not included in this list.

The list of dealers in cement includes those in all cities, villages and towns of more than 2,000 population. It is exceptionally complete and accurate. The information is absolutely new and is believed to be strictly accurate. It has all been received directly from the towns themselves since January 1, 1901. This feature makes it one of the most reliable and most complete lists of this nature which has ever been published.

The same may be said of the lists of cement users. It has not been possible in all cases to make a complete differentiation of contractors and workers in cement, nor has it always been possible to separate the names of architects and engineers strictly, according to their professions. In the first case the list of contractors contains all the names of contractors using cement in their work and the names of such workers in cement as are at the same time contractors.

The list of workers in cement contains the names of those who are to be classed strictly under this heading. In the same way the list of engineers contains the names of engineers supervising the use of cement, including city engineers, and also the names of those who are not definitely known to belong strictly to the class of architects. The list of architects contains this latter class.

The list of cement testing laboratories will be found to be a convenience when tests of material are desired. There are many municipal laboratories and small school and college laboratories where tests can be made, but which can hardly be considered ready for work on short notice or open to the general public. The list given is reliable and distributed through the country so that at least one laboratory in the list is within easy reach from any point.

The list of manufacturers of machinery contains a representative list of the makers of machinery for use in the manufacture of cement and of the makers of tools for the manipulation of cement, from concrete mixers to cement workers' tools. The extension of the cement field and the large number of plants under construction and contemplated is extending this list almost daily. No line of machinery used in a cement mill is omitted.

The fact that in the smaller cities and towns the dealers in cement are also dealers in lime, plaster and other building materials, led, rather late in the preparation of the book to a decision to include such materials in the directory lists. This decision was reached so late that a complete list could not be prepared in time for this first edition. A very comprehensive list is presented, however, and it will be largely extended in future editions. It may be said that the dealers in cement in cities and towns of about 30,000 population or less are also dealers in lime, plaster and similar materials. This is true to some extent also in the larger cities, so that the list of cement dealers may fairly be used where the list of dealers in the other materials mentioned is wanting.

INTRODUCTION

Strictly speaking, the title of this book, Directory of American Cement Industries, confines it to the consideration of American made cements and this is practically the case, but little space being taken up with foreign cements. A still further restriction is made so far as the amount of detail is concerned, since the cements sold under the name of Portland are those which are most carefully and fully treated. The general distribution of small natural cement plants throughout the many districts containing cement rock, which produce cement almost entirely for local consumption, and the practical uniformity of methods used, make it unnecessary to use much space in their consideration, beyond the larger works with extended reputation for excellence of product.

One of the first questions which arises is that of definition. Since this is a book which takes the market as it exists, it is necessary to list all the cements using the name Portland under that classification. Care is taken to make the reference from the lists of brands and manufacturers in the Directory to the descriptions of works, materials, and processes so clear and so convenient that it is easy to determine the character of materials used, and the processes used, and thus to form a good judgment of the kind and quality of the product. In general it will be found that under the heading of some one factory a full description of the materials and methods is given and that others using practically the same materials and methods are described in more condensed statements, but with sufficient fullness to be interpreted without further reference by one who has carefully gone over the entire list of descriptions. Many varieties of materials are used and a number of different processes.

Those cements which are produced by burning a natural cement rock directly are all in the class of natural hydraulic cements. In such districts as Rosendale and Louisville, and in such cases as Utica, Akron, Milwaukee, Fort Scott, etc., where the name of the district is a distinguishing mark, it is added to the name of the brand.

In some cases, notably some of the factories in the Rosendale district, some selection and mixture of rocks of somewhat different composition is made, without the care and expense incident to regular chemical analysis to insure absolute uniformity and maximum quality of product. These are classed as natural hydraulic cements.

In the Lehigh region it is a common practice to improve the quality of the natural cement manufactured by adding to it inferior portions of the product of the Portland cement departments, or a proportion of the regular Portland cement where the uniformity of the rotary kiln product obtains. This produces an "Improved" brand which will be found in the alphabetical list of natural hydraulic cement brands under "Improved." Some of the works in the same region place upon the market second and third grades of Portland cement, some of which are made from the inferior portions of the clinker produced by the kilns and some are mixtures of a portion of natural hydraulic cement with the product of the Portland cement process. If marketed under the name of Portland cement they will be found in that list, although adulterated. The manufacturers turning out these brands are usually careful to distinguish between them in their advertising literature, and the tables of results of tests will also give some indication of the difference in quality. The names of brands given under the entry of the company in the list of manufacturers are as nearly as possible in the order of their value.

Perhaps the only definition of Portland cement which will fit all the American brands marketed under that name is the following: A Portland cement is one made from an artificial mixture of materials containing lime, silica and alumina in proper proportions. With a very few exceptions, which are distinguished wherever necessary in this book by the word (pozzuolana) in parenthesis, this definition may be restricted profitably by adding the requirement that the mixture shall be made by finely grinding the materials together and shall then be burned to a hard clinker at a high temperature. With this restriction all the American cements which have been considered as belonging to this class are included under the definition, and also those which, made from slag and lime, are treated by the Portland cement process of mixing, calcining and grinding. These cements can be distinguished in the descriptions of the works. There are good authorities upon both sides of the controversy over the admission of these "calcined slag" cements to the class of Portland cements, and not perfect consistence in the various statements of the same authorities. The writer prefers to leave the high quality of the cements made by this process to speak for them, believing that as their value is demonstrated the question will settle itself.

The definitions of Portland and pozzuolana cements recently recommended by a commission of engineer officers of the United States Army seem likely to be accepted as the standard definitions and are here given. They are on the whole the most satisfactory practical statements of the differences which have been formulated. The board consisted of Maj. Wm. L. Marshall, Maj. Wm. H. Bixby and Capt. Charles S. Riche, of the Corps of Engineers, United States Army.

Portland cements are products obtained from the heating or calcining up to incipient fusion of intimate mixtures, either natural or artificial, of argillaceous with calcareous substances, the calcined product to contain at least 1.7 times as much of lime by weight as of the materials which give the lime its hydraulic properties, and to be finely pulverized after said calcination, and thereafter additions or substitutions, for the purpose only of regulating certain properties of technical importance, to be allowable to not exceeding 2 per cent. of the calcined product; otherwise additions or substitutions, after calcination, are adulterations, necessitating a change of name.

Pozzuolana cements are products obtained by intimately and mechanically mixing, without subsequent calcination, powdered hydrates of lime with natural or artificial materials, which generally do not harden under water when alone, but do so when mixed with hydrates of lime (such materials being pozzuolana, santorin earth, trass obtained from volcanic tufa, furnace slag, burnt clay, etc.), the mixed product being ground to extreme fineness.

Rock from which to make natural hydraulic cement is said to have been first discovered in this country by Canvass White in 1818, when an engineer on the construction of the Erie canal. As hydraulic cement was needed on other canals, other deposits were found at Rosendale, N. Y., about 1823; Lockport, N. Y., 1824; Louisville, Ky., 1829; Cumberland and Round Top, Md., 1836; Utica, Ill., 1838, and later in Virginia and the Lehigh Valley district of Pennsylvania. Hydraulic cement was first made at Fort Scott, Kan., in 1868, at Milwaukee in 1875.

The development of the natural cement industry is indicated by the following statements of the amounts manufactured in various years:

Year.	No. of Works.	Product.	Value in cts. a bbl.
1880		2,030,000 bbls.	
1885		4,100,000 "	
1890		7,082,204 "	51.37
1895	67	7,741,077 "	50.32
1898	76	8,418,924 "	46.19

The general distribution of the industry over the country and the variation in price in different districts is shown by the following table for 1898:

State.	No. of Works.	No. of Barrels.	Value.
Florida....	1	7,500	$7,500
Georgia..................	1	18,000	13,500
Illinois..................	3	630,228	220,580
Indiana and Kentucky...	19	2,040,000	816,000
Kansas..................	2	160,000	120,000
Maryland	4	297,475	118,989
West Virginia...........	1	42,874	17,150
Minnesota..............	2	128,436	64,218
New York..............	29	4,157,917	2,065,658
Ohio.....	3	26,724	13,362
Pennsylvania............	5	499,956	249,978
Tennessee..............	1	10,000	8,000
Texas..................	1	11,000	16,500
Virginia................	3	8,835	5,301
Wisconsin..............	1	379,979	151,992

The usual process used in making natural hydraulic cement is to reduce the rock to kiln size by crusher or otherwise, and burn it in a continuous vertical kiln into which it is fed in alternate layers with the coal or coke used as fuel. The product is taken out cold at the bottom of the kiln, run through crusher and cracker and then ground between buhr stones, the fine material being separated and that refused by the screens returned to the stones for further grinding. But slight variations from this program are made, variations in plants being mainly in details of handling. One natural cement plant is considering the installation of Portland cement grinding machinery. The ordinary product of the natural cement kiln is not burned so hard as is necessary with Portland cement, so that the stone mills are ordinarily able to grind the clinker satisfactorily.

The materials used for making Portland cement are quite various. In the Lehigh region and those of the same geological horizon two kinds of rock are used. One is an argillaceous limestone making a good quality of natural hydraulic cement when burned in the ordinary kiln. The composition of this rock is very uniform in the deposits which are used for cement making and the beds are very deep, in some cases approximating 300 feet. To this rock there must be added a certain proportion of limestone, approximately 20 per cent., to produce the proper mixture to stand the high heat of the kilns and produce a true Portland cement. These materials are mixed and ground, the composition of the two kinds of stone being watched very closely that necessary changes may be made in the proportions. Gradual reduction by rock crushers, crackers, and mill stones, Griffin mills or ball and tube mills, is the rule. Several new grinding mills are now entering the field, differing but little in principle from some of those in use, but claiming special excellence in details.

The powdered stone from the grinding mills is moistened and made into bricks when burned in vertical kilns, the bricks being dried thoroughly by hot air. There are a few modified Shofer, Johnson and Dietzsch continuous kilns in use and a very few dome kilns. When the latter kiln is used the cold kiln is filled with alternate layers of the bricks of slurry and the coal or coke used as fuel. The kiln is then ignited and kept burning until the fuel is consumed. The amount of fuel to produce the proper degree of calcination must be determined before hand. When the kiln has had time to cool the clinker is taken out, carefully sorted and the good material sent to the crusher. Counting the time for sorting and cooling the kiln the capacity of the intermittent kiln is about 25 barrels of cement a day when well managed, and it requires fuel amounting to 25 per cent or more of the weight of cement produced. The continuous vertical kilns for burning Portland cement must be capable of attaining a much higher temperature than the ordinary lime or natural cement kiln. The various patterns produce the same effect in somewhat similar manner to the Shofer kiln. It is three stories in height. The slurry bricks are put into the kiln on the upper floor through charging doors at the foot of the stack. The heat arising from the combustion below thoroughly dries the bricks and heats them. The fuel is put in through stoke holes on the floor below, and may be of the cheaper kinds of coal. The combustion takes place in a section of the shaft which is very much less in cross section than either above or below, that the draft may be concentrated and the heat as intense as is necessary. The clinker is removed below from an enlarged section of the kiln, and as it is removed the material above drops down, thus making the action of the kiln continuous. The draft of air for the fire being through the hot clinker, serves to cool that material and itself becomes heated and thus aids combustion. These kilns are economical of fuel, requiring about 12 per cent of the weight of the cement product in coal. They may be run as high as 75 barrels of cement a day. The product is more uniform than with the intermittent kiln, but still requires careful selection, as the process is not absolutely under the constant control of the operator.

The rotary kiln was invented in England, but was made successful in this country. In the Lehigh region the powdered stone, having been thoroughly dried before grinding, is fed into the upper end of the rotary kiln, which is a steel cylinder, lined as necessary, about 6 feet in diameter and from 50 to 75 feet long, depending somewhat upon the form of the material to be burned, revolving slowly. It is set on a slight incline so that the raw material gradually runs to the lower end. Gas, oil or powdered coal is used as fuel, the one used being forced under pressure into the lower end, all three burning at the point of entrance with about the same character of flame. The force of blast, amount of fuel, and rate of rotation of the cylinder being under the instantaneous control of the operator, the character of the product depends entirely upon his attention to the work, and practically every particle of the resulting clinker is capable of making the highest grade of cement of which the material is capable. The rotary kiln burns in fuel a little more than one-third the weight of the cement produced, and kilns are made capable of turning out 100 to 150 or even 175 barrels of cement a day. The effect of this kiln upon the development of the cement industry is considered later.

The clinker may be run through crushers and crackers if large enough to need it. That from rotary kilns is, however, so small, say the size of peas or a little larger, that this is not necessary. A few mills use buhr-stones for grinding, but most Portland cement clinker is too hard to grind economically in this manner. The Griffin mill, an American invention, consists of a steel ring against the inside surface of which a heavy steel roll revolving on a vertical shaft presses by centrifugal force. A separator drops the fine material into conveyors for transfer to the stock room and returns the coarser material to the mill for further grinding. Other mills on similar principle but differing materially in design are entering the field. The ball mill is approximately a cylinder partly filled with steel balls or round pebbles of very hård stone and arranged with screens for separating the fine product and returning the coarse product to the mill. It was originally used in the same manner as the other mills mentioned, but is now generally used as a first reducer, the material when it is reduced to the required size passing to a tube mill, which has a continuous cylindrical surface, is much longer, and set on a slight inclination so that the material passes slowly from one end of the mill to the other. The size of the particles of clinker fed to the tube mill, the amount of pebbles with which it is charged, the rate of rotation and the length of the tube are variable quantities, the resulting design in any particular case giving a uniform fineness of product. The clinker from the ball mill is fed into the tube mill through the axis at the upper end and drops out at the circumference or otherwise as desired at the lower end. If the mill is properly designed, a separator to return partly ground material is not necessary. There are also closed pebble mills into which the material to be ground is introduced in charges, each charge being run a definite length of time, as determined by experience. The finely ground material is then removed, and a new charge put in. With any of the apparatus mentioned any desired degree of fineness can be secured. The particular apparatus to be used, and the length of time the material must be retained, depend upon the hardness of the material, the fineness desired, and the cost of operation allowable.

In some factories the raw materials are limestone and clay or shale, which may be treated by the dry or the semi-wet processes already described.

In most of the factories of Ohio, Indiana and Michigan the wet process of mixing the materials, or some modification of it is used. The marl is excavated from the lake or marsh at the bottom of which it has been deposited and pumped or otherwise conveyed to a bin or basin in the factory. The clay or shale is brought in from the bank and the two materials are mixed in edge runner mills with water enough to allow the mixture to flow into another basin and be pumped through wet grinding mills, and kept moving in tanks where it is analyzed and the mixture corrected. Thence the wet material is pumped into the upper end of rotary kilns similar to those mentioned above, dropping out at the lower end as well burned Portland cement clinker. The process of mixing varies somewhat in different mills, but is in principle that followed in the best European plants. The material variations are noted in the descriptions of works.

One or two factories in this country use chalk and clay.

The manufacture of a cement from blast furnace slag is a recent development in this country. Two factories are now taking the slag from furnaces using suitable ore, cooling it suddenly with water and mixing the resulting slag sand with limestone or lime. The materials are thoroughly dried and mixed and then pulverized and fed to a rotary kiln according to the dry process. The resulting clinker is ground and produces a cement with similar constituents and characteristics, and made by a similar process to other American Portland cements, so that it can not be excluded by definition of process or product from the list of Portland cements.

Several factories are producing a cement properly classed as pozzuolana by mixing blast furnace slag, prepared as described, with slaked lime and grinding to the desired fineness. Although sold under the name of Portland cement and available for many of the same purposes, it is not a true Portland cement according to the more restricted definition given. It is distinguished in the subsequent descriptions and lists by the added word pozzuolana.

A short statement of the principal reasons for the enormous development of the American cement industry may be of interest. It is largely due to two causes. One is the increase in density of population and the consequent increase in the amount of work in which cement has long been used in the great extension of the number of uses to which cement can be put; and the other is the development of labor-saving processes for manufacture which reduce the cost, so that cement can be used for many constructions from which it has been largely excluded on account of the relative cheapness of other materials.

The intermittent vertical kiln, similar to the lime kiln, was first used in burning natural cement, perhaps as early as 1823, in this country. It was soon followed by the continuous kiln, of similar type, but with more than double the capacity, because no time was lost in cooling the calcined material and recharging and refiring the kiln. The comparatively low temperature in these kilns is sufficient for the calcination of the natural cement rock; in fact, a higher temperature injures the product from some deposits of cement rock.

The Portland cement industry developed in other countries, notably in England, France and Germany, using chalk or limestone and clay as materials. Intermittent kilns like the dome kilns, continuous kilns like the Dietzsch, and ring kilns like the Hoffman were used, the high temperatures necessary for complete calcination of the exact mixture necessary for Portland cement being obtainable in the special combustion chambers or by the methods of charging and burning. With the very best of care, however, it was impossible to secure uniform calcination of all the products of the furnace, and very careful selection of clinker was necessary that the cement be uniform. This necessitated much hand labor with a certain expertness, and with the vast amount of labor necessary in making bricks, drying them and depositing them in the kiln and the many handlings between, made a total which, under American conditions of labor, insured a price too high to compete with cement produced with the cheaper labor of Europe.

Notwithstanding this and the entire difference in materials, Mr. D. O. Saylor conceived the idea of making Portland cement by European methods, modified to make them fit the materials he had, viz.: the natural cement rock of the Lehigh region and limestone. After years of experimenting he succeeded in making a high grade of Portland cement by mixing the two kinds of rock in proper proportions, and by introducing labor-saving devices and improved machinery was able to compete in the American market with foreign cements, with some help from the tariff, except where the prejudice in favor of foreign cement at any price could not be overcome.

Ten years after Mr. Saylor made his first Portland cement Ransome patented in England and the United States the rotary kiln, using gas for fuel, but with the small kilns used and the previous treatment of raw material it was a failure. The Atlas Portland Cement Company took up the kiln, and with the more favorable hard and dry materials of the Lehigh valley finally made a success of it. Crude oil was later introduced for fuel and the present tendency is to use finely powdered coal.

Mention should be made of earlier use of the kiln with reasonable success by Duryee and Sanderson at Montezuma and Wallkill, N. Y., in works which are not now in operation.

With the success of this kiln the development of the Portland cement industry in this country began in earnest. It is possible to carry the material from the raw material cars to the finished package of cement without any handling, and this great reduction in the cost of labor enables the American manufacturer to compete successfully in price with any country in the world.

In 1892 the Warner Portland Cement Company tried the perfected kiln upon wet slurry, obtained by the mixture of marl and clay in pug mills, instead of drying and pulverizing bricks made of it and attempting to calcine this dust according to the method which failed in England. This was successful, and the development of the manufacture of cement in Northern Ohio and Indiana, and in Michigan, is due to this success, the wet material fed in at one end of a 60-foot kiln coming out at the other perfectly calcined Portland cement clinker of the size of peas.

One feature of the rotary kiln process is the absolute uniformity with which the clinker can be calcined. The introduction of variable speed apparatus puts the kilns under the absolute control of the expert in charge of them, and he can determine exactly the rate and amount of calcination the material shall receive.

The capacity of the rotary kilns in use averages about 125 barrels a day, say six times the capacity of the old intermittent kiln. They require more than twice the fuel of the continuous vertical kiln per barrel of product, so that there is some offset to the saving in labor cost.

Another branch of the process in which there has been great improvement is the grinding of clinker and, where required, of the dry raw materials. There are two general classes of mills; those in which the fine dust is separated from the partly ground material, the latter being returned to the mills; and those in which the process is continued long enough to turn out the finished product of sufficient fineness. There are indications of still further improvement in this direction in the near future in regard to cheapness of operation. It is difficult to conceive of a better result so far as fineness and uniformity of grinding is concerned, any desired degree of pulverization being attainable.

The amount and the rapidity of the development are indicated by following figures, most of them from the reports of the United States Geological Survey:

Year.	No. of Works.	Product.	Value.*
1890	16	335,500	$704,050
1892	16	547,440	1,152,600
1893	19	590,652	1,158,138
1895	22	990,324	1,586,830
1896	26	1,543,023	2,424,011
1897	29	2,677,775	4,315,891
1898	31	3,692,284	5,970,773
1899	..	5,146,064†	
1900	50	9,900,000†	

*The value includes packages prior to 1895. The value in bulk is given in 1895 and later.
†Estimated.

The distribution of the manufacture of Portland cement and the development in the regions named is shown in the following table:

District.	1890. No. Works.	Barrels.	Per Cent.	1898. No. Works.	Barrels.	Per Cent.
New York..............	4	65,000	19.4	7	554,358	15
Lehigh Co., Pa., and.. Phillipsburg, N. J....	5	201,000	60	9	2,674,304	72.4
Ohio..................	2	22,000	6.5	6	265,872	7.2
All other sections.......	5	47,500	14.1	9	197,750	5.4

The principal materials used are the mixtures of cement rock or clay and limestone and the mixtures of clay and marl. The development of the two is proceeding by nearly equal steps. The great majority of the new works are in the Lehigh and related regions of the first class and in the marl region of Ohio, Indiana and Michigan.

The tendency to change in the proportion of cement used of each of the great classes, natural hydraulic, foreign Portland and American Portland is shown by a comparison of the figures for 1893 and 1898, as follows:

Year.	Natural Hydraulic. Barrels.	Per Cent.	Imported. Barrels.	Per Cent.	American Portland. Barrels.	Per Cent.
1893......	7,411,815	69.4	2,674,149	25.1	590,652	5.5
1898......	8,418,924	59.6	2,013,818	14.3	3,692,284	26.1

The gain in the use of American Portland cement on the use of imported Portland cements is shown more clearly thus:

Year.	Per Cent. of American Portland Used.	Per Cent. of Imported Cement Used.
1891	13	87
1896	35	65
1898	65	35
1899	74	26
1900	80*	20

*Estimated.

That this increase in percentage for American cement is due to the increase in the manufacture of American cement is shown by the table of the growth in the American cement industry and by the following, showing the uniformity in the rate of importation of foreign cements:

Year.	Barrels Imported.
1890	2,584,125
1892	2,686,921
1893	2,674,149
1895	2,997,395
1896	2,989,597
1897	2,090,924
1898	2,013,818
1899	2,269,023
1900	2,500,000*

*Estimated.

The rapid development in the use of the rotary kiln is shown as follows, the figures being in thousands of barrels manufactured:

Year.	Barrels by Rotary Kilns.	Barrels by Vertical Kilns.
1893	149,000	441,000
1894	242,000	556,000
1895	400,000	589,000
1896	632,000	910,000
1897	1,311,000	1,366,000
1898	2,170,000	1,521,000

The development in the three or four years next following 1898 is almost entirely by the use of the rotary process, so that when the reports from the factories completed in 1899 and 1900 and to be completed in 1901 and 1902 are available the vertical kiln will be left far in the rear.

The export of cement has but just begun. As the increase in supply becomes equal to the demand competition reduces prices and new markets will be sought. The economies in manufacture which have been introduced recently will enable some factories to compete successfully with cements of other countries in price, as they are now able to compete in quality, and exports may be expected to increase at a satisfactory rate.

TESTING OF CEMENT

The methods of testing cement which are usually considered standard by American engineers are those adopted by the American Society of Civil Engineers in 1885, being recommended by a strong committee with full theoretical and practical knowledge ot the subject. The report of this committee is given almost in full as on the whole the most satisfactory statement of the tests which should be required and the methods of making them. Some special tests which have been developed since 1885 are appended, as well as some comments on the various tests brought out by a committee of the American Society of Civil Engineers in 1898 and 1899:

The testing of cement is not so simple a process as it is sometimes thought to be. No small degree of experience is necessary before one can manipulate the materials so as to obtain even approximately accurate results. The first tests of inexperienced though intelligent and careful persons, are usually very contradictory and inaccurate, and no amount of experience can eliminate the variations introduced by the personal equations of the most conscientious observers. Many things, apparently of minor importance, exert such a marked influence upon the results, that it is only by the greatest care in every particular, aided by experience and intelligence, that trustworthy tests can be made.

The test for tensile strength on a section area of one square inch is recommended, because, all things considered, it seems best for general use. In the small briquette there is less danger of air bubbles, the amount of material to be handled is smaller, and the machine for breaking may be lighter and less costly.

The tensile test, if properly made, is a good, though not a perfect indication of the value of a cement. The time requisite for making this test, whether applied to either the natural hydraulic or the Portland cements, is considerable (at least seven days, if a reasonably reliable indication is to be obtained), and, as work is usually carried on, is frequently impracticable. For this reason short time tests are allowable in cases of necessity, though the most that can be done in such testing is to determine if the brand of cement is of its average quality. It is believed, however, that if a neat cement stands the one-day tensile test, and the tests for checking and for fineness, its safety for use will be sufficiently indicated in the case of a brand of good reputation; for, it being proved to be of average quality, it is fair to suppose that its subsequent condition will be what former experiments, to which it owes its reputation, indicate that it should be. It cannot be said that a new and untried cement will by the same tests be proved to be satisfactory; only a series of tests for a considerable period, and with a full dose of sand, will show the full value of any cement; and it would be safer to use a trustworthy brand without applying any tests whatever, than to accept a new article which had been tested only as cement and for but one day.

The test for compressive strength is a very valuable one in point of fact, but the appliances for crushing are usually somewhat cumbersome and expensive, so much so that it seems undesirable that both tests should be embodied in a uniform method proposed for general adoption. Where great interests are at stake, however, and large contracts for cement depend on the decision of an engineer as to quality, both tests should be used if the requisite appliances for making them are within reach. After the tensile strength has been obtained, the ends of the broken briquettes, reduced to one inch cubes by grinding and rubbing, should be used to obtain the compressive strength.

Fineness.—The strength of a cement depends greatly upon the fineness to which it is ground, especially when mixed with a large dose of sand. It is, therefore, recommended that the tests be made with cement that has passed through a No. 100 sieve (10,000 meshes to the square inch), made of No. 40 wire, Stubbs' wire gauge. The results thus obtained will indicate the grade which the cement can attain, under the condition that it is finely ground, but it does not show whether or not a given cement offered for sale shall be accepted and used. The determination of this question requires that the tests should also be applied to the cement as found in the market. Its quality may be so high that it will stand the tests even if very coarse and granular, and, on the other hand, it may be so low that no amount of pulverization can redeem it. In other words, fineness is no sure indication of the value of a cement, although all cements are improved by fine grinding. The finer the cement, if otherwise good, the larger dose of sand it will take, and the greater its value.

Checking or Cracking.—The test for checking or cracking is an important one, and, though simple, should never be omitted. It is as follows:

Make two cakes of neat cement 2 or 3 inches in diameter, about ½ inch thick, with thin edges. Note the time in minutes that these cakes, when mixed with water to the consistency of a stiff plastic mortar, take to set hard enough to stand the wire test recommended by Gen. Gilmore, 1-12 inch diameter wire loaded with ¼ of a pound, and 1-24 inch loaded with one pound. One of these cakes, when hard enough, should be put in water and examined from day to day to see if it becomes contorted, or if cracks show themselves at the edges, such contortions or cracks indicating that the cement is unfit for use at that time. In some cases the tendency to crack, if caused by the presence of too much unslacked lime, will disappear with age. The remaining cake should be kept in the air and its color observed, which for a good cement should be uniform throughout, yellowish blotches indicating a poor quality; the Portland cement being of a bluish-gray, and the natural cements being light or dark, according to the character of the rock of which they are made. The color of the cements when left in the air indicates the quality much better than when they are put in water.

Tests Recommended.—It is recommended that tests for hydraulic cements be confined to methods for determining fineness, liability to checking or cracking, and tensile strength; and for the latter, for tests of 7 days and upward, that a mixture of 1 part of cement to 1 part of sand for natural cements, and 3 parts of sand for Portland cements, be used, in addition to trials of the neat cement. The quantities used in the mixture should be determined by weight.

The tests should be applied to the cements as offered for sale. If satisfactory results are obtained with a full dose of sand, the trials need go no further. If not, the coarser particles should first be excluded by using a No. 100 sieve, in order to determine approximately the grade the cement would take if ground fine, for fineness is always attainable, while inherent merit may not be.

Your committee thinks it useful to insert here a table showing the average minimum and maximum tensile strength per square inch which some good cements have attained when tested under the conditions specified elsewhere in this report. Within the limits given in the following table, the value of a cement varies closely with the tensile strength when tested with the full dose of sand.

American natural cement, neat:

One day, 1 hour or until set in air, the rest of the 24 hours in water, from 40 pounds to 80 pounds.

One week, 1 day in air, 6 days in water, from 60 pounds to 100 pounds.

One month (28 days), 1 day in air, 27 days in water, from 100 pounds to 150 pounds.

One year, 1 day in air, the remainder in water, from 300 pounds to 400 pounds.

American and foreign Portland cements, neat:

One day, 1 hour, or until set in air, the rest of the 24 hours in water, from 100 pounds to 140 pounds.

One week, 1 day in air, 6 days in water, from 250 pounds to 550 pounds.

One month (28 days), 1 day in air, 27 days in water, from 350 pounds to 700 pounds.

One year, 1 day in air, the remainder in water, from 450 pounds to 800 pounds.

American natural cement, 1 part of cement to 1 part of sand:

One week, 1 day in air, 6 days in water, from 30 pounds to 50 pounds.

One month (28 days), 1 day in air, 27 days in water, from 50 pounds to 80 pounds.

One year, 1 day in air, the remainder in water, from 200 pounds to 300 pounds.

American and foreign Portland cements, 1 part of cement to 3 parts of sand:

One week, 1 day in air, 6 days in water, from 80 pounds to 125 pounds.

One month (28 days), 1 day in air, 27 days in water, from 100 pounds to 200 pounds.

One year, 1 day in air, the remainder in water, from 200 pounds to 350 pounds.

Standards of minimum fineness and tensile strength for Portland cement have been adopted in some foreign countries.

Mixing, Etc.—The proportions of cement, sand and water should be carefully determined by weight, the sand and cement mixed dry, and all the water added at once. The mixing must be rapid and thorough, and the mortar, which should be stiff and plastic, should be firmly pressed into the molds with the trowel, without ramming, and struck off level; the molds in each instance, while being charged and manipulated, to be laid directly on glass, slate or some other non-absorbent material. The molding must be completed before incipient setting begins. As soon as the briquettes are hard enough to bear it, they should be taken from the molds and be kept covered with a damp cloth until they are immersed. For the sake of uniformity, the briquettes, both of neat cement and those containing sand, should be immersed in water at the end of 24 hours, except in the case of one-day tests.

Ordinary, fresh clean water, having a temperature between 60 and 70 degrees F., should be used for the water of mixture and immersion of samples.

The proportion of water required varies with the fineness, age, or other conditions, of the cement, and the temperature of the air, but is approximately as follows:

For briquettes of neat cement: Portland, about 25 per cent.; natural, about 30 per cent.

For briquettes of 1 part cement, 1 part sand: about 15 per cent of total weight of sand and cement.

For briquettes of 1 part cement, 3 parts sand: about 12 per cent. of total weight of sand and cement.

The object is to produce the plasticity of rather stiff plasterer's mortar.

An average of 5 briquettes may be made for each test, only those breaking at the smallest section to be taken. The briquettes should always be put in the testing machine and broken immediately after being taken out of the water, and the temperature of the briquettes and of the testing room should be constant between 60 and 70 degrees F.

The stress should be applied to each briquette at a uniform rate of about 400 pounds per minute, starting each time at 0. With a weak mixture one-half the speed is recommended.

Weight.—The relation of the weight of cement to its tensile strength is an uncertain one. In practical work, if used alone, it is of little value as a test, while in connection with the other tests recommended, it is unnecessary, except when the relative bulk of equal weights of cement is desired.

We recommend that the cubic foot be substituted for the bushel as the standard unit, whenever it is thought best to use this test.

Setting.—The rapidity with which a cement sets or loses its plasticity furnishes no indication of its ultimate strength. It simply shows its initial hydraulic activity.

For purposes of nomenclature, the various cements may be divided arbitrarily into two classes, namely: quick-setting, or those that set in less than half an hour; and slow-setting, or those requiring half an hour or more to set. The cement must be adapted to the work required, as no one cement is equally good for all purposes. In submarine work a quick-setting cement is often imperatively demanded, and no other will answer, while for work above the water line less hydraulic activity will usually be preferred. Each individual case demands special treatment. The slow-setting natural cements should not become warm while setting, but the quick-setting ones may, to a moderate extent, within the degree producing cracks. Cracks in Portland cement indicate too much carbonate of lime, and in the Vicat cements too much lime in the original mixture.

Sampling.—There is no uniformity of practice among engineers as to the sampling of the cement to be tested, some testing every tenth barrel, others every fifth, and still others every barrel delivered. Usually, where cement has a good reputation, and is used in large masses, such as concrete in heavy foundations, or in the backing or hearting of thick walls, the testing of every fifth barrel seems to be sufficient; but in very important work, where the strength of each barrel may in a great measure determine the strength of that portion of the work where it is used, or in the thin walls of sewers, etc., etc., every barrel should be tested, one briquette being made from it.

In selecting cement for experimental purposes, take the samples from the interior of the original packages, at sufficient depth to insure a fair exponent of the quality, and store the same in tightly-closed receptacles impervious to light or dampness until required for manipulation, when each sample of cement should be so thoroughly mixed, by sifting or otherwise, that it shall be uniform in character throughout its mass.

Sieves.—For ascertaining the fineness of cement it will be convenient to use three sieves, viz.:

No. 50 (2,500 meshes to the square inch), wire to be of No. 35 Stubbs' wire gauge.

No. 74 (5,476 meshes to the square inch), wire to be of No. 37 Stubbs' wire gauge.

No. 100 (10,000 meshes to the square inch), wire to be of No. 40 Stubbs' wire gauge.

The object is to determine by weight the percentage of each sample that is rejected by these sieves, with a view not only of furnishing the means of comparison between tests made of different cements by different observers, but indicating to the manufacturer the capacity of his cement for improvement in a direction always and easily within his reach. As already suggested in another connection, the tests for tensile strength should be applied to the cement as offered in the market, as well as to that portion of it which passes the No. 100 sieve.

For sand, two sieves are recommended, viz.:

No. 20 (400 meshes to the square inch), wire to be of No. 28 Stubbs' wire gauge.

No. 30 (900 meshes to the square inch), wire to be of No. 31 Stubbs' wire gauge.

Standard Sand.—The question of a standard sand seems one of great importance, for it has been found that sands looking alike and sifted through the same sieves gives results varying within rather wide limits.

The material that seems likely to give the best results is the crushed quartz used in the manufacture of sand paper. It is a commercial product, made in large quantities and of standard grades, and can be furnished of a fairly uniform quality. It is clean and sharp. As it would be used for tests only, for purposes of comparison with the local standards, and with tests of different cements, not much of it would be required. The use of crushed quartz is recommended by your committee, the degrees of fineness to be such that it will all pass a No. 20 sieve and be caught on a No. 30 sieve. Of the regular grade, from 15 to 37 per cent. of crushed quartz No. 3 passes a No. 30 sieve, and none of it passes a No. 50 sieve. A bed of uniform, clean sand of the proper size of grain has not been found, and it is believed that to wash, dry, and sift any of the available sands would so greatly increase its cost, that the product would not be much cheaper than the crushed quartz, and would be much inferior to it in sharpness and uniform hardness of particles.

Molds.—The molds furnished are usually of iron or brass. Wooden molds, if well oiled to prevent their absorbing water, answer a good purpose for temporary use, but speedily become unfit for accurate work. A cheap, durable, accurate, and non-corrodible mold is much to be desired.

Clips.—In using the clips recommended in the preliminary report, it was found in some instances that the specimens were broken at one of the points where they were held. This was undoubtedly caused by the insufficient surface of the clip, which, forming a blunt point, forced out the material. Where the specimens were sufficiently soft to allow this point to be imbedded, they broke at the smallest section, but when hard enough to resist such imbedding they showed a wedge-shaped fracture at the clips. To remedy this the point should be slightly flattened, so as to allow of more metal surface in contact with the briquette. Clips made in this way have been used, and good results obtained.

There should be a strengthening rib upon the outside of the clips to prevent them from binding or breaking when the specimens are very strong.

The clips should be hung on pivots, so as to avoid, as much as possible, cross strains upon the briquettes.

Machines.—No special machine has been recommended, as those in common use are of good form for accurate work, if properly used, though in some cases these are needlessly strong and expensive. Machines with spring balances are to be avoided, as more liable to error than others.

It is by no means certain that there exists any great difference in well-made machines of the standard forms.

Amount of Material.—The amount of material needed for making five briquettes of the standard size recommended is, for the neat cements, about one and two-thirds pounds, and for those with sand, in the proportion of three parts of sand to one of cement, about one and one-quarter pounds of sand and six and two-thirds ounces of cement.

Accelerated Tests.—Several tests have been used by various authorities which accelerate the action of the ingredients of the cement and thus make it possible to determine its soundness without waiting the long periods of time which are necessary under ordinary conditions. The simplest test of these is the boiling test, and while it is a test which is considered to be rather hard for a cement to pass, most of the American Portland cements and many of the natural hydraulic cements can pass it. In the case of the latter class of cements, however, inability to pass this test does not always prove unsoundness of the cement, for some very excellent natural hydraulic cements have ingredients which can not be expected to pass this test, and still the cement may be entirely satisfactory for the work required of it. With the understanding, therefore, that failure to pass the test should call for further study of a cement rather than for its absolute rejection, the test is one of much value. As presented by Prof. Tetmajer, the pats are put in cold water as soon as possible after gauging, the water is raised in about one hour to boiling temperature and the boiling is continued for three hours. Some slow-setting cements can not be put into the water until they have set. The pats should not have thin edges but should be rolled into balls and carefully flattened. Le Chatelier makes the pats in cylindrical form, 3 centimeters long and the same diameter. An American would make the dimensions each one inch. Needles are set in each end and observations on the distance apart of their points show the amount of swelling. The water is raised to boiling point in fifteen to thirty minutes and maintained there for six hours. The pats are allowed to cool before final measurements are taken. The pats are allowed to set and the test is made within 24 hours after the time of final set. Other accelerated tests use moist hot air, steam and hot water, steam or water under pressure, dry closets under a temperature above boiling point, and a gas flame. The steam and hot water tests are most uniform and satisfactory and the boiling test is much the easiest of application.

Chemical Analysis.—This is of much value in determining the probable characteristics of a new cement and in testing from time to time the freedom of the cement from adulterations. These tests should be intrusted to chemists of experience in analysis of cement, though any competent chemist can make them if necessary.

Adulterations.—Microscopic examination may detect adulteration. Slag adulterant may be detected by stirring the cement into a mixture of methylene iodide and benzine. When allowed to stand the cement will settle to the bottom, with the slag on top. The density of the mixture must be carefully fixed at the desired amount, say 2.95, by adding the proper amount of benzine. Machines are made for tests of abrasion of cement and concrete. A number of other tests are proposed for special purposes, but they need not be considered here, as the tests given are those which are of most value for commercial purposes, and those not mentioned are of little value unless made and interpreted by experts.

In a paper by Prof. W. K. Hatt before the Indiana Engineers' Society occurs the following paragraph, indicating a method of detecting slag adulteration of cement:

The appearance of the slag cement is characterized by a delicate lilac color, in some cases almost white. When cement is made from slag by a process involving roasting the cement is of a dark color like that of ordinary dark colored Portland. It has not the coarse or gritty feeling which characterizes most Portland cement. It works fat, sets slowly and passes ordinary tests of permanence of volume.

A pat of the cement exposed to the air has to be well covered to prevent the surface from cracking. After drying out, it will exhibit discolorations, yellowish or brown, whereas the pat hardened under water will not exhibit such discolorations. The characteristic color of the fracture of a water-hardened briquette is green, but when the briquette dries out the fracture becomes white. The writer has noticed this green color with a subsequent change to white in the case of a well known Portland cement, and also the discolorations in the pat, indicating slag adulteration. The green color is due to the presence in slag cement of sulphide of iron or sulphide of calcium. This sulphide becomes oxidized on exposure to the air and changes color. Slag cements usually contain from 1 to 1½ per cent. of sulphides. It is this tendency to oxidization on exposure to air which is destructive to mortar made of slag cements containing an excess of sulphides and makes it necessary to use the product in underground situations or the interior of thick walls. A parallel test of briquettes hardened in air and water should be made to check up presence of sulphides. This disintegration does not occur in case of all slag cements. It is not a necessary defect.

A committee of the American Society of Civil Engineers had the question of the adoption of standard methods of manipulation of the tests above described under consideration nearly two years, and issued a circular asking for suggestions and criticisms. Forty-five replies were received, which number, in the opinion of the committee, does not indicate a very general interest in the subject, while on many points the replies differ so greatly that the committee has not yet decided upon the formulation of a set of recommendations. It is probably true that the small number of replies is not due so much to the lack of interest in the subject as to the fact that very few persons, aside from the experts who did reply, are able or willing to answer any large number of the questions. The average of the opinions offered may be stated as follows:

Sampling.—The amount of cement to be accepted on the results obtained from a single sample is dependent on the kind and reputation of the cement. The amount and kind of work should also be considered. The amounts mentioned by various engineers vary from a sample from one barrel in three to one in a carload, the preference being for one barrel in ten. The auger or sugar trier is generally used to secure a sample from the center of the package, and nearly all keep samples from the different packages distinct. This is correct, for variation is what is to be detected.

Chemical Analysis.—This is needed only in selecting a new cement for acceptance and in securing data for final condemnation of a brand which is not keeping up to the standard. The elements or compounds which should be determined are magnesia, sulphates and adulterations. Some determine also lime, silica, alumina and iron, making the analysis as complete as that of the manufacturer. Except for use in sea water or in other peculiar surroundings, the whole analysis is not usually required.

Microscopical Tests.—These are generally considered to be unnecessary, but they are of some value in determining adulterants and the character of the grains of cement, thus giving some check on burning and grinding. From a hand-microscope to magnifying powers of 80 to 600 diameters are recommended by various engineers.

Fineness.—Riehle sieves made according to the requirements stated above, with 50, 74 and 100 meshes to the inch, are suggested for natural cement, and those with 74, 100 and 200 meshes for Portland cements. About four ounces is the popular amount to be subjected to test. Hand-shaking is said to be preferable to machine-shaking.

Apparent Density or Weight per Cubic Foot.—There are so many variables that this determination is considered to be of little value. One engineer presents a description of an apparatus for determining the weight of a briquette, correcting it by subtracting the water used.

True Density or Specific Gravity.—A few think this determination is of some value, especially in an investigation of the mode of manufacture, one engineer stating that it is the only test by which the proper calcination of the clinker can be determined.

Standard Sand.—Quartz sand of the standard set above is preferred for tests to be compared with those made by others. For ordinary watch test on accepted brands, the local natural sand, properly sifted to secure uniformity in size, should be sufficient. The size is that passing a No. 20 sieve and refused by a No. 30 sieve.

Preparation of Pastes.—This is the field in which the personal equation of the operator has most effect upon the results of tests and is also that in which conditions for the moment of mixing, of moisture of atmosphere and of materials before mixing, of cement as measured or weighed, of sand and of temperature, are of considerable importance. The general opinion seems to be that the same method of preparation should be used for each test, but the answers in the negative are from persons whose opinions have sufficient weight to leave the question open as yet. The German official rules provide for neat tests for time of setting and soundness, and for tests of sand and cement mortar for strength. The American practice seems to have been to test the cement neat for strength, but the addition of the test of mortar has become popular, and should be provided for in the standard rules. Experience indicates that the results of such tests are the more valuable, when properly made, but that they should not entirely displace the neat cement tests.

Eighty per cent. of the answers say that the proportions of sand, cement and water should be stated by weight. This is unquestionably the safest way to get uniform mixtures, the volume of cement varying so much with the method of handling. Water varies so slightly in weight per unit volume that it can be measured in the most convenient manner. The proportions will be measured by volume in actual work, but they should be fixed originally for the given materials by weight, and the corresponding proportions by volume can then be determined for the working conditions within reasonable limits of variation. As small an amount of water as possible should be used in preparation of the paste. Apparently slight differences in moistness of sand make considerable differences in the amount of water required. If the laboratory is always dry and warm the sand will become so and remain so, while if the laboratory is in a damp cellar or even in a basement dry but cool, in weather with air full of moisture the sand will absorb more or less moisture and the variation in condition of sand will require a variation in the amount of water. It is well known that different brands of cement require materially different proportions of water to make mixtures of the same consistency. Exact proportions of water for all conditions and cements can not be fixed, therefore. The precise temperature of materials and of air is not important, the preference being for temperatures between 60 and 80 degrees Fahrenheit. The hygrometric condition of the air is more important than its actual temperature. The cement and sand should be thoroughly mixed dry and the water added afterward. Some add the water all at once and others add it little by little. Trowels, spatulas, spoons and hands are used for mixing. No machine is comparable for uniformity of results with intelligent hand work by experienced operators. The time required for mixing is as much a matter of judgment as the exact amount of water required to make the stiffest possible paste, and must be learned by varied experience. Mr. Richardson estimates the time at about five minutes for slow-setting cements and less for quick-setting brands.

In all these points the question is not so much what is the best method as what method shall be followed in order to secure uniformity. In each case there is doubless a best method, and if the experts, or any large number of them, can be brought to agreement as to what is the best method, that one should be selected.

But, for example, the strongest briquette is made by using the smallest possible amount of water. This amount can not be exactly determined in advance for all cements and sands under all conditions, and must be left to the individual operator. A lower tensile strength will be found if more water is used, but in such case the exact proportion of water can be fixed by rule, and slight differences in consistency of mortar on account of peculiarities of the materials used will make only slight differences in strength.

Time of Setting.—The standard needles are best, and neat cement pats. Most operators keep the pats under a damp cloth or in damp air. Mr. Richardson says the dampness seriously delays time of setting and change in temperature changes rate of set. Very few would keep the pats in water.

Soundness—Tests for soundness are of great value, some placing them on a par with tests for tensile strength. The standard methods are most popular, but a few recommend the hot water or boiling tests. They hasten the determination. Natural and Portland cements can not be treated alike. Thus pats of natural cement can usually be put in water as soon as made without disintegrating, while some first grade Portland cements will crumble immediately, if so treated. Natural cement may not stand the hot water test, but any normal Portland will do so and nearly all such will stand the boiling test. Pats of Portland cement should remain uniform in color and the edges should remain sharp. Mr. Gowen suggests the bottle test, filling a bottle with a small neck with a cement grout, the sample to be watched for checks and cracks, as well as for cracking of the bottle by expansion. Only a few recommend the boiling test, and they seem to prefer that it be left to the well equipped special laboratory, indicating that failure under the conditions of the ordinary city laboratory should not be taken as certain condemnation of the cement.

Compressive Strength.—With reference to tests of compressive strength, nearly all advise them, one or two depending upon them to the exclusion of those of tensile and transverse strength. The opinion seems to be general that the tests can not be made in a temporary laboratory, must be made in permanent commercial or college laboratories having the necessary machines and experience. Too few have used the method to have any fixed idea as to form and dimensions of test pieces. All would treat the mortar the same as for tension tests. There are several methods of getting a true bearing in the press, truing with trowel, setting against glass and the use of sheets of lead, thick paper or cardboard, plaster of paris, or fine sand. All the prominent machines are mentioned, and the rate of applying the stress varies up to 1,000 pounds a minute.

Tensile Strength.—Opinions are in better accord on these tests than on most others. Most persons are favorable to tests of Portland cement mortar in proportions of 1 to 3, and of natural cement mortar in proportions of 1 to 2. Many are in favor of neat tests only, at least one arguing that mortar tests are little more than tests of fineness of grinding and relative value of different samples of sand. The society's standard form of briquette is satisfactory.

A non-absorbent smooth surface is demanded for mixing cement, marble, slate, glass, or smooth metal. Many finish with trowel on upper side only, but very good reasons are given for compressing the briquette with trowel or knife on both sides. Some fix the consistency of mortar by fixing the percentage of water to be added, nearly all using as little water as possible. A few prefer machine molding of briquettes, the majority preferring handwork, some ramming the cement into the mold and others claiming uniform results from pressing the cement in with fingers or trowel.

The cement is left in the molds until set, then taken out and covered with a damp cloth, or placed in damp air for 24 hours fore placing in water. It is desirable to test briquettes imme ately after removal from water. As to renewal of water, tempe ture and uniformity of temperature, there are many opinions. Co stant temperature, and renewal of the water from time to tin are advisable.

For acceptance tests on ordinary work the general opinion fav breaking briquettes at end of twenty-four hours for natural a of seven days for Portland cement. Longer time tests should made if the short-time tests are unsatisfactory for any reason a more information is desired. A few consider that weighi briquettes before testing gives data as to density, which may of value in giving the reasons for discordant results. Most repli favor the Fairbanks or Riehle form of clip, with rubber bearing as being more certain to cause breaks at the smallest section the briquette, and not at the clip, the latter occurring when the is crushing under the bearing of the clip, bending or twisting of t sample. Uniform rate of application of 400 pounds of stress minute is recommended. With strong cements, the rate at fir may be more rapid, but the latter half or fourth must be appli slowly at a uniform rate. Fairbanks, Riehle, Olsen and Michael machines are recommended. The special precautions to be take are in adjusting the clips, in avoiding the sudden application stress and in breaking briquettes immediately after removal fro the water.

Other Tests.—Bending, adhesion, abrasion, resistance to free ing and resistance to action of sea water are all advised by a fe experts, but there are no settled opinions as to their general val and the methods of making them.

SPECIFICATIONS FOR CEMENT

The general principles upon which specifications for the acceptance or rejection of cement should be prepared may well be stated, and the practical application of these principles exemplified by selections from various specifications in use in various parts of the country. The great variations in specifications for cement for the same uses would seem to be due largely to the failure to recognize such principles, though, when stated, they seem to be axiomatic.

The cement should be suited to the work in which it is to be used. This will decide whether natural hydraulic, or Portland cement shall be used and the grade of the latter. Economy should be one of the elements considered and may turn the decision to a natural cement in one locality while some grade of Portland cement would be used in another. The decision regarding the cement to be used affects the specifications for mortar and concrete also.

The exposure of the work to the weather or its protection from external conditions by position in the interior of piers or foundations or in rock or deep excavations under constant conditions of temperature, moisture, etc., will be prominent in deciding what specification to adopt for the cement to be used.

For external work the conditions of variation in temperature, drainage, possibility of shocks, blows and abrasion, appearance, determine the grade of Portland cement to be used. Here, too, the specifications for mortar and concrete are closely connected with the specification for cement.

In cases of joint action of concrete with other materials, as in Melan arch or fireproofing or other combination structures, other qualities than the tensile or compressive strength may make the decision.

Cement for mortar for laying stone must often be selected for its non-staining qualities.

The rate of setting is frequently a prime factor in making the decision, especially in sidewalk, curb and facing work, and in structures under water.

The extent of the variations in requirements may be seen fro the following table, giving specifications in use in 1898 by variou officers in the U. S. Army, Corps of Engineers, with a few other added for comparison. The information was compiled by Maj C. A. P. Hatfield and put in tabular form by *Engineering News*

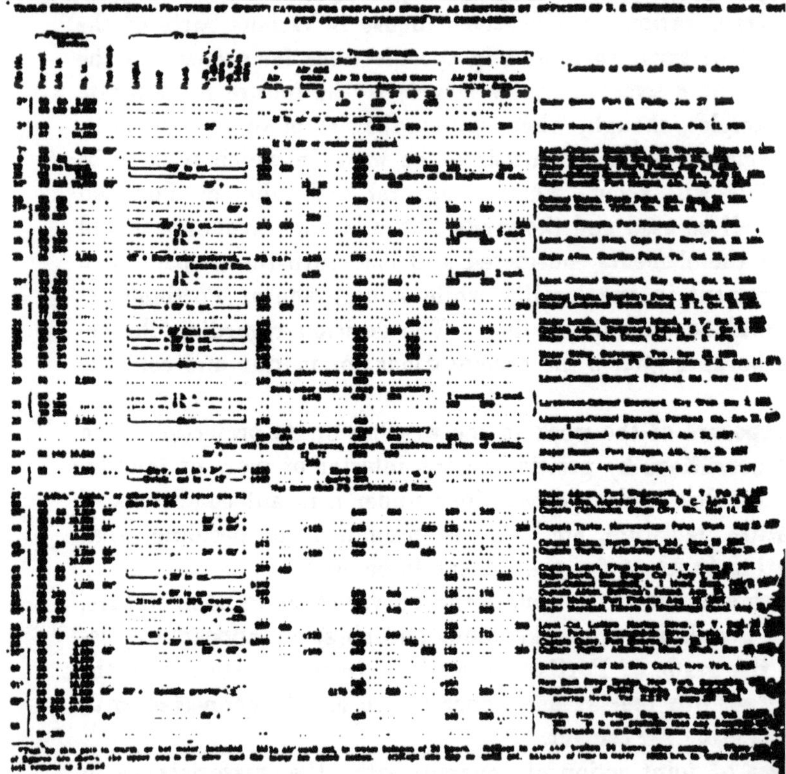

So far as the Corps of Engineers is concerned, many of variations, aside from those necessary to fit the works, have b reduced in amount on account of this comparison, but in muni pal, railroad and other work not under common managem the variations still continue. When averages of numerous spec cations are taken, however, the agreement is quite remark Thus the tensile strengths of neat Portland cement in the aver of European governments, the average of various specification United States government engineers and the average of abo

ment, especially in fineness of grinding and uniformity of calcination have a tendency to raise the standards. The Philadelphia specifications, given below, are perhaps the extreme in municipal work.

The selections from specifications which follow are intended to give the good practice of the day. With two or three exceptions the strictest specifications are not given, and those which indicate a lack of study of the questions involved are also omitted. All of those given have been in use for a sufficient length of time to prove their value under the local conditions.

The following is an abstract of the specifications for the Portland cement in use by the

U. S. NAVY DEPARTMENT.

Quality.—The cement to be of the best grade or quality.

Aeration.—Contractor shall give a certificate to the effect that the cement furnished has been seasoned or subjected to aeration for at least thirty days before leaving the works.

Packing.—The cement is to be packed in strong and well coopered barrels, lined with moisture-proof paper. The gross weight of the barrels is not to be less than 400 pounds; the weight of the cement is not to be less than 375 pounds.

Storage.—Immediately upon receipt, the cement is to be stored in a dry, well-covered and well ventilated place and thoroughly protected from the weather.

Chemical Analysis.—Of every lot of eight hundred barrels or more, the contractor shall supply an abstract of the chemical analysis of a mixed sample of the cement taken from any ten barrels of the lot. Specific gravity shall not be less than 3.

Samples for Test.—Samples of the cement are to be taken from the interior of the barrels with a suitable instrument. Samples are to be taken from every fifth barrel, in lots of twenty or more, [illegible] to one hundred barrels. If less than one hundred barrels are to [illegible] tested, the samples are to be taken from at least three barrels. [illegible] separate quantities so taken shall be mixed thoroughly together, while dry, and the compound regarded as the sample for [illegible]

[illegible]ness.—Ninety-five per cent. by weight must pass through a [illegible] 100 sieve having 10,000 meshes per square inch, the wire to be [illegible] 40 Stubbs' wire gauge, and 75 per cent. by weight must pass through a No. 200 sieve having 40,000 meshes per square inch, the [illegible] to be No. 48 Stubbs' wire gauge.

[illegible] *Qualities.*—Cakes of the paste, mixed as specified in the [illegible] paragraph, are to be moulded on glass; these cakes to be circular in shape, three inches in diameter, one-half inch thick i center and drawn down to one-eighth inch at circumference. Or cake is to set in air, and one cake is to set immersed in water. Tw wires are to be used to determine setting qualities: The firs called wire A, is to be one-twelfth inch in diameter at the lowe extremity and loaded with ¼ lb. at the upper end; and the seconc called wire B, is to be one twenty-fourth inch in diameter at th lower extremity and loaded with 1 lb. at the upper end. Cemen will be considered as quick-setting if it bears needle A withou making an indention during any time between one hour and si hours after having been mixed. The slow-setting cement mus have its final set at the end of eight hours—that is, it must bea needle B without being indented by it.

Neat Cement Paste for Test.—All neat cement for test is to b mixed on glass with clean, fresh water of a temperature betwee 60 degrees and 70 degrees F.; the quantity of the water to var between 20 per cent. and 25 per cent. by weight of the quantit of cement used.

Change of Volume.—A small quantity of the same cemen specified above is to be mixed with only sufficient water to give i the consistency of wet sand, and it is to be immediately presse into a glass tube of about one-half inch in diameter. Within tw or three days any swelling will be shown by the glass bursting; o shrinkage, by the cement becoming loose in tube; either defect is cause for rejection of the cement.

Checking and Cracking.—Three cakes of neat cement are to b prepared as specified in paragraph for setting quality. One cake after having set hard on the glass on which it was moulded, is to b placed in cold water and examined from time to time during period covering seven or twenty-seven days. If it warps, checks or surface, cracks at the edge, or leaves the glass, such defects ar cause for the rejection of the cement. One cake is to be placed in air, and one cake in water kept at a temperature of 212 degrees fo 24 hours and similarly examined.

Sand.—The sand that is to be mixed with the neat cement fo compounding mortar briquettes for test shall be No. 4 standard crushed quartz, passing through a No. 20 sieve (400 meshes to th square inch) wire to be No. 31 Stubbs' wire gauge.

Making the Briquettes.—Neat Briquettes: moisten the cemen with 20 per cent. to 22 per cent. of water, mixing and kneading i quickly by hand, using rubber gloves as protection. When thorough ly worked fill the moulds at once, having first wiped them on th inside with an oily cloth to prevent sticking. Mortar Briquettes one part by weight of cement to three parts by weight of the kin of sand specified in the preceding section shall be thoroughly in corporated while dry and then moistened with 10 per cent. to 12 pe cent. of water in the manner specified above for neat briquette Both the neat and mortar briquettes shall be prepared by the Bohm

Hammer Apparatus, which is a tilt hammer with automatic action. The hammer is driven by a cam wheel of ten cams actuated by simple gearing. The steel hammer weighs 4¼ lbs., and when the intended number of blows has been delivered the mechanism is automatically checked; the proper setting having been made for this purpose before beginning the work. The number of blows for each briquette shall be 150. The briquettes while drying in air should be covered with a damp cloth to prevent rapid surface drying, and to conduce to a uniform set.

Tensile Strength.—The neat briquettes prepared as specified above, shall stand a minimum tensile strain per square inch, without breaking, as follows:

For 12 hrs. in air and 12 hrs. in water..................200 lbs.
For 1 day in air and 6 days in water..................550 lbs.
For 1 day in air and 27 days in water..................650 lbs.

The mortar briquettes, prepared as specified above, shall stand a minimum tensile strain per square inch, without breaking, as follows:

After 12 hrs. in air and 12 hrs. in water...............150 lbs.
After 1 day in air and 6 days in water.................200 lbs.
After 1 day in air and 27 days in water................250 lbs.

Notes.—The boiling water test is designed to ascertain the durability of the cement, and is intended to show in a few hours what would take a long period otherwise. This test is supposed to show whether an excess of free lime is in the cement. Some cements stand well for short periods, but disintegrate after three or four months, due to an excess of free lime.

In making the mortar bricks, the sand and cement should be thoroughly mixed while dry, and then the specified percentage of water added quickly.

The neat tests are of less value than those of briquettes made of sand and cement. The fineness of cement is important; for the finer it is the more sand can be used with it.

Good cement should be a uniform bluish grey color throughout; yellow checks or places indicate an excess of clay or that the cement has not been sufficiently burned; and it is then probably a quick-setting cement of low specific gravity and deficient strength.

Cement that will stand a high test for seven days may have an excess of lime, which will cause it to deteriorate. The twenty-eight day test is, therefore, very useful.

The trip hammer machine for making the briquettes removes all variability in their preparation.

The most dangerous feature in Portland cement is the presence of too much magnesia and an excess of free lime, the latter indicated by the cracks and distortions in the test cakes, and the former in the deficiency of tensile strength of the briquettes. Over 3 per cent. of magnesia is excessive and dangerous.

The cement that is to be made into briquettes and cakes shc not be sifted, but it is to be used exactly as it comes from barrels.

Five briquettes should be broken to test the tensile strength, the extra variation from the mean of the five should not be (15 per cent.

The test for change of volume is very important, for expan in any work into which the cement enters would be fatal to re bility.

The test cakes should be made by rolling the cement into b and then flattening.

The expanding, cracking, and disintegrating of the cemen technically called blowing.

If the cake at the end of three days in water shows no sigr cracking or disintegrating at the edges, it can be considered s

In examining cakes for cracks, the fine air cracks found on surface, that cross and recross each other, are not due to blow but are merely the result of changes of temperature. The cra due to blowing are wedge shaped, running from the center usually accompanied by a certain amount of disintegration, es ially at the edges.

Either Fairbanks or Riehle machines should be used for bre ing briquettes in a test for tensile strength.

The weight per barrel and the weight of barrel vary and specification given above is a valuable one. Thus in 25 barrels standard American and foreign cements the average weight cement per barrel of the seven brands tested varied from 370 to pounds, the weight of barrel varied from 21 to 29 pounds and weight of unbroken package varied from about 394 to 410 pounc

The following is from the specifications in use in the

U. S. ENGINEER'S OFFICE, ST. PAUL, MINN.

The cement shall be first quality Portland cement, fresh, c finely ground, and free from lumps.

The cement must be put up in strong, durable bags, well li with paper, so as to be reasonably secure from air and moistı Each bag shall be labeled with the name of the brand and of manufacturer. Any bags torn or not properly sewed or tied at time of the delivery will be rejected.

No cement will be considered which shows final set in less tl one hour, of which less than 90 per cent. will pass through a si of 100 meshes to the inch, the wire being No. 40 Stubbs' wire gau or which does not show the following strength:

Standard briquettes prepared from neat cement must deve tensile strength per square inch as follows:

After being kept in the air twenty-four hours, 200 pounds.

After being kept in the air twenty-four hours and in water six days, 375 pounds.

After being kept in the air twenty-four hours and in water twenty-seven days, 500 pounds.

Briquettes prepared from one part of cement and three parts sand (by weight) must develop tensile strength per square inch as follows:

After being kept in air twenty-four hours and in water six days, 125 pounds.

After being kept in air twenty-four hours and in water twenty-seven days, 175 pounds.

The sand used in preparing test specimens will be standard crushed quartz sand, of such fineness that it will pass a No. 20 sieve and be retained on a No. 30 sieve. The standard sand shall be supplied free of all charge by the contractor.

A cement that cracks or checks when made into thin pats on a piece of glass, or which develops undue heat when mixed with water, will not be accepted. The cement may be subject to such other tests for soundness as the engineer officer in charge may direct, including the "boiling test."

The cement must not have its initial set within thirty minutes, nor its final set within one hour of the time water is first added to it, and when the pat is kept in a moist air at a temperature of between 65 degrees Fahr. and 70 degrees Fahr. The "initial set" and "final set" as used above being interpreted to mean the time when the pat of cement will allow a wire one-twelfth of an inch in diameter, weighted to one-fourth of a pound, and wire one twenty-fourth of an inch in diameter, weighted to one pound respectively, to rest upon it without penetration.

For railroad work the specifications are very discordant. Of forty-two railroads the few listed in the following table are the only ones having a cement specification, and these vary between wide limits in the qualities required. The table is for Portland cements. A like variation is found in the specifications for natural hydraulic cements.

ABSTRACT OF PORTLAND CEMENT SPECIFICATIONS.

Tensile Strength Required—Neat						Tensile Strength: 1 Cement, 3 Sand.				Tensile Strength: 1 Cement, [illegible] Sand.				Fineness.				Soundness.		Time of Setting as per Am. Soc. C. E. Requirements.		
No. requiring	24 hours [illegible]	No. requiring	7 days, 1 in air, 6 in water	No. requiring	28 days, 1 in air, 27 in water	No. requiring	7 days, 1 in air, 6 in water	No. requiring	28 days, 1 in air, 27 in water	No. requiring	7 days, 1 in air, 6 in water	No. requiring	28 days, 1 in air, 27 in water	No. requiring	No. 50 sieve	No. requiring	No. 100 sieve	No. requiring	Test.	No. requiring	Initial.	Final.
	Lbs.		Lbs.		Lbs.		Lbs.		Lbs.		Lbs.		Lbs.									
[illegible]	[illegible]	1	[illegible]	1	[illegible]	1	125	1	175	1	90	1	145	4	97%	2	[illegible]	4	Cold Pat	1	Not less than 30 Min.	1 hour.
[illegible]	[illegible]	[illegible]	[illegible]	2	[illegible]					1	121	1	175			6	90%	3	Boiling	1	Not less than 35 Min.	[illegible]
[illegible]	[illegible]	[illegible]	[illegible]	1	[illegible]					1	150					1	[illegible]			1	Not less than 1½ h'rs	[illegible] hours
		[illegible]	[illegible]																			
		[illegible]	[illegible]																			
		[illegible]	[illegible]																			

Fuller abstract is made of the specifications for cement used by two roads as an evidence of the requirements made for good railroad work. It will be seen that the number of honest cements which would be rejected by these specifications is small, but that they are sufficient to rule out those which would prove unsatisfactory.

The following are the specifications for cement of the engineering department of the

NEW YORK CENTRAL AND HUDSON RIVER RAILROAD.

Tests.	*Natural Rock.*	*Portland.*
Sieve— No. 50 of 2,500 meshes per square inch of No. 35 Stubbs' wire gauge.	95 % "Fine."	97 % "Fine."
Light Wire— Cement to bear 1/12" diameter wire, weight 4 oz., without imprint, in not less than........................	25 minutes.	25 minutes.
Heavy Wire— Cement to bear 1/24" diameter wire, weight 1 lb., without imprint, in not less than........................	50 minutes.	50 minutes.
Checking, Cracking, and Hot Tests— Flat cakes or "pats" of stiff plastic neat cement paste, two to three inches diameter by half inch thickness, with thin edges to be immersed in water not less than two days.	Must not crack nor become contorted along the edges.	Shall withstand without cracking a temperature of steam or water at 212° Fahr. after 24 hours set in cold water.

Tensile Strength.—Standard briquettes of one square inch of breaking section. Stress applied at a uniform rate, from zero, of about 400 lbs. per minute.

Neat.	*Natural Rock.*	*Portland.*
1 hour in air 23 hours in water.....	60 lbs.	100 lbs.
24 hours in air 6 days in water.................... .	90 "	260 "
24 " 13 "	115 "	350 "
24 " 20 "	132 "	410 "
24 " 27 "	143 "	450 "
Average...	108 lbs.	314 lbs.
Standard Sand.	*1 to 2.*	*1 to 3.*
1 hour in air 23 hours in water.....	27 lbs.	60 lbs.
24 hours in air 6 days in water.........	35 "	90 "
24 " 13 "	43 "	115 "
24 " 20 "	50 "	132 "
24 " 27 "	56 "	143 "
Average............	42 lbs.	108 lbs.

Weight.	*Natural Rock.*	*Portland.*
1 barrel shall contain of neat cement, not less than.....	300 lbs.	386 lbs.

The following are selected from the standard specifications of the maintenance of way department of the

PENNSYLVANIA RAILROAD COMPANY.

Sampling.—The cement for testing shall be selected by taking from each of six well-distributed barrels in each car-load received, sufficient cement to make five to ten briquettes; these six portions, after being thrown together and thoroughly mixed will be assumed to represent the average of the whole car-load.

Fineness.—Not more than 10 per cent. of any cement shall fail to pass through a No. 50 sieve (2,500 meshes per square inch, wire to be No. 35 Stubbs' wire gauge), and not more than 10 per cent. of Portland cement shall fail to pass a No. 100 sieve.

Cracking.—Neat cement mixed to the consistency of stiff plastic mortar and made in the shape of flat cakes, 2 or 3 inches in diameter and one-half inch thick with thin edges, when hard enough shall be immersed in water for at least two days. If they crack along the edges or become contorted, the cement is unfit for use.

Tensile Strength.—The test for tensile strength shall be made with briquettes of standard form recommended by the American Society of Civil Engineers, in moulds furnished by the engineer of maintenance of way. They must have an average tensile strength not less than that given in the table below:

	1 Day.	1 Week.	4 Weeks.
Natural Hydraulic Cement—			
Neat	**70**	**95**	**150**
1 sand to 1 cement	...	**50**	**120**
2 sand to 1 cement	...	**30**	**60**
American and Foreign Portland Cement—			
Neat	**100**	**320**	**450**
2 sand to 1 cement	...	**120**	**175**

Proportion of Water.—The proportion of water used in making briquettes varies with the fineness, age and other conditions of the cement and the temperature of the air, but is approximately as follows: Neat cement, Portland, 20 per cent. to 30 per cent.: 1 sand, 1 cement, about 15 per cent. total weight; 2 sand, 1 cement, about 12 per cent. total weight.

Mixing.—The cement and sand in proper proportions shall be mixed dry and all the water specified added at one time, the mixing to be as rapid as possible to secure a thorough mixture of the materials, and the mortar, when stiff and plastic, to be firmly pressed to make it solid in the moulds without ramming, and struck off level.

Moulding.—The moulds to rest directly on glass, slate, or other non-absorbent material. As soon as hard enough, briquettes are to be taken from moulds and kept covered with a damp cloth until immersed. In the one-day test, briquettes shall remain on the slab for one hour after being removed from mould and twenty-three hours in water. In one week or more test, briquettes shall remain in air one day after being removed from moulds and balance of time in water. Briquettes are to be broken immediately after being taken from the water. Stress to be applied at a uniform rate of 400 pounds per minute, starting each time at zero. No record to be taken of briquettes breaking at other than the smallest section.

Sand.—The sand used in test shall be clean, sharp, and dry, and be such as shall pass a No. 20 sieve (400 meshes per square inch, wire to be No. 28 Stubbs' wire gauge), and to be caught on a No. 30 sieve (900 meshes per square inch, wire to be No. 31 Stubbs' wire gauge).

Water.—Ordinary fresh, clean water having a temperature between 60 degrees and 70 degrees Fahrenheit, shall be used for the mixture and immersion of all samples.

Proportions.—The proportions of cement and sand and water shall in all cases be carefully determined by weight. In preparing briquettes for test, sufficient material is to be taken to make one briquette at a time, and enough of water being added to make a stiff plastic paste as above stated.

The temperature of the testing room shall not be below 45 degrees Fahrenheit.

For concrete work to take the place of stone masonry, Mr. V. K. Hendricks, engineer on one of the western lines of the Pennsylvania system, makes the following requirements in addition to those made above for ordinary work.

Portland Cement.—The cement shall be a true Portland cement, made by calcining a proper mixture of calcareous and clayey earths, and if desired a certified statement shall be furnished of the chemical composition of the cement, and the raw materials from which it is manufactured. Without written authority no Portland cement will be accepted which contains more than two per cent. of magnesia in any form.

The fineness shall be such that at least ninety-nine per cent. shall pass through a standard brass cloth sieve of 50 meshes per linear inch, at least ninety per cent. shall pass through a sieve of 100 meshes per linear inch, and at least seventy per cent. shall pass through a sieve of 200 meshes per linear inch.

Samples for testing may be taken from each and every barrel delivered.

Specimens prepared from neat cement shall after seven days develop a tensile strength of not less than 450 pounds per square inch. Specimens prepared from a mixture of one part of cement and three parts sand, by weight, shall, after seven days, develop a tensile strength of not less than 160 pounds per square inch.

Cement mixed neat with about 27 per cent. of water to form a stiff paste, shall, after thirty minutes, be appreciably indented by the end of a wire one-twelfth inch in diameter, loaded to weigh one quarter pound. Cement made into thin cakes on glass plates shall not crack, scale or warp under the following treatment: Thre pats shall be made and allowed to harden in moist air at from 60 to 70 degrees Fahrenheit: One of these shall be subjected to water vapor at 176 degrees Fahrenheit for three hours, after which it shall be immersed in hot water for forty-eight hours; another shall be placed in water from 60 to 70 degrees Fahrenheit, and the third be left in moist air.

Natural Cement.—Natural cement shall be of such fineness that not less than 90 per cent. shall pass through a standard brass cloth sieve of 50 meshes per linear inch.

Neat cement briquettes shall have a tensile strength of not less than 120 pounds after remaining one day in air and six days in water and shall gain in strength with age. Briquettes of one part of cement and one part sand, by weight, shall at the end of seven days develop a tensile strength of not less than 85 pounds per square inch.

A boiling test will also be made by mixing cakes as above, placing them at once in cold water, raising the temperature of the water to boiling in about an hour, continuing boiling for three hours, and then examining for checking and softening.

Three specifications are given for the cement for concrete arch construction to show the variations in requirements in first-class structures. The specifications for the work are given in a subsequent chapter. The first is for a concrete bridge at Pine Road over Pennypack Creek, Philadelphia, built in 1893, Monier construction, and said to be the first concrete arch highway bridge in the United States. It was designed and construction superintended by the Bureau of Highways of Philadelphia. After careful examination of various brands of cement a single brand of German Portland cement was specified and used, without further specification.

MELAN ARCH BRIDGE, TOPEKA, KAN., 1893.

The second, for a Melan arch bridge constructed at Topeka, Kansas, in 1896, is as follows: The Portland cement shall be a true Portland cement, made by calcining a proper mixture of calcareous and clayey earths; and the contractor shall furnish one or more certified statements of the chemical composition of the cement and of the raw materials from which it is manufactured. Only one brand of Portland cement shall be used on the work, except with permission of the superintendent, and it shall in no case contain more than 2 per cent. of magnesia in any form. The fineness of the cement shall be such that at least 98 per cent. shall pass through a standard brass cloth sieve of 74 meshes per linear inch, and at least 95 per cent. shall pass through a sieve of 100 meshes per linear inch. Samples for testing may be taken from each and every barrel delivered as superintendent may direct. Tensile tests will be made on specimens prepared and maintained until tested at a temperature of not less than 60 degrees F. Each specimen shall have an area of 1 square inch at the breaking section, and, after being allowed to harden in moist air for twenty-four hours, shall be immersed and retained under water until tested. The sand used in preparing the test specimens shall be clean, sharp, crushed quartz, retained on a sieve of 30 meshes per lineal inch, and passed through a sieve of 20 meshes per lineal inch, and shall be furnished by contractor. No more than 23 to 27 per cent. of water by weight shall be used in preparing the test specimens of neat cement and in making the test specimens, 1 of cement to 3 of sand, no more than 11 or 12 per cent of water by weight shall be used. Specimens prepared from neat cement shall after seven days develop a tensile strength not less than 400 pounds per square inch. Specimens prepared from a mixture of 1 part cement to 3 parts sand (by weight), shall, after seven days, develop a tensile strength of not less than 140 pounds per square inch, and after twenty-eight days not less than 200 pounds per square inch. Specimens prepared from a mixture of 1 part cement and 3 parts sand (by weight), and immersed after twenty-four hours in water to be maintained at 176 degrees F. shall not swell or crack, and shall after seven days develop a tensile strength of not less than 140 pounds per square inch. Cement mixed neat with about 27 per cent. of water to form a stiff paste, shall, after 30 minutes, be appreciably indented by the end of a wire 1-12 inch in diameter, loaded to weigh 1-4 pound. Cement made into thin cakes on glass plates shall not crack, scale or warp under the following treatment: Three pats shall be made and allowed to harden in moist air at from 60 degrees to 70 degrees F.; one of these shall be subjected to water vapor at 176 degrees F. for three hours, after which it shall be immersed in hot water for forty-eight hours; another shall be placed in water at from 60 degrees to 70 degrees F., and the third shall be left in moist air. Samples of 1 to 2 mortar and of concrete shall be made and tested from time to time as directed by the superintendent. All cement shall be housed and kept dry till wanted in the work.

A statement is inserted in the specifications calling attention to the severity of the requirements and adding that "it is not probable that any American natural Portlands (so-called) will meet these requirements," a statement which caused considerable unfavorable comment.

MELAN ARCH BRIDGE, AT INDIANAPOLIS, IND., 1900.

The third specification given is for Melan arch bridges constructed in Indianapolis, in 1900.

All cement used for the arches shall be either (one of four brands of German and Danish cement mentioned). Cement for the other parts of the work shall be such as is satisfactory for cement sidewalks, class "B," standard specifications form Q, and must also conform to the general specifications for cement (form H).

The specification for class "B" sidewalks is as follows:

For class "B" sidewalks, the following brands of cement will be allowed: (Fourteen German, Danish and Belgian cements and four American Portland cements are named).

The general specifications for cement (form H) are as follows:

1. Any cement without maker's name and brand on the barrel or package will be rejected without test.

2. All required samples for testing must be furnished by the contractor.

3. A supply of accepted cement must be kept on hand by the contractor.

4. Rejected cement must be removed by the contractor from the work at once.

5. Cement shall be subject to reinspection, test and rejection, if necessary, at any time.

6. All desired information as to place, materials and method of manufacture, and name of makers and agents, shall be furnished whenever desired by the Board of Public Works and City Engineer.

7. Hydraulic cement shall be of the best quality of natural cement, newly manufactured, well housed and preserved dry until required for use. It shall be finely ground, not less than 80 per cent. passing through a sieve of 80 meshes to the lineal inch. When tested neat in the usual manner, it must stand a proof tensile strain of 60 pounds per square inch on specimens allowed to set 30 minutes in air and twenty-four (24) hours under water. It shall also stand 100 pounds when allowed to set one day in air and six days in water, and 150 pounds per square inch when allowed to set one day in air and 27 days in water. When mixed one part of cement and two parts of sand, by weight, it shall stand 30 pounds when allowed to set one day in air and six days in water, and 70 pounds when allowed to set one day in air and 27 days in water, Cakes one-half inch in thickness, with thin edge, shall show no cracks or softness after seven days in water. Certificates of inspection at the mills that the cement fulfills these requirements may be required by the Board of Public Works, the cost of said inspection to be paid by the contractor.

8. Portland cement for concrete, plastering catch-basins and other miscellaneous purposes, shall be equal to the best quality of Portland cement made from selected rock, carefully manufactured, which has been well seasoned and housed and kept dry until required for use. It shall be finely ground, not less than 90 per cent. passing through a sieve of 80 meshes to the lineal inch. Neat cement shall not set in less than one hour unless quick-setting cement is specifically called for, when it shall not set in less than 10 minutes.

When tested in the usual manner it must stand a proof tensile strain of 125 pounds per square inch when allowed to set in air until hard, and the remainder of 24 hours in water. It shall also stand 350 pounds when allowed to set one day in air and six days in water, and 500 pounds when allowed to set one day in air and 27 days in water. When one part of cement is mixed with three parts of sand, by weight, it shall stand 100 pounds per square inch when allowed to set one day in air and six days in water, and 200 pounds when allowed to set one day in air and 27 days in water. Cakes one-half inch in thickness, with thin edges, shall show no cracks, blowing or softness after seven days in water.

9. Portland cement for sidewalks and other work requiring special qualities shall be equal to the best quality of German Portland cement, made from an artificial mixture of proper materials and according to the best methods of mixing, burning and grinding. It must be well seasoned and have been thoroughly well protected from injury by moisture and otherwise. It shall be finely ground, not less than 95 per cent. passing through a sieve of 80 meshes to the lineal inch, and 90 per cent. through a sieve of 100 meshes to the lineal inch. When tested neat in the usual manner, it must stand a proof tensile strain of 475 pounds per square inch when allowed to set one day in air and six days in water, and 550 pounds when allowed to set one day in air and 27 days in water. When mixed one part of cement with three parts of sand, by weight, it shall stand 150 pounds when allowed to set one day in air and six days in water, and 250 pounds when allowed to set one day in air and 27 days in water. Cakes of cement left 24 hours in boiling water shall show no signs of cracks, blowing or softness. Any brand of Portland cement which at any time appears inferior or shows a backward tendency, signs of deterioration or blowing, will be at once rejected, no matter how good previous tests may have been, and any work done with such cement must be at once removed and replaced as the engineer may direct, and without extra allowance to the contractor therefor. Uniformity in quality is essential in this grade of cement, and any cement which fails to give uniform results under uniform and approved treatment will be rejected even if it complies with the specifications in other respects. Evidence of the actual conduct of cement in sidewalks will also be required in case of cements not now in use in the city.

10. Brands of Portland cement which have been tested in the laboratory and are satisfactory for sidewalk construction are more specifically mentioned under specifications for "Cement Sidewalks, Form O." The brands of cement specified under "Cement Sidewalks, Form Q," as may be tested and found to comply with these specifications, can be used provided the following conditions are fulfilled:

First. All cement shall be shipped here in barrels.

Second. The cement companies shall send with every shipment of cement a sworn statement, showing the length of time the cement has been stored, the result of seven-day, twenty-eight-day, and fifty-six-day tests, using one part of cement to three parts of sand, by weight, in making briquettes. Cement from one barrel out of each lot of ten barrels of a shipment shall be tested. The test shall be made by a firm of cement testers, satisfactory to the City Civil Engineer, and each barrel of a shipment shall be stamped with the initials of the cement tester, the date when cement was tested, and the number of the barrel.

Third. A chemical analysis of the cement shall be made by a chemist, satisfactory to the Board of Public Works and the City Civil Engineer; all expense of said analysis shall be borne by the cement company furnishing the cement, or its agent.

The following specification for cement used in sea-water is taken from those for

WALLABOUT IMPROVEMENT, BROOKLYN, N. Y.

All the cement to be furnished under this contract must be of the class of such material known as high-grade Portland cement, free from lumps, dry and finely ground, and *unless as otherwise specified* must be of one or more of the following brands (three German brands named). Cement of other brands may be furnished provided the contractor submits proof satisfactory to the engineer that it has been used in making large masses of concrete, which have been exposed to the action of sea-water for at least two years previous to the date of this contract, and that such concrete now shows no signs of deterioration which might be imputed to defective qualities in the cement.

All the cement shall be composed of lime, silica and alumina in their proper forms and proportions, be as free as possible from all other substances and contain no adulterant in injurious proportions. The ratio of the weight of silica and alumina to the weight of the lime in the cement shall not be less than 45 to 100. The cement shall not contain more than 3 per cent. of magnesia nor more than 1 per cent. of sulphuric acid.

The cement shall not have a lower specific gravity than 3.10.

All the cement shall be of a fineness so that 99 per cent. by weight shall pass through a No. 50 sieve of No. 35 wire; 90 per cent. shall pass through a No. 100 sieve of No. 40 wire; and 70 per cent. shall pass through a No. 200 sieve of No. 45 wire, Stubbs' gauge.

The cement must not take its initial set in less than 30 minutes after mixing. It shall take its hard set in not less than 3 hours, and in not more than 8 hours.

The cement will be said to have attained its initial and its hard set when it bears without indentation respectively a wire 1-12 inch in diameter loaded to weigh 1-4 pound, and a wire of 1-24 inch in diameter loaded to weigh 1 pound, it having been previously mixed neat with about 25 per cent. of its weight of water and worked for from 1 to 3 minutes into a stiff plastic paste.

All the cement shall be capable of developing a tensile strength under various conditions as follows:

	Age.	Tensile Strength.
Mixed neat with about 25% of water by weight and worked to stiff plastic paste.	24 hours, in water after hard set...............	150
	7 days, 1 in air 6 in water 70°.................	400
	28 days, 1 in air 27 in water 70°................	600
Mixed with 3 parts sand by weight and 12% water to stiff plastic paste.	7 days, 1 in air 6 in water 70°.................	150
	28 days, 1 in air 27 in water 70°................	240

To determine the tensile strength four briquettes of the cement under each of the above conditions will be broken in a Riehle or Fairbanks or other testing machine satisfactory to the engineer.

The sand to be used in making briquettes will be clean, dry, crushed quartz, trap-rock or granite, passing a No. 20 sieve of No. 28 wire and caught on a No. 40 sieve of No. 31 wire, Stubbs' gauge. The briquettes will be of the form recommended by the American Society of Civil Engineers.

All cement must be sound in every respect and show no indications of distortion, change of volume or blowing when subjected in the form of pats to exposure in air and fresh and sea water of temperature from 60 degrees to 212 degrees, as follows: The pats will be made of neat, unsifted cement, mixed with fresh water to the same consistency as before stated for briquettes, and will be about 3 inches in diameter, having a thickness at the center of about ½ inch, tapering to about ⅜ inch at the edges. They will be moulded on plates of glass and kept thereon during examination. (a) One or more of these pats will, when set hard, be placed in fresh water of temperature between 60 degrees and 70 degrees for from 1 to 28 days. (b) One or more of these pats will be allowed to set in moist air at a temperature of about 200 degrees for about 3 hours. It will then be placed and kept in boiling water for a period of from 6 to 24 hours. (c) One or more of these pats will be allowed to set in moist air at a temperature of about 100 degrees for 3 hours; it will then be placed and kept in water of temperature of 110 degrees to 115 degrees for a period of from 24 to 48 hours. (d) One or more of these pats may be subjected to any or all of the above indicated tests (a, b and c) using sea water instead of fresh water. (e) One pat will be kept in the air for 28 days and its color observed, which shall be uniform throughout, of a bluish gray, and free from yellow blotches. A failure to pass test (b) will not necessarily cause the rejection of the cement, provided it passes the other tests for soundness as noted in (a, c, d and e) and is satisfactory in other respects to the engineers.

All the above tests may be modified and other tests in addition thereto or in substitution therefor required at the discretion of the engineer to practically determine the fitness of the cement for its intended use.

The contractor pays the cost of tests of cement which are to be made by the engineer of the work or by one or more of three testing laboratories mentioned.

As many tests as desired by the engineer must be made for composition and specific gravity and one sample shall be tested for each 100 barrels for fineness, set, tensile strength and soundness.

All the cement must be furnished in the original package in strong, substantial barrels, which shall be plainly marked with the brand or mark of the maker of the cement. Each barrel must be properly lined with paper or other material so as to effectually protect the cement from dampness. Any cement damaged by water to such an extent that the damage can be ascertained from the outside will be rejected *in toto* and the barrels unopened. Barrels containing a large proportion of lumps will also be rejected. Broken barrels of cement, if otherwise satisfactory, will be counted as half-barrels.

The engineer makes the tests upon such proportions of the whole amount of cement as he sees fit and his decision is final. He can refuse to accept cement without test and without giving his reasons.

There are one or two interesting points in the following from the specifications for the

PENNSYLVANIA AVENUE SUBWAY, PHILADELPHIA.

All the brick work of the sewers except that in the wellholes was laid in natural hydraulic cement mortar. In the wellholes Portland cement was specified. In all cases the proportions were 1 of cement to 2 of sand. All concrete used was composed of 1 part natural hydraulic cement, 2 parts sand and 4 parts of stone or furnace slag.

Briquettes, 1 square inch in section made from the natural hydraulic cement mortar in the mixing box on the work were required to develop tensile strength of 40 pounds after 1 day in air and six days in water. Portland cement mortar under like conditions must show 150 pounds, tensile strength.

The other requirements of natural hydraulic cement were as follows: Weight shall not be less than 112 pounds per imperial bushel; residue on No. 50 sieve not over 4 per cent., by weight, on a No. 100 sieve 25 per cent., on a No. 200 sieve 50 per cent. Pats of cement ½ inch thick, 60 degrees to 70 degrees F., shall develop initial set in not less than 10 minutes and hard set in not less than 30 minutes, the amount of water being just sufficient to form a stiff plastic paste. The tensile strength required was 75 pounds in 24 hours, in water after hard set; 150 pounds, 1 day in air and 6 days in water; 250 pounds, 1 day in air and 27 days in water. Mortar of 1 cement to 1 of standard quartz sand must show 75 pounds tensile strength in 7 days.

For municipal work the city of Philadelphia has the strongest specifications for cement. The city has a complete testing laboratory under the Bureau of Surveys, Department of Public Works, and a complete organization for keeping close watch of the materials in use, and can do so at comparatively slight expense.

DEPARTMENT OF PUBLIC WORKS, PHILADELPHIA.

1. *Inspection.*—All cements shall be inspected, and those rejected shall be immediately removed by the contractor. The contractor must submit the cement, and afford every facility for inspection and testing, at least twelve (12) days before desiring to use it. The engineer in charge of testing laboratory shall be notified at once upon the receipt of each shipment of cement on the work.

2. *Packages.*—No cement will be inspected or allowed to be used unless delivered in suitable packages properly branded.

3. *Storage.*—On all main sewers, bridges (unless otherwise ordered), and such branch sewers or other work as the chief engineer may designate, shall be provided a suitable house for storing the cement.

4. *Protection.*—Accepted cement, if not used immediately, must be thoroughly protected from the weather, and never placed on the ground without proper blockings, and may be re-inspected at any time.

5. *Failure.*—The failure of a shipment of cement on any work to meet these requirements may prohibit further use of the same brand on that work.

The acceptance of a cement to be used shall rest with the chief engineer, and will be based on the following requirements:

Natural Cement.

6. *Specific Gravity and Fineness.*—Natural cement shall have a specific gravity of not less than 2.9, and shall leave, by weight, a residue of not more than two (2) per cent. on a No. 50 sieve, fifteen (15) per cent. on a No. 100 sieve, and thirty (30) per cent. on a No. 200 sieve. The sieves being of brass wire cloth, having approximately 2,400, 10,200 and 35,700 meshes per square inch; the diameter of the wire being .0090, .0045 and .0020 of an inch respectively.

7. *Constancy of Volume.*—Pats of neat cement one-half (½) inch thick with thin edges, immersed in water after "hard" set, shall show no signs of "checking" or disintegration. Similar pats in air shall show no signs of blotching, checking, or disintegration.

8. *Time of Setting.*—It shall develop "initial" set in not less than ten (10) minutes, or "hard" set in less than thirty (30) minutes. This being determined by means of the Vicat needle from pastes of neat cement of normal consistency, the temperature being between 60 degrees and 70 degrees F.

9. *Tensile Strength.*—Briquettes, one (1) square inch in cross section, shall develop the following ultimate tensile strengths:

Age.	Strength.
hours (in water after "hard" set)	100 lbs.
days (1 day in air, 6 days in water)	200 lbs.
days (1 day in air, 27 days in water)	300 lbs.
days (1 day in air, 6 days in water) 1 part of cement to 2 parts of standard quartz sand	120 lbs.
days (1 day in air, 27 days in water) 1 part of cement to 2 parts of standard quartz sand	200 lbs.

Portland Cement.

10. *Specific Gravity and Fineness.*—Portland cement shall have a specific gravity of not less than 3.1, and shall leave, by weight, a residue of not more than one (1) per cent. on a No. 50 sieve, ten (10) per cent. on a No. 100 sieve, and twenty-five (25) per cent. on a No. 200 sieve. The sieves being the same as previously described.

11. *Constancy of Volume.*—Pats of neat cement one-half (½) inch thick with thin edges, immersed in water after "hard" set shall show no signs of "checking" or disintegration. Similar pats in air shall show no signs of blotching, checking or disintegration.

12. *Time of Setting.*—It shall require at least twenty (20) minutes to develop "initial" set under the same conditions as specified for natural cement.

13. *Tensile Strength.*—Briquettes of cement one (1) inch square in cross section, shall develop the following ultimate tensile strengths:

Age.	Strength.
hours (in water after "hard" set)	175 lbs.
days (1 day in air, 6 days in water)	500 lbs.
days (1 day in air, 27 days in water)	600 lbs.
days (1 day in air, 6 days in water) 1 part of cement to 3 parts of standard quartz sand	170 lbs.
(1 day in air, 27 days in water) 1 part of cement to 3 parts of standard quartz sand	240 lbs.

Sulphuric Acid.—It shall not contain more than one and three-quarters (1¾) per cent. of anhydrous sulphuric acid, (SO_3).

15. *Additional Requirements.*—All cements shall meet such additional requirements as to "hot water," "set," and "chemical," tests, as the chief engineer may determine. The requirements for "set," may be modified where the conditions are such as to make it

and the briquettes so formed placed upon a glass plate and k there until put in water.

Sand for Briquettes.—The sand used in preparing briquet shall be, unless otherwise specified, clean, sharp, crushed quar crushed so that the whole of it will pass through a No. 20 sie and be retained on a No. 30 sieve.

Pats for Tests.—Round pats of neat cement, about three (inches in diameter, one-half an inch thick at the center a tapering to a feather edge, mixed in the same manner as the ne cement briquettes and placed on a glass plate, shall not show a signs of warping or cracking after twenty-eight (28) days either air or water.

Cement that Swells to be Rejected.—Any cement which sho signs of swelling, after being mixed, will be rejected.

Fineness of Portland Cement.—Portland cement shall ground to such a degree of fineness that not less than 98 per cen by weight shall pass a No. 50 sieve, and not less than 90 per cen by weight pass a No. 100 sieve.

Tensile Strength of Portland Cement—Neat.—The ultima tensile strength of briquettes, one square inch in cross sectio made of neat Portland cement, shall be as follows:

One day in air and six days in water, 375 pounds.

One day in air and 27 days in water, 510 pounds.

Tensile Strength of Portland Cement—3 to 1.—The ultima tensile strength of briquettes one square inch in cross section, ma of one part by weight of Portland cement and three parts of san shall be as follows:

One day in air and 6 days in water, 120 pounds.

One day in air and 27 days in water, 190 pounds.

Fineness of Natural Cement.—Natural cement shall be grou to such degree of fineness that not less than 88 per cent. by weig will pass a No. 50 sieve, and not less than 77 per cent. by weig pass a No. 100 sieve.

Tensile Strength of Natural Cement—Neat.—The ultimate te sile strength of briquettes one square inch in cross section, made neat natural cement, shall be as follows:

One hour in air and 23 hours in water, 70 pounds.

One day in air and 6 days in water, 110 pounds.

One day in air and 27 days in water, 180 pounds.

Tensile Strength of Natural Cement—2 to 1.—The ultimate te sile strength of briquettes, one square inch in cross section, ma of one part, by weight, of natural cement and two parts of san shall be as follows:

One day in air and 6 days in water, 50 pounds.

One day in air and 27 days in water, 80 pounds.

Additional Tests.—In addition to the tests above specified, cement used on city work shall be subject to such other tests as w necessary to determine whether the cement possesses the proper alities for the particular work for which it is designated.

Should there be discovered at any time, any characteristics in y cement being used on any city work that are objectionable in at or any similar work, the further use of cement of this same and on all work of the same class will be prohibited, regardless of e fact that it has successfully withstood the tests hereinbefore ecified.

The city of Detroit does not require so much in variety of test nd may secure cement under its specifications which, while passing he tests required, is deficient in a marked degree in other respects

BOARD OF PUBLIC WORKS, DETROIT, MICH.

Cement to be put up in cloth or paper sacks, original packages, ach sack to be branded with the name of the manufacturer or anufacturers, and to contain 95 pounds net of Portland cement, r 132½ pounds net of natural cement, and to be delivered in such antities and at such times as the Board of Public Works ma rect, unloaded in a warehouse which shall be located on the rail ad, between 12th and Riopelle streets, south of Michigan avenue, Gratiot avenue, in the city of Detroit, and no extra charge shall made for storage or delivery.

A man satisfactory to the Board of Public Works shall be furshed by the contractor to assist in loading.

The sacks to be the property of the city of Detroit, and each bidr shall state in connection with his bid, the price per cloth sack he ll pay for each empty sack delivered at the warehouse aforesaid.

The Board of Public Works reserves the right to reject any ment considered by said Board not equal in quality to the standd above mentioned.

Portland Cement shall be of American manufacture, and shall and a test of 130 pounds per square inch tensile strain, when made to briquettes and exposed in air until final set and the balance of hours immersed in water. One day in air and 6 days in water all show a tensile strength of 380 pounds; 1 day in air and 27 in ter shall show a tensile strength of 520 pounds, and when mixed proportion by weight of one of cement to two of sand, in 7 days all stand a tensile strain of 146 pounds, and in 28 days a n of 216 pounds.

fineness, 95 per cent. shall pass through a No. 50 sieve.

Natural Cement shall be of American manufacture, and shall the test of sixty (60) pounds per square inch tensile strain hen made into briquettes, exposed 1 hour in air and immersed for enty-three (23) hours in water; and when mixed in proportions y weight of 1 of cement to 2 of sand, and exposed 1 day in air and days in water, it shall stand a tensile strain of at least fifty (50) unds per square inch; and in fineness not less than 90 per cent.

must pass through a sieve of twenty-five hundred (2500) meshes to the square inch.

The following cement specifications for 1901, from a city of 90,-000 inhabitants are presented as an unsatisfactory set, which will permit the use of poor cement of both kinds unless arbitrary rejections are made outside the letter of the specifications.

INSUFFICIENT SPECIFICATIONS.

Cement shall be of the best quality of Louisville cement or of cement equal in all respects thereto, fine ground, quick setting, capable when made into testing blocks of withstanding a tension of 60 pounds per square inch of section, when mixed pure and exposed in air 1 hour and 23 hours in water.

Cement shall be kept under cover until used and samples given in such manner as may be directed. Any cement exposed to water after testing will not be used. All cement not accepted must be immediately removed from the works.

The contractor must furnish the cement in strong, perfect paper sacks to any part of the works and in such quantities as the Commissioner of Public Works may direct and only upon the written order of said Commissioner. Bids to specify the price per hundred pounds at which the cement is to be furnished. To be weighed on the public scales.

The cement used for the curbing and tiling shall be of the best quality of American or imported Portland cement, capable of withstanding a tensile strength of 500 pounds to the square inch when mixed neat and allowed to stand 1 day in air and 6 days in water.

For sewer work the following are given as examples of practice:

DEPARTMENT OF SEWERS, READING, PA.

Composition.—Magnesia not over 2½ per cent.; sulphuric acid not over 2 per cent.

Fineness.—Ninety-five per cent. through a No. 100 sieve; 80 per cent. through a No. 200 sieve.

Checking and Cracking.—Two cakes of neat cement to be moulded on glass. One to be immersed in cold water, after having set hard, and examined from day to day for surface checking and warping, the other having been set hard to be immersed in water at 212 degrees F., and allowed to remain in water of that temperature for 24 to 36 hours. Examination of the pat at the end of that time for constancy of volume and checking. Should the pats become contorted or show signs of warping or cracking the cement

CITY ENGINEER'S OFFICE, PEORIA, ILL

Natural Hydraulic Cement.—All cement shall be what is commonly known as American natural hydraulic cement, of quality equal to the best obtainable in the market. It will be subject to rigid inspection and must be able to stand the following tests: Two cakes 3 inches in diameter and ½ inch thick with thin edges, will be made. One of these cakes as soon as set will be placed in water and examined from day to day. If the cake exhibits checks, cracks or contortions, the cement will be rejected. The other cake described will be used for setting and color tests. The time will be noted when the cake has become hard enough to sustain a wire 1-12 inch in diameter loaded with 1-4 pound. When the wire is sustained the cement has begun to set and this time shall not be less than 30 minutes. When the cake will sustain a wire 1-24 inch in diameter loaded with 1 pound, the test is complete, and this time must not be less than 1 hour nor more than 3 hours. The cake used for setting test will be preserved and when examined from day to day must be of uniform color, exhibiting no blotches or discolorations. The cement must be evenly ground and when tested with the following standard sieves must pass at least the following percentages: No. 20 sieve, 100 per cent.; No. 50 sieve, 90 per cent.; No. 74 sieve, 80 per cent. All cement for test briquettes, whether to be used neat or with sand, will be mixed with barely sufficient water to make a stiff dough or mortar. The sand for cement tests will be of such fineness that all will pass a sieve of 20 meshes per lineal inch, and none of it pass a sieve of 30 meshes per lineal inch. It will be the best quality obtainable of washed river sand. The required tensile strength per square inch shall be as follows: Neat cement, 1 day, till set in air, remainder of time in water, 60 pounds; 1 day in air, 6 days in water, 100 pounds; cement 1 part and sand 2 parts, 1 day in air, 6 days in water, 65 pounds.

A few samples of specifications for cement for foundations are given; first for foundation of standpipe.

WATER WORKS DEPARTMENT, ST. LOUIS, MO.

All cement for the work herein specified shall be of the best quality of American Portland. Cement without the manufacturer's brand will be rejected without test. All cement furnished will be subject to inspection and rigorous tests of such character as the Water Commissioner shall determine, and any cement which in the opinion of the Water Commissioner is unsuitable for the work herein specified, will be rejected.

If a sample of the cement shows by chemical analysis more than 2 per cent. of magnesia (Mg O) or more than 1½ per cent. anhydrous sulphuric acid (SO) the shipment will be rejected.

To secure uniformity in cement of approved brands all ce[ment] received on the work shall be subject to tests for checking or cracking and to the following tests for fineness and tensile strength.

All cement shall be fine ground and 85 per cent. shall pa[ss] a sieve having 10,000 meshes to the square inch.

All cement shall be capable of withstanding a tensile stress of [illegible] pounds per square inch of section when mixed neat, made into b[riquettes] and exposed 24 hours in air and 6 days in water.

All cement shall be put up in well-made barrels and all sh[ort] weight or damaged barrels will be rejected. Samples for tes[ting] shall be furnished at such times and in such manner as may be [re]quired. On all barrels of rejected cement inspection marks wil[l be] placed, and the contractor shall in no case allow these barrels t[o be] used.

In measuring cement for mortar or concrete, the standard vol[ume] of a barrel of cement shall be determined by comparing its n[et] weight with the weight of one cubic foot of thoroughly compa[cted] neat cement.

All cement for use on the works shall be kept under co[ver,] thoroughly protected from moisture, raised from the ground [by] blocking or otherwise, and dry until used. The contractor s[hall] keep in storage a quantity of accepted cement sufficient to se[cure] the uninterrupted progress of the work.

Accepted cement may be re-inspected at any time and if found [to] be damaged or of improper quality will be rejected. All reje[cted] cement shall be at once removed from the work.

PHILADELPHIA ARCHITECTS

Portland Cement.—Chemical Composition.—The cement m[ust] show less than 2 per cent. of sulphuric acid and less than 2½ [per] cent. of magnesia.

Fineness.—Ninety per cent. shall pass a No. 70 sieve; 85 to [?] per cent. shall pass a No. 100 sieve; 68 to 70 per cent. shall pa[ss a] No. 200 sieve.

Checking, Cracking and Color.—Three cakes of neat cement [are] to be moulded on glass 2 or 3 inches in diameter and about ½ i[nch] thick at the center, the edges being very thin. These cakes ar[e to] be made from a mixture of the cement and water to the consiste[ncy]

ined from day to day to ascertain if it becomes contorted, or if cracks show themselves at the edge.

Tensile Strength.—Neat cement, 7 days, 400 to 500 pounds; 28 days, 600 pounds; mortar, 3 to 1, 7 days, 150 pounds; 28 days 250 pounds.

THE USES OF CEMENT

The expansion of the field occupied by cement construction is so great and so rapid that such a chapter as this requires frequent revision to keep it up to date. Many of the uses to which cement is put are considered in detail in the following chapter on Specifications for the Use of Cement. Some others may be mentioned here as well as some methods of modifying the quality, characteristics and appearance of cement for various reasons.

The first and most important use of cement is in making mortar, for brick and stone masonry and concrete. There are so many variations in materials and proportions that the chapters on Specifications can give but a part of them, those in most common use, and those chapters contain, perhaps, sufficient detail regarding the proper places to use the various mixtures. Some consideration of the cost of mortars of various proportions and of concrete may be of value, not as giving exact figures for such cost, but as giving the principle upon which an investigation may be made in any particular case. The following is from a consideration of some experiments in this line by L. C. Sabin, U. S. Assistant Engineer, in *Municipal Engineering Magazine*:

INGREDIENTS OF A CUBIC YARD OF CEMENT MORTAR AND OF CONCRETE AND THE COST.

1. The character of the ingredients used in making cement mortar varies so much that it is difficult to accurately determine the cost of a proposed mortar except by experimenting with the materials that are to be employed. The weights per cubic foot of both cement and sand vary greatly according to the conditions of packing, the moisture, etc. The percentage of voids in the sand is one of the most important variations affecting the amount of mortar made with certain materials mixed in given proportions. The consistency of the mortar also has a marked effect, and different cements show a considerable variation in the volume of mortar that a given weight will yield. In any general treatment of the question, then, we may expect only approximate results, and the discussion here given must be considered in this light.

2. The experiments, from which tables 1 and 2 were derived,

were made with a natural sand weighing 100 pounds to the cubic foot, dry, and having about three-eighths of the bulk voids. The grains varied in size from 0.01 inch to 0.1 inch in diameter, with a few grains outside of these limits. The consistency of the mortar was such that when struck with the shovel blade the moisture would glisten on the smooth surface thus formed. In the experiments the proportions were determined by weight, and the results for proportions by volume were deduced from them. The results for neat, natural cement mortar and for the natural cement mortars containing more than four parts sand by weight were derived by analogy.

EXPLANATION OF TABLES.

3. The first section of table 1 gives the amount of materials required for Portland cement mortar when the proportions are stated by weight; the second and third sections refer to proportions by volume of loose sand to packed cement when the size of the cement barrel is assumed at 3.65 cubic feet and 3.33 cubic feet respectively. The fourth section gives the materials required when the proportions are given in terms of volume of loose sand to loose cement. Likewise, the first section of table 2 for natural cement refers to proportions by weight; the second, third and fourth sections, to proportions by volume of loose sand to packed cement when the cement weighs 265 pounds, 280 pounds and 300 pounds net per barrel respectively; while the fifth section refers to proportions of loose sand to loose cement.

The method of stating proportions by weight is the most accurate, but when the sand does not approximate the weight of 100 pounds per cubic foot when shoveled dry into a measure, the sections of the tables referring to weight proportions may require a correction, and it may be simpler to use the sections giving proportions by volume of loose sand to packed cement. The method of stating proportions by volume of loose sand to loose cement is to be deprecated, but since it is occasionally used provision is made for it in the tables.

In using those portions of the tables where the proportions are stated by volume it should be borne in mind that if the sand is damp when used it will weigh less per cubic foot; hence more, by measure, will be required to make a cubic yard of mortar.

COST OF MORTAR.

4. With the data given in tables 1 and 2 and a knowledge of the prices of the materials used in the mortar, one may estimate the cost of the materials in a given quantity of mortar. The cost of mixing will, of course, depend upon the cost of labor, the method employed, etc., and may vary from fifty cents to a dollar and fifty cents per cubic yard. If we assume for illustration that natural cement can be delivered on the mixing platform for $1.10 per barrel of 280 pounds net, that sand costs 60 cents per cubic

TABLE 1.—INGREDIENTS REQUIRED FOR ONE CUBIC YARD OF MORTAR—PORTLAND CEMENT.

[Sand weighs about 100 pounds per cubic foot. Voids ⅜ of volume.]

Parts sand to 1 of cement.	Proportions by weight, dry sand and cement.			Proportions by volume, dry loose sand to packed cement; packed cement assumed at 104 pounds per cu. ft. or 380 pounds per bbl. of 3.65 cu. ft.			Proportions by volume, dry loose sand to packed cement; cement assumed at 114 pounds per cu. ft. or 380 pounds per bbl. of 3.33 cu. ft.			Proportions by volume, dry loose sand to loose cement; loose cement assumed at 85 pounds per cu. ft.		
	Cement.			Cement.			Cement.			Cement.		
	Pounds.	Bbls. of 380 pounds net.	Sand, cu. yard.	Pounds.	Bbls. of 380 pounds net.	Sand, cu. yard.	Pounds.	Bbls. of 380 pounds net.	Sand, cu. yard.	Pounds.	Bbls. of 380 pounds net.	Sand, cu. yard.
a	b	c	d	e	f	g	h	i	j	k	l	m
0	2,810	7.40	0.00	2,810	7.40	0.00	2,810	7.40	0.00	2,810	7.40	0.00
1	1,555	4.08	0.57	1,585	4.17	0.56	1,640	4.32	0.54	1,440	3.79	0.64
2	1,050	2.76	0.78	1,080	2.84	0.77	1,140	3.00	0.74	980	2.46	0.81
3	760	2.00	0.84	785	2.06	0.84	850	2.24	0.82	660	1.74	0.87
4	600	1.58	0.88	615	1.62	0.88	665	1.75	0.87	515	1.36	0.90
5	490	1.29	0.91	505	1.33	0.90	550	1.45	0.89	425	1.12	0.92
6	420	1.10	0.93	435	1.14	....	470	1.24	0.91	....	....	....
7	....	....	....	....	....	....	410	1.08	0.93	....	....	....

TABLE 2—INGREDIENTS REQUIRED FOR ONE CUBIC YARD OF MORTAR—NATURAL CEMENT.

[Sand weighs about 100 lbs. per cu. ft. Voids ⅜ of volume.]

Parts sand to 1 of Cement	Proportions by weight, dry sand and cement.					Proportions by volume, dry loose sand to packed cement; cement assumed at 71 lbs. per cu. ft. or 265 lbs. net per bbl.			Proportions by volume, dry loose sand to packed cement; packed cement assumed at 75 lbs. per cu. ft. or 280 lbs. net per bbl.			Proportions by volume, dry loose sand to packed cement; cement assumed 80 lbs. per cu. ft. or 300 lbs. net per bbl.			Proportions by volume, dry loose sand to loose cement; loose cement assumed at 60 lbs. per cu. ft.				
	Cement.					Cement.			Cement.			Cement.			Cement.				
	Pounds.	Bbls. of 265 lbs. net.	Bbls. of 280 lbs. net.	Bbls of 300 lbs. net.	Sand cubic yard.	Pounds.	Bbls. of 265 lbs. net.	Sand cubic yard.	Pounds.	Bbls. of 280 lbs. net.	Sand cubic yard.	Pounds.	Bbls. of 300 lbs. net.	Sand cubic yard.	Pounds.	Bbls. of 265 lbs. net.	Bbls. of 280 lbs. net.	Bbls. of 300 lbs. net.	Sand cubic yard.
a	b	c	d	e	f	g	h	i	j	k	l	m	n	o	p	q	r	s	t
0	2,240	8.45	8.00	7.47	0.00	2,240	8.45	0.00	2,240	8.00	0.00	2,240	7.47	0.00	2,240	8.45	8.00	7.47	0.00
1	1,380	5.21	4.93	4.60	0.51	1,180	4.45	0.61	1,210	4.82	0.60	1,250	4.17	0.58	1,080	4.08	3.86	3.60	0.67
2	970	3.66	3.46	3.23	0.72	750	2.58	0.78	780	2.79	0.77	825	2.75	0.76	660	2.49	2.36	2.20	0.81
3	730	2.72	2.57	2.40	0.80	540	2.04	0.85	570	2.08	0.84	600	2.00	0.83	470	1.77	1.68	1.57	0.87
4	570	2.15	2.03	1.90	0.84	425	1.60	0.89	450	1.60	0.88	470	1.57	0.87	.....	.....	.....	.....	.....
5	470	1.77	1.68	1.57	0.87	.....	.....	.....	.....	.....	.....	390	1.30	0.90	.....	.....	.....	.....	.....
6	400	1.51	1.43	1.33	0.89	.....	.....	.....	.....	.....	.....	.....	.....	.....	.....	.....	.....	.....	.....

yard and the mixing costs $1.00 per yard of mortar, then we have for the cost of a mortar composed of one part cement to two parts sand by weight:

3.46 bbls. cement at $1.10	$3 80
.72 cu. yd. dry sand at .60	43
Cost of mixing per cu. yd.	1 00
Total cost of one cu. yd. of mortar	$5 23

5. For approximate results diagrams 1 and 2 give the cost of be materials used in a cubic yard of mortar for different prices of ement. In diagram 1 the proportions by weight only are indicated, nce, for Portland, the proportions by volume of loose sand to acked cement vary so little from proportions by weight. In diaram 2 the proportions of natural cement mortars are given by olume of packed cement (280 pounds net per barrel) and loose nd, as well as by weight. The diagrams are made upon the asmptions that the sand is similar to that used in the experiments corded in tables 1 and 2, and that the cost of sand is fifty cents r cubic yard.

Example.

6. To indicate the use of these diagrams let us determine the ost per cubic yard of mortar containing two parts sand to one of atural cement by weight when cement costs $1.30 per barrel of 300 ounds net, and sand is thirty cents per cubic yard. One dollr and thirty cents per barrel of 30 pounds is equivant to 0.43 cent per pound, and entering diagram 2 with this quantity, we follow the corresponding abcissa till e reach the line marked 1 to 2 by weight; we find this to he the rdinate four dollars and fifty cents per cubic yard. But in the iagram the sand is assumed to cost fifty cents per cubic yard intead of thirty cents as in the example, and as .72 cubic yard sand is sed (see table), we must subtract .72 of twenty cents, or fourteen nts, from this result, making the materials for the mortar cost 4.36 per cubic yard of mortar. If the proportions were by volme of packed cement and loose sand the cost of the materials per ubic yard of mortar would be $3.75 less twenty times .78, or $3.59. It is understood that the cost of the materials alone is given by e diagrams; the cost of mixing the materials must be added to btain the total cost.

7. The rules given for determining the proportions of ingreients to use in concrete are not all to be commended, and while is article is concerned chiefly with the quantities of materials reuired when the proportions have been decided upon, we may sugt briefly the principle which should underlie the determination of se proportions.

8. Concrete is simply a class of masonry in which the stones are all and of irregular shape. The strength of the concrete is largely

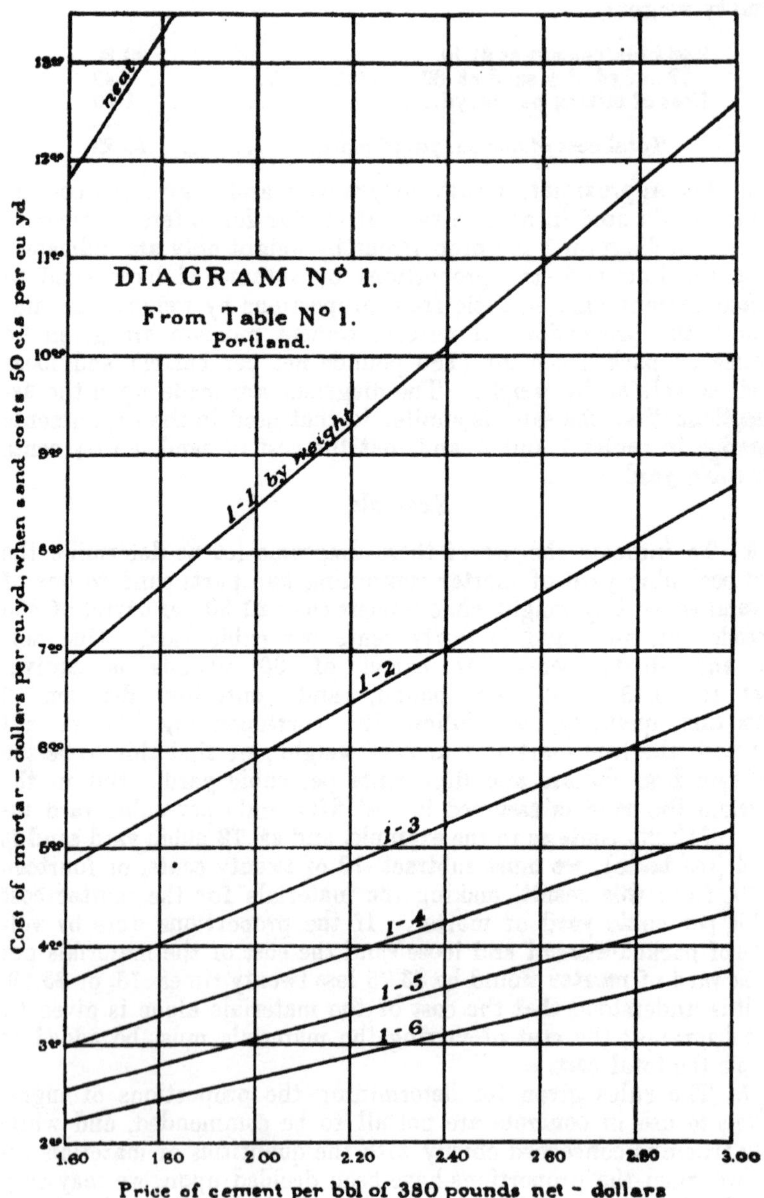
DIAGRAM N° 1.
From Table N° 1.
Portland.
neat
1-1 by weight
1-2
1-3
1-4
1-5
1-6
Cost of mortar - dollars per cu. yd., when sand costs 50 cts per cu yd
13.00
12.00
11.00
10.00
9.00
8.00
7.00
6.00
5.00
4.00
3.00
2.00
1.60
1.80
2.00
2.20
2.40
2.60
2.80
3.00
Price of cement per bbl of 380 pounds net - dollars

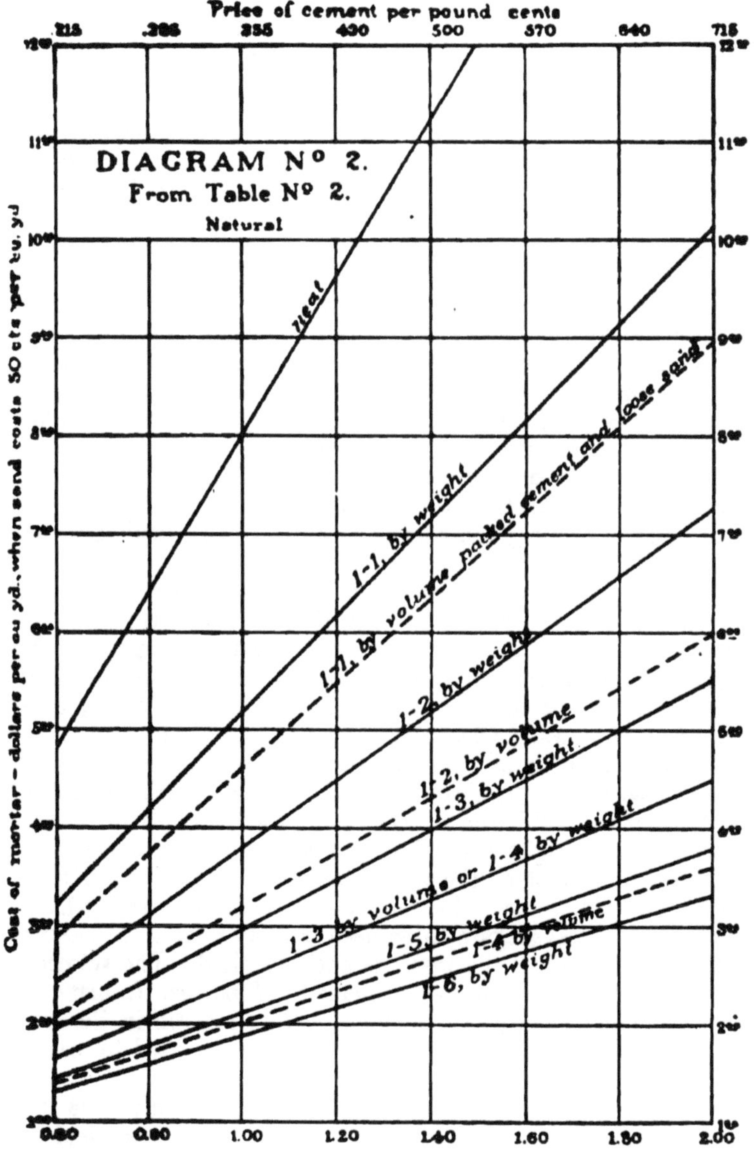
Price of cement per pound cents
DIAGRAM No 2.
From Table No 2.
Natural
neat
1-1, by weight
1-1, by volume packed cement and loose sand
1-2, by weight
1-2, by volume
1-3, by weight
1-3 by volume or 1-4 by weight
1-5, by weight
1-4 by volume
1-6, by weight
Cost of mortar - dollars per cu yd. when sand costs 50 cts per cu. yd.
Price of cement per bbl. of 280 pounds net - dollars.

dependent upon the strength of the mortar; in fact, this dependence will be much closer than in other classes of masonry, since it may be stated, as a genera rule, that the larger and more carefully cut are the stone, the less will the strength of the masonry depend on the strength of the mortar. In deciding, then, upon the proportions of ingredients to use in a given case, the quality of the mortar should first be considered. If the concrete is to be subjected to a moderate compressive stress, the mortar may be comparatively poor in cement; but if great transverse strength is required, the mortar must be of sufficient richness; while, if the concrete is to be impervious, the mortar must possess this quality as well.

9. In making concrete the general rule should be that enough mortar be used to just fill the voids in the stone. If either less or more mortar than this amount be employed the concrete will in general be weakened thereby. This last statement is subject to one exception: If the mortar becomes stronger than the stone then an excess of mortar does not weaken the concrete; this case, however, should never be permitted to occur, the aggregate used should have a strength at least equal to that required of the concrete. It is a simple matter then to determine the required amount of mortar for a given volume of broken stone or aggregate, and the amount of cement and sand for a given volume of mortar has already been considered.

10. The bulk or volume of a given mass of broken stone is not so variable a quantity as the volume of sand. The volume of the aggregate will vary considerably with the degree of packing, but the packing is influenced appreciably by the amount of moisture present. The percentage of voids in the aggregate may be determined as follows: Obtain the weight per cubic foot of the broken stone in the condition in which the percentage of voids is sought. Also obtain the specific gravity, and hence the weight per cubic foot, of the solid stone. Then one, less the quotient obtained by dividing the weight per cubic foot of the broken stone by the weight per cubic foot of the solid stone will be the proportion of voids in the former. Another method is to fill a vessel of known capacity with the aggregate to be used, and to pour in a measured quantity of water until the vessel is entirely filled. The volume of water used indicates the necessary quantity of mortar. In using this method the stone should be moistened before placing in the vessel to avoid an error from the absorption of the water used to measure the voids.

11. As to the degree of jarring or packing to which the ston should be subjected in filling, if the stone is put in loose, and it i

al, the voids obtained will be less than tl
t should be used, because it is not possibl
ibution of mortar in a mass of concrete, si
occupy only the same space as did the brol
ly shaken. And again, for perfect conc
ld be separated one from another by a thir
e the volume of the concrete will be grea
e aggregate measured in compact conditio
iency of mortar is usually more detrimenta
herefore, safer to measure the voids in
tly jarred and make the amount of mort
s so obtained.

. We may say, then, that the rational metl
rete is to let the duty required of the con
e mortar, and let the quantity be sufficien
ggregate. Knowing the percentage of voi
consequently the percentage of mortar whi
cubic yard of the finished concrete, we
imate cost per cubic yard of the latter fo
ar and given unit prices.

hus, suppose we have stone in which the voi
ar will amount to 40 per cent. of the finish
to have the mortar composed of two par
ral cement, by weight, unit prices being as

Cement,	$1.30 per bbl. of 300 pounds
Sand,	.30 per cubic yard.
Stone,	1.25 per cubic yard.

s in paragraph 6 we find the ingredients
mortar to cost $4.36. Since 40 per
e is to be mortar, the mortar in one cubi
cost 40 per cent. of $4.36, or $1.75, and o
5 will make the total cost of the materials
cubic yard.

. Diagram No. 3 may be used to get the a
concrete after having obtained the cost o
diagram 1 or 2. Thus, if we enter diag
$4.36, and follow the abscissa to the diago
., we find this to be on the ordinate $2.
edients in a cubic yard of the concrete when
cubic yard. Hence, $2.75+$0.25=$3, the
e materials in a cubic yard of the finished c
qualification "approximate" is used advisedl
that since the amount of concrete made f
ingredients is subject to slight variatio
accurate estimates of cost are not possible

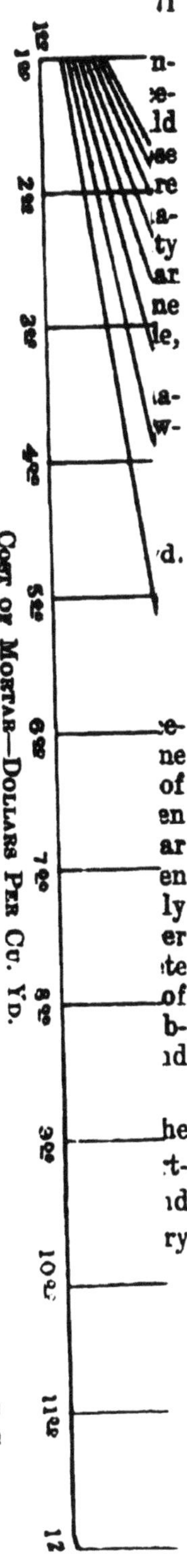

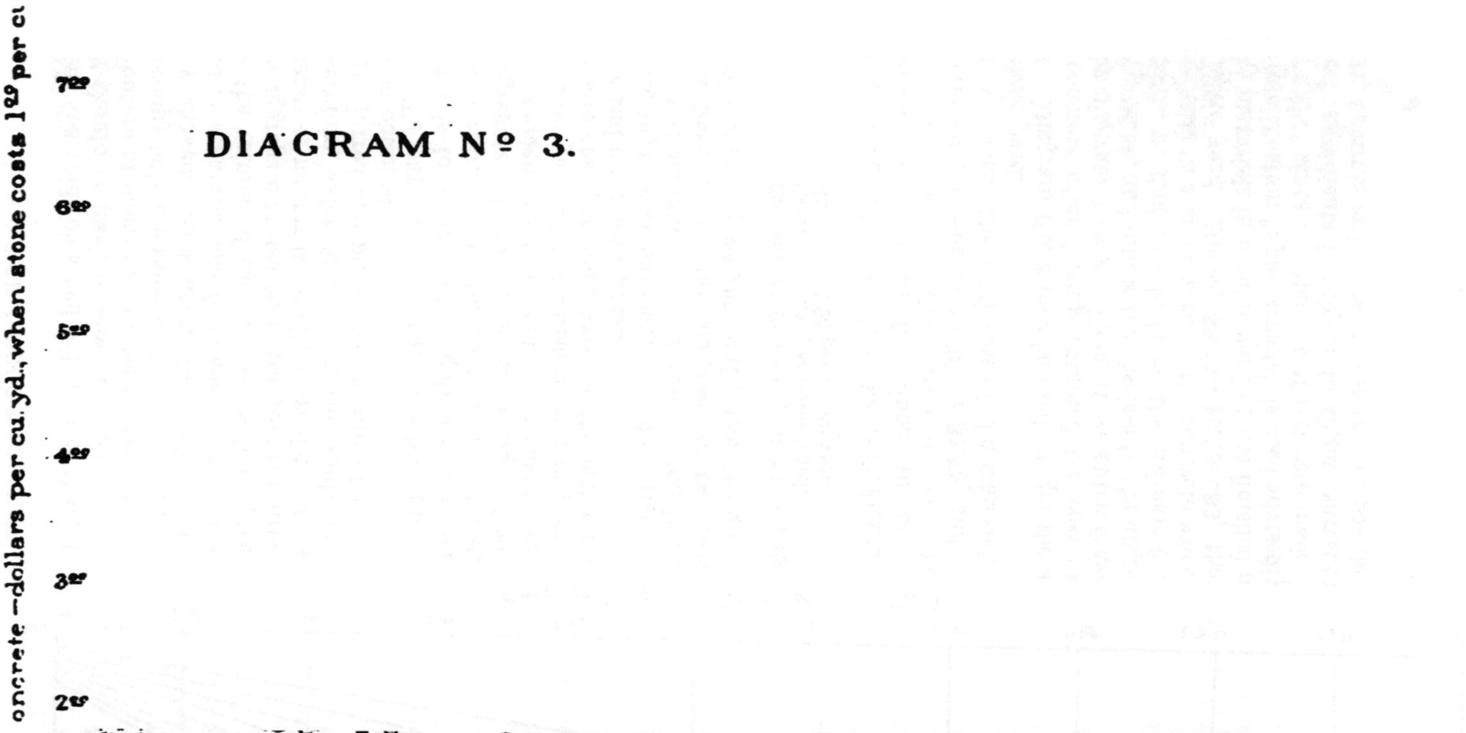

oncrete —dollars per cu. yd., when stone costs 1.00 per cu

2.00 3.00 4.00 5.00 6.00 7.00

DIAGRAM Nº 3.

14. The usual method, however, of stating proportions in concrete is to give the volume of sand and stone to one volume of cement. Thus, one of cement, three of sand and six of stone, would usually mean one volume of packed cement, three volumes of loose sand and six volumes of loose broken stone. When proportions are thus arbitrarily stated, we may determine, from the tables and diagrams already given, the amount of water which a given quantity of dry ingredients will make, and the consequent cost of the mortar per cubic yard. Then a knowledge of the voids in the broken stone will permit of a close estimate of the amount of concrete made, whence the cost of the latter.

For example, suppose it is desired to determine the cost of materials in a cubic yard of natural cement concrete under the following conditions:

One bbl. cement containing 280 pounds net at $1 per bbl.
Three bbls. sand weighing 100 pounds per cu. ft. at $0.75 per cu. yd.
Six bbls. loose broken stone having 45 per cent. voids at $1.25 per cu. yd.

1 bbl. cement=3.75 cu. ft.=0.139 cu. yd. cost..........	$1.000
3 bbls. sand=11.25 cu. ft.=.417 cu. yd. cost............	.313
6 bbls. stone=22.50 cu. ft.=.833 cu. yd. cost............	1.041
Total cost..	$2.354

From table 2 we find that it requires 2.03 barrels of cement to make one cubic yard of one to three mortar; then one barrel of cement would make 0.493 cubic yard. As 45 per cent. of the stone is voids the amount of solid stone in six barrels of broken stone would be $.833 \times .55 = .458$ cubic yard. Then the mortar plus solid stone would be $.493 + .458 = .951$ cubic yard. It has been found by experiment that the amount of concrete made will usually exceed the sum of the mortar and solid stone by from two to five per cent., hence we may assume in this case that .98 cubic yard concrete resulted from the above materials and $2.354 \div .98 = \$2.40$, the cost of the material in one cubic yard of finished concrete. To obtain the actual cost of concrete in place, the cost of mixing and deposition must be added.

The following table prepared by Mr. C. E. Fowler shows the amounts of each material required to make one cubic yard of Portland cement concrete with various proportions of cement, sand and stone. It is made by comparison with actual cases and gives very satisfactory results in practice.

Proportions.	Barrels Cement.	Cu. Yds. Sand.	Stone 0.4 voids.	Stone 0.5 voids.
1-2-3	1.77	0.51	0.87	1.05
1-2-3½	1.68	0.49	0.91	1.10
1-2-4	1.59	0.47	0.95	1.15
1-2-4½	1.48	0.44	1.00	1.20
1-2-5	1.39	0.42	1.04	1.26
1-2-5½	1.30	0.40	1.08	1.30
1-3-4	1.30	0.57	0.83	1.00
1-3-4½	1.22	0.54	0.89	1.06
1-3-5	1.16	0.52	0.92	1.11
1-3-5½	1.09	0.50	0.97	1.16
1-3-6	1.04	0.48	1.00	1.20
1-4-6	1.00	0.55	0.91	1.09
1-4-6½	0.96	0.53	0.94	1.13
1-4-7	0.92	0.51	0.97	1.17
1-4-7½	0.88	0.49	1.00	1.21
1-4-8	0.83	0.47	1.03	1.25

The heavy lines are put in the table to aid in selecting those m tures in which the voids of the stone are completely filled those which are but partly filled.

The following conclusions are drawn by various persons in discussion of a paper on the Theory of Concrete, by George Rafter, before the American Society of Civil Engineers. Conc blocks made part with mortar equal to 33 per cent. of the stone part with 40 per cent. were made, part with the dryest mixt possible, part with enough water to make the mixture plastic, part with an excess of water. Four brands of natural cement two brands of American Portland cement were used. In all, blocks of the concrete, each one cube foot, were made and crush

The blocks made with 40 per cent. of mortar and an excess water averaged 2,227 pounds crushing strength per square in with plastic mortar 2,329 pounds, with dry mortar 2,532. A sim ratio exists in the case of 33 per cent. mortar. The 40 per ce concrete averaged 4 per cent. stronger than the 33 per cent. T excess of strength was as high as 7 per cent. with mortar made one part cement to two parts sand, and there was no excess w mortar of 1 to 4.

The excess in cost of laying a cubic yard of concrete with mortar over that with wet mortar is shown by Herman Conrow figures from actual experience, as follows:

	Cost of Laying Wet Concrete.	Cost of Laying Dry Concrete.
Cement (1 barrel Portland)	$1.50	$1.50
Sand	.50	.50
Stone	1.00	1.00
Labor	1.13	2.12
Totals	$4.13	$5.12

The gang for wet concrete was 1 foreman, 9 mixers, 1 rammer, laying 15 cu. yds. a day. For dry concrete, 1 foreman, 6 mixers, 4 rammers, laying 8 cu. yds. a day. The foreman received $2 and the men $1.50 a day.

Comparison of the relative cost of hand mixing and of machine mixing is not easy so far as the discussion under consideration is concerned, the reported results being so various and so few. The general opinion is that machine mixing may, with proper machine and supervision, produce better mixed and therefore stronger concrete than hand work, especially in hot weather. The contradictions of figures of cost prevent any conclusion as to the relative economy of the two methods.

Concrete is more quickly mixed by machine and more thoroughly, as stated. A smaller amount of cement, say ten per cent., can, therefore, be used to secure the same strength of concrete. The uniformity of the concrete makes expansion and contraction of all parts of the mass the same under the same conditions, thus preventing disintegration on this account. With improved machinery and methods the question of cost is frequently solved in favor of machine mixing, in a few cases very decidedly so.

Machines for mixing concrete may be roughly divided into three classes: those which are intermittent, each charge being inserted, mixed and discharged into some conveyance ready for deposit on the work; those in which the materials are mixed in the course of falling by gravity through the machine; and those in which the materials are mixed by the motion of stirring and of conveying the materials. The last is continuous in its action, and the second may be. The first machine usually consists of a cubical box hung on trunnions at its opposite corners, or a cylinder or semi-cylinder with moving arms inside, into which the proper proportions of cement, sand, gravel or broken stone and water are introduced, the box then being turned slowly a few times until the contents are thoroughly mixed.

The second or gravity mixer, consists of a chute studded wit steel pins so placed that the materials dropping into it are we mixed while passing through, the water being added usually whe the other materials have had time to mix thoroughly.

The third is provided with screw conveyers in tubes, mixing th materials for the concrete by the process of pushing them alon The water is added toward the end of the journey. The accura of the last two methods depends upon the accuracy of the feedin of materials, a slight delay in depositing one of the ingredien giving opportunity for a shortage in the concrete for the tim and a delay in the deposit of all materials, causing an excess water for a time. Careful attendance is therefore necessary f good results.

Some very successful portable plants for performing all the ope ations of mixing for street work and for railroad work have bee designed, most of them originating for special purposes, but lat developing into machines for general use. The names of manufa turers of such machines and plants will be found in the lists cement machinery manufacturers in the directory section of th book.

Some experiments reported, where clean limestone screenin were used instead of sand in making mortar, indicate an increa in the strength of concrete.

The question of the use of gravel in place of broken stone in co crete frequently arises. Experiments reported in the report of t Engineer Commissioner of the District of Columbia for 1897 inc cate that with natural cement the gravel concrete has one-half three-fourths the strength of broken stone concrete, and with Po land cement there is but little difference, the experiments bei somewhat in favor of broken stone. It is noticeable that there is material increase in the relative strength of gravel concrete wi age so that if the concrete is not to receive its load for some mont it will be very nearly as good as that made with broken stone.

A discussion of the effect of size of sand upon the strength mortar by Mr. A. S. Cooper leads him to the conclusion, based experiments by himself and several others, that coarse sands pr duce stronger mortar than fine sands up to the size passing a No. sieve and refused by a No. 16. Sand passing a No. 50 sieve is practically without variation in its effect upon the strength mortar. The shape and condition of the surfaces of the grains different sands has as much to do with their value for cement mortar as the size, rough grains like crushed trap rock and granite being better than those with smooth surfaces, and river sand being better than beach sand. The proportions of mortar used in the tests were usually one to one.

The effect of increase in amount of sand in mortar was shown by a series of experiments at the Holyoke dam, Massachusetts, upon an American Portland cement of the highest grade. The results for tensile strength of mortar of various proportions at the end of 28 days set in water were as follows:

Sand to Cement.	Lbs. per sq. in.	Sand to Cement.	Lbs. per sq. in.
Neat cement	889	5 to 1	133
1 to 1	805	6 to 1	121
2 to 1	589	7 to 1	71
3 to 1	343	8 to 1	53
4 to 1	204	9 to 1	44

The effect of concrete on iron was shown by embedding a piece of galvanized iron in cement for six months. It was then found that the galvanizing had all disappeared but the iron was clean and bright.

The use of concrete and steel in combination is becoming very popular, and there are numerous adaptations of the principle, some patented and some free. The combination of the two materials was originally justified by the statement that the expansion of Portland cement is 0.0000143 per degree Centigrade increase in temperature, and that of iron is 0.0000145, practically the same. Cement mortar has strong adhesion to iron and protects it from oxidization.

The Monier construction was invented by a French gardener in 1876 to strengthen his flower pots, benches and fountains. It consists in the use of a netting of wire or of sets of steel rods at right angles to each other to carry tension or compression and aid the cement concrete or mortar in doing its duty and retaining its shape. It has been applied to the construction of tanks or reservoirs for the storage of water, wine, oil, pulp, grain, cement, etc., in bridges in place of buckle plates and to protect steel from corrosion, in arches, in the floors and partitions of buildings, in culverts and flumes, in fortifications, etc. Bordenave modifies it by using small sized channels, angles, I- or T-beams instead of rods, giving greater rigidity during construction. The Hyatt system uses vertical flat parallel bars with horizontal rods passing through holes in the bars. Ransome uses square rods which are twisted about the longitudinal axes, to give more thorough bond of the steel and concrete and to increase the stiffness of the rods. The Melan system uses curved beams, rolled or built I-beams usually, following the lines of the arches in which it is principally used. Cottancin, Hennebique and Bonna use special forms of wire, rod or shaped iron in floors, partitions, sewers, etc. Thacher uses steel bars in pairs, embedded in the concrete, with numerous rivets, lugs or similar projections to reinforce the adhesion of the steel and concrete. There is no connection between the bars of a pair other than the concrete. The bars act as the flanges of a beam, which takes the form designated for the arch of which it forms a part.

These constructions are sometimes used in place of steel for the cylindrical piers for bridges so often used where good foundation is far below the surface, the interior being filled with concrete in similar manner in both cases.

Expanded metal is another form of steel reinforcement of concrete which is used for facing of walls, partitions and floors. A recent successful test of a section of water conduit built of concrete and expanded metal indicates its value for this class of work. Fire proof vaults are also constructed of combined steel and concrete.

Concrete, without any reinforcement, was used as long ago as 1860 in Germany for a factory chimney about 160 feet high.

The street railway company in Minneapolis, Minn., made a novel use of concrete in reconstructing some of its lines and making the rails continuous by welding the joints. A longitudinal beam of concrete was constructed, to which the rails were spiked before the cement was set, thus making a continuous support for the rails, and a tight fastening for them. Concrete is frequently used as a foundation for the wooden ties of street railroads, but in this case the ties are displaced entirely. The usual concrete foundation for an asphalt street was laid over the street, and the pavement completed by laying the asphalt.

Development of the use of cement in sidewalks has been very rapid, and hundreds of miles of new walks are constructed each year. As a single example, the City of Indianapolis has 83 miles of improved streets, 125.08 miles of cement walks, practically all constructed within the last twelve years, 7.34 miles having been constructed in 1900.

The City of Bellefontaine, Ohio, has constructed several blocks of cement concrete street pavement, which, after a number of years' use, is in good condition. The objection made to it is that it is unusually slippery, but it would seem possible to obviate this by a different form of surface. If this objection is removed a large new field for the use of cement will open.

The use of cement for concrete floors in stables, cattle and hog pens, breweries and factories, where a smooth, durable, easily cleaned surface is required, has developed equally with its use for sidewalks. It makes an ideal floor for almost all such purposes, is easily repaired when cut into for any purpose, and is practically indestructible when properly constructed, except for wear of traffic. Special care must be taken to allow for expansion and contraction when there are great variations in temperature, and special construction to insure water-tight joints is necessary in such cases.

Street crossings of cement concrete are made in some smaller cities whose streets are not paved, and they are a sufficient improvement over the usual wood or flag stone crossing to repay the increase in cost.

Pavements for driveways to public and private stables, to railroad freight stations, factories, storehouses, etc., are equally valuable and their use is rapidly increasing.

Fences and ornamental gateways in cement concrete are very suc-

Since the invention of the Parkhurst combined curb and gutter, the use of cement for making street curbing has increased very rapidly. Over 120 miles of the Parkhurst curb and gutter alone have been constructed during the last ten years, and many miles of concrete curb and gutter and of curbing alone. The combination of curb and gutter solves a problem for macadam streets by giving a smooth gutter for drainage, and for asphalt by removing the danger of injury to the asphalt surface by water standing in flat or in obstructed gutters. The appearance of well-constructed curb is much in its favor, and it is more durable than most kinds of natural stone, the use of which is popular in some districts. The addition of strips of steel to take the wear on edges and face is made with success where the amount or character of traffic makes this precaution necessary for either stone or concrete curb, and the metal is most easily put in place and kept there when the cement curb is

The Parkhurst curb, now laid by D. C. Duntin of Indianapolis, was the pioneer and long the only combined curb and gutter manufactured. Its special features of protection and strengthening of the junction between curb and gutter and the uniformly high character of the work done and the materials used in its construction give it a deservedly good reputation.

For such small uses as cistern tops, horse blocks, steps, caps and sills, plastering cisterns, basins and manholes, Portland cement is the best material. Specifications for sidewalk mixtures are applicable to most of these uses, with slight modifications.

The use of concrete and cement mortar for lining subways is rapidly extending. The surface can be made non-absorbent, smooth and light colored where distribution of light is desirable, is quite as durable as stone or brick and usually more pleasing to the eye.

Concrete has been used in Europe for building sewers for many years. The city of Brooklyn is the only one in the United States which has used the material for this purpose extensively. Reading, Pa., and some other cities have used it to a slight extent.

Cement mortar has been used with more or less success as a lining for light steel or iron water pipes, the cement preserving the steel from corrosion and keeping the pipe constantly of the same area of cross section. Owing to errors of design, difficulty in keeping the layer of cement intact when making connections, and other similar reasons, this construction has never been very popular and it is now seldom used.

Bridge piers are frequently constructed with a heart of cement concrete and in some instances have been constructed entirely of such material, the exterior receiving a coating of Portland cement mortar specially prepared with the best of materials.

The success attained years ago in facing stone piers with a coating of cement mortar to preserve them from threatened disintegration should have more effect that it has heretofore. A facing that will show the marks of the forms after twenty years of exposure to weather, to the wear of water, and the shock of driftwood is certainly beyond criticism. There are several examples of this kind of construction to serve as object lessons for further application of the principle.

The conservative railway managers are rapidly extending the use of cement and concrete for all railway structures, and it is not mpossible that within a comparatively short term of years nearly ll structures from pipe culverts to station buildings on some railoads will be at least externally of concrete.

There are several notable examples of the use of monolithic concrete for such structures as the walls of canal locks, and some instances of the use of blocks made of concrete and set in place after mpletion.

In the construction of piers and breakwaters cement has been ed very largely in recent years. Very large blocks of concrete one are built, sometimes in place and occasionally elsewhere and en laid in place as natural stone blocks would be. Heart walls d filling may then be constructed of concrete laid in place. Some ecifications for this class of work follow in the next chapter.

The use of cement concrete for buildings in place of brick and one is gradually extending, its use as a facing for buildings perps more rapidly. For the latter use it is specially adapted, and aborate ornamentation can be indulged in at very small expense comparison with carved stone. The walls may be built entirely f concrete, especially if some of the various combinations of steel d concrete are used, being built in place. Blocks of artificial one may also be used and laid in the same manner as the natural one.

Many handsome buildings have recently been constructed in Florida of a concrete made of Portland cement and coquina shells from the vast deposits of that material on the seacoast of that State.

Cement can be used for statuary, fountains, monuments, where he color is satisfactory, and is frequently very effective.

Portland cement tile for floors, bases of walls, and special uses ave been made for a number of years. Colors are readily used as esired, and no heat being necessary, form and color may be as exact s is desired. Roofing tile of Portland cement are also very successful. They are light, durable, fire-proof, not breaking on contact with water when white-hot, and frost-proof. They are compressed under very heavy pressure and can be made of any desired hape or color.

During the construction of the Holyoke dam in Massachusetts was made to illustrate the effect of dumping concrete place under water. A batch of concrete was mixed, 1 part cement, 2½ parts sand and 5 parts broken stone, as required on the rk, and dropped before setting into a pail of water. At the end of 12 months it was examined. About ¾ in. of nearly neat cemen hard set, was found as a top layer, then about 2½ inches of san with enough cement to hold it together and a few stones, then 2 ' 3 inches of sand and stone nearly separate and perfectly clean, wi no adhesion whatever. This indicates that separation of materi dropped into place through water is too serious to be neglecte

It is a common belief among cement workers that cement mc tar is improved by allowing it to take a partial set and then re-tei pering it. Notwithstanding the fact that there are a few statemei of results of tests which seem to bear this out, the weight of tes mony is to the effect that this process is detrimental to the streng of the mortar. This is perhaps shown on the work by the fact th the re-tempered mortar sets more slowly than the fresh mortar.

The effect of frost upon the quality of cement mortar is vario In the case of natural hydraulic cement mortar, it seems to preve the setting of the cement and to disintegrate the mortar so th concrete frozen before full set has taken place is not reliable. It also true that frost has some effect upon old natural cement concre so that its life when exposed is not indefinite. With Portland (ment the same is true to a much less extent. Concrete is affected some extent by the action of the frost upon the surface. Mort used in laying stone seems to be practically unaffected if it remai frozen long enough to obtain its set, which is very materially (layed by the cold. Even successive freezing and thawing does n have very serious effect except where the mechanical effect of t expansion of particles of water in freezing forces off granules the mortar. It is, therefore, necessary to point the joints of su masonry. Salt is sometimes added to the mortar in sufficie quantities to keep the water liquid, if the temperature is below fre ing point, but above 0° F. This delays the setting of the ceme somewhat, but in reasonably steady weather this delay need not considered. About one pound of salt with 18 gallons of water wh the temperature is 30°, the quantity being increased about 3 oun for each degree of lower temperature will give good results if t masonry is free from ice.

Some experiments on freezing of mortar at the Holyoke da showed that freezing reduced the strength about 50 per cent. exc in the case of quick-setting Portland cements, which were affect

delayed by adding adulterants. A small amount of sulphate of lime (less than 2 per cent.) is sometimes added to the cement for this purpose. Lime may be added in the mortar for a similar reason and also to enable a small amount of a high grade Portland cement to be used with a large proportion of sand.

Fire-proof mortars are made by using hard-burned furnace cinders, say 1 part Portland cement, 2 parts sand, and 5 parts cinders. Natural hydraulic cement should not be used.

Sugar has been reported to increase the strength of cement mortars when the work is located in dry places, but careful experiments with various proportions of sugar fail to show this; on the other hand, any considerable proportion of sugar reduces the strength of the mortar.

For coloring cement work mineral colors are generally used. Nearly all coloring matters reduce the strength of cement, but ultramarine in small quantities increases it. Red oxide of iron, if it contains sulphuric acid, may cause swelling. Black and bluish gray are produced by using different quantities of lamp-black or peroxide of manganese; red, by the best raw iron oxide; bright red, by caput mortuum (expensive); a cheaper red by venetian red; brown, by the best roasted iron oxide; buff, by ochre; blue by ultramarine; bright blue, by prussian blue.

Cement manufacturers recommend the following quantities per 100 pounds of cement:

Black, 2 pounds excelsior carbon black.
Blue, 5 to 6 pounds ultramarine.
Brown, 6 pounds roasted iron oxide.
Gray, ½ pound lampblack.
Green, 6 pounds ultramarine.
Red, 6 to 10 pounds red iron oxide.
Bright red, 6 pounds Pompeian red.
Yellow or buff, 6 to 10 pounds yellow ochre.

The following list from a cement manufacturer's circular is inserted as a summary of the more prominent uses to which Portland cement is put in this country:

I. RAILROAD WORK.

Permanent culverts and tunnels.
Abutments, piers and retaining walls.
Foundations for buildings and machinery.
Freight platforms.
Passenger depot floors and pavements.

Construction of buildings with expanded metal lath and cen plaster.

II. MUNICIPAL AND GOVERNMENT WORK.

Irrigation and water works dams.
Conduits and sewers.
Street crossings.
Street paving.
Sidewalks, curb and gutter.
Bicycle paths.
Retaining walls.
Reservoirs and cisterns.
Culverts and bridges.

III. PRIVATE ENTERPRISES.

Manufacture or construction in the following specialties:
Cement wares.
Fence and hitching posts and corner stones.
Mounting blocks and steps.
Laundry tubs.
Burial cases.
Mangers and troughs.
Silos, steep tubs and tannery vats.
Gas and water tanks.
Swimming pools.
Vaults.
Bicycle race tracks.
Caps, sills and columns.
Artificial building stone.
Art figures.
Inlaid multi-colored tile for floors, roofs and facings.

IV. MINES AND MILLS.

Foundations of all kinds.
Boiler-house and engine-house floors.
Water-proof pits.
Water-tight passages.
Permanent walls.

V. INDIVIDUAL USE.

Floors for stables, cellars and milk houses.
Brewery and chemical works floors.
Fountains, pools, walks and driveways.
Veranda and kitchen floors of tile.
Roofing tile, facing and hearth tile.
Fire-proof construction.

SPECIFICATIONS FOR THE USE OF CEMENT

A number of sample specifications for the use of cement will be given in this chapter. The list could be very largely increased without entirely covering all the corners of the field, but it is believed that enough forms for all the principal kinds of work have been given to make it possible to determine the average specifications for good work and to prepare specifications for any particular class of work which will conform to the standards of good work which it is believed to present.

Special uses, such as statuary, tiling, etc., and its use in large work requiring special study and special machinery are not considered, as the space at command is more than full of the requirements for uses which are general in their character. It is not possible to follow any single program in arranging these specifications, but they will be found to be grouped as nearly as possible according to similarity of use or of composition of material, and the index will serve to locate any particular specification which is desired.

METHOD OF CONCRETING. MONIER ARCH BRIDGE, PHILADELPHIA.

After the entire mason work of the old stone bridge was torn down to low-water mark, substantial wooden cofferdams were built from rock bottom up to the elevation of the springing line of the new bridge around the center pier and both abutments, properly anchored to the ground, braced, and sheet piled at the inside and outside with clay puddle between, to make a solid and water-tight caisson for the whole concreting, and at the same time to serve as support for the centering and casing of the arches; 12" x 12" yellow pine timbers were used for the frame work of the coffer-dams and for the adjustable trusses of the centerings, and 3" planks also of yellow pine, for the covering and sheet-piling. To prevent any adhesion of the concrete to the wood-work, the corresponding surfaces were planed, oiled and sanded. In order to discharge the surplus water at any rate accumulated at the bottom of the concrete after its setting, small holes about $\frac{3}{8}$ of an inch in diameter were made in the planks when and wherever required.

As soon as the coffer-dams were completed and all water pumpe out, the old mason-work below low-water mark was excavated t said bottom, the top surface then first thoroughly cleaned, wette and slushed with neat Portland cement; and then the first layer concrete placed in a thickness not exceeding 12 inches, so as to s cure a thorough level base for all subsequent layers, 9 inches thic up to the springing line of the arches, laid in uninterrupted conti uation, until one layer was placed always through on either part the bridge.

Then the arches were concreted in the same manner in subseque equal layers of concrete, each one closing 9 inches thick at t crown. The concrete was applied from a movable platform by re ular tight mortar barrows, in equal portions central to the arch beginning at the haunches and continuing towards the crown of t arches at the same time, so as to secure a uniform setting of t concrete. After the first setting of each layer (requiring from to 2 hours after its bedding), a subsequent layer was placed, and on. To obtain a proper binding between the layers, during hi temperature, the top surface of each layer was kept damp; during the interruption of the work at night-time and on Sunda the top surface was covered with damped canvas, and during hea rain-storms with planks.

Wire nets, á la system "Monier," were placed between each lay 12 inches apart square, of $\frac{1}{8}$ inch galvanized iron wires, anchored upright rods to the haunches and abutments.

The following are similar to the specifications for Melan arch Topeka, Kan.:

SPECIFICATIONS FOR CONCRETE STEEL BRIDGE. KEEPERS & THACH

Plans.—The work shall be constructed complete in accordan with the general plans, sections and diagrams herewith submitte and these specifications. The specifications and drawings are i tended to describe and provide for the complete work. They are i tended to be coöperative, and what is called for by either is as bin ing as if called for by both. The work herein described is to be co pleted in every detail, notwithstanding that every item necessar involved is not particularly mentioned. The contract price sh be based upon these specifications and drawings, which are here signed and made a part of the contract.

Conditions of Calculation.—

Modulus of elasticity of concrete...............	1,400,000 l
Modulus of elasticity of steel....................	28,000,000 l
Maximum stress per square inch on steel........	10,000 l
Maximum compression per square inch on concrete..	500
Maximum shear per square inch on concrete.......	100 l
Maximum tension per square inch on concrete......	50 l

exclusive of temperature stresses. The steel exceeding their elastic limit must be capable ›ending moment of the arch, ·without aid d have a flange area of not less than 1-150 concrete at crown.

the event of any discrepancies between the es written on them, the figures are to be taken ›e of any discrepancy between the drawings the specifications are to be adhered to.

'oundations shall be shown on plans, and cons marked thereon. Foundations on rock shall ng all sand, mud, or other soft material, and rock in such manner as may be described or Foundations on hardpan, gravel and clay, ›r material intended to carry the load without ›d to the depths shown on plans.

›s, when not otherwise described, shall be en-; coffer-dam or crib, and be excavated to the s, and the piles shall be driven after the ex-'he spaces between the piles shall be filled with t is found necessary to lay the concrete under es must be used to insure its being deposited as possible. The piles shall be oak, yellow ›t will stand the blow of the hammer, straight, live timber, trimmed close, cut off square at . bark taken off. The piles shall not be less › than 16 ins. in diameter at the large end, ‹ diameter at the small end for piles having a ınder. For greater lengths the diameter of ıced 1 in. for each 10 ft. of additional length ›f 7 ins. The piles shall not be loaded with than ·given by the following formula: -1), in which L = safe load in pounds; er in pounds, h = fall of hammer in feet, n inches. The number and arrangement of ındation shall be shown on plans, and they he elevation shown.

ənt shall be a true Portland cement, made mixture of calcareous and clayey earths; and ctor shall furnish a certified statement of the of the cement, and the raw materials from ured. The fineness of the cement shall be per cent. will pass through a sieve of 50 ; least 90 per cent. will pass through a sieve ı. in., and at least 70 per cent. will pass) meshes per lin. in.

Samples for testing may be taken from each and every barrel delivered, unless otherwise specified. Tensile tests will be made on specimens prepared and maintained until tested at a temperature of not less than 60 degrees F. Each specimen will have an area of 1 sq. in. at the breaking section, and after being allowed to harden in moist air for 24 hours, will be immersed and maintained under the water until tested. The sand used in preparing the test specimens shall be clean, sharp, crushed quartz, retained on a sieve of 30 meshes per lin. in. No more than 23 to 27 per cent. of water shall be used in preparing the test specimens of neat cement, and in the case of test specimens of 1 cement and 3 sand, no more than 11 or 12 per cent. of water by weight shall be used.

Specimens prepared from neat cement shall after seven days develop a tensile strength of not less than 450 lbs. per sq. in. Specimens prepared from a mixture of 1 part cement and three parts sand, parts by weight, shall after seven days develop a tensile strength of not less than 160 lbs. per sq. in., and not less than 220 lbs. per sq. in. after 28 days. Specimens prepared from a mixture of 1 part cement and 3 parts sand, parts by weight, and immersed after 24 hours in water maintained at 176 degrees F., shall not swell nor crack, and shall, after seven days, develop a tensile strength of not less than 160 lbs. per sq. in. Cement mixed neat with about 27 per cent. of water to form a stiff paste, shall after 30 mins. be appreciably indented by the end of a wire 1-12 in. in diameter loaded to weigh ¼ lb. Cement made into thin cakes on glass plates, shall not crack, scale nor warp under the following treatment: Three pats will be made and allowed to harden in moist air at from 60 degrees to 70 degrees F.; one of these will be subjected to water vapor at 176 degrees F. for three hours, after which it shall be immersed in hot water for 48 hours; another shall be placed in water at from 60 degrees to 70 degrees F., and the third shall be left in moist air. All cement shall be kept housed and dry until wanted in the work.

Portland Cement Concrete.—The concrete shall be composed of clean, hard broken stone, or gravel, with irregular surface; clean, sharp sand, and cement, mixed in the proportions hereafter specified. Whenever the amount of work to be done is sufficient to justify it, approved mixing machines shall be used. The ingredients shall be placed in the machine in a dry state, and in the volumes specified, and be thoroughly mixed, after which clean water shall be added and the mixing continued until the wet mixture is thorough and the mass uniform. No more water shall be used than the concrete will bear without quaking in ramming. The mixing must be done as rapidly as possible and the batch deposited in the work without delay.

If the mixing is done by hand, the cement and sand shall first be thoroughly mixed dry in the proportions specified. The stone previously drenched with water shall then be deposited on this mixture. Clean water shall be added and the mass be thoroughly mixed and turned over until each stone is covered with mortar, and the batch shall be deposited without delay, and be thoroughly rammed until all voids are filled. The grades of concrete to be used are as follows: For the arches between skewbacks—1 part Portland cement, 2 parts sand, and 4 parts broken stone, or gravel, that will pass through a 1½-in. ring; for the foundations, abutments, piers and spandrels—1 part Portland cement, 4 parts sand, and 8 parts broken stone, or gravel, that will pass through a 2-in. ring.

Concrete Facing.—If concrete facing is used, it shall be composed of 1 part Portland cement, and 2½ parts sand, and shall have a thickness of at least 1 in. on all arch soffits, arch faces, abutments, piers, spandrels or other exposed surfaces. There must be no definite plane or surface of demarkation between the facing and the concrete backing. The facing and backing must be deposited in the same layer, and be well rammed in place at the same time. If the arch faces, quoins or other exposed surfaces are marked to represent masonry, such division marks shall be made by triangular strips 2 ins. wide and 1 in. deep fastened to the casing in perfectly straight and parallel lines, and all projecting corners will be beveled to correspond.

Plastering.—No plastering will be allowed on the exposed faces of the work, but the inside faces of the spandrel walls covered by the fill may be plastered with mortar having the same composition as specified for facing.

Stone Facing.—If stone facing is used, the ring stones, cornices and faces of spandrels, piers and abutments shall be of an approved quality of stone. The stone must be of a compact texture, free from loose seams, flaws, discolorations, or imperfections of any kind, and of such a character as will stand the action of the weather. The spandrel walls will be backed with concrete, or rubble masonry, to the thickness required. The stone facing shall in all cases be securely bonded or clamped to the backing. All stones shall be rock-faced with the exception of cornices and string [illegible] which shall be sawed or bush-hammered. The ring stones [illegible] dressed to true radial lines, and laid in Portland cement [illegible] with ½-in. joints. All other stones shall be dressed to true [illegible] vertical joints. No joint shall exceed ½ in. in thickness, nd shall be laid to break joints at least 9 ins. with the course below. All joints shall be cleaned, wet and neatly pointed. The aces of the walls shall be laid in true line, and to the dimensions given on plans, and the corners shall have a chisel draft 1 in. wide carried up to the springing lines of the arch, or string course. All cornices, moldings, capitals, keystones, brackets, etc., shall be built into the work in the proper positions, etc., and shall be of th forms and dimensions shown on plans.

Brick Facing with Concrete Trimmings.—The arch rings, co nices, string courses and quoins, shall be concrete-faced as describe above, the arch rings and quoins being marked and leveled to re resent masonry. The piers, abutments and spandrels shall b faced with vitrified brick as shown on plans. The brick facing sha be plain below the springing lines of the arches, and rock-face above these lines. All rock-faced brick shall be chipped by han from true pitch lines. All brick facing shall be bonded as show on plans, at least one-fifth of the face of the wall being header The brick must be of the best quality of hard-burned paving bric and must stand all tests as to durability and fitness required b the engineer in charge. The bricks must be regular in shape an practically uniform in size and color. They shall be free from lim and other impurities; shall be free from checks or fire cracks, an as nearly uniform in every respect as possible; shall be burned as to secure the maximum hardness; so annealed as to reach th ultimate degree of toughness; and be thoroughly vitrified so as make a homogeneous mass. The backing shall be carried up simu taneously with the face work, and be thoroughly bonded with it.

Artificial Stone.—All keystones, brackets, consoles, dentils, pe estals, hand-railing posts, and panels, and other ornamental wo when used, also curbs and gutters, shall be of the designs show on plans, and be molded in suitable molds. The mortar for at lea 1-in. thick shall consist of 1 part Portland cement and 2½ par sand, and when the size of the molding will admit, the interi may be composed of concrete of the same composition as spec fied for the arches. When pedestals, posts or panels carry lam posts, a 4-in. wrought-iron pipe shall be built into the concrete fro top to bottom, and at bottom shall be connected with a 3-in. pi extending under the sidewalk, and connected with a gas-pipe electric wire conduit. The pipes shall have no sharp bends, a changes in direction being made by gentle curves.

Sprinkling.—During warm and dry weather, all newly built co crete shall be well sprinkled with water for several days, or until is well set.

Mixtures.—The volumes of cement, sand, and broken stone all mixtures of mortar or concrete used in the work shall be mea ured loose.

Connections.—In connecting concrete already set with new co crete the surface shall be cleaned and roughened, and mopp with a mortar composed of 1 part Portland cement and 1 pa sand, to cement the parts together.

Arches.—The concrete for the arches shall be started simu taneously from both ends of the arch, and be built in longitud nal sections wide enough to inclose at least two steel ribs, and sufficient width to constitute a day's work. The concrete shall be deposited in layers, each layer being well rammed in place before the previously deposited layer has had time to set partially. The work shall proceed continuously day and night, if necessary, to complete each longitudinal section. These sections while being built shall be held in place by substantial timber forms, normal to the centering and parallel to each other, and these forms shall be removed when the section has set sufficiently to admit of it. The sections shall be connected as specified above, and also by steel clamps or rib connections built into the concrete.

Drainage.—Provision for drainage shall be made at each pier as follows: A wrought-iron pipe of sufficient diameter shall be built into the concrete, extending from the center of each space over pier to the soffit. The surface of concrete over piers shall be so formed that any water that may seep through fill above will be drained to the pipes. The line of drainage will be covered with a layer of broken stones, and the top of pipes will be provided with screens to prevent clogging.

Steel Ribs.—Steel ribs shall be imbedded in the concrete of the arch. They shall be spaced at equal distances apart, and be of the number shown on plans. Each rib shall consist of two flat bars of the sizes marked on plans. The bars shall be in lengths of about 30 ft., thoroughly spliced together, and extending into the abutments as shown. Through the center of each bar shall be driven a line of rivets spaced 8 ins. c. to c., with heads projecting about $\frac{1}{2}$ in. from each face of bar, except through splice plates, where ordinary heads will be used. The bars shall be in pairs with their centers placed 2 ins. within the inner and outer lines of the arch respectively as shown. All steel must be free from paint and oil, and all scale and rust must be removed before imbedding in the

The tensile strength, limit of elasticity and ductility shall be determined from a standard test piece cut from the finished material and turned or planed parallel. The area of cross-section shall not be less than $\frac{1}{2}$ sq. in. The elongation shall be measured after breaking on an original length of 8 ins. Each melt shall be tested for tension and bending. Test pieces from finished material prepared as above described shall have an ultimate strength of from 60,000 to 68,000 lbs. per sq. in.; an elastic limit of not less than one-half of the ultimate, shall elongate not less than 20 per cent. in 8 ins., and show a reduction of area at point of fracture of not less than 40 per cent. It must bend cold 180 degrees around a curve whose diameter is equal to the thickness of piece tested without crack or flaw on convex side of bend. In tension tests the must be entirely silky.

...el.—Test pieces from finished material, prepared as ...ed, shall have an ultimate strength of from 54,000 to

62,000 lbs. per sq. in., an elastic limit of not less than one-half of the ultimate strength, shall elongate not less than 20 per cent. in 8 ins., and show a reduction at point of fracture of not less than 50 per cent. It must bend cold 180 degrees and close down on itself without fracture on convex side of bend. In tension tests the fracture must be entirely silky.

Inspection.—The contractor shall furnish a testing machine of the proper capacity and shall prepare and test without charge such specimens of steel as may be required to prove that it comes up to the requirements mentioned above.

Workmanship.—The rivet holes for splice plates of abutting members shall be so accurately spaced that when the members are brought into position the holes shall be truly opposite before the rivets are driven. When members are connected by bolts, the holes must be reamed parallel and the bolts turned to a driving fit. Rivets must completely fill the holes, have full heads concentric with the rivets, and be machine driven when practicable.

Centering.—The contractor shall build an unyielding false work or centering. The lagging shall be dressed to a uniform size so that when laid it shall present a smooth surface, and this surface shall conform to the lines shown on the drawings. The center shall not be struck until at least 28 days after the completion of the arch. Great care shall be used in lowering the centers so as not to throw undue strains upon the arches. The tendency of the centers to rise at the crown as they are loaded at the haunches must be provided for in the design, or if not, the centers must be temporarily loaded at the crown, and the load be so regulated as to prevent distortion of the arch as the work progresses.

Casing.—When concrete facing is used, all piers, abutments, and spandrel walls shall be built in timber forms. These forms shall be substantial and unyielding, of the proper dimensions for the work intended, and all parts in contact with exposed faces of concrete shall be finished to a perfectly smooth surface, by plastering or other means, so that no mark or imperfection shall be left on the work.

Waterproofing.—After the completion of the arches and spandrels, and before any fill is put in, the top surface of arches, piers, and abutments, and the lower 6 ins. of the inner surface of the spandrel walls shall be covered with a suitable waterproof material, so as to exclude water effectually.

Fill.—The space between spandrel walls shall be filled with sand, earth, cinders, or other suitable material, and be thoroughly compacted by ramming, steam road roller, saturating with water or other effective means, and be finished to the proper grade to receive the curbing and pavements.

Granitoid Sidewalks.—The spaces over which the sidewalks are to be laid shall first be covered with 6 ins. of cinders well compacted. On this shall be laid 4 ins. of concrete, consisting of 1 part Portland cement, 3 parts sand, and 6 parts broken stone or gravel—small size—well rammed. The flag divisions shall then be marked off to the desired size. On the surface of the concrete shall then be laid a wearing surface 1 in. thick, composed of 2 parts Portland cement and 3 parts broken granite or other acceptable stone, in size from ⅜ in. downward. It shall be well rammed and troweled to a perfectly even surface and rolled with a toothed roller. This wearing surface must be spread on the concrete while the latter is still soft and adhesive, and neat connections must be made with cornices and curbs.

Roadway Pavement.—The pavement shall be of the kind shown on plans or mentioned in proposal, and shall be built according to the specifications adopted in the locality where used, unless otherwise mentioned.

Retaining Stone.—There shall be set at each end of roadway pavement a line of stones of approved quality, 4 ins. in thickness and 18 ins. deep, with top surface conforming to contour of pavement.

Balustrades and Hand-Railings.—The balustrades shall be of the material, and of the form and dimensions shown on plans, and shall be brought to true alignment and be firmly fastened to the outside of each sidewalk in the position shown. If an iron hand-railing is used, it shall receive two coats of approved paint after erection.

Erection.—The contractor shall employ suitable labor for every kind of work, and all stone work shall be laid by competent masons. The contractor will furnish all staging, piling, cribbing, centering, casing and material of every description required for the erection of the work; also all plant, including dredges, engines, pumps, derricks, barges, mixing machines, pile drivers, conveyors, or other appliances necessary for carrying on all parts of the work. The contractor shall assume all risks for loss or damage incurred by ice, floods, fire, or other causes during the construction of the work, and shall sufficiently watch and light the work at night during construction.

Cleaning Up.—Upon completion of work, and before final acceptance thereof, the contractor shall remove all temporary work from the river and all rubbish from the streets.

Maintaining Public Travel.—If public travel is to be maintained during the construction of the new bridge, by the removal of old bridge, construction of temporary bridge or otherwise, special mention of the same shall be made.

Removal of Old Bridge.—If the site of the proposed structure is occupied by an old bridge, the same shall be removed by the contractor. The iron work shall be piled on the bank, and the timber and stone shall become the property of the contractor.

Work Embraced by Contract.—The work embraced by contra will be for the structure complete from out to out of abutments retaining walls, as per plans and specifications, and will embra fill, pavement, sidewalks and balustrades complete for this lengt

Approaches.—The approaches will commence where the wo above mentioned ends, and if all or any part of them is included contract the same shall be specially mentioned.

Changes.—The committee in charge shall have power to dir changes which they may consider necessary or advisable in a part of the work, and such changes shall not in any way viol the contract, but the value of such changes shall be added to deducted from the contract price, and any dispute as to their val shall be settled by arbitration in the usual way.

Inspection.—All material furnished by the contractor shall subject to the inspection and approval of the committee in char

Lamp Posts, Trolley Poles and Name Plates.—If used these sh be shown on plans, or be specially mentioned.

Interpretation of Plans and Specifications.—The decision the committee in charge or their engineer shall control as to t interpretations of drawings and specifications during the executi of the work thereunder, but this shall not deprive the contractor his rights to redress, after the completion of the work, for any i proper orders or decisions.

Estimates.—Approximate estimates of work done and mater delivered shall be made on or about the last day of every mon and a valuation of the same in proportion to contract prices for t completed work will be made by the committee in charge or th engineer, which sum shall be paid to the contractor in cash, on before the 10th day of the following month, less a deduction of per cent. upon said valuation, which shall be retained until the fi completion of the work.

Final Payment.—Upon the final completion of the work, t contractor shall be promptly paid any balance of the contract pri which shall then remain due and unpaid.

SPECIFICATIONS FOR CONCRETE AND STEEL ARCH BRIDGES AT MERI IAN STREET AND ILLINOIS STREET OVER FALL CREEK, INDIANAPOLIS.

1. The work shall be constructed complete in accordance wi the general plans, sections herewith submitted and these speci cations.

2. In calculating strain for the arches and piers the followi conditions will be assumed:

1. Modulus of elasticity of concrete............ 1,400,000 lbs.
2. Modulus of elasticity of steel..............28,000,000 lbs.
3. Maximum unit stress of steel................ 12,000 lbs.
4. Maximum compression per sq. in. on concrete.. 500 lbs.
5. Maximum shear per sq. in. on concrete...... 100 lbs.
6. Maximum tension per sq. in. on concrete...... 50 lbs.
(The above to be exclusive of temperature stresses.)
7. Live load per square foot................. 150 lbs.
8. Concentrated moving load, 15-ton steam roller.

3. All foundations are shown on plans and must conform to dimensions marked thereon.

Foundations on hardpan, gravel, gravel and clay, cemented sand or other material intended to carry the load without piles, shall be excavated to the depth shown on plan.

The contractor shall construct suitable coffer-dams for the piers and abutments. The earth inside thereof shall be excavated to the depth shown on plan. During the placing of the concrete therein, the water shall be kept out of the coffer-dams, unless the bottom is so porous that it is impracticable to do so, in which case the concrete shall be placed in position by means of shutes until the bottom is made water-tight, after which the water shall be pumped out and the remaining concrete placed in position.

The contractor will be required to make the sides and ends of the coffer-dams water-tight, and no leak through them will be considered sufficient cause to require any concrete to be placed by means of shutes.

4. The piers, abutments and spandrel walls shall be built in timber forms. These forms shall be substantial and unyielding, of the proper dimensions for the work intended. And all parts in contact with the exposed faces of concrete shall be finished to a perfectly smooth surface by plastering or other means, so that no mark or imperfection shall be left in the work.

5. The contractor shall build an unyielding false work or centering. The lagging shall not be less than two inches thick and dressed to a uniform size, so that when laid it shall present a smooth surface and this surface shall conform to the line shown on the drawings.

The contractor must provide against the tendency of the centers to rise at the crown as they are loaded at the haunches. The centering must be built to allow for a settlement of one inch at the crown of the arches. The centers shall not be struck until at least thirty days after the completion of the arches. Great care shall be used in lowering the centers so as not to throw undue strains upon the arches. It is probable that three centers will be in use at the same time. The steel ribs in the bridge will be of the number, weight and length shown on plan. They must be carefully stored and put into place entirely free from oil or paint. All scale or rust must be removed immediately before placing the arch concrete about the ribs by scraping them thoroughly with sandpap or stiff wire brushes. The ribs shall consist of ten-inch stand I-beams, twenty-five pounds per foot, each rib to be made in thr sections, fully spliced with top and bottom flange plates and tw web plates on each side. The ends of the steel ribs in the abu ments shall be securely riveted to a ten-inch channel runni transversely through each abutment. In the piers the end of ea rib shall be connected with a corresponding one in the adjoini arch by two web plates. All ribs shall be connected by thre quarter-inch tie rods at intervals of about twelve feet. At th crown of the arches the lower flanges of the ribs shall be two inch distant from the top of the lagging.

6. In lieu of I-beams steel ribs may be imbedded in the co crete, consisting of flat bars thoroughly spliced together with ri ets driven through the center of each bar and spaced eight inche center to center, with heads projecting about seven-eighths of a inch from each face of bar, except through spliced plates. The ba shall be in pairs with their center plate two inches within the i ner and outer lines of the arch respectively. If bars are used i stead of the I-beams, the contractor shall submit plans showi sections and method of construction.

7. All steel shall be uniform in quality. Finished part m be free from seams, flaws or cracks and have a workmanlike fini The phosphorus not to exceed 0.08 per cent. Test pieces fr finished material shall have an ultimate strength of from 60,0 to 68,000 pounds per square inch and elastic limit of one-ha the ultimate, shall not elongate less than 20 per cent. in eig inches, and show a reduction of area at point of fracture of n less than 40 per cent. It must bend cold one hundred and eigh degrees around a curve whose diameter is equal to the thickness the piece tested, without crack or flaw on convex side of bend. tension test the fracture shall be entirely silky. Sections shall n vary more than two and one-half per cent. from those ordered.

8. *Concrete.*—The concrete shall be composed of clean, ha broken stone with irregular surface, clean, sharp sand, and Po land cement, mixed in the proportions hereinafter specified. T stone must be free from earth or foreign matter and the dust m be entirely removed. The sand must be free from earth and loa sharp but not too fine. If the mixing is done by hand the cem and sand shall first be thoroughly mixed in a dry state in the p portions specified. The stone, after being thoroughly drench with water, shall then be deposited on this mixture. Clean wa shall then be added and the mass thoroughly mixed and turn over until each stone is covered with mortar, and the batch shall deposited without delay, and thoroughly rammed until all vo are filled. No more water shall be used than the concrete bear without quaking in ramming. The mixing must be done rapidly as possible and the batch deposited on the work with

y. Approved mixing machines may be used. The ingredients l be placed in the machine in a dry state in the volume speci- and thoroughly mixed, after which clean water shall be added the mixing continued until the wet mixture is thorough and mass uniform; otherwise the method used in the hand-mixing be followed.

. For cement specification, see chapter on Specifications for nent.

0. The abutments and piers will be of concrete made in the portion of one part of Portland cement, two parts of sand and n parts of broken stone that will pass through a two-inch ring rts by volume). The abutments and pier concrete will termi- in a hidden irregular line approximately at right angles to the of thrust as shown on plan.

1. The concrete for the arches will be made in the proportion one part of Portland cement, two parts of sand, four parts of ken stone. The concreting of the arches shall be started simul- eous from both haunches in longitudinal sections wide enough east to include two steel ribs, each layer being well rammed in e before the previously deposited layers shall have had time to tially set. The widths of the sections shall be symmetrical and l be uniform in the several arches. The work shall proceed and night continuously if necessary to complete each longitu- l section. The sections while being built shall be held in place substantial timber forms perpendicular to the center and the s parallel to each other and to the axis of the bridge, and these ns shall be removed after the sections have set sufficiently to it of it.

2. The spandrel and abutment walls shall be of concrete as ified for the abutments and piers. Each spandrel wall between ansion joints, each abutment wall and each section of the es must be completed as continuous work. The abutments and s may be built each in several days' work, leaving the com- ed work of each day approximately at right angles to the line hrust, which in the piers may be taken as vertical. In con- ing old concrete with new, or one section of concrete with ther, the section previously placed shall be thoroughly wet and n slushed with pure cement, and this must be done immediately dvance of the new work.

3. *Sprinkling.*—All concrete after taking its initial set must cept moist by sprinkling water on it for at least ten days.

4. Expansion joints will be provided at the ends of the span- walls.

5. *Waterproofing.*—The upper surface of the arches and tments and the lower six inches of the spandrel and abutment ls shall be painted with coal-tar pitch of the grade used for ing cement. The expansion joints shall be covered with lapped ets of tar paper painted and held in place by the same pitch.

Any other suitable waterproof material which will effectually e clude water, and satisfactory to the Board of Public Works ai City Engineer, can be used in place of the coal-tar.

16. *Drainage.*—Provisions shall be made for draining arches and piers in a manner satisfactory to the Engineer.

17. *Earth Fill.*—The space between the spandrel walls will filled with sand, earth or other suitable material and be thorough compacted by ramming or by steam road roller or other effecti means and be finished to the proper grade to receive the cur ing and pavements.

18. *Paving.*—All curbing, sidewalks and asphalt paving sh be executed according to the plans and according to the standa specifications on file in the office of the Board of Public Worl

19. *Stone Facing.*—The ring stones, cornices and faces spandrel piers and abutments shall be of the best quality of Be ford limestone. The spandrel walls will be backed with concre or rubble masonry to the thickness required. The stone faci shall in all cases be securely bonded or clamped to the backi All stone shall be rock-faced with the exception of cornices a string courses, which shall be sawed or bush-hammered. The ri stones shall be dressed to true radial lines and laid in Portla cement mortar with joints not to exceed one-quarter of an in All other stones shall be dressed to true beds and vertical join No joint shall exceed one-quarter of an inch in thickness a shall be laid to break joints at least nine inches with the cou below. All joints shall be cleaned, wet and neatly pointed. T faces of the walls shall be laid on true lines and to the dimensio given on plan, and the corners shall have a chisel draft one in wide carried up to the springing line of the arch, or string cour All cornices, keystones, brackets, etc., shall be built into the wo in proper position and shall be of the form and dimensions sho on plan.

20. *Railing.*—The railing shall be of depth of stone as sho on plan and shall be brought to true alignment and be firmly fa ened to the outside of each sidewalk in the position shown.

21. *Cleaning Up.*—Upon the completion of the work and fore final acceptance thereof, the contractor shall remove all te porary work from the creek and all rubbish from the street.

22. *Removal of Old Bridge.*—The old bridge shall be remo by contractor. The iron trusses shall be piled up on the bank a the timber and the stone shall become the property of the contract

23. *Temporary Foot Bridge.*—The contractor shall, at his o expense, erect a temporary foot-bridge six feet wide across creek during the construction of the bridge.

24. For all patented appliances or methods used in the c struction of these bridges the contractor shall protect the c against any and all claims on account of such patents and sh himself be held liable for such claims.

The contractor shall bid a lump sum for each bridge complete. stimates shall be made monthly on the amount of work done, but) per cent. of the entire cost of the bridge shall be retained by the ty until the entire bridge has been constructed, tested and ac- pted by the city. The contractor shall file a guarantee bond tisfactory to the Board of Public Works for the sum of five thou- nd dollars ($5,000.00), the same to be in force for three years 'ter the date of the final acceptance of the work. Before the nal acceptance of the work, the contractor shall show a receipt in ıll that all bills have been paid.

(TRACTS FROM SPECIFICATIONS OF ILLINOIS CENTRAL RAILWAY FOR CONCRETE WORK.

Concrete materials may be classed as follows:

A.—Crushed limestone, which shall be stone not larger than two ches in any dimension, properly crushed, and passed through a tary or other screen having holes two inches in diameter. This ay be mixed with smaller crushed stone and stone dust in the ual proportions as it comes from the crusher, but shall have no rthy or clayey matter mixed with it. * * * Large pieces of t stone must not be mixed with the crushed limestone. * * *

B.—*Crushed Granite.*—This shall generally be used of two sizes: fine crushed granite to be used as a substitute for sand, and a arser size, particles of which are not larger than ¾ inch in eatest dimension, and to be used as a substitute for crushed nestone in making bridge seats, pedestal stones, etc. All crushed anite shall be clean, entirely free from dust and earthy or clayey atter, and each grade shall be of practically uniform size. * * *

C.—Sand for concrete shall consist of clean, sharp sand. * * * nd shall not be rejected if containing occasionally pieces of nall gravel. A sand is preferred which will not pass through a having thirty meshes to the inch. Sand shall be free from rth or alluvial matter; and, when tested by stirring with water by rubbing in the hands, shall not show the existence of more an one-half of one per cent. of loam, clay, or earth.

Natural cement concrete may be used where foundations are tirely submerged below low-water mark or where there is no sk of the same being exposed to the action of the water by cut- ng away the surrounding earth. Natural cement concrete, how- er, shall be used only where a firm and uniform foundation is und to exist after excavations are completed. In all cases where undations are liable to be exposed to the action of the water, or here the material in the bottom of the excavations is soft or of nequal firmness, Portland cement concrete must be employed for undation work.

Natural cement concrete shall usually be made in the propor- ons (by measure) of one part of approved cement to two parts of sand and five parts of crushed stone, all of character as ab specified. For Portland cement concrete foundations one part approved cement, three parts of sand and six parts of crusl stone may be used. Wherever * * * a stronger concrete is quired than is above specified * * * a natural cement concrete one, two, and four, and a Portland cement concrete of one, t and five may be substituted for the above.

Portland cement concrete shall generally be made for the bo of piers and abutments, for all wing-walls of same, and for bench walls of arch culverts, in the proportions (by measure) one part of cement, two and one-half parts of sand and six p of crushed stone. Where special strength may be required any of this work, concrete in the proportions of one, two, and may be used. * * *

For arch rings of arch culverts and for parapet head walls copings to same, Portland cement concrete, in proportions of two, and five, shall generally be used. Concrete of these pro tions shall also generally be used for parapet walls behind bri rests of piers or abutments, and for the finished copings (if us on wing walls of concrete abutments.

Bridge seats of piers and abutments and copings of conc masonry, which are to carry pedestals for girders or longer sp of iron work, shall generally be made of crushed granite and P land cement, in the proportion (by measure) of one part of proved cement, two parts of fine granite screenings, and three p of coarser granite screenings, the larger of which shall not excee inch in greatest dimension.

Mixing Concrete.—All concrete must be mixed on substan platforms of boards securely fastened together, so that the vari materials of the concrete can be kept entirely free from mixt of foreign matter. Hand-mixed concrete shall not be made batches of more than one yard in each batch. The proper amo of the several kinds of material shall be measured in some w * * * The measurement of sand and broken stone in the ordin shallow, round bottom wheelbarrow will not be considered sa factory, and shall not be permitted.

The detail of mixing concrete by hand shall be generally as lows: The proper amount of sand shall be measured out spread upon the concrete platform, and the proper amount cement shall be delivered and spread upon the same; the sand cement shall be turned over dry, either by means of shovels hoes, until they are evenly mixed. They shall then be wet made into a rather thin mortar, and shall then again be spr into a uniform and thin layer on the platform. The stone (p viously drenched with water) shall be spread upon the mortar, the whole shall be turned over at least twice * * * bef

p as sprinkler used. The inspector shall insist that the re-
at mixture of sand, cement and stone is as nearly as possible
im in character, the mortar being equally distributed through-
he mass of the stone. Also that the mixture is neither too wet
oo dry. It should be of such a consistency that, when thor-
ly rammed, it will quake slightly, but it should not be thin
gh to quake in the barrow or before ramming. * * *
achine-mixed concrete shall be of the same general consistency
o hand-mixed concrete above specified. Proper precautions
be taken to see that the requisite proportions of the different
dients are used. If machines are used which are not provided
devices to deliver each of them, the process of making con-
shall be as follows: The proper amount of sand, cement,
stone for a batch not to exceed one yard of concrete shall be
ered on the platform and roughly mixed together, so that when
ry mass is cut down and delivered to the mixer by means of
ls, proper amounts of each of the ingredients are handled in
shovelful.

will not be regarded as a satisfactory process to deliver crushed
, sand and cement at random to the mixer, without taking
special means, as above described, to insure the delivery of
roper quantities of each ingredient as nearly as may be simul-
ously.

ulds.—Moulds of substantial character shall be made in which
nstruct all concrete work. * * * The face of the mould
to the concrete shall be finished smooth, plank which are
ed at least on one side being employed for this purpose. Ma-
l for the moulds shall be of sufficient thickness, and the frame
g them shall be of sufficient strength, so that they shall be
ically unyielding during the process of filling, tamping, etc.
ifferent parts of the frame work * * * may be fastened
her by tie rods extending through the concrete. If such tie
are used they shall be so designed that no iron work will be
tside of the concrete or within less than two inches from the
of the same when the moulds are removed. This may be ac-
lished by sleeve nut connections which will permit the removal
e projecting ends of bolts, or rods, etc. * * * Another
factory method of bracing moulds is to construct them with
ties between the front and back, these ties to be placed at
ent intervals above the lower portion of the mould and to be
ed as the concrete is built up, the studding, out of which the
s are constructed, being sufficiently long to extend above the
the finished masonry, and at least one set of ties being used
his level. In general 2-inch plank, sized to approximately
thickness, shall be used for the facing of the moulds, and
for frames shall be placed at intervals not more than 4
. The planking forming the lining of the moulds shall
be fastened to the studding in perfectly horizontal lines,

the ends of these planks shall be neatly butted against each oth and the inner surface of the mould shall be as nearly as possil perfectly smooth, without crevices or offsets between the sides ends of adjacent planks. Where planks are used a second tis they shall be thoroughly cleaned, and, if necessary, the sides a ends shall be freshly jointed so as to make a perfectly smooth fini to the concrete.

Placing Concrete.—Concrete shall generally be placed in t work in layers not exceeding six inches in thickness, and, in ge eral, one layer shall be entirely completed before another one commenced. If delivered by wheelbarrows, it shall be dumped closely as possible where required, so as to avoid as much as p sible the handling or turning over the same by means of show within the excavation or mould. Where it is not practicable entir to complete one layer before commencing a second one, a plar six inches wide or more, shall be securely fastened into the ex vation or mould, against which the end of the layer of concrete sh be rammed, thus providing for a vertical joint in this layer concrete, and if a second layer has to be stopped short of the f length of the work, a second cross plank, placed at least one f back from the end of the first layer, shall be secured to the cavation or to the mould, against which to ram the second la of concrete. Layers of concrete masonry must not be tapered in wedge-shaped slopes, but must be built with square ends in t method above described, and the surface of each projection must finished hard and smooth, and flushed full of mortar, no porosit or loose stone being left thereon. Layers must not be made greater thickness than six inches unless specially permitted, a each layer must be thoroughly rammed, and the concrete must of such consistency that heavy ramming will produce a slig quaking action. In other words, the concrete must be so thorougl compacted that there will be no pores or open spaces between t stone of which it consists, which are not thoroughly filled wi mortar. * * *

A facing of mortar, consisting of one part cement (by measur to two parts of sand, shall be put in next to the moulds, for Portland cement concrete work for piers, abutments, arches, wi walls, parapet walls, and any other places where directed * * to form a finish for all such parts of the above classes of work are to be exposed to the weather, or which are liable to become exposed. A similar facing shall be used for the top surface of concrete masonry not finished with granitoid work, and such s faces shall be finished in the style of sidewalk work.

The exact thickness of one and one-half inches for this faci shall be secured in the following manner: A piece of sheet ir six inches in width (the height of one course of concrete), and any convenient length, say from six feet upwards, having sm angle irons, the projecting leg of which shall be 1½ inches in wi riveted to its face, at intervals of about two feet, and provided with handles standing above the upper edge at or near each end shall be furnished. * * * This piece of iron plate, if placed with the projecting angles against the face of the mould, will leave a space of 1½ inches between it and the mould. This space shall be filled with mortar required for facing, which mortar shall be mixed in small batches from time to time as needed for the work. When the space between the iron plate and the mould is filled and tamped with a shovel or other tool to insure complete filling of the whole space between the iron plate and the face of the mould, and when the layer of ordinary concrete is backed up against this iron plate, it is to be withdrawn by means of the handles and the whole mass of concrete rammed in one uniform layer. * * * Mortar should be of a consistency so that it will flow somewhat freely. At the same time this mortar must not be made so thin that the crushed stone may be forced through it in the process of ramming.

26. *Expansion Joints.*—Where masonry structures are more than 100 feet in length, such provision for expansion joints shall be made as may be specified. * * * Generally in the construction of large arches, or of smaller, long concrete arches, the work shall be subdivided into sections of approximately 25 feet in length, each section being separated from the adjacent one by a vertical joint extending entirely through the bench walls, arch rings, etc.; but the foundation work shall be stepped as previously explained, and made in one continuous monolithic mass. Temporary vertical partitions shall be put into the moulds, against which the concrete shall be thoroughly rammed, where arch culverts are subdivided into short lengths as above specified, these partitions being removed as each section is completed, and the next adjacent section being rammed against the concrete already constructed and set. The joints thus made shall not be flushed with mortar, nor shall any attempt be made to make the fresh concrete adhere to the older work, it being the intention that any contraction shall open, or that settlement shall effect a sliding action at such vertical joints, rather than to break up the concrete in the separate sections.

EXTRACTS FROM THE SPECIFICATIONS FOR A CONCRETE WALL BUILT BY THE HANNIBAL & ST. JOSEPH R. R. CO.

Sand.—Sand will be clean, coarse, and sharp, and will be screened on the site of the work, if necessary.

Cement.—Cement will be of the best quality of freshly ground hydraulic cement, and will be equal in quality to the best brand of Louisville cement.

Cement will be subject to test by the railroad company and must stand a tensile stress of fifty (50) pounds per square inch of sectional area on specimen of neat cement allowed a set of thirty minutes in air and twenty-four (24) hours under water.

Cement will be delivered on the work in original packages and must be carefully protected from moisture.

Broken Stone.—Stone will be hard, sound, and durable; will be thoroughly screened over a three-fourths (¾) inch mesh wire screen, and will be free from mud, clay, dust, or any earthy admixture whatever.

Eighty (80) per cent. of the stones will pass through a ring two (2) inches in diameter, and the remainder through a ring three (3) inches in diameter.

Concrete.—Concrete will consist of one measure of cement, two measures of sand, and about four measures of broken stone. Cement and sand will first be thoroughly mixed dry in a clean, tight box with hoes or by shovels; water will then be added to make a good stiff mortar and will be thoroughly worked to ensure a good mixture; broken stone thoroughly wet will then be added to the mortar, and the materials turned with shovels until the mixture is uniform and each stone covered with mortar.

After mixing, concrete will be quickly laid in horizontal layers not exceeding nine (9) inches in thickness, and will be thoroughly rammed until the water rises freely to the top.

Mortar must be used immediately after being mixed, and under no pretext will mortar be used which requires retempering.

In freezing weather all ice will be removed from the materials composing the concrete, and warm water will be used, containing one pound of salt for each gallon of water when the temperature is at 32 degrees F., and one ounce of salt in addition for every degree of temperature below 30 degrees F.

Contractor will furnish such necessary lumber or other materials as will ensure that all lines and corners will be preserved true and sharp. No portion of the mould will be removed until the concrete resting against it has been in place thirty-six (36) hours.

Finish.—All that portion of the wall above the footing course excepting the post-holes, and all the floor of the manhole and the inside face of inlets will be floated up with a mortar composed of one part of Alsen's German Portland cement and one part of clean, coarse, sharp sand, thoroughly mixed and made into mortar by the addition of water.

EXTRACTS FROM THE RULES AND INSTRUCTIONS FOR MASONS ON "COMPANY WORK" OF NEW YORK CENTRAL & HUDSON RIVER RAILROAD.

Concrete Mixing.—Mix the cement and sand as follows: Spread about one-half of the sand to be used in a batch of mortar evenly over the bed of the mortar box, then spread the cement evenly over the top of the sand, and finally spread the remainder of the sand on top. The sand and cement should then be thoroughly mixed by turning and returning at least six times with a shovel. The mixture is then drawn to one end of the box and water poured in at the other end. Then draw the mixture down to the water with a hoe, small quantities at a time, and mix vigorously until there is a good stiff mortar. Enough water should be used so that the mortar will work well under the trowel. Then level off the mixture and spread over it the required amount of broken stone or gravel, which should be first moistened; then thoroughly mix the whole mass by turning and returning it with shovels in rows, at all times preserving the same thickness of the mass until the mortar thoroughly fills all the interstices.

A thorough mixture of the ingredients is the first condition of a good concrete.

A mortar box with detachable sides will be found economical and convenient for concrete mixing.

Concrete Laying.—After the concrete is mixed it should be quickly laid in sections, in layers not exceeding 8 inches in thickness; and shall be thoroughly rammed with 2-man rammers, weighing not less than 30 pounds each, until the water flushes to the surface. It shall be allowed at least twelve hours to set before any work is laid on it. Concrete mixed for over one hour will not be allowed in the work.

Forms of timber shall be used wherever necessary to maintain the dimensions of the concrete shown on the plans.

Facing Concrete.—Concrete for facing old masonry shall consist of 1 part best quality Portland cement, 2 parts clean, coarse, sharp sand, and 4 parts of ¾-inch broken stone, with outer facing consisting of a mortar of the proportions of one part Dyckerhoff, Germania, or other approved imported Portland cement, to 2 parts clean, coarse, sharp sand of an average thickness of 1 inch deposited simultaneously with the backing; to be securely fastened to the old masonry with anchors and twisted rods as shown on the standard plan. Use moulds as specified below.

Moulds.—The concrete shall be deposited in moulds made from dressed matched siding firmly held in place by exterior braces, joists, etc.; or by bolts or ties so made as to be removed from the work and leave no iron within 1 inch of the face of the finished work. The siding shall be set truly horizontal, with butt-joints truly vertical and with the faces against which the concrete is to be [illegible], dressed, and set to true planes, and covered with soft soap or other approved material to prevent "sticking." After the moulds are removed, any open or porous places shall be neatly stopped with pointing mortar; and if so directed by the engineer, the exposed faces of the work shall be washed with neat Portland cement to give a uniform smooth finish to the exposed surfaces.

Temperature Changes.—In large structures, provision for expansion and contraction shall be made by tarred paper, vertical joints not less than 50 feet apart extending through the mass. Wet down all outside surfaces each day until the expiration of two weeks after the entire work is completed.

CEMENT WALKS.

Some general instructions and specifications for laying cement walks are given, and they are followed by samples of full specifications from St. Louis, Pittsburg and Indianapolis as examples of the variations in specifications which produce good walks.

It is especially important in this class of work to use the best materials, carefully selected, and to exercise great care in every part of the work.

Thorough drainage of the foundation course of gravel, broken stone or cinder must be assured, and this foundation must be at once firm and porous, and well compacted. It is well to do the excavating and filling some time before the concrete is put in, thus securing thorough setting. But cross boards should be placed on the fill and plank laid lengthwise on these to prevent packing of one portion more than another, where the walk is much used.

The thickness of the porous bed is not important if it be certain it is sufficient to insure solidity and perfect drainage at every part.

The bed should be well wet down before putting in the concrete.

Two by four inch strips should be firmly staked on edge with upper edge to grade, and braced apart to desired width with cross pieces between.

A thoroughly mixed body of concrete composed of one part cement, two parts sand and four parts gravel, pebbles or broken stone, is shoveled between the strips, having been tempered to such degree of dampness that when rammed solidly to place some water will be forced to the surface.

Sufficient concrete is used that about three-quarters inch space remains uniformly between the surface of grade and the surface of concrete. The concrete is then cut into blocks with an ax or wedge-shaped tool which leaves a V opening or groove between the blocks. The blocks should not be larger than 4 x 6 feet.

The position of the grooves should be carefully located on the strips or otherwise.

Finally a coat of cement mortar of one part cement and one and one-half parts sand (of excellent quality—coarse, sharp and clean), so tempered that it can be worked to a surface with a straight-edge shifted on the surface of the side strips, is applied to the surface of the concrete. A thin film of mortar is troweled on to the concrete in advance of the main body, being spread over by the straight-edge.

After the straight-edge, a float is used. This is applied just as the surface film of water is being absorbed, and immediately after it a slight troweling to a smooth surface is applied. The troweler then cuts entirely through the walk, in the lines of the joints already formed, with his trowel and bevels the edges of the cut or rounds them with an edging tool. The outer edges are also rounded or beveled.

The walk is then covered with sawdust, fine sand or canvas to protect it from the sun and air, and kept well wet for at least 48 hours, when it may be uncovered and allowed to dry out slowly, with frequent wettings for several days. The strips may then be removed.

Do not dust the surface or trowel very long.

Inside of yards or lawns less thickness of concrete and less proportion of cement may be used.

Lampblack may be mixed with cement to give dark shades when desired.

GRANITOID SIDEWALKS, ST. LOUIS, MO.

The sidewalks shall be of three separate and distinct thicknesses and kinds, and shall be classified as follows: "Ordinary Single Flagging," "Extra Double Thick Flagging" and "Driveway or Entrance Flagging," and shall be laid in the different localities within the prescribed limits at the discretion of the Street Commissioner, who shall determine which of the above named kinds shall be laid.

Grading.—All grading which may be necessary to be done in re- airing or constructing sidewalks in consequence of the adjustment f the grade of any pavement, or in order to protect the work, shall e made of such dimensions as shall be ordered, and all the filling quired shall be spread in thin layers, and must be well rammed, as to render it perfectly compact. All surplus earth shall be uled away, and all borrowed earth, which may be required, shall furnished by the contractor.

Ordinary Single Flagging.—After the grading and shaping is one, a foundation of cinders not less than eight (8) inches thick all be placed upon the sub-grade, which shall be well consolidated ramming to an even surface, and which shall be moistened just fore the concrete is placed thereon.

After the sub-foundation has been finished, the artificial stone gging shall be laid in a good, workmanlike manner.

The same to consist of two parts: 1st. A bottom course, to be ree and one-half ($3\frac{1}{2}$) inches in depth. 2d. A finishing or wear- course, to be one-half ($\frac{1}{2}$) inch in depth.

The bottom course shall be composed of crushed granite and the t Portland cement, equal to the Dyckerhoff brand, and capable withstanding a tensile strain of 400 pounds to the square inch er having been three hours in the air and seven days in water, d shall be mixed in the proportion of one part cement to three rts of crushed granite.

The crushed granite shall consist of irregular, sharp-edged ces, so broken that each piece will pass through a three-fourths

(¾) of an inch ring in all its diameters, and which shall be entirely free from dust or dirt.

The crushed granite and the cement in the above-mentioned proportions shall first be mixed dry, when sufficient clean water shall be slowly added by sprinkling, while the material is constantly and carefully stirred and worked up, and said stirring and mixing shall be continued until the whole is thoroughly mixed.

This mass shall be spread upon the sub-foundation and shall be rammed until all the interstices are thoroughly filled with cement.

Particular care must be taken that the bottom course is well rammed and consolidated along the outer edges.

After the bottom course is completed, the finishing or wearing course shall be added. This course to consist of a stiff mortar composed of equal parts of Portland cement and the sharp screenings of the crushed granite, free from loamy or earthy substance, and to be laid to a depth of one-half (½) of an inch and to be carefully smoothed to an even surface, which, after the first setting takes place, must not be disturbed by additional rubbing.

When the pavement is completed, it must be covered for three days and be kept moist by sprinkling.

Extra Double Thick Flagging.—After the grading and shaping is done, a foundation of cinders not less than six (6) inches thick shall be placed upon the sub-grade, which shall be well consolidated by ramming to an even surface and which shall be moistened just before the concrete is placed thereon. After the sub-foundation has been finished the artificial stone flagging shall be laid in a good, workmanlike manner.

The same to consist of two parts: 1st. A bottom course to be five (5) inches in depth. 2d. A finishing or wearing course to be one (1) inch in depth.

The bottom course shall be composed of crushed granite and the best Portland cement, equal to the Dyckerhoff brand, and capable of withstanding a tensile strain of 400 pounds to the square inch after having been three hours in air and seven days in water, and shall be mixed in the proportion of one part of cement to three parts of crushed granite.

The crushed granite shall consist of irregular, sharp-edged pieces, so broken that each piece will pass through a three-fourths (¾) of an inch ring in all its diameters, and which shall be entirely free from dust or dirt.

The crushed granite and the cement in the above-mentioned proportions shall first be mixed dry, then sufficient clean water shall be slowly added by sprinkling, while the material is constantly and carefully stirred and worked up, and said stirring and mixing shall be continued until the whole is thoroughly mixed.

This mass shall be spread upon the sub-foundation and shall be rammed until all the interstices are thoroughly filled with cement.

Particular care must be taken that the bottom course is well rammed and consolidated along the outer edges.

After the bottom course is completed, the finishing or wearing course shall be added. This course to consist of a stiff mortar composed of equal parts of Portland cement and the sharp screenings of the crushed granite, free from loamy or earthy substances, and to be laid to a depth of one (1) inch and to be carefully smoothed to an even surface, which, after the first setting takes place, must not be disturbed by additional rubbing.

When the pavement is completed, it must be covered for three days and be kept moist by sprinkling.

Driveway or Entrance Flagging.—After the grading and shaping is done, a foundation of crushed limestone and hydraulic cement mortar shall be laid to a depth of six (6) inches on the subgrade. The stone used in this concrete shall be broken so as to pass through a two (2) inch ring in its largest dimensions. The same shall be cleaned from all dust and dirt and thoroughly wetted and then mixed with mortar, the general proportion being: one part of cement, two parts of sand and five parts of stone. It shall be laid quickly and then rammed until the mortar flushes to the surface. No walking or driving over it shall be permitted when it is setting, and it shall be allowed to set for at least twelve hours, and such additional length of time as may be directed by the Street Commissioner or by his duly authorized agent before the pavement is put down.

Pavement.—After the sub-foundation has been finished, the artificial stone flagging shall be laid in a good, workmanlike manner. The same to consist of two parts: 1st. A bottom course to be five (5) inches in depth. 2d. A finishing or wearing course to be one (1) inch in depth.

The bottom course shall be composed of crushed granite and the best Portland cement, equal to the Dyckerhoff brand, and capable of withstanding a tensile strain of 400 pounds to the square inch after having been three hours in air and seven days in water, and shall be mixed in the proportion of one part cement to three parts of crushed granite.

The crushed granite shall consist of irregular, sharp-edged pieces, so broken that each piece will pass through a three-fourths (¾) of an inch ring in all its diameters, and which shall be entirely free from dust or dirt.

The crushed granite and the cement in the above-mentioned proportions shall first be mixed dry, then sufficient clean water shall be slowly added by sprinkling, while the material is constantly and carefully stirred and worked up, and said stirring and mixing shall be continued until the whole is thoroughly mixed.

This mass shall be spread upon the sub-foundation and shall be rammed until all the interstices are thoroughly filled with ce-

Particular care must be taken that the bottom course is well rammed and consolidated along the outer edges.

After the bottom course is completed, the finishing or wearing course shall be added. This course to consist of a stiff mortar composed of equal parts of Portland cement and the sharp screenings of the crushed granite, free from loamy or earthy substances, and to be laid to a depth of one (1) inch and to be carefully smoothed to an even surface, which, after the first setting takes place, must not be disturbed by additional rubbing.

When the pavement is completed, it must be covered for three days and be kept moist by sprinkling.

CEMENT SIDEWALKS, PITTSBURG, PA.

Description.—Pavements of this class shall consist of a foundation of coarse cinder, or broken stone, six (6) inches deep; a layer of Portland cement concrete, three (3) inches thick, and a wearing surface of Portland cement mortar, one (1) inch thick, making the total thickness of the completed pavement at least ten (10) inches.

Broken Stone for Foundation.—The broken stone or cinder to be used in the foundation shall be of approved quality, broken so that the largest dimension of any piece will not exceed three (3) inches, nor the smallest dimension of any piece be less than one (1) inch, and must be free from dust, dirt or other foreign matter

Broken Stone for Concrete.—Broken stone for concrete shall be a good, hard stone that will not be affected by the weather, broken so that the longest dimension of any stone will not exceed one and one-half (1½) inches, nor the least dimension of any stone be less than one-quarter (¼) of an inch, and must be free from dust, dir or other foreign matter.

Gravel for Concrete.—Gravel used for concrete shall be washed river gravel of such sizes that the greatest diameter of any pebble will not exceed one and one-half (1½) inches, nor the least dimension of any pebbles be less than one-quarter (¼) of an inch, and must be free from dust, dirt or other foreign matter.

Sand.—The sand shall be of the best quality of coarse, sharp clean Allegheny river sand, free from dust, loam or other foreign matter, or a sand equal in quality thereto.

Portland Cement.—Portland cement shall be equal in every respect to that described in the specifications for "Portland cement."

Water.—Water shall be fresh and free from earth, dirt or sewage

Width.—The width of the pavement shall be such as the director may specify.

Sub-Grade.—This shall be prepared as specified for "slag."

Foundation.—The foundation shall be of cinder or broken stone as hereinbefore specified, and shall be drained to the curb ditch b

Concrete.—The concrete shall consist of 1 part in volume of Portland cement, 3 parts of sand and 6 parts of broken stone or gravel.

Mixing Sand and Cement.—The cement and sand in the specified proportions shall be thoroughly mixed dry, on a tight platform with shovels or hoes until no streaks of cement are visible.

Mortar.—Water shall be added to the sand and cement, mixed in accordance with the foregoing directions, in sufficient quantities to produce a mortar of the desired consistency, and the whole thoroughly mixed with shovels or hoes until a homogeneous mass is produced.

Mixing Concrete.—The mortar, prepared as hereinbefore specified, shall be spread upon the platform, the proper quantity of broken stone or gravel, after having been thoroughly wetted, shall then be spread over the mortar and the mass thoroughly turned over with shovels or hoes not less than three (3) times, or until every pebble or piece of broken stone is completely coated with mortar.

Sprinkling.—Water shall be added by sprinkling during the process of mixing if required to secure a better consistency.

Surfaces to be Cleaned and Dampened.—All surfaces on or against which concrete is to be laid shall be thoroughly cleaned and dampened, by sprinkling with water, just previous to placing the concrete.

Spreading Concrete.—The concrete shall be evenly spread upon the foundation, as soon as mixed, in a layer of such depth that after having been thoroughly compacted with rammers of approved pattern it shall not be in any place less than three (3) inches thick, and the upper surface of it shall be parallel with the proposed surface for the completed pavement.

Marking Flags.—The slab or flag divisions shall be formed by cutting the concrete clear through, on the required lines, as soon as [illegible]. The space made by the cutting tool shall be immediately filled with dry sand and well rammed.

Size of Batches.—Concrete shall not be mixed in larger quantities than is required for immediate use, and no batch shall be larger than can be made of one barrel of cement with the proper proportions of sand and stone.

Concrete Not to be Thrown from a Distance.—Concrete shall not be dropped from too great a height or thrown from too great a distance when being placed upon the work.

Wearing Surface.—The wearing surface shall be composed of one part in volume of Portland cement and two (2) parts of sand.

Mixing.—The cement and sand in the specified proportions shall be thoroughly mixed dry, on a tight platform, with shovels or hoes, until no streaks of cement are visible.

Mortar.—Water shall be added to the sand and cement, mixed in accordance with the foregoing directions, in sufficient quantities to produce a mortar of the desired consistency, and the whole thoroughly mixed with shovels or hoes until a homogeneous mass is produced.

Laying.—The mortar, while fresh, shall be spread upon the concrete base before the latter has reached its first set, in such quantities that after being thoroughly manipulated and spread over the concrete it will make a layer one inch thick, conforming to the required grade and cross-section.

Top Dressing.—A coating of equal parts of Portland cement and dry, fine sand, thoroughly mixed, shall be swept over the surface and the surface dressed and smoothed. On steep grades the top dressing shall consist of coarse granite screenings and cement.

Flag Markings.—The surface shall then be cut into flags, the markings to be made directly over the joints in the concrete and cut clear through the wearing surface.

Marking of Surface.—The flags shall then be trued up and marked over, with the exception of a border of about an inch in width along the edges, with a toothed roller.

Protection of Top.—The pavement shall be kept moist and protected from the elements and travel until it has set.

Entrances to be Preserved.—Entrances from adjoining streets or walks to all private or public premises shall be preserved by the contractor.

Cross Section.—The completed pavement shall, unless otherwise ordered, have a rise of one-quarter (¼) of an inch to the foot rising from the curb.

Forms.—Board or timber forms shall be provided by the contractor to mould the concrete and mortar to the required shape, and shall be left in place until the concrete or mortar is set.

Retempering Not Permitted.—Retempering of concrete or mortar will not be permitted, and mortar or concrete that has begun to set before ramming is completed shall be removed from the work.

Mortar and Concrete That Has Not Set.—Concrete or mortar that fails to show a proper bond or fails to set, after, in the opinion of the director, it has been allowed sufficient time, shall be taken up and replaced with new concrete or mortar, of the proper quality, by the contractor.

Pavement to be Maintained.—If at any time during the guarantee period any cracks, scales or other defects develop in the pavement, the pavement at that point shall be taken up and relaid with new materials, in accordance with these specifications, by the contractor.

CEMENT SIDEWALKS, INDIANAPOLIS, IND.

1. Stakes will be set by the Engineer to define the line of one edge of the walk, and the grade marks will indicate the top of the walk at said line. The transverse slope of the walk will be one-

fourth inch per foot, and will be determined with level and grade board made according to drawing in Engineer's office.

2. The sidewalk shall be graded to the width as shown on plan for the entire length of the improvement, including all wings and crossings, as shown on plan, and sixteen inches below the finished surface of the walk. The grading must be smoothly and neatly done, all large stones, bowlders, roots, sods and rubbish of every description being removed from the grade, and the entire work must be made to conform fully to the profile and the grade of the walk when finished. Soft, spongy or loamy spots in the sub-grade must be taken out and refilled with good material and the grade solidified by ramming.

3. Trees shall not be injured, cut down or otherwise disturbed except by order of the Engineer. Roots of trees which are not removed, but which are contiguous to the line and grade of the walk or in any way interfere therewith, must be trimmed and cut away as the Engineer shall direct, and where the Engineer directs the stones shall be fitted to the trees and roots covered with earthenware half-pipes. Any tree removed must be grubbed for the entire width of the sidewalk and also all its roots that rise above the level of the sub-grade. No extra compensation for such work will be allowed.

4. Upon the sub-grade thus prepared and after inspection and acceptance of the same, a foundation of sand and fine gravel, or broken stone, in such proportions as, when rammed, will form a solid and compact mass, shall be spread to a uniform depth of twelve inches, all to be rammed and tamped until it presents a hard, smooth surface. It shall be sprinkled with water as required, enough remaining to render the surface as moist as the concrete at the time the latter is laid.

5. Wooden frames four inches in height will be placed in the manner necessary to outline both external edges of the walk accurately, the top of the frames being located to coincide with the established grade of the walk. Gauges must be used to render surface of foundation layer and of concrete parallel to the top of the walk. Concrete will be made as follows: One measure of Portland cement as hereafter specified for sidewalks, and two measures of clean, sharp sand or granite mixed thoroughly, while dry, and then made into mortar with the least possible amount of water; broken stone or gravel not over one inch in any dimension, thoroughly cleansed from dirt and dust, and drenched with water, but containing no loose water in the heap, will then be mixed immediately with the mortar in such quantities as will give a surplus of mortar when rammed. This proportion, when ascertained, will be regulated by measure. The Engineer may accept a clean, natural mixture of sand and gravel if it is uniform and contains no dirt, clay or stones larger than above specified. The proportions will be one part of cement to five parts of the mixture. Each batch of con-

crete will be thoroughly mixed, and the Engineer may prescribe the number of times it shall be turned over, wet and dry, to accomplish this result. In general it shall be turned (or cut) four (4) times dry and three (3) times wet. It will then be spread to fill the frames even full and be at once compacted thoroughly by ramming until free mortar appears on the surface and until a one and one-fourth (1¼) inch gauge, furnished by the inspector, shall pass over the concrete. It is the intention that the surface of the concrete, when thoroughly rammed, shall be at least one and one-fourth (1¼) inch below the top of the frame. The whole operation of mixing and laying each batch of concrete will be performed as expeditiously as possible.

6. After each batch of concrete is laid, as required, it shall be immediately covered with the wearing surface. Any portion of the foundation which has been left long enough to have any appearance of setting, shall be taken up and relaid before the top is put on, and under no circumstances will concrete be allowed to remain over night before top is put on. The wearing surface on top shall be composed of one part of the same cement used in the concrete and one part of clean, sharp sand, thoroughly mixed dry and made into mortar with the least possible amount of water. It shall be evenly and compactly spread to the finished surface of the walk and made smooth and even by troweling and floating. The top and concrete foundation shall be cut into blocks of dimensions approved by the Engineer. The pavement shall be properly fitted around all fixtures in the sidewalks, the edges of the pavement to be beveled from top surface to bottom of concrete with the material used on the top. When finished, the work shall be kept covered from the sun for three days and kept moist by sprinkling until thoroughly set.

7. Coloring matter of quality and quantity approved by the Engineer will be required for the top surface. On business streets the Engineer may require the surface to be carefully rolled with a toothed roller when the finish is completed.

8. Where walks of any description that now exist on the street shall be accepted by the Board of Public Works or the Engineer, they shall be relaid if the Engineer deems it necessary, to the grade and line established, and if the price therefor is not fixed in the contract, it shall be determined by adding fifteen per cent. to the actual cost of the work as determined by the Engineer. Similar procedure will be taken for extra work in resetting area ways and similar structures to grade and line. When a driveway occurs in the line of the walk, the walk will be increased in thickness and laid according to plans furnished by the Engineer, the additional expense to be paid by the owner.

9. All blocks used shall be perfect and of good quality in all respects, free from cracks, warps and similar imperfections. Special care shall be taken to protect the walk at night. If found

ot to comply with the specifications in any respect at any time p to the end of the guarantee period, they shall be taken out imnediately and replaced by the contractor at his own expense. All lisfigured walks shall be taken up and replaced by the contractor t his own expense.

10. Embankments shall be formed of compact earth free from arge stones or perishable materials, and shall be raised to such a eight as to conform to the grade and line after such embankment hall have become well settled by properly tamping, ramming or olling the same.

11. The lawns shall be graded to conform to walk and curb rades and dressed with fine earth, raked and left smooth. If aleady in grass, they shall be left in proper condition, satisfactory o the Engineer, and any unnecessary damage shall be repaired. Traffic on the street must not be interfered with, and the walk nust be laid in sections which will interfere as little as possible vith foot passengers. As soon as the walk has been completed n front of any lot, the contractor shall clean street in front of ompleted sidewalk of all surplus material, cement, sand, gravel, arrels, etc., used in its construction, and permanently improved treets shall be swept each night in front of completed sidewalk.

12. For class "A" sidewalks, the following brands of cements vill be allowed: (Nine brands of German and Danish cements re named.) For concrete, one part of cement to five parts of clean ravel and sand as before specified shall be used. The top shall e composed of one part of cement to one part of equal parts of lean, coarse sand and granite.

13. For class "B" sidewalks the following brands of cement vill be allowed: (Fourteen German, Danish and Belgian cenents, and four American Portland cements are named). For the oncrete one part of cement to five parts of clean gravel and sand hall be used. The top surface shall be composed of one part of ement to one part of clean, sharp sand.

14. For class "C" cement sidewalks: All such Portland cements nay be used which comply with Section 9 of Specifications for Cenent Form H, as regards test and provided that conditions mentoned in Section 10 of said Specifications be fulfilled.

15. The lawns shall be sodded, as shown on plans, with bluerass sod, free from weeds, and of such quality as approved by the ity Engineer. All joints shall be broken in laying and the sod hall be rolled to a uniform and even surface.

16. All old walks shall be removed by the contractor unless laimed by the property owner, according to Section 38 of the eneral Specifications.

The following notes on typical specifications for concrete sidealks, by Sanford E. Thompson, Asso. M. Am. Soc. C. E., in *ement*, are of interest and value in this connection:

The specifications for the construction of concrete sidewalks in various localities throughout the United States show considerable uniformity, and yet vary sufficiently so that an outline of methods employed in different places may be of interest.

It is not intended to draw from these fragmentary notes a set of ideal specifications, for the difference in construction followed in different cities may be due partly to the character of the soil upon which the walk is to be laid, partly to the climate—that is, to the extent to which the sidewalk may be affected by frost, and in part to the kinds of material which can be most readily obtained. The amount of wear which the pavement is to receive may also influence the thickness or the construction. It is believed that the data given, however, will furnish hints of value to those interested in this line of work.

In the cities selected to illustrate the different methods of paving throughout the country scarcely two of them designate concrete sidewalks in their specifications by the same terms. They are variously called "Artificial Stone Sidewalks," "Portland Cement Flag Stonewalks," "Granolithic Cement Concrete," "Cement Sidewalks," "Portland Cement Concrete Sidewalks," "Artificial Stone Flagging," or simply "Artificial Walks."

The styles of construction in the several cities vary less than the names by which the sidewalks are designated. The following table gives a very meagre outline of the dimensions and the character of the materials employed in several cities selected in different parts of the United States.

City.	Foundation.		Base.		Wearing Surface.			Dry Coating		Size of Blocks.	Guarantee.
	Thickness.	Material.	Thickness.	Proportions	Thickness.	Proportions Cement.	Proportions Sand.	Proportions Cement.	Proportions Sand		Yrs.
Boston	12"	Broken stone, gravel or cinders	3"	1:2:5	1"	1:1		......		Bet. 3½–6 ft. sq.	10
Rochester, N.Y.	6"	Sand, gravel, broken stone or cinders	**	1:5	1"	2:3		......		......	5
Phil'd'phia, Pa.	3"	Sand, gravel, broken brick stone or cinders	3"	......	2"	1:2		1:1		......	..
Wash'gt'n, D.C.	0		4"	1:2:5	1"	2:3		1:1		......	5
Chicago, Ill.	0 or 12"*	Cinders	4¼" av.	1:2:5	¾"	1:1		......		5 ft. × 6 ft.	20
Milwaukee, Wis	4"	Cinders or broken stone	2½"	1:3:5	1"	1:1		......		Bet. 36–38 sq. ft.	...
St Louis, Mo.	8"	Cinders	3½"	1:3	½"	1:1		......		......	1
Omaha, Neb.	4"	Gravel, slag or stone	3"	1:2:4	1"	1:2		3:1		......	5

* 12" cinders required where the soil is not clean sand.
** Specified for each contract.

This table merely ilustrates some of the differences in construction. To show more clearly some of the special methods followed, the various divisions of the work will be considered more in detail, using for sake of uniformity the same cities classified in the table.

Foundation.—In all of the cities the specifications require that excavation, or fill, shall be made to a definite sub-grade, and that all insecure or spongy material below this sub-grade shall be dug out and refilled with gravel, or its equivalent, and thoroughly puddled, rammed or rolled. Foundation to be placed upon this sub-grade varies considerably in different localities, both in the character of the material and the thickness of the layer. The character of the sub-soil and the climate influence the thickness necessary for good work. Many places require that the material used shall pass through a 1½-inch or 2-inch ring. All cities require that it shall be thoroughly rammed, and sometimes puddling is specified.

Concrete Materials.—Portland cement is always required, and in general the selection of the brand is limited to the best German or American cements. Some cities specify only German Portland; others give a list of German and American Portlands from which selection may be made; while others give representative brands and allow some discretion to the Superintendent.

The specifications for the cement in most of the cities require that when sifted through a sieve of 10,000 meshes per square inch, there shall not be left over 10 per cent. residue. St. Louis allows 15 per cent. residue, and Chicago allows only 8 per cent. In addition to this test, Boston and Cambridge, Mass., require that when sifted through a sieve of 32,500 meshes per square inch, there shall not be left over 45 per cent. residue. Chicago requires that, when mixed with 20 per cent. of water by measure, the initial set shall not take place in less than 45 minutes. Chicago also requires that the cement shall meet the requirements of the "boiling" test.

For tensile strength part of the cities require 500 pounds per square inch for neat briquettes which have remained twenty-four hours in air and six days in water, while others require 400 pounds, with the same test. Some of the cities require an additional test of cement mixed with sand or screenings. In Chicago one part of cement and four parts fine granite screenings, exposed one day in air and six days in water, must show a tensile strength of 200 pounds per square inch and a gradual increase of strength of 15 per cent. a the end of twenty-eight days. In the District of Columbia the specifications for the cement must conform to the current specifications for the Engineering Department of the District of Columbia.

The sand for use in the base is generally a clean, sharp sand. In Chicago clean torpedo sand is specified, ranging from ⅛ inch in size down to the finest. Voids there are not to exceed 30 per cent., and the weight must be not less than 109 pounds per cubic foot. Washington requires that sand shall range from fine to coarse, and shall be free from impurities, but may show when shaken with water and after subsidence not more than 3 per cent. by volume of silt or loam.

The kind of material used for the coarse stuff of the concrete base varies considerably in different places. Boston requires that it shall consist of sharp gravel or broken stone, not exceeding ¾ inch in size. Rochester, N. Y., specifies that fine, clean gravel, not over ¾ inch in size, shall be delivered on to the work and sift through an inclined screen having 16 meshes per square inch. For the base of the pavement is taken the clean, medium, fine gra from the front of the screen, and for the wearing surface is us the sand from behind the screen. In Philadelphia the stone mu be solid trap rock, or other approved hard slag or stone, and m pass through a 1½-inch ring. Chicago specifies crushed limesto not more than 1 inch in any direction. Milwaukee states th there shall be used cubical broken limestone, not over ¾ inch any direction. Omaha allows broken stone or slag up to 1½ in in greatest diameter.

The material for the wearing surface also varies largely in d ferent localities. Boston requires one part of fine crushed tr or granite rock, screened through ¼-inch mesh, or one part of Ne buryport sea sand to one part of Portland cement. In Philad phia two parts of crushed granite to one part imported Portla cement are used, and the granite must be free from dust and such size that the largest particles shall pass through a ¼-in sieve. In Washington the same sand is used for the surface coat is used for making the concrete of the base. Chicago uses part Portland cement to one part torpedo gravel. Milwaukee quires one part Portland cement to one part finely crushed grani which shall have square or cubical fracture and not measure o ¼ inch in any direction. Omaha requires substantial stone or gra ite which will pass through ½-inch mesh screen, mixed one p cement to two of crushed stone.

A few other cities require that dry cement shall be floated on of the surface when finishing. In Philadelphia this dryer is to one part cement to one part sharp flint sand. In Omaha, N three parts Portland cement to one part sand.

Concrete Curb.—In Boston the foundation for a curb is inches thick and consists of broken stone, screened gravel or s coal cinders thoroughly rammed. Upon this foundation is la concrete 12 inches wide and 8 inches deep, and before this is a layer of concrete 7 inches wide at the bottom and 11 inches de is placed, tapering on the outside to 6 inches wide at the top. T inside face is vertical. On the face and top a 1-inch wearing su face is laid. The exposed face is brushed with a brittle bru before becoming entirely dry.

Combined Curb and Gutter.—In Milwaukee a combined c and gutter is often laid. This consists of a curb 5 inches wide the top, having 7 inches of face above the gutter and a gutter inches in width. It is constructed in alternate sections of sto 6 feet in length. The face corner of the curb is rounded to radius of 1½ inches. The gutter flag is laid to a pitch correspo ing to the crown of the street. Excavation is made to a depth 11 inches below the gutter flag, except where a sub-soil drain required, when a 3-inch drain tile is placed below this sub-gra

foundation consists of cinders or broken stone 6 inches thick, upon this is laid the concrete core of the combined gutter and which is 4 inches thick on the bed and 4 inches in width in moulds set for the curb. A 1-inch finishing layer is placed the surface of the gutter and the face of the curb before it is troweled as usual, and then finished with a broom.

riveways.—Driveways are sometimes made of the same thick- as the regular sidewalk and sometimes thicker. In Rochester, Y., the total thickness for driveways is 6 inches, 4½ inches of being base and 1½ inches the top. In this city the contract for a driveway is 1½ times the contract price for the walk. aces of driveways are usually marked off in 6-inch squares.

lauses.—Several of the cities have special clauses which are of rest. Some of these apply particularly to the locality of the while others might generally be adopted to advantage.

Boston the specifications require that no work shall be done November 15th, or in freezing weather. In this city a metal bearing the name and the address of the contractor and the of the year in which the sidewalk is laid must be placed in sidewalk. Boston requires that no adjoining blocks shall be within six hours of each other, and the requirement is also made where spalling, splitting off, or other defects occur after com- the entire block or division must be replaced with a new or division, no patching being allowed.

hiladelphia specifies that no concrete shall be kept over half our after mixing before it is laid.

ashington specifications state that only one barrel of cement be used to a batch. In Washington, after leveling off the surface finishing coat or wearing surface, it is beaten with wooden to break any air cells and make surfacing perfectly solid. long walks transverse expansion pieces of dressed white pine x 6 inches are provided at intervals of about 200 feet.

Louis requires that the bottom course, which is 3½ inches and is composed of one part Portland cement to three parts granite, shall receive no less than one barrel cement to 36 square feet of sidewalk.

most of the cities a uniform thickness of walk is required, in Chicago the thickness is 5½ inches in the center, sloping to inches at each edge. Chicago requires that the walks shall re- at the original grade for ten years, and thus makes its con- tors responsible for the foundation. Many cities build their s with a slope of about ¾ inch to the foot toward the gutter. A specifications require that the walk shall be covered with moist until the cement is set; some specify that the length of time be three days. In some cases it is specified that the walks , or may, when required, be rolled with a metal roller to give indented finish. In one or two of the cities the authorities keep back 10 per cent. of the contract price to have a guarantee that repairs will be satisfactorily made. In the district of Columbia this amount may be invested in government bonds, if desired by the contractor.

The specifications for cement curb and gutter in Indianapolis, under which over fifty miles have been laid, are as follows:

CEMENT CURBING, INDIANAPOLIS.

1. The curb stone must be of the best quality of granite, blue oolitic limestone, stratified limestone or Berea sandstone, Parkhurst or other artificial combined curb and gutter.

2. The contractor must make good any disturbance of sidewalk or lawn and any unnecessary disturbance of trees in setting curb. Special construction to protect trees shall be made when deemed necessary by the Engineer.

3. The curb shall be under the same guarantee as the street surface.

4. Combined curb and gutter shall be set to stakes set by the Engineer at points necessary to accurately designate the line and grade of the proposed curb and gu e and any variation in the height of the same between grade points and catch-basin inlets.

5. The material to be used shall be Portland cement as specified in "Class A" for sidewalks (see Cement Sidewalk Specifications), clean, sharp, coarse sand, crushed granite and granite screenings with no stone with any dimensions over one inch.

6. The combined curb and gutter, whether Parkhurst or otherwise, shall be constructed upon a two and one-half inch concrete foundation before the concrete has become firmly set, so as to secure complete adherence between the two. The combined curb and gutter shall consist of a curb six (6) inches wide at the top and generally seven (7) inches high above the gutter where it joins the curb, and a gutter sixteen (16) inches wide and six (6) inches deep so constructed that the curb and gutter shall be monolithic. It will be composed of a concrete core or backing faced with one inch in thickness of facing or finishing mortar as shown by drawing on file in the office of the City Engineer. The core or backing will be constructed of concrete composed of

Portland cement	1	
Clean sharp sand	2½	part.
Crushed granite, crushed bowlders, or screened gravel	5	parts.

The crushed granite or bowlders shall be clean and sound, broken so that every fragment will pass through a screen with meshes one inch square, and all dust and particles smaller than a grain of corn shall be screened out. The Portland cement and sand shall be first well mixed dry and then sufficient water added, and the mixing continued until mortar of uniform composition and of the proper consistency is produced.

The crushed stone shall then be added and thoroughly mixed with the mortar until every fragment of stone is coated with mortar. The concrete will then be put in place and well compacted by ramming. The whole operation must be completed before the mortar begins to set.

The facing or finishing mortar shall be composed of

Portland cement	2 parts.
Clean sharp sand	1 part.
Crushed granite	3 parts.

The crushed granite screenings shall be made from hard, sound stone, and the fragments shall be of such size that all will pass through a screen having one-fourth-inch meshes, and all fine dust shall be screened out. The facing mortar shall be mixed in the same manner as the concrete described above.

If ordinary artificial combined curb and gutter is used it shall be constructed as specified, and there shall be no projections on back and bottom, nor shall there be any other infringement on the Parkhurst patent. If Parkhurst curb is used a projection of one inch on back and bottom according to Parkhurst patent shall be constructed as approved by the City Engineer.

7. Concrete, immediately after being mixed as above specified, shall be placed in the necessary forms or moulds as rapidly as it can be thoroughly compacted by ramming with a twenty-pound rammer until the moulds are full and the curb is ready for surfacing.

8. The entire exposed surface of the curb and gutter shall be faced by floating and troweling a coat of neat cement so as to give it a uniform color throughout.

9. The work shall be carried on uniformly and the whole curb and gutter completed while in a soft and plastic state, so that it will become a homogeneous solid when set.

10. Sections in the curb shall not be less than seven feet long.

PARKHURST COMBINED CURB AND GUTTER.

First. The gutter and curb must be so combined as to form one ...tinuous and solid stone, and the combined curb and gutter stone ...st be of the same general dimensions shown in diagram on file.

Second. No additional allowance will be made for round cor... nor for cutting holes for catch-basins, and the price paid for ...bing shall be per lineal foot in place complete.

1. The materials to be used shall be Portland cement, and ...arp, coarse sand, medium-sized gravel, or stone crushed to ...er size, all subject to the approval of the City Engineer.

... One part Portland cement, 2½ parts sand, and 5 parts ... crushed stone, shall be used in the backs and bottom ...e curb. The exposed surface of both curb and gutter shall ... with two (2) parts Portland cement, and three (3) parts fine crushed granite, or trap-rock, and sand sufficient to make a smooth and even finish, but not to exceed one (1) part.

Fifth. Portland cement must be used which shall stand a tensile strength of 300 pounds per square inch after seven days, six days in water and one day in air, and which shall have a crushing strength of 2,000 pounds per square inch after having been immersed in water seven days, and then exposed to the air thirteen days, and the contractor shall furnish for testing a sample of each and every barrel of cement to be used in the construction of artificial stone curb and gutter whenever the Engineer may request it.

Sixth. The material—of the quantity and in the proportions herein specified—shall be mixed while dry, and until the mixture has an even color. Water shall then be added slowly while the materials are being constantly and thoroughly mixed, and stirred until an evenly tempered and complete mortar suitable for moulding is obtained. The mortar thus obtained shall be immediately placed in the moulds as rapidly (but not more rapidly) as it can be thoroughly rammed, until the mould is full and the top is finished in the manner herein specified.

Seventh. The entire exposed face of the curb and gutter shall be faced by floating and troweling, so as to give it a uniform color throughout.

Eighth. The curbing is to be set to the true line and grade of the street, on a bed of six inches of fine gravel, sand or broken stone, or cinders thoroughly tamped. At the street and alley corners the curb to be made on a curve of such radius as the Engineer may direct, with true and even joints, and to be of the same description and set in the same manner as the curb before described.

STREET CROSSINGS AND DRIVE PAVEMENTS.

Excavate street 6 in. below grade line if sub-stratum is gravel, [illegible] or porous soil; if clay or an impervious soil, excavate 4 inches [illegible] and fill that with cinders, gravel or broken stone. Thoroughly ro[illegible] to proper section, lay sub-drains of 3-inch tile inside each curb lin[illegible] Pavement is laid in two courses: 1st layer, 4 inches thick, consi[illegible] of 1 part Portland cement and 4 parts clean gravel or broken st[illegible] and sand. Proportion of gravel to sand, 2 to 1. Materials are th[illegible] oughly mixed by machine; just enough water being added so [illegible] when well rammed, water will show at surface.

Second layer, or top, 2 inches thick, which takes the wear, co[illegible] sists of equal parts Portland cement and clean, sharp sand, [illegible] crushed granite including all grains to the size of a pea. Only [illegible] best of cement should be used for this purpose. The top layer [illegible] thoroughly rammed. Both bottom and top layers are divided d[illegible] ing construction into rectangular blocks about 5 feet square, w[illegible] edges neatly finished. The joints of blocks coming directly o[illegible] pipes are made like the keystone of an arch, so they can be li[illegible] up without disturbing neighboring blocks, when repairs to pipes [illegible] necessary. To secure a positive foot-hold for horses, the surface can have v-shaped grooves 1 inch wide and 3-16 in. deep, 4 inches apart and running at right angles with the street. Surface should be finished with an ordinary plasterer's wooden float. Curbs are part of outer blocks and consist of 1 part cement to 3 parts fine gravel.

aterials for one square yard equal 144 lbs. cement and 3 cu. ft. of gravel.

PREPARATION OF CONCRETE FLOORS.

For the construction of durable cement floors or sidewalks the foundation must be suitably prepared. For outdoor work on yielding ground a porous layer, at least 10 inches thick, of coarse gravel or slag should be laid, well rammed down and leveled. For indoor work on dry ground it is sufficient to level the surface and stamp it down firmly. Floors and sidewalks are generally built in two layers; a lower bed of concrete 2½ to 4 inches thick, and a surface coat of richer mortar of a thickness of ¾ to 1½ inches.

The concrete layer may be made richer or poorer, according to the service which the work must undergo. For heavy duty a mixture of cement 1, sand 3 and gravel 6 is recommended. In less important work cement 1, sand 5 and gravel 10 will answer. A suitable mixture for ordinary requirements is, cement 1, sand 4 and gravel 8 or broken stone 6.

The surface layer consists of cement 1, sand 1, and must be spread over the concrete before the latter has set. Before spreading the top layer the concrete should be freed from loose material and its surface roughed up. The mortar is spread with a straight-edge and when sufficiently hardened is finished with a wooden tool. A grooved roller is used to produce a ribbed surface, especially in sidewalk work.

When the work is finished and the cement is well set, the surface is carefully covered with a layer of sand 4 inches in thickness. This is moistened and kept in place for several weeks if possible. Only in this way can the formation of hair-cracks be prevented and a well hardened surface obtained.

Cement expands and contracts with changes of temperature, in the same way as iron, wood, sandstone and other materials. From this cause, if the necessary care has not been taken in the work, cracks will result, especially in wide surfaces. These may be avoided by dividing the flooring into smaller blocks, which should not exceed 4 to 5 square yards in area, and should be separated by strips of tar paper or by sand joints ⅜ inch in width. The joints in the concrete must correspond with those cut in the surface layer. The division of the work into blocks is also to be recommended in concrete walls and curbs.

If necessary, lay weeping drain round the inside of all outside walls, fill in over drain with brick or stone chips; then level off the bottom of cellar to an even surface, and fill in 4 inches or 6 inches of broken stone, bricks, or cinders, making the excavation enough deeper to allow this foundation below the concrete work described.

FLOORS FOR WET CELLARS.

When water flows into a cellar and can not be drained by terra cotta pipe, it is necessary to make a very strong floor to resist the outside water pressure.

1st. Prepare the bottom of the cellar in the shape of a shallow dish with the lowest part in the center.

2d. Dig a shallow well in the center and lead all the water to this well by cutting shallow ditches from the four corners of the cellar and laying 2-inch drain tile to the well or fill the ditches with loose broken stone. Keep the cellar pumped dry.

3d. Pave the cellar with hard-burned bricks, set on edge, laid in cement mortar, working from the four sides towards the center, keeping the well open in order to pump out the water.

4th. On this foundation lay the cement concrete floor.

5th. When the floor is hard plug up the hole in the center with bricks and quick-setting cement.

PORTLAND CEMENT STEPS, STAIRS, WINDOWSILLS AND CURBING.

Same as floors, except that they should be put in frames and allowed to become hard before frames are removed.

Specifications for cement mortar for sidewalks, foundations, masonry, etc., in Philadelphia, Pa., are as follows:

CEMENT MORTAR, PHILADELPHIA.

1. *Sand and Water.*—Sand shall be sharp, silicious, dry-screened, tide-washed bar sand—or approved flint bank sand, free from loam or other extraneous matter. The water must be fresh and free from dirt. When so directed by the Chief Engineer salt water may be required to prevent mortar from freezing when absolutely necessary to lay masonry in cold weather.

2. *Composition.*—Portland cement mortar shall be composed of one part of cement and three parts of sand. Natural cement mortar shall be composed of one part of cement and two parts of sand.

Mortar for pointing, grouting, bedding coping stones and bridge seats, shall be composed of one part Portland cement and two parts sand. A greater proportion of cement shall be used when required.

3. *Mixing.*—The ingredients, properly proportioned by measurement, must be thoroughly mixed dry in a tight box of suitable dimensions, and the proper amount of clean water added afterwards. No greater quantity is to be prepared than is required for immediate use, and any that has "set" shall not be retempered or used in any way.

4. *Tensile Strength.*—Mortar taken from the mixing box, and

moulded into briquettes one square inch in cross-section, shall develop the following ultimate tensile strengths:

Age.	Strength.
7 days (1 day in air, 6 days in water), 1 part of natural cement to 2 parts of sand	50 lbs.
28 days (1 day in air, 27 days in water), 1 part of natural cement to 2 parts of sand	125 lbs.
7 days (1 day in air, 6 days in water), 1 part of Portland cement to 3 parts of sand	125 lbs.
28 days (1 day in air, 27 days in water), 1 part of Portland cement to 3 parts of sand	175 lbs.

Specifications for cement mortar and concrete in Buffalo are as follows:

MORTAR AND CONCRETE, BUFFALO.

Sand and Mortar.—(62.)—All sand used in the mortar must be clean, sharp, coarse, lake sand, free from loam or vegetable matter. The proportion of sand and cement for natural cement mortar will be two (2) of sand to one (1) of cement by measure. Sufficient water will be used to make a plastic mass. Pointing mortar will be mixed, one (1) of sand to one (1) of Portland cement. All cement mortars shall be used immediately after mixing, and any that has been mixed more than half an hour, or has commenced to set, shall be rejected and thrown away.

Concrete.—(63.)—Concrete will consist of above described quality of cement, clean, sharp, coarse, lake sand, and clean stone broken so that no dimension is larger than two (2) inches.

The cement and sand shall be mixed as required for mortar, and then thoroughly mixed by use of shovels with broken stone, in the proportion of one (1) cement, two (2) of sand, five (5) of broken stone immediately before using. When put in place it will at once be leveled off, and tamped as directed by the Engineer, but must not be touched afterwards.

When it is impossible to finish the concrete in one day, the surface and ends thereof to be left, and also the method of continuing such concrete to form good bond or union to be as the Engineer may direct. No masonry to be built on the concrete until the Engineer permits.

Following are the specifications for mortar for all uses, prescribed by the City of Indianapolis, and the specifications for its use in laying sewer pipe, brick masonry, plastering and concrete for sewers and street foundations.

CEMENT MORTAR AND ITS USE IN SEWERS, MASONRY AND CONCRETE, INDIANAPOLIS.

Mortar.—1. A rectangular box shall be provided for mixing mortar, which, if required, shall be marked with cleats or otherwise to give quantities of cement and sand.

2. Mortar for brick and stone masonry and concrete shall cc sist of one part by measure of hydraulic cement, as specified, a two parts of clean, sharp sand, free from pebbles and vegeta matter. When properly measured into the box the sand and ment shall be thoroughly mixed dry until the mixture shows uniform color. When wanted for use it must be wet with t smallest quantity of water possible, and be thoroughly mixed a tempered. The Engineer may prescribe the number of times t mixture shall be turned over, dry and wet, if he considers it nec sary. The mortar must be used immediately, and none remaini on hand so long as to have set shall be re-mixed and used.

3. For pointing and for wet ditches the proportions shall one of cement to one of sand.

4. Neat cement may be required for pipe-laying in wet ditch

5. Mortar for Portland cement concrete shall be mixed as abo prescribed, using the proportions by measure of one of Portla cement, such as specified for this work, and three (3) parts of clea sharp sand free from pebbles and vegetable matter.

6. Mortar for plastering catch-basins and pointing outside sto or brick masonry shall be mixed as above prescribed, using one pa of Portland cement such as specified for this work, and one pa clean, sharp sand, not of excessive coarseness, and free from pe bles and vegetable matter.

7. In any of the above mixtures the Engineer may increase t proportions of cement for special reasons in particular places. T proportions shall all be by measure in the mortar box prescribe If other methods of measurement are permitted, the measuremen shall be based on the measurement of the cement in the origin package, and not after being removed therefrom.

Brick Sewer.—The bricks shall be clean and thoroughly saturat with clean water immediately before laying. Every brick shall neatly and truly laid to line, in full joint of mortar at one oper tion, and in no case shall mortar be slushed or grouted in after t brick is laid, except when so directed by the Engineer. All bri must break joints with those in adjoining courses.

All joints below the springing line of the arch shall be neat struck, and the joints of the arch shall be cleaned off to the face the brick work after the centers have been removed. The joints tween the courses of the inner ring shall not be more than o quarter inch and the outer rings not more than one-half inch thickness, and between the rings or shells there shall be one-h inch of mortar.

The centers of the intercepting sewer being struck, and all ru bish removed from the inside of the sewer, and the whole of the terior of the sewer being washed perfectly clean, it shall recei while wet, a thin and perfectly smooth plastering of Portland ment mortar, $\frac{3}{4}$ inch thick, laid on with plasterer's finishing trow over the whole surface of the inside. This plastering must not or disturbed or trodden upon for at least forty-eight (48) after its application. Only intercepting sewers shall be ...

outside surface of all catch-basins must be covered with cemortar ¼ inch thick. The inside surface shall be plastered thickness of ½ inch with mortar composed of one part of sand ne part of Portland cement.

outside surface of all manholes shall be covered by a coat of t mortar ¼ inch thick.

sh-tanks shall be built, plastered and tested as provided for basins and of form and dimensions shown on plans.

Sewers.—Each pipe shall be laid in a firm bed and in perconformity with the lines and levels given. The bottom of ench under each socket must be excavated so as to give the solid bearing for its whole length. The pipes must (if re-) be fitted together and matched before lowering into the , so as to secure the truest possible line on the bottom of the of pipes. They must be marked when in this position and laid trench as marked. No chipping of socket or spigot other cutting off projections will be permitted, and any pipe inn this process shall be rejected. Unless otherwise specifically d, the pipe shall be laid from the lower end of the line up. The Engineer may require the pipe to be laid with level, line ight-edge or in other manner that will produce the result required, and may require that a light be set in the last man- lamp-hole and each pipe laid so that this light shall always ble through the section of pipe under construction.

n laid in the trench as above specified, the joint shall be tely filled with mortar of one of sand and one of cement (see specifications) in a manner fully satisfactory to the En-. If he is not satisfied with the methods used by the con-, he may prescribe the method and the materials to be used ing the joints. Extra precautions shall be taken in wet . Any excess of mortar on the inside of the pipe shall be d out immediately after laying the joint.

crete.—Broken stone shall be sound, hard limestone, broken rly regular as practicable, which shall not measure more than hes in any direction, and which shall be screened through a ng screen. It shall be free from dust, loam or dirt. When ed on the line of the work, it shall be deposited on platforms for the purpose, and the sub-grade of pavement must be ed from injury by teams in hauling. All stone must be l or broken before being hauled upon the street, and under mstances will any stone be allowed to be hauled and depos- the street and then broken.

te for sewer work shall be composed of about 1½ measures as specified, and four of broken stone, as above specified, , screened gravel satisfactory to the Engineer. The mortar and stone shall be so mixed in a box, or on a platform, according to the directions of the Engineer, that every stone shall be completely covered with mortar. It shall be laid immediately and carefully placed in layers about six inches in thickness, and shall be settled in place by gentle ramming, only sufficient to flush the mortar to the surface. Before any layer is covered by another, its surface shall be scored so as to make a bond between the layers.

Concrete for foundations of pavements shall be made of either broken stone or screened gravel, as specified in resolution. The stone or gravel shall be thoroughly drenched, but contain no loose water in the heap. It shall then be mixed with mortar in such proportions as will completely fill the voids in the stone. When proper proportions are determined for the stone in use, they will be adhered to. The general proportions will be about 1 part cement to 2 parts of clean, sharp sand to 4½ broken stone or gravel. The mortar and stone shall be so thoroughly mixed, as directed by the Engineer, that every stone shall be completely coated with mortar. It shall then be deposited in place and rammed until the mortar flushes to the surface. The proportions of materials used in concrete may be varied by the Engineer as found necessary to produce the best result. Portland cement mortar will be used if distinctly specified, otherwise hydraulic cement mortar will be used.

No walking or driving over the uncovered concrete foundation will be permitted, and it shall be allowed to set for eight days, or such time as the Engineer may direct, before any further work shall progress on the same. Concrete shall be planked at street and alley crossings to permit travel to cross it without injury.

Concrete shall be sprinkled at night, when considered necessary by the Engineer, and he may require it to be protected from the sun in hot weather, and from frost in cold weather, by covering with suitable material.

The thickness of concrete foundation shall be 6 inches, unless otherwise specifically stated.

The surface of the concrete shall be parallel to the finished surface of the street, and templets shall be used as directed by the Engineer.

The Engineer shall be notified before concrete laying is begun, and no work shall be done until he has examined and accepted the sub-grade.

If at any time, for violation of these specifications, any concrete shall, in the opinion of the Engineer, prove entirely, or in any portion, inferior, it shall be removed by the contractor and replaced in a suitable manner.

A trial will be made of the following specifications for street foundations, that the relative cost may be determined.

If natural cement is used the proportions for concrete shall be one nt of natural hydraulic cement, two parts of sand and 4½ parts f broken stone.

If Portland cement is used the proportions for concrete shall be ne part of Portland cement, three parts of sand and six parts gravel.

FILLERS FOR BRICK PAVEMENTS.

Portland cement is now very generally used as a filler for the ints in brick and other block pavements. Perhaps the Murphy out was the first application to this purpose, this grout being a oprietary mixture of Portland cement and finely ground slag high silicate of alumina, with water and sand in proper proportions bstantially the same as used with Portland cement.

The Indianapolis specifications for cement filler are as follows:

9. The joints shall then be filled as nearly as possible from botm to top with a paving cement or grout as specified in the bid and ntract, and according to a formula for composition and consisncy of same approved by the Board of Public Works and the Enneer. Sand may be used as a filler in alleys when specifically ated in specifications, to be applied as directed by the Engineer.

10. When grout is used it must be equal or superior to a grout mposed of one part of Portland cement by measure and 1½ parts fine sand, which will pass through a 3-16-inch mesh. It shall be such consistency as to run readily into the joints and shall be ept in rapidly. The pavement shall be gone over a sufficient umber of times to fill every joint. When the foundation is of oken stone, the Engineer may require the grout to be put on in o coats, the first coat to be of such proportions as he may direct.

Opinions vary regarding the method of applying the grout, some st applying a coat richer in cement than above specified and folwing with one similar to that specified. Experiment has shown at, with a broken stone foundation, likely to absorb a coat put on o thin, the first application may be with advantage of a mixture one cement to three sand, well mixed with sufficient water to ake it run freely, and applied in small quantities with sufficient pidity to get it into the joints without too much separation of e sand and cement. This serves to fill the lower part of the joints d the top of the sand cushion. When it has stood a short time, it n be followed up with the specified mixture applied often enough fill the joints completely. Some cement is saved in this way, as e joints are filled without at the same time filling a good share the foundation.

CONCRETE MIXING.

The following specifications by A. P. Boller show good practice i mixing cement concrete:

In general all cements must be subject to the usual standard o inspecting and testing as recommended by the Am. Soc. C. E. Th contractor must keep on hand under proper shelter and convenien of access sufficient stock of cement ahead of his wants to afford reasonable time for its proper examination and testing. (Additional tests are provided for when necessary.)

The sand used must be clean, sharp, not too fine, free from pebbles and must not soil white paper.

The water used must be clean, fresh water.

The concrete will be mixed either by hand or machine, according to quantity needed and rapidity of requirements. Any machin used must be one of proved efficiency and reliability for uniforn product. All component parts of a concrete batch must be accu rately gauged as to relative volume. Cement and sand must thoroughly mixed dry, and be thoroughly wetted, broken stone corporated therewith, and only enough water added by sprinkling uniformly dampen the mass without wetting it, as may be direct The amount of water required will depend upon atmospheric conditions of heat and moisture, and due allowance must be made therefor. In hand-mixing, the broken stone will be spread out upon tight platform within a movable frame of gauged dimensions, holding an exact manageable batch of stone, 9 to 12 inches deep. Th stone to be flushed off uniform with edge of frame and thorough wetted, allowance being made when stone has become highly heat from the sun, when the water quickly evaporates. The sand an cement, mixed dry on an adjacent platform, to be then uniform spread over the stone prepared as above. The frame will then b lifted off, and the mass shoveled over in rows, the men workin from opposite sides towards each other, care being exercised not t heap the mass, but simply turn it over, keeping the original thickness. During this process the sprinkling to be kept up to obtain th required dampness. The operation to be repeated rapidly and onl so often as may be necessary to obtain a uniform homogeneous mas of concrete, which must be used as rapidly as possible. All concrete must be thoroughly rammed in layers, as may be directed, wit metal rammers of any approved pattern, weighing from 30 to 3 pounds each. Corners inaccessible to direct long-handled rammin as in air chambers of caissons, to have special devices provided t insure solid contact work. All concrete stone to be trap-rock, or dense, fine-grained blue limestone, or may be clean, screened, coars gravel, when used with Rosendale cement. All concrete stone mus be clean and free from dust. There will be three grades of concret required, designated by numbers:

No. 1. Concrete mass on roof of caissons and filling of air cham bers: 1 part Portland cement, 2 parts sand, and 4 parts of ½-inch clean, broken stone, i. e., passing a ¾-inch screen and retained on a ¼-inch screen.

No. 2. Concrete for footings and hearting of piers: 1 part Portland cement, 2 parts sand, and 4½ parts broken stone, miscellaneous sizes, none over 2 inches in any diameter.

No. 3. Common concrete: 1 part Rosendale cement, 2 parts sand, 5 parts gravel or broken stone.

An American Portland cement manufacturer gives the following proportions for concrete for various purposes when best quality of Portland cement is used:

1 part Portland cement.
2 parts clean, sharp sand.
4 parts broken stone. (Pass through 2-inch ring.)

Mix the sand and cement thoroughly together. Add the least possible amount of water, and turn the same over twice. After thoroughly wetting the stone add same to mixture of cement and sand. Put at once into mould and ram well. This mixture is only used where the ground may be moist and extreme weight must be carried.

1 part Portland cement.
3 parts clean, sharp sand.
6 parts broken stone.

This combination, when mixed as above, will give you a concrete strong enough to carry the tallest building.

1 part Portland cement.
4 parts clean, sharp sand.
8 parts broken stone.

This combination, mixed as above directed, gives you a concrete strong enough for all ordinary construction.

1 part Portland cement.
5 parts clean, sharp sand.
10 parts broken stone.

This combination is stronger and cheaper than you could get by using the so-called common or Rosendale cements.

After concrete is once set it is a good plan to keep it wet for three or four days.

CEMENT STUCCO FOR WALLS.

First coat, one-half inch thick.

For best results, the wall should be furred off with spruce lath put on vertically, 12 inches apart and well nailed.

On these fasten firmly expanded metal lath.

Add fibre to the mortar for lathwork.

Wet thoroughly the surface to be plastered.

Mix 1 part non-staining Portland cement with 2 parts medium sand, 1 part fine sand and one-half part lime flour. When this coat has set hard, wet the surface thoroughly and apply the second coa (one-quarter inch thick) with a wooden float.

Mix 1 part cement as above, 1 part fine sand and 2 parts mediun sand or crushed granite.

Before the second coat has set hard, it may be jointed to presen the appearance of stonework.

A small addition of lime flour increases the adhesion of th mortar.

The finished surface should be protected for at least two week with canvas curtains or bagging saturated with water.

Defects are liable to appear on cement plastered walls when (1) too much cement is used; (2) not supplied with sufficient moisture (3) not troweled sufficiently; (4) not protected from variations in temperature and drafts of air.

Plastering work should be done in the spring and never durin freezing weather.

PLASTERING CISTERNS.

For plastering cisterns, one part Portland cement to two part sand will make a job that will be impervious to water, resist fros and if well done, last for generations.

In cistern and cellar work, if there is any tendency of water t come in while the cement work is being done, that tendency mus be removed by drainage or otherwise, as the water will press th cement aside before it is hard.

WATER-TIGHT CEMENT MORTAR.

By the use of lime putty, cement mortar is made more thoroughly water-proof, due to the great density of the mortar obtained, which hardens in the water, provided the water is not moving and not to cold or impregnated with acids.

The following proportions are best for water-tight mortar:

Cement.	Lime Putty.	Sand.
1 part.	½ part.	1 part.
1 part.	1 part.	3 parts.
1 part.	1½ parts.	5 parts.
1 part.	2 parts.	6 parts.

In making cement lime mortar, it is best to thoroughly mix th sand and cement dry, then screen the lime putty, mixed with wate into a mortar box and mix the whole, adding more water if nece sary till a uniform mortar of proper consistency is obtained.

The coating may be about ¾ inch thick.

To render the surface of cement concrete impervious to air an water, the double silicate of soda and potash may be used.

Sylvester's process consists in the application of a coat made ¾ pound of castile soap to 1 gal. of water, applied at as near boilin temperature as possible and rubbed to a lather with a stiff brusl fter drying 24 hours a second coat of ½ pound alum to 4 gals. of ater is applied. Three applications of the double coating at inter- ıls of 24 hours between each coat are sufficient to render brick, one or concrete masonry impervious.

Several artificial stones are made which owe their impervious ıalities to ingredients which produce the same effect as these ashes.

PORTLAND CEMENT FOR SEWER PIPE AND BUILDING STONE.

Mixture of one part Portland cement to four parts sharp, clean nd; put in mould and tamp well. Care should be taken to see that o much water is not added.

MORTAR FOR BRICK AND STONE LAYING.

For common mortar that will harden quickly, reach greater rength at less cost than any other cement mortar, Portland ce- ent should be used with slaked lime in the proportions given low.

The addition of slaked lime in small proportions makes the mor- r "fat," "rich" and pleasant to work.

It greatly increases its adhesiveness and density, and contrary to neral belief, also adds to the strength of such mixtures.

Any greater or any less proportion of lime to the mixtures given, ill lessen the density, the tensile strength, the crushing strength nd the adhesiveness.

The proper proportions are as follows:

Portland Cement.	Sand.	Lime Paste.
1 part.	5 parts.	½
1 part.	6 parts.	1
1 part.	8 parts.	1½
1 part.	10 parts.	2

This lime paste or slaked lime is more than half water.

Soak the brick well before laying them in cement or the cement will have no water to make it harden.

SPECIAL MONIER CONSTRUCTIONS.

A special application of the Monier system is the Renton fire- oof floor, which, except where an arched form is desired, con- ts of cinder concrete, with barbed wire imbedded about one-half h from the bottom of the slab, the number of the strands per eal foot being proportioned to the span between beams and the ngth desired in the floor. The concrete used is made with the t grades of Portland cement, clean, sharp sand and hard coal eam cinders, free from ash, generally mixed in the propor- n of 1 part cement to 2½ parts of sand and 5½ parts of cinder, thoroughly and uniformly mixed by special machinery. Different types of floor construction, adapted to different classes of bui ıngs and to different thicknesses of floors, are used.

The weight of cinder concrete, composed of 1 part cement, of sand and 5½ of screened cinders, tamped on a wood center, will erage ninety-five pounds per cubic foot. Eighty pounds per cu foot is often given as the weight of cinder concrete, and this is pr ably about right where the concrete is not tamped; but for all c crete tamped on wood centering, ninety-five pounds per cubic f should be used in computing the weight of the floor and the stren of the steel beam.

Lime mortar and ordinary concrete will average 120 pounds cubic foot.

Another application of the Monier system is to the covering piles exposed to the ravages of the *teredo navalis* in sea water. T casings are made of cement mortar about cylinders of wire cl and slipped down over the piles until they reach the bottom. not subject to shocks or blows from vessels or floating debris, tl are durable and promise to be a sufficient protection.

Portland cement has been used in California for lining irri tion ditches to make them more nearly water-tight. The follow is a description of the process:

In preparing for the cementing work, sand is first hauled fr nearby river beds, or washes as they are called, and dumped alc the line of the ditch where it will be required for mortar. Cem is hauled by six-horse teams from the cement works, about miles distant. The laborers are boarded in temporary tent cam in order to be near the work as it advances. With the except of a foreman and two trowelers ordinary day laborers are employ A mortar-bed on wheels is drawn by a horse along the edge of canal, keeping pace with the plasterers. Shovelers in advance the plasterers clean out and even off the surface, and a man wit hose follows and sprinkles the surface so that it is thoroughly before plastering.

The sand is not screened, but is selected to contain a good p portion of coarse as well as fine grains and to be clean. It is mi on the portable bed in the proportion of one of cement to four sand. It is mixed with hoes, first dry then wet. The morta then slid down the chute onto a bed from which the shovelers spr it along the bottom and sides as fast as the trowelers can sprea to a surface. This coat of plaster is generally made from ½-inch thick on canal work, but on this work the coat was fro to ¼-inch thick. Within fifteen minutes after water has been ad to the mortar, the last of it is plastered on the ditch. The p tered surface is sometimes washed over with a wash of pure cem and water applied with a brush to make it more imperviou water. After standing a couple of days, water is allowed in nished section, but is kept stagnant by means of temporary dirt

From these reservoirs temporary lines of ¾-inch iron pipes arry water to the mortar bed as it keeps pace with the construc-

STREET RAILWAY FOUNDATIONS.

For street railway work Chicago has the following form of conete construction under ties and of making junctions of track ith various kinds of pavements:

Concrete.—The depth should be determined by the engineer in arge, but will vary from four to twelve inches, according to the igencies of the case, or solidity of the foundations. The concrete dth is usually one foot outside the ties at each side, or nine feet width for a seven-foot tie. The constituent parts of the conete are one part of cement, two parts of sand—sharp—and four five parts of broken stone or gravel, small enough to pass rough a two-inch ring. Mix the sand and cement dry, and turn er four times before using water. Wet the stone before adding it the sand and cement and mix thoroughly on a board platform ith tight joints. After spreading concrete, ram it thoroughly, unl water appears on the top, keeping it uniform and smooth. pread one inch of coarse sand or gravel over the concrete for tie ed. The space between the ties should be filled with concrete, roken stone, gravel or sand, as the engineer decides, thoroughly amped or rolled and brought to an even surface, ready for the paving, which should be impervious to water.

Paving.—In cities the paving may be Belgian block, brick, concrete or asphalt, and in the suburbs ordinary earth is used, if ballast of broken stone, gravel, screenings or cinders is too expensive.

Much trouble is occasioned by the loosening of the pavement long the rails and over the ties. It should be laid close and compact, with the interstices filled with paving pitch or grout, so as to nsure its being impervious. Where macadam, concrete or asphalt is used, there should be next the rail a toothing of block paving of stone or brick, to prevent disturbance of the pavement by the rail vibration.

Fine cement is used on each side of the rail web to allow the paving to fit against the lip of the rail. The usual depth of Belgian blocks is six inches, and they rest on a bed of sand one inch deep. There should be no projections to prevent the pavement from fitting close to the rail.

Concrete is much preferred abroad for foundation to broken stone; in fact, the latter is never allowed to be used.

With brick paving, the concrete should be brought to within one inch of the bottom of the bricks, then one inch of sand, spread very evenly, and lastly the bricks, laid very true, no brick the least bit higher than the adjoining ones.

DATA FOR ESTIMATES OF CEMENT WORK

Experience of engineers and the comparison of various table of amount and cost of materials required for various classes of wor in which cement is an ingredient demonstrate that there are n exact rules by which the quantities required for a given work unde a given specification can be definitely computed. It is easy to deter mine theoretically the amount of cement required for a mass o concrete, given the number of cubic yards to be filled, the percent age of voids in stone and sand, and the proportions of cement, san and stone. The actual result may vary materially either in exces or deficiency from this theoretical quantity for many such reason as the following:

The condition of the stone when voids are determined may var as to moisture and compactness, the method and force used in con solidating the stone and its previous exposure to rain or sun no being uniform. The same may be true of the sand. The measure ment of cement in original package or after emptying into a bo will make some difference. The method of mixing materials is a important consideration, in general the more thorough the mixtur the less the volume of the resulting concrete. The method of pu ting in place and the amount of tamping are also very importa factors. The proportion of mortar to the voids in the stone is no an exact measure of the resulting volume. The most thorough wo shows a shrinkage in volume of concrete from the volume of broke stone, unless the mortar is more than enough to fill the voids i the compacted stone. The same is true to some extent of gravel.

The following estimates of quantities are therefore simply ap proximate and may be exceeded or not attained, according to th local circumstances. While most of them are the result of actua experiments under practical conditions, the writer has checked b few of them in his practice, and presents them as being corre under a single set of conditions only, and approximately correct others. For rough estimates they will answer satisfactorily. Eac engineer or contractor is soon able to estimate his own quantiti under the conditions of the methods he adopts better than he ca from any statements of average results.

PACKING AND SHIPPING CEMENT.

Cement is packed in barrels, cloth sacks or paper bags, as ordered.

A barrel of Portland cement weighs about 400 pounds gross, and ould contain 380 pounds net of cement.

A barrel of eastern natural hydraulic cement weighs about 320 ounds gross and should contain 300 pounds net of cement.

A barrel of western natural hydraulic cement weighs about 285 unds gross and should contain 265 pounds net of cement.

Slag cement weighs about 350 pounds gross, or 330 pounds net.

Cloth sacks ordinarily contain one-third of a barrel of natural draulic cement, but may contain but one-fourth of a barrel of ortland cement. Paper sacks contain one-fourth of a barrel.

A carload of Portland cement usually means 100 barrels (40,000 s.); 75 barrels is the minimum carload, or the same quantity by eight in cloth or paper bags.

When cement is ordered in cloth sacks, the sacks are charged at st, viz: 10 cents each, in addition to the cost of the cement; but hen the sacks are returned to the works in good condition, freight epaid, 10 cents is allowed for each, with a deduction of 2 cents r wear and tear in some cases.

For paper bags there is no charge, as they are not to be returned.

Empty sacks to be returned, should be safely tied in bundles of n or fifty—giving the name of the sender.

Lime requires about 50 per cent. of its weight of water in slak- g; natural hydraulic cement, 28 to 31 per cent.; silica-Portland ment, 22 per cent.; Portland cement, 20 to 25 per cent.; slag ce- ent, 22 to 28 per cent.; cement and sand mortars, 10 to 23 per nt. to complete the process of crystallization.

Sand weighs from 80 to 100 pounds per cubic foot dry and loose, om 90 to 115 pounds dry and well shaken.

Gravel weighs from 100 to 120 pounds per cubic foot loose and bout 20 pounds more when well rammed.

Crushed limestone weighs about 90 pounds per cubic foot, varying mewhat either way with the size and amount of fine dust.

Concrete weighs about 140 pounds per cubic foot.

Quicklime weighs 64 pounds per cubic foot.

Lime paste, about 50 per cent. water, one cubic foot of quicklime nd one cubic foot of water make 1⅛ to 1¼ cubic feet of stiff lime ste.

Portland cement, loose, weighs 70 to 90 pounds per cubic foot; cked, about 110 pounds per cubic foot. One barrel is 3½ cubic t. weighing 380 pounds net, or 400 pounds gross. Foreign ce- nt barrels contain 3 1-3 or less cubic feet.

N-tural hydraulic cement, loose, weighs about 50 to 57 pounds bic foot; packed, about 80 pounds per cubic foot. One barrel, unds, western cement; 300 pounds, eastern cement. Weights ent and volumes of barrels are not uniform. Nearly all nat- ydraulic cement is sold in sacks as given above.

To make one cubic yard of Portland cement mortar the following quantities of cement and sand are required for the proportions stated, the cement being given in barrels, packed, and the sand in cubic yards:

Proportions.	Barrels of Portland Cement.	Cu. Yds. of Sand.
Neat cement	7.14	0
1 cement 1 sand	4.16	0.67
1 " 2 "	2.85	0.84
1 " 3 "	2.00	0.94
1 " 4 "	1.70	0.98
1 " 5 "	1.25	0.99
1 " 6 "	1.18	1.00

The following table shows the variations in amount of ingredients necessary to make a cubic yard of concrete. The table appears in the report of a committee on the use of cement made to the Association of Railway Superintendents of Bridges and Buildings, and is made up from reports of such superintendents for various railways, giving their actual practice and observation:

PROPORTIONS.						AMOUNTS OF INGREDIENTS.					
Natural Cement.	Portland Cement.	Sand.	Crushed Stone.	Gravel.	Rubble.	Natural Cement.	Portland Cement.	Sand.	Crushed Stone.	Gravel.	Rubble.
						Bbls.	Bbls.	Yds.	Cu. Yds.	Cu. Yds.	Cu. Yds
1		1½	4			1.5		0.35	0.95		
1		2	4			1.9					
1		2	4½ or 5			1.5					
1		2	5 or 6 and	1 or 2 screenings.		1.0			1.00		
	1	1	2				8	0.39	0.79		
							1.5	0.45	0 96		
	1	2	4				1.4				
							1.6	0.42	0.83		
	1	2									
	1	2									
	1	2	5 or 6 and	1 or 2 screenings.			1.0		1.00		
	1	2	6						1.00		
	1	2½	6				1.0				
	1	3	4				0.92	0.36	1.00		
							1.0	0.51	0.87		
	1	3	5				1.1				
							1.2	0.5	0.9		
							0.96				
	1	3	6				1.2				
							1.0	0.5	1.00		
							1.2	0.55	1.00		
	1	3	6				0.82	0.37	0.72		.25
	1	3	6½				0.96	0.43	0.94		
	1	3	7½				0.9	0.35	0.95		
	1	4	7½				0.68	0.35	0.96		.25

The following table of approximate quantities of materials to make 100 cubic feet of finished concrete shows the reduction in amount of cements used if the ingredients are measured in the mixing box rather than in the original package:

Proportions of Cement to Aggregate.	Barrels of Cement When Proportioned by Barrels.	Barrels of Cement When Proportioned by Measurements.	Yards of Aggregate.
1 to 1	18.3	15.8	2.75
1 " 2	11.6	10.	3.85
1 " 3	8.7	7.5	3.95
1 " 4	6.9	5.9	4.15
1 " 5	5.6	4.7	4.30
1 " 6	5.0	4.3	4.40
1 " 7	4.4	3.7	4.45
1 " 8	3.9	3.3	4.46
1 " 9	3.4	2.9	4.47
1 " 10	3.0	2.6	4.48
1 " 11	2.8	2.4	4.50
1 " 12	2.5	2.2	4.53
1 " 13	2.4	2.0	4.55
1 " 14	2.3	1.9	4.57
1 " 15	2.2	1.8	4.59
1 " 16	2.1	1.7	4.62
1 " 17	2.0	1.6	4.63
1 " 18	1.9	1.5	4.65
1 " 19	1.8	1.4	4.68
1 " 20	1.7	1.3	4.70

This table is given in the California Portland Cement Company's handbook.

The volume of mortar in fractions of a cubic yard necessary to lay a cubic yard of masonry is as follows:

For Brickwork, 1/8 inch joints	.15
" " 1/4 " "	.25
" " 1/2 " "	.40
" Ashlar, 20-inch courses	.06
" Squared Stone Masonry	.20
" Rubble Masonry	.25
" Concrete, broken stone	.55

One barrel of Portland cement will cover the following areas when used as plastering, with the various proportions of sand noted. These areas are slightly less than would be computed from the volumes of cement mortar in a preceding table on account of waste, filling of cracks and voids, etc.:

Proportions in Barrels.	Thickness of Coating.	Square Feet of Area Covered.
1 cement 1 sand	1 inch.	67
	3/4 "	90
	1/2 "	134
1 cement 2 sand	1 "	104
	3/4 "	139
	1/2 "	208
1 cement 3 sand	1 "	140
	3/4 "	187
	1/2 "	280

From the Buckeye Cement Company's handbook is taken the following table of materials required for cisterns:

Diameter in Feet.	Capacity Gallons for Each Foot Depth.	For this Column Use Diameter Digging.	For Each Foot Depth. For these Columns Use Diameter in Clear of Lining.			Bottom.	
						Bricks in Bottom.	Plastering in Bottom, Sq. Yds.
		Cu. Yds. of Digging.	Stone Lining 1 Ft. Thick (25 Cu. Ft.)	No. Bricks in Lining—1 Thick.	Sq. Yards Plastering.	Use Diameter of digging.	Use Diameter in Clear of Lining.
5	146	.73	.75	230	1.74	148	2.18
6	211	1.04	.88	275	2.09	215	3.14
7	288	1.42	1.00	320	2.44	292	4.27
8	377	1.86	1.13	365	2.79	382	5.58
9	476	2.36	1.26	410	3.14	483	7.06
10	587	2.91	1.38	460	3.49	596	8.72
11	710	3.52	1.51	500	3.84	722	10.56
12	846	4.19	1.63	550	4.19	859	12.56
13	992	4.92	1.76	590	4.54	1008	14.74
14	1152	5.70	1.88	640	4.89	1170	17.10
15	1325	6.54	2.01	680	5.24	1343	19.63

One barrel of Portland cement will lay about 60 square feet of cement walk under the first or general specification for cement walks given in the chapter on Specifications for the use of Cement.

From the California Cement Company's handbook is taken the following table of quantities required for making cement pipe, as follows:

Inside Diameter Pipe.	Thickness of Pipe.	Approximate Proportions Cement to Sand and Gravel. 1 to 3	1 to 3½	1 to 4	Number Feet Pipe to Cubic Yard Sand and Gravel.
		Number of Lineal Feet of Pipe 1 Barrel of Portland Cement Will Make.			
8 in.	1 in.	61.11	71.30	81.48	137.50
10 in.	1 in.	50.00	58.00	66.66	112.50
12 in.	1⅛ in.	37.25	43.47	49.67	83.81
14 in.	1¼ in.	28.85	33.66	38.47	64.91
16 in.	1⅝ in.	19.20	22.40	25.60	43.20
20 in.	1¾ in.	14.45	16.85	19.21	32.51
24 in.	2 in.	10.58	12.34	14.10	23.80
30 in.	2½ in.	6.77	7.89	9.02	15.23
36 in.	3 in.	4.70	5.48	6.27	10.57

In sewer work, one barrel of natural hydraulic cement used neat will lay the following lengths of pipe of the various sizes, pipe being in 3-foot lengths:

Size of Pipe.	Length 1 Bbl. of Cement Will Lay.	Size of Pipe.	Length 1 Bbl. of Cement Will Lay.
4	500	12	100
6	350	15	75
8	200	18	65
9	175	20	60
10	150	24	50

CEMENT LABORATORIES

Space is given for a description of a cement laboratory in each of three general classes, private, municipal and college, that an idea of the facilities available for the examination of cement and of materials and processes for making cement may be formed. Completeness of equipment is not an indication of reliability of reports, since the character and experience of the operators are the controlling factors, but other things being equal, the more complete the equipment the more complete the report can be made

LATHBURY AND SPACKMAN, PHILADELPHIA, PA.

The laboratory of Lathbury and Spackman, at 1619 Filbert street, Philadelphia, is very fully equipped for the study of raw materials for making cement, the process of making, and the testing of the finished product.

The cement laboratory is fitted up with a view to eliminate, as far as possible, all errors of personal equation and those due to changing temperature. There is an especially arranged system of piping and tanks for the maturing of briquettes, so that tests can be made at any interval, from one day to three years. The briquettes in the meantime are carefully maintained in changing water at a constant temperature. This laboratory also contains 2,000-pound tensile briquette machine for determining the tensile strength of cement, and a 200,000-pound automatic compression machine for crushing cubes of cement and concrete.

The mechanical laboratory is equipped with all the machines necessary for the manufacture of cement, including crushers, tube-mills, a rotary and a set-kiln, allowing quantities of cement to be made from raw materials under the conditions similar to those occurring in the regular manufacture. This plant is, in fact, complete miniature cement plant. All the machinery in both the mechanical and cement laboratories is driven by electrical power thus giving perfect and independent control of each machine.

The chemical laboratory is thoroughly supplied with all the paratus necessary for the analysis of clays, limestones, r

ments, and all the materials entering into the manufacture of ment.

New and approved apparatus is constantly being added in order at the laboratory may always be abreast of the times, and the ost accurate and scientific results may be obtained.

The records of these laboratories are carefully filed and inxed, and extend back over many years, being an almost complete cord of the cement industry of this country.

Tests of cement are made for persons desiring the same, and very large share of the business of the firm is the study of ceent materials and the design and superintendence of construcon of cement plants to utilize materials found to be favorable, ith the necessary preliminary estimates of cost of plant and cost manufacture of cement.

Names of other engineers designing cement plants, examining ment properties and analyzing and testing cement and materials r making cement will be found in the Directory lists.

MUNICIPAL TESTING LABORATORY, PHILADELPHIA, PA.

The cement laboratory of the city of Philadelphia is under the Department of Public Works in the Bureau of Surveys, in charge of a specially appointed engineer. From a paper by R. L. Humphreys, formerly in charge of the office, have been made some selections describing the methods and apparatus. Mr. W. Purvis Taylor is at present the engineer in charge of the testing laboratory.

A set of specifications, adopted as the city standard, forms the basis for the acceptance or rejection of a shipment of cement.

The tests are made from samples taken from actual shipments n the work, and not from samples furnished indiscriminately.

Samples are obtained by taking a small quantity from one barrel in every five or ten, depending on the size of the shipment, the cement being taken from the heart of the barrel in order to secure a fair sample of its fineness and quality from which the sample is drawn by means of a sampling auger. The notification card is placed on this sample.

The sample is brought to the laboratory in special collection cans made of japanned tin in four compartments, each holding about seven pounds.

The data on the notification card are entered in the Record ok, which eventually contains all the information relative to this mple, a record being kept of the number of the sample, the brand, date and place of collection, whether the shipment was in bags barrels, the fineness in per cent., date and hour of moulding the briquettes, time of setting and the temperature of the air, specific gravity, the results of the hot water tests, and the ten and compressive strength, both neat and with various proporti of sand for different periods of time.

For weighing the material to be used for making the tests, laboratory is provided with a pair of scales sensitive to ½ gran under a load of 2 kilogrammes in each pan. The mixing moulding is done on a specially-designed table, consisting of parts, each having a plate glass top, one 24 inches long by 18 inc wide, on which the mixing and moulding is done; and the ot which is 3 inches above the level of the former, is 4 feet lon feet wide, and is used for making the tests for time of setting, for markingland removing the briquettes from the moulds.

The samp e of cement collected as just described, composed portions taken from various barrels, is now thoroughly mixed passing it through what is known in the laboratory as a No. sieve. A small portion is then weighed out and made into a p by gradually adding clean water from a graduate. The quan of water required to produce a stiff, plastic paste, of about consistency of moulding clay, is thus obtained.

Having determined, by the above test, the proper percentag water required for the neat tests, 1,000 grammes of the sample weighed out, and placed upon the mixing table; a basin is t formed with this material, into which the proper percentage clean water is poured, the material is turned into the basin by aid of a trowel, and the mixing is completed by thoroughly kn ing the mass to the proper consistency with the hands. It is t firmly pressed into the moulds with a trowel and the sur smoothed. The mould is then turned over, and the same opera is repeated. The briquettes are kept in the moulds until they be removed without injury.

Moulds.—The moulds are of brass, both single, and in gang three and five, in two parts, to facilitate the removal of briquette, the parts being held together by means of a clamp. gang-moulds are usually used, the briquettes being moulded t or five at a time, according to the rate of setting.

The form is that recommended by the American Society of (Engineers, except that the corners have been rounded by curve ½ inch radius. This form has been found to be more ea moulded, and afterwards more easily adjusted in the testing chine.

The moulds are kept clean, and, before the briquettes moulded, are wiped with a cloth moistened with machine oil.

The sand is crushed quartz, all of which passes a No. 20 s and is retained on a No. 30 sieve.

Mixing and moulding by hand has been found to produce r uniform results than can be obtained with any of the mach

briquettes, prior to their immersion in water, are kept in air for a period of twenty-four hours, except in the case of enty-four hour tests, in which they are immersed after hard

this purpose there has been designed a moist closet, which placed the old method of covering briquettes with a damp This closet, which is made of soapstone 1¼ inches thick, is ted by a wooden frame and is 3 feet long, 2 feet high, and ies wide. Along the front is a strip of soapstone, 3 inches forming a basin of the bottom of the closet in which the s placed for keeping the air moist. The doors are made of covered with planished sheet copper, and are rabbeted to fit . There are two sets of shelves, the lower being a wooden nd the upper is formed of strips of plate glass, 33 inches inches wide. When closed, the closet is perfectly tight, the n the bottom keeping the air moist, preventing the briquettes rying out and thus checking the process of setting.

uettes which have been removed from the moulds are placed ge on the glass shelves, while the moulds containing the ttes too soft to be removed are placed on the rack.

in layer of neat cement is spread over one end of briquettes ning four or more parts of sand, to make a smooth surface mbering on.

preserving the briquettes in water, small agate pans were ly used, which have now been replaced by large soapstone six in number, each 7 feet long, 2½ feet wide, and 7 inches outside measure, having a capacity for over 10,000 briquettes. y are supported by two frames, formed of steel shapes. Each supplied with a continuous stream of water, at a tempera- ever less than 70° F., which enters at one end near the bot- rough two pipes, and overflows through two pipes at the end; the pipes being so arranged that the water flows uni- through the tanks. The rate of the flow through the tanks rolled by a valve on each supply pipe. The main feed pipe plied with hot and cold water, from pipes provided with by which the temperature of the mixture is regulated.

tanks were made of soapstone because it is non-absorptive, rrosive, and easily cleaned. The water is previously filtered entering the tanks, and is always clean and pure. It has he experience in the laboratory, that where briquettes are sed in pans the water becomes strongly alkaline unless it is ntly changed and the pans cleaned. Inasmuch as these tanks eplaced three dozen small pans (22 inches x 15 inches x 3) it is evident that besides the advantage of having all ttes immersed under perfectly uniform conditions, a very mount of time and labor is saved.

e briquettes are immersed on edge, and placed a slight dis- apart so as to permit the free circulation of water around them. On the outside of the tank opposite each row, celluloid cards are glued, on which are marked in pencil the inclusive numbers of the row. The briquettes being arranged in the tanks in consecutive order, they are easily located.

For determining the time of setting, the laboratory is provided with a Vicat needle and Gilmore's wires.

The Vicat needle consists of a frame bearing a movable rod having a cap at one end and a needle having a circular cross-section of one square millimetre at the other. A screw holds the needle in any desired position. The rod carries an indicator which moves over a scale (graduated to centimetres) borne by a frame. The rod with the needle and cap weighs 300 grammes; the paste is held by a conical hard rubber ring 7 cm. in diameter at base, 4 cm. high, resting on a glass plate 15 cm. square.

To determine if the paste is of normal consistency, the needle and cap are replaced by a rod 1 cm. in diameter and a cap. The rod then weighing 300 grammes shall stop sinking 6 mm. from the bottom of the ring, 4 cm. deep, filled with paste.

For neat pastes the setting is said to have commenced when the polished steel needle weighing 300 grammes does not completely traverse the mass of normal consistency, confined in the rubber ring, and the setting is said to be terminated when the same needle gently applied to the upper surface of the mass does not sink visibly into it.

A thermometer graduated to 1-5° C. is stuck into the mass and the increase of temperature of mass during setting can be thus observed. The paste is kept in the moist closet during the operation, being removed only to make trial tests of the setting.

This is the apparatus adopted by the French Commission and the Society of German Cement Manufacturers.

Gilmore's wires are commonly used in this country for determining the time of setting. They consist of two brass balls, each bearing a wire having a circular section. For the initial set the section is 1-12 of an inch in diameter, the ball and wire weighing ¼ of a pound. For hard set the section is 1-24 of an inch in diameter, and the weight is one pound.

For determining the time of setting by this method, cakes of neat cement, 2 or 3 inches in diameter, ½ inch thick, with thin edges, are made on small pieces of glass. When the paste resists the gentle application of the ¼ pound wire, the cement has attained its initial set, and when the pound wire, gently applied to the surface of the paste, ceases to make an impression, the cement has its hard set. For quick determinations these wires give sufficiently accurate results for practical purposes. For more accurate determinations the Vicat needle is used.

In determining the fineness of a cement, three sieves are employed, and are known in the laboratory as the No. 50, No. 100 and

›. 200, they having approximately 2,500, 10,000 and 40,000 ıshes per square inch; the sieve is made of brass wire cloth, the ameter of the wire being .0090, .0045 and .0020 of an inch, respectively. In addition there is a No. 20 and a No. 30 sieve for termining the relative sizes of various sands. These have 400 ıd 900 meshes per square inch respectively, the diameters of the ıres being respectively .0165 and .0123 of an inch. The sieves e provided with a tightly fitting cover and pan, which prevents ıe loss of the fine powder during the operation of sieving.

The scale for ascertaining the fineness has a capacity of 500 ammes in each pan, and is sensitive to one decigramme under ıll load. This scale, together with that for weighing the material r making the briquettes, rests on a table 3 feet long, 2 feet wide, ving a soapstone top.

The fineness (expressed in the percentage of residue left on the eve) is determined by passing 100 grammes of cement successely through the No. 50, No. 100 and No. 200 sieves. The sieve gently tapped and shaken with the hand or in an automatic mane until, after a few minutes' shaking, no appreciable quantity ısses through the sieve.

The specific gravity has replaced the old weight per bushel test. There are two forms of apparatus in the laboratory: one accordıg to Candlot and the other according to Le Chatelier.

The hot water test apparatus serves a dual purpose in this ıboratory: (1) It is used in the determination of the specific ravity and absorption of blocks of stone, bricks, concrete, etc., ıd (2) for seeking evidence of unsoundness in cements.

It consists of two tanks, made of 22-ounce copper, and placed ıe within the other, the inner tank being supported by three yelow pine scantlings (3 inches × 1½ inches) running the length of ıe tank. These are supported by a frame formed of steel shapes. The cover, provided with steam vents and an opening for the inertion of a thermometer, is made of two sheets of copper, separated by a one-inch layer of hair felt, and fits tightly into the inner ank. The cover is supported and counterbalanced by means of eights and pulley attached to the upper frame.

Both tanks are filled with water, the levels being maintained by ottles which automatically supply the loss due to evaporation or ther causes. The inner tank is provided with two sets of shelves f tinned copper wire cloth with a one-inch mesh, supported by eavy copper angles; the lower shelf is always submerged and covrs the whole area of the tank, while the upper shelf covers one-half his area and is always in the steam.

The tanks are heated by means of a copper coil supplied with team, at about 80 pounds pressure, from a one-inch pipe. The ater in the tanks (about 30 gallons) can be raised to boiling in bout 3 minutes. The temperature of the water in the inner tank controlled by means of a regulator, which can be set and constantly maintains the water in the tank at any desired tempera between 100° and 212° F. Cements are placed in hot water m tained at various temperatures for different lengths of time, the results obtained are being carefully studied.

Tensile Strength.—Briquettes are broken at regular stated riods, each sample being tested for tensile strength, both neat with standard proportions of sand, for 24 hours, 7 and 28 d Additional briquettes are made, and are systematically distrib for breaking at intervals of 2, 3, 4, 6, 12, 18 months, 2, 3, 4 ar years.

For this purpose two books are kept, a distributing book an diary. The briquettes to be broken at longer intervals than 28 are distributed in the former of these books. Each brand of ment occupies a page of this book, which is divided into colur running up and down, and across each page; the former colu have headings appropriate for the various compositions (neat, 1, 1 to 2, etc.), whether made in laboratory or on work, and met of preservation, etc.; the cross columns are headed 2, 3, 4, 6, 18 months, 2, 3, 4 and 5 years.

In the diary is entered under the proper date on which briquettes are scheduled to be broken, the sample number, number of the briquettes, and the hour.

By this means, it is readily known what briquettes are to broken each day. As a rule, the average result of three brique is taken as the tensile strength; in important tests, however, average of five briquettes is taken.

For determining the tensile strength, the laboratory posse a Riehle and a Fairbanks cement testing machine, each of 1, pounds capacity. These types of lever machines are too well kn to merit special description.

Plans have been prepared for an entirely automatic cement ing machine of 2,000 pounds capacity.

A great deal of attention is paid to the results of the test mortar taken from a mixing-box. The briquettes are made f the actual mortar on the work (1) as soon as mixed, and (2) before it goes into the work. Experience has shown this to be of the best aids in judging the actual merits of any brand of ment. Concrete cubes are also made on the work, and their we per cubic foot and crushing strength is determined, the crusl strength giving an excellent idea of the adhesiveness of any br of cement.

All cements are from time to time submitted to a chemical an sis. For this purpose the chemical laboratory has been equip with every facility for making complete chemical analyses. detail apparatus is such as will be found in any well equipped oratory, and does not require further description.

In addition to the regular tests, a great deal of experime work is being carried on. Among the many studies may be n the strength of cement in air, in hot water, mixed with s adulterants, and with various proportions of different sands. ides the standard sand the laboratory is provided with Ger-normal and various kinds of natural sands.

temperature of the laboratories is usually between 60° and . It is never permitted to fall below 60° F.; this being regu-by steam heat. In summer the windows are kept closed, and mperature rarely rises above 80° F.

the end of each year the results of the year's tests are aver-each brand of cement being rated according to this average. quirements of the specifications for the ensuing year being in accordance with these results.

city of Philadelphia, as a direct result of maintaining this tory, is using much stronger cement at a less cost than for-. The city consumes approximately each year about 100,000 of natural cement, and 30,000 barrels of Portland cement. be safely assumed on the basis of the prices prevalent in (when the laboratory was permanently established), and prevalent in 1896, that the city has saved in the four years 70,000. The cost of maintenance, exclusive of salary during me, has been less than $500 per year. In other words, the as saved $70,000, at a cost of less than 10 per cent. by the enance of this laboratory.

PURDUE UNIVERSITY, LAFAYETTE, IND.

cement laboratory, which is a part of the general engineer-boratory, contains a complete supply of small apparatus such as for testing fineness, briquette moulds, scales, etc.

re is an Olsen cement testing machine of 1,000 pounds ca-, and a Fairbanks "shot" cement testing machine, also of pounds capacity. For testing compressional and flexural th of concrete, there are four machines running from 30,000 s capacity up to 300,000 pounds capacity. There is a ma-for testing concrete under the blow of the falling weight.

orts are furnished of the results of tests of samples of ce-or concrete submitted by city engineers or others. Commu-ons should be addressed to Prof. W. F. M. Goss, Director of ngineering Laboratory.

st of cement-testing laboratories containing names and loca-f many private, municipal, governmental and college labora-will be found in the directory in its proper place. It has en easy to determine in all cases whether some of the labora-named are open to commercial work. Some of the college ries and practically all of the municipal laboratories cannot be called upon for tests beyond their own requi in many cases it is possible to arrange for the use c tained in their own work or for the use of the app proper restrictions when commercial testing laborat convenient to access.

INTS SHOWN BELOW.

ions from Quotations by Railway Freight Agents.

Providence, R. I.	New York, N. Y.	Albany, N. Y.	Buffalo, N. Y.	Philadelphia, Pa.	Pittsburg, Pa.	Baltimore, Md.	Washington, D. C.	Wilmington, Del.	San Francisco, Cal.	Portland, Ore.	Dallas, Texas.	Galveston, Texas.
15	10	†150	2	10	10	10	15	10	80	80	60	40
15	13	10½		13	13	13	18	13	80	80	60	40
17	15	12½	6½	13	7½	18	11½	10	80	80	60	40
15	13	10½	7	13	12	13	18	13	80	80	60	40
15	10	10½	7	10	10	†225	†325	†225	80	80	60	40
....	......	......	......	......	..	......	......	......	80	80	60	40
....	......	......	......	......	......	......	......	......	80	80	60	40
......	......	......	......	....	†188	......	......	......	80	80	60	40
......	......	......	......	....	†200	......	......	......	80	80	60	40
$24	$18	$12	$25½	$27	$35	$32	$47	$32	80	80	60	40
......	......	......	......	$27	......	$32	......	......	80	80	60	40
......	......	10	12	....	14	......	......	......	80	80	60	40
†175	......	......	†240	†135	14	†173	†200	......	80	80	60	40
15	9½	†260	†200	†135	14	†173	†175	†150	80	80	60	40
15	......	......	......	....	14	......	......	......	80	80	60	40
15	......	.. ..	†200	†135	12	†173	†175	†150	80	80	60	40
†175	†140	†160	†170	†135	12	†173	†175	†150	80	80	60	40
†175	†140	†225	†170	†135	12	†173	†175	†150	80	80	60	40
†175	†140	†160	†170	†135	12	†173	†175	†150	80	80	60	40
†175	...	..	......	....	......	......	†175	......	80	80	60	40
15	.....	..	......	......	12	......	......	......	80	80	60	40
†180	†145	†230	†175	†140	12	†178	†180	†155	80	80	60	40
†180	†145	†280	†175	†140	†205	†178	†180	†155	80	80	60	40
†180	†140	†160	†170	†135	14	†173	†200	†150	80	80	60	40
..	......	......	......	......	12	......	......	......	80	80	60	40
17	14	15	10	13	......	12	12	13	80	80	52½	38
17	..	13	12	†140	11	......	......	......	......	......	......	......
18	16	15½	7½	14	8	13	12½	13½	80	80	48½	34
17½	15½	15	7¼	13½	8	12½	12½	13½	80	80	48½	34
18	16	15½	6½	14	4½	13	10½	11½	80	80	52½	38
......	......	......	†140	......	†130	... ..	......	......	80	80	48½	34
18½	16½	16	8½	14½	8	13½	13½	14½	80	80	48½	34
21	19	18	11	17	11	16	16	17	80	80	46½	32
......	......	..	.	......	......	......	......	... ..	80	80	46½	32
	......	......	......	......	......	......	......	......	80	80	48½	34
30½	28½	27½	18	26½	18	25½	25½	21	80	80	......	......
24½	22½	21½	12½	20½	.....	19½	......	......	......	......	......	......
25	23	22	9	21	11	20	20	21	......	......	......	......
17½	15½	15	7½	13½	10	12½	. .	......	80	80	48½	34
...	......	......	......	......	......	......	......	......	80	80	48½	34
21	19	18	11	17	11	16	......	......	80	80	48½	34
......	......	......	......	......	......	......	......	......	80	80	48½	34
21	19	18	11	17	11	16	......	......	80	80	48½	34
......	......	......	......	......	......	......	......	......	75	75	......	......
22	20	19	12	18	12	17	17	18	75	75	42½	28
......	27½	26½	17	25½	17	......	24½	......	75	75	42½	28
29½	27½	26½	17	25½	15	24½	24½	....	75	75	......	......
29½	27½	26½	17	25½	15	24½	24½	.. ..	75	75	42½	28
22	20	19	12	18	14	17	17	18	75	75	49	49

le, Ind., 26 cents per 300 lb. barrel, minimum 100 barrels. **Jeffersonville,**

THE NEW YORK
PUBLIC LIBRARY

ASTOR, LENOX AND
TILDEN FOUNDATIONS.

FREIGHT RATES ON CEMENT

An important part of the question of cost of cement is the rate of freight which must be paid from the factory to the consumer. A knowledge of the freight rates prevailing is of value to the purchaser of cement in many ways, besides the simple knowledge of the amount he must pay out on this account.

Thus it will sometimes enable him to determine whether inferior cements from a distance are being offered, the subtraction of freight rate from the price delivered showing the actual cost of the cements and permitting comparison of such cement figures as a basis of comparison of qualities, which is frequently of much value.

The table of freight rates on cement is constructed on the following plan: In the vertical column at the right of the table is a list of the prominent localities at which cement is manufactured. The headings of the columns across the page contain the names of certain prominent distributing points. At least one such point for each State is given, and in some cases more than one. At the intersection of a horizontal line and a vertical column will be found the rate upon cement in carload lots from the factory located at the place named on the horizontal line to the city named at the head of the column. Thus the rate on cement from Akron, N. Y., to Indianapolis, Ind., is found to be 12 cents per hundred pounds. The rates in the table are all in cents per hundred pounds, except those marked with a dagger, (†) which are per ton, and those marked with a section mark, (§) which are per barrel.

The table has most of it been prepared from the records on file in the office of the Interstate Commerce Commission, under the direction of the Assistant Secretary, M. S. Decker, and that it is complete and accurate is beyond question. Our thanks and those of the users of the table are due to the Commission and its officers.

A few rates within the borders of the same State, the filing of which with the Commission is not required by law, have been determined otherwise and inserted. These rates are subject to more fluctuation than the interstate rates, but the average remains about as stated.

In many cases it was found that there were no published through rates, and some of the rates shown in the table were arrived at by combinations of existing rates. In a few cases where there are no published through rates and the manner of determining through rates was not entirely clear, no rates are shown. In cases the distance to which cement must be shipped is such shipments are not likely to be made.

The local purchaser of cement can determine the rate to his own city, if not in the table, by procuring from his local freight agent the rate on his local road to the proper distributing point given in the table, and by adding the tabular rate to this local rate he will determine the rate of freight he must pay.

Parkhurst Combined Curb and Gutter

THE BEST

There is no limestone or sandstone equal to it in durability.

There is nothing equal to it for ornamentation and beauty.

It is water-tight.

It is made with joints which take care of contraction and expansion.

Sections can be removed without marring adjoining sections.

It is stronger in construction than any other form of curb and gutter.

The owner of the Parkhurst Curb and Gutter confines his business to this form of work — it is the best of its kind, and his sole aim is to uphold its pre-eminent reputation by the most careful and reliable work.

WHERE IT IS IN USE

Ten years ago over five miles of Parkhurst Combined Curb and Gutter was constructed on Louden road, Lakeside, Minn., a suburb of Duluth, on a most treacherous clay soil. The only foundation was sand and gravel (6 inches thick), and no drain tile. It is today in perfect preservation. Over a hundred miles of Parkhurst Combined Curb and Gutter has also been in use for years in the following cities, and I refer with pride to its present condition and established reputation :

Indianapolis, Ind.	Franklin, Ind.	Kokomo, Ind.	Evansville, Ind.
Terre Haute, Ind.	Noblesville, Ind.	Brooklyn, N. Y.	Wabash, Ind.
Duluth, Minn.	Albany, N. Y.	Utica, N. Y.	Columbus, Ind.
Kansas City, Mo.	Rochester, N. Y.	Worthington, Ind	Anderson, Ind.
Dayton, O.	Pittsburg, Pa.	Bluffton, Ind.	Marion, Ind.
Muncie, Ind.	Syracuse, N. Y.	Owensboro, Ky.	Lafayette, Ind.
Rome, N. Y.	Minneapolis, Minn.	Fort Wayne, Ind.	

Parkhurst Combined Curb and Gutter can and should be used in connection with gravel, macadam, brick, wooden block and asphalt pavements.

CORRESPONDENCE INVITED.

D. C. BUNTIN, 17 Claypool Block, INDIANAPOLIS, IND.

EXPLANATION OF REFERENCE NOTES

A. The existence of companies marked thus is reported, but letters to them have neither been answered nor returned undelivered.

B. No information has been received directly from the companies marked thus, but that given is received from authoritative sources and is believed to be entirely correct. Ample opportunity for corrections, if necessary, has been given and no corrections have been received.

C. Companies marked thus have furnished the information given and have failed to respond to requests for further statements.

D. Companies marked thus have furnished a small amount of information. Additional information given is believed to be correct, as ample opportunity for correction if erroneous has been given and no corrections have been received.

E. Information regarding amount of capital stock of companies marked thus has been withheld by their officers.

F. Partnerships or individuals conduct business under the names marked thus. All others in the list are incorporated companies.

DESCRIPTIONS OF WORKS AND OF PROCESSES FOR THE MANUFACTURE OF CEMENT

The descriptions of works and processes which follow have been made as brief as possible, but are believed to give valuable indications of the character of the materials and the processes used. It is evident that but few manufacturers who have spent money and time in developing new methods and in working out economies of time and materials will be ready to give full descriptions of all steps of the process, thus losing the advantage of the experience which has cost them so much. It is also evident that a sufficient description of process and materials to enable a judgment to be formed as to the probable quality and uniformity of quality of product is of material benefit to the reputation of a manufacturer of good material, when it appears in such a book as this.

In one or two cases under each process used there will therefore be found a description long enough to give one slightly familiar with cement making processes an idea of the proper steps to be taken, while the descriptions of other works are reduced to the lowest terms consistent with clearness.

Without a completed chapter to exhibit, it has been impossible to convince some manufacturers of the benefit of the shorter description, giving general statements of methods and full statements of materials so that some plants are represented but slightly in this chapter. Every manufacturer mentioned has had an opportunity to furnish such items for the description as he would be willing to appear and a proof of each description has been sent to the manufacturer for his correction and extension.

Our thanks are due to the officers of nearly all the companies for their courtesies in furnishing information and in correcting and supplying deficiencies in descriptions.

A very few companies have failed to respond, and one or two have requested the suppression of all information. In the descriptions which follow all these facts will be stated as fully as seems necessary.

The value of the book depends so largely upon its independence of any influences which would suppress unwelcome facts or which would unduly exalt particular methods, that it has not been possible to accede to all the requests of the few companies alluded to, and the information given is set forth as the best judgment of the editor as to the actual facts. Where other authority is necessary, it is freely quoted and basis for the statements is given.

Reference should be made to the list of companies in the following pages of the directory for information regarding officers, capitalization, capacity, agencies, etc.

AMERICAN CEMENT COMPANIES.

ACME PORTLAND CEMENT COMPANY, Camden, N. J. See Note A, page 152.

AJAX PORTLAND CEMENT COMPANY, Jersey City, N. J. See Note A, on page 152.

AKRON CEMENT WORKS, Akron, N. Y.—These works manufacture the Akron Star Brand of natural hydraulic cement by the usual methods of making such cement, described elsewhere, the product being marketed by the Union Akron Cement Company, of Buffalo, N. Y., to which reference should be made for further details.

THE ALABAMA PORTLAND CEMENT COMPANY, Demopolis, Ala.—The works are under construction and information regarding them is withheld by the officers at this time. Sturtevant mills are being installed for pulverizing the limestone to be used. The brand will be the letters A P C in a diamond.

THE ALAMO CEMENT COMPANY, 207 Main avenue, San Antonio, Texas.—This company manufactures Portland and natural hydraulic cements which have been used in buildings in various cities of Texas. F. L. Smidth & Co.'s Davidsen tube-mills are used for grinding raw materials and natural cement clinker. Information regarding raw materials and process of manufacture has been withheld. The works have a capacity of 250 barrels a day and have been in operation since 1880.

THE ALMA PORTLAND CEMENT COMPANY, Wellston, Ohio, is a corporation organized under the laws of the State of Ohio, with works at Wellston, Jackson county, Ohio, and main office at Philadelphia, Pa. The company manufactures a true artificial Portland cement from a mixture of limestone and clay by the rotary

Parkhurst Combined Curb and Gutter. See pages 77, 119 and 151.

Modern Cement Machinery

ROTARY KILNS

Tube mills of various sizes for both wet and dry grinding.

TUBE MILLS, MIXERS,

BALL MILLS, GRINDING PANS,

CRUSHERS, AGITATORS,

PULVERIZERS, PUMPS, ETC.

We are prepared to furnish rotary kilns in FIVE different designs, and adapted for electrical transmission. Our line is complete for manufacturing on either the WET or DRY process, and we respectfully solicit the correspondence of those about to engage in the manufacture of cement.

THE BONNOT COMPANY

CANTON, OHIO, U. S A.

... The works were designed by Lathbury & Spackman. The ... machinery throughout the plant is driven by electrical motors. The machinery is most modern, having been in operation since 1898. Cement is burned with pulverized coal dust in rotary kilns. Smidth ball and tube-mills are used for grinding raw materials and Portland cement clinker and for pulverizing coal. This is the first plant erected in this country to manufacture Portland cement by the rotary system and using limestone and clay. It is also the first plant to use a complete electrical installation for the transmission of power. The entire plant is designed and constructed in order to make the system of manufacture as nearly automatic as possible. The Webster Manufacturing Company's elevating, conveying and power transmission machinery is used. Keystone Electric Company's motors are installed, there being one 50 horse-power, two 33 horse-power, one 25 horse-power, one 15 horse-power and one 10 horse-power motors.

The company secures their supply of limestone, clay and coal from large deposits owned by them close to the mill. The works are located at Grand Crossing, just outside of Wellston. Shipments are made over the Baltimore & Ohio railroad, Hocking Valley railroad, Cincinnati, Hamilton & Dayton railroad, and Ohio Southern railroad.

Chemical analysis of the finished product shows:

Lime (CaO), 65.88 per cent.: Silica (SiO_2), 21.63; Alumina (Al_2O_3), 6.70; Iron (Fe_2O_3), 4.75; M 1.10: Sulphuric Acid (SO_3), 1.15.

THE ALPENA PORTLAND CEMENT COMPANY, Alpena, Mich., a Michigan corporation, began operations about March 1. The materials used are soft limestone and clay shales. The semi-wet process is used. The Bonnot Company's rotary kilns and ball and tube-mills are used for calcining and grinding. Chemical analyses of the raw materials give results as follows:

	Limestone.	Shales.
Carbonate of Lime	98.14	
Lime		9.69
Alumina and Iron	0.58	20.68
Silica	0.35	55.68
Magnesia	0.65	2.35
Alkalies		1.20
Loss		10.04

The Bonnot Co., Canton, O., manufacture cement machinery.

Only laboratory samples of cement were available in time for publication in this book.

THE ALPHA PORTLAND CEMENT COMPANY is a New Jersey corporation with offices at Easton, Pa., and works at Alpha, N. J., on the main line of the Lehigh Valley railroad. The company owns 140 acres of cement rock lying from 0 to 5 feet below the surface, quarried 85 deep and extending down 185 feet from the surface without change in nature as shown by borings. About 4 per cent. of limestone must be added, and this is obtained from the Lebanon valley. The two kinds of rock are mixed at the crushers, where the first reduction in size is made. The mixture then goes to four crackers and thence to a dryer, whence it goes to nine of the Bradley Pulverizer Company's Griffin mills and ball and tube-mills. Each Griffin mill requires 25 horse-power to run it, the ball mill 30 horse-power and the tube-mill 70 horse-power. The capacity of the ball and tube-mills is three times that of a Griffin mill. From these mills the material goes to ten rotary kilns with a capacity of 150 barrels a day. One hundred tons a

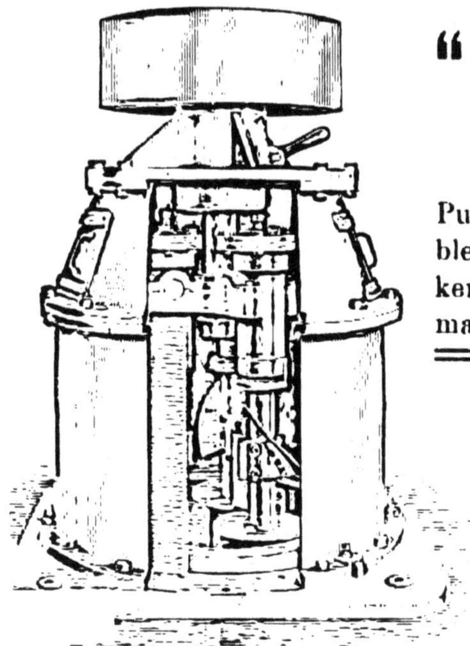

"NAIAD"

Pulverizes to an impalpable powder, cement, clinker, limestone or any hard material in one operation.

NO BETTER MILL MADE

Send for Our Reduced Price-List.

NEWELL MANUFACTURING CO., 149 Broadway, NEW YORK

day of pulverized coal are burned in the kilns. From the kil the burned clinker is elevated to the coolers, vertical iron cyli ders with air-blast through them. Thence the clinker pas through crackers, Griffin mills, fifteen in number, and F. Smidth & Co.'s Davidsen tube-mill. The American Blow Company's apparatus supplies the draft for dryers and coal burnin in kilns. The Robins conveying belts distribute the materials required and the S. Howes Company's packers are used for puttin cement in shape for shipment. The motive power consists of 1,000 horse-power engine, a 125 horse-power air compressor, an six auxiliary engines. The large engine drives the machinery the raw material mill by one shaft and eleven Griffin mills in th clinker department by another. One of the larger auxiliary e gines drives the remainder of the clinker-grinding machinery, an another the coal-grinding machinery. Steam is furnished by elev boilers, requiring 50 tons of coal a day. The water supply pumped to a reservoir from the Delaware river. Testing an chemical laboratories well equipped are in constant use. Electr transmission of power is planned, the current to be generated water-power at Raubsville, two miles distant, where 1,800 hors power can be developed. A new cement plant is under constru tion using ball and tube-mills and rotary kilns. The two will ha a capacity of 3,500 to 3,700 barrels of cement a day. Analyses the raw ground material (mixture) and of the finished product a as follows:

	Raw Material.	Cement.
SiO_2	11.96	20.38
Fe_2O_3	2.72	
Al_2O_3	4.64	
$Al_2O_3+Fe_2O_3$		10.58
CaO	42.12	63.30
MgO	2.11	2.86
CO	35.44	
SO_3		1.13
Water, graphite, and organic matter	1.01	1.75

The product has been used in many important works in all pa of the country. Some large undertakings, using 10,000 barrels more each, are the Philadelphia Bourse, Odd Fellows' Ha Archæological Museum in Philadelphia; new Fair building a Eiffel tower, the Illinois Central subways, walks and retaini walls, and walks, curbs, tunnels, cribs and other public works

Buhr Mills are made by Nordyke & Marmon Co., Indianapolis, Ind.

Chicago; United States Government work in New York harbor and Florida; the Holyoke and Meridian dams, in Massachusetts.

ALSEN'S AMERICAN PORTLAND CEMENT WORKS are under construction at West Camp, near Catskill, N. Y., upon designs made by Lathbury and Spackman. The dry process will be used. Davidsen tube-mills will be used in grinding Portland cement clinker and in pulverizing coal. The works will cost about $1,600,000, and the capitalization of the American company is about $2,250,000. A single brand of Portland cement will be made. Sinclair and Babson, 143 Liberty street, New York, are agents for the foreign and for the American company. Further information is withheld until the completion of the works. The company is reported to have acquired cement lands in the vicinity of Nazareth, Pa., also.

THE AMERICAN CEMENT COMPANY OF NEW JERSEY, with main offices at No. 22 South Fifteenth street, Philadelphia, Pa., is a New Jersey corporation owning the American Cement Company of Pennsylvania, with works at Egypt, Pa., and the Jordan Portland Cement Works at Jordan, N. Y., the manufacturing

GRINDING MACHINES
Single and double shaft mixers.

Brick Machinery

Machines for moulding plastic materials

THE CHAMBERS SELF-CONTAINED DRY-PAN.
(Patented Dec. 26, 1893, and Oct. 11, 1898.)

CHAMBERS BROS. COMPANY
Fifty-Second and Media Sts., PHILADELPHIA, PA.

branches of the business, also the Lesley & Trinkle Co., of 22 South Fifteenth street, Philadelphia, Pa., and the Uni Building Material Company, of 13-21 Park Row, New York C the sales departments of the business. The five works located Egypt, Lehigh County, Pa., are the Egypt Portland Cem Works, the Pennsylvania Portland Cement Works, the Colum Portland Cement Works, the Giant Portland Cement Works, a the Giant Rotary Portland Cement Works. The total capacity the six works at Egypt, Pa., and Jordan, N. Y., is about 5,000 b rels per day for all brands. Three brands of cement are ma factured, the Giant brand of Portland cement, the Union bra of natural hydraulic cement and the Improved Union brand, wh is a mixture of natural hydraulic cement with Portland cement

Portland cement was first made at the works in 1884, beginn with dome kilns, which are still in use at four of the plants. tary kilns were put into the new plant erected in 1898 and ad tional ones again in 1900. Lathbury & Spackman were the desi ers. The ordinary upright kiln is used in the manufacture of n ural cement. The mills are supplied with mill stones, the Brad Pulverizing Company's Griffin mills, crushers, engines and n chinery of most approved patterns. In all mills the dry proc is used.

The American Cement Company was established in 1883, John W. Eckert and Robert W. Lesley, who had been for ma years connected with the manufacturing and selling department the old Coplay Cement Company during the early years of the tablishment of the American Portland cement industry by the l David O. Saylor.

The new plant, being practically the second of the Portl cement works in the United States, naturally became the ow of some of the most valuable quarries and lands in the cement gion, and the introduction of American Portland cement into portant work was largely due to the efforts of those connected w the American Cement Company. The quarries of the comp are among the largest in the State of Pennsylvania, being fou number and embracing very large and uniform deposits of cem rock and limestone, all in close connection with the mills of company.

The quarries are large, open-faced quarries, from which the r

Griffin Mills are made by the Bradley Pulverizer Co., Boston, Mass asily mined in large quantities and in this way uniformity is ıred and the analyses of the raw material vary but slightly. 'borough chemical laboratories are connected with the works, 're daily reports are made on the raw material, as well as on 'tures going through the manufacturing process.

[']he total sales of the company for 1900 were about 1,000,000 rels, an increase from 870,000 in 1899. The company also ıs a large amount of cement land and water frontage near New-t News and Norfolk, Va., where it is planned to erect works supplying export and coastwise trade.

The Giant Portland cement is in use in the Cornell dam and Jerome Park reservoir of the New York water supply system, new East River bridge, the power house of the Metropolitan ection Company, the underground electric and cable work of Metropolitan and Third avenue street railway systems and the id transit underground railway in New York, the Reading sub-y in Philadelphia, the Niagara Falls tunnel and the new Wa-sset dam of the Boston metropolitan water system. These are, rhaps, the nine largest works of their kind ever constructed.

Improved Union cement is used in sewer construction in Phila-lphia, Pa., Newark and Orange, N. J., in paving in Philadelphia, the Baltimore & Ohio, Pennsylvania, and Philadelphia & Read-g railroads, in the Broad street station, Philadelphia, in the dams East Jersey, N. J., and Scranton, Pa., Water Companies, in the ntral Stores, New York, and other large and important work. Union cement is used in many large buildings, in street paving, rer construction, etc., including those named above, and also on ny important bridges on the railroads of the country, among m the celebrated Johnstown, Pa., bridge of the Pennsylvania rail-

odern Cement Machinery

We are prepared to design and contract for

mplete Machinery Equipment

for Hydraulic and Portland Cement Mills of any capacity. Also examine and report upon marl lands, etc. Correspondence invited.

DODGE MANUFACTURING CO., Mishawaka, Ind., U. S. A.

ENGINEERS—FOUNDERS—MACHINISTS

road, which within a month after its completion stood the gre flood of May, 1889.

ANTIETAM CEMENT COMPANY, Hagerstown, Md. S Note A, page 152.

THE ART PORTLAND CEMENT COMPANY'S works, Sandusky, Ohio, were started to make a white cement for work and other special purposes, but are now engaged in the ma ufacture of Bull Dog brand Portland cement. Smidth ball a tube-mills are used in grinding Portland cement clinker. Inf mation regarding materials, process and character of product been withheld by the company. See Note D, page 152.

THE ATLAS PORTLAND CEMENT COMPANY, 143 I erty street, New York City.—The works belonging to this co pany are located at Northampton and Coplay, Pa., and prod 3,500,000 barrels of Portland cement a year. The capacity shortly be increased to 4,500,000 barrels. The quarries of cem stone have been carefully selected to furnish the most unifo raw material possible, of the proper constitution to produce high grade of Portland cement. Rotary kilns are used for bu ing. Careful watch is kept upon the material by the laborat force to insure uniformity and the highest quality possible in product. The Robins Conveying Company's conveyors are u in distributing the materials and the American Blower Co pany's ventilating fans. The Atlas cement is shipped in barr weighing 400 pounds gross, 380 pounds net, and in duck or pa bags, of one-fourth barrel each. The cooperage department is v complete, and each barrel is lined with a specially prepared pa Analysis of the cement shows the following composition: Sili 21.30 per cent.; alumina, 7.65; iron sesquioxide, 2.85; lime, 60. magnesia, 2.95; sulphuric acid, anhydrous, 1.81; carbonic ac 1.14; potash, 0.517; soda, 0.631; moisture, 0.270.

AUSTIN PORTLAND CEMENT COMPANY, Austin, Tex See Note A, page 152.

BANGS & GAYNOR, Fayetteville, New York, manufact their Star brand of natural hydraulic cement at Fayetteville, Y., near the place where cement rock was first discovered in t country in 1818.

THE BANNER CEMENT COMPANY, Chicago, Ill.,

Electric Machinery—Keystone Electric Co., Erie, Pennsylvania.

at Cementville, Indiana, for the manufacture of Banner of Louisville natural hydraulic cement. The usual natural processes of burning and grinding are used, except that Bradley Pulverizer Company's Griffin mills are used. A special process of aerating cement is used upon the product.

VID BATTLE ESTATE, Thorold, Ont., Can. See Note ge 152.

E BEAVER PORTLAND CEMENT COMPANY, Ltd., nk, Ont., Can., manufactures Portland cement in a plant ed by Lathbury & Spackman, using the wet process. The conveying belts are used for conveying the materials and Smidth & Co.'s Davidsen tube-mills for grinding the Portland cement clinker. See Note B, page 152.

E JAMES BEHAN ESTATE, John J. Costello, Superintendent, has works for the manufacture of natural hydraulic at Manlius, N. Y., with capacity of 1,000 barrels a day.

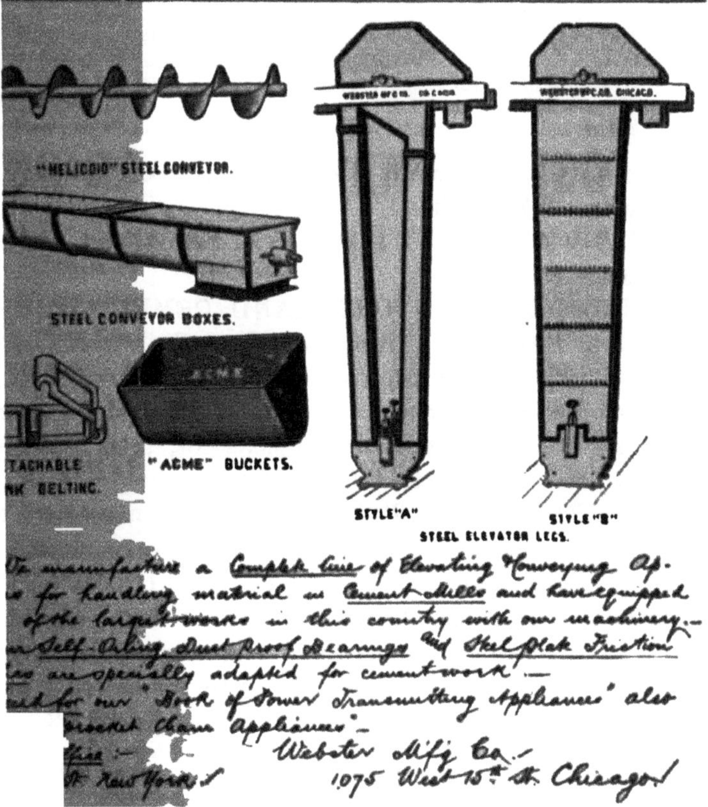

BELMONT CEMENT WORKS, Bellefonte, Pa.—See Not A, page 152.

THE BIRMINGHAM CEMENT COMPANY, of Ensley, Ala. is a New Jersey corporation manufacturing the Southern Cros brand of Portland cement from blast furnace slag. The capitali zation is $300,000, the capacity 800 barrels a day. The work are now ready to furnish cement, having been rebuilt after the destruction by fire. The slag is cooled suddenly by means of stream of water, is then dried and pulverized, lime and other con stituents being added when necessary. The S. Howes Company' packers are in use. The company thinks the definition of pozzuo lana cements made by the commission of United States enginee and given in the introductory chapter of this handbook, should no be applied too strictly to their product, as they attempt to mak all necessary additions in the furnace stack.

Analyses of the finished product lie between the followin limits:

Lime	50 to 55 per cent.
Silica	28 to 30 per cent.
Alumina and Iron	12 to 14 per cent.
Magnesia Maximum	1.50 per cent.
Sulphur	1.00 per cent.

BLUE RIDGE CEMENT AND LIME WORKS, Blue Rid Springs, Va. Works idle.

BLUE ROCK CEMENT COMPANY, New Albany, Ind. Se Note A, page 152.

THE BONNEVILLE PORTLAND CEMENT COMPAN of 1233 and 1237 R. E. Trust Building, Philadelphia, Pa., ha works at Siegfried, Pa., with a capacity of 1,500 barrels a day f Star brand Portland cement. Griffin mills are used for grindi materials. Information regarding materials, process and quali of product has been withheld.

BRIDGES & HENDERSON, Hancock, Md., manufacture Cu berland natural hydraulic cement for the neighboring markets.

THE BRIER HILL IRON AND COAL COMPANY, Youngstown, Ohio, manufactures the Brier Hill brand of Portla cement (pozzuolana) by mixing and grinding together proper prepared blast furnace slag and slaked lime substantially accor ing to process in use at other works making the same kind of c

Plasticon, a plastering cement. The Alabastine Co., Grand Rapids, Mic

BUHR MILLS

French Buhr or Esopus Stones—
Under Runner and Vertical Mills
(ALL SIZES)

Especially adapted for grinding cement, plaster of paris, crushed limestone, brickbats, etc.

Bolting Reels
Dust Collectors
Packers, Elevators
Conveyors
Mill Appliances and Supplies

IGH-GRADE POWER CONNECTIONS

Turned Wrought Iron Shafting.
Journal Boxes and Hangers.
Ring Oiling Bearings.
Pulleys, Belt Tighteners, etc.

OPE DRIVES—

Gearing,
rockets, Chain, etc., etc.

Our work in this line is way above the average. We want to bid on your work and ask you for the opportunity.

Catalogues and Prices Promptly on Request.

ORDYKE & MARMON CO.,

104 Day Street.... INDIANAPOLIS, IND.

ment. Griffin mills are used for grinding, and the Dodge Man facturing Company's rope transmission, clutches, quills, and du tight bearings are installed.

THE BRITISH COLUMBIA PORTLAND CEMEN WORKS are situated on False Creek, Vancouver, B. C., and e produce 100 tons a week. The materials used are limestone a clay, the limestone being crushed and then ground in edge-ru ner mills weighing 20 tons, and the clay in a separate mill of si ilar nature. The Sturtevant mills are used. The dry powders a mixed in screw conveyors and a cylindrical dry mixer revolvi on its axis and fitted with continuous conveyors running in o posite directions. Samples of the mixture are tested for prop tions and they are corrected if necessary. The material then g to a wet mixer, where 5 per cent. of water is added, and the mixtu is thoroughly pugged and run through a brick machine. Af drying on the drying floor, to which they are carried on an e less band, the bricks are elevated to the top of the vertical c tinuous kilns, burning 300 pounds of coal slack per ton of cem produced. The clinker taken out at the bottom is ground in bu stone mills. See Note B, page 152.

THE BRONSON PORTLAND CEMENT COMPANY, Bronson, Mich., is a Michigan corporation with a capitalization $500,000, manufacturing the Bronson brand of Portland cem Cement was first manufactured at these works in 1897.

Analyses of materials and product show:

	Marl.	Clay.	Cement.
Silica	1.60	63.75	22.90
Alumina	1.55	16.40	6.80
Iron Oxide		6.35	3.60
Carbonate of Calcium	88.90		
Oxide of Calcium		2.40	63.90
Carbonate of Magnesium	0.94		
Oxide of Magnesium		1.42	0.70
Sulphuric Acid (Anhydride)	0.16	0.14	0.40
Organic Matter	6.00	3.50	
Loss on Ignition			0.60
Carbonic Acid		3.39	
Alkalies			1.10

These analyses are made by W. H. Simmons, head chemist, Walter Banks, assistant, and are average results. The marl is tained on the 700 acres of land belonging to the company, which the works are situated, adjacent to the Lake Shore & Mi

See F. L. Smidth & Co.'s Advertisement on Page 187.

igan Southern railroad. The land is low and wet, the top three feet being of peat. This is removed by the dredge used, which then excavates the marl, the stratum of which averages 40 feet deep. The dredge boat floats on the pond or lake thus formed.

The clay used is a surface plastic clay, of which an ample supply is found on the company's property. This clay is brought in cars and dumped in a shed provided for the purpose, from which it is conveyed to the edge-runner mills, which do the preliminary grinding. Next the clay is elevated to hoppers above the mixing floor. The marl is brought in cars and dumped into pug mills, which discharge directly into storage tanks. At this point careful analyses of the marl are made. Next the marl is elevated by pumps to the mixing floor, where it is measured and the requisite amount of clay added and both together thoroughly pugged. These pug-mills discharge into a basin, from which the mixture is pumped into tube-mills, which perform the final slurry grinding and discharge the slurry into a last basin. From this basin the slurry is pumped into large dosage tanks, where corrections are made, if analysis shows the slurry of incorrect composition, and from which the corrected slurry is conveyed into the rotary kilns. From the time the marl is dumped from the cars, it is kept in constant agitation, and is continually mixed until as slurry it is pumped into the rotaries.

The rotary kilns are six feet in diameter and sixty feet long, with linings graduated in thickness and of material to suit the temperature of the various parts of the kiln. Each weighs about

Frisbie Friction Clutch Pulleys,

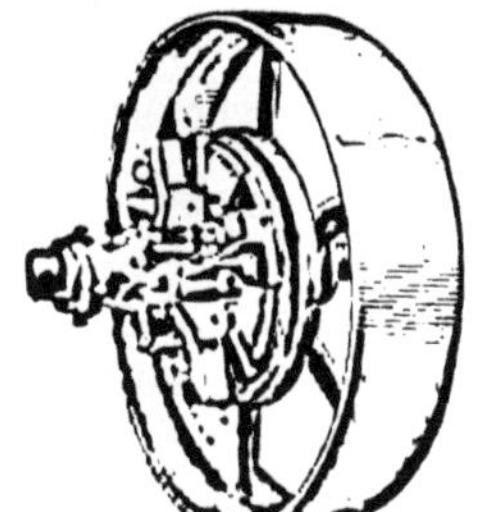

Friction Cut-Off Couplings

and Friction Winding Drums

ARE UNEQUALLED FOR SERVICE IN CEMENT MANUFACTORIES::::::: *THOUSANDS IN USE*

SEEK INFORMATION OF

THE EASTERN MACHINERY CO.

NEW HAVEN, CONN.

fifty tons, and will burn from 120 barrels to 140 barrels per da The fuel is pulverized coal, delivered by special machinery an an air blast. The slurry, about 50 per cent. water, is pumped at the higher end of the kilns, falls on wing plates and is turn over and dried, slowly descending until it is discharged from t lower end as thoroughly burned clinker.

As the clinker falls from the kilns it is taken by a conveyor a elevator to a cooler of special design, which delivers the clink of proper temperature for the final grinding and finishing, whi is done in Griffin mills. The finished product is elevated and co veyed to the storehouse to await shipment, after the final tes for fineness, tensile strength and soundness prove that it is read

There is a full equipment of boilers, electric lighting machine a number of pumps of water, slurry and oil, air compressors, e A 250 horse-power engine runs the finishing mills, the Bradl Pulverizer Company's Griffin mills. The American Blower Co pany's exhaust fans are in use. Several rope transmissions with a purtenances have been installed by the Dodge Manufacturing Co pany.

There are chemical and physical laboratories with compl equipment, also a machine shop. The capacity of the works now 1,200 barrels a day. The cement is used very largely in middle west.

THE BUCKEYE PORTLAND CEMENT COMPANY, Bel fontaine, Ohio, constructed works at Harper, Ohio, in 1889, a plans of German expert engineers and chemists for cement pla The materials used are marl and clay. The main bed of marl about 40 feet deep and covers over 400 acres. The clay is north the marl bed and dips under it. Average analyses of the raw terials and the finished product show as follows:

	Marl.	Clay.	Cement.
Carbonate of Lime	93.0	20.0	
Lime			62.50
Carbonate of Magnesia	1.5		
Magnesia			1.20
Silica	3.0 (Silica, Alumina, Oxide of Iron)	52.0	21.30
Alumina		17.0	6.95
Oxide of Iron		5.0	2.00
Sulphuric Acid		1.0	0.98
Loss on Ignition	2.5 (Loss on Ignition, Alkalies)	3.0	4.62
Alkalies		2.0	

The original process was a semi-wet process forming the m

Cement Making Motors—Northern Electric Mfg. Co., See page 181

ture into bricks, drying them in the air and in tunnel dryers, and burning in shaft kilns. A rotary kiln has been installed and both processes are at present in use. For both processes marl cars are brought into the mill on an inclined plane and dumped into cars on a track below, where the marl is weighed and the proper amount of clay added from bins adjacent. For the rotary process the material is dumped into dry pans, whence it goes through pug-mill mixers to the kilns with about 40 per cent. of water. Oil has been used for fuel, but powdered coal will be used hereafter.

The cooled clinker from the kiln is run up an inclined plane in cars to a crusher, thence through two roller crackers, passing a separator on the way to the bin and being handled by elevators and conveyors from mill to mill. From the bin it is dropped into French buhr stone mills and thence it passes through tube-mills. An interesting comparison can be made between the product by the different methods of burning. The double Dietzsch kiln first installed will turn out 75 to 80 barrels of cement a day with a fuel consumption of 20 per cent. of the weight of the cement produced; the continuous shaft kilns turn out 50 barrels each and consume 30 per cent. and the rotary kilns will turn out 120 to 160 barrels a day with a coal consumption of 30 per cent. of the weight of cement produced. There are three return tubular boilers of 150 horse-power each, a chemical filter for softening water, and a 250 horse-power engine. A blower using exhaust steam for heating air supplies the tunnel dryers. There is a very thorough chemical and testing laboratory in which continuous analyses of the material at the wet mill are made, to control the proportions of the raw materials.

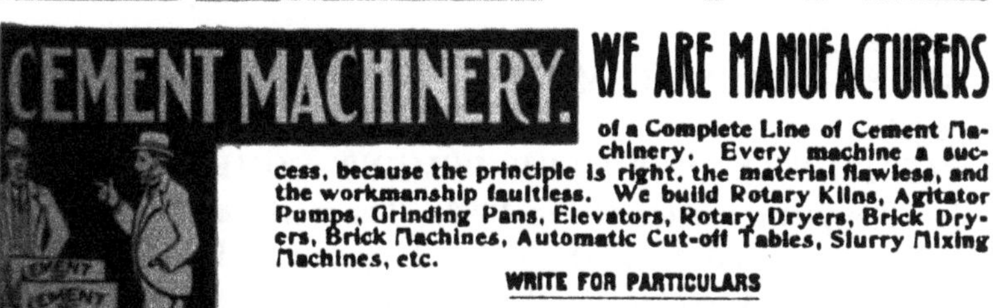

CEMENT MACHINERY.
WE ARE MANUFACTURERS
of a Complete Line of Cement Machinery. Every machine a success, because the principle is right, the material flawless, and the workmanship faultless. We build Rotary Kilns, Agitator Pumps, Grinding Pans, Elevators, Rotary Dryers, Brick Dryers, Brick Machines, Automatic Cut-off Tables, Slurry Mixing Machines, etc.
WRITE FOR PARTICULARS
The American Clay-Working Machinery Co.
BUCYRUS, OHIO, U. S. A.
NEW YORK OFFICE, - - - - 39-41 Cortlandt Street.

The plans are completed for considerably enlarging this pl this year.

THE BUCKHORN PORTLAND CEMENT COMPANY a West Virginia corporation with offices in the Real Estate Tr Building, Philadelphia, Pa., and works at Manheim, Pres county, West Virginia. The product is Buckhorn Portland ment, the capacity of the works being 1,000 barrels a day. rotary kiln method of burning is used. Sturtevant Mill Compa crushing and grinding machinery and Smidth ball and tube-m are used on raw materials and on Portland cement clin Smidth's Davidsen tube-mills are used for pulverizing the used as fuel in the kilns. See Note D, page 152.

BUFFALO CEMENT COMPANY, Limited, is a New Y State corporation. Its offices are located at No. 110 Fran street, and the quarries and works are at the intersection of M and Amherst streets, Buffalo, N. Y. The nominal capitaliza is one hundred thousand dollars ($100,000.00).

Buffalo natural hydraulic cement has been manufactured si 1874. The capacity of the works is 240,000 barrels annually.

Buffalo Portland cement has been manufactured since 18 and the capacity of the works is 40,000 barrels annually. material employed is a natural rock deposit, the average of wh when burnt produces a cement which analyzes as follows: Sil acid, 82.86 per cent.; alumina, 8.36; lime, 52.60; magnesia, 6

The noticeable features at their plant are the large contin kilns, disintegrating and grinding mills, and mixing and sepa ing appliances, patents for which they control. Bradley Pulve ing Company's Griffin mills are in use for grinding. This comp also produces a ground limestone, which analyzes as follows: bonate of lime, 90.50 per cent.; silica, 6.82; iron, .56; carbonat magnesia, .30.

BURNS CEMENT COMPANY, Burns, Kansas. See [illegible] page 152.

CALIFORNIA PORTLAND CEMENT COMPANY [illegible] Cal.—The plant was erected in 1893. The works are ab[illegible] quarters of a mile from the railroad station and the [illegible] Pacific and the Atchison, Topeka & Santa Fe railroads [illegible] to the doors of the warehouse. The location, on the slope of Sl

The Standard Plaster Co., Buffalo, N.Y., makes Calcined Plaster or St

Mt., enabled the constructors to utilize gravitation for conveying materials.

An extensive ledge of calcite stands on edge in the heart of the hill and this furnishes the lime constituent of the cement. The quarries are half-way up the hill. At the quarry the rock is loaded into cars, hauled by burros through a tunnel four hundred feet long, then dumped into a chute three hundred and seventy feet long down the side of the hill, that delivers it at the crusher on the upmost terrace of the mill. The limestone is put through a jaw crusher first, then passed over a jig-conveyor with a gridiron screen that removes the finely crushed rock, while the coarser rock gravitates to a small crusher. After reduction to nut size all the rock is delivered to a storage bin located below the crusher terrace, but above the mixing and grinding room.

The clay pits are at Perris, on the Santa Fe railroad, about thirty miles from the works. The clay is air-dried at the pits by plowing up large patches and exposing it for weeks to the dessicating California atmosphere. It is delivered at the works in cars and unloaded into large storage bins of 5,000 yards capacity. A small car and incline serves to elevate the clay as required to a small bin alongside the bin for crushed rock. On account of the dryness of the climate and materials, drying kilns are not used either for rock or clay.

In the mixing room is a battery of four Griffin mills for grinding the raw materials. A steelyard of fifteen hundred pounds capacity, with a dumping hopper, is swung under the rock bin, a charge drawn, then under the clay bin, a charge of clay drawn,

The "Howes" Automatic Friction Drive Packer

Swiftest, strongest and most durable. Dust-proof gears and bearings. Cement mixing and blending apparatus. "Eureka" Magnetic Separators for extracting metallic particles from any material such as fertilizers, lime, etc. Packers for packing all kinds of materials.

THE S. HOWES CO.

ESTABLISHED 1856

Eureka Works SILVER CREEK, N. Y.

then over a hopper below the floor, that discharges into an ele vator boot. The first mixing is done in discharging the rock an clay into this elevator boot. The elevator spouts the material int feeding hoppers above the Griffin mill. The mills reduce the ra mix to the required degree of fineness and deliver it to the screw mixing conveyors that discharge into large storage bins under neath the floor of the mixing room. Beneath the raw mix storag bin is a screw conveyor feeding the raw mix to the kiln at an rate desired by the burner in charge, the regulation being effecte by shifting a belt on a coned pulley.

The next lower terrace has a kiln shed with two rotary kiln each seventy-five feet long and of special design. Petroleum i used for fuel. It is fed into a gas producer opposite the end o the rotary. The blast is from individual fan blowers that requi but little power to run and admit of using a hot blast. These an other features of the process are covered by the Duryee patents.

On a level with the kiln building is the clinker cooling she Descending ten feet more, the level of the engine, boiler and d namo house is reached. Both steam and electric power are use A portion of the electric power is taken from the Redlands Ele tric Light and Power Company, and part is generated at th works.

The kilns and blowers are run by individual steam engines, th crushers and mills in the raw material department are run by motor set in an adjoining room. The shaft of the clinker-grin ing room is run either by the engine or dynamo, the shaft bein so coupled that a change from one power to the other can be ma instantaneously. The dynamo is also run as a motor when takin power from the Redlands Power Company. The buildings are l by electricity.

Ball and tube-mills are used in reducing the clinker. Th original and only invoice of Greenland pebbles received cost $4 per ton delivered at the works. Afterward California pebbl were found at a short distance from the works. They are quart not so perfect in shape or size as the Greenland pebbles, but th have proven equally satisfactory for grinding purposes and th cost $6 per ton for the hand-selected quality. The stockhouse bi are on a level with the mill room and have a storage capacity 40,000 barrels in bulk in eight bins.

Parkhurst Combined Curb and Gutter. Apply to D. C. Buntin, Indianapol

A screw conveyor takes the cement from the stockhouse to the shipping warehouse, where it is sacked.

The capacity of the plant is three hundred and seventy-five barrels a day.

CALUMET PORTLAND CEMENT COMPANY, 3901 Lowe avenue, Chicago, Ill.—This company is reported to be making a brand of silica Portland cement, using F. L. Smidth & Co.'s Davidsen tube-mills for grinding the product and the Webster Manufacturing Company's elevating, conveying and power transmission machinery. See Note B, page 152.

CAMPANIA MEXICANA DE CEMENTO PORTLAND, Dublan, Mexico.—On account of lack of time no information could be received before going to press. Smidth ball and tube-mills are used for grinding Portland cement clinker.

THE CANADIAN PORTLAND CEMENT COMPANY, Ltd., Deseronto, Ont., takes over the interests of the Rathbun Cement Company of Napanee Mills and Marlbank, Ont., the Beaver Portland Cement Company of Marlbank, Ont., and the St. Lawrence Cement Company of Montreal, P. Q., Canada. Information is not furnished regarding materials, processes or product, except that Smidth ball and tube-mills are used in grinding Portland cement clinker and raw materials. See Note D, page 152. Silica Portland cement is reported as manufactured at the Strathcona Works, and those of the St. Lawrence Portland Cement Company of Montreal, Davidsen tube-mills being used in grinding.

CANON CITY CEMENT COMPANY, Canon City, Colo. See Note A, page 152.

CASSADAGA CEMENT COMPANY, Cassadaga, N. Y. —No information has been received concerning this company, except that F. L. Smidth & Co.'s Davidsen tube-mills are use grinding both raw materials and Portland cement clinker Note **B**, page 152.

THE CASTALIA PORTLAND CEMENT COMPANY Pennsylvania corporation with offices at 701-702 Publication Building, Pittsburg, Pa., and works at Castalia, Ohio. Their T brand of Portland cement was first introduced to the trade September, 1898, and the sales have been so satisfactory that works have been increased to a capacity of 1,500 barrels a The capitalization of the company is $300,000. It owns from to 600 acres of marl and clay in Erie county, Ohio. The p was designed by Lathbury & Spackman. The wet process rotary kilns are used in the manufacture. Eleven kilns have installed, using powdered coal for fuel and the American Bl Company's draft system.. The Bradley Pulverizer Company's (fin mills are used in grinding and the S. Howes Company's p ers put the cement into packages. C. O. Bartlett & Co.'s four c partment dryer is in use for drying coal.

THE CATSKILL CEMENT COMPANY, Smith's Land New York, is constructing works for the manufacture of Cat brand of Portland cement, with a capacity of 300 barrels a

Chemical analyses of the finished cement show an average c position as follows, according to the reports of the comp Silica, 23.44 per cent.; alumina, 6.35; iron peroxide, 3.99; l 63.21; magnesia, 1.15; sulphuric acid anhydrous, 1.25.

Information regarding materials used and process has withheld.

CAYUGA LAKE CEMENT COMPANY, Ithaca, N. Y. Note **C**, page 152.

CHAUTAUQUA CEMENT COMPANY, Burnhams, N. See Note **A**, page 152.

CHELSEA PORTLAND CEMENT COMPANY, Ltd., troit, Mich., is reported as incorporated to construct cement w See Note **A**, page 152.

THE CHICAGO PORTLAND CEMENT COMPANY, 513 Stock Exchange Building, Chicago, Ill., has constr works at Oglesby, Ill., for the manufacture of AA Chi brand of Portland cement, with a capacity of 1,000 barrels a

For "Modern" Cement Machinery, see adv. on page 155.

(View of train bearing fourteen Griffin Mills to Iola Cement Company.)

"MOST SATISFACTORY AND ECONOMICAL"

IOLA PORTLAND CEMENT COMPANY

DETROIT, MICH., October 16, 1900.

BRADLEY PULVERIZER COMPANY, Boston, Mass.:

Gentlemen—Your inquiry as to the satisfaction the Griffin Mills are giving us duly received. We have forty-two 30-inch Griffin Mills in our plant. The writer has had a large experience with most kinds of grinding machinery, and is prepared to say that for grinding Portland cement clinker the Griffin Mill is the most satisfactory and economical grinding machine on the market. Each of the above mills has at times run over ten barrels per hour, and on long runs has averaged nine and a half barrels each per hour.

Yours truly,

IOLA PORTLAND CEMENT COMPANY,

(Signed), Per JOHN T. HOLMES, *Managing Director.*

We invite everyone interested in reducing refractory substances to an even degree of fineness to write for descriptive catalogue of this remarkable mill. It will surely interest you and may save you money.

THE

BRADLEY PULVERIZER COMPANY

92 STATE STREET, BOSTON

Lime rock and shale clays are the materials used. Fourteen fe of the latter, in two layers separated by a thin coal seam, unde lie twenty-two feet of the former, on the company's property, o which there is about 2,000 acres. Analyses of the raw materia show as follows:

	Limestone.	Clay.
Silica	6.06	53.12
Alumina	3.92	20.60
Iron Oxide		4.09
Lime	49.46	4.02
Magnesia	0.91	2.24
Sulphuric Anhydride	0.10	
Ignition Loss	39.06	13.70

The dry process is used. From the quarry crusher-house th rock and clay are taken by an aerial tramway into the mill build ing and directly to two revolving dryers. The dried material i stored in great storage bins, from which, as required, it is auto matically drawn and delivered by elevator, conveyors and auto matic feeders to Smidth ball-mills. By elevator and conveyor the partially pulverized material then goes to a storage and equal izing bin from which it is drawn by automatic machinery an conveyed to the Davidsen raw tube-mills, which reduce it to ver fine powder that flows continuously by elevator and conveyors int the large feed bins above the kilns. Rotary kilns receive this d powder from mechanical feeders and produce the cement clink by means of heat maintained day and night at a temperature about 3,000 degrees Fahrenheit, using pulverized coal blown in b air pressure fans. Automatic machinery cools the clinker, whi is mechanically stored by conveying machinery. From the clink storage bins conveyors take the cold clinker to Smidth ball-mill fed automatically, and the partially pulverized clinker is then el vated to a storage bin over the Davidsen cement tube-mills, whi finally pulverize it to the required fineness for Portland cemer The finished cement is automatically conveyed by machinery and distributed in the stockhouse, where the bins have a c pacity of 40,000 barrels. Sacking and barreling machinery the stockhouse insure uniform weight and perfect package.

The Bradley Pulverizer Company's Griffin mills, also ball a tube-mills are used in grinding raw materials and Portland c ment clinker. The Robins Conveying Belt Company's belt co veyors and the Webster Manufacturing Company's elevating, co

High Grade Power Connections by Nordyke & Marmon Co., Indianapo

veying and power transmission machinery are in use. The plant is operated very largely by electricity, the Northern Electrical Manufacturing Company's motors being used. The laboratory is fully equipped for making analyses and physical tests.

THE CHICKAMAUGA CEMENT COMPANY, Rossville, Ga., four miles from Chattanooga, Tenn., has begun the construction of works for the manufacture of the Chickamauga brand Portland cement and Dixie brand of natural hydraulic cement.

THE CLARK COUNTY CEMENT COMPANY, Sellersburg, Ind., is an Indiana corporation with a plant capable of making 900 barrels a day of Mason's Choice Hammer and Trowel brand of Louisville natural hydraulic cement from the natural rock calcined with coal in upright kilns and ground in stone mills.

THE CLINTON CEMENT COMPANY, P. O. Box., 177, Pittsburg, Pa., is a Pennsylvania corporation manufacturing the Clinton brand of Portland cement. The capacity of the works is 150 barrels a day. The cement is made by mixing limestone and properly treated blast furnace slag in due proportions, calcining the mixture in rotary kilns and grinding the resulting clinker. This is the first factory using this method of manufacturing Portland cement to be erected in this country. It was designed by Lathbury & Spackman. F. L. Smidth & Co.'s Davidsen tube-mills are used to grind the Portland cement clinker.

"ABC" Fans and Blowers
For pulverized fuel outfits.
For "waste heat" dryers.
For removing dust, and numerous other applications.
AMERICAN BLOWER COMPANY
DETROIT, MICH.

THE COLORADO PORTLAND CEMENT COMPANY has constructed works at Portland, Colo., for the manufacture of Portland cement from a mixture of cement rock and limestone similar to that used in the Lehigh district of Pennsylvania. Analysis of the finished cement shows, silica, 21.88 per cent.; alumina, 7.14; sesquioxide of iron, 2.85; calcium oxide, 64.94; magnesia, trace; alkalies, 1.18; sulphuric acid, 0.73; carbonic acid and

water, 1.08. A Griffin mill is used for grinding. Information regarding process of manufacture, capacity of plant and capitalization has been withheld.

THE COLUMBIA PORTLAND CEMENT COMPANY, Cleveland, Ohio., is reported to have been incorporated in Delaware by Cleveland and Pittsburg capitalists. See Note A, page 152.

THE CONSOLIDATED CEMENT COMPANY, 509 Goldsmith Building, Milwaukee, Wis., is constructing a plant concerning which no information has been received except that the Webster Manufacturing Company's elevating, carrying and power transmission machinery is being installed. See Note B, page 152.

THE COPLAY CEMENT COMPANY, Allentown, Pa., is a Pennsylvania corporation with works at Coplay, Pa. The first works of the company were established in 1866 for the manufacture of natural hydraulic cement by the usual vertical kiln method of calcination and mill-stone method of grinding, and now have a capacity of about 600 barrels a day. Mr. D. O. Saylor, the president of the company, after some study, decided that a product comparing favorably with foreign Portland cements could be made from the natural rock available. During the five years, 1890-1895, experiments were made upon methods of combining rocks of different chemical composition to secure the proper proportion for a high quality of Portland cement, and in the latter year the first Portland cement manufactured in the United States was turned out. The cost of manufacture was so great that competition with the foreign cements and with the prejudice in their favor was very difficult, but the uniformly high quality of cement put on the market and the introduction of improvements reducing the price have practically removed both these difficulties. The first continuous kiln was built in 1893, a Danish development of the Dietzsch kiln, and eleven are now in use. The raw material is run through crushers and crackers into bins, from which they are mixed in proportions determined by analyses made frequently. Sturtevant crushing and grinding machinery is used. The mixture, weighed out in automatic scales, is put through mill-stones and is kneaded in pug-mill and brick machines. A small amount of natural cement is used to give consistency to the bricks. Chambers Brothers' brick and clay working machinery is in use. After drying in tunnel dryers the bricks

For information about Griffin Mills address Bradley Pulverizer Co., Boston

re elevated to the top of kilns. The fuel is fed in through stoke-holes on the floor below the top. The clinker cools as it passes down from the combustion chamber and is ready to handle when removed below. The clinker is ground in Smidth ball and tube-mills and the finished product is stored in bins. The capacity of the mills is 500 barrels a day. Recently a third plant, with a capacity of 1,600 barrels a day, has been constructed upon the latest designs. A comparison of the three plants gives an excellent view of the progress of the cement industry in this country. The quarry is about one-fourth mile from the plant, and the rock is handled in cars by locomotive to an elevator, raised to the storage floor and dumped in separate piles. Crushers on the floor below and rotary dryers prepare the rock for Smidth ball-mills. There are ample storage bins at each stopping point, and the machinery is so arranged that it can be run on either cement rock or limestone as desired. Automatic weighing machines weigh out the mixture from the Smidth ball-mills in proportions determined by analyses and drop it into Davidsen tube-mills, from which it is elevated and conveyed to bins over the rotary kilns, of which there are eight. Pulverized coal is used for fuel, Smidth & Co.'s tube-mills being used as pulverizers. The clinker falls from spouts at the lower ends of the kilns into cars placed to receive it, each car being provided with a perforated pipe, which can be attached by hose to water tap, the clinker being cooled by the spray of water thus supplied. From the clinker storage floor the material is dropped into Smidth ball-mills, thence to Davidsen tube-mills, and thence to the stock-house.

Four 300 horse-power boilers furnish steam for two 600 horse-power engines, driving the raw material and the finishing mills.

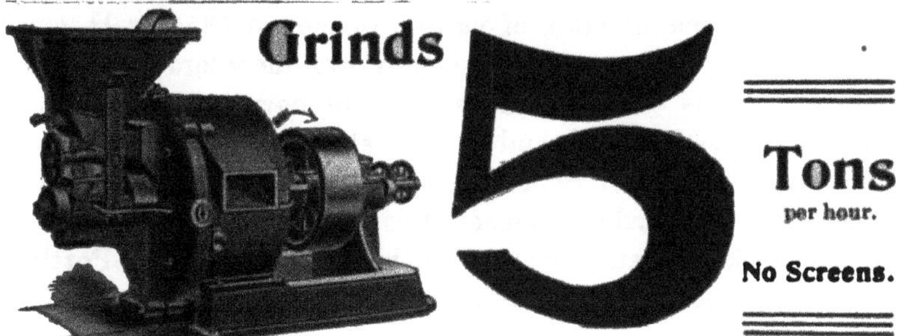

Grinds
5
Tons
per hour.
No Screens.
New Emery Mill for Limestone, Clay, etc. Price, $750. Send for circular.
STURTEVANT MILL CO., 103 Clayton St., BOSTON, MASS.

The kilns are run by two engines, and variable speed countershafts are used. This description is condensed from articles by F. H. Lewis and Henry C. Meyer, Jr. See Note B, page 152.

CRESCENT CEMENT WORKS, Long Point, Hochelaga county, Canada. These works, owned by Thos. M. Morgan, manufacture the Crescent and Diamond brands of cement. Further information regarding the works is not furnished.

CRESCENT WHITE LIME COMPANY, Fayetteville, Ark. See Note A, page 152.

CROWN CEMENT COMPANY, Allegheny City, Pa. The works of this company at Bellaire, Ohio, are not in operation at this time.

CROWN PORTLAND CEMENT COMPANY, Lansdowne, Md. See Note A, page 152.

CUMBERLAND AND POTOMAC CEMENT COMPANY, Cumberland, Md., is reported to have let the contract for its proposed new works at Pinto, to replace a plant recently burned, for $40,000. See Note A, page 152.

CUMBERLAND HYDRAULIC CEMENT AND MANUFACTURING COMPANY, P. O. Box 264, Cumberland, Md.—These works were burned in July, 1900. New works are now nearly ready to supply the market with Cumberland natural hydraulic cement. Smidth ball-mills will be used in grinding natural clinker.

CUMBERLAND VALLEY CEMENT COMPANY, Washington, D. C. See Note B, page 152.

THE CUMMINGS CEMENT COMPANY is a Connecticut corporation with main office and works at Akron, N. Y. The capitalization of the company is $300,000. The works were established for the manufacture of natural cement in 1854 by H. Cummings & Sons. The present company was incorporated in 18[illegible] and two brands of Portland cement are now manufactured, in addition to the Obelisk brand of natural cement. The capacity of the works for natural cement is 2,000 barrels a day; for Stone King brand of Portland cement it is 500 barrels a day, and for Roman Rock Portland cement, 500 barrels a day. The Portland cements are made from natural rock selected and mixed in proper proportions.

Use Keystone Generators in Cement Plants.—Keystone Electric Co

HE DEFIANCE HYDRAULIC CEMENT COMPANY, ed by Wilhelm & Gorman, has its office at Defiance, Ohio, and works at a short distance from the city. Hydraulic cement has manufactured at these works at intervals since 1846. Conous vertical kilns are used, the clinker being crushed and und on mill-stones. The cement has been used extensively in io and in parts of Michigan and Indiana. The present capacof the works is 100 barrels a day. Chemical analysis of the ent rock made by R. C. Kedzie, of the State Agricultural Colat Lansing, Michigan, shows: Organic matter, bituminous sappears on burning), 14 per cent.; silica, 42; carbonate of e, 17.7; carbonate of magnesia, 12.2; alumina, 7.0; oxide of n, 7.1.

HE DETROIT PORTLAND CEMENT COMPANY, Union ust Building, Detroit, Mich., is constructing works for the manecture of Portland cement, at Fenton, Mich, which will not be dy to turn out cement regularly before July, 1901. The works designed by Lathbury & Spackman, and the wet process will

THE BEST MOTOR
FOR
Cement—
—Making

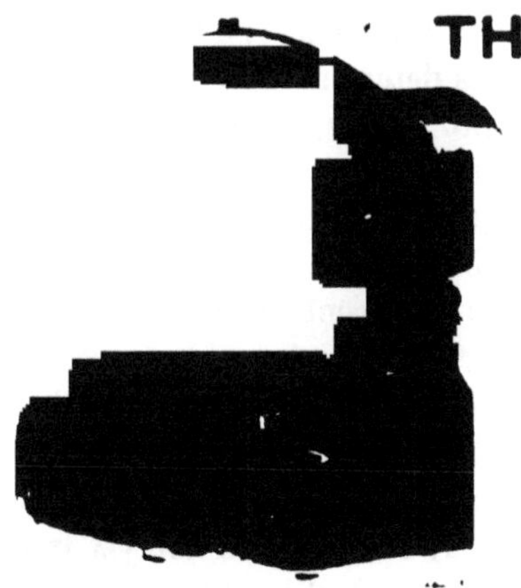

NORTHERN STEEL-CLAD MOTOR

Dust and dirt-proof. A regular bull dog for tackling the hardest kind of work, but it never growls or snarls—just plugs right along with its job. Can be belted, geared or direct connected to any machine you want to run. We build the most compact, powerful and nomical motor on the market, in sizes from 1 to 500 H. P. Also Generafor Lighting and Power from 1 K. W. to 1000 K. W.

COMPLETE EQUIPMENTS FOR POWER AND LIGHTING. GET OUR CATALOGUE AND ESTIMATES BEFORE BUYING.

RTHERN ELECTRICAL MANUFACTURING COMPANY

Engineers and Manufacturers. MADISON, WIS., U. S. A.

be used. Smidth ball and tube-mills will be used for grinding slurry and Portland cement clinker, and also in pulverizing coal for the rotary kilns. Further details are withheld pending completion of the works.

THE DEXTER PORTLAND CEMENT COMPANY, Nazareth, Pa., is a Pennsylvania corporation, which has located a new plant with a capacity of 800 to 900 barrels per day at Nazareth, Pa., to manufacture the Dexter brand of Portland cement. The first cement was turned out in January, 1901. The materials used are the usual cement rock and limestone of the Lehigh district, which is put through the dry rotary kiln process and ground in Smidth ball and tube-mills. The Robins conveying machinery is used. F. L. Smidth & Co.'s Davidsen tube-mills are used to pulverize the coal used in the rotary kiln as fuel.

THE DIAMOND PORTLAND CEMENT COMPANY, Cleveland, Ohio, is an Ohio corporation with offices on Perkins avenue at the crossing of the C. & P. railroad, and works at Middle Branch, Ohio, for the manufacture of Diamond brand of Portland cement. The works were established in 1892. The materials used are limestone and clay, which are ground separately to an impalpable powder and mixed in correct proportions as determined by chemical analyses. The mixture is moulded into bricks, which are dried and burned in Dietzsch Etagen ovens. After selection the clinker from the ovens is crushed and ground to the desired fineness in Sturtevant mills and Smidth ball-mills. Analyses of the cement show as follows: Ignition loss, 1.32 per cent; alumina, 7.85; lime, 63.22; sulphuric anhydride, 1.11; phosphoric acid, trace; silica, 21.24; iron oxide, 4.14; magnesia, 0.28; alkalies, 0.68; titanic acid, trace.

DURYEE PORTLAND CEMENT COMPANY, Montezuma, N. Y.—The works were destroyed by fire and are not yet in operation again. The company has purchased about 500 acres of marl land in central New York, and expects to erect a large plant at Montezuma. This mill was the first one that used wet slurry in the rotary kiln in the manner now used so successfully in many of the works in Ohio, Indiana and Michigan. The use of the process was begun in 1891. See Note D, page 152.

THE EDISON PORTLAND CEMENT COMPANY, New

Plasticon, a plastering cement. The Alabastine Co., Grand Rapids, Mich.

PLASTICON

HARD MORTAR PLASTER

A Plastering Cement for All Walls

Sets hard as a rock.
Works uniformly, reliably and easily.
Simple to mix—avoiding all liability of mistakes.
Gives a superior surface for decorating in any material.
Dries quickly, permitting a saving of over one-half the time required to do the same work in ordinary mortar.
Sets dense and solid, making strongest possible protection against fire, cold and heat.
Does not crack, expand or contract, and will never come loose and drop.
Plastering can be done with it the whole year, as it is not subject to freezing after having been applied for a few hours.

PLASTICON

Is best for the dealer because it works to the satisfaction of the plasterer and results to the satisfaction of the building owner; hence the dealer can handle it at a good profit.

MADE ONLY BY

HE ALABASTINE COMPANY

GRAND RAPIDS, MICH., U. S. A.

Girard Building, Philadelphia, Pa., is constructing works at Ste artsville, N. J., for the manufacture of Portland cement, wi capacity of 4,000 barrels a day at first—parts of plant being bu with a capacity of 10,000 barrels per day.

THE EGYPTIAN PORTLAND CEMENT COMPANY, inco porated in Michigan with a capitalization of $1,050,000, has i main offices in Detroit and is constructing works at Fenton, Mic They will be ready to supply the market with their brand in Augu 1901. Further information is withheld pending completion works.

THE ELK RAPIDS PORTLAND CEMENT COMPAN Elk Rapids, Mich., has just completed works for the manufactu of Elk Rapids brand of cement, with a capacity of 600 barrels day. The materials used are marl and clay, which are treated l the wet process. The Bonnot Company's machinery for manipu lating raw materials and cement clinker is installed, with Griffi mills in addition and the Webster Manufacturing Company's sy tem of elevating, conveying and power transmission machiner Dodge Manufacturing Company's rope transmissions are also in us

THE EMPIRE PORTLAND CEMENT COMPANY, Wa ners, N. Y.—The works are located on the Erie canal. The m terials from which the cement is made are found on the opposi side of the canal, about a half-mile distant. A bed of marl eig to fifteen feet in thickness is found immediately below the su face, which is underlaid by a bed of clay, in which is a large amou of carbonate of lime. The cement is made from a mixture of m terial from these two beds, equal parts from each. Cement w first made by the present process early in 1890. The capacity the works is 150,000 barrels a year. A clam-shell dredge is use to raise the materials from their beds. The cars in which th are deposited are hauled by a locomotive to the foot of the i cline to the overhead bridge over the canal, whence they are haul into the mill by cable. There being too much water in the ma for proper working, the clay is deposited in front of two revol ing dryers, into which it is regularly discharged. The dried cl drops out below and is carried by an elevator and conveyor to buh stone mills and ground. An elevator discharges it into weig ing hoppers. The wet marl is dumped into edge-runner mills

See F. L. Smidth & Co.'s Advertisement on Page 187.

Calcined Plaster

... OR ...

STUCCO

Manufactured by our new patented process, making a very strong plaster and guaranteeing an absolutely uniform product. . . . .

Capacity, 300 TONS PER DAY

Also, LAND PLASTER, manufactured from Gypsum Rock. Write for samples and price. . . . . .

STANDARD PLASTER COMPANY

BUFFALO, N. Y.

low the track level, the proper proportion of the dried clay added and the two materials are thoroughly mixed. It is sor times necessary to reduce the proportion of water in this m ture. A dryer is used to dry a part of the slurry, which is th used to stiffen the material next following. Each charge from t edge-runners is elevated to two vertical pug-mills. The slurry still too moist for making bricks. A workman receives the d charge from the mill on wooden slats, which are stacked on ca run for 24 hours through drying tunnels, and elevated to the k doors. The slurry when dry is usually in lumps of proper s for dumping into the kiln. The empty cars of slats are lowered another elevator and returned to the pug-mill. There are 18 do kilns, each 13 feet in diameter and 45 feet high, encased in she iron. The charge is made up of alternate layers of slurry a coke, the charge is allowed to burn out, when air is drawn throu the hot clinker by means of a fan, and the air thus heated is us to help the work of the furnaces supplying heat to the drying tu nels. The cooled clinker is carefully sorted, and underburnt m terial is reburned. The good clinker is loaded on barrows, elevat to the second floor and dumped into the crusher hopper. Af passing through the crushers it is run through one of ten roc emery mill-stones of the Sturtevant Mill Company. Smidth b and tube-mills are also used for grinding. Two vacuum sepa tors insure a very finely ground product. Two brands are man factured, the first grade being called Empire, and the seco Flint. Chemical analysis of raw materials and product sho as follows:

	Marl.	Clay.	Cement.
Silica	0.26%	40.48%	22.04%
Alumina	0.10	20.95	6.45
Iron Oxide			3.41
Carbonate of Lime	94.39	25.80	
Lime			60.92
Carbonate of Magnesia	0.38	0.99	
Magnesia			3.53
Loss on Ignition	4.64	8.50	
Sulphuric Anhydride			2.25

THE FORT SCOTT HYDRAULIC CEMENT COMPA Fort Scott, Kan., is a Missouri corporation of Kansas City, M with works at Fort Scott, Kansas, having a capacity of 600 bar in ten hours, making the four star brand of Fort Scott natu hydraulic cement. A chemical analysis of the cement rock r

Electric Motors and Generators See Northern Electric Mfg. Co., page r material shows: Silica, 17.26 per cent.; oxide of iron, alumina, 2.05; calcium carbonate, 61.51; magnesium car-, 11.09; undetermined, 2.64. The usual calcination and al reduction process is used in preparing the cement for t.

WLER & PAY, Mankato, Minn., own works at Austin, , with a capacity of 100 barrels a day of Austin natural hy-r cement. The works first made cement in 1894, and the ty sold has increased each year. Chemical analyses of the t rock used as raw material show: Silica and alumina, per cent.; iron, 2.09; carbonate of magnesia, 28.99; car- of lime, 49.20; sulphuric anhydride, 0.06; undetermined, The rock is calcined in the usual manner and pulverized in rushers, dry-pans and buhr-stones, with the usual screens. roduct is marketed in Minnesota, Iowa, North and South Da- Kansas, Nebraska and Missouri.

E GEORGIAN BAY PORTLAND CEMENT COMPANY, Owen Sound, Ontario, Canada.—No information has been ed concerning this company except that the Sturtevant Mill

TWO LEADERS

for grinding and pulverizing cement rock and clinker, are Smidth Ballmills and Davidsen Patent Tubemills. Both are simple, durable and efficient, with maximum output and uniform product. We are always ready to offer suggestions, make plans, or submit estimates for any cement plant or equipment.

SUPPOSE WE SEND A CATALOG?

Company's machinery is used for grinding the limestone used and that Smidth ball and tube-mills are used for grinding the Portland cement clinker. See Note B, page 152.

THE GERMAN-AMERICAN PORTLAND CEMENT WORKS, LaSalle, Illinois, are owned largely by German capitalists also interested in German Portland cement works. See Note C, page 152.

THE GLASGOW CEMENT WORKS has been known for some time as the James River Cement Works, and is incorporated under that name. Reference should be made to the latter for description of plant.

THE GLENS FALLS PORTLAND CEMENT COMPANY, Glens Falls, N. Y.—The works of the company are located on the Glens Falls Feeder Canal, where it is crossed by the tracks of the Delaware & Hudson Company railroad, thereby affording water and rail transportation for the shipment of their cement. These works during the past year have been entirely rebuilt, greatly enlarged, and remodeled so as to conform to the best cement engineering practice of the present day. Through the entire plant the construction has been of brick and iron. The permanent character of the buildings, with the numerous economies that have been introduced throughout the work, makes this plant a model one. The raw materials from which the cement is made surround the factory, and embrace a large tract extending on both sides of the Glen Fall Feeder, and on both sides of the Hudson river. These materials consist of limestone and an overlying clay. The limestone is found as usual in layers of varying thickness, differing slightly in their chemical analysis. But by care in the selection and combination of these layers, an extremely uniform product is obtained for the average, which does not vary more than one per cent. in the amount of carbonate of lime it contains. The clay is found in large deposits over the limestone, and is singularly favorable to cement making on account of its freedom from coarse sand and the uniform character of its constituents. The raw materials are treated by the dry process. The limestone and clay are first dried and partially reduced by crushers and rolls. They are then accurately weighed in the proper proportions in automatic scales. After being weighed, the materials are thoroughly mixed, then still further reduced to a fine powder by grinding mills, from which the mixture is elevated to a large bin, and then in turn it is fed to the wet mixers, where it is properly tempered with water to allow it to be made into bricks. The bricks are then run into drying tunnels, and are heated by waste heat carried in a duct from the boiler, and driven by blowers through the tunnel system.

After being thoroughly dried, the bricks are elevated to the top floor of the kiln building, where they are fed into Schöfer kilns, and properly burnt. These Schöfer kilns are an improvement on the Dietzsch kiln, and are very economical in fuel. Like all the improved German kilns, while very simple and uniform in their working when properly controlled, many disastrous failures have taken place from attempting to operate them theoretically with inexperienced men. In the Glens Falls Portland Cement Works it was found necessary to employ head burners trained in the old works of Europe. From the kilns, the clinker is conveyed to the ball-mills, where the first reduction is made with steel balls. From these it passes to the tube-mills, where the final reduction is made with flint pebbles. The finely ground cement is now ready for storing, and is conveyed to the store-house, where it is deposited in separate bins, each holding from four hundred to twenty-five hundred barrels, where the cement is carefully sampled and then tested. Average analyses of the Iron Clad brand show, lime, 63.50 per cent.; silicic acid,

Requires no floor space, does perfect work, needs no skilled mechanic to operate, ...en placed always ready, built with the best material, has rawhide gears, paper friction, ...ller bearings, with forged iron and steel, makes it very durable and for quick, hard ...ork it has no equal. Is automatic in holding or throwing out its load at any point; ...hen hoisting or lowering will carry at the same time. Descriptive catalogue and prices ...rnished upon application. Address

C. S. HARRIS & CO., ROME, N. Y.

21.50 per cent.; clay and iron oxide, 10.50 per cent.; magnesia, 1.80 per cent.; alkalies, 0.40 per cent.; sulphuric acid, 1.50 per cent.; loss, 0.80 per cent.

THE GLOBE CEMENT COMPANY, Sellersburg, Ind., manufactures the Globe brand of Louisville natural hydraulic cement by the process described under Louisville Cement Company.

THE GOLDEN RULE CEMENT COMPANY, Sellersburg, Ind., is an Indiana corporation manufacturing the Arm and Hammer brand of Louisville natural hydraulic cement by the usual process of the district. See Louisville Cement Company for description. Cement was first made at these works August 8, 1898.

THE GOSHEN PORTLAND CEMENT COMPANY, Goshen, Ind., is constructing works a short distance from Elkhart, Ind., but has not replied to requests for information.

THE GRAYLING PORTLAND CEMENT COMPANY is reported as organized with Wm. M. Courtis, of Detroit, as consulting engineer, and C. A. Campbell, 407 North Linn street, West Bay, Mich., as an interested party.

THE GREAT NORTHERN PORTLAND CEMENT COMPANY, Detroit, Mich., is a New Jersey corporation with an authorized capitalization of $5,000,000, which is constructing works at Baldwin, Mich., for the manufacture of Portland cement. It is proposed to build the plant in units of 1,000 barrels capacity per day, increasing the size of the plant from year to year as may be desired. The first unit of 1,000 barrels capacity is now under construction.

THE HANOVER PORTLAND CEMENT COMPANY, Hanover, Ontario, Canada.—No information has been received concerning the works except that a large additional building has recently been erected and that the Sturtevant Mill Company's machinery is used for grinding marl and Davidsen tube-mills in grinding Portland cement clinker. See Note B, page 152.

THE HECLA PORTLAND CEMENT AND COAL MINING COMPANY will soon be incorporated to build works for making cement at West Bay City, Mich., and will operate coal mines near the plant. The present address of those interested in the company is, U. R. Loranger, 505 Crapo Block, Bay City, Mich. The office

Parkhurst Combined Curb and Gutter is the best. See pages 77, 119, 151

of the incorporated company will be in Union Trust Building, Detroit, Mich.

THE HELDERBERG CEMENT COMPANY, Albany, N. Y., in its works at Howe's Cave, N. Y., uses the wet or semi-wet process in making Portland cement, although the raw material is the usual hard cement rock. The company also makes a brand of natural cement. The two plants at Howe's Cave have been under the same management for several years. The Bonnot Company's installation of cement-making machinery is in the Portland cement works, also the Bradley Pulverizer Company's Griffin mills and F. L. Smidth & Co.'s Davidsen tube-mills for pulverizing raw material and Portland cement clinker. The American Blower Company's draft system is in use, including a powdered coal burning outfit for ten rotary kilns. Further information is withheld. See Note D, page 152.

THE HERCULES CEMENT COMPANY, Catasauqua, Pa., has constructed works at Coplay, Pa., for the manufacture of Portland and natural hydraulic cements. Information as to raw materials, process, character of product, has been withheld.

THE HOOSIER CEMENT COMPANY, Sellersburg, Ind., manufactures Louisville natural hydraulic cement by the usual natural cement process, using vertical continuous kilns, buhrstone mills and screens. The works were put in operation in December, 1899, and have a capacity of 500 barrels a day.

HOUSTON BROS., Thirty-second street and Pennsylvania railroad, Pittsburg, Pa.—This firm reports that they are large stockholders in cement factories, and two brands, Rex Portland and

Samson Portland, are marketed as their manufacture. They also market Flint Rock, Rosendale and Cumberland Valley brands of natural hydraulic cement, and Vulcanite brand of Portland cement. No information concerning materials, methods of manufacture and quality of product has been received, except concerning Vulcanite Portland cement, which see.

HOWARD HYDRAULIC CEMENT COMPANY, Cement, Ga. See Note A, page 152.

THE ILLINOIS PORTLAND CEMENT COMPANY, Chicago, Ill. See Note A, page 152.

THE ILLINOIS STEEL COMPANY, Rookery Building, Chicago, Ill., have two plants for the manufacture of cement in connection with their blast furnaces, manufacturing both a slag or puzzolan cement, and a true Portland. . Mr. Edward M. Hagar is manager of the cement department. The cement plant at the North Works of the Illinois Steel Company was started in 1895, and has a capacity of 500 barrels per day. The new cement plant at the South Chicago Works of the Steel Company was started in 1900, with a capacity of 1,500 barrels per day. It cost $500,000. The first plant constructed was for the manufacture of a slag cement exclusively, known as the Steel brand, which is a product obtained by grinding together to exceeding fineness an intimate mixture of slag and properly prepared slaked lime. The manufacture of the cement commences with the use of properly selected ores and limestones in the blast furnaces. Slag of the proper composition is chilled as it comes from the furnace by a stream of cold water under high pressure. This breaks up and disintegrates the slag, and eliminates a large proportion of its sulphur, changing it chemically in such a way as to render it suitable for the manufacture of cement. This slag is subjected to chemical test before being fed into rotary dryers. After thorough drying, it receives its preliminary grinding in Griffin mills. It is then mixed with prepared lime and ground together in F. L. Smidth & Co.'s Davidsen tube-mills to a fineness so great that not over 4 per cent. is retained on a 40,000 mesh sieve. The product is then conveyed into bins, from which it is drawn and packed for the market. At the South Chicago plant are manufactured both the Steel brand of slag cement and the Universal brand, a true Port-

Write The Bonnot Co., Canton, O., when in need of any cement machinery

land cement under the definition of the United States Engineer Department. The process of making Universal Portland cement consists of grinding together slag of a certain composition with limestone in the right proportions, to a fineness of 95 per cent. through a 10,000 mesh sieve. This mixture is then burnt to a clinker at a high temperature, in rotary kilns. This clinker is then ground to the same fineness as before burning, and constitutes finished cement. In detail, the granulated slag of a slightly different composition than that used for Steel cement is dried in rotary dryers and ground in ball-mills, and then mixed by weighing machine in certain proportions with limestone which has already been crushed, dried and ground. This mixture of the slag and limestone is then ground together and intimately mixed in Davidsen tube-mills, from which it is conveyed to the burner building, and there fed into the rotary kilns, which are 60 feet long and 7 feet in diameter. The fuel used in these kilns is pulverized coal. The clinker is cooled in cooling tanks and carried by belt conveyor to the Smidth ball-mills and thence to Davidsen tube-mills, which finish the grinding. The Robins conveying belts and the Webster Manufacturing Company's elevating, conveying and power transmission machinery are in use. The cement is then carried to the stock-house and held in bins until ready to be shipped. The total output of both works is about 50,000 barrels a month, about equally divided between the two brands.

Following is an analysis of Universal Portland Cement by Robert W. Hunt & Co., of Chicago, made December 26, 1900:

Silica (SiO_2), 23.62 per cent.; Alumina (Al_2O_3), 8.21; Oxide of Iron (Fe_2O_3), 2.71; Lime (CaO), 61.92; Magnesia (MgO), 1.78; Sulphuric Anhydride (SO_3), 1.32; Sulphur as Sulphides, none; Loss on Ignition, 0.52.

HARRISON CONVEYOR

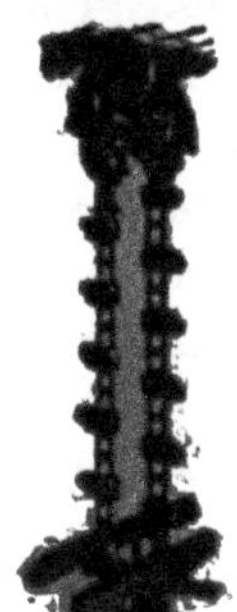

Elevating, Conveying and Power Transmission Machinery for handling material of all kinds, such as Cement, Ashes, Coal, Barrels, Boxes, Packages, etc. Made of Wrought Iron and Steel. Roller, Steel and Special Chains.

Howe Standard Scales
Howe Gas & Gasoline Engines to 60 H. P.

Catalogues

BORDEN & SELLECK CO.
Engineers & Machinists
CHICAGO, ILL.

WM. M. COURTIS, A. M.,
Mining Engineer & Metallurgist
CHEMIST
Consulting Engineer Grayling Cement Co.
Reports on Cement Properties.
Laboratory, 449 Fourth Ave.
Office, 412 Hammond Building.
DETROIT, MICH.

CEMENT INLAID ART TILE
Especially adapted to hotels, banks, libraries, vestibules, porch floors and ornamental walks.
Hollow Concrete Building Blocks,
High-Grade Cement Work of all kinds.
THE AMERICAN ART TILE CO.
COLUMBUS, OHIO.

THE IMPERIAL CEMENT COMPANY, Ltd., of Owen Sound, Ont., is constructing works concerning which no information has yet been received, except that Smidth ball and tube-mills are used in grinding Portland cement clinker and Davidsen tube-mills in grinding raw materials.

THE IMPERIAL PORTLAND CEMENT COMPANY, with offices at 1114 Real Estate Trust Building, Philadelphia, Pa., are constructing works at Nazareth, Pa., with a capacity of 1,000 barrels a day, for the production of Imperial brand Portland cement. The rock used is said to be naturally correct, so that no mixture is necessary, analyses showing, silica, 18.71 per cent.; alumina and oxide of iron, 6.30; carbonate of lime, 72.14; magnesia, 0.50. The rotary kiln process will be used.

THE INDIANA CEMENT COMPANY, Charlestown, Ind., manufactures Lion brand Louisville natural hydraulic cement by process similar to that described for the Louisville Cement Company.

THE INDIANA PORTLAND CEMENT COMPANY is a New Jersey corporation capitalized at $5,000,000, with offices at Detroit, Mich., which proposes to build works at Milford, Kosciusko county, Indiana, for the manufacture of Portland cement from marl and clay, and at Milltown, Harrison county, Indiana, for its manufacture from limestone and clay. Large purchases of land at both places are reported. The headquarters will shortly be removed to Indianapolis.

THE IOLA PORTLAND CEMENT COMPANY is a Kansas corporation with works at Iola, Kan., for the manufacture of Portland cement. The company controls several hundred acres of land underlaid with limestone, having 95 per cent. of carbonate of lime, and shale having 75 per cent. of silica and alumina. It also owns a gas well which furnishes fuel for all purposes. The buildings are well designed for the fuel used and the power transmission employed. The rock is crushed in three crushers, burned in 21 rotary kilns and ground in 42 Griffin mills. There are chemical and physical laboratories, power-house, machine shop and store-room. There are six 300 horse-power gas engines and three of 150 horse-power, using 5,000,000 cubic feet of gas a day, the equivalent of about 250 tons of coal. These engines drive the

For Cement Machinery address Nordyke & Marmon Co., Indianapolis, Ind.

achinery of the mill and the electrical equipment. The latter includes a 75-k. w. 250-volt dynamo, furnishing light at night; 2½-k. w. 250-volt generator, furnishing power for the laboratory and light in the day time; a 15-volt 125-ampere sparking dynamo, furnishing sparks to the gas engines; two storage batteries and a spare dynamo giving reserve power to prevent interruption in case of accident. The Dodge Manufacturing Company has installed 35 rope drives in the works, with the accompanying friction clutches, shafting, floor stands, dust-tight bearings, pulleys and gearing. The American Blower Company's fans are in use. Water for daily supply is pumped to reservoir and standpipe, and there is a Keystone Electric Company's motor and pump at the river at a distance of a mile, for fire service. The mill cost $1,000,000. Cement was first made in June, 1900.

IROQUOIS PORTLAND CEMENT COMPANY, Cleveland, Ohio, is a Delaware corporation with principal offices at Cleveland, and works at Caledonia, N. Y.

The lands owned by this company consist of about four hundred acres of marl and clay deposits, beginning one mile east from

KRUPP BALL MILLS AND GRIT MILLS

THE BEST MACHINERY FOR GRINDING PORTLAND CEMENT CLINKER AND RAW MATERIALS FOR MAKING SAME, COAL, ORES, ETC. BUY THE BEST SO YOU WILL NOT "HEAR THE CHIMES" IN YOUR WORKS

THOMAS PROSSER & SON

5 GOLD STREET NEW YORK

OLD COLONY BUILDING CHICAGO, ILL.

Caledonia, N. Y., and extending along the tracks of the N. Y. C & H. R. R. R. and the Lehigh Valley R. R. for a distance of abou two miles.

The marl comprising this deposit has been thoroughly sample and analyzed at all points, and consists of a fine white carbonat of lime, practically free from all impurities, being especially fre from magnesia, which, on an average, amounts to only about thre tenths of one per cent. The deposit is so near the surface as to re quire little or no stripping, and has an average depth of eight fee

The deposit of clay is free from pyrites, sand and grit, and con tains the proper ratio of alumina to silica to insure a slow settin cement.

The clay and marl are conveyed to the works by a trolley roa both materials being here stored until thoroughly air dried. Fro the storage bins, the materials are taken by a bucket convey to the drying kilns. The dried materials, after proper proportio ing, are mixed and ground dry in Smidth tube-mills, and the stored in bins ready for burning. The burning is effected b powdered coal in three rotary kilns, built and installed by the Bo not Company, of Canton. The clinker, after cooling in a pit belo the kilns, is crushed in ball-mills and ground fine in Smidth tub mills, being carried thence to the stock-house for proper aging.

The mill being located on a considerable hill, most of the tran fers above mentioned are effected by gravity.

The power plant consists of three 200 horse-power boilers, tw 250 horse-power engines, tandem compound, directly connected two 200 k.-w. alternating current generators, by which power is di tributed to all parts of the plant where it is to be applied. Alte nating motors are used, for the most part, directly connected. The motors are all enclosed in dust-proof cases.

All the buildings are entirely fire-proof, being constructed of ste frames, and brick curtain walls, with slate roofs. The works a furnished with separate buildings for machine shop and laborato each of which is fully equipped for the purpose for which it w designed.

Average analyses of the marl, clay and cement are as foll

See Indorsement of Griffin Mills by Iola Portland Cement Co.

	Marl.	Clay.	Cement.
Lime	53.5%	0.8%	64.1%
Silica	0.4	62.5	23.0
Iron Oxide	0.2	7.5	3.4
Magnesia	0.3	1.8	0.7
Sulphur SO_3	1.7	0.4	0.4

THE JAMES RIVER CEMENT WORKS is a Virginia cor-
ration with works for the manufacture of James River natural ydraulic cement at Locher, Rockbridge county, Virginia. This ment has been manufactured since 1848, when the works were arted by C. H. Locher to make cement for the locks and dams the James river and Kanawha canal. The quarries are located Locher P. O., about one mile west of Glasgow, Va., on the hesapeake & Ohio railroad and the James river. The mines and lns are on the opposite side of the river from the railroad. The ment has been ground at various times at Balcony Falls, two iles east, by water-power, at Lynchburg and at Holcombe's Rock. 1896 the present steam mill was built, and the cement clinker now conveyed across the river on a cableway. Power is gener-ed by a 100 horse-power boiler and Corliss engine.

The continuous vertical kiln is used with coal as fuel. The inker is drawn from the bottom of the kiln, crushed in ordinary t crushers, ground in French buhr-stones, the fine material run-ing through separators and being conveyed thence to the stock-om. Chemical analyses of rock and cement made some years go show:

	Rock.	Cement.
Carbonic Acid	30.40%	
Potash	0.12	
Silica	34.22	49.53%
Alumina and Oxide of Iron	7.80	11.29
Lime	17.38	25.15
Magnesia	9.51	13.77
Undetermined	0.57	0.26

Other analyses differ somewhat from these. The cement is sed in engineering works in Washington, D. C., for railroad ork, canals, dams, tunnels, reservoirs in Virginia and the adjoin-g States.

EAVY BROOMS SPECIAL BRUSHES OF ALL KINDS FOR CEMENT MANUFACTURERS

JOSEPH LAY & CO., RIDGEVILLE, INDIANA

THE KANSAS CITY AND FORT SCOTT CEMENT COMPANY is the corporate name under which cement is manufactured by the C. A. Brockett Cement Company, of Kansas City, Mo. The works are located at Fort Scott, Kan., and manufacture the double star brand of Fort Scott natural hydraulic cement. The deposit of cement rock was discovered in 1867. The ordinary vertical kilns and mills for grinding natural cement clinker are used. The cement is used in Kansas and the adjoining States in large quantities.

THE KENTUCKY AND INDIANA CEMENT COMPANY, of Jeffersonville, Ind., with mills at Watson, Ind., on the B. & O. S. W. Ry., is an Indiana corporation with a capitalization of $65,000, which manufactures the Eagle brand of Louisville natural hydraulic cement. The Western Cement Company, of Louisville, Ky., is the general sales agent. The capacity of the works is 1,500 barrels daily.

THE KINDERHOOK PORTLAND CEMENT COMPANY, Indianapolis, Ind., is reported to have been incorporated for the manufacture of brick, cement and tiling. See Note A, page 152.

THE KNICKERBOCKER CEMENT COMPANY, Poughkeepsie, N. Y.—No information regarding this company has been received except that the S. Howes Company's packers are in use. It is reported that the raw materials used are blast furnace slag and lime. See Note B, page 152.

THE WILLIAM KRAUSE & SONS CEMENT COMPANY, 1621-1623 North Fifth street, Philadelphia, Pa., has its distributing warehouse at 2119-2127 American street, and has located its works at Martin's Creek, Pa. (Application was made in March, 1901, to change the name of the company to the Martin's Creek Portland Cement Company.) The materials used are the cement rock and limestone of the Lehigh region, the cement rock being obtained from quarries on the company's property adjacent to the mills, and the limestone from their quarry about a mile distant on the Bangor & Portland railroad. A chemical analysis of the completed cement shows silica, 22.24 per cent; alumina, 7.17 per cent.; ferric oxide, 4.05 per cent.; lime, 64.13 per cent.; magnesia, 2.01 per cent. The stone is brought from the quarries in cars and dumped on the floor of the stone-house, where the two kinds are

Use Keystone Motors in Cement Plants.—Keystone Electric Co., Erie, Pa.

ed in proper proportions as shown by chemical analyses, and ped into a crusher, from which it is elevated to a storage bin, eled to an elevator, and discharged into a dryer, which uses the s from the cement kilns, an exhaust fan maintaining the proper ft for the kilns. From the dryer the material is elevated and veyed to storage bins over the ball-mills. The fine material goes to storage tanks in the kiln building. Coal is used for l in the kilns, being dried, crushed and then pulverized in a e-mill. From the storage tanks it is forced into the kiln by blast, the ground stone entering the other end of the kiln by veyor. The kilns and connected conveyors are variable in feed, operated by electric motors. The burned clinker falls into a ker cooling pit and is thence elevated and conveyed to the ce- it ball and grit-mills, the finished product being conveyed to storage bins in the stock-house, which has a capacity of 35,000 rels. Conveyors carry the cement for packing to a central at, where it is elevated to a bin for distribution to S. Howes npany's bag and barrel packers. The Webster Manufacturing npany's elevating, conveying and power transmission machin- is in use. There is a cooper-shop in the stock department. power is supplied by three 250 horse-power boilers and a 600 se-power Corliss engine. There is a 150 horse-power engine as iliary, which drives the dynamo when the large engine is not operation. Besides lighting, the dynamo furnishes power for ring kilns, blowers, the stone-house and stock-house. There also air compressors for the quarry and high-pressure air-blast. buildings are substantial brick structures, with timber roofs. stock-house walls are litholite. The capacity of the works is r 500 barrels a day, and they have been constructed so that the acity can be doubled at comparatively small expense.

THE LAKEFIELD PORTLAND CEMENT COMPANY, Ltd., en Sound, Ont., is reported to have been incorporated to con- ict a large plant at Lakefield, near Petersboro, Ont., Can. See le A, page 152. C. O. Bartlett & Co. are erecting one of their compartment dryers for drying coal.

[illegible] STANDARD STEEL CRUSHING ROLLS ....
[illegible] BREAKERS, PULVERIZING MACHINES, for Cement Clinker, Etc.,
[illegible], Dry Kilns and Plans for Crushing and Pulverizing Mills.
[illegible], 113-115 Plymouth St., Jersey City, New Jersey

THE LAWRENCE CEMENT COMPANY operates tories making Rosendale natural hydraulic cement, at ville, on the Rondout Creek, Hickory Bush, and Binnewat the Wallkill Valley railroad, near Kingston, N. Y. Cemen been made, practically, after the process now used, since 183 provements being made from time to time in details and i chinery. At Hickory Bush are located quarries and kiln product being run by tramway to Eddyville, where it is gr packed and shipped. At Binnewater are quarries, kilns and making a plant complete in itself. The material used is the lime of the lower Helderberg group of the upper Siluria mation. There are many layers of similar rock, two being successfully in making cement. The so-called light and dark are usually mixed to make the best quality of cement. The ries being in very rough and hilly country, it is possible to the kilns below the outlet of the quarry, so that the rock c dumped directly into them. The quarries usually become very shortly on account of the heavy dip of the strata. The are continuous, being fed with alternate layers of rock and layers of anthracite pea-coal, and yielding about 100 barr clinker a day each, when over-burned and under-burned cl has been sorted out. The clinker is dropped into crackers passes to mill-stones running over separator screens between tions until fine enough to drop through. The side-hill lo enables most of the movements to be by gravity.

THE LAWRENCE CEMENT COMPANY OF PENN VANIA has a large Portland cement plant at Siegfried, Pa the Central railroad of New Jersey. The original plant wa of the first erected in this country. The material used is th ment rock and limestone of the Lehigh region. The cement underlies the property of the company, and is mined, thus s the expense of stripping. The limestone is quarried at a about four miles south of the plant. The cement rock is loaded cars at the mines, hauled to the opening of the galleries and r gravity or locomotive to crushers, from which it passes to pu izers just below, and is reduced to coarse grit. After passing thr dryers it is elevated and conveyed to the hopper-shaped bins. limestone is similarly treated and stored in adjoining bins. Ana

Plasticon, a plastering cement. The Alabastine Co., Grand Rapids,

A LITTLE TALK ABOUT BUSINESS

"I like a proposition that pays."
—C. P. HUNTINGTON.

THIS PAYS!

THERE are certain things that a man in business must do. He must have an office, he must put out a sign, and he must advertise.

He must make himself known to the people who may be interested in his kind of business. The better he does this the more successful he will be.

Some of the most successful men make it a rule to spend one-fifth of their income in advertising, and they find it pays.

It makes poor business good.

It makes good business better.

The best way to advertise is to put your advertisement where it will go directly to the people who want what you sell.

We give the kind of advertising that goes directly to the right spot.

If your business is not in line with the kind our readers are interested in, we don't want you to advertise in our magazine.

If it is, we can help you, and we can give you more for your money than you can get from any other expenditure of it.

From Sacramento (Cal.) Record-Union:

"MUNICIPAL ENGINEERING has often been pronounced in these columns the most useful, practical magazine of the age, and we adhere to that judgment."

MUNICIPAL ENGINEERING MAGAZINE

Awarded Grand Prize by Paris Exposition of 1900
Holds Medal from the Chicago World's Fair

are here made and the contents of the bins are combined in proper proportions, being dropped into tunnels underneath and elevated and conveyed to automatic scales. The mixture goes to ball-mills and thence to tube-mills and thence to large bins with a capacity for 48 hours' running of each kiln. Powdered coal is used for fuel in calcination. It is automatically weighed and registered, and then passes through a rotary dryer and a 20-foot Smidth coal-grinding tube-mill, then being elevated to bins in front of kilns and fed to them by air blast. The raw material enters the kiln through water-jacketed chutes. The clinker is conveyed to storage bins with capacity of 20,000 barrels, where it is cooled by air blast from pipes in the tunnel underneath, the arrangement of bottoms being similar to that of the other storage bins. Smidth ball and tube-mills finish the cement, which is stored in a stock-house of 72 bins with a total capacity of 125,000 barrels. Between the ball and tube-mills there is an opportunity to divert the clinker to an automatic weighing and mixing apparatus, when it is desired to add natural cement to produce a second-grade Portland or an improved natural hydraulic cement. The conveyors from this point are arranged in twin lines, so that the mill can be engaged on cement of two qualities at the same time.

The cement rock from the mine may be run directly to vertical continuous kilns for the manufacture of natural hydraulic cement. The clinker from these kilns runs through a Mosser crusher and thence through one of the sets of ball and tube-mills in the raw material department, which is arranged for this purpose.

Steel and masonry construction is used throughout, except the wooden storage bins for raw material and for finished cement. The power plant includes one 1,200 horse-power and one 175 horse-power engine, a 400 horse-power air-compressor for mine power, a 75-kilowatt generator for electric light and power for cooper-shop, packing room and machine shops, which are quite complete. A 180-k. w. 220-volt belted generator of the Keystone Electric Company has also been installed. There are six 250 horse-power boilers. The Webster Manufacturing Company's elevating and conveying machinery is in use. The plant was designed and built by Lathbury & Spackman.

See F. L. Smidth & Co.'s Adve tisement on Page 67.

THE LAWRENCEVILLE CEMENT COMPANY, Binnewater (Town of Rosendale), N. Y., maker of Beach's Rosendale cement, is a New York corporation, having its sales office at 26 Cortlandt street, New York City, its works at Binnewater, in the town of Rosendale, Ulster county, New York. This is one of the oldest and largest of the companies manufacturing genuine Rosendale cement. The present plant, built a few years since to replace the old plant at Lawrenceville, which had become somewhat out of date, is very compact and so arranged as to turn out cement with a minimum amount of labor at a very low cost. The position of the strata of cement rock in the quarries necessitates working only one gallery and the almost level strata allow the stone to be taken out very rapidly.

The operations of manufacture are the same as those in general use throughout the Rosendale district. The burning is done with anthracite coal in upright continuous kilns. Direct hoists carry the burned rock from the kiln shed to the cracker room, where it is reduced in pot crackers for the mills. The grinding machinery consists of 12 sets of 4-foot mill-stones of Esopus grit, quarried in the immediate vicinity, supplemented by a double system of screens. The capacity of the works is 2,500 barrels daily.

The company makes its own barrels and sacks. A special feature of this company's equipment is its facilities for shipment; the tracks of the West Shore railroad run into its store-house and the company's private cable railroad connects with its dock for tidewater deliveries by its large fleet of steamers and barges.

Power is generated in six horizontal tubular boilers, supplying steam for the main, compressor, hoisting and dynamo engines, which are respectively of 2,100, 250 and 25 horse-power.

Air drills are in use in the quarries and hoisting engines in the quarry and on the company's cable railway.

THE LEHIGH PORTLAND CEMENT COMPANY, Allentown, Pa., is a Pennsylvania corporation organized in October,

FLINT PEBBLES
Carefully Selected and Assorted by Sizes. Also Flint Stone Lining for Cement Pulverizing Mills.
CASIMIR THORON, Importer,
Room 5, Floor K,
N.Y. Produce Exchange Annex, New York, N.Y.

ELECTRIC TRANSMISSION
OF POWER
D'OLIER ENGINEERING CO., Philadelphia
MECHANICAL AND ELECTRICAL ENGINEERS

1897. The company owns two works, situated in the heart of the cement regions. Mill A is located at Ormrod, Pa., a few miles from Coplay, on the Ironton railroad, a branch of the Lehigh Valley railroad, and has a capacity of 1,800 barrels daily. Mill B is located at West Coplay, Pa., about two miles from the Ormrod plant, and also on the Ironton railroad. This works has a capacity of 2,200 barrels daily, total capacity for the two mills being 4,000 barrels daily. The works are most modern in construction, the machinery adopted for manufacturing of the best that can be obtained, such as Griffin mills, Webster elevators and conveyors, Howes packers, etc. All engines are cross-compound-condensing, and the boilers are fitted up with mechanical stokers, making the plant most economical, systematic and practical. The company owns some 600 acres of land underlaid with cement and lime rock, the two combined giving them the necessary material for making a high-grade Portland cement. The company has store-houses sufficiently large for carrying 500,000 barrels of cement in stock, which enables it to run all through the winter months. This company enjoys a large demand for its product throughout the United States and abroad. During the past two years the government has been a large user of the "Lehigh" brand, and the company now has a large number of contracts on hand which it is filling for the government.

LOUISVILLE CEMENT COMPANY, of No. 331 West Main street, Louisville, Ky., has two plants for the manufacture of natural hydraulic cement, one located at Speeds, Indiana, and the other at Louisville, Ky.

The cement rock used is a similar argillaceous limestone to that found in New York and Pennsylvania. Analysis shows an average composition about as follows: Silica, 15 per cent.; alumina and iron oxide, 6 per cent.; calcium carbonate, 61 per cent.; calcium sulphate, 5 per cent; magnesium carbonate, 10 per cent. loss on ignition, alkalies, etc., 3 per cent. It is quarried or mined according to the amount of other rock and soil found upon the stratum of cement rock. At Speeds the quarry is about 1½ miles from the works and the face is 15 feet deep. Steam drills and high explosives are used to loosen and break up the rock which is loaded into skips placed by a locomotive jib-crane and loaded on cars, which are hauled by a small locomotive to the

For Electric Light and Power—See Northern Electric Mfg. Co., page 18[illegible]

breaker at the beginning of the mill process. The breaker is provided with screens for separating the rock into three sizes, which are burned in separate kilns, thus saving fuel and increasing the uniformity in the burned clinker. The rock is dropped into cars hauled by cable up an inclined plane over the top of the kilns, and is dumped directly into them. The coal pockets are located under a trestle, from which the railroad cars are dumped, and they in turn dump into small cars below, which are drawn by cable up an inclined plane and dump into bins. It is drawn from the bins into coaling cars equipped with swivel spouts for spreading the coal uniformly.

At the bottom of the kilns the clinker is drawn by means of inclined planes into cars, hauled up an inclined plane and dumped into chutes leading to the crushers. The material is thus handled entirely by machinery from the time it is loaded on the skips in the quarry. From the crushers the clinker goes to the crackers and mill-stones, passing over separators after each reduction to remove the fine material, which is conveyed to the packers, where it is weighed and packed into bags automatically, through the Cook Duplex Automatic weighers, the packers and bag-holders having some novel and advantageous features.

The power plant includes 750 horse-power boilers, a 300 horse-power and a 600 horse-power Corliss engine, besides the locomotive and crane mentioned.

At Louisville, Ky. (Falls mill), the quarry is located in the bed of the Ohio river, and can only be worked during low stage of water in the summer season. The character of the rock and the process of manufacture is practically identical with that which obtains at the Speed mill, located at Speeds, Ind.

Lathbury & Spackman

ENGINEERS AND CHEMISTS

CEMENT PROPERTIES EXAMINED AND REPORTED ON.
PARTICULAR ATTENTION GIVEN TO THE ANALYSES OF RAW MATERIALS USED IN THE MANUFACTURE OF PORTLAND CEMENT AND THE MAKING OF EXPERIMENTAL BURNINGS.

ANALYSES AND TESTS OF CEMENT, CONCRETE, PAVING BRICK, ASPHALT AND ALL OTHER ENGINEERING MATERIALS.

and Laboratories, 1619 Filbert St., PHILADELPHIA.

Speeds Star and J. Hulme Star brands of Louisville natural hydraulic cement are manufactured, also Horse-Shoe and S*S brands slow-setting Louisville natural hydraulic cement.

THE LUPTON PORTLAND CEMENT COMPANY, Lupton, Mich., is reported to have been incorporated in New Jersey in January, 1901, for the purpose of erecting a plant at Lupton, Mich., with a capacity of 1,200 barrels and costing about $400,000. See Note **A**, page 152.

THE MANKATO CEMENT WORKS, Mankato, Minn., manufacture natural hydraulic cement, the capacity of the works being 1,200 barrels a day. The cement is largely used by railroads cities, the United States government and others in Minnesota Wisconsin, Iowa, Montana, Nebraska, Colorado. Two brands are marketed, Mankato and U. S. G. Clifford Richardson reports the analyses of the various strata in the quarry:

Stratum.	1	2	3	4	5
Silica, SiO_2	12.14	10.10	16.80	8.90	11.8
Soluble Iron, Fe_2O_3	1.58	1.14	trace	1.02	trac
Soluble Alumina, Al_2O_3	.80	1.18	4.20	1.50	1.[illegible]
Insoluble Iron, Fe_2O_3	.26	.20	trace	trace	trac
Insoluble Alumina, Al_2O_3	3.82	1.60	4.56	1.80	2.2
Soluble Lime, CaO	22.66	25.96	22.20	24.85	24.6
Insoluble Lime, CaO	.00	.00	.00	.00	.[illegible]
Soluble Magnesia, MgO	16.41	13.70	11.57	15.60	16.0
Insoluble Magnesia, MgO	.43	1.21	.42	2.89	.6
Sulphuric Acid, SO_3	.13	.26	.22	.18	.2
Potash, KaO	2.02	1.74	2.83	1.15	1.8
Soda, Na_2O	1.50	1.76	1.92	.38	.7
Loss on Ignition, CO_2	39.07	41.29	35.90	41.80	40.8
	100.62	100.14	100.62	100.07	100.1

MANLIUS LIME, PLASTER AND CEMENT COMPANY Manlius, New York, is reported as making natural hydraulic cement as a part of its business. No information has been received See Note **A**, page 152.

MARQUETTE PORTLAND CEMENT COMPANY. LaSalle Illinois. See Note **B**, page 152. No information has been received concerning this company, except that the works are located in Deer Park Glen. The Webster Manufacturing Company's elevating, conveying and power transmission machinery and Dodge Manufacturing Company's rope transmissions have been installed

Analyses of the limestone and clay used as raw materials are given in the U. S. Geol. Survey Reports, as follows:

The Standard Plaster Co., Buffalo, N.Y., makes Calcined Plaster or Stucc

	Limestone.	Clay.
Calcium Carbonate	88.16	
Magnesium Carbonate	1.78	
Magnesia		2.57
Silica	8.20	54.30
Iron Oxide and Alumina	1.30	
Alumina		19.33
Iron		5.57
Lime		3.29
Sulphur		2.36

THE MARYLAND CEMENT COMPANY, Baltimore, Md., constructed at Sparrow's Point, Md., the second plant established in this country for the manufacture of cement from blast furnace slag. Cuban iron ores and oyster-shells are the materials used in the blast furnaces, and most of the resulting slag is suitable for making cement, when properly treated. The slag to be used in making cement is run from the furnace into a trough with a large stream of cold water, the resulting thin porous flakes being retained in a car as the water drains away. The remaining water is removed in a Ruggles-Coles dryer, through which the material is passed, and then elevated to the second floor. Here the proper amount of slaked lime is added and the mixture is deposited in charges of fixed size in closed pebble-mills, where it is ground for a fixed period of time. Owing to the difference in specific gravity of the materials, it is not considered possible to use continuous mills. When the grinding is completed the finished product is discharged into a conveyor in the basement and elevated to the packing department, where it is put into barrels by Howes packers. Four brands of pozzuolana cement are made, Penn, Toltec, Patapsco and Rhinoceros. A chemical analyses of the cement shows silica, 27.15 per cent.; alumina, 10.80; lime, 51.57; magnesia, 2.70; sulphur, 1.38; oxide of iron, 0.90; combined water

BOOTH, GARRETT & BLAIR

ESTABLISHED IN 1836

Analytical and Engineering Chemists

Chemical analyses of waters, minerals, ores and metals: cement testing: investigation of cement properties and materials.

404 and 406 Locust Street, - PHILADELPHIA, PA.

3.50; undetermined, 2.00; specific gravity, 3.10. See Note D, page 152.

THE MICHIGAN ALKALI COMPANY, Wyandotte, Mich., in its process of making caustic soda, uses much limestone and has a waste product amounting to more than 100 tons a day. In looking for a method of disposing of this refuse, the use of it for making Portland cement was suggested. The limestone formerly used contained too much magnesia to make good cement, and when this was discovered the limestone was changed and the present supply, obtained from Bellevue, Mich., contains 96 per cent. calcium carbonate, 1 per cent. magnesium carbonate and 2 per cent. silica. Clay is found on the grounds of the works at Wyandotte, which are located on the bank of the Detroit river. It has some small pebbles in it which are utilized to supply a deficiency of silica in the clay. It is hauled in cars to the clay storage building, where it is broken up in a combined conveyor and disintegrator, whence it is elevated to a rotary dryer. It is then pulverized and elevated to storage bins in the second floor. The waste from the caustic soda plant, practically precipitated chalk with about 40 per cent. of water, is brought on a traveling crane to the second floor of the cement plant, where the proper proportion of clay is added and the mixture run into a long pug-mill, where more water is added. It drops thence into tanks provided with agitators, which thoroughly mix the ingredients before discharge into a tube-mill for grinding. Tanks below the floor, also provided with agitators, receive the ground slurry and give opportunity for correction of the mixture. Thence the material is pumped to steel tanks in the second floor, provided with agitators, and can be pumped directly into the rotary kilns or to a standpipe, from which it flows into the kilns. The kilns are 60 feet long and 6 feet in diameter, with water-jacketed inlet pipes and lined with aluminous fire-brick. The clinker discharged at the lower end drops into a hopper-shaped concrete pit, which discharges into an elevator, by which it is carried to a cooling bin having a succession of metal floors, each with one opening. Arms revolving about a central shaft push the clinker around so that it drops successively from floor to floor, a supply of air aiding the cooling process. American Blower Company's exhauster draws air through the cooler and furnishes blast for coal feed to kilns, coal

Parkhurst Combined Curb and Gutter is in use in leading cities.

pulverized in F. L. Smidth & Co.'s Davidsen tube-mills being the fuel used. This clinker is then elevated and conveyed to Smidth ball-mills and tube-mills in succession, and thence to the stock-house, which is conveniently designed for storage and for packing. The process is practically automatic from beginning to end. The boiler-room contains three 350 horse-power water-tube boilers, and the engine-room a 600 horse-power engine. The works were designed by Lathbury & Spackman. The Detroit river and the Lake Shore & Michigan Southern and Michigan Central railways give the best of shipping facilities.

Detailed analyses of the limestone obtained from Bellevue, of Bellevue clay, which is also used, and of the completed cement, show as follows:

	Bellevue Limestone.	Bellevue Clay.	Wyandotte Portland Cement.
Silica	2.50%	68.10%	23.20%
Oxides of Iron } Oxide of Alumina }	1.20	21.00	2.40
			8.00
Carbonate of Lime	94.80	0.75	
Lime			62.10
Magnesia	1.50	0.80	2.00
Sulphate of Lime			1.50
Combined Water		9.35	
Alkalies and Moisture			0.80

Large quantities of Wyandotte Portland cement have been used in public buildings and in public work, in foundations of machinery and in the construction of several of the new cement plants in the Michigan district, 50,000 barrels having been used in public work in Chicago, 8,500 barrels in Detroit public work. Cement was first made in the works September 1, 1899. F. B. Holmes & Co., Hammond Building, Detroit, are the general sales agents.

ALL ABOUT CEMENT
UP-TO-DATE AND
ALL THE TIME

The best way to keep informed about everything relating to Cement the year round is to read

MUNICIPAL ENGINEERING MAGAZINE

The publication which stands foremost in representation of Cement interests.

Subscription price, $2.00 per year.

Address MUNICIPAL ENGINEERING CO.

THE MICHIGAN PO TLAND CEMENT COMPANY, Coldwater, Mich., is a Michigan corporation, with factories at Coldwater and Quincy, Mich. Two brands are now manufactured. The Wolverine brand has been on the market for over two years. That it gives satisfaction is shown by an increase of over 60 per cent. in the sales of 1900 over that of 1899, the total sales for the two years being 275,903 barrels. The capacity of the works producing this brand is now 1,500 barrels a day. This brand is used throughout the States of Indiana, Michigan, Ohio, largely in Illinois, Iowa and Minnesota, and sales are made in most of the States from Texas to Wisconsin and Idaho to West Virginia, including also Cuba and Canada. The capacity of the works making the Eclipse brand is also 1,500 barrels a day. The marl used is obtained by dredging. The wet process of manufacture is followed, the clay or shale being ground in dry pans, the clay and marl being mixed in pug-mills, ground in tube-mills, burned in rotary kilns and the clinker ground in Griffin mills on the same general plan followed by the Bronson Portland Cement Works, and given in the description of their works. Bonnot Co.'s machinery has been installed and American Blower Company's fans, also one of their heaters for warming and drying marl pile in winter. Dodge Manufacturing Company's full transmission plant has been installed at both plants, that at Coldwater including two 750 horse-power, one 200 horse-power, and two 50 horse-power rope transmissions, with quills, clutches, cut-off couplings, line-shafting, etc. The Quincy plant has the same with several more rope transmissions. Chemical analyses of the materials and product show as follows:

	Clay.	Marl.	Cement.
Loss on Ignition	7.75 to 8.50%		[illegible]
Organic Matter		1,0 to 7.0%	
Silica	58.75 to 60.50		[illegible]
Titanium Oxide	0.75 to 0.85		
Ferric Oxide	7.95 to 8.45		[illegible]
Aluminum Oxide	18.83 to 19.40		[illegible]
Silicates, including Ferric Oxide, Aluminum Oxide and Silica		1.5 to 10.0	
Calcium Oxide	0.95 to 1.25	83.0 to 98.0	[illegible]

canal, in bridge piers, etc., and sidewalk and curb and gutter in Chicago and elsewhere, as well as in foundation of buildings and concrete arches.

THOMAS MILLEN & SONS, Wayland, N. Y., began the manufacture of Portland cement at Wayland, N. Y., in 1892, having removed from South Bend, Indiana. Marl and clay are the materials used and dome kilns are used for burning. See Note B, page 152. It is reported that New York capitalists have recently purchased the works and will enlarge them.

THE MILWAUKEE CEMENT COMPANY, No. 7, Plankinton Building, Milwaukee, Wis., is a Wisconsin corporation with works about one mile north of the city limits. The company was incorporated in 1875, and began the manufacture of cement the following year. The first mill was entirely rebuilt in 1893. In 1888 mill No. 2 was built and has a daily capacity of 2,600 barrels. The works as a whole can turn out 3,800 barrels a day. The rock is quarried on the company's property hauled to the incline by steam locomotive and the top of the Campbell kilns by cable. The feature of the kilns is the grating at the bottom and the uniform distribution of draft. The calcined rock from the bottom of the kilns is hauled up an incline to the crusher in the mill building. From the crusher it enters the Berthelet separator, which consists of screens for separating the fine dust, which goes by conveyor to the packers; the fine tailings, which drop into the finishing buhr-stone mill and go thence by elevator to the screens above, to repeat the process; and the coarse tailings, which drop into a cracker stone and are carried thence to the elevator from the

Every Mill Man
Should Keep Posted by Reading
Power and Transmission
unique publication in trade literature exclusively devoted to
MODERN POWER TRANSMISSION ENGINEERING
illustrated with typical installations. Other articles of interest to the up to date factory
also contained in each issue. Sample copy free by applying to
DODGE MANUFACTURING CO. ENGINEERS FOUNDERS MACHINISTS MISHAWAKA, IND. U.S.A.
BOSTON NEW YORK CHICAGO CINCINNATI ATLANTA LONDON, ENG.

crusher to repeat the process. The finished product is run through packers into bags, sacks or barrels as desired.

THE MONOLITH PORTLAND CEMENT COMPANY, Ltd., Battle Creek, Mich., is constructing works for the manufacture of Portland cement at Bristol, Ind., which will be completed early in 1902.

NATIONAL CEMENT COMPANY, 15 Second National Bank Building, Pittsburg, Pa.—No information regarding this company has been received, except that the secretary and manager are also officers in the Castalia Portland Cement Company of Pittsburg. See Note A, page 152.

NATIONAL PORTLAND CEMENT COMPANY, Ltd., Toronto, Ont., is reported as formed to develop cement properties in Canada. See Notes A and B, page 152.

THE NAZARETH CEMENT COMPANY, Nazareth, Pa.—The Nazareth Cement Company is a Pennsylvania corporation with works at Nazareth, Pa., the product being placed on the market by the Charles Warner Company, of Wilmington, Del., Philadelphia, Pa., and 66 Maiden Lane, New York. The quarry from which the raw stone is obtained contains layers of stone of uniform chemical composition, and continuous analyses aid in making a mixture which will produce a uniform grade of cement. The rock is conveyed by a cable way about a thousand feet to the floor of the raw material storage building, where the cement and lime are weighed out in proper proportions and dumped into crushers and thence dropped into the dryers. The location of the works on a side hill allows these movements to be by gravity. The stone from the dryers is elevated slightly and conveyed to bins over Smidth ball-mills, whence it is elevated and conveyed to a like number of Smidth tube-mills. Thence the material is elevated to bins over the rotary kilns, of which there are seven. A check chemical analysis is made before burning. The coal for the kilns is crushed outside the coal mill building and elevated into the coal dryer and again elevated and conveyed to hopper over the pulverizer, again elevated to the separator and the coal dust conveyed and elevated to the 40-ton storage bin or directly to the kilns. The clinker from the kilns is dropped into coolers. When cool it is conveyed into Smidth ball-mills located on the floor be ow, thence conveyed and elevated to bins over pulverizers to tube-mills. From the tube-mills the finished product is elevated and conveyed to the stock-house, 250 x 150 feet in size, dropping from the conveyor through chutes as desired into the storage bins. Webster Manufacturing Company's conveying and elevating machinery is in use. After seasoning a proper length of time, the cement is drawn off through Howes packers into packages for the market.

The grinding departments are driven by an 800 horse-power engine. The kilns and coal-feeding machinery are driven by a 0 horse-power engine. The works are located on the Bangor & Portland division of the D. L. & W. railroad. Their capacity is about 1,400 barrels a day.

Chemical analysis of the finished product shows lime, 61.23 per cent.; silica, 19.06; alumina, 7.47; iron, 2.29; magnesia, 2.83; potash and soda, 1.41; sulphuric acid, 1.34; loss on ignition, 4.52.

NEW ALBANY CEMENT COMPANY, New Albany, Ind., has works at Haussdale for the manufacture of Louisville natural hydraulic cement by the usual process of the district.

THE NEWARK AND ROSENDALE LIME AND CEMENT COMPANY has its directors' office at 821 Prudential Building, Newark, N. J., and its sales office at 39 Cortlandt street, New York. The mills of the company, located at Whiteport, Ulster county, New York, manufacture Newark-Rosendale brand of natural hydraulic cement from the rock and by the process in use in that district. The shipping wharf of the works is at Eddyville, N. Y., on Rondout Creek. This brand of cement has been manufactured since 1848.

THE NEWARK LIME AND CEMENT MANUFACTURING COMPANY is a New Jersey corporation, with office in Newark, N. J., and works for the manufacture of Rosendale natural hydraulic cement at Rosendale, N. Y. The natural cement rock of the Rosendale region is the material used, and the methods of

INFORMATION FOR EVERYBODY

If you want to know anything about Cement, Cement work or Cement machinery we will furnish the information, if possible, on request.

MUNICIPAL ENGINEERING CO.

burning and grinding are practically the same as when the work were first established in 1837. See description of other Rosendale plants.

THE NEWAYGO PORTLAND CEMENT COMPANY, of Newaygo, Mich., have completed their plant and will be in full operation about May 1, 1901. The plant is all steel and brick construction, and has a capacity of 1,000 barrels per day. Their marl and clay deposits, aggregating over 1,000 acres, are of unusual purity and uniformity. All raw material is received in storage bins under the receiving track of a trestle. The marl is fed from the bins upon separators, and thence pumped by compressed air into large tanks. From these tanks the chemist takes his samples for analysis, to determine the proper proportion of clay to be added. The marl then flows by gravity into measuring tanks. The clay is first analyzed and then brought from storage by conveyors into disintegrating machines, to chop it up fine, and thence into a large Cummer dryer. From the dryer it is elevated into two buhr-mills, where it is ground fine, and thence into a large mixing pug, into which the marl also flows by gravity. The slurry is then pumped into three tanks, where the chemist takes his second samples. If the mixture is not exactly right, the percentage of discrepancy is determined at this point, and either pure clay or pure marl is added. The slurry then runs into the automatic feeders over the tube-mills, in which latter the material is ground the second time. From there the slurry is fed automatically into Bonnot rotaries whence, after it has been burned into clinker, it is discharged into McCaslin conveyors, which conduct it through the cooling tower into the Griffin mills. Flowing from these by gravity into screw conveyors, the finished cement is conveyed to the warehouse, and from there into the packing house, where it is drawn off through packers into packages for the market.

All of the machinery is of the most modern type and of unusually substantial build, and much of it was made after special designs. All power is furnished by the Muskegon river by means of eight huge water-wheels under a 15-foot head, and is electrically distributed throughout the plant. The machinery has been individualized as much as possible, and shafting has been almost en

Many Cement Manufacturers use Griffin Mills.

ly eliminated. Under such circumstances, perfect and uni- m grinding, mixing and burning are insured.

The Newaygo Portland Cement Company have been making ce- nt from their raw materials in small experimental kilns, etc., the last 18 months, and have shown that they can produce a t excellent product.

'HE NEW ENGLAND PORTLAND CEMENT COMPANY, Stamford, Conn., is making extensive alteration and is not now in king order, but expects to be ready some time in 1901. Lime from the Berkshire hills and silica from Long Island, with a added, are the materials to be used. Griffin mills for grind- are to be used.

'he product will be a perfectly white hydraulic cement, and probably be marketed as White and Pure brand. The infor- ion received is not sufficient to determine whether this brand uld be classed as pozzuolana under the definitions adopted.

EW JERSEY PORTLAND CEMENT COMPANY, Perth boy, N. J.—The Climax brand of Portland cement manufac- ed by this company is made by mixing granulated blast furnace and slaked lime without subsequent calcination, substantially described for other similar plants. See Note D, page 152.

The brand is classed as pozzuolana without authority from the ipany, which has read the above description and has not pro- nced it incorrect.

. L. & W. C. NEWMAN, Akron, N. Y., is a partnership manu- turing Akron natural hydraulic cement for the Union Akron ment Company of Buffalo, to which reference may be made for ther details.

THE NEW YORK AND ROSENDALE CEMENT COM- NY, of No. 280 Broadway, New York, manufactures one nd of Rosendale natural hydraulic cement known as the rooklyn Bridge" brand, at its works at Wilbur and at Rosendale, ter county, N. Y. The justly celebrated Rosendale cement t was discovered at Rosendale about the year 1823, and this

-to-Date formation

Any buyer of this book desiring supplemental information will be furnished it if possible on application to the publishers —

Municipal Engineering Company

company's works are located where the first cement was made. The dip of the strata is not so great as in some of the cement rock mines, and the cars are run easily to the mouth of the mine and thence over the top of the kilns. Some of the large kilns, elliptical in cross section, have a capacity of 250 barrels a day each. The clinker is drawn in cars up an incline to the crushers, thence it enters the separator system and the grinding mills. The works are located on the Delaware and Hudson canal and the Wallkill Valley railroad.

THE NEW YORK CEMENT COMPANY, Rosendale, New York, is incorporated under the laws of the State of New York, with its principal office or place of business at Rosendale, Ulster county, New York, and sales office at No. 29 Broadway, New York City, N. Y. The mines and manufacturing plant are situated at Lefever Falls, Township of Rosendale, Ulster county, New York, on the line of the Delaware and Hudson canal, with a present capacity of over 2,000 barrels per day. The property of this company consists in part of four hundred acres of very pure hydraulic limestone and a substantial modern plant in operation. The utmost care is exercised in the selection of the natural rock and its manufacture, and all shipments are fully tested for tensile strength, setting qualities, fineness, uniformity and weight before leaving the mills. It has been in general use for over forty years on the most important works ever attempted in this country, and has always met with the approval of the engineers and architects in charge of construction. As a Rosendale hydraulic cement its reputation for excellence is established.

THE NORTHAMPTON PORTLAND CEMENT COMPANY, 26 Broadway, New York, is constructing works at Stockertown, Pa., for the manufacture of Portland cement from the usual materials of the Lehigh region. The Webster Manufacturing Company's elevating, conveying and power transmission machinery is being installed. Further information is withheld at present.

THE F. O. NORTON CEMENT COMPANY, 92 Broadway, New York, has plants at Binnewater and at High Falls, N. Y., for the manufacture of Norton Rosendale Brand of natural hydraulic cement. The usual process of mining, burning in continuous up-

The Keystone Electrical Transmission is Best for Cement Machinery

ight kilns and grinding in buhr-stone mills is used. See Note B, page 152.

OHIO VALLEY CEMENT COMPANY, Cementville, Ind. See Note B, page 152.

THE OMEGA PORTLAND CEMENT COMPANY, Jonesville, Mich., is a Michigan corporation with office at Jonesville, Mich., and works at Omega Station, near Mosherville, Mich., where Omega brand Portland cement is manufactured. Marl and clay are the materials used, tube-mills being used to grind the raw material, rotary kilns for burning and Smidth ball and tube-mills for grinding the clinker. F. L. Smidth & Co.'s Davidson tube-mills are also used for pulverizing the coal used as fuel in the kilns. As prepared for market, the cement shows upon chemical analysis, silica, 22.24 per cent.: alumina, 7.26; iron oxide, 2.54; lime, 64.96; magnesia, 2.26; sulphuric acid, anhydride, 0.41; water and carbon dioxide, 0.33.

THE OWEN SOUND PORTLAND CEMENT COMPANY, Ltd., Shallow Lake, Ontario.—Capacity of the works, 180,000 barrels per year. The cement is made from marl and clay found in Shallow Lake, the deposit covering about 500 acres. The raw materials are mixed into a slurry and burned in Batchelor and rotary kilns, the clinker being ground in ball and tube-mills. The cement has been in use for more than ten years in the erection of tanks and power houses, in canal, railroad and street foundation work, sidewalks, etc. It is also being used largely in government work, where only cements of the highest standard are permitted to be used.

THE PEERLESS PORTLAND CEMENT COMPANY has passed into new hands and the works at Union City, Mich., are being improved and enlarged. The Bonnot Company's machinery for the wet process, Bradley Pulverizer Company's Griffin Mills, the American Blower Company's discharge fans, one of them for drying briquettes, and the Webster Manufacturing Company's elevating, conveying and power transmission machinery are being in-

ROSSENDALE REDDAWAY BELTING & HOSE CO.

Newark, N. J.

MANUFACTURERS OF . . . .

AMEL HAIR BELTING "Camel Brand" For Transmitting Power.

STITCHED COTTON BELTING "Sphinx Brand" For conveying Sand, Clay, Ores, Dirt, Etc.

LINEN FIRE HOSE

. FENWICK, 46 W. LAKE ST., CHICAGO, ILL.
AMES W. BYRNES BELTING & HOSE CO., ST. LOUIS, MO. } SELLING AGENTS

stalled, also the Dodge Manufacturing Company's rope transmi sions, with accessories. The works have manufactured Portla cement for several years, and the new company will shortly be rea to supply the market in larger quantities. Information regardi the works is withheld until the improvements are completed.

PEMBINA PORTLAND CEMENT COMPANY, Grand Fork N. D.—This company has completed works at Milton, on t Tongue river, in Cavalier county, North Dakota, for the man facture of Portland and natural hydraulic cements. The dry p cess is used. Lathbury & Spackman designed the works. T Webster Manufacturing Company's elevating, conveying and pow transmission machinery is installed. Further information co cerning materials, process and product has been withheld. S Note D, page 152.

THE PENINSULAR PORTLAND CEMENT COMPAN Jackson, Mich., is constructing works at Woodstock, Mich., for t manufacture of cement. The Bonnot cement machinery and t Bradley Pulverizer Company's Griffin mills are being install See Note B, page 152. The name of the railroad station, on t Cincinnati & Northern railway, has been changed to Cement Ci

THE PENNSYLVANIA CEMENT COMPANY has been o ganized by the same persons who control the Lawrenceville Ceme Company and is constructing works for the manufacture of Po land cement at Bath, Northampton county, Pennsylvania. T general sales office of the company is at 26 Cortlandt street, N York City.

THE PHOENIX CEMENT COMPANY, Nazareth, Pa., is a Pen sylvania corporation. The products of the works are the Phœn and Clover Leaf brands of Portland cement, for which the capac is 800 barrels a day, and the IXL Rosendale brand of natural h draulic cement, for which the capacity is 500 barrels a day. T works are capable of turning out cheaper grades of Portland ment, also. The Phœnix brand of cement is made of a care mixture of natural rock to give the proper proportions for a hi grade Portland cement. The supply of material is apparently exhaustible, one drill having been driven 286 feet through rock, analyses of which taken each 15 feet of length of drill h show a remarkable uniformity in constitution.

Plasticon, a plastering cement. The Alabastine Co., Grand Rapids

The proportion of Silica varies from	8.42 to 15.55
Iron and Alumina from	4.92 to 9.20
Carbonate of Lime from	72.19 to 84.12
Magnesia from	0. to 3.08

Samples taken from the different parts of the quarry and surrounding property show similar results, the variations being between somewhat wider limits. Perhaps two feet of soil overlies the rock. The close approximation of a large portion of the rock to the composition required for high-grade Portland cement makes the labor and trouble of mixing different kinds of rock a minimum, thus saving considerable expense in manufacture.

Steam drills are used in drilling holes for blasting. The rock thus broken up is loaded in cars running on tracks distributed conveniently about the quarry and centering at the foot of an inclined plane. The cars are hoisted by a hoisting engine into the stone house (60x93 feet), where there is storage capacity for inclement weather. A crusher with a capacity of 25 to 40 tons per hour, and requiring 30 horse-power to operate it, receives the rock and drops it on the dryer floor. A dryer 4 feet in diameter and 35 feet long is used, in which otherwise waste heat is utilized. The stone is run through the raw material end of the milling department (40x60 feet), where there are two Smidth ball-mills, one Gates and one Smidth tube-mill, the ball-mills being fitted with automatic feeders. The tube-mills are lined with silax. There is a full complement of elevating and conveying machinery for taking the material from mill to mill and then to the kiln room (60x100 feet) in a straight and continuous process. The kiln room has a storage capacity for 24 hours running of kilns. There are four rotary kilns 60 feet long by 6 feet in diameter, each supplied with a 42-inch stack 50 feet high, lined with fire-brick. The kilns are fitted with variable speed counter shafting. In one end of the kiln room is storage for pulverized coal. Two sets of blowers are also located here. The coal used for fuel runs through a coal disintegrator and a tube-mill, whence it is elevated and carried by a screw conveyor to the storage bins. The furnace of the

BOOKS ON CEMENT

	PRICE
Hydraulic Cement. By F. P. Spalding	$2.00
Portland Cement. By Charles D. Jamieson	1.50
Clark's Hand-Book on Cements	1.00
Portland Cement: its Manufacture, Testing and Use. By D. B. Butler. 360 pages, 85 illustrations	6.00
American Cements. By Uriah Cummings	3.00

Send remittance with order. Address

MUNICIPAL ENGINEERING COMPANY

dryer is outside of the building. The mill is 38x48 feet. Th clinker is dropped from the kiln into the cooler, through whic a pressure blower forces air, thus heating it on the way to the com bustion chamber of the kiln. Water supplied to the clinker is co verted into steam, cooling the clinker and increasing the combu tion. The clinker is thus disintegrated somewhat, with a savi of labor in handling. It is then elevated to the clinker end of t milling department, 60x60 feet, which is supplied with thr Smidth and one Gates ball-mill, three Gates and one Smidth tul mill, so arranged that either of the mills can run on Portland ment or in separate batteries or on two kinds of cement at t same time. The stock-house is a stone building 60x160 feet vided into bins with conveyors for distributing the cement as sired. There are two sets of conveyors and elevators, so that t kinds of cement can be handled at the same time. The capacity the storage bins is 20,000 barrels. The bins discharge into au matic packers beneath. A second stock-house arranged to han a single kind of cement is 80x280 feet and has a capacity of 60,0 barrels. There is a line of railroad track on each side of the sto house.

The natural cement department consists of four vertical kil 16 feet in diameter and 31 feet high, lined with fire-brick. T cement rock is carried in the cars to the top of the kilns on an i clined plane by the same hoisting engine used in the Portla cement department, and dumped into the kilns without handli The coal is elevated and conveyed along the other side of the kil deposited on the floor and shoveled into the kilns in required p portions. Belt conveyors carry the clinker from the bottom of t kilns to the crusher, whence it goes to the ball and tube-mills a the stock-house. The mills are arranged to make straight natu cement or any desired mixture of Portland and natural ceme

There is a machine shop (76x32 feet), a blacksmith shop, physical laboratory for testing cement and a cooper shop (90x feet) conveniently located near the packing department. T coal storage is extensive and notably convenient. The water su ply is partly from an artesian well and partly from the town wa supply, with a storage dam under construction. The office buildi contains the main office, reception room, superintendent's roo chemical laboratory and directors' room.

See F. L. Smidth & Co.'s Advertisement on Page 187.

BACON'S HOISTING ENGINE

EARLE C. BACON

ENGINEER

Hoisting, Crushing and Mining Machinery

Havemeyer Building - NEW YORK

THE FARREL ORE AND ROCK CRUSHER

SEND FOR COMPLETELY ILLUSTRATED CATALOGUES

The engine room, 110x30 feet, and the boiler house, 74x48 feet, contain 2,200 horse-power of water-tube boilers, a 250 horse-power safety boiler and three 100 horse-power horizontal tubular boilers and their appurtenances; also a 35 horse-power Corliss engine supplying power for the raw material end of the mill, a 450 horse-power engine for the clinker milling department, the fuel mill engine and the engine operating the kilns: also the electric light plant, consisting of an automatic cut-off engine and 15-k. w. generator, 125 volts, running eight enclosed arc lights and 150 incandescent lights. All the power being in one room reduces the cost for attendance to a minimum. In the machine shop is an automatic engine to run the machine shop, cooper shop and packing room of one stock-house.

THE PORTLAND CEMENT COMPANY OF UTAH, Limited, Salt Lake City, Utah, is an English corporation manufacturing Red Diamond brand of Portland cement. The materials used are two grades of argillaceous limestone, which are mixed by the dry process, using crushers, rolls and rotary pulverizers on the raw material, powdered coal for fuel in rotary kilns, and rotary pulverizers and Davidsen tube-mills for finishing cement. A Griffin mill is used for grinding coal. Electric transmission of power is used, there being separate motors for main shaft, kilns, coal-grinding apparatus and coal-drying apparatus. The works were designed by Lathbury & Spackman. Chemical analysis of the rock used shows carbonate of lime, silica, alumina and oxide of iron. Cement was first made in the works in 1896 and the present process was installed in October, 1898. The cement is used in water works, pavements, sidewalks, sewers, buildings, railroad structures, mines, government fortifications, etc., in Montana, Idaho, Wyoming, Utah, Nevada, Colorado and California. In 1897, 15,000 barrels were sold and the sales have increased each year to 75,000 barrels in 1900.

POTOMAC CEMENT COMPANY, Antietam, Md. See Note A, page 152.

THE PYRAMID PORTLAND CEMENT COMPANY, No. 65 Moffat Block, Detroit, Mich., is constructing works at Spring Arbor, Mich., for the manufacture of Portland cement. The works will be ready to supply cement in 1902 and further information will not be available until that time.

Electric Motors for Cement Makers- See North'n Elec. Mfg. Co., [illegible].

THE READING CEMENT COMPANY, Reading, Pa., is a New Jersey corporation with works near Evansville, Pa., for the manufacture of Reading Portland cement and Improved Rosendale natural hydraulic cement. The usual cement rock and limestone of Lehigh region is used and the machinery includes the latest designs of Smidth mills and kilns, the first cement being turned out in September, 1900.

RIDGEMONT CEMENT & MANUFACTURING COMPANY, Ridgemont, Va.—Works idle.

ROCKLAND CEMENT COMPANY, Jones' Point, N. Y. See Note A, page 152. American Blower Company's fan is used for circulating air through dryer.

ROUND TOP HYDRAULIC CEMENT COMPANY, Hancock and Round Top, Md. See Note B, page 152.

ST. LAWRENCE PORTLAND CEMENT COMPANY, 2664 Notre Dame street, Montreal, P. Q., Canada. See Canadian Portland Cement Company.

THE SANDUSKY PORTLAND CEMENT COMPANY, Sandusky, Ohio, is an Ohio corporation. The first plant of the company was constructed at Bay Bridge, Sandusky, using marl and clay as materials. The wet process with rotary kilns and Griffin mills for making them into cement has been developed. It has a capacity of 600 barrels. Webster Manufacturing Company's elevating and power transmission machinery is in use. The American Blower Company's fan removes dust from the mills. The company now has a second plant ready for operation at Syracuse, Indiana, using similar materials and process as the result of the expensive experiments conducted at the first plant. Powdered coal is used for fuel. The new works have six kilns, giving a capacity of 1,000 barrels a day. A 750 horse-power rope drive, with accessories, has been installed by the Dodge Manufacturing Company.

Any information on **Cement or Cement Machinery**

will be furnished on request by the publishers of this book—

Municipal Engineering Company

Further information is withheld by the company. See Note B, Page 152.

SILVER CREEK CEMENT COMPANY, Louisville, Ky., has works for manufacture of Louisville natural hydraulic cement at Cementville, Ind. See Note B, page 152.

HIRAM SNYDER, 229 Broadway, New York., has works at Rosendale, New York, for the manufacture of Rosendale natural hydraulic cement by the usual process.

THE SOUTHERN CEMENT COMPANY, North Birmingham, Ala., has recently completed a plant for the manufacture of cement from blast furnace slag (pozzuolana). See Note B, page 152. An American Blower Company's fan is used for circulating air through the dryer.

THE STANDARD CEMENT COMPANY has works at Charlestown, Ind., for the manufacture of Louisville natural hydraulic cement according to the usual process. See Note B, page 152.

THE STANDARD PORTLAND CEMENT COMPANY, Hammond Building, Detroit, Mich., is a Michigan corporation capitalized at $1,000,000, which is constructing works at Hamburg Junction to have a capacity of 1,000 to 2,000 barrels of Portland cement a day. The works are not yet completed and in operation, but will be ready to supply the Standard brand of Portland cement to the market in a short time.

THE STANDARD SILICA CEMENT COMPANY is a New York corporation with capital of $100,000, offices at No. 66 Maiden Lane, New York City, and works at Long Island City, Borough of Queens, New York. Silica Portland cement is made by a process which is intended by the inventor, Mr. F. L. Smidth, to be the perfected economical method of using Portland cement. The process consists in grinding artificial Portland cement with some inert material, such as sand or limestone, to a greater fineness than the original Portland cement. The Davidsen tube-mill is used. The mill is a hollow steel cylinder 4 feet in diameter and 16 feet long, half filled with flint pebbles, set horizontally and revolved by a gear and pinion at one end. The sand and cement are mixed and fed into the revolving cylinder by a screw conveyor through the trunnion at one end. The ground cement is delivered

cement and one part sand, so that 96 per cent. of the resultant Silica Portland cement will pass through a No. 200 sieve. The best brands of the cement are made of equal parts of such cement as the Glens Falls Portland Cement Company's Iron Clad brand of Portland cement and Rockaway Beach sand. All the cement passes the No. 200 sieve after the grinding, the 4 per cent. remainder on the sieve being all hard sand. The cement has been used in many buildings in the city of New York for foundations, floors, fireproofing, in concrete foundation for asphalt walks, in such hydraulic work as the pool in Central Park, the retaining walls and subways of the Harlem river speedway, and the testing canal at Cornell University, in addition to the use in the Dock Department.

THE TEXAS PORTLAND CEMENT COMPANY, Dallas, Texas, manufactures the Live Oak brand of Portland cement. The capitalization is $20,000. The capacity of the works is 100 barrels a day, but is being increased to 300 barrels. Cement was first made in December, 1899. The Bonnot Company's wet process machinery is used. The machinery used includes rotary kilns 72

HOW TO BUILD UP BUSINESS

The cardinal point in business success is to make yourself known to every person who can add anything to your business.

It is not possible for you to know all these people, but they can be made to know about you. This is your advantage.

Advertising does this. It opens the field. Success depends on how wisely this advertising is done. If it reaches people in your line it pays.

If you want business from the field represented by MUNICIPAL ENGINEERING MAGAZINE it will pay you to advertise in it.

Don't You Want Equal Advantage in this Field

inches in diameter and 60 feet long, crusher, dryer, dry pans, pug-mills, wet ball and tube-mills, storage tanks with agitators, ball-mills and tube-mills for clinker grinding. A 300 horse-power engine, a 350 horse-power engine, 4 tubular boilers each 72 inches by 16 feet, furnish power. The analyses of the materials used and the cement show as follows:

	Limestone.	Clay.	Cement.
$CaCO_3$	1.42%	2.05%	
CaO			62.35%
Al_2O_3	0.23	22.75	8.35
Fe_2O_3	2.05	4.10	4.25
SiO_2	6.10	60.25	22.50
SO_3	trace	trace	
Ignition Loss		8.73	
Sulphur			1.75
Alkalies			trace

The proportion of raw materials used is 5½ to one.

The cement has been used in street paving and sidewalks in Fort Worth and in foundations and fireproofing of buildings in Dallas, Fort Worth, etc., and in railroad work on T. & P. Ry.

THE THREE RIVERS CEMENT COMPANY, Three Rivers, Mich., is reported to have been incorporated to construct a plant on Pleasant Lake, about three miles from Three Rivers. See Note A, page 152.

TWENTIETH CENTURY PORTLAND CEMENT COMPANY, Fenton, Mich. See Note A, page 152.

THE UNION AKRON CEMENT COMPANY, office No. 141 Erie street, Buffalo, N. Y., is the sales agent for the Akron star brand natural hydraulic cement, manufactured by H. L. & W. C. Newman and the Akron Cement Works, at Akron, N. Y. The capacity of the works together is 2,000 barrels a day. Cement has been manufactured in these works since 1840 and has been used in many public works, by many railroads and in the construction of many bridges and buildings in Massachusetts, Connecticut, Maryland, New York, Pennsylvania, Ohio, Indiana, Illinois, Iowa, Missouri, Arkansas, and other States, to the extent of about 300,000 barrels a year at present time. The ordinary vertical kilns, buhrstones and pebble-mill are used in the process of manufacture.

THE UNION CEMENT AND LIME COMPANY, 421 Main street, Louisville, Ky., has works for the manufacture of Louisville natural hydraulic cement by the usual process, at Cement-

Coal Tar and Asphalt Products—Warren Bros. Co., 143 Federal St., Boston ville and Sellersburg, Ind., and on the falls of the Ohio at Louisville, Ky. Cement was first made by the company in 1866. In 1900 the sales of the two brands made by the company amounted to 913,000 barrels.

THE UNITED STATES CEMENT COMPANY, Sellersburg, Ind., manufactures Louisville natural hydraulic cement by the usual process.

THE UNITED STATES PORTLAND CEMENT COMPANY is reported as a Delaware corporation with an authorized capital of $12,500,000, and Sheldon H. Bassett, of Chicago, as the agent. See Note A, page 152.

THE UTICA CEMENT MANUFACTURING COMPANY, and the **UTICA HYDRAULIC CEMENT COMPANY**, Utica, Ill., are now under the same ownership and management, with Meacham & Wright, of Chicago, Ill., as sales agents. The processes used heretofore are the same as in other natural hydraulic cement plants, the rock being mined and burned in continuous vertical kilns and ground in buhr-stone mills. A new mill is under construction. The crusher building, 30 by 54 feet, will contain the crushers; the mill building, 54 by 62 feet and 24 feet high, will contain two Smidth ball and two Davidsen tube-mills of the largest size for grinding natural cement clinker, heretofore in use exclusively in Portland cement mills. The Sturtevant mills are used for crushing and grinding also. The boiler room will contain three 200 horse-power boilers, and the engine room a 575 horse-power Corliss engine. Air compressor and electric light plant for quarries and mill buildings are also provided. The warehouse is 70 by 200 feet and contains 32 bins with a storage capacity of 80,000 barrels. The weighing and loading is done automatically and by electrical machinery. Full equipment of Dodge Manufacturing Company's shafting, clutches, etc., is provided.

THE VIRGINIA PORTLAND CEMENT COMPANY, 81 Fulton street, New York, is a New Jersey corporation, with works

CHARLES CARROLL BROWN, M. Am. Soc. C. E.

. . *Consulting Engineer* . .

83 Commercial Club Bldg. - - INDIANAPOLIS, IND.

Water Supply and Purification. Sewerage and Sewage Disposal.
Paving. Cement and Its Uses.

at Craigsville, Va., on the Chesapeake & Ohio railroad. The capitalization of the company is $1,000,000. Its property consists of about 1,200 acres, and the cement plant is located on a flat area of about 25 acres at the railroad. The materials used are limestone and clay, taken from open quarries. Analyses of the raw materials and the finished products show as follows:

	Limestone.	Clay.	Cement.
Lime	54.30%	5.94%	63.14%
Silica		53.63	21.20
Alumina		24.47	7.90
Magnesia	0.66	1.79	2.40
Volatile Matter	43.63	10.03	
Insoluble	1.46		2.82
Sulphuric Acid			1.37

The limestone is crushed at the quarry and stored under a track leading from the quarry. From storage it is fed into an elevator which discharges into a dryer, whence it is elevated and conveyed to bins over ball-mills in the raw material mill. The shale is similarly treated and runs through a roll crusher, and thence through Sturtevant rock emery mills. Stone and clay are elevated to bins over an automatic weighing machine, the clay passing first through sampling bins, where it remains long enough to be tested The proper proportion being weighed out on the scales the mixture is conveyed to grit mills and thence passes by a conveyor and elevator to a large steel tank back of the kilns. Rotary kilns are used, each driven by a 10 horse-power motor. Pulverized coal is used for fuel, prepared in a coal mill with a dryer, a crusher and a tube-mill. From the kilns the clinker is dumped on the clinker pit floor, from which it is elevated and conveyed to the finishing mill and run through ball and tube-mills and thence elevated and conveyed to the stock-houses and distributed to the storage bins. Conveyors carry the cement to the packing department as desired and deposit it in the distributing bins, from which it is drawn through Howes packers into bags and barrels. The Webster Manufacturing Company's elevating, conveying and power transmission machinery is used. There is a cooperage department and a fully equipped machine shop. Nearly all of the buildings are of brick, with slate roofs. The power consists of a 725 horse-power Corliss engine, driving the machinery in both raw material and finishing mills and the coal mill.

For Cement Testing Machinery address Fairbanks Co., New York.

A shaft in an extension of the power-house is run by the large engine, or by a 250 horse-power engine, and furnishes power for running the stone, kiln and stock-houses and the electric light plant, also an air compressor for the coal plant. An independent air compressor for the quarry drills is located in the main power-house. Steam pump for water supply is located in the boiler room. There are well-equipped testing and chemical laboratories. The company has also constructed houses for operatives and a general store. The capacity of the plant is in process of increase from 800 to 1,600 barrels a day.

THE VENTNOR STONE AND BRICK COMPANY, Atlantic City, N. J., is reported to manufacture silica Portland cement, using Davidsen tube-mills for grinding. See Note B, page 152.

THE VULCANITE PORTLAND CEMENT COMPANY is a New Jersey corporation with offices in the Vulcanite Building, 1712 Market street, Philadelphia, Pa., and works at Vulcanite, N. J., the post-office being Phillipsburg, N. J.

There are two independent plants in the works, one established in 1895, and the other but recently put in operation. The materials used are the usual Pennsylvania cement rock and limestone, quarried in the immediate vicinity. The cement rock is conveyed to the works by cable tramways and the limestone is brought in by rail. The mixture is made by weight from the stock of raw stone, sufficient stock being kept on hand to permit the necessary analyses. The mixture runs through two crushers and over a plate screen between them. Thence it is carried through the dryers and

CEMENT MANUFACTURERS

When considering the issue of a prospectus, advertising booklet, or other matter requiring first-class illustrations, and plates of tests, analysis, testimonials, etc., write to us for prices and samples of our work.

We also design and make cuts for LABELS, TRADE BRANDS, etc.

We have ample facilities, expert workmen and moderate prices.

Condit Block. H. C. BAUER ENGRAVING CO., Indianapolis, Ind.

elevated to Griffin mills, thence to the rotary kilns, of which there are five in the old mill and six in the new. From the kilns the clinker is elevated to the top of cooling tanks with an artificial draft. The cooled clinker runs through crackers and Griffin mills from which it runs to the stock-house. Smidth tube-mills are also used in grinding Portland cement clinker. The size of the plant is indicated by the statement that the stock-house of the new plant is 80x590 feet and will store 70,000 barrels of cement. The capacity of the entire plant is 2,000 barrels a day. The power plant includes 500 horse-power Corliss engines, each driving independently a raw material or a finishing mill. There is a small auxiliary engine in the boiler house for the coal handling machinery, also an air compressor, an electric lighting plant and pumps. Pulverized coal is used for fuel in the rotary kilns. The Robins conveying belts are in use.

THE WABASH PORTLAND CEMENT COMPANY, 912 Union Trust Building, Detroit, Mich., is an Indiana corporation, with works at Stroh, Ind., on the Wabash railroad, about midway between Detroit and Chicago, for the manufacture of Turkey brand of Portland cement. The materials used are comparatively dry and unusually uniform marl, and a clay well adapted for cement manufacture. The plant was designed by Lathbury & Spackman. The wet process is used and four rotary kilns are used, with a daily capacity of about 500 barrels a day. Smidth ball and tube-mills are used in grinding raw material and cement clinker. A Davidsen tube-mill is used to pulverize the coal used for fuel, which is fed to the kiln by blast created by an American Blower Company's fan. The Webster Manufacturing Company's conveying and power transmission machinery is installed. The works have been in operation since August, 1900, and plans are in preparation for an increase in the capacity of the works to about 1,000 barrels a day. Analysis of the cement shows, silica, 21.35 per cent; insoluble silica (clay), 0.43; alumina, 7.31; iron oxide, 2.65; lime, 62.35; magnesia, 2.88; sulphuric anhydride, 1.78; carbonic anhydride, 0.23; water, 0.55; potash, soda and loss, 0.47.

THE WAYLAND PORTLAND CEMENT COMPANY, Rochester, N. Y., has works at Wayland and Portway **(Perkinsville)**, New York, for the manufacture of Portland cement. **No infor-**

The Standard Plaster Co., Buffalo, N.Y., makes Calcined Plaster or Stucco

MUNICIPAL ENGINEERING MAGAZINE

Is known
as the foremost in the world
in the field to which
it is devoted.
It is the Authority
for Authorities.

ONE OF THE LARGEST SPECIAL MAGAZINES PUBLISHED AT THE PRICE—140 PAGES, MONTHLY, AND $2.00 PER YEAR

SOME EXPRESSIONS REGARDING IT

FROM LEADING NEWSPAPERS

MUNICIPAL ENGINEERING is one of the most valuable technical magazines of the age. —*Sacramento (Cal.) Record-Union.*

MUNICIPAL ENGINEERING is a model high standard publication that steadily improves. —*Milwaukee Sentinel.*

MUNICIPAL ENGINEERING is an excellent magazine.—*Hartford Courant.*

MUNICIPAL ENGINEERING is always practical in its solution of problems. —*Detroit Free Press.*

HOW IT IS PRAISED BY READERS

William Newman, City Engineer of Windsor, Ont.:
"I could not get along very well without MUNICIPAL ENGINEERING."

J. H. Healy, Consulting Engineer for Municipal and Sanitary Work:
"I find MUNICIPAL ENGINEERING MAGAZINE most useful: in fact, indispensable."

Alex Thomson, Jr., Oil City, Pa.:
"I have gained much valuable information from MUNICIPAL ENGINEERING."

Robert Y. Ogg, Secretary Board of Public Works, Detroit, Mich.:
"MUNICIPAL ENGINEERING MAGAZINE is so highly appreciated by aldermen and other visitors to this office that we have to keep our copies of them under lock and key to keep them from being spirited away."

Joseph Withington, Mattoon, Ill.:
"MUNICIPAL ENGINEERING MAGAZINE is the best of its kind."

Scott Hayes, Chamberlain, S. D.:
"You are doing a splendid service and putting out a fine work."

Geo. D. Jenkins, Washington, Pa.:
"MUNICIPAL ENGINEERING MAGAZINE is a good thing. Sorry I did not know of it before this."

From Sacramento (Cal.) Record-Union:
MUNICIPAL ENGINEERING has often been pronounced in these columns the most useful, practical magazine of the age, and we adhere to that judgment."

$2.00 per year. The sooner you order it the more you gain.

MUNICIPAL ENGINEERING CO.

mation has been received except that an American Blower Company's fan and Sturtevant crushing and grinding mills has been installed. See Note B, page 152.

THE WELLSTON PORTLAND CEMENT COMPANY, Detroit, Mich., capitalized at $100,000, is constructing works at Wellston, Ohio, which will be ready for operation about June 1, 1901.

THE WESTERN PORTLAND CEMENT COMPANY, Yankton, S. D., established works in 1890 about four miles west of Yankton, S. D., for the manufacture of Portland cement from chalk and the plastic clay forming the subsoil of much of South Dakota, which overlies the chalk, with a thin layer of waste material between. A modification of the English process is used. The works are located on a hillside below the quarries and clay beds, and the raw materials are run down to the mixing platform, where the ingredients are weighed out in the proper proportions and dropped through chutes into crushers. Thence the mixture passes through beaters, where it is thoroughly worked into a wet slurry and passed out through a wire screen, from which it passes into dosage tanks, where it is kept moving by revolving arms. The slurry is elevated to a second set of heaters with finer screen and drops into another large tank, from which it is elevated into a third tank. From this it is pumped into drying chambers, to be dried by the waste heat from the kilns, or to open-air drying areas. Johnson intermittent kilns are used, charged with alternate layers of dried slurry and Milwaukee gas coke, capacity 310 barrels of clinker for each charge. Buckets running on an overhead rail and hauled by rope, run around the drying yard and over the kilns for charging the air-dried material. The clinker is crushed, run through roller crackers and mill-stones, Berthelet separators like those in the Milwaukee Cement Works being used. Four horizontal return tubular boilers furnish steam for a 500 horse-power Corliss engine. Much of the power transmission is by rope drives. There is a complete physical and chemical laboratory to keep watch of raw material and finished product. See Note B, page 152.

Analyses of the raw material and the finished cement are as follows:

For Electric Equipment for Cement Plants Address Keystone Electric Co.

	Chalk.	Clay.	Cement.
Carbonate of Lime	88.0		
Lime		2.4	60.0
Alumina	4.8	27.1	7.7
Oxide of Iron			4.3
Carbonate of Magnesia	0.2		
Magnesia		2.7	0.8
Sulphuric Acid	1.3	2.0	2.8
Alkalies	0.2	1.3	1.2

WHITE CLIFFS PORTLAND CEMENT COMPANY, White Cliffs, Ark. See Note A, page 152.

WHITE CLIFFS PORTLAND CEMENT AND CHALK COMPANY, Texarkana, Ark. See Note B, page 152.

The reports of the United States Geological Survey state that the factory is modeled after German factories, the materials, chalk and clay being ground by dry process, moulded into brick and burned in Shofer kilns. The capacity in 1896 was 300 barrels a day. Analyses of the materials show:

For the chalk, carbonate of lime, 90.23 per cent.; carbonate of magnesia, 1.15; silica, 5.33; alumina and iron oxide, 3.03.

For the clay, silica, 73.62 per cent.; alumina and iron oxide, 19.30.

THE WHITEHALL PORTLAND CEMENT COMPANY'S WORKS, Cementon, Pa., were built in 1899 on a modern design upon the principle of carrying on the various processes in a straight line without unnecessary transfers or interference. The property includes about 67 acres, and the manufacturing plant is located adjacent to the Lehigh Valley railroad. The usual Lehigh valley cement rock is used. The material is loaded on automatic side-dumping cars at the quarry, and hauled by cable to the crusher,

THE COMING LIGHT

The "Cleveland" Automatic Acetylene Gas Generator

Perfectly automatic, absolutely safe.
Approved by all Underwriters' Associations.
Has stood the test for the past three years.
Entirely new and recently patented purifying process.
Absolutely no carbonizing or blocking of burners.
Made in all sizes for lighting homes, churches and factories. Machine uses commercial size carbide, insuring 5¼ cubic feet of gas per pound.
Recently adopted by the Lake Shore & Michigan Southern R. R. Co for lighting stations.
Most durable, simplest and easiest to install of any generator on the market.
State rights for sale to manufacture bordering on the Gulf of Mexico and Pacific Coast.
Agents wanted. Exclusive territory given.
For full particulars write for catalogue.

THE HARRIS MFG. CO., Cleveland, Ohio, U.S.A.

each car coming up meeting an empty car going to quarry. Crushers can be used on either cement rock or limestone by changing slides in spouts to deliver to proper bins. There are four crushers located 29 feet above the ground, and all driven by one line-shaft. The stock-bins underneath have a capacity of 4,000 to 5,000 tons. The cement rock and limestone are mixed in proper proportions by hand and carried by elevators to the dryers, of which there are three sets of two each. Each set is run by a separate motor. From the dryers a small belt conveyor and an elevator carry the material to the raw stone grinding mill, which is equipped with six batteries, each containing one ball and one tube-mill. These batteries are divided into three sets, each set having its independent motor. A short screw conveyor and an elevator carry the material to the stock-bins over the kilns in the kiln building. There are two kiln departments, two finishing mill departments and two stock-houses, located one on each side of the power and boiler rooms, machine shop and cooper shop, thus making two independent lines from the kilns to the end. In each kiln building there are ten kilns, 6 feet in diameter and 45 feet long, controlled by variable speeders. The feed pipes are water-jacketed. At each end of the kiln buildings is a coal-grinding department, each containing a dryer and a tube-mill. Each set of kilns, dryers and tube-mills is driven by a separate motor. The clinker storage bins are 18 feet below the level of the kiln floor. Two kilns discharge into one bin at any one time. The heat from the clinker bins is taken off by large exhaust fans and used under the boilers for forced draft, culm being the fuel used. The clinker is left here long enough to cool and then taken by elevators to the finishing mills. In the two finishing mill buildings are eight batteries of ball and tube-mills like those used in the raw stone mill, divided into four sets, each set being driven by its own motor. Elevators carry the material from the ball-mills to the hoppers above the tube mills, where the final mixture of materials is made. Conveyors and elevators carry the finished product from the tube-mills to the bins in the stock-houses. Each stock-house has 10 bins, each bin having a capacity of 3,000 to 4,000 barrels of cement. Each pair of bins has its own elevators and packer, to which the cement is carried part by gravity and part by wheeling.

Cement Machinery—Earle C. Bacon, Havemeyer Bldg., New York City.

The machine shop is a five-storied building. On the first floor is the machine shop, with four small engines for driving the packers and elevators in the stock-houses, the freight elevator and the machinery in the cooper-ship on the second floor. The third, fourth and fifth floors give storage for cooper stock and barrels. In the boiler room are four 500 horse-power batteries of boilers, each battery having two units and each unit its separate smoke-stack. The coal pockets are well located to obviate rehandling. In the engine room are four large Keystone Electric Company's generators, each of 225-k. w. capacity, in two sets, each set driven by cross-compound Corliss engines; also the motive power for the machinery in the kiln building and the coal grinding department. There is an independent auxiliary power building containing an engine driving a set of generators, for emergency use. In the electric light building are three automatic engines, each driving a dynamo, also a supply room and an air compressor to furnish power for the drills used in the quarry. In all there are six 250 horse-power motors, 220 volts, one 100 horse-power motor and two 60 horse-power motors, installed by the Keystone Electric Company. The switchboard from which all are started is 38 feet long and has 21 panels. The works can be run night and day by 164 men. The works will produce 2,000 barrels of cement a day and can be run at a rate of 2,500 barrels or more. The mill cost about $700,000.

THE ZENITH PORTLAND CEMENT COMPANY, Majestic Building, Detroit, Mich., is constructing works at Grass Lake, Mich., with a capacity of 1,000 barrels a day, which will probably be ready to furnish cement in August, 1901.

Complete Equipments Furnished for Cement Manufacturing Plants.
Cement Pulverizing Machinery, Crushers, Dryers, Etc.

WEST PULVERIZING MACHINE CO. 220 BROADWAY NEW YORK

FOREIGN CEMENT WORKS.

A few hints as to processes used in some of the foreign cement works will be of interest by way of comparison with American methods. It should be remembered, however, that the rotary kiln is being introduced quite rapidly and that within a few years there will be a material change in methods of burning and handling cement. A number of descriptions of works which do not export cement to this country are available, but are not given, as it is necessary to restrict the space occupied, and only those descriptions which may be of assistance in forming a judgment upon cements found in this market can be given.

ALSEN'S PORTLAND CEMENT FABRIK, Itzehoe and Lägerdorf, Germany. One Alsen mill, designed by Lathbury & Spackman, is located at Itzehoe, adjoining the clay deposit used in the plants, and two mills are located four miles away, at Lägerdorf, at the chalk deposit used. A railroad connects the two places and carries materials back and forth. The grinding of cement clinker and packing of cement is done at Itzehoe. The wet process is used with wash mills and settling basins, without agitators. The slurry is made into balls or bricks, dried in tunnel dryers and calcined in Dietzsch or other continuous vertical kilns. Buhr-stones are used for grinding.

DYCKERHOFF & SON, Amone, near Biebrich, Germany.—These works use limestone from a quarry containing layers of hard and soft limestone of uniform composition and a layer of soft marl, which varies somewhat. Clay and fuel are brought to the works on the river Rhine, on the banks of which the works are situated. The hard limestone and clay are mixed by the dry process, the limestone being corrected if necessary by the addition of proportions of the soft limestone and marl. The materials are dried, crushed and pulverized as in the American dry process, except that mill-stones are used for grinding instead of ball and tube-mills. The soft limestone and clay are prepared by the wet process, with wash-mills provided with edge-runner mills for grinding the wet slurry and drying basins. The mixtures prepared by the two processes, being of the same composition, are mixed in brick machines in proper proportions to produce bricks of proper consistency, which are further dried by the exhaust heat of the kilns. Hoffman ring kilns are used. These kilns are arranged around a circle, about twenty

Warren's Kiolithic Cement—Warren Bros. Co., 148 Federal St., Boston

kilns completing the round. The kilns are filled with layers of slurry bricks and fuel in order, and the burning proceeds from kiln to kiln around the circle. Thus the group is in continuous action though each kiln is intermittent. The round is made about twice a month, producing about 10,000 barrels in that time. The resulting clinker is ground on buhr-stones.

HILTON, ANDERSON, BROOKS AND COMPANY, Halling, Faversham and Upnor, England.—This company has four plants for making Portland cement, two large and two small, located on the Thames and Medway rivers. The materials are chalk from neighboring chalk cliffs and clay dredged from the Medway. They are mixed in wash-mills, ground wet in buhr-stones and dried in the long drying chamber of Johnson kilns. Modified forms of these kilns are in use at the Western Portland Cement Works, Yankton, S. D., and reference is made to the description of these works. The grinding is done on millstones. Bradley Pulverizer Company's Griffin mills are also used in the process of pulverizing.

LAGERDORFER PORTLAND CEMENT FABRIK.—Eugene Lion & Co., of Hamburg, Germany, have owned cement works at Lägerdorf since 1889, the works having been started in 1876.

The factory is situated in Holstein on the banks of a shipping canal, which, through the river Stor, is connected with the river Elbe. The lighters, which are freighted at Lägerdorf directly from the stores of the factory, deliver the cement in Hamburg to ocean vessels. The raw materials used are pure chalk, found on the grounds of the factory, and clay of excellent quality, supplied also from its own pits, in inexhaustible quantities. The raw materials are treated in wash-mills with plenty of water, in order to reduce them most finely, and to insure their most intimate mixture. The slurry thus attained is very thin and liquid; by sifting it, sand, coarse particles and vegetable matter are removed. It is then passed on to millstones, where the operation of blending and mixing is continued. Thence the slurry is conveyed in conduits, in which impurities, and those parts of chalk and clay that have escaped re-

Ransome's Concrete Mixers...

Everybody is simply astonished at the performance of the Mixers. They are surely the greatest machines for the purpose ever invented.
(Signed) JAMES D. SCHUYLER, M. A. S. C. Eng'rs.

RANSOME & SMITH CO. 17 and 19 Ninth St., Brooklyn, N. Y.

duction, are deposited and removed from time to time. None of the washed liquid is permitted to settle in the backs until its components are in the most perfect state of amalgamation, as described before. In the backs or settling basins the superfluous water is drawn off, and the washed materials are left to settle until they are in a fit condition for removal to the brick presses. During the process of washing a great many samples of slurry are taken to ascertain its chemical composition. The quality of cement being affected first by the accuracy of the raw cement mixture and the perfect blending of its ingredients, it will be seen at once that variations in the composition must be found out and set right without any loss of time. By means of exact control, the variation in the percentage of carbonate of lime in the slurry can be made less than half of one per cent. To finish the mixing of chalk and clay, the stiffened slurry is conveyed by cable cars to a pug-mill, and thence to brick presses. The bricks delivered by the latter machine are dried in drying flues and conveyed in a perfectly dry state to the Dietzsch kilns, where they are burnt.

The product of these kilns, the clinker, is wheeled to the mill, crushed by stone breaker and rollers and reduced to an impalpable powder by mill-stones.

The ground cement is passed on to a large magazine of 80,000 barrels capacity, kept in store for some weeks, and does not leave the factory before it is thoroughly tested in the laboratory.

There are four steam engines of altogether 675 horse-power; a fifth one, of 225 horse-power, is being mounted, a proof of the increasing appreciation of the excellent qualities of the brand.

The backs or settling basins cover an area of several acres, and there are ten double kilns of Dietzsch design.

MANNHEIMER PORTLAND CEMENT FABRIK, Mannheim and Weisenau, Germany.—At Mannheim hard limestone and clay are dried, ground and mixed by the dry process, made into bricks with a small amount of water. At Weisenau the same materials are used in the Dyckerhoff works, nearby, the hard and soft limestone and marl being powdered dry and the clay made into a slurry wet enough to make bricks of proper consistency when the two are mixed in proper proportions. At both plants the bricks are dried and burned in Dietzsch or in Hoffman kilns.

For illustrated pamphlet, "Cement Testing," write Fairbanks Co., N. Y.

MISBURGER PORTLAND CEMENT WORKS, Hanover, Germany.—The materials used here are a bed of marl mixed with clay and an underlying bed of clay mixed with marl quarried, and analyzed as quarried, that proper mixtures may be made. At some places in the beds the proportions are correct as the material comes from the quarry. An American revolving dryer takes the mixture of the weighed materials made by an edge-runner mill and passes it to mill-stones for further dry mixing and grinding, which is continued in the conveyors which carry the cement to storage bins. A chemical analysis is made here to insure correct proportions. A small percentage of water is added to the powder, which is then run through a brick machine in as dry a state as possible. The bricks are air dried before final drying and burning in Hoffman kilns. The grinding is done on buhr-stones.

PORTLAND CEMENT FABRIK, Hemmoor, Posthof 14, Hamburg, Germany.—These works are located at Hemmoor, have a capacity of 12,000,000 barrels a year and are prompt in their adoption of improvements in methods. Chalk and clay are the materials used and they are mixed by the wet process. Griffin mills of the Bradley Pulverizer Company are used in grinding (as in nineteen other German mills) and rotary kilns have recently been installed for burning, with very satisfactory results.

SHEWAN, TOMES & CO., Hong Kong, manufacture the Emerald brand of cement, which is imported by F. J. Crowe & Co., of Tacoma and Seattle, Wash.

JOSEPH SHARPE
Concrete Specialties
Contractor of
"RANSOME SYSTEM"
Concrete and Twisted Steel
FIRE-PROOFING
647-49 East 18th St., PATERSON, N. J.

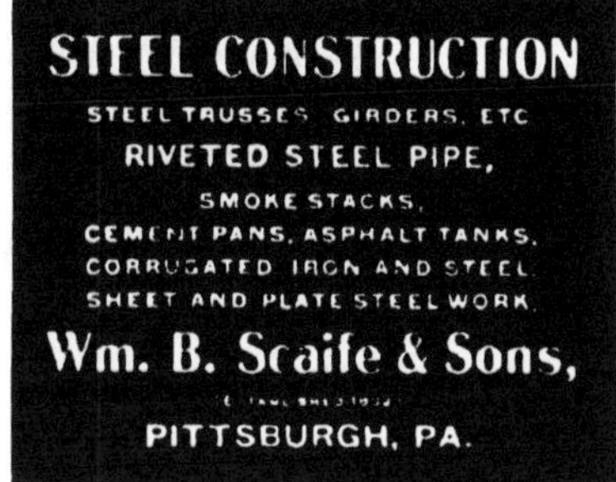

STEEL CONSTRUCTION
STEEL TRUSSES, GIRDERS, ETC
RIVETED STEEL PIPE,
SMOKE STACKS,
CEMENT PANS, ASPHALT TANKS,
CORRUGATED IRON AND STEEL
SHEET AND PLATE STEEL WORK
Wm. B. Scaife & Sons,
PITTSBURGH, PA.

DIRECTORY OF CEMENT MANUFACTURERS

The following list gives the names and addresses of all manufacturers of Portland cement which have been obtainable, of all the important manufacturers of natural hydraulic cement and of the manufacturers of the principal brands of foreign cement found in the market. All reliable information obtained regarding officers, capitalization, location and capacity of works, brands manufactured, capacity, general sales agents and shipping facilities is given. For nearly all works of importance this information is complete.

In the list are also included some plants which are not now in operation, a number which are not yet completed, and such recent incorporations as show evidence of early beginning of construction of plants. Completeness in this last class is not expected and additions are made to the manuscript list weekly or oftener. More than 160 entries will be found, exceeding the number reported annually by the United States Geological Survey.

Reference should be made for further particulars regarding the manufacturing operations of the companies to the chapter on Descriptions of Works and Processes for Making Cement preceding.

The list of American companies, including Canada and Mexico, is followed by a list of the prominent European companies exporting cement to the United States. The kind of cement manufactured is stated with the name of brand. As some companies manufacture both natural hydraulic and Portland cements, no division into classes has been made, to avoid unnecessary repetition.

AMERICAN MANUFACTURERS.

ACME PORTLAND CEMENT COMPANY, Camden, N. J. See Note A, page 152.

The Standard Plaster Co., Buffalo, N.Y., makes Calcined Plaster or Stucco

AJAX PORTLAND CEMENT COMPANY, Jersey City, N. J. H. W. Menn, W. J. Baldwin, C. M. Perkins, E. D. Hawkins, A. G. Brown, all of Jersey City, incorporators. See Note **A**, page 152.

AKRON CEMENT WORKS, Akron, N. Y. See Note **F**, page 152.
UNION AKRON CEMENT COMPANY, Sales Agents, 141 Erie St., Buffalo, N. Y.
Manufacturers of Red Star brand natural hydraulic cement.
On New York Central & Hudson River railroad.

ALABAMA PORTLAND CEMENT COMPANY, Ltd., Demopolis, Ala.—Under construction.
THOMAS C. CAIRNS, Gen'l Mgr.
Capitalization, $500,000.
Capacity, 1,000 barrels per day.
On Southern railway.

ALAMO CEMENT COMPANY, San Antonio, Texas.—
C. BAUMBERGER, Pres. and Chemist, San Antonio, Texas.
DR. F. J. HULTMYER, Vice-Pres., San Antonio, Texas.
F. W. COOK, JR., Sec'y, San Antonio, Tex.
NIC. BEHLAS, Supt., San Antonio, Tex.
Capitalization, see Note **E**, page 152.
Capacity, 250 barrels a day.
Manufacturers of Alamo Portland and natural hydraulic cements.
On International & Great Northern, San Antonio & Aransas Pass, Galveston, Hamburg & San Antonio, and San Antonio & Gulf railroads.

ALMA PORTLAND CEMENT COMPANY, Wellston, Ohio.—
B. B. LATHBURY, Pres., Philadelphia, Pa.
D. W. GRAFLY, Treas., Philadelphia, Pa.
F. D. EWING, Sec'v, Jackson, Ohio.
SAMUEL FOWDEN, Supt., Wellston, Ohio.
WM. G. HARTRANFT Co., Sales Agents, R. E. Trust Building, Philadelphia, Pa.
Capital, $150,000.
Capacity, 450 barrels a day.
Manufacturers Alma brand Portland cement.
On Columbus, Hocking Valley & Toledo, Cincinnati. Ham. & Dayton, Baltimore & Ohio Southwestern and Ohio Southern railroads.

THE **ALPENA PORTLAND CEMENT COMPANY**, Alpena, Mich.
FRANK W. GILCHRIST, Pres. and Dir., Alpena, Mich.
WM. B. COMSTOCK, Vice-Pres. and Dir., Alpena, Mich.
GEO. J. ROBINSON, Sec'y and Dir., Alpena, Mich.
WM. H. JOHNSON, Treas. and Dir., Alpena, Mich.

The Alpena Portland Cement Company—Continued.

Allen Fletcher, Auditor and Dir., Alpena, Mich.
John Monaghan, Dir., Alpena, Mich.
Chas. H. Reynolds, Dir., Alpena, Mich.
Joseph H. Colt, Dir., Alpena, Mich.
Walter S. Russell, Dir., Detroit, Mich.
Frank M. Haldeman, Supt., Alpena, Mich.
Stephen Ludlow, Frank Monaghan, Chemists, Alpena, Mich.
F. R. Potter, Business Mgr., Alpena, Mich.
Capitalization, $500,000.
Capacity, 800 barrels a day.
Manufacturers of Alpena brand Portland cement.
On Detroit & Mackinac railroad and Lake Huron.

ALPHA PORTLAND CEMENT COMPANY, Easton, Pa., works at Alpha, N. J.—
W. M. McKelvy, Pres. and Dir., Pittsburg, Pa.
A. F. Gerstell, Vice-Pres. and Gen'l Mgr. and Dir., Easton, Pa.
G. S. Brown, Sec'y and Treas., Easton, Pa.
J. M. Lockhart, Dir., Pittsburg, Pa.
J. H. Lockhart, Dir., Pittsburg, Pa.
Chas. E. Pope, Dir., Pittsburg, Pa.
Howard Riegel, Dir., Riegelsville, N. J.
Harry Dreul, Chemist, 623 High street, Easton, Pa.
W. J. Donaldson, Sales Agent, Betz Bldg., Philadelphia, Pa.
Dickinson Cement Company, Sales Agents, 931 Marquette Bldg., Chicago, Ill.
Capitalization, $1,000,000.
Capacity, 2,000 barrels a day.
Manufacturers Alpha brand Portland cement.
On Lehigh Valley railroad.

ALSEN AMERICAN PORTLAND CEMENT COMPANY. See Note B, on page 152. Works at West Camp, N. Y.
Sinclair & Babson, Agents, No. 143 Liberty St., New York City.
Capitalization, $2,250,000.
On West Shore railroad and Hudson river.

THE AMERICAN CEMENT COMPANY OF NEW JERSEY.— Offices, 22 and 24 South Fifteenth street, Philadelphia, Pa.

MANUFACTURED IN STETTIN, GERMANY.
Stettin Portland Cement—Stettin Bredower Portland Cement
(BLUE ANCHOR BRAND) (BLUE EAGLE BRAND)
Unsurpassed for sidewalks, artificial stone. Always uniform in color and quality.
WILL NOT CONTRACT OR EXPAND.
F. BEHREND, - 54 FRONT ST., NEW YORK

GIANT PORTLAND CEMENT

Manufactured since 1883, by men associated with D. O. SAYLOR, the founder of the

AMERICAN PORTLAND CEMENT INDUSTRY

USED ON THE

TWELVE ENGINEERING WONDERS OF THE WORLD

The celebrated JOHNSTOWN BRIDGE (built with "Giant" and "Union" cement), which stood the great flood of May, 1889, within six months after it was built.

The RAPID TRANSIT UNDER-GROUND RAILWAY in New York, the largest sub-way ever constructed, and which the Chief Engineer states will require 1,500,000 barrels of cement, and is the largest single contract for cement ever let in the world.

The CORNELL DAM, of the New Croton aqueduct, the largest masonry dam in the world.

JEROME PARK RESERVOIR, of the New York Croton Aqueduct System, the largest artificial reservoir in the world.

The READING SUB-WAY in Philadelphia, one of the most important sub-ways ever constructed in this country.

The NIAGARA FALLS TUNNEL, of the Niagara Falls Power Company. The largest water-power now in existence.

The ROCKVILLE BRIDGE of the Pennsylvania Railroad, at Rockville, Pa., 3,820-foot four-track stone arch, the largest masonry bridge in the world.

The POWER-HOUSE of the Metropolitan Traction Company, in New York, with its 70,000 horse-power—the largest power building in the world.

The NEW EAST RIVER BRIDGE between Brooklyn and New York. The largest bridge now building in the world.

The UNDERGROUND ELECTRIC and CABLE WORK of the Metropolitan and Third Avenue Railway Systems in New York. The greatest mileage of electric and cable roads under a single control in the United States.

The NEW WACHUSETTS DAM of the Boston Metropolitan Water System, which will have the biggest water storage capacity of any masonry dam in the world, the amount of water stored being some 60,000,000,000 gallons in all, or twice the water storage of the new Croton Dam of the New York Aqueduct System.

The CHIMNEY of the Ninety-Sixth Street Power-House of the Metropolitan Street Railway, New York—the highest chimney in the United States—353 feet high.

With this array of work now going on and coming from customers and engineers who have been buying "Giant" cement for the past sixteen years, and who still continue to buy and use it, it is unnecessary to publish letters of commendation of a brand that so well speaks for itself.

THE AMERICAN CEMENT CO.

OWNERS OF

The Egypt Portland Cement Works.	The Giant Portland Cement Works.
The Pennsylvania Portland Cement Works.	The Giant Rotary Portland Cement Works.
The Columbian Portland Cement Works.	The Jordan, N. Y., Portland Cement Works.

Office, 22 and 24 South Fifteenth St., PHILADELPHIA, PA.

The American Cement Company of New Jersey—Continued.

ROBERT W. LESLEY, Pres., 22 S. Fifteenth St., **Philadelphia.**
GEORGE W. NORRIS, Vice-Pres., "The Bourse," **Philadelphia.**
F. J. JIGGENS, Treas, 22 S. Fifteenth St., **Philadelphia.**
H. B. WARNER, Sec'y, 22 S. Fifteenth St., **Philadelphia.**
JOHN W. ECKERT, Pres. Mfg. Dept., Egypt, Lehigh Co., Pa.

Capitalization—Stocks, $2,000,000; bonds, $965,000.

Owns the Jordan Portland Cement Works, at Jordan, Onondaga county, New York.

Capacity, 400 barrels daily.

Brand, Jordan Portland cement.

On New York Central railroad.

Also owner of all the stock of the American Cement Company of Pennsylvania (see below); of the Lesley and Trinkle Company, and of the United Building Material Company. It is also developing the Tidewater Cement Works, near Newport News, Virginia.

Sales agents, Lesley & Trinkle Co., 24 South Fifteenth street, Philadelphia, Pa.; United Building Material Company, 13-21 Park Row, New York.

AMERICAN CEMENT COMPANY OF PENNSYLVANIA.—Offices, No. 22 South Fifteenth street, Philadelphia, Pa.

JOHN W. ECKERT, Pres., Egypt, Lehigh Co., Pennsylvania.
ROBERT W. LESLEY, Vice-Pres. and Treas., S. Fifteenth St., Philadelphia, Pa.
HARRY B. WARNER, Sec'y, 22 S. Fifteenth St., Philadelphia, Pa.
LESLEY & TRINKLE Co. Sales Agents, 24 S. Fifteenth St., Philadelphia, Pa.
UNITED BUILDING MATERIAL Co., Sales Agents, 13-21 Park Row, New York.

Owners of Egypt Portland Cement Works, Pennsylvania Portland Cement Works, Columbia Portland Cement Works, Giant Portland Cement Works, Giant Rotary Portland Cement Works all at Egypt, Lehigh county, Pennsylvania.

Manufacturers of "Giant" brand Portland cement, "Improved Union" brand (mixture of natural and Portland cement) and "Union" brand natural hydraulic cement.

On Ironton railroad branch from Lehigh Valley railroad.

Capacity for all brands, 5,000 barrels per day.

All of the capital stock of the American Cement Company of Pennsylvania is owned by the American Cement Company of New Jersey. (See above.)

Warren's "Kiola" Asphalt—Warren Bros. Co., 148 Federal St., Boston

Long-Time Tests.

Tests of over Five Hundred Thousand Barrels "Giant" Portland, on six of the largest dams in the United States; on the Niagara Falls Power-Tunnel, on the Boston Aqueduct; the Philadelphia Docks, Sewers and Bridges; the Washington, D. C., Sewers; and the Reading Terminal Railroad and Station, in Philadelphia, for periods up to nine years.
The only records of long-time tests on Portland Cement now published in the United States.

Test periods (each with "Number of Briquettes" and "Average, in pounds"): 1 Day, 1 Week, 1 Mo., 3 Mos., 6 Mos., 9 Mos., 1 Year, 18 Mos., 15 Mos., 2 Years, 3 Years, 4 Years, 5 Years, 6 Years, 7 Years, 8 Years, 9 Years. Fineness: [illegible].

BRAND "Giant" Portland	Neat or Mortar	Test results (1 Day – 9 Years)	Fineness		
"Sodom and Bog Brook Dams, New York Aqueduct. About 90,000 bbls.	Neat / 2 to 1 / 3 to 1	[illegible]			13.0
Titicus Dam, New York Aqueduct. About 120,000 bbls.	Neat / 2 to 1 / 3 to 1	[illegible]			11.7
Cornell and Croton Dams, New York Aqueduct. About 60,000 bbls.	Neat / 2 to 1 / 2 to 1 from Mortar Box / 3 to 1 / 3 to 1 from Mortar Box	[illegible]			14.7
Reading Terminal Railroad and Station, Philadelphia. About 80,000 bbls.	Neat / 3 to 1 / 3 to 1 from Mortar Box	[illegible]	.000	10.06	14.79
Niagara Falls Tunnel, Niagara Power Co. [illegible]	Neat / 2 to 1 / 3 to 1	[illegible]			14.5
[illegible] Dam, [illegible] Aqueduct [illegible] in the world [illegible]	Neat / 2 to 1 / 3 to 1	[illegible]			
[illegible] Giant (Cargo)	Neat / 3 to 1	[illegible]			
Metropolitan Water Board of Boston, Mass. [illegible]	Neat / 2 to 1	[illegible]	1.0		9.0
[illegible] Public Works, [illegible] Giant. [illegible]	Neat / 3 to 1	[illegible]	1.2		6.6
[illegible]	Neat / 3 to 1	[illegible]			

infor- about CEMENT AND ITS USES
is given more fully in
MUNICIPAL ENGINEERING MAGAZINE
than any other publication.
rice, $2.00 Per Year.

American Cement Company of Pennsylvania—Continued.

[*Manufacturer's Statement.*]

The "Giant" Portland cement is manufactured by the American Cement Company, whose officers, Messrs. John W. Eckert and Robert W. Lesley, were connected as far back as 1876 and 1877 with Mr. David O. Saylor in the manufacture and sale of the first successful American Portland cement.

The "Giant" Portland and "Union" natural cements have been made by the American Cement Company since 1883 to the extent of nearly 10,000,000 barrels, and the table on page 245 tells the tale of the permanence and stability of the "Giant" brand of Portland cement.

ANTIETAM CEMENT COMPANY, Hagerstown, Md. See Note **A**, page 152.

On Baltimore & Ohio, Cumberland Valley, Norfolk & Western, and Western Maryland railroads.

THE ART PORTLAND CEMENT COMPANY, Sandusky, Ohio. See Note **C**, page 152.

G. JARECKI, JR., Pres. and Gen. Mgr., Sandusky, Ohio.
P. G. WALKER, Sec'y and Treas., Sandusky, Ohio.
E. CABLE, Dir., Sandusky, Ohio.
R. E. SCHNEK, Dir., Sandusky, Ohio.
Capitalization. See Note **E**, page 152.
Manufacturers of Bull Dog brand Portland cement.

On Lake Shore & Michigan Southern, Lake Erie & Western, Baltimore & Ohio, Cleveland, Cincinnati, Chicago & St. Louis, and Columbus, Sandusky & Hocking railroads.

THE ATLAS PORTLAND CEMENT COMPANY, No. 143 Liberty St., New York, N. Y. Works at Coplay and Northampton, Pa.

J. ROGERS MAXWELL, Pres., No. 143 Liberty St., New York.
ALFONSO DE NAVARRO, 2d Vice-Pres., No. 143 Liberty St., New York.
HENRY GRAVES, JR., Sec'y, No. 153 Liberty St., New York.
HOWARD W. MAXWELL, Treas., No. 143 Liberty St., New York.
J. R. MAXWELL, JR., Ass't. Treas., No. 143 Liberty St., New York.
L. J. H. GROSSART, Engr., Northampton, Pa.
Capitalization. See Note **E**, page 152.
Capacity, 3,500,000 barrels, increasing to 4,500,000 annually.
Manufacturers Atlas brand Portland cement.

On Lehigh Valley railroad and Central railroad of New Jersey.

Cement Testing Machinery. Fairbanks Co., 311 Broadway, New York.

The Atlas Portland Cement Company—Continued.

TESTS OF ATLAS PORTLAND CEMENT

From March 1, 1894, to March 1, 1895.

Office of City Engineer, Youngstown, Ohio. F. M. Lillie, City Engineer.

Neat.	7 days.	1 mo.	6 mos.
Number of tests	65	1	3
Per cent. water	21	21	21
Average tensile strength	585	760	818
One part cement, three parts sand.			
Number of tests	57	2	4
Per cent. water	10	10	10
Average tensile strength	252	417	497

[*Manufacturer's Statement.*]

The Atlas Portland Cement Company's works are situated at Northampton and Coplay, Pa., and produce 3,500,000 barrels of Portland cement per year. The rapid rise and steady continuance in favor of Atlas is in itself a sufficient recommendation of the uniform quality of the cement. The old formula in the specifications of leading architects and engineers calling for the best imported cements, has long since given way to the new standard of "Atlas or equal." The manufacturers of this brand being aware of the responsibility of maintaining this position have adhered to the policy of allowing no cement to leave the works which is not perfect as to packages, weight and quality, subject to their absolute guarantee, thus insuring:

To the architect or engineer, that his responsibility ceases when Atlas is specified.

To the contractor, that he will be subjected to no delays owing to the rejection or questioning the quality of the cement.

To the exporter, the knowledge that his distant customer will have no cause for complaint.

And to the owner, the satisfaction of knowing that the highest grade of cement manufactured has been used on his work.

AUSTIN PORTLAND CEMENT COMPANY, Austin, Texas.— See Note A, page 152.

On Austin & Northwestern, Houston & Texas Central and International & Great Northern railroads.

BANGS & GAYNOR, Fayetteville, N. Y. See Note F, page 152.

William T. Gaynor, Partner and Supt., Fayetteville, N. Y.

Anson M. Bangs, Partner, Fayetteville, N. Y.

Capacity, 200 barrels a day.

More Cement Companies

advertise in Municipal Engineering Magazine

than in any other American publication. It reaches more of the people who buy or influence the buying of cement than any other American publication.

Bangs & Gaynor—Continued.

Manufacturers Bangs & Gaynor Star brand natural hydraulic cement.

On Elmira & Cortland branch of Lehigh Valley railroad.

BANNER CEMENT COMPANY, Masonic Temple, Chicago, Ill.

Works at Cementville, Ind.

A. NEWTON, Pres. and Gen'l Mgr., 1105 Masonic Temple, Chicago, Ill.

WM. B. HILL, Vice-Pres., Kansas City, Mo.

C. C. BISHOP, Sec'y and Treas., 1105 Masonic Temple, Chicago, Ill.

MARBLEHEAD LIME CO., Sales Agents, Masonic Temple, Chicago, Ill.

WESTERN WHITE LIME CO., Sales Agents, Kansas City, Mo.

Capitalization. See Note **E**, page 152.

Manufacturers Banner brand Louisville natural hydraulic cement.

On Pittsburg, Cincinnati, Chicago & St. Louis railroad.

DAVID BATTLE ESTATE, Thorold, Ont., Can. See Notes **A** and **F**, page 152.

On Grand Trunk railroad.

BEAVER PORTLAND CEMENT COMPANY, Ltd., Marlbank, Ont., Can. See Note **B**, page 152. Owned by Canadian Portland Cement Company, Deseronto, Ont.

On Kingston, Napanee & Western railroad.

JAMES BEHAN ESTATE, Manlius, N. Y. See Note **F**, page 152.

JOHN J. COSTELLO, Supt., Manlius, N. Y.

Capacity, 1,000 barrels a day.

Manufacturers Manlius natural hydraulic cement.

On Chenango branch of West Shore railroad.

BELMONT CEMENT WORKS, Bellefonte, Pa. See Note **A**, page 152.

BIRMINGHAM CEMENT COMPANY, Ensley, Ala.—

T. C. BALDWIN, Pres. and Dir., 18 Wall St., New York, N. Y.

J. D. CHEEVER, Treas and Dir., 18 Wall St., New York, N. Y.

W. H. PATTERSON, Dir., 100 Broadway, New York.

ANDREW ONDERDONK, Dir., New York City, N. Y.

A. W. HASKELL, Dir., Birmingham, Ala.

J. L. GIVEN, Supt. and Engr., Ensley, Ala.

Capitalization, $300,000.

Capacity, 800 barrels per day.

Manufacturers Southern Cross brand Portland cement (pozzuolana).

On Louisville & Nashville and Kansas City, Memphis & Birmingham railroads.

Consult Keystone Electric Co. on Best Method of Driving Cement Mchn'y.

BLUE RIDGE CEMENT AND LIME WORKS, Blue Ridge Springs, Va. Works idle.
On Norfolk & Western railway.

BLUE ROCK CEMENT COMPANY, New Albany, Ind.—See Note **A**, page 152.

BONNEVILLE PORTLAND CEMENT COMPANY, 1233 and 1237 Real Estate Trust Building, Phialdelphia, Pa. Works at Siegfried, Pa.
W. H. Harding, Pres., Baltimore, Md.
E. B. Grimes, Sec'y and Treas., Philadelphia, Pa.
F. F. Comstock, Agent, New York office.
Capitalization, $600,000.
Capacity, 1,500 barrels a day.
Manufacturers Star and Standard brands Portland cement.
Manufacturers Bonneville natural hydraulic cement.
On Central Railroad of New Jersey.

BRIDGES & HENDERSON, Hancock, Md.—See Note **F**, page 152.
W. W. Clarke & Son, Sales Agents, 115 Gay St. S., Baltimore, Md.
Manufacturers B. & H. brand natural hydraulic cement.
On Baltimore & Ohio railroad.

THE BRIER HILL IRON AND COAL COMPANY, Youngstown, O.
George Tod, Pres., Youngstown, Ohio.
H. H. Stambaugh, Sec'y, Youngstown, Ohio.
J. G. Butler, Gen. Mgr., Youngstown, Ohio.
David Tod, General Sales Agent, Youngstown, Ohio.
Capitalization—No separate capitalization for cement department.
Manufacturers Brier Hill brand Portland cement (pozzuolana).
On Erie, Lake Shore & Michigan Southern, Erie & Ashtabula division of Pennsylvania, Pittsburg & Lake Erie, and Pittsburg & Western railroads.

BRITISH COLUMBIA PORTLAND CEMENT COMPANY, Vancouver, B. C. See Note **B**, page 152. Not in operation.
Manufacturers of Portland cement.
On Canadian Pacific railroad.

THE BRONSON PORTLAND CEMENT COMPANY, Bronson, Mich.
J. F. Townsend, Pres. and Gen. Mgr., Akron, Ohio.
Chas. Smith, Vice-Pres., Bronson, Mich.
J. F. Hutton, Sec'y and Treas., Bronson, Mich.
Eber Davis, Supt., Bronson, Mich.
W. H. Simmons, Chemist, Bronson, Mich.

Parkhurst Combined Curb and Gutter—Write D. C. Buntin, Indianapolis

The Bronson Portland Cement Company—Continued.

EBER DAVIS, Engr., Bronson, Mich.
Capitalization, $500,000.
Capacity, 1,200 barrels a day.
Manufacturers Bronson Portland cement.
On Lake Shore & Michigan Southern railroad.

BUCKEYE PORTLAND CEMENT COMPANY, Bellefontaine, Ohio. Works at Harper, Ohio.
H. S. BARTHOLOMEW, Pres., Bellefontaine, Ohio.
G. W. BARTHOLOMEW, Treas., Bellefontaine, Ohio.
H. I. BARTHOLOMEW, Sec'y, Bellefontaine, Ohio.
Capitalization, $500,000.
Capacitv, 400 barrels per day.
Manufacturers of Buckeye Portland cement.

[*Manufacturer's Statement.*]

Tests of Buckeye Portland cement made under superintendence of S. A. Buchanan, C. E., chief engineer bridge department of the Champion Iron Company, Kenton, Ohio, and of James Wonders, C. E., city and county engineer. The cement, sand, lime paste and water were proportioned by weight. The briquettes were all of equal density, being made by a Boehme Hammer apparatus. They were kept in air twenty-four hours and in water several years.

BRAND.	Parts of sand to 1 part cement.	Tensile strength per square inch—averages of many tests.							
		7 days.	4 weeks.	1 year.	4 years.	7 years.	8 years.	10 years.	12 yrs.
Buckeye Portland	9	110	139	314					474
	6	160		(417)					605*
	3	198	291	600	725	805	890	920	1001
	2	(250)	(400)	710		957			
	1	310		(746)		1105	1 briq. stood pounds and did not break.		1286
Stern (Star), German.	3	172	210	395					665
Louisville	3	37							225
		Parts of lime putty.							
Buckeye Portland	6	4	100	245		425			
	6	2		300	420	530			
	5	1		410		700			

***Other tests show this particular test to be low.**

BUCKHORN PORTLAND CEMENT COMPANY, 413 Girard Building, Philadelphia, Pa. Works at Manheim, W. Va. See Note D, page 152.
JOHN F. STORER, Pres. and Dir., Germantown, Philadelphia, Pennsylvania.
WINTHROP SMITH, Vice-Pres. and Dir., 439 Chestnut St., Philadelphia, Pa.
CHAS. H. WORTHMAN, Sec'y and Treas., 2123 Green St., [illegible]adelphia, Pa.
WILLIAM F. HARRITY, Dir., Eq. Trust Bldg., Phila[illegible]
ABRAM C. MOTT, Dir., American and Dauphin Sts., [illegible]delphia, Pa.
WM. G. HARTRANFT CEMENT COMPANY, Sales Agents, Philadelphia, Pa.
Capitalization, $500,000.
Manufacturers Buckhorn brand Portland cement.
On Baltimore & Ohio railroad.

BUFFALO CEMENT COMPANY, Ltd., No. 110 Franklin street, Buffalo, N. Y. Works at intersection of Main and Amherst streets, Buffalo, N. Y.

LEWIS J. BENNETT, Pres., No. 110 Franklin St., Buffalo, N. Y.

JAMES P. WOOD, Vice-Pres., No. 110 Franklin St., Buffalo, N. Y.

LESLIE J. BENNETT, Sec'y, No. 110 Franklin St., Buffalo, N. Y.

Capitalization, $100,000 (nominal).

Manufacturers Buffalo brand natural hydraulic cement.

Capacity, 240,000 barrels annually.

Manufacturers Buffalo Portland cement.

Capacity, 40,000 barrels annually.

(See description of works.)

On the Lake Shore & Michigan Southern; Michigan Central; Buffalo, Rochester & Pittsburg; New York Central & Hudson River; Western New York & Pennsylvania; West Shore; Erie; New York, Chicago & St. Louis; Lehigh Valley; Delaware, Lackawanna & Western; Grand Trunk, and Wabash railroads.

BURNS CEMENT COMPANY, Burns, Kan. See Note A, page 152.

On Atchison, Topeka & Santa Fe railroad.

CALIFORNIA PORTLAND CEMENT COMPANY, 104 South Broadway, Los Angeles, Cal. Works at Colton, Cal.

S. H. MOTT, Pres., Los Angeles, Cal.

S. W. LITTLE, Vice-Pres., Los Angeles, Cal.

J. R. TOBERMAN, Sec'y, Los Angeles, Cal.

JOSEPH BROWN, Dir., Los Angeles, Cal.

FRANK H. JACKSON, Dir. and Sales Agent, Los Angeles, Cal.

C. W. SMITH, Dir., Pasadena, Cal.

ROBERT STRONG, Dir., Pasadena, Cal.

GEO. E. TALCOTT, Supt., Colton, Cal.

EDW. DURYEE, Chemist, Colton, Cal.

Capitalization. See Note E, page 152.

The highest grade of Natural Rock Hydraulic Cement manufactured in the United States.

Buffalo • Cement

Awarded diploma and medal over all competitors at the World's Columbian Exposition for excellence of raw material and material after being prepared.

MANUFACTURED BY

BUFFALO CEMENT CO. (Ltd.)

BUFFALO, N. Y.

California Portland Cement Company—Continued.

Capacity, 375 barrels a day.

Manufacturers Colton brand Portland cement.

On Southern Pacific and Atchison, Topeka & Santa Fe railroads.

CALUMET PORTLAND CEMENT COMPANY, 3901 Lowe avenue, Chicago, Ill. See Notes **B** and **E**, page 152.

Manufacturers of silica Portland cement.

On Chicago & Alton; Pittsburg, Ft. Wayne & Chicago; Chicago, Milwaukee & St. Paul; Chicago, Burlington & Quincy; Pittsburg, Cincinnati, Chicago & St. Louis; Atchison, Topeka & Santa Fe; Grand Trunk; Chicago & Eastern Illinois; Wabash; Chicago & Erie; Chicago, Indianapolis & Louisville; Chicago, Rock Island & Pacific; Lake Shore & Michigan Southern; New York, Chicago & St. Louis; Baltimore & Ohio; Wisconsin Central; Michigan Central; Chicago Great Western; Cleveland, Cincinnati, Chicago & St. Louis; Chicago & West Michigan, and Chicago & Northwestern railroads.

THE CANADIAN PORTLAND CEMENT COMPANY, Ltd., Deseronto, Ont., Can. See Note **B**, page 152. Works at Strathcona, Napanee Mills and Marlbank, Ont.; also owns the St. Lawrence Portland Cement Company, of Montreal.

E. W. Rathbun, Pres., Deseronto, Ont.
F. G. B. Allen., Managing Dir., Napanee Mills, Ont.
Jas. Dobson, Dir., Philadelphia, Pa.
C. A. Masten, Dir., Toronto, Ont.
B. B. Osler, Dir., Toronto, Ont.
M. J. Haney, Dir., Toronto, Ont.
W. D. Matthews, Dir., Toronto, Ont.
W. E. Rathbun, Dir., Deseronto, Ont.
C. J. Webb, Dir., Philadelphia, Pa.
W. Richards, Supt. Strathcona Works.
The Rathbun Co., Sales Agents, Deseronto, Ont.

Capitalization, $450,000.

Capacity, 1,200 barrels a day.

Manufacturers of Rathbun's Star, Beaver and Ensign brands of cement.

On Kingston, Napanee & Western and Grand Trunk railroads.

CAMPANIA MEXICANA DE CEMENTO PORTLAND, Dublan, Mexico. See chapter on Descriptions of Works.

THE CANON CITY CEMENT COMPANY, Canon City, Colo. Conrad Meyers, J. G. Locke, B. G. Woodford, Truman Plancett, incorporators. See Note **A**, page 152.

Capital, $50,000.

On Atchison, Topeka & Santa Fe; Canon City & Cripple Creek, and Denver & Rio Grande railroads.

See Nordyke & Marmon Co.'s advertisement of Cement Machinery.

[C]ASSADAGA CEMENT COMPANY, Cassadaga, N. Y. See Note **A**, page 152.

On Dunkirk, Allegheny Valley & Pittsburg railroad.

[C]ASTALIA PORTLAND CEMENT COMPANY, 701-702 Publication Building, Pittsburg, Pa. Works at Castalia, Ohio.

W. J. PRENTICE, Pres. and Dir., Pittsburg, Pa.
J. S. CRAIG, Vice-Pres. and Dir., Pittsburg, Pa.
GEO. W. HACKETT, Sec'y and Dir. and Gen. Mgr., Pittsburg, Pa.
GEO. J. GORMAN, Treas. and Dir., Pittsburg, Pa.
J. M. PORTER, Dir., Pittsburg, Pa.
S. W. CUNNINGHAM, Dir., Pittsburg, Pa.
C. C. BOYLE, Dir., Pittsburg, Pa.
I. D. KRAMER, Dir., Pittsburg, Pa.
S. C. APPLEGATE, Dir., Pittsburg, Pa.
Capitalization, $300,000.
Capacity, 1,500 barrels a day.
Manufacturers Tiger brand Portland cement.

On Lake Erie & Western and Cleveland, Cincinnati, Chicago [&] St. Louis railroads.

[C]ATSKILL CEMENT COMPANY, Smith's Landing, N. Y.—

P. GARDNER COFFIN, Pres., Catskill, N. Y.
J. W. KITTRELL, Sec'y and Treas., Smith's Landing, N. Y.
HERMAN C. COWEN, Supt., Smith's Landing, N. Y.
JNO. W. CUMMING, Chemist, Smith's Landing, N. Y.
FRED J. WRIGHT, Engr., Smith's Landing, N. Y.
WM. A. BASSETT, Engr., Smith's Landing, N. Y.
Capitalization, $237,000.
Capacity, 300 barrels a day.
Manufacturers Catskill brand Portland cement.

On West Shore railroad and Hudson river.

[C]AYUGA LAKE CEMENT COMPANY, Ithaca, N. Y. Under construction. See Note **C**, page 152.

M. E. CALKINS, Pres. and Gen. Mgr., Ithaca, N. Y.
L. H. SMITH, Vice-Pres., Ithaca, N. Y.
C. E. TREMAN, Sec'y and Treas., Ithaca, N. Y.
Capitalization, $100,000.

[C]HAUTAUQUA CEMENT COMPANY, Burnhams, N. Y. See Note **A**, page 152.

On Dunkirk, Allegheny Valley & Pittsburg railroad.

[C]HELSEA PORTLAND CEMENT COMPANY, Ltd., Detroit, Mich. See Note **A**, page 152.

Incorporators, Jas. D. Butterfield, Merle B. Moon, Daniel J. Smith, Lewis G. Gorton, John L. Steele.

[Gr]iffin Mills—Address Bradley Pulverizer Co., 92 State Street, Boston

CHICAGO PORTLAND CEMENT COMPANY, No. 513 Stock Exchange, Chicago, Ill. Works at Oglesby, Ill.
NORMAN D. FRASER, Pres., Stock Exchange Bldg., Chicago.
D. R. FRASER, Vice-Pres., Stock Exchange Bldg., Chicago, Ill.
RALPH GATES, Sec'y and Treas., Stock Exchange Bldg., Chicago, Ill.
D. D. DRUMMOND, Supt., Oglesby, Ill.
GARDEN CITY SAND CO., 1201-1205 Security Bldg., Chicago, Ill., Sales Agents.
Capitalization, $400,000.
Capacity, 1,000 barrels per day.
Manufacturers AA Chicago brand Portland cement.
On Illinois Central and Chicago, Burlington & Quincy railroads.

CHICKAMAUGA CEMENT CO., Rossville, Ga.—
URIAH CUMMINGS, Pres., Akron, N. Y.
W. P. D. MOROSS, Treas. and Gen. Mgr., Rossville, Ga.
Capitalization, $150,000.
Manufacturers Chickamauga brand Portland cement.
Capacity, 300 barrels per day.
Manufacturers "Dixie" brand natural hydraulic cement.
Capacity, 500 barrels per day.
On Chattanooga, Rome & Southern railroad.

CLARK COUNTY CEMENT COMPANY, Sellersburg, Ind.—
F. LAWSON MOORES, Pres., Cincinnati, Ohio.
LEONARD KRANZ, Sec'y and Treas., Supt., Sellersburg, Ind.
W. K. SMITH, Dir., Sellersburg, Ind.
JACOB KRANZ, Dir., Sellersburg, Ind.
EMANUEL KRANZ, Dir., Sellersburg, Ind.
THE WESTERN CEMENT Co., Sales Agents, Louisville, Ky.
Capitalization, $30,000.
Capacity, 1,000 barrels a day.
Manufacturers Mason Choice Hammer and Trowel brand Louisville natural hydraulic cement.
On Pittsburg, Cincinnati, Chicago & St. Louis railroad.

CLINTON CEMENT COMPANY, P. O. Box 177, Pittsburg, Pa.
J. W. FRIEND, Pres., Pittsburg, Pa.
F. N. HOFFSTOT, Sec'y and Treas., Pittsburg, Pa.
T. W. FRIEND, Asst. Treas., Pittsburg, Pa.
A. B. HARRISON, Chemist, Pittsburg, Pa.
F. H. ZIMMERS, Engineer, Pittsburg, Pa.
Capitalization. See Note E, page 152.
Capacity, 150 barrels a day.
Manufacturers Clinton Portland cement.
On Pittsburg, Cincinnati, Chicago & St. Louis; Allegheny Valley; Pennsylvania; Pittsburg & Lake Erie; Pittsburg, Chartiers & Youghiogheny; Baltimore & Ohio, and Pittsburg & Castle Shannon railroads.

Electric Machinery—Keystone Electric Co., Erie, Pennsylvania.

COLORADO PORTLAND CEMENT COMPANY, Portland, Colo. Express and telegraph office, Florence, Colo. General office, Denver, Colo. See Note D, page 152.

W. H. JAMES, Pres., Denver, Colo.

W. F. GEDDES, Gen. Man., Denver, Colo.

Manufacturers Pike's Peak brand Portland cement.

On Denver & Rio Grande and Atchison, Topeka & Santa Fe railroads.

COLUMBIA PORTLAND CEMENT COMPANY, Cleveland, Ohio. See Note A, page 152.

Incorporators: H. E. Hackenberg, H. J. Davies, N. C. Cotabish, M. M. Zellers, C. T. Richmond, of Cleveland, Ohio; D. D. Dickey, of Pittsburg, Pa.; J. S. Crider, of Allegheny, Pa.

THE CONSOLIDATED CEMENT COMPANY, 509 Goldsmith Building, Milwaukee, Wis. See Notes B and E, page 152.

COPLAY CEMENT COMPANY, Allentown, Pa. Works at Coplay, Pa. See Notes B and E, page 152.

COMMERCIAL WOOD AND CEMENT Co., Sales Agents, 156 Fifth Ave., New York City.

JOHNSON & WILSON, Sales Agents, 150 Nassau St., New York City.

Manufacturers of Saylor's and Commercial brands of Portland cement, Anchor and Commercial brands Rosendale natural hydraulic cement.

On Lehigh Valley railroad.

CRESCENT CEMENT WORKS, Long Point, Hochelaga County, Canada. See Notes C and F, page 152.

THOS. M. MORGAN, Owner.

Manufacturers Crescent and Diamond brands of cement.

For sidewalks, curb and gutter and all concrete work requiring the **Highest Grade of Portland Cement. Excels** in fineness of grinding. We manufacture **one grade** only.

CHICAGO PORTLAND CEMENT COMPANY

CRESCENT WHITE LIME COMPANY, **Fayetteville, A**
See Note **A**, page 152.
On St. Louis & San Francisco railroad.

CROWN CEMENT COMPANY, Allegheny City, Pa. Works Bellaire, Ohio.
F. SWINNER, JR., Treas.
Not in operation.

CROWN PORTLAND CEMENT COMPANY, Lansdowne, M
See Note **A**, page 152.

CUMBERLAND AND POTOMAC CEMENT COMPAN
Cumberland, Md. See Note **A**, page 152.

CUMBERLAND HYDRAULIC CEMENT AND MANUFACTU ING COMPANY, P. O. Box 264, Cumberland, Md. See N **E**, page 152.
W. L. SPERRY, Supt.
Works burned July, 1900. New works now ready.
Manufacturers Cumberland natural hydraulic cement.
On Baltimore & Ohio, Cumberland & Pennsylvania, Georg Creek & Cumberland, Pennsylvania, and West Virginia Central Pittsburg railroads.

CUMBERLAND VALLEY CEMENT COMPANY, Washi ton, D. C. Works at Cumberland, Md. See Note **B**, page 1
S. DANA LINCOLN, Pres., Ralston Bldg., Washington, D.
Manufacturers Cumberland Valley brand natural hydrau cement.
On Baltimore & Ohio, Cumberland & Pennsylvania, Georg Creek & Cumberland, Pennsylvania, and West Virginia Central Pittsburg railroads.

THE CUMMINGS CEMENT COMPANY, Akron, N. Y.—
URIAH CUMMINGS, Pres., Akron, N. Y.
RAY P. CUMMINGS, Vice Pres., Akron, N. Y.
PALMER CUMMINGS, Gen. Mgr. and Treas., Akron, N. Y.
HOMER S. CUMMINGS, Sec'y, Stamford, Conn.
Capitalization, $300,000.
Manufacturers Storm King brand Portland cement.
Capacity, 500 barrels.
Manufacturers Roman Rock brand Portland cement.
Capacity, 500 barrels.
Manufacturers Obelisk brand natural hydraulic cement.
Capacity, 2,000 barrels.
On New York Central & Hudson River railroad.

DEFIANCE HYDRAULIC CEMENT WORKS, Defiance, Oh
WILHELM & GORMAN, Owners. See Note **F**, page 152.
FRANK WILHELM, Supt., Defiance, Ohio.
Capacity, 100 barrels a day.

Plasticon, a plastering cement. The Alabastine Co., Grand Rapids, Mi

Advantages of Advertising in Municipal Engineering Magazine

MUNICIPAL ENGINEERING is the largest and most influential magazine in the field it represents. It is read by more people directly interested in this field than any other publication.

It contains more advertisements of this kind of business than any other publication, because it is the best medium.

It is kept on file for reference by interested people in most of the cities and towns in the United States and Canada.

It does for its advertisers a kind of missionary work that can not be done for them so successfully in any other way.

It not only introduces them to all the people they want to know about them, and whom they can not reach through any other facilities, but it also keeps its advertisers advised by special bulletin of the opportunities for them to get business.

It is the special aim of the management of the magazine to help its advertisers, and it does this with all the facilities of a complete and well-established organization covering the entire country.

It makes advertising pay advertisers seeking business in its field.

If that is the kind of help you want, there is no reason why it should not be as profitable to you as to others.

Defiance Hydraulic Cement Works—Continued.

Manufacturers of Diamond brand natural hydrauli cement.

On Baltimore & Ohio railroad, Wabash railroad and Wabash Erie canal.

DETROIT PORTLAND CEMENT COMPANY, 614-615 Unio Trust Building, Detroit, Mich. Works under construction a Fenton, Mich.

E. H. PAINE, Pres., 9-15 Murray St., New York City.
B. STROH, Vice-Pres., Detroit, Mich.
H. J. PAXTON, Sec'y and Treas., Detroit, Mich.
H. M. SADLER, Asst. Treas., 9-15 Murray St., New York City
L. R. SHELLENBERGER, Supt. of Construction, Fenton, Mich
Capitalization.—See Note E, page 152.

On Chicago & Grand Trunk railroad.

DEXTER PORTLAND CEMENT COMPANY, Nazareth, Pa

GEO. E. BARTOL, Pres. and Dir., 258 The Bourse, Philadelphia, Pa.
CONRAD MILLER, Vice-Pres. and Dir., Nazareth, Pa.
JOSEPH BROBSTON, Sec'y and Treas., Nazareth, Pa.
WM. B. NEWBERRY, Gen. Mgr., Chemist and Dir., Nazareth
G. A. SCHNEEBELE, Dir., Nazareth, Pa.
DR. I. A. BACHMAN, Dir., Nazareth, Pa.
JOHN P. CROZER, Dir., Upland, Pa.
SAM'L FRENCH & Co., Sales Agents, Fourth and Callowhill Sts., Philadelphia.
Capitalization, $300,000.
Capacity, 800 to 900 barrels per day.
Manufacturers Dexter brand Portland cement and French's Rosendale brand natural hydraulic cement.

On Bangor & Portland branch of Delaware, Lackawanna & Western railroad.

THE DIAMOND PORTLAND CEMENT COMPANY, Perkins Ave., at C. & P. R. R. Cleveland, Ohio. Works at Middle Branch, Ohio.

Z. W. DAVIS, Pres., Perkins Ave., at C. & P. R. R., Cleveland, Ohio.
F. L. BOARDMAN, Vice-Pres., Perkins Ave., at C. & P. R. R., Cleveland, Ohio.
W. H. BOARDMAN, Treas., Perkins Ave., at C. & P. R. R., Cleveland, Ohio
L. A. REED, Sec'y, Perkins Ave., at C. & P. R. R., Cleveland, Ohio.
JAMES F. CLARK, Supt., Middle Branch, Ohio.
E. DAVIDSON, Chemist, Middle Branch, Ohio.

See F. L. Smidth & Co.'s Advertisement on Page 187.

DIAMOND

Portland Cement

A High-Grade Portland Cement Made from Rock for All Purposes

AVERAGE of all Cement Made and Tested at the Laboratory of

THE DIAMOND PORTLAND CEMENT CO.

DURING THE YEAR OF 1900

1 Day Neat,	403.75 Lbs.
7 Day Neat,	600.65 Lbs.
28 Day Neat,	669.68 Lbs.

SAND-CEMENT, - 3 to 1

7 Day Sand,	225.34 Lbs.
28 Day Sand,	293.00 Lbs.

FACTORY, MIDDLE BRANCH, OHIO

MAIN OFFICE, CLEVELAND, OHIO

The Diamond Portland Cement Co.

The Diamond Portland Cement Company—Continued.

Capitalization, $300,000.

Capacity, 750 barrels per day.

Manufacturers Diamond brand Portland cement.

On Cleveland, Canton & Southern railroad.

Average of all cement made and tested at the laboratory of the Diamond Portland Cement Company during the year 1900:

RESULTS OF TESTS.

Neat.		1 sand, 3 cement.	
1 day	403.75 lbs.		
7 days	600.65 "	7 days	225.34 lbs.
28 days	669.68 "	28 days	293.00 "

[*Manufacturer's Statement.*]

Diamond Portland cement is made from limestone and clay carefully selected to give the best proportions, and mixed by a most thorough process to produce perfectly homogeneous quality. It is burned in Dietzsch-Etagen ovens, which have proved to be the most perfect Portland cement kilns. They are in charge of experienced men who learned their business in some of the largest mills in Germany. The clinker is carefully selected and ground to such fineness that only five per cent. is left on a No. 100 sieve. Magnesia and sulphate of lime are practically absent from the raw materials and the finished cement. The results of tests given above show its great strength. A peculiar and recommending quality of Diamond cement is the gloss, resembling a coat of varnish, which forms on the upper surface of pats as they dry. Tests made of the cement all over the country confirm the results given above and endorse our claim that we supply a superior article and a Portland cement unexcelled in quality anywhere. Each day's production of finished cement is received in a bin by itself and not permitted to leave the works until pronounced by our experts to be faultless.

THE DURYEE PORTLAND CEMENT COMPANY, Montezuma, N. Y.

Geo. W. Duryee, Sec'y, Montezuma, N. Y.

Works burned; will rebuild.

On West Shore and New York Central & Hudson River railroads.

THE EDISON PORTLAND CEMENT COMPANY, Girard Bldg., Philadelphia, Pa. Works at Stewartsville, N. J.

Works under construction.

Wm. H. Shelmerdine, Pres., Philadelphia, Pa.

W. S. Mallory, Vice-Pres., Edison Laboratory, Orange, N. J.

W. S. Pilling, Treas., Philadelphia, Pa.

Theron I. Crane, Sec'y, Philadelphia, Pa.

Thomas A. Edison, Gen. Mgr., Orange, N. J.

E. A. Darling, Engineer of Construction, Stewartsville, N. J.

Capitalization, $11,000,000.

Capacity, 4,000 barrels a day.

On Delaware, Lackawanna & Western railroad.

Cement-Making Motors—Northern Electrical Mfg. Co., page 181.

[E]GYPTIAN PORTLAND CEMENT COMPANY, Detroit, Mich.
Works at Fenton, Mich., will be ready August, 1901.
Geo. A. Foster, Pres. and Dir., Detroit, Mich.
J. F. Williams, Vice-Pres. and Gen. Mgr., Detroit, Mich.
C. B. Shotwell, Sec'y and Dir., Detroit, Mich.
C. A. Wilson, Dir., Holly, Mich.
D. S. Frackelton, Dir., Flint, Mich.
Capitalization, $1,050,000.
Capacity, 1,000 barrels daily.
On Chicago & Grand Trunk railroad.

[E]LK RAPIDS PORTLAND CEMENT COMPANY, Elk Rapids, Mich.—
Oswald F. Jordan, Pres., Dir. and Gen. Mgr., Elk Rapids.
F. R. Williams, Vice-Pres. and Dir., Elk Rapids, Mich.
Frank B. Moore, Sec'y, Treas. and Dir., Elk Rapids, Mich.
S. B. Collins, Dir., Elk Rapids, Mich.
S. S. Olds, Dir., Jackson, Mich.
Thos. A. Wilson, Dir., Lansing, Mich.
M. B. Lang, Dir., Jackson, Mich.
E. M. Bunce, Supt., Elk Rapids, Mich.
Dr. W. Michaelis, Jr., Chemist, Elk Rapids, Mich.
Louis Quinby, Engr., Elk Rapids, Mich.
Capitalization, $400,000.
Capacity, 600 barrels a day.
Manufacturers Elk Rapids brand Portland cement.
On the Pere Marquette railroad and Lake Michigan.

[EM]PIRE PORTLAND CEMENT COMPANY, Warners, N. Y.—
Thomas Brown, Pres., Franklin, Pa.
J. E. French, Vice-Pres., New York City.
Chas. Miller, Treas., Franklin, Pa.
Chas. A. Lockard, Mgr., Warners, N. Y.
E. Bravender, Supt., Warners, N. Y.
C. E. Schauffler, Res. Mgr., 737 Monadnock Blk., Chicago.
Capital, $650,000.
Capacity, 150,000 barrels a year.
Manufacturers of Empire and Flint brands of Portland cement.
On New York Central & Hudson River railroad.

[FT.] SCOTT HYDRAULIC CEMENT COMPANY, Kansas City, Mo.
Works at Ft. Scott, Kans.
Walter S. Halliwell, Pres., Kansas City, Mo.
David P. Thomas, Vice-Pres. and Gen. Mgr., Ft. Scott, Kans.
John S. Taft, Sec'y.
Ft. Scott Cement Association, Sales Agents, Kansas City, Mo.

The Standard Plaster Co., Buffalo, N.Y., makes Calcined Plaster or Stucco

Ft. Scott Hydraulic Cement Company—Continued.

Capital, $100,000.

Capacity, 600 barrels in 10 hours.

Manufacturers Four Star brand Ft. Scott natural hydraulic cement.

On Missouri Pacific and Missouri, Kansas & Texas railroads.

FOWLER & PAY, Mankato, Minn. Works at Austin, Minn. See Note **F**, page 152.

Capacity, 1,000 barrels a day.

Manufacturers Austin brand natural hydraulic cement.

On Chicago Great Western and Chicago, Milwaukee & St. Paul railroads.

GEORGIAN BAY PORTLAND CEMENT COMPANY, Ltd., Owen Sound, Ontario, Canada. See Notes **B** and **E**, page 152.

Felix Guenther, Jr., Chemist, Owen Sound, Ontario, Can.

On Canadian Pacific and Grand Trunk railroads.

GERMAN-AMERICAN PORTLAND CEMENT COMPANY. Office. 1511 Marquette Building, Chicago, Ill. See Note **C**, page 152. Works at La Salle, Ill.

Carl Prussing, Pres. and Gen. Mgr., Hamburg, Germany.

Geo. C. Prussing, Vice-Pres. and Treas., Chicago.

Fritz Worm, Sec'y, La Salle, Ill.

Edward L. Cox, General Sales Agent.

A. B. Helbig, Supt., La Salle, Ill.

Dr. Otto Strebel, Chemist.

Walter Prussing, Chemist.

Capitalization, $450,000.

Capacity, 500 barrels per day.

Manufacturers Owl Cement brand Portland cement.

On Chicago, Burlington & Quincy; Chicago, Rock Island & Pacific, and Illinois Central railroads.

GLASGOW CEMENT WORKS—Removed to Locher, Va. See JAMES RIVER CEMENT WORKS.

THE GLENS FALLS PORTLAND CEMENT COMPANY, Glens Falls, N. Y.—

W. W. Maclay, Pres. and Dir., Glens Falls, N. Y.

Byron Lapham, Vice-Pres. and Dir., Glens Falls, N. Y.

Arthur W. Sherman, Treas. and Dir., Glens Falls, N. Y.

John E. Parry, Sec'y and Dir., Glens Falls, N. Y.

S. B. Goodman, Dir., Glens Falls, N. Y.

For Cement Machinery, address Earle C. Bacon, Havemeyer Bldg., N. Y.

The Glens Falls Portland Cement Company—Continued.

GEO. H. PARKS, Dir., Glens Falls, N. Y.
F. W. WAIT, Dir., Glens Falls, N. Y.
WM. E. SPIER, Glens Falls, N. Y.
COMMERCIAL WOOD AND CEMENT COMPANY, Sales Agents, 156 Fifth Ave., New York.

Capacity, 350 barrels a day.

Manufacturers Iron Clad and Victor brands Portland cement.

RESULTS OF TESTS OF IRON CLAD BRAND PORTLAND CEMENT.

Report of the Aqueduct Commission on Iron Clad cement delivered at New Croton Dam:

Briquette exposed.			Tensile strength. Pounds per square inch.		
Air. Hours.	Water. Days.	Total. Days.	Neat.	1 cement, 2 sand.	1 cement, 3 sand.
6	18 hrs.	1	176		
24	Boiling. 1 day.	2	538	246	
24	6	7	792	585	302
24	27	28	819	645	370
		MONTHS.			
24		3	876	757	463
24		6	861	682	496
24		12	955	684	561

Fineness (10,000 mesh) 5.3. Wire test: Light, 260.7; heavy, 371.2.

Signed. CHARLES S. GOWEN, Division Engineer.

It is Our Business

TO HELP

Your Business

IF YOU MAKE, SELL OR USE

CEMENT

'rite to us and we will tell you what we can do for you.

You ought to know

Municipal Engineering Co.

The Glens Falls Portland Cement Company—Continued.

Tests of Victor Portland cement, made by Department of Do(
New York City, briquettes seven days old:

Date of test, 1899.	Neat cement.	1 part cement, 2 parts sand.
Jan. 16.	533 lbs.	222 lbs.
Jan. 31.	470 "	203 "
....	531 "	290 "
April 12.	514 "	275 "
April 13.	550 "	274 "
May 4.	516 "	222 "
May 9	526 "	270 "
June 7.	522 "	242 "
June 22.	458 "	224 "
July 5.	512 "	247 "
July 24.	470 "	227 "
July 27.	486 "	258 "
Aug. 7.	499 "	217 "
Aug. 14.	463 "	192 "
Aug. 14.	463 "	192 "
Aug. 21.	445 "	204 "
Jan. 11.	587 "	256 "
Averages	502 lbs.	236 lbs.

Pats left in air, immersed as soon as hard, and steamed a
boiled, all passed the tests satisfactorily.

Time of set, 240 minutes.

[*Manufacturer's Statement.*]

Glens Falls "Iron Clad" cement is one of the most finely-ground ceme in the market, thus giving much more cement to the standard barrel of pounds than others. It is a slow-setting cement, usually taking four to hours. This is convenient for many purposes. It soon surpasses in stren quicker setting cements. Shipments of Iron Clad brand will be guai teed to stand 600 lbs. tensile strain neat briquettes one day in air and se days in water and 175 pounds one cement to three sand; to stand boi test: 85 per cent. to pass through No. 200 sieve and 96 per cent. thro No. 100 sieve. Cement barrels will be tight, of great strength, and form. Bags will be superior cotton and all weights guaranteed. The process of manufacture was chosen as giving absolute certainty regard proper mixture, thus insuring perfect uniformity of product. A compari of the results of tests shown above demonstrates the correctness of choice. The sand-carrying power of the cement, augmented by the extr fineness and uniformity of grinding, is shown by sand tests. The econ in the use of Iron Clad cement on this account is very marked.

The Glens Falls Portland Cement Company's Victor Portland cemen a favorite for concrete and masonry work. **Its fine** is guaranteed to be 90 per cent. through a **No. 200 s** and 97 per cent. through a No. 100 sieve, **and its ten** strength to be 500 pounds per square inch neat, one in air and six days in water, and 125 **pounds one** cement to three parts sand, same time. **These q** ties make it strong and economical, both **essentials** good engineering work. Boiling test is **also guarant** The Mechanicsville dam shows the high **quality of Vi** cement concrete. The portion **containing the w** gates was built of Victor cement one part, sand two, **broken** stone

Warren's "Puritan Brand" Coal Tar Cements. Warren Bros. Co., Bo

The Glens Falls Portland Cement Company—Continued.

The river was turned through these gates when concrete was but ten days old. After several heavy freshets and a year's time had passed coffer dams were put in and the work examined. The concrete was found practically uninjured, surfaces unchanged and corners sharp, though the bedrock of the river had been worn away until some of the piers overhung the resulting cavities in the bed of the stream several feet. Such tests are fortunately rare, but Victor cement shows its ability to stand them.

THE GLOBE CEMENT COMPANY.—See Note **C**, page 152.

Works at Sellersburg, Indiana.

HERMAN PREEFER, Pres., Sellersburg, Ind.

JOHN F. FRY, Vice-Pres., Sellersburg, Ind.

HARRY H. BEAN, Sec'y and Treas., Sellersburg, Ind.

WESTERN CEMENT COMPANY, Sales Agents, Louisville, Ky.

Capacity, 800 barrels daily.

Manufacturers Globe brand Louisville natural hydraulic cement.

On Pittsburg, Cincinnati, Chicago & St. Louis railroad.

GOLDEN RULE CEMENT COMPANY, Sellersburg, Ind.—

FRED. AUG. KOEHLER, Pres. and Dir., New Albany, Ind.

JACOB WEBER, Vice-Pres. and Dir., Louisville, Ky.

WM. SCHLEICHER, Sec'y and Treas., Dir. and Sup't., Sellersburg, Ind.

JOHN J. WEBER, Dir., Sellersburg, Ind.

ED. ALEXANDER, Engr., Sellersburg, Ind.

Capitalization, $15,000.

Capacity, 500 barrels a day.

Manufacturers Arm & Hammer brand Louisville natural hydraulic cement.

On Pittsburg, Cincinnati, Chicago & St. Louis railroad.

GOSHEN PORTLAND CEMENT COMPANY, Goshen, Ind.—

Works three and one-half miles northeast of Elkhart, Ind. See Note **A**, page 152.

GRAYLING PORTLAND CEMENT COMPANY. Works proposed.

C. A. CAMPBELL, 407 N. Linn St., W. Bay City, Mich.

WM. M. COURTIS, Cons. Engr., 412 Hammond Bldg., Detroit, Mich.

GREAT NORTHERN PORTLAND CEMENT COMPANY, 82-84 Griswold St., Detroit, Mich.

Works under construction at Baldwin, Mich. A New Jersey corporation.

GEO. ANDERSON, Pres. and Dir., Detroit, Mich.

CHAS. A. STRELINGER, Vice-Pres. and Dir., Detroit, Mich.

BURTON W. YATES, Second Vice-Pres. and Dir., Detroit, Mich.

HOWARD H. PARSONS, Chairman Ex. Com. and Dir., Detroit, Mich.

Use Keystone Generators in Cement Plants.—Keystone Electric Co.

Great Northern Portland Cement Company—Continued.

DAVID OGILVIE, Treas. and Dir., Detroit, Mich.
CHARLES B. PARSONS, Sec'y and Dir., Detroit, Mich.
LEMUEL H. FOSTER, Gen. Counsel and Dir., Detroit, Mich.
ALEXANDER B. SCULLY, Dir., Chicago, Ill.
WM. FILLINGHAM, Dir., East Orange, N. J.
ARTHUR E. BARLEY, Auditor, Detroit, Mich.
R. C. CARPENTER, Consulting Engr., Ithaca, N. Y.
Capitalization, $5,000,000.
Capacity, 1,000 barrels a day, increasing later.
On Pere Marquette and Chicago & West Michigan railroads.

HANOVER PORTLAND CEMENT COMPANY, Hanover, Ont. See Note A, page 152.
On Grand Trunk railroad.

HECLA PORTLAND CEMENT AND COAL MINING COMPANY, West Bay City, Mich. Soon to be incorporated.
U. R. LORANGER, 505 Crapo Blk., Bay City, Mich.

HELDERBERG CEMENT COMPANY, Albany, N. Y. Works at Howe's Cave, N. Y. See Notes D and E, page 152.
T. H. DUNMARY, Pres., Albany, N. Y.
FRED W. KELLEY, Vice-Pres., Albany, N. Y.
EDWARD L. PRUYN, Sec'y.
JAS. C. FARRELL, Treas., Albany, N. Y.
CHAS. H. RAMSEY, Asst. Gen. Mgr. and Gen. Sales Agent, 38 State St., Albany, N. Y.
Manufacturers Helderberg Portland cement.
Manufacturers Rosendale natural hydraulic cement.
On Delaware & Hudson Company's railroad.

THE HERCULES CEMENT COMPANY, Catasauqua, Pa. Works at Coplay, Pa.
JOHN CRAIG, Dir., Catasauqua, Pa.
F. M. HORN, Vice-Pres. and Dir., Catasauqua, Pa.
JOHN T. WILLIAMS, Treas. and Dir., Catasauqua, Pa.
EDWARD D. BOYER, Sec'y, Supt. and Dir., Catasauqua, Pa.
N. D. CORTRIGHT, JR., Dir., Catasauqua, Pa.
GEO. H. WILLIAMS, Dir., Catasauqua, Pa.
JAMES W. WEAVER, Pres. and Dir., Catasauqua, Pa.
A. R. FRY, Chemist, Coplay, Pa.
JAS. DOUGHERTY, Engr., Cementon, Pa.
HOUSTON & Co., Sales Agents, 26 Cortland St., New York City, N. Y.
BRYANT & KENT, Sales Agents, Boston, Mass.
ROBINSON & Co., Sales Agents, Philadelphia, Pa.
Capitalization, $75,000.

See advertisement of Fairbanks' Cement Testing Machine.

vl.

a year.
and Granite brands Portland ce-

Lehigh, Improved Rosendale and
ids natural hydraulic cement.

MPANY, Sellersburg, Ind.—
Dir., Pittsburg, Pa.
ind Dir., Sellersburg, Ind.
, Sellersburg, Ind.
Sellersburg, Ind.
ir., Cementville, Ind.
onville, Ind.
v Albany, Ind.

ay.
Shovel brand Louisville natural

:ago & St. Louis railroad.
l St. and Pennsylvania railroad,
descriptions of works.
ind and Samson brands Portland

IENT COMPANY, Cement, Ga.

ENT COMPANY, Chicago, Ill.

TY, Cement Department, No. 1060
g., Chicago, Ill.
M. Hagar, Mgr., No. 1060 The
, Chicago, Ill.
oquist, Supt., South Chicago, Ill.
ll, Sales Agent, No. 140 Nassau
v York.
Wheelock, Sales Agent, Cooper
Denver, Colo.
gent, Havana, Cuba.
curity Bldg., St. Louis, Mo.

Engineering Magazine

bscription Price, $2.00 Per Year.

The Illinois Steel Company—Continued.

Capitalization.—No separate capitalization for cement department.

Manufacturers Universal brand Portland cement.

Manufacturers Steel brand cement (pozzuolana).

Capacity of works for each brand, 1,000 barrels a day.

The following tests of Universal brand cement were made by Robert W. Hunt & Co.:

Fineness on 100 sieve.......................................93.90
Fineness on 200 sieve.......................................75.50
Initial set ....2 hours, 5 minutes
Final set ....6 hours, 50 minutes
Boiling and cold water tests, O. K.
Specific gravity, 3.216.

Sample tested.	24 hours.	7 days.	28 days.	3 months.
Neat............	557	727	854	1023
Cement 1, sand 3	130	247	385	391

(Above figures are averages of five briquettes.)

[*Manufacturer's Statement.*]

Steel cement has been on the market for five years, and has come to be recognized by architects and engineers as a most reliable cement for work in moist locations, such as concrete or foundation construction beneath the surface of the ground or water. It is especially adapted to foundations of street pavements, heavy buildings and machinery foundations, conduit and sewer construction. It possesses peculiar qualities that impart unusual toughness and homogeneity to concrete made therefrom, and its exceeding fineness gives it great capacity for carrying sand and stone. Steel cement, in common with all slag or pozzuolana cements, is not suitable for sidewalks, floors or work exposed to dry air or subject to attrition. The care and scientific accuracy exercised in the selection of the slag, and the precise methods employed in its treatment make this, admittedly, the best slag cement manufactured, and investigation by the United States government engineers has demonstrated that it is more uniform than any cement manufactured from natural deposits.

In order that their field should not be bounded by the limitations of Steel cement, the Illinois Steel Company in 1896 undertook an extensive series of experiments with a view to manufacturing from blast furnace slag a true Portland cement that would compete in every respect with the best brands of foreign and American Portlands, and especially in those classes of work for which Steel cement was not adapted. These experiments were successful in the highest degree, and in 1900 the company placed on the market Universal Portland cement, which, as its name implies, is suitable for all purposes. This is a true Portland cement, its method of manufacture, chemical composition, fineness and specific gravity being strictly in accordance with the definitions of the most prominent cement authorities in the United States and Europe. On account of the entirely artificial character of the process employed, the mixtures are under complete control and most remarkable uniformity is obtained in the finished product.

In 1900 the new cement plant at the south works of the Illinois Steel Company at South Chicago was completed, at a cost of $500,000. At this plant both Steel and Universal Portland cements are manufactured. The

Parkhurst Combined Curb and Gutter. Apply to D. C. Buntin, Indianapolis

SOUTH CEMENT PLANT

ILLINOIS STEEL COMPANY

SOUTH CHICAGO, ILLINOIS

---

niversal Portland

For sidewalks, floors, and all work requiring the highest possible grade of Portland Cement.

teel Cement . . .

For concrete, foundation and masonry construction.

The Illinois Steel Company—Continued.

location of this plant admits of direct shipment by rail or water, and as it has only the latest and most improved machinery, low prices, high quality and quick shipment are insured. The cement plant at the north works of the Illinois Steel Company, started in 1895, is devoted exclusively to the manufacture of Steel cement. The total output of both plants is 50,000 barrels per month, divided about equally between the two products.

IMPERIAL CEMENT COMPANY, Ltd., Owen Sound, Ont. See Note B, page 152.

IMPERIAL PORTLAND CEMENT COMPANY, 1114 Real Estate Trust Bldg., Philadelphia, Pa. Works (under construction) at Nazareth, Pa.

F. H. D. BANKS, Pres., Real Estate Trust Bldg., Philadelphia, Pa.
JEROME KEELEY, Vice-Pres. and Dir. and Chemist, 421 Chestnut St., Philadelphia, Pa.
J. CHESTER WILSON, Sec'y and Dir., Real Estate Trust Bldg., Philadelphia, Pa.
JOHN D. NEWBOLD, Dir., Norristown, Pa.
JAMES W. SHEPP, Dir., 723 Chestnut St., Philadelphia, Pa.
JOHN T. DYER, Dir., Room A, Harrison Bldg., Philadelphia.
R. O. BEITEL, Dir., Nazareth, Pa.
GEO. W. LAUB, Dir., Nazareth, Pa.
WM. H. PARSONS, Dir., Phœnixville, Pa.

Capitalization, $400,000.
Capacity, 1,000 barrels a day.
Manufacturers Imperial brand Portland cement.

On Bangor & Portland railroad.

INDIANA CEMENT COMPANY, Charlestown, Ind. See Note B, page 152.

WESTERN CEMENT COMPANY, Sales Agents, Louisville, Ky.
Manufacturers Lion brand Louisville natural hydraulic cement.

On Baltimore & Ohio railroad.

INDIANA PORTLAND CEMENT COMPANY, Majestic Bldg., Detroit, Mich. (Offices will shortly be removed to Indianapolis, Ind.) Factories at Milford, Kosciusko County, Indiana, proposed; Milltown, Harrison County, Indiana, proposed.

NEIL MCMILLAN, Pres. and Dir., Detroit, Mich.
PRESTON F. MILES, Vice-Pres. and Dir., Milford, Ind.
GEORGE JOHNSTON, Treas. and Dir., Detroit, Mich.
VANTON O. FOULK, Sec'y and Att'y and Dir., Detroit, Mich.
JOHN H. SMEDLEY, Dir., Detroit, Mich.
EDWIN T. ALLEN, Dir., Detroit, Mich.
R. H. EVANS, Dir., Detroit, Mich.
KENNETH K. MCLAREN, Dir., Jersey City, N. J.

Capitalization, $5,000,000.

Proposed capacity of both mills, 6,000 barrels a day.

IOLA PORTLAND CEMENT COMPANY, Iola, Kans.—
SHELDON H. BASSETT, Pres., 827 Marquette Bldg., Chicago, Ill.
JOHN T. HOLMES, Treas., Detroit, Mich.
OSCAR GERLACH, Chemist.
SHELDON H. BASSETT, Sales Agent, Marquette Bldg., Chicago.
Capitalization. See Note E, page 152.
Capacity, 4,500 barrels a day.
Manufacturers Iola brand Portland cement.
On Atchison, Topeka & Santa Fe and Missouri Pacific railroads.

IROQUOIS PORTLAND CEMENT COMPANY, West Madison and Highland Aves., Cleveland, Ohio. Works under construction at Caledonia, N. Y.

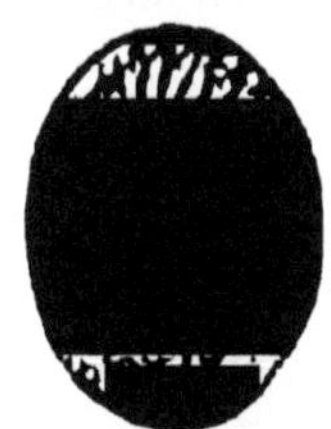

C. T. RICHMOND, Vice-Pres. and Dir., Cleveland, Ohio.
H. J. DAVIES, Sec'y and Dir., Cleveland, Ohio.
H. E. HACKENBERG, Treas. and Dir., Cleveland, Ohio.
W. V. HAMILTON, Dir. and Gen. Mgr., Caledonia, N. Y.
S. T. WELLMAN, Dir., Cleveland, Ohio.
A. W. SMITH, Dir., Cleveland, Ohio.
E. G. TILLOTSON, Dir., Cleveland, Ohio.
H. A. TREMAINE, Dir., Fostoria, Ohio.
D. D. DICKEY, Dir., Pittsburg, Pa.
JAMES VIRDIN, Dir., Dover, Del.
M. J. HOLLINGER, Supt., Caledonia, N. Y.
C. S. RICHARDS, Chemist, Caledonia, N. Y.
WELLMAN-SEAVER ENGR. COMPANY, Engrs., Cleveland, Ohio.
Capitalization, $250,000.
Capacity, 375 barrels a day.
Manufacturers Iroquois brand Portland cement.
On Erie, Genesee & Wyoming, Lehigh Valley, and New York Central & Hudson River railroads.

[*Manufacturer's Statement.*]

Iroquois Portland Cement Company is a Delaware corporation, with principal offices at Cleveland, Ohio, and works at Caledonia, N. Y. The lands owned by this company consist of about 400 acres of marl and clay deposits beginning one mile east from Caledonia, N. Y., and extending along the tracks of the N. Y. C. & H. R. R. R. and the Lehigh Valley R. R. for a distance of about two miles. The marl comprising this deposit has been thoroughly sampled and analyzed at all points, and consists of a fine white carbonate of lime, practically free from all impurities, being especially free from magnesia, which, on an average, amounts to only about three-tenths of one per cent. The deposit is so near the surface as to require little or no stripping, and has an average depth of eight feet. The deposit of clay is free from pyrites, sand and grit, and contains the proper ratio of

Use Keystone Motors in Cement Plants.—Keystone Electric Co.

Iroquois Portland Cement Company—Continued.
alumina to silica to insure a slow-setting cement. The cement is guaranteed to stand the usual standard tests, and to be equal in all respects to that of the best brands. It is especially adapted for work where it is essential that there be no shrinkage or expansion.

JAMES RIVER CEMENT WORKS, Locher, Rockbridge Co., Va.
Telegraph and Express Office, Glasgow, Va.
CHAS. H. LOCHER, Pres., Locher, Va.
H. O. LOCHER, Sec'y and Treas., Locher, Va.
EBEN LOCHER, Gen. Mgr. and Supt., Locher, Va.
CHAS. M. BLACKFORD, Dir., Lynchburg, Va.
JOHN D. HORSLEY, Dir., Lynchburg, Va.
W. T. RUCKER, Chemist, Locher, Va.
ADAMS BROS-PAYNES COMPANY, Sales Agents, Lynchburg, Va.
Capitalization, $30,000.
Capacity, 200 barrels a day.
Manufacturers James River brand natural hydraulic cement.
On Norfolk & Western and Chesapeake & Ohio railroads.

KANSAS CITY & FT. SCOTT CEMENT COMPANY, Kansas City, Mo. Works at Ft. Scott, Kans.
C. A. BROCKETT, Pres., Kansas City, Mo.
HOWARD MCCUTCHEN, Sec'y and Treas., Kansas City, Mo.
P. R. JORDAN, Dir., Kansas City, Mo.
CHAS. H. GARDINER, Supt., Ft. Scott, Kans.
H. GARDINER, Chemist, Ft. Scott, Kans.
CHAS. WAIDELICH, Engr., Ft. Scott, Kans.
FT. SCOTT CEMENT ASSOCIATION, Sales Agents, Kansas City, Mo.
Capital, $50,000.
Capacity, 700 barrels a day.
Manufacturers Double Star brand Ft. Scott hydraulic cement.
On Kansas City, Ft. Scott & Memphis; Missouri, Kansas & Texas, and Missouri Pacific railroads.

THE KENTUCKY & INDIANA CEMENT COMPANY, Jeffersonville, Ind. Works at Watson, Ind.
W. H. COOK, Pres. and Dir., Indianapolis, Ind.
C. B. ROUS, Sec'y, Treas. and Dir., Jeffersonville, Ind.
J. C. ROUS, Supt. and Dir., Jeffersonville, Ind.
W. F. CURRYER, Dir., Indianapolis, Ind.
H. L. ROUS, Dir., Frankfort, Ind.
WESTERN CEMENT COMPANY, Sales Agent, Louisville, Ky.
Capital, $65,000.
Capacity, 1,500 barrels daily.

For Cement Machinery, address Earle C. Bacon, Havemeyer Bldg., N. Y.

The Kentucky & Indiana Cement Company—Continued.

Manufacturers Eagle brand Louisville natural hydraulic cement.

On Baltimore & Ohio Southwestern railroad.

THE KINDERHOOK PORTLAND CEMENT COMPANY, Indianapolis, Ind. See Note **A**, page 152.

Incorporators, C. A. Kenyon, F. A. Joss and H. G. Branden. Capital, $2,500; authorized, $900,000.

KNICKERBOCKER CEMENT COMPANY, Poughkeepsie, N. Y. Reported manufacturers of pozzuolana. See Note **B**, page 152.

WM. KRAUSE & SONS CEMENT COMPANY, 1623 North Fifth St., Philadelphia, Pa. District Warehouse, 2119 American St., Philadelphia, Pa. Works, Martin's Creek, Pa. See Note **B**, page 152. (Application has been made for change of name to Martin's Creek Portland Cement Company.)

BERNARD J. KRAUSE, Pres.
WM. KRAUSE, Vice-Pres.
D. C. MURTHER, Sec'y.
F. B. BANKS, Gen. Mgr.
CABLE, THORN & CO., Sales Agents, New York City.
WM. WIRT CLARKE & SON, Agents, 11 Gay St. S., Baltimore, Md.

Capitalization—See Note **E**, page 152.
Capacity, 500 barrels per day.
Manufacturers Krause brand Portland cement.

On Bangor & Portland and Pennsylvania railroads.

THE LAKEFIELD PORTLAND CEMENT COMPANY, Owen Sound, Ont., Can. See Note **A**, page 152. Works under construction at Lakefield, near Petersboro, Ont., Can.

Incorporators: John M. Kilbourn, Rob't P. Butchart, W. H. E. Brevender, F. H. Kilbourn, H. B. Smith.

THE LAWRENCE CEMENT COMPANY, No. 1 Broadway, New York City, Harrison Bldg., Philadelphia, Pa. Works at Eddyville, Hickory Bush, Binnewater, N. Y.

E. R. ACKERMAN, Pres., No. 1 Broadway, New York City.
HENRY McMURTRY, Gen. Supt.

Manufacturers Hoffman, Shield and Improved Shield brands Rosendale natural hydraulic cement.
Capitalization. See Note **E**, page 152.

On the Wallkill Valley railroad and Rondout Creek (Hudson River).

DYCKERHOFF PORTLAND CEMENT

On application, E. Thiele, 99 John Street, New York, will mail to you a letter explaining the defect most frequently occurring in Portland Cement, and stating good reasons why for important work the Dyckerhoff brand should be selected, notwithstanding its higher price.

THE LAWRENCE CEMENT COMPANY OF PENNSYLVANIA, 1 Broadway, New York. Works at Siegfried, Pa.
Capitalization. See Note **E**, page 152.
T. B. Osborne, Office Sales Agent, No. 1 Broadway, New York.
C. D. Stout, Office Sales Agent, No. 1 Broadway, New York.
The Frank E. Morse Co., Exchange Sales Agents, 17 State St., New York.
Manufacturers Dragon, Paragon, Monarch brands Portland cement.
On Central Railroad of New Jersey.

LAWRENCEVILLE CEMENT COMPANY, Binnewater, N. Y.—
W. N. Beach, Pres., No. 26 Cortlandt St., New York.
U. C. Brewer, Sec'y, No. 26 Cortland St., New York.
D. A. Barnhart, Supt., Binnewater, N. Y.
Berry & Ferguson, Sales Agents, Boston, Mass.
Smith, Green Company, Sales Agents, Worcester, Mass.
Capitalization. See Note **E**, page 152.
Capacity, 2,500 barrels per day.
Manufacturers Beach's Rosendale brand natural hydraulic cement.
On Walkill Valley railroad.

LEHIGH PORTLAND CEMENT COMPANY, Allentown, Pa. Works at West Coplay and Ormrod, Lehigh Co., Pa.
Harry C. Trexler, Pres. and Dir., Allentown, Pa.
George Ormrod, Vice-Pres. and Dir., Allentown, Pa.
E. M. Young, Treas. and Dir., Allentown, Pa.
Alexander S. Shimer, Dir., Allentown, Pa.
James K. Mosser, Dir., Allentown, Pa.
George G. Sykes, Sec'y, Allentown, Pa.
Charles A. Matcham, Supt., Allentown, Pa.
Capitalization. See Note **E**, page 152.
Capacity, 4,000 barrels daily.
Manufacturers Lehigh brand Portland cement.
On Ironton railroad, branch of Lehigh Valley railroad.

Combined Curb and Gutter—Warren Bros. Co., 148 Federal St., Boston

Lehigh Portland Cement Company—Continued.

[*Manufacturer's Statement.*]

The Lehigh Portland Cement Company have an annual production of 1,500,000 barrels of Portland cement. Their works are located at Ormrod and West Coplay, in the Lehigh Valley, and are equipped with the most modern and up to date machinery. Their brand "Lehigh" is well established and known to the trade as one of the highest grades of Portland cement manufactured. The government is a large user of this brand of cement, and the testimonials given this company by government engineers testify to the high quality and satisfactory results obtained from Lehigh Portland cement. The company enjoys a large demand for their cement throughout the United States, and during the past year have made large shipments abroad. The Kelley Island Lime and Transport Company, of Cleveland, Ohio, are the distributers for the Lehigh Portland cement throughout the west and south, and will cheerfully answer all correspondence relative to this brand in their territory.

LOUISVILLE CEMENT COMPANY, 331 W. Main St., Louisville, Ky. Works at Speeds and Watson, Ind., and Louisville, Ky.

J. B. Speed, Pres., Louisville, Ky.

Western Cement Company, Sales Agents, Louisville, Ky.

Capitalization. See Note E, page 152.

Capacity, 5,000 barrels per day.

Manufacturers Speed's "Star" brand, Louisville natural hydraulic cement, J. Hulme "Star" brand, "Horse Shoe" slow setting, "S*S" brand, slow setting.

On Pittsburg, Cincinnati, Chicago & St. Louis railroad (Speed's Mill).

On Louisville & Nashville; Pittsburg, Cincinnati, Chicago & St. Louis; Chicago, Indianapolis & Louisville; Baltimore & Ohio Southwestern; Cleveland, Cincinnati, Chicago & St. Louis; Chesapeake & Ohio; Illinois Central; Louisville, Henderson & St. Louis; Southern, and Louisville, Evansville & St. Louis railroads (Louisville mill).

On Baltimore & Southwestern railroad (Watson mill).

LEHIGH BRAND

Is strongly recommended and used by United States Government Engineers, Architects, Builders and Contractors.

GUARANTEED FOR UNIFORMITY, STRENGTH AND DURABILITY.

Write for Catalogues.

Lehigh Portland Cement Co.

Capacity, 4,000 barrels daily. ALLENTOWN, PA.

THE LUPTON PORTLAND CEMENT COMPANY, Lupton, Mich. See Note A, page 152.

GEO. T. STANLEY, Pres., Lupton, Mich.
EDWARD A. WORTHINGTON, Vice-Pres. and Treas., Chicago.
WALTER HIGGS, Sec'y, Chicago, Ill.
WM. C. EDGAR, Asst. Sec'y, Chicago, Ill.
Authorized capitalization, $1,250,000.
Proposed capacity, 1,200 barrels a day.

MANKATO CEMENT WORKS, Mankato, Minn. See Note F, page 152.

P. H. CARNEY, Lessee and Mgr., Mankato, Minn.
H. E. CARNEY, Asst. Mgr. and Sec'y, Mankato, Minn.
P. H. JORDAN, Supt., Mankato, Minn.
Capacity, 60 barrels per hour.
Manufacturers Mankato and U. S. G. brands natural hydraulic cement.

On Chicago, St. Paul, Minneapolis & Omaha; Chicago & Northwestern; Chicago, Milwaukee & St. Paul, and Chicago Great Western railroads.

MANLIUS LIME, PLASTER AND CEMENT COMPANY, Manlius, N. Y. See Note A, page 152.

MARQUETTE PORTLAND CEMENT COMPANY, LaSalle, Ill. Works in Deer Park Glen. See Notes B and E, page 152.

DICKINSON CEMENT CO., Sales Agents, 931 Marquette Bldg., Chicago, Ill.

On Chicago, Burlington & Quincy railroad.

MARYLAND CEMENT COMPANY, Builders' Exchange, Baltimore, Md. Works at Sparrow's Point, Md. See Note D, page 152.

FRANK H. SLOAN, Pres., Baltimore, Md.
ROBERT C. COLE, Sec'y, Baltimore, Md.
B. G. BOILLEAU, Treas. and Gen. Mgr., Baltimore, Md.
JOHN L. GIVEN, Engr., Baltimore, Md.
WM. WIRT CLARKE & SON, 115 Gay St., Baltimore, Md., Sales Agents.
Capitalization. See Note E, page 152.
Manufacturers Penn, Toltec, Patapsco and Rhinoceros brands Portland cement (pozzuolana).

ANY QUESTION RELATING TO CEMENT
WILL BE ANSWERED ON REQUEST. IT IS A PART OF OUR BUSINESS TO KNOW ALL ABOUT CEMENT
MUNICIPAL ENGINEERING CO.

GENERAL SALES AGENTS

Wyandotte Portland Cement

FOR SIDEWALKS

BEST COLOR OF ANY CEMENT ON THE MARKET, PROVED BY MANY MILES OF THE BEST SIDEWALKS IN THE COUNTRY

GUARANTEED EQUAL TO ANY

A HIGH-GRADE PORTLAND CEMENT

EXTENSIVELY IN USE, STRONGLY INDORSED BY LEADING CONTRACTORS AND USED BY A NUMBER OF PORTLAND CEMENT COMPANIES IN THE CONSTRUCTION OF THEIR OWN PLANTS. FOR INFORMATION AND PRICES WRITE TO

F. B. HOLMES & CO., DETROIT, MICH.

MICHIGAN ALKALI COMPANY, Wyandotte, Mich.—

EDWIN FORD, Pres., Wyandotte, Mich.
J. B. FORD, JR., Vice-Pres. and Gen. Mgr., Wyandotte, Mich.
E. L. FORD, Sec'y and Treas., Wyandotte, Mich.
O. S. BUTTON, Chemist, Wyandotte, Mich.
F. B. HOLMES & Co., Gen. Sales Agents, Hammond Bldg., Detroit, Mich.

Capitalization, $2,500,000.
Capacity, 500 barrels a day.
Manufacturers Wyandotte brand Portland cement.

On Michigan Central, Lake Shore and Michigan Southern, and Detroit & Lima Northern railroads, and the Detroit river.

RESULTS OF TESTS.—The following tests were made (1) by H. C. Bailey, cement tester, city of Chicago, report dated February 13, 1901, and (2) by R. H. McCormick, city engineer, Detroit, Mich., report dated February 15, 1901. In the latter case no tamping was done in making briquettes.

TENSILE STRENGTH.

	Neat. (1)	Neat. (2)	1 cement to 3 sand. (1)	1 cement to 3 sand. (2)
7 days	618	597	351	224
28 days	859	733	481	343

Fineness.

	(1)	(2)
On No. 100 sieve	96.2 per cent.	98 per cent.

[*Manufacturer's Statement.*]

F. B. Holmes & Co., general sales agents for Wyandotte Portland cement, present the product on its merits. The use of the cement for more than a year and a half on public work in Chicago, in Detroit and other cities of Michigan, including sidewalks, and in foundations for machinery, has been eminently satisfactory. The thorough manner in which the manufacture of the cement is conducted, the uniformity and high quality of the raw materials insure a uniform product of the high quality shown by the above tests. Fifty thousand barrels of Wyandotte cement have been used in public work in the city of Chicago; 6,000 barrels were used in foundations for machinery in Edward Ford plate glass works, Toledo; 4,000 barrels in sidewalk work in Wyandotte and Rochester, Mich.; 4,000 barrels in foundations for Detroit water-works pumps; 5,000 barrels in all by the Detroit board of public works; 3,500 barrels in court-house, Detroit, mosaic work; large quantities in constructing several of the large new cement plants in Michigan and Indiana. A booklet telling what is said about Wyandotte cement by those who have used it will be sent on request to the office, Hammond building, Detroit, Mich.

MICHIGAN PORTLAND CEMENT COMPANY, Coldwater, Mich. Works at Coldwater and Quincy, Mich.—

L. W. WING, Pres., Mgr. and Dir., Coldwater, Mich.
S. H. BASSETT, Vice-Pres. and Dir., Chicago, Ill.
W. L. HOLMES, Treas. and Dir., Detroit, Mich.

See illustrated advertisement of Fairbanks' Cement Testing Machine.

E. R. Root, Sec'y, Coldwater, Mich.
L. B. Taylor, Dir., Adrian, Mich.
J. T. Holmes, Dir., Detroit, Mich.
J. C. Smallshaw, Supt. of Factories, Coldwater, Mich.
H. E. Brown, Chief Chemist, Coldwater, Mich.
F. I. Post, Asst. Chemist, Coldwater, Mich.
H. F. Dibbert, Chief Engr., Coldwater, Mich.
P. Tafel, Chief Chemist, Quincy, Mich.
A. Heyman, Asst. Chemist, Quincy, Mich.
J. L. Clark, Chief Engr., Quincy, Mich.
S. H. Bassett, Mgr. Sales Dept., 827 Marquette Bldg., Chicago, Ill.

Capitalization, $2,500,000.

Manufacturers Wolverine and Eclipse brands Portland cement.

Capacity, 1,500 barrels of each brand per day.

On Lake Shore & Michigan Southern railway.

THOS. MILLEN & SONS, Wayland, N. Y. See Notes B and F, page 152.

A. J. McBean & Co., Agents, Chicago, Ill.

Manufacturers Wayland brand Portland cement.

On Delaware, Lackawanna & Western; Erie & Pittsburg; Shawmut & Northern railroads.

L. M. Wing, Pres. S. H. Bassett, Vice-Pres. Wm. L. Holmes, Treas. E. R. Root, Sec.

Michigan Portland Cement Co.

MANUFACTURERS OF

High-Grade Portland Cement

General Sales Offices ... Marquette Building,
CHICAGO, ILL., U. S. A.

Factories—Branch County, Mich.

Our "Wolverine" and "Eclipse" brands of American Portland Cement are being extensively placed on the market under the Guarantee of this Company, as to their being equal, if not superior, to any other grade of American or foreign Portland cement; that they will stand all tests to which Portland cement is usually subjected—both being particularly adapted for sidewalk purposes: they are uniform, finely ground and with sand-carrying qualities unsurpassed.

It affords us pleasure to refer to the fact that they were largely used on the drainage canal at Chicago, where each and every car had to undergo rigid inspection and tests, and our results were highly satisfactory as compared to the other cements offered for use on that work.

We desire our extensive facilities and experience to redound to the benefit of our customers in every way, and any information or suggestions we can offer them for the profitable and economical handling of Portland cement, will be cheerfully furnished on request. We constantly carry in stock a heavy quantity of aged cement, which places us in position at any and all times to make prompt shipment.

MILWAUKEE CEMENT COMPANY, No. 7 Plankinton Bldg., Milwaukee, Wis.

SAMUEL MARSHALL, Pres. and Dir., 7 Plankinton Bldg., Milwaukee, Wis.
J. R. BERTHELET, Vice-Pres., Supt. and Dir., 7 Plankinton Bldg., Milwaukee, Wis.
JOHN JOHNSTON, Treas. and Dir., 7 Plankinton Bldg., Milwaukee, Wis.
GEO. S. BARTLETT, Sec'y, 7 Plankinton Bldg., Milwaukee, Wis.
B. K. MILLER, JR., Dir., 7 Plankinton Bldg., Milwaukee, Wis.
F. A. HINMAN, Dir., 7 Plankinton Bldg., Milwaukee, Wis.
HOWARD GREENE, Dir., 7 Plankinton Bldg., Milwaukee, Wis.
WM. PLANKINTON, Dir., 7 Plankinton Bldg., Milwaukee, Wis.
Capitalization, $350,000.
Capacity, 3,800 barrels daily.
Manufacturers Keystone brand natural hydraulic cement.
On Chicago, Milwaukee & St. Paul; Chicago & Nortwestern, and Wisconsin Central railroads.

Analysis of the cement shows:

Silica	23.16%
Alumina	6.33
Iron Oxide	1.71
Lime	38.08
Magnesia	18.38
Potash and Soda	5.27
Carbonic Acid, Water, etc.	7.07

[*Manufacturer's Statement.*]

The Milwaukee Cement Company, founded in 1875, has the unequaled resources of the largest and deepest-faced quarries known to this country and two mills of 1,500 and 2,500 barrels daily capacity, filled with the latest improved machinery. All of the railroads entering Milwaukee are connected to both plants by several miles of sidetracks owned and controlled by the company. Of the many millions of barrels of this cement used throughout the middle and western states in different constructions, all stand as monuments to its quality. The company is recognized as one of the most substantial and progressive of its kind, always in line for improvement and advancing the proper use of this important material. Its management takes pleasure in extending a cordial invitation to all engineers, architects, contractors, and others interested, to visit the mills, as a thorough investigation will convince the most skeptical of the natural advantages possessed by this company, of its intelligent and up to date manufacture, assuring the quality of its product as one of the best of natural hydraulic cements.

MONOLITH PORTLAND CEMENT COMPANY, Ltd., Battle Creek, Mich. Works at Bristol, Ind., under construction.
GEN. JAS. S. CLARKSON, Pres., New York City.
LYCURGUS McCOY., Vice-Pres., Battle Creek, Mich.
HARRIE T. HARVEY, Sec'y, Battle Creek, Mich.

The Keystone Electrical Transmission is Best for Cement Ma[illegible]

Milwaukee Hydraulic Cement

"KEYSTONE" BRAND

DAILY
CAPACITY
4,000
BARRELS

Shipping
Facilities
Unsurpassed
. . .
Supply
Unlimited

In successful use for the past twenty-five years in most of the important constructions, Government, Municipal and Private, in the middle and western states. The accepted standard of the U. S. Government.

MILWAUKEE : CEMENT : COMPANY

ROOM 7, PLANKINTON BUILDING,

MILWAUKEE —————————— WISCONSIN

Monolith Portland Cement Company—Continued.

WM. M. WHITE, Treas., Chicago, Ill.
C. L. CARMAN, Gen. Supt., Bristol, Ind.
Capitalization, $1,500,000.
Capacity, 1,000,000 barrels a year.
Manufacturers Monolith brand Portland cement.
On Lake Shore & Michigan Southern railroad.

NATIONAL CEMENT COMPANY, 15 Second National Bank Building, Pittsburg, Pa. See Note A, page 152.
GEO. W. HACKETT, Sec'y.
W. J. PRENTICE, Mgr.

NATIONAL PORTLAND CEMENT COMPANY, Ltd., Toronto, Ont. See Note A, page 152.
WM. F. COWHORN, Dir., Jackson, Mich.
P. W. STANHOPE, Dir., Toronto, Ont.
WM. PINKERTON, Dir., Toronto, Ont.
ALBERT CARMAN, Dir., Stratford, Ont.
R. H. McWILLIAMS, Dir., Owen Sound, Ont.

NAZARETH CEMENT COMPANY, Nazareth, Pa. See Note E, page 152.

F. A. STRATTON, Pres., Mt. Vernon, N. Y.
H. L. MERRY, Vice-Pres., 100 Broadway, N. Y.
GEO. F. COFFIN, Treas. and Sec'y, Easton, Pa.
P. H. HAMPSON, Mgr. and Asst. Treas., Nazareth, Pa.
ELVIN U. LEH, Supt., Nazareth, Pa.
W. ELWOOD SNYDER, Chemist, Nazareth, Pa.
CHARLES WARNER CO., Sales Agents, Wilmington, Del., Philadelphia, Pa., 66 Maiden Lane, N. Y.
Capacity, 1,400 barrels a day.
Manufacturers of Nazareth brand Portland cement.
On Bangor & Portland branch of Delaware, Lackawanna & Western railroad.

RESULTS OF TESTS.—The following results of test are published: In the tables (1) gives the results of tests at the laboratory of the Philadelphia water-works, G. S. Webster, chief engineer. Chas. H. Clifton, engineer in charge of tests, April, 1900; (2) by Booth, Garrett & Blair, Philadelphia, December, 1899; (3) at engineer's office, United States Army, Fort Delaware, Del., F. C. Warner, assistant engineer, February, 1900; (4) Lathbury & Spackman, 1619 Filbert street, Philadelphia, Pa., December 5, 1899, *et seq.;* (5) ditto, August 11, 1899, (6) ditto, February 6, 1900, *et seq.;* (7) Dr. Henry Froehling, 17 South Twelfth street, Richmond, Va., March, 1900.

Fineness.	No. 50 Sieve.	No. 100 Sieve.	No. 200 Sieve.
(1)	100. per cent	96.7 per cent	81. per cent.
(2)	99.9 "	98.6 "	83. "
(3)	100. "	99.0 "	"
(4)	"	99.3 "	87.2 "
(5)		97.4 "	84.1
(6)		99.5 "	87.7
(7)	99.6 "	98.6 "	"

For anything used in a cement factory, write The Bonnot Co., Canton, O.

Nazareth Cement Company—Continued.

TIME OF SETTING.

	Initial.	Final.
(1)	50 minutes	6 hours, 35 minutes.
(2)	2 hours, 10 "	5 " 20 "
(4)	3 "	4 " 30 "
(5)	3 " 38 "	5 " 45 "
(6)	2 "	4 " 10 "
(7)	4 " 45 "	7 "

SOUNDNESS.—(2) Hot and cold air, cold, warm and boiling water, good; (3) satisfactory; (4) hot and cold water good at 7, and 28 days and 3 months; (6) hot and cold water good at 3 months; (7) hot and cold water satisfactory at 1 and 28 days.

SPECIFIC GRAVITY.—(2) 3.02; (5) 3.04.

TENSILE STRENGTH.

NEAT.

Age.	(1)	(2)	(3)	(4)	(5)	(6)	(7)
1 day	365	189*	288	...	...	264*	...
2 days	...	...	...	...	...	...	486¶
7 "	796	874*	696‡ / 342	896*	810§	806*	855¶
28 "	838	...	...	734*	...	860*	1,077¶
3 months	...	...	...	778*	...	824*	...

ONE CEMENT—THREE SAND.

Age.	(1)	(2)	(3)	(4)	(5)	(6)	(7)
7 days	304	375†	217	298†	237†	286†	211
28 "	340	...	...	404†	...	423†	352
3 months	...	...	...	461†	...	428†	...

*20 per cent. water. †10 per cent. water. ‡7 days in air. §21 per cent. water. ¶18.5 per cent. water.

All briquettes were kept one day in air and remainder of time in water, except as noted.

[*Manufacturer's Statement.*]

The Conditions Imposed and the Results of One of the Foundation Jobs Wherein Nazareth Was Used.

The work was located at the plant of the Cedar Hollow Lime Company, Chester Valley, Pa., where a crusher plant of 800 tons daily capacity was constructed. The ledge of rock on which the crusher foundations must be located extended diagonally upward at about forty-five degrees. This plant was located about 150 feet from the face of the quarry and upon the same stratum. Two Blake crushers, manufactured by the Farrell Foundry and Machine Company, of Connecticut, were used, each weighing twenty tons, and each capable of crushing forty tons of stone per hour. The foundations were erected of proportions, one part Nazareth Portland Cement, two parts bar sand, four parts limestone screenings and six parts 1½-inch crushed limestone, making a total of one part cement to twelve parts of the aggregate by volume. These are about the proportions of the block shown in our advertisement, page 284. Since their erection one year ago, the crushers have been operating steadily, the main shaft turning at 300 revolutions per minute, and heavy blasting going on continually at the face of the quarry, 150 feet from the foundations. The construction stands today as strong and substantial as the day it was completed.

NEW ALBANY CEMENT COMPANY, New Albany, Ind. Works at Haussdale, Ind. See Note B, page 152.

WESTERN CEMENT Co., Sales Agents, Louisville, Ky.

Manufacturers of Crown brand Louisville natural hydraulic cement.

On Pittsburg, Cincinnati, Chicago & St. Louis railroad.

See Nordyke & Marmon Co.'s advertisement of Cement Machinery.

FOR ECONOMY IN CONCRETE

Use NAZARETH PORTLAND CEMENT

This Slab of Concrete was sawed from a block of the following proportions:

1 part Nazareth, { 2 parts bar sand.
4 " screenings (stone).
8 " 1½-inch stone. }

CRUSHING TEST AFTER 28 DAYS 202 TONS per cubic foot.

Write for Lime and Cement Note Book — *FREE*

CHARLES WARNER CO.

NEW YORK — PHILADELPHIA — WILMINGTON

THE NEWARK AND ROSENDALE LIME AND CEMENT COMPANY, 821 Prudential Bldg., Newark, N. J.
Sales office, 39 Cortlandt St., New York.
Works at Whiteport, Ulster county, New York.
Shipping wharf at Eddyville, Ulster county, New York.
H. F. BALDWIN, Pres., Newark, N. J.
W. L. LYMAN, Vice-Pres., Newark, N. J.
O. B. MOCKRIDGE, Treas., Newark, N. J.
A. DELANO, Sec'y, Newark, N. J.
F. H. DOREMUS, Supt. of Works, Whiteport, N. Y.
THOS. M. MAGIFF, Gen. Sales Agent, 39 Cortlandt St. N. Y.
Manufacturers Newark-Rosendale brand natural hydraulic cement.
On Walkill Valley branch of West Shore railroad.

THE NEWARK LIME AND CEMENT MANUFACTURING COMPANY, Newark, N. J. Works at Rondout, N. Y.
CALVIN TOMKINS, Pres., 120 Liberty St., New York City.
WALTER TOMKINS, Sec'y, 120 Liberty St., New York City.
CALVIN TOMKINS, 120 Liberty St., New York City, Sales Agt.
Capitalization. See Note E, page 152.
Capacity, 300,000 barrels a year.
Manufacturers Old Newark brand natural hydraulic cement.
On Ulster & Delaware railroad and Hudson river.

NEWAYGO PORTLAND CEMENT COMPANY, Newaygo, Mich.
Works under construction.

D. McCOOL, Pres., Newaygo, Mich.
WM. WRIGHT, Vice-Pres., Newaygo, Mich.
B. T. BECKER, Treas, Newaygo, Mich.
F. C. BIGELOW, Dir., Milwaukee, Wis.
H. D. HIGINBOTHAM, Dir., Chicago, Ill.
GERHARD BECKER, Dir., Milwaukee, Wis.
W. NORTHUP MCMILLAN, Dir., St. Louis, Mo.
Capitalization, $2,000,000.
Capacity, 1,000 barrels a day.
Manufacturers Gibraltar brand Portland cement.
On Pere Marquette railroad.

RESULTS OF TESTS.

Fineness.

No. 50 sieve	99%
No. 100 sieve	95.3
No. 200 sieve	77

Time of Setting.

Initial set	10 minutes.
Final set	5 hours, 10 "

Tensile Strength.

Time.	Neat.	1 cement, 3 sand.
1 day	285 lbs.	....
7 days	769 "	277 lbs.
28 days	819 "	342 "
9 months	872 "	400 "

NEWAYGO
PORTLAND CEMENT CO.

Capacity, 1,000 Barrels Per Day.

We Produce But One Grade

That is of the very Highest Quality

MANUFACTURERS OF

GIBRALTAR
BRAND
PORTLAND CEMENT

It Stands the Severest Tests.

Gibraltar Portland Cement is the Best for **SIDEWALKS**
It has the Gray Color.

WE HAVE ADVANTAGES FOR QUICK SHIPMENTS.
Ask us for Prices or Information.

NEWAYGO PORTLAND CEMENT CO.

NEWAYGO, MICH.

[Newaygo Portland Cement Company—Continued.]

[Manufacturer's Statement.]

The works of the Newaygo Portland Cement Company have a capacity of [illegible] barrels per day, and are the product of the best engineering skill obtainable. The buildings are steel and brick construction throughout, and equipped with nothing but the most modern and substantial machinery. They are operated under the company's own 2,000 horse-power hydraulic plant, which distributes the power electrically, thus insuring in a simple and convenient manner at a minimum cost, the most perfect grinding, mixing and calcining possible. The unique feature of the plant is its double check system of testing raw material as well as slurry and finished product. The raw material is unsurpassed for purity and uniformity. The Newaygo Portland Cement Company produces but one grade of cement, and that of the very highest quality. It is called the Gibraltar brand. One of the marked characteristics of this brand is its beautiful gray color, so much sought after by sidewalk builders. The shipping facilities from Newaygo are unsurpassed, the factory being located on a main line of railroad to all points. The Newaygo Portland Cement Company will be pleased to quote prices upon request, and promise prompt and courteous replies to all inquiries.

NEW ENGLAND PORTLAND CEMENT COMPANY, Stamford, Conn.

Not yet in operation.

Capitalization. See Note E, page 152.

Manufacturers White and Pure brand hydraulic cement. (pozzuolana?)

On New York, New Haven & Hartford railroad and Long Island Sound.

NEW JERSEY PORTLAND CEMENT COMPANY, Perth Amboy, N. J. See Note D, page 152; also descriptions of works.

Capitalization, $60,000.

Capacity, 100,000 barrels a year.

Manufacturers of Climax brand Portland cement (pozzuolana).

L. L. & W. C. NEWMAN, Akron, N. Y. See Note F, page 152.

UNION AKRON CEMENT CO., 141 Erie St., Buffalo, N. Y., Sales Agents.

Manufacturers Akron Red Star brand natural hydraulic cement.

On New York Central & Hudson River railroad.

NEW YORK AND ROSENDALE CEMENT COMPANY, Rondout, N. Y. Sales office, 280 Broadway, New York City. Works at Wilbur & Rosendale, N. Y.

WM. C. MORTON, Asst. Treas., Rondout, N. Y.

Capitalization, $250,000.

Capacity, 5,000 barrels a day.

Manufacturers Brooklyn Bridge brand natural hydraulic cement.

Delaware & Hudson canal and Walkill Valley railroad.

Plasticon, a plastering cement. The Alabastine Co., Grand Rapids, Mich.

HOW TO HELP BUSINESS

In plans for building up business reputation—really the first essential step—and for getting business, the best help at the least expense is in good advertising.

In the matter of advertising we have all that is good.

Look through MUNICIPAL ENGINEERING MAGAZINE and you will see that we have good advertisers—we don't want any other kind.

The service to them is so good that many of them think it is all they need.

If you seek business in our field you need our help.

In our field we know what we can do. We don't hesitate to say that we can do about all that can be done.

We cover the field thoroughly, we study it constantly, we are closely in touch with it everywhere.

Our organization embraces the best ability and the most thorough service.

This is the help you need—it is the kind that will do more for you than all other at less expense.

Write to us and ask us what we can do for you—if we can't help you we will tell you so—if we can we will tell you how, and that is what you want to know if you are progressive and wide awake.

Municipal Engineering Co.

See What Others Say About Our Service

What An Advertisement Did in Ten Days

Chicago, Ill., Nov. 24, 1900.

Municipal Engineering Co.

Gentlemen: Last month we placed an advertisement in your Magazine, which appeared for the first time in the November number, and which gave us the benefit of your advance information bulletin service. From this bulletin we obtained information which led to the sale of two of our concrete mixing machines, within ten days after the advertisement first appeared.

We are much pleased at the promptness with which returns have been realized, and beg to express our appreciation of your Magazine as an advertising medium, and also the great help which your bulletin service has proved to us. Yours very truly,

McKELVEY CONCRETE MACHINERY CO.

One Job That More Than Repaid Them

Chicago, Ill., Oct. 31, 1900.

The Municipal Engineering Magazine.

Dear Sirs: The first of January last, we placed an advertisement in your Magazine, and also subscribed to same. Believing that credit should be given when due, we desire to write and advise you that we have secured, through the advance information on contemplated work, very valuable information to us the past year, and in fact, we have secured through your Magazine one job of which we knew nothing before, which more than repays us for the cost of the advertisement.

In our business we are desirous at all times of securing recommendations for our material and feeling that possibly you have the same desire in this line, we write you as above. If this is of any service to you you are at liberty to make use of it.

Yours truly,

THE CLEVELAND STONE CO.

(Signed) C. W. Walters,
Western Agent.

[NE]W YORK CEMENT COMPANY, No. 29 Broadway, New York City. Works at Lefever Falls, Ulster county, New York.

JOHN MILLER, Pres., 29 Broadway, New York City.

BENJAMIN COCHRAN, Sec'y, 29 Broadway, New York City.

THOMAS MILLER, JR., Treas. and Gen. Supt., 29 Broadway, New York City.

J. M. MILLER, Dir., 28 Broadway, New York City.

A. MCLAUGHLIN, Supt. Mining and Manufacturing, Lefever Falls, New York.

THOS. CRAIG, Chief Engr., Lefever Falls, N. Y.

Capitalization. See Note E, page 152.

Manufacturers Rosendale hydraulic cement brand natural hydraulic cement.

On Delaware & Hudson canal, near Walkill Valley railroad.

[N]ORTHAMPTON PORTLAND CEMENT COMPANY, 26 Broadway, New York. Works at Stockertown, Pa. Nearly ready for operation. See Note C, page 152.

JAMES H. SNOW, Pres., 26 Broadway, New York.

B. SHERWOOD DUNN, Sec'y and Treas., 26 Broadway, N. Y.

DANIEL PIERSON, JR., Vice-Pres. and Gen. Mgr., 26 Broadway, New York.

Capitalization. See Note E, page 152.

Northampton Portland Cement Company—Continued.

On Bangor & Portland branch of Delaware, Lackawanna & Western railroad.

F. O. NORTON CEMENT COMPANY, No. 92 Broadway, New York. Works at High Falls and Binnewater, N. Y. See Note B, page 152.

Manufacturers Norton's Rosendale brand natural hydraulic cement.

On Delaware & Hudson canal, near Walkill Valley railroad.

OHIO VALLEY CEMENT COMPANY, Jeffersonville, Ind., Works at Cementville, Ind. See Notes B and E, page 152.

WESTERN CEMENT Co., Sales Agents, Louisville, Ky.

Manufacturers Fern Leaf brand Louisville natural hydraulic cement.

On Pittsburg, Cincinnati, Chicago & St. Louis railroad.

THE OMEGA PORTLAND CEMENT COMPANY, Jonesville, Mich. Works at Omega, P. O. Mosherville, Mich.

FRANK M. STEWART, Pres. and Dir., Hillsdale, Mich.
ISRAEL WICKES, Vice-Pres. and Dir., Jonesville, Mich.
CHAS. F. WADE, Sec'y and Treas., Jonesville, Mich.
GEO. H. SHARP, Supt., Jonesville, Mich.
WALTER H. SAWYER, Dir., Jonesville, Mich.
LYMAN J. BYERS, Dir., Jonesville, Mich.
LOUIS P. HALL, Dir., Jonesville, Mich.
WM. M. EATON, Dir., Jonesville, Mich.
F. A. ROETHLISBERGER, Dir., Jonesville, Mich.
CHAS. B. STOWE, Dir., Jonesville, Mich.
CHAS. S. RICHARDS, Head Chemist, Jonesville, Mich.
H. F. TREADWAY, Sales Agent, No. 298 Stock Exchange Bldg., Chicago, Ill.

Capitalization. See Note E, page 152.
Capacity, over 150,000 barrels a year.
Manufacturers Omega Portland cement.

On Lake Shore & Michigan Southern railroad.

THE OWEN SOUND PORTLAND CEMENT COMPANY, Ltd., Owen Sound, Ontario. Works at Shallow Lake, Ontario.

JOHN LUCAS, Pres. and Dir., Toronto, Ont.
J. E. MURPHY, Vice-Pres. and Dir., Hepworth, Ont.
R. P. BUTCHART, Mgr. and Dir., Shallow Lake, Ont.
GEO. S. KILBOURN, Sec'y-Treas. and Dir., Owen Sound,
W. H. PEARSON, Dir., Toronto, Ont.
JOHN LUCAS, Sales Agent, No. 377 Spadina Ave., Toronto, Ont.
BUCHANAN & GORDON, Sales Agents, Winnipeg, Manitoba.

Capitalization, $200,000.
Manufacturers Samson and Magnet brands Portland cement.
Capacity, 600 barrels per day for both.

On Canadian Pacific and Grand Trunk railways.

PEERLESS PORTLAND CEMENT COMPANY, Union City, **Mich.**
A. A. WRIGHT, Pres., Alma, Mich.
S. O. BUSH, Vice-Pres., Battle Creek, Mich.
WM. M. HATCH, Sec'y and Treas., Union City, Mich.
J. R. PATTERSON, Gen. Mgr., Union City, Mich.
A. LUNDTEIGEN, Asst. Mgr. and Chemist, Union City, Mich.
Manufacturers Peerless brand Portland cement.
Capitalization, $250,000.
Capacity, 1,000 barrels a day.
On **Michigan Central railroad.**

PEMBINA PORTLAND CEMENT COMPANY, Grand Forks, N. D. See Note D, page 152.
E. J. BABCOCK, Pres. and Dir., Grand Forks, N. D.
WEBSTER MERRIFIELD, Sec'y, Treas. and Dir., Grand Forks, N. D.
OTTO BABCOCK, Gen. Mgr. and Dir., Grand Forks, N. D.
Capitalization, $75,000.
Capacity, 150 barrels a day.
Manufacturers Pembina brand Portland cement.
Manufacturers Northern brand natural hydraulic cement.
On Great Northern railroad.

PENINSULAR PORTLAND CEMENT COMPANY, Jackson, Mich. Works under construction at Woodstock (R. R. Sta. Cement City), Mich. See Notes B and E, page 152.
W. R. REYNOLDS, Pres.
C. A. NEWCOMB, Vice-Pres.
W. F. COWHAM, Sec'y.
N. S. POTTER, Treas.
On Cincinnati Northern railroad.

PENNSYLVANIA CEMENT COMPANY, 26 Cortlandt St., New York. Works under construction at Bath, Northampton county, Pa.
WILLIAM N. BEACH, Pres.
URBAN C. BREWER, Sec'y and Treas.
Manufacturers Portland cement.
On Central Railroad of New Jersey.

PHOENIX CEMENT COMPANY, Nazareth, Pa.—
ISAAC HERZBERG, Pres., 603 N. Marshall St., Philadelphia, Pa.
I. L. SHOEMAKER, Vice-Pres., Ridge Ave. and Broad St., Philadelphia, Pa.
CHAS. F. KOLB, Sec'y and Treas., Ridge Ave. and Broad St., Philadelphia, Pa.
GEORGE W. LAUB, Nazareth, Pa.
[illegible] SHAFFER, Supt., Nazareth, Pa.
H. J. DETWILLER, Chemist, Allentown, Pa.

[illegible] Equipment for Cement Plants Address Keystone Electric Co.

PHŒNIX CEMENT CO.

Works, NAZARETH, PA.

MANUFACTURERS

PHŒNIX PORTLAND

CLOVER LEAF PORTLAND AND IXL ROSENDALE

CEMENTS

PHŒNIX PORTLAND CEMENT is guaranteed to be a high-grade Portland Cement—especially adapted for artificial stone work.

AVERAGE TESTS FOR YEAR 1900

ON CEMENT USED BY ENGINEERING DEPARTMENT, MINNEAPOLIS, MINN.

Test on one inch Briquettes of one-part Cement to three parts Sand.

Brand.	24 hrs. in air, 6 days in water.	24 hrs. in air, 27 days in water.	Brand.	24 hrs. in air, 6 days in water.	24 hrs. in air, 27 days in water.
Vulcanite	208 lbs.	270 lbs.	Giant	191 lbs.	256 lbs.
Saylors..........	164 "	220 "	Marquette......	184 "	240 "
Sandusky	197 "	265 "	Wolverine......	198 "	251⅕ "
Atlas	178 "	233 "	Clover Leaf....	168 "	224 "
Peerless	150 "	213 "	Dragon.........	128 "	169 "
PHŒNIX........	219 "	296 "	Wyandott	168 "	231 "
Lehigh	176½ "	241 "	Chicago AA	151½ "	191 "

WM. G. HARTRANFT CEMENT COMPANY

SOLE SELLING AGENT

Real Estate Trust Company Building, - PHILADELPHIA, PA.

Phœnix Cement Company—Continued.

WILLIAM I. ERNST, Chemist, Nazareth, Pa.

ROBERT F. WENTZ, Engr., Nazareth, Pa.

WM. G. HARTRANFT CEMENT COMPANY, Sales Agents, Philadelphia, Pa.

Capitalization, $250,000.

Capacity, 800 barrels a day Portland, 500 barrels a day natural.

Manufacturers Phoenix and Clover Leaf brands Portland cement.

Manufacturers IXL brand natural hydraulic cement.

On Bangor & Portland branch of Delaware, Lackawanna & Western railroad.

Tests made on Phœnix Portland cement in laboratories of Lathbury & Spackman, Philadelphia, August 9, 1900.

Fineness.

Passing No. 100 sieve....................98.26%
Passing No. 200 sieve....................81.49

Setting Time.

Initial set....................1 hour, 45 minutes.
Final set....................6 hours, 15 minutes.

Michaelis' Boiling Test—The pats showed no sign of checking or warping.

Average Tensile Strength of Five Briquettes One Inch Square.

24 hours in air (neat)....................402 lbs.
24 hours in air, 6 days in water (neat)....................766 "
24 hours in air, 27 days in water (neat)....................885 "
24 hours in air, 6 days in water (1 cement, 3 quartz sand).260 "
24 hours in air, 27 days in water (1 cement, 3 quartz sand).305 "

Tests made on Phœnix Portland cement in laboratory of Julian O. Hargrove, Washington, D. C., October 15, 1900.

Fineness.

Residue on 50-mesh sieve....................None.
Residue on 100-mesh sieve....................4 per cent.

Setting Time.

Initial (wire test)....................3 hours, 45 minutes.
Hard....................5 hours, 20 minutes.

Average Tensile Strength of Three Briquettes One Inch Square.

24 hours in air (neat)....................516 lbs.
24 hours in air, 6 days in water (neat)....................811 "
24 hours in air, 27 days in water (neat)....................900 "
24 hours in air, 6 days in water (1 cement, 3 quartz sand).360 "
24 hours in air, 27 days in water (1 cement, 3 quartz sand).395 "

Specific gravity, 3.0581.

Pat tests in air and water: Good.

Chemical analysis of Phœnix Portland cement made in laboratory of Julian O. Hargrove, Washington, D. C., October 15, 1900.

Silica (SiO_2)....................21.10%
Alumina (Al_2O_3)....................8.61
Iron (Fe_2O_3)....................3.21
Lime (CaO)....................61.62
Magnesia (MgO)....................2.84
Sulphur (SO_3)....................1.69
Carbonic Acid (CO_2)....................0.75

Phœnix Cement Company—Continued.

[*Manufacturer's Statement.*]

The Phœnix Portland cement is manufactured by the Phœnix Cement Co., at Nazareth, Northampton county, Pa., from composition made of an admixture of lime and argillaceous rocks. This material is quarried from large deposits of uncommon uniformity on the property of the company, adjacent to the factory. The capacity of the above plant is 1,200 barrels of cement daily. It is equipped with the most improved type of machinery and rotary kilns known to the cement industry, and is in charge of an experienced chemist, who has been identified with the manufacture of Portland cement in the Lehigh valley for the past twenty years. The cement produced has proven to be of the best quality, and is guaranteed to meet the requirements of all government and municipal specifications. Owing to its fine grinding and great bulk per barrel, it is the most economical for sidewalk and other artificial stone work. For prices, tests, etc., apply to Wm. G. Hartranft Cement Co., Real Estate Trust Building, Philadelphia, Pa.

PORTLAND CEMENT COMPANY OF UTAH, Ltd., Salt Lake City, Utah.

Frank Richardson, Sec'y, London, England.
Thomas C. Cairns, Gen. Mgr., Salt Lake City, Utah.
Ledyard M. Bailey, Accountant, Salt Lake City, Utah.
Daniel L. Blyth, Supt., Salt Lake City, Utah.
Anaconda Copper Mining Company, Sales Agents, Anaconda, Mont.
Thomas Finegan, Sales Agent, Boise, Idaho.
Newton Lumber Company, Sales Agents, Pueblo, Colo.

Capitalization, $450,000.
Capacity, 450 barrels a day.
Manufacturers Red Diamond brand Portland cement.

On Oregon Short Line, Rio Grande Western, Salt Lake & Los Angeles and Salt Lake & Ogden railroads.

POTOMAC CEMENT COMPANY, Antietam, Md. See Note A page 152.

PYRAMID PORTLAND CEMENT COMPANY, No. 65 Moffat Blk. Detroit, Mich. Works under construction at Spring Arbor Mich.

A. E. F. White, Pres.
A. C. Raymond, Vice-Pres. and Mgr.
C. W. Parsons, Sec'y and Treas.

Capitalization, $525,000.
Capacity, 1,400 barrels a day.

On Michigan Central railroad.

READING CEMENT COMPANY, 536 Penn St., Reading, Pa Works near Evansville, Pa.

M. C. Aulenbach, Pres., Reading, Pa.
F. W. Hanold, Sec'y and Treas., Reading, Pa.

For Cement Testing Machinery address Fairbanks Co., New York.

Reading Cement Company—Continued.

J. C. ILLIG, Dir., Reading, Pa.
GEO. W. BEARD, Dir., Reading, Pa.
J. L. REPPLIER, Dir., Reading, Pa.
GEO. H. DUNSFORD, Dir., William Penn, Pa.
GEO. H. B. MARTIN, Dir., Camden, N. J.
R. G. BUSH, Gen. Mgr., Fleetwood, Pa.
HENRY MULLER, Chemist, Fleetwood, Pa.
J. L. REPPLIER, Gen. Sales Agent, 536 Penn St., Reading, Pa.
THE WALTER T. BRADLEY CO., Gen. Sales Agents, Ninth and Girard Ave., Philadelphia, Pa.

Capitalization, $200,000.

Capacity, 1,500 barrels a day.

Manufacturers Reading brand Portland cement and Improved Rosendale brand natural hydraulic cement.

On Philadelphia & Reading railroad.

RIDGEMONT CEMENT AND MANUFACTURING COMPANY, Ridgemont, Va. Works idle.

On Norfolk & Western railroad.

ROCKLAND CEMENT COMPANY, Jones' Point, N. Y. See Note A, page 152.

On West Shore railroad and Hudson river.

ROUND TOP HYDRAULIC CEMENT COMPANY, Hancock and Round Top, Md.

Manufacturers Round Top brand natural hydraulic cements.

On Baltimore & Ohio railroad.

ST. LAWRENCE PORTLAND CEMENT COMPANY, 2664 Notre Dame St., Montreal, P. Q., Canada. See CANADIAN PORTLAND CEMENT COMPANY.

SANDUSKY PORTLAND CEMENT COMPANY, Sandusky, Ohio. Works at Bay Bridge, Ohio, and Syracuse, Ind. See Note C, page 152.

A. ST. J. NEWBERRY, Pres. and Treas., Cleveland, Ohio.
S. B. NEWBERRY, Mgr., Sandusky, Ohio.
DAN. P. EELS, Dir., Sandusky, Ohio.
J. POTTER, Dir., Sandusky, Ohio.
C. F. BRUSH, Dir., Sandusky, Ohio.
J. COLWELL, Dir., Sandusky, Ohio.

CEMENT WORKERS Who want information of practical help, either as to materials or methods can get it from

Municipal Engineering Magazine

the publication which stands as the leading authority on American Cement.

Subscription Price, $2.00 Per Year.

Sandusky Portland Cement Company—Continued.

A. C. DUSTIN, Dir., Sandusky, Ohio.

P. B. BEERY, Asst. Mgr. and Sales Agent, Sandusky, Ohio.

ARNOLD DOLL, Supt., Sandusky, Ohio.

JOHN F. DAVIS, Chemist, Sandusky, Ohio.

Capitalization.—See Note E, page 152.

Capacity, 1,600 barrels a day.

Manufacturers Medusa brand Portland cement.

Sandusky is on Lake Shore & Michigan Southern; Lake Erie & Western; Cleveland, Cincinnati, Chicago & St. Louis; Columbus, Sandusky & Hocking, and Baltimore & Ohio railroads. Syracuse is on Baltimore & Ohio railroad.

SILVER CREEK CEMENT COMPANY, Louisville, Ky. Works at Cementville, Ind. See Notes B and E, page 152.

WESTERN CEMENT COMPANY, Sales Agents, Louisville, Ky.

Manufacturers Acorn brand natural hydraulic cement.

On Pittsburg, Cincinnati, Chicago & St. Louis railroad.

HIRAM SNYDER, 229 Broadway, New York. Works at Rosendale, N. Y. See Note F, page 152.

A. W. VAN TASSELL, Supt., Rosendale, N. Y.

Capacity, 800 barrels a day.

Manufacturers XXX Rosendale brand natural hyd[illegible] cement.

On Walkill Valley railroad.

SOUTHERN CEMENT COMPANY, North Birmingham, Ala.—

CALDWELL BRADSHAW, Pres.

T. C. CURTIN, Vice-Pres. and Supt.

T. M. BRADLEY, Sec'y and Treas.

Capitalization.—See Note E, page 152.

Capacity, 400 barrels a day.

Manufacturers of pozzuolana.

On Louisville & Nashville and Southern railroads.

STANDARD CEMENT COMPANY, Louisville, Ky. Works [illegible] Charlestown, Ind. See Notes B and E, page 152.

Manufacturers Best 4 brand Louisville natural hydrau[illegible] cement.

WESTERN CEMENT COMPANY, Louisville, Ky., market.

On Baltimore & Ohio railroad.

STANDARD PORTLAND CEMENT COMPANY. Offi[illegible] Hammond Bldg., Detroit, Mich. Works at Hamburg Juncti[illegible] Mich.

GEORGE H. BARBOUR, Pres., Detroit, Mich.

JOHN CURRY, First Vice-Pres., Windsor, Ont.

JOSEPH HARRIS, Second Vice-Pres., Detroit, Mich.

Griffin Mills—Address Bradley Pulverizer Co., 92 State Street, Bost[illegible]

Standard Portland Cement Company—Continued.

GEORGE E. MOODY, Sec'y, Detroit, Mich.
MORRIS L. WILLIAMS, Treas., Detroit, Mich.
WM. E. MACKLEM, Asst. Treas., Detroit, Mich.
TITUS F. HUTZEL, Dir., Ann Arbor, Mich.
ROBERT R. HOWARD, Dir., Detroit, Mich.
Capitalization, $1,000,000.
Capacity, 1,000 to 2,000 barrels per day.
Manufacturers Standard brand Portland cement.

THE STANDARD SILICA CEMENT COMPANY, No. 66 Maiden Lane, New York. Works in Long Island City.
STEPHEN G. WILLIAMS, Pres., No. 30 Broad St., New York.
W. W. MACLAY, Vice-Pres., Glens Falls, N. Y.
FRANK E. SMITH, Sec'y, No. 66 Maiden Lane, New York.
GEO. M. NEWCOMER, Treas., No. 66 Maiden Lane, New York.
Capitalization, $100,000.
Manufacturers Champion brand silica Portland cement.

THE TEXAS PORTLAND CEMENT COMPANY, Dallas, Texas.

LEON BLUM, Pres. and Dir., Galveston, Tex.
JOSEPH LEVY, Vice-Pres. and Dir., Galveston, Tex.
E. R. CHESEBROUGH, Treas., Galveston, Tex.
JAS. L. TAYLOR, Gen. Mgr. and Dir., Dallas, Tex.
M. MARX, Dir., Galveston, Tex.
H. D. RAFF, Supt. and Dir., Dallas, Tex.
WM. PARR & Co., Sales Agents, Galveston, Tex.
Capitalization, $120,000.
Capacity, 300 barrels a day.
Manufacturers of Live Oak brand Portland cement.

On Gulf, Colorado & Santa Fe; Missouri, Kansas & Texas; Texas & Pacific; Houston & Texas Central, and Texas Trunk railroads.

[Manufacturer's Statement.]

We guarantee our "Live Oak" brand of Portland cement to be equal to any Portland cement made in the world. Our motto is to lead all others in strength, purity and uniformity of color. This we can only accomplish by additional labor and a decreased output; this means an additional cost of twenty-five cents per barrel to us over the cost of other manufacturers. The architects, engineers, builders and the trade can rely absolutely upon the "Live Oak" cement giving perfect satisfaction. Its setting time is very slow. This gives the mechanic ample time to use the material after mixing before same becomes set. This is a quality admired by all, and found in very few cements.

TESTS MADE IN OUR OWN LABORATORY FEBRUARY 2, 1901.

Fineness through 200 sieve	80%
Fineness through 100 sieve	95
Initial set	2 hours, 13 minutes.
Final set	6 hours, 30 minutes.

Boiling test, O. K.

The Texas Portland Cement Company—Continued.

Sample tested	24 hours.	3 days.	7 days.	14 days.	21 days.	28 days.
Neat............	312	456	670	720	774	845
1-3 normal sand.	....	....	227	240	284	330

The above is average of 5 briquettes broken.

THE THREE RIVERS CEMENT COMPANY, Three Rivers, Mich. See Note **A**, page 152. Works proposed on Pleasant Lake, Mich.

C. M. Harris, Pres.
W. J. Willits, Vice-Pres.
Geo. E. Miller, Sec'y.
E. B. Linsley, Treas.

TWENTIETH CENTURY PORTLAND CEMENT COMPANY, Fenton, Mich. Works proposed. See Note **B**, page 152.

C. L. Corrigan, Sec'y, Fenton, Mich.
J. C. Edsall, Gen. Mgr., Fenton, Mich.
Capitalization, $750,000.
Capacity, 1,000 barrels a day.

UNION CEMENT AND LIME COMPANY, 421 W. Main St., Louisville, Ky. Works at Cementville and Sellersburg, Ind., and Louisville, Ky.

Wm. A. Robinson, Pres., 421 W. Main St., Louisville, Ky.
J. T. Cooper, Vice-Pres. and Treas., 421 W. Main St., Louisville, Ky.
John L. Wheat, Sec'y, 421 W. Main St., Louisville, Ky.
Lewis Girdler, Supt., Jeffersonville, Ind.
Western Cement Company, Sales Agents, Louisville, Ky.
Capitalization, $450,000.
Capacity, 4,500 barrels a day.
Manufacturers Black Diamond and Anchor brands Louisville natural hydraulic cement.

On Pittsburg, Cincinnati, Chicago & St. Louis; Louisville & Nashville; Chicago, Indianapolis & Louisville; Baltimore & Ohio Southwestern; Cleveland, Cincinnati, Chicago & St. Louis; Chesapeake & Ohio; Illinois Central; Louisville, Henderson & St. Louis and Southern railroads.

UNITED STATES CEMENT COMPANY, Sellersburg, Ind. See Note **B**, page 152.

Manufacturers Flag brand Louisville natural hydraulic cement.

On Pittsburg, Cincinnati, Chicago & St. Louis railroad.

UNITED STATES PORTLAND CEMENT COMPANY.—

Authorized capital, $12,500,000. See Note **A**, page 152.
Sheldon H. Bassett, Agent, Marquette Bldg., Chicago, Ill.

Consult Keystone Electric Co. on Best Method of Driving Cement Mchn'y.

UTICA CEMENT MANUFACTURING COMPANY, Utica, Ill.

M. J. CLARK, Pres., Utica, Ill.
C. A. CARY, Vice-Pres., Utica, Ill.
N. J. CARY, Sec'y and Treas., Utica, Ill.
J. F. BLAKESLEE, Dir. and Supt., Utica, Ill.
SAM'L E. ELMORE, Dir., Hartford, Conn.
F. D. MEACHAM, Dir., Chicago, Ill.
MEACHAM & WRIGHT, Sales Agents, Chicago.
Capitalization, $150,000.
Capacity, 275,000 barrels a year.
Manufacturers Black Ball brand natural hydraulic cement.
On Chicago, Rock Island & Pacific railroad.

UTICA HYDRAULIC CEMENT COMPANY.

M. J. CLARK, Pres., Utica, Ill.
C. A. CARY, Vice-Pres., Utica.
M. J. CARY, Sec'y and Treas., Utica, Ill.
J. F. BLAKESLEE, Dir., Utica, Ill.
F. S. MEACHAM, Dir., Chicago.
MEACHAM & WRIGHT, Sales Agents, Chicago, Ill.
Capitalization, $300,000.
Capacity, 350,000 barrels a year.
Manufacturers Clark brand hydraulic cement.
On Chicago, Rock Island & Pacific railroad.

RESULTS OF TESTS.—(1) Mill tests average of samples taken May, 1894; (2) A. D. Thompson, city engineer, Peoria, Ill., 1899; (3) Robert W. Hunt & Co., the Rookery, Chicago, bureau of inspection, tests and consultation; (4) mill tests, 1891.

Fineness.

(2) 93.8 per cent. passed No. 50 sieve.
(3) 94.0 per cent. passed No. 50 sieve.

TENSILE STRENGTH.
Neat cement.

Age.	(1)	(2)	(3)	(4)
1 day	76	85	71	96
7 days	163	199	174	191
14 days	..	...	224	...
28 days	..	...	...	278
30 days	255	283		...
56 days	..	...		340
60 days	274			...
90 days	293			424
120 days	310			...
1 year	321			
2 years	340			
3 years	371			
4 years	390			
5 years	412			

Electric Motors and Generators Northern Elec. Mfg. Co., page 181

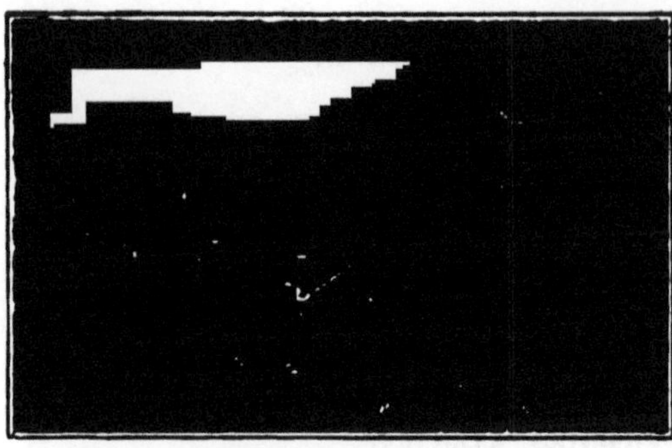

Capacity, 1,800 barrels daily.

M. J. Clark, President.
N. J. Cary, Sec. and Treas.

Utica Cement Mfg. Company

UTICA, ILLINOIS

Manufacturers of the Celebrated Black Ball Brand of

UTICA CEMENT

J. F. BLAKESLEE, Gen'l Supt.

Used throughout the United States for the past forty years. Especially adapted for tunnels, sewerage and drainage. Used exclusively in over 800 miles of sewers in the city of Chicago. Utica Cement is universally acknowledged to be the best brand in the market.

Compressive Strength in Pounds Per Square Inch.

	7 days.	14 days.	28 days.	56 days.	91 days.
Neat	1,670	2,030	2,460	2,500	2,635
1 cement to 1 sand	1,760	2,710	2,920	3,190	3,700
1 cement to 2 sand	1,440	1,540	1,960	2,160	2,720
1 cement to 3 sand	1,220	1,400	1,470	1,540	2,000

Tests made by Prof. C. N. Brown, Ohio State University, Columbus, O., from samples of Utica Cement purchased in open market. Cubes made on a Boehme hammer and given 120 blows. **Sales in 1899, 230,000 barrels.**

MEACHAM & WRIGHT, General Sales Agents

308-309 Chamber of Commerce, CHICAGO, ILL.

Capacity, 2,000 barrels daily.

M. J. Clark, President.
N. J. Cary, Sec. and Treas.
J. F. Blakeslee, Gen'l Supt.

Utica Hydraulic Cement Company

UTICA, ILLINOIS

Manufactures of the Celebrated Clark Brand of

UTICA CEMENT

Established by James Clark in 1846.

With superior facilities for prompt and careful shipment, we are enabled to meet every demand upon us promptly, and we believe to the entire satisfaction of the trade.

Tensile Strength in Pounds Per Square Inch.

	7 days.	14 days.	28 days.	2 mos.	3 mos.	6 mos.
Neat	210	255	270	283	300	340
1 cement to 1 sand	136	269	290	302	...	313
1 cement to 2 sand	76	114	162	164	172	176
1 cement to 3 sand	...	98	112	124	131	138

Tests made during 1899 by Prof. W. H. Creighton, Tulane University, New Orleans, La. Samples taken from the cement used in the construction of the new drainage system at New Orleans, La. **Sales (1900), 328,000 barrels.**

MEACHAM & WRIGHT, General Sales Agents

308-309 Chamber of Commerce, CHICAGO, ILL.

Utica Hydraulic Cement Company—Continued.

	(1)	(2)	(3)	(4)
One part cement and one part sand.				
7 days	..	...	130	113
14 days	..	...	156	...
One part cement and 1.5 parts sand.				
7 days	..	183	...	
30 days	..	264	..	...
One part cement, two parts sand.				
28 days	..	...	..	132
One part cement, three parts sand.				
28 days	..	...	..	102
One part cement, four parts sand.				
28 days	..	...	..	67
One part cement, five parts sand.				
28 days	..	...	...	48

COMPRESSIVE STRENGTH.—Made by W. K. Hatt, Purdue University, Lafayette, Ind.

Age.	Neat.	1 to 1.	1 to 2.	1 to 3.
7 days	1317	885	728	515
14 days	1655	1207	997	627
28 days	1876	1654	1428	935
60 days	2312	1832	....	1025
90 days		2015	....	1062

[*Manufacturer's Statement.*]

The natural cement mills owned and operated by us are located at Utica, La Salle county, Ill., 94 miles from Chicago, on the line of the C., R. I. & P. Ry. These mills have been in continual operation for the past forty years, during which time over 10,000,000 barrels of cement have been made and used in important work throughout the middle and western states. The rock from which Utica hydraulic cement is manufactured is very carefully examined before and after burning, thus insuring a uniform product that can be thoroughly relied upon at all times. Furthermore, each car of finished product is tested before the same leaves our works, which places us in position to know absolutely the quality of our material at all times, and which tests will gladly be furnished upon application. It is our greatest endeavor to make a strictly high grade natural cement and maintain the excellent reputation the cement has established. Our mills are always open to inspection by architects and engineers, and we are satisfied that a visit to our works and careful examination of our product will convince anyone that the Utica hydraulic cement has no superior in the natural cement field.

VIRGINIA PORTLAND CEMENT COMPANY, 81 Fulton St., New York, N. Y. Works at Craigsville, Va.

W. R. WARREN, Pres. and Dir., 81 Fulton St., New York.
H. R. BRADBURY, Sec'y and Dir., 81 Fulton St., New York.
F. W. WHITE, Treas. and Dir., 81 Fulton St., New York.
D. E. RIANHARD, Auditor and Dir., 81 Fulton St., New York.
WM. BURNHAM, Dir., 81 Fulton St., New York.
KENNETH K. MCLAREN, Dir., 81 Fulton St., New York.
F. H. LEWIS, Mgr. and Supt., Craigsville, Va.
F. D. WOOD, Asst. Supt., Craigsville, Va.

The Standard Plaster Co., Buffalo, N.Y., makes Calcined Plaster or Stucco

Virginia Portland Cement Company—Continued.

H. L. SCHOCK, Chemist, Craigsville, Va.
R. V. PARR, Engr., Craigsville, Va.
WM. G. HARTRANFT Co., Sales Agents, Philadelphia, Pa.
Capitalization, $1,000,000.
Capacity, 800 barrels a day.
Manufacturers Old Dominion brand Portland cement.
On Chesapeake & Ohio railroad.

VENTNOR STONE AND BRICK COMPANY, Atlantic City, N. J. See Note B, page 152.
Manufacturers silica Portland cement.

VULCANITE PORTLAND CEMENT COMPANY, Vulcanite Bldg. 1712 Market St., Philadelphia, Pa. Works at Vulcanite, N. J Post office, Phillipsburg, N. J.
GEO. W. ELKINS, Pres. and Dir., Philadelphia, Pa.
JOHN B. LOBER, Vice-Pres., Treas. and Dir., Philadelphia, Pa
MICHAEL EHRET, Dir., Philadelphia, Pa.
L. S. FILBERT, Dir., Philadelphia, Pa.
H. S. EHRET, Dir., Philadelphia, Pa.
B. F. STRADLEY, Sec'y and Gen. Sales Agent, Philadelphia.
WM. R. DUNN, Supt., Easton, Pa.
GEO. W. DESMET, Western Sales Agent, Chamber of Commerce Bldg., Chicago, Ill.
Capitalization, $750,000.
Capacity, 2,000 barrels a day, increasing to 4,000.
Manufacturers Vulcanite brand Portland cement.
On Lehigh Valley; Lehigh & Hudson River; Central of New Jersey; Delaware, Lackawanna & Western, and Pennsylvania railroads.

WABASH PORTLAND CEMENT COMPANY, 912 Union Trust Bldg., Detroit, Mich. Works at Stroh, La Grange county, Indiana.
A. L. STEPHENS, Pres. and Dir., Detroit.
JAS. H. MCMILLAN, Vice-Pres. and Dir., Detroit, Mich.
BETHUNE DUFFIELD, Sec'y and Dir., Detroit, Mich.
M. C. BORGMAN, Treas., Detroit, Mich.
EMIL STROH, Mgr. and Dir., Stroh, Ind.
E. W. COTTRELL, Dir., Detroit, Mich.
J. B. BROOK, Dir., Detroit, Mich.
FRED. W. HODGES, Dir., Detroit, Mich.
M. J. DRISCOLL, Supt., Stroh, Ind.
Capitalization, $600,000.

Warren Bros. Co., Boston, are Contractors for Cement Structural Work

WABASH PORTLAND CEMENT COMPANY

FACTORY

STROH (LAGRANGE COUNTY), INDIANA

(On Wabash R. R. between Chicago and Detroit)

STRENGTH
UNIFORMITY } UNEXCELLED
COLOR

Best Cement on the Market

Stands Highest Test

Every Package Guaranteed

Large Stock Ready for Immediate Shipment

General Offices, Suite 912 Union Trust Building

DETROIT, MICH.

Wabash Portland Cement Company—Continued.

Capacity, 500 barrels, increasing to 1,000 a day.

Manufacturers Turkey brand Wabash Portland cement.

On Wabash railroad.

The following are the results of tests made by **Robert W. Hun** & Co., dated December 26, 1900. Six samples of cement, marke "Wabash," received from Stroh, Indiana, November 22, 1900, wer mixed and tested as one:

Initial set............................2 hours, 40 minutes.
Final set............................7 hours, 50 minutes.
Fineness on 100 mesh....................96.05%
Fineness on 200 mesh....................80.90
Boiling test, O. K.

TENSILE STRENGTH.

24 hours. Neat.	7 days. Neat.	7 days. 3-1.	28 days. Neat.	28 days. 3-1.
403	757	330	947	409
474	796	372	909	396
473	763	309	894	431
416	738	338	883	445
456	764	311	877	417

[*Manufacturer's Statement.*]

Wabash Portland cement is manufactured by what is known as the we process. Both the marl and clay owned by this company are particularl adapted to the manufacture of a high grade of Portland cement, the ma being of exceptional uniformity and entirely free from sand and any of th impurities which are injurious to the raw material for cement makin The clay is also especially suitable as a material for mixing with the mar Analysis not only shows it to be free from sand, but also sufficiently low i magnesia as to maintain a magnesia content in the finished cement whic comes within the limits specified for a high grade Portland cement. Wabash Portland cement is always thoroughly seasoned before shippin thereby insuring its reliability before putting it in work. By careful atten tion to detail and daily analyses of the raw material during the entir process of manufacture (marl, clay, coal and slurry), and complete chem ical analysis and physical tests of the finished product, we are enabled t produce a high grade of Portland cement of unusual fineness, strength an durability and which will successfully pass every test in the specification of the American Society of Civil Engineers.

WAYLAND PORTLAND CEMENT COMPANY, Rochester, N Y. Works at Wayland and Portway (Perkinsville), N. Y. See Note B, page 152.

V. N. WHITMORE, Pres., Rochester, N. Y.

Manufacturers Genesee brand Portland cement.

On Delaware, Lackawanna & Western; Erie, and Pittsburg Shawmut & Northern railroads.

WELLSTON PORTLAND CEMENT COMPANY, Detroit, Mich.

Works under construction at Wellston, Ohio.

J. A. BOWDEN, Pres., Detroit, Mich.

FRANK J. TOWAR, Vice-Pres.

For Cement Machinery, address Earle C. Bacon, Havemeyer Bldg., N. Y

Williston Portland Cement Company—Continued.

Geo. E. Lane, Sec'y, Detroit, Mich.
Ralph M. Dyar, Treas., Detroit, Mich.
Capitalization, $100,000.
Capacity, 300 barrels per day.
On Cincinnati, Hamilton & Dayton; Baltimore & Ohio Southwestern; Ohio Southern, and Hocking Valley railroads.

WESTERN PORTLAND CEMENT COMPANY, Yankton, S. D. Milwaukee office, 135 Grand Ave. See Notes **B** and **E**, page 152.
Wm. Plankinton, Pres., Milwaukee, Wis.
D. J. Whittemore, Vice-Pres., Milwaukee, Wis.
John Johnston, Sec'y and Treas., Milwaukee, Wis.
Joseph Wilde, Gen. Mgr., Yankton, S. D.
G. W. Frostensen, Chemist, Yankton, S. D.
Capacity, 225 barrels per day.
Manufacturers Yankton Portland cement.
On Chicago & Northwestern; Chicago, Milwaukee & St. Paul, and Great Northern railroads.

WHITE CLIFFS PORTLAND CEMENT COMPANY, White Cliffs, Ark. See Note **A**, page 152.

WHITE CLIFFS PORTLAND CEMENT AND CHALK COMPANY, Texarkana, Ark. See Note **A**, page 152, and above.
On Kansas City, Pittsburg & Gulf railroad.

WHITEHALL PORTLAND CEMENT COMPANY, Cementon, Pa.
J. S. Wentz, Pres., 712 Reading Terminal, Philadelphia, Pa.
Oliver Williams, Vice-Pres., Catasauqua, Pa.
Thomas Richter, Dir., Mt. Carmel, Pa.
A. C. Leisenring, Dir., Upper Lehigh, Pa.
M. S. Kemmerer, Dir., Mauch Chunk, Pa.
B. F. Fackenthal, Dir., Easton, Pa.
H. E. Kiefer, Acting Supt., Cementon, Pa.
T. A. Hicks, Chemist, Cementon, Pa.
Sears, Humbert & Co., Sales Agents, New York, Buffalo, Philadelphia and Chicago.
Capitalization, $500,000.
Capacity, 1,500 barrels a day.
Manufacturers Whitehall brand Portland cement.
On Lehigh Valley railroad.

Municipal Engineering Magazine reaches more people who constitute the cement field of business than any other American publication. It is, therefore, the best advertising medium for this field.

THE ZENITH PORTLAND CEMENT COMPANY, Majestic Building, Detroit, Mich. Works under construction at Grass Lake, Mich.

EDWIN T. ALLEN, Pres. and Dir., Detroit Mich.
R. H. EVANS, Vice-Pres. and Dir., Detroit, Mich.
R. R. BANE, Sec'y and Dir., Detroit, Mich.
GEO. JOHNSTON, Treas. and Dir., Detroit, Mich.
B. H. ROTHWELL, Dir., Detroit, Mich.
T. E. BEEBE, Consulting Engr. and Dir., Detroit, Mich.
E. J. FOSTER, Dir., Grass Lake, Mich.
C. B. STOWE, Consulting Engr., Detroit, Mich.
Capitalization, $700,000.
Capacity, 1,000 barrels a day.
On Michigan Central railroad.

FOREIGN MANUFACTURERS.

ALSEN'S PORTLAND CEMENT FABRIK, Itzehoe, Germany.
SINCLAIR & BABSON, U. S. Agents, 143 Liberty St., New York.
Capacity, 1,000,000 barrels a year.
Manufacturers Alsen's German Portland cement.

ANTWERP PORTLAND CEMENT WORKS, Ltd., 14 Canal St. Pierre, Antwerp, Belgium. Works at Vaulx, Belgium.
ELPHEGE DENY, Mg. Dir., 14 Canal St. Pierre, Antwerp, Belgium.
FAIJA & Co., Chemists, London, Eng.
ROBT. ZIESMER & Co., Agents, Antwerp, Belgium.
Capitalization, $100,000.
Capacity, 250,000 barrels a year.
Manufacturers Hand brand Belgian natural Portland cement.

BREMER PORTLAND CEMENT FABRIK, Porta Bremen, Germany. Works in Porta Westphalica, Westphalia, Germany.
O. MATERNE, Dir., Porta Westphalica.
H. STUBBE, Dir., Porta Westphalica.
NATIONAL BUILDING SUPPLY Co., American Agents, N. Lexington St., Baltimore, Md.
Capitalization, 1,275,000 marks.
Capacity, 250,000 barrels a year.
Manufacturers Key brand German Portland cement.

COMPAGNIE GENERALE DES CIMENTS PORTLAND DE L'ESCAUT, Tournai, Belgium.
E. THIELE, U. S. Agent, 99 John St., New York.
Manufacturers Royal Crown brand Belgian Portland cement.

DUMON & CO., Belgium.
ANTHONY MENG & Co., U. S. Agents, 109 S. Front St., Philadelphia, Pa.
Manufacturers Dagger brand Belgian Portland cement.

DYCKERHOFF & SOEHNE, Amoneburg, near Biebrich, Germany.
E. THIELE, Sales Agent, 99 John St., New York.
Capacity, 700,000 barrels a year.
Manufacturers Dyckerhoff German Portland cement.

THE HAMMER SOCIETY, Tournai, Belgium.
Capacity, 100,000 barrels a month.
Manufacturers Hammer brand Belgian Portland cement.

HILTON, ANDERSON, BROOKS & CO., London, England.
E. THIELE, Agent, 99 John St., New York.
GIRVIN & EYRE, Sales Agents, 307 California St., San Francisco, Cal.
WALDO BROS., Agents, 102 Milk St., Boston, Mass.
Capacity, 800,000 barrels a year.
Manufacturers Hilton, London and B. S. & Co. London brands English Portland cement.

I. C. JOHNSON & CO., Gateshead-on-Tyne, England.
WM. WIRT CLARKE & SON, Baltimore, Md., Agents.
Manufacturers Elephant brand English Portland cement.

KNIGHT, BEVAN & STURGES, London, England.
BALFOUR, GUTHRIE & Co., U. S. Agents, Portland, Ore.
Manufacturers K., B. & S. Pyramid brand English Portland cement.

LAGERDORFER PORTLAND CEMENT FABRIK, Hamburg, Germany. Works at Lägerdorfer, Germany.
EUG. LION & Co., Owners, Hamburg, Germany.
KELLEY ISLAND LIME & TRANSPORT Co., U. S. Sales Agents, Cleveland, Ohio.
Capacity, 400,000 barrels a year.
Manufacturers Lägerdorfer Eiffel Tower brand German Portland cement.

PORTLAND CEMENT FABRIK HEMMOOR, Hamburg, Postof 14, Germany. Works at Hemmoor (Ost.).
CARL PRUSSING, Dir., Hamburg.
CARL JACOBI, Dir., Hamburg.
EDWARD L. COX, Sales Agent, Chicago, Ill.
MEYER, WILSON & Co., Sales Agents, San Francisco, Cal.
Capacity, 1,200,000 barrels a year.
Capitalization, 5,400,000 marks.
Manufacturers Hemmoor brand German Portland cement.

PORTLAND CEMENT FABRIK, Lueneburg, Germany.
E. THIELE, U. S. Agent, 99 John St., New York.
Manufacturers Heyn Bros. brand German Portland cement.

PORTLAND CEMENT FABRIK STERN, Stettin, Germany.
E. THIELE, U. S. Agent, 99 John St., New York.
Manufacturers Star Stettin brand German Portland cement.

SOCIETE ANONYME UNION FRATENELLE.
CHAS. WARNER Co., Wilmington, Del., Philadelphia and New York, Sales Agents.
Manufacturers Triton, Black Eagle and Star brands Belgian Portland cements.

MANNHEIMER PORTLAND CEMENT FABRIK, Mannheim, Germany.
MORRIS EBERT, Sales Agent, 302 Walnut St., Philadelphia, Pa.
Capacity, 600,000 barrels a year.
Manufacturers Mannheimer German Portland cement.

THE MISBURGER PORTLAND CEMENT WORKS, Hanover, Germany.
W. W. CLARKE & SON, Baltimore, Md., Sales Agents.
GIRVIN & EYRE, Sales Agents, San Francisco, Cal.
Capacity, 300,000 barrels a year.
Manufacturers Teutonia brand German Portland cement.

POMMERSCHER INDUSTRIE VEREIN AUF ACTIEN, Stettin, Germany.
F. BEHREND, U. S. Agent and Sole Importer, 54 Front St., New York.
Capacity, 500,000 barrels a year.
Manufacturers Blue Anchor Stettin brand German Portland cement.

PORTLAND CEMENT FABRIK, Hamburg.
WALTER T. BRADLEY Co., Ninth St., below Grand Ave., Philadelphia, Pa., Sales Agents.
Manufacturers Saturn brand German Portland cement.

SHEWAN, TOMES & CO., Hong Kong.
F. T. CROWE & Co., U. S. Agents, Seattle and Tacoma, Wash.
Manufacturers Emerald brand cement.

CABLE ADDRESS: EBERT, PHILADELPHIA

REGISTERED TRADE-MARK

MORRIS EBERT
302 WALNUT STREET
PHILADELPHIA, PA.
Importer and Sole Agent of
MANNHEIMER
PORTLAND CEMENT
Direct Shipments to All Available Ports.

STETTIN BREDOWER PORTLAND CEMENT FABRIK, A. G., Stettin, Germany.

F. Behrend, U. S. Agent and Sole Importer, 54 Front St., New York.

Capacity, 200,000 barrels a year.

Manufacturers Stettin Bredower, Blue Eagle brand German Portland cement.

VORWOHLER PORTLAND CEMENT FABRIK, Prussing, Planck & Co., Holzminden, Germany.

Gabriel & Schall, 205 Pearl St., New York, Sales Agents.

Manufacturers Vorwohler Lion brand German Portland cement.

DIRECTORY OF CEMENT BRANDS

The following list gives the brands or names under which cement is sold in the American market. In nearly every case the name of the manufacturer is given and the names of general sales agents, if any. In a few cases a sales agent for cement sells one or more brands under names of his own selection, not wishing the name of the manufacturer to appear. In a very few cases full information regarding brands of cement manufactured in Canada and in Europe has not been obtained in time to appear in this list. This list will be convenient in locating any brand of cement found in the market, and reference to the chapter on Descriptions of Works and the Directory list of manufacturers will give detailed information regarding the materials used and the method of manufacture.

Immediately following the name of the brand is the statement of the general class to which it belongs, whether natural hydraulic, and from what district, Portland, silica or pozzuolana. It should be noted that manufacturers apply the term Rosendale to natural hydraulic cements manufactured in the Lehigh region of Pennsylvania as well as to those made in the Rosendale district itself. The location of the works will make the distinction if it is desired.

The list of brands of American cements is given first and is followed by the list of brands of foreign cements.

AMERICAN CEMENTS.

AA CHICAGO BRAND PORTLAND CEMENT.—

Chicago Portland Cement Co., Manufacturers, 513 Stock Exchange Bldg., Chicago, Ill.

Garden City Sand Co., Sales Agents, 1201 Security Bldg., Chicago, Ill.

ACORN BRAND NATURAL HYDRAULIC CEMENT.—

Silver Creek Cement Co., Manufacturers, Louisville, Ky.

Western Cement Co., Sales Agents, Louisville, Ky.

See F. L. Smidth & Co.'s Advertisement on Page 187.

A LITTLE TALK ABOUT BUSINESS

"I like a proposition that pays."
—C. P. HUNTINGTON.

THIS PAYS!

THERE are certain things that a man in business must do. He must have an office, he must put out a sign, and he must advertise.

He must make himself known to the people who may be interested in his kind of business. The better he does this the more successful he will be.

Some of the most successful men make it a rule to spend one-fifth of their income in advertising, and they find it pays.

It makes poor business good.

It makes good business better.

The best way to advertise is to put your advertisement where it will go directly to the people who want what you sell.

We give the kind of advertising that goes directly to the right spot.

If your business is not in line with the kind our readers are interested in, we don't want you to advertise in our magazine.

If it is, we can help you, and we can give you more for your money than you can get from any other expenditure of it.

From Sacramento (Cal.) Record-Union:

"MUNICIPAL ENGINEERING has often been pronounced in these columns the most useful, practical magazine of the age, and we adhere to that judgment."

MUNICIPAL ENGINEERING MAGAZINE

Awarded Grand Prize by Paris Exposition of 1900
Holds Medal from the Chicago World's Fair

AKRON RED STAR BRAND NATURAL HYDRAULIC CEMENT.—

H. L. & W. C. NEWMAN AND AKRON CEMENT WORKS, Manufacturers, Akron, N. Y.

UNION AKRON CEMENT CO., Sales Agents, 141 Erie St., Buffalo, N. Y.

WM. WIRT CLARKE & SON, Sales Agents, 115 Gay St. S., Baltimore, Md.

ALAMO NATURAL HYDRAULIC CEMENT.—

ALAMO CEMENT CO., Manufacturers, San Antonio, Tex.

ALAMO PORTLAND CEMENT.—

ALAMO CEMENT CO., Manufacturers, San Antonio, Texas.

ALMA BRAND PORTLAND CEMENT.—

ALMA PORTLAND CEMENT CO., Manufacturers, Wellston, O.

WM. G. HARTRANFT CO., Sales Agents, R. E. Trust Bldg., Philadelphia, Pa.

ALPENA BRAND PORTLAND CEMENT.—

ALPENA PORTLAND CEMENT CO., Manufacturers Alpena, Mich.

ALPHA BRAND PORTLAND CEMENT.—

ALPHA PORTLAND CEMENT CO., Manufacturers, Easton, Pa.

W. J. DONALDSON, Sales Agent., Betz Bldg., Philadelphia, Pa.

DICKINSON CEMENT CO., Sales Agents, 935 Marquette Bldg., Chicago, Ill.

ANCHOR BRAND LOUISVILLE NATURAL HYDRAULIC CEMENT.—

UNION CEMENT AND LIME CO., Manufacturers, Louisville, Ky.

WESTERN CEMENT CO., Sales Agents, Louisville, Ky.

ANCHOR BRAND ROSENDALE NATURAL HYDRAULIC CEMENT.—

COPLAY CEMENT CO., Manufacturers, Allentown, Pa.

COMMERCIAL WOOD & CEMENT CO., Sales Agents, 156 Fifth Ave., New York.

JOHNSON & WILSON, Sales Agents, 150 Nassau St., New York.

A. P. C. BRAND PORTLAND CEMENT.—

ALABAMA PORTLAND CEMENT CO., Manufacturers, Demopolis, Alabama.

ARM AND HAMMER BRAND LOUISVILLE NATURAL HYDRAULIC CEMENT.—

GOLDEN RULE CEMENT CO., Manufacturers, Sellersburg, Ind.

WESTERN CEMENT CO., Sales Agents, Louisville, Ky.

ATLAS BRAND PORTLAND CEMENT.—

ATLAS PORTLAND CEMENT CO., Manufacturers, 143 Liberty St., New York City.

THORN & HUNKINS LIME & CEMENT CO., Sales Agents, St. Louis, Mo.

WALDO BROS., Agents, 102 Milk St., Boston, Mass.

AUSTIN BRAND NATURAL HYDRAULIC CEMENT.—
FOWLER & PAY, Manufacturers, Mankato, Minn.

B. & H. BRAND NATURAL HYDRAULIC CEMENT.—
BRIDGES & HENDERSON, Manufacturers, Hancock, Md.
WM. WIRT CLARKE & SON, Sales Agents, 115 Gay St. S., Baltimore, Md.

BANGS & GAYNOR'S STAR BRAND NATURAL HYDRAULIC CEMENT.—
BANGS & GAYNOR, Manufacturers, Fayetteville, N. Y.

BANNER BRAND LOUISVILLE NATURAL HYDRAULIC CEMENT.—
BANNER CEMENT CO., Manufacturers, Cementville, Ind.
MARBLEHEAD LIME CO., Sales Agents, 1105 Masonic Temple, Chicago, Ill.
WESTERN WHITE LIME CO., Sales Agents, Kansas City, Mo.
WESTERN CEMENT CO., Sales Agents, Louisville, Ky.

BEACH'S ROSENDALE BRAND NATURAL HYDRAULIC CEMENT.—
LAWRENCEVILLE CEMENT CO., Manufacturers, Binnewater, New York.

BEAVER BRAND OF PORTLAND CEMENT.—
THE CANADIAN PORTLAND CEMENT CO., Ltd., Manufacturers, Deseronto, Ont.
THE RATHBUN CO., Sales Agents, Deseronto, Ont.

BEST 4 BRAND LOUISVILLE NATURAL HYDRAULIC CEMENT.—
STANDARD CEMENT CO., Manufacturers, Charlestown, Ind.
WESTERN CEMENT CO., Sales Agents, Louisville, Ky.

BLACK BALL BRAND UTICA NATURAL HYDRAULIC CEMENT.
UTICA CEMENT MANUFACTURING CO., Manufacturers, Utica, Illinois.
MEACHAM & WRIGHT, General Sales Agents, Chicago, Ill.

BLACK DIAMOND BRAND LOUISVILLE NATURAL HYDRAULIC CEMENT.—
UNION CEMENT AND LIME CO., Manufacturers, Louisville, Ky.
WESTERN CEMENT CO., Sales Agents, Louisville, Ky.

BLANC BRAND STAINLESS PORTLAND CEMENT. (Pozzuolana.)
CHAS. WARNER CO., Sales Agents, Wilmington, Del., Philadelphia and New York.

BRIER HILL BRAND PORTLAND CEMENT. (Pozzuolana.)—
BRIER HILL IRON AND COAL CO., Manufacturers, Youngstown, Ohio.

BRONSON BRAND PORTLAND CEMENT.—
THE BRONSON PORTLAND CEMENT CO., Manufacturers, Bronson, Mich.

BROOKLYN BRIDGE BRAND ROSENDALE NATURAL HYDRAULIC CEMENT.—
NEW YORK AND ROSENDALE CEMENT CO., Manufacturers. Sales Office, 200 Broadway, New York.

BUCKEYE BRAND PORTLAND CEMENT.—
THE BRONSON PORTLAND CEMENT CO., Manufacturers, Brontaine, Ohio.

BUCKHORN BRAND PORTLAND CEMENT.—
BUCKHORN PORTLAND CEMENT CO., Manufacturers, R. E. Trust Bldg., Philadelphia, Pa., and Manheim, W. Va.
WM. G. HARTRANFT CEMENT CO., Sales Agents, R. E. Trust Bldg., Philadelphia, Pa.

BUFFALO BRAND NATURAL HYDRAULIC CEMENT.—
BUFFALO CEMENT CO., Ltd., Manufacturers, 110 Franklin St., Buffalo, N. Y.

BUFFALO BRAND PORTLAND CEMENT.—
BUFFALO CEMENT CO., Ltd., Manufacturers, 110 Franklin St., Buffalo, N. Y.
(See description of works.)

BULL DOG BRAND PORTLAND CEMENT.—
THE ART PORTLAND CEMENT CO., Manufacturers, Sandusky, Ohio.

CATSKILL BRAND PORTLAND CEMENT.—
CATSKILL CEMENT CO., Manufacturers, Smith's Landing, New York.

CHAMPION BRAND SILICA PORTLAND CEMENT.—
THE STANDARD SILICA CEMENT CO., Manufacturers, 66 Maiden Lane, New York.

CHICKAMAUGA BRAND PORTLAND CEMENT.—
CHICKAMAUGA CEMENT CO., Manufacturers, Rossville, Ga.

CLARK BRAND UTICA NATURAL HYDRAULIC CEMENT.—
UTICA HYDRAULIC CEMENT CO., Manufacturers, Utica, Ill.
MEACHAM & WRIGHT, Gen. Sales Agents, Chicago, Ill.

CLARKE'S IMPROVED ROSENDALE BRAND NATURAL HYDRAULIC CEMENT.—
HERCULES CEMENT CO., Manufacturers, Catasauqua, Pa.
WM. WIRT CLARKE & SON, Sales Agents, 115 Gay St. S., Baltimore, Md.

CLIMAX BRAND PORTLAND CEMENT. (Pozzuolana.)—
NEW JERSEY PORTLAND CEMENT CO., Manufacturers, Perth Amboy, N. J.

CLINTON BRAND PORTLAND CEMENT.—
Clinton Cement Co., Manufacturers, Box 177, Pittsburg, Pa.

CLOVER LEAF BRAND PORTLAND CEMENT.—
Phoenix Cement Co., Manufacturers, Nazareth, Pa.
Wm. G. Hartranft Cement Co., Sales Agents, R. E. Trust Bldg., Philadelphia, Pa.

COLTON PORTLAND CEMENT.—
California Portland Cement Co., Manufacturers, Colton, California.
Frank H. Jackson, Sales Agent, 104 S. Broadway, Los Angeles, Cal.

COLUMBIA BRAND CEMENT.—
American Cement Co., Manufacturers, Philadelphia, Pa.
W. G. Nash, N. E. Agent, 220 State St., Boston, Mass.

COMMERCIAL BRAND NATURAL HYDRAULIC CEMENT.
Coplay Cement Co., Manufacturers, Allentown, Pa.
Commercial Wood & Cement Co., Sales Agents, 156 Fifth Ave., New York.

COMMERCIAL BRAND PORTLAND CEMENT.—
Coplay Cement Co., Manufacturers, Allentown, Pa.
Commercial Wood & Cement Co., Sales Agents, 156 Fifth Ave., New York.
Johnson & Wilson, Sales Agents, 150 Nassau St., New York.

CONTINENTAL BRAND PORTLAND CEMENT.—
The Frank E. Morse Co., Sales Agents, 17 State St., New York.

CRESCENT BRAND CEMENT.—
Crescent Cement Works, Manufacturers, Long Point, Hochelaga county, Canada.

CROWN BRAND LOUISVILLE NATURAL HYDRAULIC CEMENT.—
New Albany Cement Co., Manufacturers, Jeffersonville, Ind.
Western Cement Co., Sales Agents, Louisville, Ky.

CUMBERLAND BRAND NATURAL HYDRAULIC CEMENT.
Cumberland Hydraulic Cement and Manufacturing Co., Manufacturers, P. O. Box 264, Cumberland, Md.

CUMBERLAND VALLEY NATURAL HYDRAULIC CEMENT.—
Cumberland Valley Cement Co., Manufacturers, Washington, D. C.
Houston Bros., Thirty-Second St. and Pennsylvania railroad, Pittsburg, Pa.

DEXTER BRAND PORTLAND CEMENT.—

DEXTER PORTLAND CEMENT CO., Manufacturers, Nazareth, Pennsylvania.

SAMUEL H. FRENCH & CO., Sales Agents, Fourth and Callowhill Sts., Philadelphia, Pa.

DIAMOND BRAND CEMENT.—

CRESCENT CEMENT WORKS, Manufacturers, Long Point, Hochelaga county, Can.

DIAMOND BRAND LOUISVILLE NATURAL HYDRAULIC CEMENT. (See Black Diamond.)

DIAMOND BRAND PORTLAND CEMENT.—

THE DIAMOND PORTLAND CEMENT CO., Manufacturers, Perkins Ave. and C. & P. railroad, Cleveland, Ohio.

DIAMOND P BRAND NATURAL HYDRAULIC CEMENT.—

DEFIANCE HYDRAULIC CEMENT CO., Manufacturers, Defiance, Ohio.

DIXIE BRAND NATURAL HYDRAULIC CEMENT.—

CHICKAMAUGA CEMENT CO., Manufacturers, Rossville, Ga.

DOUBLE STAR BRAND FORT SCOTT NATURAL HYDRAULIC CEMENT.—

KANSAS CITY AND FT. SCOTT CEMENT CO., Manufacturers, Kansas City, Mo.

FT. SCOTT CEMENT ASSOCIATION, Sales Agents, Kansas City, Missouri.

C. A. BROCKETT CEMENT CO., Agents, Ætna Bldg., Kansas City, Mo.

DRAGON BRAND PORTLAND CEMENT.—

THE LAWRENCE CEMENT COMPANY OF PENNSYLVANIA, Manufacturers, Siegfried, Pa.

THE FRANK E. MORSE CO., Sales Agents, 17 State St., New York.

T. B. OSBORNE, Sales Agent, 1 Broadway, New York.

C. D. STOUT, Sales Agent, 1 Broadway, New York.

EAGLE BRAND LOUISVILLE NATURAL HYDRAULIC CEMENT.—

KENTUCKY AND INDIANA CEMENT CO., Manufacturers, Jeffersonville, Ind.

WESTERN CEMENT CO., Sales Agents, Louisville, Ky.

ECLIPSE BRAND PORTLAND CEMENT.—

MICHIGAN PORTLAND CEMENT CO., Manufacturers, Coldwater, Mich.

S. H. BASSETT, Sales Agent, 827 Marquette Bldg., Chicago.

EDISON BRAND PORTLAND CEMENT.—

THE EDISON PORTLAND CEMENT CO., Manufacturers, 615 Girard Bldg., Philadelphia, Pa.

EGYPT BRAND PORTLAND CEMENT.—
Reported discontinued by AMERICAN CEMENT Co., Manufacturers, Philadelphia, Pa.

EGYPTIAN BRAND PORTLAND CEMENT.—
THE EGYPTIAN PORTLAND CEMENT Co., Manufacturers, Fenton, Mich.

ELK RAPIDS BRAND PORTLAND CEMENT.—
ELK RAPIDS PORTLAND CEMENT Co., Manufacturers, Elk Rapids, Mich.

EMPIRE BRAND PORTLAND CEMENT.—
EMPIRE PORTLAND CEMENT Co., Manufacturers, Warners, New York.
C. E. SCHAUFFLER, Res. Mgr., 737 Monadnock Blk., Chicago.

ENSIGN BRAND OF CEMENT.—
THE CANADIAN PORTLAND CEMENT Co., Ltd., Manufacturers, Deseronto, Ont.
THE RATHBUN Co., Sales Agents, Deseronto, Ont.

FERN LEAF BRAND LOUISVILLE NATURAL HYDRAULIC CEMENT.—
OHIO VALLEY CEMENT Co., Manufacturers, Jeffersonville, Ind.
WESTERN CEMENT Co., Sales Agents, Louisville, Ky.

FLAG BRAND LOUISVILLE NATURAL HYDRAULIC CEMENT.—
UNITED STATES CEMENT Co., Manufacturers, Sellersburg, Indiana.
WESTERN CEMENT Co., Sales Agents, Louisville, Ky.

FLINT BRAND PORTLAND CEMENT.—
EMPIRE PORTLAND CEMENT Co., Manufacturers, Warners, New York.
C. E. SCHAUFFLER, Res. Mgr., 737 Monadnock Blk., Chicago.

CEMENT SIDEWALK TOOLS.

FULL LINE OF
Contractors' Supplies
Send for Illustrated Catalogue and Price List.

Orr & Lockett Hardware Co. 71 & 73 Randolph St., Chicago, Ill.

FLINT ROCK BRAND ROSENDALE NATURAL HYDRAULIC CEMENT.

Houston Bros., Thirty-Second St. and Pennsylvania railroad, Pittsburg, Pa.

FOUR STAR BRAND FT. SCOTT NATURAL HYDRAULIC CEMENT.—

Fort Scott Hydraulic Cement Co., Manufacturers, Fort Scott, Kan.

Fort Scott Cement Association, Sales Agents, Kansas City, Mo.

FRENCH'S ROSENDALE BRAND NATURAL HYDRAULIC CEMENT.—

Dexter Portland Cement Co., Manufacturers, Nazareth, Pennsylvania.

Samuel H. French & Co., Sales Agents, Fourth and Callowhill Sts., Philadelphia, Pa.

GENESEE BRAND PORTLAND CEMENT.—

Wayland Portland Cement Co., Manufacturers, Rochester, New York.

GIANT BRAND PORTLAND CEMENT.—

American Cement Co., Manufacturers, 22 S. Fifteenth St., Philadelphia, Pa.

Lesley & Trinkle, Sales Agents, 22 S. Fifteenth St., Philadelphia, Pa.

United Building Material Co., Sales Agents, 13 Park Row, New York.

GIBRALTAR BRAND PORTLAND CEMENT.—

Newaygo Portland Cement Co., Manufacturers, Newaygo, Mich.

GLOBE BRAND LOUISVILLE NATURAL HYDRAULIC CEMENT.—

The Globe Cement Co., Manufacturers, Sellersburg, Ind.

The Western Cement Co., Sales Agents, Louisville, Ky.

GRANITE BRAND PORTLAND CEMENT.—

The Hercules Cement Co., Manufacturers, Catasauqua, Pa.

Houston & Co., Sales Agents, 26 Cortlandt St., New York.

Bryant & Kent, Sales Agents, Boston, Mass.

Robinson & Co., Sales Agents, Philadelphia, Pa.

HELDERBERG BRAND PORTLAND CEMENT.—

Helderberg Cement Co., Manufacturers, Howes Cave, N. Y.

Chas. H. Ramsey, Sales Agent, 38 State St., Albany, N. Y.

HERCULES BRAND PORTLAND CEMENT.—

The Hercules Cement Co., Manufacturers, Catasauqua, Pa.

Houston & Co., Sales Agents, 26 Cortlandt St., New York.

Bryant & Kent, Sales Agents, Boston, Mass.

Robinson & Co., Sales Agents, Philadelphia, Pa.

IOD AND SHOVEL BRAND LOUISVILLE NATURAL HYDRAULIC CEMENT.—

HOOSIER CEMENT CO., Manufacturers, Sellersburg, Ind.

WESTERN CEMENT CO., Sales Agents, Louisville, Ky.

IOFFMAN BRAND ROSENDALE NATURAL HYDRAULIC CEMENT.—

THE LAWRENCE CEMENT CO., Manufacturers, 1 Broadway, New York.

THE FRANK E. MORSE CO., Sales Agents, 17 State St., New York.

T. B. OSBORNE, Sales Agent, 1 Broadway, N. Y.

C. D. STOUT, Sales Agent, 1 Broadway, N. Y.

IORSESHOE BRAND LOUISVILLE NATURAL HYDRAULIC CEMENT.—

LOUISVILLE CEMENT CO., Manufacturers, 331 W. Main St., Louisville, Ky.

WESTERN CEMENT CO., Sales Agents, Louisville, Ky.

IOWE'S CAVE NATURAL HYDRAULIC CEMENT.—

HELDERBERG CEMENT CO., Manufacturers, Howe's Cave, N. Y.

CHAS. H. RAMSEY, Sales Agent, 38 State St., Albany, N. Y.

. HULME STAR BRAND LOUISVILLE NATURAL HYDRAULIC CEMENT.—

LOUISVILLE CEMENT CO., Manufacturers, 331 W. Main St., Louisville, Ky.

WESTERN CEMENT CO., Sales Agents, Louisville, Ky.

MPERIAL BRAND PORTLAND CEMENT.—

IMPERIAL PORTLAND CEMENT CO., Manufacturers, 1114 Real Estate Trust Bldg., Philadelphia, Pa.

MPROVED BONNEVILLE BRAND NATURAL HYDRAULIC CEMENT.—

BONNEVILLE PORTLAND CEMENT CO., Manufacturers, 1233-7 R. E. Trust Bldg., Philadelphia, Pa.

THORN CEMENT CO., Agts., 112-18 Church St., Buffalo, N. Y.

IMPROVED LEHIGH BRAND NATURAL HYDRAULIC CEMENT.—

THE HERCULES CEMENT CO., Manufacturers, Catasauqua, Pa.

HOUSTON & CO., Sales Agents, 26 Cortlandt St., New York.

BRYANT & KENT, Sales Agents, Boston, Mass.

ROBINSON & CO., Sales Agents, Philadelphia, Pa.

IMPROVED ROSENDALE NATURAL HYDRAULIC CEMENT.—

THE HERCULES CEMENT CO., Manufacturers, Catasauqua, Pa.

HOUSTON & CO., Sales Agents, 26 Cortlandt St., New York.

BRYANT & KENT, Sales Agents, Boston, Mass.

ROBINSON & CO., Sales Agents, Philadelphia, Pa.

IMPROVED ROSENDALE BRAND NATURAL HYDRAULIC CEMENT.—
READING CEMENT Co., Manufacturers, Reading, Pa.
J. L. REPPLIER, Sales Agent, 536 Penn St., Reading, Pa.
WALTER T. BRADLEY Co., Gen. Sales Agents, Ninth and Girard Aves., Philadelphia, Pa.

IMPROVED SHIELD BRAND NATURAL HYDRAULIC CEMENT.—
THE LAWRENCE CEMENT Co., Manufacturers, New York.
THE FRANK E. MORSE Co., Sales Agents, 17 State St., N. Y.
T. B. OSBORNE, Sales Agent, 1 Broadway, New York.
C. D. STOUT, Sales Agent, 1 Broadway, New York.

IMPROVED UNION BRAND NATURAL HYDRAULIC CEMENT.
AMERICAN CEMENT Co., Manufacturers, 22 S. Fifteenth St. Philadelphia, Pa.
LESLEY & TRINKLE, Sales Agents, 22 S. Fifteenth St., Philadelphia, Pa.
UNITED BUILDING MATERIAL Co., Sales Agents, 13 Park Row, New York.

IOLA BRAND PORTLAND CEMENT.—
IOLA PORTLAND CEMENT Co., Manufacturers, Iola, Kan.
SHELDON H. BASSETT, Sales Agent, Marquette Bldg., Chicago.

IRON CLAD BRAND PORTLAND CEMENT.—
GLENS FALLS PORTLAND CEMENT Co., Manufacturers, Glens Falls, N. Y.
COMMERCIAL WOOD & CEMENT Co., Sales Agents, 156 Fifth Ave., New York.

IROQUOIS BRAND PORTLAND CEMENT.—
IROQUOIS PORTLAND CEMENT Co., Manufacturers, Cleveland, Ohio.

IXL BRAND ROSENDALE NATURAL HYDRAULIC CEMENT.—
PHOENIX CEMENT Co., Manufacturers, Nazareth, Pa.,
WM. G. HARTRANFT Co., Sales Agents, Broad and Chestnut Sts., Philadelphia, Pa.

JAMES RIVER BRAND NATURAL HYDRAULIC CEMENT.
JAMES RIVER CEMENT WORKS, Manufacturers, Locher, Va.
ADAMS BROS.-PAYNES Co., Sales Agents, Lynchburg, Va.

KEYSTONE BRAND MILWAUKEE NATURAL HYDRAULIC CEMENT.—
MILWAUKEE CEMENT Co., Manufacturers, 7 Plankinton Bldg. Milwaukee, Wis.

KEYSTONE BRAND PORTLAND CEMENT.—
COPLAY CEMENT Co., Manufacturers Coplay, Pa.
JOHNSON & WILSON, Sales Agents, 150 Nassau St., New York
BERRY & FERGUSON, N. E. Sales Agents, 102 State St., Boston, Mass.

KRAUSE BRAND PORTLAND CEMENT.—
Wm. Krause & Sons Cement Co., Manufacturers, 1621 N. Fifth St., Philadelphia, and Martin's Creek, Pa.
Wm. Wirt Clarke & Son, Sales Agents, 115 Gay St. S., Baltimore, Md.

LEHIGH BRAND PORTLAND CEMENT.—
Lehigh Portland Cement Co., Manufacturers, Allentown, Pa.
The Kelley Island Lime and Transport Co., Agents, Cleveland, Ohio.

LIBERTY BELL BRAND PORTLAND CEMENT.—
The Frank E. Morse Co., Sales Agents, 17 State St., N. Y.

LION BRAND LOUISVILLE NATURAL HYDRAULIC CEMENT.—
Indiana Cement Co., Manufacturers, Charlestown, Ind.

LIVE OAK BRAND PORTLAND CEMENT.—
Texas Portland Cement Co., Manufacturers, Dallas, Tex.
Wm. Parr & Co., Sales Agents, Galveston, Tex.

MAGNET BRAND PORTLAND CEMENT.—
Owen Sound Portland Cement Co., Ltd., Manufacturers, Shallow Lake, Ont.
John Lucas, Sales Agent, 377 Spadina Ave., Toronto, Ont.
Buchanan & Gordon, Sales Agents, Winnipeg, Man.

MANKATO BRAND NATURAL HYDRAULIC CEMENT.—
Mankato Cement Works, Manufacturers, Mankato, Minn.

MANLIUS BRAND NATURAL HYDRAULIC CEMENT.—
Jas. Behan Estate, Manufacturers, Manlius, N. Y.

MASON'S CHOICE HAMMER AND TROWEL BRAND LOUISVILLE NATURAL HYDRAULIC CEMENT.—
Clark County Cement Co., Manufacturers, Sellersburg, Ind.
Western Cement Co., Sales Agents, Louisville, Ky.

MEDUSA BRAND PORTLAND CEMENT.—
Sandusky Portland Cement Co., Manufacturers, Sandusky, Ohio.
P. B. Beery, Sales Agent, Sandusky, Ohio.

KEYSTONE PORTLAND CEMENT

Especially suitable for heavy masonry, abutments, machinery and building foundations.

JOHNSON & WILSON
130 Nassau St., New York City

MONARCH BRAND PORTLAND CEMENT.—

THE LAWRENCE CEMENT CO. OF PENNSYLVANIA, Manufacturers, Siegfried, Pa.

THE FRANK E. MORSE CO., Sales Agents, 17 State St., N. Y.

T. B. OSBORNE, Sales Agent, 1 Broadway, New York.

C. D. STOUT, Sales Agent, 1 Broadway, New York.

MONOLITH BRAND PORTLAND CEMENT.—

MONOLITH PORTLAND CEMENT CO., Manufacturers, Battle Creek, Mich.

MUNICIPAL BRAND PORTLAND CEMENT.—

CHAS. WARNER CO., Sales Agents., Wilmington, Del.; Philadelphia and New York.

NAZARETH BRAND PORTLAND CEMENT.—

NAZARETH CEMENT CO., Manufacturers, Nazareth, Pa.

CHARLES WARNER CO., Sales Agents, Wilmington, Del.; Philadelphia and New York.

NEWARK-ROSENDALE BRAND NATURAL HYDRAULIC CEMENT.—

THE NEWARK AND ROSENDALE LIME AND CEMENT CO., Manufacturers, Newark, N. J.

THOS. M. MAGIFF, Gen. Sales Agent, 39 Cortlandt St., N. Y.

NORTHERN BRAND NATURAL HYDRAULIC CEMENT.—

PEMBINA PORTLAND CEMENT CO., Manufacturers, Grand Forks, N. D.

NORTON'S ROSENDALE BRAND NATURAL HYDRAULIC CEMENT.—

THE F. O. NORTON CEMENT CO., Manufacturers, 92 Broadway, New York.

OBELISK BRAND NATURAL HYDRAULIC CEMENT.—

THE CUMMINGS CEMENT CO., Manufacturers, Akron, N. Y.

OLD DOMINION BRAND PORTLAND CEMENT.—

VIRGINIA PORTLAND CEMENT CO., Manufacturers, Craigsville, Va.

WM. G. HARTRANFT CEMENT CO., Sales Agents, Philadelphia, Pa.

OLD NEWARK ROSENDALE BRAND NATURAL HYDRAULIC CEMENT.—

NEWARK LIME AND CEMENT MANUFACTURING CO., Manufacturers, Newark, N. J.

CALVIN TOMKINS, Sales Agent, 120 Liberty St., New York.

SAM'L H. FRENCH & CO., Agents, Fourth and Callowhill Sts., Philadelphia, Pa.

OLYMPIA BRAND ROSENDALE NATURAL HYDRAULIC CEMENT.—

JAS. A. DAVIS & CO., Sales Agents, 92 State St., Boston, Mass.

OMEGA BRAND PORTLAND CEMENT.—

OMEGA PORTLAND CEMENT Co., Manufacturers, Jonesville, **Mich.**

H. F. **TREADWAY**, Sales Agent, 928 Stock Exchange Bldg., **Chicago, Ill.**

OWL **CEMENT** BRAND PORTLAND CEMENT.—

GERMAN-AMERICAN PORTLAND CEMENT WORKS, Manufacturers, **1511 Marquette** Bldg., Chicago, Ill., and La Salle, Ill.

EDWARD L. Cox, Sales Agent, 1511 Marquette Bldg., Chicago, Ill.

PARAGON BRAND PORTLAND CEMENT.—

THE **LAWRENCE** CEMENT Co. OF PENNSYLVANIA, Manufacturers, **Siegfried, Pa.**

THE **FRANK** E. MORSE Co., Sales Agents, 17 State St., N. Y.

T. B. **OSBORNE, Sales** Agent, 1 Broadway, New York.

C. D. **STOUT, Sales** Agent, 1 Broadway, New York.

PATAPSCO BRAND PORTLAND CEMENT. (Pozzuolana.)—

MARYLAND CEMENT Co., Manufacturers, **Sparrow's** Point, Md.

PATRIOT BRAND CEMENT.—

THE FRANK E. **MORSE** Co., Owners, 17 State St., New York.

PEERLESS BRAND PORTLAND CEMENT.—

PEERLESS PORTLAND CEMENT Co., Manufacturers, Union **City, Mich.**

PEMBINA BRAND PORTLAND CEMENT.—

PEMBINA PORTLAND CEMENT Co., Manufacturers, Grand **Forks,** N. D.

PENN BRAND PORTLAND CEMENT. (Pozzuolana.)—

MARYLAND CEMENT Co., Manufacturers, Sparrow's Point, Md.

PHOENIX BRAND PORTLAND CEMENT.—

PHOENIX CEMENT Co., Manufacturers, Nazareth, Pa.

WM. G. HARTRANFT CEMENT Co., Sales Agents, Philadelphia.

PIKE'S PEAK BRAND PORTLAND CEMENT.—

COLORADO PORTLAND CEMENT Co., Manufacturers, Portland, **Colo.**

RATHBUN'S STAR BRAND OF CEMENT.—

THE CANADIAN PORTLAND CEMENT Co., Ltd., Manufacturers, **Deseronto,** Ont.

THE RATHBUN Co., Sales Agents, Deseronto, Ont.

READING BRAND PORTLAND CEMENT.—

READING CEMENT Co., Manufacturers, Reading, Pa.

J. E. REPPLIER, Sales Agent, 536 Penn St., Reading, Pa.

THE WALTER T. BRADLEY Co., Gen. Sales Agents, Ninth and **Girard** Ave., Philadelphia, Pa.

RED CROSS BRAND PORTLAND CEMENT.—
JACOB H. BLOOM, Sales Agent, 15 Whitehall St., New York City.

RED DIAMOND BRAND PORTLAND CEMENT.—
PORTLAND CEMENT CO. OF UTAH, Ltd., Manufacturers, Salt Lake City, Utah.

REX-PORTLAND BRAND PORTLAND CEMENT.—
HOUSTON BROS., Thirty-second St. and Pennsylvania R. R., Pittsburg, Pa.

RHINOCEROS BRAND PORTLAND CEMENT. (Pozzuolana.)—
MARYLAND CEMENT CO., Manufacturers, Sparrow's Point, Md.
WM. WIRT CLARKE & SON, Sales Agents, 115 Gay St., Baltimore.

ROMAN ROCK BRAND PORTLAND CEMENT.—
THE CUMMINGS CEMENT CO., Manufacturers, Akron, N. Y.

ROSENDALE HYDRAULIC CEMENT BRAND NATURAL HYDRAULIC CEMENT.—
NEW YORK CEMENT CO., Manufacturers, 29 Broadway, N. Y.

ROSENDALE NATURAL HYDRAULIC CEMENT.—
HELDERBERG CEMENT CO., Manufacturers, Howe's Cave, N. Y.
CHAS. H. RAMSAY, Sales Agent, 38 State St., Albany, N. Y.

ROUND TOP BRAND NATURAL HYDRAULIC CEMENT.—
ROUND TOP HYDRAULIC CEMENT CO., Manufacturers, Round Top, Md.

ROYAL BRAND PORTLAND CEMENT.—
CHARLES WARNER CO., Sales Agents, Wilmington, Del.; Philadelphia and New York.

SAMSON BRAND PORTLAND CEMENT.—
HOUSTON BROS., Thirty-second St. and Pennsylvania R. R., Pittsburg, Pa.

SAMSON BRAND PORTLAND CEMENT.—
OWEN SOUND PORTLAND CEMENT CO., Ltd., Manufacturers, Shallow Lake, Ont.
JOHN LUCAS, Sales Agent, 377 Spadina Ave., Toronto, Ont.
BUCHANAN & GORDON, Sales Agents, Winnipeg, Man.

SAYLOR'S BRAND PORTLAND CEMENT.—
COPLAY CEMENT CO., Manufacturers, Coplay, Pa.
JOHNSON & WILSON, Gen. Agents, 150 Nassau St., New York.
COMMERCIAL WOOD AND CEMENT CO., Sales Agents, 156 Fifth Ave., New York City; Girard Bldg., Philadelphia.

SHIELD BRAND NATURAL HYDRAULIC CEMENT.—
THE LAWRENCE CEMENT CO., Manufacturers, New York.
THE FRANK E. MORSE CO., Sales Agents, 17 State St., N. Y.
T. B. OSBORNE, Sales Agent, 1 Broadway, New York.
C. D. STOUT, Sales Agent, 1 Broadway, New York.

SOUTHERN CROSS BRAND PORTLAND CEMENT. (Pozzuolana.)—

Birmingham Cement Co., Manufacturers, Ensley, Ala.

SOVEREIGN BRAND PORTLAND CEMENT.—

Charles Warner Co., Sales Agents, Wilmington, Del.; Philadelphia and New York.

SPEED'S STAR BRAND LOUISVILLE NATURAL HYDRAULIC CEMENT.—

Louisville Cement Co., Manufacturers, 331 W. Main St., Louisville, Ky.

Western Cement Co., Sales Agents, Louisville, Ky.

*S BRAND LOUISVILLE NATURAL HYDRAULIC CEMENT.—

Louisville Cement Co., Manufacturers, 331 W. Main St., Louisville, Ky.

Western Cement Co., Sales Agents, Louisville, Ky.

STANDARD BRAND PORTLAND CEMENT.—

Bonneville Portland Cement Co., Manufacturers, 1233-7 R. E. Trust Bldg., Philadelphia, Pa.

JUST WHAT CONTRACTORS NEED

To know all the best ideas, the most successful methods, the latest news regarding all contracting work in American cities, is information of great value to progressive contractors engaged in doing that kind of work.

That is just what contractors get from Municipal Engineering Magazine.

If they don't find in the Magazine the information they want, it will be furnished on request to any subscriber. In answering a single question the Magazine often incurs expense greater than a subscription amounts to for life.

This information service alone is worth to contractors many times the subscription price.

The subscription price is only $2.00 per year. No progressive contractor can afford to be without the Magazine.

I am pleased with Municipal Engineering.—*Geo. H. Smarden, Sidewalk Contractor, Portland, Me.*

Municipal Engineering is to my mind the best for men employed in municipal work.—*J. H. Stubbs, West Roxbury, Mass.*

Municipal Engineering is worth its weight in silver.—*Salt Lake Tribune.*

MUNICIPAL ENGINEERING CO.

No. 1 Broadway, New York City, N. Y. :::::: No. 28 South Meridian St., Indianapolis, Ind.

STANDARD BRAND PORTLAND CEMENT.—
STANDARD PORTLAND CEMENT Co., Manufacturers, Hammond Bldg., Detroit, Mich.

STAR BRAND PORTLAND CEMENT.—
BONNEVILLE PORTLAND CEMENT Co., Manufacturers, 1233-1 R. E. Trust Bldg., Philadelphia, Pa.

STEEL BRAND CEMENT (POZZUOLANA).—
CEMENT DEPARTMENT ILLINOIS STEEL Co., Manufacturers 1060 Rookery, Chicago, Ill.

STORM KING BRAND PORTLAND CEMENT.—
THE CUMMINGS CEMENT Co., Manufacturers, Akron, N. Y.

TIGER BRAND PORTLAND CEMENT.—
CASTALIA PORTLAND CEMENT Co., Manufacturers, 701-2 Publication Bldg., Pittsburg, Pa.

TOLTEC BRAND PORTLAND CEMENT (POZZUOLANA).—
MARYLAND CEMENT Co., Manufacturers, Sparrow's Point, Md

TURKEY BRAND WABASH PORTLAND CEMENT.—
WABASH PORTLAND CEMENT Co., Manufacturers, 912 Union Trust Bldg., Detroit, Mich.

UNION BRAND NATURAL HYDRAULIC CEMENT.—
AMERICAN CEMENT Co., Manufacturers, 22 S. Fifteenth St. Philadelphia, Pa.
LESLEY & TRINKLE, Sales Agents, 22 S. Fifteenth St., Philadelphia, Pa.
UNITED BUILDING MATERIAL Co., Sales Agents, 13 Park Row New York City.

UNIVERSAL BRAND PORTLAND CEMENT.—
CEMENT DEPARTMENT ILLINOIS STEEL Co., Manufacturers 1060 Rookery, Chicago, Ill.

U. S. G. BRAND NATURAL HYDRAULIC CEMENT.—
MANKATO CEMENT WORKS, Manufacturers, Mankato, Minn

VICTOR BRAND PORTLAND CEMENT.—
GLENS FALLS PORTLAND CEMENT Co., Manufacturers, Glens Falls, N. Y.
COMMERCIAL WOOD AND CEMENT Co., Sales Agents, 156 Fifth Ave., New York.

VULCANITE BRAND PORTLAND CEMENT.—
VULCANITE PORTLAND CEMENT Co., Manufacturers, Philadelphia, Pa.
B. F. STRADLEY, Sales Agent, 1712 Market St., Philadelphia, Pa.
GEO. W. DESMET, Western Sales Agent, Chamber of Commerce Bldg., Chicago, Ill.

'ARNER'S IMPROVED BRAND NATURAL HYDRAULIC CEMENT.—

Charles Warner Co., Sales Agents, Wilmington, Del.; Philadelphia and New York.

'AYLAND BRAND PORTLAND CEMENT.—

Thos. Millen & Co., Manufacturers, Wayland, N. Y.

A. J. McBean & Co., Agents, Chicago, Ill.

'HITE AND PURE BRAND HYDRAULIC CEMENT. (Pozzuolana?) See description of works.

New England Portland Cement Co., Manufacturers, Stamford, Conn.

'HITEHALL BRAND PORTLAND CEMENT.—

Whitehall Portland Cement Co., Manufacturers, Cementon, Pa.

Sears, Humbert & Co., Sales Agents, New York, Buffalo, Philadelphia and Chicago.

'OLVERINE BRAND PORTLAND CEMENT.—

Michigan Portland Cement Co., Manufacturers, Coldwater, Mich.

S. H. Bassett, Sales Agent, 827 Marquette Bldg., Chicago, Ill.

'YANDOTTE BRAND PORTLAND CEMENT.—

Michigan Alkali Co., Manufacturers, Wyandotte, Mich.

F. B. Holmes & Co., Gen. Sales Agents, Hammond Bldg., Detroit, Mich.

XX ROSENDALE BRAND NATURAL HYDRAULIC CEMENT.—

Hiram Snyder, Manufacturer, 229 Broadway, New York, and Rosendale, N. Y.

'ANKTON PORTLAND CEMENT.—

Western Portland Cement Co., Manufacturers, Yankton, S. D.

FOREIGN CEMENTS.

LSEN BRAND GERMAN PORTLAND CEMENT.—

Sinclair & Babson, Agents, 143 Liberty St., New York.

Waldo Bros., Agents, 102 Milk St., Boston, Mass.

LACK CROSS BRAND FOREIGN PORTLAND CEMENT.—

Fleming & Co., Sales Agents, 123 Liberty St., New York.

LACK EAGLE BRAND BELGIAN PORTLAND CEMENT.—

Societe Anonyme Union Fraternelle, Manufacturers.

Charles Warner Co., Sales Agents, Wilmington, Del.; Philadelphia and New York.

BLUE ANCHOR STETTIN BRAND GERMAN PORTLAND CEMENT.—

POMMERSCHER INDUSTRIE VEREIN AUF ACTIEN, Manufacturers, Stettin, Germany.

F. BEHREND, Sales Agent and Sole Importer, 54 Front St., New York City.

BLUE EAGLE STETTIN BREDOWER BRAND GERMAN PORTLAND CEMENT.—

STETTIN-BREDOWER PORTLAND CEMENT FABRIK A. G., Manufacturers, Stettin, Germany.

F. BEHREND, Sales Agent and Sole Importer, 54 Front St., New York City.

B. S. & CO. LONDON BRAND ENGLISH PORTLAND CEMENT.—

HILTON, ANDERSON, BROOKS & CO., Ltd., Manufacturers, London, England.

E. THIELE, Sales Agent, 99 John St., New York.

WALDO BROS., Agents, 102 Milk St., Boston, Mass.

BULL BRAND GERMAN PORTLAND CEMENT.—

JACOB H. BLOOM, U. S. Agent, 15 Whitehall St., New York City.

BURHAM BRAND ENGLISH PORTLAND CEMENT.—

SEARS, HUMBERT & CO., Importers, 1310 Chamber of Commerce, Chicago, Ill.

CASTLE BRAND BELGIAN NATURAL HYDRAULIC CEMENT.—

WALTER T. BRADLEY CO., Agents, Ninth St., below Girard Ave., Philadelphia, Pa.

GIRVIN & EYRE, Sales Agents, 307 California St., San Francisco, Cal.

MEYER, WILSON & CO., Importers, Portland, Ore.

CATHEDRAL BRAND BELGIAN CEMENT.—

BALFOUR, GUTHRIE & CO., Importers, Portland, Ore.

CLOCK BRAND BELGIAN NATURAL HYDRAULIC CEMENT.—

WALTER T. BRADLEY CO., Agents, Ninth St., below Girard Ave., Philadelphia, Pa.

DAGGER BRAND BELGIAN PORTLAND CEMENT.—

DUMON & CO., Manufacturers, Belgium.

ANTHONY MENG & CO., U. S. Agents, 109 S. Front St., Philadelphia, Pa.

DIANA BRAND GERMAN PORTLAND CEMENT.—

ANDRES BROS., Importers, 507 John Hancock Bldg., Boston, Mass.

YCKERHOFF BRAND GERMAN PORTLAND CEMENT.—
DYCKERHOFF & SOEHNE, Manufacturers, Amoneburg, near Biebrich, Germany.
E. THIELE, Sales Agent, 99 John St., New York.
LESLEY & TRINKLE, Importers, Philadelphia, Pa.

AGLE BRAND BELGIAN PORTLAND CEMENT.—
WM. PARR & Co., Importers, Galveston, Tex.

LEPHANT BRAND ENGLISH PORTLAND CEMENT.—
J. C. JOHNSON & Co., Manufacturers, Gateshead-on-Tyne, England.
WM. WIRT CLARKE & SON, Agents, Baltimore, Md.

MERALD BRAND FOREIGN CEMENT.—
SHEWAN, TOMES & Co., Manufacturers, Hong Kong.
F. T. CROWE & Co., U. S. Agents, Seattle and Tacoma, Wash.

ERMANIA BRAND GERMAN PORTLAND CEMENT.—
MEYER, WILSON & Co., Importers, Portland, Ore., and San Francisco, Cal.
GLENCOE LIME AND CEMENT Co., Agents, 1400a Old Manchester road, St. Louis, Mo.

IANT BRAND BELGIAN CEMENT.—
BALFOUR, GUTHRIE & Co., Importers, Portland, Ore.

LOBE BRAND BELGIAN PORTLAND CEMENT.—
SPARROW, FRIDENBERG & Co., Sales Agents, 15-25 Whitehall St., New York.

IAMMER BRAND BELGIAN PORTLAND CEMENT.—
THE HAMMER SOCIETY, Manufacturers, Tournai, Belgium.

IAND BRAND BELGIAN "NATURAL PORTLAND" CEMENT.—
ANTWERP PORTLAND CEMENT WORKS, Ltd., 14 Canal St. Pierre, Antwerp, Belgium.

IANOVER BRAND GERMAN PORTLAND CEMENT.—
OLAND CEMENT Co., Agents, 160 Fifth Ave., New York.

IEIMBERGER BRAND GERMAN PORTLAND CEMENT.—
E. M. BURKE, Dealer, 814 Commerce Ave., Houston, Tex.

IEIDELBERG BRAND GERMAN PORTLAND CEMENT.—
MEYER, WILSON & Co., Importers, San Francisco, Cal., and Portland, Ore.

CORONET BRAND ENGLISH
KEENE'S · CEMENT
It is of great hardness, non-absorbent, takes a mirror polish, and is unrivalled for istering moulded work and making artificial marble.
LEMING & CO., Importers, 123 Liberty St., New York City.

HEMMOOR CROWN BRAND GERMAN PORTLAND CEMENT.—

Portland Cement Fabrik Hemmoor, Manufacturers, Hamburg, post hof 14, Germany.

Edward L. Cox, Sales Agent, Chicago, Ill.

Meyer, Wilson & Co., Sales Agents, San Francisco, Cal.

Sparrow, Fridenberg & Co., Sales Agents, 15-25 Whitehal St., New York.

Walter T. Bradley Co., Sales Agents, Ninth St., belo Girard Ave., Philadelphia, Pa.

Wm. Parr & Co., Importers, Galveston, Tex.

HERCULES BRAND (BREITENBURGER) GERMAN PORTLAND CEMENT.—

Sam'l H. French & Co., Sales Agents, Fourth and Callowhill Sts., Philadelphia, Pa.

HEYN BROS.' BRAND GERMAN PORTLAND CEMENT.—

Portland Cement Fabrik Lueneburg, Manufacturers Lueneburg, Germany.

E. Thiele, Sales Agent, 99 John St., New York.

Lesley & Trinkle, Importers, Philadelphia, Pa.

HILTON, LONDON, BRAND ENGLISH PORTLAND CEMENT.—

Hilton, Anderson, Brooks & Co., Ltd., Manufacturers, London, England.

E. Thiele, Sales Agent, 99 John St., New York.

Girvin & Eyre, Sales Agents, 307 California St., San Francisco, Cal.

Lesley & Trinkle, Importers, Philadelphia, Pa.

HOXTER BRAND GERMAN PORTLAND CEMENT.—

Sparrow, Fridenberg & Co., Sales Agents, 15-25 Whitehal St., New York.

JOSSON BRAND BELGIAN PORTLAND CEMENT.—

Sears, Humbert & Co., Importers, 1310 Chamber of Commerce, Chicago, Ill.

KAISER BRAND GERMAN PORTLAND CEMENT.—

National Building Supply Co., Agents, N. Lexington St Baltimore, Md.; 413 Carondelet St., New Orleans, La.

KARLSTADT BRAND GERMAN PORTLAND CEMENT.—

Meyer, Wilson & Co., Importers, San Francisco, Cal., an Portland, Ore.

K., B. & S. PYRAMID BRAND ENGLISH PORTLAND CEMENT.—

Knight, Bevan & Sturges, Manufacturers, London, England

Balfour, Guthrie & Co., U. S. Agents, Portland, Ore.

[K]EY BRAND GERMAN PORTLAND CEMENT.—
BREMER PORTLAND CEMENT FABRIK, PORTA, Manufacturers, Bremen, Germany.

[K]NIGHT BRAND BELGIAN PORTLAND CEMENT.—
NATIONAL BUILDING SUPPLY CO., Agents, N. Lexington St., Baltimore, Md.; 413 Carondelet St., New Orleans, La.

[L]A FARGE BRAND.—
SEARS, HUMBERT & CO., Importers, 1310 Chamber of Commerce, Chicago, Ill.

[L]AGERDORFER EIFFEL TOWER BRAND GERMAN PORTLAND CEMENT.—
EUG. LION & CO., Manufacturers, Hamburg and Lägerdorf, Germany.
KELLEY ISLAND LIME AND TRANSPORT CO., U. S. Sales Agents, Cleveland, Ohio.

[L]AUFFEN BRAND GERMAN PORTLAND CEMENT.—
SPARROW, FRIDENBERG & CO., Sales Agents, 15-25 Whitehall St., New York.

[M]ANNHEIMER BRAND GERMAN PORTLAND CEMENT.—
MANNHEIMER PORTLAND CEMENT FABRIK, Manufacturers, Mannheim, Germany.
MORRIS EBERT, Sales Agent, 302 Walnut St., Philadelphia, Pa.
MEYER, WILSON & CO., Importers, San Francisco, Cal., and Portland, Ore.

[M]EIER'S PUZZOLAN CEMENT. (Pozzuolana.)—
H. H. MEIER & CO., Manufacturers, Bremen, Germany.
SAM'L H. FRENCH & CO., Agents, York, Fourth and Callowhill Sts., Philadelphia, Pa.
WALDO BROS., Agents, 102 Milk St., Boston, Mass.

[N]ORTH'S CONDOR BRAND BELGIAN CEMENT.—
BALFOUR, GUTHRIE & CO., Pacific Coast Agents, Portland, Ore.

[O]LAND BRAND SWEDISH PORTLAND CEMENT.—
OLAND CEMENT CO., Agents, 160 Fifth Ave., New York.

[P]ORTA BRAND GERMAN PORTLAND CEMENT.—
BREMER PORTLAND CEMENT FABRIK, PORTA, Manufacturers, Bremen, Germany.
NATIONAL BUILDING SUPPLY CO., Agents, N. Lexington St., Baltimore, Md.; 413 Carondelet St., New Orleans, La.

[R]OOSTER BRAND FOREIGN PORTLAND CEMENT.—
E. M. BURKE, Dealer, 814 Commerce Ave., Houston, Tex.

ROYAL CROWN BRAND BELGIAN PORTLAND CEMENT.—

COMPAGNIE GENERALE DES CEMENTS PORTLAND DE L'ESCAUT, Manufacturers, Tournai, Belgium.

E. THIELE, Sales Agent, 99 John St., New York.

ROYAL EAGLE BRAND BELGIAN PORTLAND CEMENT.

WALTER T. BRADLEY CO., Agents, Ninth St., below Girard Ave., Philadelphia, Pa.

SATURN BRAND GERMAN PORTLAND CEMENT.—

PORTLAND CEMENT FABRIK, Manufacturers, Hamburg, Germany.

WALTER T. BRADLEY CO., Sales Agents, Ninth St., below Girard Ave., Philadelphia, Pa.

SCHIFFERDECKER BRAND GERMAN PORTLAND CEMENT.—

SEARS, HUMBERT & CO., Importers, 1310 Chamber of Commerce, Chicago, Ill.

STAR BRAND BELGIAN PORTLAND CEMENT.—

SOCIETE ANONYME UNION FRATERNELLE, Manufacturers.

CHARLES WARNER CO., Sales Agents, Wilmington, Del.; Philadelphia and New York.

STAR, STETTIN, BRAND GERMAN PORTLAND CEMENT.—

PORTLAND CEMENT FABRIK STERN, Manufacturers, Stettin, Germany.

E. THIELE, Sales Agent, 99 John St., New York.

STETTIN-BREDOWER PORTLAND CEMENT.—

F. BEHREND, Sales Agent, 54 Front St., New York.

STETTIN-GRISTOWER PORTLAND CEMENT.—

SEARS, HUMBERT & CO., Importers, 1310 Chamber of Commerce, Chicago, Ill.

TEUTONIA BRAND GERMAN PORTLAND CEMENT.—

THE MISBURGER PORTLAND CEMENT WORKS, Manufacturers, Hanover, Germany.

SPARROW, FRIDENBERG & CO., Sales Agents, 15-25 Whitehall St., New York.

GIRVIN & EYRE, Sales Agents, 307 California St., San Francisco, Cal.

TRITON BRAND BELGIAN PORTLAND CEMENT.—

SOCIETE ANONYME UNION FRATERNELLE, Manufacturers.

CHARLES WARNER CO., Sales Agents, Wilmington, Del.; Philadelphia and New York.

TROWEL BRAND FOREIGN PORTLAND CEMENT.—

MEYER, WILSON & CO., Importers, San Francisco, Cal., and Portland, Ore.

VORWOHLER LION BRAND GERMAN PORTLAND CEMENT.—

VORWOHLER PORTLAND CEMENT FABRIK, PRUSSING, PLANCK & Co., Manufacturers, Holzminden, Germany.

GABRIEL & SCHALL, Sales Agents, 205 Pearl St., New York.

VULTUR BRAND BELGIAN PORTLAND CEMENT.—

NATIONAL BUILDING SUPPLY Co., Agents, N. Lexington St., Baltimore, Md.; 413 Carondelet St., New Orleans, La.

ZEBRA BRAND FOREIGN PORTLAND CEMENT.—

E. M. BURKE, Dealer, 814 Commerce Ave., Houston, Tex.

MANUFACTURERS

THE GLENS FALLS PORTLAND CEMENT CO.

GLENS FALLS, N. Y.

W. W. MACLAY, President, ... Glens Falls, N. Y.
BYRON LAPHAM, Vice-President, ... Glens Falls, N. Y.
A. W. SHERMAN, Treasurer, ... Glens Falls, N. Y.
J. A. PARRY, Secretary, ... Glens Falls, N. Y.
S. S. GOODMAN, Director, ... Glens Falls, N. Y.
F. W. WAIT, Director, ... Glens Falls, N. Y.
G. H. PARKS, Director, ... Glens Falls, N. Y.
W. E. SPIER, Director, ... Glens Falls, N. Y.

COMMERCIAL WOOD AND CEMENT CO.

Sole Selling Agents. 156 Fifth Ave., New York.

Capacity 1,200 bbls per day. Manufacturers of The Iron Clad Brand of Portland Cement; Victor Brand of Portland Cement.

GUARANTEES—IRON CLAD BRAND

THE GLENS FALLS PORTLAND CEMENT COMPANY is willing to guarantee all of its shipments as follows: 1st. The cement will stand a minimum tensile strain of 600 lbs. to the square inch section of neat briquettes kept 1 day in air and 6 days in water. 2d. The cement will stand a minimum tensile strain of 175 lbs. per square inch section, 3 parts of sand and one part of cement, the briquettes kept 1 day in air and 6 days in water, standard crushed quartz used in testing. 3d. The cement will stand what is known as the boiling test. 4th. 85 per cent. of this cement will pass through No. 200 sieve. 96 per cent. will pass through 100 seive. All of the barrel cement will be put up in tight packages of great strength and uniformity. The bag cement will be put up in cotton bags of superior quality, and all the weights are strictly guaranteed.

GUARANTEE—VICTOR BRAND

THE GLENS FALLS PORTLAND CEMENT COMPANY is willing to guarantee all of its shipments of Victor Portland Cement as follows: 1st. The cement will stand a minimum tensile strain of 500 lbs. to the square inch section of neat briquettes kept one day in air and 6 days in water. 2d. The cement will stand a minimum tensile strain of 125 lbs. per square inch section, 3 parts of sand and 1 part of cement, the briquettes kept 1 day in air and 6 days in water, standard crushed quartz used in testing. 3d. The cement will stand what is known as the boiling test. 4th. 90 per cent. of this cement will pass through No. 200 sieve. 97 per cent. will pass through No. 100 sieve.

All of the barrel cement will be put in tight packages of great strength and uniformity. The bag cement will be put up in cotton bags of superior quality and all the weights are strictly guaranteed.

DIRECTORY OF GENERAL SALES AGENTS

The following list contains the names of the General Sales Agents for American cement companies and of the principal distributing agents and importers of foreign cements who have responded to requests for information. A definite line can not be drawn between the General Sales Agents and the ordinary dealers in cement. All who might be considered as belonging to the former class are included in this list. The list of Cement Dealers, which is given farther on, contains all the names in this list as well as those of local cement dealers.

ABEL LIME AND CEMENT COMPANY, Davenport, Iowa.—
Agents BONNEVILLE PORTLAND CEMENT CO., 1233-7 R. E. Trust Bldg., Philadelphia, Pa.
Manufacturers Star and Standard brands Portland cement and Improved Bonneville brand natural hydraulic cement.

ADAMS BROS.-PAYNES CO., Lynchburg, Va.—
Sales Agents JAMES RIVER CEMENT WORKS, Locher, Va.
Manufacturers of James River brand natural hydraulic cement.

ANACONDA COPPER MINING COMPANY, HARDWARE DEPARTMENT, Anaconda and Butte, Mont.—
Agents PORTLAND CEMENT CO. OF UTAH, Ltd., Salt Lake City, Utah.
Manufacturers Red Diamond brand Portland cement.
Agents ALSEN'S PORTLAND CEMENT FABRIK, Itzehoe, Germany.
Manufacturers Alsen's brand German Portland cement.

ANDRES BROS., 507 John Hancock Bldg., Boston, Mass.—
Importers Diana brand German Portland cement.

BALFOUR, GUTHRIE & CO., Portland, Ore.—
U. S. Agents KNIGHT, BEVAN & STURGES, London, England.
Manufacturers K., B. & S. Pyramid brand English Portland cement.
Importers Cathedral and Giant brands Belgian cement.
Pacific Coast Agents North's Condor brand Belgian cement.

BASSETT, SHELDON H., Marquette Bldg., Chicago, Ill.
Sales Agent MICHIGAN PORTLAND CEMENT Co., Coldwater, Mich.
Manufacturers Wolverine and Eclipse brands Portland cement.
Sales Agent IOLA PORTLAND CEMENT Co., Iola, Kans.
Manufacturers Iola brand Portland cement.
Agent UNITED STATES PORTLAND CEMENT Co., Dover, Del.

BATCHELDER & COLLINS, Norfolk, Va.
Agents BONNEVILLE PORTLAND CEMENT Co., 1233-7 R. E. Trust Bldg., Philadelphia, Pa.
Manufacturers Standard and Star brands Portland cement and Improved Bonneville brand natural hydraulic cement.

BEERY, P. B., Sandusky, Ohio.
Sales Agent SANDUSKY PORTLAND CEMENT Co., Sandusky, Ohio.
Manufacturers Medusa brand Portland cement.

BEHREND, F., 54 Front St., New York.
Sales Agent and Sole Importer from POMMERSCHER INDUSTRIE VEREIN AUF ACTIEN, Stettin, Germany.
Manufacturers Blue Anchor Stettin brand German Portland cement.
Sales Agent and Sole Importer from STETTIN BREDOWER PORTLAND CEMENT FABRIK, A. G., Stettin, Germany.
Manufacturers Blue Eagle Stettin-Bredower brand German Portland cement.

BERRY & FERGUSON, 102 State St., Boston, Mass.
Sales Agents LAWRENCEVILLE CEMENT Co., Binnewater, N. Y.
Manufacturers Beach's Rosendale brand natural hydraulic cement.
Sales Agents COPLAY CEMENT Co., Coplay, Pa.
Manufacturers Saylor's and Keystone brands Portland cement.

BLAIR, REED F., CO., Lewis Blk., Pittsburg, Pa.
Sales Agents BRIER HILL IRON AND COAL Co., Youngstown, Ohio.
Manufacturers Brier Hill brand Portland cement (pozzuolana).

BLOOM, JACOB H., 15 Whitehall St., New York City.
Sales Agent Red Cross brand Portland cement.
Sales Agent Bull brand German Portland cement.

BORGNER CEMENT COMPANY, Philadelphia, Pa.
Sales Agents LEHIGH PORTLAND CEMENT Co., Allentown, Pa.
Manufacturers Lehigh brand Portland cement.

BOSTON FIRE BRICK COMPANY, 164 Devonshire St., Boston, Mass.
Agents BONNEVILLE PORTLAND CEMENT CO., 1233-7 R. E. Trust Bldg., Philadelphia, Pa.
Manufacturers Standard and Star brands Portland cement and Improved Bonneville brand natural hydraulic cement.

BRADLEY, WALTER T., CO., Ninth St., below Girard Ave., Philadelphia, Pa.
Sales Agents READING CEMENT CO., Reading, Pa.
Manufacturers Reading brand Portland cement and Improved Rosendale brand natural hydraulic cement.
Sales Agents HEMMOOR PORTLAND CEMENT FABRIK.
Manufacturers Hemmoor German Portland cement.
Sales Agents Saturn German Portland cement.

BROCKETT, C. A., CEMENT COMPANY, Aetna Bldg., Kansas City, Mo.
Agents KANSAS CITY & FT. SCOTT CEMENT CO.
Manufacturers Brockett's Double Star brand Ft. Scott natural hydraulic cement.

BRYANT & KENT, 30 Kilby St., Boston, Mass.
Sales Agents THE HERCULES CEMENT CO., Catasauqua, Pa.
Manufacturers Hercules and Granite brands Portland cement and Improved Lehigh and Improved Rosendale brands natural hydraulic cement.

BUCHANAN & GORDON, Winnipeg, Man.
Sales Agents THE OWEN SOUND PORTLAND CEMENT CO., LTD., Owen Sound, Ont.
Manufacturers Samson and Magnet brands Portland cement.

BULLOCK, JOHN, & SON, Baltimore, Md.
Sales Agents Norton's Rosendale cement.

BUTTE COAL COMPANY, 19 E. Broadway, Butte City, Mont.
EDWIN L. MAYO, Proprietor.
Sales Agents WESTERN PORTLAND CEMENT CO., Yankton, S.D.
Manufacturers Yankton brand Portland cement.

CABLE, THORN & CO., New York.
Sales Agents WM. KRAUSE & SONS' CEMENT CO.
Manufacturers Krause's brand Portland cement.

CARRERE, J. MAXWELL, 66 Maiden Lane, New York.
Mgr. New York Office CHAS. WARNER CO., Wilmington, Del.

CHICAGO CRUSHED STONE COMPANY, Chicago, Ill.
Agents BONNEVILLE PORTLAND CEMENT CO., 1233-7 R. E. Trust Bldg., Philadelphia, Pa.
Manufacturers Standard and Star brands Portland cement and Improved Bonneville brand natural hydraulic cement.

CLARK, JAS. G., New Orleans, La.
Sales Agent LEHIGH PORTLAND CEMENT Co., Allentown, Pa.
Manufacturers Lehigh brand Portland cement.

CLARKE, WM. WIRT, & SON, 115 Gay St. South, Baltimore, Md.
Sales Agents UNION AKRON CEMENT Co., Buffalo, N. Y.
Manufacturers' Agents for Akron Red Star brand natural hydraulic cement.
Sales Agents BRIDGES & HENDERSON, Hancock, Md.
Manufacturers B. & H. brand natural hydraulic cement.
Sales Agents MARYLAND CEMENT Co., Sparrows' Point, Md.
Manufacturers Rhinoceros brand Portland cement (pozzuolana) and Clarke's brand hydraulic cement.
Sales Agents HERCULES CEMENT Co., Catasauqua, Pa.
Manufacturers Clarke's Improved Rosendale brand natural hydraulic cement.
Sales Agents WM. KRAUSE & SONS' CEMENT Co., Martin's Creek, Pa.
Manufacturers Krause's brand Portland cement.
Agents I. C. JOHNSON & Co., Gateshead-on-Tyne, England.
Manufacturers Elephant brand English Portland cement.

COMMERCIAL WOOD AND CEMENT COMPANY, 156 Fifth Ave., New York; Girard Bldg., Philadelphia, Pa.
RALPH PEVERLEY, Pres.; J. F. TWAMLEY, Vice-Pres.; J. C. DETWILER, Treas.; F. M. HOOVER, Sec'y.
Sales Agents COPLAY CEMENT Co., Allentown, Pa.
Manufacturers Saylor's and Commercial brands Portland cement and Anchor and Commercial brands Rosendale natural hydraulic cement.
Sales Agents GLENS FALLS PORTLAND CEMENT Co., Glens Falls, N. Y.
Manufacturers Iron Clad and Victor brands Portland cement.

COMSTOCK, F. F., 261 Broadway, New York City.
Agent BONNEVILLE PORTLAND CEMENT Co., 1233-7 R. E. Trust Bldg., Philadelphia, Pa.
Manufacturers Standard and Star brands Portland cement and Improved Bonneville brand natural hydraulic cement.

COX, EDWARD L., 1511 Marquette Bldg., Chicago, Ill.
Gen. Sales Agents GERMAN-AMERICAN PORTLAND CEMENT WORKS.
Manufacturers Owl cement brand Portland cement.

CROWE, F. T., & CO., 740 Pacific Ave., Tacoma, Wash., and 76 Starr Boyd Bldg., Seattle, Wash.
U. S. Agents SHEWAN, TOMES & Co., Hong Kong.
Manufacturers Emerald brand cement.

GLENS FALLS PORTLAND CEMENT CO.

GLENS FALLS, N. Y.

THE works of the Glens Falls Portland Cement Company are located on the Glens Falls Feeder Canal, where it is crossed by the tracks of The Delaware and Hudson Company Railroad, thereby affording water and rail transportation for the shipment of their cement. These works during the past year have been entirely rebuilt, greatly enlarged, and remodeled so as to conform to the best cement engineering practice of the present day. Through the entire plant the construction has been of brick and iron, with the Expanded Metal and Roebling systems of fireproofing for the floors, roofs, and large hoppers.

The raw materials from which the cement is made surround the factory, and embrace a large tract extending on both sides of the Glens Falls Feeder, and on both sides of the Hudson River. These materials consist of a limestone and an overlying clay peculiarly adapted to cement making. The limestone is found as usual in layers of varying thickness, differing slightly in their chemical analysis. But by care in the selection and combination of these layers, an extremely uniform product is obtained for the average, which does not vary more than one per cent. in the amount of carbonate of lime it contains.

The clay is found in large deposits over the limestone, and is singularly favorable to cement making on account of its freedom from coarse sand and the uniform character of its constituents.

The raw materials are treated by the dry process, whi:h is a satisfactory and favorite method both in this country and abroad. An outline of it is as follows: The limestone and clay are first dried and partially reduced by crushers and rolls. They are then accurately weighed in the proper proportions in automatic scales. After being weighed, the materials are thoroughly mixed, then still further reduced to a fine powder by grinding mills, from which the mixture is elevated to a large bin, and then in turn it is fed to the wet mixers, where it is properly tempered with water to allow it to be made into bricks. The bricks are now run into drying tunnels, which are heated by waste heat carried in a duct from the boiler, and driven by blowers through the tunnel system.

After being thoroughly dried, the bricks are elevated to the top floor of the kiln building, where they are fed into Schöfer kilns, and properly burnt. These Schöfer kilns are an improvement on the Dietzsch kiln, and are very economical in fuel. Like all the improved German kilns, while very simple and uniform in their working when properly controlled, many disastrous failures have taken place from attempting to operate them theoretically with inexperienced men. In the Glens Falls Portland Cement Works it was found necessary to employ head burners trained in the old works of Europe.

From the kilns, the clinker is conveyed to the ball mills, where the first reduction is made with steel balls. From these it passes to the tube mills, where the final reduction is made with flint pebbles. The finely ground cement is now ready for storing, and is conveyed to the storehouse, where it is deposited in separate bins, each holding from four hundred to twenty-five hundred barrels, where the cement is carefully sampled and then tested.

CUTLER & GILBERT, Duluth, Minn.
Sales Agents LEHIGH PORTLAND CEMENT Co., Allentown, Pa.
Manufacturers Lehigh brand Portland cement.

DABOLL, F. A., Land Title Bldg., Philadelphia, Pa.
Mgr. Philadelphia Office CHAS. WARNER Co., Wilmington, Del.

DAVIS, JAS. A., & CO., 92 State St., Boston, Mass.
Sales Agents LEHIGH PORTLAND CEMENT Co.
Manufacturers Lehigh brand Portland cement.
Sales Agents ALPHA PORTLAND CEMENT Co.
Manufacturers Alpha brand Portland cement.
Sales Agents Olympia brand Rosendale natural hydraulic cement.

DEE, WM. E., 219 Royal Ins. Bldg., Chicago, Ill.
Sales Agent AMERICAN CEMENT Co., Philadelphia, Pa.
Manufacturers Giant brand Portland cement.
Sales Agent BRONSON PORTLAND CEMENT Co., Bronson, Mich.
Manufacturers Bronson Portland cement.
Sales Agent MARQUETTE PORTLAND CEMENT Co., La Salle, Ill.
Sales Agent ZENITH PORTLAND CEMENT Co., Detroit, Mich.

DEFREES, C. H., 315 S. Taylor St., South Bend, Ind.
Sales Agent T. MILLEN & Co., Wayland, N. Y.
Manufacturers Wayland brand Portland cement.

DE SMET, GEO. W., 317 Chamber of Commerce Bldg., Chicago, Ill.
Western Sales Agent VULCANITE PORTLAND CEMENT Co.
Manufacturers Vulcanite brand Portland cement.

DICKINSON CEMENT COMPANY, 931 Marquette Bldg., Chicago, Ill.
Sales Agents MARQUETTE PORTLAND CEMENT Co., Deer Park Glen, Ill.
Sales Agents ALPHA PORTLAND CEMENT Co., Easton, Pa.
Manufacturers Alpha brand Portland cement.

DONALDSON, W. J., Betz Bldg., Philadelphia, Pa.
Sales Agent ALPHA PORTLAND CEMENT Co., Easton, Pa.
Manufacturers Alpha Portland cement.

EASTON LIME COMPANY, Easton, Pa.
Sales Agents LEHIGH PORTLAND CEMENT Co., Allentown, Pa.
Manufacturers Lehigh brand Portland cement.

EBERT, MORRIS, 302 Walnut St., Philadelphia, Pa.
Agent MANNHEIMER PORTLAND CEMENT FABRIK, Mannheim, Germany.
Manufacturers Mannheimer Portland cement.

EGLESTON, HOWARD, Havana, Cuba.
Sales Agent for Cuba, CEMENT DEPARTMENT ILLINOIS STEEL Co., Rookery, Chicago, Ill.
Manufacturers Universal brand Portland cement.
Manufacturers Steel brand cement (pozzuolana).

IELD, H. K., & CO., Alexandria, Va.
Agents BONNEVILLE PORTLAND CEMENT CO., 1233-7 R. E. Trust Bldg., Philadelphia, Pa.
Manufacturers Standard and Star brands Portland cement and Improved Bonneville brand natural hydraulic cement.

INEGAN, THOS., Boise, Idaho.
Agent PORTLAND CEMENT CO. OF UTAH, Ltd., Salt Lake City, Utah.
Manufacturers Red Diamond brand Portland cement.

LEMING & CO., 123 Liberty St., New York.
Sales Agents Black Cross brand Portland cement.

T. SCOTT CEMENT ASSOCIATION, Kansas City, Mo.
Sales Agents for FT. SCOTT HYDRAULIC CEMENT CO., Kansas City, Mo.
Manufacturers Four Star brand natural hydraulic cement.
Sales Agents KANSAS CITY & FT. SCOTT CEMENT CO., Kansas City, Mo.
Manufacturers Double Star brand natural hydraulic cement.

RENCH, SAM'L H., & CO., Fourth and Callowhill Sts., Philadelphia, Pa.
Sales Agents DEXTER PORTLAND CEMENT CO., Nazareth, Pa.
Manufacturers Dexter brand Portland cement and French's Rosendale brand natural hydraulic cement.
Agents NEWARK LIME AND CEMENT MANUFACTURING CO., Newark, N. J.
Manufacturers Old Newark Rosendale brand natural hydraulic cement.
U. S. Agents Hercules brand Breitenburger German Portland cement.
U. S. Agents H. H. MEIER & CO., Bremen, Germany.
Manufacturers Meier's Puzzolan cement (pozzuolana).

GABRIEL & SCHALL, 205 Pearl St., New York.
Sales Agents VORWOHLER PORTLAND CEMENT FABRIK, PRUSSING, PLANCK & CO., Holzminden, Germany.
Manufacturers Vorwohler Lion brand German Portland cement.

GAMAGE & WALLER, Norfolk, Va.
Sales Agents LEHIGH PORTLAND CEMENT CO., Allentown, Pa.
Manufacturers Lehigh brand Portland cement.

FLEMING & CO.
123 Liberty Street, NEW YORK.
Estimates on Application.
Adamantine, Clinker, Terra Metallic, Brick, Cement FLOORING AND PAVING

GARDEN CITY SAND COMPANY, 1201-1205 Security Bldg., Chicago, Ill.

Sales Agents CHICAGO PORTLAND CEMENT Co., 513 Stock Exchange Bldg., Chicago, Ill.

Manufacturers AA Chicago brand Portland cement.

Sales Agents LEHIGH PORTLAND CEMENT Co., Allentown, Pa.

Manufacturers Lehigh brand Portland cement.

Sales Agents VULCANITE PORTLAND CEMENT Co., Philadelphia, Pa.

Manufacturers Vulcanite Portland cement.

Sales Agents BONNEVILLE CEMENT Co., Philadelphia, Pa.

Manufacturers Star Portland cement.

GIRVIN & EYRE, 307 California St., San Francisco, Cal.

Sales Agents HILTON, ANDERSON & BROOKS, Faversham, Upnor and Halling, England.

Manufacturers Hilton brand English Portland cement.

Sales Agents MISBURGER PORTLAND CEMENT WORKS, Hanover, Germany.

Manufacturers Teutonia brand German Portland cement.

Sales Agents Castle brand Belgian natural hydraulic cement.

GLENCOE LIME AND CEMENT COMPANY, 1400a Old Manchester Road, St. Louis, Mo.

C. W. S. COBB, Pres.; T. W. C. BOHN, Sec'y; E. S. HEALEY, Treas.

Sales Agents LEHIGH PORTLAND CEMENT Co., Allentown, Pa.

Manufacturers Lehigh brand Portland cement.

Sales Agents SANDUSKY PORTLAND CEMENT Co., Sandusky Ohio.

Manufacturers Medusa brand Portland cement.

Sales Agents UTICA CEMENT MANUFACTURING COMPANIES.

Manufacturers Black Ball and Clark brands natural hydraulic cement.

Sales Agents Louisville natural hydraulic cements. (See WESTERN CEMENT Co. for list of brands.)

Sales Agents Germania brand German Portland cement.

GOETZ, CHAS. W., LIME AND CEMENT COMPANY, 352 Gratiot St., St. Louis, Mo.

Agents BANNER CEMENT Co., Chicago, Ill.

Manufacturers Banner brand Louisville natural hydraulic cement.

Sales Agents CASTALIA PORTLAND CEMENT Co., Pittsburg, Pa.

Manufacturers Tiger brand Portland cement.

HALL, C. W., 140 Nassau St., New York City.

Sales Agent CEMENT DEPARTMENT ILLINOIS STEEL Co., 106 The Rookery, Chicago, Ill.

Manufacturers Universal brand Portland cement.

HALLACK & HOWARD LUMBER COMPANY, THE, Denver, Colo.
J. H. HOWARD, Pres.; O. H. BARR, Sec'y; B. COLDREN, Treas.
Sales Agents COLORADO PORTLAND CEMENT Co., Portland, Colo.
Manufacturers Pike's Peak brand Portland cement.

HARTRANFT, WM. G., CEMENT COMPANY, Real Estate Trust Bldg., Philadelphia, Pa.
WM. G. HARTRANFT, Pres.; JOS. W. ZIPPERLEIN, Vice-Pres.; A. W. NASH, Sec'y and Treas.
Sales Agents ALMA PORTLAND CEMENT Co., Wellston, Ohio.
Manufacturers Alma brand Portland cement.
Sales Agents BUCKHORN PORTLAND CEMENT Co., Manheim, W. Va.
Manufacturers Buckhorn brand Portland cement.
Sales Agents PHOENIX CEMENT Co., Nazareth, Pa.
Manufacturers Phœnix and Clover Leaf brands Portland cement and IXL brand natural hydraulic cement.
Sales Agents VIRGINIA PORTLAND CEMENT Co., Craigsville, Va.
Manufacturers Old Dominion Portland cement.

HAWES, S. H., & CO., Richmond, Va.
Agents BONNEVILLE PORTLAND CEMENT Co., 1233-7 R. E. Trust Bldg., Philadelphia, Pa.
Manufacturers Standard and Star brands Portland cement and Improved Bonneville brand natural hydraulic cement.

HOLMES, F. B., & CO., Hammond Bldg., Detroit, Mich.
Gen. Sales Agents MICHIGAN ALKALI Co., Wyandotte, Mich.
Manufacturers Wyandotte brand Portland cement.

HOUSTON & CO., 26 Cortlandt St., New York.
Sales Agents THE HERCULES CEMENT Co., Catasauqua, Pa.
Manufacturers Hercules and Granite brands Portland cement and Improved Lehigh and Improved Rosendale brands natural hydraulic cement.

HOUSTON BROS., Thirty-second St. and Pennsylvania Railroad, Pittsburg, Pa.
Manufacturers Rex-Portland and Samson brands Portland cement.
Agents VULCANITE PORTLAND CEMENT Co.
Manufacturers Vulcanite brand Portland cement.
Agents Flint Rock Rosendale and Cumberland Valley brands natural hydraulic cement.

HUNT & CONNELL CO., Scranton, Pa.
Agents BONNEVILLE PORTLAND CEMENT Co., 1233-7 R. E. Trust Bldg., Philadelphia, Pa.
Manufacturers Standard and Star brands Portland cement and Improved Bonneville brand natural hydraulic cement.

JACKSON, FRANK H., 104 S. Broadway, Los Angeles, Cal.
Sales Agent CALIFORNIA PORTLAND CEMENT Co.
Manufacturers Colton brand Portland cement.

JACKSON, J. H., Albany, N. Y.
Agent BONNEVILLE PORTLAND CEMENT Co., 1233-7 R. E. Trust Bldg., Philadelphia, Pa.
Manufacturers Standard and Star brands Portland cement and Improved Bonneville brand natural hydraulic cement.
Agent NAZARETH CEMENT Co., Nazareth, Pa.
Manufacturers Nazareth brand Portland cement.

JENKINS & MACY, Rochester, N. Y.
Agents EMPIRE PORTLAND CEMENT Co., Warners, N. Y.
Manufacturers Empire brand Portland cement.

JOHNSON & WILSON, 150 Nassau St., New York.
Gen. Agents COPLAY CEMENT Co., Allentown, Pa.
Manufacturers Saylor's brand Portland cement.
Sales Agents Keystone brand Portland cement.
Sales Agents Anchor brand natural hydraulic cement.

JONES & GOLD, Maquoketa, Iowa.
Agents BONNEVILLE PORTLAND CEMENT Co., 1233-7 R. E. Trust Bldg., Philadelphia, Pa.
Manufacturers Standard and Star brands Portland cement and Improved Bonneville brand natural hydraulic cement.

KELLER, LUTHER, Scranton, Pa.
Sales Agent LEHIGH PORTLAND CEMENT Co., Allentown, Pa.
Manufacturers Lehigh brand Portland cement.

KELLEY ISLAND LIME AND TRANSPORT COMPANY, Cleveland, Ohio.
U. S. Sales Agents EUG. LION & Co., Hamburg and Lägerdorf, Germany.
Manufacturers Lägerdorfer Eiffel Tower brand German Portland cement.
Western Distributing Agents LEHIGH PORTLAND CEMENT Co., Allentown, Pa.
Manufacturers Lehigh brand Portland cement.

KENNEDY, D. J., 150 Frankstown Ave., Pittsburg, Pa.
Sales Agents LEHIGH PORTLAND CEMENT Co., Allentown, Pa.
Manufacturers Lehigh brand Portland cement.

KNOX, J. P. & E. A., Allegheny, Pa.
Agents BONNEVILLE PORTLAND CEMENT Co., 1233-7 R. E. Trust Bldg., Philadelphia, Pa.
Manufacturers Standard and Star brands Portland cement and Improved Bonneville brand natural hydraulic cement.

he Kelley Island Lime
& Transport Company

CEMENT DEPARTMENT

SOLE WESTERN AND SOUTHERN DISTRIBUTORS OF

Lehigh Portland Cement

High Tensile Strength.
Finely Ground.
Light and Uniform in Color.
Recommended for
High-Class Engineering Work.

MANUFACTURED BY

EHIGH PORTLAND CEMENT COMPANY

ALLENTOWN, PA.

SOLE AGENTS AND IMPORTERS FOR UNITED STATES OF

agerdorfer German
Portland Cement Co.

Write us for prices before placing orders.

ain Office, Mercantile Bank Bldg., - CLEVELAND, OHIO

LESLEY & TRINKLE CO., 22 S. Fifteenth St., Philadelphia, Pa.
R. W. LESLEY, Pres.; R. E. GRIFFITH, Vice-Pres.; WM. TRINKLE, Treas.; GASTON DAVIS, Sec'y.
Sales Agents AMERICAN CEMENT Co., Philadelphia, Pa.
Manufacturers Giant brand Portland cement and Improved Union and Union brands natural hydraulic cement.
Importers from DYCKERHOFF & SOEHNE, Amoeneburg, Germany.
Manufacturers Dyckerhoff brand German Portland cement.
Importers from PORTLAND CEMENT FABRIK, Lueneburg, Germany.
Manufacturers Heyn Bros.' brand German Portland cement.
Importers from HILTON, ANDERSON, BROOKS & CO., Ltd., London, England.
Manufacturers Hilton London brand English Portland cement.

LEWIS, DAVID W., 192 Devonshire St., Boston, Mass.
Sales Agent UNION AKRON CEMENT Co., Buffalo, N. Y.
Manufacturers Akron Red Star brand natural hydraulic cement.
Sales Agent F. O. NORTON CEMENT Co., New York.
Manufacturers Norton's Rosendale brand natural hydraulic cement.
Sales Agent GLENS FALLS PORTLAND CEMENT Co., Glens Falls, N. Y.
Manufacturers Iron Clad and Victor brands Portland cement.
Sales Agent WM. KRAUSE & SONS CEMENT Co., Martin's Creek, Pa.
Manufacturers Krause's brand Portland cement.

LITTLE, C. H. CO., THE, Detroit, Mich.
Agents BRIER HILL IRON AND COAL COMPANY, Youngstown Ohio.
Manufacturers Brier Hill brand Portland cement (pozzuolana).

LUCAS, JOHN, 377 Spadina Ave., Toronto, Ont.
Sales Agent OWEN SOUND PORTLAND CEMENT Co., Ltd., Owen Sound, Ont.
Manufacturers Samson and Magnet brands Portland cement.

LYLE, R. B., Security Bldg., St. Louis, Mo.
Sales Agent CEMENT DEPARTMENT ILLINOIS STEEL Co., 106 Rookery, Chicago, Ill.
Manufacturers Universal brand Portland cement.
Manufacturers Steel brand cement (pozzuolana).

MAGIFF, THOS. M., 39 Cortlandt St., New York.
Gen. Sales Agent NEWARK AND ROSENDALE LIME AND CEMENT Co., Newark, N. J.
Manufacturers Newark-Rosendale brand natural hydraulic cement.

MARBLEHEAD LIME COMPANY, 1105 Masonic Temple, Chicago, Ill.
Sales Agents BANNER CEMENT Co., Cementville, Ind.
Manufacturers Banner brand Louisville natural hydraulic cement.

MARTIN & SULLIVAN, Syracuse, N. Y.
Agents EMPIRE PORTLAND CEMENT Co., Warners, N. Y.
Manufacturers Empire brand Portland cement.

MARYLAND LIME AND CEMENT COMPANY, Baltimore, Md.
Sales Agents LEHIGH PORTLAND CEMENT Co., Allentown, Pa.
Manufacturers Lehigh brand Portland cement.

McALARNEY, GEO. L., Wilkes-Barre, Pa.
Agent BONNEVILLE PORTLAND CEMENT Co., 1233-7 R. E. Trust Bldg., Philadelphia, Pa.
Manufacturers Standard and Star brands Portland cement and Improved Bonneville brand natural hydraulic cement.

McBEAN, A. J., & CO., Chicago, Ill.
Agents THOS. MILLEN & Co., Wayland, N. Y.
Manufacturers Wayland brand Portland cement.
Agents LAWRENCE CEMENT Co. OF PENNSYLVANIA, Siegfried, Pa.
Manufacturers Dragon brand Portland cement.

MEACHAM & WRIGHT, Chicago, Ill.
Gen. Sales Agents UTICA HYDRAULIC CEMENT Co., Utica, Ill.
Manufacturers Clark brand Utica natural hydraulic cement.
Gen. Sales Agents UTICA CEMENT MANUFACTURING Co., Utica, Ill.
Manufacturers Black Ball brand Utica natural hydraulic cement.

MENG, ANTHONY, & CO., 109 S. Front St., Philadelphia, Pa.
Sales Agents DUMON & Co., Belgium.
Manufacturers Dagger brand Belgian Portland cement.

INFORMATION FOR EVERYBODY

If you want to know anything about Cement, Cement work or Cement machinery we will furnish the information, if possible, on request.

MUNICIPAL ENGINEERING CO.

MEYER, A. B., & CO., 19 N. Pennsylvania St., Indianapolis, Ind.
Sales Agents CASTALIA PORTLAND CEMENT CO., Pittsburg, Pa.
Manufacturers Tiger brand Portland cement.
Sales Agents COPLAY CEMENT CO., Allentown, Pa.
Manufacturers Saylor's and Commercial brands Portland cement.
Sales Agents MICHIGAN PORTLAND CEMENT CO., Coldwater, Mich.
Manufacturers Wolverine and Eclipse brands Portland cement.
Sales Agents NAZARETH CEMENT CO., Nazareth, Pa.
Manufacturers Nazareth brand Portland cement.

MEYER, WILSON & CO., San Francisco, Cal., and Portland, Ore.
Sales Agents PORTLAND CEMENT FABRIK, Hemmoor, Hamburg, Germany.
Manufacturers Hemmoor brand German Portland cement.
Importers Germania, Heidelberg, Karlstadt, Mannheimer brands German Portland cements, Trowel and Castle brands foreign cements.

MOBILE COAL COMPANY, Mobile, Ala.
Sales Agents LEHIGH PORTLAND CEMENT CO., Allentown, Pa.
Manufacturers Lehigh brand Portland cement.

MOORE, WARNER, & CO., Richmond, Va.
Sales Agents LEHIGH PORTLAND CEMENT CO., Allentown, Pa.
Manufacturers Lehigh brand Portland cement.
Agents ALPHA PORTLAND CEMENT CO., Easton, Pa.
Manufacturers Alpha brand Portland cement.
Agents Dyckerhoff brand German Portland cement.
Agents LAWRENCE CEMENT CO., New York.
Manufacturers Hoffman Rosendale brand natural hydraulic cement.

MOORES & CO., Cincinnati, Ohio.
Agents BONNEVILLE PORTLAND CEMENT CO., 1233-7 R. E. Trust Bldg., Philadelphia, Pa.
Manufacturers Standard and Star brands Portland cement and Improved Bonneville brand natural hydraulic cement.

MORSE, THE FRANK E., CO., 17 State St., New York.
Exchange Sales Agents THE LAWRENCE CEMENT CO. OF PENNSYLVANIA, Siegfried, Pa.
Manufacturers of Dragon, Paragon and Monarch brands Portland cement.
Exchange Sales Agents LAWRENCE CEMENT CO., New York.
Manufacturers of Shield, Improved Shield and Hoffman brands Rosendale natural hydraulic cement.
Sales Agents of Continental and Liberty Bell brands Portland cement.
Sales Agents Patriot brand cement.

NASH, W. G., 220 State St., Boston, Mass.
Northeastern Agent AMERICAN CEMENT Co., Philadelphia, Pa.
Manufacturers Giant, Egypt, Columbia, Improved Union brands of cement.

NATIONAL BUILDING SUPPLY COMPANY, N. Lexington St., Baltimore, Md.; 413 Carondelet St., New Orleans, La.
Agents Porta and Kaiser brands German Portland cement.
Agents Vultur and Knight brands Belgian Portland cement.

NEWHALL, H. M., & CO., 309 Sansome St., San Francisco, Cal.
Sales Agents PORTLAND CEMENT CO. OF UTAH.
Manufacturers Red Diamond brand Portland cement.

NEWTON LUMBER COMPANY, Pueblo, Colo.
Agents PORTLAND CEMENT CO. OF UTAH, Ltd., Salt Lake City, Utah.
Manufacturers Red Diamond brand Portland cement.
Agents DYCKERHOFF & SOEHNE, Amoeneburg, Germany.
Manufacturers Dyckerhoff brand German Portland cement.

NOBLE & CO., Detroit, Mich.
Agents BUFFALO CEMENT CO., Ltd., Buffalo, N. Y.
Manufacturers Buffalo brand Portland and natural hydraulic cements.

OLAND CEMENT COMPANY, 160 Fifth Ave., New York.
Agents Oland brand Swedish Portland cement.
Agents Hanover brand German Portland cement.

OSBORNE, T. B., 1 Broadway, New York.
Sales Agent LAWRENCE CEMENT CO. OF PENNSYLVANIA, Siegfried, Pa.
Manufacturers Dragon, Paragon, Monarch brands Portland cement.
Sales Agent LAWRENCE CEMENT CO., New York.
Manufacturers Hoffman, Shield and Improved Shield brands Rosendale natural hydraulic cement.

PARR, WM., & CO., Galveston, Tex.
Importers Eagle brand Belgian, Hemmoor Crown brand German Portland cement.
Gen. Sales Agents TEXAS PORTLAND CEMENT CO., Dallas, Tex.
Manufacturers Live Oak brand Portland cement.
Sales Agents IOLA PORTLAND CEMENT CO., Iola, Kans.
Manufacturers Iola brand Portland cement.

PATTERSON, J. E., & CO., Wilkes-Barre, Pa.
Sales Agents LEHIGH PORTLAND CEMENT CO., Allentown, Pa.
Manufacturers Lehigh brand Portland cement.

PITTSBURG AND BUFFALO COMPANY, Pittsburg, Pa.
Agents BUFFALO CEMENT CO., Ltd., Buffalo, N. Y.
Manufacturers Buffalo brand Portland and natural hydraulic cements.

POLLARD, W. H., & CO., Galveston, Tex.
Sales Agents LEHIGH PORTLAND CEMENT Co., Allentown, Pa
Manufacturers Lehigh brand Portland cement.

RAMSAY, CHAS. H., 38 State St., Albany, N. Y.
Sales Agent HELDERBERG CEMENT Co., Howe's Cave, N. Y.
Manufacturers Helderberg brand Portland cement.
Manufacturers Rosendale natural hydraulic cement.
Manufacturers Howe's Cave natural hydraulic cement.

RATHBUN CO., THE, Deseronto, Ont.
Sales Agents THE CANADIAN PORTLAND CEMENT Co., Ltd Deseronto, Ont.
Manufacturers Rathbun's Star, Beaver and Ensign brand of cement.

REPPLIER, J. L., 536 Penn St., Reading, Pa.*
Gen. Sales Agent READING CEMENT Co., Reading, Pa.
Manufacturers Reading brand Portland cement and Improved Rosendale brand natural hydraulic cement.

ROBINSON & CO., Philadelphia, Pa.
Sales Agents THE HERCULES CEMENT Co., Catasauqua, Pa.
Manufacturers Hercules and Granite brands Portland cement and Improved Lehigh and Improved Rosendal brands natural hydraulic cement.

SAYRE-NEWTON LUMBER COMPANY, THE, Denver, Colo
Agents ALSEN'S PORTLAND CEMENT WORKS, Hamburg, Germany.
Manufacturers Alsen's brand German Portland cement.
Agents COLORADO PORTLAND CEMENT Co., Portland, Colo.
Manufacturers Pike's Peak brand Portland cement.

SCHAUFFLER, C. E., 737 Monadnock Blk., Chicago, Ill.
Res. Mgr. EMPIRE PORTLAND CEMENT Co., Warners, N. Y.
Manufacturers Empire and Flint brands Portland cement.

SEARS, HUMBERT & CO., 83 Fulton St., New York; 434 Prudential Bldg., Buffalo, N. Y.; 1310 Chamber of Commerce, Chicago, Ill.; Fidelity Mutual Life Bldg., Philadelphia, Pa.
Western Sales Agents AMERICAN CEMENT Co., Philadelphia, Pa.
Manufacturers Giant brand Portland cement and Union and Improved Union brands natural hydraulic cement.
Sales Agents WHITEHALL PORTLAND CEMENT Co., Cementon, Pa.
Manufacturers Whitehall brand Portland cement.

SHENANDOAH LIME COMPANY, Brockett, Va.
Agents BONNEVILLE PORTLAND CEMENT Co., 1233-7 R. E. Trust Bldg., Philadelphia, Pa.
Manufacturers Standard and Star brands Portland cement

INCLAIR & BABSON, 143 Liberty St., New York.
Sales Agents Alsen's German Portland cement, Germany.
Agents Alsen's American Portland Cement Works, West Camp, N. Y.

MITH, GREEN COMPANY, Worcester, Mass.
Sales Agents Lawrenceville Cement Co., Binnewater, N.Y.
Manufacturers Beach's Rosendale brand natural hydraulic cement.

NYDER, HIRAM, & CO., 229 Broadway, New York.
Sales Agents Lehigh Portland Cement Co., Allentown, Pa.
Manufacturers Lehigh brand Portland cement.
Sales Agents Alpha Portland Cement Co., Easton, Pa.
Manufacturers Alpha brand Portland cement.
Sales Agents XXX brand Rosendale natural hydraulic cement.

OUTHEASTERN LIME AND CEMENT COMPANY, Charleston, S. C.
Sales Agents Lehigh Portland Cement Co., Allentown, Pa.
Manufacturers Lehigh brand Portland cement.
Sales Agents New York and Rosendale Cement Co., New York.
Manufacturers Brooklyn Bridge brand Rosendale natural hydraulic cement.
Importers Hemmoor brand German Portland cement.
Importers Hammer brand Belgian Portland cement.

PARROW, FRIDENBERG & CO., 15-25 Whitehall St., New York.
Sales Agents Portland Cement Fabrik, Hamburg, Germany.
Manufacturers Hemmoor Crown brand German Portland cement.
Sales Agents The Misburger Portland Cement Works, Hanover, Germany.
Manufacturers Teutonia brand German Portland cement.
Sales Agents Hoxter and Lauffen brands German Portland cements.
Sales Agents Globe Belgian Portland cement.

STOUT, C. D., 1 Broadway, New York.
Sales Agent Lawrence Cement Co., New York.
Manufacturers Hoffman, Shield and Improved Shield brands Rosendale natural hydraulic cement.
Sales Agent The Lawrence Cement Co. of Pennsylvania, Siegfried, Pa.
Manufacturers Dragon, Paragon and Monarch brands Portland cement.

STOWE-FULLER COMPANY, Arcade Bldg., Cleveland, Ohio.
Agents Brier Hill Iron and Coal Co., Youngstown, Ohio.
Manufacturers Brier Hill brand Portland cement (pozzuolana).

STRADLEY, B. F., 1712 Market St., Philadelphia, Pa.
Gen. Sales Agent and Sec'y VULCANITE PORTLAND CEMENT Co.
Manufacturers Vulcanite brand Portland cement.

TAYLOR BROS., Camden, N. J.
Sales Agents LEHIGH PORTLAND CEMENT Co., Allentown, Pa.
Manufacturers Lehigh brand Portland cement.
Sales Agents ALPHA PORTLAND CEMENT Co., Alpha, N. J.
Manufacturers Alpha brand Portland cement.

THIELE, E., 99 John St., New York.
Sales Agent DYCKERHOFF & SOEHNE, Amoeneburg, Germany.
Manufacturers Dyckerhoff brand German Portland cement.
Sales Agent PORTLAND CEMENT FABRIK STERN, Stettin, Germany.
Manufacturers Star Stettin brand German Portland cement.
Sales Agent PORTLAND CEMENT FABRIK, Lueneburg, Germany.
Manufacturers Heyn Bros.' brand German Portland cement.
Sales Agent HILTON, ANDERSON, BROOKS & Co., Ltd., London, England.
Manufacturers Hilton, London, and B., S. & Co., London, brands English Portland cement.
Sales Agent COMPAGNIE GENERALE DES CEMENTS PORTLAND DE L'ESCAUT, Tournai, Belgium.
Manufacturers Royal Crown brand Belgian Portland cement.

THORN & HUNKINS LIME AND CEMENT CO., Eighteenth and Austin Sts., St. Louis, Mo.
F. P. HUNKINS, Pres. and Treas; GORDON WILLIS, Vice-Pres. and Sec'y.
Southwestern Distributing Agents ATLAS PORTLAND CEMENT Co., 143 Liberty St., New York City.
Manufacturers Atlas brand. Portland cement.

THORN CEMENT COMPANY, 112-118 Church St., Buffalo. N. Y.
Sales Agents LEHIGH PORTLAND CEMENT Co., Allentown, Pa.
Manufacturers Lehigh brand Portland cement.
Agents BONNEVILLE PORTLAND CEMENT Co., 1233-7 R. E. Trust Bldg., Philadelphia, Pa.
Manufacturers Standard and Star brands Portland cement and Improved Bonneville brand natural hydraulic cement.
Agents ALPHA PORTLAND CEMENT Co., Easton, Pa.
Manufacturers Alpha brand Portland cement.

TOMKINS, CALVIN, 120 Liberty St., New York.
Sales Agent NEWARK LIME AND CEMENT MANUFACTURING Co., Newark, N. J.
Manufacturers Old Newark Rosendale brand natural hydraulic cement.

TOMKINS BROS., 74-94 Passaic St., Newark, N. J.; 257 Broadway, New York.

Sales Agents NEWARK AND ROSENDALE LIME AND CEMENT CO., Newark, N. J.

Manufacturers Newark Rosendale brand natural hydraulic cement.

Sales Agents DEXTER PORTLAND CEMENT CO., Nazareth, Pa.

Manufacturers Dexter brand Portland cement.

TREADWAY, H. F., 928 Stock Exchange Bldg., Chicago, Ill.

Gen. Sales Agent OMEGA PORTLAND CEMENT CO., Jonesville, Mich.

Manufacturers Omega brand Portland cement.

UNION AKRON CEMENT COMPANY, 141 Erie St., Buffalo, N. Y.

DANIEL N. LOCKWOOD, Dir.; WM. C. NEWMAN, Dir. and Treas.; EDWIN PUZEY, Salesman and Mgr. of office.

Sales Agents for H. L. & W. C. NEWMAN, Akron, N. Y., and AKRON CEMENT WORKS, Akron, N. Y.

Manufacturers Akron Red Star brand natural hydraulic cement.

UNITED BUILDING MATERIAL COMPANY, 13-21 Park Row, New York City.

R. W. LESLEY, Pres.; WALLACE KING, JR., Sec'y; FRED'K J. JIGGENS, Treas.

Sales Agents for THE AMERICAN CEMENT CO. OF NEW JERSEY, 22 S. Fifteenth St., Philadelphia, Pa.

Manufacturers of Giant brand Portland cement and Improved Union and Union brands natural hydraulic cement.

VOLLMER & REGISTER, 716-7 Harrison Bldg., Fifteenth and Market Sts., Philadelphia, Pa.

Sales Agents ATLAS PORTLAND CEMENT CO.

Manufacturers Atlas brand Portland cement.

Sales Agents UNION AKRON CEMENT CO.

Manufacturers' Agents Akron Star brand natural hydraulic cement.

WALDO BROS., 102 Milk St., Boston, Mass.

Agents ATLAS PORTLAND CEMENT CO., New York.

Manufacturers Atlas brand Portland cement.

Importers Alsen brand Portland cement.

Agents HILTON, ANDERSON, BROOKS & CO., Ltd., London, England.

Manufacturers B., S. & Co., London, brand English Portland cement.

Agents H. H. MEIER & CO., Bremen, Germany.

Manufacturers Meier's Puzzolan cement.

Agents THE LAWRENCE CEMENT CO., New York.

Manufacturers Hoffman brand natural hydraulic cement.

WARNER, CHARLES, COMPANY, Equitable Bldg., Wilmington, Del.; Land Title Bldg, Philadelphia, Pa.; 66 Maiden Lane, New York.

E. T. WARNER, Pres.; ALFRED D. WARNER, Vice-Pres.; JOHN RICHARDSON, JR., Treas.; CHAS. C. BYE, Sec'y.

Sales Agents for NAZARETH CEMENT CO.

Manufacturers Nazareth brand Portland cement.

Sales Agents for Sovereign, Royal, Municipal brands Portland cement.

Sales Agents for Warner's Improved hydraulic cement.

Sales Agents for SOCIETE ANONYME UNION FRATERNELLE.

Manufacturers of Triton, Black Eagle and Star brands Belgian Portland cements.

Sales Agents for Blanc Stainless Portland cement (pozzuolana).

WARNER, MILLER & CO., New Haven, Conn.

Agents BONNEVILLE PORTLAND CEMENT CO., 1233-7 R. E. Trust Bldg., Philadelphia, Pa.

Manufacturers Standard and Star brands Portland cement and Improved Bonneville brand natural hydraulic cement.

WASHBURN BROS. & CO., Jersey City, N. J.

Agents BONNEVILLE PORTLAND CEMENT CO., 1233-7 R. E. Trust Bldg., Philadelphia, Pa.

Manufacturers Standard and Star brands Portland cement and Improved Bonneville brand natural hydraulic cement.

WATERS, J. G., & SON, Washington, D. C.

Agents BONNEVILLE PORTLAND CEMENT CO., 1233-7 R. E. Trust Bldg., Philadelphia, Pa.

Manufacturers Standard and Star brands Portland cement and Improved Bonneville brand natural hydraulic cement.

Sales Agents LEHIGH PORTLAND CEMENT CO., Allentown, Pa.

Manufacturers Lehigh brand Portland cement.

WELLIVER HARDWARE COMPANY, Danville, Pa.

Agents BONNEVILLE PORTLAND CEMENT CO., 1233-7 R. E. Trust Bldg., Philadelphia, Pa.

Manufacturers Standard and Star brands Portland cement and Improved Bonneville brand natural hydraulic cement.

WESTERN CEMENT COMPANY, Louisville, Ky. Chicago Office, 718 Chamber of Commerce Bldg.

Sales Agents of the following companies and brands of Louisville natural hydraulic cement:

BANNER CEMENT CO., Sellersburg, Ind. Manufacturers Banner brand.

CLARK CO. CEMENT CO., Sellersburg, Ind. Manufacturers Mason's Choice Hammer and Trowel brand.

GLOBE CEMENT CO., Sellersburg, Ind. Manufacturers Globe brand.

Western Cement Company—Continued.

GOLDEN RULE CEMENT CO., Sellersburg, Ind. Manufacturers Arm and Hammer brand.

HOOSIER CEMENT CO., Sellersburg, Ind. Manufacturers Hod and Shovel brand.

INDIANA CEMENT CO., Charlestown, Ind. Manufacturers Lion brand.

KENTUCKY AND INDIANA CEMENT CO., Jeffersonville and Watson, Ind. Manufacturers Eagle brand.

LOUISVILLE CEMENT CO., Louisville, Ky. Manufacturers Speed's Star, J. Hulme Star, Horseshoe and S*S brands.

NEW ALBANY CEMENT CO., New Albany and Haussdale, Ind. Manufacturers Crown brand.

OHIO VALLEY CEMENT CO., Jeffersonville and Cementville, Ind. Manufacturers Fern Leaf brand.

SILVER CREEK CEMENT CO., Louisville, Ky., and Cementville, Ind. Manufacturers Acorn brand.

STANDARD CEMENT CO., Louisville, Ky., and Charlestown, Ind. Manufacturers Best 4 brand.

UNION CEMENT AND LIME CO., Louisville, Ky., and Cementville, Ind. Manufacturers Black Diamond and Anchor brands.

UNITED STATES CEMENT CO., Sellersburg, Ind. Manufacturers Flag brand.

HOW TO BUILD UP BUSINESS

The cardinal point in business success is to make yourself known to every person who can add anything to your business.

It is not possible for you to know all these people, but they can be made to know about you. This is your advantage.

Advertising does this. It opens the field. Success depends on how wisely this advertising is done. If it reaches people in your line it pays.

If you want business from the field represented by MUNICIPAL ENGINEERING MAGAZINE it will pay you to advertise in it.

Don't You Want Equal Advantage in this Field

WESTERN LIME AND CEMENT COMPANY, Milwaukee, Wis.
Agents for States west of Lake Michigan to Montana for ATLAS CEMENT Co., 143 Liberty St., New York.
Manufacturers Atlas brand Portland cement.

WESTERN WHITE LIME COMPANY, Kansas City, Mo.
Sales Agents BANNER CEMENT Co., Cementville, Ind.
Manufacturers Banner brand Louisville natural hydraulic cement.

WHEELOCK, S. W., Cooper Bldg., Denver, Colo.
Sales Agent CEMENT DEPARTMENT ILLINOIS STEEL Co., 1060 Rookery, Chicago, Ill.
Manufacturers Universal brand Portland cement.
Manufacturers Steel brand cement (pozzuolana).

WHITMORE, RAUBER & VICINUS, Rochester, N. Y.
Agents BUFFALO CEMENT Co., Ltd., Buffalo, N. Y.
Manufacturers Buffalo brand Portland and natural hydraulic cements.

WHITNALL & RADEMAKER CO., Milwaukee, Wis.
Agents BONNEVILLE PORTLAND CEMENT Co., 1233-7 R. E. Trust Bldg., Philadelphia, Pa.
Manufacturers Standard and Star brands Portland cement and Improved Bonneville brand natural hydraulic cement.

YOUNGSTOWN ICE COMPANY, THE, Youngstown, Ohio.
Agents BRIER HILL IRON AND COAL Co., Youngstown, Ohio.
Manufacturers Brier Hill brand Portland cement (pozzuolana).

SIFIED DIRECTORY OF CEMENT DEALERS AND USERS

DEALERS IN CEMENT

ALABAMA.

N—
ouser.
LE—
h Lumber & Milling Co.
ER—
r Cornice Works.
ay.
Hardware Co.
GHAM—
Baldwin.
y Hardware Co.
Hardware Co.
PORT—
Bros. & Co.
R—
Jones.

Perdue.
CE—
Planing Mill Co.
Hudson, Court and Tusca- Sts.
& Co.
ILLE—
ckerman.
ly Bros.
& Jones.
alkenburg & Matthews.
—

ton.
—
Coal Co., A. C. Danner Pres.
MERY—
& Teague.
Vandiver & Co.
as Lumber Co.
ECATUR—
Malone.
CITY—
City Lumber Co.
Coal, Iron & R. R. Co.
-
s Hardware Co.
n Bros. & Co.
Robbins & Son.
Schuster.
ELD—
& Co.
Freeman.

TUSCALOOSA—
Allen & Jamison Co.
TUSCUMBIA—
B. J. Brinkley Grocery Co.
UNION SPRINGS—
C. C. Clark.
W. B. Doples.
Hanson Bros.
WOODLAWN—
M. F. Wood.

ARIZONA.

PHOENIX—
J. B. Dougherty.
W. I. Horner.
Henry W. Ryder.
E. M. Skinner.
Ezra W. Thayer.
The Valley Lumber Co.
TUCSON—
J. Knox Corbett.
Thomas Wilson.

ARKANSAS.

BATESVILLE—
Theo. Maxfield & Bros.
Talley Lumber Co.
CAMDEN—
J. P. Wright.
CONWAY—
Cole & Co.
Frauenthal & Schwarz.
FORT SMITH—
Dyke Bros.
Kenney Bros., 20 S. 6th St.
J. M. Tenney & Co., 201 S. 9th St.
HELENA—
Herman Carville Co.
D. F. Hargraves & Co.
Straub Pressed Brick Co.
HOT SPRINGS—
S. A. Sammons & Son.
LITTLE ROCK—
M. R. Denie, 104 E. Markhan St.
D. E. Jones, 413 E. Markhan St.
PARAGOULD—
Paragould Lumber Co.
TEXARKANA—
Chatfield & Buhrman.

CALIFORNIA.

ALAMEDA—
E. M. Derby & Co.

AUBURN—
H. H. Buhring.
R. J. Hancock.

BERKELEY—
F. L. Foss & Co.
J. A. Marshall.
H. L. Whitney.

CHICO—
J. A. Walker.

FRESNO—
Barrett Hicks & Co.
Donahoo Emmens Co.
L. Einstein & Co.
Kutner Goldstein Co.
W. R. Madary Mill Co.
C. S. Pierce Lumber Co.
Valley Lumber Co.

GRASS VALLEY—
Elam Biggs Hdw. Co., 14 Hill St. Elam Biggs, Pres. and Manager; A. Bunney, Secy.; N. E. Biggs, Treas.
Brady & Cassidy.
Richard Noell.

HANFORD—
Central Lumber Co.
L. Davis.
J. P. English.
Wendling Lumber Co.

LONG BEACH—
San Pedro Lumber Co.

LOS ANGELES—
Frank H. Jackson, 104 S. Broadway.
Sprekels Bros. Commercial Co. (J. B. Alexander, Agt., 200 S. Spring St.)
Union Lime Co.

MARYSVILLE—
W. T. Ellis & Son
J. R. Garrett Co.

MODESTO—
The Modesto Lumber Co.

NAPA—
A. Hatt Warehouse & Lbr. Co.
F. G. Moyse.

OAKLAND—
C. W. Emery, 1155 23d ave.
Howard Co, Howard's Wharf, 1st & Market St.
C. J. Jacobson, 860 Union St
Pierce Hardware Co., 1108 & 1110 Broadway.
Remillard Brick Co., Clay N. W. Cor. 2d St.
E. B. & A. L. Stone Supply Co., 900 Broadway.

PASADENA—
The L. W. Blinn Lumber Co.
Kerckhoff Cuyner Mill & Lumber Co
Patten & Davies Lumber & Fuel Co

PETALUMA—
A. Kahn.
Geo. P. McNear.

POMONA—
Blinn Lumber Co.
Kirckhoff & Cuzner.

RED BLUFF—
Holt & Gregg.

REDLANDS—
Newport Lumber Co.

RIVERSIDE—
Gill Norman Co.
Newport Lumber Co.
Russ Lumber and Mill Co.

SACRAMENTO—
Cowell & Co., 509 I St.
W. P. Fuller Co, 1078 Second St.
Kreuzberger, 513 I St.
Shaw Ingram Batcher Co., 217 J St.

SAN BERNARDINO—
John G. Eikleman.
Gill Norman Lumber Co.
Adolph Johnson.
Wilcox & Rose Co.

SAN DIEGO—
Henry Cowell Lime & Cement Co.
J. S. Schirm, foot of 3d and 4th Sts.
Spreckles Bros.' Commercial Co., Atlantic and G Sts.
Wyman Greundike & Co.

SAN FRANCISCO—
Alsana Cement Co., 634 Mission St.
Alsen's Portland Cement Wks., Mills Bldg.
Asbestos Fire Proof Co., 112 First St.
Balfour, Guthrie & Co.
California Cement Co., Tenth and Brannan St.
S. R. Church, 307 Sansome St.
Henry Cowell, 211 Drumm St.
Forbes Bros., 307 Sansome St.
Girvin & Eyre, 307 California St.
W. R. Grace & Co., California and Battery.
H. T. Holmes Lime Co., 24 Sacramento St.
Meyer, Wilson & Co.
H. M. Newhall & Co., 309 Sansome St.
J. J. North, 343 Berry St.
Joseph Scheerer & Co., Tenth and Brannan Sts.
John Tuttle, 516 Haight st.
Usona Portland Cement Co., Parrott Building

SAN LEANDRO—
N. L. Hansen.
J. Larsen
Fred Schmidt.

SANTA ANA—
H. E. Frielster.
C. E. Granard.
Frank Hiel.
Chris McNeill.
H. E. Smith

SANTA CLARA—
J. C. McPherson.
Pacific Mfg. Co

SANTA CRUZ—
Henry Cowell & Co.

ONICA—
: Nebeker.
OSA—
igley.
rka.
ller.
rrow.
agel.
IVERSIDE—
ros.
N—
Henery.
d & Yardley.
uin Brick Co.
Ice & Fuel Co.
—
Aden.
A—
Lumber Co.
County Lumber Co.
ILLE—
esser, 337 Main St.
ND—
a.
umber Co.
lley Lumber Co.

COLORADO.

nn.
Hdw. Co.
.. Tomkins Hdw. Co.
—
ays.
ar Lumber & Supply Co.
aylor.
hiteley.
ITY—
imber Co.
l Lumber Co.
bson Lumber Co.
O SPRINGS—
Fowler Lumber Co.
Lumber Co.
Lumber Co.
Lumber Co.
—
Barrows Lime Co., 1928 15th.
Lumber & Mfg. Co., 15th, cor Sts.
J. Fisher & Co., 1700 15th St.
& Howard Lumber Co., Cor. Larimer and 7th St. Howard Pres.; O. H. Secy.; B. Colden, Treas.)
Lumber & Supply Co., N. W. lpin and 39th Ave.
Steel Co. (S. W. Wheelock, gt.), 625 Cooper Bldg.
McBride, 2046 Stout St.
& McGinnity, 18th and St.
nton Fire Roofing Co., 1815 Are St. (J. B. Hinchman, E. W. Hinchman, Secy.; W. nton, Mgr.)

Denver—Continued.
Edward W. Robinson, N. E. cor W. Iowa Ave. and S. Evans.
Rocky Mountain Fuel Co., 1010 16th St.
The Sayre-Newton Lumber Co., 23d and Blake Sts.
Seubert & Heimbecker, 729 15th St.
B. F. Threewit, 19th and New Haven.
FLORENCE—
Albert Brown.
FORT COLLINS—
Corbin-Black-Wilson L. Co.
R. R. McGregor.
S. B. Purdy.
GRAND JUNCTION—
Mayo & Endner.
Ramey-Perce L. Co.
P. A. Rice.
GOLDEN—
J. H. Linder & Co.
H. T. Quick.
GREELEY—
W. L. Clayton.
Wm. Mayher.
Neill Bros.
JULESBURG—
C. F. Iddings.
LA JUNTA—
James McNeen.
LEADVILLE—
The John Harvey Fuel & Feed Co., cor. 12th and Hemlock Sts.
LONGMONT—
D. C. Donovan & Co.
Longmont Lumber Co.
H. Riddiford & Co.
OURAY—
E. H. Taylor, Box 393.
PUEBLO—
Hughes Bros.
Newton Lumber Co.
Pueblo Lumber & Mfg. Co.
Standard Fire Brick Co.
ROCKY FORD—
English Lumber Co.
Gibson Lumber Co.
SALIDA—
S. M. Jackson Lumber Co.
Salida Lumber Co.
TELLURIDE—
Stubbs & Jakway.
Tomkins-Hunt Hardware Co.
TRINIDAD—
O. L. Davis.
Hughes Bros.
VICTOR—
Colo. T. & T. Co.

CONNECTICUT.

ANSONIA—
Ansonia Flour & Grain Co.
Royal Halbrook.
Lockwood Hotchkiss.
Charles B. Wooster.

BRIDGEPORT—
The H. M. Purdy Co.
Wheeler & Howes.
BRISTOL—
D. B. Judd & Co.
Saxton & Strong.
Stedman & Co.
S. A. Wilder & Son.
DANBURY—
Robt. S. Hiscock, 11-13 Centre.
DANIELSON—
J. A. Nichols & Co.
C. A. Young & Co.
DERBY—
F. Hallock & Co.
FARMINGTON—
N. O. Keyes.
GREENWICH—
James Maher.
Smith & Maher.
Waterbury & June.
HARTFORD—
Seth Belden & Son, 69 Commerce St.
Billings' Sidewalk & Masons' Supply Co., 415 Sheldon St.
Chas. Coburn, 154 State St.
Van Name & Co., 278 Asylum St.
Watson & Jackson, 283 Sheldon St.
JEWETT CITY—
R. R. Church.
NAUGATUCK—
Naugatuck Lumber & Coal Co.
NEW BRITAIN—
City Coal & Wood Co., 246 Main St.
New Britain Lumber & Coal Co.
People's Wood & Coal Co.
T. B. Wilcox.
NEW HAVEN—
E. A. Chatfield & Co.
The Warner, Miller Co.
NEW LONDON—
Bishop & Co., 61 Water St.
The F. H. & A. H. Chappell Co., 286 Bank.
Moses Darrow, 81 Water St.
The Fishers Island Mfg. Co., 81 State St.
Wm. Higgins, 366 Bank St.
NORWALK—
John H. Ferris.
Charles T. Leonard.
A. J. Meeker & Co.
Raymond Bros.
NORWICH—
Carpenter & Williams.
Peck, McWilliams & Co.

S. J. OSBORN, JR. & CO.
Asphalt and Granitoid
ROOFING, FLOORS AND WALKS
Combined Curb and Gutter
Pearl and Eggleston Ave., CINCINNATI, OHIO

PUTNAM—
John A. Fox & Co.
Perry & Blom.
The Wheaton Building & L[illegible] Co. E. M. Wheaton, pres. & [illegible] E. M. Corbin, sec'y. & treas.
ROCKVILLE—
Frank Grant.
George W. Hill.
SHELTON—
D. W. Clark.
SOUTHINGTON—
Southington Lumber & Feed Co.
SOUTH NORWALK—
Raymond Bros.
STAFFORD SPRINGS—
E. C. Dennis.
W. E. Dimond.
Glover & Son.
STAMFORD—
L. Blondel.
A. E. Bounty.
Dean & Horton.
STONINGTON—
Wm. P. Bindloss.
TORRINGTON—
Bronson Bros.
Hotchkiss Bros.' Co.
UNIONVILLE—
The Parsons Lumber and Hard[illegible] Company. Dan'l Mason, Pr[illegible] Luke A. Parsons, Secy.; John Parsons, Treas.
Sanford & Hawley.
WALLINGFORD—
Horace Batsford.
Dickerman Hdw. and Sup. Co.
H. B. Todd & Son Co.
C. F. Wooding.
WATERBURY—
Apothecaries Hall Co.
C. V. & T. F. Atwood.
Gaffney & Martin.
Chas. Jackson & Son.
J. W. Jaffney & Co.
WILLIMANTIC—
C. L. Boss.
Hillhouse & Taylor.
Geo. K. Nason.
WINSTED—
Bronson Bros.
J. C. Burwell.
Culver & Borstol.
J. W. Roe.

DELAWARE.

DOVER—
Slaughter & Bice.
GEORGETOWN—
W. J. Thoroughgood.
MIDDLETOWN—
G. E. Hukill.
MILFORD—
A. K. Hall & Son.
Hearn, Adkins & Powell.

ASTLE—
Eliason.
astle Brick and Lime Co.
IGTON—
I. Solomon.
Warner Co., Equitable

STRICT OF COLUMBIA.

NGTON—
Portland Cement Co., 11th St.
Y. Ave., N. W.
& Ross, 614 11th St., N. W.
, Geo. M., 641 New York Ave.,

Harry W., 1559 31st St., N. W.
n Construction Co., 902 F St.,

Edward T., Delaware Ave. &
, N. E.
g, John Herbert, 520 13th St.,

rland Valley Cement Co., 602
., N. W.
& Co., Washington Savings
Bldg.
Lime & Coal Co., N. Capi-
E Sts.
, Gustav, 509 H St., N. E.
, Louis, 1001 7th St., N. W.
Henry A., New Jersey Ave.
Sts., N. W.
ne Plaster Co., 6th St., Wharf,

n F. Lewis, 1501 7th St., N. W.
James H., McGill Bldg.
al Mortar Co., 612 F St., N. W.
ac Hydraulic Cement Co., 930
. N. W.
Thomas W., 902 F St., N. W.
Robert P., 610 13th St., N. W.
f, Alexander M., 1413 G St.,

f, W. Kelsey, 1413 G St., N.

Fernando H., 490 Louisiana

and Bros., Washington Sav-
Bank Bldg.
, Noble J., Florida Ave. &
t., N. W.
. J. T., Sons, 204 10th St.,

, J. G., & Son, 1045-1047 32d St.,

ley, Joseph M., 314 10th St.,

FLORIDA.

NDINA—
Hoyt & Co.
Bros.
VILLE—
Hardware Co.
ddins.
Thomas.

JACKSONVILLE—
George R. Foster, Jr.
Chas. R. Tyson.
KEY WEST—
Wm. Curry's Sons.
John W. Johnson.
Wm. A. Johnson & Bro.
LAKE CITY—
A. B. Hart.
OCALA—
McIver & McKay.
PALATKA—
W. R. Merryday.
Vertrus & Co.
PENSACOLA—
W. F. Lee, Cy. Eng.
TALLAHASSEE—
Gilmore & Davis Co.
L. C. Yaeger.
TAMPA—
Burton E. Coe Co.
I. S. Giddins & Co.
Knight & Wall Co.
So. Lbr. & Supply Co

GEORGIA.

ALBANY—
Cruger & Pace.
J. D. & B. L. Weston.
AMERICUS—
L. G. Council.
P. L. Holt.
Johnson & Harrold.
ATHENS—
J. H. Huggins & Son.
E. L. Lyndon.
Moss Mfg. Co.
W. J. Smith & Bros.
ATLANTA—
Dunning & Son, 14 N. Forsyth St.
Holdt & Bullington, 836 Equitable Bldg.
V. H. Kriegshaber, 6 N. Forsyth St.
C. P. Murphy & Son, 6 N. Forsyth St.
Byron Sanders, 24½ Whitehall St.
Sciple Sons, 8 Loyd St.
AUGUSTA—
Burum Miller & Co.
Nixon & Co.
W. J. Rutherford & Co., 102 Washington St.
BAINBRIDGE—
Johnson Hardware Co.
I. Kroliecki.
E. J. Willis & Co.
BARNESVILLE—
Turner & Prout.
BRUNSWICK—
Coney & Parker.
CARTERSVILLE—
Ladd Lime Works.
CEDARTOWN—
J. H. Dodds.
Hall & Barr.

COLUMBUS—
Wm. Beach.
Bush Hardware Co.
T. L. Gruyard, 1318-1320 First ave.
CORDELE—
Cordele Sash, Door & Lumber Co.
DAWSON—
W. W. Farnum.
Variety Works Co.
ELBERTON—
Elberton Hardware Co.
GAINESVILLE—
J. R. Canning.
C. L. Deal.
GRIFFIN—
W. H. Newton & Co.
Newton Coal & Lumber Co
LA GRANGE—
H. C. Butler.
Pike Bros.
MACON—
T. C. Burke, 358-362 Third St.
Marsee & Felton.
Willingham Sash and Door Co.
MARIETTA—
Anderson Bros.
L. Black & Son.
C. E. Henderson.
MILLEDGEVILLE—
Cook Lumber Co.
J. R. Hines.
MOULTRIE—
J. W. Dukes.
A. Huber.
NEWNAN—
W. S. Askew & Co.
R. D. Cole Mfg.
QUITMAN—
G. W. Aurett.
J. H. Wade.
ROME—
N. S. Bale.
N. J. Huffaker.
SANDERSVILLE—
C. A. Adams.
SAVANNAH—
C. M. Gilbert & Co., Bay & W. Broad Sts.
Andrew Hanley Co. (T. J. Dinkins, sec'y. & treas.).
THOMASVILLE—
J. W. Dillen.
J. F. Evans & Son.
VALDOSTA—
Boothe & Kent.
C. B. Peeples.
WAYCROSS—
D. J. Crawley.
S. A. Marshall, 9 Lott St.

IDAHO.

BOISE CITY—
Eagleson Lumber Co.
Thos. Finegan.
Goodwin Lumber Co.
Ridenbaugh Lumber Co.
Shaw Lumber Co.
MOSCOW—
Nels Jensen.
W. C. Lauder.
POCATELLO—
J. W. Harvey.
R. Sevice & Co.
WALLACE—
Anderson & Potter.
Joseph Turner.

ILLINOIS.

ALTON—
Henry Watson.
ANNA—
Finch & Schick.
ARCOLA—
The Central Lumber Co. (F. H Jones, Pres., Tuscola; Geo. Bent V. Pres., Chicago; H. W. Patten, Treas. & Mgr.).
W. W. Hawkins & Co.
AURORA—
J. E. Salisberg & Co.
White & Todd.
BEARDSTOWN—
Beardstown Lbr. & Grain Co.
Borchardt & Steins.
W. H. Rhineberger.
Schmoldt Bros.
BELLEVILLE—
Fred C. Daab.
Reeb Bros.
Christian Schaefer.
BELVIDERE—
O. H. Wright & Co.
BLOOMINGTON—
T. F. Harwood & Sons.
Parker Bros.
CAIRO—
H. H. Halliday.
Kelly Bros'. Lbr. Co., 1911 Com Ave.
Chas. Lancaster.
P. T. Langan.
CANTON—
Andrews Bros
Dan Mackret & Co.
CARLINVILLE—
C. F. Barrick & Co.
McClure, Hemphill & Ross.
Jno. Moody & Son.
Shale, Brick & Tile Wks.
CARROLLTON—
L. S. Bushwell.
CARTHAGE—
M. J. Helfrich & Co.
W. E. Lyon & Co.
D. S Strader.
CENTRALIA—
H. Condit & Son.
Chas. A. Glore.
J. W. Tate.
CHAMPAIGN—
Alexander Lumber Co.
Jno. W. Stipes.
W. W. Walls & Co.

N—
r, Allen & Co.
ESTON—
Bros.
·r & Son.
Griffin.
ı & Son.
GO—
Portland Cement Co., 1210
ıber of Commerce.
ican Cement Co. 1310, 138 hington St.
· Backman, 8143 Muskegon Ave.
er Cement Co., 1105 Masonic ple.
. Barker, 2487 W. Twelfth St.
t Mfg. Co., 1216 Merchants' ı & Trust Bldg.
on H. Bassett, Marquette r.
lerk, Biglow & Co., 1635, 84 buren.
l S. Brandon, 115 W. 65th.
et Portland Cement Co. 1310, Washington.
go Ballast Co., The Rookery.
:o Cement Coating Co., 737 adnock.
:o Crushed Stone Co., 928, 108 alle.
go Portland Cement Co., k Exchange.
ıs Connelly, 311 Oxford Bldg.
rd L. Cox, 1511 Marquette dg.
Culmer & Son, 7325 Woodlawn.
E. Dee, 219 Royal Ins. Bldg.
ge W. DeSmet, 317 Chamber ommerce Bldg.
ıson Cement Co., 931 Marquette
.
: & Shepard Co., 184 LaSalle St.
Druecker, 109 N. Canal St.
'e Portland Cement Co., 737 adnock.
Mfg. Co., 731-33 S. Ashland Ave.
& Bruckner, 806 N. Ashland.
en City Sand Co., 1203, 88 ison.
an-American Port. Cement ·ks, 1511 Marquette Bldg.
Haynes, 317 Chamber of Com- ce Bldg.
ıs-Reynolds Co., 1210 Chamber Commerce.
Johnson Cement & Lime Co., 188 Madison.
Bros., 1615 Belmont.
ehead Lime Co., 1105 Masonic ple.
ıette Cement Co., 931, 204 Dear-
..
McBean & Co. 1, 78 LaSalle St.
ham & Wright, 309 Chamber Commerce.

Chicago—Continued.
Milwaukee Cement Co., 803. 188 Madison.
Monolith Port. Cement Co., 928, 204 Dearborn.
Thomas Moulding Co., 1007 Chamber of Commerce.
John Munch, 118 11th.
E. B. Myers, 605 Chamber of Commerce.
Otley Cement Co., 611, 138 Washington.
Peerless Cement Co., 928, 108 LaSalle.
C. H. Rose Co., 89, 159 LaSalle.
C. E. Schauffler, 937 Monadnock Blk.
Fred Schultz, 658 S. Halsted.
Sears Humbert & Co., 1310 Cham. of Com.
Stearns Lime & Stone Co., 165 E. Randolph.
Henry F. Treadway, 928, 108 LaSalle.
Utica Cement Ass'n, 308 Chamber of Commerce.
Utica Cement Co., 98 Market St.
I. A. Viall, W. 1188 S. Halstead St.
Western Cement Co., 718, 138 Washington.
N. A. Williams Co., 219 Washington.
Wisconsin Lime & Cement Co., 605 Cham. of Com. Allen B. Cook, Pres.; N. J. Druecker, V. Pres.; E. B. Myers, Secy.; W. L. Wood, Treas.
Wm. Wright, 1635, 84 Vanburen.

CHILLICOTHE—
Chillicothe Lbr. Co.
H. & E. F. Hunter.

CLINTON—
R. B. Day & Co.
Kent & Co.
Walter Taylor.

COLCHESTER—
S. D. Mills.
J. O. Moon.

DANVILLE—
M. Gunor.
N. E. Holden.
Hooton Bros.
S. Q. & E. C. Lamm.
McMillan & Hill.
Fred Prast.

DECATUR—
F. C. Betzer.
Decatur Hard. P. Co.
V. H. Parke & Son.

DEKALB—
Carter & Mosher.
E. F. Nichols.
John Nichols.
L. C. Schermerhorn.
Geo. Tervistege.

DIXON—
E. H. Crabtree.
Dan'l Curran.

DOWNER'S GROVE—
C. S. Hughes & Co.
Geo. T. Hughes.
Mertz & Mochel.
DWIGHT—
W. H. Conrad.
Geo. W. Flagler.
John Stewart.
EAST ST. LOUIS—
W. H. Hill Lime & Cement Co.
EDELSTEIN—
H. & E. F. Hunter.
EDWARDSVILLE—
Frank J. Barnett.
Geo. Hotz & Son.
John Stolze & Son.
EFFINGHAM—
Austin Lumber Co.
Wildi Leddy Lumber Co.
ELGIN—
Adams & Seymour, 200 Douglas Ave.
Edward Bell, 451 Enterprise.
Wm. Bell, Room 2, McBride Blk.
Elgin Brick & Tile Co., 162 Douglas Ave.
E. I. Gerry, 517 Chicago.
David H. Heger, 111 Division.
Knickerbocker Ice Co., 10 River St.
Henry McBride, 7 S. State St.
John S. Wilcox, 108 Douglas Ave.
ELMHURST—
E. W. Fischer & Co.
W. Overkamp & Co.
EVANSTON—
Geo. Brignall.
Carrier, Cement Dealer.
Evanston Elevator & Coal Co.
Leonhardt Bros.
B. B. Noyes.
FAIRBURY—
W. H. Bartlett.
Jesse Stevens & Co.
FAIRFIELD—
Dickey, Summers & Kramer.
Fairfield Lumber Co.
FREEPORT—
R. L. Cummings.
Mrs. Jennie Grant.
FULTON—
W. C. & J. C. Snyder.
GALENA—
M. Friesenecker.
F. Linenfelser.
Wm. Siniger.

T. W. SPINKS
SEWER PIPE, CEMENTS
AND BUILDING MATERIALS
phone 49 South. COVINGTON, KY.

GALESBURG—
J. E. Hinchliff.
Thomas Keefe.
Hiram Mars.
J. C. Simpson & Co.
Terry & Lewis.
GALVA—
E. W. Houghton Lumber Co.
J. C. Simpson Lumber Co.
GENESEO—
J. W. Goss & Co.
Turner & Brown.
F. L. Winsor.
GENEVA—
Leindecker & Hawkins.
GIBSON CITY—
Keiser & Holmes El. Co.
Spaulding Lumber Co.
GIRARD—
Boston & Thompson.
Flood & Lowe Lumber Co.
GRANITE CITY—
J. R. Ewing.
GRAYVILLE—
J. M. Blood & Bro.
GREENVILLE—
J. O. Allen.
E. H. Bigard.
C. Chapple.
H. B. Heninger & Co.
S. Leppard.
L. J. Meyer.
J. Reed.
Urban Willman.
HARRISBURG—
J. B. Ford.
Robt. King.
HARVARD—
W. D. Hall.
Lake & Harris.
HARVEY—
Harvey Coal Co. (not inc.). A. W. Campbell & Mrs. M. M. Wood.
Wausau Lumber Co.
HENRY—
H. and E. F. Hunter.
HIGHLAND—
S. Marti.
F. B. Suppiger.
HIGHLAND PARK—
John Middleton.
Raffen & Baker.
Alex. Robertson.
HILLSBORO—
H. M. Howell.
HINSDALE—
Geo. Boger.
HOOPESTON—
J. H. Dyer Lumber Co.
Hoopeston Lumber Co.
JACKSONVILLE—
B. P. Andrews & Sons.
J. S. & G. S. Russel.
Smith & Stimpson.

:YVILLE—
Christy.
ockrell Lumber Co.
Jacobs.
T—
en Buck, 511 Cass St.
go Ballast Co.
V. Hayes, 571 Cass St.
AKEE—
ton & Kern.
ufault.
Hawkins.
akee Stone & Lime Co.
man & Son.
Risser.
iehle, 12-15 West Ave.
.NEE—
r & Trask.
t F. Whiffen.
e A. Wyatt.
VILLE—
er & Lacy.
Weeks.
Y—
er, Allen & Co.
d Peintner.
Shaw.
e F. Wightman.
.NGE—
Lagrange Sand Co.
Lyon.
LLE—
ndyke Bros.
Gibson.
. Hunter & Co.
r. Stevens & Co.
IT—
Derby.
Helbig.
Y—
Evans Son's Co.
Pierce & Co.
TOWN—
. Simpson.
t Yemfel.
.N—
nder Lumber Co.
Ottz.
.. Simpson.
an & Spitly.
ORT—
n & Co.
Ryan.
:B—
e & Simeral.
Gamage.
Hannan.
ALL—
rnesberger.
Booth.
CTAH—
W. Lischer.
ON—
s & R[illegible]
POLIS CITY—
Gibbons.

MOLINE—
Beder Wood.
MOMENCE—
J. J. Kirby & Co.
B. L. Tabler.
MENDOTA—
Jack & Conkey.
Miller & Schmidt.
P. Yockey.
MINONK—
A. B. Kipp.
MONMOUTH—
E. A. Lord Fuel & Ice Co.
Monmouth Lumber Co.
A. A. Rogers.
Andrew W. Ryan.
J. W. Sipher & Co.
MONTICELLO—
Geo. Blain & Co.
Jno. Maier.
A. L. Starkey.
MORRISON—
J. M. Burtch.
Perault & Son.
Potter & Johnson.
MOUND CITY—
G. F. Meyer & Co.
Mound City Crystal Ice Mfg. Co. (Thos Boyd, Pres.; E. A. Wilson, Secy. & Treas.; G. J. Murphy, Mgr.).
G. J. Murphy.
Parks & Higgins.
MOUNT CARROLL—
W. H. Wildey.
MOUNT OLIVE—
Niemann Bros.
NAPERVILLE—
A. H. Beidelman
M. Schwartz & Co.
NASHVILLE—
Deucker & Smith
W. O. Welbe.
NORMAL—
H. W. [illegible]hammer & Co.
E. E. Van Hook
OAK PARK—
Bryant Bros
A. [illegible]
OLNEY—
Olney Paving & T[illegible] M[illegible] Co.
OTTAWA—
[illegible]
[illegible]
PANA—
[illegible]
[illegible]
PARIS—
[illegible]
[illegible]
[illegible]
PAXTON—
[illegible]
[illegible]
PEKIN—
[illegible]

PEORIA—
B. Bushnell.
C. E. Butts & Co.
Dolan & Maher, 100 Cedar St.
G. Janssen & Sons, 230 Deckman Ave.
W. M. Lyons.
J. W. Mackemer & Co., 2212 W. Adams.
Peoria Fuel Co., 513 S. Washington.
T. J. Wasson, 403 S. Washington.

PERU—
Christian Zimmerman.

PETERSBURG—
Fred Apken.
E. S. Cheaney & Co.

PINCKNEYVILLE—
B. P. Murphy.
H. R. Schulze.
Gustav Wangelin.

PITTSFIELD—
Alexander Lumber Co.
Dutton & Co.
Loyd Hardware Co.

PLANO—
Boston & Jiler.

PORT BYRON—
Port Byron Lime Association. E. B. Stone, mgr.

PRINCETON—
J. H. Brown.
A. L. Davis & Son.
J. H. Delano & Son.

QUINCY—
Campbell Bros., 920 Hampshire.
The Flack Lumber Co., 438 Bway.
Knoch & Meyer, 115 Delaware.
Middendorf Bros., 926 Bway.
Quincy White Lime & Cement Co., 237 S. Front.

ROCHELLE—
M. J. Braiden.
C. A. Hizer.
Southworth & Pool.

ROCK FALLS—
Coe & Van Sant.
Hubbard Bros.
Smith & Grater.

ROCKFORD—
A. L. Bartlett.
Hart & Page.

ROCK ISLAND—
E. G. Frazer.
Port Byron Lime Ass'n. E. B. Stone, Mgr.

RUSHVILLE—
C. G. Munroe & Co.
J. G. Nolan & Co.

ST. CHARLES—
St. Charles Lumber Co.
West Side Lumber & Supply Inc. W. H. Townsend, Pres. (8 more); J. E. Switzer, Secy., & Mgr.

SAVANNA—
J. D. Fulrath.

SHAWNEETOWN—
Chas. Carroll.
Goetzman Bros.
Krebs & Shaw.
A. K. Lowe's Son.

SHELBYVILLE—
S. W. & J. W. Conn.
Parker & Roberts.

SPARLAND—
H. & E. T. Hunter.

SPARTA—
Robt. Allen.
J. S. Brown.
W. P. McLaughlin.

SPRINGFIELD—
Baker & Baker.
A. Eielson.
H. C. Irwin.
J. H. Schuck & Son.
Peter Vredenburgh.

STAUNTON—
H. C. Buchterkirchen.
Darlington Lumber Co.

STERLING—
Moses Dillon.
John Peck.

STREATOR—
J. C. Ames Lumber Co.
G. A. Schmid.
Streator Lumber Co.

SULLIVAN—
Alexander & Co.
O. J. Ganger.

SYCAMORE—
Holcomb Bros.
N. Side Lumber Co.
Sycamore Lumber Co.

TOLUCA—
J. E. Porterfield.

TUSCOLA—
The Alexander Lumber Co.
F. H. Jones Lumber Co.

URBANA—
C. A. Besore.
J. F. Gensel.

BOOKS ON CEMENT

PRIC
Hydraulic Cement. By F. P. Spalding............ $2.(
Portland Cement. By Charles D. Jamieson........ 1.
Clark's Hand-Book on Cements..................... 1.(
Portland Cement; its Manufacture, Testing and Use. By D. B. Butler. 360 pages, 85 illustrations 6.(
American Cements. By Uriah Cummings........... 3.(
Send remittance with order. Address
MUNICIPAL ENGINEERING COMPAN

—
bbott.
& Selb.
Niemann.
IA—
Kiles.
Sharpe.
W—
& Diehl.
Kranshaw.
KA—
Bros.
ierce.
GAN—
stow.
ON—
tcliffe.
HALL—
ter Lumber Co., F. F. Wor-
. Pres. and Mgr.; H. H.
on, Secy.; W. A. Dillman,
.
TTE—
n Bros.
ESTER—
Allen & Co.
TOCK—
Lumber Co.
Hall.

INDIANA.

—
nick & Sons.
& Ayres Lumber Co.
NDRIA—
m Lumber Co., 602-616 S. Curve
F. L. Mercer, Pres.; W. S.
num, Secy., Chicago; J. G.
num, Treas. and Mgr.)
avis Lumber Co.
SON—
Bailey & Co., Jackson St.
Big Four R. R.
Vernon & Son.
—
Gilbert.
Hendry.
Miller.
Shank.
—
Hardware Co.
—
Martin & Co.
Stearnes & Son.
N—
Lumber Co.
is & Co.
Trush.
A—
Heed.
angley.
Maffey.
Spaeth & Co.
Wright.

BEDFORD—
W. E. Harvey.
Laus-Fry Lumber Co.
N. R. Lowder.
BLOOMINGTON—
H. S. Ansted.
Gillam & Co.
David Hughes.
BLUFFTON—
Studabaker, Sale & Co.
BRAZIL—
Kattman, Tilley & Morgan.
Gordon G. Kerfoot.
McCrea, Brown Co.
D. O. Stone.
BREMEN—
J. H. Steineck.
J. F. Weiss & Co.
BROOKVILLE—
Jos. Fieber.
John Fries.
J. H. Master & Son.
Peter Weist & Co.
BROWNSBURG—
Greer-Wilkinson Co
CANNELTON—
P. Clemens & Sons.
Jacob Heck & Co.
Mrs. T. Irvin.
COLUMBIA CITY—
Jos. Champion.
W. W. Kessler & Son.
COLUMBUS—
Hege & Co.
Geo. Moyer & Son.
CONNERSVILLE—
E. A. Enos, East Connersville.
Ready & Showalter.
COVINGTON—
M. H. Clark.
CRAWFORDSVILLE—
Jos. Binford & Son.
The Hall Coal Co.
Fred Hoffman.
Smith & Duckworth.
J. W. Stroh & Co.
CROWN POINT—
Paul E. Raasch.
DANVILLE—
Danville Lumber Co.
DECATUR—
J. D. Hale.
Calvin Miller.
J. K Niblick.
DELPHI—
Christian Bros.
Delphi Lime Co.
Charley & G. P. Harley.
W. B. Wason & Co.
DUNKIRK—
Edwin Hoover.
Wm. L. Skinner.
J. L. Slough.

ELKHART—
Godfrey & Livengood.
Independent Coal Co., M. U. Demorest, propr.
J. P. Sanders.

ELWOOD—
Winters Lumber Co.

EVANSVILLE—
L. M. Baird, 220 W. Water.
Wm. Eichel, 215 W. 1st St.
Espenlaub & Johann, 1401 E. Delaware St.
Gearing-Haller Planing Mill Co., 816-830 W. 6th St.
Klenck Bros. 621 Fulton Ave.
H. A. Lensing, 422 Sycamore St.
John S. McCorkle, 500 W. 8th St.
Wm. Meyer, 400 Edgar St.
Louis Oehlmann, 933 E. Columbia.
Theo. E. Rechtin, 27 L. 7th St.
Swormstedt & Sonntag, 516 Main St.

FAIRMOUNT—
Lindsey & Swain.
Mercer Branan Lumber Co.
W. H. Minnich.

FORTVILLE—
Greer-Wilkinson Co.

FT. WAYNE—
Edward M. Baltes & Co., 27 N. Harrison St.
E. H. F. Brennier, 207 W. De Wald.
Jos. Derheimer, 177 E. Jefferson St.
E. H. Ehle, 529 Broadway.
John Evers & Son, 323 Hanna.
Wm. Geahe, 76 Pearl.
H. A. Grothitman, 28 E. 4th.
Hattersly & Son, 46 & 48 E. Main.
Keller & Braum, 84 Pearl St.
E. C. Moellering & Co., 53 Murray St.
Wm. Moellering & Son, 53-59 Murray.
C. L. Olds Const. Co., Elekron Bldg.
Trentman Supply Co., 9 N. Calhoun.
Warrenburg & Busching, E. Superior.
F. J. Zimmerly & Co., 141 Calhoun.

FRANKFORT—
Given Campbell & Co.
Wm. G. Morris & Bro.

FRANKLIN—
J. M. Dunlap, Agt.
Robt. Waggener.

GARRETT—
Garrett Lumber Co.
Emil Hill.
Julius Hill.

GAS CITY—
J. C. Crawford & Co.

J. L. VAN NATTA & CO.
WHOLESALE AND RETAIL
Coal, Wood, Lime, Cement, Etc.
LAFAYETTE, IND.
OFFICE—First and Columbia Streets
YARD—Cor. L. E. & W. Ry. and 2d Street

GOSHEN—
Goshen Fuel & Supply Co.
J. D. Hebert.
Freeman Poyser.
C. S. Swank.

GREENCASTLE—
C. S. Eiteljorg.
Daniel Kelley.

GREENFIELD—
J. D. Conklin & Son.
Greenfield Lbr. & Ice Co.

GREENSBURG—
Geo. G. Bussell.
Chas. H. Johnson.
O. L. Pulse & Co.

HAMMOND—
Wm. Ahlborn.
Erie Coal Co.
Hammond Coal Co.
John Laws & Son.

HARTFORD CITY—
J. S. Newbauer & Co.

HUNTINGBURGH—
Christ W. Roettger.
Adam Stratman.

HUNTINGTON—
E. O. Allman.
C. E. Bash.
Martin Mindnich.
Western Lime Co.

INDIANAPOLIS—
Aikman & Schwert, 30th & Ca
Balke & Krauss Co., cor. Ma Mo.
Columbia Coal Co., State Deloss.
Consolidated Coal & Lime Virginia Ave.
Frank M. Dell, 730-40 E. W
R. S. Foster & Co., 47 B'd'[illegible] Bldg.
Fred Goepper, 429 Holmes Haughville.
Greer-Wilkinson Co.
Hoosier Transfer & Coal Co., Delaware.
Ingalls Lime & Stone Co., 18 bard Blk.
A. B. Keeport & Co., 314 W. N
Julius Keller & Son.
Malott Coal & Lime Co., cor. & Peru Aves.
A. B. Meyer & Co., 19 N. Pe
Morgan & Jackson, 350 W. 13
Wales Coal & Lime Co., 911-13 Ave.

JEFFERSONVILLE—
Silas Carr.
Thos. J. Lindley.
Lindley & Carr.

KENDALLVILLE—
Adolph Adams.
Jno. Deibele.
Stinson & Cawley.

KNIGHTSTOWN—
Henry Watts.

—
lbaugh & Son.
g-Landon Co.
TE—
man, 110-112 N. 2d St.
ader.
Van Natta & Co., 110 Co-
St.
E—
Wigton.
—
Richter.
Kirk.
umber Co.
—
ves.
—
nning & Son.
es.

lkinson Co.
ORT—
ley & Co., 515 Market St.
Johnson, S. E. Cor. Berk-
pencer.
eport & Co., 515 Market St.
rt Cement Wk., N. Mar-
. Peoria Junc.
Lux.
Johnston, S E Cor. Berk-
Spencer.
orhees, 400 Sycamore.
—
Miller.
hite.

lkinson Co.
& Baldwin.
outhall.
VILLE—
adeville.
aites.
Lumber Co.
CITY—
kinson Co.
itschmidt.
Lbr. & Coal Col.
awlings.
A—
& Rankart.
gtling & Son.
—
ow.
me Co. A. L. Beck, Pres.
Williams, Secy. & Treas.
Klee, Mgr.
—
ney.
ll.
e.

kinson Co.
ndlton, 115 S. Wash. St.
Builders' Supply Co., Cor.
& Franklin.
Kirby Ave.

NEW ALBANY—
L. Hammersmith & Co., 1403 E. Elm.
E. T. Slider, 306 Pearl.
NEW TRENTON—
Louis Brow.
NOBLESVILLE—
H. M. Caylor & Son.
Clark Supply House.
Griffin Brothers.
W. E. Longley.
Pinnell & Dulin.
NORTH MANCHESTER—
North Manchester Lbr. Co. (F. L. Mercer, Pres., Chicago; O. S. Knudson, V. Pres., Chicago; W. S. Brannum, Secy., Chicago; W. R. Oyler, Treas. & Mgr).
Ulrey Hurter & Co.
NORTH VERNON—
J. B. Miller.
North Vernon Pump & Lumber Co.
Tripp Bros.
OAKLAND CITY—
Creek & Heldt.
J. S. Evans.
W. N. Stewart.
Thompson & Co.
PLYMOUTH—
L. Linkerhelt.
Conrad Sult.
H. G. Thayer & Co.
PORTLAND—
E. W. Buck, Box 291.
Cartwright & Hiadington.
Holmes Bros.
Sanders Bros.
PRINCETON—
Epperson, Herriott & Co.
Alfred S. Ford.
James M. Scantlin.
RENSSELAER—
Bales Lumber Co
Hiram Day.
J. C. Gwin & Co.
John H. Jessen.
Warren & Rush.
RICHMOND—
Philip Brookens, 39 S. 6th St.
Wm. Cain, S. E. Cor. 11th & Main.
Charles S. Farnham, 170 Ft. Wayne Ave.
Hackman & Kletfoth, 112 S. 7th St.
Mather Bros., 1008-1020 N. F.
Shera & Starr, 272 Ft. Wayne Ave.
RISING SUN—
Geo. B. Gibson's Sons.
Hunter, Harris Co.
ROCHESTER—
G. F. Barcus.
A. F. Bowers.
ROCKVILLE—
J. A. Joiner.
Ott & Boyd.
RUSHVILLE—
John P. Frazee.
Pinnell & Root.

SALEM—
W. R. Alexander.
W. J. Hauger.
McCowen & McCowen.
SANFORD—
Claude Hill Lumber Co.
SELLERSBURG—
Barnett, Bottorff & Snodgrass.
Emmett Cuddy.
Sellersburg Clay Co.
SEYMOUR—
A. W. Mills.
R. F. White.
SHELBYVILLE—
J. O. Parrish.
SOUTH BEND—
C. H. Defrees, 315 S. Taylor St.
Miller & Lontz.
SPENCER—
J. A. McHaley.
J. L. Pierson Lbr. Co.
TELL CITY—
Frank Basedow.
Ferd Becker.
Henry H. Bielefeld.
TERRE HAUTE—
August Fromme, 7th and Hulman Sts.
Reiman & Steeg Co.
Terre Haute Coal & Lime Co. J. S. Talley, Pres.; R. W. Rippetoe, V. P.; J. W. Landrum, Secy., Treas & Mgr., 629 Wabash Ave.
THORNTOWN—
Emmins & Riley.
TIPTON—
F. J. Fralich & Co.
Tipton Lumber Co.
UNION CITY—
The Knapp Supply Co., L. C. Huesmann, Mgr.
VALPARAISO—
C. W. Dickover.
Chas. F. Lemoke.
VEVAY—
A. V. Danner.
Jas. K. Pleasants.
VINCENNES—
M. A. Bostworth.
John Cox.
John Hartigan.
H. R. McIlvaine.
W. H. Moore, 232 S. Fifth St.
WABASH—
Duck & Pressler.
Smith Hubbard Lumber Co.
WARSAW—
Eschbaugh & Weimer.
Warsaw Lumber Co.
WASHINGTON—
The M. J. Carnahan Co.
O. M. Crosby.
John W. Feagan.
The Hatfield & Palmer Co.
Joseph Kretz.
WHITING—
F. W. Dargling.
Jas. J. Donegan.
Allen Steilinger.
W. E. Vates.
WINAMAC—
H. Kittinger.
Williams & Hathaway.
WINCHESTER—
Stephen Clevenger.
George Yeager.

IOWA.

ALBIA—
W. B. Ballew Lumber Co.
ALGONA—
L. Lamb Lumber Co.
F. S. Norton & Co.
W. Wheeler & Turner Co.
ANAMOSA—
Braisted & Prentice.
Shaw & Dutton.
ATLANTIC—
Green Bay Lbr. Co.
C. P. Meredith.
BELLE PLAINE—
Francis Guthrie.
Relling & Co.
BURLINGTON—
Bernard Bros. & Mercer.
L. C. Harper.
CARROLL—
Green Bay Lbr. Co.
W. T. Joyce Co.
CEDAR FALLS—
R. K. King.
M. D. Philleo.
C. A. Wise & Sons, 315 Main St.
CEDAR RAPIDS—
Key City Roofing Co.
Wm. King & Co.
CHARLES CITY—
W. E. Holbrook.
F. A. Thomas.
CHEROKEE—
Cherokee Lumber Co.
T. W. Fans.
Weart & Lyought.
CLARINDA—
Green Bay Lbr. Co.
G. Wm. Richardson.
CLINTON—
M. I. Mead, 126 Water St.
Smith & Oakes, 6th Ave. & 1st.
CORNING—
H. H. LaRue.
Ralph Newcomb.
W. Newcomb & Co.
COUNCIL BLUFFS—
G. A. Hoagland, 716 S. Main.
J. H. Queal & Co., 115 W. B'way
CRESCO—
Lomas & Son.
Wm. F. Rathert.
CRESTON—
G. S. Rex & Son.

PORT—
ime and Cement Co., 1841
ingham Road.
aussen, 103 Ripley St.
avenport Fuel Co. (H. O.
rt, Pres.; A. C. Fredick, Sec.
as.)
& Co., 308-312 E. 3rd. St.
ick, 425 Brady St.
H—
Adams.
handler & Son.
Lumber Co.
INES—
ines Fuel & Lime Co.
E—
Point Lime Co.
ty Lime Wks.
ty Roofing Co.
& Molo, 472 Main St.
Bros.
GROVE—
Lbr. Co.
inesh & Co.
—
& Moser.
Esgen Lumber Co.
VILLE—
Janson & Co.
Vilcox & Co.
ELD—
W. Cable Lumber Co.
Jordan Lumber Co
GE—
Hdw. Co.
DISON—
Abel.
C. Atlee.
Lumber Co.
spanjer & Son.
OOD—
ay Lumber Co.
LL—
arney.
& Jenkins.
outts.
N—
hane.
ITY—
umber Co.
Lembaugh.
usser.
ALLS—
Biggs.
ll & McDowell Co. (H. B.
Pres. and Mgr.; W. H. Woods.

& Griffith.
& Foote.
lusser.
K—
n & McManus.
us & Tucker.
Namara & Sons.
oal & Ice Co.

KNOXVILLE—
J. S. Bellamy.
Moody & Parsons.
LE MARS—
Knoor & Schafer.
M. A. Moore & Co.
W. H. Perry.
MALVERN—
Green Bay Lumber Co.
George Palmer & Co.
MAQUOKETA—
Jones & Gold.
MARENGO—
McKnight Bros.
MARSHALLTOWN—
C. A. Buchwald, 109 N. Center.
J. C. Dunn, 204 E. Main.
Gregory-Brown Coal Co., 117 E. Main.
Marshalltown Coal & Ice Co., 202 E. Main.
MASON CITY—
J. W. Barlow Coal Co.
A. T. Lien.
Smith & Cole.
Williams Coal Co.
MONTICELLO—
Eastwood & Chase.
J. S. Hall.
MT. PLEASANT—
Bowman & Kauffman.
C. M. Clark.
MUSCATINE—
W. D. Goldsberry, 312 Iowa Ave.
NEW HAMPTON—
Bigelow & Donovan.
John Foley.
OELWEIN—
Cole & King Bros.
G. W. Jamison.
Ricker & Bratnober.
OSAGE—
James A. Smith.
OSCEOLA—
W. R. Ballew Lumber Co.
McAuley Lumber Co.
OSKALOOSA—
H. D. Browning.
G. H. Carlon & Son.
E. H. Little.
C. P. Sipes.
OTTUMWA—
C. W. Major & Co.
M. B. Root & Son.
Shewry & Fulliner.
PELLA—
D. S. Huber.
A. N. Kuyper.
PERRY—
McColl Lumber Co.
J. R. Swearingen & Co.
J. E. Wilson.
RED OAK—
Green Bay Lumber Co.
George Palmer Lumber Co.

SHENANDOAH—
Green Bay Lumber Co.
George Palmer & Co.

SIOUX CITY—
G. H. Hollandsworth.
Hopper & McNeil Co., 308 Jackson.
H. C. McNeil & Son.
J. H. Queal & Co.
W. Sanborn & Co.
Webb Bros. Co. Jas. D. Webb, Pres. W. P. Webb, Secy & Treas.
Chas Weller & Co.

SPENCER—
Floete Lumber Co.
John Paul Lumber Co.
A. C. Perine.

STUART—
F. E. Ball.
Green Bay Lumber Co.
Holmes & Williams.

TAMA—
B. F. Hill.

TIPTON—
C. M. Cook.
Grassel & Hambright.
Laubscher & Jacobs.
Reichert & Gellar.

VILLISCA—
Green Bay Lumber Co.
Rand Lumber Co.

VINTON—
Boggs & Conner Co.
Ricker & Bratnober.
W. H. Thompson.

WASHINGTON—
Samson & Montgomery.
Shields & Son.

WATERLOO—
Key City Roofing Co.
Wangler Drug Co.
Waterloo Lumber Co. Warren Brown, Pres., Secy & Mgr.; W. W. Miller, Treas.

WAVERLY—
W. F. Fritz.
Ricker & Bratnober Lumb. Co.

WEBSTER CITY—
B. L. Willis Lumber Co.
C. E. Younkee Lumber Co.
J. W. Young.

WHAT CHEER—
Willis Stanley.
Valley Lbr. Co.

THE ACME PAVING COMPANY
MANUFACTURERS OF
Acme Combined Curb & Gutter, Asphalt Floors, Artificial Stone.
WHEELING, W. VA. AKRON, OHIO.
Main Office, - 408-420 West State St., COLUMBUS, OHIO.

KANSAS.

ABILENE—
Badger Lumber Co.
Kruger & Cramer.
Rice & Johntz.

ARGENTINE—
Badger Lumber Co.
Jasper & Boeke.
J. B. Smith & Co.

ATCHISON—
B. L. Brockett.
Donnellan & Rossger.
C. A. Wright.

BELOIT—
Chicago Lumber & Coal Co.

BURLINGTON—
Cogshead Lumber Co.

CHANUTE—
Chanute Lumber Co.
F. B. Dubach & Co.
Geo. W. Williams.

CHERRYVALE—
W. C. Dicus & Co.
Long-Bell Lumber Co.
W. O. Whitney Lbr. & Grain Co.

CHETOPA—
H. H. Long.
J. F. Shields.

COLUMBUS—
C. G. Metyler.

CONCORDIA—
Chicago Lumber & Coal Co.
Dudley Lumber Co.
Long-McCue Lumber Co. (R. A. Lon Pres., Kansas City, Mo.; Thos. McCue, Sec. Treas., Mgr.).

DE SOTO—
Hedges Bros.

EL DORADO—
R. W. Long.
M. M. Vandenberg.

EMPIRE CITY—
Williams & Robeson.

EMPORIA—
Emporia Lumber Co.
Evans & Thomas.
J. C. Kirkwood.
E. F. Sprague.
Watson-Ballweg Lumber Co.

EUREKA—
Houston Lbr. Co.

FORT SCOTT—
T. H. Ford.
Ft. Scott Hydraulic Cement Co
C. H. Gardiner.
A. C. Penniman & Son.
D. P. Thomas.

GALENA—
Lowdermilk & Wass.
McClung Cement Co.
L. K. Moeller.
J. H. Smith.

GARNETT—
S. Crum.
Galley & Rice.

—
'hristian
CHA—
Brown Lumber Co.
ha Lumber Co.
Moore Lumber Co.
ullivan Lumber Co.
Y—
& Brown.
Y—
ghey & Son, J. Greene, Mgr.
NSON—
Snyder.
White.
NDENCE—
Horstick.
sland Lumber & Mfg. Co.
eyrrell.
regemba.

ortland Cement Co.
'aylor.
White.
ON CITY—
Lumber Co.
olson & Co.
Vadleigh.
White.
CITY—
Enright, 1024 S. 18th St.
nfield Sand & Fuel Co., Cen-
Ave. & Kaw R.
'. Horsman, 905 N. 5th St.
ate Sand Co., 610 Minn Ave.
Fames & Son, 349 Minn. Ave.
t Peck Sand Co., Kaw R.,
sage.
NCE—
ce & Son.
NWORTH—
Geiger.
McDonald.
TTAN—
'. Higinbotham.
VILLE—
ice Lbr. Co.
Webber.
SON—
ardt & Suderdorf.
uperior Lumber Co.
wney.
N—
Lbr. Co.
1 Lbr. Co., John Olinger, Prop.
Lbr. Co.
& McGraw.
E—
Cosgrove.
Bros.
Lanter.
1 & Haven Lumber Co.
CITY—
Heizer.
Lumber Co.

OSWEGO—
J. C. Richcreek Lumber Co.
O. E. Woods & Co.
OTTAWA—
S. Bohrbaugh.
John Halloren.
M. R. Harris.
PAOLA—
John F. Merrill, Wea & Gold Sts.
M. A. Schroeder.
PARSONS—
Clark & Bates.
E. H. McCreery.
Parsons Lumber Co.
P. S. White.
PITTSBURG—
J. H. Kitchen.
Fred Mossmann.
Pittsburg Lime & Cement Co.
ROSEDALE—
Current River Lumber Co.
SALINA—
C. Eberbardt.
H. H. Jack Lumber Co.
Kansas Lumber Co.
Leidigh & Havens Lumber Co., J. H. Leidigh, Pres. (Kansas City, Mo.); W. F. Grosser, Secy.; H. R. Banks, Treas. (Kansas City, Mo.); A. P. Havens, Mgr. (Minneapolis, Kas.).
H. H. Sudendorf.
STANLEY—
Hedges Bros.
STERLING—
D. J. Fair.
Irish & Quigley.
TOPEKA—
The Builders' Supply & Material Co. (Wm. Rynerson, Mgr.).
Chicago Lbr. Co.
Ewart Lbr. Co.
Hanley & Co., 426 W. Gordon St.
W. I. Miller.
J. Thomas.
WEIR CITY—
Long Bell Lbr. Co.
WELLINGTON—
F. A. Amsden.
Long Bell Lbr. Co.
Rock Island Lbr. & Mfg. Co.
WICHITA—
American Cement Plaster Co., 700 Mass.
M. S. Hinman, 218 W. Second.
L. C. Jackson, 112 S. Market.
J. W. Laidlaw, 575 W. Douglass.
O. B. Stocker, 143 N. Water.
J. H. Turner, 535 W. Douglass.

KENTUCKY.

ASHLAND—
Ashland Feed & Produce Co.
Bush, Watson & Co.
CARROLLTON—
J. W. Easterday.
O. M. Wood & Son.

COVINGTON—
Covington Stone & Sand Co.
Edward Spinks, 1718 Madison.
Anthony Volmering, 1720 Madison Ave.
Brake Wilding, 423 Greenup.

CYNTHIANA—
Frank Asbury.
J. R. Poindexter.
J. W. Smiser.

DANVILLE—
E. R. Dillehay.
Dunham Bros.
W. H. Lillard.
Taylor Terhune.

DAYTON—
M. R. Hunter, jr., 513 7th St.
A. Walter, jr., 6th & Boone Sts.

EARLINGTON—
St. Bernard Coal Co.

FRANKFORT—
C. E. Collins.
M. A. Collins.
P. C. Sower & Co.
Stagg & Bacon.
E. M. Williams.

FRANKLIN—
T. H. Ford.

GEORGETOWN—
J. A. Shropshire.
J. P. Wayts & Co.

GLASGOW—
Dickinson Bros.
Smith & Cook.

HARRODSBURG—
Mitchell & Sallee.
Rue & Sullivan.
H. C. & M. L. Vanarsdall.

HENDERSON—
P. A. Blackwell & Co.
Norris, Lockett & White.

HOPKINSVILLE—
Dagg & Richards.
Dalton Bros.
Forbes & Bros.

LEBANON—
J. L. Hilpp.
C. B. Johnston.

LEXINGTON—
L. des Cognets & Co.
T. T. Justice & Co., Spring & Vine Sts.
Geo. Land.
Jno. B. Payne.

LOUISVILLE—
C. J. Comstock, 2026 Lytle St.
Fall City Artificial Stone Co., 146 E. Main St.
Louisville Cement Co., 333 W. Main St.
Ohio Valley Cement Co., 133 Third St.
J. B. Speed & Co., 331 W. Main St.
Standard Cement Co., 338 W. Main St.
Owen Tyler, 608 Equitable Bldg.

Louisville—Continued.
Union Cement & Lime Co., [illegible] Main St.
Utica Lime Co., [illegible] W. [illegible]
Western Cement Co., 2[illegible] W. [illegible]

MADISONVILLE—
C. E. Owen.
L. H. Page.
J. B. Ross's Sons.
Ruby & Co.

MAYFIELD—
R. E. Foster.
R. D. Robertson & Co.
Jack Webb.

MAYSVILLE—
Omer Dodson.
M. C. Rorsell & Son.

MORGANFIELD—
Newman & Richards.
B. G. Waller & Co.
Young, Waller & Young.

NEWPORT—
M. M. Allen.
Charles Spinks.

NICHOLASVILLE—
B. Wolf.

OWENSBORO—
W. G. Burnett.
F. T. Guenther.
W. A. Guenther & Sons.
A. Steitler, Jr.
Venable & McJohnston.

PADUCAH—
Barry & Henneberger.
Covington Bros. & Co.
R. G. Terrell.

PARIS—
Ford & Co.
E. F. Spears & Sons.
G. W. Stuart & Co.

RICHMOND—
L. R. Blanton.
Covington, Arnold & Bro.
E. Deatherage & Co.
Higgins & Luxon.
Letcher & Witt.
Samuel Rice.

SHELBYVILLE—
John P. Allen, Jr.
L. H. Gruber & Sons.
W. H. Hall & Son.
J. J. Ramsey & Bro.
D. N. Shaup.

WINCHESTER—
Perry & Evans.

LOUISIANA.

ALEXANDRIA—
C. N. Adams.
Hoffman & Wilson.
L. A. Stafford.

BATON ROUGE—
John J. Capdeville.
Garig, Wilson & Co.
Jones & Whitaker.
Ronaldson-Puckett Co., Ltd.

LDSONVILLE—
ine.
mann Bros.
L. Maurin.
KLIN—
Delahoussaye.
A—
Daigle.
& J. C. Dupont.
ON—
y Bros.
. McKowen & Co.
CHARLES—
Buck & Son.
. Stanford.
DE—
r Grocer Co., Ltd.
Bros.
e Grocer Co., Ltd.
e Hardware Co., Ltd.
ern Grocer Co., Ltd.
Bros. Co., Ltd.
IITOCHES—
Ducournau & Son.
IBERIA—
Erath.
ORLEANS—
tt Mfg. Co., 910 Hennen Bldg.
Baylen, 826 Union St.
V. Bierce, Ltd.
G. Clark, 408 Magazine St.
Clark Co., Ltd., 1111 Julia St.
Demourelle & Sons, 602 N. n St.
F. Dow, 421 Carondelet St.
e Eike, 1801 Carondelet St.
her & Estalotte, 1519 Canal St.
ce Feitel, 834 Magazine St.
Flanagan, 311 Barome St.
dman Ford, 304 Barome St.
hncke, 816 Howard Ave.
ke Navigation & Improvet Co., 816 Howard St.
Jamison, 415 Carondelet St.
tts Kearny & Sons, 423 Gra- St.
e & Flauders, 630 Gravier St.

New Orleans—Continued.
Lagarde Lime & Stone Co., 226 Carondelet St.
George M. Leahy, 512 Camp St.
R. McWilliams, Ltd., 342 Camp St.
National Bldg. Supply Co., 412 Carondelet St.
New Orleans Roofing & Metal Works, 92 Lafayette St.
Ong-Hiller Co., Ltd., 534 Magazine St.
Peter E. G. Pleasworth, 2311 N. Rampart St.
Harry Stevens' Sons Co., 826 Union St.
Edward Thompson, 530 Natchez St.
Allen Tupper, 713 Union St.
Tupper & Sargent, 713 Union St.
A. H. White Co., Ltd., 532 Grovier St.
OPELOUSAS—
The C. Deitlein Gro. Co. Ltd.
A. C. Skiles.
J. T. Stewart.
SHREVEPORT—
W. A. Pleasants Hardware Co.

MAINE.

AUBURN—
Bearce, Wilson & Co.
Jno. Dingley & Co.
AUGUSTA—
A. M. Brown.
Chas. N. Cunningham.
L. Haskell Co.
E. J. Philbrick.
BANGOR—
H. F. Bailey.
A. Chapin & Co.
R. B. Dunning & Co. (George W. Dunning, Pres.; James A. Dunning, Secy.; John G. Dunning, Treas. and Mgr.)
A. R. Hopkins Co.
BATH—
Read Nichols Co.
BELFAST—
Cooper & Co., 22 Front St.

L ABOUT CEMENT
UP-TO-DATE AND
ALL THE TIME

The best way to keep informed about everything relating to Cement the year round is to read

MUNICIPAL ENGINEERING MAGAZINE

The publication which stands foremost in representation of Cement interests.

ription price,
)0 per year.

Address MUNICIPAL ENGINEERING CO.

BERWICK—
Oscar C. Davis.
John Mathews.
BOOTHBAY HARBOR—
C. F. Dodge.
BRIDGTON—
Fred C. Knight.
Wales, Hamblen & Co.
BRUNSWICK—
Chas. E. Hacker.
Larkin D. Snow.
BUCKSPORT—
E. B. Gardner & Co.
CALAIS—
Boardman Bros.
Chase, Barker & Co
Todd Bros.
DEXTER—
W. H. Carr.
G. A. Dustin.
F. W. Parsons.
DOVER—
Sawyer & Gifford.
EASTPORT—
Geo. W Capen.
E. S. Martin & Son.
S. L. Wadsworth & Son.
FAIRFIELD—
F. J. Savage.
FOXCROFT—
Babson & Co.
A. W. Gilman & Co.
E. A. Ireland Co.
W. M. Steward & Son.
GARDINER—
Dingley & Decker.
G. H. Harrington.
A. N. Potter & Co.
Wm. Wiley.
HALLOWELL—
Frank G. Wingate.
MACHIAS—
Crane Bros.
W. C. Holway,
E. I. White.
MADISON—
J. R. Emery & Co.
MILLTOWN—
S. S. Pineo.
NORWAY—
C. B. Cummings & Son.
Chas. L. Hathaway.
H. L. Horne.
C. N. Tubbs & Co.
OAKLAND—
H. A. Burrell.
OLD TOWN—
Oscar T. Brown
George A. Gray.
Elem T. Hartwell.
Andrew J. Sampson.
ORONO—
A. J. Durgin.
F. C. Park.
PITTSFIELD—
Getchell & Chandler.
T. G. Lancey & Co.
PORTLAND—
Chas. S. Chase.
Cox & Ward Co.
Lord Bros. & Co.
Portland Pipe Co.
SKOWHEGAN—
Blunt Hardware Co.
C. A. Ross.
R. D. Rowles & Co
THOMASTON—
J. A. Creighton & Co.
J. O. Cushing & Co.
WALDOBORO—
J. T. Gay & Son.

MARYLAND.

ANNAPOLIS—
S. & M. Basil, 308 Pearl St.
ARLINGTON—
Chas. T. Cockey, Jr.
BALTIMORE—
J. A. Aller's Sons, Charles & West Sts.
American Cement Co., 112 St. Paul. St.
Edward Brady & Son, 915 Park Ave.
Jno. Bullock & Sons, 229 Smith Wharves.
Henry Clark, Fremont & Winchester Sts.
Wm. Wirt Clarke & Son, 115 Gay St. S.
Samuel J. Diggs & Sons, 707 S. Caroline St.
T. M. Dinsmore & Co., 416 O'Donnell St.
Wm. C. Ditman, 540 E. Monument St.
Fredrick Ellenbrok, 2104 Frederick Ave.
J. T. Flautt & Co., 1224 Penn Ave.
Geo. A. Gegner, Eastern & Clinton Aves.
M. F. Gore, 608 Law Bldg.
Robt. S. Green, 853 Frederick Ave.
S. M. Hamilton & Co., 413 Water St.
Geo. M. Hay, 14 N. Green St.
John Hertel & Sons, Chester & Boston Sts.
The Lime & Cement Exchange of Baltimore City, Builders' Exchange Bldg. Chas. H. Classen, Pres; Benj. Wallis, V. Pres.; Addison H. Clarke, Secy.; Wm. A. Allers, Treas.
Maryland Cement Co., 18 Builders' Exchange.
Maryland Lime & Cement Co., 219 Bowly's Wharf.
National Building & Supply Co., Mfrs. Record Bldg.
H. Noble & Co., 18 S. Gay St.
J. L. Robinson, 302 Fidelity Bldg.
Walbrook Coal & Supply Co., Mont Ave. & W. Md. R. R.
Benjamin Wallis, 210 E. Lexington St.
L. J. Warren, 213 Falls Ave.

BEL AIR—
Hanway & Keen.
CAMBRIDGE—
J. B. Brown, Race St.
Cambridge Mfg. Co., Mill No. 8.
J. H. Hubbard, Race St.
CHESTERTOWN—
J. D. Bacchus.
W. S. Culp.
S. F. Smith.
CRISFIELD—
A. B. Cochran & Co.
CUMBERLAND—
Cedar Cliffs Cement Co.
Cumberland Hydraulic Cement and Manufacturing Co.
The Kemeweg Co.
The J. C. Orick Son Co.
Potomac Cement Co.
HAGERSTOWN—
Victor Cushmer & Son.
Victor Cushwa & Son.
J. V. Jamison.
HAMPDEN—
J. P. Benson's Sons.
HAVRE DE GRACE—
C. C. Pusey & Co.
POCOMOKE—
Thos. J. Veasey.
F. M. Wilson & Co.
PORT DEPOSIT—
J. M. Campbell & Co.
Port Deposit Store Co.
ROCKVILLE—
Oscar L. Johnson.
Wm. W. Welsh.
SALISBURY—
Wm. A. Crew.
Farmers' & Planters' Company.
Salisbury Lime & Coal Co.
WESTMINSTER—
Gilbert & Gehr.
Westminster Hdw. Co.
WILLIAMSPORT—
V. Cushwa & Sons.

MASSACHUSETTS.

ADAMS—
L. J. Follett & Son.
AMESBURY—
H. H. Bean & Son.
ARLINGTON—
Pierce & Winn Co.
ATTLEBORO—
C. L. Bowen.
E. O. Dexter.
William Fales.
A. H. Tucker.
BEVERLY—
Independent Coal Yard.
Pickett Coal Co.
BOSTON—
Andres Bros., 507 John Hancock Bldg.
Berry & Ferguson, 102 State St.
Boston Fire Brick Co., 164 Devonshire St.
Boston Rubber Cem. Co., 50 Lincoln.

Boston—Continued.
Bryant & Kent, 30 Kilby, Rm. 14.
Chandler & Barker, 124 Summer St.
Curtis & Pope Lbr. Co., 774 Albany.
Davis, James A. & Co., 92 State.
Dorchester Building Material Co., 250 Freeport.
Fiske & Co., 164 Devonshire.
Geo. E. Frost, 488 Neponset Ave., Nep.
Golding & Co., 177-199 Ft. Hill sq.
Hamm & Carter, 560 Albany St.
Holmes & Blanchard Co.
T. W. Hoxie & Co., 234 State St.
D. W. Lewis, 192 Devonshire Sa.
W. B. Mullen, 95 Milk, Rm. 15.
W. A. Murffeldt Co., 192 Devonshire.
Willard G. Nash, 220 State, Cambridge.
William C. Morcross Co., 484 Albany.
A. T. Nute & Son, 151 Swett.
Puritan Brick Co., 9th St., opp. Old Harbor St.
Waldo Bros., 102 Milk.
Warren Brothers Co., 143 Federal.
S. A. White, 85 High.
E. H. Whitney, 35 Arch St.
Windsor Cement Co., 446 Albany St.
Geo. H. Wood Co., 431 Medford.
Wm. H. Wood & Co., Broadway and 3d, Cambridgeport.
BRAINTREE—
B. H. Woodsum Co.
BROCTON—
Isham Mitchell & Co., 338 Montello St.
CAMBRIDGE—
Burdett & Bynner, 674 Mass. Ave.
David F. Burns, 5 Blackstone St.
A. A. Elston & Co., 99 Broadway.
Geo. W. Gale Lumber Co., 640 Main St.
T. J. Murphy & Co., 473 Main St.
Hycent Purcell, 441 Main St.
M. F. Tracy & Son, 74 Boylston St.
Warren Bros. Co., Potter St. near 3d St.
W. F. Webster Cement Co., Albany St.
Wm. H. Wood & Co., 13 Broadway.
CHELSEA—
Richardson & Co., 341 Broadway.
S S. Tuksey, 191 Winnisimmett St.
CHICOPEE—
Dennis G. Canty.
Patrick Rourke.
DEDHAM—
A Fisher.
EVERETT—
Green & Warrington
D. P. Murphy.
FALL RIVER—
Byron W. Anthony
Samuel Benoit
Borden & Remington
Covel & Osborn Co

Fall River—Continued.
Staples Coal Co.
James H. Wilson.

FITCHBURG—
B. A. Cook.
E. N. Cummings & Co.
Damon & Gould Co. W. B. Damon, Pres.; W. T. Hidden, Sec'y; R. D. Gould, Treas.
Lawrence Sons & Co.

FLORENCE—
Chas. O. Parsons.

GLOUCESTER—
Frank O. Griffin.
L. B. Nauss & Sons.

GREAT BARRINGTON—
James A. Brewer.
Burget & Lewis.

GREENFIELD—
J. E. Lamb.

HAVERHILL—
D. D. Chase Lumber Co., 9 Washington St.
M. S. Holmes, 148 Washington St.
E. A. Messinger, 10 Pleasant St.
A. H. Saltmarsh, 24 Arch St.
A. T. Stearns Lumber Co., 166 Devonshire St.
Taylor-Goodwin Co., 16 Main St.
Frank P. Woodsum, 62 Fleet St.

HOLYOKE—
Geo. L. Bosworth.
Dennis J. Landers..
Lynch Bros.
John J. Prew.
Richards & Goddard.

IPSWICH—
W. G. Brown.
John S. Glover.

LAWRENCE—
James Chambers, 8 Broadway Ave.
George L. Gage, 594 Essex St.
D. J. O'Mahoney & Co., 151 Hampshire St.
M. O'Mahoney, 8 West St.
O. E. Runnells, 8 Jackson St.

LOWELL—
Edward Cawley.
Connors Bros.
Phillip P. Connors & Co.
Chas. E. Howe.
Wm. E. Livingston, 15 Thorndike St.
W. E. Livingston, Pres.; H. R. White, Secy.; Wm. Livingston, Treas.

LYNN—
John W. Blaney & Co.
J. B. & W. A. Lamper.
James H. Ryan, 797 Washington St.
William C. Whittredge.

MALDEN—
Elmore E. Locke.
Malden Coal Co.
Talbott Bros., Bell Rock Sta.

MARBLEHEAD—
M. Gilbert & Son.
J. S. Martin & Co.

MEDFORD—
F. E. Foster & Co., 89 Riversi[de] Ave.
Highland Coal Co., Harvard C[or.] Winchestor St.
E. E. Locke, 74 Florence St.
Medford Moulding & Mantle C[o.] Winchester nr. Harvard St.
New Hampshire Lumber Co., 590 B[os]ton Ave.
J. E. Ober & Son, 492 High St.
Thatcher & Littlefield, 616 Bost[on] Ave.

MELROSE—
Seth E. Benson & Co., 20 Tremo[nt] St.
C. B. & F. H. Goss, 158 Essex St.
Samuel H. Hellen, Renwick Road.
Newell & Walker, Wyoming Ave.

MILFORD—
H. A. Barney.
L. A. Cook.
P. P. Field.
Williams Bros.

NATICK—
W. D. Parlin.
C. and J. A. Underwood.

NEW BEDFORD—
Chas. S. Paisler, 160 N. Water St.
S. S. Paine & Bro.

NEWBURYPORT—
James C. Colman.

NEWTON CENTER—
Arthur Muldoon.

NORTH ADAMS—
Alderman & Carlisle.
Burlingam & Darby's Co.
Potter Brothers.

NORTHAMPTON—
W. N. Potter & Sons.
John A. Sullivan.

PITTSFIELD—
J. H. Butler Lumber Co., 108 Tenn. S[t.]
Dodge & Devanny, 180 Columbus A[ve.]
Gale Lumber Co., Oak near Li[n]coln St.
C. C. Gamwell, 65 Columbus Ave.
Glentz & Cheney, 45 Clapp St.
Howard & Morrow, 59 North St.
J. W. Kirchner, 156 North St.
Z. A. Ward, Center & West Sts.

PLYMOUTH—
Anthony Atwood.

QUINCY—
Geo. E. Frost, 488 Neponset Ave.
Theo. Salstein, 39 Quarry St.
Wm. Shea & Son, 12 Common St.
Wm. Westland, 36 Hancock St.

READING—
Bancroft, Wendell & Co.

SALEM—
James Fairfield.
Geo. W. Lane.
Geo. W. Pickering.

ILLE—
d Coal Co., 367 Highland Ave.
Sanborn, ft of N. Union.
FIELD—
S. Noble Co., 202-208 Lyman

AM—
Emerson & Co.
ON—
Coal Co.
AM—
nk Frost.
m Coal Co.
TOWN—
Pevear & Co.
Sprague & Co.
ER—
Schumurey.
ELD—
Hildreth.
ahony.
& Galvin.
EWTON—
ddy & Co.
N—
Lumber Co.
Vinn & Co., 375 Main St.
STER—
. Carr.
Crane.
Marsh.
Powers.
aith-Green Co.
& Foster.

MICHIGAN.

—
& Washburn.
Imbert.
Bros., 58-60 N. Main.
—
rown & Co.
Dean.
er.
Steele.
N—
Phillips.
yden.
Dunning.
Green.
s.

Produce Co.
& Hannah.
—
Portland Cement Co.,
son Blk.
Collins, 151 Water St.
Fox, 116 E. Chisholm St.
BOR—
Rohde.
CREEK—
Dibble.
Lewis.
Giles.
Y—
Bros. & Co.
Young.

BAY SHORE—
Bay Shore Lime Co.
BELDING—
E. Chapple.
Wilson & Co.
BENTON HARBOR—
Jas. McDonald.
W. P. Robbins.
Stevens & Morton Co.
BESSEMER—
C. Hansen.
BIG RAPIDS—
Reynolds & Co.
W. J. Sloss.
BLISSFIELD—
The Phillips Company, Ltd.
BRONSON—
Nichols & Reynolds.
CADILLAC—
William Cassler.
C. J. Manklelow.
Stewart & Anderson.
CALUMET—
Armstrong & Thielman.
Bajari & Ulseth.
CARO—
T. E. Kelsey.
Vantine & Gardner.
CASSOPOLIS—
Hayden & Tompsett.
CEDAR RAPIDS—
Wm. King & Co.
CHARLEVOIX—
Brown Bros.
H. Widdifield.
CHARLOTTE—
Miller & Hamilton.
Webster Cobb & Co.
CHEBOYGAN—
Cheboygan Mfg. Co.
G. C. Dodd & Co.
W. & A McArthur & Co., Ltd.
COLDWATER—
Adams & Davis.
S. Pollock & Son.
CONSTANTINE—
The Constantine Lumber Co.
DELRAY—
Jas. Burk.
Wm. J. Frasier.
Joe Kinnell.
Jalle Miller.
David Spicer.
DETROIT—
Bolton Lime & Stone Co., 104 Lafferty Place.
Brady & Co., 11 Woodward Ave.
Horace H. Dickinson, 418 Grand River Ave.
Jas. T. Eaman Coal Co., 75 Woodbridge St., West.
Egyptian Portland Cement Co., 712 Union Trust Bldg.
Great Northern Portland Cement Co., 84 Griswold St.
George Heal, 669 Baker St.

Detroit—Continued.
W. E. Heames & Co., 75 Woodbridge St., West.
F. B. Holmes, 306 Hammond Bldg.
Henry Houghton, 806 Hammond Bldg.
Iola Portland Cement Co., 1111 Majestic Bldg.
F. P. Jones, 202 Beaubien St.
Lewis & Wickey, 926 Grand River Ave.
C. H. Little Co., 340 Atwater St., East.
Michigan Portland Cement Co., 1111 Majestic Bldg.
Noble & Co., foot 1st St.
Ortmann & Co., 1099 Wabash Ave.
Pittsburgh Artificial Stone Co., 429 6th St.
Standard Portland Cement Co., 811 Hammond Bldg.
F. B. Stevens, 12 Griswold St.
G. A. Stewart, 148 Grand River Ave.
Thomas Bros. & Co., 711 Hammond Ave.
Wabash Portland Cement Co., 912 Union Trust Bldg.

DOWAGIAC—
G. E. Bishop.

DURAND—
Hamlin Bros.
McBride & Son.

EATON RAPIDS—
Spears & Scofield.
Webster, Cobb & Co.

FENTON—
B. Potter.
Fred Welch.

FLINT—
Hall & Co.
S. C. Randall & Co., F. & P. M. R. R., bet. N. 2d & N. 3d E.
E. W Reid, 313 Beach St.

GLADSTONE—
L. E. Folsom.
W. I. Ely & Co.

GRAND HAVEN—
N. Robbins.

GRAND LEDGE—
E. C. Astley & Son
J. M. Burtch & Co.

GRAND RAPIDS—
Albert Himes, 65 Pearl-st.
A. B. Knowlson, under Natl City Bk.
T. E. Wykes, S. Ionia-st

Office, 721 Wainwright Bldg.
Telephones: Bell Main 35, Kinloch A. 270.

GILSONITE CONSTRUCTION Co

Asphalt, Cement and Granitoid Work.

Brewery Work a Specialty. Asphalt and Tile Roofs, Concrete Foundations.

Hollow Tile and Concrete FIREPROOFING.

St. Louis, Mo.

GREENVILLE—
M. Ludlow.
Miller & Miller.

HANCOCK—
J. S. Stringer.

HASTINGS—
F. H. Barlow & Co.
Covert O. Freer.
R. K. Grant.

HILLSDALE—
E. H. Cunningham.
L. C. Wright.

HOLLAND—
T. Keppel's Sons.
Scott & Lugers.

HOUGHTON—
Elm & Bowdin.
M. Van Orden.

HOWELL—
O. O. Hutchins & Sons.
Wright & Co.

HUDSON—
R. F. Birch.
Cruse & Blood.
E. Mayes & Co.

IONIA—
W. C. Page & Co.

IRON MOUNTAIN—
J. R. Halfelty.
E. Harvey.

IRONWOOD—
F. J. Hager Lumber Co.

ISHPEMING—
F. W. Read & Co.

ITHACA—
N. Church.
O. B. Churchill, Box 63
O. H. Heath & Son.
Ithaca Lumber Co.
Will Naldret.
Wilbur Nelson.
Pinney & Horr.

JACKSON—
J. E. Bartlett Co., Columbu Liberty Sts.
C. A. Howind, 15 Dwight Bldg.
Robert Lake Co., Liberty & waukee Sts.
E. J. Tobin & Co., 145 W. Pearl

KALAMAZOO—
J. D. Bixby & Son.
Dewing & Sons.
A. H. Humphrey.

LAKE LINDEN—
Calumet & Hecla Mining Co.

LANSING—
P E. Lacy & Co.
Lansing Artificial Stone Co.
A. H. Whitehead.

LAPEER—
T. B. Flanagan.
E. C. Roberts.

LUDINGTON—
Chas. Genia.
John Kieswalter.

MANISTEE—
Thomas Kenney, Foot of Smith

STIQUE—
›r & Bassford.
.e Marble Lime Co.
NE CITY—
: Bros.
nerman Bros.
!UETTE—
E. French.
. Spear & Sons.
HALL—
er & Cater.
se & Blood.
. Day.
MINEE—
.s Bros. & Co., 1106 Main St.
. Monack, 1316 Main St.
AND—
. Baker.
. Hawks.
'AY—
ner & McCann.
en Bros.
:OE—
F. Finzel.
. Kibble.
& Baier, 14 and 16 Front St.
Steiner.
'LEMENS—
Lema, Front St.
er & Smith, foot of Park Ave.
LEASANT—
Audlin.
Butcher & Co.
Hidey.
edy Bros.
. Newton.
Skelton.
SING—
ll & Stebbins.
Coates
Manley.
EGON—
Kanitz.
egon Stone Sidewalk Co.
JNEE—
Johnson.
—
L. Reddick.
illes Smith.
I ADAMS—
Arnold.

ile Lumber Co.
O—
m Healy.
D. Kelley.
Siple & Co.
O—
Brooks & Son, 1003 W. Main-

Woodard.
Todd & Co.

PETOSKEY—
Darling & Beahan.
D. M. McDonald.
D. C. Osborne.
H. O. Rose & Co.
PONTIAC—
Robt. T. Knight.
Colin MacCallum.
Wm. H. Osmun.
Fred Poole.
PORT HURON—
Boynton & Thompson.
Cameron & Co.
F. D. Jenks & Co.
J. W. Thompson, jr.
READING—
Geo. Worden.
REED CITY—
H. J. Crocker.
Curtis Bros.
SAGINAW—
Morley, Ewen & Co., N. Tilden-st.
E. E. Johnson.
Remer Bros., West Side.
ST. CLAIR—
W. R. Kemp.
ST. IGNACE—
D. J. Chambers & Bros.
Stellwagon & Kynoch.
ST. JOHNS—
Jno. Hicks.
L. G. McKnight.
J. S. Osgood.
ST. JOSEPH—
W. A. Preston.
Wallace & Sons.
SAULT STE. MARIE—
Union Dock & Coal Co.
Port Royal Dock Co., Ashmun St.
W. P. Arms, Pres. (Youngstown, O.); H. H. Stambaugh, Secy. (Youngstown, O.); J. C. Barnhisel, Mgr.
SOUTH HAVEN—
W. G. Packard.
A. M. Prouty.
Volney Ross.
South Haven Lumber Co.
TECUMSEH—
Chas. A. Slayton.
THREE RIVERS—
F. M. Case & Co.
Jno. Griffiths.
TRAVERSE CITY—
Wilhelm Bartak & Co.
Prokep Kyselks.
H. & L. Meir Co.
VICKSBURG—
Vicksburg Lumber Co.
WEST BAY CITY—
McLaughlin & Co.
WYANDOTTE—
H. A. Eberts.
Wayman Coal Co.

YPSILANTI—
Chas. E. King.
O. E. Thompson & Sons.
Webster, Cobb & Co.

MINNESOTA.

ALBERT LEA—
D. M. Dominick.
ALEXANDRIA—
M. Fifield.
Page Bros.
ANOKA—
J. A. Chesley.
Geo. A. McCaully.
AUSTIN—
A. N. Decker.
J. F. Fairbanks.
BLUE EARTH—
Anthony Anderson.
South & Sasse.
BRAINERD—
Fisher & Walters.
John Larson.
CHASKA—
M. H. Muyres.
Herman Nicoli.
Henry Simons.
CROOKSTON—
Crookston Lumber Co.
Robertson Lumber Co.
A. M. Smitson.
Stewart Lumber Co.
DETROIT—
Reid & Woekman.
Wilcox Lumber Co.
DULUTH—
Cutler & Gilbert.
Paine & Nixon Co., 116 W. Mich St.
Thomson & Dunlop, 31 W. Mich. St.
FARIBAULT—
Carpenter Glass Co.
Faribault Cement Pavement Works.
E. M. Leach & Son.
Wisconsin Lumber Co., A. Blodgett, sr., Pres.; A. Blodgett, jr, Secy. and Treas.; W E. Blodgett, V. P.
FERGUS FALLS—
E. Barbeau.
T. H. Grady.
GLENCOE—
L. P. Albrecht.
Betcher Lumber Co.
Classen Bros.
John Davis.
H. Wadsworth & Co.
HIBBING—
W. G. Close.
Itasca Mer. Co.
Peter McHardy.
B. O'Rourke
HUTCHINSON—
R. C. Libby & Co
KENYON—
Wisconsin Lumber Co., A Blodgett, sr., Pres.; W E. Blodgett, V. P.; A. Blodgett, Jr., Sec. Treas.
LAKE CITY—
Richardson Hardware Co., (not inc.) inc.)
C. Sinclair.
Charles Wire & Sons.
LITCHFIELD—
J. Esbjornsson.
F. Koplin.
J. W. Simpson.
LITTLE FALLS—
J. W. Berg.
T. J. Mathieson.
H. F. Schleusner.
MANKATO—
T. R. Coughlan.
Fowler & Pay.
Mankato Lime and Stone Co.
MINNEAPOLIS—
H. L. Braesch, 28 Washington-ave., N.
Mads. Christenson, 10 N. Third-st.
S. J. Hewson Co., 10 N. Third-st.
R. F. Jackson, 829 Lumber Exch.
Harold Johnson, 342 Lumber Exch.
J. C. Landers & Co., 1013 Lumber Exch.
G. H. Lawes & Co., 842 Lumber Exch.
J. F. Manchester, 130 N. E. Seventh-st.
Minneapolis Cedar Co., 1013 Lumber Exch.
Minneapolis Lime and Cement Co., 216 Third-ave., south.
Northwestern Hydraulic Cement and Stone Co., 418 Guaranty Loan bldg.
W. H. Page, 17 S. Fourth-st.
Paine & Nixon Co., 834 Lumber Exch.
Plymouth Paving Co., 728 Plymouth-ave.
Proctor Plaster Co., 315 S. Fifth-st.
Selenite Cement and Plaster Co., 1029 Lumber Exch.
Standard Stone Sidewalk Co., 222 N. Y. Life bldg.
Superior Mfg. Co., 734 N. First-st.
Union Railway Storage Co., 26 S. Washington-ave., H. E. Carpenter, Sec.-Treas.
Warehouse & Builders' Supply Co., 734 N. First-st.
MONTEVIDEO—
Chas. Betcher Lumber Co.
G. Eliason.
MOORHEAD—
V. Fischer.
T. Goodsell & Co.
P. H. Lamb.
Moorhead Hardware Co.
NEW ULM—
Fullerton Lumber Co.
F. Nagel & Co.
NORSTRAND—
Wisconsin Lumber Co. A. Blodgett, Sr., Pres.; W. Blodget, V. P.; A. Blodgett, Jr., sec.-Treas.
NORTHFIELD—
Wisconsin Lumber Co. A. Blodgett, Sr., Pres.; W. Blodgett, V. P.; A. Blodgett, Jr., Sec.-Treas.

NNA—
Lucas Lumber Co.
Norton Co.
sin Lumber Co.
)NE—
ı Lumber Co.
rost.
ING—
ielson.
eyblad.
Osterlind.
Sheldon & Co.
STER—
Dodge.
Haagenson.
Lumber Co.
UD—
& Porwall.
wart & Co.
L—
Bell, 274 Jackson St.
Blake & Co., 540 Endicott

Mfg. Co., S. E. Cor. Arcade
ells Sts.
olondar, 148 8th St.
City Furniture Co., 639 Jack-
st.
. Stone Co., 709 Wabash St.
g & Shepley, 217 W. Universi-
re.
ı Lumber Co., 194 E. 7th St.
. Lawes & Co., 49 E. 5th St.
Hoff Mfg. Co., W. S. Levee
it W. Roberts.
restern Lime Co., 71 Lower
.
restern Stone Co., 186 W. Uni-
y Ave.
ee Cement Lime Mfg. Co., 219
nut St.
oates & Co., 764 E. 3rd St.
il Lime & Cement Co., 156 E.
t.
ER—
t Lumber Co.
Bros.
rber & Lampman.
'ENTER—
ros. & Co.
:—
Batcher.
Klem
Miller.
'ATER—
elly.
ARBORS—
. Lunz.
arbors Lumber Co.
HA—
Tones Co.
A—
Lucus Lumber Co.
umber Co. A. Blodgett, Sr.,
; W. Blodgett, V. P.; A.
ett, Jr., Sec.-Treas

WATERVILLE—
Wisconsin Lumber Co.
WEST CONCORD—
Wisconsin Lumber Co. A. Blodgett, Sr., Pres.; W. Blodgett, V. P.; A. Blodgett, Jr., Sec.-Treas.
WILLMAR—
F. O. Peterson.
Peterson & Quale.
J. S. Robbins.
WINDOM—
Lambert Lumber Co.
Strunk-Sherwin Co.
J. W. Tuthill Lumber Co.
WINONA—
J. O'Dea.
H. J. Willis.
WORTHINGTON—
Albinson & Broberg.
St. Croix Lbr. Co.
J. W. Tuthill Lbr. Co.

MISSISSIPPI.

BILOXI—
E. Glennan.
J. V. Hagan.
L. Loper & Co.
Chas. Redding.
BROOKHAVEN—
C. B. Perkins.
E. M. Price & Co.
CANTON—
M. Alexander & Co.
G. D. Leitch.
C. Olsen & Co.
COLUMBUS—
Morgan, Walker & Co.
Ratatson & Co.
CORINTH—
McCord & Brakeman.
GREENVILLE—
Greenville Brick and Improvement Co.
GREENWOOD—
Greenwood Brick and Lumber Co.
GRENADA—
Gabbott Moore & Co.
Jennings Sainson.
Kimbrough & Perry.
HOLLY SPRINGS—
J. E. Anderson.
JACKSON—
W. W. Morrison.
D. G. Patton & Co.
MERIDIAN—
J. A. & J. H. Hister.
C. M. Rubush.
NATCHEZ—
L. M. Dalgarn & Bro.
I Lowenburg & Co
Charles Meeks
Charles Miller.
Rumble & Wensel Co
OXFORD—
Lewis & McKee.
Oxford Hardware Co.
PASS CHRISTIAN—
Brandt & Dempf.
Guy Northrop.

PORT GIBSON—
S. Bernhermer & Son.
Wm. Cahn & Co.
L. Levy's Sons.

VICKSBURG—
R. L. Crook & Co.
P. P. Williams.
W. C. Worrell & Co., N. Wash. St.

WATER VALLEY—
F. A. Pearce.

WESSON—
Atkinson & McDonald.
J. E. Patterson.

WEST POINT—
G. W. Braine.
West Point M'f'g. Co.

WINONA—
Turner & Timson.
Winona Hardware Co.

YAZOO CITY—
Quekmeyer & Gardner.
Montgomery Land Co.
J. F. Powell.

MISSOURI.

AURORA—
M. L. Coleman.

BOONVILLE—
Chas. Meierhoffer.
E. H. Roberts.

BRUNSWICK—
Chas. D. Marshall.
B. Muehring.
Jasper Perry.

BUTLER—
Logan & Moore Lumber Co.
H. C. Wyatt & Son.

CALIFORNIA—
Hart Lumber Co.
W. H. Mengel.

CAMERON—
Russell & Russell.
R. De Steigner.

CANTON—
Joshua Ellis.
Wm. Schuetz.

CARROLLTON—
Badger Lumber Co.
T. W. Ballew & Co.

CARTHAGE—
Harrison, Calhoon & Harriso
Home Lumber Co.
S. H. Regan Lumber Co.
B. F. Thomas.

CARUTHERSVILLE—
Caruthersville Hardware Co.
Caruthersville Lumber & Mi
Cunningham Bros.
F. T. Jackson.
F. W. Phleiger.
Riverside Lumber Co. J. P. G
Pres. (Fredericktown, Mo.);
Russell, Sec., Treas. & Mgr.
G. E. Zimmerman.

CENTRALIA—
Lacrosse Lumber Co.
J. L. Thomas Lumber Co.

CHILLICOTHE—
Grace & Sons.
Hannibal Saw Mill Co.
Hoge Bros. Lumber Co.
Saunders-Turner Lumber Co.

CLINTON—
Anderson & Co.
J. F. Brown & Co.
Conyers & Taylor.
Hurley Lumber Co.

COLUMBIA—
Terrell & Crouch Lumber Co., Broadway.
McAllester Lumber Co.
Tandy Lumber Co.

DEEPWATER—
R. J. Hurley Lumber Co.

DESOTO—
W. H. Blank.

ELDORADO SPRINGS—
Logan & Moore.

FULTON—
La Crosse Lumber Co.
W. P. Records.

GALLATIN—
G. H. Fitzgerald.
C. W. Hitchcock.
S. R. Simpson & Son.

GLASGOW—
Rall Bros.

GREENFIELD—
S. W. Japes.

Any information on **Cement or Cement Machinery** will be furnished on request by the publishers of this book—

Municipal Engineering Compa[ny]

[BAL—
shank Lumber & Coal Co.
ibal Lime Co.
McCooey & Co.
r Lime Co.

NSVILLE—
sse Lumber Co.
le & Schoppenhorst.

EN—
Chappell.
E. Starkey.

VILLE—
Dulany.
Richeson.

ENDENCE—
r Lumber Co.
E. Lewis.
cDonald.

RSON CITY—
Lohman.
H. Morelock.
Tanner.

I—
Chickering, 513 Va. Ave.
Cement & Coal Co., McKinley

S CITY—
Cement Plaster Co., 121 W. th-st.
can Mason Safety Thread Co., unction bldg.
Brockett Cement Co., 121 W. th-st.; C. A. Brockett, Treas. Genl. Mgr.; Howard McCutch- Secy. and Treas.
rs' Material Supply Co., 407 al Tel. bldg.
Deardorff, Twentieth and Vine-
Dickey Clay Mfg. Co., 715 Wal- st.
Scott Cement Assn, 121 W. th-st.
enfield Sand and Fuel Co., ral-ave. and Kaw River.
Halliwell, 107 E. Tenth-st.
ational Trading Co., 618 Wyan- -st.
s City & Ft. Scott Cement Co., '. Eighth-st.
-Watkins Lime and Cement 1900 Walnut St.
Merrill, S. W. Boulevard and nit-st.
ri Lime and Cement Co., 201 l Tel. bldg.
oal and Lime Co., 1900 Grand-
Cement Plaster Co., 308 Pos- el. bldg.
Sutermeister, Twenty-first-st. Main-ave.
Hallliwell Cement Co., 107 E. 1-st.
n White Lime Co.

KING CITY—
J. W. Liggett.
Miner & Frees.

KIRKSVILLE—
W. P. Foster.
Kirksville Lumber Co.
V. Miller & Son.
W. S. Murphy, 104 S. Maine St.

LAMAR—
Houston & Shelton.

LATHROP—
B. B. Beery & Co.

LEBANON—
Hinds & Wussgerber.
J. G. Lingsweiler.

LEXINGTON—
Harris-Anderson Lumber Co.
J. R. Moorehead.
Triumph Press Brick Co. G. W. Hyde, Pres.; John T. Bush, Treas.

LOUISIANA—
Crystal Carbonate Lime Co.

MARCELINE—
D. Brown.
W. H. Rosenbery.

MARSHALL—
La Crosse Lumber Co.
Page & Mitchell.

MARYVILLE—
Conrad & Totterdale.
Ridgway Lumber Co.
F. H. Rowley.

MEMPHIS—
W. W. Eckman.
T. H. Weigner.

MEXICO—
Coatsworth & Co.
Houston & Crow.
LaCross Lumber Co.

MOBERLY—
W. W. Babcock & Co.
Moberly B. & T. Co.
D. H. Mornice & Co.

MONETT—
August Othenin.
J. H. Otterman.

MONROE CITY—
C. D. Everhart & Co.
P. W. Hilston.

MONTGOMERY CITY—
LaCrosse Lbr. Co.

NEOSHO—
Neosho Planing Mill Co., Jas Robinson, Pres.; J. B. Robinson, Secy.-Treas.; R. H. Robinson, Mgr.

NEVADA—
Clark & Bates Lumber Co.
Home Lumber Co.
Logan-Moore-Boyd Lumber Co.

NORBORNE—
Badger Lumber Co.
Cunningham, Beckemere & Co.

PALMYRA—
J. F. Heinze & Son.
Geo. A. Noble.
W. J. Jackson & Co.

PIERCE CITY—
Pierce City Lime Co.
PLATTSBURG—
T. W. Ballew.
P. J. O'Malley.
PLEASANT HILL—
Clark Lumber Co.
J. C. Jones.
RICH HILL—
R. J. Hurley Lumber Co.
Williamson & Montgomery.
RICHMOND—
Davis & Child.
ROLLA—
A. S. Long & Son.
T. E. Dyer.
ST. CHARLES—
Bruns Machine Co.
C. & H. Hafer.
J. Phil Hoehn.
Dubach Lumber Co.
Ocks-Rohlfing & Co.
ST. GENEVIEVE—
Chas. H. Biel & Co.
John L. Boverie.
Jakerst Bros. & Yealy.
ST. JOSEPH—
S. W. Nieweizer.
Chas. Nowland.
ST. LOUIS—
Acme Cement Plaster Co., 313 N. 9th St.
Arkansas Portland Cement Co., 313 N. 9th St.
Berry-Horn Coal Co., 308 N. 6th St., Al Berry, Secy.
Centaur Lime Co., 3852 Manchester.
Chas. W. Goetz Lime & Cement Co., 3627 Gratiot, P J Dauernheim, Pres.; Louisa A. Goetz, Secy and Treas.
W. H. Hill Lime & Cement Co., 11 N. Main St.
Johannes Lime & Cement Co., 2438 Kosciusko.
Lawrence Martin & Co., Parnell & Nat. Bridge Road.
Meacham & Wright, 721 Olive St.
Metal Core Cement Tie Co., 313 W. 19th St.
Royal Cement & Plaster Co., 18th, near cor. Austin.
St. Louis Contracting Co., 32 Turner Bldg.
Henry M. Schultz & Co., 7920 Pennsylvania Ave.
Thorn & Hunkins Lime and Cement Co., 18th and Austin Sts.
William Wedemaier, Rm. 824 Wainwright Bldg.
SALEM—
Clark Merc. Co.
SALISBURY—
J. H. Green.
Salisbury Lumber Co.
SEDALIA—
Babcock Lumber Co.
Gallie Lumber Co., Kentucky St.
Mo. Central Lumber Co.
SENECA—
P. G. Browning & Co.
SHELBINA—
Cotton & Boettcher.
C. P. Dobyns & Co.
Hannibal Saw Mill Co.
SLATER—
Dulaney Bros.
La Crosse Lumber Co.
SPRINGFIELD—
Bunker Bros.
Campbell Lumber Co.
W. L. Garrett.
Marblehead Lime Co.
Nichols & Co.
Vaughan Coal & Sand Co.
STANBERRY—
Gromer & Co.
Kimball Lumber Co.
THAYER—
H. J. F. Davis.
Hopkins & Emmons.
TIPTON—
Wm. Ferguson.
Wm. Schmidt & Co.
TRENTON—
Badger Lumber Co.
F. W. Ballew.
WEBB CITY—
Corwin & Matthews.
Webb City Lumber Co.
WEBSTER GROVE—
W. W. Alter.
Robt. Horspool.
A. N. Winthers.
WEST PLAINS—
J. E. Johnson.
Lewis-Faly Commission C[o.]
WINDSOR—
Brown Lumber Co.
Hudson & Son.

MONTANA.

ANACONDA—
Anaconda Copper Mining [Co.,] Hardware Dept.
BILLINGS—
T. R. Hines & Co.
BOZEMAN—
Jonas Henderson.
S. C. Kenyon, 320 Main-st.
Lansing & Wells.
Isaac Oldritt.
BUTTE—
Anaconda Copper Mining [Co., Hard]ware Dept. D. H. G[...] Mgr.; J. A. Dunlap, Pur. [...]
Butte Coal Co. Edwin L. M[...]
Butte Sewer Pipe & Tile C[o.]
Western Fuel Co.
GREAT FALLS—
W. L. Martin & Co.
J. O'Neil.

A—
Holter Hardware Co., 113 N.
.
STON—
ıghnow.
Miles.
—
Rowland.
.TTAN—
ttan Fuel & Lumber Co.
LA—
la Merc. Co.
la Brick & Cement Co.
.V CREEK—
Woodward.

NEBRASKA.

ND—
McLeran.
Parkhurst.
A—
Bell.
Green.
Lysinger.
ICE—
Graff.
ıannah.
H. Von Steen.
Wiebe.
—
l Lumber and Grain Co.
ds & Bradford Lumber Co.
McQuaine.
ON—
t Hood.
BUS—
& Smith.
Iogland.
Hughes.
ıfman.
—
Lumber Co.
& Smith.
erman.
RY—
ry Lumber Co.
Gellatly.
witzer.
CITY—
Easley & Co.
on & Stuart.
NT—
ds & Bradford Lumber Co.
d Lumber Co.
Schneider Co.
A—
& Boleton.
hler Co.
ISLAND—
o Lumber Co.
Harrison.
Hoagland.
GS—
n Lumber Co.
Schneider Co.
Oliver & Co.

HOLDREGE—
D. T. Cornell & Co.
C. A. Galloway.
Johnson & Norlin.
KEARNEY—
Bradford Krisler Lumber Co.
F. H. Gilchrist Lumber Co.
Scott Bros.
Chas. Seeley.
LINCOLN—
W. I. Bailey.
Searle & Chapin Lumber Co., 737 N. St., J. G. Chapin, Pres.; J. F. S.arle, Secy.-Treas.
Whitebreast Coal & Lime Co.
R. S. Young.
NEBRASKA CITY—
L. E. Cornsett & Son.
Edwards, Bradford Lumber Co.
D. P. Rolfe & Co.
NORFOLK—
Chicago Lumber Co.
Edwards & Bradford Lumber Co.
L. C. Mittelstadt.
NORTH PLATTE—
W. W. Birge.
G. F. Field.
C. F. Iddings.
OMAHA—
Adams & Keely Co., 1529 Sherman Ave.
Bullard & Hoagland, Izard & 20th Sts.
M. A. Desbrow & Co., 1202 Izard St.
Hampton Lumber Co., 1242 South 10th St.
Geo. A. Hoagland, 9th & Douglas.
C. W. Hull Co., 20th & Izard Sts.
A. L. Patrick Lumber Co., 1501 Military Ave.
Wagner & Buchanan, 23d & Paul.
Welshans & Holbrook, 309 S. 17th.
O'NEILL—
Galena Lumber Co.
O. O. Snyder.
PAWNEE CITY—
Neil Duncan.
Pawnee Lumber Co.
PLATTSMOUTH—
C. D. Cummins.
F. M. Richey.
Jno. Waterman.
SOUTH OMAHA—
Louis Bradford Lumber Co., 319 N. R. R.-ave.
Bradford Kinsler Lumber Co., 501 N. Twenty-fourth-st.
Broadwell-Rich Coal Co., 2418 N-st.
Cuddington & Wilcox, 2417 N-st.
E. H. Howland Lumber and Coal Co., 438 N. Twenty-fourth-st.
Ed. Munshaw & Co., 602 N. Twenty-seventh-st.
J. B. Watkins & Co., 2420 N-st.
SUTHERLAND—
C. F. Iddings.

TECUMSEH—
Estate of W. H. Hassett, G. W. Hassett, Mgr.
YORK—
Charles Anderson.
A. F. Bloomer.
Geo. Fair.
W. Moist.
Smith & Rogers Lumber Co.

NEVADA.

CARSON CITY—
Geo. H. Meyers.
Virginia & Truckee R. R. Co.
RENO—
J. R. Bradley Co.
Nevada Hardware & Supply Co.
Reno Mercantile Co.
Edward Schmitt.
VIRGINIA CITY—
David Crosby.

NEW HAMPSHIRE.

BERLIN—
Berlin Mills Co.
Chas. Jolbert.
Esobel & Co.
H. C. Rowell.
CONCORD—
Dickerman & Co., 14 Bridge St.
James H. Rowell, 45 School St.
D. W. White, Phenix Hotel.
Woodworth & Co., Hills Ave. & R. R. Square.
DOVER—
A. Converse Place Lumber Co., 17 Cocheco St.
FRANKLIN—
J. D. Kirk.
KEENE—
Knowlton & Stone.
Spencer Hardware Co.
LACONIA—
T. J. Guay.
J. P. Pitman & Co.
John Parker Smith.
LAKEPORT—
C. F. Locke.
MANCHESTER—
Adams Bros., 754 Elm St.
Head & Dowat Co., 97 Granite, Cor. Canal.
J. Hodge, 485 Elm St.
Mead, Mason & Co., 215 The Kenard.
Clarence R. Merrill, 412 Merrimack.
Henry W. Parker, 30 Granite, Cor. Franklin.

J. L. LUDLOW **Municipal, Sanitary & Hydraulic Engineer**
M. Am. Soc. C. E. 434 Summit Street, WINSTON, N. C.
Consultations, reports, plans, specifications, estimates of cost and superintendence of construction for water-works, sewerage systems, electric lighting, and other municipal improvements; water filtration and sewage disposal; expert examinations, tests and reports on water supplies and the value and efficiency of water-works plants.

NASHUA—
L. P. Dunklee & Son, 34 Summer St.
O. B. Tilton, 233 Main St.
Geo. A. Willard, 115 Vine St.
PORTSMOUTH—
John H. Broughton.
J. A. & A. W. Walker.
ROCHESTER—
Chas. W. Bradly.
Morrill & Greenfield.
SOMERSWORTH—
Francis Fordiff.
Albert Hanson.
Joseph Perron.

NEW JERSEY.

ASBURY PARK—
Asbury Park Building Supply Co.
Buchanan & Smock.
Geo. E. Farmer, 51 S. Main.
Chas. S. Lewis, S. Main, near Broadway.
L. M. Taylor, 1107 Main.
ATLANTIC CITY—
Atlantic City Lumber Co., 22 N. Ill. Ave.
D. K. Donnelly, N. C. & Baltic Aves.
G. Garrison, California Ave.
J. M. Frere, 16 N. Ill. Ave.
D. B. Ingersoll, 16 N. Fla. Ave.
Lake & Risely, Pleasantville, N. J.
Edwin Smith, Baltic & Tenn. Aves.
J. Summerville Smith, Ohio & Mediteranean Aves.
Somers Lumber Co., Arctic & Mo. Aves
ATLANTIC HIGHLANDS—
P. S. Conover, jr.
Corning Lumber Co.
Hopping & Ely.
BAYONNE—
Baldwin & Figneira, Garfield-ave. and Grand-st.
BELVIDERE—
S. M. Gordon & Co.
D. Perry & Son.
Widenor Bros.
BEVERLY—
A. L. Perkins.
BLOOMFIELD—
Ogden & Cadmus.
BOONTON—
Theo. Ringlieb.
BORDENTOWN—
Howard L. Newell.
W. H. Shreve.
BRIDGETON—
Daniel Bacon & Son.
Wm. O. Garrison.
BURLINGTON—
Jonathan Goodheer.
Thos. Milnor & Sons.
John A. Vandegrift, jr.
Wm. R. Vandegrift.

N—
ı Lime Co., 127 Federal-st.
Coles & Sons Co., Front, cor,
ın-ave.
ersey Supply Co.
us Reeve, 31 Market-st.
Rudderow & Son, Market, cor
t-st.
Bros.
, Harbison & Co., 1131 S.
t-st.
RTOWN—
· & Simmons.
—
Lumber Co.
W. Hill.
Union Lumber Co.
Smith.
)RANGE—
& Genung Co.
T. Pierson.
ETH—
& Carlton.
& A. Heidritter.
ter & Horre.
& F. C. Sayre.
—
e Bostwick.
WOOD—
Bros.
NGTON—
Bodine & Sons.
B. Hopewell.
A. Kline.
y Kuhl.
OLD—
t Combs & Co.
Stutesen.
ELD—
Construction & Supply Co.,
ırt Place. Jas. W. Finnegan,
.; John T. Harrop, Sec. &
s.; R. N. Billings, Engr.
ESTER CITY—
Gloucester Feed Co.
n & Pettit.
ENSACK—
nsack Coal & Lumber Co.
. G. Demarest, Pres., (New
ord, N. J.); M. G. Demarest,
; Elmer Blauvelt, Treas., (Ora-
N. J.).
· & Smith.
rvelt Bros.
ONFIELD—
Bros.
ONTON—
H. Bernshouse.
KEN—
· H. Vanderbilt, 1628 Willow
.
Y CITY—
·in & Figueira, Garfield Ave. &
nd St.
ngham Cement Co., 55 Mont-
ery St.
Brooks, 168 17th St.

Jersey City—Continued.
Continental Cement Co., 55 Montgomery St.
Jas. P. Hall, 588 Central Ave.
International Rock Plaster Co., 259 Wash'n St.
National Lime Co., 530 Grand St.
Arthur P. Roy, 399 Jackson Ave.
The United Building Material Co., Foot Jersey Ave.
Van Keuren & Son, Grand & Prior St.
Washburn Bros. Co.

LAMBERTVILLE—
A. C Gamdey.
Jacob Heins.

LONG BRANCH—
Chandler & Maps.
Cloughley, Nichol & Co.
L. & D. Edwards & Co.

MADISON—
Bruen & Morris.
Green & Pierson.
Joseph M. Smith & Co.

MANASQUAN—
E. S. Van Leer.

MATAWAN—
Cartan & Devlin.
W. A. Close T. and M. Co.
Chas. A. Geran.

MILLVILLE—
C. F. Cory.
Kimball, Prince & Co.

MONTCLAIR—
Chas. T. English, 112 Park St.
Wm. O. Peersons, 14 Forest St.

MORRISTOWN—
Dalrymple-Hastings Co.
C. W. Ennis & Co.

NEWARK—
Commonwealth Roofing Co., 10 Division St.
Cook & Genung Co., 16 Jersey St.
Builders' Material & Supply Co., 5 Badger Ave.
Eureka Cement Co., 2 Ave. A.
Knickerbocker Cement Works, Foot of Brill St.
Leinhardt & Guenther, 312 Littleton Ave.
Thomas W. McNally, 31 Fillmore St.
Fred L. Morrison, 309 S. 6th St.
Thos. Morrison, Van Buren St.
Newark & Rosendale, 763 Broad St.
Phillips White Rock Lime Co., 133 Front St.
James R. Sayre, Jr., & Co., River, near Center St. Depot.
Marcus Sayre Co., Front St., Adj. Center St. Bridge.
Tomkins Bros., 74-94 Passaic St.
E Willetts, 4 Waydell St.
Windsor Lime Co., Center St.
Stewart Wolf & Co., 304 Waverly Place.

NEW BRUNSWICK—
John H. Conger, 62 New St.
R. R. Outcalt, 261 George St.
Rolfe & Son, 181 Burnet St.
Philip Weigel, Jr., 2 Peace St.

NEW MILFORD—
Cooper & Demarest.

NEWTON—
Hart & Iliff.
Hopkins, Williams & Co.
W. F. Howell.
W. W. Woodward.

ORANGE—
Conover Bros., 51 Lincoln Ave.
Cook & Genung Co., Main & Clinton Sts.
A. M. Matthews & Co., 68 Freeman St.
A. F. Pierson, Pierson's Alley, near Main.

PALMYRA—
Palmyra Ice & Coal Co.

PASSAIC—
The Anderson Lumber Co.

PATERSON—
John Agnew, Prince, cor. Slater.
T. J. Brogan.
C. R. Forbes, 735 Main St.
Christopher Kelley, R. R. Ave., cor. Green St.
John R. Lee.
Morley & Forbes.
A. H. Smith, 41-47 Lafayette.

PAULSBORO—
D. R. Ackley.
E. G. Miller.

PENNGROVE—
Barber & Turner.
E. G. Brick.
John Sumerill & Bro.
C. C. Turner.

PERTH AMBOY—
Farrington & Runyon.
Samuel Heall.
N. J. Portland Cement Co.

PHILLIPSBURG—
Geo. Cole.
M. T. Hagerty.
Jordan Shafer.
Stacy & Shafer.
Clarence Walters.

PLAINFIELD—
Boice, Runyon & Co., 242-260 Park Ave.
J. S. Irving Co., 91 Central Ave.
J. D. Loiseaux.

PLEASANTVILLE—
Lake & Risley.

PRINCETON—
Fielder, Beekman & Co.

RAHWAY—
G. M. Friese.
Elmer Oliver.

RED BANK—
J. Trafford Allen.
Jas. T. Burrowes.
J. A. Throckmorton.

RIDGEFIELD PARK—
Brewster & Son.

RIVERSIDE—
Haines Bros.

ROCKAWAY—
B. K. & G. W. Stuble.

RUTHERFORD—
E. T. Galloway.
Julius Jaeger.

SALEM—
Clarkson Lippincott.
Benj. Stratton.

SOMERVILLE—
A. G. Anderson & Co.
Sargeant Bros.
David J. Smith.

SOUTH AMBOY—
Jas. Bloodgood.
Thomas Downs.
Sexton & Donnell.
Slover & Disbrow.

SOUTH ORANGE—
H. B. Halsey Co.
Roll & Sickley.

SUMMIT—
D. W. Day & Son, Spring R. R. Avues.
Geo. V. Muchmore, Park

TRENTON—
Samuel Heath, 334 Perry
W. L. Phillips, 607 Cass St
J. B. Richardson & Son, 12 ton St.
P. B. Richardson, 111 E. St

VINELAND—
Kimball, Price & Co.
Leach & Bro.

WESTFIELD—
J. S. Irving.
Tuttle Bros.

WEST HOBOKEN—
Thos. Keynton, 201 Clinton

WOODBURY—
L. Brown & Co.
Chas. Walton.

NEW MEXICO.

ALBUQUERQUE—
J. C. Baldridge.
John A. Lee.

CARLSBAD—
A. N. Pratt.

ROSWELL—
Burton Linge Lumber Co
Lewis & Wells.
Seay, Gill & Morrow Co

SANTA FE—
W. H. Goebel.
Wm. McKenzie.

NEW YORK.

ADDISON—
Geo. C. Howard.

Y—
Blake, 173 1st St.
owe Granite Co., 13 N. Pearl

. Brumaghim, 285 Wash. Ave.
illiam H. Burton Co., Centre &
ie.
on & Hawn, 288 Central Ave.
Dwight.
d N. Fuller, Chapel, cor. Carol

elderberg Cement Co., 28 State

H. Jackson, 92 3d Ave.
Kurtz, 336 Central Ave.
Kurtz, Jr., & Wendy, 352 Cen-
Ave.
d & Youngman, 256 State St.
McCabe, 122 State St.
H. Ramsay, 28 State St.
Woodruff, 142 Broadway.
—
n & Linson.
s Bros.
. Waterman.
ONT—
Sons.
—
s & Eaton.
ILLE—
Wood.
RDAM—
Seold.
r & Davy.
S—
nd & Son.
—
ooks & Ranger.
venue Mills Co.
N—
Barnes & Son, 23 Wall St.
Clark, 173 State St.
ha Bros., 39 Water St.

Babcock.
Watkins & Co.
A—
. Dawson.
. Smith.
r & Winslow.
Worthington & Son Co.

& R. J. Davison.
Faucett.
Shannon.
MTON—
W. Ballard & Co., 21 Jarvis

& Stewart, 120 State St.
E. Ensign, 200 Chenango St.
Lumber Co., Jarvis St.
LO—
Cement Co., 50 River.
Berrick & Sons, 1151 Main.
Hunt, 3 Builders' Exchange.
Rhinehan, 179 Ellicott.
Cement Co., 110 Franklin.

Buffalo—Continued.
Buffalo Mortar Works, Builders' Exchange.
Buffalo Sewer Pipe Co., 77 Tonawanda.
Philip Carey Mfg. Co., 33 W. Seneca.
Carroll Bros., Virginia and Fourth.
Charles Dehn, Louisiana and Perry.
Durkine & Merkle, 26 Builders' Exchange.
Diamond Fire Clay Co., 176 Ellicott.
G. Elias & Bro., 965 Elk-st.
German Rock Asphalt and Cement Co., 304 D. S. Morgan bldg.
Gibraltar Wall Plaster Co., 21 Builders' Exchange.
J. B. King & Co., 322 W. Genesee.
John Lyth & Sons, 48 W. Eagle.
Monarch Mfg Co., 534 Main.
H. L. & W. C. Newman, 50 River.
Louis Pfohl & Son, Dock and Water.
Portland Cement Co., 112 Church.
M. A. Reeb, 599 Michigan.
J. H. Ross, 141 Erie.
Sears, Humbert & Co., 434 Prudential bldg.
Thorn Cement Co., 112 Church.
Union Akron Cement Co., 141 Erie.
Walbridge & Co., 392 Main.
Williamsville Quick Lime Co., Broadway and Elm.
Weed & Co., 292 Main.
G. W. Williams, 598 Mastern.

CAMBRIDGE—
J. D. Hall.
Amos Konkey.

CAMDEN—
Geo. Abbott's Sons.
Giles Coy.
W. H. Dorrance & Son.

CANAJOHARIE—
W. H. Bain.

CANANDAIGUA—
Frank R. Beecher.
Alexander Davidson.
Geo. T. Thompson.

CANISTEO—
Burrell Bros.
W. T. Goff.
O. O. Laine.
J. H. Strait.

CANTON—
L. W. Eldredge.
Hoare Bros.

CARTHAGE—
Noah Chamberlain.
Chanfty Bros.
Jones & Simmons.
J. A. Loomis.
J. E. Strickland & Son.

CATSKILL—
Jas. Cooke.
Geo. W. Holdridge.
E. Lampman.

MUNICIPAL ENGINEERING MAGAZINE

Is known as the foremost in the world in the field to which it is devoted. It is the Authority for Authorities.

ONE OF THE LARGEST SPECIAL MAGAZINES PUBLISHED AT THE PRICE—140 PAGES, MONTHLY, AND $2.00 PER YEAR

SOME EXPRESSIONS REGARDING IT

FROM LEADING NEWSPAPERS

MUNICIPAL ENGINEERING is one of the most valuable technical magazines of the age.
—*Sacramento (Cal.) Record-Union.*

MUNICIPAL ENGINEERING is a model high standard publication that steadily improves.
—*Milwaukee Sentinel.*

MUNICIPAL ENGINEERING is an excellent magazine.—*Hartford Courant.*

MUNICIPAL ENGINEERING is always practical in its solution of problems.
—*Detroit Free Press.*

HOW IT IS PRAISED BY READERS

William Newman, City Engineer of Windsor, Ont.:
"I could not get along very well without MUNICIPAL ENGINEERING."

J. H. Henly, Consulting Engineer for Municipal and Sanitary Work:
"I find MUNICIPAL ENGINEERING MAGAZINE most useful; in fact, indispensable."

Alex Thomson, Jr., Oil City, Pa.:
"I have gained much valuable information from MUNICIPAL ENGINEERING."

Robert Y. Ogg, Secretary Board of Public Works, Detroit, Mich.:
"MUNICIPAL ENGINEERING MAGAZINE is so highly appreciated by aldermen and other visitors to this office that we have to keep our copies of them under lock and key to keep them from being spirited away."

Joseph Withington, Mattoon, Ill.:
"MUNICIPAL ENGINEERING MAGAZINE is the best of its kind."

Scott Hayes, Chamberlain, S. D.:
"You are doing a splendid service and putting out a fine work."

Geo. D. Jenkins, Washington, Pa.:
"MUNICIPAL ENGINEERING MAGAZINE is a good thing. Sorry I did not know of it before this."

From Sacramento (Cal.) Record-Union:
MUNICIPAL ENGINEERING has often been pronounced in these columns the most useful, practical magazine of the age, and we adhere to that judgment."

$2.00 per year. The sooner you order it the more you gain.

MUNICIPAL ENGINEERING CO.

RAUGUS—
Benson.
Rich.
AM—
W. Boright.
KILL—
n Courter.
Karker & Co., Main St.
m W. Summons.
S—
& T. W. Neary, 13 Broadway.
ıd & Munro, 72 Remsen St.
ıs Slavin & Co.
idman, 220 Mohawk St.
PRING—
Cornell.
Crookston.
H. La Due.
es E. McClary.
RSTOWN—
F. Brady & Co.
TH—
I. Mason & Son.
NG—
Comosh, W. Market St.
Farr & Co.
AND—
& Warfield.
n & Starin.
& Hall.
CKIE—
ix Lumber Co.
—
& Bromley.
n & Kiff.
ld Milling Co.
IT—
Q. Clark.
& C. E. Martin.
Putnam & Co.
FERRY—
n & Co.
VILLE—
Gow.
Guile.
e & Snyder.
RK—
trong & Fleischman.
S M. Hamilton.
G. McCarthy.
BRIDGE—
Bros.
AURORA—
Adams.
Geib.
s & Ball.
HAMPTON—
Hampton Coal Co.
Hampton Lumber Co.
VILLE—
& Deyo.
W. Donaldson.

ELMIRA—
Barker Bros.
Costello & Neagle.
Diver & Copley.
Holmes & Co.
W. H. Lee & Son.
FAIRPORT—
Dobbin & Moore.
C. L. Fuller.
G. S. Holman.
A. M. Loomis.
A. Van Norman.
FAR ROCKAWAY—
Thomas Kane.
F. R. Smith.
A. C. Walton.
FISHKILL-ON-THE-HUDSON—
W. H. & W. F. Weston.
FORT EDWARD—
L. E. Montgomery, Notre Dame St.
James G. Kinne.
FORT PLAIN—
Will J. Diefendorf, 52-56 Canal St.
FRANKFORT—
W. W. Crosby.
FREDONIA—
Cobb & Pritchard.
F. E. Cooke.
Sly & Coddington.
FREEPORT—
A. J. & J. M. Southard.
FULTON—
Gage, Porter & Co.
GENESEO—
N. W. & C. D. Neff.
Purtiss, Carpenter & Co.
GENEVA—
Beard & Son.
Geneva Lumber Co.
Goble Bros.
R. J. Rogers Lumber Co.
H. A. Torrey.
GLENS FALLS—
M. H. Bradt & Co.
Finch, Pruyn & Co.
GLOVERSVILLE—
Peter Chevalier.
Mayfield Lime & Cement Co.
L. A. Phelps.
GOSHEN—
Conklin & Cummins.
Fancher Bros.
GOUVERNEUR—
W. T. Carbin.
H. H. Noble.
A. S. Whitney.
GOWANDA—
J. E. Van Densen.
GREEN ISLAND—
M. Smith.
GREENPORT—
C. L. Corwin.
HAMILTON—
N. R. Wickwise.
HARRIETSTOWN—
Starks, Goss, Caffrey Co.
Trombley & Hatch.

HAVERSTRAW—
I. M. Hedges.
H. F. Johnston.
HEMPSTEAD—
W. G. Adams.
Jos. Griffin.
Molineaux Bros.
G. D. Van Vranken.
HERKIMER—
C. W. Palmer & Co.
C. R. Snell.
HICKSVILLE—
Julius Augustin.
F. Herzog & Son.
HOMER—
Maxon & Starin.
HOOSICK FALLS—
Easton, Rising & Worden.
Francis Riley.
A. H. Sherwood.
HORNELLSVILLE—
James Fahy, 37 Cass St.
S. Hollands, 169 Main St.
James Kingkade, 2 Delaware Ave.
Simmons & Honell.
HORSEHEADS—
H. H. McQueen.
Hathaway & Bundy.
HUDSON—
Charles W. Macy.
Wm. H. Travis & Son.
IRVINGTON—
Dinkel & Jewell Co.
ITHACA—
Campbell Bros.
Driscoll Bros. & Co.
Joseph Fowles.
JAMESTOWN—
W. H. Endress.
Jamestown Coal & Coke Co.
W. L. Slotboom.
JOHNSTOWN—
John G. Ferres, 118 W. Main St.
Frank Miller.
Levi Stephenson.
James I. Younglove.
KEESEVILLE—
A. W. Shields & Co.
KINGSTON—
Abbey, Stephen & Sons.
F. H. Griffith.
H. W. Palen's Sons.
A. S. Staples.
LAKE PLACID—
Walton Bros.
LANCASTER—
J. C. Garretsee.
Samuel Walter.
LANSINGBURGH—
J. B. Madden & Co., 617 First Ave.
LEROY—
J. A. Collins.
N. B. Keeney & Son.
Geo. F. Lowe.
F. C. Rogers, Lake St.
LEISTERSHIRE—
E. L. Baldwin
M. S. Hotchkiss
LITTLE FALLS—
W. B. Newell.
James Van Allen.
LOCKPORT—
M. J. Crowe.
C. N. Stainthorpe.
C. B. Whitmore.
LOWVILLE—
Louis Bush.
C. F. Yousey.
LYONS—
B. F. Lockwood.
MALONE—
Howard & Shert.
Thompson Bros.
MAMARONECK—
Foshay & Brewer.
L. Moffatt.
MASSENA—
Garvin & Rutherford.
Keyes & Moore.
Hubert Trefly.
MATTEAWAN—
S. M. Davidson.
MECHANICSVILLE—
Barnes & Ladow.
R. Moore & Son.
Robinson & Ferris.
MEDINA—
Filkins & Gorman.
John Horan.
MIDDLETOWN—
Buck Bros.
G. W. & G. H. Galloway.
Gordon, Horton & Co.
Spooner & Ayres.
G. A. Swalm & Co.
MOHAWK—
Broomhall & Co.
MONTOUR FALLS—
Joseph E. Barbour.
D. C. Blair.
Samuel J. Brown.
S. W. Sterrett.
MT. VERNON—
Builders' Supply Co., 16 E. First
NELSONVILLE—
Martin Adams.
NEWARK—
L. G. Mattison.
Chas. E. Seggett.
NEWBURGH—
Jno. J. E. Harrison, 490 Broadw
Samuel A. Wilson, 173 Washin St.
Frank G. Wood, 134 Washington
NEWMAN—
Starks, Goss, Caffrey Co.
NEW ROCHELLE—
New Rochelle Coal and Lumber Echo Bay Dock.

ORK CITY, BOROUGH OF
KLYN—
& Howe, 6?? Manhattan Ave.
Burroughs & Co., Newtown
k.
Canda Co., 184 3d St.
e & Kreheler Co., 1227 Grand St.
Bros., 59 Lott St.
y Clarke, Gowaner's Canal.
Cohn, Pitkin Ave., cor. Stone.
Colyer, 95 Plymouth St.
y & Doody Co., 407 Hamilton

f P. G. Hughes, 182 Douglass St.
Jump & Co., 97 Milton St.
& Adams, 610 Kent Ave.
r & Killian, 356 Stockholm St.
Maher, 97 9th St.
Mahnken, 632 Kent Ave.
Masset Co., 486 Flatbush Ave.
ughlin & Furman, Foot Bay 17

Neely & Sons, 9 Adelphia St.
Meserole, 45 Greenpoint Ave.
Morton Sons Co., 287 Carroll St.
ber & Co., 984 Lee Ave.
Reimer Co., 1107 Metropolitan

ph Reimer, 2814 Atlantic Ave.
Stroeber, 416 Johnson Ave.
roeber, 416 Johnson Ave.
Steel Cement Co., 240 Kent Ave.
Wens, 2432 Atlantic Ave.

YORK CITY, BOROUGH OF
IATTAN AND BRONX—
Cement Plaster Co., 161st St.
Jerome Ave.
m Co., 200 E. 98th St.
Portland Cement Co., 143 Lib-
St.
sbestic Co., 45 Broadway.
Portland Cement Co., 124
rty St.
Baber, 26 Cherry St.
Baldwin & Co., 11 Broadway.
ir, Williamson & Co., 27 Wm.

Beach, 26 Cortlandt St.
hrend, 54 Front St.
Bell & Son, 127th St. and Ger-
Ave.
Blaso Co., 156 5th Ave.
H. Bloom, 15 Whitehall St.
velle Cement Co., 261 Broadway.
R. Brigham, 261 Broadway.
Brook's Sons' Co., 615 W. 49th
rs' Supply Co., Fishers Lane.
Thorn & Co., 258 Broadway.
& Smith, 26th St. and E.
r.
xwell Carrere, 66 Maiden
.
re Lime Co., 217 W. 125th St.
s Coffey, 345 E. 117th St.
bian Fireproofing Co., 1123
dway.

New York City—Manhattan—Continued.

Commercial Wood and Cement Co., 156 Fifth Ave.
F. F. Comstock, 261 Broadway.
Connelly & Shafer, 74 Cortlandt St.
Consolidated Wheatland Plaster Co., 120 Liberty St.
Coplay Cement Co., 156 5th Ave.
William Coogan, Park and Pelham Ave.
Curtin & Ver Valen, 66 Maiden Lane.
Rufus Darrow, Foot W. 47th St.
Dearing & Co., 60 Liberty St.
J. P. Duffy & Co., 4th Ave. & 189th
A. G. Duysters, 45 Broadway.
Dyckerhoff Portland Cement Co., 78 William St.
Eastern Cement Co., 1133 Broadway.
Eureka Cement Co., 1 Madison Ave.
Faucett Ventilated Fire Proof Building Co., Ltd., 1133 Broadway.
Fleming & Co., 123 Liberty St.
Flint, Eddy & Co.
Francklyn & Ferguson, Cotton Exch.
Gabriel & Schall, 205 Pearl St.
Gardner Building Material Co., 68 Broad St.
E. C. Gates & Co., Webster Ave. & S. Blvd.
John Gleason, 24 Goerch St.
Glens Falls Portland Cement Co., 156 5th Ave.
Goss & Edsall, 358 W. St.
Haebler & Co., 71 Wall St.
Chas. Ward Hall, 140 Nassau St.
Hammill & Gillespie, 240 Front St.
C. B. Hewett & Bro., 48 Beekman St.
W. N. Hoagland, 1123 Broadway.
E. A. Holmberg, 160 5th Ave.
W. T. Hookey, 2407 3d Ave.
Houston & Co., 26 Cortland St.
Hyde Bros., 113 E. 27th St.
Irvine & Co., 217 W. 125th St.
R. H. Jaffray & Co., 160 5th Ave.
Johnson Cement Coating Co., 156 5th Ave.
Johnson & Wilson, 150 Nassau St.
J. P. Kane Co., 287 4th Ave.
Alexander Keller, 81 New St.
L. E. Kennedy & Co., 61 Broadway.
Alex Kellier, 81 New St.
T. A. Keyes, 81 New St.
J. B. King & Co., 1 Broadway.
Knickerbocker Cement Co., 66 Maiden Lane.
Lawrence Cement Co., 1 Broadway.
Lawrenceville Cement Co., 26 Cortlandt St.
George Livingston, 1123 Broadway.
Thos. M. Magiff, 39 Cortlandt St.
Major Cement Co., 461 Pearl St.
Manhattan Brick and Terra Cotta Co., 284 South St.
Marquardt, H. & Co., 21 S. William.
Mason's Supplies Co., 284 South St.

New York City—Manhattan—Continued.

Henry Maurer & Son, 420 E. Twenty-third St.
Meeker, Carter & Booraem, 1 Madison Ave.
Ludwig Meyerstein, 136 Liberty St.
Clifford L. Miller, E. One Hundred and Sixty-first St. and Jerome Ave.
Moen Asphaltic Cement Co., 103 Maiden Lane.
Moffat & Barto, 1123 Broadway.
The F. E. Morse Co., 17 State St.
Morse Steel Wire Tire Co., 131 W. Twenty-fifth St.
Murtagh & McCarthy, Rivington and East Sts.
Newark & Rosendale Lime and Cement Co., 30 Cortlandt St.
G. M. Newcomer, 66 Maiden Lane.
N. E. Cement Coating Co., 156 Fifth Ave.
New York Cement Co., 29 Broadway.
N. Y. & Rosendale Cement Co., 280 Broadway.
New York Pottery Co., W. Thirty-sixth St. and Twelfth Ave.
New York Wood Vulcanizing Co., 71 Broadway.
N. Y. and N. J. Fireproofing Co., 156 Fifth Ave.
F. O. Norton, 92 Broadway.
Oland Portland Cement Co., 160 Fifth Ave.
E. I. Olmsted, 17 Park Row.
T. B. Osborne, 1 Broadway.
Overbaugh & Camp, Kingsbridge.
N. & W. J. Peck, 430 E. Forty-eighth
O. D. Person, 160 Fifth Ave.
J. A. Philbrick, 1889 First Ave.
Platt Plaster Co., 130 Fulton St.
Charles Plock, 543 W. Twenty-second
G. Quaile, 396 Broadway.
Edward Records, 17 Park row.
Reliance Brick & Cement Co., 145 Broadway.
Roebling Construction Co., 121 Liberty St.
H. P. Robinson, foot W. Forty-ninth
Rock Plaster Co. of N. Y. & N. J., 11 Broadway.
James Rogers, Twelfth Ave. and W. One hundred and thirty-second St.
Rose Brick Co., 645 W. Fifty-second
Sackett Wall Board Co., 116 Nassau
Sayre & Fisher Co., 207 Broadway.
W. H. Schmohl, 814 E. Fourteenth

F. H. KIRCHNER & CO.

GENERAL CONTRACTORS

For all kinds of Heavy Masonry, Foundations, Railroad Grading, Tunneling, Paving and Sewering. TELEPHONE 450 MAIN.

General Offices,
Temple Court, Eighth & Plum Sts., CINCINNATI, O.

New York City—Manhattan—Continued.

Sears, Humbert & Co., 81 Fulton St.
H. R. Sellers, 1 Madison Ave.
Sinclair & Babson, 143 Liberty St.
F. L. Smidth & Co., 66 Maiden Lane.
Hiram Snyder & Co., 120 Broadway.
Sparrow, Fridenberg & Co., Whitehall St.
Standard Silica Cement Co., 66 Maiden Lane.
E. G. Soltman, 164 W. Forty-sixth St.
C. D. Stout, 1 Broadway.
Terry & Holmes, 643 W. Fifty-second
Emil Thiele, 99 John St.
Thompson & Starrett, Battery Park Bldg.
Calvin Tomkins, 120 Liberty St.
Tomkins Bros., 257 Broadway.
W. G. Tucker Mfg. Co., foot E. One hundred and sixteenth St.
Tucker & Vinton (Inc.), 156 Fifth Ave.
Union Metal Corner Co., 131 W. Twenty-fifth St.
United Building Material Co., 6[illegible] Broadway.
U. S. Mortar Supply Co., 1123 Broadway.
Frank Vernon, 160 Fifth Ave.
Virginia Portland Cement Co., 8[illegible] Fulton St.
Charles Warner Co., 66 Maiden Lane.
C. R. Weeks & Bro., 542 W. 14th St.
White Brick & Terra Cotta Co., 1[illegible] 5th Ave.
G. W. White & Co., 1133 Broadway.
Nathaniel Wise, 1133 Broadway.
T. C. Wood, 616 Greenwich St.

NEW YORK CITY, BOROUGH QUEENS—

G. A. W. Brown & Co., Spruce and Seward Ave., Richmond Hill.
Clonin & Messenger, 757 Boulevard, L. I. City.
L. I. Hill.
Jamieson & Bond, Boulevard Oceanus.
D. S. Jones & Co., 15 Vernon Ave., L. I. City.
Kraemer Bros., 10th & 5th Ave., College Point.
J. H. L'Hommendieu, 7 Vernon Ave., L. I. City.
F. C. Norton, Franklin Ave., Far Rockaway.
Rudolph Reimer & Son, Ocean Ave., Ozone Park.
G. S. Roe, Park Ave., **Bay Side.**
A. M. Ryon, 89 Main St., Flushing.
Styler & Dougherty, 59 Flushing Ave., Flushing.
Wotherspoon & Son, 725 Vernon Ave., L. I. City.

City—Queens—Continued.
:hneider, 324 Jackson Ave.,
:ity.
d Silica Cement Co., 110
ng Ave.
ORK CITY, BOROUGH OF
OND—
os., Tottenville.
Havens, New Brighton.
McRoberts & Co., Tompkins-

C. Seguin & Co., Princes Bay.
ompson, West New Brighton.
ompson & Sons, Stapleton.
Van Clief, Port Richmond.
Whitford, Port Richmond.
A FALLS—
Humbert.
TONAWANDA—
Berger.
Rose.
-
: & Sherman.
White & Co.
BURG—
Barr.
Brittan.
kett.
-
Supply Co.
Taylor.
—
rcellus.
Ruby.
A—
Butts.
& Pruyn.
)—
arwell & Co.
Quinlan.
-
s' & Builders' Supply Co., C.
ller, Pres. L. H. Tuthill, Secy.
Tuthill, Treas. & Mgr.
erwilliger.
)—
ustin.
Few.
BAY—
Hammois.
RA—
Anderson.
essions
OGUE—
ey & Sons.
ILL—
n's Son's Company, H. P.
Pres. F. M. Dain, Secy. &
.
mith, Jr.
AN—
rs & Sristock.
onklin & Son.
otter Lumber Co.
-
White.

PHILMONT—
Walter Ham.
PLATTSBURG—
Dock and Coal Co.
Henry, Wood & Marshall.
Nichols & Co.
Sowly Hardware Co.
PORT CHESTER—
W. E. Peck.
Wm. Ryan & Co.
Chas. Tibbits.
PORT JEFFERSON—
T. F. Darling & Son.
O. T. Fanning & Co.
Loper Bros.
PORT JERVIS—
W. H. Coonrod Co.
H. O. Rosenkrans.
Rueling & Cole.
POTSDAM—
H. K. Baldwin & Co.
O. E. Bonney & Son.
R. L. McAllister.
POUGHKEEPSIE—
C. N. Arnold.
E. B. Layton.
D. W. Wilbur.
PULASKI—
Frary & Sage
Wm. Peach.
QUEENSBURY—
M. Brandt & Co.
Finch, Pruyn & Co.
RENSSELAER—
James Gray, 371 Broadway.
RHINEBECK—
Frank Herrick.
RICHFIELD SPRINGS—
L. S. Chase.
C. H. Evans.
L. McCredy & Son.
Geo. Monahan.
W. B. Ward.
RIVERHEAD—
Corwin & Young.
John E. Young.
ROCHESTER—
Wm. A. Franklin, 65 Main East.
James W. Hutchison, 322 Brown.
Jenkins & Macy.
Lamson & Leason, Cottage & Seward.
Joseph J. Mandery.
Thomas Oliver, 328 South Ave.
Rochester Lime Co., 209 W. Main.
Whitmore, Rauber & Vicinus, 279
South Ave.
ROME—
W. J. Cromond.
Parry & James.
SAG HARBOR—
East Hampton Lumber & Coal Co.,
Ltd.
SALAMANCA—
J. A. Andrews & Son.
Gallagher Bros.
McCann, Hubbell & Co.
Fred Miller.

SALEM—
Charles W. Button.
Wm. J. Cruikshank.
E. W. Philo.

SANDY CREEK—
S. H. Barlow.
Miles Blodgett.
Henry C. Crandall.
Hydorn & Snyder.
Samuel Sadler.
Edward Williams.

SANDY HILL—
Griffin Lumber Co.
Kenyon Lumber Co.

SARANAC LAKE—
Starks, Goss, Caffrey Co.
Trombley & Hotch.
Walton & Tousley.

SARATOGA SPRINGS—
Russell M. Choate, 245 East Ave.

SAUGERTIES—
Finger & Lewis.
Saugerties Coal & Lumber Co.

SCHAGHTICOKE—
Empire Mill & Coal Co.

SCHENECTADY—
Barhyte & Devenpeck.
C. F. Rankin.
Rankin & Cary.
N. I. Schermerhorn.

SENECA FALLS—
A. P. Haney, Clinton St.
F. Maier, Fall St.
S. S. Palmer, Clinton St.

SIDNEY—
C. W. Burnside.

SILVER CREEK—
W. E. Blanding Co.
G. P. Brand & Sons.
Geo. Shafner.

SING SING—
J. E. Barlow, Main St.
Barlow & Co., Main St.
I. Terwilliger's Son, Central Ave.
Washburn & Todd, Depot Sq.
A. L. Young, Main St.

SKANEATELES—
Richard Carver.
W. G. Stuart.

SOUTHAMPTON—
Hampton Lumber Co.

SPRINGVILLE—
Conger & Ware.
Herbold & Kessler.

SYRACUSE—
J. E. Britton, 201 N. Onondaga St.
Burhans & Black Co., 136 N. Salina
George R. Clark, 541 S. Clinton.
The Eureka Plaster Co., 64 Wieting Blk.
Martin & Sullivan, 112 W. Genesee.
New York Brick & Paving Co., S. A. & K. Bldg.
Geo. W. Park & Son, 417 E. Water St.

Syracuse—Continued.
Paragon Plaster Co., [illegible] St. Jacob Amos, Pres.; [illegible] Squier, Secy.-Treas., Mgr. —

TARRYTOWN—
Dinkel & Jewell Co. (Not Inc
A. & F. C. Husted.
A. P. Husted.
Jacob Odell's Sons.

TONAWANDA—
Henry Barnes.

TROY—
Crandall, Knight & Richard, River St.
Max Guinn, [illegible] River St.
Geo. D. Slade, Division St.
Troy Paint & Color Works, [illegible] St.
Young & Halstead, foot of Gran

TUPPER LAKE—
McDonald & Son.
C. H. Simon.

UTICA—
American Hard Wall Plaster C
W. H. McCann.
Munson Bros.
D. D. Winston.

WALDEN—
D. C. Domminck.
Hasbrouck & Sloan.
C. W. Hill.
E. S. Sayer.

WALTON—
Ells & Reynolds.
S. P. Olcott.
H. B. Olmstead.

WARSAW—
Cheney & McGee.
S. J. Crawford.

WARWICK—
Cankling & Strong.

WATERFORD—
F. B. Peck.
W. A. Sale.
Geo. D. Slade.

WATERLOO—
Edwin Clarke.
A. H. Terwilleger & Son.

WATERTOWN—
C. P. Englehart, 14 Polk St.
Albert L. Rice, 28 B Arsenal St
C. D. Riggs & Co., 73 River St.
Robbin & Hotchkin, 16 River

WATERVILLE—
F. W. Putnam.

WATKINS—
J. H. Drake estate.

WAVERLY—
H. J. Baldwin.
A. Mullock.

WEEDSPORT—
Caywood, Stickle & Co.
W. H. Eldredge.

WESTFIELD—
John R. Fay.
Westfield Lumber and Coal Co

HALL—
Martin.
Sullivan, 35-37 Canal St.
PLAINS—
V. Young & Sons Co.
ng & Bro.
BORO—
Raymer.
RS—
ice Bros.

NORTH CAROLINA.

LLE—
. Scott & Co.
Westall.
OTTE—
Ward & Co.
Withers.
ON—
Ralph.
ETH CITY—
Flora & Co.
r Bros. & Co.
rimer & Co.
on & Co.
Woodley.
ORO—
& Eason.
oro Hardware Co.
Huggins.
& Johnston.
se & Bros.
BORO—
Hardware Co.
Woodroffe.
RSON—
Parker & Co.
Watkins.
ETTA—
Haynes.
enrietta Mill Co.
RY—
Ingohl.
l Hardware Co.
RSVILLE—
Davis & Son.
: Linville.
N—
Canady.
& Hooker.
NTON—
nton Hardware Co.
AIRY—
Toyce.
Merritt.
ERN—
Hardware Co.
Smallwood.
Whitby & Co.
UTH—
Brinkley.
Hampton.
Honithal.

RALEIGH—
T. H. Briggs & Sons.
Julius Lewis Hardware Co., 224 Fayetteville St.
S. M. and W. J. Young.
REIDSVILLE—
W. P. Ware.
P. H. Williamson & Co.
ROCKINGHAM—
W. I. Everett.
Pu Du Hardware Co.
SALEM—
Fogle Bros.
SALISBURY—
J. Allen Brown.
Geo. R. Martin & Bro.
TARBORO—
C. J. Austin.
Howard & Co.
Tarboro Hardware Co.
WILMINGTON—
Roger Moore's Sons & Co.
J. T. Riley & Co.
The Worth Co.
WILSON—
Geo. D. Green Hardware Co.
Mayo & Watson.
WINSTON—
Miller Bros. Co., G. L. Miller, Pres. and Mgr.; J. J. Leight, V. P.; W. L. Harper, Sec.-Treas.
Shepherd & Nonfleet.

NORTH DAKOTA.

DICKINSON—
Walton & Davis.
FARGO—
Fargo Lime & Fuel Co.
North Dakota Tile Works, S. Birch, Prop.
N. Stanford.
GRAFTON—
Nollman & Lewis.
Robertson Lumber Co.
St. Hillair Lumber Co.
GRAND FORKS—
Dinnie Bros.
P. S. Houston.
Robertson Lumber Co
JAMESTOWN—
Gull River Lumber Co.
W. C Hooelick.
Lutz Lumber Co.
C. D. Shurlock.
WAHPETON—
L. E. Horton & Co.
John Rischard.

OHIO.

AKRON-
Akron Supply Co., 615 E Mill St.
G. A. Bisbee, 229 S. Main St.
Botzum Bros., 113 & 115 S Main St.
N. W. Brown, 355 S. Main St.
J. H. Case & Co., 132 Wooster Ave.
Cramer & Logan, 716 & 718 S. Main
Geo. Crisp & Son, 500 E. Main St.

Akron—Continued.
John G. Haury, 705 Broadway.
Inman Bros. Cement Co., 1184-1186 E. Market St.
L. Kryder & Sons, 112 S. Main St.
Peterson & Wright, 128 N. Main St.
H. H. Sperry, 134-148 S. Canal St.
ALLIANCE—
John Auld & Sons.
J. C. Craven.
Milner & Sopher.
F. J. Poto.
I. G. Tollerton & Son.
ASHLAND—
Wm Boren.
Clugston & Harvey.
ASHTABULA—
Crosby Hardware Co.
Hall & Salisbury.
Paine Bros.
J. A. Paisley.
ATHENS—
Athens Lumber Co.
Rardin Bros.
BARBERTON—
American Clay Mfg. Co.
Barberton Hardware Co.
C. S. Johnson.
Miller Bros.
Paul & Herry.
Prentiss & McCoy.
Morris Young.
BELLAIRE—
Carter Bros.
BELLEFONTAINE—
Bellefontaine Stone & Lime Co.
J. H. Bush.
Robt. Roberts.
BELLEVUE—
F. Creech.
BEREA—
Fred Brown.
Lawrence & Brightman.
BOWLING GREEN—
Geo. Brothers.
Geo. E. Mercer.
H. G. Mercer.
The Snow Flake Lime Co.
Starr Supply Co.
BRIDGEPORT—
Meister Bros.
Jesse Moore.
BRYAN—
Christman Bros.
Henry Keck.
J. P. Long.
BUCYRUS—
Samuel Bonebrake.
Wm. Reed.
CADIZ—
John Aukerman.
E. M. Long & Sons.
J. B. Rogers.
W. T. Wood & Son.
CAMBRIDGE—
The Cambridge Hardware Co.
Carlisle & Grimes.
R. V. Orme.
CANAL DOVER—
Wible, Enck & Co.
CANTON—
Artificial Ice & Storage Co.
Wm. Barber & Sons.
Canton Feed Store.
Harrison Ave. Feed Store.
John S. Rohrer.
Hiram Shaub.
CARTHAGE—
L. McCammon Bros.
CELINA—
J. W. Desch.
CHICAGO—
R. Heath.
W. A. Willams.
CHILLICOTHE—
George Borst, Jr.
Chillicothe Coal Co.
Chas. Coppel.
Chas. Snyder.
Union Coal Co.
CINCINNATI—
Alex. J. Baker, 1037 Gilbert Ave.
Wm. Bindley, 3rd & Eggleston Ave.
Fred Brewe, 1698 Montrose Ave.
Builders' Supply & Tiling Co., 4 W. 4th St.
Building Material Supply Co., 136 W. 4th St.

More Cement Companies

advertise in **Municipal Engineering Magazine**

than in any other American publication. It reaches more of the people who buy or influence the buying of cement than any other American publication.

—Continued.
harles, 1265 Harrison Ave.
mes G. Christie Lime & Ce-
Co., 824 Ready St.
ati Sewer Pipe Co., Water &
lts.
ney Supply Co., 1434-1440
e St.
Conkling, Gilbert Ave., near

tors' & Builders' Supply Co.,
anton Ave.
rd & Co., 1097 Walnut St.
M. Crosby, 711 Plum.
afe, 1686 Bremen St.
Granbery & Co., 425 Plum.
Hirsch, 4098 Eastern Ave.
olley, 309 Johnston Bldg.
Howe, 225 Stark.
olling Co., 717 Reading Road.
harles Kuhl Artificial Stone
W. Canal.
McCammon Bros., 854 W. 6th

H. McCracken Supply Co., 629
ont St.
m. Mayer Co., 644 W. 3d St.
e, Mills & Co., 652 W. 3d St.
& Co., 954 W. 5th.
Lime Co., 964 W. 5th.
Moss, Dumont & McCullough

born, Jr. & Co., Pearl and
ston Ave.
ase Co., 3237 Fredonia Ave.
Ross Raff, 23 E. 3d St.
Settle & Co., Station M.
Stritzinger, Lick Run Pike,
Tp.
Stuene, 1610 John St.
as. Taylor's Sons Co., Burns,
n 6th and 8th.
ber & Co., Blue Rock & Apple.
Wolf, 2187 Central Ave.
VILLE—
ales.
ein Bros.
B. Niles.
Mill Co.
AND—
& Bradley, 231 The Arcade.
Bros., Pennington.
Builders' Supply Co., 323 Co-

Builders' Supply Co., 729
Bldg.
& Peck, 720 Williamson Bldg.
nd Portland Cement Co,
na Ave.
or Plaster Co., Kirkland.
le Portland Cement Co.
P. James, 126 Elm.
Island Lime and Trans-
Co., Mercantile Bk. Bldg.
Supply & Seed Co., 19 Main.
ugh & Co., 221 Cuyahoga

Cleveland—Continued.
Pope Cement & Brick Co., Cuyahoga Bldg. Chas. E. Pope, Pres. (Pittsburg, Pa.).
Rowebling Construction Co., 88 Superior Bldg.
Sandusky Portland Cement Co., 42 Atwater Bldg.
Stowe-Fuller Co., 513 Superior Bldg.

CLYDE—
F. P. Hurd & Sons.

COLD SPRING—
Moores & Co.

COLLINWOOD—
Baldwin Bros.

COLUMBUS—
Acme Paving Co., 408-420 W. State St.
American Art Tile Co., 52-54 E. Lynn St.
American Clay Mfg. Co., 315 N. High St.
Jas. P. Carlisle, 10 Amboa St.
The Central Supply Co., 306-308 N. High St.
The Columbus Coal & Lime Co., 347 S. High St.
The Columbus Macadam Co., 319 Dublin Ave.
Ferris Steam Mortar Wks., 626 Galloway Ave.
Haydenville Mining & Mfg. Co., 190 W. Long St.
Pennsylvania Fuel Co., 9 Naghten St. (A. Hamilton, Mgr.; E. W. Parker, Treas.)
Jacob Rapp & Co., 375 S. High St.
Rock Plaster Mfg. Co. E. T. Bingham, V. P.
F. S. Stimmel, 606 S. High St.
R. L. Watson, 71½ E. State St.

CONNEAUT—
Wm. Babbett.
Weldon & Babbett.

COSHOCTON—
A. H. Thompson.

CUYAHOGA FALLS—
Bates & James.
Howe & Co.

DAYTON—
T. D. Eichelberger & Sons.
W. S. Hawthorn.
C. A. Starr, 125-131 Wayne Ave.

DEFIANCE—
M. B. Gorman.
Peter. Weigarding.

DELAWARE—
Geo. Clark & Son.
J. F. Gardner.
Wm. Mathews & Co.
H. J. McCullough & Co.
E. E. Naylor Co.

DELPHOS—
Keremann Lumber Co.
H. Ricker & Sons.

DENNISON—
Romig Feed Co.
EAST LIVERPOOL—
W. H. Adams.
Diamond Hardware Co.
Eagle Hardware Co.
The J. T. Smith Lumber Co.
Union Planing Mill Co.
EAST PALESTINE—
L. D. Crowl.
H. J. Fraser.
Smith & Crawford.
ELMWOOD PLACE—
Elmwood Place Supply Co.
Fred Mauthe.
ELYRIA—
Hyland & Monbach.
Elyria Coal & Sewer Pipe Co., E. F. Sanford, Prop.
FAYETTE—
L. A. Baker.
FINDLAY—
Rhamy & Miller, 538 S. Main St.
FOSTORIA—
Fostoria Stone & Lime Co.
D. P. Lloyd & Co.
Seneca White Lime Co.
FRANKLIN—
P. P. Maxwell.
A. T. Meeker.
FREMONT—
Q. Burgoon & Son.
Gottron & Cook.
GALION—
E. A. Bryan & Co.
GALLIPOLIS—
Charles Frankenberg.
Daniel Henry.
Jas. H. Karnes.
Racoon Coal and Fuel Co.
John C. Rue.
Geo. Schneider.
Adolphus Viney.
GENEVA—
C. W. Anderson & Son.
M. F. Rose.
GIRARD—
A. E. Hartzell.
Henry Hartzell.
GLENVILLE—
Engelhart Fulton Co.
C. C. Schellentrager.
GREENFIELD—
Rucker Co.
HAMILTON—
Anderson & Shaffer.
J. F. Bender Bros.
August Benninghofen, Court St. & C., H. & D. R. R.
Chas. Diefenbach & Co.
Eugene Hunter.
Sieffe & Wirtz.
F. J. Straub & Co.
HICKSVILLE—
Clay Crowe & Co.
W. O. Hughs & Co.
F. N. Jeffries.
Warner & Rose.
HILLSBORO—
John Fallon.
IRONTON—
Hayward & Murdock.
W. A. Murdock.
JACKSON—
S. H. Hardin.
T. W. Grose.
McKitterick Bros.
KENTON—
John Callam & Co.
Robinson & Gage.
LAKEWOOD—
Builders' Central Supply Co.
W. H. Wing.
LANCASTER—
N. R. Butler & Co.
Henry Carter.
Louis J. Snyder.
LEBANON—
Barrett & Jameson.
J. M. Lambert.
Lewis Bros.
Warren Coal Co.
LEETONIA—
M. O. Lodge.
LIMA—
Fidelity Coal and Supply Co.
Lima Coal and Sewer Pipe Co.
Watson & Co.
LISBON—
P. M. Armstrong & Co.
Bye & Bye.
LOCKLAND—
Jno. Mueller.
LOGAN—
Eisele & McLain.
LONDON—
Galligher & Murray.
John B. Van Wagener. W. High
LORAIN—
Lorain Lumber and Mfg. Co.
Penney Bros.
South Lorain Coal and Supply Co.
LOUISVILLE—
Keim & Son.
Pierson & Metzger.
MADISONVILLE—
Geo. S. Payne.
W. H. Settle & Co
MANSFIELD—
Barton & Willis, 38 N. Main St.
Fred Beeg, 299 Spring Mill St.
M. L. Branyan & Bro., 107 Main St.
Dill & Dille, 8 W. Third St.
Oberlin & Leutsy.
Voegele Bros., 197 N. Main St.
MARION—
T. E. De Wolf.
Leffler & Bland.
Marion Lbr. & Coal Co.
Prendergast Lbr. & Coal Co.
MARTINS FERRY—
L. L. Sheehle.
Scott Lumber Co.

VILLE—
Jones.
rass & Fullington.
LON—
water & Son, 1-3 Exchange St.
Clementz, 57-59 Canal St.
Segner, 74 S. Erie-st.
A—
Wood & Co.
SBURG—
& Catrow.
EPORT—
T. McElhenny.
ETOWN—
Cooch & Sons, E. Third St.
etrich & Co., Fourth St.
Gillham, E. Third St.
Kemp & Sons, Park St.
Smith, W. Third St.
—
et Lumber, Coal & Feed Co.
JUNCTION—
Risher.
ERNON—
rson & McCreary.
t R. Smith.
LEON—
s & Hildred.
NVILLE—
King & Co.
Landis.
I. Vorhes & Co.
RK—
T. Evans & Son, 35 S. 13th St.
URGH—
let Lumber, Coal & Feed Co.,
es P. O., Ohio.
COMERSTOWN—
Barnett & Co.
PHILADELPHIA—
ing & Yeiser.
Royal Sewer Pipe & Fire Brick
, B. F. Cotter, Supt.
A. Zeeb.
STRAITSVILLE—
R. Calkins.
C. & I. Co.
Hedges.
& Co.
—
V. Eaton.
Head & Co.
H BALTIMORE—
ster & Rogers.
D. Stoffer.
ner A. Young.
VALK—
E. Bell, Woodlawn Ave.
ins & Stryker, Whittlesey Ave.
l & Woodward, Linwood Ave.
Tuttle, N. Prospect St.
VOOD—
L. Lang.
LIN—
I. Cole.
lin Coal & Lumber Co.

OTTAWA—
G. C. Williams & Sons.
OXFORD—
J. E. Chatten.
Johnston Bros. & Co.
H. S. Thobe.
PAINESVILLE
The Downs Co.
The S. R. King Co.
J. E. Metzger & Co.
PAULDING—
E. M. Hawkins.
PIQUA—
A. A. Huber.
H. C. Reed & Co.
S. Zollinger & Co.
POMEROY—
W. G. Downie.
John Epple.
John Geyers.
PORT CLINTON—
Edw. Bertsch.
Granite Wall Plaster Co. G. W. Beemer, Pres. (Clarks Summit, Pa.), F. S. Culver, Secy. & Mgr.; M. S. Knight, Treas. (Scranton, Pa.).
Peter Johnson.
PORTSMOUTH—
J. B. Gibson, 82-86 W. 3d.
Alex M. Glockner, 206 Market.
J. C. Hibbs & Co., 130-132 W. 2d.
Jno. Kaps, W. 10, head Court.
Clyde E. King, E. 7 & Kendall.
Frank McGowan, E. 5 & Broadway.
Portsmouth Pressed Br. Co., 111 Market.
Smith Lumber Co., 1001 Lincoln.
Webster Fire Brick Co., S. Webster, Ohio.
RAVENNA—
J. A. Bennett.
H. K. Van Meter.
READING—
W. L. Comer.
Koehl Bros.
RIPLEY—
Thos. Buchanan.
Robt. Carr.
W. H. Reinert.
Thompson & Lewis.
ROCKY RIVER—
W. J. Geiger & Co.
Watkins Bros'. Co.
SALEM—
Jas. Brown & Co.
Chas. Campbell & Son.
Hensellwood & Kling.
Salem Hardware Co.
SALINEVILLE—
Stephen Bunn.
SANDUSKY—
Art Portland Cement Co.
P. B. Beery, Sandusky Cement Co.
Marsh & Co.
The Wagner Lake Ice & Coal Co.

SHELBY—
W. H. Morris.
Wills & Meyers.

SIDNEY—
E. J. Griffis & Co.
Jno. Heisen.
O. S. Marshall & Son.
Geo. H. Worch Co.

SOUTH BROOKLYN—
Gates Elevator Mills Co.

SPRINGFIELD—
Edward H. Ackerson, 138 Limestone.
Edward H. Ackerson, 138 S. Limestone.
Jno. M. Berger, 1022 Lagonda Ave.
Mills Bros., 107 S. Limestone.
Moores & Co., P. O. Address, Cold Springs, O.
The Moores Lime Co., N. W. C. Linden Ave & Washington.
M. C. Russell, N. W. C. Limestone and Warder.
Chas. T. Shepard, 101 E. Pleasant.
The Springfield Coal & Ice Co., 93 S. Limestone.
The Springfield Stone & Lime Co., 207 N. Plum.
Ulrick & Williams, 141 S. Limestone.
J. J. Webb, 263 Cedar.

STEUBENVILLE—
W. F. Davidson.
McGowan Bros.
John Orr's Sons.

STRYKER—
The Stryker Mfg. Co.

TIFFIN—
Crobaugh & Dahm Hdw. Co.
Phil Grummel.
Park Bros.
Geo. Stewart.

TOLEDO—
The Fred Boice Co., 15 St. Clair St.
The Buckeye Lime Co., 209-210 Cham. Com. Bldg. John Noble, Fostoria, O., Pres.; E. F. Gregg, Sec. & Mgr.
P. & T. Degnan, Builders' Furnishing Co., 417 Water St.
J. Hartman & Son, Superior & Swan Creek.
W. O. Holst & Co., S. Erie, between Creek & M. & E. Canal.

Toledo—Continued.
Kind & Kulmann Builders' [illegible] ply Co., 153 S. St. Clair St. R. Kulmann, Pres.; [illegible] Kind, Secy. and Treas.)
The Lime City Co., 422 The Spitz[illegible]
New Process Lime Co., Cor. Mc[illegible] & L. S. & M. S. Ry.
Ohio Lime & Cement Co., 305 C[illegible]ber Commerce.
H. H. Pierce, 227 The Nasby.
Poinier & Lester, 204 Water St.
James Rooney, 118 Collingwood A[illegible]
Toledo White Lime Co., 56 Pro[illegible] Exch.

TROY—
Geo. W. Conrad & Co.
E. J. Eby.
The Troy Tile & Brick Co.

UHRICHSVILLE—
C. V. McCluskey.
Jacob Pearch.

UPPER SANDUSKY—
W. A. Gibson.

URBANA—
J. J. Anderson.
Joel Bates.
C. C. Creager.

VAN WERT—
Jones & Tudor.
Kauhe & Alspach.
Lowrey, Hiestand & Co.

WAPAKONETA—
John Whiteman.

WARREN—
The Cereal Supply Co.
Greenwood & Co.
Grenamyer & Co.
Thomas Murray.

WASHINGTON COURT HOUSE
A. C. Henkle.
Geo. F. Robinson.

WAUSEON—
Palmer & Palmer.
F. R. Smallman.

WAVERLY—
Geo. Bauersachs.
Gehres Bros.
Pee Pee Milling Co.

WELLINGTON—
Bowlby & Hall.
J. H. Shelley.
J. R. Sherman, Jr.

WELLSTON—
A. B. Leach.
Ohio Building Co.
Wellston Lumber Co.

WELLSVILLE—
S. L. Dennis.
C. V. Shoub.

WILMINGTON—
Adams Hardware Co.
Tom Darbyshire.
Joshua Jefferies.
W. J. Slack.
J. W. Sparks.

M. C. RUSSELL CEMENT PAVING COMPANY

Sidewalks, driveways, stable floors, brewery floors, cellar bottoms, engine beds, artificial stone fence bases, steps of all kinds, also combination curb and gutter.
Excels all others in beauty and durability. All work promptly and satisfactorily done.

PHONE 10642. 80 COLLEGE AVE. SPRINGFIELD, O.

Works on Warder St. bet. Fountain and Limestone Sts.

[illegible]ed 1880. All Work Guaranteed.

'ER—
& Son.
›wood Coal Co.
Smith & Son.
›r Bros.
—
& Casad.
Farrell.
ıx & Co.
ˌSTOWN—
Hill Iron & Coal Co.
Buehrle, W. Federal St.
ˌranite Wall Plaster Co., Geo.
ıer, Pres. (Clark's Summit
; F. S. Culver, Sec. and Mgr.
t Clinton, O.)
Vitch Hazel Coal Co., 362 Fed-
St.
Youngstown Ice Co., 120 W.
merce St.
VILLE—
ı Bros.
Harris & Bros.
Moorehead.
Townsend.

KLAHOMA TERRITORY.

OMA CITY—
DeBolt.
. Green.
—
Buller.
Edwards.
Lumber Co.
Bell Lbr. Co.
CITY—
Bell Lumber Co.
Pond.

OREGON.

Y—
/ & Mason.
ıs Bros.
't & Lox Hdw. Co.
/orth Drug Co.
Young & Son.
ND—
Evans.
CITY—
che.
LLIS—
Kline.
'S PASS—
Ridder Hardware Co.

Comp.
ETON—
& Light.
ester.
Taylor.
AND—
ır, Guthrie & Co. (Walter
ırns, res. partner.)
McCraken Co., 401-7 Irving St.
McCraken, Pres., Jas. R. Mc-
en, Sec.-Treas., E. H. Mc-
en, Mgr.

Portland—Continued.
Meyer Wilson & Co., 1st Natl. Bank bldg.
C. W. Nottingham.
SALEM—
D. S. Bentley & Co.
John Hughes.
THE DALLES—
Hugh Glenn.
Joseph T. Peters.
Wasco Warehouse Co.

PENNSYLVANIA.

ALLEGHENY—
Champion Wall Plaster Co.
A. U. Corde, Nixon and Manhattan sts.
Barrett Mfg. Co., 1131 Rebecca St.
Duncan & Porter, 315 Sandusky St.
Fitzgerald Plaster Co., 212 Anderson St.
J. P. & E. A. Knox, Juniata St. and Preble Ave.
Murray Bros., 20 Lacock St., E. A.
ALLENTOWN—
John Berry & Son, Union, opp. Jordan St.
Jas. F. Butz, Gordon & Jordan Sts.
Coplay Cement Co., B. & B. bldg.
M. C. Ebbecke Hardware Co., 606 Hamilton St.
Lehigh Portland Cement Co.
Albert S. Weiler, L. V. & Terminal R. R.
ALTOONA—
Canan Building Supply Co.
Canan-Knox Supply Co.
John Halton.
AMBLER—
J. Watson Craft.
L. Y. Davis.
David Knipe.
Geo. W. Niblock.
APOLLO—
G. J. Bortz.
S. W. Hamilton.
H. P. Wood.
ASHLAND—
P. E. Buck & Sons.
C. & J. Leibig.
McConnell & Bro.
H. J. Stief.
ASHLEY—
Flory & Hemmel.
J. E. Marcey.
Aaron Seorfors.
W. W. Vincent & Son.
ATHENS—
D. J. Macafee.
BANGOR—
Bangor Lumber & Mfg. Co.
Snyder & Houck.
C. C. & F. S. Wise.
BEAVER—
Simpson & Ingram.

BEAVER FALLS—
F. F. Brierly.
W. J. Davidson.
Pearson & Son.
BEDFORD—
Cleaver & Gailey.
David Holderbaum.
BELLEFONTE—
Dan'l Irvin's Sons.
McCalmont & Co.
Potter & Hoy.
BETHLEHEM—
Black Diamond Coal Co., Main, S. E. Cor. River St., W. B.
E. J. Gerlach, 60 Water St.
Geo. F. Stahr, 59 S. Main St., W. B.
BIRDSBORO—
Miller Bros.
John W. Slipp.
BLAIRSVILLE—
C. F. Murray.
T. G. Murray.
BLOOMSBURG—
Moyer Bros.
H. G. Supplee.
BLOSSBURG—
Clark & Jones.
BRADDOCK—
McCrady & Rosser.
BRADFORD—
L. A. Fisher & Co., 92 Main St.
Louis Langworthy, 71 High St.
W. S. Robison, 143 Main St.
BRISTOL—
E. M. Peirce.
BROOKVILLE—
McKnight & Son.
G. A. Pearsall & Son.
Geo. L. Sandt.
BUTLER—
H. J. Klingler & Co., 139 E. Jefferson St.
W. S. McCrea.
Geo. Schaffner.
CALIFORNIA—
California Builders' and Supply Co.
C. W. Savage & Co.
CAMBRIDGE SPRINGS—
Bolard Bros.
Smith & Wilber.
CANONSBURG—
W. J. Elliott.
Munnell & Young.
CARBONDALE—
Mills Bros.
CARLISLE—
H. A. Barr, 3 Hanover St.
Bixler & Sons.
Wagoner Bros., N. Hanover St.
CARNEGIE—
C. A. Foster.
J. J. Smith.
CATASAUQUA—
G B. F. Deily.
Daniel Milson.
CHAMBERSBURG—
Coyle & Diehl.
W. C. Finney.
H. S. Gilbert.
Hiteshew & Co.
CHARLEROI—
Lee Lutes.
A. R. Mountser.
CHESTER—
D. M. Bunting.
Chester Lumber and Coal Co.
Stacy G. Glauser.
L. W. Wood & Bro.
CLEARFIELD—
F. Johnson & Bro.
McCullough & Co.
Powell Bros. & Jowell.
CLIFTON HEIGHTS—
Walter Jones.
COATESVILLE—
N. Lukens.
W. W. Mast.
V. S. Pownell.
COLUMBIA—
Stoner & Hall Hdw. Co.
Hiram Wilson.
CONFLUENCE—
V. M. Black & Co.
C. W. Kurtz.
CONNELLSVILLE—
J. R. Balsley.
Calhoun & Co.
Fayette Lumber Co. Ltd.
South Connellsville Lumber Co.
CONSHOHOCKEN—
Wm. Davis, Jr., & Co.
Evan D. Jones & Co.
Wm. Potts Jones.
S. and J. Pugh.
CORRY—
Barlow Hdw. Co.
COUDERSPORT—
Doane & Barnes.
H. J. Olmstead & Sons.
CURWENSVILLE—
Jacob Bilger.
Fred J. Dyer & Co.
DANVILLE—
S. Failey & Co.
Welliver Hardware Co., F. C. Der Pres.; W. W. Welliver, Secy. Mgr.
DARBY—
Darby Mortar Co.
Gottshall & Morgan.
Oscar Thurston.
DERRY—
Ballantyne & Co.
Derry Hdw. Co.
Geo. Mowry.
S. B. Piper.
DOYLESTOWN—
James Barrett.
W. H. Randall.

ǂ—
ǂ Hardware Co.
ǂ Iron Works.
& Hoover, Long Ave. and St.
ay Bros.
?rothero.
)WNINGTON—
& Wollerton.
–
Lime Co.
ROUDSBURG—
'oudsburg Lumber Co., Ltd.
.oder & Sons.
JM—
ockley.
A—
Von Nieda.

ırton, 9 West 8th St.
McCarty, cor. 16th & Wayne

rd Wall Plaster Co., foot of ı St.
Walther, cor. 19th & Parade

n & Austin, 13th & Sassafras

hayer & Son, Chester St. &

T—
Planing Mill Co.
.IN—
Ioward.
King.
ND—
rkbeck.
l Lumber Co.
Martin.
RT—
Long.
High Wallace.
IN—
McGovern.
& Dawson.
TOWN—
Bowditch, Haines & Boynton

VILLE—
Liebig.
BURG—
Good & Co.
ıoemaker.
R. Young.
ILLE—
Emery.
on & Moyer.
l Hardware Co.
EAD—
3. Roosa.
BURG—
& Lutz, 812 Market St.
:hoads, 7th & Briggs Sts.
thoads, Cowden & Forster

hoads, Foster, near 2d St.
:hlayer, 999 N. 3d St.

HASTINGS—
Stuttmatter Bros.
HAWLEY—
Guinn Bros.
Hawley Glass Co.
HAZELTON—
J. C. Bright & Co.
S. Y. Frederick.
Hazelton Machinery & Supply Co.
HOLLIDAYSBURG—
J. B. Condron.
John H. Law.
HOMESTEAD—
Samuel Hall.
Kennedy & West.
HONESDALE—
Dodge & Erk.
W. W. Weston.
HUGHESVILLE—
J. J. Brenholtz.
Jeremiah Kelly.
J. J. Malony & Son.
HUNTINGDON—
Africa Bros.
S. B. Chaney & Co.
B. F. Fink.
C. H. Miller Hardware Co.
INDIANA—
Keller & Jamison.
J. L. Orr.
J. M. Stewart & Co.
IRWIN—
L. C. Fox.
JENKINTOWN—
Thos. Nicholson & Son.
Smith & Schively.
JERMYN—
Peck Lumber Mfg. Co.
JOHNSTOWN—
A. J. Haws & Son.
R. D. Jones, 117 Haynes St.
R. R. Thomas & Kinzey.
John W. Walters.
KINGSTON—
Thos. Wright, Cy. Engr.
KITTANNING—
Daugherty Bros.' Brick Co.
Heilman Bros.
E. E. Hileman.
R. A. Hileman.
McConnell & Luker.
Jas. McCullough, Jr.
KUTZTOWN—
Walt B. Bieber.
Eugene P. De Turk.
N. S. Schmehl.
LANCASTER—
Flinn & Breneman.
E. O. Henry.
Herr & Snavely.
Marshall & Rengier.
Reilly Bros & Raub.
Steinnan Hdw. Co.
Stoner, Shreivor & Co.
W. D. Spreetor, Son & Co.

LANSDALE—
James Brady.
G. Jenkins & Co.
G. L. Thompson.
LANSDOWNE—
Garrett H. Lewis.
LATROBE—
P. H. Doherty.
Kiser & Kline.
Pores Hardware & Plumbing Co., 226 Railroad St.
P. H. Saxman.
A. J. Steele & Bro.
LEBANON—Gamber & Failer.
Geo. Krause & Co.
B. F. Patschke.
LEHIGHTON—
Lehigh Coal & Hardware Co.
LEWISBURG—
C. Dreisbachs' Sons.
LEWISTOWN—
F. G. Franciscus.
J. B. Selheimer.
LINDSEY—
W. T. Rodgers.
LOCK HAVEN—
Joseph Candor.
LYKENS—
Rumberger & Son.
MAHANOY CITY—
Ball Bros.
Seligman & Co.
MANHEIM—
Abram Kline.
MANSFIELD—
Asa Cleveland.
A. R. Decker.
Myron Mills.
Morgan E. Rose.
MARIETTA—
Miller & Co.
Stump & Mueller.
MAUCH CHUNK—
P. J. A. Binder.
Chas. Neast.
Nathan Sterner.
M'DONALD—
McCarty & Robb.
M'KEESPORT—
Bowman Bros.
John Hurrell's Sons Co.
Kelly & Dry.
W. D. Reed & Co.
John Serena & Co.
M'KEES ROCK—
J. E. Digby & Co., 10 Chartiers Ave.
MEADVILLE—
Marcus Ellis & Son.
E. L. Irvin.
C. P. Harris.
MEDIA—
Ball & Rhodes.
Hawley & Snowden.
C. Frank Williamson.
MERCER—
Carter Bros.
A. J. McKean.
Mercer Milling & Lbr. Co.
A. Newhall.
MIDDLETOWN—
A. B. Croll.
Hoff & Raymond.
MILTON—
John W. Brevy.
H. Judson Raup.
MINERSVILLE—
Geo. Ball.
Geo. Y. Brown.
Lytle Stove Co.
MONONGAHELA CITY—
Downer Bros.
Albert M. Gregg.
T. S. McCurdy.
Moore Saw & Planing Mill Co.
Yohe Bros.
MONTROSE—
Billings & Ryan.
Cooley & Son.
MOUNT JOY—
J. H. Buohl.
Gabriel Mover.
H. S. Newcomer.
MOUNT PLEASANT—
Kalp & Mechling.
W. H. Smith & Son.
J. A. Stevenson & Co.
NATRONA—
N. Hoohey.
R. S. M. Co.
NAZARETH—
Franklin J. Hahn.
Jacob Messinger.
Phoenix Cement Co.
Edward J. Unangst, Broad and Belvidere Sts.
Franklin P. Wunderly.

Up-to-date information about CEMENT AND ITS USES is given more fully in MUNICIPAL ENGINEERING MAGAZINE than any other publication.

Subscription Price, $2.00 Per Year.

BRIGHTON—
Hunter & Co.
olf Bros.
Martsolf.
Riehl.
ASTLE—
, McFarland & Co.
& Smith Co.
all Bros.
KENSINGTON—
Klingensmith.
rs, Robison & Hardy.
McKean & Son.
ORT—
Jones.
Ficke.
STOWN—
Sigler.
EAST—
& Mackay.
Scouller.
UMBERLAND—
Boust.
Deihl.
LE—
le Lumber Co.
llace & Bro.
TY—
ell & Borland, 243 Elm St.
& Kelley Lumber Co., 275 Elm
ield Coal & Lumber Co. (not
& Co.
Roess.
Roess.
Lumber & Coal Co. (not inc.)
ANT—
Brown & Co.
Bros.
D—
Dickey & Co.
Passmore.
ALL—
Kyle.
—
Good.
Clay Mfg. Co.
RGYL—
Carrell.
rald, Speer & Co.
YN—
Lutz.
Mathias.
DELPHIA—
Portland Cement
te Trust Bldg.
Portland Cem
Bldg.
Ambler, P. & R.
squehanna.
gh Bitumastic
Walnut St.
ean Cement C

Philadelphia—Continued.

American Mason Safety Tread Co., 628 Mutual Life Bldg.
American Stone & Builders' Supply Co., 2101 N. American St.
Amies Cement Paving Co., Broad & Arch Sts.
Atlas Portland Cement Co., 716 Harrison Bldg.
James Beatty, 211 York St.
James E. Beatty, 173 E. Chelten Ave.
Bonneville Portland Cement Co., 1307 Real Estate Trust Bldg.
Cyrus Borgner Co., 23d, ab. Race St.
Harris Bortel & Co., 2013 Market St.
Bourse Exhibition, S. Fourth & S. 5th, bel. Chestnut & Market.
Walter Bowditch, 205 E. Haines Gtn.
Walter T. Bradley & Co., 9th bel. Girard Ave.
Samuel P. Budd, 1019 Passyunk Ave.
Builders' Specialty Mfg. Co., Ltd., 136 S. 4th St.
Builders' Storage & Supply Co., 1547 N. Hutchinson.
Philip Carey Mfg. Co., 223 S. 6th St.
Robert Coane, 307 Fidelity Bldg.
Commercial Wood & Cement Co., Girard Bldg.
James Corr & Co., 211 York.
C. A. Cox's Sons, 2137 N. American.
Coplay Cement Co., 305 Girard Bldg.
F. A. Daboll, Land Title Bldg.
Paul A. Davis, Jr., 136 N. Water St.
Wm. J. Donaldson, 503 Betz Bldg.
Cornelius Dougherty, 1207 S. 7th St.
Drehmann Pacing Co., 2629-31 Parrish St.
Morris Ebert, 302 Walnut St.
Edgar J. Ellis, 74 S. Broad St.
Edison Portland Cement Co., 615 Girard Bldg.
Eclipse Cement & Blacking Co., 1238 Belmont Ave.
P. H. Fairlamb & Co., 115 S. 30th St.
Henry Ferrall, 1117 S. 47th St.
Peter J. Foley, 2618 N. 6th St.
M. M. Fox & Co., Christian St., whf. ach.
Samuel H. French & Co., York Ave., 4th and Callowhill.
Frederick R. Gerry Co., 1835 Market St.
Globe Fireproofing Co., 449 Philadelphia Bourse.
Hanley, White & Co., 2730 N Broad St.
Alex. Y. Hanna & Co., 405 West End Trust Bldg.
Wm. G. Hartranft Cement Co., 1112 Real Estate Trust Bldg.
J. H. Hinkle & Co., American & Cambria Sts.
George Halzbaur, 1340 Seltzer St.
Louis A. Kellich, 500 Betz Bldg.
Chas. Kelley, 1612 French St.

Philadelphia—Continued.

I. W. Kenderdine & Bro., 24 S. 7th St.
O. W. Ketcham, 409 Builders' Exchange.
Fred King, 3424 Chestnut St.
Knickerbocker Lime & Mortar Co., 366 Ninth St.
James Knowlan, 45 N 13th St.
Wm. Krause & Sons, 2129 American.
Lawrence Cement Co., Harrison Bldg.
Lee & Edge, 14 S. Broad St.
Lesley & Trinkle Co., 22 S. 15th St.
John Lucas & Co., 4th & Race St.
Lukens & Yerkes, 204 Girard Bldg.
Mannheimer Portland Cement Co., 302 Walnut St.
Hugh Martin, 1133 Winton St.
Henry Maurer & Son, 24 S. 7th St.
Geo. W. McCaully & Son, 2030 Market St.
Anthony Meng & Co., 109 S. Front St.
Merritt & Co., 1024-34 Ridge Ave.
Howard M. Murphy, 1543 Newkirk St.
Geo. F. Murray, 905 Oxford St.
National Supply Co., 703 Witherspoon Bldg.
Eugene E. Nice, 272 S. 2d St.
B. H. Nicholas, 3214 Columbia Ave.
Parrott & Miller, 526 S. 8th St.
Howard Plucker.
Robert Patterson & Son, Cherry St., whf.
Philadelphia Clay Material Co., 48th and Merion Ave.
Phoenix Cement Co., 1112 Real Estate Trust Bldg.
Quaker City Mortar Co., 50 N. 23d St.
John W. Rapp, 911 Harrison bldg.
Rigby Cement Co., 1232 S. Penn Sq.
Thomas Robinson & Co., 201 Church St
F. H. Roney & Co., 519 Crozer bldg.
J. W. Rutan, 315 Head Bldg.
Sears, Humbert & Co., Fidelity Mutual Life Bldg.
B. F. Stradley, 1712 Market St.
Jacob Schwartz, 2306-8 N. 27th St.
Ernst Scholz, 1407 N. Camac ST.
Smedley Construction Co., 711 Stephen Girard Bldg.
Chas. E. Smith, 426 E. Girard Ave.
Edwin A. Smith & Son, 1017 Frankfort Ave.
Rufus R. Thomas & Co., 1801 Market St.
Standard Plastic Mfg. Co., 404 Girard Bldg.
S. A. Stoneback, 1328 N. 9th St.
E. H. Thomas, Builders' Exchange.
Chas. P. Tomlinson, 1237 Arch St.
Jacob L. Tyson, 900 Jefferson St.
U. S. Fireproof Wood Co., 2218 Race St.

Philadelphia—Continued.

Van Stan's Stratena Co., 810 [illegible] St.
Victor F. Van stan, [illegible]
G. R. Vogles, 309 Builders' [illegible]
Vollmer & Register, [illegible] Bldg.
Vulcanite Portland Cement [illegible] 1712 Market St.
E. A. Waddy & Co., [illegible]
Henry Wagner, [illegible]
Chas. Warner Co., [illegible] Title Bldg.
Warren-Ehret Co., 1210 [illegible] Bldg.
Wm. E. Willams, 1545 N. [illegible]

PHOENIXVILLE—

N. H. Benjamin Co.
Caswell & Moore.
Harry Morris.
John M. Wilkinson.
Albert Yerkes.

PITTSBURG—

Allegheny Co. Builders' Sup[illegible] 1806 Josephine St.
W. J. Baughman, Smallman [illegible] 28th St.
Mrs. W. J. Baughman, [illegible] St.
Reed F. Blair, Lewis Block[illegible]
Buray & McNeill, [illegible] Standard [illegible]
Castalia Portland Cement [illegible] 701 Publication Bldg.
Cook & Fair, 317 Smith Blk.
East End Supply Co., 125 Fran[illegible] Ave.
C. A. Foster, 1st St. & R. R. [illegible]
The Granite Wall Plaster Co. [illegible] W. Beemer, Pres., Clark[illegible] Pa.; C. Graham, Vice-Pres[illegible] Culver, Secy. & Treas., Por[illegible]ton, Ohio.
Heppenstall & Marquis, Liber[illegible] & 32d St.
Houston Bros., 32d st and F[illegible]
D. J. Kennedy, 150 Frankstow[illegible]
William T. Leggett Co., 10[illegible]erty Ave.
Logan-Gregg Hardware Co., [illegible] St.
McDowell Mfg. Co.
L. S. McKallip & Co., 12th & [illegible]
Miller, Mason & Co., 627 Park [illegible]
A. G. Morris Lime & Limesto[illegible] 18 2d National Bank Bldg.
H. A. Noah Co., 20 Schmidt Bl[illegible]
Patterson & Co., 1222 Grant Av[illegible]
James R. Pitcairn, 805 Ha[illegible] Bldg.
Pittsburg & Buffalo Co. [illegible] Bldg.
Pittsburg Builders' Supply [illegible] German Nat'l Bank Bldg.
Pope Cement & Brick Co[illegible] Wood St., 6th floor. [illegible] and, Mgr. Cement Dept.
West & Wilson, 7458 Finance S[illegible]

y—Continued.
ms & Co., 304 Water St.
. William & Co., 308 Duquesne
Young, 34th St. & A. V. Ry.
TON—
Patterson & Co., 274 N. Main
TOWN—
gely & Son.
VILLE—
Bright & Co.
Esterley Sons.
W. Miller.
Thompson, Center & Market
SUTAWNEY—
Nordstrum.
sutawney Hdw. Co.
son Hdw. Co.
Williams.
ERTOWN—
Acney.
O'Brien.
Wain & Bro.
ING—
t & Co.
Fox & Co.
Bros.
& Bro.
es D. Miller & Son, foot Chest-
st.
ne Lime Co.
Reppiler, 536 Penn-st.
ter Hardware Co.
VO—
Baird.
Stevenson.
Swain.
OLDSVILLE—
les E. Evans.
ohner.
lex Stoke.
. Young.
VAY—
, Murphy & Co.
Bros. & Co., Ltd.
Y PARK—
. Jones, tr.
RSFORD—
walter, Grater & Co.
se & Son.
ARY'S—
& Russ.
& Hall Lumber Co.
Schimm.
e Wolf.
—
Maney.
Lumber Co.
SKILL HAVEN—
Meyers.
Bros.
Saylor.
TON—
Senaze, 706 Scranton St.
Stone Co., 726 Scranton St.
& Shear Co., 119 N. Washing-
Ave.

Scranton—Continued.
Hunt & Connell Co.
Luther Keller, 813 W. Lackawanna Ave.
Paragon Plaster & Supply Co., 1500 Albright Ave.
Peck Lumber Mfg. Co., 101 E. Market St.
Price & Howarth, 1001 N. Washington Ave.
Scranton Fire Brick Co., Nay Aug Av. N. Green Rdy.
Scranton Vitrified Brick Mfg. Co.
Ehret, Warren & Co., 321 N. Washington Ave.
Washburn, Williams & Co., 119 Merden St.
J. B. Wooslsey & Co., 312 Forest Ave.
SEWICKLEY—
S. A. Chamberlin.
Alden Hays.
SHAMOKIN—
Boughner, Goodwill & Co.
J. H. Conley & Sons.
Jos. W. Kessler.
Fred Kumer, 542 Diamond St.
Shamokin Hdw. Co.
Warren Unger.
SHARON—
Wallis & Carley.
A. Wishart & Sons.
SHARPSBURG—
Henry Ferla.
SHARPSVILLE—
James Blaney.
Simon Sheasley.
SHENANDOAH—
M. P. Fowler.
Glenn & O'Hearn.
SHIPPENSBURG—
B. A. Betz.
M. G. Hale.
George H. Stewart.
G. F. Walters & Son.
SLATINGTON—
Dettmer & Handwerk.
Gross, Eritzinger & Co.
SOMERSET—
H. F. Barnett.
Cook & Beerits.
D. W. Saylor.
SOUTH BETHLEHEM—
Brinker & Wagner.
Cyrus Jacoby.
Edwin Laufer.
SOUTH FORK—
Justus Volk.
SPRING CITY—
Mowrey Latshaw Hardware Co.
STEELTON—
Keller & Mumma, 136 N. Front St.
STROUDSBURG—
East Stroudsburg Lumber Co.
Shiffer Bros.
Jos. Wallace.

SUNBURY—
G. W. Hackett.
Wm. H. Heim.
Geo. W. Simpson.
Sunbury Supply Co.

SUSQUEHANNA—
E. W. Jackson.
M. Millane.

TAMAQUA—
Weaver's Son & Haldeman.

TARENTUM—
W. F. Goodwin.
A. J. Marlarkey & Co.
Tarentum Hdw. Co.
Wm. O. Wood.

TITUSVILLE—
Eduards Bros.
W. I. Hale.

TOWANDA—
B. F. Myer.

TREMONT—
Sanner Bros.
F. B. Wheeler.

TYRONE—
F. D. Beyer & Co.
Franciscus Hardware Co.
E. P. Irwin & Co.
Grazier Bros. & Stine.
D. A. Smith & Son.
J. S. Smith.

UNION CITY—
Thompson & Hipple.
Union Coal & Supply Co.

UNIONTOWN—
W. C. McCormick.
J. T. Sternbower & Co.

WARREN—
Pickett Hardware Co.
Wm. Spinner.
H. J. Thomas.

WASHINGTON—
R. T. Hallam & Sons, 77 E. Bean St.
Brit Hart, E. Malden Lane.
Chas. H. Spriggs, 100 W. Maiden St.

WATSONTOWN—
F. H. Knight.

WAYNE JUNCTION—
Charles Fredericks.

WAYNESBORO—
Daniel Hess.

WEATHERLY—
Charles Cassler.

WEST CHESTER—
Bennett & Lean.
E. Malin Hooper.
Serrill J. Sharples.

[illegible] and Buffalo Co.
[illegible], Manufacturers and Shippers of
[illegible], Coke, Brick, Lumber, Sand
and Builders' Supplies
Via all Railroads Centering Pittsburg, Pa.
and Buffalo, N. Y. General Offices,
Park Building. Warehouses and Yards,
[illegible] Liberty Ave.
[illegible]TTSBURG, PA.

WESTGROVE—
S. K. Chambers & Bro.
Solomon J. Pusey.

WEST NEWTON—
E. C. Leightty & Co.
Fred Schoaf.
M. F. Scholl.

WHITE HAVEN—
John Donnelly.
Geo. K. Kocher.
Geo. W. Moyer.
John Shaffer.
E. A. Stehly.

WILKESBARRE—
Fred A. Guard.
Geo, L. McAlarney.
J. E. Patterson & Co.

WILKINSBURG—
Hays Coal and Supply Co., ton Ave. & P. R. R.
J. B. Hill & Co., Pen Ave. & P. R.

WILLIAMSPORT—
Central Commission Co.
Diamond Wall Cement Co.
Gohl & King.
F. H. Kellar & Co., 27 W. Third
Kline & Co.
David Stuempfle, 332 Penn St.

WILLIAMSTOWN—
Amos Lebo.

WRIGHTSVILLE—
S. M. & C. H. Branstock.
Geo. W. Moore.
Wrightsville Supply Co.

YORK—
McClellan & Gotwalt.
Reichley & Allison.
P. A. Small & Son (Ltd).

RHODE ISLAND.

BRISTOL—
Eugene Le Clair.
Seth Paull.
Wardwell Lumber Co. W. T. Wa well, Pres. F. F. Gladding, S & Treas.

CENTRAL FALLS—
H. B. Wood & Co.

EAST GREENWICH—
Wm. L. Sharpe.
Lodowick C. Shippee.
Jos. S. Thornley.

NARRAGANSETT—
J. C. Tucker, Jr.

NEWPORT—
A. N. Barker, 205 Thames & Lo Wharf.
Albert Hammett, 321 Thames St.
Swinburne, Perkins & Co., 215 Tha

PAWTUCKET—
Newell Coal Co.
Olney & Payne Bros., 30 East Av

ENCE—
C. Goff, 31-49 Point St.
. H. Grant, 25 Stanton Ave.
Olneyville, R. I.)
Harris, 77 Dyer St.
ster & Hudson, 55 Point St.
IELD—
ucker, Jr.
LY—
x & Wilcox.
Kenyon & Co.
& Co.
herman, 139 Main St.
OCKET—
umber Co., River St.
cket Lumber Co., 189 N. Main

SOUTH CAROLINA.

LLE—
le Cotton Mill.
le Lumber Co.
Hammond & Co.
Drug Co.
ON—
nderson & Bro., 26 Depot St.
& Ledbetter.
ELL—
Moore.
RT—
istensen.
Legare, P. O Box 217.
Schefer.
I—
m & Co.
lan.
& Shannon.
STON—
on Lumber Co., W. End
.
randt, 118 Church.
a Portland Cement Co., 194-6
y.
Hughes, 82 Mary.
ohnson & Co., East End
ens.
stendorff, 92 Washington.
**astern Lime and Cement
76 E. Bay.**
R—
Machine & Lumber Co.
BIA—
rown & Bro.
& Lawrence.
ICE—
oenist & Co.
Gregg.
Hudson.
EY—
one Springs Lime Co.
Richardson & Co.
VILLE—
Brown, Wardlaw and Birnil
& Speights, 113 W. Washing-
t
& Austin, 115 W. Washing-
t.

NEWBERRY—
A. L. Davis & Co.
William Johnson.
Newberry Hardware Co.
ORANGEBURG—
L. E. Williams.
PIEDMONT—
Piedmont Mfg. Co.
SPARTANBURG—
S. B. Ezell.
Gower, Speights & Co.
SUMMERVILLE—
Rufus Knight.
O. C. Sires & Bro.
John W. Taylor.
SUMTER—
W. B. Boyle.
H. Harby.

SOUTH DAKOTA.

ABERDEEN—
S. H. Brooman Lumber Co.
St. Croix Lumber Co., Second-ave. and Lincoln-st. W. Chalmers, Pres. (Stillwater, Minn.); F. W. Raymond, local manager.
J. S. Hart & Co.
BROOKINGS—
I. S. Binford.
Laird-Norton Lumber Co.
Yeomans Bros. & Hodgins.
DEADWOOD—
Fish & Hunter Co.
Smith & Hatch Lumber Co. (not inc.), Smith Blk.
Stearns Co.
FLANDREAU—
A. G. Nevins.
LEAD—
Fisher, Hunter & Co.
Phillips & Bartlett.
MADISON—
C. L. Colman Lumber Co.
L. Lamb Lumber Co.
A. G. Nevins.
MITCHELL—
Robert Burns.
Davis & Daniels.
Fullerton Lumber Co.
SIOUX FALLS—
Miracle & Miracle.
Sioux Falls Lumber Co. W. F. Wider, Pres.; John Parker, Sec., Treas. and Mgr.
WATERTOWN—
Hayes, Lucas Lumber Co.
Hess & Raes, Maple St.
Laird-Norton Lumber Co.
YANKTON—
Harry Call.
Fred Donaldson.
Loonan & Smith.
McCaull, Webster & Co.
St. Croix Lumber Co.
W. B. Valentine.

ATHENS—
Bayless & Moody.
McKeldin & Watson.
Reed Bros.

BRISTOL—
Barker Hdw. Co.
V. Keebler.

CHATTANOOGA—
C. A. Moross Co., 121 Cherry St.

CLARKVILLE—
Jno. Hurst & Co.
Kisser & Northington.

CLEVELAND—
Hall Bros.
W. A. Lillard & Co.
S. W. Marshall & Co.

COLUMBIA—
Jas Andrews & Co.
Dobbins & Ewing.
E. W. Gamble.
J. P. Street & Co.

DAYTON—
Dayton Coal and Iron Co.
W. C. Godsey.
A. Johnson & Sons.

FAYETTEVILLE—
J. W. Barnett.

HARRIMAN—
W. L. Doane.
Tenn. Building Co.

HUMBOLDT—
W. H. McKnight & Son.

JACKSON—
R. S. Fletcher & Co.
C. M. Thompson & Co.
Jno. L. Wisdom.

JOHNSON CITY—
C. K. Lide & Co.

KNOXVILLE—
Chandler & Co.
Geo. P. Chandler.
Chapman, White, Lyons & Co.
Sanford, Chamberlain & Albers, 43 Gay St. E. J. Sanford, Pres.; W. P. Chamberlain, Sec.-Treas.; A. J. Albers, Mgr.

LEBANON—
Page Bros.
Woolard & Williams.

MARYVILLE—
King & Caldwell.
McNutt, Chandler & West.

McMINNVILLE—
Biles & Smith.
Morfoul & Rogers.

MEMPHIS—
Jno. A. Denie & Sons.
J. F. Forsythe, 316 Front St.
Wright Lime & Cement Co.

MORRISTOWN—
Brown & Stubblefield.
East Tenn. Wood Working Co.

MOSSY CREEK—
Z. T. Godwin.
B. E. Tallant.

MURFREESBORO—
Street & Spain.

NASHVILLE—
Cooper & Co., [illegible]
W. T. Hardison & Co.
Thos. Nolan.

ROGERSVILLE—
G. D. Hale & Co.
Miller, Lea & Co.
Rogan, Nice & Smith.

SODDY—
New Soddy Coal Co.

SOUTH PITTSBURG—
W. F. McDaniel & Co.

UNION CITY—
T. L. Bramford.

TEXAS.

ABILENE—
G. M. Bowie & Son.
Burton, Lingo Co.

AUSTIN—
Geo. Brush.
A. F. Martin & Bro.

BASTROP—
J. L. Wilbarger & Co.

BEAUMONT—
E. L. Wilson & Co.

BELTON—
H. Andrews.
J. H. James & Son.
Smith, Peyton & Co.

BONHAM—
O. T. Lyon & Sons.
E. D. Steger & Co.

BROWNSVILLE—
J. S. & M. H. Cross.
H. M. Field.
F. Yturria.

BROWNWOOD—
Borwnwood Lumber Co.
Wm. Cameron & Co.
M. T. Jones Lumber Co.

BRYAN—
Garth, Howell & Webb.
G. S. Parker.
Peter Winter.

CALDWELL—
Jenkins & Jenkins.
Sillman & McClain.

CALVERT—
Calvert Lumber Co.
F. M. Lumber Co.

CAMERON—
Wm. Jeter & Co.
Milborn Co. Lumber Co.

CLEBURNE—
Cameron, Williams & Co.

CORPUS CHRISTI—
C. C. Lumber Co.
E. D. Sidbury.

CORSICANA—
Corrall & Cobb.
M. T. Jones Lumber Co.
McCammon & Lang.
C. A. Sammons.
J. E. Whiteselle & Co

S—
hs & Cowser, 500 Commerce.
& Dow.
& Rawlins, 271 Elm.
Summerfield.
Portland Cement Co.
Waespi, 861 Elm.
TUR—
Smith.
DN—
nna.
-Leeper Lumber Co.
N—
s Bros. & Co.
N—
Smith & Co.
Spencer & Co.
SO—
so Fuel Co., 411 S. Santa Fe St.
T. Roe, Secy.; W. W. Fink,

m Coal Co.
-Badger Co.
ORTH—
trong Lumber Co.
n Lingo Co. J. P. Waples.
(Denver, Col.); R. C. Gal-
th, Secy.; W. Burton, Treas.
gr.
ron Lumber Co.
Roe.
RICKSBURG—
Priess.
SVILLE—
Lyon & Son.
s, Painter & Co.
Iridge & Bro.
STON—
y & McVitie.
L Henchman, 2410 Mechanic St.
Parr & Co.
Pollard & Co.
ETOWN—
Lumber Co.
Lumber Co.
E—
Allen & Son.
rson Bros.
ETTA—
Mayfield Lumber Co.
SORO—
trong Bros.
Dowlen & Co.
Lyon & Son.
& Campbell.
ON—
Burke, 814 Commerce Ave.
e & Co., 501 Washington St.
McLaughlin & Co., 810 Willow

SSON—
& Meyer.
Mfg. Co.
D—
w Tillison.

LULING—
Luling Lumber Co.
MARLIN—
J. W. Robinson & Co.
R. B. Spencer & Bro.
MARSHALL—
Cock & Harris.
Jas. Higgins.
M'KINNEY—
G. W. Owens & Co.
J. M. Wilcox & Son.
NAVASOTA—
Navasota Lumber and Mfg. Co.
J. Youens & Co.
NEW BRAUMFELS—
Connel Lumber Co.
Louis Henne.
Geo. Pfeuffer Lumber Co.
ORANGE—
L. Miller.
SAN ANTONIO—
Alamo Cement Co., 207-209 Main Ave. (G. H. Kalteyer, Pres.; C. Bamberger, Secy. and Mgr.)
L. P. Boettler.
J. C. Deelman.
Henry Pauly, 102 Goliad & Peach Sts.
SAN MARCOS—
J. H. Gary.
San Marcos Mercantile Co.
SHERMAN—
A. A. Fielder.
O. T. Lyon & Sons.
J. B. Wilson & Bro.
SULPHUR SPRINGS—
O. M. Pate.
W. D. Pruitt.
G. H. Wilson.
TAYLOR—
Evens Burke Lumber Co., S. F. Evens, Pres.; J. B. Burke, Sec. Treas. & Mgr.; 501-11 W. 2d St.
Holder & Barge.
J. A. Thompson.
TEMPLE—
C. M. Campbell & Sons.
TERRELL—
Abes & Walton.
Powers Lumber Co.
Wraten Grain & Lumber Co.
VICTORIA—
Bailey Mills Co.
A. Goldman.
A. Levi & Co.
WACO—
Brazelton & Johnson.
Wm. Cameron & Co., Inc. W. W. Cameron, Pres. & Treas.; W. T. League, Secy.; C. R. Sherrill, Mgr.
Carlton Bros
Nash, Robinson & Co.
WEATHERFORD—
Leeper Conway Co.
Mike Salon.
Weatherford Lumber Co.

UATH.

AMERICAN FORK—
Chipman Merc. Co.
J. E. Jenson.

BRIGHAM CITY—
J. F. Merrell & Co.
W. C. Mortensen & Son.

HEBER—
F. O. Buell.
H. Hatch & Co.
Mark Jeffs.

LEHI—
Kirkham & Sons.
People's Coop. Store.
Ross & Ross.

MT. PLEASANT—
B. Hansen & Co.

OGDEN—
Co-op. Wagon & Machine Co.
Geo. A. Lowe Co.
Sidney Stevens Implement Co. Sidney Stevens, Pres. & Mgr.; C. H. Stevens, Secy.; F. J. Stevens, Treas.

PARK CITY—
W. E. Boyd.
Gregg & Co.
W. H. Harris.
Pape & Lets.
Summit Lumber Co.
Welch & Co.

PAYSON—
Geo. W. Hancock.
John E. Hulsh.
Payson Co-operative Store.

PROVO CITY—
John Grier, sr.
Smoot Lumber Co.
E. J. Ward & Sons.

RICHFIELD—
Lewis & Nuteer Hdw. Co.

SALT LAKE CITY—
Culmer Bros.
Langton Lime and Cement Co.
Elias Moris & Sons' Co.
Morrison Merrill & Co.
Portland Cement Co. of Utah.

VERMONT.

BARRE—
Allen & Richardson, Depot Sq.
L. M. Averill, N. Main St.
R. L. Clark, Prospect St.

BELLOWS FALLS—
Eaton & Norwood.
Howard Hdw. Co.

BENNINGTON—
J. H. Loring & Co., 113 Depot St.

BRATTLEBORO—
Mellen & Proctor.
Robbins & Cowles.

It is Our Business

TO HELP

Your Business

IF YOU MAKE, SELL OR USE

CEMENT

Write to us and we will tell you what we can do for you.

You ought to know

Municipal Engineering Co.

NGTON—
Booth, Lake St.
igton Grocery Co.
n Bros., Lake St.
ng, Kimball & Co.
r Grocery Co.
AVEN—
. Campbell.
PELIER—
t & Bailey.
Hyde.
ND—
affee's Sons.
el P. Curtis & Son.
Landon & Co.
Noyes.
nd Fire Clay Co.
HNSBURY—
Colbeck & Son.
& H. K. Ide. E. T. Ide, Pres.
Treas.; Geo. M. Gray, V. P.
Sec.
GFIELD—
Kenney.
m, La Fountain & Co.
Riehn.
OSKI—
& Catlin.

VIRGINIA.

NDRIA—
K. Field & Co., 115 N. Union
Robinson's Sons, 121 King St.
LEY—
Jacocha.
OL—
r Hardware Co.
ebler.
ENT—
ndoah Lime Co.
ESTON—
n Brethers, Capitol & Piedmont
Crawford & Co., South End of
awha Bridge.
Gates, 21 Summers St.
an & Gardner, Clendennin &
River.
Hardware Co., 111 3rd St.
. Smith Hdwre. Co., 117 3rd St.
ber & Maloy, 104 Charleston St.
LOTTESVILLE—
P. Carver.
s & Carroll.
Porter.
y Williamson.
l. Vest & Co.
ON FORGE—
. Moody & Co.
n & McKinney Co.
ILLE—
es L. Pritchett, 207 and 209
erside Block.

FREDERICKSBURG—
E. Dorsey Cole.
W. S. Embrey.
O. D Foster.
G. J. Marshall.
HAMPTON—
Jacob Heffelfinger.
HARRISONBURG—
Coffman Bros.
Snell, Beery & Co.
C. A. Sprinkel & Son.
H. N. Whitesel & Bro.
LEESBURG—
Norris Bros.
Shroff & Co.
LEXINGTON—
Owen Hardware Co.
LOCHER—
James River Cement Co.
LURAY—
A. L. Jameson.
Luray Lime Co.
LYNCHBURG—
Adams Bros.—Paynes Co., 901 Main
Adams Monroe Mfg. Co., 70 Adams
C. S. Hutter, 1008 Church St.
Lynchburg Box Co., 1112 Clay St.
Pierce & Akers Co., 715 Main St.
W. O. Taylor, 214 Ninth St.
Williams & Barnett, 917 Main St.
S. S. Wright, 822 Church St.
MARION—
Look & Lincoln.
NEWPORT NEWS—
Benson, Phillips & Co.
Booker Poarch Co.
B. D. Chandler.
James River Supply Co.
NORFOLK—
Batchelder & Collins.
Gamage & Waller.
PETERSBURG—
Booth & Co.
PORTSMOUTH—
Lindsay & Co., 801 Crawford St.
PULASKI—
I. R. Albert.
RADFORD—
James Mercantile Co.
R. J. Naul.
Radford Grocery Co.
W. R. Roberts & Co.
Virginia Iron, Coal & Coke Co.
RICHMOND—
S. H. Hawes & Co.
Warner, Moore & Co.
ROANOKE—
Catogni Bros.
Central Mfg. Co.
J. H. Marsteller, 21 E. Campbell Ave.
J. H. Wilkinson & Co.
SALEM—
D. T. Martin—
W. S. Oakley & Son.

SOUTH BOSTON—
Easley & Lawson.
R. W. Lawson & Co.
STAUNTON—
Baker Bros.
J. A. Fauver & Co.
M. E. Miller & Bro.
R. L. Stratton.
SUFFOLK—
R. R. Allen.
E. L. Foulk & Co.
Shoof, Weithers & Co.
WEST POINT—
Ned Bland & Bro.
R. & J. L. Bland & Bell.
W. C. Davis.

WASHINGTON.

CENTRALIA—
A. L. Atkins.
CHEHALIS—
O. F. Sainton.
ELLENSBURG—
Alsip & Sons, Walnut, north of 4th.
NEW WHATCOM—
W. M. Frizell.
PORT TOWNSEND—
Lion & Barthop Co.
SEATTLE—
Balfour, Guthrie & Co., Bailey Bldg.
F. T. Crowe & Co., 76 Starr Boyd Bldg.
Dodwell & Co., Ltd.
Schwabacher Hardware Co.
Seattle Hardware Co.
Smythe, Wakefield & David.
SPOKANE—
Washington Brick, Lime and Mfg. Co.
TACOMA—
Balfour, Guthrie & Co.
F. T. Crowe & Co., 740 Pacific Ave.
P. J. Fransioli & Co., 1111 Commerce Ave.
Tacoma Trading and Transportation Co., 1715 Dock St. C. S. Barlow, Pres.

WEST VIRGINIA.

BLUEFIELD—
Georgia Lumber Co.
Geo. N. Speiden & Co.
CHARLESTON—
Brown Bros., Capitol and Piedmont
E. T. Crawford & Co., S. End of Kanawha Bridge.
J. H. Gates, 31 Summers St.
Morgan & Gardner, Clendennin and Elk River.
Wagner & Maloy, 164 Charleston.
CLARKSBURG—
The Hornor Gaylord Co.
Ruhl Koblegard & Co.
The Williams & Davisson Co.
GRAFTON—
Geo. Brew.
J. W. Caveney.
HUNTINGTON—
Sam Beswick.
T. M. Carr & Co.
C. C. Dusenberry.
Mossman Bros.
NEW CUMBERLAND—
C. S. Bradley.
New Cumberland Water & Gas Co
PARKERSBURG—
Rex Hardware Co., 111 3d St.
W. H. Smith Hardware Co., 117 3d S
POINT PLEASANT—
Filson Bros.
SHEPHERDSTOWN—
A. S. Dandridge.
G. T. Hodges.
SISTERSVILLE—
Lazear Bros.
WELLSBURG—
J. S. Liggett.
G. W. Miller.
J. M. Walker & Co.
WESTON—
A. M. Baily.
A. A. Warren.
WHEELING—
Lewis & Haslett.

WISCONSIN.

ANTIGO—
A. F. Brehmer.
D. Clements.
APPLETON—
P. Leonhardt.
Marston Bros.
L. A. Rose.
G. D. Rowell & Son.
ASHLAND—
Ashland Lime, Salt & Cement O. A. Quam, Pres.; Thos. Edwa Secy., Treas. & Mgr.
J. H. Younker.
BARABOO—
H. M. Johnston Lumber Co., Broadway and Third Ave. Al Stewart, Pres. (Wausau, Wis.); M. Johnston, Sec., Treas., Mgr.
J. L. Stewart.
BELOIT—
Beloit Lbr. Co.
City Fuel Co.
Keeler Lbr. Co.
L. O. Stardosh.
BERLIN—
H. D. Lawrence.
G. S. Morris.
BLACK RIVER FALLS—
Black R. F. L. & M. Assn.
BOSCOBEL—
T. Carrier & Co.
Ruka Bros. Mfg. Co.
BURLINGTON—
Home Lumber Co.
Wilbur Lumber Co.

ıan Lumber Co. E. W. East-
, Mgr. (Mineral Point, Wis.)
'AN—
r Lumber Co.
RE—
Garvey.
:VILLE—
tler.
ıan Lumber Co., E. W. East-
, Mgr., (Mineral Point, Wis.),
:astman, local mgr.
ND—
ıan Lumber Co. E. W. East-
, Mgr. (Mineral Point, Wis.)
—
E. Hart.
Huntley & Co.
Loveland.
:VILLE—
.ville Lbr. Co.
Lovejoy Lbr. Co.
DU LAC—
·r Milling Co.
Bros.
ATKINSON—
x & Morris Co.
er & Hoffman Sons.
BAY—
ousen & Hathaway.
l Coal Co.
rlbert.
RIVER—
Pettingill & Co.
Russell.
grodt.
VILLE—
Bros.
H. Macloon.
theram, 56 Linn St.
er & McKey Lumber Co.
RSON—
Brown.
ıon Brick & Tile Co.
DALE—
an Lumber Co. E. W. East-
Mgr. (Mineral Point, Wis.)
LUNA—
ıdaur.
Lumber & Mfg. Co. John Jan-
Pres.; John M. Jansen, Secy.,
s. & Mgr.
HA—
Burr, 214 Park St.
Gottfriedsen, 79 N. Main St.
Lothrop, Park St.
anner, First. St.
OSSE—
Hart Implement Co. H. C.
, Sr., Pres., Treas., Mgr.; H.
art, Jr., Secy.
nb Lumber Co.
Marden.
Paul Lumber Co.
GENEVA—
· Lumber Co.

LANCASTER—
Eastman Lumber Co. E. W. Eastman, Mgr. (Mineral Point, Wis.)

MADISON—
Conklin & Sons.
C. F. Cooley.
Chr. Lawrence.
Troan & Erdall.

MANITOWOC—
Peter Endries & Co.
J. G Johnson Co.
Manitowoc Land & Salt Co.

MARINETTE—
Lyon Bros. & Co.
Moore Bros & Co.

MARSHFIELD—
Ebbe & Thompson.
John A. Hoffman.

MENASHA—
H. H. Plummer.

MENOMINEE—
F. C. Michaels.
John Hopwood.

MERRILL—
H. Allen.
W. R. Bryan.
C. M. Howard, 204 Cottage St.
R. Trontrow & Co.

MILWAUKEE—
Adamant Mfg. Co., 480 Virginia St.
Berthelet Sewer Pipe Co., 152 W. Water St.
Bond Lime & Cement Co., 421 3rd St.
Chicago Ballast Co.
Consolidated Milwaukee Cement Co., 509 Goldsmith St.
Durr Plaster Co., 311 Grove St.
Hugh L. Gaffney Co., 302 Germania Bldg.
Illinois Leather Co., Canal St. Vogel's Island.
Val Jesion & Co., 718 Clinton St.
George Lund, 180 Clinton St.
Daniel Mayer, 469 3rd St.
Milwaukee Cement Co., 7 Plankinton Bldg.
Perkins & Co., 147th St.
W. H. Pipkorn & Co., 417 11th St.
Pipkorn & Tews, Humboldt Ave. & Commerce.
Ricketson & Schwartz, 35 University Bldg.
Sarnow Lime Co., N. W. cor. Vliet & 33d St.
W. G. Taylor Co., 432 Broadway.
Whitnall & Rademaker Co., 211 Grand Ave.
Western Portland Cement Co., 135 Grand Ave.
Julius Wettendorf, 189 Lloyd St.
Western Lime and Cement Co., 211 Grand Ave.

MINERAL POINT—
Eastman Lumber Co., E. W. Eastman, Mgr.; W. Eastman, Pres., Platteville, Wis.

MONROE—
Carroll Bros.
Dodge Lumber Co.
James Lumber Co.

MONTFORT—
Eastman Lumber Co., E. W. Eastman, Mgr., (Mineral Point, Wis.)

NEENAH—
Neenah Sewer Pipe Co.
Defnet & Jensen.

NEILLSVILLE—
Denis Towrigny.

NEW LONDON—
E. E. Consins.
Merton & Mack.
John P. Thorn.

OCONTO—
James Megar.

OSHKOSH—
Cook & Brown Lime Co.
Chris Johnson.
Kusche & Bro. Lime Co.

PLATTEVILLE—
Eastman Lumber Co.; N. Eastman, Pres.; M. Eastman, Sec.; O. A. Eastman, Treas.

PORTAGE—
C. F. Mohr.

PORT WASHINGTON—
C. A. Mueller.
Frank Schumacher.

PRESTON—
Eastman Lumber Co., E. W. Eastman, Mgr. (Mineral Point, Wis.).

PRINCETON—
Frank Giese.
Elmer Morse.
Frank Jahr.

RACINE—
David Lawton.

REEDSBURG—
Morgan Bldg. Co.
Reedsburg B. & L. Co.
Townsand Bros.
West Side Lumber Co.

REWEY—
Eastman Lumber Co. E. W. Eastman, Mgr. (Mineral Point, Wis.)

RICHLAND CENTER—
A. H. Krouskop.

RIPON—
Barnett & Anderson.
Gillett & Son.
Horner & Middleton.
Ed Pedrick.

Mem. Am. Soc. C. E. Mem. Am. Soc. M. E.
OLIN H. LANDRETH
Engineering Laboratory:
Union College: Schenectady, N. Y.
CONSULTING ENGINEER
Expert Tests, Investigations and Reports on
Cements, Cement Rock and
Building Materials.

RIVER FALLS—
A. F. Cargill.
F. D. [illegible].
Ulnch & Anderson.

SHAWANO—
Schweers Bros.
Upham & Russell Co.
A. Wipperman.

SHEBOYGAN—
Sheboygan Lime Works.
Henry Schaetle, jr., 112 N. 8

SHELL LAKE—
W. B. Curtis.
Shell Lake Lumber Co.
J. H. Shields.

SHULLSBURG—
Eastman Lumber Co. E.
man, Mgr. (Mineral Pt.,

SPARTA—
Brittingham & Hixon Lum
J. D. Young Lumber Co.

STOUGHTON—
E. H. Gerard.
H. T. Hanson.
Heddles Lumber Co.

SUPERIOR—
Superior Supply & Fuel Co.,
Ave.
Warehouse & Builders' Su
E. S. Tower, Bay Slip.
W. J. Wheeler, 8th & Nettle

TOMAH—
E. A. Dakers.
W. Earle & Co.

TOMAHAWK—
Bradley Co.
Evenson Bro.

TWO RIVERS—
Henry Koppelman.

VAUGHN—
Daniel Reid Harley.

WASHBURN—
P. A. Oscar.

WATERTOWN—
J. Burns.
P. J. Euper.
Tatzlaff & Co.

WAUKESHA—
A. J. Gittner & Co.
Palmetier & Abell.
Wilbur Lumber Co.

WAUPACA—
K. T. Chandler.
Hans Ebbe.

WAUPUN—
Caldwell & Loomans.
Crowley Lumber Co.

WAUSAU—
W. R. Bryan.
Henry Goebel.
August Klosterman.
F. W. Krause.
Wm. Paff.

WYOMING.

CHEYENNE—
Morrison, Merrill & Co.

ı & Employes Co.
liday Co.
,E—
Mer. Co.
ining Co.

Box 90.
-
umber Co.
nber Co.
ımber Co.
CANADA.
N. S.—
rry & Co.

Sarjeant.

E—
n Co.
ker.
MAN.—
O'Hara.
itchell.
Ifg. Co.
Long.
Co.
& McDearmid.
E. ONT.—
ynolds.
n Co.
rt.
y.
ALBERTA—
lw. Co.
: Co.
& Co.
ORD, ONT.—
)wen.
ıglas.
ın Co.
PLACE, ONT.—
ıead.
eton.
s. & Co.
TOWN, P. E. I.—
s.
dgers.
NT.—
owland.
Bro.
)NT.—
ım.
et.
.
son.
ONT.—

& Son.
H, N. S.—
inson.
y.
os.
), ONT.—
ın Co.

DRESDEN, ONT.—
Joshua Wright.
DUNNVILLE, ONT.—
Congdon & Marshall.
James Rolston.
John Taylor.
FORT WILLIAM, ONT.—
W. H. MacKuerot & Co.
W. S. Piper.
FREDERICTON, N. B.—
R. Chestnut & Sons.
James S. Neill.
Gus Tweedale & Co.
GLENCOE, ONT.—
Gillespie & Co.
Huston & Co.
I M. Kellar.
GODERICH, ONT.—
F. B. Holmes.
Charles Reid & Co
GUELPH, ONT.—
John M. Bond & Co
John Kennedy.
George B. Morris.
George A. Richard & Son.
HALIFAX, N. S.—
Black Bros. & Co., 49 Upper Water St.
T. A. S. De Wolfe & Son, 135 Upper Water St.
William Stairs, Sons & Morrow, 174 Lower Water St.
HULL, QUE.—
Wright & Co.
JOLIETTE, QUE.—
Charles Leblanc.
M. H. Leprohon.
J. H. Renaud.
J. C. Theriault.
KENTVILLE, N. S.—
T. P. Calkin & Co.
T. L. Dodge & Co.
KINGSTON, ONT.—
Jno. Corbett, 95 Princess St.
Dalton & Strange, 177 Princess St.
W. A. Mitchell, 85 Princess St.
G. W. Sears, 69 Princess St.
Simmons Bros., 211 Princess St.
Archibald Stracham, 198 Princess St.
LINDSAY, ONT.—
R. Bryans & Co.
J. G. Edwards & Co.
McLennan & Co.
W. G. Woods.
LONDON, ONT.—
Bowman & Co.
W. J. Element.
LONG POINT, CAN.—
Thos. M. Morgan.
MADOC, ONT.—
S. Rollins.
MAGOG, P. Q.—
Ambroise Hamel.
David Pepin.
MILTON, ONT.—
Mr. Clements.
Mr. Dewar.

MONCTON, N. B.—
Robertson & Givan.
Summer & Co.

MONTREAL, QUE.—
Bellhouse, Dillon & Co., 30 St. Frs. Xavier.
Alex. Bremner, 50 Bleury St.
F. P. & W. Currie, 134 McGill St.
The Forsyth Granite and Marble Co., Ltd., 552 Williams St. Robt. Forsyth, Pres. & Mgr.; John Duthie, Sec. & Trea.
W. McNally & Co., 38-50 McGill St.
The St. Lawrence Cem. Co., 2664 Notre Dame St.

MOUNT FOREST, ONT.—
J. P. Noonan.
Scott & Murphy.
C. J. Thornhill.
L. H. Yoemans.

NANAIMO, B. C.—
A. R. Johnson & Co.
W. McCape.

NEW WESTMINSTER, B. C.—
R. F. Anderson & Co.
Bellysa & Co.
Cunningham Hardware Co.
Gilley Bros.

NIAGARA FALLS, ONT.—
R. Coulson.
J. E. Hutchings & Co.
Cole & McMurray.
W. E. Thomas.

NORWICH, CAN.—
Chas. E. Boyd.

ORANGEVILLE, ONT.—
Adamson, Heath & Sproul.
F. J. Marshall.

OSHAWA, ONT.—
T. Brathwaite.
J. E. Hawkins.
Lander Bros.

OTTAWA, ONT.—
T. Sidney Kirby & Co., Sussex St.
E. G. Laverdure & Co., 71 William St.
McCullough & Cowan, 39 Sparks St.
Dan'l O'Connor, jr., 298 Bank St.
The Ottawa Fireproof Supply Co., 514 Sussex St.
Wright & Co., 43 Besseur St.

PAISLEY, ONT.—
A. Sinclair.

PEMBROKE, ONT.—
Dunlap & Co.
G. M. M. Hunter.

PETERBOROUGH, ONT.—
The Kingan Hardware Co.
Micks & Co.
Peterborough Hdwe Co.
The Rathbun Co.

PICTON, N. S.—
Barry Bros.
I. Carson & Sons.
J. and J. Yorston.

PICTON, ONT.—
Carter Bros.
R. Haddon.
A. W. Hepburn.
The Rathbun Co.

PORTAGE LA PRAIRIE, MAN.—
T. M. Bearnish.

PORT ARTHUR, ONT.—
The Marks & Clavet Lobie Co.
Wells & Emmerson.

PRESCOTT, ONT.—
R. W. Ross & Co.
N. Willard & Co.

RENFREW, ONT.—
P. S. Stewart Co.

ROSSLAND, B. C.—
Hunter Bros.
Red Star Storage & Trans. Co.
Steen & Co.

ST. ANDREWS, N. B.—
W. D. Forster.
G. D. Grinmer.
Hartt & Greenlaw.
J. A. Shirley.

ST. CATHARINES, ONT.—
Samuel Boyd.
Coy Bros.
McEdward & Moore.
Newman Bros.
John Nicholls.
H. J. Riddle.

ST THOMAS, ONT.—
F. M. Griffin.

SARNIA, ONT.—
James Lockhart.

SAULT STE. MARIE, ONT.—
I. J. Downey.
Moore & Brown.
Northern Hardware Co.
W. H. Plummer & Co.

SHALLOW LAKE, ONT.—
Owen Sound Portland Cement Co.

SHERBROOK, QUE.—
Codere Fils, et Cie.
Loomis & Sons.
Mitchell & Co.

SIMCOE, ONT.—
Charles Allen.
J. B. Jackson.

STRATFORD, ONT.—
Brigham & Ingram.

TILSONBURG, ONT.—
C. M. Brookfield.
T. Crawford.

TORONTO, ONT.—
C. G. Collins, 11 George St.
A. I. Ferguson, 215 Queen St., E
W. H. Knowlton, 36 King St., E.
John Lucas, 377 Spadina Ave.
Maguire Bros., 84 Adelaide St., W.
Ontario Lime Assoc., 118 Esplanade St., E.
Paterson Mfg. Co., 361 King St., E.

YFIELD, QUEBEC—
on & Cie.
ngevin.
Leger.
Morond.
Wilson.

UVER, B. C.—
Portland Cement Co.
np & Co.
, Coleman & Evans.

ERTON, ONT.—
Bros.
Vigan.

Y, ONT.—
& Granger.
& Bro.

WINGHAM, ONT.—
Jno. Clegg & Co.
Smith & Pethick.

CITY OF WINNIPEG, MAN.—
Buchanan & Gordon.
Dobson & Jackson.
Kelly Bros. & Co.
W. F. Lee.

WOODSTOCK, N. B.—
H. E. Burtt.
W. F. Dibble & Son.

YARMOUTH N. S.—
S. A. Crowell & Co.
E. K. Spinney.

CUBA.

HAVANA—
Howard Egleston.

A LITTLE TALK ABOUT BUSINESS

"I like a proposition that pays."
—C. P. HUNTINGTON.

THIS PAYS!

HERE are certain things that a man in business must do. He must have an office, he must put out a sign, and he must advertise.

He must make himself known to the people who may be interested in his kind of business. The better he does this the more successful he will be.

Some of the most successful men make it a rule to spend one-fifth of their income in advertising, and they find it pays.

It makes poor business good.

It makes good business better.

The best way to advertise is to put your advertisement where it will go directly to the people who want what you sell.

We give the kind of advertising that goes directly to the right spot.

If your business is not in line with the kind our readers are interested in, we don't want you to advertise in our magazine.

If it is, we can help you, and we can give you more for your money than you can get from any other expenditure of it.

From Sacramento (Cal.) Record-Union:

"MUNICIPAL ENGINEERING has often been pronounced in these columns the most useful, practical magazine of the age, and we adhere to that judgment."

MUNICIPAL ENGINEERING MAGAZINE

Awarded Grand Prize by Paris Exposition of 1900
Holds Medal from the Chicago World's Fair

CONTRACTORS AND LARGE USERS OF CEMENT.

ALABAMA.

)N—
ıke.
ser.
& Wolsoncraft.
Iudson.
.LE—
)aniel.
Moore.
GHAM—
Burkhalter & Co.
Cornish, 1235 S. 21st. St.
n & Colvin.
& Lallande Bros.
ulmer.
. Krebs.
La Coste.
:Poland.
n Construction Co.
—
ee Coal, Iron & Railroad Co.
ILLE—
kerman.
Bost.
Brandon.
Hutchens.
—
ormby.
—
Chamberlain.
y Paving Co., 56 S. N. Mich-

Manville.
:Adory, 413 St. Francis.
Paving Co., 57 St. Francis.
Robinson Contracting Co.
Worthington.
MERY—
Crombie & Williams.
Ford & Co.
ewman & Co.
Talbot & Co.
CITY—
ılpepper.
agan.

ennett.
ELD—
Brick & Lumber Co.
Hagler.
ohnson.

TUSCALOOSA—
Finnell Bros.
Finnell & McCalla.
TUSCUMBIA—
Aaron Bresler.
Franke Gautman.
UNION SPRINGS—
H. O. Foster.
WOODLAWN—
J. L. Burns.
Gibson Mfg. Co.
J. R. Griffith.
E. L. Quironet.

ARIZONA.

DUNCAN—
Ward & Courtney.
PHOENIX—
J. D. Brooks.
M. Beverly Cox.
Clinton Campbell.
Fifield & Gallagher.
Goff & Galpin.
H. B. Kersting.
James O'Conner.
Charles Peterson.
TUCSON—
Tucson Cement & Sidewalk Co.

ARKANSAS.

ARKANSAS CITY—
Whitehall & Co.
BATESVILLE—
Frank Joblin.
M. M. Stuart.
CAMDEN—
James Mendenhall.
CONWAY—
J. M. Courtney.
G. W. Donaghey.
FORT SMITH—
Andrew Elefson, 1015 North Seventh
J. L. Girard, 717 Garrison Ave.
L. S. O'Neil, 607 North Thirteenth
Southwestern Engineering & Construction Co.
HELENA—
Allen Bros. Paving Co.
Edwin Miller Paving Co.
T. H. Rice.

HOT SPRINGS—
Mike Jodd.
John Kelly.
H. N. Weideman.
LITTLE ROCK—
John Bethuns, 2600 Cumberland St.
J. R. Blalock, 614 Center St.
Julius Brandt, 1209 Barber Ave.
E. J. Fisher, 823 W. Fourth St.
J. G. Huber, 2004 West Seventeenth
J. C. Hutton, 1419 Poplar N. L. R.
W. H. Lambert, N. L. R.
W. H. Lambertson, N. L. R.
H. Weideman, 1401 Izard St.

CALIFORNIA.

ALAMEDA—
B. F. Corry, 2222 Buena Vista St.
L. V. Corry, 2222 Buena Vista St.
Emil Kirchoff, 1710 Grand.
A. Kynock, 1248 Versailles Ave.
A. Le Plant, 840 Oak St.
D. G. Mackenzie, 2020 Clinton.
Jas. Potts, 2066 Alameda Ave.
Powell Bros., 2260 Central Ave.
V. C. Stanguist, 3249 Encinal St.
BAKERSFIELD—
J. S. Carroll.
C. J. Lingren.
Peck Bros.
C. H. Quincey.
BERKELEY—
R. J. Carter.
Herman Eruska.
J. A. Marshall.
M. Murphy.
DUARTE—
B. R. Davisson.
FRESNO—
Edward C. Bacon.
Thomas Barrett.
W. S. Betteridge.
Lewis Cook.
C. J. Craycroft.
Jos. Spinney.
LONG BEACH—
M. S. Cummings.
Jas. Dovey.
J. Driskill.
Chas. Mushrush.
GRASS VALLEY—
D. E. Matteson.
L. E. Pingree.
HANFORD—
Central Lumber Co.
L. Davis.
Wendling Lumber Co.
LOS ANGELES—
A. M. Austin, 1422 Bush St.
L. Brodie, 1006 E. 18th St.
G. S. Brown, 419 N. Burlington Ave.
W. F. Burnham, 949 E. 33d St.
F. W. Caley, 512 Crocker.
A. E. Chaffey, Stowell Blk.
Clemens & Son, 1216 Catalina.
M. A. Cumming, 299 N. Ave.
J. A. Daniels, 1626 Palo Alto.

Los Angeles—Continued.
J. A. Fairchild, 837 S. Burlington Ave.
J. Flood, 208 Wilmington.
French & Reed, 107 N. Broadway.
Frick Brothers, 315 Requena.
J. M. Gardner, 40 Douglass Bldg.
F. Gillespie, 202 Nolan.
Grant Bros., 155 Wilson Blk.
Gray Brothers & Ward, 107 N. Broadway.
J. Hein, 1471 W. 25th St.
W. Hooker, 556 S. Hill St.
Hughes & Edwards, Gordon Blk.
R. Keating, 402 Douglass Bldg.
C. Leonardt, 438 Burne Bldg.
Frank Lindinfield, 310½ S. Los Angeles.
W. A. Link, Schumaker and Normandy.
Los Angeles City Water Company.
D. Madigan, 734 Jackson.
C. L. McCombs, Wilson Blk.
P. J. McCormack, 250 S. Bunker Hill.
S. McCrary, 905 E. 28th.
Wm. O. Newcomb, 2307 Romeo.
F. Niemann.
W. A. Norman, 626 San Pedro.
Odemar Brothers & Co., 213 W. 1st.
A. Olsen, 1821 W. Pico.
W. A. Paramore, 1619 Council.
E. C. Peck, 1321 Girard.
W. L. Peck, 210 E. 25th.
J. M. Piltlabo, 622 S. Hope.
J. A. Rhodes, 2122 E. 8th.
E. C. Rice, 2818 Maple Ave.
P. J. Richmond, 1622 Winfield.
F. L. & L. D. Rogers, 2907 Penn. Ave.
San Gabriel Electric Co., 254 S. Los Angeles St.
A. Sedine, 318 Court.
Edward Sheehan, 116 S. Flower.
Conrad Sheerer & Co., 237 W. 1st St.
P. C. Smith, 1543 Council.
Smith & Gavin, 937 Stanford.
A. Swensen, 225 Stinson Blk.
W. E. Thornton & Co., Wilson Blk.
F. B. Tilden, 477 N. Quebec.
J. B. Ware, 1128 S. Hill.
J. H. Watson, 438 E. Rice.
J. E. White, Fulton Blk.
Frank W. Whittier.
L. Wiedenman, 143 N. Daly.
W. L. Younger, 442 Victor.

MARYSVILLE—
I. Luke.
Swain & Hudson.

MODESTO—
Jas. Willison.

NAPA—
G. Errington.
C. H. Gildersleeve.
G. Knox.
J. M. Wetmore.
J. E. Wiedburger.

ND—
Arnott, 1722 San Pablo Ave.
Badgly, 1118 Broadway.
Burr, 421 Edward.
'arr, 806 Alice St.
'anaugh, 1408 Tel Ave.
Childs, 563 27th St.
ıbb, 1182 18th St.
ı. Coates, 526 2d St.
Brothers, 478½ 10th St.
ıney, 1463 3d St.
Dunlevey, Fruitvale, near
ıins.
)akland Contracting & Paving
1016 Broadway.
ı & Wilson, Macdonough Bldg.
Estey, 458 E. 17th St.
& Son, 467 10th St.
ry, 513 25th St.
ılavin, 126 4th St.
ıdman, 576 William St.
ıney, 828 Lydia St.
kett, 362 7th St.
Hagan, 2234 Andover St.
ey, 814 Brush St.
·afy, 466 24th St.
ıerin, 862 21st St.
tkes, 1172 7th St.
use & Reardon, 353 13th St.
Hord, 936 Filbert St.
hoe, 59 20th St.
ınedy, 819 22d St.
ian, 663 28th St.
ight, 1517 Brush St.
Matthews, 1307 Market St.
'arthy, 701 Brush St.
lvihill, 872 Mead Ave.
ıd Asphalt Paving Co., 11 and
acdonough Bldg.
ıd Concrete Co., 1203 Broadway.
ıd Construction Co., 458 9th St.
)akland Paving Co., Central
ı Bldg.
Artificial Stone Co. 468 10th
Phipps, 630 E. 12th.
ont Paving Co., Macdonough
.
ı Putnam, 1930 Broadway.
ıansome Concrete Construction
1016 Broadway.
temington, 2067 Market.
ırd Improvement Co., Central
ı Bldg.
nton, 1318 Tel Ave.
Stone, 900 Broadway.
Wicker, 1457 12th St.
ENA—
ı H. Dovey.
Edwards.
·w & Geo. Halloway.
lton & Phillips.
Hughes.
Smith.
& Roberts.
ΊA—
& Carson.
Fleming.

REDLANDS—
Southern California Power Co., 14-16 State St.

RIVERSIDE—
Concrete Pipe & Construction Co.
Fleck & Ormand.
C. P. Hancock.
Chas. Quast.

SACRAMENTO—
T. M. Burns, 22 & N St.
Carl & Crobey.
T. E. Clark, 617 15th St.
Henry Dehn, 2802 J St.
M. Kenny, Windsor Hotel.
Jas. McGillwray, 23 & F St.
R. W. Parker, 1908 M St.
Jas. Scholefield, 2213 L St.
J. D. Shearer, 2316 O St.
A. Teichert, 24th & J St.
Jas. Touhey, 1423 6th St.

SAN BERNARDINO—
Jno. Driver.
Nathan Philbrook.
Ernest Vinoger.

SAN DIEGO—
John Engelbret and Olaf Nelson.
Goodbody & Sons.
Goodbody & Roisner.
Jos. Kelly.
Jas. McNair.
Frank Mesner.
Wm. Osborne.
J. Frank Over.
Over & Nagle.
Simpson & Perine.
W. S. Waterman.

SAN FRANCISCO—
Alcatraz Asphalt Co., 206-7 Crocker Bldg.
Jas. H. Bingham, 406 Buchanan.
Bonnot Bonnot, 100 Montgomery St.
Buckman Contracting Co., 508 California.
Martin Buzzini, 4045 26th St.
California Concrete Co., 220 Montgomery St
Alex L. Campbell, 40 New Montgomery St.
City Street Improvement Co., Mills Bldg.
Cushing-Wetmore Co., 19 Montgomery.
Bryan Diggins, 2416 Sutter St.
Philip S. Fay, 124 Sansome St.
J. W. Ferris, 320 Sansome St.
Richard Flaherty, 35 Post St.
Flinn & Treacy, 303 Montgomery.
S. Gilletti System Co., 49 City Hall.
Geo. Goodman, 307 Montgomery.
Grant Bros., Chronicle Bldg.
Gray Bros., 228 Montgomery.
Carl Griese, 40 New Montgomery.
H. H. Grussel, 718 Valencia.
C. C. W. Haum, 313 28th St.
Healy, Tibbets & Co., 42 Stewart St.
Jas. A. Hulling, 229 9th Ave.
Dennis Jordan, 633 Webster.
Richard Keatinge, 40 New Montgomery.

San Francisco—Continued.

Pacific Paving Co., 118 Phelan Bldg.
Thos. B. Roche, 318 Bush.
San Francisco Construction Co., 308 California St.
San Francisco Paving Co., 508 California St.
Santa Cruz Contracting Co., 11 Montgomery St.
Peter Sexton, 406 McAllister.
Steiger Terra Cotta and Pottery Works, 155 Market St.
F. M. Stevens, Larkin and Market Sts.
Geo. Stone, Claus Spreckles Bldg.
E. R. Thomason, 20 Phelan Bldg.
Union Paving and Contracting Co., 80 Flood Bldg.
Clarence D. Vincent, Mills Bldg.
C. A. Warren, 232 Montgomery St.
Williams, Belser & Co., 302 Montgomery St., room 2.
L. G. Young, 1 8th St.

SAN JOSE—
T. A. Brookbanks, 357 S. 1st.
C. E. Colahan, 398 W. Santa Clara.
Thos. P. Doyle, 70 Delmar Ave.
S. Fisher, 10th & Wash.
G. W. Hanson, 36 S. 2d.
Jno. McReynolds, 243 N. 13th.
L. C. Otto, 36 S. 2d.
J. Riechers & Son, 36 S. 2d.
Peter Rosenbaum, 167 N. 7th.
Smith & Stadler, 54 N. 1st.
J. Stanley, Mission St.

SAN LEANDRO—
J. R. Faulkes.
E. B. Stone & Co.

SANTA ANA—
J. Dawson.
H. E. Finester.
C. E. Gronard.
Frank Hiel.
Chris McNeill.
H. E. Smith.

SANTA BARBARA
J. C. Phillips.
John Williamson.

SANTA CLARA—
T. P. Cunningham.

SANTA MONICA—
C. L. Powell.

SANTA ROSA—
W. L. Nagel.
J. W. Swank.

STOCKTON—
H. E. Barber.
Clark & Henery.
Hammond & Yardley.
Hedges & Buck.
Smith & Rice.
Southworth, Cratton & Co.
Turner Bros.

VALLEJO—
P. McDonnell.
John McManus.

VENTURA—
H. A. Giddings.

WATSONVILLE—
James Haigard.
A. R. Wilson.

WOODLAND—
H. T. Barnes.
John Campbell.
H. Ervin.

COLORADO.

CENTRAL CITY—
Quigley & Co.

COLORADO CITY—
E. C. Strott.
E. & R. W. Waycott.

COLORADO SPRINGS—
A. W. Atkinson, 230 E. Da
Lynn S. Atkinson, 23 W. H
Colorado Springs Stone & Co., 115 E. Bijou.
L. E. Davie, 25 E. Pike's Pe
S. M. Goshen, 122 N. Tejon
C. H. & H. G. Grimwood, Bijou.
Hart & Son, 115 E. Bijou.
Ord & Swope, 120 E. Verm
Schlessinger & Strott, 26 E fano.

DENVER—
The American Monolith Co.
Bermudez Blake Contracting Boston Bldg.
W. C. Bradbury & Co., 5 road Building.
Brown Contracting Co., 1135 1
Colorado Mantel and Tile Stout St.
Colorado Paving Co., 52 Bldg.
T. W. Cook & Co., 1623 Trem
Combs & Sess, 522 15th St.
Denver Mantel and Tile C Court Place.
Denver Mosaic and Tile Co., Colfax Ave.
Denver Paving Co., Railroad
Denver Sewer Pipe and Clay
Denver Terra Cotta Lumber
Denver Wire and Iron Work
Geo. Freund & Co.
Willam Hayden, P. O. Box
Hughes & Stewart, 804 People Bldg.
Johnson & Sorenson.
Frank Kirchof, 1942 Curtis St.
Chas. McBride, 2426 Stout St.
Chas. M. McCabe, 1849 Emers
John A. McIntyre, 402 Cooper
Z. E. Moncrief, rear 1119 19th
John H. Nooney Tile Co., 34 fax Ave.
John M. O'Rourke Construct 1115 Larimer St.
Renton Fire Proofing Co., 1 pahoe St.
Sayre-Newton Lumber Co.
Senbert & Heimbecher, 729 15t
William Simpson, 1642 Champ

:ontinued.
. Teller, 706 Equitable Bldg.
Valdo, 1246 Curtis St.
n Realty and Paving Co., 304 House Blk.
NCE—
& Welsh.
ce Water Dept. H. E. Kil- Supt.
man & Hendritsh.
vart.
:OLLINS—
Button.
Conley.
Fuller.
Loveland.
Pierce.
Walker.
N—
H. Gow.
JUNCTION—
Lumsden.
& Dexter.
EY—
& Garden.
Nusbaum.
ILLE—
H. Saum.
J. Moran, 411 W. Eighth St.
V. Turpin, 431 E. Ninth St.
ONT—
Brown.
Hall.
Schoolcraft.
Wiggins.
—
's Carney.
Taylor.
Whinnerah.
O—
do Stone and Flagging Co., ral Blk.
ng Trading Co.
& Powers.
Summers & Co.
FORD—
Blomgren.
ley & Gobin.
—
& Turner.
RIDE—
n Anderson.
. Cameron.
Reed.
AD—
Carlson.
Henry.
Krug & Co.
Pierce.
V. Poole.
llivan.
Wilkins.
IA—
ally.

CONNECTICUT.

ANSONIA—
A. B. & C. Co.
Wm. Bothwell.
Royal Halbrook.
Thos. Hennessey.
W. N. Houghtaling.
Wm. Potter.
C. B. Wooster.

BETHEL—
E. T. Andrews.
P. Dolan.
P. McDonald.

BRIDGEPORT—
W. S. Bullard.
Burns & Co.
Oliver B. Cole.
E. T. Doolittle.
M. O'Connor.
B. D. Pierce, Jr., Co.
Standard Asphalt Co.
Stillman & Godfrey.
The Williams & Dewhurst Co.

BRISTOL—
Geo. C. Arms.
P. J. Coleman.
Ira Gaylord.
T. H. Keirns.
Wm. Linsted.
J. M. White.

DANBURY—
John P. Beard, 43 Spring St.
F. C. Benjamin & Co., 11-13 Spring St.
Jas. L. Sherman, 10 Balmforth Ave.
Wardell Bros. & Co.

DANIELSON—
J. G. Gilbert.

DERBY—
F. H. Fagan Co.
J. C. Gilligan.
R. T. Patchen & Son.

GREENWICH—
Banks & Brush.
Thos. Eagan.

HARTFORD—
Daniel Ahern, 38 Crown St.
Charles B. Andrus, 902 Main St.
William Angus, 110 Oak St.
Angus & Chesebro, 31 Warner St.
Billings Sidewalk and Masons' Supply Co., 154 Charter Oak St.
Barrett Bros., 10 Trumbull St
Hiram Bissell, 43 Wadsworth St.
Watson H. Bliss, 17 Lewis St.
S. B. Bosworth, 42 Front St.
William J. Bray, 35 Imlay St.
Henry A. Budde, 103 Hungerford St.
E. W. Clarke & Son, 32 Village.
George E. Dennison, 168 Pearl St.
E. F. Ede, 3 Pawtucket St.
John P. Hills, 754 Main St.
Hills & Fox, 50 John St.
D. W. Hollis & Son, 212 Asylum St.
Robert Moore, Sheldon and Taylor Sts.
Michael O'Neil, 24 Pawtucket St.

Hartford—Continued.
William F. O'Neil, 172 Farmington Ave.
A. W. Scoville, 902 Main St.
Michael Sheedy, 75 Franklin Ave.
Southern New England Paving Co., 141 Trumbull St.
Watson, Tyron & Son, 720 Main St.
Watson & Jackson, 283 Sheldon St.

JEWETT CITY—
F. H. Gilbert.
John E. Green.
Richard Howard.

MERIDEN—
John F. Dahill.
John S. Lane & Son.

MIDDLETOWN—
A. Brazos & Sons.
Roger Kennedy.

MILFORD—
Edw. N. Clark.

NAUGATUCK—
J. H. Dunn.
Ham & Tuttle.
Chas. M. Potter, P. O. Box 276.
M. F. McCabe.

NEW BRITAIN—
M. S. Austin.
Geo. A. Cadwell.
John Canfield.
Doolittle Bros.
John Hanna's Son.
A. A. Lyman.
John Nolan.
R. G. Ramage.
W. B. Sparks & Son.

NEW HAVEN—
C. W. Blakeslee & Son, 58 Waverly St.
Geo. Bohn & Sons, 470 Congress Ave.
A. Brazos & Sons, 808 Elm St.
D. G. Carmichael, 11 Cassius St.
C. W. Clark & Son, 173 Long Wharf.
Connecticut Concrete Co., 40 Church St.
Coyne Bros. Concrete Co., 250 Blatchley Ave.
J. A. Doolitle & Co., 179 Church St.
Fair Haven Concrete Co., 2 Cedar Hill Ave.
The Geo. M. Grant Co., 133 Union St.
C. W. Kellog & Co., 506 State St.
Chas. B. Kinney Co., 61 Orange St.
J. N. Leonard & Co., 21 Sylvan Ave.
Patrick Maher, 283 Sherman Ave.
Laurence O'Brien, 70 Beach St.
R. Redfield & Sons, 800 George St.
C. Dwight Robinson, 442 State St.
Sperry & Treat, 39 Church St.
John P. Thompson, 962 Grand Ave.
Vermont Construction Co.
Jos. B. Whitby, 29 Auburn.

NEW LONDON—
Benjamin Andre, 88 Williams St.
H. O. Burch & Co., 410 Grand St.
Frank P Driesbach.
Michael H. Fitzgerald, 6 Truman.

New London—Continued.
Elisha Post, Gardner Ave., nea Montauk.
H. E. Rogers, 41 Grand St.

NORWALK—
Salvator Charriot.
Frank F. Clark, Newton Ave.
H. O. Clark.
John W. Edmunds, 13 Wall St.
Lathrop & Shea.
C. T. Leonard & Co.
John B. Morton, 58 Taylor Ave.
Raymond Bros.
Henry A. Sanders.
Wm. Sheldon.

NORWICH—
Carpenter & Williams.
Chas. W. Burton.
Cruthers & Lillibridge.
Chas. S. Fiske.
A. B. Nickerson.
Peck, McWilliams & Co.
Frank G. Rice.
Ringland Bros.
Torrance & Matthews.

ORANGE—
L. A. Brown.
O. W. Dutcher.
John L. Sherman.
H. P. Wheeler.

PLAINVILLE—
R. G. Hart.

PLANTSVILLE—
Luther Barnes.
T. W. Conles.

PUTNAM—
A. L. Arnold & Co.
C. H. Kelly.
Wheaton Bldg. and Lbr. Co.

ROCKVILLE—
R. Farrell.
Jos. Fitzgerald.
A. E. Harris.
Chas. Raw.

SHELTON—
S. O. Daniell.
P. Murphy.

SOUTHINGTON—
Luther Barnes.
J. W. Francis.
J. F. Knapp.
Thomas & Nolan.
A. N. Woodruff.

STAFFORD SPRINGS—
A. E. Converse.

STAMFORD—
Elam Ballard.
Bell & Suly.
Leonard Blondel.
A. E. Bounty.
M. S. Brown.
F. A. Buttrey.
Corbo Bros.
Dean & Horton.
Cornelius Holly.
Frank Hook.

d—Continued.
Hornshaw.
& Whitehead.
McAdams.
Connell & **Sons.**
Paul.
: Shea.
Troy.
Vitt.
'ozella.
ie A. Wust.
NGTON—
Brayton.
y Budlon.
Vilcox.
FORD—
rs & Collins.
NGTON—
x.
Croft.
eson.
VILLE—
Jones.
NGFORD—
Crockett.
e Botsford.
mack Heating Co.
Ranford.
Redmond Co.
Ward.
tBURY—
t Bros. Co.
ew D. Byrnes, 90 Bank St.
eld & Chatfield, 55 Benedict St.
ity Contracting Co., 58 Centre

is Dooling, 64 Stone St.
ior Concrete Co.
. Gaffney & Co., 16 E. Main.
's Jackson & Son, 312 Bank

th & Son, 26 Magill St.
d McManus, 120 Bridge St.
Riggs, 107 Locust.
Bros. Co., 52 Benedict St.
bury Concrete Co., 283 Bank.
IANTIC—
Comins.
'd A. Jackson.
Jordan.
el Sullivan.
Sullivan.
ED—
Carey.
Johnson.
Adams.
Beers.

DELAWARE.

L—
& Bro.
—
s W. Johnston.
RD—
nin T. Collins.

WILMINGTON—
Davis & Bro., 827 Lombard.
Delaware Construction Co.
Diamond State Steel Co.
Harlan & Hollingsworth Co.
John Jacoby.
Lenderman & Bro.
Jas. M. Malloy.
Geo. W. McCaulley & Son, 103 W. 8th St.
Jas. McColgan, 1019 Lancaster Ave.
A. S. Reed & Bro. Co., 815 Shipley St.
Simmons & Bro.

DISTRICT OF COLUMBIA.

WASHINGTON—
Geo. W. Acorn, 1315 11th St., N. W.
Wm. C. Allard, 314 5th St., N. E.
Richard G. Alvey, 1251 K St., S. E.
James A. Anderson, 76 P St., N. W.
Max H. Andrae, 1532 10th St., N. W.
Wm. L. Argue, 503 7th St., N. W.
Wm. J. Babbington, 913 7th St., N. E.
Isaac M. Baker, 8 3d St., N. E.
John W. Baker, 715 3d St., N. E.
Barber & Rose, 614 11th St., N. W.
George M. Barker, 641 New York Ave., N. W.
George W. Barkman, 21 7th St., N. E.
William Barstow, 12 Hanover St., N. W.
Warren F. Basim, 612 M St., N. W.
John W. Beha, 619 N St., N. W.
Wm. F. Blaydes, 715 3rd St., N. E.
Francis A. Blundon, 67 S St., N. W.
John F. Blundon, 3900 T St., N. W.
Joseph A. Blundon, 1006 F St., N. W.
William L. Blunt, 1059 31st St., N. W.
Richard Bogan, 247 Pomeroy Ave.
George B. Boland, 101½ L St., N. W.
Thomas M. Bond, 2108 18th St., N. W.
Frederick W. Booth, 1640 Columbia Rd., N. W.
Orlando Bradt, Tunlaw Rd., N. W.
John W. Brashears, Winthrop Heights.
Warren F. Brenizer, 63 R St., N. W.
Brennan Construction Co., 902 F St., N. W.
Aloysius P. Brosnahan, 811 10th St., N. E.
Austin P. Brown, 1416 F St., N. W.
William Brown, 238 Oriel Ct., N. E.
Arthur C. Burch, 42 N. Y. Ave., N. W.
Michael Burke, 495 L St., S. W.
Herman Burgess, Brookland.
John N. Burlew, 2d and N, N. W.
James Burns, 1420 A St., S. E.
Henry T. Burrows, River Rd.
Robert Burrows, Murdock Mill Rd.
Orlando W. Butler, 16 Fillmore St., Anacosta.

Washington—Continued.

Bartholomew A. Callan, 301 McLean Ave., S. W.
James S. Capps, 402 Florida Ave., N. W.
Frank S. Carmody, 339 1st St., N. E.
John P. Carmody, 324 Massachusetts Ave.
Simon Carmody, 339 1st. St., N. E.
Wm. Carr, 2212 2d St., N. W.
Wm. B. Catching, 1925 G St., N. W.
John S. Catts, 1211 D St., S. W.
Michael H. Cavanaugh, 521 13th St., N. W.
Fred'k H. Chaffee, 1079 32d St., N. W.
Robert Clarkson, 1238 5th St., N. W.
Wm. M. Clayton & Co., 508 11th St., N. W.
Anthony M. Clegg, 908 G St., N. W.
Colburn Paving Co., 1425 N. Y. Ave., N. W.
James M. Coleman, 621 Florida Ave., N. W.
Joseph W. Collins, 1016 T St., N. W.
Robert Collins, 820 North Carolina Ave., S. E.
William P. Collins, 628 H St., S. W.
Benj. P. Connick, 1225 I St., S. E.
George O. Cook, 10 B St., N. E.
James H. Cooper, 1348 Wallach Pl., N. W.
John Herbert Corning, 520 13th St., N. W.
Arthur Cowstill, 1110 F St., N. W.
Cranford Paving Co., 1418 F St., N. W.
Geo. W. Daut, 520 7th St., S. W.
Geo. W. Darby, 830 9th St., N. W.
Rezin W. Darby, 1062 32d St., N. W.
Washburn E. Davis, 615 C St., N. E.
Samuel W. Deckman, 210 D St., S. E.
Edmund J. De Lacy, 1810 5th St., N. W.
John Devine, 1240 32d St., N. W.
Wm. B. Douglass, 323 Maryland Ave., N. E.
Geo. W. Dove, 1329 T St., N. W.
James A. Dowrick, 1625 1st St., N. W.
Fredk. Drew, 1814 4th St., N. W.
Alexander Duehay, 1215 Vermont Ave., N. W.
Daniel A. Duffy, 1905 4th St., N. W.
James M. Dunn, 1324 5th St., N. W.
Nicholas Eckhardt, 1140 18th St., N. W.
Beverly H. Ellett, 220 12th St., S. W.
John H. Ellis, 1118 6th St., N. W.

Washington—Continued.

Wm. H. Ellis, 1425 New York Ave., N. W.
Louis H. Emmert, 1419 G St., N. W.
Henry W. Eno, 34 Harrison St., Anacostia.
Charles Ernst, 22 Q St., N. E.
Charles H. Eslin, 3531 13th St., N. W.
Ferdinand Espey, 412 10th St., S. E.
Frank J. Ettinger, 207 12th St., N. W.
Frank D. Evans, 1214 21st St., N. W.
Fahey & Co., Washington Sav. Bank Bldg.
Andrew J. Fisher, 921 Virginia Ave., S. W.
Wm. B. Fowler, 12th St. & Mt. Olivet Ave.
Geo. F. Freeman, 405 21st St., N. W.
Wm. F. Garber, 1337 N St., N. W.
Charles E. Getz, 621 I St., N. W.
Henry P. Gilbert, 1062 32d St., N. W.
Andrew Glesson, 1216 N. Capitol St.
Charles E. Goodman, 1837 6th St., N. W.
Wm. C. Goodwin, 737 Steuben St., N. W.
Philip N. Gottwals, 18 N St., N. W.
Lawrence J. Grant, 1005 1st St., N. W.
Percival B. Grant, 1635 New Jersey Ave., N. W.
Edward G. Gunnell, 612 F St., N. W.
Frank L. Hanvey, 213 12th St., N. W.
Gustav Hartig, 509 H St., N. E.
Louis N. Hays, Deanewood. N. W.
Louis Hays, 1001 7th St., N. W.
Robert C. Head, 1539 Columbia St., N. W.
George W. Heisley, 425 12th St., N. W.
Melvin H. Herriman, 224 12th St., S. E.
William Holmead, 3531 13th St., N. W.
Holtzclaw Bros., 1705 Penna. Ave., N. W.
Thomas C. Hoover, 835 4th St., N. E.
David Horan, 1013 3rd St., N. E.
William M. Horstkamp, 809 M St., N. W.
Geo. C. Hough, 508 F St., N. W.
Edward Howe, 1713 Florida Ave., N. W.
John H. Howlett, 1313 Wallach Pl., N. W.
John Hughes, Jr., Washington Sav. Bank Bldg.
Thomas Hughes, 58 New York Ave., N. W.

The Foremost Representative of American Cement Interests is Municipal Engineering Magazine
Subscription Price, $2.00 Per Year.

n—Continued.

y Hutchinson, 1331 G St.,

B. Iardella, 424 11th St., S. E.
Jackson, 923 L St., N. W.
W. Jones, Brookland.
ι. Jones, New Jersey Ave. &
, N. W.
F. Jones, 1613 Lincoln Ave.,

F. Jones, Jr., 1613 Lincoln
N. E.
Jones, 2043 Seaton St., N. E.
yce, 1142 18th St., N. W.
Joyce, 1142 18th St., N. W.
Kearn, 29 R St., N. W.
. Keene, Brightwood Park.
V. Kennedy, 1123 21st St., N.

. Keyes, 909 22nd St., N. W.
. Keyser, 618 G St., N. E.
llen, 3327 P St., N. W.
King, 751 Sheridan St., N.

J. King, 933 G St., N. W.
Kinney, 2000 N St., N. W.
Knight, 1015 C St., S. W.
Knighton, 922 2d St., N. E.
L. Kolb, 703 6th St., N. E.
I. Lamb, 615 15th St., N. E.
Landvoight, 2100 1st St.,

os., 112 12th St., S. E.
J. Lane, 1010 1st St., S. E.
A. Langley, 310 12th St.,

H. Lansdale, 1214 S St.,

ary, 1201 11th St., N. W.
Leathers, 623 4th St., N. W.
.. Lewis, Tennallytown.
F. Lewis, 1501 7th St.,

R. Lindsey, Kenilworth.
Lipscomb, 1416 F St., N. W.
Lloyd, 308 H St., N. W.
W. Loeffler, 2409 Brightwood
N. W.
V. Lowrey, 1512 6th St., N. W.
. Lukei, 812 5th St., N. E.
. Lyons, Metropolis View,

:Devitt, 40 R St., N. W.
cDonald, 3314 16th St., N. W.
I. McGill, McGill Bldg.
McGraw, 1837 L St., N. W.
:Gregor, 729 12th St., N. W.
McIntyre, 3221 Q St., N. W.
McNamara.
. Macarty, 1419 G St., N. W.
Maudley, 1638 12th St., N. E.
D. Manning, 440 8th St., S. W.
L. Marshall, 303 Massachu-
ιve., N. E.
V. Martin, 224 7th St., N. E.
ι. Masson, 26 Arthur St., Ana-

Washington—Continued.

William H. Matthews, 2113 E St., N. W.
Meads & Reynolds, 934 F St., N. W.
Frank E. Metcalf, 32 Quincy St., N. W.
Alexander Millar, 1215 Ohio Ave., N. W.
Julian J. Miller, 1385 Georgia Ave., S. E.
Henry C. Mockabee, 482 G St., S. W.
Peter J. Morris, 1137 C St., N. E.
Joseph Mullen, 420 11th St., N. E.
John A. Mulloy, 322 B St., S. E.
James K. Murphy, 509 7th St., N. W.
John Murphy, 1322 9th St., N. W.
John H. Murphy, 2082 35th St., N. W.
Murray Bros., 1944 2d St., N. W.
Luk E. Murtaugh, 1712 32d St., N. W.
Mathews Myers, 2338 Brightwood Ave., N. W.
Thomas F. Myers, Conduit Road.
John A. Narjess, 555 15th St., S. E.
National Contractors' Agency Co., 1413 G St., N. W.
John J. Neumeyer, 1305 5th St., N. W.
James F. Nolan, 1709 New Jersey Ave., N. W.
John H. Nolan, 1413 G St., N. W.
Timothy O'Brien F S N
Daniel O'Connor, 3319 R St., N. W.
James O'Day, 2436 K St., N. W.
Charles J. Ortlip, 1139 5th St., N. E.
Gilbert J. Osterman, 507 E. St., N. W.
James L. Parsons, 1425 New York Ave., N. W.
William A. Pate, 308 10th St., N. W.
Edwin Perry, Brightwood Park.
William M. Plummer, 412 7th St., S. E.
Thomas H. Power, 825 6th St., S. W.
Sam'l J. Prescott & Co., 507 12th St., N. W.
Franklin M. Proctor, 1232 6th St., N. W.
Samuel S. Richardson, 1335 N. St., N. W.
Richardson & Burgess, 613 14th St., N. W.
Richard W. Ricketts, Wisconsin Ave., N. W.
Luther W. Riley, 229 10th St., S. E.
Thos. W. Riley, foot 11th St.
John Roche, 23 P St., N. E.
Robert V. Rusk, 472 Louisiana Ave., N. W.
Edward O. Sanderson, 1106 7th St., S. E.
Edmund Saxton, 123 G St., N. E.
Henry Schneider, 1607 New Jersey Ave., N. W.
William Scooler, 2112 Ward Pl., N. W.
Samuel C. Scott, 425 7th St., S. E.
Franklin P. Serrin, Conduit R-

Daniel M. Shehan, 613 14th St., N. W.
W. H. Shoemaker, 229 Elm St., N. W.
Lewis N. Simpson, Brightwood Park.
William R. Skinner, Reno City.
F. S. Smith & Co., 1217 F St., N. W.
Richard H. Sorrell, 329 N St., S. W.
William W. Souder, 3413 Holmead Ave., N. W.
Wm. E. Spear, 20 Bliss Bldg.
Thos. M. Steep, 24th St., N. W.
Wm. H. B. Stout, 501 Stanton Pl., N. E.
John B. Stubbs, 1134 Florida Ave., N. E.
John W. Swainson, 627 H st., N. W.
Thomas W. Swart, 322 Mass. Ave., N. E.
Maurice F. Talty, 300 M St., N. E.
Stephen Talty, 300 M St., N. E.
Talty & Allen, 612 F St., N. W.
James Tenly, 511 S St., N. W.
Columbus Thomas, 1709 35th St., N. W.
Archibald Thompson, 1220 I St., N. E.
Jeremiah E. Thorne, 1627 16th St., N. W.
Bartley Thornton, 1130 23d St., N. W.
James F. Tilley, 525 13th St., N. W.
Charles V. Trott, 329 T St., N. W.
Wm. A. Vaughn, 1006 Conn. Ave., N. W.
Robert H. Voutz, 11 N St., N. W.
Noble J. Walker, Florida Ave. and 8th St., N. W.
John T. Walker & Sons, 1920 N St., N. W.
John T. Walker & Sons, 204 10th St., N. W.
Edward R. Walton, 139 E St., S. E.
Edward E. Ward, 1015 20th St., N. W.
Joshua N. Warfield, 472 Louisiana Ave., N. W.
E. G. Wates, 721 12th St., N. W.
Roderick D. Watson, 1212 C St., S. W.
Watts & Taylor, 523 9th St., N. W.
George Webster, Brightwood Park.
William J. Wells, 513 13th St., N. W.
Francis Wickline, 328 B St., N. E.
Wilfong & Fawcett, Amer. Univ. Park, N. W.
George Woodruff, Eckington Pl., N. E.
George E. Wyne, 417 11th St., S. W.
James M. York & Son, 912 G St., N. W.
Wm. Yost & Bro., 1002 Penna. Ave., S. E.
Thomas G. Young, 247 Elm St., N. W.
Emory W. Yount, 411 9th St., S. W.

Thos. Eastmore.
John Mann.
James McGiffin.
O. S. Oakes.
W. H. Stevens.

GAINESVILLE—
E. J. Baird.
J. R. Eddins.
E. C. McMahan.

JACKSONVILLE—
Bisbie & Foster.
Jos. Bryan.
Wm. T. Cotter.
Winchell French,
Jacksonville Pavi
S. S. Leonard Co.
W. A. MacDuff.
R. G. Ross.

KEY WEST—
Wm. A. Johnson &
Wm. R. Kerr.
Alfred B. Sawyer
W. F. V. Scott.
D. B. Walker.

OCALA—
McIver & MacKa

TALLAHASSEE—
Gilmore & Davis
Taylor & Childs.

TAMPA—
James Brown.
S. S. Leonard.
Levick & Moore.
A. L. Shaw.
Chas. Wright Pav

GEO

ATHENS—
E. Borry.
J. A. Soye.
J. W. **Watson.**

ATLANTA—
Atlanta Terra Co
Bluff Sts.
Atlanta Tile Co.,
Wm. J. **Bishop, I**
V. H. Kriegshaber
C. P. Murphy &
Byron Sanders, 2
Southern Roofing

AUGUSTA—
W. F. **Barne.**
T. O. **Brown.**
McKinzie **& Son.**
C. L. **Rounds.**
Albert J. **Twiggs.**

BAINBRIDGE—
J. W. Barney.
W. H. **Carr.**

BARNESVILLE—
A. O. Bennett &

BRUNSWICK—
J. C. **Baldwin.**
W. H. **Bowen.**

SVILLE—
Caves.
Ilburn.
'OWN—
gan.
riffin.
:US—
Bros.
Iardaway.
ray, Jones & Co.
.E—
Bensen.
:omer.
.achels.
N—
artlett.
rch.
Pittman.
TON—
Long.
Wallis.
VILLE—
Hudson.
'. Pierce.
N—
Cunningham.
Hindsman.
Vestbrook.
NGE—
Butler.
Bros.
—
Berland.
Burke, 358-362 34th St.
Hendrix.
Jones.
TTA—
ck & Son.
rson & Austin.
DGEVILLE—
Alling.
McMillan.
RIE—
Dukes.
Harris.
ber.
AN—
Askew & Co.
Cole Mfg. Co.
AN—
Fitzgerald.
ne.
Weisenborn.
—
ll Lumber Co.
ll Mfg. Co.
n Sash, Door & Bldg. Co.
Watson.
NNAH—
tic Contracting Co.
LE—
Choate.
ASVILLE—
y Arnold.
Gribbin.
Miller.

VALDOSTA—
S. W. Booker.
Boothe & Kent.
Hester & Hall.
WAYCROSS—
Jeff Darling.
G. N. Elliston.
J. R. Weed.

HAWAIIAN ISLANDS.

HONOLULU—
Ripley & Dickey.

IDAHO.

BOISE CITY—
John Bartok.
Thos. Finnegan.
J. E. Rankin.
MOSCOW—
Nels Jensen.
W. C. Lander.
POCATELLO—
J. F. Murrey.
WALLACE—
John H. Hanson.
M. C. Murphy.

ILLINOIS.

ALTON—
Charles A. Degenhardt.
Golike & Rust.
Henry Watson.
Wolf, Maufit & Curdie.
ANNA—
Geo. W. Davis.
C. C. Kelley.
Chas. O'Neal.
ARCOLA—
Wm. Lough.
Chas. Wesch.
AURORA—
H. D. Hallett.
R. S. Safford & Son.
BATAVIA—
John Hendrickson.
BEARDSTOWN—
Beardstown Lbr. & Grain Co.
Barchardt & Steins.
Peter Flanery.
Ivemeyer & Greshmeyer.
Chas. Kimple.
W. H. Rhimeberger.
John Schafer.
Schmoldt Bros.
BELLEVILLE—
Moritz Hoefken.
Reeb Bros.
Peter Stander.
Chas. A. Stookey.
Geo. P. Uhl.
BELVIDERE—
John Fair.
Frank Howard.

BLOOMINGTON—
Geo. Bowman.
J. H. Burnham.
John Cherry, Jr.
Pat McDonald.
Geo. McIntosh.
S. R. White.

BLUE ISLAND—
Rexford Bros.
Wilson, Jackson & Co.

CAIRO—
Thos. Ferguson.
Kelly & Kusener.
John Madden.
James Miller.
Wm. Schatz.

CANTON—
H. Dougherty & Co.
John Hallor.
W. H. Hallor.
Jno. P Lingenfelter.

CARLINVILLE—
John Flori & Sons.
Harry Hillier.
H. Kuester & Co.
Frank Lynch.
John Ross.
Henry Winters.

CARTHAGE—
J. M. Foulds.
Richard Miller.
Richard Stowe.
Frank Vertner.

CENTRALIA—
Jno. Clark.
T. C. Douthit.
Jas. Spring.
A. J. Sligar.

CHAMPAIGN—
Polland, Goff & Co.
Jno. W. Stipes.

CHARLESTON—
C. D. Mitchell.
Geo. P. Muchmore.

CHESTER—
W. C. Swannick.

CHICAGO—
George Adgate, 734 Stock Exchange Bldg.
John P. Agnew, 100 Washington St.
Alcatraz Paving Co., 400, 123 LaSalle St.
American Ballast Co., 1008, 188 Madison.
American Railway Construction Co., 1203 Monadnock Blk.
Adolph Anderson, 204, 145 LaSalle St.
A. W. Anderson, 320 W. 61st St.
Chas. J. Anderson, 5414 5th Ave.
Chas. M Anderson, 5951 Henry (A).
John A. Anderson, 488 27th St.
John C. Anderson, 847 W. Polk.
Richard Andrews, 6052 Langley Ave.
Simon P. Andrus, 1081 W. Lake.
Angus & Gindele.
Appel & Ryder, 503, 172 Washington.

Chicago—Continued.
Geo. Archer, 652 Noble Ave.
Clyde Armstrong, 6735 Lafayette Ave.
Robert H. Atkinson, 5008 State.
Magnus Augustine, 502, 145 LaSalle.
Soren J. Bach, 618 N. Artesian Ave.
Arthur W. Bairstow, Cor. W. Lawrence & N. Spaulding.
James Bairstow & Co., 78 LaSalle St.
D. A. Baker, 3841 S. Campbell.
Baldwin & Snyder, 9, 159 LaSalle St.
Herman Balz, 828 S. Horman Ave.
Barber Asphalt Paving Co., 1209 Stock Exchange Bldg.
Peter Barbian, 811 Nelson.
John Barnes, 39 N. Artesian.
Jas. B. Barnett, 2, 78 LaSalle St.
The Barnett & Record Co.
John C. Barrett, 6824 St. Lawrence Ave.
Peter Bartzen, 311 W. St. Lawrence.
Bates & Rogers, 1603 Manhattan Bldg.
Christian Baum, 3638 Wallace.
Peter Becker, 344 Larabee.
Philip Becker, 1229 Perry.
John W. Bennett, 3405 Indiana Ave.
Andrew Berg, 7019 Emerald Ave.
Wm. F. Bergemann, 597 N. Wood.
Peter Berghins, 6224 S. Morgan.
Bermudez Asphalt Paving company, 1210, 153 LaSalle St.
Biernolt & Carter, 121 Edgemont.
P. F. Bieson, 606, 145 LaSalle.
Frank S. Billmeyer, 835 Perry.
Harry A. Bishop, 1120 The Rookery.
Rudolph Blome, Bank Floor, Unity Bldg.
Bloodgood & Stone.
Edw. Bloom, 6645 Lowe Ave.
Ferdinand L. Blunck, 52 Wilmot Ave.
Edw. J. Bode, 1119 N. 40th Ave.
Frank Boeing, 1675 N. Humbolt.
Wm. H. Boone, 1249 Sixty-ninth place.
Herman Boonemann, 1472 Grand.
Jay B. Boulton, 425 W. 69th St.
B. F. Bowman & Son, 6814 S. Park Ave.
J. Boydell, 4339 Prairie Ave.
Lars J. Braben, 708 Augusta.
James D. Bradley, 36-34 Wabash Ave.
Edw. R. Brainerd, 350 Wabash Ave.
Thos. F. Brennan, 27 Hastings.
Briscle Bros., 425 S. Fairfield.
Fred S. Brown, 95, 240 LaSalle.
John Brown, 482 42d Place.
The Brownell Improvement Co., 1220 Chamber of Commerce.
Valentine Bueckermann, 1004 Wilcox Ave.
August Buettner, 1068 S. Robey.
Conrad Buhmann, 624 W. 21st St.
Fred Bulley, 412, 115 Dearborn St.
Frank Burke, 573, 62d St.

—Continued.

Buschmer, 120 Racine Ave.
& Sherrill, 21 Washington.
Caldwell & Son Co., Western 17th & 18th Sts.
. Cameron's Sons, 8, 177 La-St.
F. Camp, 402 S. Kedzie.
M. Campbell & Co., 745 Marle Bldg.
tan P. Campton, Alley, Rear Wabash.
Bros., 6069 S. Green.
Carlsen, 542 W. Erie St.
A. Carlson, 1672 Fletcher.
se Carter, 482 Adams St.
o Ballast Co., Rookery Bldg.
o Belting Co.
o Cement Coating Co., 1641 adnock Blk.
o Ship Bldg. Co., 925 The ery.
o Telephone Co.
en Christianson, 974 60th St.
Christianson, 845 69th St.
houtka, 1224 Turner Ave.
A. Christy, 810, 879 Dearborn

an Clark & Sons Co., 2 Sher-St.
& McVeigh, 1268 Monadnock.
ing Clark, 908, 134 Monroe.
Hauss, 9611 Parnell Ave.
. Coleman, 1041 W. Superior St.
bian Kiln & Construction com-, 68A, 84 Adams St.
ian Construction company, 610, ackson Boulevard.
& Co., 6870 LaSalle.
onlan, 510, 172 Washington.
onley, 5021 Calumet Ave.
H. Conley, 1482 W. Ohio St.
Connelly, 285 Walnut.
Connelly, 311 Oxford Bldg., 184 alle.
Conway Co., Chamber of Com-e.
s H. Cooke, 2062 Harvard.
e Cook, 11916 Lowe Ave.
orcoran, 6209 Seipp Ave.
ouler, 619 N. Maplewood.
Courtney, 11, 92 LaSalle.
Crane, 30 W. Randolph.
Crilly, 208, 167 Dearborn St.
Dabelstein, 845 W. Huron St.
J. Deegling, 1172 Grensham.
Daffin, 301, 145 LaSalle.
Daley.
Demerer's Sons, 95½ 159 La-St.
D. Danielson, 10061 Avenue L.
M. Darling, 4233 Chamberlain

Davidson, 270 N. Avers.
Harvester Works.
Winder, 965 Horman Ave.

Chicago—Continued.

Julian DeLaby, 776 N. Fairfield.
Anthony F. Delfosse, 5, 56 Washington.
Jos. Denton, 3564 Cottage Grove Ave.
Despatch Constroustion Co., Fisher Bldg.
John P. Dickey, 232 W. 48th Ave.
Dillon & Conlan, 510, 172 Washington.
Dolese Bros. & Co., G 178 LaSalle.
Dolese & Shepard Co., 184 La Salle.
Thos. L. Dooley & Co., 315, 145 La Salle.
John H. Dorothy, 520, 108 La Salle.
John Dowdle, 212, 145 La Salle.
August Dranert, 3035 Parnell Ave.
Jos. J. Duffy & Co., Chamber of Commerce.
Frank M. Dub, 3319 Lowe.
August Eich, 466 Thomas.
Albert D. Elmers, 5330 Ellis Ave.
Peter Enders, 331 Mohawk.
Frank Engel, 12007 Union Ave.
Nels. V. Erlandson, 8839 Princeton.
E. T. Evans & Son Co., 4487 State.
Thos. Fahy, 1446 W. 51st St.
Falkenau Construction Co., Chicago Stock Exchange Bldg.
Victor Falkenau, 1116, 108 La Salle.
John Fanning, 25 Walton Place.
Farley & Green Co., Chamber of Commerce.
Henry Farsbinder, 5007 Armour Ave.
John Feudl, 350 N. Hermitage Ave.
Nathan Ferguson, 4359 Champlain.
Martin Finn, 433 Forty-seventh St.
Paul F. Finster, 377 Maxwell.
John E. Fitzgerald, 537 S. Sangamon.
Fitzgerald & Son, 732 Elk Grove Ave.
Fitzsimmons & Connell Co., 1012-1014 Tacoma Bldg.
James Flaska, 1472 W. Thirteenth Pl.
John P. Flich, 1240 Montana.
Robert J. Forrester, 6251 Greenwood Ave.
Charles Foss, 743 Cornelia Ave.
Thomas D. Foster, 291 Millard Ave.
George H. Fox, 3156 Prairie Ave.
Henry F. Friederichs, 279 W. Huron.
George A. Fuller Co., 1027 Marquette Bldg.
The J. L. Fulton Co., 1118 Monadnock Block.
Gaffney & Long Construction Co., 1107, 131 LaSalle.
James Galvin, 30, 84 Wash. St.
John Gallagher, 5321 Shields Ave.
Garden City Construction Co., 610, 169 Jackson Boulevard.
Garden City Paving & Post Co., 504, 167 Dearborn.
Garden City Sand Co., 188 Madison.
Matthew Garth, 739 Carroll Ave.
John Gebhardt, 160 Orchard.

Chicago—Continued.

John Gerten, 561 Cleveland Ave.
E. C. Gettins, 811, 188 Madison.
Harry S. Gilbert, 232 Lunt Ave.
Gildemeister & Bro., 151 Rhine.
Charles W. Gindele, 3333 LaSalle.
George A. Gindele, 1400, 188 Madison.
E. F. Gobel Co., 47, 140 Dearborn.
Rudolph Goetzler, 900 S. Lawndale.
Ambrose M. Goldsmith, 2821 Emerald.
Aaron J. Goodrich, 807 W. 87th St.
Chester H. Goodrich, 8833 Wallace.
Michael Goodrich & Co., 3232 Wentworth.
Edward P. Gorman, 140 Locust.
John Gorman, 3841 Wentworth.
Grace & Hyde C., 1408 Wabash Ave.
Albert Graff Co., 13, 177 La Salle.
Graham Pressed Concrete Co., 709 Royal Insurance Bldg.
John Griffiths, 135 Adams St.
Gus. A. Gunggoll, 155, 185 Dearborn St.
Lucius Guptill, 6817 S. Halstead.
Gurley-Howard Co., 822 Opera House Blk.
August Hagedorn, 418 W. Jackson Boulevard.
James P. Halls, 1032 W. Madison.
Sam Halls, 218 La Salle.
John Hammond & Co., 28, 159 La Salle.
Wm. Hancox, 16 Campbell Park.
Christian Hanke, 121 Canalporte Ave.
Michael D. Hanley, 408 Maxwell.
Daniel Hannan, 2957 State.
Arthur F. Hanson, 9639 Avenue M.
Hards Brothers, 261 N. Clarke.
David H. Harper, 3963 Michigan Ave.
Gustav A. Harper, 4406 Langley.
Hauser Co., 315, 272 Madison.
Wm. F. Haussen, 2702 Milwaukee.
Hayes Brothers, S. Kedzie Ave., Cor. W. 34th.
Herman W. Hazenberg, 6311 S. Halstead.
Philip Hedrich & Son, 119 Homer.
E Lee Heidenreich, 541 Rookery.
The Heidenreich Construction Co., 539 Rookery.
Philip Heil, 4171 Central.
Franz Hein, 586 S. California.
Adolph Heinkel, 10437 Avenue N.
Fred M. Heinkel, 9242 Ontario Ave.
J. A. Heineman & Co., 803, 84 LaSalle.
Herman Hey, 938 School.
Jasper M. Higginbotham, 2831 Armour.
Fred Hildebrandt, 256 Seminary Ave.
Thos. Hillary, 4600 Champlain Ave.
Geo. Hinchliffe, 9, 159 LaSalle.
Hoeffer & Co., 315, 138 Washington.
H. C. Hoff & Co., 5, 78 La Salle.
E. J. Hoffman & Co., 1320, 138 Washington.

Chicago—Continued.

W. L. Hoffman.
Fred J. Hoppe, 400 S. Morgan.
M. Hughes, 243 S. Lincoln.
David Hurd, 251 Ogden.
Hurlbut Portland Cement Paving company, 507 Chamber of Commerce.
Edward Hulmsted, 319 N. Fifty-second Ave.
Morris Hurwitz, 556 S. Sangamon.
Illinois & Georgia Improvement company, 1018 Monadnock.
Illinois Portland Cement Paving company, 626, 218 La Salle.
Illinois Telephone Construction company, 754 The Rookery.
George W. Jackson, 44 Lafayette Building.
August Jacobi, 43 Seldon.
Aaron Jay, 47 S. 40th.
Treikin Jensen, 6319 S. Paulina.
Adolph A. Johnson, 376 W. Ohio.
Franz Johnson, 717 Carmen Ave.
Frederick Johnson, 1909 Milwaukee Ave.
John Johnson, 817 N. Maplewood.
John B. Johnson, 811, 160 Washington.
John W. Johnson, 5607 Indiana.
Nels Johnson, 120 Sedgwick.
Thomas Johnson, 804 W. 62d St.
Jones & Jones, 254 W. Congress.
John H. Jones, 76, 36 Bond Ave., Sta. S.
Thomas Jordan, 313 W. Clybourn Place.
Meyer Kadeskewitz, 9, 159 La Salle.
Charles Kaestner, 241 S. Jefferson St.
John Karlberg, 287 Division.
Alexander Karlsteen, 144 Edgewood Ave.
Karstens & Robrahn, 760, 125 La Salle.
Joseph F. Kavanagh, 2615 Line.
C. W. Kearns & Co., 928 Stock Exchange Building.
Wm. J. Keeson, 701 S. Wood.
Gottfried Kehl, 625 N. Campbell Ave.
James T. Kelly, 741 W. 43d St.
Michael Kelley, 812 W. 61st St.
John W. Kennedy, 440 Dayton.
Kilstofte & Peterson, 1028 Augusta.
F. Kipp & Co., 1459 Newport Ave.
Henry Kirchner, 928 Millard Ave.
John S. Kirkpatrick, 648 W. 68th.
Christian Kish, 796 Fulton.
Kitchell & Webb, 55 S. Morgan.
Charles F. Klambach, 145 W. Jackson Boulevard.
Fred Klippel, 947 W. 50th Place.
Knickerbocker Improvement Co., 58, 92 LaSalle.
John F. Knopp, 13409 Superior Ave.
Peter Knowe, 34 N. Canal.
Wm. S. Knox, 328 W. Harding Ave.
Albert J. Koch, 2068 Lexington.
Henry Koehncke, 13774 Leyden.

—Continued.
e Kopfsiller, 355 W. Huron.
t Kreyls, 77, 92 LaSalle.
s W. Lábinsky, 227 Cuyler Ave.
Laffer & Co., 914, 185 Dearborn

La Moines, 4045 Calumet.
ch C. Lane, 177 Coblentz.
lquist, 494 W. Dearborn St.
s W. Larsen, 5164 LaSalle.
arson, 323 W. Sixty-first.
Laschetzke, 2118 Lowe Ave.
l. Leander, 3834 Rhodes Ave.
C. Leyer, 1227 Millard Ave.
Leach, 1402, 304 Dearborn St.
een Brothers, 815, 138 Washington.
n Lemke, 832 Thomas.
& Haldeman, 827 Monadnock Building.
Lindon, 871 N. Artesian.
e Lindstrom, 6605 La Fayette.
Link, 6420 Emerald St.
s Lonergan & Co., 906, 272 Dearborn St.
R. Long, 833 Ogden Ave.
Loss & Co., 623-5 Pullman Building.
Lota, 610, 60 Wabash Ave.
Louis, 4736 Justine.
Luedke, 1835 N. Central Park

Lund, 231 W. Huron.
& Co., 1105 The Rookery.
S. Lusk, 1208, 355 Dearborn St.
Lyman & Co., 1409, 52 Dearborn St.
J. Lynch, 319, 138 Washington.
Lynch & Co., 157 La Salle.
n & Drews Co., 1822 Chamber of Commerce.
Making, 6558 Rhodes.
Maloney, 1234 Diversey.
[illegible]
[illegible] Co., 1105 Masonic Temple.
Marquardt, 623 N. Lincoln.
h Marsh, 5129 Superior.
Mast, 1805 W. 19th.
. Masolouski, 676 N. Oakley.
Mavor, 705, 167 Dearborn St.
Mayer, 55 S. Sangamon.
Mayhew, 6324 Justine.
W. Maynard, 439 W. 69th St.
[illegible] Bros. Co., 1410, 77 Jackson Boulevard.
L. McCall, 83, 119 La Salle.
McCall, 82, 119 La Salle.
McCarthy, 610 32d St.
F. McCaughey, 1512 W. 19th.
McClintock, Jr., 67 S. 44th.
McCoy, 189 Superior St.
F. McDonald, 463 S. Marshfield.

McGrath, 604 S. Paulina.
[illegible] & Co., 180 W. Adams.

Chicago—Continued.
Donald McKay, 1365 S. Harding Ave.
James H. McMahon, 5521 W. Ontario.
Neil McMillan, 703, 167 Dearborn.
Michael McNamara, 3621 S. Paulina.
Thomas McQuarry & Son, 2945 Cottage Grove Ave.
Arthur Meagher, 6543 Drexel.
Edward Meisel, 1734 Lincoln Ave.
Louis L. Meister, 142 Fry.
Thomas J. Mellone, 1564 Fulton.
Edward Melville, 361 W. 63rd.
George Messermuth, 315, 56 5th Ave.
J. S. Metcalf Co.
Wm. Meyne, 482 N. Robey.
John F. Michalski, 1006, 172 Washington.
Francis Mills, 6038 S. Halstead.
James H. Mitter, 919 S. Hoorman.
Morris & Wait, 208 Grand Cent. Pass. Sta.
W. H. Mortimer, 730, 189 LaSalle.
Charles A. Moses, 506 Chamber of Commerce.
E. H. Moore, 213, 145 LaSalle.
Felix Montenie, 1446 Lexington.
Hugh D. Moreland, 733, 107 Washington.
George Morrison, 1921½ 5th St.
Edson Morse, 102 Segwick.
Solomon J. Mas, 1477 70th St.
Albert Motschman, 9, 159 LaSalle.
August Mueller, 9, 159 LaSalle.
Carl R. Mueller, 39 Clifton.
Chas. Mueller & Sons, 1635 N. Halstead.
Hermann Mueller, 221 Pine Grove Ave.
Oscar Mueller, 485 Belden.
Paul Mueller, 178 Lewis.
John F. Muldon, 1537, 79 Dearborn.
John W. Mullen, 494 S. Wood.
Charles G. Mueller, 1860 Surf St.
Alois Munch, 144 Cleveland.
Daniel J. Murphy, 396 Dearborn.
The Murphy Grout Co., 473 Dearborn.
Nash Brothers.
Nash & Dowdle.
F. C. Neagle & Son Co.
Fred Nehls, 209 Blackhawk.
A. Nelson & Son, 315 W. Ohio.
Ernest P. Nelson, 1062 Osgood.
Nelson & Peterson, 612, 84 LaSalle.
Thomas M. Nelson, 656 The Rookery.
C. M. Netterstrom & Son, 403, 84 La Salle.
Charles F. Newman, 859 Cortez.
H. F. Newman, 87 Dearborn.
T. Nicholson & Son's Co., 315 Dearborn St.
Soren N. Nielson, 132 W. Erie.
Swan J. Nihlean, 3629 Forest Ave.
Edward J. Nordie, 827 Lincoln Ave.
North American Ry. Construction Co., 1320 Monadnock Block.
Thomas O'Brien, 6528 Parnell.
Ockerhind & Son, 2771 N. Seeley.

Chicago—Continued.

O'Day & Farwell, 214, 145 LaSalle.
James Oliver, 3813 Aldine.
James F. Olmstead, 6548 Normal.
Oscar Olson, 832 Edgewater.
Thomas O'Neill, 3732 S. Lincoln.
Theo. Ostrowski, 711 Dickson.
Andrew Ouderdonk, The Rookery.
John Owne, 6519 Champlain.
H. S. Palmer & Co., 8904 Houston Ave.
Chas. Papsline, 59 McLean.
Wm. Z. Partello, 2908 N. Hermitage.
J. S. Paterson Construction Co., 1364 Monadnock Block.
William Peterson, 606 W. Madison.
Henry Paull, 206 North.
Edward Paulson, 1109 W. 13th St.
Frank J. Pease, 2767 N. Forty-second St.
John Pedgrift, 2507 Chamber of Commerce.
Samuel E. Pedgrift, 2507 Evanston.
John Pierce, Cor. Clark and Adams.
Herman Pekholz, 6335 Bishop.
Riley E. Perham, 7952 Union.
E. B. Perkins, 663 Flournoy St.
L. B. Perkins, 663 Flournoy St.
Joseph Peroutka, 1125 S. Whipple.
Andrew Person, 1657 W. Spaulding.
John W. Peterson, 645 W. North.
Peterson & Olson, 777 N. Maplewood.
Otto Peterson, 757 N. Maplewood.
Vorin A. Peterson, 1134 Otto.
Thomas Phee, 230 Grand Central Pass. Sta.
Pillinger Brothers, 109 N. Park Ave.
Julian Pischke, 1341 N. Artesian Ave.
Alex. W. Pohlman, 476 S. Wood.
Jos. Polowsky, 193 Armitage.
Chas. M. Porter, 702, 84 La Salle St.
Clement Porter, 1358 S. Central Park Ave.
Portland Cement Cem. Pav. Co., 507 138 Wash.
Portland Cem. Pav. Asphalt Co., 60, 92 La Salle.
Herman Potratz, 968 N. Halsted.
Nathan A. Paull, 61 W. Vanburen.
Thomas A. Pound, 3841 Elmwood.
Wm. Pound, 3841 Elmwood.
Powell Brothers, 310, 138 Washington.
Michael F. Powers, 17, 132 La Salle.
John B. Preant, 23 Plum.
John Prescher, 828 Girard.
Abner Price, 2219 Prairie Ave.
Alex. Price, 3641 Vernon.

Chicago—Continued.

James S. Price, 1836 Indiana.
William D. Price, 3427 W. 56th.
Gottlieb Prieewe, 19 Gardner.
John Proesel, 261 Larrabee.
Philip Quinn, 468 N. Erie.
Frank Radzinski, 57 Clifton.
Railway Construction Co., 1214, 155 LaSalle.
Henry Ramm, 1155 S. Central Park Ave.
S. M. Randolph, 217, 134 Wash. St.
Henry Rath, 2 Webster.
Gustav Raum, 665 W. 21st.
Joseph M. Reardon, 1518 Noble Ave.
Wm. Reiman, 5542 Drexel.
Wm. Reinert & Son, 4845 Indiana.
Rennacker Construction Co., 316, 16 LaSalle.
Republic Chemical & Creosoting Co., 1116, 138 Washington.
Henry Rieper, 632 N. Hoyne.
Wm. Ritchie, 4543 St. Lawrence.
Mark G. Roby, 993 Warren.
George R. Rockefeller, 3732 Calumet.
Jacob Rodatz, 414 Rookery.
Fred H. Roessler, 693 Fullerton.
Romheld & Gallery Co., 91 Dearborn.
Pearson Rooke, 2442 Cottage Grove Ave.
Edw. G. Roquemore, 637 N. Harding.
Henry Rosewell, 110 Quincy.
Jos. Rus, 1150 S. Kedzie.
Wm. J. Rycraft, 1067 W. Congress.
James A. Sackley, Chamber of Commerce.
Sammis Mosaic Tile & Gravel Co.
Gustaves Schaetz, 1506 W. 15th Place.
Schillinger Brothers Co., 192 N Morgan St.
Charles Schleyer, 6919 Elizabeth.
Geo. A. Schneider, 2441 Wentworth Ave.
Christian Schnur, 775 Girard.
Chas. Schroeder, 41 Janssen.
Herman Schoenning, 303 W. 18th.
Richard T. Schofield, 7008 Lowe Ave.
Wm. Schwerin, 975 W. 21st St.
Scoviller & Bierworth.
Gilbert H. Scribner, Jr., 136 Adams St.
Adolph Seaborg, 7045 Emerald.
John B. Seidler, 1043 N. Sawyer.
Sennott Construction Co., 38, 81 Washington.
James Serovy, 602 S. Fairfield.
P. J. Sexton, 301, 164 Dearborn St.

ANY QUESTION RELATING TO CEMENT
WILL BE ANSWERED ON REQUEST. IT IS A PART
OF OUR BUSINESS TO KNOW ALL ABOUT CEMENT
MUNICIPAL ENGINEERING CO.

Continued.

& Shinglaw Co., 609 Western Bldg.

Shedd, 7125 Railroad Ave.

Sherwin Co., 693, 47th.

ibbett, 420 W. 63rd.

& Neunkirchen, 1635 Roscoe.

Sikorski, 646 Holt.

mpson, 1172 S. Central Park.

n Brothers Co., 704, 138 .

clair Construction Co.

H. Skoglund, 937 Edgewater.

ski & Sikarski, 133 W. Divi-

E. Skreve, 504, 185 Dearborn

A. Slack, 3149 S. 41st.

Slama, 970 W. 18th Place.

Slattery, 4044 Indiana.

T. Slattery, 540 S. 41st.

Sloan, 3, 708 Vincennes.

G. Smith, 6027 S. Green.

Moss & Brown, 78 La Salle.

Sodren, 311 W. 109th St.

ollitt, 104, 140 Dearborn St.

Sollitt & Sumner, 103-4, 140 orn.

ouka, 1011 S. California.

Specker, 5648 La Salle.

V. Sproul, 312, 138 Washington.

. Stradler, 1073 S. Hamlin.

. Stradler, 1983 Greenshaw.

I. Stafford, 3440 Cottage

n & Blome, 79 Dearborn.

d Concrete Construction Co., 4 La Salle.

d Paving Co., 716, 172 Wash- St.

Construction Co., 402, 108 orn.

N. Stearn, 4645 Calumet Ave.

Steenmueller, 343 Hudson Ave.

I. Stephens, 5729 La Salle.

Steven, 3118 Wallace.

Stoe, 1654 87th.

Streeter, 1208, 355 Dearborn.

C. Stuckmaier, 83 W. Van

E. Sweiberg, 5743 Princeton.

B. Swift Co., Security Bldg.

Taunnler, 5544 Shields.

aylor, 6832 Yale.

Thiels, 476 N. Wells.

Thompson, 713, 167 Dearborn.

G. Tieman, 825 W. 65th.

A. W. Tieman, 1810 W. 9th.

imblin, 30 Penn.

odd, 604, 145 La Salle.

odd, 604, 145 La Salle.

P. Treat, 1106 The Rookery.

Tubbs, 7359 Vincennes Rd.

Uebelmesser & Co., 82 W.

Construction Co., 402, 108 Dear- St.

Chicago—Continued.

U. S. Repair & Guaranty Co., 467 The Rookery.

Universal Bldg. Sup. & Jobbing Co., 654 W. Madison.

F. P. Updike, 704 Chamber of Commerce.

Valley Construction Co., 402, 108 Dearborn St.

Gysbertus Van Gulden, 6717 S. Green.

Cornelius Van Mourick, 828 W. Congress.

Henry Veich, 1427 S. Homan.

Emil Vermash, 1177 N. Spaulding.

Charles M. Vibert, 351 S. Oakley.

Olaf P. Vider.

William Walk, 978 N. Halsted.

Thomas S. Walker, 138 29th.

Jacob Walters, 67 W. 22d Pl.

William Walters, 862 Racine St.

Walter Wardrop, 1302, 215 Dearborn St.

Wm. W. Ware, 876 W. Erie.

Robert Warnock, 361 W. Washteman.

Washburn & Washburn.

Joseph Watry, 32 Iowa St.

H. F. Watson Co., 192 5th Ave.

Wm. E. Weale, 7020 St. Lawrence.

Sam'l E. Webbe, 214, 169 Jackson Boulevard.

Louis E. Weick, 451 Cleveland.

W. A. & A. E. Wells, 1014 Monadnock Blk.

Wells & Campbell, 499 W. 19th St.

William Wendorff, 404 W. North.

Charles J. Westphal, 1653 W. Leavitt.

Western Paving & Supply Co., 1011-191 LaSalle St.

George A. Wheatman, 930 S. Hamlin.

W. W. Wheeler, 114 W. Washington.

Eugene De F. Wheelock, 5224 Lake.

John White, 7015 Indiana.

Edwin White, 3512 Parnell.

Peter White, 678 W. 14th St.

Thomas N. White, 760 S. Sawyer St.

Wm. Wiegrefe & Son, 572 Thomas.

Henry Wilke, 5003 Armour.

E. Will & P. Lutsch, 18, 88 LaSalle St.

Williams Construction Co., 804, 153 LaSalle.

Hugh R. Williams, 178 S. Albany.

John Williams, 138 W. 59th.

John Winblad, 6349 S. Peoria.

George J. Witt, 954 W. Artesian.

Albert E. Wood, 85 S. Wood.

George Wood, 4540 Prairie.

Walter Woodley, 693, 47th St.

Frank Zandler, 1460 34th Place.

Jacob Zeinel, 1900 N. Marshfield.

Julius Zuenhlke, 247 W. Belmont.

John Zulewsky, 5845 Drexel.

CHILLICOTHE—

Frank Hayden.

Ellis Kiser.

CLINTON—
Jas. Kirk.
Wood Seats.
COLCHESTER—
S. D. Mills.
J. O. Moon.
DANVILLE—
Day & Jones.
E. G. Dickerson.
R. Knickerbocker & Co.
J. H. Palmer.
Stratton Co.
W. H. Wright.
M. Yeager.
Phil Yeager.
DECATUR—
Bachman & Tuttle.
Theo. Brinkoetter.
Culver Electric Co.
Geo. Dempsey.
John Giblin.
Adam F. Gilbert.
O. W. Kincaid.
Lunn & Lunn.
E. L. Martin Paving Co.
Moffitt & Ammann.
Randall & Troutman.
S. A. Tuttle & Co.
DEKALB—
Adolf Peterson.
Raymond Rolfe.
A. F. Rylan.
DIXON—
J. W. Kelly.
W. J. McAlpine.
DOWNERS GROVE—
Beidelman Bros.
H. H. Woelfersheim.
DWIGHT—
Ames L. Orr.
De Witt Miller.
Mumson & Co.
EAST ST. LOUIS—
Anderson & Co.
Burke & Keely.
W. H. Hill & Co.
Frank Keating & Co.
M. J. Keeley & Co.
H. C. Lake & Co.
M. McCabe.
Southern Ill Const. Co.
EDWARDSVILLE—
John Childs.
B. H. Richards.
EFFINGHAM—
Henry Sanders.
G. F. Volkman.
ELGIN—
Frank Anderson, 503 Enterprise.
Elhanan Bundy, 432 Fulton St.
John Fluck, 166 Hill Ave.
Chas. E. Giertz, 326 W. Crystal Ave.
Geo. A. Hall, 170 Centre.
Willis W. Hauser, 132 W. Channing.
Fred W. Juby, 530 St. Charles.
Jacob Lind & Son, 340 W. State.

Elgin—Contin
Frank Lind
Ralph McC
Marckhoff
L. E. Pal
Peter M. S
John G. St
ELMHURST-
Barrensche
C. R. Dunn
EVANSTON-
C. T. **Bartl**
E. R. Brad
Axel Carls
M. Foley.
James Hux
Voigts & G
Jas. Wiggi
FAIRBURY-
F. M. Bak
Ide Harris.
Matt Kam
Joe Patern
FREEPORT-
H. W. Han
Gus Rohle
Jas. Stuart
FULTON—
W. A. Buel
A. D. Cha
Ernest Hu
GALENA—
William A.
James Jac
William Le
Carson Sco
Edward To
GALESBUR
A. P. Ande
John Bassl
Ferry & L
John B. M
James O'C
P. T. Olson.
J. A. Rean
Charles Ru
M. E. Swe
E. J. Zette
GALVA—
J. P. Gibb
Charles Wi
GENESEO—
G. W. Cro
Alfred Joh
C. C. Mart
GIBSON CIT
W. E. Arr
A. Clark.
M. J. Hoffn
GIRARD—
Alec Crawf
Jas. McCar
John McCa
Jeff Parks.
Geo. Robins
GRANITE C
M. Heller.

VILLE—
Allen.
Bigard.
apple.
›pard.
Meyer.
eed.
Willman.
SBURG—
Ford.
King.
.RD—
Breitenfeld.
.erce.
Roach.
Wellington.
:Y—
Bloodgood.
Van Alstine.
AND—
ttner.
Fentz.
ich.
:k.
AND PARK—
Ditmer.
indbloom.
Noerenberg.
Obee.
Rectenwald.
ORO—
Fourer.
nnemeyer.
'otter.
.LE—
ı & Drallmer.
STON—
Sappington.
Stratton.
›NVILLE—
:herry.
ell & Co.
Smith.
'VILLE—.
Hansell.
—
M. Campbell, 3 Auditorium

Lockhart, 5 Scott St.
t McHugh, 809 N. Chicago St.
Monahan, 519 Baker Ave
KEE—
'ault.
Harpin.
'pin.
kee Artificial Stone Co.
Iatur & Co.
McGillis.
ghlin Construction company.
hle.
Sinclair.
EE—
nquist.
ag & Tesch.
& Smith.
:Keon.
Sinclair.

KNOXVILLE—
B. O. Krotter.
LACON—
Conrad Peintner.
John Shaw.
Geo. F. Wightman.
LAGRANGE—
Albert Anderson, 235 Kensington Ave.
J. H. Esson.
D. A. Lyon.
LA SALLE—
Chris Awe & Co.
Charley Bros.
L. C. Gibson.
Matthiessen & Hegeler Zinc Co.
LEMONT—
A. J. Helbig.
John McGrath.
LE ROY—
Harry Lamont.
P. J. Lamont.
T. W. Vanatta.
A. S. White.
LEWISTOWN—
C. V. Hughes & Bros.
LINCOLN—
T. B. Davy.
Eugene McCord.
A. L. Ottz.
Jno. A. Simpson.
LOCKPORT—
John Effting.
Jerry Gilldo.
James Gregory.
Herman Lintner.
MACOMB—
Johnson Bros.
Tiernan & Holden.
MARSEILLES—
Barron & Peace.
William McIvor.
MASCOUTAH—
John Bueltner.
Charles Clement.
George W. Lisher.
MATTOON—
C. E. Kinser & Son.
J. B. Kinser & Co.
Loomis & Rose.
W. E. Miller.
MELROSE PARK—
J. W. Barker.
MENDOTA—
Bierworth & Co.
Law & Barber.
Henry Zolper.
METROPOLIS—
J. C. Ferrell.
Dick Green.
MOLINE—
Wm. O. Cressy.
Gainy & Resser.
Ed Gust.
Ludwig Hammerquist.
Huey & Stouffer.
Pierce & Lundquist.

MONMOUTH—
John H. Baldwin.
Brodin & Dungan.
E. A. Lord Fuel & Ice Co.
Silas Pillsbury.
A. W. Ryan.
O. D. Wilcox & Son.
MONTICELLO—
Dan Householder.
Scott Miller.
W. F. Lodge.
A. L. Starkey.
MOUND CITY—
The Mound City Crystal Ice Mfg. & Coal Co.
MOUNT CARROLL—
W. E. Wiler.
MOUNT OLIVE—
Peter Nischivitz.
NAPERVILLE—
A. H. Beidelman.
Benj. Beidelman.
Lieber Bros.
NASHVILLE—
Wiese & Gewe.
NORMAL—
F. A. Leighton.
Thos. Sylvester.
NORTH HARVEY—
C. W. Stevens.
OAK PARK—
Harper & Buttendorf.
H. D. Maize.
J. J. Marrison & Co. & O'Brien.
J. W. Smith.
OTTAWA—
A. B. Bradish.
Colburn & Myers.
T. & H. Colwell.
W. A. Jeffery.
Sanders Bros. Mfg. Co.
Sinnott Bros.
J. J. Wafer.
John Walter.
PANA—
Geo. Bickel.
Wm. McFall.
PARIS—
John Curtis.
Tobias Hipple
S. Safford & Sons.
PAXTON—
D. D. Dunnan.
N. P. Neilson.
H. Pearson.
Turner Bros.
PEORIA—
Jas. S. Allen, 713 Hamilton Ave.
William M. Allen, 531 Woolner Bldg.
Nicholas Becker, 226 Taylor St.
E. E. Bull, 12 S. Jefferson.
A. W. Bushnell, 403 S. Wash. St.
Albert Coleman & Son, 508 5th Ave.
Crescent Stone Co., 117 N. Jefferson Ave.
Frederick E. Derby, 734 Howett.

Peoria—Continued.
Dolan & Maher, S. Adams and Oak Sts.
Wm. H. Ebaugh, 701 7th Ave.
John W. Fay, 108 Windom.
Frank B. Hasbrouck, 323 Ellis.
Frank Hoeppner, 149 Proctor.
G. Janssen & Sons, 230 Wash. Ave.
Val Jobst & Son.
Charles Kammerer, 815 5th Ave.
John J. McDonald, 207 Louisa.
Fred Meints.
O'Connor Brothers, 205 S. Jefferson.
Peter J. Philbower, 712 Wash. St.
Adam Saal.
J. H. W. Schwerm, 106 McReynold.
Fred Siefert, 212 S. Orange.
T. J. Wasson, 403 S. Wash. St.
D. A. Wells & Son, 512 7th Ave.
Albert L. Wookey, 1006 S. Adams.
PERU—
Schweikert Bros.
J. L. White.
PETERSBURG—
Joseph Bath.
J. R. Carver.
J. W. Carver.
C. P. Hadsall.
A. T. White.
PINCKNEYVILLE—
Harry Grover.
A. T. Jenner.
T. E. Turner.
PITTSFIELD—
A. V. Wills & Son.
PLANO—
Lige Kendall.
W. G. Van Kirk.
PRINCETON—
C. A. Brown.
J. H. Brown.
A. H. Peterson.
QUINCY—
Robert P. Ahern, 823 Jersey.
Joseph E. Ball, 116 W. 10th St.
Campbell Brothers, 920 Hampshire.
Ebert & Shanahan, 609 W. Fourth St.
Conrad J. Eikleman, 1007 Lind.
The Flack Lumber Co., 438 Broadway.
John Guesen, 1825 Oak.
Wm. F. Hummert, 1311 W. 9th.
Col. Davis James, 811 W. 9th St.
Herman H. Kampling, 720 W. 15th St.
Koch & Meyer, 115 Delaware.
William Menke, 709 Payson Ave.
August B. Menke, 121 W. 8th.
F. W. Menke Stone & Lime Co., W. S. Front, ft. State.
Middendorf Brothers, 926 Broadway.
Quincy White Lime Cement Co., 237 S. Front St.
Peter Simons, 1400 Vine St.
Henry B. Terstegge, 1818 Lind.
Joseph P. Terstegge, 1322 W. 11th St.
Theo. H. Vonder Haar, 736 W. 14th St.
Bernard J. Weners, 832 W. 11th St.

ELLE—
. Hizer.
h Opdyler.
FALLS—
Burdick.
k Hardesty.
Jensen.
FORD—
C. Allen, 414 N. Winnebago.
rich Construction Co.
Larsen.
affioli, 211 E. State St.
elson, 1227 Seventy-third Ave.
'ord Art. Stone Sidewalk Co.,
Fifth Ave.
as Tole, 1124 Rock.
ISLAND—
Larkin.
McConochie & Sons.
Nevins.
nfield Bros.
l Sears.
ity Construction Co.
'ARLES—
. Alexander.
Anderson.
Dalquist.
R. Long.
n Smith.
Welch.
NEETOWN—
Ash.
Bellamy.
W. Jenkins.
. Jermains.
BYVILLE—
· Bros.
'A—
Lewis.
Stumpe.
GFIELD—
& Son.
F. Culver.
r (The) Construction Co.
Cunningham.
olithic Pavement Co.
Irwin.
Ryan.
Taintor.
. Vance.
e & Lawson.
n, Patterson & Striffler.
ING—
McBride.
O'Hare & Son.
TOR—
Allen.
Davidson.
Davis.
er & Son.
'wartz.
n Western Co.
VAN—
man Bros.
Jones.

SYCAMORE—
S. T. Armstrong.

TAYLORVILLE—
The Taylorville Marble & Granite Works.

TOLUCA—
John Gannon.
J. E. Poterfield.

TUSCOLA—
J. Bruhn.
William Burrgraff.
S. S. Goehring.

URBANA—
Wm. Beasley.
Jno. B. Bennett.
R. J. Gill.
Jobst & Co.

VENICE—
Frank Kraft.
Chas. Pope Co.
Jno. Williams.

VIRGINIA—
John Dobson.
Sam'l Suffern.
Jas. Turner.

WARSAW—
John D. Critchfield.
Ed Louden.
Pluene Bros.
Wm. Raleigh.

WATSEKA—
Martin & Igou.
Jas. M. Strate.
Wagner Bros.

WAUKEGAN—
Frank Miller.

WHEATON—
H. D. Compton.
J. De Grasse.
Irving Ingraham.
Sam'l Welden.

WHITE HALL—
Thos. J. Grant.
Wm. H. Pritchard.
Chas. Sturdevant.

WILMETTE—
James Crabb.
Joseph Heinzen.
John A. McGarry & Co.

WOODSTOCK—
John Connell.
S. E. Cunningham.
John Hauck.
C. Johnson.
J. T. Johnson.
P. J. McCauley.
Fred Schneider.

INDIANA.

ALBANY—
W. W. Furrow.

ALEXANDRIA—
Saml J. Brandon.
Pete L. King.

ANDERSON—
Wm. Cronin.
Dalton & Tappen.
C. H. Daniels.
T. P. Kelly.
B. Lukens & Son.
Lyst & Son.
M. E. Pearson.

ANGOLA—
Irving Stocker.

ATTICA—
J. A. Foster & Co.

AUBURN—
J. F. Aber Co.
Long & Brandon.
Picker Bros.
Scott Walker & Co.

AURORA—
William Platt.
John Scott.
J. C. Wright.

BEDFORD—
R. D. Gyger.
William Hilton.
Thomas Whitted, Jr.

BLOOMINGTON—
W. A. Pike.
L. M. Shoemaker & Co.
Henry H. Voss.

BRAZIL—
Pat Fitzpatrick.
Hawkin Hawkins.
O. C. Hawkins.
Thomas Keegan.
W. F. Loyd.
Reese Phillips.
Thomas Phillips.

BREMEN—
Van Skyhawk & Grunewalt.
I. F. Wine.
Lawrence Yost.

BROOKVILLE—
Frank Gagle.
Charles Horn.
Wm. West.

CANNELLTON—
Henry Heim.
Frank Paulin.
John Uehlein.

COLUMBIA CITY—
Erdman & Wynkoop.

COLUMBUS—
Everroad & Son.
Gilbert & Everroad.
Moyer & Son.

CRAWFORDSVILLE—
Buchanan Bros
M. J Carroll
Henry Clements.
J. A. Harding.
Fred Hoffman.
John Johnson.
Ira McConnell, 219 W. College St.
Jas. M. Waugh.

CROWN POINT—
F. Hagadorn.
Jos. Heinrich.
Rudolph & Crowell.

DECATUR—
E. Fritzinger.
Miller & Williams.
E. Woods & Co.

DELPHI—
John C. O'Connor.
Ira Rinehart.

DUNKIRK—
R. S. Allen.
M. D. Wood.

ELKHART—
Frank Brumbaugh.
Isaac Grimes.
Chas. D. Kinney.
Jno. W. L. Moran.
Jno. H. Williams.

ELWOOD—
J. A. Dehority.
P. T. O'Brien.
James Pauley.

EVANSVILLE—
Alcorn, Craft & Idol, 15 2d Ave.
W. Allen, 1049 W. 3rd St.
Anchor Paving Co., 128 W. Water St.
J. Richard Anderson, 510 U. 8th St.
Bedford, Weikel & Nugent, River front near foot of Division.
Jacob J. Bippus, 116 E. Illinois.
John T. Bullen, 300 Olive St.
Caden Stone Co., 425 E. Ohio.
Cottage Bldg. Co., 301 S. Water St.
Charles H. Davies, 503 Oakley St.
Wm. H. Dedrick, 103 Clark St.
Michael Elpers, 408 Adams Ave.
Espenlaub & Johann, 1401 E. Delaware.
Evansville Artificial Stone Co., 422 Sycamore St.
Evansville Contract Co., Cor. Water & Pine.
Henry G. Farr, 1001 Division.
Gearing & Haller Planing Mill Co., 816 W. 6th St.
George W. Goodge, 1308 Walnut.
J. J. Groeninger, 100 Walker St.
Robert J. Hyde, 1615 Main St.
Christ Kanzler, 917 E. Illinois.
Patrick Kelley, 14 Stahlhefer St.
Chas. A. Koerner, 19 W. Maryland.
Lannert & Rickwood, N. E. Cor. Pennsylvania & Oakley.
H. A. Lensing, 420 Sycamore St.
H. Lohse & Co., 7-9 2nd Ave.
Benj. F. Mayhorn, Jr., 406 U. 3rd St.
Jno. S. McCorkle & Son, 500 Upper 8th St.
John Oakley, 436 Jefferson Ave.
Louis Reichert, 316 Madison Ave.
Theo. E. Richtin, 7th & Ingle Sts.
William T. Seymour, 508 4th Ave.
Edw. F. Sonntag, 516 Main St.

...le—*Continued.*
Stinchfield & Son, 1115 W. ...sylvania St.
C. Struchen, 1001 Cherry St.
A. Swope, 1000 Vine St.
C. Tinnemeyer, 607 U. 9th St.
...Voelkel, 1904 1st Ave.
...el Weber, 321 Olive St.
...Veiss, 525 S. Garvin.

...YNE—
F. Brenneler, 207 W. DeWald.
...erheimer, 177 E. Jefferson.
Ehle, 529 Broadway.
...Evers & Son, 323 Hanna.
...ayne Roofing & Paving Co., 152 ...Main.
...Geake, 76 Pearl.
Grothaltman, 28 E. 4th.
...sly & Sons, 46 and 48 E. Main.
& Braun, 84 Pearl.
...Moellering & Co., 53 Murray.
Olds Const. Co., Elecktron ...
Remus, 442 Broadway.
...nburg & Busching, E. Superior ...
Ziemendorf, 19 Wagner St.

...FORT—
Condon.
Hinds.
...s & Brown.
...d H. Morris.
...A. Ross.

...LIN—
...on Balser.
...Crowel.
Crowel.
Davis.
...Halstead.

...TT—
...Hill.
Hill.
...ber.

...TY—
McCormack.
...Stine.

...S—
...Corpe.
...rant.
...I. Grant.
Hatch & Sons.
...Klopfenstein.
Larimer.
...Bros. & Co.
Aust.
...ler.

...CASTLE—
...Earlie.
...Schilimeyer.
...Steele & Son.

...FIELD—
...s J. Fawcett.
...effries.
...ohnson.
...Kirkpatrick.

GREENSBURG—
Peter Plckett.
O. L. Pulse & Co.
Thomson & Kessing.

HAMMOND—
H. Ahlborn, 740 State St.
Henry Otto, 297 Sohl St.
William Pepperdine, 242 Plummer Ave.

HUNTINGBURG—
Christ W. Roettger.

HUNTINGTON—
John Barrett.
Fisher, Keefer & Bailey.
Peter Foster.
Henry Keller.
Martin Koch, 102 Cline St.
W. H. Patterson.
James W. Shock, 82 E. Market St.
Julius Weeling.

INDIANAPOLIS—
Wm. H. Abbett, 1724 S. Meridian St.
Aikman & Schwert, 30th and Canal.
Wm. C. Allen 516 N. New Jersey.
Wm. Bossert, 216 W. 11th St.
Joseph Brennan, 1719 N. Senate Ave.
Henry J. Bowen, 606 W. 10th St.
Davis C. Bustin, 17 Claypool Bldg.
Wm. Burch, 1419 Cornell Ave.
Jas. Buskel, 2234 N. Arsenal
August Bothe, 116 Evison.
Capitol Paving and Construction Co., 1 Hubbard Blk.
Wm. R. Carlin, 1901 Brighton Boul.
Richard M. Cash, 40 E. Wash St.
Albert Cline, 302 Lemcke Bldg
Horace G. Coldwell, 129 E. Market.
J. K. Cooper & Co.
Frank B. Dearinger, 610 Bates St.
Henry L. Dedman, 146 E. Market St.
Dorran Brothers 1117 Ottawa
Wm. H. [illegible] 1522 Lexington.
Henry [illegible] 221 N. State
[illegible]
[illegible]
[illegible]
[illegible]
[illegible]
[illegible]
[illegible]
[illegible]
[illegible]
[illegible]
[illegible]
[illegible]
[illegible]
[illegible]
[illegible]
[illegible]
[illegible]

Indianapolis—Continued.

Thomas H. Jameson, Builders' Exchange.
Peter Jochum, 216 Detroit.
Richard Jones, 809 Torbet.
Rufus S. Judd, 1924 Highland Place.
Wm. P. Jungclaus Co., 825-27 Mass. Ave.
August Kaiser, 222 N. Adelaide.
Wm. Kattau & Son, 464-6 Cedar St.
Julius Keller, 127 Fulton.
R. L. King, 2248 Indiana Ave.
Ernest A. Kottlowski, 525 S. Pine.
Fred H. Laakman, 606 W. St. Clair.
Frank Lawson.
Lewis & Graham, 23 Ingalls Blk.
Henry Maag, 11 Regent.
George W. McCray, 2137 N. Senate.
Meridian Construction Co., 26 Virginia Ave.
Elihu W. Millikan, 2401 Martindale.
John N. Millikan, Sherman House.
Lynn B. Millikan, 921 Stevenson Building.
Moon & Whitsell.
Thomas J. Morse, 317 N. West.
Wm. Newton, 1019 Oakland.
Cornelius S. Niemier, 1543 Lexington.
I. H. Norman, 128 E. Market.
Chas. Nuerge & Co., 1217 E. Ohio.
Charles Pearce, 714 N. Illinois.
Wm. Petrie, 1834 Highland Place.
J. C. Pierson & Son, 503 Majestic Bldg.
Beverly C. Porter, 607 W. 11th St.
Jacob F. Prensch, 1115 Olive.
Wm. Prosser, 1440 E. Tenth.
Henry E. Reinking & Son, 1016 E. Market.
Riverside Construction Co., 7 Claypool Bldg.
Benj. F. Rogers, 223 N. Arsenal.
Rogers & Dunlop, 116 N. Delaware.
Henry C. Roney, 1618 Park Ave.
W. R. Rubush & Sons, 1223 Woodlawn Ave.
Benedict J. Schlanzer, 1338 Charles.

Indianapolis—Continued.

Fred Schreiber, 158 Palmer.
John A. Schumacher Co., 820 E. St Clair.
Walter P. Scott & Co., 27 Kentucky Ave.
Geo. W. Seibert, When Blk.
Eugene Sheehan, 602 N. Oriental.
Edward Shingler, 1010 Sterling.
Jas. E. Shover, 21 N. Alabama.
Wm. E. Shover, 219 N. Alabama.
Shover & Austin, 322 E. Market St.
Hiram T. Sink, 609 E. Michigan.
Smith & Larrison, Hartford Blk.
Henry C. Smithers, 319 W. Maryland
Ferd C. Smock & Co., 427-8 Lemcke Bldg.
J. L. Spaulding.
Henry Spielhoff & Son, Box 100 Builders' Exchange.
Geo. W. Stanley, 323-331 N. Adelaide
Wm. P. Stewart & Co., 11 N. Alabama.
H. H. Symmes Co., Room 2, Board of Trade.
Peralfon F. Tall, 3062 N. Capitol Ave
Robert Thomas, 1798 Northwestern.
Van Camp Burial Vault Co.
Benj. F. Wade, 117 N. Missouri.
Western Paving & Supply Co., 2 Claypool Bldg.
The P. C. Weyenberg Co., 911 Stevenson Bldg.
White & Harrison, 1135 E. Pratt.
Joel Williams, 72 Ingalls Block.
Edward R. Wolf, 311 Lemcke Building.
Luke Woods, 2011 Yandes.

IRVINGTON—
John Moore.

KENDALLVILLE—
Adolph Adams.
John Deibele, S. Main St.

KOKOMO—
A. R. Bowker.
David Frazee.
J. C. Rayle.

ALL ABOUT CEMENT UP-TO-DATE AND ALL THE TIME

The best way to keep informed about everything relating to Cement the year round is to read

MUNICIPAL ENGINEERING MAGAZINE

The publication which stands foremost in representation of Cement interests.

Subscription price, $2.00 per year.

Address MUNICIPAL ENGINEERING CO.

'ontinued.
Record.
tuddell.
n & Son.
TTE—
I. Budge.
ton.
Eaton.
ey.
ckson..
umper.
Moore.
& Yeagy.
lon.
chardson.
& Jamison.
& Son.
odders.
nstruction Co.
NGE—
Shattick.
TE—
truss.
Vankirk.
N—
e & Downes.
ves.
oves.
ER—
iddle.
Iays.
issey.
Tutt.
PORT—
illey (Plastering), S. S. Shultz,
Kloenne (S. T.).
rnes (Cement), 219 Plum St.
. Barnes & Sons (Brick and
, 228 Front St.
. Bush (Stone), 611 North St.
H. Ellison (Street), 1417
way.
J. Gallion (Cement), 4 Oak

F. Gleitze (Brick and Stone),
Market.
F. Heitzman (Brick and
, 1713 George St.
upp (Street), 318 Linden Ave.
bson & Co. (Brick and Stone),
rth.
W. Knight (Cement), 1203 To-
t.
. Lingguist (Brick and Stone),
. Market St.
Talbot (Stone), 3 Elliott Bldg.
ld McDonald (Cement), 1400
t St.
McElheny (Plastering), 1503
t St.
Iedland & Sons (Brick and
, 38 Eel River Ave.
E. Morehead (Plastering), N.
r. Bartlett and Kloenne (S T).
. Price (Brick and Stone),
) and State Sts.

Logansport—Continued.
Wm. E. Shafer (Street), 2211 High St.
M. A. Talbott & Co. (General), Room 3 Elliott Bldg.
Henry Weigand (Brick and Stone), 613 Miami.
Orlando M. Werner (Plastering), N. S. Bartlett 1 E Kloenne (S T).
Eden E. Williams (Plastering), 1408 Market St.
Andrew Winters (Cement), 34 Michigan Ave.
Henry J. Wolf (Mason), 76 Bates St.
Leonard Wolf (Stone), 16 Columbia St.

MARION—
Chas. W. Barley.
S. M. Grandy.
Lewis Hartshorn.
Wm. Hartshorn.
Leffler & Bland.
L. C. Lillard.
John McDonald.
Miller & Williams.

MARTINSVILLE—
Burton & Prather.
S. J. Mandeville.
Henry Russ.

MICHIGAN CITY—
Judson Alexander, 217 E. 4th St.
Chas. De Witt.
Ohming Bros.
Aug. Schneider.
Jas. Southard.
Aug. Schneider & Son.

MISHAWAKA—
A. S. Hess.
Henry Schmidt.

MITCHELL—
Reuben Bareford.
J. A. Coleman.
Daniel Lee.

MUNCIE—
John A. Brown, 707 E. Main St.
Wm. Bussard.
James Carpenter, 919 E. Washington St.
William Dakin, 217 W. Willard St.
Thomas P. Duke, 521 S. Grant St.
J. M. Gee, 122 N. Dill N. C.
Michael Glaser, 1005 Center St.
Lee M. Glass, 210 E. 8th St.
J. W. Golenor, 1307 S. Beacon St.
O. J. Hager, S. W. Cor. Elm & Highland Ave.
Hamilton & Snyder, 310 E. Gilbert St.
Grant Hancock, 1345 Kirby Ave.
Marion Hathaway, 305 N. Jackson St.
Philip Hedrick, 622 W. Howard St.
W. H. Hickman, 719 Powers.
Geo. H. Higman, 117 E. Seymour St.
Indiana Bridge Co.
Chas. E Kellir,.
Oscar Kieble, 708 W. Main St.
S. T. Kiser, 612 E. Charles St.

Muncie—Continued.
E. A. Leatherman, 413 S. Jefferson St.
George Lowe.
James B. Ludlow, 217 E. Howard St.
John W. Max, 1501 S. Madison St.
D. C. Mitchell, 214 E. Howard St.
J. S. Moore.
Wm. H. Moore, 807 S. Monroe St.
Morrow & Morrow, 516 E. Washington St.
Chas. E. Nicewander, 307 E. Jackson St.
John W. Norris, 202 Riverside Ave., Riverside.
E. J. Pearson, alley between Main & Jackson, west of Franklin.
N. B. Powers, 305 Wheeling Ave., Riverside.
John D. Ridge, 1127 E. Washington St.
H. C. Russey.
Isaac W. Sayler, 417 S. Council St.
Ezra Searles, 816 E. Washington St.
Martin Shafer, 1101 E. Willard St.
Leander Shaver, 521 S. Grant St.
Samuel G. Sheller, Cor. Berlin and Powers.
E. Shopbell, 105 E. Gilbert St.
Albert N, Shuttleworth.
John W. Souders, 1111 E. Jackson.
Stahle & Riegle, 216 W. Main St.
L. Stogdell, 1201 Powers St.
John H. Stover, 510 W. Howard St.
Chas. Ferd Van Deveer, 626 N. Jefferson St.
Isaac W. Whitemyre, 804 W. Main St.
L. G. Williams, 517 E. Charles St.
Simeon Wright, 1122 W. 22d St.
D. V. Zimmerman, 1103 W. 1st St.

NEW ALBANY—
Squire Beattie, 1514 N. 1st St.
Louis Biel, 1915 Charlestown Rd.

NEW TRENTON—
Louis Brow.

NOBLESVILLE—
Hiram Avery.
E. F. Cottingham.
H. D. Gray.
Heinzmann Bros.
Isaac P. Keiser.
L. B. Lanham.
Cal. Stafford.

NORTH MANCHESTER—
Jonas Grossnickle.
J P. Noftzger.
Jno. D. Spurgeon.

NORTH VERNON—
J. B. Miller.

OAKLAND CITY—
Chas. Alexander.
T. J. Bacon.
Jo. Beardsley
Frank Linzy.

PENNVILLE—
Phillips & Palley.

PERU—
Michael Burke.

PLYMOUTH—
Wm. McDuffie.
Jacob Ness.
E. Price & Sons.
Chas. Rasenberry.

PORTLAND—
E. W. Buck, Box 291.
Geo. Loyd.
William Stephens.

RENSSELAER—
Hiram Day.
John H. Jessen.
Norman Bros.
Warren & Rush.

RICHMOND—
Christian E. Burkhardt (artif. 226 S. 7th St.
James Carrell (street pavin N. 17th St.
John T. Cronin (street pavin N. Ninth St.
Frederick Grottendick (street 51 S. 23d.
Henry J. Hasecoster (general) 12th St.
Joseph N. Hodgin (general) 17th & N. B.
Wm. Lee, 406 N. 6th St.*
Henry Miller (street paving), 6th St.
Daniel F. O'Neal (general), 5 13th St.
Wm. Rehling (cement w'k'rs), 6th St.
George W. Simmons (cement w 210 N. 7th St.
G. W. Sumption.
Aug. A. Turner.
Wm. Wagner.
Fredk. Waking.

RISING SUN—
James Harris.
Geo. W. Gibbs.

ROCHESTER—
A. F. Bowers.
Carter & Onstott.
D. L. Gaskill.
Jno Hill.
Marsh Hill.

ROCKVILLE—
Jos. A. Britton.
L. W. Brown.
Edgar Jerome.
Ferguson & Co.
Patton & Lang.

RUSHVILLE—
Samuel A. Glore.
Oglesby & Kelley.
J. Hill Vance.

SALEM—
Geo. Carroll.
Ambrose Shrum.
Hiram Smock.
R. N. Owens.

3URG—
ırnett.
Bottorff & Snodgrass.
ıodgrass.
.—
. Short.
itewart.
Bros.
'ILLE—
. Smith.
END—
nderson.
rnes & Sons.
. Barnes & Co.
. Bruce.
efrees, 315 S. Taylor St.
Bros.
& Shank.
:—
Babbs.
. Green.
Massey.
linkard.
'Y—
ɜarwater.
ɔoper & Son.
ller.
ichoenberger.
HAUTE—
. Abbott.
lood.
rler.
Fromme, 7th & Hulman

iebel.
Construction Co.
Judd.
ıdd.
& Earl.
P. McGinnis.
Miller.
Miller.
t Miller.
& Coplin.
Morton & Co., 629 Wabash Ave.
Peters.
ele.
& Steig Co.
Haute Artifical Stone Works.
oorhees & Co.
Vallace.
'OWN—
Carmack.
Young.
—
Bowlin & Hadley.
:AISO—
ndahl.
ındy & Hugart.
—
Г. Gordon.
. Plew.
Sabberton.
abberton.
ıbberton.

VINCENNES—
Jas. Friese.
Casper & Wm. Heyman.
John Hartigan, 12 S. 2d St.
J. D. LaCroix.
W. H. Moore.
John Seligman.
Ben Vatchett.

WABASH—
Thos. Bridges Son.
Philip Hipskind & Sons.
Lambert Bros.
Edward Smith.
Valentine Smith.
Thorne & Williams.

WARSAW—
A. W. Bates.
Thos. M. Le Hew & Son.

WASHINGTON—
Noah Bogard, 1400 E. Grove.
Brown Bros.
John W. Feagans, 704 W. Walnut St.
Reister Bros.

WEST LAFAYETTE—
Nathanial B. Moore, N. Vine St.
Sanders & Jamison.
Samuel Snyder, Grant & State Sts.
Byron Sowders, Vine & Columbia St.

WHITING—
W. F. Brunt.
G. H. Hilliard.
Mahon & Laverty.
Jerry O'Neil.
Wm. Schniderwent.

WINAMAC—
Stephen Parcel.

WINCHESTER—
Geo. Yeager.

WOLCOTTVILLE—
H. C. Brown.

IOWA.

ALGONA—
A. M. Coan.
Cowan & McMurray.

AMES—
A. L. Gardner.

ANAMOSA—
E. C. Holt.
J. E. Powers.

ATLANTIC—
Con Enright.

BELLE PLAINE—
Palmer Bros.

BURLINGTON—
O. M. Burris, 608 Jefferson St.
Fesemin & Miller.
Fred Hoppman.
Geo. Kriechbaum.
Frank Landell.
Lyda & Co.
Isaac Pearson.

CARROLL—
Hart & Mohler.
V. Hinricks.

CEDAR FALLS—
Jeff Bishop.
Coombs & Son, 1401 W. 8th St.
Philpot & Carrigan.
Jas. Robinson.
W. A. Robinson.
CEDAR RAPIDS—
John Anderson.
R. L. Bowe.
Boynton & Warriner.
F. M. Brown.
W. A. Edgar.
Ford & Dela Hunt.
Jackson Construction Co.
W. O. Johnson.
Murray Bros.
Budd Snoufer.
L. Wallace & Son.
Wardle & Yeager.
CHARITON—
S. H. Malloy.
CHARLES CITY—
W. C. Collins.
Henry Craig.
J. L. Johnson.
C. Kuhnle.
Charles Schroeder.
CHEROKEE—
T. W. Faus.
Millard & Symmes.
COUNCIL BLUFFS—
L. C. Besley, 1501 N. Broadway.
J. B. Connor, 1107 S. 4th.
Martin Hughes & Son, 903 S 3rd.
McMahon Roofing Co.
S. W. Reynolds & Sons, 901 7th Ave.
Welshans & Holbrook, 309 S. 17th.
E. A. Wickham & Co., 19 Scott.
Wickham Bros. 19 Scott.
CLINTON—
S. Shoecraft & Son.
Smith & Ockis.
CORYDON—
J. C. Brazil.
CRESCO—
Seth Pearson.
DAVENPORT—
P. Connelly, 307 E. 10th.
Corry & Wernentin Co.
Davenport Granitoid Co., 205 Brady St.
Flick & Johnson Const. Co., 53 Schmidt Bld.
D. A. McGirgin, 228 N. 12th.
Tri City Const. Co, 35 Masonic Temple.
Walsh Const. Co., Masonic Temple.
DES MOINES—
J. E. Allen.
Butcher & Storey, 527 E. Walnut.
J. W. Campbell, Rollins Blk.
Capital City Brick & Pipe Co.
J. H. Chenoweth, 1615 Lyon.
Des Moines Asphalt Co., 213 5th St.
Flint Brick Co., 210 5th St.
Timothy O'Brien & Co., 948 10th St.

Des Moines—Continued.
N. W. Stark & Co., Equitable Bld
J. E. Toussaint, 616 High.
Fremont Turner.
DUBUQUE—
Wm. Baker.
Blake Roofing Co.
Byrne & Saul.
T. J. Donahue.
P. Eisbach.
E. J. Evans.
Jno. Liley.
O'Farrell & Norton.
Portland Paving Co. Jas. Lee, M 207 W. Locust St.
Stenck & Lineham.
J. Y. Streek.
Matthew Tschirgi, Jr., 46 Henion
EAGLE GROVE—
Joe Witzel.
ELDORA—
W. S. Allison & Son.
Wm. A. Kyle.
M. M. Mullford.
Shirley & White.
ESTHERVILLE—
F. Miller.
Ed. Nourse.
FAIRFIELD—
William Cook.
William Donaldson.
Archie Gilchrist.
Richard Way.
Jno. Z. Wildman.
FT. DODGE—
Frank McCann.
FT. MADISON—
B. Lantry Sons.
Ft. Madison Construction Co.
GRINNELL—
R. G. Coutts.
INDEPENDENCE—
D. C. Sheehan.
IOWA CITY—
John L. Berry.
J. S. Farrell.
Thos. Hanlon.
Wm. Horrabin.
John B. Lauer.
J. Osborne.
Sam'l Tomlin.
KEOKUK—
Cameron & McManus.
Tom Dwyer.
Jno. Eastline & Co.
McCutcheon Bros.
McManus & Tucker.
Jas. McNamara & Sons.
F. E. Stamms.
LE MARS—
L. B. Faus.
Barney Kramer.
Chas. D. Symmes.
MALVERN—
J. W. Bartley.
R. L. Hammond.

ALLTOWN—
tkinson.
ilman.
CITY—
& White.
abler.
Gardiner & Co..
& Kropf.
Hillmar.
elson, 322 W. 11th St.
ore & Co.
mes.
bsing.
Wells.
ELLO—
& Lightfoot.
EASANT—
& Norman.
TNE—
er.
Murphy.
AMPTON—
Roberts.
N—
Eller.

mett.
A—
Schropp.
OSA—
Blake.
Carlon & Son.
Mathews.
Nelson.
Sipes.
Wareham.
VA—
onstruction & Mfg. Co.
-
Burnett.
ourtney.
McDevitt.
N—
Vade.
NDOAH—
Burkhard.
CITY—
Angess.
Rabue.
Baker Co., 412 Brown Blk.
stianson & Co.
Palace Cement Works, P. P.
ll, Prop. Box 297.
Hanlon & Co.
Bros.
—
Herron.
Morrison.

Foundry & Machine Co.
—
Bossert.
Irmis.
Leefers.
Wickman.

VILLISCA—
J. S. Dahuff.
R. Hale.
F. W. Swanson.
WATERLOO—
F. N. Eastman.
D. P. Faus.
L. B. Faus.
Wm. Hetts.
Jno. Moothart.
Nathan Moothart.
M. L. Newton, 617 Mulberry St.
J. F. Schifferdaker, 127 N. Mulberry St.
WAVERLY—
Frank W. Russell.
WEBSTER CITY—
C. E. Atkinson.
Brigg & Klareland.
W. J. Zitterall.
WINTERSET—
Harry Clearwater.
A. L. Foster.

KANSAS.

ABILENE—
J. L. Kruger.
ARCADIA—
A. H. Bourne.
ARGENTINE—
Brown & Dodson.
Drollinger & Barrett, 417 W. Metropolitan Ave.
G. W. Gully.
ARKANSAS CITY—
J. H. Brown.
ATCHISON—
Thomas Beattie.
M. J. Clozes.
R. W. Kelly.
McAuly & Bryning.
E. S. Wills.
L. Wines.
CHERRYVALE—
Adams & Behner.
J. H. Brewster.
G. W. Brewster.
Thos. Pettigrew.
L. S. Skelton.
CONCORDIA—
J. H. Cleary.
T. P. Larson.
A. Linville.
W. T. Short.
COUNCIL GROVE—
Joseph Axe.
J. W. Colyer.
P. S. Martz.
L. Peterson.
EL DORADO—
T. B. Appleman.
M. M. Baker.
W. W. Lentz.
I. A. Rich.
Small & Sanford.
L. D. Stewart.

EMPORIA—
J. M. Anderson.
E. Daniels.
E. F. Sprague.
D. L. Thomas.
EPHRATA—
Ephrata Electric Co.
EUREKA—
C. E. Chandler.
FORT SCOTT—
E. P. Bowen.
Goodlander Lbr. Co.
E. J. March.
John McDonald, 582 S. Main.
E. E. Strother.
GALENA—
Barker & Son.
Wm. Goff.
B. Lillard.
J. W. McClung.
Geo. W. McCullough.
J. W. Rupert.
W. H. Stephenson.
C. H. W. Sturtridge.
GARNETT—
J. W. Barndt.
Jno. Stump.
Wheelon & Dockendorf.
GIRARD—
Girard Brick Co.
HIAWATHA—
John Krebs.
Wm. Helter.
J. K. Hirth.
INDEPENDENCE—
T. D. Brewster.
Jas. Carter.
J. W. Glass.
W. H. Kiney.
S. A. Smith.
IOLA—
American Construction Co.
KANSAS CITY—
Allen & Allen, 637 Osage St.
Allen & Dumas, 608 S. 6th St.
C. J. Anderson, 844 Ohio St.
J. H. Babbitt, 1024 Barnett St.
H. W. Bachman, 712½ Lyon St.
N. D. Bass, 2028 Darby St.
I. N. Bennett, 1606 N. 5th St.
I. D. Blackburn, 820 Everett St.
J. L. Bright, 737 Tauromore St.
H. R. Brown, 1302 N. 3d St.
J. W. Brown, 2115 N. 5th St.
J. F. Buckley, 1015 Balt. St.
Robert Burton, 26 N. 6th St.
W. J. Butler, 528 Minn. Ave.
D. E. Caswell, 443 Washn. St.
D. N. D. Clark, 634 Sandusky St.
J. C. Consaul, 728 Parallel Ave.
W. H. Criswell, 1310 N. Third St.
J. H. Crow, 262 S. Tremont St.
S. J. Davidson, 1411 N. Fifth St.
M. H. Deavey, 731 Armstrong St.
J. T. Dempsey, 650 S. First St.
Joseph Diamond, 36 N. Second St.
Thomas Downs, 534 Ann St.

Kansas City—Continued.
Eugene Dreier, 311 N. Ninth St.
M. G. Ela, 2002 N. Sixth St.
R. B. Elliott, 238 N. Sixteenth S
C. A. Ellis.
T. S. Evans, 647 Orville St.
M. J. Faubion, 837 S. Balt. St.
J. W. Ferguson, 518 N. Seventh
L. G. Ferguson, 570 S. Park St.
William Fletcher, 1600 Armstrong
F. C. Foster, 2 Perry St.
F. L. Funk, 645 Tauromore St.
E. N. Garcelon, 731 Homer St.
Jeremiah Grindrod, 344 Ann St.
P. A. Hager, 226 N. 8th St.
T. F. Hannan, 511 New Jersey
I. L. B. Henderson, 817 S. 6th St.
J. M. Hines, 860 Orville St.
W. P. House, 720 Ferry St.
James Howison, 1137 Locust St.
C. H. Inge, 1235 Orange St.
P. J. Johnson, 53 S. 8th St.
J. W. Jones, 1000 Osage St.
Kansas City Cement Sidewalk C
Leonard Kemp, 508 N. 5th St.
P. H. Kreisher, 739 Armstrong
John Lahey, 413 Miami St.
William Ledbetter, 713 Everett
A. H. Lytte, 902 Miami St.
H. J. McCashin, 534 Barnett St.
J. T. McCaulley, 529 Sandusky
T. M. McCaulley, 1043 Neb. Ave.
Proctor McCormick, 1608 N. 5th
F. A. Melvin, 630 S. 8th St.
J. M. Miller, 746 Sandusky St.
William O'Connell, 644 Barnett St
C. S. Otto, 619 New Jersey St.
C. L. Peterson, 427 Dugarro St.
Prather & Rowe, 747 Minn. Ave.
G. M. Reeds, 250 N. 8th St.
T. C. Russell, 2111 N. 5th St.
E. D. Ryan, 914 S. 5th St.
Charles Schlosser, 1300 Ohio St.
C. A. Schogren, 272 N. 6th St.
S. S. Sharpe, 2210 N. 10th St.
A. H. Sibley, 4 Franklin St.
Joseph Small, 822 Tauromore St
D. F. Smith, 837 Splitlog St.
J. A. Smith, 1720 N. 5th St.
J. F. Stanley, 817 Barnett St.
F. H. Taylor, 748 Sanford St.
J. W. Taylor, 827 S. Mill St.
G. W. Thompson, 616 S. 6th St.
C. M. Thorpe, 835 S. 10th St.
W. H. Weaver, 740 Barnett St.
T. J. Williams, 616 N. 9th St.
Eugene Woodcock, 719 Lyon St.
LEAVENWORTH—
Chapin & Greever.
Owen Duffy.
A. M. Geiger.
John McGuire.
MARYSVILLE—
Wm. Dougherty.
Theodore Hammett.
Theodore Hahn.
Peter Rozine.

o.

on.

n, 962 Lincoln St.
521 Johnson St.
14 Morgan St.
1161 Johnson St.
Belmont St.
r, 1731 Forest St.

ent.
W. Gordon St.

WELLINGTON—
W. P. Seaton.
Chas. Cooper.
D. Murphy.

WICHITA—
J. W. Burton.
J. W. Koontz.
A. L. Laird.
C. H. Sumption.

KENTUCKY.

ASHLAND—
Charles D. Boggess.
Davidson & King.
J. J. Gates & Co.
Jno. O'Kelly.
Ed White.

BOWLING GREEN—
R. Underwood.

COVINGTON—
Artificial Stone & Tile Co., 206 Park.
Carl Bros., 813 Crescent.
Covington Artificial Stone Co., 822 Main.
John McKenna & Son, 1807 Greenup.
Jas. Steffen.
T. W. Spinks.
Jerry Sullivan, 86 Howell St.
Elsworth L. Woods, Edwards & George.
Robert Woods, 1660 Edward.

CYNTHIANA—
Frank Asbury.
J. R. Poindexter.
J. A. Smiser.

DANVILLE—
E. K. Dillehan.

DAYTON—
Fred Gerrein, 313 6th St.
John Trapp, 1st and Clay Sts.
Frank E. Walter.

EARLINGTON—
Geo. Farnsworth.
Lee Oldham.
M. McCord.

FRANKFORT—
W. E. Bosworth.
Mason, Hoge, King & Co.
Ben. F. Morrison.
E. Power, Agt.

FRANKLIN—
Thos. H. Ford.

GLASGOW—
E. R. Davis.
Geo. H. Mansfield.

HARRODSBURG—
Robt. Edgers.
J. W. Robards.
J. M. Smith.

HENDERSON—
P. C. Kyle.
Ed Manion.
R. P. Farmsworth.

HISEVILLE—
Welby Ebert.

HOW TO HELP BUSINESS

In plans for building up business reputation—really the first essential step—and for getting business, the best help at the least expense is in good advertising.

In the matter of advertising we have all that is good.

Look through MUNICIPAL ENGINEERING MAGAZINE and you will see that we have good advertisers—we don't want any other kind.

The service to them is so good that many of them think it is all they need.

If you seek business in our field you need our help.

In our field we know what we can do. We don't hesitate to say that we can do about all that can be done.

We cover the field thoroughly, we study it constantly, we are closely in touch with it everywhere.

Our organization embraces the best ability and the most thorough service.

This is the help you need—it is the kind that will do more for you than all other at less expense.

Write to us and ask us what we can do for you—if we can't help you we will tell you so—if we can we will tell you how, and that is what you want to know if you are progressive and wide awake.

Municipal Engineering Co.

See What Others Say About Our Service

What An Advertisement Did In Ten Days

Chicago, Ill., Nov. 24, 1900.
Municipal Engineering Co.

Gentlemen: Last month we placed an advertisement in your Magazine, which appeared for the first time in the November number, and which gave us the benefit of your advance information bulletin service. From this bulletin we obtained information which led to the sale of two of our concrete mixing machines, within ten days after the advertisement first appeared.

We are much pleased at the promptness with which returns have been realized, and beg to express our appreciation of your Magazine as an advertising medium, and also the great help which your bulletin service has proved to us. Yours very truly,

McKELVEY CONCRETE MACHINERY CO.

One Job That More Than Repaid Them

Chicago, Ill., Oct. 31, 1900.
The Municipal Engineering Magazine.

Dear Sirs: The first of January last, we placed an advertisement in your Magazine, and also subscribed to same. Believing that credit should be given when due, we desire to write and advise you that we have secured, through the advance information on contemplated work, very valuable information to us the past year, and in fact, we have secured through your Magazine one job of which we knew nothing before, which more than repays us for the cost of the advertisement.

In our business we are desirous at all times of securing recommendations for our material and feeling that possibly you have the same desire in this line, we write you as above. If this is of any service to you you are at liberty to make use of it.

Yours truly,
THE CLEVELAND STONE CO.
(Signed) C. W. Walters,
Western Agent.

NSVILLE—
s & Bro.
& Richards.
ı Bros.
ON—
Daisey.
Fowler.
Gooodin.
Goodin.
Goodin.
Strong.
ΞTON—
y & Haney.
Justice.
Construction Co.
Winter.
ILLE—
Alsmeier, 2509 W. Market St.
Bailey, 1204 Preston.
Butterhoff, 1318 E. Jacob Ave.
nridge Asphalt Co., 358 14th St.
Carwell, 561 3d.
Colston, 55 Bismarck Ave., W. h St.
ıyne, 314 W. Main St.
Cornell, 1226 18th St.
Cornell, 561 3d St.
Crowley, 1219 7th St.
Davison, 1052 2d St.
onahue, 1320 W. Main St.
Everett, 1123 W. Market St.
'ity Artificial Stone Co., 144 E.

'igg, 453 W. Jeff. St.
'. Fitch, Main cor. Wenzel.
'. Fitsch, 2715 Virginia Ave.
ıalson, 544 W. Jeff. St.
Inau, 1311 21st St.
Gosnell, 327 5th St.
Iosnell, 1, 327 5th St.
Hairkins, 1546 Prentice St.
Houser, 630 Clay St.
Jones, 2705 High Ave.
King, 1013 Ash St.
lle Artificial Stone Co., 253

le Contracting Co., 915 Columbia Bldg.
Lewman & Co., 816 Columbia

'. Mehler, 345 5th St.
. Miller, 543 26th St.
Montgomery, 2428 Park Ave.
cCarty, 1220 13th St.
ıl Roofing & Supply Co., '. Main St.
'in, 1717 W. Chestnut St.
'ugent & Bro., 238 5th St.
wens, 606 Equitable Bldg.
ıte, 1820 W. Walnut.
Yates, 1127 W. Main.
edman, 1812 Hancock.
ffran, 512 E. Ky.
nahan & Co., 510 Columbia

ıon, 1800 12th St.

Louisville—Continued.
Charles Stilger, 1817 W. Walnut St.
R. E. Warren, 1927 W. Walnut St.
Willard & Cornwell, Columbia Bldg.
W. A. Wilson, 1810 W. Jeff.
B. S. Witton, 2543 Beech St.
Jeremiah Williams, 780 W. Walnut.
Whitney Artificial Stone Co., 315 5th.

MADISONVILLE—
W. C. Mann.
M. C. Reynolds.

MAYFIELD—
J. C. Belote.
Jacob Hooper.

MAYSVILLE—
Purnell Bros.

NEWPORT—
Peter Ader
Harry E. Brawley.
Thos. C. Brown, 210 York.
Joseph Collspy.
Fitzsimmons Bros., 12th & Brighton.
Geo. B. Smith.
Chas. Spinks & Son, 121 E. 6th.

OWENSBORO—
C. E. Dawson.
Badger & Welch.
J. N. Grady.
C. C. Hooper.
Geo. C. Littell.
J. J. Williams.

PADUCAH—
Jacob Briderman.
Chamblain & Murray.
Joseph Dringle, Jr.
Al. Hymarsh.
F. W. Katterjohn & Sons.
J. E. Williamson.

PARIS—
The Art Stone Work Co. B. F. Monday & Son, Props.

RICHMOND—
L. R. Blanton.
D. H. Myers.
G. H. Myers.
Samuel Rice.
D. Shanahan & Co.
Turpin, Stone & Co.

SHELBYVILLE—
Morris Brown.
L. H. Gruber & Sons.
Timothy Megane.
Daniel O'Leary.

WINCHESTER—
Marshall Bates.
H. Brent.
Horace Colerane.
M. A. Donohue.
Henry Judy.
J. & B. White.

LOUISIANA.

ALEXANDRIA—
Hoffman & Wilson.
Jno. Runshang.
L. A. Stafford.

BATON ROUGE—
H. J. Allen.
Jas. D. Brown.
Geo. Legg.
R. L. Pruyn.
DONALDSONVILLE—
J. Deslattes.
J. Dudenhoffer.
J. E. Hebert.
D. Landry.
FRANKLIN—
W. B. Cook.
HOME PLACE—
Victor Adema.
Joseph Dringle, Jr.
ILLAWARA—
R. Nicholson.
KENNER—
Frank Burke.
Jourdan Bros.
HOUMA—
Bonvillain & Bergeron.
J. E. Naquin.
KLOTZVILLE—
Donovan & Daly.
MANCHOC—
M. Hanick.
MILLIKEN'S BEND—
A. S. Calthar.
MONROE—
I. T. Davis.
H. C. Voss.
J. F. Wetzell.
J. W. Wright.
MOUND—
F. A. Maxwell.
NEW IBERIA—
Jules Dryfus.
J. W. Taylor.
NEW ORLEANS—
C. J. Babst, 1205 S. Franklin St.
Barber Asphalt Paving Co., 708 Hennen Building.
Belden & Seelay, 616 Commercial.
George Blanchin, 316 Baronne St.
Henry W. Bond, 350 Baronne St.
Sidney A. Calougne, 806 Perdido St.
Walter T. Carey & Bro., 630 Camp St.
J. Catrano, 1022 Toulouse St.
A. Chevalier Pavement Co., 523 St. Louis St.
Joseph F. Codifer, 806 Grover.
Charles F. Collom & Co., 320 Carondolet St.
Gabriel Correjollies, 817 Union St.
Craven & Co., 320 Carondolet St.
J. A. Craven & Co., Carondolet and Union Sts.
J. B. Craven, 531 Canal St.
C. J. Cullom, Carondolet & Union Streets.
Gasper Cusachs, 316 Baronne St.
John Dempsey, 1028 Jackson Ave.
Eastwick Engineering Co., 531 Canal St.
Fabacher & Estalotte, 1519 Canal St.
Philip Fath, 536 Sixth St.

New Orleans—Continued.
Maurice Feitel, 824 Magazine St.
James M. Ferguson, 826 Union St.
John H. Gardner, 505 Tchoupi St.
George J. Glover, 311 Baronne St.
Gulf Dredging & Timber Co., Gravier St.
Adolph H. Hanemann, jr., 817 Uni St.
Edward Hely, 513 Canal St.
John B. Honor & Co., 213 Delta St.
Hunter & Frey, 531 Canal St.
F. Jahncke, 816 Howard St.
John J. Keegan, 3607 Magazine St
John M. Kelly, 321 Carondolet St.
E. F. Keplinger, 822 Union St.
A. M. Lockett & Co., 339 Carond St.
Louisiana Improvement [illegible] Hennen Building.
Sheldon Lynne, 326 S. Dorgenois S
John McCoy, 1433 Melpomene
Robert McNamara, 219 Excha Place.
R. G. Memory, 117 S. Derbigny.
Metropolitan Building Co., 217 ronne St.
Mississippi Levee Construction (513 Canal St.
J. D. Moody & Co., Ltd., 606 Co mercial Place.
National Contracting Co., 713 H nen Bldg.
John J. Navo, 2202 Cleveland St.
Peter Navo, 2202 Cleveland St.
Josiah B. Outland, 337 St. Charles
Caesar Prola, 722 Toulouse St.
Payne & Joubert, 423 Carondolet
Robert R. Rifenberick.
Rosetta Gravel Paving & Impro ment Co., 808 Perdido St.
Nathanial G. Scott, 806 Gravier St
Aug. F. Slaugerup, 204 Godcha Bldg.
Hugh Smith, 2414 S. Franklin St.
Southern Asphalt Paving Co., Perdido St.
Charles Spinks & Son, 121 Caron let.
Harry C. Spinks, 531 Canal St.
R. S. Stearnes & Co., 302 Hen Building.
William R. Taylor, 806 Common S
D. & J. Trauchina, 1104 Sixth St.
G. D. Von Phul, 229 Magazine St.
W. L. Whitlow, 425 Gravier St.
Harry W. Wright, 866 Carondolet
OPELOUSAS—
J. E. Allen.
Geo. Pulford, Jr.
ST. ROSE—
J. M. Lambert.
E. H. Williford.

'EPORT—
in Bros.
o. Chachere.
VISTA—
: Nicholson.
ꝛPROOF—
McLaughlin.

MAINE.

ıR—
& Grady.
Luriet.
Robinson.
M. Sawyer.
-
P. Healey.
rd ·Landrigan.
Nichols Co.
·. Reed.
·l H. Rogers.
.ST—
ıald & Morrison.
:CK— •
ın Lord.
ws Bros.
BAY HARBOR—
Becker.
Dodge.
Dolloff.
PORT—
Ames & Co.
WICK—
H. Barnes.
E. Hacker.
—
Walker.
LLTON—
Kelley.
Robinson.
Shaw.
R—
Cobb.
ORT—
oast Packing Co.
OFT—
ay Babson.
r Dexter.
. Folsom.
d P. Martin.
Nichols.
)WELL—
Haines.
W. Howard.
Lundey.
TON—
e & Clifford.
ı Howard, 36 Lisbon.
AS—
Gilson.
Preble. .
)N—
ɔn & Johnson.
)WN—
Winchell.
DEXTER—
Flanders.

NORWAY—
C. H. Adams.
Horace Pike.
OLD ORCHARD—
Duff Construction Co.
OLD TOWN—
Elem T. Hartwell.
J. B. Morin & Son.
Andrew J. Sampson.
Rufus D. Wadleigh.
ORONO—
Elmer Littlefield.
S. McPheters.
Patrick Wall.
PITTSFIELD—
Bryant & Co.
Arthur Libby.
PORTLAND—
Ephriam Dyer, Cape Elizabeth.
D. F. Griffin & Bro., 122 Exchange.
Portland Pipe Co., 23 Pearl.
Thos. Shannahan, 221 Franklin.
Geo. H. Smardon & Co., 22 Exchange.
Joseph Westcott, 191 Middle.
ROCKLAND—
W. H. Glover & Co.
W. S. White.
SANFORD—
W. J. Philpot.
SKOWHEGAN—
Jas. A. Hoxie & Sons.
N. P. Reed.
H. E. Reed.
THOMASTON—
F. A. Atkins.

MARYLAND

BALTIMORE—
Jas. H. Atkinson, 14 North.
H. S. Best, 702 2d Ave. N. Pulaski.
Jas. Biden, Cor. Pratt and Parkin.
Ernest P. Brandt, 30 Washington St., Homestead.
Filbert Paving and Const. Co., 1310 Block St.
Thos. Garner, 1715 Aisquith.
Jas. F. McCabe & Co., Equitable Bldg.
Jas. P. McGovern, 209 E. Fayette.
Maryland Construction and Contracting Co., Equitable Bldg.
Maryland Pavement Co., Equitable Bldg.
Max B. Miller, 1430 Patapsco S.
John W. Paxton, 18 Maple Ave., W.
Peach Bottom Cement, Tile and Brick Co.
Patrick Reddington, 1344 Asquith.
John L. Robertson, 302 Fidelity Bldg.
Roland Park Co.
Sanford & Brooks, 21 S. Gay.
John Schaffner, 1008 Ridgley.
Schwind Quarry Co., Fidelity Bldg.
Arthur L. Shreve, 202 E. Chase St.
Stevens Litholite Stone Co.
John H. Thorman & Co., 12 McClellan St.

CAMBRIDGE—
J. B. Brown, Race St.
J. H. Hubbard, Race St.
Henry Patchell, Travers St.

CHESTERTOWN—
W. S. Carroll.
W. S. Culp & Son.
F. E. Dwyer.
R. K. Pippin.
W. T. Pippin.

CRISFIELD—
E. C. Furniss.
Fred Gibbons.
S. C. Gibbons.
S. J. Gibbons.
C. W. Goldsborough.
H. Hayman.
A. L. Webb.

CUMBERLAND—
G. H. Martz.

FROSTBURG—
Fuller Bros
Henry Williams.
Peter Whetstone.

HAGERSTOWN—
March & Keedy.

HAVRE DE GRACE—
Geo. V. Mitchell.
Sam'l Touchton.

ROCKVILLE—
Thomas C. Groomes.
Alfred C. Warthen.
Edwin M. West.

POCOMOKE—
H. B. Pritchard.
James Richards.

PRINCESS ANNE—
Jas. McAllen.

ROCKVILLE—
Thos. C Groomes.
Alfred C. Worthen.
Edwin M. West.

SALISBURY—
Wm. N. Bounds.
W. A. Crew.
W. J. Johnson.
T. M. Shumens.

WILLIAMSPORT—
J. Frank Kreps.
Miller Bros.
Smaltz & Drake.

MASSACHUSETTS.

AMESBURY—
Andrew Wilson.

AMHERST—
John Wrigley.

ARLINGTON—
Geo. H. Lowe.
Richard A. Welch & Co.

ATTLEBORO—
Attleboro Concrete & Roofing Co.

BEVERLY—
Thos. Fitzgibbon.
McSweeney & Cahill.

BEVERLY FARMS—
Beverly Water Dept.
Connolly Bros.
Linehan & Co.

BOSTON—
Aberthaw Construction Co., 7 Exchange Place.
American Fire Proofing Co., 166 Devonshire, Room 49.
American Sewage Disposal Co., 89 State, Room 57.
P. R. Bailey, 70 Kilby, Room 86.
Barnes Ruffin Co., 218 Tremont.
Bay State Fire Proofing Co., 1 Beacon.
Beacon Construction Co.
Edwin L. Booth, 79 Columbia Rd.
Boston Asphalt Co., 54 Kilby, Room 17.
Boston Tile & Mantel Co., 361 Boylston.
Louis G. Bragdon, 113 Devonshire.
Austin D. Brown, 55 State, Room 634.
J. L. Byrne, 131 Devonshire.
Walter F. Burke, 95 Milk.
Ethan R. Cheney, 166 Devonshire.
John C. Coleman & Son, 1536 Columbus Ave.
Collins & Ham, 119 Boston.
Coughlin & Ryan, 280 Columbus Ave.
Cork Floor & Tile Co., 17 Milk, Room 11.
George E. Crawley, 7 Tremont Place.
Patrick Cushing & Son, 215 Wash. St.
John J. Doyle, 3 Hollis.
Eastern Expanded Metal Co., 39 Court & 166 Devonshire.
C. H. Eastwick, 113 Devonshire.
Walter M. Evatt, 186 Devonshire.
George E. Fenn, 94 Blackstone.
H. Gore & Co., 54 Kilby.
Joseph W. Grigg, 24-26 Charlestown.
R. Gustavino Co., 19 Milk St., Room 53.
Aaron A. Hall, 23 Central.
Harries & Letteney Co, 1014 Tremont Bldg.
Charles Harris, 70 Kilby.
Geo. Hayes & Co., 95 Milk.
T. J. Hind, 19 Milk St.
Holbrook, Cabot & Daly, 1140 Tremont Bldg.
David H. Jacobs & Son, 166 Devonshire St.
John S. Jacobs & Son, Herald Bldg.
Jones & Meehan, 1 Beacon, Room 83.
W. H. Keyes & Co., 95 Milk.
John T. Langford, 70 Kilby.
D. W Lewis, 192 Devonshire.
A. A. Libby & Co., 79 Milk.
C. C. Litchfield, 69 Pearl.
Lord Bros, 40 State St.
Lombard Fireproofing Co., 166 Devonshire.
Low Art Tile Co., 129 Portland.
James McGraw & Co.
Metropolitan Contracting Co., 95 Milk.

'ontinued.
olitan Fire Proofing Co., 166
ıshire.
& Co., 93 Milk.
Murtfeldt Co., 192 Devonshire.
al Fire Proofing Co., 166 Dev-
re.
;ngland Fire Proofing Co., 178
nshire, Room 307.
ı & Maley, 16 City Hall Sq.
B. O'Rourke, 449 Dorchester

ıd Stone Ware Co., 42 Olive.
'ray, 166 Devonshire St.
ıg Construction Co., 178 Devon-
.
.eagan & Co., 971 Tremont.
us C. Richmond, 209 Wash.
Ryan, 16 E. Bos.
Shaw & Co., 8 Congress.
n Brothers, Corp., 166 Devon-

Smith, 2 A Park.
Dillingham & Co., 8 Oliver St.
ı & Waterman, 90 Canal.
. Carr & Andrews, 64 Federal

Trainer Mfg. Co., 89 and 91
.
:rumbull & Co., Tremont Bldg.
Turner & Co., 19 Milk St.,
ı 34.
Ufheil & Co., 25 Fanueil Hall

States Paving Co., 50 State
.
ı Brothers. 102 Milk.
'n Brothers Co., 143 Feder-
.
ən & Co., 43 Milk.
H. Whitney, 34 Hawley.
ɔr Cement Co., 446 Albany and
əvonshire.
'ON—
McBride.
TON—
Baldwin, 744 Montello St.
'assidy, 57 Perkins St.
Carpenter, 37 Belmont St.
W. Cornwell, 221 Ames.
:ribben, 16 Roan Court.
n Finn, 69 Otis St.
v Gale, 43 Pine St.
Iayward, 131 Clifton Ave.
Bros., 243 Howard St.
Jackson, 560 Summer St.
ınson, 43 Foster St.
'rie, 223 Warren Ave.
McDermott, 388 Pleasant St.
'll, Isain & Co., 338 Montello St.
W. Moury, 213 Prospect St.
n O'Connor, 57 River St.
1. Strauss, 122 Arthur St.
'd T. Fremaine, 24 E. Elm St.
White, 88 Main St.
n White, 24 Washburn Ave.
Williams, 33 Pearl St.

BROOKLINE—
Philip S. Allen, 81 Green.
J. Driscoll & Co.
CAMBRIDGE—
Barber Asphalt Paving Co., 246 First St.
Burditt & Bynner, 674 Mass. Ave.
David F. Burns, 5 Blackstone St.
Chandler & Barber, 124 Summer St.
William Condon, 351 Putnam Ave.
John T. Culhane, 18 Flagg St.
J. Culhane, 35 Boylston St.
John Doody, 9 Sparks.
John Dooly, 269 Mt. Auburn St.
John J. Donahue, 20 Decatur.
A. A. Elston & Co., 99 Broadway.
Geo. W. Gale Lumber Co., 640 Main St.
Heffernan Bros., 404 Columbia St.
Thomas J. Hind, 19 Milk St.
Frank Larner & Son, 14 Mill St.
Chas. Linehan, 1480 Cambridge St.
Geo. H. Lowe, 177 Mass. Ave.
Samuel McCullock, 49 Erie St.
T. J. Murphy & Co., 473 Main St.
Michael O'Sullivan, 11 Riverview Ave.
Hycent Purcell, 441 Main St.
John T. Scully & Bro., 84 First St.
Luther P. Slavin, 61 Broadway.
Jeremiah Sullivan, 25 Willard St.
Taylor, Carr & Andrews, Burney St., near First.
M. F. Tracy & Son, 74 Boylston St.
Wm. H. Wood & Co., 13 Broadway.
CHELMSFORD—
J. W. Robinson & Co.
CHELSEA—
Daniel Coughlin, 243 Webster Ave.
J. P. Morgan, 237 Spruce St.
CHICOPEE—
Patrick Beston.
Benj. F. Dotney.
Michael Hickey.
CHICOPEE FALLS—
John D. Sullivan.
CLINTON—
Devine & McBridge.
COTTAGE CITY—
F. P. Bunker.
DANVERS—
Edw. L. Kelly.
EAST HAMPTON—
Geo. W. Hendricks.
Thos Quinlan.
EAST WALPOLE—
Andrew Carberry.
EVERETT—
A. E. Blanchard.
Fessenden & Libby Co.
FALL RIVER—
William Beattie.
Beattie & Cornell.
Callahan & Daley Co.
Henry N. Cash, 522 Slade.
John Crowe.
Joseph M. Darling.

[illegible]—
[illegible]erguson.
N. Taylor.
[illegible]DFORD—
T. [illegible]man.
[illegible]ertram.
O. Brightman.
[illegible]Davis.
[illegible] & Co., 165 Hillman.
[illegible] Sullivan & Son.
[illegible]RYPORT—
[illegible]n Bros.
[illegible] Greely & Co.
[illegible]N—
[illegible] & Sons.
[illegible]N CENTRE—
[illegible] Muldoon.
[illegible]ADAMS—
[illegible] Lally, 87 Main St.
[illegible] & Hannam.
[illegible] & Co.
[illegible]y Bros.
[illegible]Wood & Co.
[illegible]MPTON—
[illegible] Bailey, 70 N. Elm St.
[illegible]ghton, 132 South.
[illegible] Layman, 25 Maple.
[illegible] Mathews.
[illegible]Mathews.
[illegible] Mather.
[illegible]earns, 80 Monroe.
[illegible]Whalen.
[illegible] Whiting.
[illegible]
[illegible]
[illegible] Smith.
[illegible]ELD—
[illegible] & Healy, 42 Bradford.
[illegible]Booth, 48 Kent Ave.
[illegible] Lumber Co., 108 Feirn [illegible]
[illegible] & Hall, 23 Hamlin St.
[illegible]Devanny, 154 Madison Ave.
[illegible] & Devanny, 180 Columbus [illegible]
[illegible]. Foote, 73 Bradford St.
[illegible]umber Co., Oak, near Lincoln [illegible]
[illegible] & Cheney, 45 Clapp St.
[illegible] Dillon, King St.
[illegible]. Halpine, Dalton Ave. and [illegible]rd St.
[illegible]aly, 18 Oak St.
[illegible] & Morrow, 59 North St.
[illegible]L. Humphrey, 15 Stoddard St.
[illegible]Kirchner, 156 North St.
[illegible]Markham, 172 First St.
[illegible]Hall & Co., 28 W. Housatonic [illegible]
[illegible]L. Petithory, 118 Alder St.
[illegible]Rabeau, 21 Pleasant St.
[illegible] H. Turner, 47 Lake St.
[illegible] Wallace, Plunkett north of [illegible]g.
[illegible]ard, Center and West Sts.
[illegible]oung, 253 River St.

PLYMOUTH—
George H. Harlow.

QUINCY—
Gilcoin Bros., 12 Quincy St.
Harkins Bros., 57 Goffe St.
C. B. Huston, Clay and Beale St.
Johann Johanson, 23 Arthur St.
Alex Kenn, 12 Columbia St.
Laurentius Klang, 10 Curtis St.
S. N. Maloney, 30 Fayette St.
Chas. W. McKenzie, 26 Intervale St.
Edw. Menhinick, 10 S. Walnut St.
Swan J. Peterson, 35 Albertina St.
Michael Shea, 30 Bunker Hill Ave.
August Siberg, 5 Nelson St.
F. A. Souther, 9 Edison St.
P. J. Williams, 5 Independence Ave.

READING—
E. H. Forbes.

REVERE—
Geo. H. Lancaster.

SALEM—
J. B. Balcomb.
Galmon & Driscoll.
Caleb M. Kelly, 57 Loring Ave.
S. S. Merrill.
E. F. Osgood.
Jos. N. Parsons.
Elijah R. Perkins, 8 Warren Court.
J. N. Peterson.
T. H. Sargent.
Tardiff & Caron, 13 Endicott St.
B. A. Touret.
J. E. Trask.
Jas. J. Welch & Co.

SOMERVILLE—
T. Allen, 187 Cedar.
Bartholomew Burke, 342 Lowell.
Christopher Burke, 116 Cedar.
Owen Cunningham, 78 Wash.
Edwin F. Cushing, 72 Central.
Theo. J. Cushing, 38 Beacon.
Daniel A. Dorey, 15 Appleton.
T. H. Gill, 22 Bonair.
W. J. McCarthy & Co., 27 Bonair.
Rutton & Woods, 89 Broadway.

SOUTHBRIDGE—
Calvin Claflin.

SOUTH FRAMINGHAM—
French Bros.
August Saucier.

SPRINGFIELD—
Geo. H. Blodget, 337 Central.
Peter Burke, 16 Osgood.
Michael Curtis, 105 Florence.
Jeremiah R. Driscoll, 385 Liberty.
Woodward Murkland, 44 Lafayette.
Vila A. Shaw, 86 Dawes.
D. D. Sprague, 342 Main.

STONEHAM—
Geo. H. Nichols.

TAUNTON—
W. R. Black, 32 Union.
Hugh F. Magee.

UXBRIDGE—
Newell & Snowling.

WALTHAM—
W. A. Cole & Co.
Wm. W. Hayes.
T. W. Kinser & Sons.
John Lally.
WARE—
P. J. Nelligan.
WARREN—
John Keenan.
WATERTOWN—
David F. Tripp.
WESTBORO—
Daniel P. Day.
WEST BERLIN—
Winston & Co.
WEST CHELMSFORD—
H. E. Fletcher.
WEST EVERETT—
Michael Talent & Co.
WESTFIELD—
William Dineen.
Geo. R. Miller.
WEST MEDFORD—
H. A. Halcomb & Co.
Louis G. Bragdon, 48 Sharon.
WEST NEWTON—
Wm. H. Mague.
Thomas P. Mague.
Gannon Bros.
WINCHESTER—
Thos. Quigley, 232 Main.
WINTHROP—
Craib & Trumbull.
Simon J. Donovan.
WOBURN—
J. M. Ellis & Co., Salem St.
Patrick Farrey, 22 Hudson St.
J. F. Kelley, 124 Arlington Road.
WORCESTER—
F. L. Allen.
Geo. W. Carr, 518 Main.
Geo. H. Cutting.
H. L. Jenks & Son, 6 Crystal.
Henry Mullen & Son.
Norcross Bros.
Nicholas R. Power & Co., 10 Merrifield.
Worcester Artificial Stone Co., 5 Sargeant.

MICHIGAN.

ADRIAN—
Thos. Gimbert.
Matthes Bros.
ALBION—
S. S. Brown & Co.
Dean & Dean.
Schumacher & Son.

HOW TO BUILD UP BUSINESS

The cardinal point in business success is to make yourself known to every person who can add anything to your business.

It is not possible for you to know all these people, but they can be made to know about you. This is your advantage.

Advertising does this. It opens the field. Success depends on how wisely this advertising is done. If it reaches people in your line it pays.

If you want business from the field represented by MUNICIPAL ENGINEERING MAGAZINE it will pay you to advertise in it.

Don't You Want Equal Advantage in this Field

›ung.
:BOR—
aumgardner, 217 5th Ave.
łros, 550 Ashley St.
Pickard.
: CREEK—
ackofen.
›empsey.
Halladay.
Lewis.
Milten.
& Munroe.
Page & Co.
leeper.
TY—
Campbell.
Fehrenbach.
Hurley.
Meagher.
›rth American Chemical Co.
& Wolfe.
Perry.
ın.
'G—
łarlow.
Pratt.
Vhitford.
V HARBOR—
Hartman. 328 Lorette Ave.
IER—
W. Eggers.
Gerhardt.
Lorson.
:. Marten.
PIDS—
h Davey, 628 S. State St.
Moore.
White.
.AC—
Cassier.
t & Anderson.
ET—
Bell.
ıohue.
Procissi.
Roehm.
'. Roehm.

Ames.
f. Thompson.
OTTE—
Campbell.
G. Riley, 480 Island St.
Warner.
'ATER—
Carpenter.
Hanna.
s & Faust.
& Raymond.
Sweet.
UR—
Keyes.

DETROIT—
Robert M. Adams, 4 Lincoln Ave.
Albert Albrecht, 1017 Union Trust Bldg.
Alcatraz Construction Co., 623 Hammond Bldg.
American Cement Tile Co., 221 Congress St. W.
American Construction Co., 1111 Majestic Bldg.
American Contracting Co., 619 Hammond Bldg.
B. Armstrong & Co., 59 Gratiot Ave.
Courtney F. Babcock, 84 Howard St.
Barber Asphalt Pav. Co., 420 Hammond Bldg.
M. W. Bartholomai, 374 Hancock Bldg.
Batchelder, Wasmund & Co., 70 Atwater St.
Wm. Beebe, 270 McGraw Ave.
Alex. Bell, 455 Campbell Ave.
P. A. Billings & Co., 234 Griswold St.
M. Bloy & Son, 12 Peninsular Bank Bldg.
John Bolin, 906 Bellevue Ave.
George M. Bolton, 430 Lincoln Ave.
Anthony Breitenback, 17 Exposition Bldg.
The E. A. Bresler Co., 26 Lafayette Ave.
Geo. A. Burch, 518 Seventeenth St.
W. J. Burton & Co., 164 Larned St. W.
Thos. Campau & Son.
J. D. Candler & Co., 177 High St. E.
H. Carew & Co., 210 Jos. Campau Ave.
Carkin, Stickney & Cram, foot of First St.
A. J. Carmichael, 11 Kauter Bldg.
Michael H. Carroll & Son, 684 6th St.
L. F. Cassidy, 790 Lincoln Ave.
Alexander Chapoton, Jr., 40 Fort St.
Chase Construction Co., 1321 Majestic Bldg.
Cleveland Silex Stone Co., 19 Woodward Ave.
Antoine Corbeille, 1059 14th St.
Geo. M. Cosper, 144 Forest Ave. E.
Cornelius J. Cronin, 267 6th St.
Crosman Gregory & Co., 49 Hodges Bldg.
Cummings Conduitt Co., 620 Union Trust Bldg.
Currie & Conn, foot Mt. Elliott Ave.
Geo. E. Currie, 1250 Jefferson Ave.
James Cutting, 184 23rd St.
J. J. Deppert, 743 Beaubien St.
Chas. J. Depuy, 978 Greenwood Ave.
Detroit Artificial Stone Walk & Floor Co., S. W. Cor. Hastings & Benton.
Detroit Cedar & Lumber Co., 504 Cham. of Com.
Detroit Cement Sewer Pipe Co.

Detroit—Continued.

Detroit Construction Co., 9 Cleland Bldg.
A. J. Dupois & Co., 619 Cham. of Com.
Louis Erard, 154 Park St.
Geo. Farwell, 150 Willis Ave.
Field & Hinchman.
John Finn, 12 Fort St., W.
Michael Finn, 136 Pine St.
Foley Bros., 716 8th St.
J. A. Foster, 359 Field Ave.
W. J. Frazier, 73 Thaddeus St.
Henry Frederic, 434 Scotten Ave.
A. D. Frings, 186 Adelaide St.
Gagnier & Dressler, 294 Catherine St.
John B. Galvon, 285 Selden Ave.
Mr. Gartner, 21 Fort St.
G. W. Gilbert, 20 Gilman St.
F. H. Goddard, 100 Theodore St.
Chas. Goddeeris & Co., 295 Townsend Ave.
David Good, 981 Russell St.
James Goodman, 153 15th St.
Peter C. Gossaert & Son., 111 Meldrum Ave.
Archibald Grant, 40 Fort St. W.
James Grant, 40 Fort St., W.
Michael J. Griffin, 104 Lafferty Pl.
Thomas P. Groat, Wabash St., N. Grand Boulevard.
Otto E. C. Guelich, 623 Hammond Bldg.
James Hanley, 40 Fort St. W.
James S. Hardie, 1086 4th Ave.
James Hartness, 499 Jos. Campau St.
J. H. Harvey, 181 Lincoln Ave.
Heard Cut Stone Co., 625 Lincoln Ave.
Richard Helson, 21 Gilman St.
Wm. H. Henderson, 21 Forest Ave.
W. M. Hibbler, 1221 Trumbull Ave.
A. G. Hollands, 1128 Vinewood St.
Huebner Mfg. Co., 226 Fort St.
Hiram H. Hunter, 26 Fort St.
J. G. Hutzel, 119 Baltimore Ave. W.
Interior Construction and Improvement Co., 33 Peninsular Bank Bldg.
International Construction Co., 1120 Cham. of Com.
Thomas Jenner, 97 Shelby St.
John W. Jones, 917 15th St.
Conrad Keller, 657 Canfield Ave.
Thomas Kennedy, Crawford Ave. N. Fort St.
Thos. J. Kennedy, 114 14th Ave.
G. R. King, 1006 Brush St.
James Kingsley, 447 Bagg St.
Aaron C. Kinner, 326 Selden Ave.
Jos. J. Koerber & Co., 68 Hale St.
George Kopp, 23 Dettloff Ct
Michael Lally, 93 High St.
Wm. P. Langley, 161 Elizabeth St. E.
Wm. Lappin, 946 Concord Ave.
John H. Laurie, 55 Montcalm St.
Louis Lemke, 30 Cleveland St.
Lennane Bros., D, Peninsular Bank Bldg.

Detroit—Continued.

Elmer T. Lever, 274 Oakland Ave.
The C. H. Little Co., 348 [illegible] E.
W. H. McCausland & Son, 129 [illegible] St. W.
Duncan H. McDonnell, 813 Dix [illegible]
John McLaughlin & Co., [illegible]
L. G. McEdwards, 808 Lincoln [illegible]
G. P. Magann, 47 Campau Bldg.
Jas. E. Marentette & Co., 121 [illegible] St. W.
J. J. Mason, 367 McKinstry Ave.
Herbert A. Meir, 490 Gratoit Ave.
Herman Mens, 208 Stanton Ave.
J. A. Mercier, 211 Hammond Bldg.
Henry Merdian & Co., 499 Chene [illegible]
Randall Mitchell, 571 Forest Ave. [illegible]
Frank Moore, 696 Warren Ave. W.
Patrick Moran, 40 Fort St. W.
Thos. Muir & Son, 1101 Union T[illegible] Bldg.
Nicholson Mfg. Co., 456 Brod[illegible] Ave.
Nutt & Clark, 40 Fort St.
H. P. O'Connell, 157 Larned St. [illegible]
Frank Odien, 657 Clifton Ave.
Hugh J. O'Donnell & Son, 40 Fort [illegible]
A. J. Orth, 166 Hastings St.
Ortman & Co., 1080 Wabash Ave.
John J. Owen, 9 Elm St.
J. R. Pearson Co., 19 Wilcox St.
Peninsular Artificial Stone Co.
Pittsburg Artificial Stone Co., [illegible] 6th St.
Ferdinand Porath, 878 25th St.
Julius Porath, 1493 18th St.
John W. Power, 104 Wayne St.
Leonard Price, 137 Longley Ave.
Putnam & Moore, 40 Fort St. W.
Raymond Bros., 236 Bagg St.
H. J. Reading Truck Co., 15 Wo[illegible] bridge St. E.
Henry Rebbeck, 265 Merrick Ave.
Wm. H. Reich, 60 Pulford Ave.
Geo. Reynolds, 842 Superior St.
E. K. Roberts & Co.
R. Robertson & Co., N. E. Hasting & Pignette.
Nelson J. Rogers, 285 23rd St.
August H. Rose, 416 Mich. Ave.
Michael Ryan & Son, 94 Iron St.
Wm. H. Savory, 924 25th St.
Hilary Schaefer, 118 Macomb St.
Edward Schafer, 369 Macomb
Schillinger Bros., S. W. Cor. & D. G. H. & M. Ry.
Scholl Bros., 40 Fort St. W.
Thos. P. Sheehan, 92 Spruce
John N. Singleton, [illegible] Frederic Ave.
G. E. Smith & Co., [illegible] Majestic Bldg.
J. E. Smith, S. W. Cor. Forest Ave and D. G. H. & M. Ry.
John M. Spaulding, 40 Fort St. W.

Continued.
peier, 270 Williams Ave.
Spicer, 7 Harrington Ave.
y Bros., 83 Beacon St.
n Starrs, 250 15th St.
. Bros., 40 Fort St.
Stevens, 12 Griswold St.
l Sullivan, 721 Cass Ave.
Pav. Co., 182 Sullivan Ave.
.. Thick Mich. Ave., W. of
ral Ave.
s Bros. & Co., 711 Hammond
H. Traves, 335 5th St.
Bros., 521 Mullett St.
H. Trumbull, 22 Sidney Ave.
an Marble Mosaic Art Co., 98
h St.
Co., 126 Woodbridge St. E.
S. Vivier, 189 Avery Ave.
Wagner, 734 St. Aubin Ave.
n Rock Asphalt Pav. & Roof-
Co., S. W. Cor. Ills. St. & D.
& M. Ry.
White, 740 8th St.
G. Whittaker, 189 Selden Ave.
ine Construction Co., 717
mond Bldg.
ald S. Wood, 362 Ash St.
Zander, 1030 25th St.
IAC—
Bishop.
Andrew.
D—
Paving Co.
dyear.
I—
ey.
Brock.
ns.
ONE—
Brant.
Call.
Folsom.
HAVEN—
lark.
LEDGE—
DeWitt.
Gillam.
earce.
RAPIDS—
nderson, 48 Alex Ave.
Boyes, 275 Stocking.
Brooks, 40 N. Union.
ell & McNabb.
Cargill.
Curtis & Co.
Grand Rapids Sidewalk Co., 40
l.
Gilner, 451 Grandville Ave.
n Glauz, 285 First.
Rapids Sidewalk Co., 109 Ot-
Stone Co., 87 Kent.
n & Appleyard.
th & Son.
, Owen & Ames, 721 Ottawa.

Grand Rapids—Continued.
J. B. Holy, 289 W. Broadway.
M. A. Lehner, 273 Watson.
Thos. Martin, 101 Central Ave.
Mathewson & Kloote, 842 E. Fulton.
H. P. Miller, 206 Sinclair.
J. C. Murray, 23 Hailley Pl.
James McDermott.
James O'Hara, 353 S. Lane Ave.
Wm. C. Osbun.
C. H. Pelton.
John Powers, 104 Hovey.
A. H. Prange, 334 N. Ioni.
H. M. Reynolds & Son, corner Louis and Campau.
Leonard Schneider, 246 Cass Ave.
E. W. Seamans, 97 N. Ottawa.
D. W. Vandermeulen, 528 Ottowa.
C. E. Williams, 30 Henrietta.
Valley City Artificial Stone Co.
GREENVILLE—
W. R. Holden.
HASTINGS—
Covert O. Freer.
Hastings Cement Walk Co.
HILLSDALE—
F. M. Stewart.
HOLLAND—
T. Ten Houten.
Frank Orting.
Peter Orting.
Wm. Wanroy.
HOMER—
R. J. Harlow.
HOWELL—
C. C. Scheffen.
John Tinnard.
HUDSON—
Wm. Coppius.
John McGinnis.
S. Pettit.
Wm. Sharr.
Joe Wolf.
IRON MOUNTAIN—
R. Meyers.
F. E. Parmalee.
W. H. Sweet.
ISHPEMING—
John Anderson.
Gustav Lindborn.
Alex. Swanson.
ITHACA—
Ira Bovee.
John Bronson.
Orrin B. Churchill, Box 63.
J. Hall.
Chas. Kerr.
JACKSON—
T. C. Brooks & Son.
Joshua M. Brooks, 110 1st.
C. A. Howind, 15 Dwight Bldg.
Louis Jagnow, 160 Johnson.
Robert Lake Co., Liberty & Milwaukee St.
E. C. Van Leuven, Bennet Bldg.
Sam'l Pickleo, 303 S. Water St.
E. J. Tobin & Co., 145 W. Pearl St.
Robert Way, 322 Backus.

KALAMAZOO—
Gahy Peters.
Kalamazoo Supply & Construction Co.
John Roe, 607 Douglas Ave.
John J. Sales, 316 W. Walnut.
Thos. Sales, 120 Burr Oak.
Daniel D. Streeter & Co.
Peter Vande Palder, 306 Burr Oak.
LAKE LINDEN—
Calumet & Hecla Mining Co.
Rohm & Richard.
LANSING—
Martin E. Fitzpatrick, 813 St. Joseph St., W.
Lansing Artificial Stone Co.
Fred'k M. Rounsville.
Woodcock & Neal.
LAPEER—
G. F. Demorest.
E. K. Earl.
C. D. Smith.
R. A. White.
LAURIUM—
Dan McLeod.
Vincent Vairo.
LUDINGTON—
Chas. Brown.
MANISTIQUE—
Jno. Larson.
W. S. Ramsey.
MARINE CITY—
Geo. Denny.
MARSHALL—
G. A. Breigel.
John Cuzzozins.
H. H. Day & Son.
Edgerton Bros.
John Rentschler.
MENOMINEE—
Wm. Bang, 812 Stephenson Ave.
MIDLAND—
Dow Chemical Co.
Midland Stone Co.
MONROE—
Geo. Dorner.
Geo. Hagg.
Chas. Kibbee.
Chas. A. Maurer.
John Maurer.
John Schmid.
MT. CLEMENS—
James Fenton.
Geo. H. Nichols, 299 N. Gratiot Ave.
MT. PLEASANT—
Wm. H. Carpenter.
J. F. Hidey.
Wm. Kennedy.
L. D. Newton.
Lewis Wells.
MUNISING—
Jos. Kaskannet.
MUSKEGON—
Z. S. Braubias.
A. W. Clark.
M. W. Decker.

Muskegon—Continued.
Thos. Hew.
W. R. Jones.
Alex McIntosh.
Robt. B. Nice.
J. J. Olson.
Putnam & Co.
Smith & Nelson.
NEGAUNEE—
S. E. Chaussee.
S. F. Pearce.
A. Sindquest.
NILES—
Wm. Evick.
W. Hilles Smith.
OTSEGO—
John Kelly.
Wm. Healy.
PETOSKEY—
Eugene Barnes.
Aug. Habner.
Frank Meginnis.
Dudley McDonald, 616 E. Mich
Phil Rikoff.
PONTIAC—
George Morris.
Peterson & Co.
PORT HURON—
J. H. Baker.
The Botsford-Jenks Co.
Garret S. German.
J. C. Kalameier, Sr.
Louis Kreutzman.
F. D. Jenks & Co.
T. McGonagle.
Jas. O'Sullivan.
A. J. Smith.
Jos. A. Thompson.
L. F. Zeils.
QUINCY—
Whitney & Co.
REED CITY—
J. C. Hamilton.
SAGINAW—
John C. Davis.
A. H. Delonjoy & Son, [illegible] L
C. L. Delonjoy, 118 Annesly.
John W. Forstner, 2043 Court
John J. Granville, 902 Morgan
Morris C. Heinemonn, 1114 (
Lamson & Crowley.
Lalonde Bros.
Kerns & Spence.
J. C. Shultz, 223 N. Fourth
Scanlan & Crowley.
Ira Vesterfelt, 1022 Emerson.
SAULT STE MARIE—
Michael Bennett.
Simond Dumond.
Hughes Bros. & Bangs.
Jas. L. Lipsett.
I. E. Miller.
Michigan Lake Superior Powe
T. H. Riddle Construction Co.
SALINA—
E. W. Ford.

Minneapolis—Continued.

Balch & Peppard, 348 Hennepin Ave.
Barnett & Record Co., 302 Corn Exch.
J. A. Benson, 2531 Dupont Ave. S.
L. C. Berg, 308 S. 3rd St.
J. A. Bohn, 332 Boston Blk.
C. F. Breitenstein, 208 19th Ave. N.
G. W. Brown, 120 S. 4th St.
L. Buhl & Co., 254 3rd Ave. S.
James Burns, 2313 18th Ave. S.
J. E. Burns, 2601 15th Ave. S.
Canney & Howe, 1013 Lumber Exch.
August Cedarstrand, 516 Central Ave.
L. L. Chaderick & Co., 2934 Nicolet Ave
J. C. Clark, 99 S. 12th St.
Columbus Paving Co., 804 N. E. Wash. St.
Columbus Stone Sidewalk Co., 1843 E. Lake St.
H. F. Comstock & Co., 125 Central Ave.
Geo. Cooke, 305 Boston Blk.
Crittenden Roofing & Mfg. Co., 704 S. 5th St.
Cronk & Eull, Globe Bldg.
Crown Iron Works, 113 2d Ave. S. E.
T. F. Curtis, 610 Bank of Com. Bldg.
Andrew Dahl, 2707 Riverside Ave.
Dissette-Crichton Co., 409 Hennepin Ave.
Harry Downs, 1707 Park Ave.
Drake Mantel & Tile Co., 510 2d Ave. S.
B. A. Eaton, 2415 N. E. Polk St.
J. & W. A. Elliott, 602 Lumber Exch.
Evensta & Hagstrom, 606 33d Ave. N.
Fagain Bros., 328 S. E. Delaware St.
John Fagerstrom, 3435 Blaisdell Ave.
A. W. Fields, 509 Humbolt Ave. N.
J. H. Fisher & Son, 15 S. 6th St.
Flour City Paving Co., 613 1st Ave. N. E.
Franklin Stone Sidewalk Co., 909 E. 21st St.
P. P. Gilmore & Son, 208 S. 4th St.
J. W. Gorman, 3400 2d Ave., S.
F. E. Graves, 1231 S. 9th St.
C. F. Haglin, 230 Lumber Exch.
W. H. Haight, 323 Ave., N.
Halvorson & Richards Co., 510 Globe Bldg.
Michael Hanley, 2633 Stevens Ave.
S. M. Hanley, 227 N. E. Polk St.
Heaton & Ellison, 1818 4 Ave., S.
Hennepin Paving Co., 1309 S. 5th St.
Christopher Hilken, 2528 N. E. Howard St.
C. H. Hille, 210 Lumber Exch.
Olaf Hoff, 230 Lumber Exch.
Forster James, 717 10th Ave., S.
John Johnson, 2732 Franklin Ave., E.
Bernard Kavenhoerster, 416 14th Ave., N.
M. J. Kelley, 1429 N. E. 6th St.
E. Kneeland & Co., 328 E. Grant St.

Minneapolis—Continued.

D. F. Kreklan, 1510 N. [illegible]
W. H. Lammas, [illegible] Ave., [illegible]
C. J. Larson & Co., [illegible]
W. M. Lasley, 3006 Bryant Ave.
Leck & Prince, 215 S. [illegible] St.
H. H. Leighton & Co., [illegible]
W. N. Leighton Co., 213 S. [illegible]
Libby & Nelson, [illegible] Ave.
Linton & Co., 501 N. Y. Life Bldg.
H. A. Lovern, 2822 Lyndale Ave.
Luttgen & Griffith Co., 745 Washington Ave., N.
A. E. McCallum, 925 20th Ave., [illegible]
J. A. McDougal, 1309 21st Ave., N.
Angus McLeod Co., 409 6th Ave
F. G. McMillan, 4 S. E. 5th St.
R. McMillan & Co., 123 N. 4th [illegible]
A. McMullen & Co., 225 Hen[illegible] Ave.
Minneapolis Paving Co., 127 S. [illegible]
Minneapolis Sidewalk & Pav. Co[illegible] Boston Blk.
Minnesota Paving Co., Temple [illegible]
Minnesota Stone & Tile Work[illegible] Kasota Bldg.
Chas. Morse, 619 S. 9th St.
Nelson Bros. Sidewalk Co., [illegible] ton Blk.
R. J. Ness, 503 Russell Ave., N.
E. L. Newell, 2716 Oakland Ave.
Erich Newell, 2716 Oakland Ave.
J. A. Nordeen, 2410 24th Ave., S.
Northern Building Co., 500 Lum[illegible] Exch.
Northwestern Brick & Fireproo[illegible] Co., 9 N. 3d St.
Northwestern Mantel Co., 419 S[illegible] St.
J. S. O'Donnell, 918 1st Ave. S.
Patrick O'Mallery, 305 Kasota B[illegible]
Matthew Otter, 1216 N. E. 2d [illegible]
J. H. Owen, 240 Lumber Exchan[illegible]
Parkhurst Paving Co., [illegible] Guar[illegible] Loan Bldg.
Paulson & Larson, 1704 11th Ave.
Peterson Bros. Sidewalk Co., [illegible] Clinton Ave.
E. D. Pierson, 2921 16th Ave. S.
Plymouth Paving Co., 728 Plym[illegible] Ave.
Peter Robertson, 325 Hennepin A[illegible]
Maglorne Rocheford, 1401 18th St[illegible]
W. F. Rourke, 2620 Bloomington [illegible]
Rydell & Carlson, 2114 Dupont Av[illegible]
S. M. Schaak & Co., 15 S. 1st [illegible]
M. J. Seymour, 1421 N. 6th St.
Edward Smith, 717 10th Ave. S.
Jeremiah Smith, 2800 S. E. 4th St[illegible]
Standard Construction Co., Lu[illegible] Exch.
Standard Stone Sidewalk Co., [illegible] ton Blk.
Star Paving Co., 12th Ave., N cor. E. 27th.

polis—Continued.

. Swan, [illegible] Irving St.
. Taylor, 1547 N. E. Jeff. St.
iel Tobin, 2761 Emerson Ave. N.
. Trossenhauser, 806 The Phoe-

City Sidewalk & Paving Co., 221
v. Ave. N. E.
el Vivial, 1813 E. 24th St.
ton Bros., 801 Globe Bldg.
Wunder, 842 Lumber Exch.
'EVIDEO—
evideo Stone Sidewalk Co.

Caldwell.
n Bros.
artel.
H. Merritt.
ULM—
agel & Co.
nan Schapekahm & Co.
ONNA—
. Anderson.
Anderson.
Burdick Paving Co.
TONE—
Redmond.
WING—
Dally.
Danielson.
sterlend.
[illegible]ER—
. Graham.
. McCormick.
[illegible]sen.
LOUD—
Kropp.
stian Schaefer.
ph Schillinger.
AUL—
[illegible] Anderson, 671 E. Geranium St.
[illegible] Andreen, 1237 Cortland St.
[illegible] Bartels, 165 Fuller St.
[illegible] Brady, 541 Selby Ave.
[illegible] & Son, 406 Endicott Bldg.
[illegible]-Ryan Co., 880 Globe Bldg.
A. Cameron, 173 E. University
e.
[illegible] & Bungardner, 501 Bank of
[illegible] Bldg.
[illegible] Daly, 36 Lawson St.
[illegible] Deeks & Co., 75 Nat. G. A.
[illegible] Bldg.
[illegible] Doherty, 606 W. 7th St.
[illegible] Donnelly, Montreal Ave., east
[illegible]
[illegible] Donovan & Son, 813 Pioneer
[illegible] Bldg.
[illegible] Englehelm, 296 Williams St.
[illegible] Stone Co., 709 Wabash St.
[illegible] Bros. & Parker, 33 Nat. G. A.
[illegible]
[illegible], [illegible] E. Page St.
[illegible] & [illegible], 217 W. Univer-
[illegible]

St. Paul—Continued.

Thos. Fitzpatrick & Son, 17 W. 9th St.
Wm. Foelsen, 336 W. University Ave.
G. R. Foley, 813 Osceola Ave.
Foley Bros., 9 Gilfillan Blk.
C. A. Fowble, 963 Burr St.
G. W. Godfrey, 356 Van Slyke Court.
G. J. Grant, 61 E. 9th St.
F. W. Grierson, 209 W. 7th St.
Joseph Guertin, 20 8th St.
A. Guthrie & Co., 62 Nat. G. A. Bank Bldg.
James Hanson, 286 E. 6th St.
H. C. Harmon, 25 E. 6th St.
Hennessy & Cox, 205 N. Y. Life Bldg.
Huebner & Son, 1061 Arcade St.
Frank Jackson, 179 E. Third St.
E. J. Johnson, 902 Thomas St.
Wm. L. Keefe, 417 N. Y. Life Bldg.
Keough & Ryan, 31 Court Blk.
Lange Bros., 537 Wabasha St.
Fredrick Leer, 581 Lafound St.
Patrick Leo, 74 Garfield St.
August Lettan, 672 Pine St.
A. P. Linden, 84 E. 5th St.
Lindquist & Lind, 34 E. 2d St.
R. J. Lisee, 791 Holly Ave.
James McClure, 606 Pioneer Press Bldg.
Peter McSherry, 623 Winslow Ave.
Gustav A. Mattson, 679 E. Geranium St.
E. E. Merrill, 118 E. Isabel St.
Minnesota Stone Co., 780 Ramey St.
Martin Moehrle, 59 E. 7th St.
David W. Moore & Co., 726 Thomas St.
Morris & Wait, Drake Blk.
K. P. Myhre, 117 Atwater St.
John Nevin, 282 Harrison Ave.
Newman & Hoy, 311 Chamber of Commerce.
Nicholson Bros., 286 W. 7th St.
Nickow & Dahlman, 160 W. 4th St.
John Norenberg & Co., 669 Western Ave. North.
Fred C. Norlander, 411 Case St.
Northwestern Stone Co., 186 W. University Ave.
Wills Peterson & Co., 156 E. 3d St.
William Porten, 569 Capitol Boulevard.
Portland Stone Co., 95½ E. 4th St.
C. D. Pruden, 300 Merrill Bldg.
Andrew Rankin, 484 Selby Ave.
A. J. Rheault, 386 Summit Ave.
O. L. Rheume, 597 Fairview St.
William Robertson, 1221 W. 3d St.
F. J. Romer, 200 Ramsey St.
A. W. Rylander, 761 York St.
St. Paul Bldg. Co., 209 W. 5th St.
St. Paul Cement Works (J. Bachman, Mgr.).
St. Paul Sidewalk Co., 726 E. 7th St.
St. Paul Stone Co., 533 Wabasha.

St. Paul—Continued.
L. E. Shields, 33 Nat. G. A. Bank Bldg.
Peter Siems, 33 Nat. G. A. Bank Bldg.
Neil Stewart, 1245 Charles St.
Leonard Stockwell, 567 N. Fairview Ave.
J. C. Stoddart, 717 Ashland Ave.
Wm. H. Stoddart, 647 Cherokee Ave.
Charles Stone, 643 Burr St.
Olaf Sundgaard, 571 Broadway.
P. H. Thornton, 22 Gilfillan Blk.
I. F. Fostevin & Son, 450 Robert St.
Thomas Wenisch, 411 Raroux St.
Winston Bros., 769 N. Prior Ave.

ST. PETER—
Brogen & Couplin.

SAUK CENTER—
E. L. Newell & Co.

STAPLES—
Chas. Batcher.
M. C. Miller.

STILLWATER—
Albert Erlitz.
Stillwater Stone Sidewalk Co., Carlson & Sandquist, Props. Burlington and S. 1st Sts.

TWO HARBORS—
Christ Carlson.
Nelson Freeburg.
Chas. F. Nordstrom.
Geo. Spurback.
John Strom.

WABASHA—
Geo. Buddy.
J. H. Evans & Sons.
H. Fuller.
Jno. Gardner.
F. H. Hard.
S. Myrtetus.
John Rafter.

WASECA—
Haugood & Honald.
W. F. Rourke.

WELLS—
Schneider, Schultz & Co.

WILLMAR—
A. P. Bergeson.
A. Bjorsell.
Chas. Dahlheim.

WINDOM—
J. A. Crane.
Carl Peterson.
Priest Building Co.

WINONA—
Philip Blasang.
S. D. Van Gorden.
H. J. Willis.
Winona Construction Co.

WORTHINGTON—
E. W. Cutler.

MISSISSIPPI.

BAY ST. LOUIS—
S. P. Driver.
G. Gardebled.
Chas. Sawyer.

BILOXI—
J. D. Barnes & Co.
Harkness & Eistetter.
Thompson & Eistetter.

BROOKHAVEN—
Chris Larsen.

CANTON—
M. Alexander & Co.
G. D. Leitch.
C. Olsen & Co.

COLUMBUS—
B. H. Atkinson.
W. T. Christopher.
L. J. Kelly.
D. S. McClanahan.
J. N. Prickett.
J. P. Stansel.
Stansel Bros.
C. Wilson.

CORINTH—
T. B. Dalton.
V. A. Grace.
McCord & Brakeman.

GREENVILLE—
J. F. Barnes.
Ernest Hyer.

GRENADA—
E. M. Whittaker.

JACKSON—
W. J. McGee.
H. M. Taylor.
Wells & Wells.

MERIDIAN—
H. Dabbs.
C. M. Rubush.
Mr. Staub.
A. Wimbush.

NATCHEZ—
A. Angeleti.
Bost & Chamberlain.
L. M. Dalgarn & Bro., 112 N. Pi St.
Geo. Ruscher.
Ruscher & Parent, 304 N. Pearl St.

CEMENT WORKERS Who want information of practical help, either as to materials or methods can get it from

Municipal Engineering Magazine

the publication which stands as the leading authority on American Cement.

Subscription Price, $2.00 Per Year.

·*Continued.*
Scudamore & Son.
n Stietenroth.
D—
W. Worley.
HRISTIAN—
McDonald.
McDonald.
IBSON—
ackson.
Jorvan.
Wilson.
URG—
Gregory.
ald & Shea.
Parent.
VALLEY—
Kelly.
Pearce.
& Alexander.
N—
Bailey.
& Ford.
sippi Mills.
POINT—
Pullington.
A—
ly.
CITY—
Davis.
Glass.
King.
Moore.
zo Newman.

MISSOURI.

AR—
Cowden.
ILLE—
Hogan.
FIELD—
Richards.
WICK—
Carlo.
Mitchell.
Penick.
r Zimmerman.
ER—
Day.
V. Ross.
ORNIA—
Inman.
RON—
Barrett.
Fawcett.
W. Hall.
Marcum.
s McClean.
A. Moore.
Pollard.
W. Sloan.
ON—
s Chinchen.
am Chinchen.
aton.
y Hinkamper.

CARROLLTON—
Sidney Kelley.
F. J. Robinson.
L. J. Shaw.
CARTHAGE—
N. L. Damon.
McNerney Bros.
Wetherell & Co.
CARUTHERSVILLE—
J. M. Argo.
G. W. Bradley.
C. W. Cratty.
F. W. Phleiger.
G. E. Zimmerman.
CENTRALIA—
Will Eaton.
CHILLICOTHE—
O. P. Glore.
Wm. Glore.
Huggett & Gier.
J. A. McCarty.
D. T. Peters.
Geo. Peters.
S. K. Richards.
CLINTON—
W. H. Donohue.
N. H. Duff.
Joseph Harness.
P. W. Morrissette.
B. Taff.
COLUMBIA—
E. F Arthur.
H. C. Bergman.
J. H. Guitar.
ELDORADO SPRINGS—
J. H. Smith.
FULTON—
Frances Boand.
GREENFIELD—
N. Butterworth.
P. H. Hull.
HANNIBAL—
Wm. Camery.
Chas. Hanes.
HIGGINSVILLE—
L. C. Mitchell.
HUNTSVILLE—
J. H. Minor.
INDEPENDENCE—
W. W. Angel.
Collier Bros.
John E. Lewis.
W. M. Randall.
Wm. Street.
Chris Tetler.
IRONTON—
R. Hatson.
JEFFERSON CITY—
Ernest Braun.
W. H. Kolkmeyer & Co.
Jos. Pope & Bro.
H. J. Wallau.
JOPLIN—
W. W. Fones, 1103 W. 7th St.
H. C. Hilsabeck, 1202 Grand Ave.
E. J. Overly, 118 W. 4th St.
C. F. Schilling, P. O. Box 731.

KANSAS CITY—
American Asphalt & Mastic Co., 305 Hall Bldg.
Adam Armstrong Contracting Co., 3904 Roanoke Boul.
J. J. Armstrong, 206 Baird Bldg.
W. D. Ashdown, 19 S. 6th St.
Atkinson Bros., 721 N. Y. Life Bldg.
J. C. Ball, 1621 Main St.
G. M. Banfield, 2828 Flora St.
G. B. Barclay, Navajo Bldg.
Barber Asphalt Paving Co., Gibraltar Bldg. Henry R. Kasson, Supt.
W. A. Boyard, 1313 Holmes St.
R. J. Boyd Paving & Construction Co., 315 Am. Bk. Bldg.
J. T. Broughal, 628 N. Y. Life Bldg.
James Burke, 722 Forest St.
J. L. Cannon, 1820 Euclid Ave.
Jas. Carney, 4020 Woodland St.
Cheatham & Stone, 512 Whitney Bldg.
Colyer Bros., Grand & 27th Sts.
T. O. Combs, 616 Ind. Ave.
Cotter, McDonald & Co., 714 Wyandotte St.
J. M. Courtney, 900 E. 17th St.
Creech & Lee, 309 N. Y. Life Bldg.
Louis Curtis, 706 E. 19th St.
Day & Son, 1511 E. 12th St.
F. A. Dodds, 2208 Charlotte St.
C. L. Dunham, 2369 Balt. Ave.
Elk Asphalt Co., 315 Am. Bank Bldg.
Silas Emerick, 411 E. 13th St.
W. M. Edwards, 216 Lyceum Bldg.
The Falk Co., 208 Nelson Bldg.
J. H. Fink, 200 Junction Bldg.
Henry Gerlach, 24th and Cypress Sts.
R. M. Gillespie Construction Co., 504 Postal Tel. Bldg.
Gilsonite Roofing & Paving Co., 716 N. Y. Life Bldg.
L. G. Gipple, 3608 Baltimore Ave.
Robt. Gray, 717 E. 9th St.
S. J. Hayde, 506 Whitney Bldg.
John Henry, 3215 Locust St.
M. C. Hogue, 618 E. 14th St.
Hollinger & Mitchell, 1214 Main St.
Thos. Hook, 1910 Kas. Ave.
Hoover & Mason, 514 N. Y. Life Bldg.
J. S. Hopkins, 1010 Union Ave.
C. T. Houlehan Contracting Co., 818 E. 9th St.
Andrew Jarcke, 209 Lyceum Bldg.
Charles Johnson, 2414 E. 22d St.
Fred'k Johnston, 3415 Vine St.
Kansas City Cement Sidewalk Co., 107 E. 10th St.
Kansas City & Oklahoma Const. Co., 817 N. Y. Life Bldg.
Kansas City Stone Sidewalk Co., Postal Tel. Bldg.
Edward Kelly, 1112 Harrison St.
W. A. Kelly, 946 N. Y. Life Bldg.
W. M. Kenefick, 1485 Inde. Blvd.
M. L. Kenlen, 3320 Flora St.
J. H. Knapp, 1226 Askem St.

Kansas City—Continued.
Knapp & Coumbe.
Latimer & Benning, 418 Am. Bk. Bldg.
H. C. Lindsley, 1423 E. 8th St.
D. W. Lynch, 525 Locust St.
Lynch-Mulholland Const. Co., 10 W. Mo. Ave.
Dennis Malloy, 606 E. 14th St.
H. L. Marks, 800 W. 30th St.
C. S. McBride, 815 E. 18th St.
J. R. McIloried, 601 Heist Bldg.
Thos. McNamara, 547 Holmes St.
T. V. McNarney, 3363 Oak St.
Matthew Mense, 201 Moss Bldg.
Adelbert Meyers, Troost Park.
W. H. Middleton, 924 E. 3d St.
Nicholas Miller, 3112 Highland St.
Missouri Sidewalk Co., Mass. Bldg.
Michael Moran, 340 W. 6th.
C. R. Munger, 924 Euclid St.
Nevins & Johnson.
D. B. Norton, 2329 Locust St.
D. C. O'Keefe, 1008 Union Ave.
Parker-Washington Co., 2309 Pa. St.
Pelletier Contracting Co., 1011 Grand St.
Portland Paving Co., 505 Postal Tel. Bldg.
Pringle & Flowerree, 311 Lyceum Bldg.
Riley & Olive, 1118 Grand Ave.
Phillip Ritchey, 1430 Cherry St.
Isaac Robinson, 206 Lyceum Bldg.
Rock Creek Natural Asphalt Co., 6 Whitney Bldg.
C. F. Rosenbury, 916 E. 14th St.
T. L. Rowland, 1225 Vine St.
T. F. Ryan, 2634 Penn. St.
J. T. Seddon, 1306 Central St.
David A. Shanholtzer, Whitney Bldg.
Wm. Shaw, 3119 E. 16th St.
L. C. Slavens, Jr., 3144 Main St.
J. J. Smith, 3300 E. 10th St.
L. J. Smith, 2411 Benton Blvd.
Standard Construction Co., 206 Hall Bldg.
V. E. Steel, 3328 Troost St.
V. E. Steen, 1512 W. 39th St.
Stewart Sidewalk Co., 104 E. 9th St.
W. H. Stripe, 1013 Tracy St.
W. A. Summet, Brighton and 27th Sts.
Taylor Construction Co., 209 Postal Teleg. Bldg.
G. R. Timms, 3831 Woodland St.
Treetrail Paving Co., 121 W. 8th St.
J. T. Wachs, 1814 E. 11th St.
Michael Walsh, 2207 Holmes St.
J. H. Waugh, 1410 Bales St.
White & Redmond Sidewalk Co., 1? W. 8th St.
W. A. Wilson, 209 Postal Tel. Bldg.
Wilson & Lonsdale Cheldley Bldg.
G. W. Youmans, Am. Bank Bldg.

KING CITY—
Frank Morton.
C. Wileman.

KIRKSVILLE—
C. C. Anderson.
W. L. Burnett.
T. J. Earhart.
Stephen Eggert.
W. S. Murphy.
Thos. Sees.
Geo. Shaw.

LAKE VIEW—
John Rhoads.

LAMAR—
Geo. Liddle.

LEXINGTON—
Hair & Hedge.
John Muligan.
Triumph Press Brick Co.

LOUISIANA—
Smashey & Roberts.

MACON—
Geo. Kohl.

MARCELINE—
B. J. Patrick.
David Porter.
H. D. Porter.
John Porter.
Jas. Wamie.

MARSHALL—
Rose Bros.
C. E. Thorp.

MARYVILLE—
Chas. Arnold.
Will Compton.
H. Elsworth.
Geo. Walker.

MEMPHIS—
Thos. Broadwater.
Witherspoon & Martin.

MEXICO—
Henry Myers.

MOBERLY—
F. M. Lambert.
John E. Lynch.
G. A. Sinclair.

MONROE CITY—
Chas. B. Anderson.
Wallace Bond.
Geo. A. Hawkins.

MONTGOMERY CITY—
C. P. Evered.
J. F. Evered.
R. A. Sharp.
Aug. Staudhardt.

NEOSHO—
Chas. Davis.
Neosho Planing Mill Co.

NEVADA—
A. L. Daly.
Joe Goodnaugh.
Theo. Lacoff.
Louis Landmann.
Shepard & Shade.

NORBORNE—
M. C. Bidwell.
Lee Montgomery.
Chas. Roeselle.
August Schrader.
John Wade.

PLEASANT HILL—
Wm. Bussard.
Press Mason.
James Prater.
James Roof.

RICH HILL—
Hiram Vail.

ROLLA—
Hunter & Lancaster.

ST. CHARLES—
Frank Bottani.
Carl Bull & Son.
H. Ehlmann.
Herman Hallrah.
John Heckmann
Jos. Kurtz.
Fred Reimer.
Hy. Schnedler.

ST. GENEVIEVE—
Robert Abernathy.
Amadie Boyen.
U. Burkhard.
Henry Morean.

ST. JOSEPH—
Daniel Donoghue.
Feeney & Whelan.
Helsey Bros. Paving Co., 118 S. 8th St.
John Marnell.
Patrick Morley.
Robt. Read.
Peter Swenson.
Waller Paving Co., 204 N. 10th.

ST. LOUIS—
Abbott-Gamble Contracting Co., 6 Chestnut.
Abel & Gerhard Plumbing Co., 909 1 6th.
American Granitoid Flagging Co., 1 Park Ave.
Asphalt & Granitoid Constructio Co., 2420 S. Broadway.
Holland W. Baker, 708 Lincoln Trus Bldg.
Bambrick-Bates Const. Co., 81 Chestnut St.
Barber Asphalt Paving Co., 121 Chemical Building.
Barrett Mfg. Co., 1097 N. 9th.
John Beiswanger, 1810 Division St.
H. G. Bohn & Co.
W. & D. Boyce Co., 721 Olive St.
Bradford Marble Co., 1211-1229 S. St.
Bryan Brady, 304 N. 8th St.
P. M. Bruner Granitoid Co., 304 N 8th.
Central Bridge Co., 720 Lincoln Trus Bldg.

:—
Smith.
Wadsworth.
N—
Blew.
)—
Murray.
:R GROVE—
.aikie.
nklin.
en.
sam.
LAINS—
Brown.
Martin.
V SPRINGS—
McLucas.
R—
idges.
elm.

MONTANA.

IDA—
acobson.
Starr.
.N—
Brown.
Ishow.
e.
Schwan.
Walsh.
.
Sewer Pipe & Tile Co.
Hinds.
Lafferty.
Reardon.
s Rowan.
Ryan.
n Asphalt & Gravel Roofing

s, Parsons & Boomer.
HELENA—
nerican Smelting & Refining

Water & Power Co.
A—
rigbaum & Co., 352 N. Main.
TON—
Hamilton.
LA—
ibson.

NEBRASKA.

ID—
he.
Moulton.
N—
Allen.
A—
Burt.
Daniels.
pker.
CE—
Hickman.
Lee.
S. Lehigh.
Thomas.

BLAIR—
Herman Shields.
H. L. Strove.

CHADRON—
Samuel Dubel.
Elmer Longear.
Ira Longear.

COLUMBUS—
Mason E. Beall.
Jacob Glurns.

CRETE—
Wm. Farley.
Jno. Kerst.
E. Martin.
Wm. Megrew.
Jno. Mullner.

FAIRBURY—
D. S. Allen.
H. J. Evans.
Rich. McLean.
Clint Richardson.

FALLS CITY—
M. N. Bair.
C. H Hineman.
W. B. Schmucker.

FREMONT—
Phil P. Mowrer.
H. A. Pierce.
C. I. Shawn.
Shawn Bros.

GENEVA—
R. Whitfield.
A. Freeman.
E. J. Evans.

GRAND ISLAND—
Otto Kirsche.
Wm. Scheffel.

HASTINGS—
Fred Butzirus.
John Hempel.
Chas. Hensel.
E. E. Ladd.
O. N. Staley.

HOLDREGE—
David Detter.
C. M. Johnson.

KEARNEY—
A. Cedarholm.
C. C. Davis.
Richard Hibberd, 3023 Avenue A.
Scott Bros.

LINCOLN—
M. R. Beman.
Miles Callanan, 913 South St.
Lincoln Artificial Stone Co.
John McDonald, 2850 O St.
Sheely & O'Shea, 609 N. 27th St.

NEBRASKA CITY—
Jos. Burr & Son.
Prue & Shannon.

NORFOLK—
E. A. Amarine.
S. A. Barnes.
J. B. Herman.
W. L. Kern.
Wm. Klug.
R. W. Mills.
A. Morrison.
R. H. Reynolds.

NORTH PLATTE—
W. H. Johnston.
Frank Martin.
Conrad Walker.

OMAHA—
E. E. Barber, 2019 Grace St.
Barber Asphalt Paving Co., 5th & Jones Sts.
Lee Baroch, 505 S. 13th St.
Bellamy & Hornung, 1614 Capitol Ave.
D. J. Creedon, 2022 Charles St.
P. J. Cummins, 50 Barker Blk.
Grant Paving Co., 306 Bee Bldg.
A. R. Hoel, 2622 Burt St.
Katz & Crandall, 802 N. Y. Life Bldg.
F. J. Lewis Roofing & Mfg. Co., 312 S. 16th St.
McGee, Kahmann & Co., Man. Bldg.
Chalmers McWilliams, 4306 Burdette St.
Hugh Murphy, Bee Bldg.
Omaha Gas Mfg. Co.
Geo. Parks & Co., 441 N. 24th St.
Frank Romans, 2210 N. 26th St.
J. B. Smith & Co., Ranege Bldg
Frank Waller, 519½ N. 16th St.
Welshans & Holbrook, 309 S. 17th St.

O'NEILL—
C. S. Davis.
John Hunt.

PAWNEE CITY—
John Coldiron.
Plummer & Lyons.

PLATTSMOUTH—
Jno. Hartman.
D. M. Jones.
Z. W. Kennedy.
Jno. Kinser.
Peter Renland.

ST. PAUL—
Chicago Lumber Co.
L. Larson & Co.

SOUTH OMAHA—
Carter Alcox, 13th and M Sts.
D. M. Click & Co., 19th and M Sts.
Flore & Co., 21st bet S and R Sts.
McDonald & Bock, 23d and J Sts.
Geo. Parks & Co., 441 N. 24th St.
Theodore Schrader, 661 S. 28th St.

TECUMSEH—
E. M. Atterberry.
W. R. Borton.

YORK—
Geo. Daugherty.
Geo. Fair.
J. W. Moist.
Jacob Zieg.

NEVADA.

CARSON CITY—
V. B. Cross.
W. G. Elliott.
J. Johnson.
R. Logan.
Z. Wilcox.

RENO—
Burke Bros.
Caine & Shadler, 202 Virginia St.
Chas. E. Clough.
Geo. E. Holesworth.
W. W. Shaff.

VIRGINIA CITY—
H. McIntosh.
Thos. Muchle.

NEW HAMPSHIRE.

BERLIN—
Napoleon Nolan.
Louis Rodwick.
H. C. Rowell.
John Steward.

CLAREMONT—
John McGrath.

CONCORD—
Concord Foundry Co., 8 Chandler
C. Le Fellows.
Ford & Kimball, 41 S. Main.
Rowell & Plummer.

DOVER—
J. S. Abbott.
E. W. Hooper.
O. J. Palmer.
A. Converse Place Lumber C 17 Cochecho St.

DURHAM—
D. Chessley & Co.

LACONIA—
G. Cook & Son.
T. J. Guay.
H. S. Stone.

LAKEPORT—
L. D. Clark.
O. T. Muzzey.

MANCHESTER—
Frank A. Gay.
Robie Consolidated Concrete Co., Elm St.

NASHUA—
Nashua Cement Sidewalk Co.
Nashua Concrete Co., 140 Main St.
Tardif & Bellavance, 106 Tolles St.

PORTSMOUTH—
Anderson & Jenkins.
W. A. Hodgdon.
J. R. Holmes.
E. N. McNabb.
Sugden Bros.
E. W. Trefethen.

ER—
Ames.
›ward.
'ORTH—
Bernier.
Burke.
Mitchel.

NEW JERSEY.

C HIGHLANDS—
Davis.
Emery.
Leonard.
ıackenbush.
ıthall & Son.
E—
ecker, 64 E. 4th St.
ros., Ave. E, cor E 22d St.
ady, 32 W. 47th St.
Buttner, 528 Boulevard.
Colgan, 98 Ave. C.
Gilbertson, 17 Dodge St.
County, 205 E 22d St.
. Cozine, 810 Ave. B.
re, 30 W. 7th St.
. Daly, 14 E. 28th St.
J. Daly, 146 Ave. C.
Donovan, 36 W. 16th St.
Downey, 41 W 27th St.
llon, 14 W. 23d St.
C. Farr, 32 E. 22d St.
Ford, 47 Andrew St.
& Cogan, 953 Garfield St.
'. Keeney, 99 W 51st St.
McCabe, Boulevard, cor. W.
..
C. Mead, 25 E. 42d St.
M. Murray, 9 W. 9th St.
& Edwards, W 54th St., nr
:.
Russell, 79 W. 22d St.
C. Ryan, 46 W. 41st St.
& Preston, 64 E. 3d St.
Sippel, 207 Ave. D.
J. Welcher, 34 E. 21st St.
ERE—
Gardner & Co.
Y—
Higgins.
IELD—
Ackerman.
allahan.
Griffith.
N—
Ringlieb.
I—
Tile Paving Co., 301 Market

te Pav. & Const. Co., Federal
bove 12th.
. Sherman, 33 Haddon Ave.
Sweeten & Son.
Ward, 821 58th St.
A. Ward, 638 Benson.
Whitecraft, 640 Benson.

CAPE MAY—
L. E. Miller.
M. C. Swan.
DOVER—
Andrew Roderer, Jr.
Smith & Fanning.
EAST ORANGE—
J. W. Baigrie.
E. I. Condit.
B. Coyne.
Jos. P. Davis.
E. Doremus & Co.
A. P. Hamblen Son Co.
Pring Bros.
ELIZABETH—
Henry T. Clark.
Donohue & McKeon.
Chas. Ellbacker.
P. Faughnan.
Fitzgerald & Potts.
Louis Quien.
Mathew Wade.
Robt. Wilson.
ENGLEWOOD—
D. L. Barrett.
Chas. Brucker.
Joseph H. Garrison.
Joseph Thomson.
John B. Vanderbeck.
FREEHOLD—
A. Brown & Son.
GARFIELD—
N. J. Construction & Supply Co., Hobart Place.
Troost & Co.
GLOUCESTER CITY—
L. Bowe.
Burt & O'Hara.
Charles F. Rincorn.
HACKENSACK—
Samuel R. Cumming.
Wm. H. Whyte.
HACKETTSTOWN—
J. H. Beatty.
G. W. Smith.
HAMMONTON—
Chas. P. Myres.
Henry Nicholia.
Edward T. Strickland.
HOBOKEN—
Barber Asphalt Paving Co., 259 Washington St.
Commonwealth Roofing Co., 58 1st St.
Jas. Waddington, 619 Jeerson St.
IRVINGTON—
John Ballard, Osborne Terrace.
JERSEY CITY—
Wm. T. Ard, 57 Bonner Ave.
Wm. H. Gautier & Co., 1 Exchange Place.
John Hopkins, 492 Central Ave.
Hudson Co. Contracting Co., 367 Communipaw Ave.
Louis Kirchner, 292 Duncan Ave.
Wm. Ormsby, 166 Hudson Boulevard.
P. T. Plunkett, 1090 [illegible]
J. W. Rehill, 369 Co[illegible]

Jersey City—Continued.
P. Sanford Ross, 277 Wash'n St.
B. M. & J. F. Shanley, 16 Exchange Place.

LAKEWOOD—
Jno. C. Brown.

LAMBERTVILLE—
Geo. W. Arnett.
Frederick Parker.

LONG BRANCH—
Wm. H. Alexander.
Christian. Brehm.
Peter Mari.

MADISON—
Daniel Burns.

MANASQUAN—
Newbury & Estell.
A. F. Vannote.

MATAWAN—
John M. Hulsart.

MILLVILLE—
Reeves & Son.

MONTCLAIR—
Wm. Doyle, Midland Ave.
James B. Dyer, Montague Place.
Owen Feeney, Valley Road.
Donato Fusco, Glenridge Ave.
Karl I. Muller, Miller St.

MORRISTOWN—
John D. Collins.
Dempsey & Cooney.
Thos. Malley.
Sturgis Bros.

NEWARK—
John C. Ahrens, 72 Fairview Ave.
William Ahrens, 13 Peshine Ave.
William Ballard, Runyon Ave & 10th St.
Barber Asphalt Paving Co., 763 Broad St.
George Brown & Co., 374 Belleville Ave.
Chert Stone Co., 238 Washington St.
A. H. Clark's Sons, 22 Clinton St.
Commonwealth Roofing Co., 19 Division St.
Conway & Co., Central Ave., cor. 7th St.
W. A. Cullen, 828 Broad St.
John S. Day & Co., 763 Broad St.
Henry Dickson, 22 Clinton St.
Henry M. Doremus, 763 Broad St.
John Doriety, 168 Ridge St.
Dowd & Olds, 27 Van Wagenen St.
Eustice Bros., 22 Clinton St.
Wm. A. Gay, 22 Clinton St.

Newark—Continued.
David Harper, 122 N. 11th St.
Harrison Construction Co., 745 Bro[ad] St.
P. H. Harrrison, 30 S. 9th St.
Eugene B. Hedden, 22 Clinton St.
V. J. Hedden & Son, 431 Ogden St.
J. G. Hetzel, 67 Main St.
Wm. J. Hughes, 112 Bergen.
Michael Kane, 57 S. 13th St.
J. W. Lansing & Son, 122 Market [St.]
Geo. C. McEwan Co., 238 Washing[ton] St.
F. W. McManus, 22 Clinton St.
Thos. J. Mackinson, 225 S. 7th St.
Jas. H. Maguire, 214 Peshine Ave.
Manufacturers' Contracting Co., [illegible] Broad St.
Charles Marsh, 308 Ogden St.
Alex Milmoe, 87 S. 6th St.
Newark Asphalt Co., 196 Market St.
Newark Paving Co., 800 Broad St.
N. J. Asphalt Co., 763 Broad St.
New York Roofing Co., 19 Divis[ion] St.
Thomas A. O'Connor, 86 Congress [St.]
Joseph Oshwald.
Jacob Peter, 127 Frelinghuysen A[ve.]
Chas. B. Pruden, 22 Clinton St.
Ford C. Pruden, 22 Clinton St.
T. J. Regan & Co., 179 Market [St.]
J. L. Reid, 763 Broad St.
S. Rizzolo & Co., 15 Lock St.
P. Sanford Ross, 75 Johnson Ave.
Geo. W. Roydhouse.
Arthur E. Sandford, 27 Kearny [St.]
David P. Sandford, 199 Garside [St.]
David C. Seymour, 164 Market [St.]
B. M. & J. F. Shanley, 867 Bro[ad St.]
Standard Paving Co., 22 Cl[inton] St.
W. H. Turrell.
Union Cut Stone Const. Co., 22 [Clin]ton St.
Peter Vanderhoff & Sons, 235 [illegible] St.
Van Steenberg & Clark, 204 Ogd[en St.]
E. M. Waldron.
Joseph Wells, 885 Summer St.

NEW BRUNSWICK—
Thos. C. Cole, Townsend & Drift.
Jas. Gilligan.
Radel & Shafer.
T. H. Riddle.

BOOKS ON CEMENT

Hydraulic Cement. By F. P. Spalding............ [illegible]
Portland Cement. By Charles D. Jamieson........ [illegible]
Clark's Hand-Book on Cements.................... [illegible]
Portland Cement; its Manufacture, Testing and Use. By D. B. Butler. 360 pages, 86 illustrations [illegible]
American Cements. By Uriah Cummings........... [illegible]

Send remittance with order. Address

MUNICIPAL ENGINEERING COMPAN[Y]

man.

on, 46 Fair St.
Cor. Slater.
ard St.
[illegible] N. 4th.
Lawrence St.
Graham Ave.
n Co., 32 Pater-

'Derrom Ave.
terson Natl. Bk.

28th Ave.
g Co., Main Cor.

brand.
[illegible]
Tiling Co., 17

R. R. Ave., cor.

k. Bldg.
ine Bldg.
17th Ave.
n, 1st Natl. Bk.

Leslie St.
Main St.

Madison Ave.
Pipe & Construc-
Broadway.

Pearl St.
[illegible] Co., Romaine

Tile Co., [illegible] Main

Sussex.
ark Ave.
[illegible] E. 18th St.
[illegible] Co., [illegible] Grand.
Lafayette St.
[illegible] Ave.
[illegible], [illegible] Jackson.
[illegible]

Chas. Denny.
John Harker.
Adam Jeso, Sr.
Eli Strimple.
Nathan Wood.

PERTH AMBOY—
Donohue & Leavy.
Jas. Growney.
Henderson Bros.
A. Hoagland.
Thos. Langan.
I. C. Ostergaard.
Woglon & Clinchey.

PHILIPSBURG—
Edw. Korp.
Adam Martin.
T. S. Pursel.

PLAINFIELD—
Patrick Christmas.

RAHWAY—
T. Covintree.
Eastman & Trembly.
Geo. W. Heath.
John Melburn.
Geo. W. Moore.
A. T. Ray.
Chas. Scrimshaw.
Peter Tillman.

RED BANK—
William Sewing.
Joseph Swannell.

RIDGEWOOD—
Wm. C. Munro.

ROCKAWAY—
Geo. E. Schofield.

RUTHERFORD—
Edwin T. Galloway.

SALEM—
Bell & Campit.
Lewis Steelman, [illegible] Wesley St.

SOMERVILLE—
John D. Hornby.
D. J. Smith.

SOUTH AMBOY—
James Collins.
James Quinlan.

SOUTH ORANGE—
John Barrett.
Henry Becker & Son.
David Roe.
John O'Reilly, Jr.

SUMMIT—
J. Chandler.
E. G. Delaney.
P. McGowan.
W. H. Smith.
S. Wright & Son

TENAFLY—
L. O. Atwood & Co.

TRENTON—
Aaron Hoarkyard, [illegible] S. Clinton St.
Michael Hurley, [illegible] Perry St.
Wm. F. Kelly, [illegible] Pennington Ave.
Lewis Lawton, [illegible] Hamilton Ave.
The N. J. Wire Cloth Co.

Trenton—Continued.
Dennis Roe, 483 W. State St.
M. F. Smith, 82 Greenwood Ave.
C. B. Walton, 107 Lamberton St.

VINELAND—
Jehiel Vaughn.

WEEHAWKEN—
Geo. Roman.

WEST HOBOKEN—
John Berkley.
Wm. Gundling, 420 Charles St.

WEST LONG BRANCH—
Monroe V. Poole.

WOODBURY—
E. P. Henry.
D. L. Pine.

NEW MEXICO.

ALBUQUERQUE—
Don Dickerson.
Dodd & Lembke.
Jas. McConiston.
Russell Bros.

ROSWELL—
B. F. Daniels.
Dunning & Rasmussen.
Thos. Howard.
Frank Le Roy.
Geo. Munro.
Pearce & Bixby.
D. Y Tomlinson.

NEW YORK.

ALBANY—
James Ackroyd, 12 James St.
Albany Construction Co., Twiddle Bldg.
Callanan Road Improvement Co., 51 State St.
Collins Bros., Benson Bldg.
S. J. Davenport & Co., 11 Tweddle Bldg.
Dollard & Holler, 66 State St.
T. Henry Dumary, 38 State St.
Macnee & Rabe, 659 Broadway.
B. F. & P. W. Mulderry, 115 1st St.
Prescott, Buckley & Callahan, 51 State St.
Anton Weller, 566 Broadway.

ALBION—
Baker & Judson.
W. S. Buell.
Arthur Harris.

AMSTERDAM—
John J. Turner.

ATHENS—
Theodore Every & Son.
Harmon Miller.

ATTICA—
Broadbooks & Ranger.
Wm. Toursett.

AUBURN—
Furniss Bros.
T. F. Walsh.

AUSABLE CHASM—
W. M. Mooney & Co.

AUSABLE FORKS—
J. & J. Rogers Co.

AVON—
Henry Chase.
Wm. Clark.
Upson & Whisker.

BALLSTON SPA—
Wm. Clements.

BATAVIA—
Chas. La Fountain.
Wm. E. Page.
Weaver & Winslow.
W. C. Wolsey.

BATH—
Thos. H. Campbell.
John Collins, 26 Geneva St.
Phil Shoemaker.

BINGHAMTON—
Chenango Engineering Co., 160 [illegible] St.
W. A. Conklin, 99 Court St.
Andrew Douglas, 109 LeRoy.
John Kelly, 193 Front St.
A. C. & E. A. Matthews, 47 [illegible] St.
A. D. Osborn, 159 Beethoven S[illegible]

BOYLSTON—
Elery Crandall.

BUFFALO—
J. L. Alberger & Son, [illegible]
American Contracting Co., [illegible]cott Sq.
Argentic Paving Co., 358 Laf[illegible] Ave.
Atlas Contracting Co., 47 Main [illegible]
Henry Author, 1410 Fillmore Av[illegible]
Wittig Ball, 52 E. North St.
Charles Ballschmieder, 49 Pete[illegible]
J. M. Barnes, 1004 [illegible] St.
C. P. Barnwell, [illegible], 14th [illegible]
W. C. Beck, 1248 Fillmore Ave[illegible]
Charles Berrick Sons, [illegible] Ma[illegible]
H. C. Biddlecome, 412 Perry.
M. Birkmeyer, 5 Glenn.
Black & Hunt, 3 Builders Ex[illegible]
Rudolph Boye, 1058 [illegible]
Arthur Bouldering, [illegible]
W. F. Boysen, 402 Ellicott, [illegible]
O. W. Bruce, 51 Best.
Buffalo Bridge & Iron Work[illegible] Ave., N. Seneca.
Buffalo Cement Co., [illegible] St.
Buffalo Concrete Paving [illegible] Northampton.
Buffalo Electric Co., [illegible]
Buffalo Engine Works, [illegible]
Buffalo Expanded Metal C[illegible]
Buffalo Engineering Co., [illegible] Bk. Bldg.
Buffalo Ferrolithic Pav. C[illegible]ers' Ex.
Buffalo Granolithic [illegible] W. Eagle.
Buffalo [illegible] Co. Bk. Bldg.

Continued.

Sewer Pipe Co., 77 Tonawanda.

Burgard, 220 Lathrop.

Bros., 827 Mooney Bldg.

r Bros., 420 Main St.

Callard, 82 Kentucky.

l Bros., 4th, cor. Virginia.

. Carter & Sons, 26 Builders' Exch.

Case & Son, 31 Main St.

Chapman & Co., 476 Ellicott

Churchyard, 648 Clinton St.

Paving Co., 74 Riverside Ave.

urn Bros. & Co., 43 Builders' Exch.

y Engineering Co., 426 Ellicott

& Hopkins, 350 Niagara St.

Cotter, 22 Myrtle.

& Fench, 61 Terrace.

r Granite & Concrete Co.

nt Pavement Co., 96 Erie Co. Bldg.

& Co., 316 Pearl St.

W. Day, 989 Main St.

Dodge & Co., 20 W. Eagle.

lly Contracting Co., 894 Ellicott Sq.

ovan, 1204 Prudential Bldg.

& Huntington, 379 Main St.

1133 Niagara.

Paving Co., 22 Pomona Place.

111 Ash St.

& H. Fogelsonger, 215 Oak St.

Fosburgh, 722 Prudential Bldg.

Frank & Bro., 44 Builders' Exch.

Frank, 1124 Genesee.

Friedman, 38 Fox.

Engine Works, Ft of Illinois.

Galle, 58 Indiana ch. rd.

1900 Filmore Ave.

Bros., 428 Dearborn St.

Rock Asp. Co., 304 D. S. Morgan Bldg.

Gael, Jr., 1 Quarry.

Gill, 265 Plymouth Ave.

Goldsmith, 205 Eaton.

Gorges, 836 Broadway.

Gpacher, 215 Genesee.

Gthie Paving Co., 71 W. Eagle.

& Jennings, Ft. of Main.

& Latimer, Ft. of Main.

Griffiths, 377 Prospect Ave.

Gruber, 223 Walden Ave.

Grupp, 51 Riley.

Gugino, 80 Trenton Ave.

Hager & Son, 141 Elm.

Hardie, 124 Peckham.

Hall, 186 West Ave.

Sons, 69 Tonawanda.

& Greenberg, 7 Erie Co. Bk.

Buffalo—Continued.

Henry Harden, 287 Northampton.

Louis Harlerecht, 814 Mutual Life Bldg.

Harrar Construction Co., 88 Coal & Iron Exch.

Henry Hartke, 252 Humboldt.

Henry Hacker, 206 Dearborn.

William Henrich & Sons, 193 Spring St.

T. L. Herman, 257 Riley.

Hilderbrandt & Frank, 192 Best.

W. Hingoton, 87 Erie Co. Bk. Bldg.

E. M. Hinman, 1570 Seneca.

E. D. Hofeller, 1655 Main St.

Daniel Hotaling, 365 Conn St.

T. L. Howells, 93 Briggs Ave.

Hughes Bros. & Bangs, 910 D. S. Morgan Bldg.

Iroquois Iron Works, 173 Maiden Ave.

Peter Jochin, 220 Johnson.

Johnson & Co., Abbott Road & Buffalo.

Louis Juhre, 308 Moselle.

William Kadan, 119 Hamilton.

Kehr & Felton, Ft. Church.

George Kempf, 99 Locust.

John Kilvington, 1420 Niagara.

J. A. Klein, 170 Lafayette Ave.

G. L. Knight, 327 W. Delaware Ave.

Albert Krause & Son, 24 Builders' Exch.

Philip Kreisher, 48 Wasmurth Ave.

Carl Kreuger, 112 Davey.

Edward Krohn, 313 Loepere.

Henry Krohn, 212 Kingsley.

John Krohn, 214 Northampton.

Michael Kruger, 74 Armbruster.

A. E. Kurchhoff, 377 Guilford.

Lake Erie Engineering Works, Chicago & Perry.

John Lannen, 667 Oak St.

Lancaster Brick Co., 93 Franklin St.

Wm. Larkin, 495 Ellicott Sq.

Josiah Leard, 299 Military St.

Leh & Co., S. Mich. & Ganson.

Frank Leppert, 91 Mills.

Herman Lohrke, 120 Sherman.

Fred Luedeman, 610 High St.

C. E. Lutsman, 409 Riley St.

G. W. Maltby, 1 Maryland.

Chas. Maguvero, 253 Court St.

P. W. McDermott, 269 Normal Ave.

McDonnell & Sons, 958 Main St.

McDonough & Eustes, Carroll, C Van Rensselaer.

George Manus, 35 Mortimer.

Louis Marburg, 31 Church.

J. L. Mehler, 287 Lemon.

Joseph Metz, 292 Elm.

W. F. Metz, 146 Sherman.

Fred Metzler, 227 Ludington.

Daniel Miller, 134 Best.

John Miller, 802 Best.

E. R. Miller, 496 Northampton.

Buffalo—Continued.
Henry Miller, 240 Kehr.
E. W. Mitchell, 158 Dewey Ave.
G. W. Moore, W. 177 Elk.
G. W. Morris, 302 Ellicott Sq.
Mosier & Summers, 1266 Seneca.
J. G. Murphy, 273 Conn.
Louis New, 58 B St.
Joseph Neumer, 2070 Del. Ave.
P. W. Norton, 62 Cary St.
Daniel O'Leary, 125 Van Rensselear.
A. O'Neill & Bros., 411 Mooney Bldg.
Michael Paradowski, 72 Beck.
George Parks & Sons, 217 15th.
F. C. Perkins, 126 Erie Co. Bk. Bldg.
F. B. Pickering, 716 7th St.
Portland Stone Co., ft. Jersey.
Power Installation Co., 203 Main St.
J. J. Pyne, 405 Cornwall St.
Queen City Engineering Co., Perry & Miss.
Queen City Cut Stone Co., 94 Goodrich.
W. A. Rappich, 2293 Main St.
C. R. Rauch, 788 Humboldt.
R. J. Reidpath, 317 Mutual Life Bldg.
Joseph Richter, 463 Glenwood Ave.
Jacob Ritzman, 1121 Ellicott Sq.
Lorentz Ritzman, 49 Eaton.
Rogers Construction Co., 81 Erie Co. Sav. Bk. Bldg.
R. C. Rohde, 48 Berlin St.
William Rohde, 52 Berlin St.
Charles Rohloff, 60 Bardol.
E. H. Roos, 364 Elm.
Chas. Rownnack, 26 Girard Pl.
Rumrill & Carter, 1 Builders' Exch.
C. A. Rupp, 47 E. Utica.
Stephen Ryall, 331 Sweet Ave.
Joseph Sageden, 499 B'way.
W. C. Sandel, 138 Mastern.
W. M. Savage, 507 Prospect Ave.
Henry Schaefer's Sons, 578 Elm.
Schirman Bros., 103 Sycamore.
Schmidt Bros., 3 Builders' Exch.
Matthew Schuster, 9 Burtis Ave.
M. L. Schwarts, 569 Main St.
Robert Seibert & Co., 1000 Prudential Bldg.
The Roebling Construction Co., 96 Erie Co. Bank Bldg.
George Shaaf, 547 E. Utica.
F. G. & G. R. Sikes, 871 Ellicott Sq.
Joseph Sirece, 107 Ash.
J. F. Stabell, 1135 Niagara.
C. E. E. Steimwachs, Del. and Fillmore Aves.
Fred Stephan, 525 Walden Ave.
James Stewart & Co., 732 Prudential Bldg.
Stokes Bros., 500 Mooney Bldg.
William Thomas, 1286 West Ave.
J. H. Tilden, 12 Henry St.
Theo. Tulikouski, 25 Kosciusko.
Anthony Vallman, 151 Purdy.

Buffalo—Continued.
Victor Paving Co., 312 Penna. St.
C. F. Waldorf, 341 Urlean.
C. J. Waldow, 535 Mooney Bldg.
Wallridge & Co., 392 Main.
James Ward, 58 Commercial.
J. C. Watson, 16 Builders Exch.
C. A. White, 367 Normal Ave.
John Wiegang, 27 Sidway.
Williams, McNaughton & Bapst, D. S. Morgan Bldg.
Thomas Wilson, 111 Grote.
Wisdom Paving Co., 240 Terrace
J. A. Wolsley, 877 Main St.
Yamerthal Stone Co., 369 Leroy Av
Charles Young, 1096 Smith.
Robert Zacher, 435 Emslie.
Andrew Ziegler, 164 Edward.

CAMDEN—
Chas. Blanchard.
Harvey Coy.
Geo. Shuster.

CANANDAIGUA—
F. X. McNulty.
Hugh Smith.

CANISTEO—
Edwin Foster.
E. L. Gray.
O. P. Jeffers.
D. S. Powell.

CANTON—
Gardner & Veitch.
Henry Robson.

CARTHAGE—
Noah Chamberlin.
Jones & Simmons.

CATSKILL—
Jas. Cooke.
Geo. W. Holdridge.
E. Lampman.

CHATEAUGAY—
High Falls Pulp Co.

CLYDE—
C. A. Lux.

COBLESKILL—
Stanton Courter.
H. D. Karkee & Co.
Charles Linster.
William Murphy.

COHOES—
John W. Flynn.

COLD SPRING—
J. M. Cornell.
Greene Crookston.
William H. La Due.
Charles E. McClary.

COOPERSTOWN—
John C. Smith.
Chas. Tuttle.

CORINTH—
E. J. Sturtevan & Son.

CORNING—
T. Bradley.

,AND—
& Warfield.
Corwin.
Meagher.
:—
. Hine.
Woodruff.
IIT—
Babcock.
ιw & Howell.
ιhon & Bisbee.
Phillips.
; FERRY—
reedon.
rancis.
Hart.
EVILLE—
s Gow.
ie & Snyder.
IRK—
Hilliard.
Maidel.
Meister & Son.
ι Rider.
Rogan.
AURORA—
Clary.
nore Pratt.
HAMPTON—
A. Eldredge.
Grinshaw, Jr.
Jones.
RA—
Allington.
llo & Neagle.
H. Fasnaught, 523 Harper St.
Fisk & Co.
'old & Maloney.
Kelley & Co.
rd & Dempsey.
T. Sadler & Co., 336 E. Water St.
'ORT—
. Howell.
:. Longley.
ILL ON THE HUDSON—
y & Ayers.
; Jones.
EDWARD—
n & Sundstrom.
PLAIN—
evendorf.
ONIA—
Fitzgerald.
ON—
er Bradley & Co.
ers & Smith.
uirk.
I. Ross.
SEO—
h Cone.
Forbes.
Leonard.
ιel Manion.
7A—
le.
Emericke.

GLENS FALLS—
James Anderson & Co.
John Reilly.
GLOVERSVILLE—
Baker & Judson, 60 N. Main St.
A. M. Banker.
J. A. Delaney.
Kirk Dutcher.
A. L. Henry.
GOSHEN—
W. C. Altman.
George Kipp.
Joseph Weir.
GOUVERNEUR—
John Campo.
H. H. Post.
GOWANDA—
A. F. Clark.
Carl P. Randall.
J. E. Van Deusen.
GRANVILLE—
P. Gravalin.
Alonzo Norton.
L. Weinberg.
HEMPSTEAD—
Jas. E. Baldwin.
HERKIMER—
Clinton Beckwith.
Harter & Lewis.
R. B. Lewis & Co.
John H. Nelson.
HICKSVILLE—
Sebastian Braun.
Adam L. Dauch.
John Elfring.
Joseph Hassemann.
August Schlimm.
HOOSICK FALLS—
L. E. Buckley.
Corneulis McCaffrey.
William Carey.
HORNELLSVILLE—
E. Y. Butler, 27 Ransom St.
John Feehan, 6 Elizabeth St.
G. W. Prentiss, 256 Canisteo St.
W. H. Shink, 5 Smeltzer Ave.
I. M. Stevens, N. Ransom.
Eugene Tucker, 86 Seneca St.
S. L. Tucker, 25 W Genesee St.
John Wing, Thacher St.
HORSEHEADS—
Ezra Howell.
Howell & Botsford.
Jackson & McKee.
Ira B. Payne.
HUDSON—
John Fitzgerald.
Dennis Hester.
Smith Patterson.
Shute & Rightmyer.
HUNTINGTON—
Bunce & Holmes.
D. S. Ireland.
IRVINGTON—
Dinkel & Jarrell Co.

ITHACA—
Joseph Campbell.
Driscoll Bros. & Co.
O. D. Edwards.
Joseph Fowler.
Reuben Gee.
S. M. Oltz.
Chas. Wanger.
JAMESTOWN—
Gus Burlin.
John W. Hassler, 106 E. 8th St.
Jamestown Construction Co.
JOHNSTOWN—
Morvin Currie.
G. H. Howarth.
J. H. Howarth.
JONES' POINT—
James A. Degroat.
KEESEVILLE—
R. J. McNally.
Prescott, Buckley & Callanan.
KINGSTON—
Campbell & Dempsey.
Darling Bros.
Wm. S. Green.
F. H. Griffith.
LAKE PLACID—
R. W. Clifford.
Seth Johnson.
LANCASTER—
J. O. Garretson.
Samuel Walter.
LANSINGBURGH—
Northern N. Y. Asphalt Pav. Co.
LE ROY—
Connors & Dillon.
E. Sherman.
LESTERSHIRE—
M. S. Hotchkiss.
LITTLE FALLS—
H. M. Boyer.
Hullinan Bros.
C. D. West.
LOCKPORT—
M. J. Crowe.
Frank J. Le Valley.
Patrick F. Niland, 204 Washington St.
C. N. Stainthorpe & Co.
C. B. Whitmore.
LOWVILLE—
James T. Campbell.
Thos. M. McCabe.
LYONS—
J. J. Finnegan.
MALONE—
C. Boardway.
Wm. Lynch.
O. Moore.
O. W. Vaughan.
MAMARONECK—
W. F. McCabe.
MASSENA—
T. A. Gillespie Co.
Keyes & Moore.
MATTEAWAN—
Taylor & Holt.
Schuyler Tillmon.
W. C. Warwick.
MECHANICSVILLE—
Fuller & Waite.
The Hudson River Power Transmission Co.
Warner & Madigan.
MEDINA—
Stanley E. Filkins.
MIDDLETOWN—
Luther Barber.
Crane & Giles.
Donoly & Deihl.
Robt. Lewis.
G. H. White.
MOHAWK—
Brown Bros.
John Morrell.
John Quackenbush.
MONTOUR FALLS—
Wm. Mallette.
W. Swarthaut.
Jos. K. Young & Son.
MOUNT VERNON—
Cartwright & Kenlon.
M. Griffin.
Johnson & Light.
Westchester Public Works Co.
NELSONVILLE—
Martin Adams.
NEWARK—
Schattner & Ginthener.
Chas. F. Schuman.
NEWBURGH—
John P. Convery, 108 Renwick St.
Steele Harrison, 97 Dubois St.
Robt. Huddleson, 60 Bay View Terrace.
Hugh McLernon, 209 3d St.
John McNeal, 161 Johnston St.
William Sager, 15 William St.
James Stewart, 304 First St.
NEWMAN—
Geo. T. Chellis.
C. N. Davis.
Edw. Kennedy.
NEW ROCHELLE—
Galgano Bros.
F. W. Molloy.
John New & Son.
NEW YORK CITY: BOROUGH OF BROOKLYN—
Andrew R. Baird, 38 Hooper St.
John Bray, 40 Court St.
Brooklyn Cement Sidewalk Co., 3d & Hoyt Sts.
Bushwick Roofing & Paving Co., 93 Grand St.
Thos. F. Byrnes, 419 Park Place.
P. J. Carlin & Co., 26 Court St.
Castle Bros., 58 Lott St.
Cody Bros., 354 Park Ave.
Cranford & Co., 534 St. Marks Ave.
Daniel J. Creem, 307 Washington St.
Chas. A. Cregin, 360 Fulton St.

k City—Brooklyn—Continued.

S. Cronin, 273 Clinton St.
zzo, 39 Sherman St.
Daily Co., 40 Court St.
n-McLean Construction Co.,
Ave. & S. 6th St.
nd Bros., 449 Columbia St.
Donovan, 614 Union St.
Dregnan, 1544 Fulton St.
k Farrel, 290 Eldert St.
Fieber, 105 Stockholm St.
ithic Stone Co., Arbuckle

Flynn, 187 Montague St.
Jenner Fire Proof Flooring
Briggs Ave. & N. 8th.
Fruh, 241 Emerson Place.
Furey, 136 Remsen St.
Gillen, 1127 Willoughby Ave.
. Graham, 25th St., near 22d

Graves, 1076 5th Ave.
Greene, 350 Fulton St.
Hanna, 815 Classon Ave.
& Maguire, 485 Flatbush Ave.
Granulate Paving Co., 1053
tic Ave.
Hart, 4th Ave. & DeGraw St.
Heilman, 105 Debevoise St.
Hennessy, 146 Troy Ave.
Hesterberg, 41 Grant St.
F. Horan, 84 Tillary St.
s & Gray, 192 Douglas St.
Jordan, 277 Keep St.
Maguire, 198 Hillary St.
F. Maillie, 1229 Prospect Pl.
McDermott, 153 Front St.
. McGarry, 136 Remsen St.
J. McKeever & Co., 371 Fulton

McNamee, 16 Court St.
politan Roofing Co., 52 Franklin

Miles & Son, E. N. Y. Ave.
B. Mitchell, 764 De Kalb Ave.
Mock, 81 Debevoise St.
Moran, 1421 Fulton St.
e L. Moyer, 1101 Park Place.
an & Co., 128 Hope St.
York Tiling Co., 70 Willoughby

York Vitrified Tile Co., 79 4th

A. Nolan, 887 Hancock St.
a & Gorman, 301 Douglas St.
O'Hara, 265 Windsor Place.
H. O'Rourke, 186 Remsen St.
Otterbein, 26 Court St.
& Fatta, 61 N. 14th Ave.
P. Paxton, 846 Putnam Ave.
Pflaum, 351 52d St.
Puckelwaldt, 725 Liberty Ave.
Putnam, 52d St. and 35th Ave.
ugh & Smith, 17-19 Ninth

Raynor, 153 Kosciusko St.

New York City—Brooklyn—Continued.

Reliable Roofing Co., 307 Prospect St.
Harrison Rockefeller, 755 Flatbush Ave.
M. Schneider & Son, 144 21st St.
Schratweiser's, 426 3d Ave.
Bernhard Schubert, 252 Tompkins St.
Matthew Smith & Son, 143 N. 8th St.
Clinton Stephens & Son, 662 Lafayette Ave.
Wm. P. Sturgis, 608 Park Ave.
Edward Thalheimer, 166 Stanhope St.
Wilson & Baillie Mfg. Co., 93 9th St.

NEW YORK CITY: BOROUGHS OF MANHATTAN AND BRONX—

Abbott-Gamble Contracting Co., Times Bldg.
American Encaustic Tiling Co., Ltd., 1123 Broadway.
Anderson-Murphy Co., 14 John St.
Atlantic Alcatraz Asphalt Co., 57 E. 59th St.
The Asbestolithic Co., 95 Nassau St.
Matthew & Jas. Baird, 337 E. 63d St.
Jas. E. Baldwin, 1123 Broadway.
Jos. W. Barton, Westchester.
Batterson & Eisle.
Behnke & Cordes, 966 Forest Ave.
Henry Belden, 31 Broadway.
John Berkery, 11 William St.
H. P. Binswanger, 1 Madison Ave.
Boller & McGaw, 71 Broadway.
Alfred Boote, 124 W. 33d St.
Wm. Bradley, 534 W. 48th St.
Bradley & Currier Co.
P. F. Brennan, 1748 Wash. Ave.
A. A. Briggs, 19 E. 130th.
F. X. Brosnan, 146 W. 74th.
Burehorn & Granger, 136 Liberty St.
F. S. Caldwell, 114 5th Ave.
Cambridge Tile Mfg. Co., 115 Worth St.
The H. B. Camp Co., Park Row Bldg.
M. Caravatta.
Cataract Construction Co., 35 Wall St.
Chapman & Fitch, 253 Broadway.
City Wastes Disposal Co., 874 Broadway.
John Claffy's Sons, 48 Dey St.
L. Russell Clapp, 52 New St.
Geo. A. Clark, 243 Broadway.
Clark & Baille, 132 Park Ave.
Clark & Co., 100 Broadway.
Chas. W. Collins, Webster Ave. and E. 166th St.
Chas. H. Colman & Co., 207 Broadway.
Commonwealth Roofing Co., 874 Broadway.
Conover Fireplace Mfg. Co., 9 W. 30th St.
Consolidated Lehigh Slate Co., 574 W. Broadway.

MUNICIPAL ENGINEERING MAGAZINE

Is known
as the foremost in the world
in the field to which
it is devoted.
It is the Authority
for Authorities.

ONE OF THE LARGEST SPECIAL MAGAZINES PUBLISHED AT THE PRICE—140 PAGES, MONTHLY, AND $2.00 PER YEAR

SOME EXPRESSIONS REGARDING IT

FROM LEADING NEWSPAPERS

MUNICIPAL ENGINEERING is one of the most valuable technical magazines of the age.
—*Sacramento (Cal.) Record-Union.*

MUNICIPAL ENGINEERING is a model high standard publication that steadily improves.
—*Milwaukee Sentinel.*

MUNICIPAL ENGINEERING is an excellent magazine.—*Hartford Courant.*

MUNICIPAL ENGINEERING is always practical in its solution of problems.
—*Detroit Free Press.*

HOW IT IS PRAISED BY READERS

William Newman, City Engineer of Windsor, Ont.:
"I could not get along very well without MUNICIPAL ENGINEERING."

J. H. Hanly, Consulting Engineer for Municipal and Sanitary Work:
"I find MUNICIPAL ENGINEERING MAGAZINE most useful; in fact, indispensable."

Alex Thomson, Jr., Oil City, Pa.:
"I have gained much valuable information from MUNICIPAL ENGINEERING."

Robert Y. Ogg, Secretary Board of Public Works, Detroit, Mich.:
"MUNICIPAL ENGINEERING MAGAZINE is so highly appreciated by aldermen and other visitors to this office that we have to keep our copies of them under lock and key to keep them from being spirited away."

Joseph Withington, Mattoon, Ill.:
"MUNICIPAL ENGINEERING MAGAZINE is the best of its kind."

Scott Hayes, Chamberlain, S. D.:
"You are doing a splendid service and putting out a fine work."

Geo. D. Jenkins, Washington, Pa.:
"MUNICIPAL ENGINEERING MAGAZINE is a good thing. Sorry I did not know of it before this."

From Sacramento (Cal.) Record-Union:
MUNICIPAL ENGINEERING has often been pronounced in these columns the most useful, practical magazine of the age, and we adhere to that judgment."

$2.00 per year. The sooner you order it the more you gain.

MUNICIPAL ENGINEERING CO.

-City—Manhattan—Continued.
-idated Telegraph & Electrical
-ay Co., 85 Duane St.
-h T. Cragin, 44 and 46 Broad-
-lf & Sons, 165 W. 32d St.
-iver Co., 170 Broadway.
-k Crimmins.
F. Cunningham, foot W. 13th
-. Cunningham, 247 E. 33d St.
Curran, 48 Dey St.
-. Cushing, 455 W. 165th St.
-na State Marble Co., 250 11th
-n & Archer, 120 E. 25th St.
-Heid & Alexander, 127 E. 23d
-H. Deans, 71 Broadway.
-f Deeves & Son, Broadway
-Duane Sts.
-h-McLean Const. Co., 1 Broad-
-ey & Konspinski, 1454 Amster-
-Ave.
-. & Co., 42 E. 23d St.
-H. Dewey, 8th St., Williams-
-b.
-. Doak, 600 W. 152d St.
Doolittle, 31 Nassau St.
-& Stratton, 71 Broadway.
-I. Dreyer, 5 Park Place.
Dunn, 26 Chambers St.
-Edlitz & Son, 489 5th Ave.
-Emerich, 1634 Park Ave.
-City Subway Co., Ltd., 15 Dey
-Contracting Co., 99 Cedar St.
-Construction Co., 171 Broad-
Paving & Construction Co.,
-roadway.
-Englehard, 39 Cortlandt St.
-ering Contract Co., 71 Broad-
-ion Contracting Co., 69 Wall
Ficklen, 272 W. 12th St.
-. Flaherty, 41 Peck Slip.
-lammer, 254 W. 23d St.
-anagan, 215 W. 125th St.
-g & Co., 123 Liberty St.
Flynn, 217 W. 125th St.
-Fogarty & Co., 48 Dey St.
Fogarty, 416 E. 62d St.
-orsham, 35 Broad St.
-rank, 734 Lex. Ave.
-& Rooney, 1605 2d Ave.
-ambrick Co., 220 Broadway.
-& Furlong, 465 E. 134th St.
-rry & Son, 416 E. 25th St.
-ildersleeve, 215 W. 125th St.
-leeve & Smith, 39 Cortlandt
A. Gillespie Co., 1308 Have-
-r Bldg.

New York City—Manhattan—Continued.

A. E. Godeffroy, 45 Broadway.
Gollick & Smith, 1133 Broadway.
Jas. Gough, 309 E. 93d St.
Grace & Hyde Co., 26 E. 42d St.
Granitic Paving & Construction Co., 96 Broadway.
Wilhelm Greisser, 11 Broadway.
Griffin & Bro., 14th St. & 10th Ave.
R. Guastawino Co., 11 E. 59th St.
Jos. J. Hardiwen, 81 E. 125th St.
Harries Bros., 100 Broadway.
Chas. Ward Hall, 140 Nassau St.
W. J. Hadden & Sons, 143 Liberty St.
Peter Handibode, jr., 770 Tremont Ave.
D. W. Hemming, 201 W. 106th St.
Wm. Hilgers Co., 205 W. 101st St.
R. H. Hood Co., 220 Broadway.
Isaac A. Hopper, 219 W. 125th St.
M. S. Hotchkiss.
Howden Tile Co., 53 W. 24th St.
Edwin L. Hunt, 27 Thames St.
Frank C. Huntley, 600 Wales Ave.
Hyde Bros., 260-266 W. Broadway.
F. A. Hyde Tiling Co., 1123 Broadway.
Willard F. Inman, 62 William St.
W. H. Jackson & Co., Broadway & 18th St.
W. Jackson's Sons, 246 Front St.
R. H. Jaffray & Co., 160 5th Ave.
J. R. F. Kelly & Co., 220 Broadway.
B. H. Lage, 313 E. 23d St.
P. & T. Larkin, 616 E. 15th St.
M. J. Leahy, 3101 3d Ave.
J. C. Leeson, foot W 143d St.
Wm. G. Leeson, 641 W 143 St.
Chas. Lehman, 31 Manhattan St.
Eugene Lentilhon, 489 5th Ave.
Henry Lipps, Jr., Elliot Ave., Williamsbridge.
Martin Lipps, 899 E. 149th St.
Frank R. Long & Co., 320 Broadway.
Henry Lyons, Stewart Bldg.
J. C. Lyons, 81 E. 125th St.
Henry Maas, 961 2d Ave.
Macknight Flintic Stone Co., 150 Broadway.
Bernard Mahan, 106 Fulton St.
Mart & Lawton, 1121 Broadway.
J. B. McDonald, 15 Park Row.
Matthew McDonald, 706 9th Ave.
P. J. McDonald, 242 4th Ave.
McDonald & Onderdonk, Jerome Park.
McGuire & Hall, Havemeyer Bldg.
M. McHugh & Son, 505 W. 42d St.
John McIver, 301 W. 128th St.
Peter McKeever, 200 E. 114th St.
T. J. McKenna, 35 Broadway.
Clarence S. McKune, 1368 Broadway.
E. J. McLaughlin, 585 E. 134th St.
Frank W. McNeal, 80 Reade St.
D. J. McNiece, 146 Broadway.

New York City—Manhattan—Continued.

McQuade & Mahoney, 1298 Lexington Ave.
Mack Paving Co., 35 Nassau St.
Manhattan Construction Co., 11 Broadway.
Mapes-Reeve Construction Co., 150 Nassau St.
A. B. Marshall, 81 E. 125th St.
W. H. Masterson, Park Ave., near 176th St.
Melan Arch Construction Co., 15 Park Row.
Louis G. Meyer, 156 5th Ave.
Joseph Moon, 170 E. 89th St.
Dennis W. Moran, 280 Broadway.
J. S. Mosher, 8 E. 42d St.
T. C. Murphy, 1725 Sedgwick Ave.
W. H. Murphy, 150 5th Ave.
Thos. F. Murray, 1426 Amsterdam Ave.
Wm. J. Murray, 147 E. 125th St.
Theo. Namuer, 15 Manhattan St.
National Conduit & Cable Co., 41 Park Row.
National Conduit Co., Times Bldg.
National Contracting Co. T. Hugh Bowman, Pres., 32 Broadway.
Naughton & Co., 258 Broadway.
Wm. Nelson, 13 Chambers St.
Henry Neus, 454 E. 116th St.
New York Dredging Co.
Patrick Norton, 1035 3d Ave.
J. P. O'Donnell, 720 Tremont Ave.
Thos. O'Leary & Sons, 235 Center St.
A. Onderdonk, 1 Broadway.
J. T. O'Rourke, 2410 Park Row Bldg.
Peter Otto, 890 Jackson Ave.
A. D. Palmer, 27 Thames St.
John H. Parker, 215 E. 94th St.
Parsmore, Meeker & Co., 11 5th Ave.
D. G. Pecora, 411 E. 114th St.
Pellarin & Co., 23 W. 28th St.
Penrhyn Slate Co., 101 E. 17th St.
Pietrowski, Keller & Co., 418 E. 91st St.
Jas. Pilkington, 73 E. 128th St.
A. C. Pucci, 340 E. 109th St.
Purcell & Fay Co., 244 W. 23d St.
Ransome Concrete Co., 26 Broadway.
Rapid Transit Construction Co., 15 Broad St.
Rapid Transit Subway Const. Co., 13-21 Park Row.
J. W. Rapp, 311 E. 94th St.
P. E. Raques, 55 Liberty St.
H. J. Reilly, 31 Broadway.
T. H. Riddle & Co., 35 Broadway.
Andrew J. Robinson Co.
Robert Rouman, 64 E. 11th St.
W. K. Ryan, 239 W. 72d St.
Rudolph Schroeder, 442 Greenwich St.
Geo. Schofield, 454 E. 138th St.
H. R. Sellers, 1 Madison Ave.
Shalack Bros., 47 W. 140th St.
Ira A. Shaler, 27 William St.

New York City—Manhattan—Continued.

John Shea, 254 E. 68th St.
John M. Sheehan, 416 E. 58th St.
Sicilian Asphalt Paving Co., 46 Times Bldg.
Sienna Marble & Tile Co., 64 E. 11th St.
Simmemayer & Parry, 509 W. 54th St.
Skilton & Son, 31 Broadway.
John Slattery, 370 Park Ave.
Chas. Smedley, 19 Whitehall St.
Terance A. Smith, 106 Fulton St.
Snare & Triest, 39 Cortlandt St.
Sooysmith & Co., Wall St.
Standard Structural Co., 11 Broadway.
D. N. Stanton & Sons, 18 Broadway.
Clinton Stevens & Son, 13 Park Row.
Stone & Thurston, 220 Broadway.
John H. Sturk & Co., 328 E. 102d St.
Roger Sullivan, 215 W. 125th St.
Sutherland Const. & Imp. Co., 15 Wall St.
John Sweatt.
Jas. Symington, 16 Exchange Place.
Herbert Tate, 21 E. 20th St.
Ronald Taylor, 156 5th Ave.
W. N. Thayer.
Thileman & Smith, 147 E. 125th St.
Tice & Jacobs, 510 Pearl St.
J. A. Toscani & Co., 215 E. 38th St.
Traitel Bros. & Co., 133 W. 42d St.
Tucker & Vinton Inc., 156 5th Ave.
David Tulloch, 308 E. 108th St.
John Twiname, 2033 Bathgate Ave.
Union Subway Construction Co., 13 Cortlandt St.
United Company, 15 Park Row.
United States Paving Co., 182 Broadway.
E. S. Vaughan, 103 Maiden Lane.
Venetian Wood Tiling Co., Inc., 280 Broadway.
Geo. J. Wallace, 121 4th Ave.
J. Ford Walter, 316 W. 19th St.
Washburn & Washburn.
Weand & McDermott, 71 Broadway.
M. F. Westergren, 485 E. 144th St.
J. Gilbert White & Co., 29 Broadway.
Geo. H. Whyte.
W. C. Whyte, 15 Cortlandt St.
Woltmann, Keith & Co., 11 Wall St.
Henry Wright, 584 E. 148th St.

NEW YORK CITY—BOROUGH OF QUEENS—

Jas. Gillies' Sons, Vernon Ave., Long Island city.
John Hansle, Metropolitan.
Thos. Kane, Far Rockaway.
Henry J. Mullen, Ozone Park.
Pietrowski & Killer, 24 Purvis, Long Island city.
Thos. Skuese, Flushing.
J. Rufus Terry, 357 Webster Ave., Long Island city.

YORK CITY—BOROUGH OF MOND—
1 & Quien, Port Richmond.
'an Bros., 398 Rich. Ter., Port ımond.
Hardy, 22 Maple St., Port ımond.
ohnson, West New Brighton.
F. McQuade, 48 Columbia St., t New Brighton.
politan Construction Co., New hton.
rd J. Pounds, Port Richmond.
Simonson & Son, Port Rich- d.
Walker, Rich Ter., near Mer- au Ave., Mariners' Harbor.
Whitforce, Port Richmond.

RA FALLS—
act Construction Co.
nt & Co.
3. Humbert, 14 Gluck Bldg.
Makin.
Rickert.
Shepperd & Co.

[TONAWANDA—
Allen, 108 Falconer St.
T. Charlton, Thompson St.
. Palmer, Oliver St.
ɔson, Hubman & Fisher, Main

:—
rrison.
Howard.
Lynch.
Magee.

'SBURG—
· & Willard.
s Lynch.
3. Norton.
Paquette.
Whalen.

—
e Fee.
Van Campen.

A—
Gay.

TA—
Barnes.
Bostwick.
& Miller.
Packer.
Woodin.

O—
: Bradley Co.
lkin & Son.
Barnett.
McLaughlin.
Ratigan.
Smith.

O FALLS—
Calkins.
Knapp.
Whitney.

OWEGO—
Ford Bros.
Geo. Jones.
A. H. Keeler.

OXFORD—
William P. Buckley.
Chas. W. Church.

OYSTER BAY—
J. T. Bennett.
O. Hendrickson—
W. S. Moore.
G. B. Powers.

PALMER'S FALLS—
Hudson River Pulp & Paper Co.

PATCHOGUE—
R. Henry Parks.
William S. Simpson.
Emerson G. Terrell.

PEEKSKILL—
James Miller.
James Nichols & Co.
John Smith, Jr.

PENN YAN—
Carey Bros.
Pat Quinn.
L. B. Worden.

PERRY—
Jas. McIntyre.
Geo. O'Brien.

PHILMONT—
Henry Christman.
Charles Ham.
Walter Ham.
Robert Shadie.

PLATTSBURG—
D. Callahan.
M. J. Fatzpatnile.
A. McQuillan.
Merrichen & Adams.
Prescott-Buckley Cons. Co.

PORT CHESTER—
Henry E. Merritt.
Wm. Ryan & Co.
Jas. Weir.

PORT JERVIS—
Matthew Heitzman.
Jacob Lehn.
Joseph Place.

POTSDAM—
Harry Delisle.
R. L. McAllister.
C. G. Rogers.

PULASKI—
Fra.y & Sage.
Wm. Peach.
D. B. Wood.

RHINEBECK—
Francis Curnan.
E. M. Haines.
Augustus Van Keuren.

RICHFIELD SPRINGS—
L. S. Chase.
Geo. Monahan.
W. B. Ward.

RIVERHEAD—
Ernest Duryea.
E. G. Duryea.
Charles Hempstead.

ROCHESTER—
Warner B. Bargy, 227 Hawley.
Brayer & Albaugh, 27 Main St. E.
F. A. Brotsch, 12 Triangle Bldg.
Chambers & Casey, 313 Powers Bldg.
Wm. H. Clark, 45 North St.
J. Commons & Son, 156 Central Park.
H. N. Cowles, 304 N. Goodman.
P. H. Curtis, 25 Favo St.
Frank E. Dyer, 34 Pearl St.
Ellsworth & Grant, 81 Insurance Bldg.
Julius Friedrich, 29 Friedrich Park.
William Fuller, 16 State St.
James Holahan, 96 Penn. Ave.
Wm. H. Jones & Sons, 85 Exchange.
Michael Krewer, 175 Wilder.
Lauer & Hagaman, 458 Clinton Ave. S.
Jacob Mather & Son, 156 Central Park.
Godfrey S. Neff, 30 Evergreen.
E. L. Oliver, 688 Clinton Ave. S.
Rochester Vulcanite Pavement Co., Alexander and Erie Canal.
Rock Asphalt Pavement Co., 31 Insurance Bldg.
S. J. Wagoner, 11 Ardmore.
Whitmore, Rauber & Vicinus, 279 South Ave.

ROME—
W. J. Cromond.
Parry & Jones.

RONDOUT—
Wm. McCullough.
Robt. Watson & Son.

SALAMANCA—
P. O. Connor.
Philo Gates.
C. D. Hickey.
Spon & Robinson.

SALEM—
Chas. W. Button.
L. P. Copeland.
Wm. J. Cruikshank.
E. W. Philo.
Charles A. Shaw.

SANDY CREEK—
Henry A. Allard.
Henry C. Crandall.
Joseph Crandall.
William Hunter.
S. E. Wheeler.

SANDY HILL—
Allen Bros'. Co.
Philippe Beaulac.
Flood & Sherrill.
McCaghey & Linehan.
Monty, Higby & Co.

SARANAC LAKE—
Branch & Callanan.
M. Danforth.
E. Norman.
Geo. Williams.

SARATOGA SPRINGS—
Saratoga Cement Sidewalk Works, **Geo. W. Winship, Propr.**

SAUGERTIES—
Frank Pidgeon.

SCHAGHTICOKE—
Thomas Bracken.

SCHENECTADY—
J. B. Bailey.
W. G. Caw.
J. H. Clements, 502 Hamilton St.
James Devine, 102 Wall St.
Samuel Dickhoff.
Kellam & Shaffer.
Andrew Kinum, 119 Park Pl.
Jas. Maloney.
John McDermott, 108 Romeyn St.
John McEncroe, 709 Union St.
Schenectady Const. Co.
B. Van Vranken.

SENECA FALLS—
Barlow & Woodcock.

SILVER CREEK—
S. W. Erdle.
Fred Gunther.

SINCLAIRVILLE—
Frank E. Shaw.

SING SING—
Stephen Brown.
Geo. H. Eldridge, Ellis Place.
Albert Emmett, Tompkins Ave.
Geo. Harris, Denny St.
Edward Rockett, Dale Ave.
J. L. Sterritt, Ellis Place.
Eli Valentine, Todd Ave.

SKANEATELES—
Richard Carver.
Platt & Loss.
J. L. Shultz & Co.
Wm. Williams.

SOUTHAMPTON—
E. J. Corrigan.
Fred Duryea.
T. G. Topping.

SPRINGVILLE—
C. W. Kellogg.

STONY POINT—
Charles W. Dykins & Son.
Edward A. Thompson.

SYRACUSE—
Geo. H. Alpeter & Son, 631 N. Salina St.
Asphaltina Const. Co., Kirk blk.
J. E. Britton, 201 W. Onondaga St.
John W. Bustin, 405 W. Onondaga.
John Dunfee & Co., Dunfee Bldg.
Empire Contracting Co., 112 E. Jefferson St.
Geo. D. Grannis, Gd. Opera House Blk.
Geo. G. Hall, 1511 Spring St.

—*Continued.*
:eltine, 100 Townsend St.
aynes, 206 N. Crouse Ave.
'. Jordan, 409 N. Valley St.
Driscoll & Co., Dunfee Bldg.
Lavelle, 712 Almond St.
t Lawson, 233 Briggs St.
J. Mack, Kirk Bldg.
Mara, Lynch Blk.
& Sullivan, 112 W. Genesee St.
Marvin, 307 Gifford St.
cCaw, 746 Harrison St.
IcDonald, 519 Wyoming St.
Millen, 706 W. Genesee St.
Pack & Son, 415 E. Water St.
y & O'Hara, 518 Jackson St.
van & Son, 112 W. Genesee St.
se Improvement Co., 1 War-
ldg.
A. Weed, 114 Seymour St.
'OWN—
. **& Jerrel Co.**
Duell.
irr.
ANDA—
'hase.
Chase.
sse.
Construction Co.

Besch, 129 Ferry St.
McKenna, 173 3d St.
'n New York Asphalt Paving
hurch & State Sts.
y & Catlin, 84 Congress St.
LAKE—
Sharhand.
Vest.

a & Son, 47 Park Ave.
Bros.
a Construction Co., 59 Arcade.
Construction Co.
& Baxter.
ohnston.
ate Paving Co.
arsden, 205 Center St.
aving Co., 62 Arcade.
guist, 2026 Bleecker St.
one Co., 20 Whitesboro St.
I—
awford.
Decker.
Hardware Co.
Rosencrans.
igh & Kidd.
—
I. Brown.
Reynolds.
rix.
. Howland.
'K—
.ton.
illoway.
& Ronnsavell.
'ros.

WATERFORD—
H. S. Eveline.
Flynn & Parker.
WATERLOO—
Robert Logan.
Wm. Murphy.
John Van Reper.
WATERTOWN—
Ironite Concrete Co., 28 Flower Bldg.
W. J. Sempler.
Wm. Walsh, 9 Boon St.
Haley, Ward & Co., Flower Bldg.
WATERVILLE—
P. Nurna.
Taft Bros.
WATERVLIET—
Thos. Benjamin, 1501 7th Ave.
WATKINS—
Robt. J. Baldwin.
A. F. Chapman.
WAVERLY—
Whalen & Higgins.
WEEDSPORT—
Caywood Stickle & Co.
M. Grace.
WESTFIELD—
John Hatsel.
C. H. Mason.
David Sutherland.
Ed Waterman.
Harry Wratten.
WHITEHALL—
A. D. Bartholomew.
WHITE PLAINS—
J. Duffey & Co.
J. Jackman & Co.
Freeman H. Merritt.
Toney Richards.
WHITESTONE—
L. Collins.
J. Geotz.
Geo. Hipple.
J. Miller.
WILLSBORO—
New York & Penn Co.
YONKERS—
John Callahan, Riverdale Ave.
Commonwealth Roofing Co.
R. A. Destrange.
Dougherty & Berrigan.
Wm. J. Flanagan.
P. J. Flannery.
Grady, Kearns & Hart, 23 Orchard St.
Geo. T. Kelly.
Denis Murphy
Pennell & O'Hern
Robt. L. Stewart.
L. K. Sutherland

NORTH CAROLINA.

ASHEVILLE
E. T. Belote
T. E. Davis
W. T. Hadlow

Asheville—Continued.
O. D. Revell.
J. A. Wagner.
J. M. Westall.
W. E. Wolfe.
BEAUFORT—
Shul & Duncan.
CHARLESTON—
Adams & Hutchinson, 14 Atlantic.
The Bailey Lebby Co., 213 Meeting St.
J. A. Bell, 2 Green.
J. A. Benson, 62 Wentworth.
W. B. Boivriest, 59 Tradd.
Martin Caulfield, 61 Laurens.
De Costa & Edwards, 4 State.
G. H. Dehrman, 249 E. Bay.
J. W. Devereaux, 44 Reid.
N. A. Devereaux, 15 Judith.
Jacob Enter, 5 Tradd.
G. Teigendrager, 206 W. Philip.
T. G. Fields, 306 Ashley Ave.
J. F. Hanley, 238 St. Philip.
R. K. Harrison, 147 Nassau.
L. J. Hollings, 255 Ashley Ave.
J. E. Keregan, 14 Glebe.
B. F. Kramer, 60 Meeting.
I. F. Lanier, 34 Shepard.
McCarrel & Sloan, 53 Broad.
Henry Oliver, 2 Mott La.
M. W. Powers, 52 Beaufaine.
R. J. Preston, 81 Smith.
H. D. Schumacher, 614 King.
J. T. Snelson, 110 Tradd.
D. L. Thompson, 295 Rutledge Ave.
M. J. Treahy, 3 Horlbeck Al.
E. T. Viett, Magnolia Ave., cor. Meeting.
H. T. Zacharias, 179 Meeting.
CHARLOTTE—
T. W. Ahrens.
Jo. Asbury.
S. J. Asbury.
W. W. Phife.
EDENTON—
Theo. Ralph.
ELIZABETH CITY—
A. L. Hawkins.
W. A. Jones.
Elisha Overton.
FAYETTEVILLE—
Poe & Co.
GOLDSBORO—
T. I. Fussel.
Porter & Goodwin.
D. J. Ross & Co.
L. G. Weddell.
HENDERSON—
Robt. Bunn.
K. W. Coghill.
H. C. Linthicum.
R. R. Pinkston.
HENRIETTA—
R. R. Haynes.
S. B. Tanner.
HICKORY—
J. D. Elliott.
MORGANTOWN—
John Campbell.
W. H. Sloan.
MOUNT AIRY—
W. A. Bolt.
PLYMOUTH—
W. J. Jackson.
B. Nurney.
RALEIGH—
A. W. Shroyer & Co.
Weir, Hunnicut & Co.
REIDSVILLE—
J. W. Jennings.
J. Robinson.
J. H. Sharpe.
ROCKINGHAM—
J. H. Williams.
SALISBURY—
George R. Martin & Bro.
TARBORO—
D. J. Rose & Co.
WADESBORO—
A. D. Dumas.
WILMINGTON—
J. A. Applegate.
R. H. Brady.
M. F. Costin.
Henry Green.
D. Hanna.
WILSON—
John B. Deans.
J. E. Wilkens.
WINSTON—
Consolidated Mining & Construct Co.
J. M. Cummings.
Chas. Loman.
I. McIver.
Miller Bros. Co.
T. Morgan.
R. H. Pitts.

NORTH DAKOTA.

FARGO—
H. Ameson.
J. H. Bowers.
Gus Erickson.
Fargo Tile Walk Co.
Casper Johnson.
E. C. Kennedy.
Edward Nelson.
North Dakota Tile Works, Birch, Prop.
G. B. Runner.
Stewart Wilson.
GRAFTON—
St. Hillair Lumber Co.
Nollman & Lewis.
Robertson Lumber Co.
GRAND FORKS—
Anderson & Hunter.
D. A. Dinnie.
Dinnie Bros.
M. J. Moran.

TOWN—
Goodman.
Bensch.
. Bensch.

TON—
Christiamo.
Rischard.
r Bros.

OHIO.

—
Supply Co., 612-615 E. Mill St.
Barnett, 428 Carroll St.
Buehrle, 317 Allyn St.
. B. Camp Co., 30 Park St.
Crisp & Son, 500 E. Mill St.
rown Fire Clay Co., 1200 E.
ket St.
Dwart & Co., 110-120 Brook St.
Ewing, 121 Kirkwood St.
Flower, 119 S. High St.
Gobel, 300 E. South St.
Haury, 407 Wheeler St.
Hugill, 626 E. Mill St.
Hugill, 114 S. College.
McCourt, 318 S. Main St.
Miller, 308½ E. Exchange St.
O'Marr, 545 W. Market St.
on & Wright, 128 N. Main St.
Bros., 104 Carmichael St.
Wildes & Son, 116 S. College

elm & Son, 204 E. Cedar St.
r Brick Co., Cor. Grant and
n.

CE—
evine.
Fitspatrick.
at.
Middleton.
Miller.
Vilson.

BULA—
Salisbury.
King.
Pulman.
tanley.
Starkweather.

S—
Bleness.
Harris.
Harris.
. Fensel.
Towsley.

RTON—
ia Chemical Co.
Bros.
Henry.

RE—
ney.
McClain.
Bros.
). Toole.
iffl.

BELLEFONTAINE—
Jas. E. McCracken.
C. C. Shank.
W. T. G. Snyder.

BELLEVUE—
W. H. Gardner & Co.
Sam Higgins.

BEREA—
John Allen.
A. J. Brown.
Chas. Golke.
Wm. Seidler.

BOWLING GREEN—
Wm. C. Blystone.
George Hodgson.
Geo. E. Mercer.
H. G. Mercer.

BRYAN—
J. C. Beaules.
Wm. Grim.
George Higgins.
O. Willett.

BUCYRUS—
A. H. Gardner.

CADIZ—
John Ankerman.
E. M. Long & Sons.

CAMBRIDGE—
Borton Bros.
Hoyle & Scott.
Jas. Jackson.
J. E. Lepage.
Linn Bros.
Wm. Wharton.

CANTON—
American Granitoid Paving Co.
Carlos Angeretti.
Harry Corl.
John D. Dunbar.
John Hadley.
F. J. Melbourne.
Geo. Oliver.
Richard Stanton.
Turnbull & Piero.
T. K. Turnbull & Son.
Wise & McCaffertv.

CARTHAGE—
August Helming.

CELINA—
Clem Barnbinger.
John B. Petrie.
Chas. Smith.
Bernard Wesker.

CHICAGO—
Joseph Beelman.
C. E. Seitlers.
W. A. Williams.

CHILLICOTHE—
John S. Butler.
M. L. Jones.
Lilter Bros.
Jerome McIntrie.
John Ogden.
Wm. N. Renick.

CINCINNATI—
August Behne, 2185 Barnard.
A. W. Bouchard, Observatory Ave. and Custer St.
J. H. Brinck, 2127 W. 8th.
H. C. Buddenberg, 1434 Main.
The Philip Carey Mfg. Co., 310 Elm.
Cincinnati Granitoid Co., 31 Carlisle Bldg.
Patrick T. Coffey, 1006 E. 3d.
Archibald Colter, 2315 Kenton St.
Columbus Fireproofing Co., 23 E. 3d.
Corbett Brothers, 713 Mound.
Cornelius Cronan, 1620 Hewitt Ave.
George Dell, 10 E. McMickon Ave.
Edward Dorsey, 963 W. 7th St.
George Douglass & Co., 800 Plum.
Duerr & Faul, 2528 Vine.
Eddison & Co., 3096 Mathers St.
George Elzenhoefer, 4173 Hamilton Ave.
Geo. Endres, 228 Mohawk St.
John W. Enright, 714 Mound.
The David Folz Asphalt Paving Co., 230 W. 8th.
Harry Feldkamp, 70 Linn.
Henry Frank, 2015 Western Ave.
Henry Frank, jr., 1638 Western Ave.
Jos. Fredrich, 2862 Corrnany Ave.
S. D. Getchell, 1109 Gilbert Ave.
Fred Gier & Co., 17 W. 13th St.
Globe Paint and Roofing Co., 50 Perin Building.
Haydenville Mining and Mfg. Co., 502 Main St.
O. J. Hazel, 106 E. 8th St.
Hugo Hengstenberg, 3106 Vine.
William Hillenbrand, 2310 W. 8th.
Walter S. Hollaender, 1342 Main.
Charles Homan, 2605 Vine.
Kieserling & Wanner, 1820 Vine.
F. H. Kirchner & Co., 8th and Plum.
Wm. Kolling Co., 717 Reading Road.
Wm. H. Kopp, 2272 Bogen.
John Kuehne, 221 W. Liberty St.
The Charles Kuhl Artificial Stone Co., 9 W. Canal.
Jacob Kuhn, 1145 Bank.
Laping Brothers, 2733 Woodburn Ave.

Cincinnati—Continued.
Thomas Larkin, 315 John.
George F. Laubly & Co., 266 Ludlow Ave.
Wm. Lawson & Brothers, 8th and Walnut.
Frank A. Moeller, 19 Calhoun.
Alex Menger, 2136 Ohio Ave.
B. A. Leonard, 1007 Walnut St.
John Lipps, Cor. Denham and Linden.
Martin Mack, 28 W. McMeckon Ave.
Charles V. Maescher Co., 520 Reading Road.
John E. Mahoney, 711 Whittier.
McCarthy Brothers, 620 Des Moines.
Henry Niemes, 4112 Hamilton Ave.
Frank Nieson, 1308 Sycamore.
The E. J. Nolan Plumbing Co., 604 Main.
J. F. Nolan, 965 E. McMillan St.
Herman Nolte, 951 Clinton.
S. J. Osborn, Jr., & Co., Pearl and Eggleston Ave.
William Peters, 837 Findlay.
Queen City Cement Pavement Co., Glenway Ave. and Austerlitz Rd.
Geo. A. Ramsey, 2349 Kenton.
S. L. Rice, 3d and Main.
Adam Ruby, 437 Carlisle Ave.
Ryan & Smith, 208 W. 3d St.
Oliver Schlemmer, 1811 Linn.
C. B. Schmidt & Co., 215 E. 4th.
Edward Scully, 1149 Bates Ave.
W. H. Settle & Co., Station M.
John Steckewelter, 2419 Vine St.
Jeremiah A. Sullivan, 518 Central Ave.
Trinidad Asphalt Co., 17 W. Water.
F. W. Trinkle, 2137 Central Ave.
Tweedie & Cluxton, 3816 Spring Grove Ave.
Van Sandt & Meeds, 60 Atlas Blk. Bldg.
Wm. F. Wagner, 2852 Colerain Ave.
David A. Walker, Beechwood Ave. and Cinnamon St.
Wanner Brothers, 1327 Vine.
Wm. Welsh & Co., 1304 Central Ave.

Any information on **Cement or Cement Machinery** will be furnished on request by the publishers of this book—

, 39 Euclid Ave.
k Wire Co.
97 Brenton.
Professor.
1314 Zoeter Ave.
2 Kenmore.
Columbus.
28 Doan.
126 Murray Hill Ave.
571 Detroit.
Co., 41 Central Ave.
ens, 41 Central Ave.
249 Quimby Ave.
ner, 45 Case Library

Montrose.
35 2d Ave.
0 Nottingham Bldg.
) Society for Savings

Hayward.
97 Broadway.
105 Brenton.
k Son, Builders' Ex-

, 8 Glen Terrace.
22 William.
3 Vincent.
rs' Supply Co.
, 545 Central.
Co., Hickox Bldg.
ad Paving Co., 209

Builders' Exchange.
ons, 81 Huntington.
219 Superior Bldg.
Crawford Rd.
36 Prosser.
35 Detroit.
8 Kirtland.
Son, 519 American

128 The Arcade.
3 Pearl.
3 Edmunds.
35 Myrtle.
ltman.
02 Lockwood Ave.
35 Woodland Ave.
Palm.
451 Jennings Ave.
Franklin Ave.
ion Co., 807 Ameri-
.
ch, 128 Star Ave.

T. H. Garland, 1 Preble.
W. J. Gawne, Ft. Kirtland.
Gick & Fry, Builders' Exchange.
John Gill & Sons, 401 Cuyahoga Bldg.
R. E. Green & Son, 573 Detroit.
D. & G. Griese, 541 Society for Savings Bldg.
Adam Grimm, 428 Garrettson Ave.
C. N. Griffin, 416 The Arcade.
A. G. Hausman, 195 Scoville Ave.
August Helm, 47 Astor Ave.
C. M. Herb, 6 Dove.
C. J. Hoffman, 687 Jennings Ave.
Henry Holocker, 142 Carran.
N. H. Humphrey, 1035 Giddings Ave.
Hunkin Bros., 302 Sawtell.
Henry J. Huntingdon, 19 Vincent St.
C. E. Jenkins, 46 Spangler Ave.
H. W. Johns Mfg. Co., 221 Savings Bldg.
Christopher Johnson, 152 Oregon.
James Kacal, 16 Ehart.
S. C. Kane, 1862 Euclid Ave.
M. E. Kavanaugh, 490 Prospect.
Keasby & Mattison Co., 117 Water.
J. J. Keiper, 1649 St. Clair.
Kelly Island Lime and Transport Co.
Albert Kerslake, 18 Itaska.
Wm. Klein, 208 S. Woodlawn Ave.
C. F. Kuentz, 330 Waverly Ave.
T. S. Kuster, S. Woodlawn.
Albert Lang, 26 Simon.
J. V. Leach, 208 Lake.
W. C. Lehmann, 219 Becker Ave.
James Loader, 38 Princeton.
H. I. Luff, 2236 Euclid Ave.
Hugh Lyle, 415 Doan.
J. D. Maclennan, 527 Garfield.
Malone Stone Co., Garfield Bldg.
H. C. Masters, Builders' Exchange.
Mathew & Libby, Chamber of Commerce.
W. B. McAllister, 20 Newton.
James McCarthy, 1 Little.
Patrick McCarthy, 194 Dodge.
C. T. McCracken, 64 Jones Ave.
Wm. McDowell, 321 Mills Ave.
J. W. McLean, 31 Rutland.
T. J. McMannus, 410 The Arcade.
J. W. Moran, 31 Rutland.
Morse, Myer, Williand & Tubman, 133 Colonial Arcade.
National Concrete Fireproofing Cor. 249 The Arcade.
T. Nicholson & Co., 302 Electric Bldg.
Norcross Bros.
Northern Ohio Paving Co., Case Library Bldg.
P. H. O'Donnell, 785 Lake.
Edward O'Neill, 163 Wade Ave.

Cleveland—Continued.

F. E. Oviatt, 14 Fern.
Tom Paige, 701 Cuyahoga Bldg.
A. R. Parker, 1438 Superior.
H. C. Patchett, 100 Florence.
W. H. Patchett, 2168 Superior.
H. A. Peterson, 814 Detroit.
Phillips & Bixel, 984 Woodland Ave.
Pope Cement & Brick Co., Cuyahoga Bldg.
Louis Poplowsky, 347 Prospect.
P. R. Putnam, 742 Crawford Rd.
J. A. Reaugh & Son, 523 Garfield.
F. J. Rehor, 29 Amos.
Reserve Construction Co., 153 Prospect.
James Rockford, Builder's Exchange.
C. C. Roehl, 187 Woodbridge.
Frederick Roehl, 140 Merchant Ave.
John Roehl, 742 Clark Ave.
William Ryan, 18 Everett.
F. B. Sager, 23 McConnell.
C. A. Sarber, 365 Case Ave.
Shailer & Schillinglaw Co., 210 W. River.
Michael Sheehan, 20 Lyon.
H. G. Slatmyer, 130 Lake.
Henry Soeder, 20 Merchant Ave.
C. F. Spahlinger, 77 Hicks.
Spence Bros., 2923 Euclid Ave.
Standard Contracting Co., Wade Bldg.
Standpipe Covering Co., 22 Michigan.
Stowe-Fuller Co., 513 Superior Bldg.
C. H. Strong & Son, 623 Cuyahoga Bldg.
Thomas Sullivan, 52½ Tracy.
Jacob Tecka, 40 Chadwick.
J. F. Terney, 61 Davenport.
W. I. Thompson, 176 Euclid.
Alexander Thorn.
I. D. Tuttle, 32 Blackstone Bldg.
U. S. Construction Co., 204 Superior.
P. Velotta, 17 Fairview Place.
Warren Chemical & Mfg. Co., Cham. of Com. Bldg.
G. E. Whitehouse, 9 Beaver.
Thomas Wood, 26 Michigan.
John Wulff, 1965 Denison Ave.
James Young, Builders Exchange.

CLYDE—
Geo. Robinson & Son.
F. Woodworth.

COLLINGWOOD—
Baldwin Bros.

COLUMBUS—
N. B. Abbott, 85 N. High St.
J. T. Adams, 307 Schultz Building.
Acme Paving Co., 408-420 W. State St.
American Art Tile Co., 52-54 E. Lynn St.
American Clay Mfg. Co., 315 W. High St.
Brust & Bauch, 336 Sycamore St.

Columbus—Continued.

Capital City Artificial Stone Co., 78 N. Princeton Ave.
Jas. P. Carlile, 10 Ambos St.
The Central Supply Co., 306-308 N. High St.
Columbus Coal & Lime Co., 347 S. High St.
The Columbus Macadam Co., 319 Dublin Ave.
Cook, Grant & Cooke.
J. P. Crowe, 457 E. Naghten St.
Charles Danegger, 132 E. Schiller.
Davis De Forest, 1412 Oak St.
Dill & Reeves, Columbia Bldg.
Ferris Steam Mortar Works, 628 Galloway St.
John Gaa & Son, 1085 Oregon Ave.
C. H. Garnes, 1273 Main St.
W. M. Graham, 185 E. Town.
Haydenville Mining & Mfg. Co., 190 W. Long St.
Huff & Eigensee, 85 N. High St.
W. B. Jones, 237 E. Spring.
M. J. Keefe, 72 N. Central Ave.
John Kuhn, 55 N. Skidmore.
T. C. Lawler, 777 W. Town.
W. H. Luchtenberg, 410 The Wyandotte.
Charles McCloud, 545 E. Main.
D. W. McGrath, 1079 Summit St.
P. R. McLaughlin, 490 E. Rich St.
Wm. Merkle, 625 S. 5th St.
The Murphy Grout Mfg. Co.
Philip Newbold, 164 N. 21st St.
F. A. Ohrstedt, McKinley & Rodgers St.
Pennsylvania Fuel Co., 9 W. Naghten St. A. Hamilton, Mgr.; E. W. Parker, Treas.
A. G. Pugh, 26½ N. High St.
Jacob Rapp & Co. 3755 High St.
G. M. Schneider, 1-2 S. High St.
Schultz & Son.
Shaffer Roofing Co., 102 W. Long.
W. F. Smith, 186 Jefferson Ave.
Stearns & Hoover, 48 Deshler Bldg.
F. S. Stimmel, 506 S. High St.
Michael Stubenrauch, 378 S. Wash'n Ave.
Herman Stutz, 324 Jackson St.
Wm. M. Taylor, 26 S 3rd St.
Warren-Scharf, 361 W. State St.
R. L. Watson, 71½ E. State.
A. W. White, 415 Western Ave.

CONNEAUT—
Fred Hawley.
Sam Ransom.

CUYAHOGA FALLS—
Bates & James.
Howe & Co.

DAYTON—
Jas. F. Archer, 124 W. Columbia St.
Ellsworth Brentlinger, 1310 N. Main St.
M. G. Cain, 453 W. 5th St.
Jas. E. Conley, 1240 W. 1st. St.

-*Continued.*
n Asphalt Roofing and Pav- Co., 18 S. Canal St.
Hemel, 374 S. Henry St.
rcher, 173 Burns Ave.
Kernan.
. Lauterbach, 156 S. Allen St.
ihns & Co., 536 E. 2d. St.
Kuhl Artificial Stone Co., 536
d. St.
. Lee, 34 S. Eagle St.
. Lockwood, 8 N. Fulton St.
larbleithic Co.
Ritty, 443 W. Holt St.
on Stinebarger, 122 S. Euclid
ior Stone Co., 122 S. Wayne
Swertman, 54 S. Bond St.
ad Asphalt Paving Co.
. Wenger, 230 N. Western Ave.
. Wroe, 449 N. Grafton Ave.
NCE—
Baltes.
ider Bros.
VARE—
Bobo.
Gardner.
Heller.
McDonald.
Miller.
IOS—
& Kollsmith.
R—
Jaeger.
Smith.
PALESTINE—
Crowl.
A—
l Eason.
l & Schultz.
Wolff.
AY—
y & Harris.
. Fassett, 531 S. Main St.
Kleinman, 335 Walnut St.
RIA—
Karg.
KLIN—
Meeker.
. Van Horne.
ONT—
Brockman.
POLIS—
Frankenberg.
l Henry.
H. Karnes.
C. Rue.
e Schneider.
hus Viney.
VA—
Waters.
D—
H. Beaver.
Hake.
Hanna.

GLANDORF—
F. N. Ellis & Co.
GREENVILLE—
Greenville Construction Co.
W. J. Irwin.
HAMILTON—
Isaac Commons, D and Webster Sts.
Hugh H. Hall, 121 S. A St.
Hamilton Architectural Portland Cement Co., 16 Beckett's Blk.
J. G. Hutcheson.
Frank Kinch.
C. F. Koehler.
Wm. H. Louthan.
Miami Cement Co.
Geo. Wilson, S. 11th St.
HICKSVILLE—
Warner & Rose.
HILLSBORO—
Jerry Foley.
IRONTON—
J. B. Black.
S. G. Black.
Frank Brawley.
Cook & Cook
T. J. Mulligan.
Wileman & Helbling.
KENT—
J. E. Kerr & Co.
KENTON—
Jno. Burkart.
J. Christ.
Eli. Lambert.
Maddux & Erwin.
Jno. Quinn.
Jno. S. Scott.
Wells Brothers.
LANCASTER—
Jas. Littrell.
Jno. Littrell.
Jas McManamy.
S. L. Conklin.
Chas. Henderson.
C. H. Jones.
Fred Quiller.
Clint Smith.
LIMA—
E. J. Cantwell, 619 E. North St.
W. P. Cantwell, 119 E. North St.
Jacob Caster, 313 W. Spring St.
W. H. Hance, 139 W. Wayne St.
John Hell, 777 W. Wayne St.
W. H. Orr, 743 W. North St.
Jacob Spyker, 500 W. Wayne St.
C. M. Vansky, 422 W. Third St.
J. M. Wulst, 206 E. Market St.
LISBON—
Carlisle & Moore.
George Forne.
Geo Plero.
Springer & March.
Levi Stackhouse.
LOCKLAND—
W. C. Bunyan.

LOGAN—
Thomas Kintz.

LONDON—
Corr & Kulp.
Jno. Ebner.
Wm. Wynne.

LORAIN—
John Stang.

LOUISVILLE—
John Jacquet.

MADISONVILLE—
J. E. Gornien.
W. H. Settle & Co.

MANSFIELD—
Jacob Cline & Co.
Gandert Bros.
Hering & Son.
Lomax and Portman.
Mansfield Cement and Paving Co., 124 W. 5th St.
Wm. Martin.
Chas. Schung.
Straub & Hamblin.

MARIETTA—
W. J. Berry.
D. W. Dye.
John Wilking.

MARION—
P. Kelly & Co.

MARTIN'S FERRY—
John Boehm.
Chas. Rothermund.
Henry Rothermund.

MARYSVILLE—
Wm. Diehl.
Geo. Fox.

MASSILLON—
Neidlinger & Kraft, 122 Wellman St.
H. Weible, 231 Duncan St.

MEDINA—
John Crofoot.
Jacob Dreiler.
Wm. Frazier.
Thos. Gower, Sr.
Geo. Gruninger.
Albert Smith.
Waters & Levet.

MIAMISBURG—
Grove & Catron.
Jay Jacobs.
Kercher & Toms.

MIDDLEPORT—
Beeson Bros.
Ed S. Grant.
J. B. Lindsley.
B. F. White.

MIDDLETOWN—
Dietrich & Cooch, 35 W. 3d St.
M. F. Kemp & Son.
Middletown Paving Co

MILES—
John Barriball.
Geo. C. Wagner.

MINGO JUNCTION—
Flato Bros.
H. A. Richer.

MT. VERNON—
S. B. Church.
Jacob Coxey.
J. A. Stoyle.

NELSONVILLE—
M. A. King & Co.
B. F. Landis.
W. H. Vorhis & Co.

NEWARK—
J. C. Brennan, 37 V
W. H. Chilcoat, R. [illegible]
J. F. Childress, 20 S.
—— Coffman, 20 [illegible]
D. T. Coffman, [illegible]
W. E. Coffman, [illegible]
Wm. T. Evans & [illegible] teenth St.
D. E. Jones, 111 W.
C. E. Moore, N. W. ta and Canal.
E. J. Maurath, 76 S.
G. C. Wilson, 64 Hi

NEWCOMERSTOWN—
W. M. Brode.

NEW PHILADELPHI
Geo. Edwards.
Samuel Miller.

NILES—
Tompkins & Smith.
Edward Wagstaff.

NORTH BALTIMORE
H. J. Everitt.
C. J. Knoke.
H. D. Pilcher.

NORWALK—
Fred Shumer, Jacks
Stewart & Simmons,

NORWOOD—
Jas. McJoynt.
John Snyder.

OBERLIN—
Chas. H. Gleuss.

OSNABURG—
Jacob Shengle.

OTTAWA—
M. H. Fisher.
Jos. Pishel.

OXFORD—
W. T. Johnston.
H. S. Thobe.

PAINESVILLE—
E. Callender.
J. D. Sargent.
Jas. Shelly.
H. A. Sutherland.

PAULDING—
Geo. Hardesty.

PIQUA—
C. E. Martin.
John H. Reid.

POMEROY—
Geo. Bauer.
C. W. Jones.

CLINTON—
Bertsch.
te Hard Wall Plaster Co.
Johnson.

MOUTH—
Gilson, 82-86 W. 3rd.
M. Glockner, 206 Market St.
Hibbs & Co., 130-132 W. 2nd.
Kaps, 77 W. 10. P. O. Pond Run.
Kaps, 77 W. 10. P. O. Pond
.
Kelly & Sons, 800 Jackson.
E. King, E. 7 and Kendall.
McGowan, E. 5 and Broad-
.
el Monroe, 314 12th St.
Neighbors, 1322 Union.
mouth Pressed Brick Co., 111
ket.
Reeg, 1127 Findlay.
Lumber Co., 1001 Lincoln.
ter Fire Brick Co., S. Webster,
.
Wright, 96 E. 2nd.

NA—
Frank.

NG—
Hunter.
Koenig.
el Roth.
st Schmidt.

Y—
arr.
Fritz.
Norris.
Thompson.
Webb.

RIVER—
ox.
Davis.
Kiddney

[illegible]—
el [illegible]
& [illegible]
D Smith

EVILLE—
[illegible]

SKY—
[illegible]
Fenz & [illegible]
[illegible]
H Smith

Y—
[illegible]
[illegible]
[illegible]
[illegible]
Huffman

Y—
Fisher
Fisher
[illegible]
[illegible]

SPRINGFIELD—
John H. Berger
Chas. J. Henry, 872 W. High
G. H. Logan, 218 N. Murray
Wm. F. Payne, 32 Chestnut St.
The M. C. Russell Cement Paving Co., 80 College Ave.
Ulrick & Williams, 141 N. Limestone.

STEUBENVILLE—
G. J. Fickes, 313 N. 5th
Floto Bros., 500 N. 7th
---- Nicholson, 331 Market

STRYKER—
The Stryker Mfg. Co.

TIFFIN—
M. Baumgartner.
John E. Kline.
John Schubacher.
Geo. Stewart.

TOLEDO—
E. Arnold, 334 St. Clair St.
A. Beauty & Sons, 410 Madison St.
Jacob Bick, 607 The Nasby
Bartoli Marble, Mosaic and Tile Co., 1010 Monroe St.
Burnap & Burnap, 602 The Nasby.
Garland & Warner, 31 The Nasby
G. H. Cole & Co., 426 The Valentine.
Edward Ford Plate Glass Co.
Garrigan Bros., 424 The Valentine.
J. J. Geghan, Hurst Block
[illegible]
M. J. [illegible]
[illegible]
[illegible]

[illegible]

Toledo—Continued.
Thacher & Shirley, 3 Marine Bldg.
Thomas Tyrrell, Cor. Lucas & 13th Sts.
J. W. Van Etten, 643 Oakwood Ave.
Ignatius Wernert, 1214 Erie St.
Alanson Wood, 612 The Nasby.
James Woods, 2013 Union St.

TORONTO—
Chas. Bray.
Joe Edwards.

TROY—
Deweese & Enyeart.
W. H. Northcott & Co.
J. C. Robins.

UHRICHSVILLE—
James Greenlees.
G. F. Hammond.
Henry Hilton.
Mack Hunt.
J. M. Lickey.
H. N. Parks.
Chas. Van Vlech.

URBANA—
Joel Bates.
C. C. Creager.
Lewis Dickinson.

VAN WERT—
Delong & Kline.
Geo. Rice.
Chas. Thornell.

WARREN—
Robert Bell.
Benjamin Bullis.
Clinite Bros.
Elliott Bros.
J. R. Sealey.
Watson & Sutherland.

WASHINGTON—
Fred Schwartz.

WAUSEON—
Palmer & Palmer.

WAVERLY—
David Armbrust.
Geo. Hoeflinger.

WELLINGTON—
Wm. Young.

WELLSTON—
Louis Barnes.
Fred W. Cook.
A. W. Downard

WILMINGTON—
Alph Anderson.
Bart Boyland.
Tom Darbyshire.
Devoe & South.
Pink Reynolds.
Joseph Wakefield.

WOOSTER—
Geo. Fultz.
Wm. Hummer.
Wm. Long.
Wm. Woodland.

XENIA—
John Farrell.
W. O. Maddux.

YOUNGSTOWN—
Davis & Caldwell, 19 N. Phelps St.
James B. Chambers, 715 Mill St.
Thos. Lightbody, 922 Himrod Ave.
Christ Mauser, 25 N. Walnut St.
Niedemeier & Restle, 109 Jefferson.
National Steel Co.
Ohio Stone Paving Co., 374 E. Federa St.
Republic Iron & Steel Co.
Vetter & Heasley, 620 Market St.

ZANESVILLE—
Adams Bros.
Ayers Asphalt Paving Co.
Evans & Dunsweiler.
Fogarty & Curtis.
The Mosaic Tile Co.
Petit & Abele.
T. B. Townsend & Co.

OKLAHOMA TER.

EL RENO—
M. J. Kane.

GUTHRIE—
Anderson & Pulse.
J. T. Blake.
J. F. Brickner.
Scott Cooper.
T. R. Cotton.
H. M. Fielding.
John Scribner.
M. White.

NORMAN—
McCoy & Bethune.

OKLAHOMA CITY—
Oklahoma Cotton Compress Co.

PERRY—
Wm. Herman.
T. J. Johnson.
J. J. Noon.
Geo. Seevy.
Wm. Shiffer

PONCA CITY—
M. Tuman.
Geo. Christman.
Chas. E. Welch.

OREGON.

ALBANY—
W. E. Baker.
A. P. Chamberlain.
W. A. Cox.
J. R. Wilson, P. O. Box 581.

ASHLAND—
C. H. Veghte.
W. K. Reeves.

ASTORIA—
Normile, Fastabend & McGregor.

BAKER CITY—
Neuhaus Bros.

CORVALLIS—
John Bier
Ed Felton.
Chas. Tower.

MORO—
J. O. Elrod.

g.

00 Shaver St.
& Contract Co.

'ard.
64 Sable Bldg.

en.

SYLVANIA.

e, 15 Park Way, E. A.
r, 21 O'Hara St.
cker, 24 Park Way,

man, 502 Avery St.
ry & Supply Co., 101
. A.
Co., 1514 Franklin St.
, 825 Washington Ave.
ris, 106 Erie St., W. A.
t, 1820 Beaver Ave.
iels, 607 Preble Ave.
120 Ohio St., E. A.
1901 Market St.
, 100 Monitor St.
Co., 2030 Chartiers

24 Franklin St.
& Son, 616 Rebecca

hill, 215 Park Way,

10 E. Diamond St.
awrence, 102 Erie St.,

M. 535 Ohio St., E. A.
& Co., 615 W. Dia-

tosh & Co., 207 Penna.

Co., 139 Federal St.
23 Belmont St.
Jr., 1004 Perry, W. A.
, 821 Penn. Ave.
t Paving Co., Alle-

2001 Perrysville Ave.
Ohio and W. Diamond

in, 401 Federal St.
, 714 3d St.
Charles St. and Nor-

l, 1315 Federal St.
& Bro., 2022 Chartiers

, 810 W. Diamond St.

James Wherry & Co., 867 North Ave., W. A.
D. Winters & Son, 801 Jackson St.
Young & Gaver, 258 River Ave.

ALLENTOWN—
Allentown Paving & Construction Co., 902 Hamilton St.
Paul Balosh, 406 Ridge Ave.
Chas. H. Edwards & Co.
Henry E. Erich, 17th & Liberty Sts.
I. L. Lehr & Son, 8 S. 7th St.
Jas. W. Stuber, 142 S. 7th St.

ALTOONA—
H. G. Allen, 933 17th St.
H. H. O'Keeon, 911 19th St.
W. L. Shellenberger, 1710 9th Ave.

AMBLER—
Alb. Beck.
Edw. C. Evans.
Morris Redifer.
B. S. Russell.

APOLLO—
Kirkwood & Willard.

ASHLAND—
C. & J. Liebig.

ASHLEY—
F. P. Blodgett.
J. E. Marcey.
Andrew Murphy.
W. J. Neeld.

ATHENS—
Botsford & Kunes.
J. M. Clark.

AXE MANN—
H. Uhl.

BANGOR—
A. H. Bruch.
John C. Miller.

BEAVER FALLS—
Chandler Bros. Co.
Simon Harrold.

BEDFORD—
Geo. C. Hawkings.
Lessig Bros.

BELLEFONTE—
Samuel Gault.
Henry Lowry.
John Noll.
Thos. A. Shoemaker.
W. H. Steele.

BETHLEHEM—
A. F. Knight.
Lehigh Valley Construction Co.

BIRDSBORO—
L. H. Focht.
A. E. Manger.
R. Mohr & Son.

BLAIRSVILLE—
C. F. Murray.
F. G. Murray.

BLOOMSBURG—
Fred Kumer.
O. B. Mellick.

BLUE BELL—
Geo. Amberg, Jr.

BRADDOCK—
Braddock Lumber Co.
Copeland Bldg. Co.
David T. James.
Jos. H. Rankin.
Union Planing Mill Co.

BRADFORD—
N. H. Bannon.
F. F. Davis.
Wm. Hanley.
Hill & Slattery.
N. I. Jacobson.
David J. Kelley.
J. J. Lane.
Sheehan & McGhaun.
E. N. Unruh.
S. D. Winter.

BRISTOL—
Jas. Banister.
Thos. Vandegrift.
Jno. S. Wright.

BRYN MAWR—
Frank M. Leacock.
Wm. Viney.

BUTLER—
W. E. Cochran.
J. A. McDowell.
Geo. Schenck.
John Shaffner.
Ed Weigand.

CALIFORNIA—
O. O. Hornbake.
John R. Powell's Sons.

CAMBRIDGE SPRINGS—
C. W. Beach.
G. D. Bunting.
Enos Brown.
Miles Crosley.
Hanchett Bros.

CARBONDALE—
Blair & Kennedy.
Collins & Kennedy.

CARLISLE—
L. C. W. Faber, South St.

CARNEGIE—
S. Gamble.
W. H. Roberts.

CATASAUQUA—
Edward J. Boyer.
David L. Emanuel.
Emanuel & Son.
Moritz Forner.
Christian Garbian.
Henry J. Leickel.
Daniel Mullen.
Harry J. Seamen.

CHAMBERSBURG—
B. F. Johns.

CHARLEROI—
T. B. Hastings.
W. B. Taylor.

JUST WHAT CONTRACTORS NEED

To know all the best ideas, the most successful methods, the latest news regarding all contracting work in American cities, is information of great value to progressive contractors engaged in doing that kind of work.

That is just what contractors get from Municipal Engineering Magazine.

If they don't find in the Magazine the information they want, it will be furnished on request to any subscriber. In answering a single question the Magazine often incurs expense greater than a subscription amounts to for life.

This information service alone is worth to contractors many times the subscription price.

The subscription price is only $2.00 per year. No progressive contractor can afford to be without the Magazine.

I am pleased with Municipal Engineering.—*Geo. H. Smarden, Sidewalk Contractor, Portland, Me.*

Municipal Engineering is to my mind the best for men employed in municipal work.—*J. H. Stubbs, West Roxbury, Mass.*

Municipal Engineering is worth its weight in silver.—*Salt Lake Tribune.*

MUNICIPAL ENGINEERING CO.

No. 1 Broadway, New York City, N. Y. :::::: No. 28 South Meridian St., Indianapolis, Ind.

R—
re County Paving & Const.

ickerson.
urraday.
. Johnson.
Bros.
rovost.
Taylor.
eigand.
IELD—
Co.
Hughes.
N HEIGHTS—
Congleton.
. Manley.
Shipley.
Winterbottom.
VILLE—
Dickinson.
D. Lynn.
BIA—
. Broome.
Daron.
D. Forry.
Upp.
Weber.
ENCE—
Fike.
Flanigan.
Stark.
LLSVILLE—
Balsley.
n & Co.
c Lumber Co., Ltd.
Connellsville Lumber Co.
—
ey Bros.
Paul & Son.
RSPORT—
A. Button.
Horton.
Bros.
NSVILLE—
nsville Contracting Co.
E. Patton.
Whittaker.
LLE—
s & Gibbs.
STATION—
Harold.
ON—
Wagner.
IS—
Betts.
DOWNINGTON—
Fisher.
Guthrie.
rnes & Zook.
N—
Brodhead & Bro.
Lesher & Son.
. Miles & Son.
STROUDSBURG—
dinger.
B. Edinger.

EMPORIUM—
W. H. Cramer.
John W. Kriner.
ERIE—
Ed Driscoll.
Kraft & Walther.
Mayer Bros.
John McCormick & Son.
Dennis O'Brien.
EVERETT—
Cottage Planing Mill Co., Spring St.
FLORIN—
J. Y. Kline.
FRANKLIN—
R. A. Bigley.
J. A. Fredericks.
John Osborn.
Daniel Sheehan.
FREELAND—
Jas. Griffith.
Lewis Lentz.
Patrick Meehan.
GIRARDVILLE—
John B. Leibig.
GREENSBURG—
Geo. W. Good & Co.
Keenan & Co.
HANOVER—
McC. Davidson.
HARRISBURG—
Matthew Flanagan.
Galbraith Bros.
Wm. Jennings.
Ward & Stucker.
HASTINGS—
Duncan & Spangler.
Philip Kline.
HAWLEY—
Henry Breed.
HAZLETON—
Fischer & Son.
James & Williams.
HOLLIDAYSBURG—
H. P. Malone & Co.
J. S. Vipond.
HOMESTEAD—
R. M. Elliott & Co.
Erbeck Bros.
HUGHESVILLE—
William A. Ball.
John Erdler.
Chas. Hughes.
HUNTINGDON—
J. C. Hall.
Strickler & Watson.
INDIANA—
E. M. Lockard.
A. F. Moreau.
Wm. L. Swanger.
JENKINTOWN—
Jas. W. Ball.
Horan & Leswing.
L. A. Nagle & Co.
G. Walter Sperry.

JERMYN—
Peck Lumber Mfg. Co.
JOHNSTOWN—
Geo. Krueger.
W. J. Rose & Sons.
Wm. Smith & Bros.
Herman Thiele.
KINGSTON—
C. J. & B. J. Coon.
Coon & Mooney.
KITTANNING—
Daugherty Bros. Brick Co.
Heilman Bros.
W. Hileman.
R. A. Hileman.
McConnell & Luker.
Jas. M. McConlough, jr.
KUTZTOWN—
Chester W. Rhode.
Daniel C. Weil.
LANCASTER—
Joseph A. Eichel.
J. U. Fritchey.
J. G. Galbraith.
F. V. Hinden.
Lancaster Cement Paving Co.
Wm. M. Oster.
C. F. Stauffer.
LANSDOWNE—
P. Mahoney.
R. Shoemaker.
LANSFORD—
Jas. R. Hall.
L. C. & Nav. Co.
Herman Riebe.
LATROBE—
James Dalton.
P. J. Dalton.
John Hermann.
John Onderzer.
Thomas Pottinger.
Daniel W. Smith.
LEBANON—
Sam'l Bells Sons, N. 10th St.
H. C. Fricke, Canal St.
LEHIGHTON—
J. H. Hottenstein.
LEWISBURG—
Jno. H. Betzer.
Chauncey Foster.
Jos. M. Nesbit.
Hervey M. Windel.
LEWISTOWN—
F. G. Francis.
R. H. Montgomery.
J. B. Seiheimer.
LIONVILLE—
Geo. Stine.
LOCKHAVEN—
Geo. S. Goode & Co
D. L. Miller & Co.
MAHANOY CITY—
Smith & Campion.
MANSFIELD—
E. N. Bentley.
Reuben Curtis.

MARIETTA—
Geo. Stecher.
M'DONALD—
D. Capitan.
Jos. G. Hunter.
M'KEESPORT—
Bowman Bros.
Hocker & Shaw.
Kelly & Dry.
Oberlin & Co.
Robert Weir.
M'KEES ROCKS—
Chas. K. Barnha
MEADVILLE—
D. W. Cochran.
Geo. Sidler.
Veith Steiss.
Keystone Paving
MEDIA—
Johnson & Wick
MIDDLETOWN—
C. W. Yost.
MILTON—
Peter J. Cristo.
Amandus Hill.
MINERSVILLE—
Geo. Ball.
Henry H. Dornt
James A. Maurer
MONONGAHELA
A. M. Able.
Clarence Haggert
Frank Haggerty.
Gus Markle.
MONTROSE—
L. P. Loomis.
MOUNT JOY—
H. W. Grosh.
NATRONA—
J. J. Muller.
M. J. Steffen.
NAZARETH—
John F. Dolan.
NEW BRIGHTON
Thos. Houlette.
R. D. Hunter &
Martsolf Bros.
R. B. McDaniel &
NEW CASTLE—
McMillin & Moo
David S. Norris
Geo. H. Van Ho
NEW KENSINGT
Joe B. Heister.
J. S. Murray.
Robt. E. Rowan.
H. S. White.
NORRISTOWN—
John D. Dyer.
Skelly & Weave
G. W. Smith &
NORTH EAST—
Alfred Nelson.
C. M. Schultz.

y.

n.

A—
ng Co., 1028 Wither-

& Scully Co., 2917 N.

icial Stone Paving and
Co., 211 S. 9th St.
Pavement Co., 2310 N.

, 1847 N. 6th St.
Bro., 24th and Locust-

, Jr., 1203 Filbert St.
3 N. Maschnter St.
Paving Co., Harrison

aw, 410 Walnut St.
, 1942 Forbes St.
ing Co., 2506 Benezit

a, 1409 Ritner St.
Son, 7 N. Juniper St.
39th and Haverford

loan, 1835 Market.
Co.
fg. Co., 223 S. 6th St.
Co., 906 Girard Bldg.
ers & Son, 1022 York St.
lor, (Inc.), 257 S. 4th.
icial Stone Paving Co.,
t.
Vest, 604 Fidelity Bldg.
evine, Haverford and

. Benezit n 25th c Hill.
nstruction Co., Betz

le, 104 N. Penn Gtn.
, 1509 Sansome St.
k Co.
ving Co., 2629 Parrish

206 E. Lehigh Ave.
tamin, 408 N. 12th So.
Artificial Stone Paving
8th St.
Co., Ferguson Bldg.
, 2618 N. 6th St.
824 Washington Ave.

Germanic Artificial Stone Paving Co., 1409 Ritner St.
Frank R. Gerry, 1835 Market St.
Globe Artificial Stone Paving Co., Betz Bldg.
Adolph Grant & Co., 210 Chestnut St.
Greenwood Brothers, 2006 Frankford Ave.
Guarantee Paving Co., Betz Bldg.
Matthew Hall, 1927-31 Market St.
Franklin M. Harris & Co., 1611 Filbert St.
I. H. Hathaway & Co.
Haupt & Franklin, 18 S. Broad St.
J. H. Hinkle & Co., American & Cambria Sts.
Holt & Schober, 378 Bourse.
Christopher L. Huber, York rd., near Haines.
Italian Marble Mosiac Co., 431 Spruce St.
Evan Jones, 36th and Liberty Sts.
Charles B. Kline, 331 N. 4th St.
Jas F. Knowlan, 45 N. 13th St.
Wm. Krause & Sons Cement Co., 1621 N. 5th St.
John R. Livezey, 128 S. 20th St.
J. H. Louchheim & Co., 1432 S. Penn Sq.
James Y. MacDonnell Co., 123 N. Franklin.
Francis S. Markland, 424 Walnut St.
Henry Maurer & Son, 29 S. 7th St.
D. J. McNichol, 704 Betz Building.
James H. McQuade, 3512 5th Ave.
Merritt & Co., 1024-1028 Ridge Ave.
Joseph S. Miller, 1808-10 Ridge Ave.
Miller Artificial Stone Pavement Co., 2440 N. Fairhill St.
Mosaic Art Co., 522 N. 10th St.
Howard M. Murphy, 1643 N. Dover St.
National Fireproofing Co., 1200 S. Girard Bldg.
Andrew F. Nett, 1234 E. Chelton Ave.
Stacy B. Opdyke, Jr., 122 Belmont Ave.
George L. Peabody.
George R. Peacock, 212 N. 13th St.
Pennsylvania Asphalt Paving Co., 114 N. Broad St.
Penn. State Construction Co., 735 Drexel Bldg.
Penn. Tile Mfg. Co., 331 N. Fourth St.
Michael Perrello, 710 Ellsworth St.
Louis Peters, Seymour & Keyser Gtn.
Petrific Paving Co., 3345 Market St.
Phoenix Paving Co., 58 N. 4th St.
Joseph Pinto, 5236 Germantown Ave.

Philadelphia—Continued.

Quaker City Paving Co., 45 N. 13th St.
Richardson & Ross, 30th & Race Sts.
George W. Roydhouse, 24 S. 7th St.
James J. Ryan, 1126 N. 40th St.
Ernest Scholz, 1407 N. Camac St.
J. Schwartz, 2306 N. 27th St.
B. M. & J. F. Shanley, 1429 Market St.
Sharpless & Watts, 1522 Chestnut St.
W. S. P. Shields, 705 Witherspoon Bldg.
Smedley Construction Co., 712 Stephen Girard Bldg.
Smedley Coonstruction Co., 711-712 Stephen Girard Bldg.
Smith & Davis Co., 334 N. Broad St.
Standard Concrete Mfg. Co., 507 Betz
Standard Plastic Mfg. Co., 405-6 Stephen Girard Bldg.
Joseph Stetwagon, 525 Commerce St.
S. A. Stoneback, 1328 N. 9th St.
S. A. Taylor, 82 Schmidt Bldg.
Tennis Construction Co., 924 Stephen Girard Bldg.
Trent Tile Co., Klagg Ave., cor. Plum.
United Gas Improvement Co., 333 Walnut St.
U. S. Fireproof Wood Co., 2218-20 Race St.
Vandegrift Construction Co., 663 Drexel Bldg.
Vulcanite Paving Co., 1710 Market St.
Michael Walsh, 1707 N. 24th St.
Warren-Ehrit Co., 1210 Land Title Bldg.
Wm. Wharton, Jr., & Co., Ltd.
J. M. Wilcox & Co., 509 Minor St.
Windsor Paving Co., 46 N. 12th St.
Joseph Yeager, 817 Spring Garden.
John Zehunder, 3508 N. Randolph St.

PHILLIPSBURG—
C. H. Lutjens & Son.

PITTSBURG—
William Allshouse, 433 4th Ave.
A. Ansell & Son, 112 4th Ave.
Thomas Atchison, 5417 Potter St.
Wm. F. Ballantyne, 718 Chestnut St.
Henry Balz, 2 Troy Hill Road.
Samel K. Beatty, 2100 Market St.
W. D. Beatty, 900 W. Diamond St.
L. Benz & Bros., 14 S. 13th St.
Bollinger Bros., 123 1st Ave.
Booth & Flinn, Ltd., 1942 Forbes St.
Kearns Bracken, 5134 Carnegie St.
C. H. Bradley, Jr., & Co.
Breitweiser & Co., 516 Market St.
Morris Broida, 1204 Clark St.
J. E. Brown, 409 Market St.
Browning Bros., 506 4th Ave.
G. R. Buchan, 911 Carnegie Bldg.
DeWitt C. Carroll, 32 Schmidt Bldg.
W. A. Cassidy, 6637 Deary St.

Pittsburg—Continued.

Charles H. Chance, [illegible]
John M. Clark, 1816 Wharton [illegible]
John Cline, 7232 Ballard Ave.
John Cline, Jr., 7232 Ballard [illegible]
George Cochrane, Jr., [illegible] Washington Ave.
George A. Cochrane, 1210 Washington Ave.
John Conley, 5107 Keystone [illegible]
J. A. Cornelius, 53 Schmidt Bl[illegible]
Cronin & O'Herron, 17th St. Muriel.
Curran & Hussey, 215 4th Ave.
Deeds Bros., 245 4th Ave.
W. J. Dow, 434 4th Ave.
Drake & Stratton Co., 34 Corr[illegible] Bldg.
F. R. Dravo & Co.
C. M. Driver, 427 5th Ave.
J. E. Dykmann, 7222 Kelby St.
Charles Egan, 1018 Locust St.
Valentine Ehmer, 141 Washi[illegible] Ave.
Eichenlamb & Madden, 105 [illegible] Ave.
John S. Elliott, 822 Webster Av[illegible]
Edward E. Erickson, 8 Garrison [illegible]
Hugh Ferguson, 3233 Penn. Av[illegible]
Frederick L. Fisher, Jumonvill[illegible] Ann Sts.
W. & J. Frances & Co., Liberty and 34th St.
Frick & Co., 51 Schmidt Bldg.
George A. C. Fuller, 408 Lewis [illegible]
G. S. Fulmer, 409 Market St.
General Engineering & Constr[illegible] Co., 52 Shannon Bldg.
T. M. Gillespie Co., 604 Westing[illegible] Bldg.
Globe Asphalt Co., 405 Bakewell [illegible]
Golden & Crick, 3512 5th Ave.
Graff & Kennedy, 11 Lemon Av[illegible]
Frederick Grinner, 1801 Market [illegible]
George Griser, 187 46th St.
Benjamin A. Groah Co., 409 M[illegible] St.
Ebenezer Hallett, 440 4th Ave.
T. J. Hamilton, 409 Market St.
Hamilton & Riffle, 8 Strawberry [illegible]
George E. Hardie, 33 Pride St.
Robert M. Hays, 413 4th Ave.
W. H. Helper, 309 Collins Ave.
Joseph M. Henderson, 150 Jancey [illegible]
Joseph L. Hersch, Sta[illegible] & L[illegible] Aves.
Heyl & Patterson, 51 Water St.
Daniel Hief, 11 Norton Ave.
James Howard, Jr., & Co., 2[illegible] Cance Blk.
W. E. Howley & Co., 1508 Park [illegible]
A. L. Huff, 148 Roup St.
Hyde Bros. & Co., 908 Lewis Bl[illegible]
Jackson & Fulton, 216 Ferguson [illegible]
Jolly Bros. & Co., 201 [illegible]
Evan Jones, Liberty Ave. & 3[illegible]

rg—Continued.

& Foley Co., 247 Water St.
fman & Byland, 94 Maple St.
ng & Ridge, Forbes & Miltenger Sts.
r & McDonald, 212 Frankstown :.
s Kellert & Son, 603 Empire g.
Kerbaugh, 1036 Penn Ave.
& Fox, 2565 5th Ave.
am Kerr's Sons, 315 Lewis Blk.
W. Keyser, 6636 Deary St.
ge W. King, 4315 Main St.
er & McClarren, 214 Ferguson ck.
. Krewsler, 3217 Penn Ave.
l Lamond, 716 Ferguson Blk.
ınder Laughlin & Co., 704 Lewis .
E. Lersch, Park Ave. & Ane St.
Lydick, 409 Market St.
Lydon, 5409 Keystone St.
ge Maismith, 6312 Butler St.
solf Bros., 412 7th Ave.
rt C. McCain, 208 Alpine Ave.
arren Construction Co., Ltd., 214 guson Blk.
E. McClellan, 429 Diamond St.
. McClure & Son Co., 201 Smith ck.
McClurg Gas Construction Co., Vater St.
s M. McCurdy, 632 Penn. Ave.
McDonald, 602 Penn Bldg.
vain, Unkefer & Co., 8 Wood St.
ınder McKnight, 4507 Forbes St.
McNally, 1007 Forbes St.
s H. McQuade, 3512 5th Ave.
McSpadden, 326 4th Ave.
elber, 530 Standard Bldg.
s Messer, 5102 Carnegie St.
ge H. Meyers, 4049 Woolslayer
· & Reed, 623 Park Bldg.
ım Miller & Sons, 1210 Carnegie g.
f. B. Milholland Co., 714 5th Ave.
Murphy, 32 Schmidt Bldg.
rtin Meyer, 2116 Sarah St.
Castle Asphalt Block Co., 1018 n. Ave.
s Omslaer, 301 Park Bldg.
tros., 1825 Wharton St.
s Owens, 411 4th Ave.
Paler, 423 N. Euclid Ave.
rson & Patton, Lowry and 2d. .
n & Gibson, 528 Standard Bldg.
ody & Filbert Co., Ltd., 5850 ter Ave.
Asphalt Paving Co., 87 Westıouse Blk.

Pittsburg—Continued.

Pittsburg Stone and Pavement Co., Hamilton Bldg
Louis Plank, 1715 Sarah St.
Pope Cement and Brick Co., 421 Wood St.
William T. Powell, 508 4th Ave.
William W. Price, 301 Ferguson Blk.
George A. Rahl, 610 Bingham St.
Charles Rath, 612 McCandless Ave.
T. W. Reilly & Co., 723 Park Bldg.
Andrew Richmond & Son, 516 Market St.
James Rodger, 3514 5th Ave.
Rodgers & Abel, 321 Water St.
Sadler, Martin & Evans, 20 Frankstown Ave.
Frank P. Sawlers, 109½ 44th St.
Wm. B. Scaife & Sons, 221 1st Ave.
George H. Schmunk, 7 Enon Ave.
John F. Scott & Co., 506 Smith Block.
John Seibert, 1700 Jane St.
Michael Senge, 5272 Keystone St.
F. E. Shallenberger, 16 Grant St.
Sheets & Fishburn, 317 Louden St.
Henry Shenk, 900 Lewis Blk.
S. R. Smythe & Co., 1429 Park Bldg.
George M. Sterling, 1900 Bedford Ave.
Wm. J. Sterling, 559 7th Ave.
A. T. Stevenson, 218 Meadow St.
James Stewart & Co., 32 2d National Bank Bldg.
Stratton, Lewis & Co., 327 1st Ave.
Sweeney & Houston, 23d St. & P. R. R.
Louis J. Unverzagt, 416 Chislett St.
Waddell & Miller, Boquet ab. 5th Ave.
Wadsworth Stone and Paving Co., 411 Tradesmen's Bldg.
Wm. Waite, 2500 Jane St.
T. M Walker, 409 Market St.
J. E. Walsh, 48 Dithridge St.
James A Watt, 5613 Kirkwood St.
Werneburg, Sheehan & Co., 413 4th Ave.
Joseph Werner, 169 Washington Ave.
Westinghouse, Church, Kerr & Co., 11 Westinghouse Bldg.
Frederick Westphal, 179 McClure Ave.
A. & S. Wilson, 541 3d Ave.
Alexander Wilson, 4507 Forbes.
Wilker & Bothwell, 63 Standard Bldg.
Thomas D. Wollett & Son, 31 Washington Ave.
R. S. Wright, 210 Ferguson Block.
John K. Wymard, 915 Gerritt St.
Gotthard Wyss, 425 Bissell Block.
Wm. J. Zahnisser, 44th & Lawrence Sts.

PITTSTON—
Geo. Andrews.
Tate & Haley.

RENOVO—
J. H. Baird.
C. C. McInerney.
REYNOLDSVILLE—
Thos. E. Evans.
Reynolds Hardware Co.
Jas. V. Young.
RIDGWAY—
Wm. Edwards.
Hyde, Murphy & Co.
W. H. Miner.
ROYERSFORD—
Sam'l Brunner.
ST. CLAIR—
W. W. Thorn.
ST. MARYS—
Thos. Ernst.
Joe Schlimm.
John Wegmer.
Peter Wegmer.
SAYRE—
Botsford & Kunes.
C. D. Carey.
Mahlon Johnson.
T. P. Maney.
SCHUYLKILL HAVEN—
Irwin Becker.
Daniel M. Phillips.
SCRANTON—
Barber Asphalt Paving Co.
Burke Bros.
M. H. Dale, 329½ Washington Ave.
Donahoe & O'Boyle.
J. J. Fahey.
Geo. Harvey, 620 Deacon St.
Luther Keller.
P. F. O'Hara.
V. H. O'Hara.
Paragon Plaster Co.

M. P. F
Glenn &
SOMERSE
F. B. G
J. S. Hi
M. H. S
SOUTH B
Owen C
SOUTH F
Wm. Mc
Justus
SPANGL
Dan Bu
SPRING
John H
John W
Jones Y
STAUNT
Hale P
STROUD
A. Y. H
H. W.
U. L. P
Shiffer
SUNBUR
Geo. W
Peter F
TARENT
John D
Dr. G.
Jas. A.
D. H.
W. H.
G. W.
TITUSVI
W. H.
M. R.
Jas. W
TOWAN
Edw.

CITY—
& Long.
—
Bros.
CITY—
Hoss.
Lewis.
N—
eck.
E. Hamon.
GTON—
Forrest.
Hallam & Sons, 77 E. Penn.

& Slater, W. Wheeling St.
TOWN—
gbee.
cRinch.
—
ohnson Co.
ORO—
ulver.
HESTER—
orcoran.
E. Farrell.
Townsend.
OVE—
. Little.
McLimens.
. Moore.
Reyburn.
A. Wilson.
EWTON—
eff.
Frank Obley.
choll.
HAVEN—
onnelly.
Kocher.
. Moyer.
haffer.
tehly.
BARRE—
Hendler.
Kuss.
Schmitt, 202 Market.
SBURG—
r & Robinson, Penn. Ave.
MSPORT—
Construction Co.
& Snyder.
mpfle & Co., 332 Penn. St.
SVILLE—
S. Flurry.
Lockard.

Birkinbine.
Engle.
Lehman, S. Geo. St.
. Wolf.

RHODE ISLAND.

—
. Barbour.
Buffum.
Dube.
Le Clair.
all & Co.

CENTRAL FALLS—
John E. Cowden, 396 High St.
Theo. F. Dixon, 6 Summer St.
J. Stephen Dolen, 181 Hadley St.
Fred Herbert, 41 Washington St.
Lescault & Monast, 73 Fuller St.
Joseph Massy, 1 Tiffany St.
George A. Simmons, 17 Illinois St.

CRANSTON—
H. B. Lockwood.

EAST GREENWICH—
James R. Murray.
Byron Roscoe.
Lodowick C. Shippee.

EAST PROVIDENCE—
Anthony R. Barney.
Orray Butts.
J. Crane & Co., 158 Fort St.
Manuel Garcia.
Daniel S. Peck.
T. A. Perry.
Fred Wareham.
Leander F. Whitmarsh.

NARRAGANSETT—
John Bristow.
J. C. Tucker, Jr.

NEWPORT—
Frederick A. Allan, 15 Gibbs Ave.
Allan H. Bishop, 31½ Farwell St.
Alex Booth, 13 Narragansett Ave.
M. Brotherson, 128 Spring St.
Brown & Douglas, 72 & 111 Connection St.
W. H. Coffyn, Langley's Wharf.
John Collon, 31 & 33 Dennison St.
Phillip F. Conroy, 183 Thames St.
Robt. W. Curry, 146 Spring St.
Sheldon H. Curtis, 220 Spring St.
Phillip Dowling, 65 Perry St.
Patrick H. Dunn, 8 Narragansett Ave.
Patrick J. Fagan, 41 Hammond St.
A. J. Fludder, Chapel Pl.
Friend & Maymor, 29 Walnut St.
James M. Gillus, 64 Roseneath St.
James Graham, 11 & 15 Webster St.
John V. Hammett, 32 Church St.
Kirwin Bros., 4 Goodwin St.
W. H. Langley, 9 Elizabeth St.
G. H. Lundgren, 38 Long Wharf.
George Mackie, Harrison Ave.
M. A. McCormick, Thames St.
R. H. McIntosh, 360 Spring St.
McLean & Mason, 13 Frank St.
Morgan Bros., 6 Dean Ave.
M. F. Murphy, 16 Callender Ave.
John Radford, 65 Mill St.
Thos. H. Reagan, 37 Dixon St.
Stoddard & Gladding, 14 Poplar St.
B. F. Tanner, Commercial Wharf.
W. J. Underwood, 32 Franklin St.
Wilber & Manchester, 24 Dennis St.
Harry Wilson, 27 Friendship St.
Herbert Wilson, 12 Friendship St.

PAWTUCKET—
F. N. Adams & Son.
Fred Hebert.
R. H. Kirk & Son.
Henry F. Lull.
Wilmarth & Mackillop.

PEACE DALE—
R. L. Baker.
Felix Doane.

PROVIDENCE—
F. M. Ballou & Co., 1823 Broad St.
J. W. Bishop & Co., 417 Butler Ex.
M. N. Cartier, 293 Canal St.
Wm. A. Chapman & Co.
Citizens' Concrete Co., 75 Westminster St.
Wm. Gilbane & Bro., 96 Harris Ave.
H. B. Hathaway, 48 Wilson St.
Johnson Concrete & Roofing Co., 654 Atwells Ave.
Nicholas Langlois, 293 Canal St.
H. B. Lockwood, 115 Wentworth Ave.
Elmer B. Mason, 33 Wendell St.
J. Wm. Moore & Co., 161 Orange St.
Narragansett Improvement Co., 122 Public St.
Prov. Concrete and Roofing Co., 35 Westminster St.
Rhode Island Cement Drain Pipe Co., 500 Valley St.
R. I. Concrete Co., 3 Custom House St.
Smith Concrete Co., 535 A. Banigan Bldg.
Union Concrete & Roofing Co., 71 Wadsworth St.

WAKEFIELD.
G. H. Bullock.

WARREN—
Jos. Adams.

WESTERLY—
C. H. Fayerweather.
Wm. Louden.
Eugene O'Neil.
Westerley Concrete Co.

WOONSOCKET—
F. M. Ballou & Co.
O. P. French & Son, 16 Deiter St.
Jos Wright, 136 High St.

SOUTH CAROLINA.

ABBEVILLE—
W. H. Long.
Yarb Madden.
C. A. Smith.

ANDERSON—
J. B. Barton.
J. M. Smith.
H. C. Townsend.
J. F. Wilson.

BARNWELL—
John Eve.
J. W. Woodward.

BEAUFORT—
N. Christensen.
R. R. Legare, P. O. Box 217.
C. O. Townsend, Beaufort Ir Works.

CHARLESTON—
Herman S. Cordes, 86 America St.
Louis E. Cordray, 5 Hempstead Sq
W. H. Crouch & Bro., P. O. Box 36
W. E. & E. L. Friday.
A. M. Manigault, 21 Broad St.
Earl Sloan, 172 Rutledge.

COLUMBIA—
Stewart Contracting Co.

FLORENCE—
Silas Bounds.
J. W. Gregg.
T. B. Reynolds.
W. J. Wilkin.

GAFFNEY—
L. Baker.
Cecil & Curry.

NEWBERRY—
W. L. Davis & Co.
E. H. Leslie & Co.

ORANGEBURG—
D. W. Ayers.
S. A. Blackmon.

PIEDMONT—
J. C. Haynes.

SUMMERVILLE—
A. J. Braid.
Jeff D. Braid.
Frank Springs.

SUMTER—
W. H. Epperson.
M. C. Kavanagh.
J. W. McKelver.

SOUTH DAKOTA.

ABERDEEN—
Aberdeen Cement & Tile Works.
E. W. Van Meter.

BROOKINGS—
Bergwin & Jerde.
I. N. Lanshe.
E. J. Ray.
Wold & Johnson.

Municipal Engineering Magazine reaches more people who constitute the cement field of business than any other American publication. It is, therefore, the best advertising medium for this field.

OOD—
arker.
Evans.
Iarland.
& Munn.
.w.
RINGS—
Bralsford.
-
Connelly.

Smith.
N—
Iall.
Lutz.
tilson.
ELL—
Bryer.
Perry.
eurenbrand.
FALLS—
Connelly, 817 W. 11th.
And.
P. Madison, Peck Ave. &
s St.
e & Miracle.
Ward, 416 S. Menlo Ave.
TOWN—
Burdich.
& Rau.
ON—
llensky.
r & Bowyer.
Connelly.
Kingsbury.

TENNESSEE.

OL—
Paving Co.
Echols.
Hobbs.
McCary.
ry Bros.
Scharf.
raft & Lowe.
& Wilson.
Lumber Co.
Trammel.
Wagner.
ANOOGA—
anooga Roof and Paving Co.,
E. Montgomery Ave.
& Co.
KEVILLE—
Eberhardt.
Manning.
Wilson.
ELAND—
. Eversaul.
Hall.
. Parks.
Parks.
MBIA—
nbia Water & Light Co.
. Oakes.
er & Worley.

Columbia—Continued.
Tom Simpson.
W. F. Vaughan.
DAYTON—
Jeff Brewer.
A. J. Erwine.
Alex Johnson.
Jeff D. Miller.
DYERSBURG—
X. B. Wickersham.
JACKSON—
J. G. McCabe & Co.
Chas. Owens.
J. T. Whitehead.
KNOXVILLE—
Geo. P. Chandler, 415 W. Depot Ave.
J. C. Kinzell.
Knoxville Supply Co.
W. P. Koon & Co.
J. C. Monday.
J. T. Wilder.
LEBANON—
Page Bros.
Woolard & Williams.
MARYVILLE—
David Jones.
McMINNVILLE—
Alpha Young.
MEMPHIS—
Granolithic Paving Co., 453 Georgia St.
W. J. Haire.
Ed Halley.
P. Koehler, 196 Main St.
M. Larkin.
Miller Paving Co., 20 Madison St.
Chas. R. Miller Paving Co., 16 Madison St.
C. J. Wagoner & Co.
MURFREESBORO—
W. C. Henry.
NASHVILLE—
Adamant Stone Co., 128 S. Front St.
J. W. Broderick. N. High St.
Cooper & Co., 144-148 S. Front St.
E. T. Lewis, N. Cherry St.
J. V. Lightman, N. Summer St.
Nashville Chemical Co., 921 N. Front St.
Nashville Roofing and Paving Co., 811 Cherry St.
Sinnott & Dyer, 441 N. Cherry.
Tennessee Tile & Paving Co., 500 N. Front St.
ROGERSVILLE—
Rogan, Nice & Smith.
SOUTH PITTSBURG—
R. A. Patton.
UNION CITY—
T. L. Bransford.

TEXAS.

ABILENE—
D. B. Anderson.
R. A. Miller.
J. B. Reese.
Tom Russell.

AUSTIN—
Francis Fischer.
C. Fuhrmann & Bro.
Frank Ilse, 109 E. 9th St.
Manfrais & Barney, 812 W. 12th St.
Jas. E. Polhemus.
Pat Rail.
Jas. Watterston.

BEAUMONT—
F. A. Hyatt & Co.

BELTON—
James O'Casner.
C. S. Fisher.
W. R. Hendrickson.
Shaw & Kingston.
Ben D. Lee.

BONHAM—
S. W. Bolton.

BROWNSVILLE—
S. W. Brooks.

BROWNWOOD—
John Chaillette.
Pat Ford.
Wm. Hood.
J. P. Messick.
Geo. Miller.
Al. Morton.
D. Sinclair.
Newt Staags.

BRYAN—
J. W. Gregg.
Geo. W. Jenkins.
M. L. Wallace.
P. E. Wellman.

CALDWELL—
Mr. Harigraves.
Mr. King.

CAMERON—
J. W. Frierson.
T. M. Sapp.

COLORADO—
Wm. D. Tubbs.
Charles Williams.
G. Y. Wilson.

CORPUS CHRISTI—
Ried & Sutherland.
John A. Smith.
Vetters Bros.

CORSICANA—
Haslum Bros.
Lockhead & Co.
Wood & Co.

CUERO—
Ward & Polmie.

DALLAS—
F. F. Gannon.
Peter Kahland, 516 Jackson St.
J. N. Ryan, 206 Portland St.
John Sheehan, 886 Elm St.
Slocum & Wood, 190 Eakins St.
J. Waespi, 861 Elm St.

DECATUR—
Robt. Clark.
Tom Dunn.
Ed Johnson.

DENTON—
Tom Lovell.

DUBLIN—
C. S. Oates.
M. White.

EL PASO—
Nick Carson.
El Paso Fuel Co., 411 S. Santa St.
W. S. Holtzman.
R. C. Lowell.

ENNIS—
T. A. Laird.
B. F. Sargeant.

FT. WORTH—
John Bardon.
Wm. Brice.
S. N. Brookshire.
Brown & Dabney.
Morgan Evans.

GAINESVILLE—
A. D. Craft.
John Gregson.
H. H. Hayden.

GALVESTON—
Wm. S. Burgess.
J. W. Byrnes & Co., 212 Tremo
Chase & Smith, 2103 Strand.
Galveston Cement Pipe Works, Market St.
Isaac Heffron, 2808 Market.
Richer, Lee & Co., 2201 Strand.

GEORGETOWN—
Belford Lumber Co.
J. Gahogan.
Jack Hutty.
J. Rymal.

HEARNE—
L. W. Carr.
Jno. Robb.
M. M. Rocke.

HILLSBORO—
Will Hatcher.
Scott Shook.
Tom Sowell.

HONEY GROVE—
Jacob Fein.

HOUSTON—
T. W. Boone, 1817 Crawford St.
Burkitt & Barnes, 1015½ Pre Ave.
Crowley & Lewis, 1020 Franklin
C. E. Donnelly, 3103 Harrisl Road.
R. H. Downey & Bro., 402 Binz B
P. H. Garrigan, 716 Capitol Ave.
F. M. Gilbert, 3606 Milam St.
Hipp & Key, 210 Binz Bldg.
Wm. E. Humphreyville, 213 L Bldg.
B. L. Jenkins, 1105 Bagby St.
James W. Kerr, 212 Fannin St.
R. Lamb, 1816 State St.
Patrick Rabbitt, 1512 35th St.
Rudersdorf & Simpson, 1910 Bell A
F. J. Shea, 1703 Texas Ave.

ontinued.
nith, 901 Congress Ave.
rrie, Baker and Walnut St.
Tierney, 3517 Commerce St.

-

& Sons.
tetter.
bett.
ynes.
ortscheller.
ert.
L—
ık.
rsythe.
gins.
Whaley.
d & Emmons.
Y—
Furr & Son.
Johnson.
Scott.
AUNFELS—
es.
Henry.
loeller.
per.
eilbacher.
—
Robinson.

. Breneman.
ONIO—
ettler.
anklin.
lson.
Washington Co.
lephone Co.
action Co.
stern Telephone Co.
RCOS—
naldson.
e.
N—
McGee.
R SPRINGS—
enton.
Pruitt.
Vilson.
—
ogan.
Struve.
—
Blankenstein.
L—
Hopkins.
& Dumgold.
McMain.

ade.
vell.
ERFORD—
Cornelious.
lon.

UTAH.

AMERICAN FORK—
Arthur Dickerson.
Nephi Elsmore.
T. A. Lee.
J. C. Miller.
J. H. Pulley.
BRIGHAM CITY—
F. W. Earl.
Jas. Frederickson.
LEHI—
Chas. Fetherson.
Elias Jones.
Chas. Ohran.
OGDEN—
M. Bucher.
J. P. O'Neill, 2763 Madison Ave.
Joseph Parry, 1743 Washington.
PARK CITY—
Mr. Drake.
PAYSON—
R. Cottrell.
Otto Erlandson.
David P. McDowell.
W. H. Pickering.
PROVO CITY—
Sidney H. Belmont.
Goodman & Tucker.
RICHFIELD—
Martin Anderson.
John Kyhl.
Oley Lund.
SALT LAKE CITY—
Frank O. Harrigan, P. O. box 1167.
Culmer-Jennings Paving Co.
Elias Morris & Sons.
Salt Lake Gilsonite Co., 5 Culmer Blk.
Utah Asphalt and Varnish Co., 404 McCormick Blk.
Wasatch Asphaltum Co., 5 Culmer Blk.
SPRINGVILLE—
C. W. Homes.

VERMONT.

BARRE—
C. A. Badger.
Orrin Simons.
Ward & Douglass.
White & Normandeau.
BENNINGTON—
Theo. Carpenter & Sons.
BURLINGTON—
Edward Callahan, 21 North St.
Duffee Levere, 121 Elmwood Ave.
E. F. Moore, 144 College St.
Charles Stone, 15 Murray St.
PROCTOR—
Vermont Marble Co.
RUTLAND—
A. L. Adams.
L. M. Pike.
Vermont Marble Co.
ST. ALBANS—
Vermont Construction Co.

ST. JOHNSBURY—
M. J. Colbeck & Son.
SOUTH HERO—
O'Brien, McHale & Co.
SPRINGFIELD—
J. E. Morse.
W. P. Morse.

VIRGINIA.

ALEXANDRIA—
Henry & Joseph Padgett.
BEDFORD CITY—
E. G. Buck.
BERKELEY—
W. J. Ballance.
Guild & Co.
CHARLOTTESVILLE—
Brand & Wenger.
Gillispie & Co.
A. P. Smith.
CLIFTON FORGE—
Towles & Pendleton.
DANVILLE—
C. H. Brommer.
W. A. Deitrick.
C. H. East.
J. H. Fitzgerald.
R. B. Graham.
H. A. Osborne.
H. T. Pearson.
FREDERICKSBURG—
A. M. Garner.
J. J. Heflin.
William Livingston.
F. P. Stearns.
G. W. Wroten.
HAMPTON—
R. H. Richardson & Son.
LEESBURG—
Norris Bros.
LEXINGTON—
Ed Johnson.
LYNCHBURG—
Virginia Paving & Construction Co.
MANCHESTER—
Jas. F. Bradley.
J. H. Middendorf.
NEWPORT NEWS—
J. W. Davis.
S. L. Foster & Son.
Wm. Furey.
W. H. Lumber.
John A. Moss.
B. J. Phipps.
W. Richardson.
NORFOLK—
John U. Addenbrook & Son.
S. L. Foster.
PETERSBURG—
C. M. Brister.
W. W. Robinson.
PORTSMOUTH—
B. F. Caraway, 111 Holladay Park View.
Porter & Page, 315 High St.
PULASKI—
Miller & Wardin.
RICHMOND—
Newton E. Ancarrow.
Colonial Construction Co.
A. W. McClay.
Jas. Netherwood.
Old Dominion Iron and Nail Wor Co.
Tredegar Iron Works.
Water P. Veitch.
ROANOKE—
Markley & Co.
J. H. Marsteller, 21 E. Campbell A
Roanoke Gas and Water Co.
Roanoke Mineral Co.
SALEM—
W. G. B. Fitzgerald.
STAUNTON—
Geo. Greaver.
Wm. Larner.
Evans Ross.
SUFFOLK—
W. H. Barnes.
Geo. L. Borum.
H. R. Culley.
WEST POINT—
A. Robinson.

WASHINGTON.

EVERETT—
Maney, Goerig & Rydstrom.
NEW WHATCOM—
E. E. Broker.
OLYMPIA—
Savage & Scofield.
PORT TOWNSEND—
Maney, Goerig & Rydstrom.
Pardee & Sheehan.
PUYALLUP—
E. A. Barrett.
SEATTLE—
Brandt Artificial Stone Co.
Mathew Dow.
T. M. McClellan.
T. Royan.
Smythe, Wakefield & David.
Stirrt & Goetz.
Whitmore Concrete Co., 54 Horton Bldg.
SPOKANE—
Adams & Hogan.
City Street Improvement Co.
J. A. Crutzer, 911 Mallon Ave.
M. Hare, Temple Court Bldg.
J. H. McAllister, S. 111 Mill St.
Thos. Olsen, 408 Indiana Ave.
John H. Stone, 514 6th Ave.
TACOMA—
J. C. Dickson, 1123 S. E St.
A. Rydstrom.
Tacoma Bituminous Paving Co.
Tweeden & Mills.
WALLA WALLA—
Dion Keefe.

WEST VIRGINIA.

IELD—
rtee & Co.
Mann.
ESTON—
Peyton, Charleston Nat. Bank

St. Clair, 61 Virginia Ave.
& Mumford Contracting Co.,
Capitol St.
rn Construction Co.
Withrow Lumber Co., 63 Capi-
t.
SBURG—
Bradford.
Freese.
Jackson.
Bros. & Bryan.
Taggert.
ON—
Diennin.
Keane.
angor.
NGTON—
Carr.
Hill.
Lallance.
alten.
RSBURG—
Brown & Son, 529 Avery St.
ell & Drake, Court Sq.
Hare, 1048 Market St.
Heydenreich, 520 Juliana St.
us Kennedy, 1927 Seventh St.
s & Young, 555 Sixth St.
PLEASANT—
L. Neighbors.
ds & Stortz.
& Munford Contracting Co.
Stortz.
ERDSTOWN—
Blondin.
Blunt.
Humrickhouse, Jr.
VILLE—
Rea.
Rice.
BURG—
Cheeks.
e Jacobs.
s & Mathews.
'eister.
N—
n Berger.
uke.
McBride.
ING—
Hallock & Co., City Bank Bldg.
D. McCarty, 30 14th St.
n & Co., 335 Main St.
M. Robrecht, 145 14th St.
Bros., 2115 Main St.

WISCONSIN.

ON—
g.
mann & Co.

Appleton—Continued.
Driscoll Sewer Pipe Co.
J. H. Green & Sons.
Hackworthy Con. Co.
Wm. Rohloff.
Robt. J. Wilson.
ASHLAND—
A. Donald & Co.
Dan Egan.
Jno. H. Foster.
A. H. Oakey.
T. E. Pugh.
BARABOO—
J. Arnott.
Baraboo Roofing & Paving Co.
J. Cummings.
Isenberg Bros.
McFarland Bros.
Otto Schadde.
BELOIT—
O. Baker
J. C. Clarke.
Cunningham Bros.
W. E. Stevens.
BERLIN—
Julius F. Caman.
Asa Rogers.
BOSCOBEL—
John McCord.
CLINTON—
W. H. Donohue.
N. H. Duff.
Jos. Harness.
P. M. Marressette.
B. Taff.
DELAVAN—
James Davidson.
N. K. Jones.
D. E. Lee.
T. Moore.
Young & Hicks.
EAU CLAIRE—
C. N. Bostwick, 464 Summit Ave.
Robert Brewer, 315 4th St.
D. A. Cameron, 470 Summit Ave.
Chappell Concrete and Tile Co., 207 Grand Ave., East.
Edward Ehrlich, 416 Spruce St.
Philip Ferderhen, 610 N. Barstow.
E. M. Fish & Co., 402 S. River St.
W. R. Harvey, 420 5th St.
Hoppner & Bartlett, 414 Grand Ave. E.
Lang Construction Co., 10 P. O. Bldg.
Andrew Larson, 1120 and 1121 Grand Ave.
Henry Laycock, 822 3d Ave.
Thomas McGowan, 421 Congress St.
W. J. Mills, 611 Bellinger St.
Arthur Mitchell, 521 Erin St.
Gilbert Oren, 533 Niagara St.
J. W. Ross, 228 Water St.
H. S. S. Keels, 303 Marston Ave.
G. O. Stiles, 1529 S. Farwell St.
ELROY—
J. W. Dunlap.

FOND DU LAC—
A. F. Boelke.
M. Drier.
J. Hulter.
Geo. Tuttle.

GREEN BAY—
Batice Rose.
Fabry & Henklemen.
D. Fitzpatrick.
Chas. Gouleke.
Koch Bros.
Peter Lagers.
Van & Co. (C. H. and J. H. Van de Sande.)

IRON RIVER—
Ben Rowe.
L. J. Russell.
B. Ungrodt.

JANESVILLE—
Geo. D. Cannon, 4 E. Oak St.
B. P. Crossman, 65 Pine St.
Jno. Peters, 101 4th Ave.
E. Ratheram, 56 Linn St.
Ezra Rice, Magnolia Ave.
James Shearer, 108 Mineral Pt. Ave.

JEFFERSON—
Hermann Fehrman.
John J. Spangler.

KAUKAUNA—
L. Lindaur.
Mulholland & Connors.

KENOSHA—
F. Gottfredsen, 79 N. Main St.
John Priddis, Ashland Ave.

LA CROSSE—
Evans & Brazee.
A. V. Fetter.
The H. C. Hart Implement Co., 105 N. Front St.
La Crosse Stone Sidewalk Co.
La Crosse Tile and Portland Cement Co.
J. H. Marden.

MADISON—
L. B. Gilbert.
J. W. Mitchell.
Nicholas Quinn.
Robt. Warnock.

MANITOWOC—
Louis Bartke, 809 S. 17th St.
George Boll, 1221 S. Main St.
Valentine Goetzler, 1217 S. 8th St.
Herman, Trastek & Co., 1231 S. Main. St.
Theodore Jorsch, 11th St. and Huron St.
Claus Jurnge, 1231 S. 7th St.
J. H. Keith, 710 York St.
G. W. Kennedy, 615 N. 5th St.
Carl Lange, Huron and 11th Sts.
Jacob Matek, 1209 S. 11th St.
James McGovern, 22nd and Western Ave.
J. D. Miller, North Western House.
Miller Sidewalk Co.
J. W. Pell, 917 S. 15th St.

Manitowoc—Continued.
W. E. Peliet, [illegible] and [illegible] Sts.
John Riederer, 1208 S. Main St.

MARINETTE—
John Crockett.
W. H. Robinson.
J. E. Utke.

MARSHFIELD—
Frank Ward.
Levi Woolsen.

MENASHA—
P. Hyland.
Mat Lambert.
John Lux.
H. H. Plummer.

MENOMINEE—
Albert Hitz.
H. H. Peck.
Mike Puhl.

MERRILL—
Geo. W. Clark.
Raefeldt & Hesterman.
V. Henrich & Co.

MILWAUKEE—
Badger State Pavement Co., [illegible] Sentinel Bldg.
Geo. Bayer, 927 29th St.
C. Beck & Co., 1150 Kinnikinic Ave.
Edward Becker, 2612 Vliet St.
Willard P. Beckwith, 712 Twenty-Ninth St.
Thomas R. Bentley, Builders and Traders' Exchange.
Herman Berg, [illegible] Buffum St.
Henry S. Berninger, [illegible] Pierce St.
C. A. Berthelet, Matthews Bldg.
Berthelet Sidewalk Co., [illegible] W. [illegible] St.
H. G. Block & Co., 812 Second Ave.
John Bluhm, 164 Burleigh St.
Joseph J. Boehm, 378 Sixth Ave.
Aug. C. Boettcher, 905 Twenty-[illegible] St.
Nicholas Boll, 410 Orchard St.
Michie Bonnett & Co., N. E. Cor. Galena and Thirty-first St.
Charles Breest, 1150 Ninth St.
S. J. Brockman, 746 Astor St.
Aug. C. Buchholz, 907 11th St.
Henry Buestrin & Sons, [illegible] [illegible] St.
Daniel Coakley, 384 Farwell Ave.
John J. Crilley, 121 19th St.
Stephen J. Croft, 3102 Galena St.
John Czaplewski, [illegible] 8th Ave.
Stephen Czaplewski, 747 1st Ave.
Herman Daehn, [illegible] [illegible] Ave.
Wm. Dallmann, [illegible] 25th St.
Chas. Danischefsky, [illegible] [illegible]
Charles Dekarski, [illegible] Central Ave.
John Dierschow, [illegible] Orchard St.
John Donohue & Son, [illegible] [illegible] Ave.
Michael Doyle, 434½ Lafayette Pl.
Charles Duchow, 2026 Brown St.

ukee—Continued.
& Kaftner Constr. Co., 81 Grand

ck H. Dunn, 777 Van Buren St.
ck J. Dunn, 909 Kramer St.
F. Ehlers, 880 4th St.
olas Engle, 837 29th St.
am Equitz, 1623 Center St.
Feldar, 559 4th Ave.
inand Felschow, 861 Burnham St.
y Filter, 2110 Cherry St.
G. Filter, 772 1st St.
N. Forrestal, 325 15th St.
ard W. Forrestal, 706 Van Buren

y Frey, 1133 3rd St.
ence Friske, 1010 Booth St.
ur C. Froemming, 1318 Hum-
Ave.
mming Bros., 1288 Humbolt Ave.
Froemming, 1444 N. Pierce St.
I. Frownfelter, 479 Park St.
Gajewski, 421 Maple St.
h Gansel, 1368 8th St.
Gassert, 1006 Central Ave.
lph Gehring, 1041 Holton St.
las Glander, 616 8th St.
Gottschalk, 829 Fourth St.
s Graham, 840 Cass St.
el M. Green, 41 Sentinel Bldg.
ory & Roberts, 812 Jackson St.
Greisler, 548 24½ St.
n W. Griese, 887 28th St.
les Grunewald, 1907 Cold Springs

& Co., 494 Commerce St.
koff Bros., 1701 North Ave.
Hathaway & Co., Voegel's
nd, S. of Canal.
Haubner, E. side 39th St., be-
en Wright & Meinecke.
s Hauboldt, 420 14th St.
nas G. Hayden, 484 S. Pierce St.
Heiden, 718 Center St.
ew Heiden, 701 9th St.
& Huebbe, 1441 23rd St.
Heuser, 950 19th St.
ard J. Hickey, 325 14th St.
erick Hildebrand, Forest Home
and 23d St.
man & Bauer, 279 Lake St.
nan Hohensel, 965 27th St.
A. Holt, 756 5th St.
y Hove & Son, 1922 State St.
ughes & Co., 325 Prairie St.
am Janke, 1214 19th St.
n G. Jennrich, 2019 Elm St.
av J. Jeske & Bro., 1089 Rich-
s St.
G. Jones, 309 Pleasant St.
P. Jones, 82 Wisconsin St.
k Kacsyuski, 720 5th Ave.
Keller, 1117 Humboldt Ave.
dore Kerner, 819 "C," 3rd St.
Kinsella, 617 Clinton St.
W. Kinsella, 617 Clinton St.

Milwaukee—Continued.
Adolph Kissner, Sr., 675 17th St.
Oscar Knie, 1298 N. Pierce St.
Rudolph Knie, 1070 Richards St.
Wm. H. Knoechel, 609 16th St.
Koch & Son, 1186 10th St.
Edward G. Komschlie, 670 American Ave.
William Kraatz, 871 10th St.
F. H. Kratzer, 845 6th St.
Albert Kroening & Son, 623 Greenfield Ave.
John Land, 645 17th St.
Frank Landgraf, 1102 13th Ave.
Albert Lehn, 429 4th St.
Frank C. Leimbach, 1414 12th St.
Frank Lesala, 688 Mitchell St.
Henry Lindert, 1716 Lloyd St.
C. E. Loss & Co., 509 Goldsmith Bldg.
Peter S. Loy, 1514 Cedar St.
Frank Malek, 584 16th Ave.
Frederick J. Mann, 947 E. 38th St.
George J. Markey, 555 Potter Ave.
Henry Marsh, 30 N. Ave.
Anton Mauk, 100 Harmon St.
George J. Markey, 30 North Ave.
J. D. McCusker & Co., 612 Grand Ave.
Wm. T. McGovern, 100 8th St.
McIntosh Bros., 513 Pabst Bldg.
Meredith Bros., 109 Lincoln Ave.
Leonhard Miller, 1176 6th St.
Milwaukee Sidewalk Co., 307 Grand Ave.
John O. Morris & Co., 411 Jackson St.
Alexander Monroe, 533 14th St.
A. Monsted & Co., 507 Pabst Bldg.
Frank H. Nakielski, 15 Walworth St.
Max Neff, 907 4th St.
H. Neidner & Co., 437 Milwaukee St.
Northwestern Tile Co., 428 Grand Ave.
E. C. Notbohn Co., 308 Iron Ave.
August Nuedling, 998 16th St.
James O'Connor, 222 Lyon St.
Robert Oldenburg Co., 1094 Island Ave.
John S. O'Neill, 885 Astor St.
Edward Pax, 82 Clark St.
H. S. Pelton & Co., 428 Grand Ave.
Peters & Grunewald, 827 Seventeenth St.
Joseph Polczynski, 342 Brady St.
Portland Cement Walk Co., 204 Grand Ave.
Conrad Raulf, 533 Twenty-fourth St.
Hubert Riesen, 882 First St.
Paul Reisen, 428 Grand Ave.
Rudolph Riesen & Son Co., 165 Lee St.
Theodore P. Riesen, 1108 N. Pierce St.
Fred Rische, 264 Eighth St.
Edwin J. Roberts, 403 Wisconsin St.
John Roehring, 1238 Humboldt Ave.
W. T. Roehring, 1234 Humboldt Ave.

Milwaukee—Continued.
Henry C. Roenaing, 1035 Newhall St.
Adam Schmidt, 650 Oakland Ave.
Henry Schmidt, 653 Twenty-first St.
Henry Schoen, 1206 Eighth St.
Christian Schopnecht, 1212 Second St.
John Schramka, 1001 Bremen St.
Schuett & Fry, 791 Weil St.
Wm. C. Schulz, 896 Buffum.
P. J. Shea & Son, 1002 Lincoln Ave.
Wm. D. Six, 164 Mason St.
David M. Sneddon, 635 Wentworth Ave.
Spahn Bros. & Co., 2309 Galena St.
Edward Spahn, 2309 Cherry St.
Joseph Spahn & Son, 340 15th St.
Sponholz & Co., 328 Grand Ave.
Edward Steigerwald, 2308 Galena St.
Charles Stieger, 1225 Center St.
Edward Stormowski, 958 Warren Ave.
Wenzel Strachota, 687 Walker St.
Gerhard F. Stuewe, 308 20th St.
Adolph Taddey, 593 24½ St.
F. W. Taddey & Son, 1705 Chestnut St.
Frederick Tegge, 598 21st St.
Robt. Tempelmann, 1824 Cherry St.
John L. Templin, 439 American Ave.
Henry F. Tesch, 82 Reservoir Ave.
Teske & Boge, 679 Lapham St.
Fred J. Thiel, 867 8th St.
Andrew Tophooven, 488 Madison St.
Ferdinand Tribus, 613 24th St.
Joseph Tuckholka, 577 6th Ave.
Carl F. Ueckert, 838 2nd. St.
Heran Villwock, 561 Union St.
August Vogt, 772 2nd. St.
Sylvester Wabiszewski, 591 Grant St.
Adolph Weidner, 539 Washington St.
John Weiher, 878 Franklin St.
August Wendt, 543 Superior St.
Frederick Werner, 346 18th St.
Jacob Werner, 555 12th St.
Western Paving and Supply Co., 770 Commerce St.
The Whitnall & Rademaker Co., 211 Grand Ave.
Willian Wiesmann, 1017 Muskeg Ave.
Louis Wilke, 840 11th St.
Winding & Gezelschap, 710 Pabst Bldg.
Ernest Winter, 752 2d St.
William Winter, 1029 2d St.
Chas Volgast, 490 Greenfield Ave.

Milwaukee—Continued.
Frederick Zeisse, 513 3d Ave.
Geo. E. Zimmerman, 947 12th St.
Frank E. Zodrow, 698 28th St.

MONROE—
Walter Coradine.
Sam Isley.
Kiester & Baumann.

NEILLSVILLE—
W. B. Campbell & Son.
S. Loy.

NEW LONDON—
Jno. Brill.
Leo. Froehlich.
Ed Polley.
Frank Schoenrock & Son

OCONOMOWOC—
H. Lorieberg.

OCONTO—
John Derks.

OSHKOSH—
John Fife Jr.
P. L. Marden.
John Martin.
Northwestern Sewer Pipe Co.
M. J. Seymour.

PORTAGE—
John Deehl.
Wm. Kutzke.

PORT WASHINGTON—
Jas. Ubink.

RACINE—
J. P. Corse & Son.
Jacob Larson.
David Lawton.
D. B. McLeod & Co.
A. Wesley Schroyer.

REEDSBURG—
H. Fauteck.
Henry J. Schroeder.

RIPON—
Chris Fry.
Peter Lambert.
A. Naylor.
Chas. Rivenburg.
Ernest Tobolt.
Fred Webster.

RIVER FALLS—
Ulrich & Andersen.

SHAWANO—
John Andrews.
Chris Fritz.
Theo Gentz.
Fred. Kruger.
Lorenz Schenk.
Wm. Regling.

Up-to-Date Information

Any buyer of this book desiring supplemental information will be furnished it if possible on application to the publishers —

Municipal Engineering Company

.o—*Continued.*
Schultz.
Thomas.
YGAN—
Ackermann.
her & Horn.
st Kraft.
mmensen.
Rathsburg.
Schaetzer.
Scheele, Jr., 712 N. 8th St.
LAKE—
Shields.
A—
Dahe.
Huschka.
Knaus.
HTON—
Hill.
Mandt.
Ovren.
I—
Dakers.
. Smith.
IVERS—
nberg Bros.
Koppleman.
Snettinzer.
Wilsman.
BURN—
Halloran.
RTOWN—
Cowen.
ff & Co.
Gorney.
laff Bros.
ESHA—
. Cahill.
st Dillman.
ACA—
niner.
UN—
Green.
AU—
W. Clark.
Goebel.
st Klosterman.
Krause.
l Bros. & Golz
SUPERIOR—
Barker.
Bros.
Cowdin.
Smith.
Bros.
Wilcox.
st Zachan.

WYOMING.

NNE—
& Bradley.
NS—
rsen, Box 90.
DAN—
Johnson.

CANADA.

AMHERST, N. S.—
Rhodes, Curry & Co.
J. N. Page.
C. J. Silliker.
AYLMER, ONT.—
Geo. Collins.
Thomas Wooster.
BARRIE, ONT.—
Edward Brown.
John Hines.
BELLEVILLE, ONT.—
Frank Dolan.
B. Trualsch.
BRANDON, MAN.—
John Forbes.
Chas. Hall.
T. M. Harrington.
Murdock McKenzie.
Chas. Miller.
Geo. Sterrett.
BROCKVILLE, ONT.—
David S. Booth.
Frank Dolan.
Abraham Hagarty.
CALGARY, ALBERTA—
Hugh McClelland.
J. C. McNeill.
Thos. Underwood, Box 91.
CAMPBELLFORD, ONT.—
James Binor.
Charles Dunk.
Wm. Hall.
John Heagle.
Rooksly & Bros.
CHARLOTTETOWN, P. E. I.—
Lowe Bros.
CHESLEY, ONT.—
Stanley & McLaggan.
CLINTON, ONT.—
Chas. Carter.
Jos. Wheatley.
COBURG, ONT.—
Geo. Bond.
Henderson Bros.
Jet Bros.
COLLINGWOOD, ONT.—
John Lockton.
H. Wynar.
CORNWALL, ONT.—
James C. Johnstone.
Williams & Fallon.
DARTMOUTH, N. S.—
S. B. Davis.
Alex Hutchinson.
Thos. Leahy.
Wm. Phillips.
J. Simmonds & Co.
DUNNVILLE, ONT.—
Robert Bennett.
FORT WILLIAM, ONT.—
Gowanbock, Magee & Co.

FREDERICTON, N. B.—
A. N. Block.
T. E. Foster.
Jno. Maxwell.
L. Stevenson.

GLENCOE, ONT.—
Gillespie & Co.

GODERICH, ONT.—
Chas. A. Reed & Co.

GUELPH, ONT.—
Thos. Dobbie.
Thos. Foster.
Guelph Paving Co.
Daniel Keleher.
John Kennedy.

HALIFAX, N. S.—
Samuel M. Brookfield, 70 Granville St.
Freeman Bros., 15 Carleton St.
Michael E. Keefe. N. Fatridge's Wharf.
Malcolm Johnston.
Samuel A. Marshall, 7 Cunard St.
Nickerson Bros., 31 Cunard St.
Rhodes, Curry & Co., 300 Robie St.

HAMILTON, ONT.—
Dominion Construction Co.
Good & Co.
Wm. Hancock.
Hannaford Bros.
Kramer-Irwin Rock Asphalt & Cement Co.
Geo. E. Mills, 612 King St. E.

HULL, QUE.—
Jos. Bourgue.

JOLIETTE, QUE.—
D. Dostaler.
E. Lanzon.

KAMLOOPS, B. C.—
Johnston & Gill.

KINGSTON, ONT.—
Robert Clugston, 396 Brock St.
Robert J. Free, 94 Division St.
William Langdon, 207 Nelson St.
William McCartney, Jr., 198 University Ave.
J. C. Mitchell, 185 William St.
Alexander Newlands, 184 Ordnance St.
George Newlands, 506 Princess St.
W. J. Turkington, 18 Patrick St.

LINDSAY, ONT.—
James M. Chalmers.
P. G. Pilkie.
Wm. Walters.

LONDON, ONT.—
Bowman & Co.
C. E. A. Carr.
P. L. Marden & Co.

MADOC, ONT.—
John Tucker.

MAGOG, P. Q.—
Albine Lavoie.
David Pepin.
Daniel Peters.

MINNEDOSA, MAN.—
S. Fairbairn.

MONTREAL, QUE.—
M. Bastien & Valiquette, Cherrier St.
Bellhouse, Dillon & Co., St. Frs. Xavier St.
I. Desormeau.
The Forsyth Granite & Marble Co., Ltd., 552 William St.; R. Forsyth, Pres. & Mgr.; John Duthie, Sec. & Treas.
T. D. Lawrence, 15 Laval Ave.
Peter Lyall & Sons, 88 King St.
The Sicily Asphaltum Pav. Co., Mill St.

MOUNT FOREST, ONT.—
Geo. Patton.
Jas. Reid.

NANAIMO, B. C.—
Alex Henderson.
W. McCape.
A. Summerhays.

NEW WESTMINSTER, B. C.—
J. C. Allen.
F. Bauer.
J. Coghlan.
Wm. Cooper.
Henry Hoy.
J. Carter Smith.

ORANGEVILLE, ONT.—
Cesar & Eart.

OSHAWA, ONT.—
James Gall.
John Stacey.

OTTAWA, ONT.—
Thos. Ashwith, 194 Queen St.
W. H. Davis, 404 Theodore St.
Foley & Co., 61 Waller St.
Alex Garvock, 167 Gilmour St.
John Heney, 66 Daly Ave.
Hodgson & Co., 15 Cooper St.
John J. Lyons, 558 King St.
Archibald McNaughton, 236 Lisgar St.
John O'Connor, 229 Theodore St.
T. A. Shore, 411 Cooper St.

PEMBROKE, ONT.—
Dowsley & Summers.
J. W. Munro.

PETERBOROUGH, ONT.—
James Bogue.
Corsey & Laverdun.
Adam Dawson.
H. Evans.
J. E. Hayes.
Wm. Langford.
R. Sheehy.

PETROLIA, ONT.—
Imperial Oil Co.
J. J. Kerr.

PICTON, N. S.—
Fred J. Cole, Jr.
Alex. Murray.
John Murray.

ONT.—
Shaw.
Smith.
Velsh, Sr.
TON, ONT.—
.on Quarry Co.
:W, ONT.—
& Young.
REWS, N. B.—
Iorsnell.
:evenson.
HARINES, ONT.—
n Bros.
icholson.
icholson.
ihan.
ley.
iddle.
ilson & Son.
PHENS, N. B.—
tevenson.
MAS, ONT.—
riffin.
TE. MARIE, ONT.—
:Crae.
'hail.
TH, ONT.—
eridge.
OOKE, QUE.—
nture.
gerald.
awkins.
& Sons.
ONT.—
Mason.
ontgomery.
Steinhoff.
rey.
DALE, QUE.—
ger & Sons.
TER, ONT.—
nested.
URG, ONT.—
rookfield.

TORONTO, ONT.—
Edmund Burke.
Constructing & Pav. Co., Ltd., 1 Toronto St.
Cumming & Co.
Excelsior Paving Co.
B. Gibson.
W. T. Grant & Co., 50 Front St., E.
R. H. Hill.
J. H. McKnight, 43 Rose Ave.
J. McBean, 163 Dowling.
J. McGuire, 48 Henry St.
Fred McKeown.
Robert Robertson, 82 Scollard St.
Hugh Ryan & Co.
D. L. Van Vlack, 108 Pembroke St.
VALLEYFIELD, QUE.—
O. Brais.
Louis Cosette.
O. Cossette.
Tremblay & Frere.
VANCOUVER, B. C.—
Edward Cook.
Cook & Dixon.
J. J. Nickson.
Ironside, Rennie & Campbell.
WALKERTON, ONT.—
R. B. Clement.
J. L. Lloyd.
WEST FORT WILLIAM, ONT.—
Gowanlock, Magee & Co.
WHITBY, ONT.—
Thos. Deverell.
Wm. Westlake.
WINNIPEG, MAN.—
Dobson & Jackson.
F. Fry.
Kelly Bros. & Co.
W. F. Lee
Thos. Sharpe.
WOODSTOCK, N. B.—
Albert Bremer.
John G. Hastay.
W. D. Steeres.
YARMOUTH, N. S.—
Pettit & Sellars.

ENGINEERS, ARCHITECTS AND OTI
PERVISORS OF THE USE OF CEM

ALABAMA.

ANNISTON—
Golucke & Co., Chas. W. Carlton, Supt.
J. D. Hunter.
AVONDALE—
W. R. Starbuck, Cy. Engr.
BIRMINGHAM—
Alber & Byrne, 1909½ 1st Ave.
Allen W. Haskell, 1916 Morris Ave.
Julian Kendrick, Cy. Engr.
Chas. Wheelock & Son.
FLORENCE—
A. G. Negley, Cy. Engr.
GADSDEN—
P. H. Fitzgerald, Cy. Engr.
LANETT—
J. B. Butler.
T. Nodaway, Cy. Engr.
MARWELL—
B. F. Thompson, Cy. Engr.
MONTGOMERY—
Abercombie & Williams, 555 N. Court.
PHENIX CITY—
R. F. Shavors.
SELMA—
G. K. McCormick.
Julien Smith, Cy. Engr.
SHEFFIELD—
L. S. Proctor, Cy. Engr.
TUSCALOOSA—
Woolsey Finnell, Cy. Engr.
Finnell & McCalla.
Wm. Toxey.
TUSCUMBIA—
W. H. Gillman.
UNION SPRINGS—
N. Harris, Cy. Engr.
WOODLAWN—
W. J. Parkes, Cy. Engr.
R. D. Betts.
J. R. Pill.

ARIZONA.

PHOENIX—
W. A. Farish, Cy. Engr.
Jas. McCreighton.
Gus. Streits.
TUCSON—
Thos. Conton, Cy. Engr.

ARKAN

FT. SMITH—
T. A. Bayley, Cy I
HOT SPRINGS—
Sam'l Hamblin, Cy.
S. P. Van Patten.
LAKE VILLAGE—
D. A. Sherfey
LITTLE ROCK—
Francis H. Conway
J. H. Haney, Cy. E
WARREN—
H. P. O'Shields.

CALIFO

ALAMEDA—
W. R. Poyser, Cy. E
BAKERSFIELD—
Chas. H. Congdon.
H. R. Macmurdo.
M. A. Macmurdo, C
BERKELEY—
F. S. Edinger, Brov
Chas. L. Huggins, (
BOWERS—
R. M. Vail.
EUREKA—
W. C. Elsemore, Cy
FRESNO—
B. G. McDougall.
A. C. Schwarts.
HANFORD—
D. Bromfield, Cy. I
R. W. French.
KERN—
W. C. Ambrose.
LONG BEACH—
D. A. Soverign, Cy.
LOS ANGELES—
Hagen E. Abs, 338 B
W. Bassell, 435 Dou
E. M. Boggs, 535 St
L. Booth & Sons, 33
G. Chaffey, 219 Stow
T. B. Comstock, 535
J. H. Dockweiler.
Fred'k. Eaton, Bur
L. Friel, 211 Wilson
Harry Hawgood, 346
Johnson & Catey, 3(
J. D. Lippincott.
Frank H. Olmsted.

eles—Continued.
rcell, 412 Wilcox Bldg.
Quinton.
Schuyler, 401 Douglas Bldg.
r & Miller, 320 Stimson Blk.
F. Stafford, Cy. Engr.
Troeger, 215 S. Hill.
VILLE—
R. Meek, Cy. Engr.
& Hudson, A.
TO—
Finney.

Buckman, Cy. Engr.
NAL CITY—
Savage.
ND—
Adams.
Bardman, 906 Bdy.
Bardman, 906 Bdy.
Clement, Macdonough Bldg.
n & Wilson, 11-12 MacDonough

Fogg, 1004 Bdy.
Gray, 923 Linden St
Miller, Macdonough Bldg.
Morgan, 1004 Bdy.
Treadwell, 970 Center.
ENA—
Allin.
Clapp, Cy. Engr.
Ramel.
A—
Sanders, City Engr.
Wright.
LUFF—
F. Lunning, County Surveyor.
NDS—
Lum, Cy. Engr
Nichols.
SIDE—
Johnson, Cy. Engr.
MENTO—
Boyd, City Engr.
Kieffer.
Mullenney.
ERNARDINO—
k.
Shepard.
EGO—
D'Hemecourt, Cy. Engr.
Hibbard.
haile.
RANCISCO—
Alberger, 315 Calif. St.
r L. Adams, Crocker Bldg.
Allardt, 420 Calif. St.
Baker & Co., 325 Montgomery

an Barth, 601 Calif. St.
Benson, 507 Montgomery St.
Besore, 927 Market.
rd Bienenfeld, Crocker Bldg.
Bowers, 101 Sansome St.
Bowie, 217 Sansome St.
n Bridges, 819 Market St.

San Francisco—Continued.
Davenport Broomfield, Mills Bldg.
R. E. Browne, Nevada Block.
E. J. Cahill, 508 Calif. St.
L. M. Clement, Crocker Bldg.
F. A. Clark, 420 Calif. St.
Cobb & Hesselmeyer, 421 Market St.
D. L. Cochorn, 531 Calif. St.
H. D. Connick, City Hall.
J. B. Cowden, 320 Sansome St.
George Davidson, 530 Calif. St.
Dillman & Wallace, 722 Montgomery St.
Robert McF. Doble, 202 Sansome St.
Donham & Herrmann, 328 Montgomery St.
W. R. Eckart, Nevada Block.
J. W. Ferris, 320 Sansome St.
H. D. Gates, 311 Lyon St.
J. T. Gibbes, 612 Clay St.
R. H. Goodwin, 240 Montgomery St.
Ewald C. Gurnee, City Hall.
C. E. Grunsky, Cy. Engr., City Hall.
E. F. Haas, 320 Sansome St.
Hemenway & Miller, Hearst Bldg.
R. J. Hillis, 531 Calif. St.
S. G. Hindes, 330 Market St.
C. H. Holcomb, 319 Parrot Bldg.
William Hood, 4 Montgomery St.
A. M. Hunt, 331 Pine
N. B. Kellogg, 420 Calif. St.
P. E. Lamar, 927 Market St.
W. G. Lockhardt, 71 Stevenson St.
Marsden Manson, 530 Calif. St.
E. W. McCormick, 240 Bush St.
Samuel McMurtrie, Claud Spreckles Bldg.
J. T. Meddock, 531 Calif. St.
D. E. Melliss, 526 Sacramento St.
G. H. Mendell, 530 Calif. St.
E. J. Molera, 606 Clay St.
R. F. Morton, 120 Sutter St.
W. Morgan & Co., 108 1st St.
Robert Munch, 606 Montgomery St.
M. M. O'Shoughnessy, Crocker Bldg.
R. A. Parker, 320 Sansome St.
Quinby & Harretson, Phelan.
M. F. Reilly, 538 Kearny St.
John Richards, 22 Calif. St.
J. G. Smith, Hearst Bldg.
S. H. Smith, Parrott Bldg.
W. H. Smythe, 101 Sansome St.
C. Z. Soule, 11 Montgomery St.
W. B. Storey, Jr., 641 Market St.
Lawrence Thompson, 915 Geary St.
C. S. Tilton, 420 Montgomery St.
Hubert Vischer, Flood Bldg.
Vivier & Leopolds, 124 Sansome St.
Otto Von Geldern, Flood Bldg.
B. Von Homever, Claus Spreckels Bldg.
A. W. Von Schmidt, 808 Montgomery St
D. D. Wass, 36 E. South St.
J D West, 531 Calif. St.
J. R. Wilkinson, 4th & Townsend St.

SAN JOSE—
C. M. Barker, Cy. Engr.
SAN LUIS OBISPO—
Geo. Story, Cy. Engr.
SANTA ANA—
H. Clay Kellogg.
L. M. Swinehart, Cy. Engr.
SANTA BARBARA—
John J. Hollister.
SANTA CLARA—
C. E. Moore.
SANTA CRUZ—
E. D. Perry, C. E.
E. L. Van Cleek, Arch.
L. B. R. Olive.
SANTA MONICA—
T. H. James, Cy. Engr.
SANTA PAULA—
W. W. Orcutt, Hardware Bldg.
STOCKTON—
Geo. Rushforth.
Geo. A. Atherton, Cy. Engr.
VENTURA—
J. A. Barry.
WATSONVILLE—
C. B. Lewis.
P. M. Andrews.
WOODLAND—
Wm. Masters.
P. N. Ashley, Cy. Engr.

COLORADO.

BOULDER—
James P. Maxwell, Cy. Engr.
CANON CITY—
Cliff Hall, Cy. Engr..
Rittenhouse & Bradbury.
COLORADO SPRINGS—
H. I. Reid, Cy. Engr.
DENVER—
George G. Anderson, 744 Equitable Bldg.
Donald W. Campbell, 744 Equitable Bldg.
Dietrich & Mitchell, 231 Cooper Bldg.
D. C. Dunlap, 1106 Lincoln Ave.
John B. Hunter, Cy. Engr.
Wm. P. Jones, Engr. B. P. W.
F. E. Kidder, A.
Edmund B. Kirby, 612 Boston Bldg.
George B. McFadden, 1534 Champa St.
Peter O'Brien, 30 Railroad Bldg.
John M. Odenheimer, 48 Tabor Blk.
William Adorno Peck, 1643 Champa St.
S. A. Rank, 514 Coooper Bldg.
Jesse Scobey, 33 Bank Block.
J. C. Ulrich, 1528 Champa St.
Henry A. Vezin, 420 Boston Bldg.
Gilbert Wilkes & Co., 510 Ernest St.
Thomas L. Wilkinson, 610 Boston Bldg.
J. W. Wilson.
Alfred F. Wuensch, 827 Equitable Bldg.
FORT COLLINS—
Wm. Rist, City Engr.
GOLDEN—
Howard H. Utley, Cy. Engr.
GRAND JUNCTION—
David R. Crosby.
Chas. W. Haskill, City Engr.
E. H. Kern.
GREELEY—
Ben Cooper.
E. M. Nusbaum.
R. F. Walter, Cy. Engr.
LA JUNTA—
F. T. Lewis, City Engineer.
LEADVILLE—
George Holland, City Engineer.
OURAY—
Rich Whinnerah, Cy. Engr.
PUEBLO—
E. W. Hathaway, City Hall.
E. P. Martin.
Wm. Peach, City Engr.
SALIDA—
Henry Silf.
TELLURIDE—
C. W. Gibbs.
TRINIDAD—
C. H. Knickerbocker, City Eng
Rapp Bros.
Norval W. Wall.
VICTOR—
F. V. Bodfish, Cy. Engr.
Davis & Byle.
Shay & Hartington.

CONNECTICUT.

ANSONIA—
Jas. S. Hall, City Engr.
J. M. Wheeler.
BRIDGEPORT—
B. H. Hull, 1022 Main.
W. B. Palmer.
H. G. Scofield, Cy. Engr.
Scofield & Ford.
BRISTOL—
A. Wm. Sperry, Cy. Engr.
DANBURY—
Chas. O. Brown, City Engr.
DERBY—
Dan'l S. Brinsmade, City Engr.
FARMINGTON—
C. Norce.
HANOVER—
Joseph P. Lyon.
HARTFORD—
Chas. H. Bunce, Cy. Engr.
Henry R. Buck.
Luther W. Burt.
Edward W. Bush.
Butts & Crosby.
Edwin D. Graves.
T. H. McKenzie.
Henry Souther.
MERIDEN—
W. S. Clark, City Engr.

TOWN—
ugur, City Engr.
. Bishop, 129 Main.
UCK—
Ham, City Engr.
EDFORD—
. Coggeshall.
RITAIN—
Caldwell.
ldershaw, Cy. Engr.
ll & Co.
AVEN—
P. Bogart, 82 Church St.
Buddington, 82 Church St.
Hill, 82 Church St.
s W. Kelly, Cy. Engr., City

Nichols, 865 Chapel St.
s & Potter, 42 Church St.
Searles, 70 Church St.
Sperry, 82 Church St.

ONDON—
. Crandall.
H. Richards.

LK—
nd Brown.

ALK—
N. Wood, Cy. Engr.

CH—
E. Chandler, Cy. Engr.

M—
Card.
ILLE—
McKnight.
ON—
Brinsmade, Cy. Engr.
INGTON—
McKenzie, City Eng.
NORWALK—
Wood, Cy. Eng.
ORD—
d A. Parsons, City Engr.
Cochrane.
NGFORD—
McKenzie, Cy. Eng.
RBURY—
A. Cairns, City Engr.
r J. Patton, 63 Bank St.
. Smith, 140 Grand St.
Thompson, 57 W. Main St.
n & Bonnett, 77 Bank.
MANTIC—
Fenton, City Engr.
. Card.
ED—
Barker, Cy. Engr.

DELAWARE.

R—
Mathews, Cy. Engr.
INGTON—
H. Boughman, Cy. Engr
k R. Carswell.
Hatton.
Rice, Jr.

DISTRICT OF COLUMBIA.

WASHINGTON—
Walter Atlee, 613 15th St., N. W.
H. K. Averill & Co., 1421 F St., N. W.
James Berrall, 930 F St., N. W.
Samuel Bootes, 1411 F St., N. W.
Alexis I. P. Coates, 613 15th St., N. W.
Richard P. Crenshaw, 1604 Q St., N. W.
Geo. W. Dorner, 607 Louisiana Ave., N. W.
Edward G. Emack, 902 F St., N. W.
Engineer Department, District of Columbia.
Engineer Department, U. S. A.
Jas. G. Hill, Corcoran Bldg.
Howell & Taylor, 605 12th St., N. W.
John C. Long, 600 F St., N. W.
W. M. Poindexter, 806 17th St.
Ewald Schmidt, 2235 13th, N. W.

FLORIDA.

DUNEDIN—
C. G. Force.
JACKSONVILLE—
Wm. F. Colter.
J. Francis Le Baron.
Philip Prioleau, Cy. Engr.
KEY WEST—
Wm. H. Gwynn.
OCALA—
Geo. McKay.
James Moorhead, Cy. Engr.
PENSACOLA—
W. F. Lee, Cy. Engr.
TALLAHASSE—
Overton Bernard.
TAMPA—
Fred T. Warren, City Engineer.
WEST TAMPA—
B. F. Bettis, Cy. Engr.

GEORGIA.

AMERICUS—
Jno. B. Ansley, City Engr.
ATHENS—
J. W. Barnett, City Engr.
ATLANTA—
R. N. Clayton, City Engr
Geo. H. Crafts, 164 Forrest Ave
Hall Bros., 415 Temple Ct
A. F. Walker, 519 Austell Bldg.
Grant Wilkins, 9½ Peachtree St
AUGUSTA—
A. H. Davenport.
Nisbet Wingfield, Cy. Engr.
BARNESVILLE
J. H Phillips, Cy. Engr
BRUNSWICK
W. C. Anderson.
C. T. [illegible], Cy. Engr
CARTERSVILLE
J. E. [illegible] Cy. Engr

CEDARTOWN—
C. R. Pittman, City Engr.
COLUMBUS—
D. W. Champayne.
Robt. L. Johnson, Cy. Engr.
GAINESVILLE—
W. Wright, Cy Engr.
GRIFFIN—
W. M. Holman, Cy. Engr.
MACON—
J. W. Wilcox, City Engr.
MILLEDGEVILLE—
O. M. Cone, Cy. Engr.
SAVANNAH—
W. W. Hegeman.
Percy Sugden, 114 Bryan.
VALDOSTA—
W. H. Gainey, Cy. Engr.

IDAHO.

BOISE CITY—
E. G. Eagleson, Cy. Engr.
MOSCOW—
D. W. Hannah, Cy. Engr.
POCATELLO—
V. Roader, City Engr.
Oscar Sonekalb.
WALLACE—
G. Scott Anderson.
H. K. Helbostad.
George R. Trask, Cy. Eng.

ILLINOIS.

ALTON—
J. W. Dickson, Cy. Engr. of Venice, Ill.
Elmer Rutledge, City Engr.
ARCOLA—
Wm. Lough.
Jerry McDaniel, Cy. Eng.
Chas. Wesch.
AUSTIN—
Harry A. Potwin.
BATAVIA—
E. K. Merideth, Cy. Engr.
BELLEVILLE—
Louis Graner.
BELVIDERE—
W. M. Marean, Cy. Engr.
BLOOMINGTON—
Bell & Melluish.
E. Folsom, Cy. Engr.
J. H. Burnham.
CAIRO—
J. S. Jenkins.
Kelly & Kersener.
Wm. Thrupp, City Engr.

CANTON—
Geo. W. Chandler, Cy. Engr.
CHAMPAIGN—
J. O. Baker.
W. H. Tarrant, Cy. Engr.
CHARLESTON—
Ed Millar.
Cole Wamsley.
CHESTER—
S. N. Thompson, City Engr.
CHICAGO—
Herman R. Abbott, 1200 Mich Ave.
Dankmar Adler, A.
H. C. Alexander, City Hall.
Alvord & Shields, Hartford Build
Charles G. Armstrong, 1508 F Bldg.
Bion J. Arnold, Marquette Bldg
Sam'l. G. Artingstall, 240 Rialto
Burton J. Ashley, 1202 Michigan
H. F. Baldwin, Chf. Engr. C. & R. R.
Bates & Rogers, 1603 Manh Bldg.
Olof Benson & Co., 401, 91 Dea
Carl Binder, 903, 100 Randolph.
Herman H. Bremer, 715, 100 Wington.
Charles A. Chapman, 1149, 204 D born.
Christie, Lowe & Heyworth, LaSalle.
G. L. Clausen, 66, 164 LaSalle.
John A. Cole, 1580, 84 Van Buren
Theo. L. Condron, 1750 Monad Blk.
Lyman E. Cooley, 713, 21 Quincy
Elmer L. Corthell, 64 Audit Bldg.
Walter W. Curtis, 547, 204 Dearb
W. E. Dauchy, Chf. Engr. C. & P. R. R.
W. S. Dawley, Chf. Engr. C. & R. R.
F. E. Davidson, 201 City Hall.
Fred H. Davies, 88 Walton Pl.
Dickman & McKenzie, 1224 Rook
Geo. W. Dorr, 804, 204 Dearborn.
Duane Doty, 40 Arcade Bldg.
Engineering Contract Co., cago Stock Exchange.
Louis Enricht, 707, 188 Madison.
John Ericson, City Engr.
Wm. B. Ewing, 1700 Marquette
Fritz Foltz, A.

INFORMATION FOR EVERYBODY

If you want to know anything about Cement, Cement work or Cement machinery we will furnish the information, if possible, on request.

MUNICIPAL ENGINEERING CO.

ntinued.

ı & Hopke, 401, 132 Clark.
Glendening, 1512 Monadnock.
ldsborough.
Howard Co., 822 Opera Blk.
raff, 606, 145 LaSalle St.
Griesser Eng. Co., 907 Bldg.
Griffith, 311, 255 Dearborn St.
& McNaugher, 1121 The
idenreich, 541 The Rookery.
Heimbucher, 1341, 204 Dear-
rant, 1640, 79 Dearborn.
Hughes, 1511 Gt. Northern
V. Hunt & Co., 121 The
ston & Co., 715, 100 Wash- St.
Jenney, A.
Knapp, 157 Michigan.
unstman, 64, 84 Adams.
La Pointe & Co., 20, 177 La
. Lee, 41 Arcade Bldg.
Libby, 1770, 84 Van Buren.
le & Nichol, 712, 21 Quincy.
Maloney, 712, 21 Quincy.
Markmann, 1013, 172 Wash.
W. Marshall, 1336, 204 Dear-
McHarg, 538 The Rookery.
er McLennan, 1405, 100
T. Mead, 605, 164 Dearborn.
Modjeski, 1742 Monadnock
ana, 1243, 1244 Marquette
ogan Morgan, 169 Jackson B.
usy, 1400, 84 Van Buren.
chols, 1538 Monadnock.
oble, 1742 Monadnock.
I. Nott, 1330, 204 Dearborn.
radis, Chf. Engr. Chic. Ter. r R. R. Co.
arkhurst, Engr. Bridges & Il. Cent. R. R.
S Patton, A. 115 Monroe St.
Testing Laboratory 1750 ock.
Chf. Engr., Ill. Tel. Const. Rookery.
otter, 1407, 3150 Dearborn
V. Powell, 1006, 138 Washing-
Henderson, 1553 Monadnock
Rideout, 26 Randolph.
Mott, 1336, 204 Dearborn.
N. Roberts, 706, 97 Clark
. Roberts, 706, 97 Clark
Roney, 760 Monadnock Blk
Rosecrans, 1401 Monadnock

Chicago—Continued.

Rowe & Rowe, 802, 225 LaSalle.
Emil Rudolph, 408 Opera House Bldg.
Salich & Co., 802 Monadnock Blk.
Sargent & Lundy, Monadnock Blk.
Julius Schaub, 1650 Monadnock Blk.
The Scherzer Rolling Lift Bridge Co., 1616 Monadnock Blk.
Carl E. Schulze, 903, 109 Randolph.
E. C. & R. M. Shankland, 816 The Rookery.
Edwin M. Smith, 3147 Vernon.
Wm. Sooy Smith, 733 Stock Exchange.
W. L. Stebbings, 113 Monadnock Blk.
August K. Stein, 1342 W. Western.
Charles L. Strobel, 1744 Monadnock.
George W. Sturtevant, Jr., 908 Fisher Bldg.
Sturtevant & Todd, 1208, 277 Dearborn.
Leland L. Summers, 441 The Rookery.
Samuel A. Treat, A., 1507 Fisher Bldg.
Alonzo J. Tullock, 1742 Monadnock Bldg.
Martin Van Allen, 6, 69 Dearborn.
J. H. Wagner, 61 Portland Blk.
Edward P. Wheeler, 1400, 84 Dearborn.
W. H. Wheeler & Co., 1400 Old Colony.
R. B. Wilcox, City Hall.
Benezette Williams, 801, 153 LaSalle.
Carl B. Williams, 801, 153 LaSalle.
Edgar Williams, 713, 21 Quincy.
Robert E. Williams, 711, 84 LaSalle.
Charles Wilmerding, 84 VanBuren.
Wilson & Marshall, A., 218 LaSalle St.
Albert H. Wolfe, 720, 22 Continental Bank.
Frank W Wood, 1538 Monadnock Blk.
Edwin S. Woods, 84 VanBuren.
August Ziesing, 1323 Monadnock.

CHILLICOTHE-
J H. Slum, Cy. Engr.

DANVILLE-
Walter H. Martin, Cy. Engr.
Chas Cottingham.

DECATUR
R O Rosen
Geo V Loring, Cy. Engr

DIXON
Chas V Kerch, City Engr.

DWIGHT
Wm Miller, Cy Engr

EAST ST LOUIS
E S Helm, Cy Engr.

EDWARDSVILLE
C H Spillman
Chas Pauley & Son
Chas Hill
J H Theuer

EFFINGHAM-
W E Lagenbeel Cy. Engr.

ELGIN—
W. W. Abell.
EVANSTON—
Chas. R. Ayers.
O. E. Blake.
F. W. Handy.
Myron Hunt.
Robert Long.
John H. Moore, Cy. Engr.
R. E. Orr.
P. C. Stewart.
FREEPORT—
Geo. A. Graham, Cy. Engr.
F. E. Josel.
FULTON—
James O'Rourke, Cy. Engr.
GALESBURG—
M. J. Blanding, City Engr.
GALVA—
C. V. Dickinson, Cy. Engr.
GIBSON CITY—
W. E. De Vore, Cy. Engr.
GILMAN—
A. D. Thompson.
GRANITE CITY—
Hill & Kishner.
GRAYVILLE—
Geo. Faiszh, Cy. Engr.
HARVARD—
J. F. Wertzel.
HARVEY—
T. D. Hobson, Cy. Engr.
HIGHLAND—
Louis Blattner, Cy. Engr.
HILLSBORO—
James A. Davis, Cy. Engr.
HINSDALE—
F. A. Seiber, Cy. Engr.
HOOPESTON—
John Ernst, Cy. Engr.
JACKSONVILLE—
C. W. Brown, Cy. Engr.
JERSEYVILLE—
A. N. Embley, A.
Wm. Embley, Cy. Engr.
JOLIET—
H. A. Stevens, Cy. Engr.
Geo. W. Brown.
KANKAKEE—
R D. Gregg, Cy. Engr.
KEWANEE—
John Eaton Shepardson, Cy. Engr.
LACON—
Geo. F. Wightman, Cy. Engr.
LAGRANGE—
W. B. Ewing.
Geo. W. Waite, Cy. Engr.
LASALLE—
C. M. Rickard, Cy. Engr.
LEMONT—
John Brankey, Cy. Engr.
LEWISTOWN—
Edward Feaster, Cy. Engr.
LINCOLN—
D L. Braucher.
J. M. Deal.
LOCKPORT—
Hiram Edus, Cy. Engr.
MACOMB—
Cephas Holmes, Cy. Engr.
MATTOON—
A. C. Loomis.
W. Ed. Millar, City Engr.
MOLINE—
Olof Z. Cervin, Arch.
H. G. Paddock, Cy. Engr.
MOMENCE—
J. I. Clark.
MONMOUTH—
Prof. T. S. McClanahan.
J. Ed. Miller, Cy. Engr.
MONTICELLO—
W. F. Lodge.
J. W. Wiley, City Engr.
MOUNT CARROLL—
W. E. Wiler.
John H. Warfield, Cy. Engr.
NORMAL—
Jas. G. Melluish, Cy. Engr.
OAK PARK—
R. A. Carpenter, City Engr.
OTTAWA—
J. F. Richardson, Jr.
W. E. Stucker.
Kesson White.
PEKIN—
D. H. Jansen.
PEORIA—
C. G. Anderson, 24 Arcade Bldg.
H. E. Beasley, Cy Engr.
Henry Cassens, 626 Keetale.
C. M. Dolan, 238 Hancock St.
W. C. Evans, 100 Y. M. C. A. Bld
Harman & Hewitt, Arcade Bldg.
D. H. Maury, Water Works Co.
Nathaniel B. Perry, 507 Niag Bldg.
PETERSBURG—
Charles Anderson.
Wm. Leatson.
Geo. W. Smith, Cy. Engr.
PONTIAC—
P. P. Knight, Cy Engr.
QUINCY—
Enoch R. Chatten, 2049 Maine.
F. A. Grocer, City Engr.
Ferguson A. Grover, City Hall.
Fred'k Hancock, 123½ S. 3d St.
George Wolcott, 2263 Hampshire.
ROCKFORD—
Edw. Main, City Engr.
C. C. Stowell.
ROCK ISLAND—
Wm. A. Darling, County Surv'r.
RUSHVILLE—
John S. Bogby, City Engr.
SANDWICH—
W. M. Hay, County Engineer.
SAVANNA—
J. P. Plattenberger.

LLE—
wn.
ELD—
s.
Hamilton, Cy. Engr.
'almer, Cy. Engr.
eeler.
en.
son.
ives.
iydon.
ec. Co.
es, City Engr.
wn.
oyer, City Engr.
N—
ven, City Engr.
Russell, City Engr.
. Prout.
ALL—
pin.
E—
ge.
berts, Cy. Engr.
CK—
bergelt.
nke, City Engr.

INDIANA.

RIA—
iphrey, Cy. Engr.
S—
I. Downey
Rogers, Cy. Engr.
Auken, Cy. Engr.
ers, Cy. Engr.
[illegible], Cy. Engr.
STON—
[illegible], Cy. Engr.
[illegible], Cy. Engr.
[illegible]
LLE—
[illegible]
[illegible], Cy. Engr.
A CITY—
N. Miller
[illegible], Cy. Engr.
[illegible], Cy. Engr.
[illegible]

CONNERSVILLE—
Karl Hanson, Cy. Engr.
CRAWFORDSVILLE—
Fred Hoffman.
W. F. Sharpe.
E. S. Simpson, Cy. Engr.
James M. Waugh.
CROWN POINT—
Geo. W. Fisher.
Frank Knight.
DANVILLE—
Wm. F. Franklin, Cy. Engr.
DECATUR—
H. B. Knoff, Cy. Engr.
DELPHI—
John W. Fawcett.
Wade P. Thompson, Cy. Engr.
DUNKIRK—
W. H. Budders, Cy. Engr.
ELKHART—
D. F. Cordrey, City Engr.
L. E. Hitchcock.
ELWOOD—
John Finan, Jr., Cy. Engr.
EVANSVILLE—
Chas. C. Genung, Court House
Miles L. Saunders, Cy. Engr., City Hall
James D. Saunders, 210 U. 3rd St.
FORT WAYNE—
F. M. Randall, Cy. Engr.
FRANKFORT—
Chas. E. [illegible], Cy. Engr.
FRANKLIN—
E. L. [illegible], Cy. Engr.
GAS CITY—
J. J. [illegible], Cy. Engr.
GOSHEN—
John L. [illegible], City Engr.
GREENCASTLE—
[illegible], Cy. Engr.
GREENSBURG—
[illegible], Cy. Engr.
GREENWOOD—
[illegible]
[illegible]
[illegible]
[illegible]
HAMMOND—
[illegible]
[illegible]
[illegible], City Engr.
HARTFORD CITY—
[illegible], Cy. Engr.
[illegible]
[illegible]
[illegible], Cy. Engr.
[illegible]
[illegible], Engr.
[illegible]
[illegible]
[illegible]
[illegible]
[illegible]

Indianapolis—Continued.
Lewis K. Davis, 113 Monument Place.
Morris M. Defrees, 62 Ingalls Blk.
W. K. Eldridge, Stevenson Bldg.
Hervey B. Fatout, Room 130½ N. Delaware.
David I. Gibson, A, Law Bldg.
John J. Hainsworth, 106 Commercial Club Bldg.
B. J. T. Jeup, City Engr.
Jos. Laycock, 25 W. Washington St.
Henry A. Mansfield, 1001 Stevenson Bldg.
A. P. McCarthy, 1518 Deloss.
W. Scott Moore & Son, A.
Jas. B. Nelson, 61 Baldwin Blk.
C. A. Paquette, Del. & South Sts.
J. Clyde Power, 13 Court House.
Adolph Scherer, A.
Wm. C. Smith, 52 When Bldg.
Wm. P. Smith, 154 E. Court St.
Vonnegut & Bohn, A.
Frank Woodbridge, 30, 120 E. Market St.

JEFFERSONVILLE—
Victor W. Lyon, Cy. Engr.

KENDALLVILLE—
Henry Bortner, Cy. Engr.

KOKOMO—
James F. Bruff.
Jackson Morrow, Cy. Engr.
A. W. Smith.

LAFAYETTE—
W. K. Hatt.
Melvin Miller.
W. D. Pence.
Geo. H. Stevenson.
C. L. Wagstoff.

LAPORTE—
A. J. Mammero, Cy. Engr.
Hiram Burner.
M. J. Henock.

LAWRENCEBURG—
G. W. Loeber, Cy. Engr.

LIGONIER—
E. B. Gerber, Cy. Engr.

LEBANON—
John Fulwider, Cy. Engr.

LOGANSPORT—
Bridge City Construction Co., Biddle Island.
Henry F. Coleman, 322 3d St.
W. A. Osmer, Cy. Engr.

MARION—
L. M. Overman, Cy. Engr.
A. R. Smith.

MARTINSVILLE—
F. A. Gageby, Cy. Engr.
C. G. H. Goss.

MICHIGAN CITY—
C. E. Combs.
H. M. Miles, Cy. Engr.

MITCHELL—
Wm. M. James, Cy. Engr.

MONTICELLO—
Web P. Bushnell.

MUNCIE—
Toney C. Hefel, Little Blk., 300½ Main.
W. H. H. Wood, Cy. Engr., Co House.

NEW ALBANY—
Samuel Mann, Cy. Engr.

NEW CASTLE—
Omer Minesinger, Cy. Engr.

NOBLESVILLE—
C. J. Cottingham, Cy. Engr.

NORTH VERNON—
W. B. Prather, Cy. Engr.

OTTERBEIN—
W. S. Vandervort, Town Engr.

PERU—
Michael Horan, Cy. Engr.

PLYMOUTH—
John Butler, Cy. Engr.

PORTLAND—
A. J. Frost, Cy. Engr.

PRINCETON—
G. M. Emmerson, Cy. Engr.

RENSSELAER—
H. L. Gamble, Cy. Engr.
J. C. Thrawls.

RICHMOND—
Sackett & Howard.
H. L. Webber, Cy. Engr.

RISING SUN—
Geo. B. Gibson's Sons.
Hunter, Harris & Co.

ROCKVILLE—
Claude Ott, Cy. Engr.

RUSHVILLE—
William Dill, Cy. Engr.
Geo. R. Kelley.

SEYMOUR—
Geo. Slagle.

SHELBYVILLE—
J. H. Phillips, Cy. Engr.

SOUTH BEND—
A. J. Hammond, Cy. Engr.
John F. Meighan.

SPENCER—
T. Guy Pierson.

TELL CITY—
J. M. Cooper & Sons.
Geo. Minto, Cy. Engr.

TERRE HAUTE—
W. H. Floyd.
Geo. R. Grimes, 521 Ohio.
Harris & Paige.
V. K. Hendricks.
B. McKeen.
Chas. Scott.
Geo. H. Simpson.
Ralph Sparks, Cy. Engr.
Vrydagh & Co., A

TIPTON—
Ira F. Crall, Cy. Engr.

UNION CITY—
S. R. Bell, City Engr.

AISO—
I. Carver.
. Lembke.
Rankin, Cy. Engr.
.
Danglade.
NES—
ershey, Cy. Engr.
rshey.
Rodgers.
piker.
piker.
I—
P. Woods, Cy. Engr.
V—
Chamberlain, Cy. Engr.
IGTON—
I C. Faith, Cy. Engr.
Faith.
Poland.
Smiley.
AFAYETTE—
Fawter, Town Engr.
G—
Bridge.
Evans.
ESTER—
. Yunker, Cy. Engr.

IOWA.

A—
Conner.
Metcalf, City Engr.
IGTON—
ght Eaton.
Steece, Cy Engr.
FALLS—
Newton, Cy. Engr.
obinson.
RAPIDS—
n & Warrimer.
Merrideth, City Engr.
& Yeager.
. Wynn.
KEE—
Pingrey, City Engr.
N—
P. Chase, Cy. Engr.
Engineering Co.
t Schnell.
IL BLUFFS—
H. Campbell.
Etnyre, Cy. Engr.
PORT—
Baker.
Beuck.
Francis.
Laurbach.
G. Olshausen.
Sheriff.
DINES—
Cross & Son.
n & Moss. Ia Loan & Trust
.
M. King, City Engr.
Lovell, Equitable Bldg.

Des Moines—Continued.
J. B. Marsh.
B. Schreiner, 1445 Maple, E. & A.
DUBUQUE—
E. C. Blake, Cy. Engr.
G. B. Strickler.
Matthew Tschirgi, Jr., 46 Henion St.
ESTHERVILLE—
R. B. Callwell, City Engr.
Jeffries & Miller.
FT. DODGE—
J. H. Albright.
GRINNELL—
D. M. Blain, Cy. Engr.
IOWA CITY—
Louis E. Lyon, 716 Van Buren.
Chas. S. Magowan, Cy. Engr.
IOWA FALLS—
Wm. Kane, Cy. Engr.
KEOKUK—
J. Ross Robertson, Cy. Engr.
G. M. Walker.
LE MARS—
J. W. Meyers, Cy. Engr.
MALVERN—
J. Deardorf, Cy. Engr.
MASON CITY—
I. E. Stanley.
F. P. Wilson, Cy. Engr.
NEW HAMPTON—
A. D. Bowen, Cy. Engr.
OSAGE—
W. Whalen, Cy. Engr.
OSKALOOSA—
John A. Shannon, Cy. Engr.
RED OAK—
E. Clever, Cy. Engr.
SHELDON—
Frank E. Wade.
SIOUX CITY—
Burkhead & Reese.
Henry Fisher.
W. W. Beach.
J. M. Lewis, Cy. Engr.
L. F. Wakefield.
STUART—
J. R. Caldwell.
VINTON—
J. A. Brown, Cy. Engr.
E. L. Stickray .
WATERLOO—
M. L. Newton, Cy Engr.
Shaw & Shaw.
WAVERLY—
H. S. Hoover, Cy. Engr.
WEBSTER CITY—
J. R. White.
E. E. Fox.
WHAT CHEER—
H. L. Campbell, Cy. Engr.

KANSAS.

ARGENTINE—
J. H. Lasley, Cy. Engr.
ARKANSAS CITY—
J. H. Matthews, Cy. Engr.

CHANUTE—
J. W. Pratt, Cy. Engr.
CHERRYVALE—
S. L. Hibbard, City Engr.
CHETOPA—
J. M. Bannon, City Engr.
CLAY CENTER—
Newton Allen, City Engr.
CONCORDIA—
S. P. McCrary, Cy., Engr.
COUNCIL GROVE—
T. B. Haslam.
EL DORADO—
Jno. H. Austin, Cy. Engr.
EMPORIA—
Matthew Brown.
A. J. Smith, Cy. Engr.
C. W. Squires.
FORT SCOTT—
James Burton, Cy. Engr.
GALENA—
F. M. Anderson.
W. H. Duncan.
J. B. Hodgdon, Cy. Engr.
GARNETT—
John A. Rankin, Cy. Engr.
GIRARD—
S. P. Christian, Cy. Engr.
HIAWATHA—
C. P. Beecher, Cy. Engr.
HOLTON—
Walker Talbert, Cy. Engr.
HUTCHINSON—
F. H. Carpenter.
INDEPENDENCE—
J. Phelan, Cy. Engr.
IOLA—
J. H. Harris, Cy. Engr.
KANSAS CITY—
Lesley & Barclay, 612 Minn. Ave.
C. L. McClung, 2112 N. 10th St.
S. G. McLoon, Cy. Engr.
LAWRENCE—
Holland Wheeler, City Engr.
LEAVENWORTH—
C. F. Greever, Cy. Engr.
M. D. Parlin.
F. C. Waite.
MARYSVILLE—
John Braly, City Engr.
OLATHE—
Fred Pickering, Cy. Engr.
OSAGE CITY—
Gust Johnson, Cy. Engr.
OSWEGO—
E. B. Bayless, Cy. Engr.
J. M. Fleming.
John McKane.
OTTAWA—
Geo. P. Washburn.
Jas. A Service, Cy. Engr.
PAOLA—
N. J. Roscoe, Cy. Engr.
PARSONS—
M. C. Gaffey, Cy. Engr.
PITTSBURG—
C. G. Waite, Cy. Engr.
ROSEDALE—
Wm. Barclay, Cy. Engr.
SALINA—
O. P. Hamilton, Cy. Engr.
STERLING—
A. L. Olmstead, Cy. Engr.
TOPEKA—
Wm. H. Barnes.
Jas. Dun.
H. V. Hinckley.
Holland & Spires.
W. B. Storey, Jr.
Wm. Tweddle.
P. L. Wise, Cy. Engr.
WELLINGTON—
C. L. Roberts, Cy. Engr.
WIER CITY—
Jno. R. Braidwood, Cy. Engr.
WICHITA—
H. L. Jackson, Cy. Engr.
WINFIELD—
J. S. Boynton, Cy. Engr.

KENTUCKY.

ASHLAND—
C. D. Boggess, Cy Engr.
BELLEVUE—
J. A. Rabbe, Cy. Eng., 113 Ta
Ave., P. O. Newport.
CARROLTON—
A. T. Mitchell.
COVINGTON—
W. E. Gunn, Cy. Engr.
E. O. Young, Cy. Engr.
CYNTHIANA—
B. F. Allen.
J. R. Poindexter, Cy. Engr.
DANVILLE—
C. Breckenridge.
DAYTON—
J. A. Rabbe, Cy. Engr., P. O. N
port.
EARLINGTON—
B. W. Robinson, Cy. Engr.
FRANKFORT—
Robt. A. Frazer, Cy. Engr.
B. Marshall.
D. M. Woodson.
HARRODSBURG—
D. Castleman, Cy. Engr.
HENDERSON—
S. H. Kimmel, Cy. Engr.
HOPKINSVILLE—
John A. Twyman, Cy. Engr.
LEBANON—
J. F. Barker.
R. W. Bickett, Cy. Engr.
R H. Carter.
E W Wise
LEXINGTON—
Clarke & Howard.
P P O'Neill, City Engr.

LE—
urtenay.
ny, 549 3d St.
eod, National Bank Bldg.
or & Son, 406 3d St.
, 16 Norton Bldg.
W. Parsons, Cy. Engr.
ter, Columbia Building.
ulhafer, 510 5th.
& Cornwell, 804 Columbia

VILLE—
mour, Cy. Engr.
D—
chfield.
rphy, Cy. Engr.
IELD—
im, Cy. Engr.
—
azier, Supt. Pub. Wks.
rton, Cy. Engr.
RO—

fley, Cy Engr.
lbott.
Whitehead.
—
vis.
opkins.
von.
lcox, Cy. Engr.
D—
aringer, City Engr.
ILLE—
n, Cy. Engr.

LOUISIANA.

RIA—
vester, Cy. Engr
OUGE—
Cy. Engr
ARLES—
lms, Cy. Engr.

ll, Cy. Engr.
EANS—
chnel, 721 Hennen Bldg
Bell, 219 Carondelet St
Brown, 741 [illegible]
& Malochee [illegible] Carondelet

Waddill, [illegible] St. Charles St
Dearborn, [illegible]
E. DeB[illegible]

DeL'Isle [illegible]
[illegible]
[illegible] & [illegible]

[illegible]
[illegible] Cy. Engr.
Kerr [illegible]
[illegible]
T [illegible]

New Orleans—Continued.
A. M. Lockett & Co., 339 Carondelet St.
Gustave Maass, 821 Hennen Bldg.
John M. Ordway, 3125 Chestnut.
Aug. F. Slangerup, 204 Godchaux Bldg.
Hunter Stewart, 225 Carondelet St.
George E. Surgi, 806 Gravier St.
G. D. Von Phul, 223 Magazine St.
F. H. Waddill, Masonic Temple
W. B. Wright, 20 City Hall
OPELOUSAS
T. George Chachere.
Willis Richard, Cy. Engr
SHREVEPORT—
J. R. Barbour, [illegible] Texas St.
W. R. De Voe, 330 Fannin St.
F. W. Kane, 221 Milam St.
T. M. Morton, 518 Milam St.

MAINE.

AUGUSTA—
W. B. Getchell, City Engr
BANGOR—
Frank L. Marston, Cy Engr
G. S. Vicery
Geo. H. Hamlin.
BATH—
Chas A. Corliss, Cy. Engr.
BOOTHBAY HARBOR
Richard Latter, Cy Engr.
CALAIS
Willis McAllister, Cy. Engr.
Benj. Gardiner
CARROLLTON
R W. Steele, Cy Engr
DEERING
J W Barbour, Cy. Engr
DOVER
C. F Hurd, Cy Engr
EASTPORT
C. B Dow Cy Engr.
FOXCROFT
Herman S Martin
GARDINER
Frederic Danforth, 20 Water.
LEWISTON
Jno A Jones Cy Engr
MACHIAS
H F Taylor Cy Engr
MADISON
C H Humphreys Cy Engr
OLD TOWN
[illegible] J Burrell Cy Engr
ORONO
C. H Hamlin
PITTSFIELD
Preston Hervey
D. M Parks Cy Engr
PORTLAND
Geo. R Fernald, Cy Engr.
[illegible] & Cummings
E. C Jordan

Advantages of Advertising in Municipal Engineering Magazine

UNICIPAL ENGINEERING is the largest and most influential magazine in the field it represents. It is read by more people directly interested in this field than any other publication.

It contains more advertisements of this kind of business than any other publication, because it is the best medium.

It is kept on file for reference by interested people in most of the cities and towns in the United States and Canada.

It does for its advertisers a kind of missionary work that can not be done for them so successfully in any other way.

It not only introduces them to all the people they want to know about them, and whom they can not reach through any other facilities, but it also keeps its advertisers advised by special bulletin of the opportunities for them to get business.

It is the special aim of the management of the magazine to help its advertisers, and it does this with all the facilities of a complete and well-established organization covering the entire country.

It makes advertising pay advertisers seeking business in its field.

If that is the kind of help you want, there is no reason why it should not be as profitable to you as to others.

Try It!

:ASTON—
. Creighton & Co.
Cushing & Co.
:RVILLE—
:. Getchell, City Engr.

MARYLAND.

IMORE—
'y Adams, Equitable Bldg.
ieth Allen, 804 Equitable Bldg.
h L. Blockwell, 229 E. German.
s Duncan, Equitable Bldg.
'. Fendall, Cy. Engr.
ert Geer, Equitable Bldg.
. Greiner, Mt. Royal Sta.
:. Hambleton, 8 South St.
es & Penniman, Atlantic Trust
lg.
& Quick, Equitable Bldg.
L. Kenly, City Hall.
. H. Latrobe, Merchants' Bk.
lg.
Parker-McCormick Co., 110 St.
ul.
FIELD—
M. Riggin, Cy. Engr.
ERLAND—
'. Lefevre, Cy. Engr.
Schmidt.
Shrion.
TBURG—
. Watson, Cy. Engr.
:RSTOWN—
Hughes, Cy. Engr.
MOKE—
ard Burdick, Cy. Engr.
BURY—
E. Suman, Cy. Engr.
MINSTER—
A. Roop, Cy. Engr.

MASSACHUSETTS.

:RLY—
. J Berry.
ON—
'thaw Construction Co., 7 Exchange Place. Room 52.
n D Adam., Box 1377, Boston, O.
ard P. Adams, 53 State, Room 4.
ry S. Adams, 53 State, Room 542.
enry Adams, 136 Congress
nwall & Lincoln, 3 Hamilton ace.
. O. Badger, 1140 Columbus Ave
:oward Barnes, 7 Water St
nes, Ruffin Co., 218 Tremont.
s. H. Bartlett, 9 Concord Sq
:. Bates, 94 Green, J. P.
'. Baxter, 15 Court Sq., Room 72
State Dredging Co., 19 High.
& Co., 24 Warren, Box R. 36
7. Bowditch 60 Devonshire.
:er Brackett, 3 Mt Vernon
. H. Bradley, 53 State, Room 642.
ner Briggs, 79 Milk, Room 27.
lerick Brooks, 31 Milk, Room 302.

Boston—Continued.

W. M. Brown, Jr., 20 Pemberton Sq.
Thos. S. Burr, 53 State, Room 639.
Edw. A. Buss, 85 Water, Room 65.
J. L. Bryne & Co., 131 Devonshire, Room 29.
J. H. Burt & Co., 1617 Blue Hill Ave.
C. H. Butting & Co., 64 Federal.
George R. Cary, 25 Old Court House.
Howard A. Carson, 20 Beacon St.
Charles Carr, 7 Exchange.
W. B. Carr, 23 Court, Room 218.
H. H. Carter.
Freeman C. Coffin, 53 State, Room 826.
Ethan R. Cheney, 166 Devonshire.
John E. Cheney.
Ed. A. Clark, 170 Summer.
Wm. L Clark, 17 Milk, Room 25.
Frank G. Coburn & Co., 926 Tremont Bldg.
John C. Coleman & Son, 1536 Columbus Ave.
Collins & Ham. 119 Boston.
John Connors, 8 Danube.
Continental Construction Co., 170 Summers.
W. W Cooley.
A. B. Corthell, 220 South Sta.
Coughlan & Ryan, 280 Columbus Ave.
J. Crane, 113 Cambridge Alls.
Henry D. Crane, Powell St., opp. 702 Dorchester Ave.
Joshua Crane, Jr., 1122 Tremont Bldg.
J. B Dacy, 110 Minot.
Charles H Davis, 14 State.
Edgar S Dorr, 30 Tremont.
Arthur Eappleyard, 50 State, room 15.
Eastern Dredging Co.., 25 Congress Room 8
Wm. C. Edwards, 113 Devonshire.
The C. H. Eggle Co., 17 Cenral.
Chas. D. Elliott, 31 Exchange Place.
Clarence S. Ellis, 53 State, Room 828.
John W. Ellis, 178 Devonshire, Room 416.
Emery & Stuart, 166 Devonshire.
George E Evans, 95 Milk St.
Arthur G. Everett, A, 62 Devonshire St.
E W Everson & Co., 166 Devonshire.
Loring N. Farnum, 53 State, Room 419.
Burton R. Felton, 1121 Tremont Bldg.
Clarence T. Fernald, 101 Milk.
Desmond FitzGerald, 3 Mt. Vernon.
Charles W. Folsom, 30 Tremont.
Frank A. Foster, 34 School, Room 43.
John R. Freeman, 31 Milk, Room 63.
Hollis French & Allen Hubbard, 3 Hamilton Pl.
French & Bryant, 4 State.
Harry Arthur Frink, 23 Pinckney.
Joseph P. Frizell, 60 Congress.

Boston—Continued.

F. L. Fuller, 12 Pearl, Room 35.
Charles H. Gannett, 53 State, Room 1102.
Frank B. Gilbreth, 85 Water, Room 23.
X. H. Goodnough, 140 State House.
James O. Goodwin, 53 State, Room 406.
Jos. L. Gooch, 166 Devonshire, Room 52.
H. Gore & Co., 54 Kilby, Room 2.
Gow & Foss, 8 Exchange Place.
E. H. Gowing, 95 Milk St.
Arthur F. Gray, 53 State.
C. G. Hall & Son, 7 Exchange Pl., Room 48.
Frederick P. Hall, 85 Devonshire, Room 13.
E. A. W. Hammatt, 53 State, Room 629.
Henry A. Hancox, 258 Wash.
W. E. Hannan, 34 School, Room 49.
H. A. Hanscom & Co., 53 State.
Harriman Brothers, 40 Water, Room 20.
Chas. Harris, 70 Kilby, Room 68.
Harris & Letterny, 1014 Tremont Bldg.
Ephraim Harrington & Co., 60 State.
Louis E. Hawes, 73 Tremont St.
George Hayes & Co., 95 Milk.
C. Atherton Hicks, 501 Tremont Bldg.
Thos. B. Hind, 19 Milk.
Arthur Hodges, 8 Exchange Place, Room 8.
Gilbert Hodges Co., 60 State.
Holbrook, Cabot & Daly, 1140 Tremont Bldg.
Albert H. Howland, 60 Congress.
Wm. E. Hoyt.
C. S. Humphreys.
Charles C. Hutchinson, 152 State.
Hyde & Sherry, 15 Court Sq., Room 44.
William Jackson, Cy. Engr., 50 City Hall.
David H. Jacobs & Son, 166 Devonshire.
Johnson Brothers, 166 Devonshire.
Jones & Meehan, 1 Beacon, Room 83.
Arthur D. Jones, 76 Kingston.
William Kelly, 366 W. Broadway.
W. H. Keyes & Co., 96 Milk St.
G. A. Kimball, 101 Milk.
Richard D. Kimball, 34 Merchants Row.
Edward H. Ketfield, 53 State, Room 1104 A.
John T. Langford, 70 Kilby, Room 39.
Lawler Brothers, 16 City Sq.
Albert A. Libby & Co., 79 Milk, Room 35.
Thomas J. Lyon, 166 Devonshire.
Angus MacDonald, 95 Milk, Room 15.
Mack & Moore, 22 Chapman Place.
Henry Manley, 51 City Hall.

Boston—Continued.

Elmer G. Mann, 12 Pearl St.
Walter H. Mansfield, 54 Kilby St.
Henry H. Marden, 25 Bloomfield [illegible]
L. K. Marston, 22 Catawba.
Elmer G. Mann, 12 Pearl.
Walter H. Mansfield, 54 Kilby.
J. W. McArdle, 95 Milk, Room [illegible]
John N. McClintock, 20 State St.
McClintock & Woodfall, 15 Court [illegible]
McHale & O'Connor, 16 City Sq.
Allen McIntosh, 166 Devonshire.
A. McMurty & Sons, 16 Shepard.
McNeill Brothers, 196 Freeport.
Charles H. Mead, 39 Court.
Mead, Mason & Co., 520 Tremont.
Leonard Metcalf, 14 Beacon St.
Metropolitan Contracting Co., 95 M[illegible] Room 68.
Franklin M. Miner, 25 Old Co[illegible] House.
Moore & Co., 95 Milk St., Room 6[illegible]
Charles Morton, 53 State, Room 828.
Moulton & O'Mahoney, 209 Washi[ng]ton.
Neale, Preble & Co., 166 Devonshi[re]
Norcross Brothers, 1143 Tremont.
O'Brien, McHale & Co., 16 City Sq.
O'Brien & Sheehan, 16 City Sq.
Orne & Lawrence, 95 Milk.
Osborn Company, 41 Ames.
W. A. Payson, 354 Blue Hill Ave.
Chas. A. Pearson, 21 City Sq.
Charles C. Perkins, 25 Old Court
Pierce & Barnes, 7 Water.
Wm. Pray, 166 Devonshire.
Wm. Gibbons Preston, A., 186 Devonshire St.
John H. Proctor, 73 Elmira.
Ralph A. Quimby, 53 State.
James H. Roberts & Co., 137 Poland.
Frederick L. Rice, 125 Milk.
George S. Rice, 95 Milk, Room 73.
John H. Rice, 79 Milk St.
Roebling Construction Co., 178 Devonshire.
Joseph Ross, 28 School & 166 Devonshire.
W. A. & H. A. Root, 42 Dulow [illegible] & 166 Devonshire.
Thomas A. Rowe & Co., 209 Wash.
Wm. L. Rutan, 71 Wareham.
Edward Sawyer, 60 Congr[ess] Room 3.
Walter H. Sawyer, 60 Congress.
Wm. H. Sayward, 166 Devonshire.
W. J. C. Semple, 25 Old Court Ho[use]
Edw. S. Shaw, 12 Pearl.
James F. Shaw & Co., 8 Congress
George W. Sherman, 53 State.
W. F. Sherman, 27 State.
Sherman & Martin, 163 Dartmo[uth]
Frank E. Sherry, 15 Court Sq. [illegible]
Simpson Bros., corp. 166 Devonshire
George E. Sleeper, 7 Deane, Room

ontinued.
n A. Snow, 166 Devonshire.
. Barbour, 1121 Tremont Bldg.
Humphreys, 85 Water, Room

nne, 68 Devonshire, Room 20.
Dillingham & Co., 6 Oliver,
33.
. Stearns, 15 Exchange.
Stearns, 3 Mt. Vernon.
H. Sutherland, 62 Murdock.
er & Cooper, 73 Exchange

Carr & Andrews, 64 Federal

A. Taylor, 719 Tremont Bldg.
inkham, City Hall.
A. Tracy, 39 Court.
Trumbull & Co., 1121 Tremont

Tudor, 95 Milk St.
l K. Turner, 53 State, Room

urner & Co., 19 Milk, Room 34.
unt & Howe, A.
Vleet, 34 Oliver.
. Varney, 46 School, Room 10.
Varney, A.
n Brothers, 143 Federal St.
& Smith, 53 State.
n & Co., 43 Milk, Room 3.
n & Howard, 85 Devonshire,
23.
O. Whitney, 25 Old Court
.
Whitten, 8 Hamilton Place.
Wheeler, 14 Beacon.
. Whitney, 15 Court Sq.
Wellcutt & Son, 166 Devon-

I. Williams, 53 State, Room

W. Wilson, 190 Dorchester.
A. Wilson, City Hall.
V. Wood Co., 2380 Wash
er Woodbridge, 4 P O Sq.
ry & Leighton, 166 Devon-
Room 51.
ter Const. Co., 53 State.
314.
R. Worcester, 53 State, Room

. Young & Co., 506 Tremont

ON—
rock, 39 Parsons St
T. Palmer, 60 Fairbank St.
'ON—
R. Felton, City Engineer.
'd & Howard, 15 Green St.
& Wetherbee.
.INE—
French, Town Engineer.
& Bryant, 334 Washington St.

CAMBRIDGE—
Frank H. Carter, Cy. Engr's office.
Louis M. Hastings, City Engineer.

CAMBRIDGEPORT—
Frank A. Bayley, 133 Austin St.
L. M. Hastings, City Engineer.

CANTON—
Frederick Endicott.

CHELSEA—
Jos. R. Carr.
Alfred L. Maggi, Cy. Engr.
J. H. Stubbs.

CHICOPEE—
Frank P. Cobb, Cy. Engr.

CLINTON—
H. A. Miller.
Parker & Bateman.
T. F. Richardson.
C. E. Wells.

EAST CAMBRIDGE—
Francis H. Kendall, court house.

EAST WALPOLE—
Edmund Grover.

EVERETT—
C. Harrison.
C. W. Mason, Cy. Engr.

FALL RIVER—
Philip D. Borden, Cy. Engr.
Walter E. Noble.

FITCHBURG—
Wm. K. Bailey.
David A. Hartwell, Cy. Engr.
Geo. Raymond.
Works & Briggs.

GLOUCESTER—
Winslow L. Webber, Cy. Engr.

HAVERHILL—
Robt R Evans, Cy. Engr.
Nelson Spofford, 14 Water St.

HOLYOKE—
E A Ellsworth, 7 Main.
J. J. Kirkpatrick.
T. W. Mann
Jas L Tighe, Cy. Engr.
Tower & Wallace.

HYDE PARK—
E. A. W. Hammatt, 10 Neponset Blk.
Addison C Nickerson.

JAMAICA PLAIN—
J. Edwin Jones.

LAWRENCE—
Arthur D. Marble, Cy. Engr.
Sjostrom & Franklin, 316 Essex.

LOWELL—
George Bowers, Cy. Engr.
F. W. Fornham, Cy Engr's office.

LYNN—
Chas. W. Gay, 25 Exchange St.
J. K. Harris, 59 Exchange St.
Geo. I Leland
Edward H. Smith, Cy. Engr.

MALDEN—
Chas. G. Waitt.
Geo. A. Wetherbee, Cy Engr.
Chas. C. Whittier.

MARLBORO—
Jas. F. Bigelow, Cy. Engr.
MEDFORD—
Howard T. Barnes, Cy. Engr.
James O. Goodwin, C. E., 28 Main St.
MELROSE—
W. Dabney Hunter, Cy. Engr.
Larrabee & Barry, 514 Main St.
Walter C. Stevens, 541 Main St.
MILLBROOK—
Lawrence Bradford.
NANTUCKET—
Jesse B. Snow.
NEW BEDFORD—
Albert B. Drake, 164 Williams St.
George H. Nye.
William F. Williams, Cy Engr.
NEWBURYPORT—
John P. Titcomb, Cy. Engr.
NEWTON—
Irving T. Farnham, Cy. Engr.
NEWTON HIGHLANDS—
Sanford E. Thompson.
NEWTONVILLE—
Percy M. Blake.
NORTH ADAMS—
John H. Emigh, City Engr.
Franklin B. Locke.
NORTHAMPTON—
E. C. & E. E. Davis.
R. F. Putnam.
Wm. F. Pratt, Jr.
L. M. Thacher, Cy. Engr.
NORTH ATTLEBORO—
Frank T. Wescott, Supt. Streets.
PITTSFIELD—
Barnes & Jenks, 28 West St.
Arthur A. Forbes, City Hall.
Geo. A. Murdock, 43 Wahconah St.
QUINCY—
E. W. Branch, 5 Adams Bldg.
H. Flood, 1 Adams Bldg.
Perry Lawton, 7 Savings Bank Bldg.
Otis D. Rice, Hancock House.
H. T. Whitman, 21 Adams Bldg.
SALEM—
Metcalf & Ashton, 39 Church.
SAUGUS—
Levi G. Hawkes.
SOMERVILLE—
E. W. Bailey, City Engr.
Frank H. Morris, 86 Hudson St.
SOUTHBRIDGE—
Arthur C. Moore, 100 Main St.
SOUTH FRAMINGHAM—
Heald, Simpson & Co.
SPRINGFIELD—
Geo. N. Merrill & Co., 292 Main.
Mace Moulton, 233 Main.
Chas. M. Slocum, City Engr.
SUDBURY—
N. Raymond Pratt.
TAUNTON—
Luther Dean.
Geo. A. King, Cy. Engr.
WALTHAM—
Bertram Brewer, Cy. Engr., 3 Mo[illegible]
St.
Alfred M. Wyman.
WATERTOWN—
W. F. Larned, Town Engr.
WESTBORO—
E. C. Appleton.
WESTFIELD—
Thayer & Magill, Parks Blk.
Oren E. Parks, Cy. Engr.
WEST MEDFORD—
H. Bissell.
WEST NEWTON—
S. Child, St. Comrs. Office.
I. T. Farnham, Cy. Engr.
Henry D. Woods, 99 Highland S
WEYMOUTH HEIGHTS—
Henry A. Nash, Jr.
WINCHESTER—
Chas. M. Thompson, Cy. Engr.
WOBURN—
Frank B. French, Cy. Engr.
WORCESTER—
C. A. Allen.
Walter A. Gleason.
Frederick A. McClure, Cy. Eng
A. C. Rice.
G. H. White.

MICHIGAN.

ADRIAN—
Jas. Blair, Cy. Engr.
ALBION—
John Welper, Cy. Engr.
ALPENA—
C. M. Stephens, Cy. Engr.
ANN ARBOR—
Geo. F. Key, Cy. Engr.
BATTLE CREEK—
E. U. Hunt, Cy. Engr.
BAY CITY—
Geo. Turner, Cy. Engr.
BENTON HARBOR—
L. Herringway, Cy. Engr.
BESSEMER—
John W. Eggen.
Benj. Gerhardt.
Geo. Rupp, Cy. Engr.
BIG RAPIDS—
L. F. June.
CADILLAC—
A. J. Teed, Cy. Engr.
CHARLOTTE—
G. W. Richardson, Cy. Engr.
DELRAY—
Merritt M. Willmarth, Cy. En
DETROIT—
W. Hy Ashwell & Co., 25 W
Opera House Block.
C. M. Barber, Demet-Solvay
Baxter & Young, 201 Wayne Co
ings Bank Bldg.
Chas. W. Beseler, 63 Henry S
C. C. Bothfield, 34 Home Bank

'ontinued.
L. Brown, 820 Chamber of
ıerce.
ıs Campau & Son, 3 Cam- Bldg.
I. Courtis, 412 Hammond

. Cram, 26 Hancock Ave., W.
& Hinchman, 1203 Majes- Bldg.
Wilkes & Co., 1112 Union Bldg.
Henry, 52 Woodward Ave.
Hickey, 41 Highland Ave., H. P.
Howard, 171 Griswold St.
:e W. Hubbell, 232 Jefferson

Jerome, 109 Washington Ave.
Barcroft, 407 Ferguson Bldg.
Keating, 149 Harrison Ave.
ynn, 301 Congress St., W.
Maxwell, 582 Champlain St.
t H. McCormick, Cy. Engr.
Raymond.
Ray, 19-20 Peninsular Bank

Sabin, U. S. Asst. Engr.
Sauer, 39 Hodges Bldg.
Thomas & Co., 42 Hodges Bldg.
Wheeler, U. S. Engr. office.
Wilkes & Co., 1112 Union Bldg.
Wilmarth, 2287 Grand River

Wilson & Co. Fort St., W. of

Wisner, 607 Wayne Co. Bank

D—
Joslin, Cy. Engr.
RAPIDS—
s, Cy. Engr.
N—
·, Cy. Engr.
eenberger.
-
Hall, 300 Saginaw, N.
n Mathewson, 109 S 1st St.,

HAVEN—
Page, Cy. Engr.
RAPIDS—
M. Ames, Cy Engr.
CK—
Stockley, Cy Engr
ND—
Price, Cy. Engr
TON—
Edwards, Cy Engr
L—
W. Bullock, Cy. Engr
N—
ton W. Grenell, Cy. Engr.
MOUNTAIN—
n I. James, Cy Engr.

IRONWOOD—
Jas. H. Gowdie, Cy. Engr.
ITHACA—
Wm. Stanton, Cy. Engr.
JACKSON—
Clare Allen, Dwight Bldg.
L. D. Grosvenor, 265 W. Main St.
R. M. Newman, Cy. Engr.
N. M. Sweet, 416 S. Gorham St.
KALAMAZOO—
Geo. S. Pierson.
G. B. Pike, Cy. Engr.
LAKE LINDEN—
John Rodda, Cy. Engr.
Norbert Sarazin.
LANETTE—
J. B. Birtler.
Tom Hadaway, Cy. Engr.
LANSING—
C. E. Bement.
H. A. Collar, Cy Engr.
LAPEER—
C. D. Burritt, Cy. Engr.
LAURIUM—
Duncan Campbell..
Carl E. Nystrom.
D M. Scott.
C. K. Shand.
LUDINGTON—
C. E. Mitchell, Cy. Engr.
MANISTEE—
E. W. Muenscher, Cy. Engr.
MARINE CITY—
Wm. Streit, Cy. Engr.
MARQUETTE—
Geo. Reichel, St. Comr.
Robert R. French.
MARSHALL—
P. A. Courtright, Cy. Engr.
MENOMINEE—
Albert Hass, Cy. Engr.
MT CLEMENS—
J. W. Irwin, Cy. Engr.
MT. PLEASANT—
E. R Coburn.
MUSKEGON—
C. S. Gamble, Cy. Engr.
NILES—
F. A. Bryan, Cy. Engr.
NORWAY—
G. A. Helberg, Cy. Engr.
OWOSSO—
H. E. Riggs, Cy. Engr.
PETOSKEY—
S M. Corson.
O S. Heydon, Cy. Engr.
L. J. Pettengill.
PONTIAC—
Wm. J. Fisher, Cy. Engr.
PORT HURON—
W. W. Philips, Cy. Engr.
SAGINAW—
H. E. Terry, Cy. Engr.
ST. CLAIR—
Mandeville Poole, Cy. Engr.

ST. IGNACE—
Ed. Forrester, Cy. Engr.
ST. JOSEPH—
C. S. Rigby, Cy. Engr.
SAULT STE. MARIE—
Jas. A. Lowrie, Cy. Engr.
R. C. Sweatt, A.
Jas. Ripley, Asst. U. S. Engr.
TRAVERSE CITY—
Irvine Watson, Cy. Engr.
WEST BAY CITY—
J. H. Bloomshield, Cy. Engr.
WYANDOTTE—
Geo. B. Palmer, Cy. Engr.

MINNESOTA.

ALBERT LEA—
F. H. Fisk, Cy. Engr.
AUSTIN—
M. N. Clausen.
BLUE EARTH—
J. A. Dean, Cy .Engr.
BRAINERD—
R. K. Whiteley, Cy. Engr.
CROOKSTON—
Alex Gray.
O. L. Hamery, Cy Engr.
Geo. A. Ralph.
DETROIT—
Mercer & Pearson.
Henry Taylor.
DULUTH—
Davis & Davis.
T. F. McGillivray, City Hall.
R. W. Nichols.
Patton & Frank.
GLENCOE—
Geo. Allen, Cy. Engr.
LAKE CITY—
Geo. Cornelius, Cy. Engr.
LITCHFIELD—
Fred Hankey, Cy. Engr.
LITTLE FALLS—
Andrew Fenn, Cy. Engr.
MANKATO—
M. B. Haynes.
Jas. R. Thompson, Cy. Engr.
MINNEAPOLIS—
F. W. Cappelen, C. E, 702 Oneida Blk.
G. W. Cooley, Court House.
W. F. Dealing, Sidewalk Engr., City Hall.
J. E. Egan, 255 Hennepin Ave.
J. T. Fanning, Kasota Block
Francis Henry, Lumber Exchange.
Olaf Hoff, 702 Oneida Blk.
Carl Illstrup, Sewer Engr., City Hall
A. H. Opsahl, 811 Sykes Blk.
Walter S. Pardee, A., City Hall.
Wm. W. Redfield, 8 City Hall.
W. H. Roberts, Supt W W.
Geo. W. Sublette, Cy Engr.
MONTEVIDEO—
S. L. Moyer
NEW ULM—
Herman Amme.
Geo. Boock.
Julian Bernett, Cy. Engr.
OWATONNA—
Harvey S. Dartt, Cy. Engr.
RED WING—
Wm. Danforth.
R. W. McKinstry.
ROCHESTER—
H. F. Gebeler, Cy. Engr.
ST. CLOUD—
S. S. Chute, Cy. Engr.
ST. PAUL—
J. H. Armstrong, 504 Globe Bldg.
R. B. C. Bement, 504 Endicott Bldg.
Oscar Claussen, Comr. Pub. Wks. & Cy. Engr.
D. L. Curtice, 337 Wabasha St.
J. D. Estabrook, 699 Lincoln Ave.
C. A. Forbes, 11 Court Blk.
Fowble & Fitz, 34 Union Blk.
C. F. Loweth, 20 First Nat'l Bk. Bldg.
N. D. Miller, 551 Westminster St.
C. J. A. Morris, 613 Goodrich Ave.
L. W. Rundlett, 605 Lincoln Ave.
W. A. Somers, 33 Metropolitan Opera House.
H. E. Stevens, 530 Grand Ave.
H. A. Swenson, 538 Endicott Bldg.
Geo. L. Wilson, Asst. Comr. Pub. Wks.
F. D. Woodbury, 2288 Doswell Ave.
SAUK CENTER—
G. C. Ingram, Cy. Engr.
STILLWATER—
H. H. Harrison.
Myron Shepard, Cy. Engr.
TWO HARBORS—
A. A. Reed, Cy. Engr.
WASECA—
O. L. Smith, Cy. Engr.
WINONA—
Geo. Z. Heuston.
J. N. Maybury & Co.
W. L. Miller, Cy. Engr.
WORTHINGTON—
M. S. Smith, Cy. Engr.

MISSISSIPPI.

BAY ST. LOUIS—
Chas. Sanger.
BILOXI—
W. R. Harkness.
Thompson & Eistetter.
BROOKHAVEN—
Geo. C. Hoskins, Cy. Engr.
COLUMBUS—
H. Wilmot, Cy. Engr.
JACKSON—
Walter G. Kirkpatrick, Cy Engr.
MERIDIAN—
Krouse & Hutchings.
W. G. Myers, Cy. Engr.

IEZ—
. Babbitt, Cy. Engr.
Dalgarn, 112 N. Pearl St.
Walton.
GIBSON—
Allair.
Butler, Cy. Engr.
:VILLE—
W. Hall.
R VALLEY—
Hessing, Cy. Engr.
N—
Wooden.
NEWTON—
T. Farnham, Cy. Engr.
CITY—
Underwood, Cy. Engr.

MISSOURI.

:A—
. Van Frank, Cy. Engr.
R—
Johnson, Cy. Engr.
)RNIA—
:e & Ross.
:ON—
e Bridge & Const. Co.
Dildine, Cy. Engr.
N—
Dittmer, Cy. Engr.
LLTON—
Steele, Cy. Engr.
AGE—
King, Cy. Engr.
V. Payne & Son
HERSVILLE—
g P. Reynolds, Cy. Engr.
ICOTHE—
addus, Cy. Engr.
Garver
Glore.
Glore.
)N—
Allen, Cy. Engr.
Highnote
IBIA—
E. Flood, Cy. Engr.
N—
. Hudgins, Cy. Engr.
H. King
TIN—
lin & Rose
BAL—
Moltz, Cy. Engr.
N—
Schidenberger, [illegible]
ENDENCE—
Pendleton, Cy. Engr.
RSON CITY—
Dewey, Cy. Engr.
C. Harding
—
Hunter, [illegible]
IcKee, Cy. Engr. [illegible]
Michaelis, [illegible]

KANSAS CITY—
S. P. Anderson, 2211 Grove St.
O. N. Axtell, 2200 E. 18th St.
E. J. Beard, 3838 McGee St.
G. J. Bell, 1819 Summit St.
S. W. Benedict, 659 Park St.
Daniel Bontecon, 404 W. 9th St.
G. M. Brockman, 1513 Penn St.
E. C. Burgess, 300 Indiana St.
Burns & McDowell, 409 Postal Tel. Bldg.
J. L. Case, 900 W. 13th St.
A. M. Church, 202 Mass. Bldg.
E. M. Collins, Brunswick Hotel.
John Donnelly, 401 Whittier Place.
B. W. Dunkard, 202 Mass. Bldg.
W. H. Dunn, 4023 Oak St.
H. H. Fillery, 2816 Campbell St.
Freygang & Tracon, 600 Gibraltar Bldg.
A. C. Fulkerson, 1609 Balto. Ave.
C. W. Gambol, 604 E. 38th St.
E. T. Gunter, 510 Brooklyn St.
W. L. Harmon, 23 W. 31st St.
E. A. Harper, 429 W. 11th St.
J. C. Herring, 2622 Spruce St.
W. E. Herring, 406 Olive St.
J. W. Heylmun, 2301 E. 6th St.
R. T. Heylmun, 2301 E. 6th St.
Hogg & Rose, A.
J. W. Hoover, 514 N. Y. Life Bldg.
Wynkoop Kiersted, Water Works Bldg.
Daniel O'Flaherty & Son, 708 Wall St.
Walter C. Root, A.
Henry Van Brunt, A., 1214 A Main St.
Rob't W. Waddell, Cy. Engr., City Hall
Waddell & Hedrick, 602 Gibraltar Bldg.
Henry A. Wise
LAMAR
Wm. Hague, Cy. Engr.
LEXINGTON
Matt. Owens, Cy. Engr.
Geo. Wade
Joseph A. Wilson
MACON
[illegible] Du Bois, Cy. Engr.
M[illegible]
[illegible] Cy. Engr.
[illegible]
[illegible] Cy. Engr.
M[illegible]
[illegible] Engr.
[illegible]
[illegible] Cy. Engr.
MEMPHIS
[illegible] Engr.
[illegible]

MONETT—
Morris Clinton, Cy. Engr.
NEOSHO—
J. M. Sherwood, Cy. Engr.
NEVADA—
Jas. M. Clack, Cy. Engr.
F. L. Lacoff.
OREGON—
C. E. Young, Cy. Engr.
PALMYRA—
H. C. Schutz, Cy. Engr.
PIERCE CITY—
Jno. Short, Cy. Engr.
POPLAR BLUFF—
Ernest Bacon, Cy. Engr.
RICHMOND—
S. L. Bay, Cy. Engr.
ROLLA—
John A. Garcia, Cy. Engr.
H. H. Hohenschild.
ST. CHARLES—
Frank J. Bull.
Carr Edwards, Cy. Engr.
ST. JOSEPH—
J. R. Rackliffe, Cy. Engr.
ST. LOUIS—
Abbot-Gamble Contracting Co., (The) 620 Chestnut St.
Holland W. Baker, 706 Lincoln Trust Bldg.
Oscar W. Bleeck & Son, 1007 Chestnut St.
Brennecke & Fay, 122 N. 7th St.
George Bruyn, 22 S. 4th St.
Wm. H. Bryan, 706 Lincoln Trust Bldg.
Bryan & Humphrey, 706-7-8 Lincoln Trust Bldg.
Samuel W. Burchard, 6726 Marmaduke Ave.
Robt. Carrick, 806½ Chestnut St.
Colby & Baker, 706 Lincoln Trust Bldg.
Columbia Electric Engineering Co., 915 Chemical Bldg.
James T. Dodds, 813 Chestnut.
Edw. Flad, Water Commissioner.
Owen Ford, Security Bldg.

St. Louis—Continued.
W. L. Garrells, 720 N. 4th St.
Jno. T. Garrett, 715 Locust St.
Geisel Construction Co., 715 L St.
E. A. Hermann, Sewer Com'r.
John F. Hinckley, 800 Fullerton
Minard L. Holman, 105 N. 7th.
Henry H. Humphreys, 313 N.
Elmer J. Irey, 4030 R Castleman
Chas. W. E. Jennings, 706½ Pi
Berkeley E. Johnson, 16 N. 8th.
Clinton Kimball, 720 N. 4th.
John A. Laird, Suite 903 Full Bldg.
Chas. H. Ledlie, 220 N. 4th St.
McGahan & Flaherty, 9-11 Ave.
R. E. McMath, Surveying Co., Lincoln Trust Bldg.
A. L. McRae, 526 Lincoln Trust
C. V. Mersereau, 3838 Shenan Ave.
A. N. Milner, 422 Fullerton Bld
Robt. Moore, 119 Laclede Bldg.
Geo. J. Percival, 418-19 Holland
Richard H. Phillips, 535-6 Li Trust Bldg.
Hiram Phillips, Pres. Bd. Pub.
Pitzman's Co. of Surveyors & E 615 Chestnut.
J. B. Quigley, Wainwright Bld
S. B. Russell, Prin. Asst. Water Dept.
Alfred Siebert, 49.4 Columbia A
Isaac A. Smith, 122 N. 7th.
Richard R. Southard, 6628 S B way.
Eugene Spangenberg, 314 N. 3d.
Chas. Stael, 915-916 Chemical B
Clinton F. Stephens, 319 N. 4th.
Hubert P. Taussig, 105 N. 7th.
Jno. S. Thurman, 416 Lincoln Bldg.
James A. Tiernan, 1719 Pend Ave.
R. L. Van Sant, 609 Commercial
Chas. Varrellman, Street Comr.

More Cement Companies

advertise in Municipal Engineering Magazine

than in any other American publication. It reaches more of the people wh buy or influence the buying of cemen than any other American publication

-Continued.
A. Wagner, 600 Am. Central

Vall, Sewer Dept., City Hall.
ells, 407 N. 12th St.
'ise, Asst. Sewer Comr., City

H. Zeller, 122 N. 7th.
JRY—
, Cy. Engr.
A—
Zoll, Cy. Engr.
FIELD—
Vhite, Cy. Engr.
'hillips.
Bisbee.
—
lark, Jr., Cy. Engr.
N—
tyan, Cy. Engr.
LAINS—
'abb, Cy. Engr.

MONTANA.

DA—
IcDonald, Cy. Engr.
IS—
Iorris.
N—
'horpe, City Hall.

ickenbach, Cy. Engr.
Blackford.
'oll.
& McDonald.
Paine.
Strasburger.
ODGE—
B. Davis.
—
Bond.
ELENA—
Robertson.
W—
Mahon.
FALLS—
rench.
Iunroe.
Swearingen, Cy. Engr.
Whitten, Phelps Blk.
A—
Cumming.
A—
Farmer.
W. Helmick, Cy. Engr.
Hovey.
eerl.
EL—
Jaqueth, Cy. Engr.
STON—
Crooks.
LA—
aburg & Catlin
Gibson.
ghes, Cy. Engr.

PHILIPSBURG—
Geo. W. Wilson.

NEBRASKA.

ASHLAND—
A. C. Urch, Cy. Engr.
AUBURN—
J. M. Hacker.
AURORA—
H. C. Wood, Cy. Engr.
BEATRICE—
Willis Ball, Cy. Engr.
Geo. A. Berlinghof.
R. W. Grant.
BLAIR—
Thos. F. Kelley, Cy. Engr.
CHADRON—
Samuel Dubel.
Ira Longcoe.
COLUMBUS—
Fred Gotshalk.
R. L. Rossiter, Cy. Engr.
CRETE—
Prof. Brown, Cy. Engr.
DAVID CITY—
E. P. Harrington, Cy. Engr.
FAIRBURY—
A. Courtney.
FALLS CITY—
M. N. Bair, Cy. Engr.
FREMONT—
J. W. Andrews, Cy. Engr.
GENEVA—
W. E. Harrison, Cy. Engr.
GRAND ISLAND—
A. C. Koenig, Cy. Engr.
HASTINGS—
C. A. Heartwell, Cy. Engr.
C. D. Richey.
J. R. Sims.
HOLDREDGE—
Hans. Karr, Cy. Engr.
KEARNEY—
E. N. Porterfield, Cy. Engr.
LINCOLN—
Adna Dobson, Cy. Engr.
NEBRASKA CITY—
A. M. Munn, Cy. Engr.
NORFOLK—
W. H. Loren, Cy. Engr.
J. C. Stitt.
NORTH PLATTE—
L. B. Isenhart.
C. P. Ross, Cy. Engr.
OMAHA—
W. G. Higgins, 318 S. 15th.
J. E. House, C. E., 415, 1st Natl. Bank.
G. T. Prince, 27 Neb. Natl. Bk. Bldg.
Andrew Rosewater, Cy. Engr.
Thos. Shaw, 526 Paxton Blk.
PLATTSMOUTH—
E. E. Hilton, Cy. Engr.
ST. PAUL—
Robt. Harvey, Cy. Engr.

SOUTH OMAHA—
Herman Beal, Cy. Engr., City Hall.
A. L. Davis, Glasgow Blk.
J. Klewitt, Jr., 4 Murphy Blk.
W. S. King.
O. M. Zander, Pioneer Blk.
SUPERIOR—
W. H. Green, Cy. Engr.
YORK—
A. B. Codding, Cy. Engr.

NEVADA.

CARSON CITY—
W. W. Coleman.
VIRGINIA CITY—
W. T. Moran.

NEW HAMPSHIRE.

BERLIN—
Edwin S. Bryant, Cy. Engr.
C. B. Gifford.
A. D. Lawrence.
CHARLESTON—
Sam'l Webber.
CONCORD—
W. B. Howe, Cy. Engr.
DOVER—
Asa M .Mattice .
W. C. Ogden, 6 Cushing St.
A. T. Ramsdell.
J. Ed Richardson.
KEENE—
Fred W. Towne.
LACONIA—
F. G. Berry.
E. R. Davis, Cy. Engr.
Wm. Nelson.
MANCHESTER—
Bartlett & Gray.
Dudley & Doherty.
Samuel J. Lord, Cy. Engr.
NASHUA—
A. W. Dean, Cy. Engr.
Chas. E. Emerson, 5 Fletcher.
Geo. B. Pearson, 262 Main.
A. H. Saunders, 70 King.
NEW CASTLE—
J. W. Walker, U. S. Govt. Engr.

NEW JERSEY.

ATLANTIC CITY—
Ashmead & Hackey, 42 R. E. & L. Bldg.
Henry H. Cross, 22 Law Bldg.
Jno. Hackney, City Engr.
H. G. Harris & Co., 1304 Atlantic Ave.
S. Lutherberg, 212 Rosemont Ave.
Elias Wright, 24 N. Penn Ave.
ATLANTIC HIGHLANDS—
T. J. Emery
A. C. Hurley, Cy. Engr.
BEVERLY—
Charles Stokes, Cy. Engr.
BLOOMFIELD—
A. H. Olmsted.
BRIDGETON—
Walter M. Sharp, Cy. Engr.
BOONTON—
Chas. F. Hopkins, Cy. Engr.
CAMDEN—
Louis F. Bodine, 305 Market St.
Levi C. Farnham, City Engr.
Henry S. Haines, 313 Temple Bldg.
Henry J. Sherman, 313 Temple
Earl Thompson, 301 Market St.
Jacob H. Yocum, 302 State St.
DOVER—
Smith & Jenkins, Cy. Engrs.
ELIZABETH—
Wm. H. Luster, Jr., Cy. Engr.
ENGLEWOOD—
Wm. V. Van Blarcom, Cy. Engr.
FREEHOLD—
N. J. Conover.
GARFIELD—
C. W. Holliday, Cy. Engr.
GLOUCESTER CITY—
A. A. Powell, Cy. Engr.
HACKENSACK—
Lemuel Lozier, Cy. Engr.
P E. Van Buskirk.
Alfred W. Williams.
JERSEY CITY—
Robert C. Bacot, 1 Montgomery St.
William Baxter, 17 Emory St.
Gustav Blau, Jr., 709 Grand St.
Charles B. Brush & Co., 1 Newark St.
Robert H. Daly, 76 Montgomery St
Earle & Harrison, 1 Montgomery St.
Ferris Garwood, 98 Hudson St.
Emil Gull, 19 Charles St.
E. W. Harrison, 1 Montgomery St.
William H. Hooker, 138 Montgomery St
Charles Hopper, 259 Washington St.
Edward W. Insley, 344 Central Ave.
John C. Payne, 1 Montgomery St.
P. Sanford Ross, 277 Washington St.
William L. Ross, 277 Washington St.
Van Keuren & Co., Gregory & Van Vorst Sts.
LAMBERTVILLE—
Frank M. Wilson, Cy. Engr.
LONG BRANCH—
J. Wesley Seaman, Cy. Engr.
MONTCLAIR—
Frank W. Crane, Cy. Engr.
MORRISTOWN—
Arthur S. Pierson, Cy. Engr.
NEWARK—
Frank E. Albinger, 164 Market St.
Charles P. Baldwin.
C. Melville Borrie, 757 Broad St.
Thos. Crenny.
J. & W. C. Ely.
A. Faber du Faur, 22 Nichols St.
Adolph Faber du Faur, jr., 127 Elm St.
W. P. Field, 763 Broad St.

-Continued.
'. Field, Prudential Bldg.
sco & Barkhorn, 748 Broad St.
H. Gardner, 784 Broad St.
d R. Halsey, 164 Market St.
e B. Hedden, 22 Clinton St.
3. Hooper, 238 Washington St.
n R. Kinsey, 10 South St.
ch Bros., 770 Broad St.
r B. Martin, 101 S. 11th St.
McMurray, 22 Clinton St.
Mitchell, 18 9th Ave.
Iueller, 810 Broad St.
Owen, 800 Broad St.
. Palm, 43 Magnolia St.
'd S. Rankin, Cy. Engr., 873
d St.
. C. Sacconi, 800 Broad St.
Scarlett, 226 Market St.
Sherrerd, City Hall.
ion Van Duyne & Son, 800
d St.
e Vanderpool, 757 Broad St.
Witzel, 839 Broad St.
RUNSWICK—
Atkinson, Cy. Engr.
E—
C. Crane, 252 Main St.
e B. Hedden, 20 Walnut St.
W. Hodgkinson, 18 Canfield St.
& Taylor, 242 Main St.
e P. Olcott, 252 Main St.
V. Reimer, 249 Main St.
RA—
S. Haines, Cy. Engr.
C—
K. Irving.
& Watson.
SON—
m W. Christie, Paterson Sav-
Inst. Bldg.
Ferguson, 152 Market St.
l J. Harder, Cy. Engr.
Smith, Passaic Water Co
AMBOY—
Homman, Cy. Engr.
PSBURG—
Smith, Cy. Engr.
AY—
H. A. Adams, Cy. Engr
ANK—
m S. Sneden, Cy. Engr.
WAY—
Jenkins, Cy. Engr.
RFORD—
Watson, Cy. Engr.
—
Acton, Cy. Engr
AMBOY—
Thomas, Cy Engr.
ORANGE—
Taylor, Cy. Engr
UNNA—
G. Force, Jr.
T—
eller, Cy. Engr

TRENTON—
R. Albert, 22 Walnut St.
J. P. Anderson, 439 Bellevue Ave.
H. W. Bradley, 201 Hudson St.
H. Barton, 41 Yard St.
R. B. Budd, 240 Hamilton Ave.
J. S. Chambers, jr., 193 Brunswick Ave.
C. B. Dahlgren, 510 W. State Ave.
C. C. Haven, City Hall.
F. J. Eppele, 530 Perry St.
G. Johnston, 418 Market St.
C. D. McClary, Riverview Cem.
N. R. Montgomery, 185 Greenwood Ave.
W. T. Morgan, 29 Charles St.
J. C. Nevins, 211 Clay St.
A. J. Swan, 21 N. Olden Ave.
E. G. Spilsbury, 216 W. State St.
H. V. Thompson, 917 Carteret Ave.
J. L. Watson, 137 E. State St.
VINELAND—
E. C. Potter, New York City.
WESTFIELD—
H. C. Van Emburgh, Cy Engr.
WEST HOBOKEN—
Robert Gaw, Cy. Engr.
WOODBURY—
Wm. M. Carter, Cy. Engr.

NEW MEXICO.

ALBUQUERQUE—
E. B. Cristy.
Hill & La Driere.
H. D. Johnson.
Pitt Ross, Cy. Engr.
CARLSBAD—
B. A. Nymeger, Cy. Engr
ROSWELL—
C. R Carr.
Mark Howell.
M. Kinney.
W. M Reed, Cy. Engr.
SANTA FE—
J L. Zimmerman, Cy. Engr

NEW YORK.

ALBANY
Horace Andrews.
Edward A Bond, State Engr.
John O'Hara, Cy Engr.
Wm Pierson Judson, State Hall.
Herman H Ross & Sons, 121 State.
ALTAMONT
W E. LaFountain.
AMSTERDAM
Frank E. Crane, Cy. Engr.
AUBURN
D F Austin Cy Engr.
BATH
Robt M Lyon, Cy. Engr.
BINGHAMTON
H E. Monroe, Cy. Engr.
Chenango Engineering Co.

BUFFALO—
Harry B. Alonson.
F. V. E. Bardol, Cy. Engr.
H. T. Buttolph, 13 City Hall.
Chas. H. Davis, 98 Cedar St.
George C. Diehl, 836 Ellicott Sq.
John F. Ellsworth, Franklin & Eagle Sts.
S. J. Fields, Ch. Engr. Exposition.
E. B. Guthrie, 436 Ellicott Sq.
L. H. Knapp, 280 Linwood Ave.
Geo. A. Ricker, 702 Ellicott Sq.
F. G. & G. R. Silkes, 171 Ellicott Sq.
O. F. Wilford, 79 Woodlawn Ave.
J. F. Witmer, 705 Ellicott Sq.

CANANDAIGUA—
Harry Welch, Cy. Engr.

CANISTEO—
J. H. Consalus, Cy. Engr.
E. W. Pearce.

CANTON—
Leslie R. Smith, Cy. Engr.

CARTHAGE—
J. P. Brownell, Cy. Engr.

COHOES—
C. H. Van Auken, Cy. Engr.

COLD SPRINGS—
Wm. Burns.

CORNING—
Robt. O. Hoyt, Cy. Engr.

CORTLAND—
Henry C. Allen, Cy. Engr.
W. B. Landreth.

DUNKIRK—
James P. Morrissey, Cy. Engr.

EAST AURORA—
Geo. Hanlisten, Cy. Engr.
Chas. P. Fink.
Geo. Olmstead.

EAST HAMPTON—
Wm. H. Barnes.

ELMIRA—
Considine & Waltz.
John C. Ingraham.
F. E. Leach, Cy. Engr.
Ransom T. Lewis, 119 Caldwell Ave.
J. E. Rawlins.

FAR ROCKAWAY—
A. J. Bogart.
Morrell Smith.

FISHKILL-ON-THE-HUDSON—
W. R. Scofield, Cy. Engr.

FULTON—
O. C. Breed, Cy. Engr.

GENEVA—
Wm. Church, Cy. Engr.

GLENS FALLS—
Jos. Michaelson.
Geo. P. Slade, Cy. Engr.

GLOVERSVILLE—
E. Brown Baker.
A. A. Beattie.
F. L. Comstock.
Chas. Fiske, Cy. Engr.

GOSHEN—
V. K. Mills.

HAMILTON—
E. L. Kingsbury, Cy.

HAVERSTRAW—
Chas. M. Hilton, Cy.

HORNELLSVILLE—
F. W. Dalrymple, Cy.

HORSEHEADS—
M. Rickey, Cy. Engr.

HUDSON—
H. K. Bishop, Cy. E
John Franklin.

HUNTINGTON—
C. P. Darling.

ITHACA—
J. F. Bradley, Cy. Eng
G. S. Williams.
A. B. Wood.

JAMESTOWN—
Geo. W. Jones, Cy. E

JOHNSTOWN—
James W. Miller, Cy.

KEESEVILLE—
A. Bigelow.

KINGSTON—
Geo. N. Bell, Cy. En
P. E. Clarke.
E. B. Codwise.
Wilgott Klingberg.
James E. Phinney.

LAKE PLACID—
Geo. T. Chellis, Cy. E

LANCASTER—
W. M. Small, Cy. Eng

LANSINGBURGH—
C. E. Hicks, 567 2d A

LEROY—
Frank Rider, Cy. Eng

LESTERSHIRE—
S. M. Baird, Cy. Eng

LITTLE FALLS—
S. E. Babcock.
E. T. E. Lansing.
John McComb, Cy. E

LOCKPORT—
Chas. H. Cornes, City
Julius Frehsee, Centr

MALONE—
H. M. Conant.

MASSENA—
E. B. Bumsted.
Joseph H. Clark, Cy. I

MATTEAWAN—
C. B. Van Slyck.

MIDDLETOWN—
Van Allen Harris.
Chas. H. Smith, Cy.

NEWBURGH—
Charles Caldwell, Cy.
Frank E. Esterbrook.
Fred M. Sneed, A, 5
J. D. Van Buren.

NEW ROCHELLE—
Clarence S. Haskell, (

, Municipal Bldg.
, Municipal Bldg.
, 189 Montague St.
, Municipal Bldg.
, Municipal Bldg.
, 189 Montague St.
, 1367 Broadway.
, 84 Broadway.
, Municipal Bldg.
, 4 Court Square.
, 4 Court Square.
sartidge, 189 Montague St.
n, 200 Bushwick Ave.
rton, Municipal Bldg.
h, Municipal Bldg.
84 Broadway.
ngham, 189 Montague St.
, 350 Fulton St.
, 361 Fulton St.
n, Municipal Bldg.
294 Montague St.
r, Municipal Bldg.
ona, Municipal Bldg.
ea, Jr., 84 Broadway.
age, 498 Leonard St.
, 168 Montague St.
ault, Borough Hall.
y, 215 Montague St.
, Municipal Bldg.
ran, Cropsey Ave. & Bay

, 916 DeKalb Ave.
ch, 189 Montague St.
Municipal Bldg.
lman, 4 Court Square.
mond, Municipal Bldg.
ond, Municipal Bldg.
ry, 84 Broadway.
, Municipal Bldg.
, 4 Court Square.
Johnson, 84 Broadway.
84 Broadway.
gsley, 84 Broadway.
ka, 4 Court Square.
, 84 Broadway.
ith, Municipal Bldg.
ey, 1091 Atlantic Ave.
n, Municipal Bldg.
, 4 Court St.
ey, 26 Court St.
role, 189 Montague St.
ton, 189 Montague St.
ken, 189 Montague St.
s., Ft. Clinton St.
ay, 26 Court St.
s, 84 Broadway.
Debevoise, 1153 Myrtle

ne, Municipal Bldg.
Municipal Bldg.
k, Municipal Bldg.
, 84 Broadway.
nd, 4 Court Square.

Richard Schermerhorn, 340 Fulton St.
Joseph Strachan, Municipal Bldg.
J. A. Tilley, 84 Broadway.
G. W. Tillson, Municipal Bldg.
A. S. Tuttle, Municipal Bldg.
C. S. Voorhees, 16 Court St.
B. M. Wagner, Municipal Bldg.
C. D. Ward, Municipal Bldg.
R. N. Wheeler, Municipal Bldg.
E. S. White, Municipal Bldg.
Lazarus White, Municipal Bldg.
J. D. Wilkens, 84 Broadway.
C. G. Williams, 84 Broadway.
R. L. Williams, 204 Montague St.
G. E. Winslow, Municipal Bldg.

NEW YORK CITY, BOROUGHS OF MANHATTAN AND BRONX—

W. I. Aims, 35 Broadway.
T. H. Alison, 39 Cortlandt St.
Anderson & Murphy, 14 John St.
C. W. Atkins, 18 Broadway.
Asher Atkinson, 203 Broadway.
W A. Aycrigg, 102 Chambers St.
E. C. Bacon, 26 Cortlandt St.
W. S. Bacot, 1 Broadway.
W. J. Baldwin, 107 W. 17th St.
Ball & Corbett, 39 Cortlandt St.
C. J. Balthasar, 396 Broome St.
O. W. Barnes, 55 Broadway.
H. P. Barr, 141 Broadway.
Barry & Co., 56 Liberty St.
L. Bartholomew, 171 Broadway.
J. Bates, 126 Liberty St.
E. L. Bauer, 68 Bible House.
Wilhelm Bauer, 82 Nassau St.
W. L. Beard, 51 W. 10th St.
W. B. Beckley, 17 Park Row.
W. D. Benedict, 31 Nassau St.
W. R. Bergholz, 15 Cortlandt St.
Gerald Barry, 200 Broadway.
W. H. Birkmire, 396 Broadway.
Joseph Bijur, 2 Broad St.
J. L. Blackwell, Inc., 20 Broad St.
Oscar Bloch, 1123 Broadway.
Harrison Blunt, 874 Broadway.
John Bogart, 40 Wall St.
A. P. Boller, 1 Nassau St.
R. P. Bolton, 35 Nassau St.
A. L. Bowman, 71 Broadway.
P. T. Brady, 81 Centre St.
Paul Brandner, 49 Liberty St.
H. W. Brinckerhoff, 45 Broadway.
W. H. Briethaupt, 66 Broadway.
J. E. Brooke,, 45 Broadway.
Thos. E. Brown, Jr., 71 Broadway.
C. C. Buckner, 11 Wall St.
Andrew Bryson, 29 Broadway.
C. G. Buchanan, 143 Liberty St.
C. W. Buchholz, 21 Cortlandt St.
Building & Sanitary Inspection Co., 874 Broadway.
C. H. Bull, 19 Park Row.
G. B. Burbank, 15 Wall St.
Burhorn & Granger, 95 Liberty St.

New York City—Manhattan and Bronx—Continued.

J. W. Burke, 45 Broadway.
W. E. Burke, 258 Broadway.
Burnett & Tainter, 111 5th Ave.
J. T. Butt, 115 Nassau St.
Cady, Berg & See, 31 E. 17th St.
F. E. Candor, 11 Pine St.
Carrere & Hastings, A.
A. A. Cary, 96 Liberty St.
Chambers & Hone, 60 New St.
J. Park Channing, 32 Park Pl.
Chimney Construction Co., 99 Nassau St.
Wm. L. Church, 874 Broadway.
J. J. Clare, 735 Summit St.
Clark & MacMullen, 42 E. 23d. St.
C. L. Clarke, 31 Nassau St.
T. C. Clarke, 1 Nassau St.
W. G. Clark, 1123 Broadway.
T. C. Clarke, 127 Duane St.
A. W. Colwell, 39 Cortlandt St.
F. A. Cokefair, 20 Broad St.
J. J. Cone, 71 Broadway.
J. V. Connell, Produce Exchange, A.20.
Constable Bros., 22 E. 16th St.
F. S. Cook, 280 Broadway.
Theodore Cooper, 35 Broadway.
Cooper & Wegand, 1133 Broadway.
F. G. Corning, 15 Broad St.
E. L. Corthell, 1 Nassau St.
Robert Crawford, 332 E. 43d St.
W. W. Crehore, 39 Cortlandt.
J. J. R. Croes, 68 Broad St.
Foster Crowell, 18 Broadway.
W. C. Culver, 136 Liberty St.
J. Y. Culyer, 68 Park Row.
B. A. Dare, 120 Broadway.
J. H. Darlington, 31 Pine St.
C. H. Davis, 7 Cedar St.
Clarence Delafield, 59 Maiden Lane.
Harold De Raaslaff, 45 Broadway.
De Raaslaff & McNulty, 181 William St.
D. H. Dixon, 27 William St.
W. J. M. Dobson, 7 Dey St.
A. L. G. Doty, 21 State St.
Drewson Co., 5 Beekman St.
James Dubois & Co., 11 Broadway.
J. G. Dudley, 29 Broadway.
P. H. Dudley, 80 Pine St.
Louis Duncan, 71 Broadway.
F. A. Dunham, 220 Broadway.
R. F. Dunham, 220 Broadway.
Eastwick Engineering Co., Ltd., 21 Park Row.
Emmens & Strong, 1 Broadway.
Engineering Contract Co., 71 Broadway.
M. E. Evans, 20 Nassau St.
Faber du Faur & Donnelly, 132 Nassau St.
F. J. Falding, 45 Broadway.
G. P. Farley, 100 Broadway.
Field & Everett, 43 Cedar St.
G. S. Field, 1 Broadway.

New York City—Manhattan and Bronx—Continued.

W. P. [illegible]
Floy & [illegible]
Ford, Bacon [illegible]
Campbell [illegible]
Foster & [illegible]
W. G. Foster, [illegible]
Geo. L. Fowler, [illegible]
A. E. Fope, [illegible]
Francis Bros. [illegible] 18th St.
W. P. Freeman, [illegible]
W. K. Freeman, [illegible]
Freeman & [illegible]
W. H. Fritchman, [illegible]
C. O. H. Fritsche, [illegible]
W. J. Fryer, [illegible]
Alphonse Fteley, [illegible]
J. H. Fuertes, [illegible]
G. W. Fuller, [illegible]
O. C. Gayley, [illegible]
W. P. Gerhard, [illegible]
R. W. Gibson, [illegible]
G. E. Gifford, [illegible]
A. C. Gildersleeve, [illegible]
R. S. Gillespie, [illegible]
F. C. Glaser, [illegible]
C. J. Goldmark, [illegible]
J. M. Goodill, 100 [illegible]
F. H. Gottlieb, 136 [illegible]
E. L. Gould, 1 Br[illegible]
Gray-Smith Engine[illegible] Ave.
E. A. Greene, [illegible]
Geo. S. Greene, [illegible]
J. S. Griggs, Jr., [illegible]
Greene & Greene, [illegible]
B. B. Guion, [illegible]
W. C. Gunnell, 125 [illegible]
Wm. S. Hallaway, [illegible]
C. A. Hague, [illegible]
S. S. Haight, [illegible]
Hallsted & McNaug[illegible]
W. J. Hammer, [illegible]
John Hankin, [illegible]
Hippolyte Hardy, [illegible]
T. B. Haring, [illegible]
Robt. L. Harris.
Haskins & Coffin, [illegible]
C. H. Haswell, 1808 [illegible]
G. S. Hayes, 111 5t[illegible]
Allen Hazen, 223 Br[illegible]
W. L. Hedenberg, [illegible]
Jno. Heerdegan, 44 [illegible]
G. C. Henning, [illegible]
Rudolph Hering, [illegible]
A. B. Herrick, [illegible]
J. M. Hicks, 19 Pa[illegible]
W. H. Hildebrand, [illegible]
R. W. Hildreth & [illegible]
Geo. Hill, 150 5th [illegible]
G. C. Hillman, [illegible]
Hill, Quick & Allen[illegible]
F. E. Hinckley, [illegible]
G. D. Hiscox, [illegible]

...Broadway.
...[illegible] Broadway.
...Glasgow, 21 Nassau St.
...& Co., 71 Broadway.
...son, 71 Broadway.
...[illegible] Broadway.
...Cortlandt St.
..., 120 Liberty St.
...Co., 1[illegible]5 Broadway.
...ryer, 26 Cortlandt St.
...es, 22 Nassau St.
...[illegible] Nassau St.
..., 41 Liberty St.
...1 Broadway.
...1 Wall St.
..., A., 150 5th Ave.
...Jr., 39 Cortlandt.
...) Broadway.
...William St.
..., 26 Cortlandt St.
...de, 20 Broad St.
...vles, 26 Cortlandt St.
..., 686 Kingsbridge Rd.
...r, 71 Broadway.
...aster, 99 Nassau St.
...72 Trinity Place.
...35 W. 51st. St.
...220 Broadway.
...Jr., 15 Cortlandt St.
...99 John St.
...ion, 11 Broadway.
...[illegible] Broadway.
...rigues, 552 W. 23d St.
...t, 129 W. 42d St.
...thal, 47 Cedar St.
...Broadway.
...ne Co., 52 Broadway.
...n, 39 Cortlandt.
...38 Park Row.
...38 Park Row.
...2 Broadway.
...42 Cortlandt St.
...Dermott, 19 Whitehall

...ott, 29 Broadway.
...ll, 26 Cortlrndt.
...nzie, 111 Broadway.
...106 E. 23d St.
...in, 237 Broadway.
...ald, 1 Broadway.
...6 Broadway.
...801 Bothgate Ave.
...ntosh, 150 Nassau.
..., 150 Nassau St.
...) Broadway.
...Wall St.
...89 Fifth Ave.
...1, 410 W. 115th St.
...17 Park Row.
...1 Broadway.

C. B. Meyers, 3 Union Squa...
Frank Miller, 39 Cortlandt...
Hew Miller, 100 Broadway.
Milliken Bros., 11 Broadway
Moffat & Hewitt, 10 E. 23d
John Monks & Son, 120 Wa...
C. K. Moore, 11 Broadwa...
E. C. Moore, 130 Pearl St.
G. S. Morison, 35 Wall St.
Otto A. Moses, 49 Exchange...
William Mueser, 17 Park ...
J. N. Murphy, 116 Nassau
C. H. Myers, 45 Broadway.
August Namur, 35 Broadw...
S. M. Neff, 120 Liberty St.
New England Engineerin...
Broadway.
H. B. Newhall, Jr., 26 Cor...
E. P. North, 150 Nassau ...
Olcott, Fearn & Peele, 18 B...
L. F. Olney, 99 Nassau St.
Andrew Onderdonk, 1 Broa...
Opdyce & Thompson, 17 Pa...
J. F. O'Rourke, 17 Park R...
Osborn Co., 45 Broadway.
Osterberg & Sutton, 11 Bro...
J. F. Padelford, 246 W. 106t...
Charles Paine & Son, 32 Pa...
G. H. Paine, 32 Park Pla...
B. H. Parsons, 97 Cedar S...
Harry de B. Parsons, 22 Wil...
W. B. Parsons, 22 William
Pattison Bros., 141 Broadwa...
C. E. Pearce, 97 Cedar St.
J. J. Pearson, 40 Wall St.
Peters & Roberts, 11 Broad...
Phillips & Worthington, 1...
way.
E. H. Phipps, 220 Broadway
Pierce Well Engineering &
Co., 136 Liberty St.
Ferdinand Pontrichet, 16 W...
Geo. B. Post, A., 33 E. 17th
R. B. Post, 51 Chamber St.
Post & McCord, 289 4th Ave.
Alexander Potter, 150 Nassa...
J. J. Powers, 44 Broadway.
John Pownall, 150 Nassau S...
Bruce Price, A.
A. B. Proctor, Jr., 111 5th A...
Purdy & Henderson, 78 5th
G. W. Randall, 1123 Broadwa...
J. C. Randolph, 15 Broad St.
P. E. Raque, 289 4th Ave.
W. B. Reed, Jr., 162 W. 121st
W. B. Reed, 621 Broadway.
Thorburn Reid, 120 Liberty ...
W. P. Reid, 220 Broadway.
Frederick Reinert, 280 Broa...

New York City—Manhattan and Bronx—Continued.

E. P. Roberts, 22 William St.
Nathaniel Roberts, 160 5th Ave.
J. M. Robinson, 15 Broad St.
C. W. Roepper, 45 Broadway.
Barnard Rolf, 39 Cortlandt St.
A. J. Rossi, 35 Broadway.
Ferdinand Ruttman, 45 Broadway.
E. S. Safford, 253 Broadway.
P. A. Sanguinette, 39 Cortlandt St.
Livingston Satterlee, 40 Broadway.
F. H. Sawyer, 160 Broadway.
N. L. Schloss, 39 Cortlandt St.
S. M. Scot, 11 Broadway.
H. E. Seaman, 40 Wall St.
A. F. Sears, 20 Broad St.
I. A. Shaler, 27 William St.
Shedd & Sarle, 52 Broadway.
J. C. Sheridan, 7 Rector St.
Jos. Simmons, 35 Nassau St.
F. W. Skinner, 100 William St.
Small & Schurmann, 265 Broadway.
Augustus Smith, 39 Cortlandt.
C. W. Smith, 31 Broadway.
F. H. Smith, 16 Exchange Pl.
T. R. Smith, 150 Broadway.
J. P. Smithers, Jr., 40 Broadway.
Snare & Triest, 39 Cortlandt.
C. H. Snow, University Hights.
Sooysmith & Co., 71 Broadway.
J. F. Sorzana (firm of), 31 Broadway.
E. G. Spilsbury Engineering Co., 45 Broadway.
T. W. Sprague, 97 Cedar St.
Standard Engineering & Contracting Co., 160 5th Ave.
Starr Engineering Co., 250 Broadway.
Henry Steers, Jr., 1 Broadway.
Stone & Thurston, 220 Broadway.
Herman A. Strauss, 29 Liberty St.
E. L. Street, 44 Wall St.
Structural Engineering Co., 39 Cortlandt St.
C. W. Stewart, 33 Broad St.
B. J. Sullivan, 220 Broadway.
James Symington, 16 Exchange Pl.
G. A. Taber, 106 E. 23d St.
Caesar Teran, 102 Fulton St.
C. F. Terney, 123 Liberty St.
E. G. Thomas, 97 Cedar St.
G. H. Thomson, 51 E. 44th St.
T. K. Thomson, 17 Park Row.
H. C. Thompson, 136 Liberty St.
R. H. Tingley, 102 Fulton St.
W. H. Titus, 3 Union Square, W.

New York City—Manhattan and Bronx—Continued.

R. P. Tomassek, 217 W. 125th St.
C. H. Tompkins, 120 Liberty St.
A. B. Tower, 1123 Broadway.
Tower & Wallace, 309 Broadway.
F. M. Towl, 26 Broadway.
C. S. Towle, 220 Broadway.
L. L. Tribus, 84 Warren St.
J. C. Trautwine, Jr., 27 Williams St.
A. W. Trotter, 71 Broadway.
B. W. Tucker, 15 Cortlandt St.
G. R. Tuska, 62 Williams St.
Oluf Tyberg, 39 Cortlandt.
United Construction Co., 17 Park Row.
United Engineering & Contracting Co., 17 Park Row.
J. G. Van Horne, 71 Broadway.
Franklin Van Winkle, 39 Cortlandt St.
H. L. Vanzile, 11 Broadway.
C. G. Vermeule, 203 Broadway.
A. L. Von Bauer, 1123 Broadway.
F. Von Emsparger, 35 Nassau St.
J. A. L. Waddell, 11 Broadway.
Waddell & Montgomery, 72 Trinity Place.
Geo. Wadman, 33 Stuyvesant St.
Walker & Stidham, 874 Broadway.
J. F. Ward, 45 Broadway.
Wm. R. Ware, A. Columbia College.
J. D. Waring, 45 Broadway.
Waring, Chapman & Farquhar, Broadway.
C. S. Warner, 468 W. 146th St.
W. H. D. Washington, 1 Broadway.
John Waterhouse, 71 Broadway.
A. L. Webster, 3 Broadway.
W. H. Weightman, 29 Broadway.
J. H. Wells, 32 Nassau St.
S. C. Weiskopf, 21 State St.
Wetmore & Lendsing, 120 Liberty.
G. A. Wheeler, 253 Broadway.
S. Whinery, 95 Liberty St.
J. T. Whistler, 52 Broadway.
W. H. White, 32 Pine St.
F. S. Williamson, 256 Broadway.
Fremont Wilson, 66 Maiden Lane.
H. G. Winn, 121 E. 44th St.
A. R. Wolff, 130 Fulton St.
Woltmann, Keith & Co., 11 Wall
E. J. Wood Co., 243 Broadway.
Chas. Wyeth, 1 Madison Ave.
A. J. Zerbe, 11 Broadway.
J. E. York, 52 Broadway.

Up-to-date information about CEMENT AND ITS USES is given more fully in MUNICIPAL ENGINEERING MAGAZINE than any other publication.

Subscription Price, $2.00 Per Year.

)RK CITY, BOROUGH OF
'S—
ns, 1 Town Hall.
:Laughlin, Co. Engr.
nd Peralta, 4 Center St., Ja-
.
:oemer, 20 Main, Flushing.
l Rutter, Rockaway Park
us.
ck Skeen, 411 Lockwood St.,
City.
mith, 24 Jackson Ave., L. I.

Tait, 5th & Jackson Ave., L.
'.
'an Alst, 702 Vernon, L. I.

)RK CITY, BOROUGH OF
OND—
'reeman, New Brighton.
Hillyer, 407 Richmond Ter.,
Brighton.
P. Morrison, 23 Rich Ave.,
Richmond.
acot, Stapleton.
Klein, 42 Harrison St., Sta-

l R. Yetman, Tottenville.
. FALLS—
C. Johnson.
Jones.
McCulloh.
ery, Cy. Engr.
'ONAWANDA—
& Snow.
nith, Cy. Engr.
3URG—
Hacket.
e, Cy. Engr.
.
'msby, Cy. Engr.
Sieber, A.
—
illips, Cy. Engr.
-
. Harris.
'nsby, Cy. Engr.
Seeber.
UE—
Son.
F. Smith, Cy. Engr.
LL—
ynolds, Cy. Engr.
RVIS—
hofield, Cy. Engr.
:EPSIE—
evoort, 54 Market.
Fowler, Cy. Engr.
URY—
lade, Cy. Engr.
AER—
lessing, Cy. Engr.
ER—
Brown, 16 State.
'rafts, 97 Glendale P'k.
ershed.

Rochester—Continued.
E. A. Fisher, Cy. Engr.
Gillette, Hay & Gillette, 751 Powers Bldg.
W. C. Gray, 418 Powers Bldg.
J. H. Grant, City Hall.
Horace Jones, 142 State.
E. Kuichling, 209 Clinton Ave., N.
Geo. W. Rafter, 63 Kenwood Bldg.
John C. Ryan, 118 Arcade.
W. R. Storey, 711 E. & B. Bldg.
W. J. Stewart.
J. N. Tubbs, 207 Wilder Bldg.

ROME—
F. A. Coleman, Cy. Engr.
G. S. Hook.
Knight & Hopkins.
Geo. C. Schillner.

RONDOUT—
Geo. N. Bell, Cy. Engr.
P. Edwin Clarke.
Jas. E. Phinney.

SALAMANCA—
K. Kelsey, Cy. Engr.

SANDY CREEK—
S. E. Wheeler, Cy. Engr.

SARATOGA SPRINGS—
J. S. Mott, Cy. Engr.

SCHENECTADY—
J. Leland Fitzgerald, Cy. Engr.
J. M. Jackson.
Olin H. Landreth.
L. B. Sebring.
D. C. Smith.

SIDNEY—
James L. Clark, Cy. Engr.

SING SING—
C. E. Cartwright, S. Highland Ave.
C. S Gowen.
W. E. Horton, James St.

SOLVAY—
James M. Gere, Cy. Engr.

SYRACUSE—
James B. Cahoon, 639 Onondaga St.
W. B. Cogswell.
Allen & Farrington.
Rhesa Griffin, 307 E. Genesee St.
Geo. E. Higgins, 84 Wieting Blk.
H. C. Hodgkins, 610 W. Onondaga.
Thomas H. Mather, 38 Nottingham Bldg.
Geo. A. Morris, 102 Holland St.
Henry T. Reach, City Hall.
H. Soule.
Russell R. Stuart, Cy. Engr.
Charles A. Sweet, 252 James St.
James G. Tracy, 405 S. A. & K. Bldg.

TARRYTOWN—
Ward Carpenter & Son.
D. S. Merritt.
E. J. Wulf, Cy. Engr.

TONAWANDA—
D. M. Greene.
J. B. Snow, Cy. Engr.

TROY—
Edward R. Cary, Cy. Engr.
Cary & Roemer, Times Bldg.
John Flynn.
W. G. Raymond.
Palmer C. Ricketts, 17 1st.
Martin Schenck.
TUPPER LAKE—
W. E. La Fountain, Cy. Engr.
UTICA—
C. W. Adams, 132 Oneida.
F. K. Baxter, 102 Blecker.
Lewis Clifford, Jr.
Paul L. Schultze, Cy. Engr.
R. W. Sherman.
WALDEN—
Chas. Caldwell, Cy. Engr., P. O. Newburgh.
WARWICK—
Henry Pelton, Cy. Engr.
WATERTOWN—
F. A. Hinds.
C. O. McComb, Cy Engr.
WHITEHALL—
A. D. Bartholomew, Cy. Engr.
WHITE PLAINS—
J. M. Farley, Cy. Engr.
YONKERS—
Wm. H. Baldwin, 45 Washurton Ave.
E. Sherman Gould.
C. V. Leliva, Cy. Engr.

NORTH CAROLINA.

ASHEVILLE—
B M. Lee, Cy. Engr.
CHARLOTTE—
Fingal C. Black.
Hayden, Wheeler & Slocum
Hook & Sawyer.
F P Milburn
C A Spratt, Cy Engr.
GREENSBORO—
Frank A Peirce
HENDERSON—
A C Linthicum
RALEIGH
W Z Blake, Cy. Engr.
ROCKINGHAM—
W L. Everett
SALISBURY
N E Scales Cy Engr.
WILMINGTON
J C Chase
Jos H McRee, Cy Engr
WINSTON
J. L. Ludlow.
J O Magruder Cy Engr.

NORTH DAKOTA.

FARGO—
Hancock Bros.
H Beebe
J O Shea
Sam F Crabbe, Cy Engr
GRAFTON—
E L Ross, Cy. Engr.
GRAND FORKS—
J. J. Smith, Cy. Engr.
W. S. Russell.
JAMESTOWN—
B. P. Tilden, Cy. Engr.

OHIO.

AKRON—
W. D. Chapman, 504 Everett Bldg
J. A. Gehres, Court House Squar
Paul Bros., 230 Main St.
John W. Payne, Cy. Engr.
ALLIANCE—
W. B. Hunt.
O. W. Pfouts, Cy. Engr.
ASHLAND—
F. L. Nied rheiser, Cy. Engr.
ASHTABULA—
L. A. Amsden.
F. E. Bissell.
H. E Mann, Cy. Engr.
Abner D. Strong.
ATHENS—
J. R. Sands, Cy. Engr.
BELLAIRE—
A. J. Norton, Cy. Engr.
BELLEFONTAINE—
Gimo & Fisher.
Jas. C. W. Wonders, Cy. Engr.
BOWLING GREEN—
E. L. Spafford.
L. B. Fraker.
BRYAN—
Schurman & Consaul.
CAMBRIDGE—
O. M. Hoge, Cy. Engr.
CANTON—
L. E. Chapin
G. M Kaufman, Central Sav. B Bldg
E. J. Landor.
Robt Ostermayer, 1211 S. Clevel Ave.
L. W. Thomas, 123 Tuscarawas St
Guy Tilden, Schaefer Blk.
Philip H. Weber, Cy. Engr.
CARROLLTON—
J. D. Lane, Cy. Engr
CARTHAGE—
E. F Layman, Cy. Engr.
CELINA—
A. W. Fishbaugh.
Martin Lutz, Cy. Engr.
CHILLICOTHE—
John F Cook
Walter M. Dawley.
H M. Read, Cy. Engr.
CINCINNATI—
Louis F Boeh, 4135 Florida Ave
Wm H Boeh, City Water Work
G Bouscaren, 2d Floor City Hall
J E Breen, County Engr
M D. Burke, 404 Pike Bldg.
Clinton Cowen, 540 Main.
C N Danenhower, 1426 Elm.
George W. Diekmeir, 211 15th St

ti—Continued.
Duwelius, 127 E. 3d.
'. Dowson, 2617 Cleinview Ave.
ıaw & Punshon, Glenn Bldg.
ınd Race.
. Engle, 1530 Lincoln Ave.
Ford, Jr., 1059 Wesley Ave.
Goldfogle, Dennison Hotel.
M. Harper, 1546 Baymiller.
Harrison, County Surveyor.
Bros., Hopkins & Linn.
W. Hill, 35 Glenn Bldg.
· S. Hobby, 610 Lincoln Ave.
Hosbrook & Son, 65 Pickering
.
'ook & Ferris, 429 Pike
'.
Huge, 9th and Main.
Knorr, County Engineer.
Krug, County Engineer.
Layman, 32 E. 3d.
. Locke, 40 E. 3d.
Mathewson, 4222 Chambers.
E. Morris, 2846 Harrison Ave.
Newcomer, 11 Masonic Temple.
B. Punshon, Chief Engineer B.
A.
F. Randolph Co., 232 E. 5th.
E. Rasinsky, 1641 Clayton.
Read, 32 E. 3d.
Rugg & Co., 340 Main.
Schmidt & Co., 215 E. 4th St.
G. Smith, Jr., M. E., 11 Ham-
Bldg.
ngel, 409 Pike Bldg.
Stanley, Chief Engineer B. of
, City Hall
A. Stewart, 517 Johnston Bldg.
Stichnath, Shaw Ave., Hyde
.
· E. Sullivan, City Hall.
lundmaker, County Engineer.
P. Tharp, 810 Neave Bldg
Tozzer, 4211 Turrill.
Wulfekoetter, Jr., 14 Hul-
Blk.
G. Wulff, Spring Grove &
ı Aves.
VILLE—
Abernethy, Cy. Engr
Fuller.
McMananry.
owery.
.AND—
S. Barnum, A., New England
Boalt, 45 Outhwaite Ave
Bogardus Osborn Eng. Co.,
rn Bldg.
L. Cobb, 2509 Euclid Ave
1 C. Cooke, 11 Hough Place.
ulley, 4 Redell St
Harrington, 509 Osborn Bldg.
H. Haupt, 73 Edgewood Place.

Cleveland—Continued.
Chas. W. Hopkinson, A., 50 Euclid Ave.
A. Lincoln Hyde, New England Bldg.
Marvin W. Kingsley, Supt. Water Works.
C. F. Lake, Osborn Eng. Co., Osborn Bldg.
Chas. F. Lewis, 307 Cuyahoga Bldg.
Walter Miller, 407 Perry-Payne Bldg.
Benjamin F. Morse, E. & A., 36 Cheshire St.
J. P. Ogden, Engr. of Pavements, City Hall.
The Osborn Engineering Co., Osborn Bldg.
J. T. Pardee, Engr. of Bridges, City Hall.
Isaac K. Pierson, 416 Cuyahoga Bldg.
Albert H. Porter, 403 Osborne Bldg.
M. E. Rawson, 762 Genesee Ave.
Walter P. Rice, Dir. P. W., City Hall.
John N. Richardson, A., 262 Prospect St.
Geo. S. Rider, 604 Century Bldg.
Jas. Ritchie, Cy. Engr., Hickock Bldg.
L. T Schofield, A., 338 Erie St.
Chas. F. Schultz, 354 Superior St.
Chas. H. Strong, 622 Cuyahoga Bldg.
Henry C. Thompson, 20 Benton St.
Joshua D. Varney, 53 Public Square.
Wellman-Seaver Eng. Co., 1404 New England Bldg.

CLYDE—
W E. Gillett

COLUMBIANA—
J G. Beatty.

COLUMBUS—
B. F. Bowen, 28 E. State St
Henry Cordes
John Courtright, 347 S. High St.
F J. Fisher, 23 E. State St.
M. H. Gates, 23½ N. High St.
Julian Griggs, City Engr.
E. A. Kemmler, City Hall.
E. E. Legg, 4½ Pioneer Blk.
R R Marble, 23 E. State St.
Chas E. Perkins, Chf. Engr. State B P W.
F J Picard, 59 Clinton Blk.
Snow & Barbour, 86 N. High.
Frank Snyder, 23 E. State.
J. A. Taft, 23 E. State.

CONNEAUT—
C. H Slater, Cy. Engr.

COSHOCTON—
John A. Hanlon.

CRESTLINE—
C. W. Babst, Cy. Engr.

CUYAHOGA FALLS—
Hosea Paul.

DAYTON—
Harry J. McDargh.
H. E. Talbot & Co.
F. M. Turner, Cy. Engr.
DEFIANCE—
Henry F. Toberen, City Engr.
DELAWARE—
J. B. Taggart, City Engr.
EAST LIVERPOOL—
A. W. Scott.
John A. George, Cy. Engr.
Adolph Fritz.
ELYRIA—
Wm. H. Searles.
C. H. Snow, Cy. Engr.
FINDLAY—
E. C. Bolton.
J. W. S. Reigle, Cy. Engr.
FREMONT—
Henry Hughes, Cy. Engr.
GALION—
J. W. Atkinson, Cy. Engr.
GALLIPOLIS—
M. F. Leonard.
Arius K. Williams, Cy. Engr.
GENEVA—
B. F. Hewet, Cy. Engr.
GLENVILLE—
The Walter P. Rice Eng. Co., Cleveland, Cy. Engrs.
GREENVILLE—
W. D. Brumbaugh, Cy. Engr.
C. O. Lucas.
HAMILTON—
L. A. Dillon, City Engr.
HARTWELL—
H. C. Innes.
IRONTON—
F. G. Leete, Cy. Engr.
JACKSON—
Solon Smith, Cy. Engr.
KENTON—
W. W. Myers, Cy. Engr.
Alex. R. Taylor.
O. P. Wilson.
LAKEWOOD—
Robt. Wager.
R. J. Wood, City Engr.
LANCASTER—
A. E. Bretz.
Jno. N. Wolfe, City Engr.
LEBANON—
Frank A. Bone.
W. R. Kemper, City Engr.
Wm. McCole.
P. O. Monfort.
Webb Smith.
LEIPSIC—
D. W. Seitz, Cy. Engr.
LIMA—
R. H. Gamble.
J. C. McCollough.
L. F. Prevost, Cy. Engr.
Geo. Taylor.

LONDON—
E. E. [illegible]
[illegible]
LORAIN—
E. C. [illegible]
C. H. Snow
MADISONVI
Asa [illegible]
MANSFIELD
Jacob [illegible]
F. F. [illegible]
V. Redding
MARIETTA—
E. F. Gebe
W. P. Mas
MARION—
J. W. Scot
MARTIN'S
Abram La
MARYSVILL
J. C. Kenn
MASSILLON
D. C. Bort
MIDDLEPO
Thos. Head
Thos. Midd
MIDDLETOV
Frank Doty
Ave.
MINGO JUN
James L. C
MT. VERNO
A. Cassill,
NAPOLEON-
C. N. Schw
NEWARK—
N. H. Brow
NEW PHIL
J. H. Boot
NILES—
Wm. Wilso
NORTH BA
D. W. Lee
NORWALK-
John Layli
L. B. Mess
NORWOOD—
Jas. A. Ste
OBERLIN—
W. B. Gerr
OTTAWA—
J. S. Cartw
OTWAY—
J. W. Smit
PAINESVIL
Frank M.
PAULDING-
Oliver Mor
PIQUA—
H. E. Whi
POMEROY—
Headly &
PORT JEFF
Chas. Coun

UTH—
Bratt, 11 Gallia.
yan, Cy. Engr., 33 E. 8th.
A—
inton, Cy. Engr.
—
oper.
osbrook, Cy. Engr., P. O.
ati.
TS—
uthan, Cy. Engr.

rench, Cy. Engr.
rawn.
Y—
wer.
Miller, Cy. Engr.
-
Weddle, Cy. Engr.

use, Cy. Engr.
KLYN—
se, City Engr.
IELD—
lds, 19 E. High St.
ever, 25½ E. Main.
aron, Cy. Engr.
Snyder, 57 W. Main.
Bird, Court House.
VILLE—
rfman, Cy. Engr.
ston, 3rd Ft. Court House.

ters, Cy. Engr.
-
Brown, Cy. Engr.
Buxton, T. & O. C. R. R.
lark, 2024 School Pl.
ok, Law Bldg.
T. Oakley, The Spitzer.
phant, 1st Asst. Cy. Engr.
Sherman, 613 Nasby Bldg.
ratton, 115 Cham. of Com.
—
hite, Cy. Engr.

alker, Cy. Engr
ANDUSKY—
reek.
—
Swisher, Cy. Engr
RT—
eatty, Cy. Engr
Rimer.
NETA—
Craig, Engr
—
ennise[illegible]
ickey [illegible]
wood
ealey
GTON—
acobs [illegible]
arker
Y—
lanbe[illegible]
Overm[illegible]

WELLSTON—
Thos. M. Davidson.
Homer Goddard.
WILMINGTON—
J. A. Brown, Cy. Engr.
Alph McKay.
WOOSTER—
J. L. Eberhardt, Cy. Engr.
XENIA—
G. A. McKay.
YOUNGSTOWN—
F. M. Lillie, Cy. Engr.
Owsley & Boucherle, A.
David M. Wise.
ZANESVILLE—
Henry I. Buell, Cy. Engr.

OKLAHOMA TER.

GUTHRIE—
J. Foucart.
Mr. Bennett.
T. C. Frazier, Cy. Engr.
SHAWNEE—
W. F. Graves.
PONCA CITY—
G. H. Brett, Cy. Engr.

OREGON.

ALBANY—
C. H. Burggraf.
CORVALLIS—
G. V. Skelton, Cy. Engr.
PORTLAND—
Wm. B. Chase, Cy. Engr.
D. D. Clarke, City Hall.
J. H. Cunningham, 610 Cham. Com.
W. H. Kennedy, Ore. R. R. & Nav. Co.
E. M. Lazarus.
Richard Martin, Jr.
Whidden & Lewis.

PENNSYLVANIA.

ALLENTOWN—
Geo. F. Goins, City Engr.
Jacoby & Weishampel.
ALTOONA—
Harvey Linton, City Engr.
AMBLER—
Albert Beck.
Edw. C. Evans.
Thomas S. Gillin, Cy. Engr.
Morris Redifer.
R. S. Russell.
ASHLAND—
Jos. B. Garner, Cy. Engr.
ASHLEY—
H. B. Smith, Cy. Engr., P. O. Wilkesbarre.
BEAVER—
I. A. Atwood.
BEAVER FALLS—
H. T. Baker, City Engr.
BELLEFONTE—
J. H. Wetzel, Cy. Engr.

BELLEVUE—
Edeburn & Cooper, Cy. Engrs.
BETHLEHEM—
Lewis J. H. Grossart, 23 S. Main St.
R. E. Neumeyer, Cy. Engr., 143 Broad St.
William B. Spengler, 23 S. Main St.
BIRDSBORO—
Samuel Rea, Cy. Engr.
BLOOMSBURG—
Jas. C. Brown, Cy. Engr.
BRADDOCK—
Wm. Howat, Cy. Engr.
BRADFORD—
E. N. Uuruh, A.
P. B. Winfree, Cy. Engr.
BRYN MAWR—
Sam'l M. Garrigues.
BUTLER—
C. F. L. McQuiston, Cy. Engr.
CAMBRIDGE SPRINGS—
H. H. Finney, Cy. Engr.
CARBONDALE—
Walter Frick, Cy. Engr.
CHAMBERSBURG—
S. D. Culbertson, Cy. Engr.
CHARLEVOI—
R. L. Barnhart.
Wm. Lloyd, Cy. Engr.
CHESTER—
W. H. Karns.
C. H. Ladomus.
CLIFTON HEIGHTS—
Thos. G. Janvier, Cy. Engr.
COATESVILLE—
H. G. Book, Cy. Engr.
COLUMBIA—
E. W. Goerke.
J. Koch.
Samuel Wright, Cy. Engr.
CONNELLSVILLE—
S M. Foust, Cy. Engr.
CORRY—
Nevin R Dickson, Cy. Engr.
G. D. Gilbert
COUDERSPORT—
Ora L. Nichols.
CRAFTON—
James S. Haring
CURWENSVILLE—
W. A Moore, Cy Engr.
DERRY STATION—
J. Jack Neil, Cy Engr.
EASTON—
A Prescott Folwell
Louis A Francisco, Cy Engr
S H Lea
EMPORIUM—
A H Shafer, Cy Engr
ERIE—
Ben E Briggs, Cy Engr
EVERETT—
G. W Cunard, Cy Engr
FRANKLIN—
T. L Kennerdell, Cy. Engr.
E. C Read

HARRISBURG—
F. C. A. G. Bergengren.
HASTINGS—
Jas. Campbell, Cy. Engr.
HAZELTON—.
A. B. Celdix, Poplar & Chestnut Sts
L. O. Emmerich, 201 N. Laurel St.
Jas. S. Haring, Cy. Engr.
E. A. Hess, 197 Peace St.
T. S. McNair, Diamond Ave. & Alter St.
I. E. Unstead. 91 N. Church St.
HUNTINGDON—
J. Murray Africa, Cy. Engr.
INDIANA—
Robt. M. Mullen, Cy. Engr.
JENKINTOWN—
Jos. W. Hunter, Cy. Engr.
JOHNSTOWN—
Geo. Krueger.
Lee Masterton, Cy. Engr.
Alex. McKeever.
Geo. Wild, A.
Wilson & Kuhn.
KINGSTON—
Thos. Wright, Cy. Engr.
KITTANNING—
R. L. Ralston, Cy. Engr.
KUTZTOWN—
A. S. Heffner, Cy. Engr.
LANCASTER—
Israel Carpenter, Cy. Engr.
D. M. Rothenberger.
C. E. Urban.
Jas. Warner.
LANSDOWNE—
Thos. G. Janvier, Cy. Engr.
LANSFORD—
Wm. J. Dornbach.
Chas A Rutter, Cy. Engr.
LATROBE—
Gebhart & Reed, Cy. Engrs
LEBANON—
Thos R. Crowell, Cy. Engr.
G W Hayes.
LYKENS—
Samuel Cox, Cy Engr.
MANSFIELD—
E. N. Bentley.
Andrew Sherwood, Cy. Engr
MARIETTA—
Casper Eates, Cy. Engr
MAUCH CHUNK—
Franz Mackl, Cy Engr
M'DONALD—
R F Hunter, Cy Engr
M'KEES ROCKS—
S. L Gardner, Cy. Engr.
MEADVILLE—
W A Doane, City Engr.
MEDIA—
C M Broomall
MIDDLETOWN—
Geo S Mish, Cy. Engr.
MONONGAHELA CITY—
Geo T Jenkins, Cy. Engr.

ᴇRTH—
Brendlinger.
ʀETH—
: J. Kunkle, Cy. Engr.
rt F. Wents.
CASTLE—
H. McConahy, Cy. Engr.
Woods.
KENSINGTON—
Ellis.
). White, Cy. Engr
STOWN—
Calhoun, 606 DeKalb St.
W. Corson, 7 E. Airy St.
; Cresson, 507 Swede St.
lm D. Patterson, Cy. Engr.
I EAST—
Hill, City Engr.
IUMBERLAND—
; G. Dieffenbach, Cy. Engr.
ʟLE—
le & Miller, Cy. Engrs.
ΓY—
field Engineering Co., 237 Elm

Roess, Cy. Engr., City Hall.
N—
Yerger, Cy. Engr.
DELPHIA—
·r Albright, 908 Land Title
·.
Alsop, 134 S. 3d St.
lliam Baist, 906 Walnut St.
Balderston, A., 411 Walnut St.
W. Barnes, 134 S. 9th St
F. Bertolett, 723 Heed Bldg.
Berthoud, 431 Odd Fellows' ple.
Birkinbine, Odd Fellow's Tem-

Boas, 14 S. Broad.
ı, Garrett & Blair, 406 ıst St.
T. Boyt, 302 Walnut St.
S. Budd, 1030 Witherspoon
·.
ıall W. Brown, 1023 Witherspoon
·
·tt B. Carter, 1202 Harrison
:.
t C Clarkson, 710 Stephen Gi- Bldg.
& Hubbard, 1414 S. Penn. ıre.
H. Clifton, Spring Garden er Works.
ɘs W. Collins, 1030 Wither- n Bldg.
Cooper, 614 N 3rd St.
Corson, 1212 Montgomery Ave
m Cox, 204 Walnut Place.
t A. Commings, 714 Girard
·
. Darlington, 1120 Real Estate ıt Bldg.
's G. Darrah, 945 Drexel Bldg

Philadelphia—Continued.
Howard Deacon, 1103 Stephen Girard Bldg.
John Jerome Deery, 1015 Betz Bldg.
Chas. F. Douglass, A. 1313 S. 19th St.
W. A. Drysdale, 415 Hale Bldg.
M. Ward Easby, 909 Grozer Bldg.
Joseph D. Ellis, 325 Walnut St.
Axel H. Engstrom, 517 Bullitt Bldg.
Henry P. Feister, 1011 Chestnut St.
Robert A. Fowden, 405 Hale Bldg.
Francis Bros. & Jellett, 704 Arch St.
John Fraser & Son, A, Imperial Bldg.
William Copeland Furber, 421 Chestnut St.
John L. Gill, Jr., 302 Walnut St
Richard Gilpin, 421 Chestnut Bldg.
William S. Gray, 1030 Witherspoon Bldg.
Robert P. Green, 1102 Stephen Girard Bldg.
Haupt & Franklin, 906 Crozer Bldg.
Joseph Hartshorne, 602 Harrison Bldg.
E. J. Hedden, 14 S. Broad St.
Magnus Hellstrom, 572 Bullitt Bldg.
E Hexamer & Son, 419 Walnut St.
Holt & Schober, 378 Philadelphia Bourse.
Griffith M. Hopkins, 302 Walnut St.
Horn & Morris, 1227 Betz Bldg.
R. M. Huston, 302 Walnut St.
Philip H. Johnson, 1123 Betz Bldg.
Emery J. Kerrick, 228 W. Hortter St., Germantown.
Keystone Engineering Co., 929 Chestnut St.
J. Geo. Klemm, Jr., 929 Chestnut St.
George R. Kurrie, 904 Walnut St.
James B. Ladd, 1127 Real Estate Trust Bldg.
Lathbury & Spackman, 1619 Filbert St.
Latta & Terry, 1001 Chestnut St.
Ambrose E. Lehman, 711 Walnut St.
Henry J. Lamborn, 704 Witherspoon Bldg.
Edward F. Lummis, 436 Walnut St.
N. S. Lynch, 308 Walnut St
Thomas B. Main, 1227 Stephen Girard Bldg.
Edward V. Maitland, 2d, 230 Drexel Bldg.
George M. Newhall, 136 S. 4th St.
Wm. H. Millard, 1103 Stephen Girard Bldg.
Edwin P. Monroe, 1345 Arch St.
Howard Murphy, 260 S. 3d St.
Ernest W. Naylor, 50th St. and Lancaster Ave.
Quimby Engineering Co., 915 Ridge Ave.
John A. Patterson, 120 Walnut St.
Alexander Rea, 800 Land Title Bldg.
S. Howard Rippey, 1301 Stephen Girard Bldg.

Philadelphia—Continued.

Frank C. Roberts & Co., 1508 Filbert.
Limo F. Rondinella, 728 Stephen Girard Bldg.
Lewis Rodman Schultz.
Coleman Sellers, 1301 Stephen Girard Bldg.
Wm. L. Simpson, 5th & Buttonwood Sts.
Steel & Wilke, 1213 Filbert.
J. Prescott Stoughton, 926 Stephen Girard Bldg.
Frederick G. Thorn, Jr., 1227 Stephen Girard Bldg.
John C. Trautwine, Jr., 257 S. 4th St.
John C. Trautwine, 3d, 257 S. 4th St.
Theodore F. Triepel, 234 Diamond St.
Harold Van Duzee, 427 Walnut St.
John A. Walton, 8218 Germantown Ave.
Robert Weaver, 532 Arch St.
G. S. Webster, Chf. Engr. Dept. Pub. Works, Bureau of Surveys.
William R. Webster, 411 Walnut St.
Albert C. Wood, 606 Girard Bldg.
Wilson Bros. & Co., Drexel Bldg.
William Wyllner, 1030 Witherspoon Bldg.
Joseph H. Young, 1203 Harrison Bldg.

PITTSBURG—

Henry Aiken, 403 Lewis Blk.
W. W. Anderson, 810 Penn Bldg.
D. Ashworth, 325 4th Ave.
J. Carroll Barr, 1117 Carnegie Bldg.
Wm. Bradford, 331 4th Ave.
C. H. Bradley, Jr., & Co., 323 4th Ave.
W. R. Brown, Cy. Engr.'s office.
John Brunnuer, Cy. Engr.
E. M. Butz & Co., 1128 Park Bldg.
J. N. Chester, 600 Lewis Blk.
Curran & Hussey, 215 4th Ave.
Samuel Diescher, 714 Hamilton Bldg.
F. R. Dravo & Co., 812 Lewis Blk.
Edeburn, Cooper & Co., 410 Grant St.
W. A. Edeburn, 412 Grant St.
Chas. Ehlers & Son, 615 W. Diamond St. A.
Edward B. Erickson, 8 Garrison Bldg.
Ernest L. Farren, 65 Fidelity Bldg.
Frease & Sperling, Ross Ave. & Wood St., Sta. D.
Frick & Co., 51 Schmidt Bldg.
G. A. Gilfillan, 78 Fidelity Bldg.
J. T. Graham, 615 Times Bldg.
G. F. Greenwood, Times Bldg.
Hallsted & McNaugher, 401 Monongahela Bk Bldg.

It is Our Business

TO HELP

Your Business

IF YOU MAKE, SELL OR USE

CEMENT

Write to us and we will tell you what we can do for you.

You ought to know

Municipal Engineering Co.

SPRING CITY—
Isaac P. Rhodes, Cy. Engr.
STEELTON—
C. H. Hoffer, Cy. Engr.
L. E. Johnson.
STROUDSBURG—
Geo. G. Shafer, Cy. Engr.
TARENTUM—
E. E. Maurhoff, Cy. Engr.
TITUSVILLE—
Jos. Smith, Cy. Engr.
TREMONT—
G. M. Beadle, Cy. Engr.
E. A. Kaercher.
WARREN—
D. F. A. Wheelock, Cy. Engr.
WASHINGTON—
John M. McAdam, Cy. Engr.
WELLSBORO—
A. Hardt, Cy. Engr.
WEST CHESTER—
W. A. MacDonald, Cy. Engr.
WILKES BARRE—
W. V. Ingham, Cy. Engr.
Albert H. Kipp, A., 77 Coal Exch.
H. S. Smith.
WILKINSBURG—
Freease & Spedling, Cy. Engrs., P. O. Sta. D, Pittsburg.
J. H. Harlow & Co., 701 Wood St., Pittsburg.
WILLIAMSPORT—
Geo. D. Snyder, City Engr.
YORK—
Henry Birkinbine.
Jas. G. Durbin.
R. B. McKinnon, Cy. Engr.

RHODE ISLAND.

BRISTOL—
Eugene Le Clair.
CENTRAL FALLS—
William Faitoute Keene, Cy. Engr., 84 Cross St.
NARRAGANSETT—
T. G. Hazard, Jr., Cy Engr.
NEWPORT—
Wm. P Buffum, 301½ Thames St.
Philip F. Conroy, 183 Thames St
Joseph P. Cotton, 201 Thames St.
W H Lawton, 24 Bellvue Ave.
PAWTUCKET—
Geo A. Carpenter, Cy. Engr.
PROVIDENCE—
W. D. Bullock, City Hall.
Chas. F. Chase, 75 Westminster.
Otis F. Clapp, Cy. Engr.
J. V. Dart, City Hall.
Sam'l M. Gray, 10 Weybosset.
Shedd & Sarle, 146 Westminster.
Alfred Stone, A., 49 Westminster St.
R H Tingley, 75 Westminster.
Edmund B Weston, 86 Weybosset.
RIVERSIDE—
J. H Armington.
WAKEFIELD—
L. L. Holland, Cy Engr.
WOONSOCKET—
J. W. Ellis.
Frank H. Mills, Cy. Engr.

SOUTH CAROLINA.

ABBEVILLE—
J. L. Johnson, Cy. Engr.
ANDERSON—
S. O. Jackson, Cy. Engr
BEAUFORT—
C. C. Townsend.
CHARLESTON—
J. H. Dingle, Cy. Engr.
Fuller, Dawson & Co., 61 Broad.
John Gadsden, Jr., 50 Broad.
Rutledge Holmes, 50-52 Broad.
Henry H. Johansen, 37 Broad.
R. B. Olney, Supt. Sewers.
Simons & Mayrant, 42 Broad.
Earle Sloan, 15 Broad.
A. W. Todd, 63 Broad.
CHESTER—
James Hamilton, Jr.
COLUMBIA—
B. Holley, Hotel Jerome.
A. Gamewell La Motte, A. & E, 1200 Main St.
D. B. Miller, Cy. Engr.
Niernsee & La Motte.
S. R. Stoney, 1235 Washington St.
FLORENCE—
J. W. Brunson, Cy. Engr.
W. J. Wilkins.
GREENVILLE—
J. R. Lawrence, 125½ S. Main St.
J. E. Sirrine, 103 S. Main St.
PIEDMONT—
Jas. Orr Haynes, Cy. Engr.
Wm. Lee.
SPARTANBURG—
Howe & Olney, 67 W. Main St.
F. H. Knox.
Ladshaw & Ladshaw, 10 Kennedy Pl.
A. Madole, 58 Morgan Sq.
SUMMERVILLE—
Henry S Burden.

SOUTH DAKOTA.

ABERDEEN—
E. W Van Meter, Cy. Engr.
ALEXANDRIA—
W. J. Hull.
BROOKINGS—
E. G Davis, Cy. Engr.
DEADWOOD—
J R. Hickox, Cy. Engr.
Francis C. Tucker.
Vincent & Jewett.
LEAD—
J. P. Crick, Cy. Engr.
MADISON—
W. R Smythe, Cy. Engr.
MITCHELL—
W. J. Hull, Cy. Engr.
RAPID CITY—
B E Lovejoy, Cy. Engr.

FALLS—
. Dow & Son, A.
Howe, Cy. Engr.
A. Pear, A.
ı Schwarz, A.
RTOWN—
Brickell, A.
W. Carpenter, Cy. Engr.
Rowe, A.
TON—
Brewer.
Bruce, Cy. Engr.
Summers.
Wilde.

TENNESSEE.

OL—
t Grey, Cy. Engr.
'ANOOGA—
rt Hooke, Cy. Engr.
Hunt.
SVILLE—
Marable, Cy. Engr.
Wilson.
N—
Daniels, Cy. Engr.
Truex.
MAN—
d Griffitt, Cy. Engr.
Pearsall.
ON—
Lancaster, Cy. Engr.
VILLE—
ann Bros.
Beaver.
Moreland.
Park, Cy. Engr.
Waters, A.
ON—
Hatcher, Cy. Engr.
Seagroves.
HIS—
Bell, Cy. Engr.
w J. Bryan.
& Lovell, Equitable Bldg.
CREEK—
Call.
ILLE—
& Creighton, 3 Berry Blk.
& Young, 79 Cham. of Com.
M. Leftwich.
Locke, 1518 McGarock St.
Donald, N. C. & St. L. Ry.
man & Brown.
Washburn.
KI—
Grigsby.
CITY—
rdner, Cy. Engr.

TEXAS.

T—
Matthews.
McDonald & Sons, 706 Colorado.
P. McFall, Cy. Engr.
N—
Rucker, Cy. Engr.

BONHAM—
W. A. Petus.
BROWNSVILLE—
S. W. Brooks, Cy. Engr.
BROWNWOOD—
C. N. Davis, Cy. Engr.
BRYAN—
M. Nagle, Cy. Engr.
P. E. Wellman, A.
CALDWELL—
M. D. Rogers, Cy. Engr.
CALVERT—
D. H. Francis, Cy. Engr.
W. H. Kirsch.
H. Osson.
CAMERON—
W. M. Crosswy, Cy. Engr.
CORPUS CHRISTI—
A. M. French, Cy. Engr.
CORSICANA—
W. M. Elliott, Cy. Engr.
A. J. Hook.
A. B. Mothershead.
DALLAS—
R. W. Havens.
B. S. Wathen.
DUBLIN—
R. T. Daniels.
J. C. Williams.
EL PASO—
Ed. Kneezel.
E. Krause.
Geo. C. Wimberly, Cy .Engr.
FT. WORTH—
S. B. Haggart.
John B. Hawley, Cy. Engr.
W. B. King.
Howard Messer.
M. R. Sanguinet.
GAINESVILLE—
Geo. Fisher.
J. G. Garrett.
H. Hulen, Cy. Engr.
GALVESTON—
C. F. W. Felt.
R. H. Peek, Cy. Engr.
HARRIMAN—
Willard Griffith.
G W. Pearsall.
HENRIETTA—
C. B. Patterson, Cy. Engr.
HOUSTON—
James H. Berry, 105½ Main St.
William Bradburn, Court House.
Abraham Cross, 1104 Preston St.
James O. Davis, 508⅛ Main St.
C. W. Lewis, City Hall.
William Mackintosh, 500 Kiam Bldg.
John W Maxcy, 203 Binz Bldg.
Geo. B. Miles, 213 Levy Bldg.
I. Austin Miller, City Hall.
Samuel E. Packard, 212 Fannin St.
William A. Polk, 212 Fannin St.
Alexander Potter, 500 Kiam Bldg.
Charles M. Staples, 614 Dallas Ave.
Patrick Whitty, 117½ Main St.

LAREDO—
Chas. E. Frees, Cy. Engr.
LYONS—
Frank Hervey.
MARLIN—
R. S. Hunnicutt, Cy. Engr.
MARSHALL—
C. G. Lancaster.
McKINNEY—
S. H. COLE, Cy. Engr.
NEW BRAUNFELS—
Alf. Rothe, Cy. Engr.
ORANGE—
J. A. Pinkston, City Engr.
SAN ANTONIO—
Thomas Franklin.
Alfred Giles.
Geo. E. Haines.
E. G. Trueheart, Cy. Engr.
J. A. Wahrenburger.
SHERMAN—
A. Q. Nash, City Engr.
SULPHUR SPRINGS—
Sig Wachholder.
TEMPLE—
F. M. Temple.
TERRELL—
S. A. Oliver.
TEXARKANA—
Sidney Stewart.
TYLER—
M. L. Lynch.
WACO—
Geo. B. Gurley, Cy. Engr.
WEATHERFORD—
N Carroll, Cy. Engr.

UTAH.

BRIGHAM CITY—
N. P. Anderson, Cy. Engr.
MT. PLEASANT—
A. Rosenland, City Engr.
OGDEN—
A. F. Parker, City Engr.
M. S. Parker.
PARK CITY—
Wilber McLellan, Cy. Engr.
Pope & Lets.
PAYSON—
Otto Erlandson.
W. C. Wightman, Jr., Cy. Engr.
PROVO CITY—
Caleb Tanner, Cy. Engr.
R. C. Watkins.
SALT LAKE CITY—
Wm. Ashton.
A. F. Doremus, 226 N. Second West St.
R. C. Gemmell, 223 Second East St.
W. P. Hardesty, Progress Bldg.
F. C. Kelsey, Cy. Engr.
W. A. Morey, Engr. Bridges and Bldgs. R. G. W. Ry.
C. L. Stevenson, Atlas Blk.

VERMONT.

BARRE—
F. A. Walker.
C. S. Currier, Cy. Engr.
P. S. Smith.
BURLINGTON—
V. J. Barbour, 96 N. Prospect St.
Frank H. Crandall, City Hall.
Albert R. Dow, 234 Pearl St.
H. M. McIntosh, Cy. Engr., City Market Bldg.
Frank O. Sinclair, 174 Main St.
J. W. Votey.
Charles L. Woodbury, 133 St. Paul St
MONTPELIER—
Currier & Smith, 43 State St.
F. A. Walker, A.
RUTLAND—
Arthur C. Grover, City Engr.
WINOOSKI—
V. K. Nash, City Engr.

VIRGINIA.

ALEXANDRIA—
J. C. Ramage, Southern Ry.
BERKLEY—
R. M. Phelps, Cy. Engr.
Chas. J. Woodsend, A.
BRISTOL—
Robert Grey, Cy. Engr.
DANVILLE—
C. A. Ballou, Cy. Engr.
FREDERICKSBURG—
S. S. Bradford, Cy. Engr.
LEXINGTON—
Hutton Engineering Co.
Wm. G. McDowell, Cy. Engr.
LYNCHBURG—
J. M. B. Lewis.
NEWPORT NEWS—
Geo. W. Fitchett.
E. A. Marye, Cy. Engr.
P. Thornton Marye.
NORFOLK—
Wm. T. Brooke, Cy. Engr.
Jno. Graham, Jr., 236 Main.
PETERSBURG—
Thos. R. Dunn, Cy Engr.
PORTSMOUTH—
H. C. Cassell, 434 High St.
PULASKI—
H. Alexander, Cy. Engr.
RICHMOND—
C. P. E. Burgwyn, 819 Main St.
W. E. Cutshaw, Cy. Engr.
H. Frasier, Chf. Engr., C. & O. R. R.
Hydraulic Engineering Co.
Noland & Baskerville.
RIO—
C. M. Bolton.
ROANOKE—
C. S. Churchill.
J. H. Wingate, Cy. Engr.
STAUNTON—
Carter H. Harrison, Cy. Engr.

WASHINGTON.

D—
ostain, Cy. Engr.
IATCOM—
Donovan.
IC—
'arner.
—
S. Fortiner.
owler.
haus, 513 Pioneer Bldg.
ud.
hompson, Cy. Engr.
GAN—
'g & Sonneman.
E—
Welle, Cy. Engr.
—
. Davis.
Wolfard, 1003 A.
g & Russell Co., Cal. Bldg.
. Taylor, Cy. Engr.
VALLA—
.rk, Cy. Engr.

WEST VIRGINIA.

ELD—
outz.
Hill, Cy. Engr.
—
e.
ard.
STON—
Campbell, Kanawha Bank
g.
hapman, Court House.
le, 237½ Kanawha.
gue, 40½ Capitol St.
enable, 56 Capitol St.
BURG—
ennis.
ndlay, Cy. Engr.
ettigrew.
ndevanter.
—
encer, Cy. Engr.
GTON—
ford.
ierce.
adburn, Cy. Engr.
wart.
BURG—
Harrison.
BURG—
nnan & C. [illegible]
Dunbar
Smith [illegible]
kson Cy. Engr.
RG—
yd.
G—
ite Cy. Engr.

WISCONSIN

APPLETON—
N. M. Edwards.
C. H. Gillett, Cy. Engr.
Chas Pride.
H. Wildhagen.
ASHLAND—
D. G. Sampson, Cy. Engr.
BARABOO—
W. G. Kachoffer, Cy. Engr.
R. W. McFarland.
BELOIT—
R. R. Caldwell, Cy. Engr.
F. H. Kemp.
W. H. Wheeler & Co.
BERLIN—
D. P. Blackston, Cy. Engr.
BLACK RIVER FALLS
H. H. Powers, City Engr.
BLUEFIELD—
W. S. Fouts.
Geo. H. Hill, Cy. Eng.
DODGEVILLE—
J. E. Jones, City Engr.
EAU CLAIRE—
Chas. A. Alderman, City Engr.
L. P. Wolff, 1013 3d Ave.
ELROY
E. Buck, Cy. Engr.
FOND DU LAC
A. D. Conover
D. A. Molitor.
E. B. Parsons, Cy. Engr
FORT ATKINSON
Frank Bisset.
GREEN BAY
Dan'l Harteau.
HUNTINGTON
E. Crawford
Jno Sandbourn, City Engr
J. B. Stewart
JANESVILLE
P. F. Brown
C. V. Kerch, Cy. Engr
KENOSHA
Robt H. Moth, Cy. Engr
LA CROSSE
Frank Powell, City Engr
MADISON
[illegible]
[illegible]
[illegible]
[illegible]
[illegible]
[illegible]
[illegible]
[illegible]
[illegible]
[illegible]
[illegible]
[illegible]

MERRILL—
Francis E. Mathews, Cy. Engr.
G. L. Sturdivant.
MILWAUKEE—
Samuel D. Austin, 307 Grand Ave.
Geo. H. Benzenberg, 436 Jefferson St.
Fred Bredel, 118 Farwell Ave.
Christ Engel & Son, 301 15th St.
Fred'k H. Ford, 82 Wisconsin St.
Melvin W. Goodhue, 204 Grand Ave.
William F. Goodhue, 204 Grand Ave.
Albert M. Patitz, 428 Grand Ave.
Chas. J. Poetsch, Cy. Engr.
R. G. Reinertsen, 458 Jefferson Ave.
Oscar Sanne, 893 Hackett Ave.
Fred Schneider, 468 Washington Ave.
Edmund F. Spalding, 106 Mason Ave.
Gustav Steinhagen, 401 Germania Bldg.
Julian V. Wright, 315 Goldsmith Bldg.
NEENAH—
L. C. Hjorth, Cy. Engr.
NEILLSVILLE—
C. S. Stockwell, Cy. Engr.
NEW LONDON—
A. W. Millard, Cy. Engr.
OCONTO—
W. B. Hall, Cy. Engr.
OSHKOSH—
Harvey W. Leach, Cy. Engr.
PORTAGE—
C. E. Corning, Cy. Engr.
PORT WASHINGTON—
H. C. Cal, Cy. Engr.
RACINE—
Orson Burlingame, City Engr.
S. G. Knignt, County Surv.
RICE LAKE—
L. A. Schade, Cy. Engr.
RIPON—
C. H. Chandler, Cy. Engr.
SHAWANO—
H. A. Brauer, Cy. Engr.
SHEBOYGAN—
C. N. Boley, Cy. Engr.
TOMAH—
Geo. J. Howard, Cy. Engr.
TOMAHAWK—
Wm. McGee, Cy. Engr.
WASHBURN—
Thos. Moore, Cy. Engr.
WATERTOWN—
G. H. Stanchfield.
WAUKESHA—
Jno. P. Dey, Cy. Engr.
Wm. Powrie
WAUPUN—
Albert Raube, Cy. Engr.
WAUSAU—
Fred Clark.
M. Deane.
Chas. Juers.
C. W. Nutter, Cy. Engr.
WEST SUPERIOR—
E. B. Banks.

Wyoming.

CHEYENNE—
W. D. Pease, Cy. Engr.
RAWLINS—
James A. Hansen, A.
ROCK SPRINGS—
F. A. Manley.
SHERIDAN—
F. C. Williams, Cy. Engr.
SHERMAN—
M. S. Parker.

CANADA.

ALMONTE, ONT.—
A. Bell.
AMHERST, N. S.—
Charles Campbell, City Engr.
BELLEVILLE, ONT.—
R. Craft Hulme, Cy. Engr.
BRANDON, MAN.—
H. H. Shillinglaw, Cy. Engr.
BROCKVILLE, ONT.—
Wm. B. Smellie, Cy. Engr.
CALGARY, ALBERTA—
G. A. Stewart, Cy. Engr.
CAMPBELLFORD, ONT.—
Wm. Hall.
CHARLOTTETOWN, P. E. I.—
C. B. Chappell.
H. C. Harnis.
Jno. P. Nicholson, Cy. Engr.
CLINTON, ONT.—
W. J. Paisley, Cy. Engr.
CORNWALL, ONT.—
F. D. McNaughton, Cy. Engr.
FREDERICTON, N. B.—
Wm. McKay, City Engr.
GLENCOE, ONT.—
James Robertson, Cy. Engr.
GODERICH, ONT.—
Jas. Reid, Cy. Engr.
GUELPH, ONT.—
W. F. Colwill.
James Hutcheon, Cy. Engr.
HALIFAX, N. S.—
F. W. W. Doane, Cy. Engr.
M. Murphy.
HAMILTON, ONT.—
John S. Fielding.
Peter Mogenson, 193 Jackson St.
Wm. Stewart, A.
E. B. Wingate.
HULL, QUEBEC—
R. W. Farley, City Engr.
JOLIETTE, QUE.—
D. Dostaler, A.
J. D. A. Fitzpatrick, Cy. Engr.
KAMLOOP, B. C.—
R. H. Lee.
KINGSTON, ONT.—
A. K. Kirkpatrick, Cy. Engr.
LINDSAY, ONT.—
James W. Chalmers, Cy. Engr.
LONDON, ONT.—
Ormsby Graydon.

, ONT.—
Rollins. Cy. Engr.
ON, N. B.—
Archibald.
Edington, Cy. Engr.
EAL, QUE.—
arlow. City Engr.
Kennedy.
Peterson.
Shanly.
' FOREST. ONT.—
Ritchie, Cy. Engr.
VESTMINSTER. B. C.—
Hill, Cy. Engr.
Keefer.
RA FALLS. ONT.—
Mitchell. Cy. Engr.
Nichols.
EVILLE, ONT.—
West.
Wheelock. Cy. Engr.
'A. ONT.—
akman.
'A. ONT.—
n J. Ker. Cy. Engr.
P. O'Hanly.
SOUND. ONT.—
Dowell, Town Engr.
OKE. ONT.—
Norris. Cy. Engr.
BOROUGH, ONT.—
rtlett.
Betcher.
ackwell.
S. Hay. Cy. Engr.
Rogers.
. ONT.—
O. Crandall.
ARTHUR. ONT.—
McDougall. Cy. Engr.
tts, A.
COLBURN. ONT.—
H. Lawlor.
C. QUE.—
Stuart.

RENFREW, ONT.—
H. E. Brownlee, Cy. Engr.
ROSSLAND, B. C.—
John Honeyman. A.
W. F. Van Buskirk, Cy. Engr.
ST. THOMAS, ONT.—
J. H. Kennedy.
SAULT STE. MARIE, ONT.—
J. Russell Halton.
Mr. Heyd.
J. A. Wilde.
SHERBROOKE, ONT.—
Cox and Amos.
Thos. Fremblay, Cy. Engr.
J. B. Verrett.
SIMCOE. ONT.—
C. C. Fairchild. Cy. Engr.
SMITH FALLS, ONT.—
J. H. Moore. C. E.
TORONTO. ONT.—
M. I. Butler, 22 Wellington Place.
Willis Chipman, 103 Bay St.
D. B. Dick, A.
Joseph A. Fowler, 121 Victoria St.
W. T. Jennings.
E. H. Keating.
Jas. McDougall.
Charles H. Rust, Cy. Engr.
Strickland & Symons. A.
TRAILL. B. C.—
J. G. Sullivan.
W. F. Tye.
VALLEYFIELD. QUE.—
J. H. Sullivan. City Engr.
VANCOUVER. B. C.—
Thos. H. Tracy. Cy. Engr.
VICTORIA. B. C.—
F. C. Gamble.
WALKERTON. ONT.—
Jas. Warren, City Engr.
WINNIPEG, MAN.—
Col. H. N. Ruttan, Cy. Engr.
YARMOUTH, N. S.—
E. [illegible] Mathews, Cy. Engr.

—In this list A [illegible] Cy. Engr. [illegible] City Engineers.

A LITTLE TALK ABOUT BUSINESS

"I like a proposition that pays."
—C. P. HUNTINGTON.

THIS PAYS!

THERE are certain things that a man in business must do. He must have an office, he must put out a sign, and he must advertise.

He must make himself known to the people who may be interested in his kind of business. The better he does this the more successful he will be.

Some of the most successful men make it a rule to spend one-fifth of their income in advertising, and they find it pays.

It makes poor business good.

It makes good business better.

The best way to advertise is to put your advertisement where it will go directly to the people who want what you sell.

We give the kind of advertising that goes directly to the right spot.

If your business is not in line with the kind our readers are interested in, we don't want you to advertise in our magazine.

If it is, we can help you, and we can give you more for your money than you can get from any other expenditure of it.

From Sacramento (Cal.) Record-Union:

"MUNICIPAL ENGINEERING has often been pronounced in these columns the most useful, practical magazine of the age, and we adhere to that judgment."

MUNICIPAL ENGINEERING MAGAZINE

Awarded Grand Prize by Paris Exposition of 1900
Holds Medal from the Chicago World's Fair

WORKERS IN CEMENT.

(See also list of Contractors and Large Users of Cement.)

)TE.—This list includes the workers in cement, except in the larger cities; the intention to include as far as possible the practical users of cement, who work on and furnish als for their own contracts. It has not been possible in cities to separate such men hose simply in the employment of contractors. In the larger cities they are nearly all ed in the list of contractors, to which list reference should be made.

ALABAMA.

VILLE—
Akerman.
'T—
n & Co.
E—
ved Wood Pavement Co., H. E. ville, Supt.
IELD—
Gray.
y Hillman.
LAWN—
Dimon.
Carson.

ARIZONA TER.

IX—
Burtis.
Chamberlain.
und Lumber Co.
Skinner.
le Plumbing Co.
N—
Hayes.

ARKANSAS.

EN—
Hollingsby.
PRINGS—
el Jodd.
Kelly.
Weidcman.

CALIFORNIA.

EN—
Kinkel.
Hammond.
RSFIELD—
Carroll.
Lindgren.
Bros.
Quincy.
LEY—
Marshall.

HANFORD—
A. M. Ashley.

MARYSVILLE—
M. T. Harrington.
I. Luke.
W. H. Plymire.

PASADENA—
James H. Dovey.
S. J. Edwards.
Andrew & Geo. Halloway.
J. B. Hughes.
Hamilton & Phillips.
E. H. Smith.
Ward & Roberts.

POMONA—
John Beaton.
R. A. Burke.
Scott Carson.
H. Cushing.
Lon Fleming.
Wm. Simmons.

RIVERSIDE—
Zeno Dernoss.
Chas. Ohlhausen.

SAN BERNARDINO—
Rialto Irrigation District.

SANTA CLARA—
T. P. Cunningham.

SANTA CRUZ—
Bryan Byrne.
James Griffin.
C. A. Logue.
G. H. Lease.
W. E. Miller.
L. S. Sherman.
W. J. Thurber.
C. L. Twiss.
Geo. Van Wagner.

SANTA ROSA—
W. P. Bagley.
W. L. Nagel.
Jos. Neumaier.

John McManus.
W. S. Wilds.
VENTURA—
Thos. Bell.
Harry Roberts.
L. F. Webster.
WATSONVILLE—
James Halward.
WOODLAND—
H. T. Barnes.
John Campbell.
H. Erwin.

COLORADO.

DENVER—
Johnson & Sorenson.
Chas. McBride, 2046 Stone St.
The Renton Fireproofing Company, 1815 Arapahoe St.
Seubert & Heinbecker, 729 15th.
GRAND JUNCTION—
Garrison & Fletcher.
FORT COLLINS—
Fred Buzzell.
J. Finger.
Benj. Franklin.
M. R. Gibbons.
Jno. Lunn.
S. E. Moore.
Wm. Metcalf.
Ed. Sulter.
J. C. Whedbee.
PUEBLO—
G. W. Roe, A.

CONNECTICUT.

BRISTOL—
Ira Gaylord.
NEW HAVEN—
Frank Brazos.
John A. Doolittle & Co.
T. J. Maher.
ORANGE—
L. A. Brown.
O. W. Dutcher.
John L. Sherman.
H. P. Wheeler.
SOUTHINGTON—
W. S. Barnes.
John Colliny.
Thomas Nolan.
UNIONVILLE—
Jos. Jeltner.

DELAWARE.

WILMINGTON—
Lenderman & Bro.
Geo. W. McCaulley & Son.
A. S. Reed & Bros. Co.
Simmons & Bro.

FLORIDA.

GAINESVILLE—
E. C. McMahan.

DAWSON—
J. S. Bartlett.
Robt. Bittman.
Jos. Burch.
GAINESVILLE—
L. F. Finger.
Robt. Edison.
MARIETTA—
J. C. Waters.
NEWNAN—
W. S. Askew
R. D. Cole Mf
ROME—
N. B. Watson
T. C. Wyatt.

ID

WALLACE—
Wilmot M. Sc

I

BELLEVILLE—
Emil Funk.
Moritz Horfke
Reeb Bros.
Geo. P. Uhl.
BLOOMINGTON
Peter Bowman
CAIRO—
W. W. Fletche
W. R. Hallida
James Quinn.
CANTON—
W. H. Hallor.
John Hallor.
CARLINVILLE-
Jno. Flori & S
Harry Hillier.
H. Kuiester &
Frank Lynch.
Jno. Ross.
Henry Winters
CHARLESTON-
Chas. Fleehart
Fuller Bros.
Rod Johnson.
Michael Millar.
Minton & Twi
Jack Van Pelt.
CHILLICOTHE-
Frank Hayden.
Ellis Kiser.
Wm. Reed.
COLCHESTER—
John Ruddle.
Lewis Underhi
DECATUR—
M. J. Cuttle.
A. Kremling.
O. H. Whitsell
Dan'l Whitsell

JRY—
Foker.
ay.
over.
onner.
ord.
3URG—
& Lewis.
—
rawford.
cCarthy.
IcCarthy.
rks.
obinson.
E CITY—
ller.
RD—
reitenfeld.
Bush.
Hogan.
ierce.
Wellington.
ND—
Bros.
LE—
& Drallmer.
VILLE—
Bros.
Nally.
son.
ILLE—
Dennis.
Penn.
Stinson.
Wilkes.
—
Peintner.
haw.
NGE—
Anderson.
Wallen.
Weseman.
T—
Herman.
Nelson.
—
Yount.
Yount.
OWN—
Hughes & Bros
B—
n Bros.
& Holden.
ALL—
eel.
m Bros.
JTAH—
ueltner.
Clement.
Lischer
ON—
Kinser.
ile.
—
Berg.
it.

MOMENCE—
F. O. Clark.
Chris Hansen.
J. Lundstrum.
P. Sharkey.
J. J. Sharky.

MONMOUTH—
John H. Baldwin.
Silas W. Pillsbury.
A. W. Ryan.
O. D. Wilcox & Son.

MONTICELLO—
Otis Jenkins.
Scott Miller.
A. L. Starkey.
Wm. Wall.

MORRISTOWN—
Theo. Collins.
Wm. Collins.
John S. Lingel.
Fred Meyer.
G. W. Mericle.
Alex. Phillips.
A. J. Quackenbush.
F. M. Quackenbush.
Frank Royer.

NORMAL—
F. A. Leighton.
Thos. Sylvester.
Jos. Wrenn.

OTTAWA—
Thomas Peattie.
O. P. Robinett.

PAXTON—
A. J. Johnson.
Turner Bros.

PETERSBURG—
Ed L. Goodman.
John Huggins.
James M. Walker.

PINCKNEYVILLE—
Harry Grover.
A. T. Jenner.
T. E. Turner.

PITTSFIELD—
Harry Anson.
John Fletcher.

PLANO—
Stewart Bros.

ROCHELLE—
C. A. Hizen.
A. Stoddard.

SHELBYVILLE—
David Bare.
Asa Manley.
Jas. E. Miller.
Geo. Moyer.
Jacob Risacker.

SPARTA—
Wm. Stumpe.

STAFFORD SPRINGS—
E. J. Sweet.
Silk Bros.

STREATOR—
James Campbell.
Chas. Lyons.

SULLIVAN—
Horshman Bros.
J. A. Jones.

SYCAMORE—
John Eddy.
Arthur Johnson.

TOLUCA—
John Gannon

TUSCOLA—
Jas. Hixson.
William Renner.
Jno. Smith.

URBANA—
V. Bearley & Co.
Wm. Bearley.
Jno. B. Bennett.
E. Fryer, Jr.

WATSEKA—
A. C. Lyman.
Clarence South.
Geo. Wright.

WHEATON—
Louis Beshler.
Mr. Doty.
Charles Gates.
Charles Vogel.

WOODSTOCK—
Jno. Connell.
Jno. Hauck.
J. T. Johnson.
C. Johnson.

INDIANA.

ALBANY—
Cub Ford.

ANGOLA—
A. E. Metzgar.
Geo. Ritter.
Simon Ritter.

ATTICA—
Joseph Clark.
Geo. Roberts.

AUBURN—
Henry Peckhart.
John Trusch.

AURORA—
M. Bailey.
Job Cosby.
Wm. Platt.

BLOOMINGTON—
Murphy & Denton.
W. A. Pipe.
Vop & Howard.

BROOKVILLE—
Dora Brown.
John Castle.
Frank Gagle.
Chas. Horn.
Wm. West.

BRAZIL—
Bud Akers.
J. M. Cutshall.
John Hughes.
H. B. McMillan.
Ben Monce.
John Rider.
Orson Vanderhoff.
Andrew Young.

CRAWFORDSVILE—
Della Deets.
Chas. Girard.
Luther Hamilton.
John Hunt.
Frank Lewsader.
J. D. Tracey.

DANVILLE—
John Berryman.
Maden & Stevensen.

DELPHI—
Geo. Bell.
John Cook.
Ira Rinehart.

FAIRMOUNT—
H. M. Crilley.
Frank Goodall.

FT. WAYNE—
Kruse & Busching, 93 E. Superio
Alfred Shrimpton, W. Main.
F. Zimmerdorf & Son, 19 Wagner

FRANKFORT—
Wm. Reed.
Joseph Speitel.

GARRETT—
Link Ober.

GREENSBURG—
J. L. Wootman.

GREENFIELD—
J. H. Johnson.
Jos. Marsh.

HAMMOND—
S. Shade.

HARTFORD CITY—
R. J. Coulson.
David Manon.

KENDALVILLE—
Adolph Adams.

LEBANON—
Chas. M. Gilmore.

MONTPELIER—
John Hamilton.
Dan'l Wood.

NORTH MANCHESTER—
Bush Bros.
W. W. For.
Thos. Leatherland.
James Wallace.

OAKLAND CITY—
Joseph Barton.
Thos. Rainey.
Jas. Stewart.

PERU—
John Lynch.

'D—
gby.
uhn.
ynes.
ephens.
AER—

essen.
Bros.
Warren.
UN—
arvis.
'reys.
nes.
Mauses.
ER—
skill.
LE—
Glore.
lore.
oore.
Stamm.
. Vance.
RS—
Wieler.
BURG—
ll.
andall.
—
ibbs.
ly.
'chner.
inkard.
AUTE—
& Grimes.
TON—
Cutter.
Mooney.
Feagans.
C—
ill.
Keys.
—
urton.

IOWA.

'ALLS—
oombs & Son.
Slade.
oot.
ier.

rown.
Quinn.
E—
'ans.
ringle.
Paving Co.
Stenck.
—
arris.
urray.
urray.
Myres.
. Tower.

ESTHERVILLE—
Hawk Bros.
Olif Johnson.
C. S. Millers.
FAIRFIELD—
James Canterberry.
Chas. Muflenix.
Joseph Small.
John Warner.
Venr. White.
GRINNELL—
R. G. Coatt.
IOWA CITY—
W. Horrabin.
J. B. Laner.
Osborne & Tomlin.
MALVERN—
R. L. Hammond.
T. E. Vanhorn.
R. B. Vandevert.
MASON CITY—
Geo. Gabler.
W. W. Naramore.
MONTICELLO—
Clark Byam.
Thos. Cassidy.
Alf. Fry.
NEW HAMPTON—
Jas. Johnson.
W. T. Mahoney.
J. S. Slatton.
M. Winter.
OELWEIN—
G. W. Eller.
OSCEOLA—
Jno. Campbell.
Henry Muchmone.
OSKALOOSA—
Chas. Blakeslee.
SAC CITY—
John Cooper.
C. S. Larimer.
SHENANDOAH—
M. V. B. Goshen.
SIOUX CITY—
P. P. Comoli.
L. Christianson & Co.
Hanson Bros.
TIPTON—
O. Frame.
W. J. Gilmore.
Wm. Milford.
John Wickman.
VILLISCA—
Henry Dennis.
Elmer Dennis.
VINTON—
S. M. Campbell.
Wm. Campbell.
Jno. Houck.
WEBSTER CITY—
C. L. Briggs
Wm. Inslay.

KANSAS.

ABILENE—
J. A. Wilkie.

CHERRYVALE—
C. M. Adams.
Geo. Behner.
D. B. Pearson.
T. J. Pearson.

CHETOPA—
H. Merrill.

EL DORADO—
F. J. Bowie.
Marian Dailey.
John Trimble.
Wm. Trimble.

EMPIRE CITY—
E. S. Cornelius.

EMPORIA—
J. P. Ross.

GARNETT—
Hill & Coppage.
W. A. Mahan.

GIRARD—
O. G. Hitch.
Thos. McKaughey.
R. M. Tiffany.

HIAWATHA—
A. Adams.
Thos. Daniels.
W. E. Richards.

MARYSVILLE—
Theodore Hammett.
Theo. Hahn.
P. Rozine.

NEWTON—
Sam'l Pauline.

OSAGE CITY—
T. B. Lamb.
W. D. Roady.
A. G. Young.

SALINA—
John A. Nelson.
August Nelson.

KENTUCKY.

ASHLAND—
J. B. Crouse.
F. C. Friend.
F. Horstmann.
Jno. Mead.
Ed White.

DANVILLE—
Wm. King.

EARLINGTON—
Geo P. Farnsworth

FRANKFORT—
D M. Woodson.

HARRODSBURG—
Robt. Edgers.
J. W. Robards.
J M. Smith.

HENDERSON—
R. P. Farnsworth
P C. Kyle.
Ed Marion.

LEBANON—
J. Daisey.
R. P. Fowler.
P. Smith.
James Sansburn.

MAYFIELD—
J. C. Belote.
Jacob Hooper.

RICHMOND—
M. F. Kuns.
Samuel Rice.

SHELBYVILLE—
Robt. Lilheart.

LOUISIANA.

ALEXANDRIA—
Hoffman & Wilson.
Jno. Runshang.

BATON ROUGE—
A. Berhel.
Paul Le Blane.
A. Pino.
Jas. Potts.

DONALDSONVILLE—
Ferdinand Delattes.
Jos. Delattes.
Desire Landry.
P. Ramirey.

HOUMA—
Eriest Chanoin.
J. E. Naquin.

JACKSON—
Thos. Arnhein.

NATCHITOCHES—
Jos. Keyser.

OPELOUSAS—
Emile Donatto.
Theo. Gilvin.

MAINE.

BRIDGTON—
Stephen G. Dow.
James Houlden.

BRUNSWICK—
Louis H. Barnes.
Chas. E. Hacker.

BUCKSPORT—
H. F. Ames & Co.

CALAIS—
Robt. Walker.

CARROLLTON—
Wm Bates.
Joe Walden.

DEXTER—
C. F. Beam.
Jos. Haines.

EASTPORT—
Chas. Hamilton.
H. Sharland.
C. H. Varney.

FOXCROFT—
B. A. Thomas.
D. M. Whittridge

MADISON—
Joseph Coughlin.

—
;lass.
hell.
D—
'ns.
:.
ιN—
xie & Sons.
.
.
'ON—
Moulton.
Moulton.
RO—
ogue.
ζ.
'ILLE—
eag.

MARYLAND.

E—
d Barnett.
rannock.
rs.
OWN—
er.
leman.
man.
nell.
.ND—
.
ran.
'aft.
er.
E—
yer.
'—
s.
or.

ASSACHUSETTS.

G—
Building Co.
arter.
wenier.
Herlihy.
Cosmer.
. N. Lawrence.
lehale.
ft.
Foss.
Varney.

ill, 102 Cleveland St.
aux, Jr., 196 Essex.
McMullen.
ueen, Mountain Ave
PTON—
Bailey.
Whiting.
Mather.
tthews.
atthews.
arten.

WOBURN—
J. M. Ellis & Co., Salem St.
Patrick Farrey, 22 Hudson St.
J. F. Kelley, 124 Arlington Road.

MICHIGAN.

ADRIAN—
Thos. Gimbert.
Matthes Bros.
ALLEGAN—
A. W. Lutts.
Julius Markey.
G. Markey.
W. Tilson.
ALMA—
Nelson Lilley.
H. F. Thompson.
BENTON HARBOR—
Chas. Hartman.
Aug. Hartman.
BESSEMER—
H. Blumenkamp.
Anton Cederberg.
Chas. Nyguest.
FARIBAULT—
Warren Smith.
GRAND HAVEN—
J. E. Clark.
GRAND LEDGE—
Fay Ward.
GRAND RAPIDS—
H. N. Cargill.
Granite Stone Co.
Kooiman Bros.
Mathewson & Kloote.
E. W. Seamans.
HASTINGS—
Hastings Cement Walk Co.
C. O. Freer.
ITHACA—
Ira Bovee.
John Bronson.
Chas. Churchill.
Orrin Churchill.
John Rupp.
JACKSON—
Sam'l Pickleo.
E. J. Tobin & Co.
E. C. Van Lewven.
LAPEER—
Ed Bousman.
S. A. Cooley.
M. Hubberd.
MANISTIQUE—
Allen Stewart.
MARQUETTE—
R. R. French.
MARSHALL—
Peter Doyle.
Chester Kidney.
Chas. Porter.
MONROE—Chas. Kibbee
Chas. A. Maurer.
John Maurer.
MUSKEGON
L. H Kanitz

PETOSKEY—
D. McDonald.
J. J. Ransom.
SOUTH HAVEN—
O. M. Foster.
Marshall & Sarager.
C. L. Webster.
TECUMSEH—
Frank Bowerman.
Walter Fink.
John Green.
James E. Lowry.
James Mitchell.
THREE RIVERS—
Peter Deaner.
J. C. Enders.
Geo. Whitesell.
TRAVERSE CITY—
Hill Bros.
John Spidding.

MINNESOTA.

ALEXANDRIA—
J. L. Alton.
AUSTIN—
Austin Cement Works.
BRAINERD—
J. H. Kallahan.
CROOKSTON—
Chas. H. Jefferson.
Louis Ruard.
Aug. Schutler.
GLENCOE—
Wm Burkhart.
John Butler.
Claus & Nubbee.
LAKE CITY—
L. S. Lutz.
Martin Olson.
PIPESTONE—
A. D. Brown.
A. Hedrick.
John Williams.
SAUK CENTER—
E. L. Newell & Co.
STAPLES—
Sid Taylor.
STILLWATER—
Stillwater Stone Sidewalk Co.
WILLMAR—
A. P. Bergeson.
WINDOM—
Ed Iverson.
Emil Quam.
Martin Quam.
S. H. Thompson.

MISSISSIPPI.

BAY ST. LOUIS—
Eug. Dupre.
Aug. Keller.
L. N. Spotorno.
BILOXI—
J. Eistetter.
Henry Eistetter.
G. A. Harkness.
CANTON—
M. Alexander & Co.
G. D. Leitch.
C. Olsen & Co.
COLUMBUS—
L. J. Kelly.
C. Wilson.
GRENADA—
Eli M. Whittaker.
OXFORD—
N. & W. Worley.
PASS CHRISTIAN—
R. W. McDonald.
Wm. Roberts.
WATER VALLEY—
S. Kelley.
C. C. Kirby.
F. A. Pearce.
WESSON—
J. A. Bailey.
J. E. McDonald.
WEST POINT—
Jas. Osborne.
WINONA—
Jules Blackwell.

MISSOURI.

BRUNSWICK—
Egbert Bruce.
Charles Jessup.
James Nickolls.
CHILLICOTHE—
G. M. Bolter.
Harry Miller.
John Miller.
D. G. Roe.
Geo. Stubbs.
GREENFIELD—
N. Butterworth.
J. B. Fruin.
P. H. Hull.
Fred Morrison.
HIGGINSVILLE—
Canterbury Bros.
L. C. Mitchell.

The Foremost Representative of American Cement Interests is .... Municipal Engineering Magazine
Subscription Price, $2.00 Per Year.

-
les.
ebel.
kson.
on.
LLE—
nor.
DENCE—
Lewis.
Randall.
LLE.
es.
avis.
Eggert.
Guire.
CITY—
Dirigo & Son.
aith.

eimberger.
RLES—
ottani.
ll & Son.
ann.
Hallrah.
eckmann.
rtz.
imer.
edler.
EVIEVE.
bernathy.
Boyer.
nard.

lmer.
oshaw.
aughn.
.
ns.
ailey.
heart.
Y—
lew.
osley.
l.
AINS—
ant.
ohnson.
R—
e Long.
s.
lm.

MONTANA.

Carroll.
TON—
amilton.

NEBRASKA.

O—
e.
oulton.
on.

CHADRON—
Samuel Dubel.
Elmer Longcoe.
Ira Longcoe.
CRETE—
Jno. Mullner.
FREMONT—
P. P. Mowrer.
KEARNEY—
A. Cedarhober.
Thos. Dunham.
P. Ryan.
Richard Hibberd.
RENO—
A. F. Niedt.
SOUTH OMAHA—
C. Bechtle, 626 N. 20th St.
Flagle & Zigler, 23d & K Sts.
Fred Lienelen, 20th St.
Frank Thomas.
TECUMSEH—
S. F. Murphy.
YORK—
Geo. Daugherty.
Geo. Fair.
W. Moist.
Jacob Zieg.

NEVADA.

CARSON CITY—
V. B. Cross.
W. G. Elliott.
J. J. Johnson.
R. Logan.
Z. Wilcox.

NEW JERSEY.

BELVIDERE—
Frank Gibbs.
Wm. Ross.
FREEHOLD—
C. R. Emmons.
A. E. Preston.
Augustus Thompson.
Geo. Vanderhoffe.
HACKENSACK—
Frank E. Hopper.
MATAWAN—
Morris Duncan.
Walter Quackinbush.
Peter Van Pelt.
W. C. Van Pelt.
MILLVILLE—
A. S. Dunham.
Wm. Vanaman.
NEWARK—
Commonwealth Roofing Co.
W. W. Schouler.
Standard Paving Co.
Wm. H. Turrell.
PATERSON—
Jno. Agnew.
T. J. Brogan
Chris Kelly.
John R. Lee.
Marley & Forbes.
Joseph Sharpe, 647 E. 18th St.
A. Smith.

PAULSBORO—
Chas. Robinson.
PENNGROVE—
Enoch Hasker.
Adam Jeso, jr.
John Jeso.
Eli Strimple.
PERTH AMBOY—
M. Kennedy.
RAHWAY—
D. M. Roll.
Washington Roll.
Alonzo Turner.
SOUTH ORANGE—
John Barrett.

NEW MEXICO.

ROSWELL—
Dunning & Rasmussen.
B. F. Daniels.
Thos. Howard.
Frank LeRoy.
Geo. Munro.
Pearce & Bixby.

NEW YORK.

BATH—
John Collins.
CANISTEO—
Geo. L. Davison.
E. P. Hayes.
John W. Saunders.
Geo. L. Saunders.
CARTHAGE—
John Leeher.
Paul Roby.
Jarvis Simmons.
CATSKILL—
Jas. Cooke.
Geo. W. Holdrige.
E. Lampman.
CATTARAUGUS—
Loren Merritt.
COLD SPRING—
Wm. Myers.
Chas. Weyant.
CORTLAND—
A. H. Decker.
G. T. Maxson & Co.
Beers & Warfield.
DEPOSIT—
P. Bisbee.
John McMahon.
DUNKIRK—
John Hilliard.
Fred Maidel.
Peter Meister & Son.
EAST AURORA—
Peter Robarg.
Chas. Wright.
Wm. Wright.
EAST HAMPTON—
T. R. Barnes.
Geo. E. South.
FAIRPORT—
Wm. Larwood.
GLOVERSVILLE—
J. A. Delaney.
Kirk Dutcher.
E. D. Filmer, Jr.
GOUVERNEUR—
John Campo.
H. H. Post.
GRANVILLE—
Thomas Brown.
Benjamin Jones.
Thos. Murray.
HICKSVILLE—
Jacob Mann, Sr.
Louis Munch.
Henry Schlimm.
Frederick Voegelle.
HORSEHEADS—
Jno. Van Order.
Ira B. Payne.
Theo. Payne.
KEESEVILLE—
A. H. Munsen.
LOWVILLE—
Hiram Gray.
MALONE—
J. Bissonette.
P. Bainode.
O. W. Vaughn.
OGDENSBURG—
N. C. Lynch.
PATCHOGUE—
John S. Parks.
Geo. Parks.
PERRY—
A. J. Hicks.
Michael Higgins.
Robert Rore.
PORT JERVIS—
Mathew Heitzman.
Jacob Lehn.
Joseph Place.
POTSDAM—
Harry Delish.
R. L. McAllister.
C. G. Rogers.
Isaac Young.
RED BANK—
Frank Manson.
Fred Thompson.
SAG HARBOR—
Edwin J. Beckwith.
Henry Beckwith.
Gilbert H. Edwards.
SALAMANCA—
Andrew Andrews.
T. A. Jamison.
Fred Miller.
J. Van Steenburg.
SALEM—
E. W. Philo.
Chas. A. Shaw.

CREEK—
ls.
nter.
er.
Vheeler.
NG—
Marks, Spring St.
Miller, Glen Ave.
Miller, Terrace Ave
POINT—
Robbins, Ann St.
iffin.
Dykins, Jr.
TOWN—
Bird.
C. Odell.
rancisco.
CK—
une.
Venden.
ELD—
atsel.
ohnston & Son.
Sutherland.
HALL—
Bosley.
Iulhollander.
Parr.

NORTH CAROLINA.

LLE—
Belote.
Wolfe.
OTTE—
Ahrens.
sbury.
ry.
Phife.
ORO—
Bros.
n Houghton Co.
& Wrenn.
TTA—
Williams.
VILLE—
Ballard.
tewart.
NTON—
Campbell.
Doll.
cGalliard.
JTH—
lford.
GHAM—
Skipper.
JRY—
. Martin & Bro.
RO—
arrison.
l & Matthewson.
atthewson.

NORTH DAKOTA.

—
h.

GRAND FORKS—
A. Dinnie & Co.
JAMESTOWN—
Rudolph Weise.
Chas. White.

OHIO.

ASHTABULA—
Geo. L. Stanley.
ATHENS—
Geo. L. Fenzel.
C. W. Harris.
C. C. Harris.
J. K. Osmond.
Wm. Sommer.
BARBERTON—
Edson Bishop.
Oliver Hoch.
Adam Gossman.
Christ Paridon.
D. M. Reed.
John Smith.
BOWLING GREEN—
George E. Mercer.
BRYAN—
Jacob Beavers.
William Riggles.
Geo. Higgins.
CADIZ—
John Aukerman.
CAMBRIDGE—
W. J. Allen
E. Dilley.
Ed Duffey.
Chas. Erven.
CANTON—
Carl Angeretti, 1519 Grant St.
Jos. J. Dehn, 430 Springfield Ave.
CHILLICOTHE—
John S. Butler.
John Ogden.
Wm. W. Renick.
CIRCLEVILLE—
Martin Donley.
John Green.
John Lust.
Chas. Meinfelter.
A. Mowery.
DELAWARE—
L. B. Denison.
Deflinger Bros.
H. D. Hessey.
Ed. Mendenhall.
J. B. Saggart.
Abel Wilson.
DELPHOS—
F. Ganshaw.
EAST LIVERPOOL—
Cook & Clark.
Hill & Wallace.
John M. Ryan.
Sears & Hunter.
FRANKLIN—
A. F. Meeker.
J. T. Parker.
Clint Stanton.
W. S. Van Horne.

GIRARD—
Chas. Anderson.
Wm. Anderson.
A. Delbrat.
Wm. Morrison.
Silas Weir.

LISBON—
Carlisle & Moore.
George Forse.
George Piero.
Springer & March.
Levi Stackhouse.

LONDON—
Edw. Bird.
Jos. Golden.

LOUISVILLE—
Joseph Gotter.

MADISONVILLE—
Settle & Co.

MANSFIELD—
Jacob Cline & Co., 184 W. 5th St.
Gandert Bros., 104 S. Diamond St.
Hering & Son, 132 S. Main St.
Ralph Lomax, 72 First Ave.
William Martin, 234 S. Diamond St.
Straub & Hamblin, East 3rd St.

MARTIN'S FERRY—
Jos. Davidson.
Gus Rothermund.
I. N. Talbott.

MASSILLON—
E. G. Miller, 80 Muskingum St.

MEDINA—
Jno. Crofoot.
Jacob Dreher.
Wm Frazier.
Thos. Gouer, Sr.

MT. VERNON—
William Champion.
James Freeman.

NAPOLEON—
Pontious & Riger.

NEW CEMENTOWN—
James Hiller.

NEW STRAITSVILLE—
Sam Emrick.
T. Spicer.
Richard Spicer.

NORTH BALTIMORE—
Jno. Bartz.
J. W. Fisher.
H. J Hindall.

OSNABURG—
A. M Rice.

OTTAWA—
J. Fuerst.
Jiss Williams.
D. Wickham.

OXFORD—
Marion Lester.
H. S. Thobe.

PARIS—
Unkefer Bros.

PORT CLINTON—
Wm. Bodenstein.
Peter Johnson.
Rickleff Richardson.

RAVENNA—
W. J. Brigham.
C. Z. Loomis.
F. J. Williams.

SALINEVILLE—
Ellsworth Randolph.

SO. BROOKLYN—
J. Boesch.

SPRINGFIELD—
M. C. Russell.

TOLEDO—
Michael Kelly, Avondale Ave.

TORONTO—
Jos. Edwards.

WAUSEON—
Geo. Eck.
A. R. Stranaham.

WAVERLY—
Chris Hanbell.
Wm. Powell.

WELLINGTON—
Wm. Dutridge.
Wm. Holmes.
Jno. Sherman, Sr.
J. R. Sherman, Jr.

XENIA—
John Farrell.
W. O. Maddux.

OKLAHOMA TER.

GUTHRIE—
Michael Cassidy.
Scott Cooper.
Phil Fray.
H. J. Vanderberg.
Michael White.

PONCA CITY—
Chas. E. Welch.

OREGON.

ALBANY—
H. C. Harkness.
J. R. Wilson.

ASHLAND—
A. D. Ferguson.
R. A. Payne.
W. K. Reeves.
Geo. Riggs.

BAKER CITY—
S. L. Schreffler.
D. T. F. Votaw.

MORO—
John Kay.
Cap. Nelson

PORTLAND—
Wm. Holz.

PENNSYLVANIA.

AMBLER—
Morris Redifer.
Edw. C. Evans.

PENNSYLVANIA.

)—
Leibig.
heele (Girardville).
)NTE—
ll,
ell.
Bell.
ɔll.
nith.
HEM—
:night.
ıcarer.
RO—
'ters.
Bros.
ILLE—
ıhn.
3URG—
.mer.
ellich.
RD—
ıvis.
nley.
:obson.
ıe.
—
Dowell.
haffner.
ıgner.
)GE SPRINGS—
Veaver.
RSBURG—
d Baltimore.
hns.

arter.
or.
oinson.
binson.
ellion.
st Woodsworth.
worth.
A—
Broome.
:NCE—
own.
e.
PORT—
·rton.
Ryan.
an, Jr.
Sullivan.
3VILLE—
hompson.
—
'ra.
-
ts.
Bros.
M—

ıe.
D—
.ner.

HASTINGS—
Frank Abel.
A. T. Miller.
HAWLEY—
Chas. Bellman.
L. Geisler.
HUGHESVILLE—
Jno. Edler.
Henry Eichernauf.
Chas. Hughes.
W. C. Miller.
Pearson Smith.
INDIANA—
A. F. Moreau.
W. L. Swanger.
KITTANNING—
A. R. Daugherty.
P. Daugherty.
LEBANON—
Granitine Plaster Co.
MANSFIELD—
Joseph Deitlin.
Hiram B. Faulkner.
MARIETTA—
David Hollinger.
McKEES ROCKS—
B. J. Barnhart.
David Richards.
MEDIA—
Thos. K. Baldwin.
MIDDLETOWN—
C. W. Yost.
MONTROSE—
H. H. Hibbard.
J. Holley.
Geo. Noll.
N. C. Roberts.
MT. JOY—
H. W. Grosh.
NAZARETH—
Harry Weitzell.
Henry Schaeffer.
NORTHUMBERLAND—
A. A. Barrett.
Jos. Vandevender.
PATTON—
Chas. Austin.
John Gagliardi.
A. T. Huber.
H. F. Lawhead.
PENLLYN—
Alan Mathias.
POTTSTOWN—
John H. Rush.
READING—
A. G. Huebner, 560 Gordon St.
L. H. Huebner, 112 Hamilton St.
C. I. Koch, 203 Spruce St.
E. Wagenblast, 622 Mulberry St.
R. L. Wilson, 720 Pear St.
REYNOLDSVILLE—
M. Mohney.
RIDGWAY—
William Edwards.

ST. MARY'S—
E. L. Willard.
SCHUYKILL—
Dan'l Fisher.
G. W. Roeder.
SCRANTON—
M. H. Dale.
SHAMOKIN—
Coates Bros.
Fred Kumer.
H. T. Roup.
SHARPSBURG—
Henry Ferla.
WATSONTOWN—
W. A. Edwards.
James Zettlemayer.
WESTGROVE—
Wm. H. Reyburn.
Harry McLimens.

RHODE ISLAND.

BRISTOL—
Israel Dube.
Nathaniel Gladding.
Eugene Le Clair.
EAST GREENWICH—
James R. Murray.
Byron Roscoe.
NARRAGANSETT—
John Bristow.
J. C. Tucker, Jr.
WESTERLY—
Eugene O'Neil.
C. H. Sayerweather.

SOUTH CAROLINA.

ABBEVILLE—
Yarb Madden.
ANDERSON—
S. O. Jackson.
Alex S. Katton.
J. P. Wilson.
Berry Wilson.
CHESTER—
M. A. Carpenter.
J. R. Simril.
FLORENCE—
Silas Brunds.
J. W. Gregg.
T B. Reynolds.
W. J. Wilkin.
PIEDMONT—
Norman Fleming.
SUMMERVILLE—
A. J. Braid.
Jeff D. Braid.
Frank Springs.

SOUTH DAKOTA.

ABERDEEN—
Aberdeen Cement & Tile Co.
E. W. Van Meter.
BROOKINGS—
J. N Davis.
O. Hanson.
Steen & Wilson.
DEADWOOD—
Nat. Hamilton.
Ed Hauschka.
Joe Marnett.
IRENE—
P. F. Connolly.
MADISON—
Peter Marquart.
WATERTOWN—
Johnson Bros. & Johnson.
YANKTON—
B. Ballensky.
Jas. Kingsbury.

TENNESSEE.

CLEVELAND—
Thomas Banks.
A. T. Bayless.
COLUMBIA—
Britton & Abbott.
C. F. Dodson.
DAYTON—
John Acuff.
John Maley.
Robt. Morgan.
Jas. Wycuff.
JACKSON—
J. F. Whitehead & Co.
KNOXVILLE—
Jos. Armstrong.
Claude Hood.
Jos. Morgan.
LEBANON—
Page Bros.
Woolard & Williams.
McMINNVILLE—
Alpha Young.
MEMPHIS—
W. J. Haire.
Edw. Halley.
M. Larkin.
Miller Paving Co.
C. J. Wagoner & Co.
MOSSY CREEK—
M. Brown.
John Patrick.
MURFREESBORO—
Green Sanson.
ROGERSVILLE—
Frank Allison.
Chas. Lackey.
Alp. Ross.
SODDY—
A. J. Brown.
UNION CITY—
W. Becker.

TEXAS.

ABILENE—
J. B. Reese.
BELTON—
Thos. Karns.
BROWNSVILLE—
S. W. Brooks.
CAMERON—
W. P. Davis.
Capt. Irwin.

/ILLE—
:raft.
·egson.
-Iayden.
ΞY—
:. Farr.
:AUNFELS—
eltner.
Moeller.
ıshorn.
enfuehr.
TONIO—
oettler.
RCOS—
Forscyth.
R SPRINGS—
'. Ashchroft.
oiner.
Wilson.
:—
ıkenstein.
L—
Hopkins.
w & Dungold.
McMain.
Worbington.

UTAH.

AN FORK—
Featherstone.
s Featherestone.
ınyder.
Wright.
.M CITY—
Earl.
·ederickson.
IM—
L. Brenholdt.
hristensen.
Christensen.
Spendrup.
Neilsen, Jr.
—
)'Neill, 2763 Madison Ave.
AKE CITY—
Morris & Sons' Co.

VERMONT.

—
Avery.
Whiting.
NGTON—
Phillips.
'hillips.
Watson.
FIELD—
ıe Bro.

VIRGINIA.

)N FORGE—
Gleason.
LLE—
Brimmer,
Orchow.

NEWPORT NEWS—
S. L. Foster & Son.
Mr. Griffin.
Mr. Temple.
ROANOKE—
J. H. Marsteller.
SWEET HALL—
Chas. Major.
WEST POINT—
Wm. Tuppence.

WASHINGTON.

SEATTLE—
Andrew Jackson.

WEST VIRGINIA.

CLARKSBURG—
Cattrell Bros.
I. A. Jackson.
Lee Mills.
Shinn Bros. & Bryan.
NEW CUMBERLAND—
A. H. McConkey.
W. J. Snowden.
Frank Thayer.
POINT PLEASANT—
Reynolds & Stortz.
W. C. Stortz.
SHEPHERDSTOWN—
Hezekiah Jones.
Thos. Leggett.
Andrew Waldeck.

WISCONSIN.

ASHLAND—
A. Donald & Co.
A. H. Oakey.
BLACK RIVER FALLS—
Wm. O. Ball.
Jno. P. Matson.
DELAVAN—
Hatch & Calkins.
DODGEVILLE—
Elliott Bros.
Kit Whilford.
ELROY—
L. Kropf.
Preuss Bros.
Chas. Sheldon.
FORT ATKINSON—
Geo. J. Becker.
Jno. V. Becker.
GREEN BAY—
J. H. Van der Sande & Co.
JEFFERSON—
Herman Fehrman.
J. G. Kurtz.
John J. Spanglers.
MADISON—
Oakey & Buser.
Parr & Lawrence.
Sharp & Son.
MENASHA—
H. H. Plummer.
MENOMINEE—
John Larson.
Jas. Mason.

MERRILL—
Geo. W. Clark.
F. Hesterman.
V. Henrich.
W. Raefeldt.

MONROE—
Kiester & Bauman.
Sam Isley.

OCONTO—
Oliver St. Peter.

RIPON—
Henry Lambert.
Job Stallird.
Gus Tobolt.

SHAWANO—
Aug. Kruger.
Fred Kruger.
Chas. Petatz.
Wm. Regling.

SHELL LAKE—
D. Chambenan.
W. Dewett.

SPARTA—
C. Muhlenbech.
Richard Peter.

WAUSAU—
G. W. Clark.
August Klosterman.

WAUPUN—
Thos. Green.

WASHBURN—
Nels. Odegaard.
N. Palen.
O. Sincraon.

WYOMING.

NEW CASTLE—
Will Holden.

CANADA.

AMHERST, N. S.—
J. N. Fage.

AYLMER, ONT.—
Geo. Collins.
Thomas Wooster.

BARRIE, ONT.—
Edward Brown
J. Stapleton.
Chas. Swinnerton.

BRANDON, MAN.—
Alex Allen.
Hurst Bros.
M. McKenzie.
A. J. Shether.

CAMPBELLFORD, ONT.—
John Chase.
Geo. Elphick.
John Lane.
S. Stephens.

CHARLOTTETOWN. P. E. I.—
Phillip P. Coyle.
Richard Duffey.
Jno. Goneulcey.

FORT WILLIAM, ONT.—
A. Cameron.
Geo. Pappin.

GODERICH, ONT.—
Chas. Reid.
Walter Sharman.

GUELPH, ONT.—
W. F. Colwill.
Wm. Day.
J. J. Mahoney.
W. T. Tanner.

MILTON, ONT—
M. Leonard.
A. McLellan.
T. McDowell.
R. McJannett.

MONTREAL, QUE.—
Robt. Forsyth, 2496 St. Catherine St., 546-570 William St.

MOUNT FOREST, ONT.—
Jas. Reid.

PICTON, ONT.—
John Dunlop.
Patrick Lynch.
William Shaw, Sr.

ST. ANDREWS, N. B.—
Chas. Horsnell.
T. McCarthy

SHERBROOKE, QUE.—
J. Gunning.

SIMCOE, ONT.—
The Sylica Barytic Stone Co.
Harry Weston.

TORONTO, ONT.—
A. Gardner & Co., 17 Toronto Arcade.
Harvard Contracting Co., Victoria St.
W. R. Payne, 8-10 Givens St.

VALLEYFIELD, QUE.—
Zipher Demers.
Etienne Tindel.

ANY QUESTION RELATING TO CEMENT
WILL BE ANSWERED ON REQUEST. IT IS A PART OF OUR BUSINESS TO KNOW ALL ABOUT CEMENT
MUNICIPAL ENGINEERING CO.

CEMENT TESTS AND ANALYSES.

LABORATORIES AND ENGINEERS MAKING ANALYSES TESTS OF CEMENT AND CEMENT MATERIALS—ENGINEERS WHO DESIGN CEMENT PLANTS.

POLYTECHNIC INSTI- ıburn, Ala., B. B. Rose, nist.

ıY CITY, PA., Municipal ʏ.

TOPEKA & SANTA FE ɪeka, Kas., Tests

GA., Municipal Labora-

E & OHIO SOUTH- ɴ RY., Maintenance of ., Cincinnati, O. Tests.

Iilwaukee, Wis., Chemist.

.ER, 1 Nassau St., New ıts.

ıARRETT & BLAIR, cust St., Philadelphia, H. Garrett, Andrew A. o. B. Garrett, J. Ed- hitfield, Frederick H. Analyses and Tests. nd Superintendence of ion of Cement Plants.

ASS., Metropolitan Water unicipal Laboratory.

'ESTING LABORATOR- ʼrt A. Sanorus, Mgr., 6 .t. Asa W. Whitney, 1017 , Philadelphia, Pa. Tests.

'ON, IOWA, Emmett . Engr. Municipal Labora-

)NT. Municipal Labora-

PENTER, Cornell Univ., Y., Designer of Cement

ʟ. CARY, 95 Liberty St., . Analyses and Tests. De- Cement Plants.

VILLER, Allentown, Pa.

& M'KENZIE, 1224-8 **ldg., Chicago,** Ill. Tests.

ɒ, Colton, Calif. Analyses **ɑms** for cement

HENRY FROEHLING, 17 S. 12th St., Richmond, Va. Tests.

G. FROSTENSEN, Yankton, S. D. Chemist.

ERNEST HANTKE, 646 Broadway, New York, N. Y. Chemist.

ROBT. W. HUNT & CO., 1121 Rookery Bldg., Chicago Ill. 71 Broadway, N. Y. Monongahela Bank Bldg., Pittsburg, Pa. Tests.

A. HUGO CEDERBERG, Catasauqua, Pa. Designer Cement Plants.

CHATTANOOGA, TENN., Robert Hooke, Cy. Engr. Municipal Laboratory.

CHICAGO, ILL., Board of Public Works. P. C. McArdle, Engineer in Charge of Tests. Street Department. H. L. Bailey, Cement Tester, Chicago Avenue Water Works, Municipal Laboratories.

CHICAGO & ALTON RAILWAY CO. H. F. Baldwin, Chief Engr., Chicago, Ill. Tests.

CHICAGO, ROCK ISLAND & PACIFIC RY. W. E. Dauchy, Chf. Engr., Chicago, Ill. Tests.

CORNELL UNIVERSITY, Ithaca, N. Y. Analyses and tests.

CORTLAND, N. Y. Municipal Laboratory.

W. M. COURTIS, 412 Hammond Bldg., Detroit, Mich. Aanlyses and Tests. Reports on Cement Properties.

DETROIT, MICH. Municipal Laboratory.

LATHBURY & SPACKMAN, 1619 Filbert St, Philadelphia, Pa. B. Bretnall Lathbury, Henry S. Spackman. Analyses and Tests. Design and Construction of Cement Plants.

LAFAYETTE COLLEGE, Easton, Pa. Dept. of Civil Engineering. Analyses and Tests.

LEDOUX & CO., 99 John St., New York. Chemists.

F. H. LEWIS, Craigsville, Va. Design and Construction of Cement Plants.

LOS ANGELES, Calif. Municipal Laboratory.

W. H. LUSTER, Elizabeth, N. J. Tests.

ILLINOIS CENTRAL R. R. H. W. Parkhurst, Engr. of Bridges & Bldgs., Chicago, Ill. Tests.

UNIVERSITY OF ILLINOIS, Urbana, Ill. I. O. Baker, Prof. Civ. Eng. Analyses and Tests.

IOWA ENGINEERING CO., Clinton, Ia. Chas. P. Chase, Mgr. Tests.

STATE UNIVERSITY OF IOWA, Iowa City, Ia. A. V. Sims, Prof. Civ. Eng. Tests.

INDIANAPOLIS, IND. B. J. T. Jeup, Cy. Engr. Municipal Laboratory.

JOSLIN, SCHMIDT & CO., Cincinnati, O. Design of Manufacturing Plants.

L. E. KENNEDY & CO., Room 50, 61 Broadway, New York. Tests and Design of Works.

KEWANEE, ILL., J. E. Shepardson, Cy. Engr. Municipal Laboratory.

WALTER G. KIRKPATRICK, C. E. Jackson, Miss. Tests.

MASSACHUSETTS INSTITUTE OF TECHNOLOGY, Boston, Mass. Anaylses and Tests.

M'GILL UNIVERSITY, Montreal, Can. Tests.

CHAS. F. M'KENNA, 231 Pearl St., New York. Analyses and Tests.

MINNEAPOLIS, MINN., G. W. Sublette, Cy. Engr. Municipal Laboratory.

F. A. MOORE, Vincennes, Ind. Chemist.

MUNCIE, IND., W. H. Wood, Cy. Engr. Municipal Laboratary.

NEW CASTLE, PA., Municipal Laboratory.

NEW YORK CITY. Croton Aqueduct Commission. Tests.

NEW YORK CITY. Department of Docks. J. A. Bensel, Engr. in Chief. Chandler Davis, Asst. Engr., in charge of Tests. Tests.

NEW YORK STATE ENGINEER AND SURVEYOR, Cement Testing Department. Russell S. Greenman, Engineer in Charge, Albany, N. Y. Tests.

NEW YORK TESTING LABORATORY, Long Island City, N. Y. Clifford Richardson, Dir. Analyses and Tests.

OHIO STATE UNIVERSIT[Y, Colum]bus, O. Prof. C. N. Brow[n, in] Charge of Cement Te[sts.] Tests.

OIL CITY, PA., G. F. Roes[...] Engr. Municipal Labor[atory.]

OMAHA, NEB., Andrew [Rose]water, Engr. Municipal [Lab]oratory.

THE OSBORN CO., Osborne [Bldg.,] Cleveland, O. A. W. Carpen[ter in] Charge of Cement Te[sts.] Analyses and Tests. W. [...]gardus and C. F. Lake, [...]ant Engineers. Design [and] Construction of Cement P[lants.]

OTTAWA, ONT., Can. Mu[nicipal] Laboratory.

OWENSBORO, KY., B. B. Sh[...] Cy. Engr. Municipal La[bora]tory.

JAS. J. PEARSON, 49 Wall-st[., New] York, N. Y. Tests.

PEORIA, ILL. H. E. Beasl[ey,] Engr. Municipal Laboratory.

PHILADELPHIA, PA. Wm Haddock, Director Dept. Works. Geo. S. Webster, Chf. Bureau of Surveys. W. [...] Taylor, Engr. in charge of t[he] laboratory. Municipal Labor[atory.] Filtration Testing Plant. Ch[...] Clifton, Engr. in Charge.

PHILADELPHIA & REA[DING] RAILWAY CO. Robert [...] Chemist. E. Chamberlain, [...] Engr. Analyses and Tests.

PITTSBURG, PA. John Bru[...] Cy. Engr. Municipal La[bora]tory.

POPE CEMENT & BRICK CO, [...] Wood St., Pittsburg, Pa. T[...]

PURDUE UNIVERSITY, L[afay]ette, Ind. W. F. M. Goss, [...] Mech. Eng. W. K. Hatt, in c[harge] of cement testing.

RANSOME & SMITH, Broo[klyn,] N. Y., Chicago, Ill. Tests.

READING, PA., Alex. Murdoc[h, Cy.] Engr. Municipal Laboratory.

ST. LOUIS, MO., Edward Flad[, Wa]ter Commissioner. A. N. M[...] Sewer Commissioner. Mun[icipal] Laboratories.

SALT LAKE CITY, UTAH. M[unici]pal Laboratory.

SCHOOL OF PRACTICAL [SCI]ENCE, Toronto, Ont. Tests.

F. L. SMIDTH & CO., 66 M[aiden] Lane, N. Y. Copenhagen. [...]ergade 20 K. Design and [Con]struction of Cement Plant[s.]

H. Q. SMITH, McKinney. [...] Chemist.

WM. SOOY SMITH & CO., 72[...] Exchange Bldg., Chicago, Ill.

HENRY SOUTHER, Har[tford,] Conn. Tests.

IERN RAILWAY CO., J. C. ıge, Supt. of Tests, Alexan- Va.

GFIELD, MASS. Municipal ratory.

E HAUTE, IND., Ralph H. ks, Cy. Engr. Municipal Labor- .

KA, KAN., P. L. Wise. Cy. . Municipal Laboratory. An- s and Tests.

NTO, ONT., CAN. Municipal ratory.

NE UNIVERSITY, New Or- , La. Prof. W. H. P. Creigh- in charge of cement testing.

COLLEGE, Schenectady, N. . H. Landreth, Prof. Civ. Analyses and Tests.

KLIN VAN WINKLE, 39 ıdt St., New York. 297 Broad- Paterson, N. J. Tests.

RSITY OF VERMONT, Burton, Vt. Engineering Laboratory. J. W. Votey, Prof. Civ. r. Analyses and Tests.

WABASH, IND. Robert P. Woods, Cy. Engr. Municipal Laboratory.

J. A. L. WADDELL, Kansas City, Mo. Tests.

WASHINGTON, D. C. Office of Engineer Comr. District of Columbia. A. W. Dow, Inspector of Asphalt and Cements.

WASHINGTON UNIVERSITY, St. Louis, Mo. J. L. Van Ornum, Prof. Civ. Eng. Analyses and Tests.

ROBERT E. WENTZ, Nazareth, Pa. Design and construction of cement plants.

WILLIAMSPORT, PA. Municipal Laboratory.

WILLIAM J. WILSON, 335 5th Ave., Pittsburg, Pa. Tests.

UNIVERSITY OF WISCONSIN, Madison, Wis. J. B. Johnson, Dean of School of Engineering. Analyses and Tests.

WORCESTER, MASS. Municipal Laboratory.

YOUNGSTOWN, O. Municipal Laboratory.

MACHINERY AND TOOLS FOR CEMENT USERS.

AGITATORS.

American Clay Working Machinery Co., Bucyrus, O.
The Aultman Co., Canton, O.
The Bonnot Co., Canton, O.

AIR COMPRESSORS.

SAN FRANCISCO, CAL.—
Fulton Engineering & Ship-Building Works, Harbor View & 15th.
Parke & Lacy Co., 21 Fremont St.
Rix Engineering & Supply Co., 519 Howard St.
The Compressed Air Machinery Co., 11 First.

SOUTH NORWALK, CONN.—
The Norwalk Iron Works Co.

DENVER, COL.—
Edward P. Allis Co., 1649 Tremont St.
W. H. Emanuel, 1711 Tremont St.
Hendrie & Bolthoff Mfg. & Supply Co., 1601 17th St.
Ingersoll-Sargeant Drill Co., 1718 California St.
J. George Leyner, 729 17th St.
Sullivan Machinery Co., 332 17th St.

CHICAGO, ILL.—
Edward P. Allis Co., 509 Home Ins. Bldg.
N. C. Bullock Mfg. Co., 1170 W. Lake.
Chicago Pneumatic Tool Co., 635 Monadnock Blk.
Clayton Air Compressor Works, Havemeyer Bldg., New York.
Fanning Mfg. Co., 153-155 W. Jackson Boul.
Fraser & Chalmers, Cor. 12th and Washtenaw.
Ingersoll-Sergeant Drill Co., 1510 Old Colony Bldg.
M. O. Kasson & Co., 702-279 Dearborn.
Rand Drill Co., 1328 Monadnock Blk.
Scully Steel & Iron Co., 130-156 Fulton.
Sullivan Machinery Co., 56 N. Clinton.
Weir & Craig Mfg. Co., 2421-2439 Wallace.
Geo. D. Whitcomb Co., 86 E Ohio.

BOSTON, MASS.—
Ingersoll-Sergeant Drill Co., 77 Ol
Stilwell-Bierce & Smith-Vaile 51 Oliver.

FITCHBURG, MASS.—
Burleigh Rock Drill Co.

BATTLE CREEK, MICH.—
American Steam Pump Co.

DETROIT, MICH.—
Fairbanks, Morse & Co., 103 Je son Ave.

ST. LOUIS, MO.—
Curtis & Co. Mfg. Co., 2201-2211 W Ave.
The Ingersoll-Seargeant Drill Co. Fullerton Bldg.
Norwalk Air Compressor, 511 Se ty Bldg.
D. W. Pratt, 211-213 Lucas Ave.
Rand Drill Co., 1311 Chemical
St. Louis Steam Engine Co., Commercial.
Sidney H. Wheelhouse, 412, 413 Lincoln Trust Bldg.

CLAREMONT, N. H.—
Sullivan Machinery Co.

MONTOUR FALLS, N. Y.—
Havana Bridge Works.

NEWBURG, N. Y.—
Newburg Ice Machine and En Co.

NEW YORK CITY. BOROUC MANHATTAN AND BRONX—
Clayton Air Compressor Work Cortland St.
The Frasse Co., 38 Cortland St.
McKiernan Drill Co., 120 Lit St.
Rand Drill Co., 100 Broadway.

TROY, N. Y.—
M. C. Hammett.

CINCINNATI, O.—
Laidlaw-Dunn & Gordon Co.
Lane & Bodley Co.
MacLeod & Clark, 457 E. Front

CLEVELAND, O.—
Cleveland Pump and Fixture Co Frankfort.

DAYTON, O.—
Stilwell-Bierce & Smith-Vaile C

ENY, PA.—
·am Pump Co.
CK, PA.—
k Machine & Mfg. Co.
ELPHIA, PA.—
Exhibition, 4th and 5th Sts., hestnut and Market.
Pumping Engine Co., 941 Bldg.
Tool Mfg. Co., 11th, cor.

ir Brake Co., 901 Harrison

-Dunn-Gordon Co., 724 Arch

Bierce & Smith-Vaile Co., h St.
RG, PA.—
Steam Pump Co., The, 317 3d

am Pump Co., Grant Ave. N, Ave., A.
Kirk & Son Co., 910 Duquesne

-Dunn-Gordon Co., 317 3d Ave.
eam Pump Works, 317 3d Ave.
R. Worthington, 317 3d Ave.
RBON, Pa.—
Iron Works.
ON, Pa.—
Mfg. Co.
BARRE, PA.—
Iron Works.
N, TEX.—
l-Sergeant Drill Co., Kiam

KEE, WIS.—
lis & Co.
g Mfg. Co.

HANDLING MACHINERY.

e & Marmon Co., Indian-, Ind.
Pulley Co, Columbus, Ind.
& Elliott, Wilmington, Del.

BALL MILLS.

rtlett & Co., 43-45 Center eveland, O.
hem Foundry & Machine o. Bethlehem, Pa.
nnot Company, Canton, O.
& Chalmers, W. 12th St. & enaw Ave., Chicago, Ill.
ron Works, Elston Ave. & ingdale Road, Chicago, Ill.
Krupp. (Thos. Prosser & 15 Gold St., N. Y.
midth & Co., 66 Maiden N. Y.

BALLS, STEEL.

Brecker & Co., 95 Reade St, York.
Cleveland Ball & Screw Co., The Arcade, Cleveland, O.
Grant Ball Co., 68 Clarkwood Ave, Cleveland, O.
Hathorn Mfg. Co., Bangor, Me
Krupp (Thos. Prosser & Son) 15 Gold St. New York.
Simonds Rolling Machine Co., Fitchburg, Mass.
Steel Ball Co., 840 Austin Ave., Chicago, Ill.

BARREL MACHINERY.

Defiance Machine Works, Defiance, O.
J. L. Dix Foundry Co., Glens Falls, N. Y.
M Garland Co., Bay City, Mich.
Peter Gerlach & Co., Cleveland, O.
E. B. Holmes Machinery Co., 59 Chicago, St., Buffalo, N. Y.
Merritt Mfg. Co., Lockport, N. Y.
Rochester Barrel Machy. Co., Rochester, N. Y.
Wickes Bros., Saginaw, Mich.

BEARINGS.

C. O. Bartlett & Co., 43-45 Center St., Cleveland, O.
The Bonnot Co., Canton, O.
Fraser & Chalmers, W. 12th and Washtenaw Ave., Chicago, Ill.
Hill Clutch Co., Cleveland, O.
Nordyke & Marmon, Indianapolis, Ind.
Reeves Pulley Co., Columbus, Ind.
Robins Conveying Belt Co., 13-21 Park Row, N. Y.
Walker & Elliott, Wilmington, Del.
Webster Mfg. Co., 1075-1097 W. 15th St., Chicago, Ill.

BELTING.

SAN FRANCISCO, CAL.—
F. R. Cork Co., Oakwood and 18th St.
H. N. Cook Belting Co., 317 Mission St.
Crane Co., 23 First St.
L. P. Degen, 105 Mission St.
Jno. D. Eby, 17 Main St.
Gorham Rubber Co., 308 Mission St.
Gutta Percha and Rubber Co., The, 30 Fremont St.
Alexander Heins, 134 Main St
Henshaw, Bulkley & Co., Fremont and Mission Sts.
D. J. Kelly, Oakwood and 18th Sts.
M. O'Brien, 509 Mission St.
Pacific Tool and Supply Co., 100 First St.
Parke & Lacy Co., 21 Fremont St.
Revere Rubber Co., 527 Market St.

DENVER, COL.—
Fairbanks, Morse & Co., 1600 17th St.
The Link Belt Machinery Co., 1328 17th St.
Mine and Smelter Supply Co., 17th St., cor. Blake.

WATERBURY, CONN.—
Novelty Mfg. Co., 121 Maple St.
The Bristol Co., Naugatuck rd. nr. Platt's Bridge.

CHICAGO, ILLS.—
W. D. Allen Mfg. Co., 151 Lake.
H. W. Caldwell & Son Co., Western Ave. & 17th St.
Chicago Belting Co.
The Diamond Rubber Co., 938-939 Marquette Bldg.
The B. F. Goodrich Co., 141 Lake.
Fraser & Chalmers, 12th & Washtenaw Ave.
The Link Belt Machinery Co., 39th St. and Stewart Ave. Edward A. Turner, Pres.; Staunton B. Peck, V.-P. and Chief Engr.; Dyke Williams, Sec. & Treas.; H. K. McLean, Gen. Supt.
Thomsas Belting Co., 46-48 S. Clinton.
Webster Mfg. Co., 1075 W. 15th St.

EAST ST. LOUIS, ILL.—
Capen Belting & Rubber Co., 104 N. 3d St.
Crescent Belting Co., 1119 N. 6th St.
Harry C. Spring Supply Co., 318 N. 2d St.

PEORIA, ILL.—
Hagerty, Graber & Co., 915 S. Washington.
Charles Johnson, 2023 S. Adams.
F. Meyer & Bro. Co., 1313 S. Adams.
Peoria Belting Co., 717 S. Adams.
H. G. Rouse & Co., 318 S. Adams.

COLUMBUS, IND.—
Reeves Pulley Co.

EVANSVILLE, IND.—
C. H. Ellert, 104 Main.
Evansville Leather & Belting, 509 Main.

INDIANAPOLIS, IND.—
E. C. Atkins & Co., 402-410 S. Ills.
W. B Barry Saw & Supply Co., 228-230 S. Penn.
Central Rubber & Supply Co., 229 S. Meridian
Duckwall Rubber & Supply Co., 123 W. Maryland.
Hide, Leather & Belting Co., 227 S. Meridian.
Indpls. Belting & Supply Co., 131 S. Illinois.
Miller Oil & Supply Co., 31-35 McNabb
Nordyke & Marmon Co., W. Morris and I. & V. R. R.
Taylor & Smith, 247 S. Meridian.

MUNCIE, IND.—
Geo. Keiser & Co., 115-117 S. High
Powers & Foorman, 511 S. Walnut
Robert Scott, 304 S. Walnut St.

MARSHALLTOWN, IA.—
A. E. Shorthill Co., 2d Ave., S. Cor. Linn.

LOUISVILLE, KY.—
Ahrends & Ott Mfg. Co., 325 Main.
W. B. Belknap & Co., 111 W. Ma
W. E. Caldwell Co., Brandeis A S. E. C. Brook.
Andrew Cowan & Co., 435 W. M
Kentucky Saw Works, 925 W. M
W. H. Neill, 507 W. Main.

NEW ORLEANS, LA.—
Chicago Belting Co., 406 Caron St.
Gibbens & Stream, 213 Canal St.
New Orleans Railway & Mill Su Co., 620 Camp St.
Revere Rubber Co., 412 Caron St.
Whitney & Sloo Co., 108 N. Peter
Woodward, Wight & Co., 406 C St.

BOSTON, MASS.—
American Leather Link Belt Co. High.
H. K. Barnes, 104 Franklin.
F. G. Barry & Co., 5 Olive Pl.
Bay State Belting Co., 119 Fran
Boston Belting Co., 256-260 De shire.
Boston Woven Hose and Rubber 170 Summer.
Carton Belting Co., 64 Federal, 13.
Chicago Raw Hide Mfg. Co., Franklin.
Choate & Brown, 134 Congress.
Fayerweather & Ladew, 228 Fran
James Foley & Co., 578-581 Atl Ave.
G. A. Gilman, 143 Federal.
Globe Leather Belting Co., 132 P
Albert Griffiths Saw Co., 40 Olive
Gutta Percha and Rubber Mfg. 71 Pearl.
Henry C. Hunt Co., 32 Oliver.
C. L. Ireson, 97 High.
Kidder Supply Co., 29 Pearl.
Leviathan Belting Co., 120 Pearl.
Main Belting Co., 120 Pearl.
Geo. T. McLaughlin Co., 120 Fu
Page Belting Co., 31 Pearl.
Revere Rubber Co., 63 Franklin.
Jas. H. Roberts & Co., 137 Portl
Chas. A. Schieren & Co., 119 Hig
Schultz Belting Co., 184 Summer
Spadone Bros. Mfg. Co., 71 Pear
Star Belting Co., 31 Pearl.

CAMBRIDGE, MASS.—
Sawyer Belting Co., 20 Thorndik

ELD, MASS.—
& Tucker, 44 West St.
. Foote & Co., 82 West St.
Irchner, 156 North St.
MASS.—
Belting Co., 19 Baxter St.
T, MICH.—
alleable Co., Cor. Wight & St.
Oak Belting Co., 11 Atwater
.
Oak Belting Co., 262 Wight

rey's Sons Mfg. Co., Cor. 1st odbridge St., W.
Walker & Son, 129 Larned St.
Vormer Machinery Co., 55 bridge St., W.
ing & Co., 15 Woodward Ave.
POLIS, MINN.—
ik Belt Supply Co.
kes & Co., 915 Washn. Ave. S
L, MINN.—
ane & Ordway Co., 248 E.

ir Rubber Co., 375 Sibley St.
CITY, MO.—
Byrnes Belting and Hose Co., nion Ave.
Chase Mercantile Co., 1408 W. t.
iks, Morse & Co., 1217 Union

Western Mfg. Co., 1221 Union

Supply Co., 1205 Union Ave.
.s & Conover Hardware Co., 5th St.
IS, MO.—
d Belting Co., 320 N. 2d St.
W. Byrnes Belting & Hose 2 Wash. Ave.
Belting Co., 214 N 2d St.
. Belting Co., 1121 N. 6th St.
bber Co., 415 N. 4th St.
man Hide & Leather Co., 1905 ndoah.
i Belting Co., 120 S. Commer-

h Rubber Co., 1009-1011 Wash.

d Supply Co., 200-202 N. 2d.
ork Belting & P. Co., Ltd., 411

Rumsey Mfg. Co., 806-820 N.

Belting Co., 402 Barton.
C. Spring Suppply Co., 318-322
.
sen Belting Co., 205-217 Destre-

tD, N. H.—
. Eastman & Co., Eastman
. Concord.

Foote, Brown & Co., 2 Main St., Penacook.
Humphrey Dodge Co., 102 No. Main.
Thompson & Hoague, 42 No. Main.
Page Belting Co., E. Penacook St.

MANCHESTER, N. H.—
Alfred K. Hobbs, 1064 Elm.
Manchester Hardware Co., 938 Elm.
John B. Varick Co., 809 Elm.

NASHUA, N. H.—
James Barnard, 70 Main St.

NEWARK, N. J.—
Banister & Pollard, 206 Market St.
E. C. Faitoute 97 Market St.
R. Gray, Jr., 190 Market St.
Macknet & Doremus, 796-798 Broad St.
Joseph Meier's Sons, 291 Market St.
Newark Leather Belting Co., 291 Market St.
Roe & Conover, 200 Market St.
Rosendale-Reddaway Belting & Hose Co., Euclid Ave.
C. W. Walker, 274 Market St.

PATERSON, N. J.—
C. C. Van Houten & Co., 37 Van Houten.
Van Riper Mfg. Co., 14 Van Houten.

ALBANY, N. Y.—
Albany Belting & Supply Co., 372 Broadway.
Wheeler & Wilson Mfg. Co., 28 N. Pearl St.

BUFFALO, N. Y.—
Bickford & Francis Belting Co., 53 Exchange.
Boston Belting Co., 90 Pearl.
Buffalo Belting Wks., 122 Washn.
Buffalo Mill Supply Co., 240 Main.
W. A. Case & Son., 31 Main.
Fairbanks Co., 210 Main.
Timothy Gingras, 59 Terrace.
Goodyear Rubber Co., 48 Exchange.
Graton & Knight Mfg. Co., 292 Main.
R. Hoffeld & Co., 63 Carroll.
F. C. Howlett & Co., 94 Pearl.
Leech, Hall & Kemp, 252 Main.
C. H. McCutcheon, 18 Ohio.
F. H. C. Mey, 64 Columbia.
Peerless Belting Co., 59 Terrace
Plumbers' and Steam Ftrs' Supply Co., 112 Exchange.
Revere Rubber Co., 94 Pearl.
Walbridge & Co., 392 Main.
Weed & Co., 292 Main.

COHOES, N. Y.—
Sweet & Doyle, 75 Mohawk St.

NEW YORK CITY, BOROUGH OF BROOKLYN—
John Walker & Son, 310 Furman St.

NEW YORK CITY, BOROUGH OF MANHATTAN AND BRONX—
Stephen Ballard Rubber Co., 123 Chambers St.
E. H. Behringer, 74 Warren St.

Boston Belting Co., 100 Reade St.
Randolph Brandt, 38 Cortlandt St.
Allan Carpenter, 103 N. Moore St.
Crescent Belting & Packing Co., 253 Broadway.
Diamond Rubber Co., 127 Duane St.
Fayerweather & Ladew, 159 E. Houston St.
M. J. Fitzgerald, 58 Center St.
The Frasse Co., 38 Cortlandt St.
Graton & Knight Mfg. Co., 112 Liberty St.
Gutta Percha & Rubber Mfg. Co., 128 Duane St.
A. B. Laurence, 113 Liberty St.
The Link Belt Engineering Co.
Leonard & McCoy, 118 Liberty St.
D. Maavatty, Jr., & Co., 69 Center St.
Mineralized Rubber Co., 18 Cliff St.
Montclair Rubber Co., 123 Chambers St.
New Jersey Foundry & Machine Co., 26 Cortlandt St.
New York Foundry & Machine Co., 84 Reade St.
George Rahmann & Co., 31 Ferry St.
Robins Conveying Belt Co., 17 Park Row.

ROCHESTER, N. Y.—
Mathews & Boucher, 26 Exchange.
Cross Bros. & Co., 114 Mill.
Machinists' Supply Co., 301 State.

SYRACUSE, N. Y.—
Frank C. Howlett, 212 S. Clinton St.
Syracuse Supply Co., ltd., 238 W. Fayette St.

AKRON, O.—
The Akron Belting Co., 206-208 S. Canal St.

CINCINNATI, OHIO—
The Am. Oak Leather Co., Kenner & Dalton Ave.
Thos. J. Bell & Co., 320 Main.
The Boebinger H'ware Co., 315 E. Pearl.
The Bradford Belting Co., [illegible] & 2d.
The A. C. Cattell Co., 604 Vine.
Cleveland Rubber Works, 612 [illegible]
Crawley & Johnston, 520 Main.
Gilbert Belting Co., 77 Elm.
Hubbard, Hall & Co., 105 E. [illegible]
The E. A. Kinsey Co., 331 W. [illegible]
J. H. Kohmescher & Co., 120 E. [illegible]
The John H. McGowan Co., 54 [illegible] tral Ave.
Machinists' Supply Co., 320 [illegible]
N. Y. Belting & Packing Co. [illegible] Y., 134 W. 2d.
Page Belting Co. of Concord, N. [illegible] 134 W. 2d.
Queen City Supply Co., Pearl & [illegible]
Revere Rubber Co., 522 Main.
Jos. Sharp Belting & Supply Co. [illegible] E. Front.
Walter M. Thompson, 835 W. 5th.
Julius Uihlein & Co., 134 W. 2d.
Wirthlin Bros., 208 W. 7th.

CLEVELAND, O.—
C. O. Bartlett & Co., 43-45 [illegible] ter St.
Cleveland Belting, Repair & [illegible] Co., 12 Long.
Manhattan Rubber Mfg. Co., Champlin.
McIntosh Huntington Co., 118 [illegible]perior.
Ohio Rubber Co., 206 Superior.
Bodifield Belting Co., 24 S. Wat[illegible]
Cleveland Oil Extraction Work[illegible] Jennings Ave.
E. B. Davidson & Co., 102 Supe[illegible]
N. Y. Leather Belting Co., Champlain.
Strong, Carlisle & Hammond C[illegible] Frankfort.
R. A. Williams & Co., 55 S. Wat[illegible]

COLUMBUS, O.—
Andrews, Knight & Barnes, 45 Broad St.
Capital City Machine Wks., 12[illegible] Spring St.

ALL ABOUT CEMENT UP-TO-DATE AND ALL THE TIM[illegible]

The best way to keep informed about everything relating to Cement the year round is to read

MUNICIPAL ENGINEERING MAGAZINE

The publication which stands foremost in representation of Cement interests.

Subscription price, $2.00 per year.

Address MUNICIPAL ENGINEERING C[illegible]

ıs Supply Co., 161 N. High St.
:rey Mfg. Co.
Miller Co., 31 W. Broad St.
FIELD, O.—
retney & Co., 114 E. Main.
OHIO—
E. Dale & Co., 136 Water St.
ırdware Co., 710 Monroe St.
Rubber Co., The, 418 Summit

'ilcox Co., The, 210 Water St.
', PA.—
Waldron & Co.
ıem Foundry and Machine
. Bethlehem, Pa.
ELPHIA, PA.—
er Bros., 410-412 N. 3rd.
.rny & Son, 228 N. 3rd.
E. Bell, 201 Church.
Billington, 113 Chestnut.
ond, 520 Arch.
Belting Co., 14 N. 4th.
& Martin, 112 S. 2d.
3oyd & Bro., 14 N. 4th.
Mfg. Co., 146 N. 2nd.
elt Co., 15 N. 9th.
Etsweiler, 230 N. 3rd.
aks Co., 701 Arch.
urner & Co., 1433 Fairmount

elt Co., 1023 Filbert St.
& Knight Mfg. Co., 132 N

Hill, 15 N. 9th.
ein & Bailey, 25 N. Front St
oughton & Co., 24? W. Som.

Hopkins & Perkins Co. [illegible]
ıut.
Mulconroy, 1?7 Market [illegible]
:hs & Son, 7? [illegible]
:lt Engineering Co. [illegible]
Ave., N. P. & R. R. N. [illegible]
:lting Co. [illegible]

Malleable Iron [illegible]

C. Paulus & [illegible]

[illegible]

Hartley-Rose Belting Co., 634 Smithfield St.
Logan-Gregg Hardware Co., 12a 4th St.
Charles Munson Belting Co., 904 Smithfield St.
J. & H. Phillips, 138 6th St.
Pittsburgh Gage & Supply Co., 319 Water St.
Revere Rubber Co., 2 Wood St.
Charles A. Schieren & Co., 240 3rd Ave.
Scully Belting & Supply Co., 301 Wood St.
Somers, Fitler & Clarke, Ltd., 327 Water St.
Speck, Marshall & Co., 110 Wood St.
Standard Scale & Supply Co., Ltd., 211 Wood St.
Charles A. Turner, 14 Market St.
SCRANTON, PA.
C. F. Beckwith & Co., 7 Dime Bank Bldg.
W. P. Connell & Sons, 118 Penn Ave.
Kingsbury & Scranton, 310 Paull Bldg.
Scranton Supply & Machinery Co., 131 Wyoming Ave.
SOUTH BETHLEHEM, PA.
Bethlehem Foundry & Machine Co.
CENTRAL FALLS, R. I.
Weatherhead Thompson & Co., 447 Mill St.
SPARTANBURG, S. C.
[illegible]
[illegible]
HOUSTON, TEX.
[illegible]

[illegible]

E. P. Allis Co., Milwaukee, Wis.
American Blower Co., Detroit, Mich., Chicago, Ill, New York,
Andrews & Johnson Co., 256-60 Washington Blk, Chicago, Ill.
Bachus Mfg., Co., 174 Penn St., Newark, N. J.
A. W. Banister, 35 Wareham, Boston, Mass.
Bethlehem Foundry & Mach. Co., So. Bethlehem, Pa.
The Bonnot Co., Canton, O.
Boston Blower Co., Hyde Park, Mass.
Buffalo Forge Co., 22-24 Randolph, Chicago, Ill.
J. B. & J. M. Cornell, 26th & 11th Ave., New York.
F. M. Crane, 179 Market St., Newark, N. J.
Dodge, Haley & Co., 218 High, Boston, Mass.
Exeter Machine Works, 32 Oliver, Boston, Mass.
Eymon-Evans Mfg. Co., 42 Oliver, Boston, Mass
Fraser & Chalmers, W 12th & Washtenaw Ave., Chicago, Ill.
Marietta Fan Co., Marietta, Pa.
Massachusetts Fan Co., 53 State St., Boston, Mass.
National Blower Works, 17th & St. Paul Ave., Milwaukee, Wis.
New York Blower Co., Bucyrus, O., 39 Cortlandt St., New York.
Nordyke & Marmon Co., Indianapolis, Ind.
P. H. & F. M. Roots Co., Connersville, Ind., 109 Liberty St., New York.
L. M. Rumsey Mfg. Co., St. Louis, Mo.
St. Louis Blower and Heater Co., 1628-1630 N. 9th St., St. Louis, Mo.
Seymour & Whitlock, 43 Lawrence, Newark, N. J.
Sommer Electrical Co., 251 Market St., Newark, N. J.
B. F. Sturtevant Co., Jamaica Plain Station, Boston, Mass.
Wm Tod & Co., Youngstown, O.
Walworth Construction and Supply Co., 100 Pearl, Boston, Mass.
Wilbraham-Baker Blower Co., 2526 Frankford Ave., Philadelphia, Pa.
Young Bros., 320 Atwater St., E. Detroit, Mich.

BOILERS.

BIRMINGHAM, ALA.—
W. M. Crellin.
Linn Iron Works.
Means & Fulton Iron Works.
Williamson Iron Works.
LITTLE ROCK, ARK.—
D. R. Wing & Co.
LOS ANGELES, CAL.——
Baker Iron Works.
Fulton Engine Works.
Llewellyn Iron Works.
Thomson & Boyle.
Union Iron Works.
SAN FRANCISCO, CAL.—
Babcock & Wilcox Co., 32 First
Baker & Hamilton, Pine & Dav
John Burke, 139 Beale St.
McIntosh & Wolpmann, 195 Fren St.
C. C. Moore & Co., 32 First St.
Novelty Iron Co., Crocker Bldg.
Pacific Coast Boiler Works, 235 I St.
Pacific Coast Machinery Co., 12 mont St.
Risdon Iron & Locomotive Wc Howard & Beale Sts.
Springfield Boiler & Mfg. Co., First St.
The Tracy Engineering Co., 151 mont St.
Union Iron Works, 222 Market S
H. S. White, 516 Mission St.
G. G. Wickson & Co., 34 Main
DENVER, COL.—
Ball Engine Co., 622 Mining Bldg.
C. S. Burt, 4 Bank Blk.
F. M. Davis Iron Works Co., I mer, cor. 8th St.
Denver Boiler & Sheet Iron W Co., N. W. cor. Wazee & 35th S
Denver Engineering Works, B cor. 30th St.
Doty & De Lange, 1434 Blake St
Jeffrey Mfg. Co., Equitable Bldg
Root Improved Water Tube Bo 1711 Tremont St.
Star Boiler & Sheet Iron Works 15th St.
Stirling Water Tube Safety Boil Bank Blk.
Weigele Pipe Works, 2949 Larime
West Denver Boiler Works, 438 mer St.
John Young, 2245 Blake St.
NEW LONDON, CONN.—
Thomas Drummond, 231 Bank.
The Morgan Iron Works, Fort N
WATERBURY, CONN.—
Randolph-Clowes Co., 384 Bank.
WILMINGTON, DEL.—
Adams & Johnson.
Harlan & Hollingsworth Co.
Hilles & Jones Co.
Pusey & Jones Co.
Remington Machine Co.
WASHINGTON, D. C.—
Warren W. Biggs Heating & tilating Co., 1416 Pa. Ave., N
H. Boswell & Co., 1229 7th Av
Hubbard Heating Co., 918 F N. W.

VILLE, FLA.—
.evens Engineering Co.
, GA.—
Machine Works.
Safety Boiler Co.
ILL.—
oiler Works, Trask & Dear-
s.
ILL.—
.ragwanath, 48-52 W. Divi-

s, Morse & Co., Franklin &

rley Down Draft Furnace
perior, Townsend & Sedg-

iester & Co., 241-61 S. Jef-

rling Company, Pullman
). C. Barfer, Pres.; J. K.
on, V. P.; E. R. Stettinuis,
J. P. Sheddon, Supt. Shops
berton, O.
LL.—
eam Boiler Wks., 250 W.

ILL.—
ody & Sons, 104 Cedar.
an Boiler Co., 801 S. Wash-

ILL.—
xman & Co., Ws. Front ft.

Michelman, 121 W. 2d St.
Boiler Co., Es. Commercial
. Hampshire & Vermont.
LLE, IND.—
Machine Wks., 127 L. 1st St.
ltz, 18-30 3d Ave.
lz, 13 3d Ave.
POLIS, IND.—
n Boiler and Sheet Iron Co.,
W. Washington.
**Engine Works, 19th and
idale.**
: & Taylor Co., 740 W. Wash.

Connaughton, 534 S. Capitol

W. Kennedy, 1019-1131 Beech-

Plake, 607 Kentucky Ave.
Davis Co., 230 S. Missouri St.
PORT,, IND—
er Bros. & Co., S. E. Cor.
nd Erie Ave.
IND.—
rozier, W. Adams, bet. Cole
anning, W. S.
Boiler and Sheet Iron Wks.,
Mulberry St.
BANY—
Hegewald & Co., Water bet.
and W. 1st St.
& Co., Pearl and Oak Sts.

RICHMOND, IND.—
Gaar, Scott & Co., 6th & Washington Ave.
Richmond Machine Works, 534-536 N. 10th St.
Robinson & Co., N. S. Main, bet. 2d and 3d Sts.
CLINTON, IA.—
Star Boiler Works, 1st. St. & 8th Ave.
MARSHALLTOWN, IA.—
A. E. Shorthill Co., 2d Ave., S. W. Cor. Linn.
MUSCATINE, IA.—
Garren & Hines, Spring, nr. Front.
Muscatine Boiler & Iron Works, Spring, nr. 2nd.
FORT SCOTT, KAS.—
Ft. Scott Foundry & Mach. Works Co.
LOUISVILLE, KY.—
American Machine Co., 524 E. Main St.
W. E. Caldwell & Co., Brandies & Brooks.
Geiger, Fisk & Co., 725 E. Main.
Henry Vogt Machine Co.
NEW ORLEANS, LA.—
Babcock & Wilcox Co., 339 Carondolet St.
Erie City Iron Works of Erie, Pa., 511 Godchaux Bldg.
SHREVEPORT, LA.—
P. Parsons, 301 Strand St.
PORTLAND, ME.—
Portland Co., 58 Fore St.
M. T. Quinn, 59 Commercial St.
BALTIMORE, MD.—
Ames Iron Works, 341 Equitable Bldg.
Ellicott Machine Co.
Robt. Poole & Son Co.
BOSTON, MASS.—
Dow, Braman & Co., 239 Causeway.
Harrison Safety Boiler Works, 77 Oliver St.
Lidgerwood Mfg. Co., 77 Oliver St.
CAMBRIDGE, MASS.—
Wm. Campbell & Co., 212 6th St., N. Broadway.
Rawson & Morrison, 31 Main St.
Roberts Iron Works Co., 180 Main St.
PITTSFIELD, MASS.—
Adison M. Chapel, 272 Fenn St.
J. W. Kirchner, 156 North St.
H. S. Russell, 92 McKay St.
ALPENA, MICH.—
John Oliver, Jr., 219 W. Oldfield.
ANN ARBOR, MICH.—
T. L. Sutter & Sons, 725 Main, N.
BATTLE CREEK, MICH.—
Brennan Boiler Works.
BAY CITY, MICH.—
Industrial Works.
Mackinnon Mfg. Co.
John Maher.

DETROIT, MICH.—
John Brennan & Co., N. W. cor. Toledo Ave. and 24th St.
Buffalo-Pitts Co., S. S. M. C. R. R. W. of Junction Ave.
Central Boiler Works, S. E. cor. 3d and Congress St.
Dearing Water Tube Boiler Co., 551 Grand River Ave.
Detroit Range Boiler Co., 607 24th St.
Detroit Screw Works, 49 Riopelle St.
East End Boiler Works, 11 St. Aubin Ave.
Stephen Pratt, N. E. cor. Foundry & M. C. R. R.
J. Sprenger & Sons, 1188 River St.
The Standard Foundry Co., 671 Atwater St.
Willis C. Turner, 441 Hubbard Ave.
Wray-Austin Machinery Co., 171 Woodbridge, S. W.

GRAND RAPIDS, Mich.—
Adolph Leitell Iron Works.

KALAMAZOO, MICH.—
Frank H. Buechner.
Clark Engine & Boiler Co.

MANISTEE, MICH.—
Manistee Iron Works Co., cor. Jones & Ashland.
Union Boiler Works, foot of Smith.

MENOMINEE, MICH.—
Menominee Boiler Works, 1208 Ogden Ave.

MINNEAPOLIS, MINN.—
The E. P. Allis Co., 416 Corn Exch.
American Radiator Co., 513 Guaranty Bldg.
Archamba Heating Co., 219 S. 3d St.
Willliams Bros., Lower Nicolett Island.
Crown Iron Works, 113 2d Ave., S. E.
D. G. Hough, 305 6th Ave., S.
Lambrex Bros., 505 13th Ave., S.
Minneapolis Iron Works, 900 S. 4th St.
Moore Heating Co., 704 S. 5th St.
Otto Gas Engine Works, 313 S. 3d St.
J. G. Robertson, 532 Guaranty Bldg.
Woolf Valve Gear Co., 912 Guaranty Bldg.

ST. PAUL, MINN.—
Davis Heating and Plumbing Co., 148 E. 4th St.
Kenny Bros., 339 E. 4th St.
A. L. Ide & Sons, 408 E. 4th St.
George R. Morton, 109 Nat. G. A. Bank Bldg.
J. G. Robertson, 409 Manhattan Bldg.
Springfield Boiler and Mfg. Co., 408 Manhattan Bldg.
South Park Foundry and Machine Co., 11 Gilfilan Blk.
Watrous Engine Works Co., 62 S. Robert St.
Western Machinery Mfg. Co., 249 E. 4th St.

VICKSBURG, MISS.—
P. J. Foley.

KANSAS CITY, MO.—
The Brownell & Co., 1216 Union
Darby Kansas City Boiler W
1026 W. 8th St.
Fairbanks, Morse & Co., 1217 Ave.
Great Western Mfg. Co., 1221 Ave.
Sherman & Lewis, 1205 Union A
Springfield Boiler and Mfg. Co Union Ave.

ST. LOUIS, MO.—
Green Engineering Co., 313 W St.
Heine Safety Boiler Co., 708 Ba Commerce Bldg.
John Nooter, 816 N. Main.
John O'Brien Boiler Wks. Co., N. W. Cor. Mullanphy.
John Rohan & Son Boiler Wks Lewis, N. W. Cor. Biddle.
Michael J. Ryan, 1301 S. Main.
St. Louis Engineering & Suppl 706 Chestnut.
Chas. H. Verbarg, 2830 S. 3d S
Jos. F. Wangler Boiler & Sheet Wrks. Co., 1535 W. 9th St.

BUTTE, MONT.—
Walsh & McGrade.

OMAHA, NEB.—
Drake, Wilson & Williams.
Omaha Boiler Works.

NASHUA, N. H.—
J. J. Crawford & Son, 4 & 6 De
C. B. Jackman & Son, 33 Cros

NEWARK, N. J.—
Automatic Rotary Stoking Co., 810 Broad St.
Chas. C. Ball & Co., 148 N. J. Ave.
Cyrus Currier & Sons, 21 R. R.
W. G. & G. Greenfield, 5th c Harrison.
Hewes & Phillips Iron W Orange & Ogden Sts.
Lambert Hoisting Engine Co. Poinier St.
L. J. Lyons & Co., 189-195 Com St.
Owen McCabe, 195 Commerce St
J. S. Mundy, 22 Prospect St.
Seymour & Whitlock, 43 Law St.

NEW BRUNSWICK, N. J.—
National Water Tube Boiler Co

PATERSON, N. J.—
Sipp Electric & Machine Co., M Van Houten.
Samuel Smith & Son, 130 Rail Ave.

7, N. Y.—
Brass & Iron Co., 165 Broad-

F. Green, 67 Church St.
Nicholson, 11 Church St.
inner & Arnold Co., 205 Broad-

veeney, 43 Liberty St.

O, N. Y.—
lberger & Son, 695 Ellicott.
am Engine Works, Norton
Vater.
Engineering Co., 9 Erie Co.
Bldg.
Machinery Co., 24, Burwell

Dempster, 24 Burwell Pl.
Boiler Works, Mary & In-

& Trefts, 56 Perry.
& Roberts Boiler Wks., 21
a.
Iron Works, 178 Walden Ave.
ohndohl, 355 Niagara.
rie Boiler Works, Perry and
ro.
Engine & Boiler Works, 530
t Sq.
& Cousins, 29 Burwell Pl.
City Engineering Co., Perry
ississippi.
ros. & Co., Mary and Indiana.

ORK CITY, BOROUGH OF BROOKLYN.

Basin Iron Works, Summit
ay Sts.
k Steam Boiler Co., 240 Lor-
St.
a Engineering Works, Wil-
nd Imla Sts.
her Cunningham & Son, 433
oint Ave.
onohue Sons, 108 Wallabout

Enderlin, Jr., & Co., 49 N.

Machine & Steam Boiler
, 18 Franklin St.
lroy, Foot 24th St
Hurlbert, Foot 24th St.
ggins, 38 Harrison St.
eyden, 227 Gold St.
Farrell & Son, 52 Commer-
.

n Bros., Foot 26th St.
McNeil, William & Imlay St.
& Long, Foot Court St.
Iron Works, 151 William St.
er Reid, 68 Commerce St.
on Works, Foot 27th St.
gt & Co, 30 Franklin St.
White, 570 Smith St.

NEW YORK, N. Y., BOROUGHS OF MANHATTAN & BRONX—

Abendroth & Root Mfg. Co., 99 John St.
Acme Boiler Co, Willis Ave. & 148th St.
D. Ahearn & Co., 263 South St.
American Radiator Co., 42 E. 20th St.
American Stoker Co., 141 Broadway.
Ames Iron Works, 149 Broadway.
Andrews, Phalon & Co., 241 West St.
Aultman & Taylor Mach. Co., 39 Cortlandt St.
Babcock & Wilcox Co., 29 Cortlandt St.
James Beggs & Co., 9 Dey St.
Charles Behlen, 72 Trinity Pl.
C. A. Bennett, 120 Liberty St.
Bigelow Co., 15 Cortlandt St.
H. J. Boes, 487 E. 138th St.
William Boes, 493 E 135th St.
Burhorn & Granger, 95 Liberty St.
G. H. Chasmar, 39 Cortlandt St.
Coatesville Boiler Works, 141 Broadway.
E. N. Cokefair, 39 Cortlandt St.
William Collins Sons, Foot of W. 21st St.
Conover Mfg. Co., 26 Cortlandt St.
P. Delany & Co., 85 Liberty.
Donegan & Swift, 6 Murray St.
J. M. Duncan, 39 Cortlandt St.
East Jersey Pipe Co., 26 Cortlandt St.
Economy Mfg. Co., 141 Broadway.
Edgemoor Iron Co., 26 Cortlandt St.
Michael Fogarty, 533 W. 33d St.
George Fox's Sons, 511 W. 34th St.
Gas Engine & Power Co., 50 Broadway.
Gem City Boiler Co. 39 Cortlandt St.
Gorton & Lidgerwood Co., 96 Liberty St.
P. R. Gray, Jr., 26 Cortlandt St.
R. J. Gray, 54 E. 132d St.
Greenlie, Wyatt & Co., 499 Water St.
E. P. Hampson Co., 26 Cortlandt St.
W. F. Haring, 141 Broadway.
Harrisburg Foundry & Mach. Wks, 203 Broadway.
Harrisburg Mfg. & Boiler Co., [illegible] Liberty St.
Harrison Safety Boiler Works, [illegible] Cortlandt St.
Hawley Down Furnace Co., [illegible] Cortlandt St.
Hazelton Boiler Co., 120 Liberty St.
Henry Heather, 462 11th Ave.
Heine Safety Boiler Co., 11 Broadway.
Heipershausen Bros., [illegible] St.
Herendeen Mfg. Co., [illegible] Cortlandt St.
Lane & Bodley Co., 120 Liberty St.
Leonard & McCoy, 113 Liberty St.
Model Heating Co., [illegible] Centre St.
Morgan Iron Works, [illegible] E. [illegible] St.
Morse Iron Wks & Dry Dock Co., [illegible] New St.

National Furnace Co., 52 Broadway.
N. Y. Central Iron Wks. Co., 17 Park Row.
N. Y. Safety Steam Power Co., 107 Liberty St.
Newburgh Steam Boiler Works, 85 Liberty St.
Julian Nicholl & Co., 126 Liberty St.
D. M. Nichols, 2 Gouverneur Slip.
Oil City Boiler Works, 39 Cortlandt St.
Olney & Warrin, 36 Dey St.
Oswego Boiler Works, 39 Cortlandt St.
W. H. Page Boiler Co, 68 Beekman St.
Payne Engineering Co., 120 Liberty St.
Walter Pendleton & Co., 17 Park Row.
Andrew Phelps' Sons, 29 West St.
Phoenix Iron Works Co. 15 Cortlandt St.
Quintard Iron Works, 742 E. 12th St.
Alexander Reid, 408 West St.
James Reilly Repair & Supply Co., 230 West St.
Richmond Stove Co., 85 Center St.
Riter Conley Mfg. Co., 39 Cortlandt St.
Roberts Safety Water Tube Boiler Co., 39 Cortlandt St.
J. F. Rogers & Co., 42 Cortlandt St.
Ross Iron Works, 81 Broad St.
Ruggles Coles Engineering Co, 39 Cortlandt St.
Albert Smith & Son, 698 11th Ave.
Francis Stickler, 69 Beekman St.
Stirling Co., 95 Liberty St.
Strutherd, Wells & Co., 26 Cortlandt St.
Superior Boiler Co., 17 Park Row.
Thayer & Co., Inc., 39 Cortlandt St.
Thorpe, Platt & Co., 97 Cedar St.
Tonkin Boiler Co, 26 Cortlandt St.
W. W. Tupper & Co., 39 Cortlandt St.
U. S. Foundry & Machine Co., 26 Cortlandt St.
F. A. Verdon & Co., 25 Pine St.
Watertown Engine Co., 39 Cortlandt St.
Wickes Bros., 95 Liberty St.
Woolston & Brew, 14 Broadway.
F. W. Wright, 131 Worth St.
E. B. Van Atta, 39 Cortlandt St.

ROCHESTER, N. Y.—
Robert Bryson, 1[illegible]7 Mill.
Sidney Hall, [illegible]75 Mill
Rochester Boiler Works, 1[illegible] River.
Rochester Machine Tool Works, 3 Frank.
Wilson & Dunn, Foot River.

AKRON, O.—
Briggs Boiler Works Co., 12
The J. C. McNeil Co., Cor and Sweitzer Ave.

CINCINNATI, O.—
Aultman & Taylor Machine Mansfield, O., 93 Perin Bld
The Chas. Barnes Co., 200 S
Thos. J. Bell & Co., 331 W.
Crawley & Johnston, 522 Mai
Economy Machinery Co., 42
The Francis Fritsch Mfg. Micken Ave., Dunlap & S
The I. & E. Greenwald Co Pearl.
Hannam-Bechtel Circulator W. 2d.
Robert Jones & Co. Pearl and Ludlaw.
The E. A. Kinsey Co., 331 W.
Laidlaw-Dunn-Gordon Co., P Plum.
The John H. McGowan Co., tral Ave.
McIlvain & Spiegel Boiler a Co., Pearl and Lawrence.
W. D. Norton, 6th and Carr.
Oil City Boiler Works of Oil C 342 Main.
J. K. Rugg & Co., 340 Main.
Smith, Meyers & Schnier, Front.
The Stirling Co., 805 Neave Bl
Tudor Boiler Mfg. Co., 716 E.
Vance & Love, 328 W. 3d.

CLEVELAND, O.—
American Shipbuilding Co., duct.
Brownell & Co., 202 Superior
Cleveland Steam Boiler V West.
Erie City Iron Works, 807 Bldg.
Kaltenbach & Griess, 1618 V son Bldg.
River Machine & Boiler Co., at E. R. R.
H. E. Teachout, Forrest at I

COLUMBUS, O.—
Eaton Machine Wks., 98 W St.
Potts Machinery Co., 162 N.

FINDLAY, O.—
The Adams Bros. Co., 421 Main Cross.
George McArthur, 129 Meek

MARIETTA, O.—
Marietta Boiler Works, Wa Seventh.
Pattin Bros. & Co., 124-126 I
H. Strecker, 709 Fort.

ELD, O.—
berts, L. S. Bridge E. of

p Mfg. Co.,, Junc. C., C., L. R. R. and Greenmount

sey Machine Co., 74 E. ton.
/ILLE, O.—
y, 204 North.
& Irwin, 610 Adams.
.—
os, 139 S. Erie St.
& Co., 1009 Water St.
iler and Engine Works, 700 t.
D, ORE.—
Iron Works.
Iron Works.
HEM, PA.—
n Boiler Works, Front and npton, S. B.
LPHIA, Pa.—
Radiator Co., 622 Arch St.
n Works, 716 Fidelity Bldg.
gine Works, 15 N. 7th St.
& Wilcox, 642-644-646 Drexel

zley Iron Works, 514 S. Del.

Basshor & Co., 608 Harrison

rchfield Co., 619 Arch St.
& Granger, 1004 Stephen Gir-g.
Carroll, 1335 Mt. Vernon St.
e Boiler Works, 701-2 Fidel-r.
Iron Works, 808 Land Title

Ervien & Co., 420 Memphis

nning, 2926 Boudinot St.
Engineering Co., 764 Swanson

Gilman, 1108 Beach St.
oldner & Son, Tasker St. Del. River.
riffing Iron Co., 382 Phila.

Safety Boiler Works, 17th legheny Ave.
fety Boiler Co., 601 Fidelity

bbs, 3d, Arch and Race St.
Holmes & Co., 612 Arch St.
Foundry & Machine Works, dge Ave.
Kane Mfg. Co., Huntingdon, tter.
Co., 612 Betz Bldg.
on Engine Works, 704 Arch

ton Machine Co., 2237 N. St.
& White, 240 Chestnut St.

Lebanon Boiler Works, 206 N. 4th St.
John McAdams, E. Susquehanna Ave. Wharf.
McGovern & Smith, 2054 E. Lehigh Ave.
McNeil Boiler Works, 1001 Chestnut St.
John S Naylor, Front & Girard Sts.
August Nuttinger, Sr., 826 N. 4th St.
John Nuttall, 1723 N. 5th St.
William H. Page Boiler Co., The, 636 Arch St.
Oswego Boiler Works, 6 N. 6th St.
Parker Engine Co. of Cal., Schuyler C. Dalamater, sales agent, 1041 Drexel Bldg.
Pennsylvania Boiler Works, 301 Arch St.
Penn. Range Boiler Co., 2010 N. 10th St.
J. K. Petty & Co., 206 N. 4th St.
Pierce, Butler & Pierce, 24 S. 7th St.
Reilly & Fearon, 1154-56 N. 3d St.
J. & G. Rich, 120 N. 6th St.
Benj. T. Scott, 206 N. 4th St.
Scott Machine Co., 2237 N. Front St.
Isaac A. Sheppard & Co., 4th & Montgomery Ave.
Sheridan & Co., 1173 S. 9th St.
H. B. Smith Co., 510 Arch St.
Standard Co., 631 Arch St.
Sterling Water Tube Safety Boiler, 205 Betz Bldg.
Struthers, Wells & Co., 501 Fidelity Bldg.
Thayer & Co., 542 Drexel Bldg.
Thompson Bros., 112 Bread St.
Thompson Iron Wks., 1825-1827 Callowhill.
Conrad Wanner, 1450 N. Delhi St.
Robert Wetherill & Co., 1213 Betz Bldg.
Wilbraham Bros.
Wilfong Bros., 52d c. P., W. & B. R. R.

PITTSBURGH, PA.—
Babcock & Wilcox Co., 1217 Empire Bldg.
Bovaird & Seyfang Mfg. Co., 546 2d Ave.
John Brennan & Co., 600 Times Bldg.
Cahall Sales Dept., 541 Wood St.
Thomas Carlin's Sons Co., 1600 River Ave., E. A.
W. J. Carlin Co., 610 Lewis Blk.
Carroll-Porter Boiler & Tank Co., 207 Penn. Ave.
Frick & Lindsay Co., 200 Wood St.
Geary Water Tube Boiler, 323 4th Ave.
Harrison Safety Boiler Works, 812 Lewis Blk.
Heine Safety Boiler Co., 902 Lewis Blk.

Iron City Boiler Works, 20th St. & Pike St.
William M. Kerr, 401 Ferguson Bldg.
James Lappan & Co., 20th & Pike Sts.
Manchester Co., 3108 Smallman St.
James F. Morrison, 41 Water St.
R. Munro & Son, 23d & Smallman St.
J. A. McCormick, 318 1st Ave.
James McNeil & Bro., 29th St. & A. V. Ry.
Oil City Boiler Works, 323 4th Ave.
John M. Pearson, 2 Mulberry A.
Pittsburgh Locomotive & Car Works, 2101 Beaver Ave., A.
William B. Pollock Co., 1217 Park Bldg.
Porter Foundry & Machine Co., ltd., 1 Darrah St., A.
S. G. Rheam & Co., 43d st. & A. V. Ry.
Wm. B. Scaife & Sons, 221 First Ave.
Sheriff Machinery Co., 131 Water St.
Somers, Fitler & Clarke, ltd., 327 Water St.
Sterling Co., 421 Water St.

SCRANTON, PA.—
Dickson Mfg. Co., Penn Ave., C. Vine St.

WILKESBARRE, PA.—
Vulcan Iron Works.

CENTRAL FALLS, R. I.—
Central Falls Boiler Repair Shop, 16 Maple Ave.

CHARLESTON, S. C.—
Charleston Boiler and Sheet Iron Works, Virginia and Clendenning.
Charleston Iron Works, 123 Pritchard.
J. F. Riley, 68 South St.
Riverside Iron Works, Concord. E. end Hasell.
Valk & Murdock Iron Works, 12, 20 Hasell.
Charles Ward, South Side.

COLUMBIA, S. C.—
V. C. Bradham, 1323 Main St.
W. H. Gibbes & Co., 804 Gervais St.
Palmetto Iron Works, 1802 L. St.
Toyers Engine Works, 711 G St.

GREENVILLE, S. C.—
Greenville Machine Works, 2 Laurence St.
Palmetto Iron Works, 402 Rhet

CHATTANOOGA, TENN.—
Casey & Hedges Mfg. Co.
Lookout Boiler & Mfg. Co.
Welsh & Weidner.

HOUSTON, TEX.—
Hartwell Iron Works, E. S. W bet Baker & Allen.
Herman H. Tofte, 109 Milam S

SALT LAKE CITY, UTAH—
Haynes & Son.
Samuel Holmes.

BURLINGTON, VT.—
W. H. Lang, Goodhue & Co.

ALEXANDRIA, VA.—
P. F. Gorman, 321 S. Union St.

SPOKANE, WASH.—
W. P. Scott.
Union Iron Works.

PARKERSBURG, W. VA.—
Fisher & Kootz, 208 1st St.

EAU CLAIRE, WIS.—
Eau Claire Mill Supply Co., 4(Claire St.

MANITOWOC, WIS.—
Manitowoc Steam Boiler Wor Quay St.

MILWAUKEE, WIS.—
Buxbaum & Miller, 287 Virgini
Davis Bros. Mfg. Co., 576 Clint
J. W. Eviston & Son, 233 Oreg
Logemann Bros., 282 Oregon
T. L. McGregor Boiler Worl Oregon St.
Mertes-Miller Co., 239 Lake St
Milwaukee Boiler Co., 220 Oreg
Seamless Structural Co., 718 over St.

BOLTING MACHINERY

C. O. Bartlett & Co., 43-45 (St., Cleveland, O.

Any information on **Cement or Cement Machinery**

will be furnished on request by the publishers of this book—

Municipal Engineering Compa

frey Mfg. Co., Columbus, O.
:e & Marmon, Indianapo-
ıd.
Waldron & Co., Muncy, Pa.

ЭTS FOR ELEVATORS.

n Co., Canton, O.
Bartlett & Co., 43-45 Cen-
., Cleveland, O.
[alleable Iron Co., Detroit.

Caldwell & Son Co., Chicago.
Mfg. Co., Mishawaka, Ind.
Mfg . Columbus, O.
:e & Marmon, Indianapo-
ıd.
& Elliott, Wilmington, Del.
Mfg. Co., 118-126 North Ave.,
ago, Ill.

(CONVEYOR, ECCENTRIC,
:NAL, STEP, TAKE UP.)

artlett & Co., 43-45 Center
eveland, O.
Mfg. Co., Mishawaka, Ind.
Mfg. Co., Columbus, O.
:e & Marmon Co., Indian-
s, Ind.
Pulley Co., Columbus, Ind.
:r Mfg. Co., 1075 W. 15th
icago; 38 Dey St., New

BRICK MACHINERY.

O, ILLS.—
Brick Machinery Co., 729,
:arborn.
lm, Boyd & White Co., Cor.
'th and Wallace.
La Dow & C., 1107 Chamber
mmerce.
APOLIS, IND.—
3. Gray, 1510 W. Wash.
Hensley, 629-630 Lemcke Bldg.
CITY, MO.—
Raymond & Co., 1205 Union

:, IND.—
[ock, 247 and 249 The Johnson.
IS, MO.—
rnholtz Brick Mchy. Co., 1214-
'oplar.
eller Brick Mch. Co., 915-916
nd Bldg.
'S, O.—
nerican Clay Working Ma-
ry Co.
7, O.—
ounot Company.
NATI, O.—
ın Creager's Sons Co , 115 W.

, O.—
Freese & Co.

PHILADELPHIA, Pa —
George Carnell, 1819 N. 5th St.
Chambers Bros. Co., 52d, below Lancaster Ave.
C. W. Raymond & Co., 101 Chestnut St.
PITTSBURG, Pa.—
C. W. Raymond Co., 1519 Park Bldg.

BRUSHES FOR CEMENT PLANTS.

Jos. Lay & Co., Ridgeville, Ind.

BUCKETS FOR ELEVATORS, CONVEYORS, ETC.

C. O. Bartlett & Co., 43-45 Center St., Cleveland, O.
Bethlehem Foundry & Machine Co., S. Bethlehem, Pa.
The Bonnot Co., Canton, O.
H. W. Caldwell & Son Co., Western Ave. & 17th St., Chicago, Ill.
The Contractors' Tool Co., 118 S. 6th St., Philadelphia, Pa.
Dodge Mfg. Co., Mishawaka, Ind.
Fraser & Chalmers, W. 12th & Washtenaw Ave., Chicago, Ill.
The Haywood Co., 97 Cedar St., New York, N. Y.
The Jeffrey Mfg. Co., Columbus, O.
Nordyke & Marmon Co., Indianapolis, Ind.
L. M. Rumsey Mfg. Co., St. Louis, Mo.
Webster Mfg. Co., 1075 W. 15th St., Chicago, Ill., 38 Dey St., New York.
Walker & Elliott, Wilmington, Del.
Weller Mfg. Co., 118-126 North Ave., Chicago, Ill.

BUHR MILLS.

C. O. Bartlett & Co., 43-45 Center St., Cleveland, O.
Nordyke & Marmon Co., Indianaolis, Ind.
Richmond City Mill Works, Richmond, Ind.
Chas. Ross & Son Co , 16-20 Stuben St., Brooklyn, N. Y.
Sprout, Waldron & Co., Muncy, Pa.
Sturtevant Mill Co., Marrison Square, Boston, Mass.
Walker & Elliott, Wilmington, Del.

CABLE TRAMWAY.

Earle C. Bacon, Havemeyer Bldg., New York, N. Y .
Borden & Selleck Co., 48-50 Lake St., Chicago, Ill.
The S. Flory Co., Bangor, Pa.
A. Leschen & Sons, Rope Co., 920 N. Main St., St. Louis, Mo.
Rawson & Morrison Mfg. Co., Boston, Mass.

CAR MOVERS.

The Aultman Co., Canton, O.
C. O. Bartlett & Co., 43-45 Center St., Cleveland, O.
Borden & Selleck Co., 48-50 Lake St., Chicago, Ill.
Dodge Mfg. Co., Mishawaka, Ind.
Nordyke & Marmon Co., Indianapolis, Ind.
Reeves Pulley Co., Columbus, Ind.
Webster Mfg. Co., Chicago, Ill.

CARS—(DUMP, DRYER, TRANSFER, ETC.)

The Atlas Bolt and Screw Co., Cleveland, O.
Bethlehem Foundry and Machine Works, South Bethlehem, Pa.
The Bonnot Co., Canton, O.
Chambers Brothers Co., 52d St., Below Lancaster Ave., Philadelphia, Pa.
Fraser & Chalmers, W. 12th and Washtenaw Aves., Chicago, Ills.
E. M. Fresse & Co., Galion, O.
The Jeffrey Mfg. Co., Columbus, O.
Arthur Koppel, 68 Broad St., New York.
New Jersey Foundry & Machine Co., 26 Cortlandt St., New York, N. Y.
C. W. Leavitt & Co., 25 Cortlandt St., New York.
Means Foundry & Machine Co., Steubenville, O.
Walker & Elliott, Wilmington, Ind.
Wonham & Magor, 29 Broadway, New York, Cleveland, O.

CASTINGS.

Earle C. Bacon, Havemeyer Bldg., New York, N. Y.
Bethlehem Foundry & Machine Co., S. Bethlehem, Pa.
Fraser & Chalmers, W. 12th & Washtenaw Aves., Chicago, Ills.
Stephen R. Krom, 113-115 Plymouth St., Jersey City, N. J.

CLINKER COOLERS.

C. O. Bartlett & Co., 43-45 Center St., Cleveland, O.
The Bonnot Co., Canton, O.
Bethlehem Foundry & Machine Co., South Bethlehem, Pa.
Wm. F. Mosser & Son, Allentown, Pa.
Vulcan Iron Works, Wilkesbarre, Pa.

CLUTCHES.

American Clay Working Machinery Co., Bucyrus and Willoughby, O.
Dodge Mfg. Co., Mishawaka, Ind.
The Eastern Machinery Co., New Haven, Conn.
Falls Rivet & Machinery Co., Cuyahoga Falls, O., and 208 Fulton St., New York.

Fraser-Chalmers, W. 12th ington Ave., Chicago, Ill.
Hill Clutch Co., Cleveland,
Jones & Laughlins, Ltd., Pa.
Link Belt Engineering town, Pa., and 49 Dey York.
Nordyke & Marmon, In lis, Ind.
Nordberg Mfg. Co., Milwau
Reeves Pulley Co., Columbu
Wm. Sellers & Co., 1600 St., Philadelphia.
Southwark Foundry & Ma Philadelphia.
Walker & Elliott, Wilming
Webster Mfg. Co., 1975 St., Chicago, Ill.
Weller Mfg. Co., 118-126 N Chicago, Ill.
Whitman Mfg. Co., Garwo & 39 Cortlandt St., New

COAL HANDLING MACI

Earle C. Bacon, 26 Cour New York
Borden & Selleck Co., 48
Jeffrey Mfg. Co., 1325 Bldg.
C. W. Leavitt & Co., 15 Co New York.
Link Belt Mach'y Co., Co and Stewart Ave., Chi Nicetown, Philadelphia, New York.
New Jersey Foundry & M 26 Cortlandt St., New Y
Rawson & Morrison Mfg. Main St.
Robins Conveying Belt Row Bldg., New York.

CONCRETE LAYING MAC

Contractors' Tool Co., St., Philadelphia, Pa.
Drake Standard Machine 300 Jackson Boulevard, C
Ransome & Smith Co., St., Brooklyn, N. Y.

CONCRETE MIXE

The American Clay Wo chinery Co., Bucyrus,
C. O. Bartlett & Co., St., Cleveland, O.
Jno. F. Byers Machine C na, O.
H. W. Caldwell & Son Co Western Ave., Chicago,
Thos. Carlin's Sons Co., Ave., Allegheny, Pa.
Chambers Bros. Co., low Lancaster Ave., phia, Pa.
The Cockburn Barrow Co., 210 11th St., Jersey

:tors' Plant Co., 172 Federal
Boston, Mass.
ontractors' Tool Co., 118 S. 6th
Philadelphia, Pa.
Foundry & Machine Co., Ni-
. Falls, N. Y.
Standard Machine Works, 298-
ickson Boulevard, Chicago, Ill.
Dunning, Syracuse, N. Y.
& Saxton, 123 G St. N. E.,
ington, D. C.
ighes Mfg. Co., Hamilton, O.
s Iron Works, Buffalo, N. Y.
ffrey Mfg. Co., Columbus, O.
bach & Griess, 1618 William-
Bldg., Cleveland, O.
F. Mosser & Son, Allentown,

**vey Concrete and Machin-
Co., 1206 Security Bldg.,
igo, Ill.**
rsey Foundry & Machine Co.,
rtlandt St., New York.
**ke & Marmon Co., Indian-
s, Ind.**
' Iron Works, 151 William St.,
klyn, N. Y.
Poole & Son Co., office and
; Woodbury Station, Balti-
Md. Branch office 233 E.
an St., Baltimore, Md.
**me & Smith Co., 17-19 9th
Brooklyn N. Y.**
**Conveying Belt Co., 13-21
Row, N. Y.**
Scholl & Co., 126 Liberty St.,
York.
Smith, 134 10th St., Milwaukee.

Vaughn & Taylor Co., Cuya-
Falls, O.
' & Elliott, Wilmington, Del.

NVEYING MACHINERY.

lso Elevating Machinery.)

an Tool & Machine Co., 109
St., Boston, Mass.
ltman Co., Canton, O.
**C. Bacon, Havemeyer Bldg.,
York.**
ailey-Lebby Co., 213 Meeting
Charleston, S. C.
Mfg. Co., Milwaukee, Wis.
**Bartlett & Co., 43-45 Center
Cleveland, O.**
em Foundry & Machine Co.,
thlehem, Pa.
Bonnot Co., Canton, O.
**& Selleck Co., 48-50 Lake
Chicago, Ill.**
Caldwell & Son Co., Western
& 17th St., Chicago, Ill.
Holsting & Conveying Ma-
Co., Cleveland, O.
Malleable Iron Co., Detroit,

Thos. Carlin's Sons Co., Alegheny, Pa.
Chain Belt Co., Milwaukee, Wis.
J. B. & J. M. Cornell, 26 & 11th Ave., New York.
Geo. V. Creeson Co., 18th St. & Allegheny Ave., Philadelphia, Pa.
Dodge Mfg. Co., Mishawaka, Ind.
Exeter Machine Works, Pittston, Pa.
S. Flory Mfg. Co., Bangor, Pa.
Fraser & Chalmers, W 12th & Washtenaw Ave., Chicago, Ill.
Gates Iron Works, Elston Ave. & Bloomingdale Road, Chicago, Ill.
Geo. D. Grannis, Syracuse, N. Y.
Fred Grotenrath, 111 W. Water St., Milwaukee.
C. W. Hunt & Co., 45 Broadway, New York.
The Jeffrey Mfg. Co., Columbus, O.
Chas. C. Klein, Marshall & Cambria Sts., Philadelphia, Pa.
Kaltenbach & Griess, 1618 Williamson Bldg., Cleveland, O.
A. Leschen & Sons Rope Co., 920 N. 1st St., St. Louis, Mo.
Lidgerwood Mfg. Co., 96 Liberty St., New York.
Link Belt Machinery Co., W. 39th, S. E. cor. Stewart Ave., Chicago; Nicetown, Pa.; 49 Dey St., New York.
Macomber & White Rope Co., 19 S. Canal St., Chicago, Ill.
Mine & Smelter Supply Co., Denver, Col.
Wm. F. Mosser & Son, Allentown, Pa.
J. W. Moyer, 125 N. 3d St., Philadelphia, Pa.
Nelsonville Foundry & Machine Co., Nelsonville, O.
New Jersey Foundry & Machine Co., 26 Cortlandt St., New York.
Nordyke & Marmon Co., Indianapolis, Ind.
Norman & Evans, Lockport, N. Y.
Rawson & Morrison Mfg. Co., Cambridgeport, Boston, Mass., & 11 Broadway, New York.
Reeves Pulley Co., Columbus, Ind.
Robins Conveying Belt Co., 13-21 Park Row, N. Y.
Walker & Elliott, Wilmington, Del.
Webster Mfg. Co., 1075 W. 15th St., Chicago, Ill., 38 Dey St., N. Y.
Weller Mfg. Co., 118-126 North Ave., Chicago, Ill.
Whitney Iron Works Co., New Orleans, La.
Wickes Bros., Saginaw, Mich.

CORBELS.

Nordyke & Marmon Co., Indianapolis, Ind.

CRUSHERS—(STONE, CEMENT, COAL AND CLAY.)

Adrian Brick & Tile Mach. Co., Adrian, Mich.

American Clay Working Machinery Co., Bucyrus and Willoughby, O.

A. J. Armstrong, W. S. Summit, bet. 30th and 31st st., Kansas City, Mo.

The Aultman Co., Canton, O.

F. C. Austin Mfg. Co., 1318, 315 Dearborn, Chicago.

Earle C. Bacon, Havemeyer Bldg., New York, N. Y.

The Bailey-Lebby Co., 213 Meeting St., Charleston, S. C.

C. O. Bartlett & Co., 43-45 Center St., Cleveland, O.

Bradley Pulverizer Co., 92 State St., Boston, Mass.

Bethlehem Foundry & Machine Co., So. Bethlehem, Pa.

The Bonnot Co., Canton, O.

H. Brewer & Co., Tecumseh, Mich. (clay).

C. G. Buchanan, 141 Liberty St., New York.

Chambers Brothers Co., 52d St. Below Lancaster Ave., Philadelphia, Pa.

Climax Road Machine Co., Marathon, N. Y.

Colyer Bros., Grand Ave., Cor. 27th, Kansas City, Mo.

Diamond Drill & Machine Co., Birdsboro, Pa. Royal Crusher.

Dickson Mfg. Co., Scranton, Pa. (coal).

The Eastern Machinery Co., New Haven, Conn.

Farrel Foundry & Machine Co., Havemeyer Bldg., New York.

Fraser & Chalmers, 12th St. and Washtenaw Ave., Chicago, Ill.

E. M. Freese & Co., Galion, O.

Gates Iron Works, Elston Ave. and Bloomingdale Road, Chicago, Ill. 237 Franklin, Boston, Mass.

Good Roads Machinery Co., Kennett Square, Pa., 36 S. Market, Boston, Mass.

Hendrick Mfg. Co., Carbondale, Pa. (coal.)

Holmes & Blanchard Co., 39 Charlestown, Boston, Mass.

J. H. Houghton, 77 Oliver, Boston Mass.

C. W. Hunt Co., 45 Broadway, N. Y. (coal.)

The Jeffrey Mfg. Co., Columbus, O., 41 Dey St., New York.

Kent Mill Co., 5 Beekman St., New York.

Stephen R. Krom, 113-115 Plymouth St., Jersey City., N. J.

N. W. Lyle, 205 Manhattan I Kansas City, Mo.

Wm. R. Martin Iron Works, La ter, Pa.

R. McCully, Philadelphia, Pa.

Geo. T. McLauthin Co., 120 F St., Boston, Mass.

J. T. Noyes Mfg. Co., Buffalo.

D. W. Pratt, 211 and 213 Lucas

Raymond Bros. Impact Pulv. Monadnock Blk., Chicago, Ill.

C. W. Raymond Co., Dayto (clay.)

Robins Conveying Belt Co Park Row, New York.

Julian Scholl & Co., 126 Libert, New York.

Sprout, Waldron & Co., Muncy,

Stevenson & Co., Wellsville (clay.)

Sturtevant Mill Co., Har Square, Boston, Mass.

Taplin, Rice & Co., Akron, O. (

Vulcan Iron Works, Wilkesbarre

Walker & Elliott, Wilmington,

The Williams Patent Crusher & verizer Co., Broadway, and M gomery Sts., St. Louis, Mo.

The West Pulv. Mach. Co. Broadway, New York.

Young-Brennan Crusher Co., 111 cock St, Brooklyn, N. Y.

CRUSHING ROLLS.

E. P. Allis Co., Milwaukee, Wis

Earle C. Bacon, Havemeyer B New York, N. Y.

C. O. Bartlett & Co., 43-45 Ce St., Cleveland, O.

The Bonnot Co., Canton, O.

Thos. Carlin's Sons, Allegheny, I

Geo. V. Cresson Co., 18th & Alleg Ave., Philadelphia Pa., & 141 erty St., New York

Fraser & Chalmers, 12th St. & W tenaw Ave., Chicago, Ill.

Gates Iron Works, 650 Elston Chicago, Ill., & 11 Broadway, York.

Jeffrey Mfg. Co., Columbus, O.

Stephen R. Krom, 113-115 P outh St., Jersey City, N. J.

Scaife Foundry and Machine Pittsburg, Pa.

Sturtevant Mill Co., Har Square, Boston, Mass.

DREDGES AND SHOVELS

The Bucyrus Co., South Milwa Wis.

H. W. Caldwell & Son Co., We Ave. & 17th St. Chicago, Ill.

Chambers Brothers Co., 52d below Lancaster Ave., Pl delphia, Pa.

ontractors' Tool Co., 118 S. 6th Philadelphia, Pa.
-y Mfg. Co., Bangor, Pa.
ayward Co., 97 Cedar St., New ..

r Bros., Sault Ste. Marie, Mich.
rial Works, Bay City, Mich.
City Engineering Co., Erie, Pa.
1 Steam Shovel Co., Marion, O.
1 Dredge Co., 37 State St., Al-. N. Y.
Souther & Co., 12 Postoffice re, Boston, Mass.
Smith & Sons Co., Jersey City,

Thew Automatic Shovel Co., in, O.
oledo Foundry & Machine Co., lo, O.

:RS—ROTARY AND TUNNEL R BRICK, COAL AND NE.

Alsip, Belleville, Ill.
merican Clay Working Ma-ery Co., Bucyrus, O.
C. Bacon, Havemeyer Bldg. York, N. Y.
Bartlett & Co., 43-45 Center Cleveland, O.
hem Foundry & Machine Co., h Bethlehem, Pa.
lonnot Co., Canton, O.
bers Brothers Co., 52d St., w Lancaster Ave., Phila-hia, Pa.
ian Creagers Sons, 115 W. 2d Cincinnati, O. (brick.)
. D. Cummer & Son Co. Cleve-. O.
' & Chalmers, 12th St. and htenaw Ave., Chicago, Ill.
ds Iron Works, 178 Walden . Buffalo, N. Y.
en R. Krom, 113-115 Plym-t St., Jersey City, N. J.
G McGann, The Rookery, Chi-. Ill
F. Mosser & Son, Allentown,

ial Blower Works, 17th St. and Paul Ave., Milwaukee, Wis.
es-Coles Engineering Co., 39 landt St., New York.
Sturtevant Co., Jamaica Plain on, Boston, Mass.
'urney Drier Co., Louisville.

1 Iron Works, Wilkesbarre, Pa.
Vest Pulv. Machine Co., 220 idway, New York.
Williams Patent Crusher & Pul-:er Co., Broadway and Mont-ery Sts., St. Louis, Mo.

DUMPS, WAGON.

Nordyke & Marmon Co., Indianapolis, Ind.

DUST COLLECTORS.

C. H. Gifford & Co., 135 N. 3d St., Philadelphia, Pa.
National Blower Works, 17th and St. Paul Ave., Milwaukee, Wis.
Nordyke & Marmon Co., Indianapolis, Ind.
Robins Conveying Belt Co., 13-21 Park Row, New York, N. Y.
Sprout, Waldron & Co., Muncy, Pa.

ELECTRIC GENERATORS AND ELECTRIC MOTORS.

SAN FRANCISCO, CAL.—
Brooks-Follis Electric Corporation, 523 Mission St.
California Electrical Works, 409 Market St.
F. F. Eggers, 134 Sutter St.
Electric Railway & Mfrs. Supply Co., 548 Mission St.
Electrical Engineering Co., 509 Howard St.
General Electric Co., 1109 Claus Spreckles Bldg.
Herzog & Dahl, 31 Main St.
Impey Bros., 927 Market St.
J. M. Klein Electrical Works, 421 Montgomery St.
Pacific Electric Motor Co., 183 Jessie St.
D. D. Wass, 36 E. South St.
Western Light & Power Co., 916 Market St.
Westinghouse Electric & Manufacturing Co., 228 Bush St.

DENVER, COL.—
Coal Machinery Co., 519 Opera House Blk.
Crocker-Wheeler Co., 311 Kittredge Bldg.
Electrical Supply & Construction Co., 429 17th St.
Flint & Lomax, 1937 Curtis St
General Electric Co., 505 16th St.

WATERBURY, CONN.—
Waterbury Battery Co., 41 Brown St.

WASHINGTON, D. C.—
Tallmadge & Wilson, Star Bldg.

CHICAGO, ILL.—
Aaron Electric Co., 181-183 S. Clinton.
Becker Bros., 39 W. Washington.
C C Electric Co., 828 Monadnock Blk.

Central Electric Co., 264-270 5th Ave.
Chicago Edison Co., 139 Adams.
Commonwealth Electric Co., 139 Adams.
Eddy Electric Mfg. Co., 837-38 Marquette Bldg.
General Electric Co., 1047 Monadnock Blk.
Gregory Electric Co., 54-62 S. Clinton.
Holtzer-Cabot Electric Co., 397 Dearborn St.
Kohler Bros., 1804-12 Fisher Bldg.
Milwaukee Electric Co., 1808 Fisher Bldg.
Northern Electric Mfg. Co., 939-40 Monadnock Blk.
Roth Bros. & Co., 88-92 W. Jackson.
Sprague Electric Co., 609 Fisher Bldg.
Triumph Electric Co., 13-15 Monadnock Blk.
Blk.
Wagner Electric Co., 1624 Marquette Bldg.
Western Electric Co., 592 S. Clinton.
Westinghouse Electric & Mfg. Co., 1220 N. Y. Life Bldg.

PEORIA, ILL.—
R. Lester Thayer Co., 5 Hamlin Bldg.
John Schneider & Co., 410 Fulton.
Wetherell Novelty Works, 309 Fulton.

QUINCY, ILL.—
Central Iron Works, 201 S. Front.

INDIANAPOLIS, IND.—
Commercial Electric Co., 220 W. Merrill St.
Indianapolis District Telegraph Co., 15 S. Meridian.
Jenney Electric Mfg. Co., P., C., C. & St. L. & Belt Rys
Chas. W. Meikel, 122-126 N. Penn.
Sanborn Electric Co., 22 E. Ohio.

LOUISVILLE, KY.—
H. C. Tafel, 333 3d St

BOSTON, MASS.—
G. M. Angier, Co., 64 Federal.
Bibber-White Co., 49 Federal St.
Boston Electric Co., 29 Harrison Ave.
Boston Motor Supply Co., 123 Pearl St.
Bringham Electric Co., 63 Oliver St.
C. & C. Electric Co., 19 High St.
Chase-Shawmut Co., 161 F. & Hill Sq.
Walter H. Chase, 611 Sudbury Bldg.
S. B. Conditt, Jr., & Co., 63 Olive.
Crocker Wheeler Electric Co., 49 Federal.
Edison Electric Illuminating Co., 3 Head Pl
Elektron Mfg. Co., 143 Federal.
General Electric Co.. 200 Summer St.
Hancock Equipment Co.
H. A Holder, 45 Warren.
James L. Kimball, 53 State.
Northern Electrical Mfg. Co Oliver.
Frank Ridlon Co., 200 Summer, 22..
Houghton Seaverns, 200 Summer
B. F. Sturtevant Co.,, Jamaica] near R. R. Station.
W. A. Toppon, 9 Haverhill.
Westinghouse Electric & Mfg. C State St.
F. E. Whitney, 65 Sudbury.

BROCKTON, MASS.—
D. K. Carpenter, 37 Belmont St
Millard Electric Co., 198 Main St.

MEDFORD, MASS.—
Waterman & Chamberlain, Me Sq.

DETROIT, MICH.—
Commercial Supply Co., 206 Gri St.
Detroit Electric Co., 47 State St.
Detroit Electrical Exchange, Gratiot Ave.
Dimmer Machine Works, 90 W bridge St., W.
Edison Illuminating Co., 18 Was ton Av.
Electric Service & Appliance Co Randolph St.
Electric Supply & Engineering Co Jefferson Ave.
Gardner Elevator Co., N. E. cor & River Sts.
Michigan Electric Co., 101 Wood Ave.
Thomas Muir & Son, 1101 Union Bldg.
Otis Elevator Co., 1102 Majestic
M. N. Rowley Co., 52 Woodward
Scott Bros. Electric Co., 59 Fa St.
Seidler & Muier Electric Co., 207 ferson Ave.
Henry L. Walker, 3 Griswold St
Wolverine Electric Co., 149 C River Ave.

MINNEAPOLIS, MINN.—
Vernon Bell & Son, 56 S. 3d St.
Electrical Engineering Co., 248 nepin Ave.
The Electric Machinery Co., 10 Ave., N.
W. I Gray & Co., 802 Sykes Bl
Minneapolis Electric & Constru Co., 17 S. 4th St.
John Trevor, 309 Century Bldg.

KANSAS CITY, MO.—
Hodge-Walsh Electrical Engine Co., 701 Delaware St.
E. M. Reed & Co , 717 Delaware

ST PAUL, MINN.—
Electrical Engineering Co., 31 Ave.
George R. Morton, 109 Nat. (Bank Bldg.

/est Engineering Co., 131 E. 5th

western Electric, Co., 131 E. 5th

s-Goss Co., 357 Rosabel St.
ıl Electric Co., 135 E. 5th St.
ıh Electric Co., 604 Globe Bldg.
JIS, MO.—
B. Electric Co., Turner Bldg.,
. 8th.
ıia Electric Engineering Co.,
Chemical Bldg.
rcial Electrical Supply Co.,
009 Market.
r-Wheeler Co., 641 Century

cal Machinery & Specialty
204-6-8 Franklin.
ayne Electric Works, 818 Lin-
Trust Bldg.
l Electric Co., 815-816 Wain-
ıt Bldg.
Electric Mfg. Co., 638 Century

s & Halske Electric Co., 116
de Bldg.
r Electric Mfg. Co., 2017-2023
st.
n Electric Co., 623 Security

A, N. H.—
ester Electric Co., 42 Hanover.
ester Heating & Lighting Co.,
Elm.
N, N. J.—
E. Morgan Co., 216 Federal St.
RK, N. J.—
Burland & Co., 200 Thames St.
Crane, 179 Market St.
F. Conroy, 81 Thames St.
Currier & Sons, 21 Railroad Pl.
). Dickson, 88 John St.
Dorris, 15½ Mechanic St.
ynamo & Motor Works, 66 N.
R. Ave.
c Motor & Equipment Co., 12
er St.
Electrical Mfg. Co., 35 N. J.
. Ave.
r Electrical Co., 251 Market St.
Zimmerman, 194 Market St.
SON, N. J.—
lectric & Machine Co., Mill, cor.
Houten.
LO, N. Y.—
lberger & Son, 695 Ellicott Sq.
E. Averill, 357 7th.
) Electric Co., 227 Pearl.
) Engine Works, 18 Perry.
, Gasoline Motor Co., Dewitt
Bradley.
Flach & Son, 70 W. Genesee.
l Electric Co., 677 Ellicott Sq.
ffeld & Co., 61 Carroll.
n & Gibson, 176 Niagara.
Jones, 128 Franklin

F. P. Little Electrical Co., 135 Seneca.
Albert Mann, 313 Mooney Bldg.
Mashinter Electrical Co., 12 Perry.
McCarty Bros. & Ford, 45 N. Division.
New Motor Co., 997 Ellicott.
Noye Mfg. Co., 50 Lakeview Ave.
F. C. Perkins, 126 Erie Co. Blk. Bldg.
Charles Plumb, 47 W. Swan.
Power Installation Co., 202 Main.
Robertson Electric Co., 13 Niagara.
H. I. Sackett, Builders' Exch. Court, Cor. Pearl.
J. C. Sterns & Co., 255 Pearl.
G. C. Woolverton, 444 Niagara.

COHOES, N. Y.—
Clute Bros., 72 Remsen St.

NEW YORK CITY—BOROUGH OF BROOKLYN, N Y.—
Columbia Machine Works, 18 Fulton St
Lundine Co., 321 Flatbush Ave.
Riker Electric Motor Co., 45 York St.
Sidney Green, 90 Pearl St.
M. R. Rodrigues, 10 Whipple St.

NEW YORK CITY—BOROUGHS OF MANHATTAN & BRONX—
Conn. Dynamo and Motor Co., 526 W. 25th St.
Crocker-Wheeler Co., 39 Cortlandt St.
Diehl Mfg. Co., 561 Broadway, N. Y.
C. & C., Electric Co., 143 Liberty St.
Durbrow & Hearne Mfg. Co., 8 Wooster St.
Elektron Mfg. Co., 126 Liberty St.
General Electric Co., 44 Broad St.
W. S. Hill Electric Co., 203 Broadway
Manhattan Machinery Co., 95 Liberty St
Paragon Fan & Motor Co., 572 1st Ave.
Palmer & Olson, 210 Center St.
Siemens & Halske Electric Co., 100 Broadway.
B. F. Sturtevant Co., 131 Liberty St.
Triumph Electric Co., 39 Cortlandt St.

ROCHESTER, N. Y.—
Maland F. Burns, 20 Spring.
Eureka Specialty Co., 14 N. Water.
Higgins-Almstead Co., 59 State.
Rochester Electric Motor Co., 3 Frank.
Standard Electric Construction Co., 32 N. Water.

SCHENECTADY, N. Y.—
General Electric Co.

SYRACUSE, N. Y.—
Paul T. Brady, 902 University Bldg.
H. P. Cameron Electrical Mfg. Co., 220 N Clinton St
Fort Wayne Electrical Works, 717 Dillaye Mem. Bldg.

General Electric Co., 603 S. A. & K. Bldg.
H. J. Gorke, 305 S. Clinton St.
Onondaga Dynamo Co., 219 Walton St.
Beardsley N. Sperry, Shannard, cor. Niagara St.

AKRON, O.—
The Akron Electrical Mfg. Co., Ira Ave., South Akron.

CINCINNATI, O.—
Bullock Electric Mfg. Co., E. Norwood.
Cincinnati Motor Co., 644 W. 7th.
Creaghead Engineering Co., 802 Plum.
Crescent Electric Co., 309 Pike Bldg.
Devere Electric Co., 430 Plum.
Gray & Co., 505 Elm.
D. J. Hauss, 426 Pike Bldg.
Jantz & Leist Electric Co., 808 Elm.
The E. A. Kinsey Co., 331 W. 4th.
Laidlaw-Dunn-Gordon Co., Pearl & Plum.
Northern Electric Co. of Madison, Wis., 607 Johnston Bldg.
John L. Nowotny, 106 E. Pearl St.
Post-Glover Electric Co., 316 W. 4th.
Queen City Electric Co., 220 W. 8th St.
H. Richter 614 Central Ave.
R. J. Russell, 607 Johnston Bldg.
A. L. Schulman, 41 Perin Bldg.
Standard Electric Co., Pearl & Elm
Stewart Electric Co., 5th & Sycamore.
John A. Stewart Electric Engineering Co., 430 Sycamore.
The Triumph Electric Co., 610 Baymiller.

CLEVELAND, O.—
S. K. Elliott, 31 Blackstone Bldg.
Elwell-Parker Co., 1066 Hamilton.
E. S. Ford, 48 Wade Bldg.
Pelton Engineering Co., 1076 Hamilton.
Triumph Co., 48 Wade Bldg.
Westinghouse Mfg. Co., 1310 N. E. Bldg.
Lincoln Electric Co., 71 Ontario.

COLMUBUS, O.—
Andrews, Knight & Barnes, 45 W. Broad.
Buckeye Electric Repair Works, 110-112 W. Spring.
Electric Supply & Construction Co., 80 E. Gay St.
Erner & Hopkins, 370 N. High St.

TOLEDO, O.—
The F. Bissell Co., 116 St. Clair St.
Eddy & McColl, 329 The Nasby.
Williams & Meyers, 502 Summit St.

JUST WHAT CONTRACTORS NEED

To know all the best ideas, the most successful methods, the latest news regarding all contracting work in American cities, is information of great value to progressive contractors engaged in doing that kind of work.

That is just what contractors get from Municipal Engineering Magazine.

If they don't find in the Magazine the information they want, it will be furnished on request to any subscriber. In answering a single question the Magazine often incurs expense greater than a subscription amounts to for life.

This information service alone is worth to contractors many times the subscription price.

The subscription price is only $2.00 per year. No progressive contractor can afford to be without the Magazine.

I am pleased with Municipal Engineering.—*Geo. H. Smarden, Sidewalk Contractor, Portland, Me.*

Municipal Engineering is to my mind the best for men employed in municipal work.—*J. H. Stubbs, West Roxbury, Mass.*

Municipal Engineering is worth its weight in silver. — *Salt Lake Tribune.*

PA.—
one Electric Co., Erie, Pa.
DELPHIA, PA.—
atic Fan & Motor Co., 1407 Filbert St.
C. Electric Co, 45 N. 7th St.
eney Irwin & Co., 1217 Filbert
er-Wheeler Electric Co., No. rican Bldg.
H. Dallett & Co., York and ely Ave.
r Engineering Co., 125-127 11th St.
Electric Mfg. Co., 506 Comce St.
ington Co., 47 S. 17th St.
al Electric Co., 206 S. 11th St.
one Electrical Exch., 130 S. on St.
Lehman & Co., 109 S. Juniper
r City Elec. Co., 237 Dock St.
e L. Richter, 1914 Columbia
lott Shaw & Co., 632 Arch St.
H. Stewart & Co., 35 N. 7th
Strang, 723 Walnut St.
R. Swope, 120 N. 7th St.
nghouse Elec. & Mfg. Co., 708 d Title Bldg.
BURG, PA.—
nghouse Electric & Mfg. Co.
ORT, R. I.—
in Hammett & Co., 32 Mill St.
ilven & Potter, 247 Thames St.
ON, TEX.—
on Plumbing Co., 713 Main St.
Miller, 12 Main St.
ON, WIS.—
tern Electrical Mfg. Co.
AUKEE, WIS.—
tern Electrical Mfg. Co., 600 st Bldg.
F. Rohn, 88 Mason St.
Engineering Co., 1001 New End Bldg.

ELECTRIC LIGHTING.

er Engineering Co., 125-127 11th St., Philadelphia, Pa.
tone Electric Co., Erie, Pa.
. Thayer, New York City.
inghouse Electric & Mfg. Co., sburg, Pa.

ELECTRIC MACHINERY.

er Engineering Co., 125-127 11th St., Philadelphia, Pa.
y Mfg. Co., Columbus, O.
tone Electric Co., Erie, Pa.
e, Williams & Co., Trust Bldg., ladelphia, Pa.
. Rumsey Mfg. Co., St. Louis,
Westinghouse Electric & Mfg. Co., Pittsburg, Pa.

ELECTRIC WIRING.

D'Olier Engineering Co., 125-127 S. 11th St., Philadelphia, Pa.
H. A. Holder, 45 Warren St., Boston, Mass.
Keystone Electric Co., Erie, Pa.
Westinghouse Electric & Mfg. Co., Pittsburg, Pa.
Henry Kroder, Katz Bldg., Paterson, N. J.
Morse, Williams & Co., Trust Bldg., Philadelphia, Pa.
Sturtevant Mill Co., Harrison Square, Boston, Mass.

ELEVATING MACHINERY.

(See Also Conveying Machinery.)
The American Clay Working Machinery Co., Bucyrus, O.
The American Stoker Co., Weld Bldg., Boston, Mass.
Chambers Brothers Co., 52d St. below Lancaster Ave., Philadelphia, Pa.
D'Olier Engineering Co., 125-127 S. 11th St., Philadelphia, Pa.
The Eastern Machinery Co., New Haven, Conn.
A. N. Fitzsimmons, 1531 Monadnock, Chicago, Ill.

ENGINES.

BIRMINGHAM, ALA.—
Birmingham Machine & Foundry Co., E. Birmingham.
Hardie-Tynes Foundry & Mach. Co.
Williamson Iron Co., 1420 1st Ave.
LITTLE ROCK, ARK.—
E. C. Wehrfritz Mach. & Supply Co.
Wing & Stephens Co.
SAN FRANCISCO, CAL.—
Baker & Hamilton, Pine and Davis Sts.
W. T. Garratt & Co., 138 Fremont St.
Jackson Byron Machine Works, 625 6th St.
Union Iron Works, 222 Market St.
DENVER, COL.—
Ball Engine Co., 622 Mining Exchange Bldg.
C. S. Burt, 4 Bank Blk.
F. M. Davis Iron Works Co., Larimer, Cor. 8th St.
Jeffrey Mfg. Co., 544 Equitable Bldg.
Weber Gas & Gasoline Engine Co., 1713 Wazee St.
HARTFORD, CONN.—
Pitkin Bros. & Co., 152 State St.
WILMINGTON, DEL.—
J. Poole Morton Co.
Benj. F. Shaw Co.
Walker & Elliott.

ATLANTA, GA.—
Atlanta Mach. Works.
DeLoach Mill Mfg. Co.
Thos. F. Seitzsinger.
Winship Mach. Co.

CHICAGO, ILL.—
Edw. P. Allis Co., 509 Home Ins. Bldg.
American Hoist & Derrick Co., 60 S. Canal.
Atlas Corliss Engines, 204 Dearborn.
Atlas Engine Works, cor. Canal & Randolph.
Ball Engine Co., 1526 Monadnock Blk.
William Baragwanth, 48-52 W. Division.
Borden & Selleck, 48-50 Lake St.
Brownell & Co., 184-86 Washington.
Buckeye Engine Co., 1249, 204 Dearborn.
M. C. Bullock Mfg. Co., 1170 W. Lake.
H. Channon Co., Market & Randolph.
Erie City Iron Works, 34-36 W. Monroe.
Erie Engines & Boilers, 57 S. Canal.
Fairbanks, Morse & Co., Franklin and Monroe.
Fraser & Chalmers, cor. 12th & Washtenaw.
Hamilton Corliss Engine Co., 46 S. S. Canal.
Chas. Kaestner & Co., 241-61 S. Jefferson.
Marine Iron Works, Clyborn & Southport Ave., ft. C St.
Lidgerwood Mfg. Co., 1510 Old Colony Bldg.
Phoenix Iron Works Co., 202-4 W. W. Bldg.
Rainier & Williams, 63 S. Canal.
Willis Shaw, 625-6, N. Y. Life Bldg.
Troy Engine & Machine Co., 1502 Monadnock.
E. H. Wachs, 158-164 Indiana.
Chas. P. Willard & Co., 49 S. Canal.

EVANSVILLE, IND.—
J. T. Foley & Co., 102 N. 3d St.
Grote Manufacturing Co., 116 Fulton Ave.
Heilman Machine Works, 127 L-1st St.
Ferd Holz, 18-30 3d Ave.
Massillon Eng. & Thresher Co., 1325 Main St.

INDIANAPOLIS, IND.—
Allfree Engine Co., 21st & Northwestern.
Atlas Engine Works, Cor 19th and Martindale.
Chandler & Taylor Co., 740 W. Washington.
Howe Engine Co., cor. Hillside & Boyd.

LOGANSPORT, IND.—
Bridge City Construction Co., I Island.

MUNCIE, IND.—
Albert Carpenter, 723 S. Liberty
Cary Crozier, W. Adams, bet. & Manning.

RICHMOND, IND.—
Gaar, Scott & Co., Washington & N. 6th St.
Richmond Machine Works, 524-10th St.
Robinson & Co., N. S. Main, b & 3d.

BURLINGTON, IA.—
Murray Iron Works Co.

KANSAS CITY, KAN.—
Riverside Iron Works Co.

LOUISVILLE, KY.—
American Machine Co., 523 E. M
W. E. Caldwell & Co.
Grainger & Co.

NEW ORLEANS, LA.—
Gardner Motor Co., Ltd., The, St., bet. St. Ann & Dumaine.
Harrisburg Foundry & Mach.
Shakespeare Iron Works, 913 St.

PORTLAND, ME.—
Jno. Lidback.
Orr & Jennings.
Portland Co.

BALTIMORE, MD.—
Ames Iron Works, Equitable I
Robt. Poole & Son Co., 233 E man St.
Wallace Stebbins & Sons, 1 German St.

BOSTON, MASS.—
American Down Draft Boiler (Congress St.
American Rotary Engine C Devonshire.
American Stoker Co., 53 State
Ames Iron Works, 8 Oliver.
Atlantic Works, 70 Border.
Babcock & Wilcox Co.
A. Bedford, 43 Milk St.
Bertelsen & Petersen, 140-146 I E. B.
Boston Hoisting Co., 54 Falmo
Boston Blower Co., Hyde Parl
Braman, Dow & Co., 239-245 (way.
Buckeye Engine Co., 178 Devon
Buerkel & Co., 28 Union Park
Byers & Smith, 103 Haverhill
Henry D. Cram, Powers St., S.
Joseph Crowther, 81 Haverhill.
Cunningham Engineering Co., 62 mont Bldg.
Cunningham Iron Co., Fargo S

vis & Co., 53 State St.
' Iron Works, 53 State St.
achine Works, 32 Oliver.
W. Field, 117 Main, Cam-
ort.
zhenry & Co., 36 Charleston.
er Engine Co., Weymouth,

. Franklin, 165-167 Ft. Hill

nt & Co., 8 Oliver.
el Economizer Co., 53 State.
r Foundry & Mchy. Co., 60

rvey, 606 Atlantic Ave.
& Co., 160 Liverpool.
: Blanchard Co., 39 Charles-

t & Co., 67 Charleston.
hattuck & Co., 45 Charles-

ughton, 77 Oliver St.
Kendricken, 80 Sudbury.
gineering Co., 61 Oliver.
Kendall & Sons, 144-178 Main

iball, 53 State St.
od Mfg. Co., 77 Oliver St.
oss, 21 S. Market St.
McLauthlin Co., 120 Fulton

son, 81 Haverhill.
s, 162 A.
Minton, 119 Summer.
ating Co., 512 John Hancock

Morse & Co., 19 Pearl.
ett, 4 Oliver St.
Power Co., 258 Wash. St.
: Safety Steam Power Co.,
nshire.
Engine Works, 19 Pearl St.
age Boiler Co., 32 Oliver St.
Paine & Son, Clayton, cor.

Percy, 212 Summer St.
amons & Co., 57 Oliver.
llips, 410 Sudbury Bldg.
att, 111 Haverhill.
Morrison Mfg. Co., 31-45
ambridgeport.
hmond & Son, 571 E. 5th.
sson Engine Co., 239 Frank-

Dynamo & Engine Co., 53

on Works, 180-198 Main St.,
geport.
berts & Co., 137 Portland.
tor Vehicle Co., 113 Devon-

tevant Co., Jamaica Plain,
R. Station.
Co., 1015 Tremont Bldg.

Walker & Pratt Mfg. Co., 31 Union.
Walworth Construction & Supply Co., 100 Pearl.
Westinghouse, Church, Kerr & Co., 53 State St.
Whittier Machine Co., 53 State St.

BROCTON, MASS.—
White & Wetherbee, 254 Main St.

CAMBRIDGE, MASS.—
Walter W. Field, 117 Main St.
J. H. Houghton, 77 Oliver St.
Rawson & Morrison, 31 Main St.

PITTSFIELD, MASS.—
J. W. Kirchner, 156 North St.
Robbins, Gamwell & Co., 68 West St.

QUINCY, MASS.—
Walworth Mfg. Co., 132 Federal St.

DETROIT, MICH.—
American Blower Co., 1400 Russel St.
John Brennan & Co., Toledo Ave. & 24th St.
Buffalo Pitts Co., S. S. M. C. R. R., W. of Junction Ave.
Detroit River Gasoline Engine Works, 665 Atwater St., E.
Dimmler Machine Works, 90 Woodbridge St., W.
Gardner Elevator Co., 21st & River Sts.
C. C. Worner Machinery Co., 55 Woodbridge St., W.
Wray-Austin Machinery Co., 171 Woodbridge St., S. W.

MINNEAPOLIS, MINN.—
The E. P. Allis Co., 416 Corn Exch.
Crown Iron Works, 113 2d Ave., S. E.
Minneapolis Iron Works, 900 S. 4th St.
Otto Gas Engine Works, 313 S. 3d St.
J. G. Robertson, 532 Guaranty Bldg.
Woolf Valve Gear Co., 912 Guaranty Bldg.

ST. PAUL, MINN.—
Geo. R. Morton, 109 Natl. G. A. Bk. Bldg.
J. G. Robertson, 409 Manhattan Bldg.
A. L. Ide & Sons, 408 Manhattan Bldg.
Western Paul Steam System Co., 136 Endicott Arcade.

CORINTH, MISS.—
W. T. Adams Machine Co.

KANSAS CITY, MO.—
Weber Gas & Gasoline Engine Co., 413 S. W. Boulevard.
Kansas City Elevator Mfg. Co., 115 W. 19th St.
Otis Elevator Co., 932 N. Y. Life Bldg.
Riverside Iron Works, Central Ave. & 4th St.

ST. LOUIS, MO.—
Brownell & Co., of Dayton, O., 502 N. 2d.
Buckeye Engine Co., 721 Olive.
Curtis & Co. Mfg. Co., 2201-2, 2211 Wash Ave.
Wm. Ellison & Sons Mfg. Co., 1020 N. 6th St.
Erie Engine Works, 521 N. 2d St.
Exeter Machine Works, The, 1311 Chemical Bldg.
Fairbank Morse & Co., 302-4 Wash. Ave.
Hooker Steam Pump Co., 1101 N. 2d.
Hoover, Owens & Rentschler Co., 319 N. 4th.
Houston, Stanwood & Gamble Co., 811 N. 2d St.
A. L. Ide & Son, 705 Olive.
Moses P. Johnson Mchy. Co., 715-717 N. 2d.
Kingsland Mfg. Co., 1521 N. 11th.
Missouri Motor Co., 5726 Vernon Ave.
N. O. Nelson Mfg. Co., 8th, S. E. cor. St. Charles.
D. W. Pratt, 211-213 Lucas.
M. Rumely & Co., 108 S. 10th.
L. M. Rumsey Mfg. Co., 806-820 N. 2d.
Rumsey & Sikemeier Co., 519-521 N. Main.
Russell Engine Co., 319 N 4th St.
St. Louis Engineering & Supply Co., 706 Chestnut St.
St. Louis Gas & Gasoline Eng Wks., 2519 S. 2d.
St. Louis Gasoline Motor Co., 824 Clark Ave.
St. Louis Iron Machine Works, 126 Choteau Ave.
St. Louis Steam Engine Co., 16 S. Commercial.
J. A. Vail, 319 N. 4th.

OMAHA, NEB —
Drake, Wilson & Williams.

NASHUA, N. H.—
Rollins Engine Co.

NEWARK, N. J.—
Cyrus Currier & Sons, 21 R. R. Pl.
Gould & Eberhardt, 113 J. R. R. Ave.
W. G. & G. Greenfield, N. 5th & Cross Sts.
Hewes & Phillips, Orange & Ogden Sts.
Lambert Hoisting Engine Co., 117 Pioneer St.
Kowalewski & Ruesch, 22 Green St.
Joseph S. Mundy, 22 Prospect St.
George A. Ohl & Co., 157 Oraton St.
Seymour & Whitlock, 43 Lawrence St.
Skinner & Leary, 5, 7 R. R. Pl.
Watts, Campbell Co., The, 298 Ogden St.

NEW YORK CITY—BOROUGH BROOKLYN—
Conrad Carlson, 1230 15th St.
Lidgerwood Mfg. Co., Foot Diken
John W. Plunkett, 476 Hamilton
South Brooklyn Steam Engine 149 Van Brunt.

NEW YORK CITY, BOROUGHS MANHATTAN AND BRONX—
E. P. Allis Co., 95 Liberty St.
Am. Engine Co., 95 Liberty St.
Ames Iron Works, 149 Broadwa
Armington & Sims, 141 Broadw
Atlas Engine Works, 26 Cortland
Earle C. Bacon, Havemeyer B
Ball Wood Co., 120 Liberty.
Bass Foundry & Machine Co., Broadway.
Joshua Baggaley, 14 James Slip.
Baxter Engine Co., 118 Liberty S
James Beggs & Co., 9 Dey St.
Charles Behlen, 72 Trinity Pl.
C. A. Bennett, 120 Liberty St.
C. H. Brown & Co., 141 Broadw
Buckeye Engine Co., 39 Cortland
A. A. Cardwell, 39 Cortlandt St.
Walter Christie, 519 E. 18th St.
Columbia Machine Works, 521 45th St.
C. & G. Cooper Co., 26 Cortland
Lancelot Copleston, 39 Cortlandt
Donegan & Swift, 6 Murray St.
J. F. Duffy, 39 Cortlandt St.
Ewing-Essick Engine Co., 62 Tr Pl.
Fischer Foundry & Machine Co. Broadway.
Fitchburg Steam Engine Co., 39 (landt St.
Frick Co., 39 Cortlandt St.
Gas Engine & Power Co. and Ch L. Seabury & Co., 50 Broadway
E. P. Hampson Co., 26 Cortlandt
Haring Steam Plant Equipment 141 Broadway.
W. F. Haring, 141 Broadway.
Harrisburg Foundry & Ma Works, 203 Broadway.
Hoover, Owens & Rentschle Cortlandt St.
Houston, Starrwood & Gamble 39 Cortlandt St.
Howard & Morse, 45 Fulton St.
C. W. Hunt Co., 45 Broadway.
International Power Co., 253 B way.
F W. Iredell, 26 Cortlandt St.
Lambert Hoisting Engine Co. Broadway.
Lane & Bodley Co., 120 Liberty
James Leffel & Co., 85 Liberty
Leonard & McCoy, 118 Liberty
Lidgerwood Mfg. Co., 96 Liberty
E. H. Ludeman, 39 Cortlandt
McIntosh, Seymour & Co., 26 landt St.

Miller & Co., 39 Cortlandt St.
ı Iron Works, 814 E. 19th St.
Central Iron Works Co., 17 Row.
Safety Steam Power Co., 107 ty St.
Yacht Launch & Engine Co., ls Heights.
& Warrin, 36 Warren St.
Co., 120 Liberty St.
Engineering Co., 120 Liberty

lvania Iron Works, 621 Broad-

k Iron Works Co., 15 Cortlandt

ay Dynamo & Engine Co., 149 lway.
Hydraulic Engine Mfg. Co., liberty St.
Rogers & Co., 42 Cortlandt St.
& F. M. Roots Co., 109 Liberty

Scholl & Co., 126 Liberty St.
Swingley & Co., Ltd., 120 Lib- St.
n Engine Co., 136 Liberty St.
Engine Co., 143 Liberty St.
s Mfg. Co., 95 Liberty St.
ers, Wells & Co., 26 Cortlandt

Sturtevant Co., 131 Liberty St.
Sullivan, 365 Front St.
n Locomotive Mfg. Co., 26 andt St.
Todd, 203 Broadway.
sal Engine Co., 52 Broadway.
Machine Co., 95 Liberty St.
Wachs & Co., 39 Cortlandt St.
town Engine Co., 39 Cortlandt

Wells, 136 Liberty St.
ghouse Machine Co., 26 Cort- St.
ghouse, Church, Kerr & Co., ortlandt St.
on & Breir, 141 Broadway.
t Steam Engine Works, 90 Broadway.
YORK CITY, BOROUGH OF ENS—
Island Machine & Marine Com- tion Co., foot East Ave. (L. I.
.
TOWN, N. Y.—
n, Hodge & O'Brien, 40 Flow- dg.
town Engine Co., 215 Main St.
OTTE, N. C.—
nburg Iron Works.
, O.—
tar Drilling Mch. Co., 145-150 lington St.
, Rice & Co., 301-403 S. Broad-

Webster, Camp & Lane, 180 N. High St.

CINCINNATI, O.—
Fairbanks, Morse & Co., 307 Walnut.
The E. A. Kinsey Co., 331 W. 4th.
Howe Scale Co., The, 129 E. 5th.
Wais & Roos Punch & Shear Co., 1422 Plum.
F. M. Watkins, 309 W. 4th.

COLUMBUS, O.—
Columbus Brass Co., 94 N. 6th St.
W. H. Miller Co., The, 31 W. Broad St.
Potts Machinery Co., 162 N. 3d St.
Rarig Engineering Co., 5th Ave., E. Alum Creek.
Weinman Machine Works, 21-23 N. Scioto St.

FINDLAY, O.—
Adams Bros.' Co., The, 421-423 W. Main Cross.
Parshall & Till, 101½ S. Main St.

MARIETTA, O.—
Waterman & Detler, 109 Second.

NEWARK, O.—
Scheidler Machine Works, N. W. cor. 1st & Franklin.

PORTSMOUTH, O.—
Jacob Brunner, 28 W. 5th.
Ports. Foundry & Machine Works, W. 3d & Jefferson.

SPRINGFIELD, O.—
The O. S. Kelly Co., N. Limestone, bet. North & Frey.
The Jas. Leffel & Co., E. of C., C., C. & St. L. Ry. bet. Lagonda Ave. and Nelson.
Trump Mfg. Co., The, Junc. C., C., C. & St. L. R. R. & Greenmont Ave.

STEUBENVILLE, O.—
Robinson & Irwin, 610 Adams.

TOLEDO, O.—
G. W. Heartley, 901 Water St.
The Lozier Motor Co., 615 Gardner Bldg.
McLin & Geck, cor. Monroe & Bancroft Sts.

PORTLAND, ORE.—
Portland Iron Works.
Willamette Iron Works.

BANGOR, PA.—
The S. Flory Co.

PHILADELPHIA, PA.—
Ames Iron Works, 716 Fidelity Bldg.
John Baizley Iron Works, 514 S. Delaware Ave.
Bates Machine Co., 631 Arch St.
T. T. Burchfield Co., 619 Arch St.
Burhorn & Granger, 1004 Girard Bldg.
P. F. Campbell, 55 Laurel St.

Chambers Bros. Co., 52d St., below Lancaster Ave.
J. F. Chuse Co., 633 Arch St.
Geo. E. Coolidge, 327 Drexel Bldg.
Corlis Engine Wks., Howard & Huntingdon Sts.
D'Olier Engineering Co., 125 S. 11th St.
Cox & Sons Co., 215 Race St.
William Eckbolds' Sons, 707-13 E. Girard Ave.
Erie City Iron Wks., 803 Land Title Bldg.
Arthur Falkenham, 109-15 N. 22d St.
Fischer Foundry & Machine Wks., 608 Harrison Bldg.
Fitchburg Steam Eng. Co., 1001 Chestnut St.
Harrisburg Foundry & Mach. Wks., 702 Betz Bldg.
John E. Holmes & Co., 612 Arch St.
Kensington Engine Wks., 704 Arch St.
Lane & Bodley Co., 333 Phila. Bourse.
John H. McGowan, 1420 Chestnut St.
John H. Naylor, Front & Girard Ave.
N. Y. Safety Steam Power Co., 15 N. 7th St.
August Nittinger, Sr., 333 Phila. Bourse.
Philadelphia Engineering Works.
Rawson & Morrison Mfg. Co., 33 Phila. Bourse.
Rider-Ericsson Eng. Co., 40 N. 7th St.
Ridgway Dynamo & Eng. Co., 807 Girard Bldg.
William F. Ruwell, 919-23 Ridge Ave.
Julian Scholl & Co., 611 Betz Bldg.
Sciple Pump Co., 107-9 N. 3d St.
Snow Steam Pump Works, 724 Arch St.
Stillwell-Bierce & Smith-Vaile Co., 612 Arch St.
Chas. W. Van Vleck, 327 Drexel St.
Watson & McDaniel Co., 146 N. 7th St.
Westinghouse, Church, Kerr & Co., 512 Girard Bldg.
Robt. Wetherill & Co., 1225 Betz Bldg.

PITTSBURG, PA.—
Brown Hoisting & Conveying Machine Co., 1112 Carnegie Bldg.

PITTSTON, PA.—
Vulcan Iron Works, 549 Exeter St.

SCRANTON, PA.—
Dickson Mfg Co., Penn Ave & Vine St.

WILKESBARRE, PA —
Vulcan Iron Works.

WILLIAMSPORT, PA.—
Valley Iron Works.

YORK, PA.—
York Mfg. Co.

PROVIDENCE, R. I.—
York Mfg. Co., York, Pa.; N Bunn, N. E. Agent, 9 Westmi St.

CHARLESTON, S. C.—
Bailey-Lebby Co., 213 Meeting.
Cameron & Barkley Co., 160 Mee
Charleston Iron Works, 123 Pr ard.
J. F. Riley, 6-8 South.
Riverside Iron Works, Concord end Hasell.
Valk & Mudrock Iron Works, Hasell.

COLUMBIA, S. C.—
V. C. Bradham, 1326 Main St.
W. H. Gibbes & Co., 804 Gervai
Palmetto Iron Works, 1802 Li St.
Tozers Engine Works, 711 Ge St.

GREENVILLE, S. C.—
Greenville Machine Works, 21 Lawrence St.
Palmetto Iron Works, 402 Rhett

EAU CLAIRE, WIS.—
Eau Claire Mill Supply Co., 402 Claire St.

MILWAUKEE, WIS.—
The Edw. P. Allis Co., Clinton bet. Florida and National Ave
The Filer & Stowell Co., Beche Ziemer St.
Milwaukee Machinery Co. (Inc. W. Water St.
O. L. Packard Machinery Co., 1 Water St.
Vilter Mfg. Co., Clinton St., Becher and Lincoln Ave.
Wisconsin Machinery Co., 125 Water St.
H. P. Yale & Co., 99 W. Water

EXCAVATORS.

(See also Dredges and Shov
M. Beatty & Sons, Welland, Canada.
The Bucyrus Co., South Milwa Wis.
Jeffrey Mfg. Co., Columbus.
Robins Conveying Belt Co., Park Row, New York.

FANS.

American Blower Co., De Mich.
Backus Mfg. Co., 174 Penn. St., ark, N. J.
J. B. & J. M. Cornell, New City.
F. N. Crane, 179 Market St., Ne N. J.
C. H Gifford & Co., 135 N. 3 Philadelphia, Pa.
B. F. Sturtevant Co., Boston,

ichusetts Fan. Co., 53 State Boston, Mass.

rke & Marmon Co., Indianalis, Ind.

Rumsey Mfg. Co., St. Louis,

ur & Whitlock. 43 Laurence Newark, N. J.

er Electrical Co., 251 Market Newark. N. J.

FEED PIPES.

r & Chalmers, W. 12th St. and htenaw Ave., Chicago, Ill.

n Iron Wrks, Wilkesbarre, Pa.

DERS FOR PEBBLE AND TUBE MILLS.

Mill Co., 5 Beekman St., New k. N. Y.

FLAT BOXES.

Bartlett & Co., 43-45 Center Cleveland, O.

rke & Marmon, Indianapo- Ind.

s Pulley Co., Columbus, Ind.

r & Elliott, Wilmington, Del.

FORGINGS.

ehem Foundry & Machine Co., Bethlehem, Pa.

GEARING.

Allis Co., Milwaukee, Wis.

Bartlett & Co., 43-45 Center Cleveland, O.

's Brass & Model Works, 312 Ave., Newark, O.

ehem Foundry & Machine Co., h Bethlehem, Pa.

n & Sharpe Mfg. Co., Provice, R. I.

. Caldwell & Son Co., Western and 17th St., Chicago, Ills.

& J. M. Cornell. 26th and 11th . New York.

V. Cresson Co., 18th and Alley Ave., Philadelphia, Pa.

e Mfg Co., Mishawaka, Ind.

Rivet & Machinery Co., Cuyaa Falls, O., and 26 Fulton St., York.

r & Chalmers. W 12th St and htenaw Ave., Chicago Ills.

al Electric Co., Schenectady, Y.

on Tool Co., 19 Browns Race, hester, N. Y.

Clutch Co., Cleveland, O.

es & Blanchard Co., 23 Charles St., Boston, Mass

es & Blanchard Co., 23 Charles n, Boston Mass.

urgh & Sons Co., Cleveland, O.

effrey Mfg Co., Columbus, O.

Jones & Sons [illegible] Mass

& Laughlin Ltd., Pittsburg, New York & Chicago

Lane & Bodley Co., Cincinnati, O.

Geo. T. McLauthlin Co., 120 Fulton St., Boston, Mass.

Morse, Williams & Co., Trust Bldg., Philadelphia, Pa.

Nordyke & Marmon Co., Indianapolis, Ind.

J. Noyes Mfg. Co., Buffalo, N. Y.

A. Plamondon Mfg. Co., 57 S. Clinton St., Chicago, Ill.

Robert Poole & Son Co., Woodbury Sta., Baltimore, Md.

Reading Foundry Co., Reading, Pa.

Reeves Pulley Co., Columbus, Ind.

Chas. Ross & Son Co., 16-20 Steuben St., Brooklyn, N. Y.; 233 E. German St., Baltimore, Md.

Sprout, Waldron & Co., Muncy, Pa.

Vulcan Iron Works, Wilkesbarre, Pa.

Walker & Elliott, Wilmington, Del.

Webster Mfg. Co., 1075 W. 15th St., Chicago, Ill.

T. B. Wood's Sons, Chambersburg, Pa.

GRATE BARS.

Bethlehem Foundry & Machine Co., S. Bethlehem, Pa.

Fraser & Chalmers, W. 12th St. and Washtenaw Ave., Chicago, Ill.

L. M. Rumsey Mfg. Co., St. Louis, Mo.

GREASE CUPS.

Reeves Pulley Co., Columbus, Ind.

Robins Conveying Belt Co., 13-21 Park Row, New York.

GRINDING MACHINERY.

(See also Pulverizers.)

The American Clay Working Machinery Co., Bucyrus, O.

Bethlehem Foundry & Machine Co., So. Bethlehem, Pa.

Geo. V. Cresson Co., 18th St. and Allegheny Ave., Philadelphia, Pa.

Nordyke & Marmon Co., Indianapolis, Ind.

Rockwood Mfg. Co., Indianapolis, Ind (clay)

Sprout, Waldron & Co., Muncy, Pa.

Whitney Foundry Equipment Co., Harvey, Ill (clay)

GRIT MILLS.

Krupp, (Thos. Prosser & Son), 15 Gold St., New York.

Sturtevant Mill Co., Harrison Square, Boston, Mass.

GUDGEONS.

Nordyke & Marmon Co., Indianapolis

Reeves Pulley Co., Columbus, Ind.

Walker & Elliott, Wilmington, Del.

HANGERS.

C. O. Bartlett & Co., 43-45 Center St., Cleveland, O.

HOW TO HELP BUSINESS

In plans for building up business reputation—really the first essential step—and for getting business, the best help at the least expense is in good advertising.

In the matter of advertising we have all that is good.

Look through MUNICIPAL ENGINEERING MAGAZINE and you will see that we have good advertisers—we don't want any other kind.

The service to them is so good that many of them think it is all they need.

If you seek business in our field you need our help.

In our field we know what we can do. We don't hesitate to say that we can do about all that can be done.

We cover the field thoroughly, we study it constantly, we are closely in touch with it everywhere.

Our organization embraces the best ability and the most thorough service.

This is the help you need—it is the kind that will do more for you than all other at less expense.

Write to us and ask us what we can do for you—if we can't help you we will tell you so—if we can we will tell you how, and that is what you want to know if you are progressive and wide awake.

Municipal Engineering Co.

See What Others Say About Our Service

What An Advertisement Did in Ten Days

Chicago, Ill., Nov. 24, 1900.

Municipal Engineering Co.

Gentlemen: Last month we placed an advertisement in your Magazine, which appeared for the first time in the November number, and which gave us the benefit of your advance information bulletin service. From this bulletin we obtained information which led to the sale of two of our concrete mixing machines, within ten days after the advertisement first appeared.

We are much pleased at the promptness with which returns have been realized, and beg to express our appreciation of your Magazine as an advertising medium, and also the great help which your bulletin service has proved to us. Yours very truly,

MCKELVEY CONCRETE MACHINERY CO.

One Job That More Than Repaid Them

Chicago, Ill., Oct. 31, 1900.

The Municipal Engineering Magazine.

Dear Sirs: The first of January last, we placed an advertisement in your Magazine, and also subscribed to same. Believing that credit should be given when due, we desire to write and advise you that we have secured, through the advance information on contemplated work, very valuable information to us the past year, and in fact, we have secured through your Magazine one job of which we knew nothing before, which more than repays us for the cost of the advertisement.

In our business we are desirous at all times of securing recommendations for our material and feeling that possibly you have the same desire in this line, we write you as above. If this is of any service to you you are at liberty to make use of it.

Yours truly,

THE CLEVELAND STONE CO.

(Signed) C. W. Walters,
Western Agent.

ıem Foundry & Machine Co., thlehem, Pa.
Caldwell & Son Co., Western & 17th St., Chicago. Ill.
ıers Bros., 32d St. below aster Ave. Philadelphia,
Mfg. Co., Mishawaka, Ind.
& Chalmers. W. 12th St. & tenaw Ave., Chicago, Ill.
uch Co., Cleveland, O.
ffrey Mfg. Co., Columbus, O.
ke & Marmon Co., Indianıs, Ind.
Pulley Co., Columbus, Ind.
Ross & Son Co., 1520 Steuben Brooklyn, N. Y.
& Elliott, Wilmington, Del.
er Mfg. Co., 1075-1097 W. St., Chicago, Ill.

HEATERS.

can Blower Co., Detroit,
Forge Co., Buffalo, N. Y., 6 Cortlandt St., New York.
ctors' Tool Co., 118 S. 6th St., delphia, Pa.
al Blower Co, 17th and St. Ave., Milwaukee, Wis.
York Blower Co., Bucyrus, O. rtlandt St., New York.
Sturtevant, Jamaica Plain Sta- Boston, Mass.

HOISTING MACHINERY.

ıan Hoist & Derrick Co., 904 ıen Bldg., New Orleans, La.
C. Bacon, Havemeyer Bldg. York, N. Y.
Bartlett & Co., 43-45 Center Cleveland, O.
n & Selleck, 48-50 Lake St., ago, Ill.
Hoisting & Conveying Co., land, O., and Pittsburg, Pa.
ctors' Plant Mfg. Co., Boston,
Mfg. Co., Mishawaka, Ind.
astern Machinery Co., New en, Conn.
Machine Works, 1311 Chemical ., St. Louis, Mo.
Flory Mfg. Co., Bangor, Pa.
& Chalmers, 568 Washtenaw . Chicago, Ill.
[. Fritz Foundry & Machine 2008 S. 3d, St. Louis, Mo.
ı Foundry & Machine Co.
S. Harris Co., Rome, N. Y.
ayward Co., 97 Cedar St., New , N. Y.
r Elevator Co., 314 E. Water Syracuse, N. Y.
d Iron Works, Chicago, Cor. ıger, Buffalo, N. Y.

Ingersoll-Sergeant Drill Co., **Boston,** Mass.
Jeffrey Mfg. Co., Columbus, O.
Moses P. Johnson Machinery Co., 715 N. 2d, St. Louis, Mo.
Kaltenbach & Griess, 1618 Williamson Bldg., Cleveland, O.
Kansas City Elevator Mfg. Co., 115 W. 19th St., Kansas City, Mo.
Keystone Electric Co., Erie, Pa.
Lidgerwood Mfg. Co., 96 Liberty St. New York, Boston, Mass., 406 Canal St., New Orleans.
Lord, Bowler & Co., 39 Center St., Cleveland, O.
Volney W. Mason & Co., Lafayette St., Newport, R. I.
Geo. T. McLauthlin Co., 120 Fulton St., Boston, Mass.
Nordyke & Marmon Co., Indianapolis, Ind.
Otis Elevator Co., 112 Church St., Buffalo, N. Y.
D. W. Pratt, 211 Lucas Ave., St. Louis, Mo.
Ransome & Smith Co., 17-19 9th St., Brooklyn, N. Y.
Rand Drill Co., 100 Broadway, New York, Monadnock Bldg., Chicago.
Riverside Iron Works, Central Ave. & 4th St., Kansas City, Mo.
Robins Conveying Belt Co., 13-21 Park Row, New York.
L. M. Rumsey Mfg. Co., 806 2d St., St. Louis, Mo.
Weber Gas & Gasoline Engine Co., 413 S. W. Boulevard, Kansas City, Mo.

HOPPERS.

Webster Mfg. Co., 1075-1097 W. 15th St., Chicago, Ill.

KILNS, ROTARY.

The American Clay Working Machinery Co., Bucyrus, O.
Bethlehem Foundry & Machine Company, South Bethlehem, Pa.
The Bonnot Company, Canton, O.
Fraser & Chalmers, 12th & Washtenaw Ave., Chicago, and 80 Broadway, New York.
Gates Iron Works, Elston Ave. & Bloomingdale Road, Chicago, Ill.
Wm. F. Mosser & Son, Allentown, Pa.
Reeves Pulley Co., Columbus, Ind.
F. L. Smidth & Co., 66 Maiden Lane, New York.
Vulcan Iron Works, Wilkesbarre, Pa.

LINING FOR KILNS.

F. L. Smidth & Co., 66 Maiden Lane, New York.

LOCOMOTIVES, SMALL.

Baldwin Locomotive Works, 500 N. Broad St., Philadelphia, Pa.

W. J. Carlin Co., Lewis Block, Pittsburg, Pa.

Jeffrey Mfg. Co., Columbus, O.

Arthur Koppel, 68 Broad St., New York.

C. W. Leavitt & Co., 15 Cortlandt St., New York.

H. K. Porter Co., 531 Wood St.

Stearns Mfg. Co., Erie, Pa.

Vulcan Iron Works, Wilkesbarre, Pa.

Westinghouse Electric & Mfg. Co., Pittsburg, Pa.

LUBRICATORS.

Robins Conveying Belt Co., 13-21 Park Row, New York.

L. M. Rumsey Mfg. Co., St. Louis, Mo.

MAGNETS.

Stephen R. Krom, 113-115 Plymouth St., Jersey City, N. J.

Nordyke & Marmon Co., Indianapolis, Ind .

Sprout, Waldron & Co., Muncy, Pa.

MECHANICAL DRAFT.

(See also Blowers.)

American Blower Co., Detroit, Mich.

The American Stoker Co., Weld Bldg., Boston, Mass.

C. H. Gifford & Co., 135 N. 3d St., Philadelphia, Pa.

National Blower Works, 17th St. & St. Paul Ave., Milwaukee, Wis.

B. F. Sturtevant Co., Jamaica Plain, Boston, Mass.

MECHANICAL STOKERS.

The American Stoker Co., Weld Bldg., Boston, Mass.

The Babcock & Wilcox Co., 29 Cortlandt St., New York.

MIXERS FOR CEMENT.

Max F. Abbe Mfg. Co., 218 Broadway, New York.

Alexander Iron Works, Syracuse, N. Y.

The Bonnot Co., Canton, O.

W. D. Dunning, Syracuse, N. Y.

Nordyke & Marmon Co., Indianapolis, Ind.

MORTAR COLORS.

Thomas Moulding Company, 1007 Chamber of Commerce Bldg., Chicago, Ill.

Wm. Wirt Cl
St., Baltimor

Cleveland Iron
land, O.

Fiske & Co., 1
ton, **Mass.**

S. H. French
& Callowhill

Rossie Iron O
burg, N. Y.

Chas. R. Week
St., New Yor

OVERH

New Jersey Fo
26 Cortlandt

G. L. Stuebne
St., Long Isl

Wilcox Mfg. C

P

Barnard & L
Ill.

C. O. Bartlett
St. Clevelan

W. D. Dunning

The S. Howe
N. Y.

The Invincible
Silver Creek,

Nordyke & M
apolis, Ind.

P

The Max F.
Broadway,

The Bonnot C

Robert Delar
France.

Kruppe (Tho
Gold St., Ne

John McGlincy
York, N. Y.

Casimir Tho
K, N. Y.
New York.

F. L. Smidth
Lane, New

B. Voigt, 138
York City.

PEB

(See also Bal

C. O. Bartlett
St., Clevela

Bethlehem Fo
So. Bethlehem

The Bonnot C

Contractors' T
Philadelphia,

Nordyke & M
apolis, Ind.

ER TRANSMISSION.

s Co., Milwaukee, Wis.
: Selleck Co., 48-50 Lake :ago, Ill.
lleable Iron Co., Detroit,

ldwell & Son Co., Western .7th St., Chicago, Ill.
Co., Lakeport, N. H.
resson Co., 141 Liberty St., ›rk; 18th St. & Allegheny iladelphia, Pa.
vis Iron Works Co., Den-

fg. Co., Mishawaka, Ind.
:ngineering Co., 125-127 St., Philadelphia, Pa.
it & Machinery Co., Cuya- ılls, O., and 226 Fulton St., rk.
Chalmers, W. 12th St. & ıaw Ave., Chicago, Ill.
h Co., Cleveland, O.
Machine Co., Holyoke, & er, Mass.
fg. Co., Columbus, O.
Laughlins (Ltd.), Pittsburg, rk & Chicago.
: Electric Co., Erie, Pa.
t Engineering Co., Nice- Philadelphia, Pa., & 49 Dey r York.
t Machinery Co., Chicago,

AcLanthlin Co., 120 Fulton ton, Mass.
& Marmon Co., Indian- Ind.
Iron Works Co., So Nor-

ole & Son Co., Baltimore,

ulley Co., Columbus, Ind.
:onveying Belt Co., 13-21 ow, New York.
ers & Co. (Inc.), 1600 Hamil- Philadelphia, Pa.
: Elliott, Wilmington, Del.
Mfg. Co., 1075 W. 15th cago, Ill., 38 Dey St., New

fg. Co., 118-126 North Ave., , Ill.
Bros., Saginaw, Mich.
. Chambersburg, Pa.

PUG MILLS.

lso Brick Machinery.)

not Co., Canton, O.
's Bros. Co., 52d St., be- ıncaster Ave., Philadel- 'a.
eese & Co., Galion, Ohio.

PULLEYS.

American Tool & Machine Co., 109 Beach, Boston, Mass.
Aultman Co., Canton, O.
C. O. Bartlett & Co., 43-45 Center St., Cleveland, O.
Bethlehem Foundry & Machine Co., So. Bethlehem, Pa.
H. W. Caldwell & Son Co., Western Ave. and 17th St., Chicago, Ill.
Chambers Bros. Co., 52d St. below Lancaster Ave., Philadelphia, Pa.
Geo. V. Cresson & Co., 18th and Allegheny Ave., Philadelphia, Pa., and 141 Liberty St., New York.
Crowell Clutch & Pulley Co., Westfield, N. Y.
Dodge Mfg. Co., Mishawaka, Ind.
The Eastern Machinery Co., New Haven, Conn.
Exeter Machine Works, Pittston, Pa.
Falls Rivet & Mchy. Co., 52 Purchase, Boston, Mass.
Fraser & Chalmers, W. 12th and Washtenaw Ave., Chicago, Ills.
Hill Clutch Co., Cleveland, O.
James Hunter Machine Co., 70 Kilby Room 67, Boston, Mass.
Chas. J. Jager Co., 174 High, Boston, Mass.
The Jeffrey Mfg. Co., Columbus, O.
W. A. Jones Foundry & Machine Co., 58 S. Jefferson St., Chicago, Ill.
Jones & Laughlins, Ltd., Pittsburg, New York and Chicago.
Geo. F. McLauthlin Co., 120 Fulton St., Boston, Mass.
Nordyke & Marmon Co., Indianapolis, Ind.
A. Plamondon Mfg. Co., 59 S. Clinton St., Chicago, Ill.
R. Poole & Son Co., Baltimore, Md.
Reeves Pulley Co., Columbus, Ind.
Robins Conveying Belt Co., 13-21 Park Row, New York.
Chas. Ross & Son Co., 16-20 Steuben St., Brooklyn, N. Y.
Sprout, Waldron & Co., Muncy, Pa.
Union Machine Co., Worcester, Mass.
Walker & Elliott, Wilmington, Del.
Webster Mfg. Co., 1075-1097 W. 15th St., Chicago Ill.
Weller Mfg. Co., 118-126 North Ave., Chicago, Ill.
T. B. Wood's Sons, Chambersburg, Pa.

PULVERIZERS.

(See also Grinding Machinery.)

Max F. Abbe Mfg. Co., 218 Broadway, New York.
J. R. Alsing Co., 75 Guernsey St., Brooklyn, N. Y.

393 Dorchester, Boston, Mass.
Co-Operative Foundry Co., S. W. cor. Congress & 5th, Detroit, Mich.
Geo. V. Cresson Co., 18th & Alleghany Ave., Detroit, Mich.
Daly & Anderson, 51 S. Clinton, Chicago, Ill.
F. H. Davis & Co., 53 State St.
E. A. Delano, 50-56 S. Clinton, Chicago, Ill.
Dodge Mfg Co., Mishawaka, Ind., 166-68 S. Clinton St., Chicago, Ill.; 137 Purchase, Boston, Mass.
J. B. Dutton, 1026 Scotten Ave., Detroit, Mich.
Fairmount Machine Co., 2106 Wood St., Philadelphia.
Falls Rivet & Mchy. Co., 52-54 Purchase St., Boston.
Dana Fitz & Co., 110 North, Boston, Mass.
Arthur C. Harvey Co., 115 Purchase, Boston, Mass.
Hill Clutch Co., Cleveland, O.
G. & A. Hodson, 226 Arch St., Philadelphia, Pa.
Holmes & Blanchard Co., 39 Charleston, Boston, Mass.
L. L. Holt & Co., 67 Sudbury, Boston, Mass.
E. F. Houghton & Co., 240 W. Somerset St., Philadelphia.
J. Hunter Mchy. Co., 70 Kilby St., Boston, Mass.
The Jeffrey Mfg. Co., Columbus, O.
Milwaukee Rice Machinery Co., 105 W. Water St., Milwaukee, Wis.
Geo. T. McLauthlin Co., 120 Fulton St., Boston, Mass.
Nordyke & Marmon Co., Indianapolis, Ind.
Purves Machinery & Iron Co., South & Water Sts., Philadelphia, Pa.
Reeves Pulley Co., Columbus, Ind.
J. & G. Rich, 120 N. 6th St., Philadelphia, Pa.
J. Roberts & Co., 137 Portland, Boston, Mass.
Roberts Poole & Son Co., Woodbury Sta., Baltimore, Md.; 233 E. German St., Baltimore, Md.
Robins Conveying Belt Co., 13-21 Park Row, New York, N. Y.
Charles Ross & Son Co., 16 Steuben St., Brooklyn, N. Y.
L. M. Rumsey Mfg. Co., St. Louis, Mo.
Seelye Mfg. Co., 111 Lincoln, Boston, Mass.
Sprout, Waldron & Co., Muncy, Pa.
Chas. A. Strelinger & Co., 110 Bates St., Detroit, Mich.
Walker & Elliott, Wilmington, Del.
Webster Mfg Co., 1075-1079 W. 15th St., Chicago, Ill.

Philadelphia, Pa.

SHEAVE

Dodge Mfg. Co.,
Fraser & Chalmers,
tenaw Ave., Chica
Jeffrey Manufacturi
bus, O.
Geo. T. McLauthlin
St., Boston, Mass.
Nordyke & Marm
apolis, Ind.
Reeves Pulley Co.,
L. M. Rumsey Mfg
Mo.
Walker & Elliott,

SPEED REG

D'Olier Engineeri
S. 11th St., Phil
Keystone Electri
Reeves Pulley Co.,

SPOU

Dodge Mfg. Co., M
Fraser & Chalmers
Washtenaw Ave.,
Walker & Elliott, W
Webster Mfg. Co.
15th St., Chicago

SPROCKET

C. O. Bartlett & C
St., Cleveland, O
Bethlehem Foundry
S. Bethlehem, Pa.
H. W. Caldwell &
Ave. and 17th St.
Dodge Mfg. Co., M
The Jeffrey Mfg. C
Nordyke & Marm
apolis, Ind.
Reeves Pulley Co.,
Walker & Elliott,
Webster Mfg. Co.
15th St., Chicago

STAC

The Contractors' T
St., Philadelphia.
Fraser & Chalmers
tenaw Ave., Chica
Vulcan Iron Works,

STEAM T

American Blower
way, New Yor
Marquette Bldg.

STRUCTURAL IRO

Bethlehem Foundry
Bethlehem, Pa.
J. B. & J. M. Co
City.

WAGONS.

Nordyke & Marmon Co., Indianapolis, Ind.

WIRE ROPE.

Jeffrey Manufacturing Co., Columbus, O.

Macomber & Whyte Rope Co., 21 S. Canal St., Chicago, Ill.

Geo. T. McLaughlin Co., 120 Fu St., Boston, Mass.

New Jersey Foundry & Machine 26 Cortlandt St., New York, N.

Nordyke & Marmon Co., Indianapolis, Ind.

L. M. Rumsey Mfg. Co., St. Lo Mo.

It is Our Business

TO HELP

Your Business

IF YOU MAKE, SELL OR USE

CEMENT

Write to us and we will tell you what we can do for you.

You ought to know

Municipal Engineering Co.

DEALERS IN LIME AND PLASTER.

(See also Dealers in Cement.)

-This list contains the names of dealers in lime who do not also deal in cement. uplicate of the list of Dealers in Cement. Nearly all those in the Cement list are ın lime, the exceptions being found in the larger cities only, so that if both lists ractically all the dealers in lime in cities of more than 2,000 population will be d very few who are not lime dealers. See Preface.

COL.—
. Bingham, 2 S. Larimer
reen 2d & 3d Sts.
vn, 1939 15th St.
ime and Fluxing Co.
Lime & Fluxing Co., 641
e Bldg.
untain Fuel Co., 1010 16th

ry & Co., 2001 Blake St.
tkins Mdse. Co., 1525 Wa-

EN, CONN.—
mant Plaster Co., 10 River

ILL.—
Mfg. Co., 517 Cham. of

os & Co., 355 31st.
Co., 1019 Chamber of Com-

Stone & Lime Wks. Co.,
ber of Commerce.
itton, 118 W. Lake.
mberlain, 908, 134 Monroe.
Inion Lime Works Co., 408
of Commerce.
ooley, 416 Hawthorne.
Pangburn, 55, 16 Pacific

. Co., 814, 115 Dearborn.
ngle, Jr., 1210, 183 Madison.
. Halleman & Co., Cor. W.
d N. Kenzie.
pkins, 50 Dearborn.
mber Co., 400 N. Halstead.
& Cement Co., 651 W. 63d.
ansen & Co., 518 W. Di-

nston & Co., 72 Ewing.
& Osborne, 344 W. Van

chleiter, 3351 State.
Lorscheider, 716 W. 63d.
Ioninger Co.
he & Son, 21 N Elizabeth.

Right Supply Co., 729 W. 63d.
J. R. Rhinehart Co., 668 W. Madison.
Rock Plaster Mfg. Co., 1019 Cham. of Com.
E. A. & C. E. Thomas, 614, 138 Washington.
Jas. C. Woodley & Co., 69, 163 Randolph.

ELGIN, ILL.—
Michael J. Lydon, 521 South.
Henry C. Otto, 218 North.
Charles Veeder, 526 Enterprise.

LINCOLN, ILL.—
John A. Simpson, Agt. Acme Cement Plaster.

PEORIA, ILL.—
Peoria Fitzgerald Plaster, 100 Cedar.
Peoria Portland Cement, 403 S. Washington.

INDIANAPOLIS, IND.—
Diamond Wall Plaster Co., 920 E. North.

NEW ALBANY, IND.—
I. A. Hardin, 505 State St.
Peter R. Stoy & Son, 109 E. Main St.

MARSHALLTOWN, IA.—
W. D. Goldsberry, 312 Iowa Ave.

BALTIMORE, MD.—
Charles T. Cockey, Jr., Arlington, Md.
J. P. Bensons' Sons, Hampden, Md.

BOSTON, MASS.—
American Fire Proofing Co., 156 Devonshire, rm. 49.
Alvin R. Bailey, 19 Congress.
Bay State Fire Proofing Co., 1 Beacon, rm. 88.
Waldo H. Bigelow, 53 State St., rm. 811.
Cerro Pulley Co., 34 Oliver.
Cobb Lime Co., 30 Kilby, rm. 14.
Timothy Crowell, 144 State St.
C. A. Dodge & Co., 79 Milk & 166 Devonshire.

Eastern Expanded Metal Co., 39 Court, rm A.
Electro Vulcan Co., 178 Devonshire.
T. A. Elston & Co., 409 Dorchester Ave.
Geo. W. Gale, Lbr. Co., 640 Main.
Lally Patent Column Co., 65 Federal.
Augustus F. Lash, 29 D St.
Leatherbee & Co., 106 Milk.
Lombard Fire Proofing Co., 166 Devonshire, rm. 32.
National Fire Proofing Co., 166 Devonshire.
N. E. Adamant Co., 79 Milk.
David P. Page, 507 Medford.
I. W. Pinkham & Son, 206 Devonshire.
Sackett Wall Board Co., 113 Devonshire.
E. D. Sawyer & Co., 166 Devonshire.
Union Metal Corner Co., 206 Summer.
W. M. Weston Co., 120 Milk and 166 Devonshire.
Weston & Bigelow (same as Waldo H. Bigelow).

GRAND RAPIDS, MICH.—
Alabastine Co.

MINNEAPOLIS, MINN.—
Cutter & Gilbert, 3 N. 3d St.
Homan Cement & Lime Co., 112 Bank of Com. Bldg.

ST. PAUL, MINN.—
M. H. Blake & Co., 540 Endicott Bldg.
Bohn Mfg. Co., S. E. Cor. Arcade and Wells St.
John Calandar, 148 8th St.
Capitol City Furniture Co., 639 Jackson St.
Gribben Lumber Co., 194 E. 7th St.
Geo. H. Lawes & Co., 49 E. 5th St.
Lee & Hoff Mfg. Co., W. S., Levee St. 1st W Roberts.

KANSAS CITY, MO.—
Deatherage Lumber Co., 1065 W. 8th St.
Louisiana & Gulf Lumber Co., 19th & Main St.

LOUISIANA, MO.—
Crystal Carbonate Lime Co.

ST. LOUIS, MO.—
Glencoe Lime and Cement Co., 1400 A Old Manchester Rd.

OMAHA, NEB.—
Baker Cemantico Co., 1404 Farnham St.
C. L. Chaffee, 3 N. Y. Life Bldg.
Celina Valley Plaster Co., 903-5 New York Life Bldg.

NEWARK, N. J.—
Newark Lime and Cement Co., 22 Clinton St.

BUFFALO, N. Y.—
Standard Plaster Co.

NEW YORK CITY, BOROUGH BROOKLYN—
Clark Bros., 202 N. 10th St.
Edward Clarke, 291 N. 9th St.
Empire Lime Kiln, 213 10th St.
P. S. Kelley, 17 Kent Ave.
J. B. King, 7 Broadway.
K. Kroner, 356 Stockholm St.
Perry Bros., Morgan Ave. & M ole.
C. H. Reynolds, 12th & Wythe A

NEW YORK CITY, BOROUGHS MANHATTAN AND BRONX—
Bloomer & Co., 82 New Chamber
F. G. Chase, 1 Madison Ave.
Glens Falls Co., 26 Cortlandt St.
Jointa Lime Co., 26 Cortlandt St.
Keenan Lime Co., 74 Cortlandt S
Morgan Lime Co., 26 Cortlandt
O'Connell & Hillery Lime & M Dust Co., 649 W. 131st.
Perry Bros., 27 Coenties Slip.
Rockland-Rockport Lime Co. Cortlandt St.
Sherman Lime Co., 26 Cortlandt

SYRACUSE, N. Y.—
Adamant Plaster Co., 210 M gomery St.

CINCINNATI, O.—
L. A. Metcalfe, 2433 Gilbert Ave.
Mills, Spelmire & Co., 652 W 3d.

EAST LIVERPOOL, O.—
Old Roman Plaster Co.

FINDLAY, O.—
Tarbox & McCall, 903 Faching S

MARIETTA, O.—
Butts & McCormick, 102 Front.
J. F. McHugh, Ohio, bet. 4th and
J. Seyler & Bro., 158, 160 Front.

PORT CLINTON, O.—
The Granite Wall Plaster Co.

PORTSMOUTH, O.—
New Process Lime Co.

TOLEDO, O.—
The Buckeye Lime Co., 208 Ch of Com. Bldg.
Doherty & Co., foot of Washin St.
The Fishack Plaster Co., 407 Cha of Commerce.
Napoleon Pulp Plaster Co., 710 Nasby.
Toledo White Lime Co., 56 Pro Exchange.

WARREN, O.—
Elastic Pulp Plaster Co.

YOUNGSTOWN, O.—
The Granite Wall Plaster Co.

ALLEGHENY, PA.—
Barrett Mfg. Co., 1131 Rebecca St
Champion Wall Plaster Co., Franklin and Preble Ave. Ricl Forde, Pres., 216 Charleston Frank J. Schellman, Secy., Beaver Ave.; Wm. A. S Treas., 1704 Beaver Ave.

'. Corde, Nixon & Mahhattan
, A.
an & Porter, 315 Sandusky
A.
erald Plaster Co., 212 Ander-
St., A.
erald Wall Plaster Co.
. & E. A. Knox, Juniata &
ble Ave., A.
LEHEM, PA.—
s J. H. Grossart, 23 S. Main St.
Neumyer, 143 Broad St.
am B. Spengler, 23 S. Main St.
DELPHIA, PA.—
x Allen, 1319 Washington Ave.
ew Blair, 900 Jefferson St.
& Co., 1021 Passyunk Ave.
r Hollow Lime Co., 1109 Land
e Bldg.
ael Dougherty, 905 Oxford St.
well Coal and Lime Co., 2736 N.
ad St.
amin Housekeeper, 1526 N. Amer-
i St.
augh Lime Co., Wash'n Ave. and
St.
s S. Lyster, 3052 Market St.
stus Reeve, 31 Market St.
lard Lime & Cement Co., 1317
sh. Ave.
s R. Thomas & Co., 1801 Mar-
St.
lland Lime Co., 1411 S. 47th St.
BURG, PA.—
. Fox, 121 Wabash St.
Granite Wall Plaster Co. Geo.
Beemer, Pres., Clarks Summit,
; C. Graham, Vice Pres; T. E.
ver, Secy. & Treas., Port Clin-
, Ohio.
Morris Lime & Limestone Co.,
d Natl. Bk. Bldg.
ay Bros., 20 Lacock St., E. A.

SCRANTON, PA.—
Paragon Plaster & Supply Co., 1500 Albright Ave.
Scranton Woodworking Co., 510 Penn Ave.

HOUSTON, TEX.—
George B. Miles, 213 Levy Bldg.

CHARLESTON, W. VA.—
Rex Hardware Co., 111 3d St.
W. H. Smith Hardware Co., 117 3d St.

EAU CLAIRE, WIS.—
Dunnville Sandstone Quarries, Railroad, near Armory Bldg.
McDonough Mfg. Co., 1500 Galloway St.
Madison St. Mfg. Co., Madison and Forest Sts.
W. O. Matteson, 654 1st Ave.
Phoenix Furniture Co., Broadway and 9th Ave.
Phoenix Mfg. Co., Forest and Wisconsin Sts.
A. H. Stevens, 312 S., River St.
Wisconsin Pipe & Fuel Co., 10 S. Dewey St.

MANITOWOC, WIS. —
Manitowoc Building Supply Co., 5th and York Sts.

MILWAUKEE, WIS.—
Adamant Mfg. Co., 480 Virginia St.
Bottom Sand Co., 535 National Ave.
Joseph Druecker & Sons, 347 E. North Ave.
Durr Plaster Co., 311 Grove St.
Milwaukee Falls Lime Co., Humboldt Ave. & Commerce.
Milwaukee Lime Co., 180 Clinton St.
Ormsby Lime Co., 511 Pabst Bldg.
Wisconsin Lime & Cement Co., 163 New Ins. Bldg.

LIME MANUFACTURERS.

ALABAMA.

ANNISTON—
Anniston Lime and Stone Co.
CALERA—
R. E. Bowden.
Calera Land and Lime Co.
C. L. O'Neal.
J. B. Randall.
CANADARQUE—
W. E. Brinkerhoff.
FT. PAYNE—
Standard Lime Co.
LIME ROCK—
Milton Gentle.
Hunt & Co.
LONG VIEW—
J. B. Adams.
Long View Lime Works.
ROCK SPRINGS—
E. G. Eaton.
SILURA—
F. H. Hardy.

ARKANSAS.

LITTLE ROCK—
M. R. Dennie.

CALIFORNIA.

LOS ANGELES—
Los Angeles Lime Co., 205 San Pedro.
W. W. Reed, 202 Nolan, Smith and Bridge Blk.
Union Lime Co., 203 San Pedro.
Western Commercial Co., 209 N. Los Angeles.

SAN FRANCISCO—
H. T. Holmes Lime Co., 34 Sacramento.
Patent Brick Co., 240 Montgomery.
Jos. Scheerer & Co., 10th and Brannan.
E. L. Snell, 16 Hayes.

COLORADO.

DENVER—
Colorado Lime and Fluxing Co., Equitable Bldg.
Leadville Lime and Fluxing Co., 641 Equitable Bldg.
LEADVILLE—
Jeremiah Irvin.

CONNECTICUT.

BROOKFIELD—
Brookfield Lime Co.
EAST CANAAN—
Canfield Brothers.
NEW HAVEN—
H. A. Stevens (oyster shell) Chapel.
NORTH CANAAN—
Anchor Lime Co.
Chas. Barnes' Sons.
Canaan Lime Co.
Pierce & Freeman.
REDDING—
John Todd.

DELAWARE.

NEW CASTLE—
New Castle Brick & Lime Mfg. (

DISTRICT OF COLUMBIA.

WASHINGTON—
John McL. Dodson, 27th & K. N.
Knott & Moler, 28th & K. N. W.

FLORIDA.

OCALA—
Ocala Lime Co.

GEORGIA.

ATLANTA—
Sciple Sons, 8 Loyd.
SAVANNAH—
Andrew Hanley Co.
TALKING ROCK—
Talona Lime Works.

ILLINOIS.

CHICAGO—
Artesian Stone & Lime Works, Washington.
Chicago Union Lime Works Co., Chamber of Commerce.
Andrew H. Halleman & Co., Kenzie Ave. & W. Chicago Ave
Indiana Lime & Cement Co., 651 23d.
Marblehead Lime Co., Masonic T ple.
FFrederick K. Schultz, 658 S. I sted.

ı Lime & Stone Co., 165 E. olph.
sin Lime & Cement Co., ber of Commerce Bldg.
/A—
a Lime Co.
)RT—
ennie Grant.
‹—
Lime Co.
KEE—
kee Stone & Lime Co.
YRON—
c G. A. Metzger.
yron Lime Association.
tyron Lime Co.
—
ity Lime Co.
: Meyer, 1015 Payson Ave.
Menke, Stone & Lime Co.
White Lime & Cement Co.

INDIANA.

YNE—
Baltes & Co., 27 N. Harrison.
oellinger's Sons, 53 Murray.
APOLIS—
Keeport & Co., 314 W. North.
CASTLE—
astle Brick, Stone & Lime Co.
IGDON—
n Lime Co.
PORT—
Keeport & Co.
Lux.
LL—
l Lime Co.
VERNON—
Miller.

IOWA.

AM—
n Lime Co.
MONT—
her & Burke.
N—
Lime Co.
PORT—
hl & Son.
INES—
oines Fuel & Lime Co., 211 erry.
ASS—
Kelley.
Strickland.
Iltgen.
UE—
Point Lime Works.
Fengler.
ty Lime Works.
rhand & Buddin.
TH—
er.
E CITY—
Valley Stone & Lime Co.

GUTTENBERG—
George Kohler.
MAYNOKETA—
A. Hurst & Co.
Maynoketa Lime Co.
MASON CITY—
A. T. Lien.
MONMOUTH—
L. B. Stuart & Co.
UNION—
Oliver Jones.
VIOLA—
Collins & Hilton.
WILTON JUNCTION—
Sugar Creek Lime Co.

KANSAS.

WICHITA—
O. B. Stocker.

KENTUCKY.

LOUISVILLE—
Utica Lime Co., 421 W. Main.

MAINE.

CAMDEN—
Carleton, Norwood & Co.
S. E. & H. L. Sheperd Co.
LINCOLNVILLE—
E. M. Coleman.
ROCKLAND—
Jas. Abbott & Sons.
Almon Bird.
Cobb Lime Co.
A. F. Crockett Co.
Cornelius Doherty.
Farrand, Spear & Co.
A. W. Gay & Co.
Perry Brothers.
Pillsbury, Jno. R.
Chas. R. Pressey.
White & Case.
ROCKPORT—
C. E. Carlton Co.
Jno. H. Eells.
THOMASTON—
Burgess, O'Brien & Co.
John A. Creighton & Co.
J. O. Cushing & Co.
E. K. O'Brien.

MARYLAND.

BALTIMORE—
John A.. Allers' Sons, Charles & West.
Wm. C. Ditman, 540 E. Monument.
Geo. A. Gegner, Eastern Ave., c. Clinton.
Gegner & Green, 2115 Aliceanne.
Robt. S. Green, 853 Fkd. Ave., Ext.
Ideal Lime Co., 540 E. Monument.
Geo. Judge (shell), Jenkins' la.
Maryland Lime & Cemnt Co., Bowey's Wharf.
National Building Supply Co., Lex. & North.

Platt & Co., Fort Clement St.
Standard Lime & Stone Co., Equitable Bldg.
Texas Lime Co., Bowey's Wharf.
Wm. Wallace, 1223 Ridgely.
Washington Building Lime Co., Equitable Bldg.

BUCKEYSTOWN—
Baker Brothers.
Standard Lime & Stone Co.
Washington Bldg. Lime Co.

COCKEYSVILLE—
Zephaniah Poteet.

LIMEKILN—
M. J. Grove Lime Co.

TEXAS—
Wm. C. Ditman.
Ideal Lime & Stone Co.
Frank M. Lee.
Wm. P. Lindsay.
Shipley Bros.

MASSACHUSETTS.

ADAMS—
L. J. Fallett & Sons.

BOSTON—
Cobb Lime Co., 30 Kilby.
Fiske, Homes & Co., 164 Devonshire.

CHESHIRE—
Cheshire Lime Mfg. Co.
A. S. Farnam & Bro.

MICHIGAN.

ALPENA—
O. Fox.

BAY SHORE—
Bay Shore Lime Co.
Petoskey Lime Co.

BELLEVUE—
Dyer & Hall.
Bellevue Lime Quarry.

DETROIT—
W. E. Heames & Co., 78 Woodbridge.
Henry Houghten, 806 Hammond Bldg.
C. H. Little Co., 340 Atwater, E.

CONTRACTORS'
TOOLS
AND SUPPLIES
WHEELBARROWS, PICKS,
SHOVELS, HOES, TAMPS,
ROLLERS, EDGERS,
MARKERS, SCREENS,
ETC., ETC.
W. H. ANDERSON & SONS
14 and 16 Macomb Street, Detroit, Mich.

MANISTEE—
S. Bedford.

MANISTIQUE—
White Marble Lime Co.

MUSKEGON—
Muskegon Lime Works.

PETOSKEY—
L. G. Grimes.
H. O. Rose.

SAGINAW—
Bay Port Quarries, 728 W. Wa
Ave.
E. Everett Johnson, 401 S. T
E. S.
Remer Brothers, 300 Madison.

MINNESOTA.

MANKATO—
Mankato Lime & Stone Co.

RED WING—
G. A. Carlson.
Glover Lime Works.
Gust. Lillyblad.

ST. PAUL—
Northwestern Lime Co., 71]
Levee.
Shakopee Cement Lime Mfg. C
Chestnut.

WINONA—
H. J. Willis.

MISSOURI.

AUXVASSE—
Marblehead Lime Co.

BOONVILLE—
Lohse & Miller.

CALIFORNIA—
Wm. Murrell.

CARTHAGE—
Ash Grove White Lime Ass'n., & Traders Ex.
Carthage Marble and White Li
Hubb & Hill Star Lime Co.
Missouri White Lime and Sto

DENVER—
Fremont Lamb.

DE SOTO—
H. W. Blank.

HANNIBAL—
Empire Lime Co.
Hannibal Lime Co.
Star Lime Co.
Waller Lime Co.

KANSAS CITY—
Ash Grove White Lime Ass'n, Tel. Bldg.
C. A. Brockett Cement Co.,]
8th.
Missouri Lime and Cement C
Postal Tel. Bldg.
Ozark Stone and Lime Co., C
and Wyandotte.
Western White Lime Co., Post
Bldg.

ANA—
l Carbonate Lime Co.
& Cash.
: CITY—
Raupp & Son.
JIS—
.ge Marble and White Lime Co.,
e Bldg.
ir Lime Co., 3852 Manchester

e Lime and Cement Co., 1400
Manchester Road.
annes Limo Co., 2436 Kosciusko.
& Hunkins Lime and Cement
S. end of 18th St. Bridge.
FIELD—
head Lime Co.

MONTANA.

—
on Lime Co., Silver Bow Blk.
FALLS—
Bros.

NEBRASKA.

CE—
Clayes.

NEW JERSEY.

N—
n Lime Co.
SON—
Phillips Lime Co.
E—
e Lime Works.
K—
Morrison, Cor. Clover & Van
1.
k Lime and Cement Co., 22
on St.
k Lime & Cement Mfg. Co.,
of Bridge.
k & Rosendale Lime & Ce-
Co., 763 Broad.
White Rock Lime Co., 133
.
RUNSWICK—
n R. Outcalt.
ON—
Richardson & Son.

NEW YORK.

OW—
Williams & Co.
LO—
nsville Quick Lime Co., Cor.
way & Elm.
.
Marble Lime Co.
ONT—
ont Co.
A—
nk.
EVILLE—
& Gaynor.

GLENS FALLS—
Glens Falls Co.
Jointa Lime Co.
Morgan Lime Co.
Sherman Lime Co.
GLOVERSVILLE—
Mayfield Lime & Cement Co.
KINGSTON—
F. W. Gross, Hasbrouck Ave. and Murray.
Newark Lime & Cement Mfg. Co.
LEROY—
Geo. H. Holmes.
LOCKPORT—
John Berkman, 35 Canal.
NEW YORK CITY, BOROUGH OF BROOKLYN—
Empire Lime Kilns, 213 N. 10th.
NEW YORK CITY, BOROUGHS OF MANHATTAN & BRONX—
Bloomer & Co., 82 New Chamber.
John J. Brooks (shell), 603 W. 55th.
Cable, Thorn & Co., Mfrs.' Agts., 253 Broadway.
Fred'k. G. Chase, 1 Madison Ave.
Cheshire Lime & Builders' Supply Co., 217 W. 125th.
Foster F. Comstock, 261 Broadway.
Glens Falls Co., 26 Cortlandt.
Irvine & Co., 215 W. 125th.
Keenan Lime Co., 74 Cortlandt.
Morgan Lime Co., 26 Cortlandt.
Newark & Rosendale Lime & Cement Co., 39 Cortlandt.
O'Connell & Hillery Lime & Marble Dust Co., 640 W. 131st.
O. D. Person, 160 5th Ave.
Dennis Reardon, 74 Cortlandt.
Rockland-Rockport Lime Co., 26 Cortlandt.
Sherman Lime Co., 26 Cortlandt.
Calvin Tomkins, 120 Liberty.
Chas. Warner Co., 66 Maiden Lane.
NIAGARA—
B. Messing.
PORT JERVIS—
Jacob Nearpass.
RICHVILLE—
Gardner Brothers.
ROCHESTER—
Lawson & Leason, Cor. Cottage and Seward.
Thomas Oliver, 328 South Ave.
Rochester Lime Co., 209 W. Main.
Whitmore, Rauber & Vicinus, 279 South Ave.

S. J. OSBORN, JR. & CO.
Asphalt and Granitoid
ROOFING, FLOORS AND WALKS
Combined Curb and Gutter
Pearl and Eggleston Ave., CINCINNATI, OHIO

SHELBY—
E. B. Simonds.
SING SING—
Sing Sing Lime Co.
SODUS CENTRE—
E. B. Mather & Co.
SYRACUSE—
Israel E. Britton, 201 W. Onondaga.
TROY—
W. E. Cheney & Son, 558 River.
TUCKAHOE—
O'Connell & Hillery Lime & Marble Dust Co.
WATERTOWN—
H. S. Cory, P. O. Box 254.

NORTH CAROLINA.

BOILSTON—
L. H. Centrell.
BREVARD—
E. M. Allison.
G. W. Young.
CATAWBA—
M. B. Trollinger.
HOLLYWOOD—
Hollywood Fertilizing Co.
HOT SPRINGS—
M. J. Flagg & Co.
LIME ROCK—
W. A. Estes.
WASHINGTON—
A. W. Styron.
WINDSOR—
B. W Askew.
YADKINSVILLE—
Consumers' Lime Co.

OHIO.

BOWLING GREEN—
Snow Flake Lime Co.
BUCYRUS—
Broken Sword Stone Co.
CAREY—
Daum & Co.
CINCINNATI—
Jas. G. Chrispin Lime and Cement Co., 826 Reedy St., and Norwood, O.
H J Conkling, Gilbert Ave.
Contractors' and Builders' Supply Co., 2849 Stanton Ave.
L. H. McCammon Bros., 854 W. 6th.
Moore & Co., 954 W. 5th.
Moores Lime Co., 927 W. 5th.
Martin Stritzinger, Lick Run Pike, Green township.

Marbleithic Floors

The *ONLY* floors for railway stations and public buildings

Clean, durable, beautiful.

Correspondence Solicited

THE MARBLEITHIC CO., Dayton, Ohio.

CLAY CENTRE—
Clark Co.
CLEVELAND—
John A. Edam, 915 Pearl.
Kelley Island Lime and Tran port Co., Mercantile Bank Bld
Ralph T. James, 126 Elm.
COLD SPRINGS—
Moore & Co.
COLUMBUS—
Columbus Macadam Co., 319 Dub Ave.
The Rock Plaster Mfg. Co.
EAST LIVERPOOL—
Old Roman Plaster Co.
FOSTORIA—
Fostoria Stone & Lime Co.
D. P. Lloyd Co.
FREMONT—
Gottron Bros.
GENOA—
E. C. Gregg.
Frank Holt.
GIBSONBERG—
Dohn Lime Co.
Zorn Horning Co.
GREENFIELD—
Rucker & Co.
LIME CITY—
Lime City Co.
LIMESTONE—
Limestone Lime Co.
LUCKEY—
N. B. Eddy & Co.
Norris Christian Lime & Stone C
MALVERN—
Canton & Malvern Tile & Clay C
MARION—
John Evans Lime & Stone Co.
PIQUA—
Levi Cofield.
Ohio Marble Co.
PORT CLINTON—
The Granite Wall Plaster Co.
PORTSMOUTH—
New Process Lime Co.
REX—
O. D. Brown.
ROCKY BRIDGE—
Human & Reaser.
SANDUSKY—
L. R. Johnson & Co.
Daniel Kunz.
Ohlemacher Lime Co.
SPRINGFIELD—
Mills Bros.
Moore & Co.
Moore's Lime Co.
SUGAR RIDGE—
Sugar Ridge Stone & Lime Co.
J. W. & J. J. Urschel.
TOLEDO—
Buckeye Lime Co., 209 Cham. of C Bldg.
Doherty & Co., ft. of Washingt

Eddy & Co.
:ity Co., 422 Spitzer Bldg.
'rocess Lime Co.
ime & Cement Co.
White-Lime Co., Produce

:N
: Pulp Plaster Co.
:ON—
Duncan.
STOWN—
ranite Wall Plaster Co.

OREGON.

AND—
:raken Co., 407 Irving.
gham & Co., ft. Wash'n.

PENNSYLVANIA.

HENY—
pion Wall Plaster Co., Frank-
ind Preble Ave.
rald Wall Plaster Co.
TOWN—
J. Clader.
E. Trexler.
NA—
:anan & Co.
ALE—
lale Lime & Stone Co.
FONTE—
mont & Co.
OCK—
Newton Ground Lime and Ce-
: Co.
EPORT—
David & Co.
R. Hagner.
y Lime Co.
ER HILL—
Krall.
SLE—
ear Bros.
IBIA—
ian Bros.
JLT—
Catanach.
Lime and Stone Co.
N—
n Lime Co.
Snyder.

er S. Burton, 9 W. 8th.
Thayer & Son.
KSTOWN—
K. McLanahan, Jr.
ER—
: & Carty.
VER—
r & Son.
ISBURG—
s Walton, 223 Market.
NNING—
Dougherty.
ASTER—
Keller, 154 N. Queen.

LEWISTOWN—
Hawk Bros.
Edw. McCoy.
LOCK HAVEN—
R. W. & G. E. Rishell.
MALVERN—
Michael Dougherty.
Knickerbocker Lime Co.
MILL HALL—
Mill Hall Lime Co.
NORRISTOWN—
Evans & Co.
W. B. Rambo.
B. F. Richardson & Co.
PHILADELPHIA—
Avondale Lime & Stone Co., 2202 Chestnut.
Cedar Hollow Lime Co., 900 Jefferson.
C. A. Cox's Sons, 2137 N. American.
Sam'l H. French & Co., 4th & Callowhill.
Benj. Housekeeper, 901 Thompson.
Kerbaugh Lime Co., 15th & Wash'n Av.
Keystone Lime Co., Christian St.
Knickerbocker Lime Co. (Inc.), 366 Wharf, Schuylkill.
Lukens & Yerkes, Stephen Girard Bldg.
Jas. S. Lyster, 3052 Market.
Standard Lime Co., 1317 Washington Av.
PITTSBURG—
Houston Brothers, 32nd & P. R.
A. G. Morris Lime & Limestone Co., Ltd., Second Natl. Bank Bldg.
PORT KENNEDY—
Blair & Co.
QUARRYVILLE—
John Rineer.
READING—
Reading Lime Co.
SCRANTON—
Cornelius B. Haslam, 118 Cliff.
Luther Keller, 813 W. Lex Ave.
SWEDELAND—
Robt. McCoy.
TYRONE—
Keystone Lime & Stone Co.
A. G. Morris Lime & Limestone Co.
UNIONVILLE—
E. D. Logan & Bro.
WAYNESBORO—
Decarbonated Lime Co.
WRIGHTSVILLE—
C. S. Budding.
Kerr Bros.

JOHN COLLINS
Cement Walk Contractor
Bath, New York

YORK—
Henry Grothe.
Henry Y. Kottcamp.
Philip J. Kottcamp.
Henry Lucking.
Wm. F. Smith.
William Witta.
William H. Witta.

RHODE ISLAND.

LINCOLN—
Harris Limerick Co.
Stephen Wright.
LONSDALE—
Dexter Limerick Co.

SOUTH CAROLINA.

GAFFNEY—
Carroll & Co.
W. H. Richardson & Co.

TENNESSEE.

BURNS—
Wright Lime Works.
CHATTANOOGA—
Gager Lime & Mfg. Co. 203 Carter.
CLARKSVILLE—
Jas. Stinchfield.
KNOXVILLE—
East Tennessee Lime & Sand Co.
Knoxville Lime & Sand Co.
Southern Lime Co.
NASHVILLE—
W. T. Hardison, 115 S. Front.
PALMYRA—
Palmyra Lime Co.
SHERWOOD—
Alden Lime Co.
Gager Lime & Mfg. Co.
TULLAHOMA—
H. McKinsey & Sons.

TEXAS.

AUSTIN—
Austin White Lime Co.
Wm. Walsh & Co.
DALLAS—
Griffith & Cowser, 590 Commerce.
F. Michil, S. end of Mkt.
Moore & Rowling, 271 Elm.
EL PASO—
J. H. Smith.

UTAH.

OGDEN—
J. T. Johnson & Co., 585 28th.
SALT LAKE CITY—
Hancock & Co.
Langton Lime & Cement Co. Ridd & Martin.
Wm. Varley.

VERMONT.

BRISTOL—
B. C. Sargent.
BURLINGTON—
Tobey & Catlin.
IRA—
Dexter D. Day.
LEICESTER—
Brandon Lime & Marble Co.
Leicester Lime & Marble Co.
NEW HAVEN—
H C. Palmer.
NORTH POWNALL—
Follett Bros.
Tarble & Johnson.
WEATHERFIELD—
Chas. Ansden.
WINOOSKI—
Tobey & Catlin.
S. H. Weston.

VIRGINIA.

BLUE RIDGE SPRINGS—
Blue Ridge Cement & Lime Wks.
RICHMOND—
Augusta Lime Co., 1110 E. Main.
A. S. Lee & Son, 28th, cor. Cary.
Moore Lime Co., 17th and Dock.
Richmond Phosphate Co., Chamber of Com. Bldg.
RIVERTON—
Carson & Son.

WASHINGTON.

SEATTLE—
Seattle and Roche Harbor Lime Co.
SPOKANE—
Washington Brick, Lime and Mfg. Co., Stevens and N. P. Ry.
TACOMA—
Tacoma and Roche Harbor Lime Co.

WEST VIRGINIA.

BAKERTON—
Washington Bldg. Lime Co.
MARTINSBURG—
Standard Lime and Stone Co.
WHEELING—
Wheeling Lime and Cement Co.

WISCONSIN.

APPLETON—
J. H. Marston & Co.
CEDARBURG—
Anschutz Lime and Stone Co.
F. Groth.
EDEN—
Nast Bros.
GRAFTON—
Milwaukee Falls Lime Co.
HAMILTON—
Western Lime and Stone Co.
MILWAUKEE—
J. Druecker & Sons, 356 E. North Ave.
Ormsby Lime Co., 511 Pabst Bldg.
Sarnow Lime Co., 3308 Vliet.
Western Lime and Cement Co., Pabst Bldg.
NEW LONDON—
Westphal Bros.
Western Lime and Cement Co.

OSHKOSH—
Cook & Brown Co.

RACINE—
C. Fox & Sons.
Horlick Lime & Stone Co.

SHEBOYGAN—
Sheboygan Lime Works.

SUPERIOR—
Warehouse & Builders Supply Co.

WYOMING.

LARAMIE—
Clark, Pelton & Employes Co.

More Cement Companies

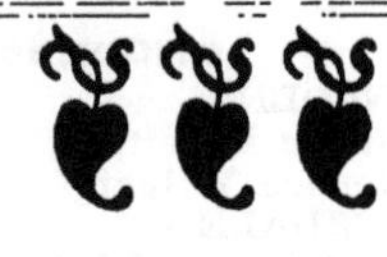

advertise in **Municipal Engineering Magazine**

than in any other American pnblica tion. It reaches more of the people who buy or influence the buying of cement than any other American publication.

PLASTER MANUFACTURERS.

Adamant **Mfg.** Co., 317 Cham. of Com. Bldg., Chicago.

Adamant Mfg. Co., Hammond Bldg., Detroit, Mich.

Adamant Mfg. Co., Minneapolis, Minn.

Adamant Mfg. Co., Superior, Wis.

Adamant Mfg. Co., Syracuse, N. Y.

Adamant Mfg. Co. of America, 156 5th Ave., New York.

Adamant Wall Plaster Co., Indianapolis, Ind.

Alabaster Co., Alabaster, Mich.; 1019 Cham. of Com. Bldg., Chicago; Union Trust Bldg., Detroit, Mich.

Alabastine Co., Grand Rapids, Mich.

Alpine Plaster Co., Los Angeles, Cal.

American Asbestos Co., 45 B'way, New York.

American Cement Plaster Co., Lawrence & Wichita, Kas.

American Plaster Co., Lawrence, Kas.

American Hard Wall Plaster Co., Utica, N. Y.

American Mfg. Co. (Eclipse), Waynesboro, Pa.

American Mortar Co., 39 N. Division, Grand Rapids, Mich.

Baker Plaster Co., Hot Springs, S. Dak.; Omaha, Neb.

Best Bros. & Co., Medicine Lodge, Kas.

Blue Rapids Plaster Co., Blue Rapids, Kas.

Blue Valley Plaster Co., Omaha, Neb.

C A. Brockett Cement Co (Aetna), 121 W 8th, Kansas City, Mo

J L Brown, 1939 15th St., Denver, Col.

Buffalo Mortar Co., Buffalo N Y

Buffalo Paragon Wall Plaster Co., Buffalo, N Y.

Californa Anti-Caloric Co , 21 Mission San Francisco, Cal

Cardiff Gypsum Plaster Co., Ft. Dodge, Ia.

Champion Wall Plaster Co , Franklin & Preble Ave., Allegheny, Pa

The E A Chatfield Co., 250 Boulevard, New Haven, Conn

Wm. E. Cheney & Son, 558 River
Troy, N. Y.

Wm. Wirt Clarke & Son, 115 Gay
S., Baltimore, Md.

Connecticut Adamant Plaster Co.
River St., New Haven, Conn.

Consolidated Plaster Mfg. Co., Lo
land, Col.

Cooper & Co., Nashville, Tenn.

Crown Wall Plaster Co., W. Br
dock, Pa.

Dayton Wall Plaster Co., Dayton,

Decatur Hard Wall Plaster Co.,
catur, Ill.

Decorators' Supply Co., 209 S. C
ton, Chicago.

Dennison Wall Plaster Co., Der
son, O.

Des Moines Fuel & Lime Co.,
Moines, Ia.

Diamond Wall Cement Co., Nya
N. Y.

Diamond Wall Plaster Co., Indi
apolis, Ind.

Dickinson Cement Co., 931 M
quette Bldg., Chicago, Ill.

Dillon Cement Plaster Works,
lon, Kas.

John Druecker, Canal & Kinzie S
Chicago, Ill.

Duncombs Stucco Co., Ft. Dodge,

Durr Plaster Co., Milwaukee, Wi

Eagle Plaster Mills, Grand Rapi
Mich

Elastic Pulp Plaster Co., Warren,

English Plaster Works, Oakfi
N. Y.

Erie Hard Wall Plaster Co., Erie

Eureka Plaster Co., Syracuse, N.

Evansville Adamant Factory, Eva
ville, Ind.

The Fishback Plaster Co., 407 Ch
of Comm., Toledo, O.

Fitzgerald Plaster Co., Allegh
Pa.; Springfield, Ill.; Peoria,
and Huntingdon, W. Va.

Forrester Plaster Co., ft. Kirtla
Cleveland, O

Ft. Dodge Plaster Co., Ft Do
Ia

Samuel H French & Co., 4th & (
lowhill, Philadelphia, Pa.

Gibraltar Wall Plaster Works,
Niagara, Buffalo, N. Y.

F. Godfrey & Bro., 100 Monroe, Grand Rapids, Mich.

Golden Gate Plaster Mills. 215 Main, San Francisco, Cal.

Grand Rapids Gypsum Works, 429 Mich. Trust Co. Bldg., Grand Rapids. Mich.

Grand Rapids Plaster Co., 65 Monroe, Grand Rapids, Mich. (W. S. Hovey, Gen. Agt.).

Granite Hard Wall Plaster, 6½ 4th, N., Minneapolis, Minn.

Granite Wall Plaster Co., Grand Rapids, Mich., and Port Clinton and Youngstown, O.

Great Western Plaster Co., Blue Rapids, Kan.

Gypsum Products Mfg. Co., Grand Rapids, Mich.

Hammill & Gillespie, 240 Front St., New York.

Hearfield, Bannister & Co., 320 Sansome, San Francisco, Cal.

Higginson Mfg. Co., Newburg, N. Y.

International Rock Plaster Co., Jersey City, N. J.

Iowa Plaster Association, Fort Dodge, Ia.

Kentucky Wall Plaster Co., Water, E of 1st., Louisville, Ky.

Keystone Plaster Co., Lock Box 676, Chester, Pa.; 16 S. Broad, Phila., Pa.; 6th St. wharf S. W., Washington, D. C., & Williamsport, Pa.

J. B. King & Co., 1 Bway., N. Y., & New Brighton, S. I., N. Y., & 322 Genesee, Buffalo, N. Y.

V. C. & C. B. King, 510 West, New York.

Lone Star Plaster Co., Quanah, Tex.

Marsh & Co., Sandusky, O.

Michigan Plaster Co., Grand Rapids, Mich.

Michigan & Ohio Plaster Co., Pythian Temple, Grand Rapids, Mich.

Midland Plaster & Cement Co., 518 Michigan Trust Bldg., Grand Rapids, Mich.

Midland Plaster Co., Bldrs. & Traders' Exch., Kansas City, Mo.

Montana Hard Wall Plaster Co., Butte, Mont.

Montana Plaster Co., Joliet, Mont.

Napoleon Pulp Plaster Co., 719 The Nasby, Toledo, O.

Newark Lime & Cement Mfg. Co., foot of Bridge St., Newark, N. J.

New England Adamant Co., 166 Devonshire, Boston.

New Jersey Adamant Mfg. Co., Newark, N. J.

Newkirk Plaster Works, Newkirk, Okla Ter.

Ohio Adamant Co., 183 Meravin, Cleveland, O.

Old Roman Plaster Co., East Liverpool, O.

Ottumwa Plaster Co., Ottumwa, Ia.

Paragon Plaster Co., Syracuse, N. Y.

Paragon Plaster & Supply Co., Scranton, Pa.

V. H. Parks & Son, Decatur, Ill.

Peoria Portland Cement Wall Plaster, Peoria, Ill.

Phoenix Plaster Mills (Wotherspoon & Son, props.), 65 9th Ave., N. Y.

Platt Plaster Co., 130 Fulton, N. Y.

Queen City Plaster Works, 7 Tonawanda, Buffalo, N. Y.

A. D. Rathbone, Grand Rapids, Mich.

Red Beach Plaster Mills, Red Beach, Me.

Rock Plaster Mfg. Co., 1019 Cham. of Com. Bldg., Chicago, Ill.

Rock Plaster Co., of N. Y. & N. J., 11 B'way, N. Y., and ft. 7th, Hoboken, N. J.

Rock Plaster Co., Dresden, O.

Rock Plaster Mfg. Co., Columbus, O.

Rock Plaster Co., Providence, R. I.

Rock Plaster (Samuel H. French & Co., agents), 4th and Callowhill, Phila., Pa.

Rockford Wall Plaster Co., Rockford, Ill.

Roman Cement Plaster Co., Springvale, Kas.

Royal Cement Plaster Co., Salina, Kas., and S. end of 18th St. Bridge, St. Louis.

Royal Plaster Co., 8th c. Culvert, Cincinnati, O.

Salina Cement Plaster Co. Salina, Kas.

Southwestern Plaster Co., Savannah, Ga.

Springfield Eureka Hard Plaster Co., Springfield, Mass.

Standard Cement Plaster Co., Laramier, Wyo.

Standard Plaster Co., Buffalo, N. Y.

Standard Wall Plaster Co., Winona, Minn.

Calvin Tompkins, 120 Liberty St. New York.

Union Mills, Grandville, Mich.

The Warner Miller Co., Railroad Ave. New Haven, Conn.

L. A. Watkins Merchandise Co., 1525 Wazee St., Denver, Col.

Windsor Cement Co., 166 Devonshire, Boston, Mass.

Wotherspoon & Son, 65 9th Ave., New York.

Wymore Plaster Co., Wymore, Neb.

Zenith Wall Plaster and Finish Co., 11 N 3d, Minneapolis, Minn.; South St Paul, Minn., and Fort Dodge, Ia.

INDEX

Warren Brothers Company

MAIN OFFICE, 143 FEDERAL STREET, BOSTON, MASS.

Manufacturers and Dealers in all kinds of Coal Tar and Asphalt Products for use in all classes of work except Asphalt Street Paving.

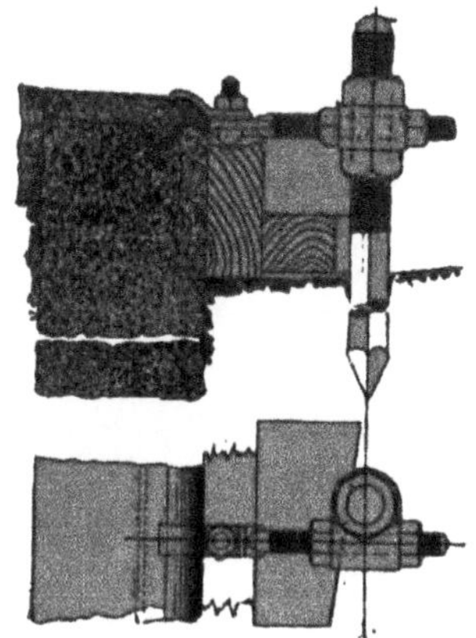

Contractors for

SIDEWALK PAVING,
CONCRETE STRUCTURAL WORK,
KIOLITHIC STONE SIDEWALKS,
BITUMINOUS MACADAM PAVEMENTS,
ASPHALT SIDEWALKS,
TAR CONCRETE SIDEWALKS,
STEEL EDGE CURBING,
COMBINED CURB AND GUTTER, ROOFING, ET.C

WARREN'S KIOLITHIC CEMENT

This cement is especially manufactured for us and develops the best qualities possible for use in surface structural work. It is not specially adapted for use under water.

WARREN'S "KIOLA" ASPHALT

is specially and differently prepared for all different uses such as sidewalks, driveways, roofing, waterproofing, block filling, rock asphalt mastic, etc. We are free to use all classes of asphalt under this trade-mark and use only that which is most suitable for the particular use for which it is intended.

WARREN'S "PURITAN BRAND" OF COAL TAR CEMENTS

are prepared for the same uses as the "Kiola," using as a basis the tar produced by the Cambridge Gas Works, which works has not changed its system of manufacturing gas in thirty years, and produces the largest quantity of straight run tar produced in New England.

Our laboratory methods of selecting Coal Tar Bitumens would exclude from use all water gas or process tars which represent over eighty per cent. of all the tars on the market.

Warren's Patent Laid Kiolithic Artificial Stone Curb with Galvanized Steel Guard is the most practical and beautiful curb in existence.

We are the only manufacturers not engaged in Asphalt Street Paving who adopt rational and careful methods in preparing bituminous materials.

WARREN BROS. COMPANY, 143 FEDERAL ST., BOSTON, MASS.

Lightning Source UK Ltd.
Milton Keynes UK
UKHW020910260119
336226UK00009B/339/P